MANAGEMENT

The New Competitive Landscape

Sixth Edition

Thomas S. Bateman

McIntire School of Commerce,
University of Virginia

Scott A. Snell

Cornell University

 **McGraw-Hill**
Irwin

Boston   Burr Ridge, IL   Dubuque, IA   Madison, WI   New York   San Francisco   St. Louis
Bangkok   Bogotá   Caracas   Kuala Lumpur   Lisbon   London   Madrid   Mexico City
Milan   Montreal   New Delhi   Santiago   Seoul   Singapore   Sydney   Taipei   Toronto

MANAGEMENT: THE NEW COMPETITIVE LANDSCAPE

Published by McGraw-Hill/Irwin, a business unit of The McGraw-Hill Companies, Inc., 1221 Avenue of the Americas, New York, NY, 10020. Copyright © 2004, 2002, 1999, 1996, 1993, 1990 by The McGraw-Hill Companies, Inc. All rights reserved. No part of this publication may be reproduced or distributed in any form or by any means, or stored in a database or retrieval system, without the prior written consent of The McGraw-Hill Companies, Inc., including, but not limited to, in any network or other electronic storage or transmission, or broadcast for distance learning.

Some ancillaries, including electronic and print components, may not be available to customers outside the United States.

This book is printed on acid-free paper.

domestic   1 2 3 4 5 6 7 8 9 0 DOW DOW 0 9 8 7 6 5 4 3
international 1 2 3 4 5 6 7 8 9 0 DOW DOW 0 9 8 7 6 5 4 3

ISBN 0-07-253865-1

Publisher: *John E. Biernat*
Executive editor: *John Weimeister*
Senior developmental editor: *Christine Scheid*
Marketing manager: *Lisa Nicks*
Producer, Media technology: *Mark Molsky*
Lead project manager: *Mary Conzachi*
Senior production supervisor: *Michael R. McCormick*
Photo research coordinator: *Judy Kausal*
Photo researcher: *PoYee Oster*
Supplement producer: *Betty Hadala*
Senior digital content specialist: *Brian Nacik*
Cover design: *Artemio Ortiz Jr.*
Interior design: *Artemio Ortiz Jr.*
Typeface: *10/12 Janson*
Compositor: *Carlisle Communications, Ltd.*
Printer: *R.R. Donnelley*

Library of Congress Cataloging-in-Publication Data

Bateman, Thomas S.
    Management : the new competitive landscape / Thomas S. Bateman, Scott A. Snell.—6th ed.
        p. cm.
    Includes bibliographical references and index.
    ISBN 0-07-253865-1 (alk. paper) — ISBN 0-07-121429-1 (international : alk. paper)
    1. Management. I. Snell, Scott, 1958- II. Title.
    HD 31 .B369485 2004
    658—dc21

                                                        2002038669

INTERNATIONAL EDITION ISBN 0-07-121429-1
Copyright © 2004. Exclusive rights by The McGraw-Hill Companies, Inc. for manufacture and export. This book cannot be re-exported from the country to which it is sold by McGraw-Hill. The International Edition is not available in North America.

www.mhhe.com

For my parents, Tom and Jeanine Bateman
and Mary Jo, Lauren, T.J., and James

and

My parents, John and Clara Snell,
and Marybeth, Sara, Jack, and Emily

About the Authors

Thomas S. Bateman

Thomas S. Bateman is Bank of America Professor and management area coordinator in the McIntire School of Commerce at the University of Virginia. Prior to joining the University of Virginia, he taught organizational behavior at the Kenan-Flager Business School of the University of North Carolina to undergraduates, M.B.A. students, Ph.D. students, and practicing managers. He also recently returned from two years in Europe as a visiting professor at the Institute for Management Development (IMD), one of the world's leaders in the design and delivery of executive education. Dr. Bateman completed his doctoral program in business administration in 1980 at Indiana University. Prior to receiving his doctorate, Dr. Bateman received his B.A. from Miami University. In addition to Virginia, UNC-Chapel Hill, and IMD, Dr. Bateman has taught at Texas A&M, Tulane, and Indiana universities.

Dr. Bateman is an active management researcher, writer, and consultant. He has served on the editorial boards of major academic journals and has presented numerous papers at professional meetings on topics including managerial decision making, job stress, negotiation, employee commitment and motivation, group decision making, and job satisfaction. His articles have appeared in professional journals such as the *Academy of Management Journal*, *Academy of Management Review*, *Journal of Applied Psychology*, *Organizational Behavior and Human Decision Processes*, *Journal of Management*, *Business Horizons*, *Journal of Organizational Behavior*, *Decision Sciences*, and *Financial Times Mastering Management Journal*.

Dr. Bateman's current consulting and research centers on entrepreneurs in the United States, Central Europe, and Southeast Asia; intrinsic motivation; and the successful pursuit of long-term work goals.

He works closely with companies that include Nokia, Singapore Airlines, Quintiles, and USPS.

Scott A. Snell

Scott A. Snell is Professor of Human Resource Studies in the School of Industrial and Labor Relations at Cornell University. He received a B.A. in Psychology from Miami University, as well as M.B.A. and Ph.D. degrees in Business Administration from Michigan State University. Dr. Snell has taught courses in human resource management and strategic management to undergraduates, graduates, and executives. He is actively involved in executive education and has conducted international programs in Europe and Asia as well as Australia and New Zealand.

Professor Snell has worked with companies such as AT&T, GE, IBM, Merck, and Shell to address the alignment of human resource systems with strategic initiatives such as globalization, technological change, and knowledge management. His research and teaching interests center on how leading companies manage their people to gain competitive advantage. This work focuses on the development and deployment of intellectual capital as a foundation of an organization's core competencies.

Dr. Snell's research has been published in a number of professional journals, including the *Academy of Management Journal*, *Academy of Management Review*, *Human Resource Management*, *Human Resource Management Review*, *Industrial Relations*, *Journal of Business Research*, *Journal of Management*, *Journal of Managerial Issues*, *Journal of Management Studies*, *Organizational Dynamics*, *Organization Studies*, *Personnel Psychology*, and *Strategic Management Journal*. He is also coauthor of *Managing Human Resources*. In addition, Dr. Snell has served on the editorial boards of *Journal of Managerial Issues*, *Digest of Management Research*, *Human Resource Management*, *Human Resource Management Review*, *Human Resource Planning*, and *Academy of Management Journal*.

Preface

The "new economy" has finally arrived. Corporate America deserves great credit for bringing prosperity to the United States and much of the rest of the world. During these last few years, which have been marked by tremendous advances in technology and globalization, some businesspeople "got it" and realized their wildest dreams, while other old-economy types didn't get it and were left behind.

No, wait: That was the turn of the century, just a few short years ago. As we write this, things are very different. The tech bubble burst and the economy slowed all over the world. Many high-flying companies went bust. Some top executives were embarrassed, arrested, and indicted and are facing jail terms. People don't just mistrust big business—they are outraged, and reforms have begun. But while many new-economy companies failed, companies that symbolize the old economy survived and appear to be the key to turning around the global recession.

Business environments, like pendulums, swing from one extreme to another. By the time you read this, some things will have changed again. These changes will contribute to the fall of some currently successful companies and managers and the rise of others who currently struggle or are now just dreaming of new business ideas.

For you, as a businessperson as in life, uncertainty will be a constant state of affairs. That is, no one knows for certain what will happen, or what to do in pursuit of a successful future. Luck and the right circumstances can help companies (and people) succeed in the short run. But in the long run good management is essential.

Fortunately, you have access to current knowledge about how to manage. We have learned a lot from the people and companies that have succeeded and failed. The continuing experiment created by the vast array of management practices that exist in the business world, combined with sound research that helps tease out what works from what doesn't, helps us to both learn from mistakes and identify the most important lessons and useful practices that managers can employ. We hope that you will not only learn as much as you can about this vital activity but also commit to applying it—by reading and learning, and also by using it in the best possible ways.

Good managers not only cope with change but thrive on change while applying the known fundamentals of good business practice. The following chapters will help you understand what is happening as the business world changes and will give you some reality-based "anchors" that remain constant despite change. These anchors will give you perspectives and ideas that we hope will always be useful. Some of those anchors are techniques for how to assess changing circumstances before making decisions and taking action. Others are essential practices that are important in any situation.

This book and the course you are taking will help you face the managerial challenges of a changing world. In doing so, they will help you identify what's important and what's not, make good decisions, and take effective action on behalf of yourself, your colleagues, and the organizations for which you work.

Our Goals

Our mission with this text hasn't changed from that of our previous editions: to inform, instruct, and inspire. We hope to *inform* by providing descriptions of the important concepts and practices of modern management. We hope to *instruct* by describing how you can take action on the ideas discussed. We hope to *inspire* not only by writing in a positive, interesting, and optimistic way but also by providing a real sense of the unlimited opportunities ahead of you. Whether your goal is starting your own company, leading a team to greatness, building a strong organization, delighting your customers, or generally forging a positive future, we want to inspire you to take positive actions.

We hope to inspire you to be both a thinker and a doer. We want you to think about the issues, think about the impact of your actions, think before you act. But being a good thinker is not enough; you also must be a doer. Management is a world of action. It is a world that requires timely and appropriate action. It is a world not for the passive but for those who commit to positive accomplishments.

Keep applying the ideas you learn in this course, read about management in sources outside of this course, and certainly keep learning about management after you leave school and continue your career. Make no mistake about it, learning about management is a personal voyage that will last years, an entire career, your entire lifetime.

Competitive Advantage

Today's world is competitive. Never before has the world of work been so challenging. Never before has it been so imperative to your career that you learn the skills of management. Never before have people had so many opportunities with so many potential rewards.

You will compete with other people for jobs, resources, and promotions. Your organization will compete with other firms for contracts, clients, and customers. To survive the competition, and to thrive, you must perform in ways that give you an edge over your competitors, that make the other party want to hire you, buy from you, and do repeat business with you. You will want them to choose you, not your competitor.

To survive and thrive, today's managers have to think and act strategically. Today's customers are well educated, aware of their options, and demanding of excellence. For this reason, managers today must think constantly about how to build a capable workforce and manage in a way that delivers the goods and services that provide the best possible value to the customer.

By this standard, managers and organizations must perform. Four essential types of performance, on which the organization beats, equals, or loses to the competition, are *cost, quality, speed,* and *innovation.* These four performance dimensions, when done well, deliver value to the customer and competitive advantage to you and your organization. We will elaborate on all these topics throughout the book.

Good managers find ways to make their organizations successful. The way to do this is to build competitive advantage in the forms of cost competitiveness, quality, speed, and innovation. Because of the importance of the four sources of competitive advantage—which really are goals that every manager should constantly try to achieve and improve on—we refer to them frequently throughout the book. The idea is to keep you focused on a type of "bottom line," to make sure you think continually about "delivering the goods" that make both the manager (you) and the organization a competitive success.

Results Orientation

An important theme of this book, then, is how to manage in ways that deliver *results*—results that customers want. When you deliver high-quality, innovative products, quickly, and at a competitive price, you are achieving the results that can give you the competitive edge. And keep in mind, these are the same results that your competitors strive for as they try to gain an edge over you.

This approach makes this book unique among management texts. Rather than offering only concepts and processes, which nonetheless are integral parts of this text, we have a clear results orientation that is essential to success. The concepts and processes are means to an end, the ways by which you can achieve the results you need.

The New Competitive Landscape

The subtitle of the book refers to the fact that managers must develop and sustain competitive advantage, and real results, in a time when the business world has been rocked by new developments. The Internet, globalization, the bursting of the tech bubble, recent business scandals, knowledge management, the need to collaborate across organizational boundaries, and other changes in the business environment and business practice dramatically cast doubt on the relevance of the "old ways" of managing. In 2000, people were saying that the old economy was gone, giving way to a new economy in which a new game is played under very different rules.

But by 2001, the dot-com shakeout and economic slowdown had people saying that the old rules—including the need for profits!—are as vital as ever. Perhaps there is no distinction between the old economy and the new. Nonetheless, the context has changed, drastically. Our goal is to teach managers and aspiring managers how to compete successfully in the new era.

Topical Currency

It goes without saying that this textbook, in its sixth edition, remains on the cutting edge of topical coverage, as updated via both current business examples and recent management research. Chapters have been thoroughly updated, and students are exposed to a broad array of important current topics.

We have done our very best to draw from a wide variety of subject matter, sources, and personal experiences.

A Team Effort

This book is the product of a fantastic McGraw-Hill/Irwin team. Moreover, we wrote this book believing that we would form a team with the course instructor and with students. The entire team is responsible for the learning process.

Our goal, and that of your instructor, is to create a positive learning environment in which you can excel. But in the end, the raw material of this course is just words. It is up to you to use them as a basis for further thinking, deep learning, and constructive action.

What you do with the things you learn from this course, and with the opportunities the future holds, *counts.* As a manager, you can make a dramatic difference for yourself and for other people. What managers do matters, *tremendously.*

Outstanding Pedagogy

Management: The New Competitive Landscape is pedagogically stimulating and is intended to maximize student learning. With this in mind, we used a wide array of pedagogical features—some tried and true, others new and novel:

- Learning Objectives, which open each chapter, identify what students will learn by reading and studying the chapter.

- Opening quotes provide a thought-provoking preview of chapter material. The quotes are from people like Peter Drucker (on management), Jack Welch (on strategy), Henry David Thoreau (on ethics), Julius Caesar (on leadership), and Charles Kettering (on change and the future).

- Setting the Stage describes actual organizational situations and provides rich introductory examples of the chapter topics. Setting the Stage is placed before the text material as a practical application.

- Boxed inserts describing current examples and controversial issues are found throughout the text.

- "From the Pages of *Business Week*" highlights recent *Business Week* articles.

- Icons representing the four running themes of the book—cost, quality, speed, and innovation—are placed at appropriate points in the text to indicate an extended example, best practice, or issue for discussion. The icons continually reinforce and enhance the learning of these important results-oriented themes.

End-of-Chapter Elements

- Key terms are page-referenced to the text and are part of the vocabulary-building emphasis. These terms are defined in the glossary at the end of the book.

- A Summary of Learning Objectives provides clear, concise responses to the learning objectives, giving students a quick reference for reviewing the important concepts in the chapter.

- Discussion Questions, which follow the Summary of Learning Objectives, are thought-provoking questions that test a student's mastery of concepts covered in the chapter and ask for opinions on controversial issues.

- Concluding Cases provide a focus for class discussion.

- Two Experiential Exercises are included in each chapter. Most of them are group-based, and some involve outside research.

End-of-Part Elements

- An Integrating Case appears at the end of each of the five parts of the book.

- Two short Case Incidents also focus on managerial problems that include issues from multiple chapters and are a stimulating arena for discussion.

- Part One has an in-basket exercise, which we believe is an excellent exercise for early in the course.

Comprehensive Supplements

For the Student

- **Interactive-Student CD-ROM**—*Free* with the purchase of a new textbook. The Student CD-ROM contains interactivities, self-assessment exercises, chapter quizzes, and links for students to go above and beyond the boundaries of the printed textbook. The "Build Your Management Skills" area of the CD utilizes Flash technology along with detailed feedback to bring exercises and concepts to life in 3-D.

- **Online Learning Center**—www.mhhe.com/bateman6e.

For the Instructor

- Instructor's Manual, prepared by Thomas Lloyd, Westmoreland County Community College, contains chapter outlines, suggested discussion questions and answers for Setting the Stage, two lecturettes for each chapter, suggested answers to end-of-chapter Discussion Questions, suggested answers to the Concluding Case discussion questions, objectives and teaching tips for the Experiential Exercises, and discussion questions and suggested answers for Case Incidents and Integrating Cases.

- Test Bank, prepared by Amit Shah, Frostburg State University, contains approximately 100 questions for each chapter and consists of true/false, multiple-choice, fill-in, matching, and essay questions.

- PowerPoint Presentation software, developed by Michael Gordon of Rutgers University, presents an outline of the text with accompanying graphs and figures, along with additional material. Downloads of text tables and figures are housed on the Instructor CD-ROM. A self-contained viewer is packaged with each disk so that those who do not have the PowerPoint software can easily view the presentation.

- Videos are available for each chapter. Corresponding video cases and a guide that ties the videos closely to the chapter can be found in their respective areas of the Online Learning Center.

- Computerized Testing enables you to pick and choose questions and develop tests and quizzes quickly and easily on the computer. Available for Windows or Mac users.

Acknowledgments

This book could not have been written and published without the valuable contributions of many individuals.

Our reviewers over the last five editions contributed time, expertise, and terrific ideas that significantly enhanced the quality of the text. The reviewers of the sixth edition are:

Rathin Basu
Ferrum College

Anthony S. Marshall
Columbia College

James C. McElroy
Iowa State University

John W. Rogers
American International College

Christina Stamper
Western Michigan University

Our thanks to these members of our focus group:

Ray Aldag
University of Wisconsin—Madison

Shawn Carraher
Indiana University—NW Campus

Al Crispo
Purdue University

Marya Leatherwood
University of Illinois—Springfield

MarySue Love
Maryville University

Granger Macy
Texas A&M—Corpus Christi

Michael Vijuk
William Rainey Harper College

Ben Weeks
St. Xavier University

We also would like to thank those who reviewed for us in previous editions:

Debra A. Arvanites
Villanova University

Robert J. Ash
Rancho Santiago College

Charles A. Beasley
State University of New York—Buffalo

Hrach Bedrosian
New York University

Charles Blalack
Kilgore College

Mary A. Bouchard
Bristol Community College

Eugene L. Britt
Grossmont College

Barbara Boyington
Brookdale Community College

Lyvonne Burleson
Rollins College—Brevard

Diane Caggiano
Fitchburg State College

Elizabeth A. Cooper
University of Rhode Island

Anne C. Cowden
California State University—Sacramento

Ron Dibattista
Bryant College

Dale Dickson
Mesa State College

Michael W. Drafke
College of DuPage

J. F. Fairbank
Pennsylvania State University

Janice Felbauer
Austin Community College

David Foote
Middle Tennessee State University

Alan J. Fredian
Loyola University—Chicago

Steve Garlick
DeVry Institute—Kansas City

John Hall
University of Florida

Donald E. Harris
Oakton Community College

Carolyn Hatton
Cincinnati State Tech Community College

Frederic J. Hebert
East Carolina University

Durward Hofler
Northeastern Illinois University

Thomas O. James
Benedictine College

William Jedlicka
William Rainey Harper College

Elias Kalman
Baruch College

Gus. L. Kotoulas
Morton College

Augustine Lado
Cleveland State University

Catherine C. McElroy
Bucks County Community College

Jim McElroy
Iowa State University

David L. McLain
Virginia State University

Dot Moore
The Citadel

Joseph B. Mosca
Monmouth College

Randy Nichols
Oakland City University

Bert Nyman
Rockford College

James J. Ravelle
Moravian College

Joseph C. Santora
Essex County College

Marc Siegall
California State University—Chico

Fred Slack
Indiana University of Pennsylvania

Carl Sonntag
Pikes Peak Community College

Christina Stamper
University of North Carolina—Wilmington

Jim Wachspress
New Jersey Institute of Technology

Many individuals contributed directly to our development as textbook authors. Dennis Organ provided one of the authors with an initial opportunity and guidance in textbook writing. John Weimeister has been a friend and adviser from the very beginning. The entire McGraw-Hill/Irwin team demonstrated continued and generous support for this book. John Biernat was a great champion for the project and is a talented publisher and a good friend. Kurt Strand is, too. Christine Scheid is the consummate developmental editor, doing all with great skill and professionalism. And Lisa Nicks, Marketing Manager, you *rock*. What a team!

Finally, we thank our families. Our parents, Jeanine and Tom Bateman and Clara and John Snell, provided us with the foundation on which we have built our careers. They continue to be a source of great support. Our wives, Mary Jo and Marybeth, demonstrated great encouragement, insight, and understanding throughout the process. Our children, Lauren (who also helped with clerical work), T. J., and Jamie Bateman and Sara, Jack, and Emily Snell, are an inspiration for everything we do.

Thomas S. Bateman
Charlottesville, VA
Scott A. Snell
Ithaca, NY

Learning Features

An important theme of this text is how to manage in ways that deliver *results*—results that customers want; how to be a "thinker and doer"; how to know when, and if, to act. Bateman and Snell have put together a rich selection of learning features that highlight companies' ups and downs, stimulate learning and understanding, and challenge students to respond.

Learning Objectives

A chapter road map for your students—the Learning Objectives will tell them what they will know after completing the chapter.

CHAPTER 1

CHAPTER 1

Managing

Management means, in the last analysis, the substitution of thought for brown and muscle, of knowledge for folklore and tradition, and of cooperation for force.
—Peter Drucker

CHAPTER OUTLINE

Managing in the New Competitive Landscape
The Internet
Globalization
Knowledge Management
Collaboration across "Boundaries"
Managing for Competitive Advantage
Innovation
Quality
Speed
Cost Competitiveness
Delivering All Four
The Functions of Management
Planning: Delivering Strategic Value
Organizing: Building a Dynamic Organization
Leading: Mobilizing People
Controlling: Learning and Changing
Performing All Four Management Functions
Management Levels and Skills
Top-Level Managers
Middle-Level Managers
Frontline Managers
Working Leaders with Broad Responsibilities
Management Skills
You and Your Career
Be Both a Specialist and a Generalist
Be Self-Reliant
Be Connected
Actively Manage Your Relationship with Your Organization
Survive and Thrive

LEARNING OBJECTIVES

After studying Chapter 1, you will know:

1. The major challenges of managing in the new competitive landscape.

2. The drivers of competitive advantage for your company.

3. The functions of management and how they are evolving in today's business environment.

4. The nature of management at different organizational levels.

5. The skills you need to be an effective manager.

6. What to strive for as you manage your career.

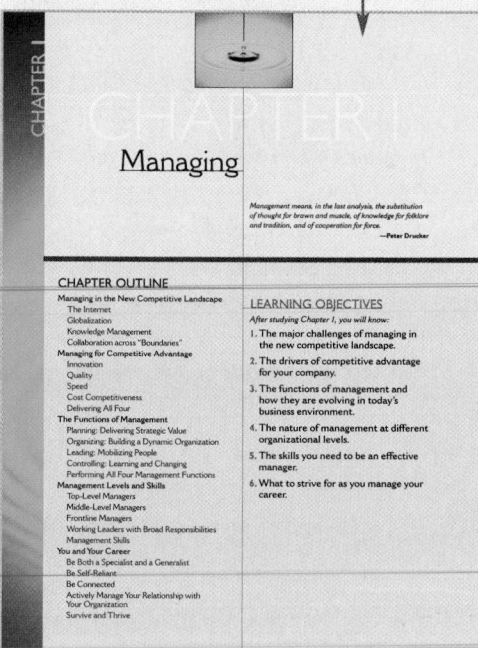

WHAT TO DO? FROM FAST ACTION TO INACTION

Sometimes managers are forced into action, and sometimes this occurs in tragic circumstances. When the World Trade Center was attacked, Merrill Lynch's offices were destroyed and three employees were killed. The firm had plans in place for potential crises such as power loss, loss of water, loss of a building, and loss of voice and data communications. It did not have a plan for all those problems occurring at once.

Management quickly set priorities: make sure people were all right; relocate 9,000 employees; put infrastructure in place; get the firm trading again. It was a tremendous challenge, and as Merrill executive Bob McCann put it, "We were calling audibles from the line of scrimmage. It didn't always go smoothly, but it worked" (p. 134). Amazingly, Merrill Lynch was trading when the U.S. market reopened on September 19.

Fortunately, most managerial decisions are not born of tragedy, and are not so frighteningly newsworthy. Here are a few recent examples of situations that you probably haven't heard about but that are important nonetheless. Consider what you would have done.

Imagine that you get a report that a folding chair that your company sells collapsed, and a customer strained a muscle. What would you do?

Or you manage a different company, one that sells smoke alarms, and a few customers tell you their alarms don't work properly. What actions would you take?

Or you learn that some removable seats on the jogging strollers you sell were not snapped onto the frame. Now what?

Or a hinge on a baby crib's drop gate is defective. What would you do?

In the last case, the Baby's Dream furniture company notified the Consumer Product Safety Commission (CPSC)—but not until nine injuries were reported—and the company was fined $200,000 for not reporting the defect promptly.

For the jogging strollers, Baby Trend's management acted decisively by contacting 120 Babies "R" Us stores, checking 2,250 strollers to make sure the snaps were fastened, and retrieving the strollers already sold.

The error in production seemed small to some, but Baby Trend acted decisively and responsibly.

For the smoke alarms, Harvey Grossblatt of Universal Security Instruments decided to collect more information, contacted an independent laboratory and the CPSC, and learned that neither could find a problem with the alarms. But whereas so many decision makers would consider the episode to be over, Grossblatt said, "Let's have an abundance of caution, and let's deal with it," and recalled 34,000 smoke alarms, at a cost of $150,000.

What about the folding chair incident? Peter Jenkins of Boston Warehouse Trading Corp. had no idea whether it was a freak accident or a flawed chair. He described it as very stressful, because he didn't know whether there really was a problem and didn't know what to do. Fortunately, he conducted tests in the company's warehouse, discovered a screw that was too small and weakened the chairs, notified the CPSC, and recalled 1,800 chairs. "I wouldn't want my mother sitting on [one]," he said.

This chapter is not about product recalls, or the CPSC, or ethics and social responsibility, which are discussed thoroughly in Chapter 5. It is about decision making, the most basic and constant managerial activity. The topics covered include decision making under crisis circumstances.

Setting the Stage

"Setting the Stage" Opening Vignette

For a description of actual organizations providing rich introductory examples, look to each chapter's "Setting the Stage."

In addition, as technology evolves, new industries, markets, and competitive niches develop. For example, the advent of computers created a huge industry. Early entrants in biotechnology are trying to establish dominant positions, while later entrants work on technological advances that will give them a competitive niche.

New technologies also provide new production techniques. In manufacturing, sophisticated robots perform jobs without suffering fatigue, requiring vacations or weekends off, or demanding wage increases. Until the U.S. steel industry began modernizing its plants, its productivity lagged far behind that of the technologically superior Japanese plants.

New technologies also provide new ways to manage and communicate. Computerized management information systems (MIS) make information available when needed. Computers monitor productivity and note performance deficiencies. Telecommunications allow conferences to take place without requiring people to travel to the same location. Consider the following discussion of changes in the field of retail sporting goods. As you can see, technological advances create innovations in business. Strategies developed around the cutting edge of technological advances create a competitive advantage; strategies that ignore or lag behind competitors in considering technology lead to obsolescence and extinction. This issue is so important that we devote an entire chapter (Chapter 17) to the topic.

FROM THE PAGES OF

BusinessWeek

Sports Gear Goes Geek

As Lance Armstrong tackles the French Alps, he's measuring his ascent with the help of an engineering marvel from Nike and the Japanese watchmaker Seiko: an altimeter built into a titanium-coated wristwatch. Armstrong's eyes are protected by sunglasses from Oakley that are precision molded to thousandths of an inch for aerodynamic efficiency and equipped with optical lenses so clear that a laser beam can pass through them without noticeable defraction. Under Armstrong's body floats a superstrong carbon fiber-epoxy bicycle frame built to cut the wind with teardrop-shaped tubing and weighing in at a pixiesque 2.27 pounds.

Mirroring changes in the manufacturing and aerospace industries over the past decade, cycling has experienced a rapid evolution from gut check to geek tech. Computerized engineering and materials science have influenced the design of everything from pedals, to shoes, to gear assemblies. In sports ranging from golf and tennis to sailing and softball, sports-equipment companies increasingly apply space-age techniques they once reserved for the pros to everyday products. It's all part of a mad scramble to win customers and improve margins in a sports-equipment market that totaled $65 billion in 2001 in the United States alone.

As computer power soared and prices sank, three dimensional (3-D) modeling quickly got cheap. A select group of sporting-goods companies took notice. Most were in areas where athletes rely heavily on technology, such as golf, cycling, tennis, and running. As they incorporated 3-D modeling into design and production, those firms found that they were able to tweak designs to unprecedented tolerances. "We're moving a nose piece a hundredth of an inch back and forth to make sure it looks the best. It's pretty obsessive," says Oakley's president, Colin Baden. The Foothill Ranch (California) company produces not only sunglasses but also wristwatches and apparel.

Computerized design also spawned a generation of machines that use digital coordinates to generate precision scale models in light-reactive plastics or wax, and those machines can receive commands from any place around the globe. Engineers could go from concept drawings to prototypes in hours, not days. Sporting-goods companies with serious design shops either own such a device or use one regularly. Oakley's Baden can input design parameters into his prototype machine in the morning, have resin sunglass models by noon, pop in premade lenses, and have mountain bikers and skiers test the models and provide feedback by 5 P.M. Nike's Boyd notes that this quick cycle is particularly important in sports where ergonomic factors are crucial to a product's sales potential.

"From the Pages of *Business Week*"

Current *Business Week* articles spotlight key issues in the text.

Up-to-Date Real-World Examples

Nothing brings material to life better than in-text examples featuring real companies, people, and situations. These examples permeate the text.

Publicly traded pharmaceutical firms, for example, face regulation both from the FDA and the SEC. When the FDA declined to review IMClone's application for approval of Erbitux, a new cancer-fighting drug, the firm's stock price plummeted and the SEC opened an investigation into whether the firm misled investors and was involved in insider trading. Bristol-Myers Squibb, which had invested $2 billion for a 20 percent stake in IM-Clone Systems, lost $875 million and faced separate SEC investigation into its accounting practices.

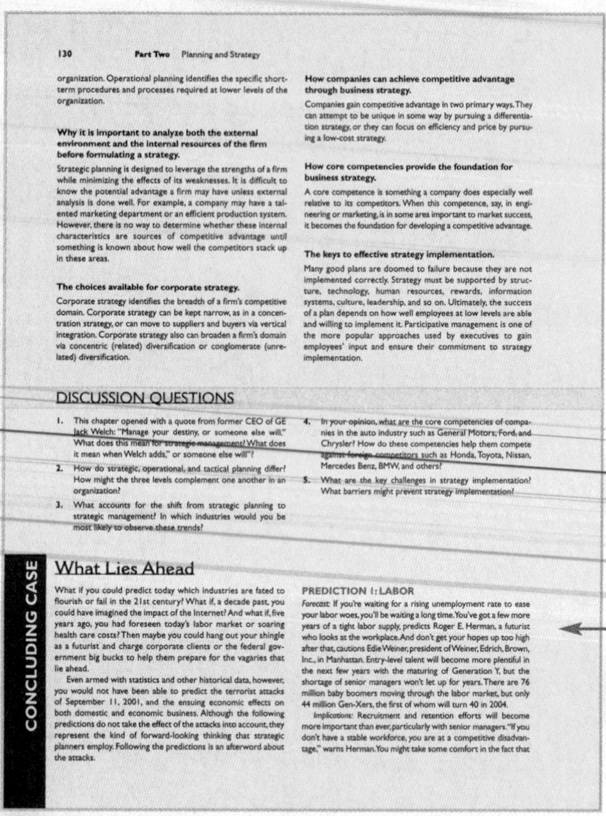

130 **Part Two** Planning and Strategy

organization. Operational planning identifies the specific short-term procedures and processes required at lower levels of the organization.

Why it is important to analyze both the external environment and the internal resources of the firm before formulating a strategy.

Strategic planning is designed to leverage the strengths of a firm while minimizing the effects of its weaknesses. It is difficult to know the potential advantage a firm may have unless external analysis is done well. For example, a company may have a talented marketing department or an efficient production system. However, there is no way to determine whether these internal characteristics are sources of competitive advantage until something is known about how well the competitors stack up in these areas.

The choices available for corporate strategy.

Corporate strategy identifies the breadth of a firm's competitive domain. Corporate strategy can be kept narrow, as in a concentration strategy, or can move to suppliers and buyers via vertical integration. Corporate strategy also can broaden a firm's domain via concentric (related) diversification or conglomerate (unrelated) diversification.

How companies can achieve competitive advantage through business strategy.

Companies gain competitive advantage in two primary ways. They can attempt to be unique in some way by pursuing a differentiation strategy, or they can focus on efficiency and price by pursuing a low-cost strategy.

How core competencies provide the foundation for business strategy.

A core competence is something a company does especially well relative to its competitors. When this competence, say, in engineering or marketing, is in some area important to market success, it becomes the foundation for developing a competitive advantage.

The keys to effective strategy implementation.

Many good plans are doomed to failure because they are not implemented correctly. Strategy must be supported by structure, technology, human resources, rewards, information systems, culture, leadership, and so on. Ultimately, the success of a plan depends on how well employees at low levels are able and willing to implement it. Participative management is one of the more popular approaches used by executives to gain employees' input and ensure their commitment to strategy implementation.

DISCUSSION QUESTIONS

1. This chapter opened with a quote from former CEO of GE Jack Welch: "Manage your destiny, or someone else will." What does this mean for strategic management? What does it mean when Welch adds," or someone else will"?
2. How do strategic, operational, and tactical planning differ? How might the three levels complement one another in an organization?
3. What accounts for the shift from strategic planning to strategic management? In which industries would you be most likely to observe these trends?
4. In your opinion, what are the core competencies of companies in the auto industry such as General Motors, Ford, and Chrysler? How do these competencies help them compete against foreign competitors such as Honda, Toyota, Nissan, Mercedes Benz, BMW, and others?
5. What are the key challenges in strategy implementation? What barriers might prevent strategy implementation?

CONCLUDING CASE

What Lies Ahead

What if you could predict today which industries are fated to flourish or fail in the 21st century? What if, a decade past, you could have imagined the impact of the Internet? And what if, five years ago, you had foreseen today's labor market or soaring health care costs? Then maybe you could hang out your shingle as a futurist and charge corporate clients or the federal government big bucks to help them prepare for the vagaries that lie ahead.

Even armed with statistics and other historical data, however, you would not have been able to predict the terrorist attacks of September 11, 2001, and the ensuing economic effects on both domestic and economic business. Although the following predictions do not take the effect of the attacks into account, they represent the kind of forward-looking thinking that strategic planners employ. Following the predictions is an afterword about the attacks.

PREDICTION 1: LABOR

Forecast: If you're waiting for a rising unemployment rate to ease your labor woes, you'll be waiting a long time. You've got a few more years of a tight labor supply, predicts Roger E. Herman, a futurist who looks at the workplace. And don't get your hopes up too high after that, cautions Edie Weiner, president of Weiner, Edrich, Brown, Inc., in Manhattan. Entry-level talent will become more plentiful in the next few years with the maturing of Generation Y, but the shortage of senior managers won't let up for years. There are 76 million baby boomers moving through the labor market, but only 44 million Gen-Xers, the first of whom will turn 40 in 2004.

Implications: Recruitment and retention efforts will become more important than ever, particularly with senior managers. "If you don't have a stable workforce, you are at a competitive disadvantage," warns Herman. You might take some comfort in the fact that

Concluding Case

Another relevant real-world company to wrap up the chapter and provide focus for class discussion.

Summary of Learning Objectives and End-of-Chapter Material

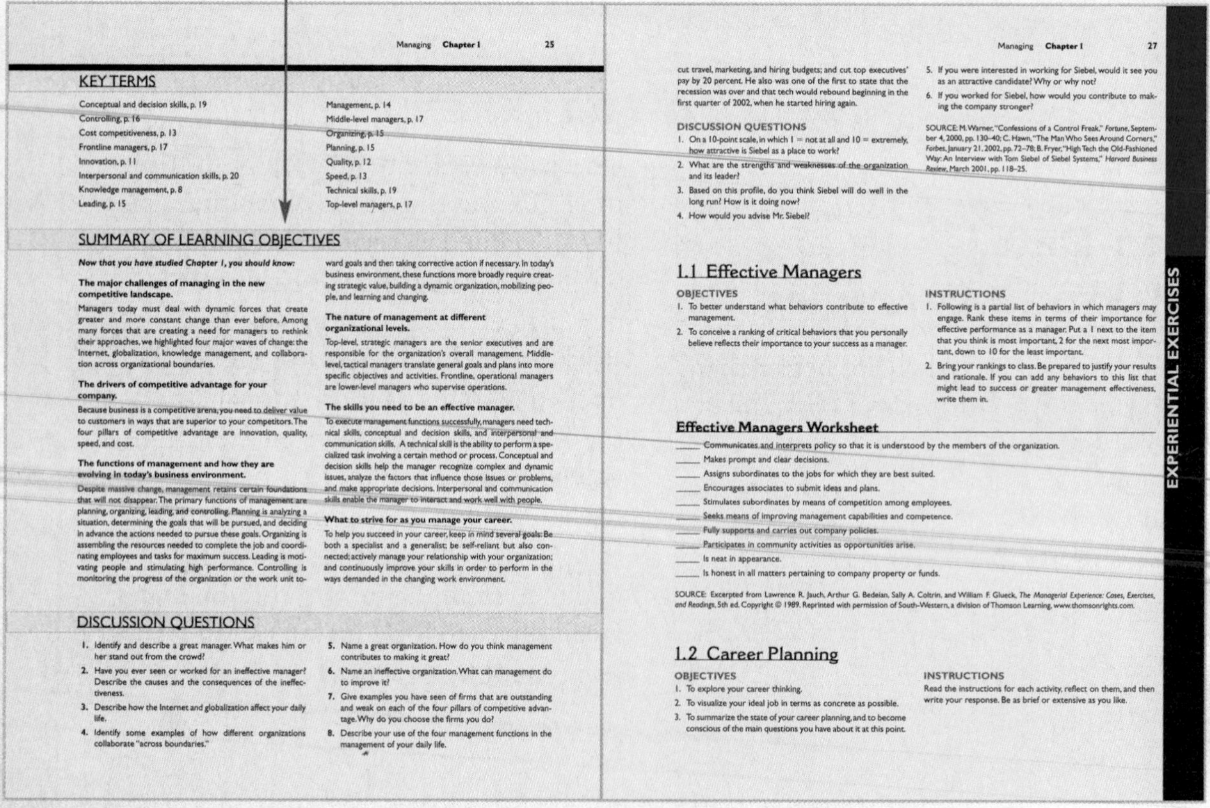

Managing **Chapter 1** 25

KEY TERMS

Conceptual and decision skills, p. 19
Controlling, p. 16
Cost competitiveness, p. 13
Frontline managers, p. 17
Innovation, p. 11
Interpersonal and communication skills, p. 20
Knowledge management, p. 8
Leading, p. 15
Management, p. 14
Middle-level managers, p. 17
Organizing, p. 15
Planning, p. 15
Quality, p. 12
Speed, p. 13
Technical skills, p. 19
Top-level managers, p. 17

SUMMARY OF LEARNING OBJECTIVES

Now that you have studied Chapter 1, you should know:

The major challenges of managing in the new competitive landscape.

Managers today must deal with dynamic forces that create greater and more constant change than ever before. Among many forces that are creating a need for managers to rethink their approaches, we highlighted four major waves of change: the Internet, globalization, knowledge management, and collaboration across organizational boundaries.

The drivers of competitive advantage for your company.

Because business is a competitive arena, you need to deliver value to customers in ways that are superior to your competitors. The four pillars of competitive advantage are innovation, quality, speed, and cost.

The functions of management and how they are evolving in today's business environment.

Despite massive change, management retains certain foundations that will not disappear. The primary functions of management are planning, organizing, leading, and controlling. Planning is analyzing a situation, determining the goals that will be pursued, and deciding in advance the actions needed to pursue these goals. Organizing is assembling the resources needed to complete the job and coordinating employees and tasks for maximum success. Leading is motivating people and stimulating high performance. Controlling is monitoring the progress of the organization or the work unit toward goals and then taking corrective action if necessary. In today's business environment, these functions more broadly require creating strategic value, building a dynamic organization, mobilizing people, and learning and changing.

The nature of management at different organizational levels.

Top-level, strategic managers are the senior executives and are responsible for the organization's overall management. Middle-level, tactical managers translate general goals and plans into more specific objectives and activities. Frontline, operational managers are lower-level managers who supervise operations.

The skills you need to be an effective manager.

To execute management functions successfully, managers need technical skills, conceptual and decision skills, and interpersonal and communication skills. A technical skill is the ability to perform a specialized task involving a certain method or process. Conceptual and decision skills help the manager recognize complex and dynamic issues, analyze the factors that influence those issues or problems, and make appropriate decisions. Interpersonal and communication skills enable the manager to interact and work well with people.

What to strive for as you manage your career.

To help you succeed in your career, keep in mind several goals: Be both a specialist and a generalist; be self-reliant but also connected; actively manage your relationship with your organization; and continuously improve your skills in order to perform in the ways demanded in the changing work environment.

DISCUSSION QUESTIONS

1. Identify and describe a great manager. What makes him or her stand out from the crowd?
2. Have you ever seen or worked for an ineffective manager? Describe the causes and the consequences of the ineffectiveness.
3. Describe how the Internet and globalization affect your daily life.
4. Identify some examples of how different organizations collaborate "across boundaries."
5. Name a great organization. How do you think management contributes to making it great?
6. Name an ineffective organization. What can management do to improve it?
7. Give examples you have seen of firms that are outstanding and weak on each of the four pillars of competitive advantage. Why do you choose the firms you do?
8. Describe your use of the four management functions in the management of your daily life.

Managing **Chapter 1** 27

cut travel, marketing, and hiring budgets; and cut top executives' pay by 20 percent. He also was one of the first to state that the recession was over and that tech would rebound beginning in the first quarter of 2002, when he started hiring again.

DISCUSSION QUESTIONS

1. On a 10-point scale, in which 1 = not at all and 10 = extremely, how attractive is Siebel as a place to work?
2. What are the strengths and weaknesses of the organization and its leader?
3. Based on this profile, do you think Siebel will do well in the long run? How is it doing now?
4. How would you advise Mr. Siebel?
5. If you were interested in working for Siebel, would it see you as an attractive candidate? Why or why not?
6. If you worked for Siebel, how would you contribute to making the company stronger?

SOURCE: M. Warner, "Confessions of a Control Freak," *Fortune*, September 4, 2000, pp. 130–40; C. Hawn, "The Man Who Sees Around Corners," *Forbes*, January 21, 2002, pp. 72–78; B. Fryer, "High Tech the Old-Fashioned Way: An Interview with Tom Siebel of Siebel Systems," *Harvard Business Review*, March 2001, pp. 118–25.

EXPERIENTIAL EXERCISES

1.1 Effective Managers

OBJECTIVES

1. To better understand what behaviors contribute to effective management.
2. To conceive a ranking of critical behaviors that you personally believe reflects their importance to your success as a manager.

INSTRUCTIONS

1. Following is a partial list of behaviors in which managers may engage. Rank these items in terms of their importance for effective performance as a manager. Put a 1 next to the item that you think is most important, 2 for the next most important, down to 10 for the least important.
2. Bring your rankings to class. Be prepared to justify your results and rationale. If you can add any behaviors to this list that might lead to success or greater management effectiveness, write them in.

Effective Managers Worksheet

____ Communicates and interprets policy so that it is understood by the members of the organization.
____ Makes prompt and clear decisions.
____ Assigns subordinates to the jobs for which they are best suited.
____ Encourages associates to submit ideas and plans.
____ Stimulates subordinates by means of competition among employees.
____ Seeks means of improving management capabilities and competence.
____ Fully supports and carries out company policies.
____ Participates in community activities as opportunities arise.
____ Is neat in appearance.
____ Is honest in all matters pertaining to company property or funds.

SOURCE: Excerpted from Lawrence R. Jauch, Arthur G. Bedeian, Sally A. Coltrin, and William F. Glueck, *The Managerial Experience: Cases, Exercises, and Readings*, 5th ed. Copyright © 1989. Reprinted with permission of South-Western, a division of Thomson Learning, www.thomsonrights.com.

1.2 Career Planning

OBJECTIVES

1. To explore your career thinking.
2. To visualize your ideal job in terms as concrete as possible.
3. To summarize the state of your career planning, and to become conscious of the main questions you have about it at this point.

INSTRUCTIONS

Read the instructions for each activity, reflect on them, and then write your response. Be as brief or extensive as you like.

enjoyed better client relations, a better service record, and a better reputation than other local agencies because of a reputation for high-quality service at a moderate cost to funding agencies. Recently, however, competitors have begun to overtake the Community Agency, resulting in declining contracts. John Cabot is expending every possible effort to keep his agency comfortably at the top.

Ron Smith, Director of the agency, reports directly to Cabot. He has held this position since he helped Cabot establish the agency 19 years ago.

Joan Sweet, Head of Client Services, reports to Smith. She has been with the agency 12 years, having worked before that for HEW as a contracting officer.

Tom Lynch, Head Community Liaison, reports to Joan Sweet. He came to the Community Agency at Sweet's request, having worked with Sweet previously at HEW.

Jane Cox, Head Case Worker, also works for Joan Sweet. Cox was promoted to this position two years ago. Prior to that time,

Jane had gone through a year's training program after receiving an MSW from a large urban university.

TODAY'S MEETING

John Cabot has called the meeting with these four managers in order to solve some problems that have developed in meeting service schedules and contract requirements. Cabot must catch a plane to Washington in half an hour; he has an appointment to negotiate a key contract that means a great deal to the future of the Community Agency. He has only 20 minutes to meet with his managers and still catch the plane. Cabot feels that getting the Washington contract is absolutely crucial to the future of the agency.

SOURCE: Judith R. Gordon, *A Diagnostic Approach to Organizational Behavior.* Copyright © 1983 Pearson Education, Inc. Reprinted by permission of Pearson Education, Inc., Upper Saddle River, NJ.

SSS Software In-Basket Exercise

One way to assess your own strengths and weaknesses in management skills is to engage in an actual managerial work experience. The following exercise gives you a realistic glimpse of the tasks faced regularly by practicing managers. Complete the exercise, and then compare your own decisions and actions with those of your classmates.

SSS Software designs and develops customized software for businesses. It also integrates this software with the customer's existing systems and provides system maintenance. SSS Software has customers in the following industries: airlines, automotive, finance/banking, health/hospital, consumer products, electronics, and government. The company has also begun to generate important international clients. These include the European-Airbus consortium and a consortium of banks and financial firms based in Kenya.

SSS Software has grown rapidly since its inception just over a decade ago. Its revenue, net income, and earnings per share have all been above the industry average for the past several years. However, competition in this technologically sophisticated field has grown very rapidly. Recently, it has become more difficult to compete for major contracts. Moreover, although SSS Software's revenue and net income continue to grow, the rate of growth declined during the last fiscal year.

SSS Software's 250 employees are divided into several operating divisions with employees at four levels: nonmanagement, technical/professional, managerial, and executive. Nonmanagement employees take care of the clerical and facilities support functions. The technical/professional staff perform the core technical work for the firm. Most managerial employees are group managers who supervise a team of technical/professional employees working on a project for a particular customer. Staff who work in specialized areas such as finance, accounting, human resources, nursing, and law are also considered managerial employees. The executive level includes the 12 highest-ranking employees at SSS Software. There is an organization chart in Figure A that illustrates SSS Software's structure. There is also an Employee Classification Report that lists the number of employees at each level of the organization.

In this exercise, you will play the role of Chris Perillo, Vice President of Operations for Health and Financial Services. You learned last Wednesday, October 13, that your predecessor,

Michael Grant, has resigned and gone to Universal Business Solutions, Inc. You were offered his former job, and you accepted it. Previously, you were the Group Manager for a team of 15 software developers assigned to work on the Airbus consortium project in the Airline Services Division. You spent all of Thursday and Friday and most of the weekend finishing up parts of the project, briefing your successor, and preparing for an interim report you will deliver in Paris on October 21.

It is now 7 A.M. Monday, and you are in your new office. You have arrived at work early so you can spend the next two hours reviewing material in your in-basket (including some memos and messages to Michael Grant), as well as your voice mail and email. Your daily planning book indicates that you have no appointments today or tomorrow but will have to catch a plane for Paris early Wednesday morning. You have a full schedule for the remainder of the week and all of next week.

ASSIGNMENT

During the next two hours, review all the material in your in-basket, as well as your voice mail and email. Take only two hours. Using the following response form as a model, indicate how you want to respond to each item (that is, via letter/memo, email, phone/voice mail, or personal meeting). If you decide not to respond to an item, check "no response" on the response form. All of your responses must be written on the response forms. Write your precise, detailed response (do not merely jot down a few notes). For example, you might draft a memo or write out a message that you will deliver via phone/voice mail. You may also decide to meet with an individual (or individuals) during the limited time available on your calendar today or tomorrow. If so, prepare an agenda for a personal meeting and list your goals for the meeting. As you read through the items, you may occasionally observe some information that you think is relevant and want to remember (or attend to in the future) but that you decide not to include in any of your responses to employees. Write down such information on a sheet of paper titled "note to self."

SOURCE: D. Whetten and K. Cameron, *Developing Management Skills,* 3rd ed. (New York: Harper Collins, 1995).

Integrated Case

Appearing at the end of each part, these cases focus on managerial problems and are a stimulating arena for discussion.

Flexible Appendices

So that professors have flexibility in structuring their course, we offer seven topical appendices such as "Managing in Our Natural Environment," "Information for Entrepreneurs," and "Operations Management in the New Economy."

The Evolution of Management

For thousands of years, managers have wrestled with the same issues and problems confronting executives today. Around 1100 B.C., the Chinese practiced the four management functions—planning, organizing, leading, and controlling—discussed in Chapter 1. Between 350 and 400 B.C., the Greeks recognized management as a separate art and advocated a scientific approach to work. The Romans decentralized the management of their vast empire before the birth of Christ. During medieval times, the Venetians standardized production through the use of an assembly line, building warehouses and using an inventory system to monitor the contents.[1]

But throughout history most managers operated strictly on a trial-and-error basis. The challenges of the industrial revolution changed that. Management emerged as a formal discipline at the turn of the century. The first university programs to offer management and business education, the Wharton School at the University of Pennsylvania and the Amos Tuck School at Dartmouth, were founded in the late 19th century. By 1914, 25 business schools existed.[2]

Thus, the management profession as we know it today is relatively new. This appendix explores the roots of modern management theory. Understanding the origins of management thought will help you grasp the underlying contexts of the ideas and concepts presented in the chapters ahead.

Although this appendix is titled "The Evolution of Management," it might be more appropriately called "The Revolutions of Management," because it documents the wide swing in management approaches over the last 100 years. Out of the great variety of ideas about how to improve management, parts of each approach have survived and been incorporated into modern perspectives on management. Thus, the legacy of past efforts, triumphs, and failures has become our guide to future management practice.

EARLY MANAGEMENT CONCEPTS AND INFLUENCES

Communication and transportation constraints hindered the growth of earlier businesses. Therefore, improvements in management techniques did not substantially improve performance. However, the industrial revolution changed that. As companies grew and became more complex, minor improvements in management tactics produced impressive increases in production quantity and quality.[3]

The emergence of *economies of scale*—reductions in the average cost of a unit of production as the total volume produced

increases—drove managers to strive for further growth. The opportunities for mass production created by the industrial revolution spawned intense and systematic thought about management problems and issues—particularly efficiency, production processes, and cost savings.[4]

Figure A.1 provides a timeline depicting the evolution of management thought through the decades. This historical perspective is divided into two major sections: classical approaches and contemporary approaches. Many of these approaches developed simultaneously, and they often had a significant impact on one another. Some approaches were a direct reaction to the perceived deficiencies of previous approaches. Others developed as the approaches attempted to explain the real issues facing managers and provide them with tools to solve future problems.

Figure A.1 will reinforce your understanding of the key relationships among the approaches and place each perspective in its historical context.

CLASSICAL APPROACHES

The classical period extended from the mid-19th century through the early 1950s. The major approaches that emerged during this period were systematic management, scientific management, administrative management, human relations, and bureaucracy.

Systematic Management During the 19th century, growth in U.S. business centered on manufacturing.[5] Early writers such as Adam Smith believed that the management of these firms was chaotic, and their ideas helped to systematize it. Most organizational tasks were subdivided and performed by specialized labor. However, poor coordination among subordinates and different levels of management caused frequent problems and breakdowns of the manufacturing process.

The systematic management approach attempted to build specific procedures and processes into operations to ensure coordination of effort. Systematic management emphasized economical operations, adequate staffing, maintenance of inventories to meet consumer demand, and organizational control. These goals were achieved through:

- Careful definition of duties and responsibilities.
- Standardized techniques for performing these duties.

30

Instructor Supplements

Bateman/Snell also features some exciting and useful supplements for instructors and students.

Instructor's Resource Guide

Located on our instructor's CD-ROM, the Instructor's Manual is a creative guide to understanding management, offering many elements such as chapter outlines, suggested discussion questions, two lecturettes per chapter, and objectives and teaching tips. Professors will have a vast assortment of possibilities for enhancing their classes.

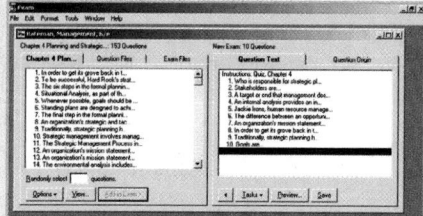

Test Bank
Computerized Test Bank

Located on our instructor's CD-ROM,

The Test Bank contains approximately 1,800 questions, with a mix of true/false, multiple-choice, and essay questions. Multiple-choice questions are ranked (easy, medium, or hard) to help the instructor provide the proper mix of questions.

Instructor's Presentation CD-ROM

ISBN 007-253872-4

This CD-ROM allows professors to easily create their own custom presentation. They can pull from resources on the CD, like the Instructor's Manual, the Test Bank, figures downloaded from the text, videos, and PowerPoint, or from their own PowerPoint slides or Web screen shots.

Instructor Supplements

PageOut

McGraw-Hill's unique point-and-click course website tool enables users to create a full-features, professional-quality course website without knowing HTML coding. With PageOut you can post your syllabus online, assign McGraw-Hill Online Learning Center or eBook content, add links to important off-site resources, and maintain student results in the online grade book. You can send class announcements, copy your course site to share with colleagues, and upload original files. PageOut is free for every McGraw-Hill/Irwin user, and, if you're short on time, we even have a team ready to help you create your site.

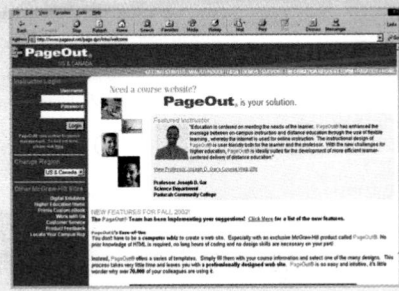

Primis Online

You can customize this text by using McGraw-Hill's Primis Online digital database. This feature offers you the flexibility to customize your course to include material from the largest online collection of textbooks, readings, and cases. Primis leads the way in customized eBooks with hundreds of titles available at prices that save your students over 20 percent from bookstore prices. Additional information is available at 800-228-0634.

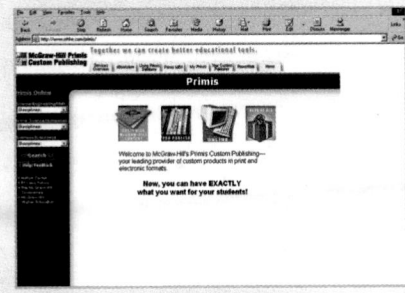

Instructor Supplements

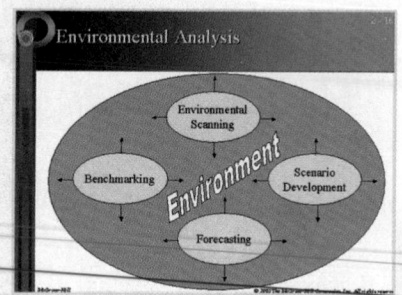

PowerPoint®

Located on our Instructor's CD-ROM, the PowerPoint presentation features approximately 20 slides per chapter for use in the classroom.

Videos

ISBN 007-253867-8

A combination of NBC file footage and PBS selections, along with our newly developed Skills videos, offers instructors the opportunity to highlight such topics as Negotiating, Conflict Management, Self-Management/ Etiquette-Diversity, Listening, and Teamwork—all for situational analysis in the classroom.

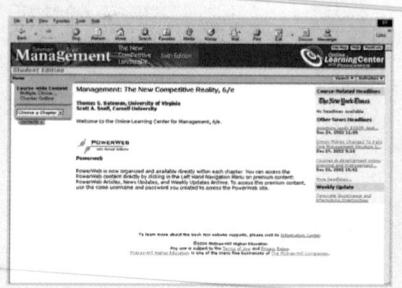

Online Learning Center

www.mhhe.com/bateman6e

The Online Learning Center (OLC) is a website that follows the text chapter by chapter, with additional materials and quizzing that enhance the text and/or classroom experience. As students read the book, they can go online to take self-grading quizzes, review material, or work through interactive exercises. OLCs can be delivered in multiple ways—professors and students can access them directly through the textbook website, through PageOut, or within a course management system (e.g., WebCT, Blackboard, TopClass, or eCollege).

Student Supplements

Student CD-ROM

All NEW copies of this text are packaged with a special Student CD-ROM. This added-value feature includes:

- Interactive modules that encourage hands-on learning about such topics as Motivation, Leadership, and Organizational Communication

- Chapter outlines

- Interactive chapter quizzes

- Videos of real-world companies

- Exercises and quizzes to enhance videos

- A special link to Bateman/Snell's Online Learning Center

McGraw-Hill's PowerWeb

Harness the assets of the Web by keeping current with PowerWeb! This online resource provides high-quality, peer-reviewed content, including up-to-date articles from leading periodical sand journals, current news, weekly updates, interactive exercises, Web research guide, study tips, and much more!
http://www.dushkin.com/powerweb

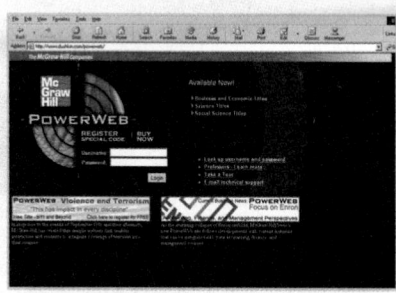

Contents in Brief

Part One

Foundations of Management 2

1 Managing 4

Appendix A: The Evolution of Management 28

2 The External Environment 40

3 Managerial Decision Making 64

Part Two

Planning and Strategy 104

4 Planning and Strategic Management 106

5 Ethics and Corporate Responsibility 136

Appendix B: The Caux Round Table Business Principles of Ethics 164

Appendix C: Managing in Our Natural Environment 166

6 International Management 176

7 New Ventures 210

Appendix D: Information for Entrepreneurs 238

Part Three

Organizing: Building a Dynamic Organization 240

8 Organization Structure 242

9 The Responsive Organization 272

10 Human Resource Management 298

11 Managing the Diverse Workforce 328

Part Four

Leading 362

12 Leadership 364

Appendix E: Classic Contingency Models of Leadership 394

13 Motivating for Performance 396

14 Managing Teams 424

15 Communicating 450

Part Five

Controlling: Learning and Changing 486

16 Managerial Control 488

17 Managing Technology and Innovation 518

Appendix F: Operations Management in the New Economy 543

18 Creating and Managing Change 552

Glossary G-1

Notes N-1

Photo Credits P-1

Name Index I-1

Subject Index I-11

Contents

Part One
Foundations of Management 2

Chapter 1
Managing 4

SETTING THE STAGE: Sometimes You Get It,
Sometimes You Don't 5

Managing in the New Competitive Landscape 6
  The Internet 6
  Globalization 6
  Knowledge Management 8
  Collaboration across "Boundaries" 9
Managing for Competitive Advantage 11
  Innovation 11
  Quality 12
  Speed 13
  Cost Competitiveness 13
  Delivering All Four 14
The Functions of Management 14
  Planning: Delivering Strategic Value 15
  Organizing: Building a Dynamic Organization 15
  Leading: Mobilizing People 15
  Controlling: Learning and Changing 16
  Performing All Four Management Functions 16
Management Levels and Skills 17
  Top-Level Managers 17
  Middle-Level Managers 17
  Frontline Managers 17
  Working Leaders with Broad Responsibilities 18
  Management Skills 19
You and Your Career 21
  Be Both a Specialist and a Generalist 21
  Be Self-Reliant 21
  Be Connected 21
  Actively Manage Your Relationship with Your Organization 22
  Survive and Thrive 23
Key Terms 25
Summary of Learning Objectives 25
Discussion Questions 25

CONCLUDING CASE: Would You Work Here? 26
EXPERIENTIAL EXERCISES 27

Appendix A: The Evolution of Management 28

Chapter 2
The External Environment 40

SETTING THE STAGE: Telecoms Face External
Pressures 41
  A Look Ahead 42
The Macroenvironment 43
  Law and Regulations 43
  The Economy 44
  Technology 44
  Demographics 46
  Social Issues and the Natural Environment 47
The Competitive Environment 48
  Competitors 48
  Threat of New Entrants 49
  Threat of Substitutes 49
  Suppliers 50
  Customers 52
Environmental Analysis 53
  Environmental Scanning 53
  Scenario Development 54
  Forecasting 54
  Benchmarking 56
Responding to the Environment 56
  Adapting to the Environment: Changing Yourself 56
  Influencing Your Environment 58
  Changing the Environment You Are In 60
Choosing a Response Approach 61
Key Terms 61
Summary of Learning Objectives 61
Discussion Questions 62
CONCLUDING CASE: Many New Airlines Will
Never Grow Old 62

Chapter 3

Managerial Decision Making   64

SETTING THE STAGE: What to Do? From Fast
Action to Inaction   65
Characteristics of Managerial Decisions   66
   Lack of Structure   66
   Uncertainty and Risk   68
   Conflict   69
The Stages of Decision Making   70
   Identifying and Diagnosing the Problem   70
   Generating Alternative Solutions   71
   Evaluating Alternatives   72
   Making the Choice   73
   Implementing the Decision   73
   Evaluating the Decision   74
The Best Decision   74
Barriers to Effective Decision Making   75
   Psychological Biases   75
   Time Pressures   77
   Social Realities   78
Decision Making in Groups   78

   Potential Advantages of Using a Group   78
   Potential Problems of Using a Group   79
Managing Group Decision Making   80
   Leadership Style   80
   Constructive Conflict   80
   Encouraging Creativity   81
Organizational Decision Making   82
   Constraints on Decision Makers   83
   Models of Organizational Decision Processes   84
   Negotiations and Politics   84
   Decision Making in a Crisis   85
   Emergent Strategies   87
Key Terms   88
Summary of Learning Objectives   89
Discussion Questions   89
CONCLUDING CASE: Trying to Move on
after a Crisis   90
EXPERIENTIAL EXERCISES   91
INTEGRATING CASE: SSS Software In-Basket
Exercise   93
CRITICAL INCIDENTS   103

Part Two
Planning and Strategy   104

Chapter 4

Planning and Strategic
Management   106

SETTING THE STAGE: Getting into the Groove at
Hard Rock Café   107
An Overview of Planning Fundamentals   108
   The Basic Planning Process   108
Levels of Planning   111
   Strategic Planning   112
   Tactical and Operational Planning   112
   Linking Tactical, Operational, and Strategic Planning   113
Strategic Planning   115
   Step 1: Establishment of Mission, Vision, and Goals   116
   Step 2: Analysis of External Opportunities and Threats   117
   Step 3: Analysis of Internal Strengths and Weaknesses   120
   Step 4: SWOT Analysis and Strategy Formulation   122
   Step 5: Strategy Implementation   127
   Step 6: Strategic Control   128
Key Terms   129

Summary of Learning Objectives   129
Discussion Questions   130
CONCLUDING CASE: What Lies Ahead   130
EXPERIENTIAL EXERCISES   132

Chapter 5

Ethics and Corporate
Responsibility   136

SETTING THE STAGE: Corporate America:
How's It Doing?   137
Ethics   138
   Ethical Systems   138
   Business Ethics   140
   The Ethics Environment   142
   Ethical Decision Making   146
Corporate Social Responsibility   147
   Contrasting Views   147
   Reconciliation   149
   Corporate Social Responsiveness   150

The Political Environment 152
   Competitive Advantage 152
   Corporate Legitimacy 152
   Strategies for Influencing the Political Environment 153
The Natural Environment 155
   A Risk Society 155
   Ecocentric Management 156
   Environmental Agenda for the Future 157
Key Terms 157
Summary of Learning Objectives 158
Discussion Questions 158
CONCLUDING CASE: Nike Controversies 159
EXPERIENTIAL EXERCISES 160

Appendix B: The Caux Round Table Business Principles of Ethics 164

Appendix C: Managing in Our Natural Environment 166

Chapter 6

International Management 176

SETTING THE STAGE: A Bumpy Ride at DaimlerChrysler 177
The Global Environment 179
   European Unification 179
   The Pacific Rim 180
   North America 181
   The Rest of the World 181
Consequences of a Global Economy 182
Global Strategy 188
   Pressures for Global Integration 188
   Pressures for Local Responsiveness 189
   Choosing a Global Strategy 189
Entry Mode 194
   Exporting 195
   Licensing 195
   Franchising 195
   Joint Ventures 196
   Wholly Owned Subsidiaries 196

Management across Borders 197
   Skills of the Global Manager 197
   Understanding Cultural Issues 200
   Ethical Issues in International Management 203
Key Terms 205
Summary of Learning Objectives 206
Discussion Questions 206
CONCLUDING CASE: Wal-Mart and Megastore Wars in Mexico 207
EXPERIENTIAL EXERCISES 207

Chapter 7

New Ventures 210

SETTING THE STAGE: Humble Beginnings and Top Honors 211
Independent Entrepreneurs 214
   Why Become an Independent Entrepreneur? 214
   The Role of the Economic Environment 214
   What Business Should You Start? 216
   What Does It Take to Be Successful? 219
   Planning 222
   Entrepreneurial Hazards 225
   Global Start-Ups 228
Intrapreneurship 228
   Building Support for Your Idea 228
   Building Intrapreneurship 230
   Organizing New Corporate Ventures 230
   Hazards in Intrapreneurship 230
   Entrepreneurial Orientation 231
   3M—A Prototype 232
Key Terms 232
Summary of Learning Objectives 233
Discussion Questions 233
CONCLUDING CASE: Enter the Competition 234
EXPERIENTIAL EXERCISES 234

Appendix D: Information for Entrepreneurs 238

Part Three
Organizing: Building a Dynamic Organization 240

Chapter 8

Organization Structure 242

SETTING THE STAGE: Adidas Enters a Three-Legged Race 243

Fundamentals of Organizing 244
   Differentiation 244
   Integration 245
The Vertical Structure 246
   Authority in Organizations 247

Hierarchical Levels   249
Span of Control   249
Delegation   250
Decentralization   255
The Horizontal Structure   256
The Functional Organization   257
The Divisional Organization   259
The Matrix Organization   260
Organizational Integration   263
Coordination by Standardization   263
Coordination by Plan   264
Coordination by Mutual Adjustment   264
Coordination and Communication   265
Looking Ahead   266
Key Terms   268
Summary of Learning Objectives   268
Discussion Questions   269
CONCLUDING CASE: Lucent: Clean Break,
Clean Slate?   269
EXPERIENTIAL EXERCISES   271

Chapter 9
The Responsive Organization   272

SETTING THE STAGE: Keeping Flextronics
Flexible   273
Today's Imperatives   274
Organizing for Optimal Size   275
The Case for Big   276
The Case for Small   276
Being Big and Small   277
Organizing for Environmental Response   279
Organizing for Customer Responsiveness   279
Organizing for Technological Response   282
Types of Technology Configurations   282
Organizing for Flexible Manufacturing   283
Organizing for Speed: Time-Based Competition   285
Organizing for Strategic Response   289
Organizing around Core Competencies   289
The Network Organization   290
Strategic Alliances   291
The Learning Organization   292
The High-Involvement Organization   293
Final Thoughts about Responsive Organizations   293
Key Terms   294
Summary of Learning Objectives   294
Discussion Questions   294
CONCLUDING CASE: The Biggest Grocery Store
You've Never Heard Of: Grabbing "Ahold" of the
Virtual Market   295
EXPERIENTIAL EXERCISES   296

Chapter 10
Human Resources Management   298

SETTING THE STAGE: The Online Dash for
Talent   299
Strategic Human Resources Management   300
The HR Planning Process   301
Staffing the Organization   304
Recruitment   304
Selection   305
Workforce Reductions   308
Developing the Workforce   312
Training and Development   312
Performance Appraisal   314
What Do You Appraise?   314
Who Should Do the Appraisal?   315
How Do You Give Employees Feedback?   316
Designing Reward Systems   317
Pay Decisions   317
Incentive Systems and Variable Pay   318
Employee Benefits   319
Legal Issues in Compensation and Benefits   319
Health and Safety   320
Labor Relations   320
Labor Laws   320
Unionization   321
Collective Bargaining   321
What Does the Future Hold?   322
Key Terms   323
Summary of Learning Objectives   324
Discussion Questions   325
CONCLUDING CASE: Boomerang Hiring:
Maybe You *Can* Go Back   325
EXPERIENTIAL EXERCISES   326

Chapter 11
Managing the Diverse Workforce   328

SETTING THE STAGE: Seeing the Benefits of
Hiring the Blind   329
Diversity: A Brief History   330
Diversity Today   330
The Size of the Workforce   332
The Workers of the Future   332
The Age of the Workforce   338
Managing Diversity versus Affirmative Action   342
Competitive Advantage through Diversity   343
Challenges of a Diverse Workforce   344
Multicultural Organizations   345

How Organizations Can Cultivate a Diverse Workforce 346
    Top Management Leadership and Commitment 346
    Organizational Assessment 347
    Attracting Employees 347
    Diversity Training 349
    Retaining Employees 350
Key Terms 352
Summary of Learning Objectives 352

Discussion Questions 353
**CONCLUDING CASE: Diversity Is in Good
Hands at Allstate 353**
EXPERIENTIAL EXERCISES 354
**INTEGRATING CASE: The Merger of Federal
Express and the Flying Tiger Line 360**
CASE INCIDENTS 360

Part Four
Leading: Mobilizing People 362

Chapter 12
Leadership 364

SETTING THE STAGE: Some Prominent Leaders 365
Vision 366
Leading and Managing 368
Leading and Following 368
Power and Leadership 369
    Sources of Power 369
Traditional Approaches to Understanding Leadership 371
    Leader Traits 371
    Leader Behaviors 372
    Situational Approaches to Leadership 377
Contemporary Perspectives on Leadership 383
    Charismatic Leadership 383
    Transformational Leadership 384
    Post-Heroic Leadership 385
    A Note on Courage 386
Developing Your Leadership Skills 386
Key Terms 387
Summary of Learning Objectives 387
Discussion Questions 388
CONCLUDING CASE: Following a Legend 388
EXPERIENTIAL EXERCISES 390

Appendix E: Classic Contingency Models
of Leadership 394

Chapter 13
Motivating for Performance 396

**SETTING THE STAGE: Two Contrasting Approaches
to Motivation 397**

Motivating for Performance 398
Setting Goals 399
    Goals That Motivate 399
    Limitations of Goal Setting 399
Reinforcing Performance 400
Performance-Related Beliefs 402
    The Effort-to-Performance Link 403
    The Performance-to-Outcome Link 403
    Impact on Motivation 404
    Managerial Implications of Expectancy Theory 404
Understanding People's Needs 405
    Maslow's Need Hierarchy 405
    ERG Theory 406
    McClelland's Needs 407
    Need Theories: International Perspectives 407
Designing Motivating Jobs 407
    Job Rotation, Enlargement, and Enrichment 408
    Herzberg's Two-Factor Theory 408
    The Hackman and Oldham Model of Job Design 410
    Empowerment 411
Achieving Fairness 413
    Assessing Equity 414
    Restoring Equity 414
    Fair Process 415
Job Satisfaction 417
    Quality of Work Life 417
    Psychological Contracts 418
Key Terms 419
Summary of Learning Objectives 419
Discussion Questions 420
**CONCLUDING CASE: In Need of Motivation at
Toys 'R' Us 420**
EXPERIENTIAL EXERCISES 421

Chapter 14

Managing Teams   424

SETTING THE STAGE: Two High-Impact Teams   425
The Contributions of Teams   426
Benefits of Groups   427
The New Team Environment   427
   Types of Teams   428
   Self-Managed Teams   429
How Groups Become Teams   431
   Group Activities   431
   The Passage of Time   432
   A Developmental Sequence: From Group to Team   432
   Why Groups Sometimes Fail   432
Building Effective Teams   434
   A Performance Focus   434
   Motivating Teamwork   435
   Member Contributions   435
   Norms   436
   Roles   437
   Cohesiveness   437
   Building Cohesiveness and High Performance Norms   439
Managing Lateral Relationships   441
   Managing Outward   441
   Lateral Role Relationships   442
   Intergroup Conflict   442
   Managing Conflict   443
   Conflict Styles   444
Key Terms   445
Summary of Learning Objectives   445
Discussion Questions   446
CONCLUDING CASE: Group Meetings: Love 'em or Hate 'em   447
EXPERIENTIAL EXERCISES   448

Chapter 15

Communicating   450

SETTING THE STAGE: The Power of Dialogue   451
Interpersonal Communication   452
   One-Way versus Two-Way Communication   453
   Communication Pitfalls   453
   Mixed Signals and Misperception   454
   Oral and Written Channels   456
   Electronic Media   456
   Communications Networks   459
   Media Richness   461
Improving Communication Skills   462
   Improving Sender Skills   462
   Nonverbal Skills   464
   Improving Receiver Skills   465
   Effective Supervision   467
Organizational Communication   468
   Downward Communication   468
   Upward Communication   471
   Horizontal Communication   473
   Informal Communication   473
   Boundarylessness   474
Key Terms   475
Summary of Learning Objectives   475
Discussion Questions   476
CONCLUDING CASE: Would You Really Do It?   477
EXPERIENTIAL EXERCISES   478
INTEGRATING CASE: Frank Perriman's Appointment   480
CASE INCIDENTS   483

Part Five

Controlling: Learning and Changing   486

Chapter 16

Managerial Control   488

SETTING THE STAGE: Chrysler Stops the Skid   489
Bureaucratic Control Systems   491
   The Control Cycle   491
   Approaches to Bureaucratic Control   494

   Management Audits   496
   Budgetary Controls   497
   Financial Controls   500
   The Downside of Bureaucratic Control   503
   Designing Effective Control Systems   506
The Other Controls: Markets and Clans   507
   Market Control   508

Clan Control: The Role of Empowerment and Culture   510
Key Terms   514
Summary of Learning Objectives   514
Discussion Questions   515
CONCLUDING CASE: Procter & Gamble Lets Go of the Reins and Goes for a Spin   515
EXPERIENTIAL EXERCISES   516

Chapter 17
Managing Technology and Innovation   518

SETTING THE STAGE: Native Americans Stake a High-Tech Claim   519
Technology and Innovation   520
   The Technology Life Cycle   521
   The Diffusion of Technological Innovations   523
Technological Innovation in a Competitive Environment   524
   Technology Leadership   524
   Technology Followership   526
Assessing Technology Needs   527
   Measuring Current Technologies   527
   Assessing External Technological Trends   527
Framing Decisions about Technological Innovation   528
   Anticipated Market Receptiveness   528
   Technological Feasibility   529
   Economic Viability   530
   Anticipated Competency Development   530
   Organizational Suitability   531
Sourcing and Acquiring New Technologies   533
   Internal Development   533
   Purchase   533
   Contracted Development   533
   Licensing   533
   Technology Trading   534
   Research Partnerships and Joint Ventures   534
   Acquisition of an Owner of the Technology   534
Technology and Managerial Roles   535
Organizing for Innovation   536
   Unleashing Creativity   536
   Bureaucracy Busting   537

Implementing Development Projects   538
Technology, Job Design, and Human Resources   538
Key Terms   540
Summary of Learning Objectives   540
Discussion Questions   541
CONCLUDING CASE: Matsushita's Creative Destruction   541
EXPERIENTIAL EXERCISES   542

Appendix F: Operations Management in the New Economy   543

Chapter 18
Creating and Managing Change   552

SETTING THE STAGE: Change Agents Talk about Change   553
Becoming World Class   554
   Sustainable, Great Futures   554
   The Tyranny of the "Or"   555
   The Genius of the "And"   556
Managing Change   556
   Motivating People to Change   557
   Harmonizing Multiple Changes   563
   Leading Change   564
Shaping the Future   566
   Exercising Foresight   566
   Learning Continuously   566
   Creating Advantage   568
   Creating the Future   570
   Shaping Your Own Future   572
Key Terms   572
Summary of Learning Objectives   572
Discussion Questions   575
CONCLUDING CASE: Making Your Mark   575
EXPERIENTIAL EXERCISES   577
INTEGRATING CASE: The Transformation at General Electric   581
CASE INCIDENTS   584

Glossary   G-1
Notes   N-1
Photo Credits   P-1
Name Index   I-1
Subject Index   I-11

MANAGEMENT

The New Competitive Landscape

PART ONE

Foundations of Management

- Managing
- The External Environment
- Managerial Decision Making

**Planning:
Delivering Strategic Value**

- Planning and Strategic Management
- Ethics and Corporate Responsibility
- International Management
- New Ventures

Strategy Implementation

Organizing: Building a Dynamic Organization

- Organization Structure
- The Responsive Organization
- Human Resources Management
- Managing the Diverse Workforce

**Leading:
Mobilizing People**

- Leadership
- Motivating for Performance
- Managing Teams
- Communicating

**Controlling:
Learning and Changing**

- Managerial Control
- Managing Technology and Innovation
- Creating and Managing Change

Foundations of Management

The three chapters in Part One describe the foundations of management. Chapter 1 describes the imperatives of managing in the new era and introduces key functions, skills, and competitive goals of effective managers. Chapter 2 describes the external environment in which managers and their organizations operate. Chapter 3 discusses the most pervasive managerial activity—decision making. Sound decision-making skills are essential for effective managerial performance.

CHAPTER 1

Managing

Management means, in the last analysis, the substitution of thought for brawn and muscle, of knowledge for folklore and tradition, and of cooperation for force.

—Peter Drucker

CHAPTER OUTLINE

Managing in the New Competitive Landscape
The Internet
Globalization
Knowledge Management
Collaboration across "Boundaries"

Managing for Competitive Advantage
Innovation
Quality
Speed
Cost Competitiveness
Delivering All Four

The Functions of Management
Planning: Delivering Strategic Value
Organizing: Building a Dynamic Organization
Leading: Mobilizing People
Controlling: Learning and Changing
Performing All Four Management Functions

Management Levels and Skills
Top-Level Managers
Middle-Level Managers
Frontline Managers
Working Leaders with Broad Responsibilities
Management Skills

You and Your Career
Be Both a Specialist and a Generalist
Be Self-Reliant
Be Connected
Actively Manage Your Relationship with Your Organization
Survive and Thrive

LEARNING OBJECTIVES

After studying Chapter 1, you will know:

1. The major challenges of managing in the new competitive landscape.

2. The drivers of competitive advantage for your company.

3. The functions of management and how they are evolving in today's business environment.

4. The nature of management at different organizational levels.

5. The skills you need to be an effective manager.

6. What to strive for as you manage your career.

SOMETIMES YOU GET IT, SOMETIMES YOU DON'T

Yahoo! was one of many incredible stock investments during a time when "they get it" was the ultimate compliment in the business world and "they don't get it" was the ultimate insult. *Getting it* referred to navigating the "new economy" successfully—usually meaning the successful business use of the Internet. *Not getting it* meant either not trying to do business via the Net or doing it badly.

Yahoo! is an excellent Internet portal and a popular one. But customers don't pay for services, don't buy products from it, and ignore the banner ads that were to be an essential source of revenues. As revenues declined in 2001 and 2002, the stock price plummeted. The details vary, but many companies during this period mirrored this spectacular success and rapid fall.

At least Yahoo! is still alive, with hopes and plans. Other Internet portals, such as Excite, Lycos, Disney's Go, and NBC's Snap, have folded or faded. On the bright side, in the face of a very challenging business environment, Wal-Mart, PeopleSoft, GE, Citigroup, Southwest Airlines, Home Depot, and FedEx have gotten so many things right that they were among America's 10 most admired companies for 2002.

It's not just companies, but also people, who sometimes get it sadly wrong and sometimes get it wonderfully right. Those who usually get it right include *Business Week*'s "Managers of the Year" Meg Whitman of eBay, Carole Black of Lifetime Entertainment, Lou Gerstner of IBM, and Reuben Mark of Colgate-Palmolive. They received these honors by doing the kinds of things you will be learning about in this book. On the other hand, some high flyers recently have fallen. Jacques Nasser was removed from the helm of Ford Motor Company (reasons: financial losses, difficulties with e-commerce, morale problems, the Firestone/Explorer crisis, corporate politics). James E. Goodwin of United Airlines lost his job

eBay Chief Executive Officer Meg Whitman opens the front door of eBay headquarters in San Jose, California. While many tech companies have moaned about hard times, eBay has continued making money.

due to the loss of money, the failure of a takeover, no backup plan to deal with that failure, and huge, costly pay hikes for pilots. One of the most notorious is Enron's Jeff Skilling, a mastermind of unethical financial maneuvering who (among other things) wiped out $60 billion in shareholder value.

Then there's Josh Harris, the founder of the streaming media company Pseudo.com. During the height of the Internet gold rush, Harris brashly told *60 Minutes* and CBS, "Our business is to take you out. I'm in a race to take CBS out of business . . . That's why we're going to make the big bucks." CBS, of course, is still around, whereas Pseudo.com is not.

Sources: Special Report, "The Top Managers of the Year," *Business Week*, January 14, 2002, pp. 52–72; Special Report, "The Fallen," *Business Week*, January 14, 2002, pp. 78–79; M. Gunther, "The Cheering Fades for Yahoo," *Fortune*, November 12, 2001, pp. 151–159; M. Boyle, "The Shiniest Reputations in Tarnished Times," *Fortune*, March 4, 2002, pp. 70–72.

No manager is always right or always wrong, but some get it right more often than others. The examples in "Setting the Stage" suggest that companies, like individuals, succeed or fail for a variety of reasons. Some of these reasons are circumstantial. Others are personal and human and include the decisions managers make and the actions they take.

In business, there is no replacement for effective management. Companies may fly high for a while, but they cannot do well for very long without good management. It's the same for individuals: *Business Week's* Managers of the Year[1] succeed by focusing on fundamentals, knowing what's important, and managing well. The aim of this book is to help you succeed in those pursuits.

Managing in the New Competitive Landscape

When this decade began, the economy was soaring. A new business terminology was replacing the old, distinguishing the new Internet managers from the established crowd.[2] *Business models* replaced *strategy*. The new buzz was about *reach* (customers), *stickiness* (repeat purchases), and *competing in a space* (market). It was as if everything had changed and the traditional essentials of business management were not important after all. Business seemed easy.

Turns out, it's not easy. As the high-tech "new economy" heated up, more and more firms competed for the same unproven markets. Profits proved hard to come by, and many high-flying companies came crashing down. But there was some good news: The bad news made people face reality and forced them to focus on basic principles of profit and cost efficiency.[3]

Why did so many companies fall so far, so fast? In little more than one year, the business world changed dramatically. The dot-com bubble burst, a recession came, September 11, 2001 brought terrorist attacks, and economic uncertainties snowballed. But changing circumstances were only part of the story. In addition, managers made a lot of bad decisions. They grew arrogant, mistreated customers, didn't worry about costs, and gave away valuable services because profits didn't seem to matter. They misapplied managerial principles, in part because they lacked managerial experience and expertise.[4]

Times may change, but managerial practices will always separate effective from ineffective organizations. According to *Business Week*, "The Darwinian struggle of daily business will be won by the people—and the organizations—that adapt most successfully to the new world that is unfolding."[5] What defines this "new world," and the competitive landscape of business? You will be reading about many relevant issues in the coming chapters, but we begin here by highlighting four key elements that make the current landscape different from the past: the Internet, globalization, the importance of knowledge and ideas, and collaboration across organizational "boundaries."

The Internet

Communication technologies are driving massive change in the world of management. The Internet changes the way managers must think and act with regard to everything from devising strategies to leading and motivating employees. Management is still strategic, and still intensely interpersonal and human, but now it also must happen via the Web.[6]

At the beginning of this decade, technology was dazzling people with returns that seemed limitless. E-business (business conducted electronically) was all the rage. But when the overheated market crashed, "profitable Internet company" became an oxymoron.[7] The term *e-business* became discredited to the point where GM dropped it and started calling its e-business efforts "digitization."

But by mid-2002, 25 percent of the publicly held Internet companies had become profitable.[8] E-travel and e-finance (shining examples: Expedia, Priceline, and Schwab) emerged as big winners. The health services company WebMD, once branded a loser, began making money. Even nonprofitable Net companies at least had potential as takeover targets for established companies, because they could provide the Internet services those companies needed.

Many Internet-only companies died, making it seem that mixing the Internet with physical stores was the only way to make money online. But as of 2002, most profitable Web companies were selling information-based products that don't require shipping, and so they didn't need physical stores[9] (as the jargon has it, "bricks" to go with their "clicks").

At the same time, old economy types, written off for dead during the heyday of the dot-com boom, have survived and are now using the Internet as a tool to solidify their future. Barnes & Noble sells successfully via the Net, not solely but as a complement to its real stores—people still like to browse the aisles, thumb through books, and have a cup of coffee.[10]

The percentage of trade that takes place on the Net is small, but it is growing, as is the number of Internet users worldwide. Some observers compare e-commerce to the automobile industry in the era of the Model T, Ford's original all-black model in the early 1900s.[11] The debate about the future of e-business continues, but the industry may now be poised for a long, steady climb for decades to come. Much of the work now will focus on helping existing companies use the Internet to cut costs, serve customers better, and open new markets.[12]

The Internet revolution is definitely here, and the real wealth creation is yet to come.[13] The Net may not be a business unto itself, but it clearly is a powerful tool for improving business. It is difficult to predict how a particular company like Yahoo!, described in "Setting the Stage," will be performing by the time you read this. It is clear, though, that its fate, like that of all companies, will derive from a combination of factors in the business environment and the decisions and actions of its managers.

Who doesn't remember the goofy, but endearing "mascot" of the now defunct website Pets.com? Pets.com spent huge advertising dollars on the concept and the ads, only to fall victim of the dot-com crash. Don't get too teary-eyed, though, because our pseudo-canine friend has landed another gig to hawk auto loans to people with bad credit for 1-800- Bar-None.

Globalization

Far more than in the past, enterprises are global, with offices and production facilities in countries all over the world. Foreign companies by the hundreds are joining the New York Stock Exchange.[14] Corporations such as Bertelsmann, Citicorp, ASEA Brown Boveri, and Nestle are "stateless": They operate worldwide without reference to national borders.[15]

For U.S. and non–U.S. managers alike, isolationism is a thing of the past.[16] This must be so for organizations to survive worldwide competition in a global marketplace. U.S. companies are no longer the unrivaled stars of the business world.

For example, since 1993, the Big Three U.S. automakers have lost market share worth $35 billion to overseas competitors.[17] *Consumer Reports'* 2001 list of the best vehicles in 10 categories includes not a single U.S. car or truck. Currently, Toyota, Nissan, and Honda are building truck plants in Indiana, Mississippi, and Alabama and will possibly cut U.S. truck profits by more than half by 2004.

On the brighter side, MTV has been extremely successful expanding overseas.[18] Eight of 10 MTV viewers live outside the United States; with its sister operations, VH1 and Nickelodeon, MTV reaches 1 billion people in 18 different languages in 164 countries. Similarly, most growth for Tricon (which owns KFC, Pizza Hut, and Taco Bell) is global.[19] KFC has 5000 restaurants in the United States and over 6,000 overseas. In China, KFC has over 500 restaurants, and opens 10 new ones per month—even though a KFC value meal costs about six hours' salary. Like other successful global companies, KFC customizes: it offers tempura crispy strips in Japan, and in Thailand it offers fresh rice with soy or sweet chili.

Intel Chairman Andy Grove believes all companies will need to evolve into Internet companies to survive.

Emotions ran high when the spin-off of Tricon Global Restaurants Inc., from PepsiCo Inc., was celebrated at the New York Stock Exchange. Chairman and CEO David Novak (with the yum cheese hat) energizes his company with this emotional style.

Competing globally is not easy. Companies often overestimate the attractiveness of foreign markets.[20] Those markets look big and untapped, but the difficulties (costs and risks) also are big. Overseas sites need local marketing, and local management builds relationships and trust.[21] EBay, Schwab, and Yahoo! established successful local sites country by country. Don't forget, the product itself must be locally desirable, a problem that AOL struggled to overcome.

Even small firms that do not operate on a global scale must make important strategic decisions based on international considerations. Many small companies export their goods. Many domestic firms assemble their products in other countries. And companies are under pressure to improve their products in the face of intense competition from high-quality foreign producers. Firms today must ask themselves, "How can we be the best in the world?"

Knowledge Management

One of the most important forces for change in management is the growing need for good, new ideas. Because companies in advanced economies have become so efficient at producing physical goods, most workers have been freed up to provide services or "abstract goods" like software, entertainment, data, and advertising. Efficient factories with few workers produce the cereals and cell phones the market demands; meanwhile, more and more workers create software and invent new products and services.[22] As top consultant Gary Hamel puts it, "We have moved from an economy of hands to an economy of heads."[23]

Chief knowledge officer will be an important job in coming years.[24] **Knowledge management** is the set of practices aimed at discovering and harnessing an organization's intellectual resources—fully utilizing the intellects of the organization's people. Knowledge management is about finding, unlocking, sharing, and altogether capitalizing on the most precious resources of an organization: people's expertise, skills, wisdom, and relationships. Knowledge managers find these human assets, help

knowledge management

Practices aimed at discovering and harnessing an organization's intellectual resources.

people collaborate and learn, help people generate new ideas, and harness those ideas into successful innovations.

Production of tangible goods remains an essential part of the economy and of effective management, but companies like GE, Dell, Toyota, and ABB owe their success in large part to intellectual capital. Whereas "capital" used to be a purely financial concept, it now has an additional meaning. Intellectual capital is the collective brainpower of the organization.[25] Today, managers must create a work environment that attracts good people, makes them want to stay, and inspires creative ideas from everyone. The ultimate goal is to turn the brainpower of their people into profitable products.

Collaboration across "Boundaries"

One of the most important processes of knowledge management is to ensure that people in different parts of the organization collaborate effectively with one another. This requires productive communications among different departments, divisions, or other subunits of the organization. For example, British Petroleum tries to create "T-shaped" managers who break out of the traditional corporate hierarchy to share knowledge freely across the organization (the horizontal part of the T) while remaining fiercely committed to the bottom-line performance of their individual business units (the vertical part). This emphasis on dual responsibilities for performance and knowledge sharing occurs at GlaxoSmithKline (the pharmaceutical giant), Siemens (the large German industrial company), and Ispat International (a London-based steelmaker).[26]

Collaboration across former "boundaries" occurs between as well as within organizations. Companies merge; competitors join forces to cooperate in pursuit of

---

WE HAVE AN OPPORTUNITY TO INVENT A NEW WORLD— COLLECTIVELY.

And we can make it better than the existing world, not just in a narrowly economic sense but also in a broader human sense: for ourselves and for our children and for our children's children.

For instance, new information technologies and new ideas about management are bringing us to a place where we can consider radically new ways of organizing work. It may be possible to create companies that give employees a better sense of achievement, of camaraderie, or of autonomy than ever before.

That's tremendously exciting.

What worries me is the possibility that we'll create a world that is much more economically efficient—but that is much less satisfying to live in—than the one that we inhabit today . . .

I'm worried that we won't bring the personal side of the equation up to the level of the financial side.

I also worry about people who live and work in developing countries. It's clear that the economy is becoming more global. But the jury is still out on whether the developing world will be integrated into the developed world in a thoughtful and fair way, or in a way that exploits and oppresses people.

We have a historical opportunity—perhaps even a historical obligation—to make wise choices about how we move forward.

I just hope we don't blow it.

Thomas W. Malone (malone@mit.edu) is the Patrick J. McGovern Professor of Information Systems at the MIT Sloan School of Management. He is also the founder and director of the MIT Center for Coordination Science and was one of the two founding codirectors of the five-year MIT research initiative "Inventing the Organizations of the 21st Century."

SOURCE: *Fast Company*, September, 2000 p. 142.

A Comment on the New Business Era

a common business interest; the Internet blurs the lines between companies as members work together to solve business problems.[27]

Companies today also must motivate and capitalize on the ideas of people outside the traditional company boundaries. How can a company best use the services of its consultants, ad agencies, and suppliers? What kinds of partnerships can it create with other companies in the same industry—even companies with which it competes? And how about customers? Companies today still need to focus on delivering a product and making the numbers, but above all they must realize that the need to serve the customer drives everything else.

Best serving the customer can start with involving the customer more in company decisions. For example, companies like P&G are getting customers to think creatively and talk with one another online to come up with new product and service ideas.[28] Bank One Corp. invites customers to help improve its services. "Our customers have a great desire to improve the bank, and we act on their ideas," says the president.[29] This isn't about the occasional comment from a customer; it's about a strategic, systematic, active approach to achieve better customer service through managing customer relationships in such a way that customers contribute their best ideas.

The Internet, globalization, the monumental importance of new ideas, collaboration across disappearing boundaries . . . what are the repercussions of this tidal wave of new forces? The magazine *Fast Company* asked 17 business leaders to consider this question. The previous page shows a complete comment by an MIT business professor. Below, Table 1.1 offers some other comments.

TABLE 1.1   Comments on Today's Competitive Landscape

Tom Peters, author and consultant: "Somebody once asked me what I wanted my epitaph to say. I want it to say, 'He was a player.' It wouldn't mean that I got rich . . . It would mean that I participated fully in these fascinating times . . . whatever this 'new economy' thing is, it is reinventing the world of commerce."

Jonathan Hoenig, founder of capitalistpig asset management: "The most valuable commodity isn't soybeans but service . . . The human touch is what's going to propel our 'commodified' business models into the next century and beyond. I feel terribly privileged to be alive at such an exciting time in history."

Patricia Seybold, author of customers.com: "A lot of people think the new economy is all about the Internet . . . it's really about customers. Customers are transforming entire industries . . . the customer is at the core of the business."

Nathan Myhrvold, cofounder and copresident of Intellectual Ventures: "The new economy is about rethinking and reshaping what has already happened. It's about producing fertile ground for radically new ideas. Workers with good ideas, or the ability to generate ideas, can write their own ticket."

Krishna Subramanian, chairwoman and CEO, Kovair Inc.: "Companies used to be structured around individual contribution. Now teamwork—presenting a seamless interface to the customer, across all points of contact and all business functions—is becoming more important . . . What do I worry about? Pace. Everything is so frenzied right now. I'm not sure that we stop—or even slow down—often enough to think about what we're doing, to try to balance our work with our lives."

Pehong Chen, chairman, president and CEO, Broadvision Inc.: "That's what is so awesome about the new economy. You have the ability to do something with your work and to know that you made a difference. You. Not your system. Not your company's policies. You."

Thomas Stewart, Fortune magazine: "We stand at the beginning of a new century, in the middle of a technological revolution, and at the end of a great stock market bubble—virgin territory, construction sites, and ruins, all at once. Let's go."

What is your reaction to these comments? Many of these issues are discussed in later chapters.

SOURCES: R. F. Maruca, "Voices," *Fast Company*, September 2000, pp. 105–44; T. Stewart, "Intellectual Capital: Ten Years Later, How Far We've Come," *Fortune*, May 28, 2001, pp. 192–93.

Managing for Competitive Advantage

The rise of the Internet turned lives upside down. People dropped out of school to join Internet start-ups or start their own. Managers in big corporations quit their jobs to do the same. Investors salivated, and invested heavily. The risks were often ignored, or downplayed, sometimes tragically.

Consider two earlier industries of similar transforming power: automobiles and aviation. There have been at least 2,000 car makers, but now there are only three car companies left in the United States—and even they have not been great investments. Similarly, hundreds of aircraft manufacturers have gone bankrupt, some very recently. And the net amount of money made by all U.S. airline companies is zero. That's right: All those companies in total have made no money whatsoever.[30]

What is the lesson to be learned from all the failures in these important transformational industries? A key to understanding the success of a company—whether traditional, Internet-based, or a combination of both—is not how much the industry in which it operates will affect society or how much it will grow. The key is the competitive advantage held by a particular company and how sustainable or renewable that advantage is.[31] Good managers know that they are in a competitive struggle to survive and win.

To survive and win, you have to gain advantage over your competitors and earn a profit. You gain competitive advantage by being better than your competitors at doing valuable things for your customers. But what does this mean, specifically? To be profitable, what must managers deliver? The fundamental success drivers are innovation, quality, speed, and cost competitiveness.

Innovation

Two Stanford business professors completed a study of 18 great companies. Impressed with all the companies, the authors still were able to choose one above them all that they believed would be the most successful over time. That company was 3M, and the reason is its extraordinary ability to innovate.[32]

Innovation is the introduction of new goods and services. Your firm must adapt to changes in consumer demands and to new competitors. When the Net allowed merchants to bypass traditional distribution channels and reach buyers directly, traditional marketers had to learn how to innovate to remain competitive.[33] Plus, products don't sell forever; in fact, they don't sell for nearly as long as they used to, because so many competitors are introducing so many new products all the time. Your firm must innovate, or it will die.

> **innovation**
>
> **The introduction of new goods and services.**

A top consultant, Gary Hamel, notes that the real competitive battle was never between the heralded new Internet economy and an old economy.[34] Instead, the competition has always been between newcomers and the old guard. The perpetual battle is between unconventional thinking and unthinking ritual. In recent years, newcomers battered incumbents with unconventional new approaches to business. Only the incumbents that keep innovating, like Wal-Mart and IBM, have continued to increase their share of wealth.

Companies that once were revolutionaries—Apple, Compaq, 3Com, Adobe—are now struggling to stay relevant. The balance of power, Hamel says, has shifted decisively in favor of the unorthodox. Not mincing words while speaking directly to successful executives, Hamel warns, "Odds are, over the next few years newcomers are going to capture most of the new wealth in your industry. Odds are, your company is going to get its ass kicked by a bunch of irreverent, tradition-defying rebels."[35]

Innovation is today's holy grail.[36] It is the most potent means of creating new wealth.[37]

Like the other sources of competitive advantage, innovation comes from people; it must be a strategic goal; and it must be managed properly. You will learn how great companies innovate in later chapters.

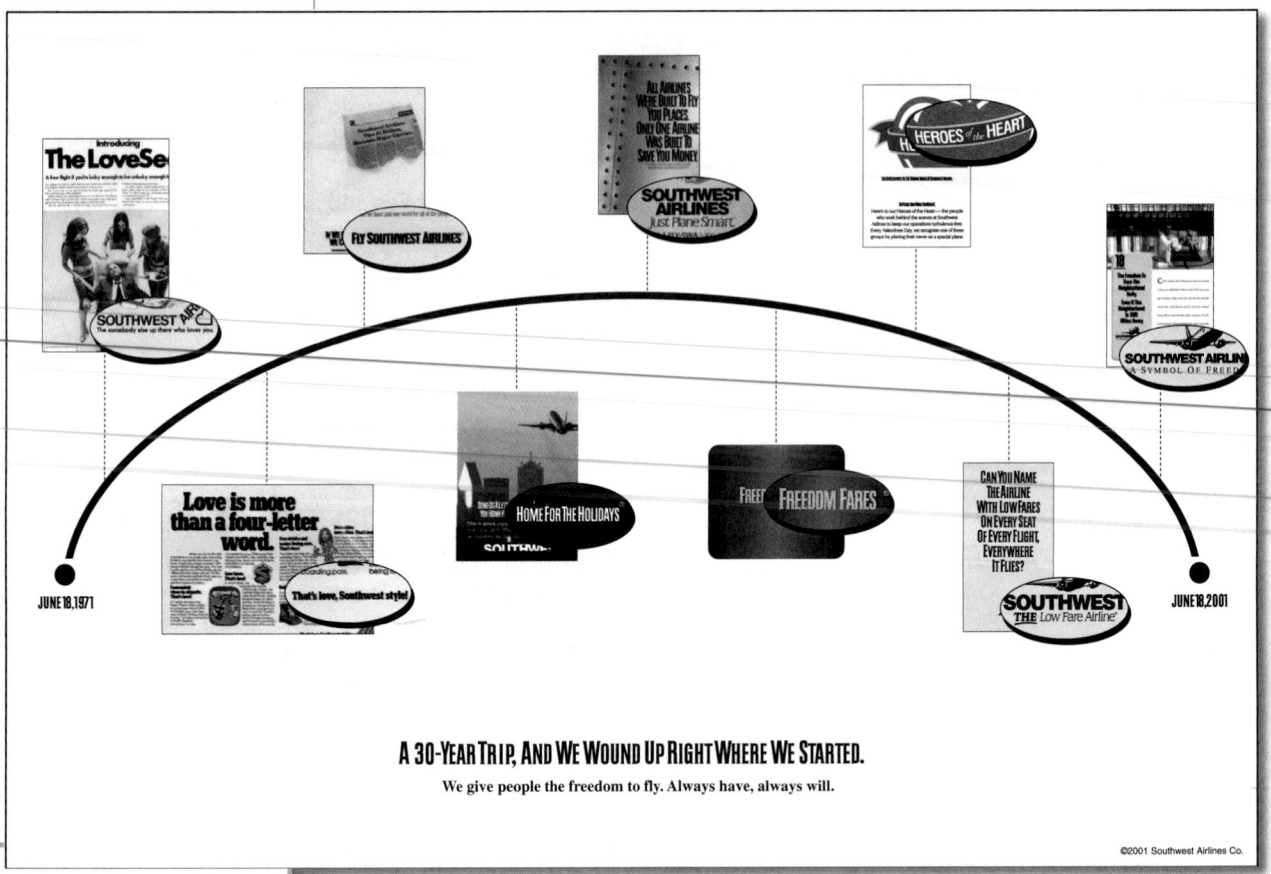

Cost competitiveness gives Southwest Airlines a big advantage over its rivals.

Quality

Quality is the excellence of your product, including its attractiveness, lack of defects, reliability, and long-term dependability. The importance of quality and standards for acceptable quality have increased dramatically in recent years. Customers now demand high quality and value, and will accept nothing less.

quality

The excellence of a product, including such things as attractiveness, lack of defects, reliability, and long-term dependability.

Historically, quality pertained primarily to the physical goods that customers bought. Today, service quality is vital as well. For example, making things easy for customers is an important dimension of quality; FedEx, Alamo, and Dell make it easy for customers to use their services. Catering to customers' other needs creates more perceived quality. Wine.com provides online access to wine information, plus the expertise of a sommelier. To provide better service, one of Lufthansa's competitive goals is "superior knowledge of customers." The airline tracks customer tastes closely, offers home pages in several dozen languages, delivers individual email, and provides account access, hotel links, travel guides, online booking for 700 airlines, and baggage tracing.[38]

Quality is further provided when companies customize goods and services to the wishes of the individual customer. Lands' End allows customers to create a "personal model" for testing the fit and look of swimwear; Chipshot.com allows golfers to configure clubs to their preferred specifications.[39] VooDoo of Sunnyvale, California, and Cannondale of Bethel, Connecticut, use websites to allow customers to create personalized, customized bicycles.[40] They link each customer to a local dealer to place the final order and receive the product.

Trying to gain both cost and quality advantages over its rivals, GM is experimenting with a factory near Lansing, Michigan.[41] The factory would assemble cars Lego-style, using large modules of parts shipped by suppliers directly to the assembly line. The goal is to sharply reduce labor costs while dramatically improving quality. The approach could enable a build-to-order system that gives customers the precise combination of options they want.

Providing world-class quality requires a *thorough* understanding of what quality really is.[42] Quality can be measured in terms of performance, various service dimensions, reliability (failure or breakdowns), conformance to standards, durability, and aesthetics. Only by moving beyond broad, generic concepts like "quality," to identifying the more specific elements of quality, can you identify problems, target needs, set performance standards more precisely, and deliver world-class value.

Speed

Speed often separates the winners from the losers in the world of competition. How fast can you develop and get a new product to market? How quickly can you respond to customer requests? You are far better off if you are faster than the competition—and if you can respond quickly to your competitors' actions.

Speed isn't everything—reliability, dependability, quality, costs, and so forth, separate winners from losers. But those things being equal, faster companies are more likely to be the winners, slow ones the losers. Even pre-Internet, speed had become a vital requirement in the 1990s. Companies were getting products to market, and in the hands of customers, faster than ever. Now, the speed requirement has increased exponentially. Andy Grove, chairman of Intel Corporation, says the Internet is a tool, and the biggest impact of that tool is speed.[43] Everything, it seems, is on fast-forward.

> **speed**
>
> **Fast and timely execution, response, and delivery of results.**

For executives at established companies who left their world and joined the "great migration" to risky Internet start-ups, one of the biggest shocks was the sheer speed of Internet life. L. Gregory Ballard of MyFamily.com said that in established companies, you should not make any major decisions in your first three months on the job, while you learn the business. But "Internet time doesn't give you three months. It gives you three days"[44] (p. 5).

You read earlier about GM and the other U.S. automakers struggling against overseas competition. One option that could help them compete is to stop performing low-margin operations like stamping and welding and concentrate on value-added processes like design and marketing.[45] This would greatly speed innovation and the time to get new products into the market.

Cost Competitiveness

Cost competitiveness means that your costs are kept low enough so that you can realize profits and price your products (goods or services) at levels that are attractive to consumers. Ebay set the standard for profitable Internet companies by having so few fixed costs—no inventory, sales force, or warehouses.[46] Marriott, hit hard by the drop in tourism and travel, is cutting costs every way it can and offering much lower room rates.[47] Needless to say, if you can offer a desirable product at a low price, it is more likely to sell.

> **cost competitiveness**
>
> **Keeping costs low in order to achieve profits and be able to offer prices that are attractive to consumers.**

Managing your costs and keeping them down requires being efficient: accomplishing your goals by using your resources wisely and minimizing waste. Little things can save big money, but cost cuts involve trade-offs. Lucent cut the number of lightbulbs per cubicle from four to one.[48] The BBC could save $400,000 per year by banning free biscuits from internal meetings. The Swedish navy, dealing with budget cuts, dropped round-the-clock operations in favor of Monday through Friday, 9 to 5. Martha Stewart, rather than throwing a big holiday party at Martha Stewart Living OmniMedia, asked her managers to host staff parties at their homes—perhaps not a popular cost-cutting step.[49]

Raw materials, equipment, capital, manufacturing, marketing, delivery, and labor are just some of the costs that need to be managed carefully. One reason so many dot-coms failed was that their huge, up-front advertising costs usually didn't translate into big sales; their customer acquisition costs were as much as four times higher than those of offline competitors. Because the cost of customer acquisition is so high, the Net is a great way to communicate with customers but a terrible way to get new customers.[50]

Consumers can now easily compare prices on the Net from thousands of competitors. If you can't cut costs, you can't compete.

From his dorm room, Michael Dell took on giants IBM, Apple, and Compaq. The amazing success of Dell Computer is due to its quality, low cost, innovation, and speed.

Delivering All Four

Don't assume you can settle for delivering just one of the four competitive advantages: low cost alone, or quality alone, for example. The best managers and companies deliver them all.

Michael Dell started Dell Computer in his dorm room and used a low-cost, direct-sales approach to making his company the driving force in the PC business. Dell says, "We will be the lowest-cost provider, period."[51] But low cost is not the only thing at which Dell excels. Dell builds and ships PCs within 36 hours of receiving an order. All of its suppliers know they must deliver parts to Dell within one hour. At the same time, Dell computers have consistently held some of the highest quality ratings in the industry. Nonetheless, Michael Dell recently became obsessed with improving quality even further.[52] He decided that the sensitive hard drive needed to be handled less during assembly. Dell innovated by revamping the production lines, which reduced the number of touches from more than 30 per drive to fewer than 15. Rejected hard drives fell by 40 percent, and the overall PC failure rate by 20 percent.

The Functions of Management

Management is the process of working with people and resources to accomplish organizational goals. Good managers do those things both effectively and efficiently.

To be *effective* is to achieve organizational goals. To be *efficient* is to achieve goals with minimal waste of resources, that is, to make the best possible use of money, time, materials, and people. Some managers fail on both criteria, or focus on one at the expense of another. The best managers maintain a clear focus on both effectiveness *and* efficiency.

These definitions have been around for a long time. But as you know, business is changing radically. The real issue is what to *do*.[53]

The context of business and the specifics of doing business are changing,[54] but there are still plenty of timeless principles that make great managers, and great companies, great. While fresh thinking and new approaches are required now more than ever, much of what has already been learned about successful management practices remains relevant, useful, and adaptable, with fresh thinking, to the 21st-century business environment.

To use an analogy: Engineering practices evolve continually, but the laws of physics are relatively constant.[55] In the business world today, the great executives not only adapt to changing conditions but also apply—fanatically, rigorously, consistently, and with discipline—the fundamental management principles. These fundamentals include the four traditional functions of management: planning, organizing, leading, and controlling. They remain as relevant as ever, and they still provide the fundamentals that are needed in start-ups as much as in established corporations. But their form has evolved.

Planning: Delivering Strategic Value

Planning is specifying the goals to be achieved and deciding in advance the appropriate actions needed to achieve those goals. Planning activities include analyzing current situations, anticipating the future, determining objectives, deciding in what types of activities the company will engage, choosing corporate and business strategies, and determining the resources needed to achieve the organization's goals. Plans set the stage for action and for major achievements.

> **planning**
>
> The management function of systematically making decisions about the goals and activities that an individual, a group, a work unit, or the overall organization will pursue in the future.

The planning function for the new business environment, discussed in Part 2 of this book, is more broadly described as *delivering strategic value*. Historically, planning described a top-down approach in which top executives establish business plans and tell others to implement them. Now and in the future, delivering strategic value is a dynamic process in which people throughout the organization use their brains and the brains of customers, suppliers, and other stakeholders to identify opportunities to create, seize, strengthen, and sustain competitive advantage. This dynamic process swirls around the objective of creating more and more value for the customer. Effectively creating value requires fully considering a new and changing set of stakeholders and issues, including the government, the natural environment, globalization, and the dynamic economy in which ideas are king and entrepreneurs are both formidable competitors and potential collaborators. You will learn about these and related topics in Chapter 4 (planning and strategic management), Chapter 5 (ethics and corporate social responsibility), Chapter 6 (international management), and Chapter 7 (new ventures).

Organizing: Building a Dynamic Organization

Organizing is assembling and coordinating the human, financial, physical, informational, and other resources needed to achieve goals. Organizing activities include attracting people to the organization, specifying job responsibilities, grouping jobs into work units, marshaling and allocating resources, and creating conditions so that people and things work together to achieve maximum success.

> **organizing**
>
> The management function of assembling and coordinating human, financial, physical, informational, and other resources needed to achieve goals.

Part 3 of the book describes the organizing function as *building a dynamic organization*. Historically, organizing involved creating an organization chart by identifying business functions, establishing reporting relationships, and having a personnel department that administered plans, programs, and paperwork. Now and in the future, effective managers will be using new forms of organizing and viewing their people as perhaps their most valuable resources. They will build organizations that are flexible and adaptive, particularly in response to competitive threats and customer needs. Progressive human resource practices that attract and retain the very best of a highly diverse population will be essential aspects of the successful company. You will learn about these topics in Chapter 8 (organization structure), Chapter 9 (responsive organizations), Chapter 10 (human resources management), and Chapter 11 (the diverse workforce).

Leading: Mobilizing People

Leading is stimulating people to be high performers. It is directing, motivating, and communicating with employees, individually and in groups. Leading involves close day-to-day contact with people, helping to guide and inspire them toward achieving team and organizational goals. Leading takes place in teams, departments, and divisions, as well as at the tops of large organizations.

> **leading**
>
> The management function that involves the manager's efforts to stimulate high performance by employees.

In earlier textbooks, the leading function was about how managers motivate workers to come to work and execute top management's plans by doing their jobs. Today and in the future, managers must be good at *mobilizing people* to contribute their ideas, to use their brains in ways never needed or dreamed of in the past. As described in Part 4, they must rely on a very different kind of leadership (Chapter 12) that empowers and motivates people (Chapter 13). Far more than in the past, great work must be done via great teamwork (Chapter 14), both within work groups and across group boundaries. Ideally, underlying these processes will be effective interpersonal and organizational communication (Chapter 15).

Controlling: Learning and Changing

controlling

The management function of monitoring progress and making needed changes.

Planning, organizing, and leading do not guarantee success. The fourth function, **controlling,** monitors progress and implements necessary changes.

Monitoring is an essential aspect of control. If you have any doubts that this function is important, consider that after the terror attacks of September 11, 2001, many Department of Agriculture laboratories could not account for dangerous biological agents supposedly in their stockpiles, including 3 billion doses of a dangerous virus. The Department of Energy could not account fully for radioactive fuel rods and other nuclear materials lent to other countries.[56] On a different note, a man with an ax (a hatchet, according to a company spokesman) entered an Oklahoma City Wal-Mart. On his way in, the greeter not only failed to alert authorities but placed a sticker on the weapon so he would not be charged for it when he left. The man, who robbed the store, had claimed he was returning it.[57] Controls failures can take many forms!

When managers implement their plans, they often find that things are not working out as planned. The controlling function makes sure that goals are met. It asks and answers the question, "Are our actual outcomes consistent with our goals?" It makes adjustments as needed.

Successful organizations, large and small, pay close attention to the controlling function. But Part 5 of the book makes it clear that today and for the future, the key managerial challenges are far more dynamic than in the past; they involve continually *learning and changing.* Controls must still be in place, as described in Chapter 16. But new technologies and other innovations (Chapter 17) make it possible to achieve controls in more effective ways, and to help all the people throughout the company, and across company boundaries (including customers and suppliers), to use their brains, learn, make a variety of new contributions, and help the organization change in ways that forge a successful future (Chapter 18).

The four management functions apply to you personally, as well. You must find ways to create value, organize for your own personal effectiveness, mobilize your own talents and skills as well as those of others, and constantly learn, develop, and change for the future. As you proceed through this book and this course, we encourage you to not merely do your "textbook learning" of an impersonal course subject, but to think about these issues from a personal perspective as well, using the ideas for personal development and advantage.

Performing All Four Management Functions

As a manager, your typical day will not be neatly divided into the four functions. You will be doing many things more or less simultaneously.[58] Your days will be busy and fractionated, spent dealing with interruptions, meetings, and firefighting. There will be plenty to do that you wish you could be doing but can't seem to get to. These activities will include all four management functions.

Some managers are particularly interested in, devoted to, or skilled in a couple of the four functions but not in the others. The manager who does not devote adequate attention and resources to *all four* functions will fail. You can be a skilled planner and controller, but if you organize your people improperly or fail to inspire them to perform at high levels, you will not be an effective manager. Likewise, it does no good to be the kind of manager who loves to organize and lead, but who doesn't really understand where to go or how to determine whether you are on the right track. Good managers don't neglect any of the four management functions. Knowing what they are, you can periodically ask yourself if you are devoting adequate attention to *all* of them.

Management Levels and Skills

Organizations (particularly large organizations) have many levels. In this section, you will learn about the types of managers found at three different levels in large organizations: top-level, middle, and frontline.

Top-Level Managers

Top-level managers are the senior executives of an organization and are responsible for its overall management. Top-level managers, often referred to as *strategic managers*, are supposed to focus on long-term issues and emphasize the survival, growth, and overall effectiveness of the organization.

> **top-level managers**
>
> **Senior executives responsible for the overall management and effectiveness of the organization.**

Top managers are concerned not only with the organization as a whole but also with the interaction between the organization and its external environment. This interaction often requires managers to work extensively with outside individuals and organizations.

The chief executive officer (CEO) is one type of top-level manager found in large corporations. This individual is the primary strategic manager of the firm and has authority over everyone else. Others include the chief operating officer (COO), company presidents, vice presidents, and members of the top executive committee.

Traditionally, the role of top-level managers has been to set overall direction by formulating strategy and controlling resources. But now, top managers are more commonly called upon to be not only strategic architects but also true organizational leaders. As leaders they must create and articulate a broader corporate purpose with which people can identify, and one to which people will enthusiastically commit. Effective top leaders treat people as valued members of the organization. As GE's legendary Jack Welch said, "A manager's job is to make people feel 10 feet tall—strong, powerful, self-confident, willing to take risks" (p. 93).[59]

Middle-Level Managers

As the name implies, **middle-level managers** are located in the organization's hierarchy below top-level management and above the frontline managers. Sometimes called *tactical managers*, they are responsible for translating the general goals and plans developed by strategic managers into more specific objectives and activities.

> **middle-level managers**
>
> **Managers located in the middle layers of the organizational hierarchy, reporting to top-level executives.**

Traditionally, the role of the middle manager is to be an administrative controller who bridges the gap between higher and lower levels. Middle-level managers take corporate objectives and break them down into business unit targets; put together separate business unit plans from the units below them for higher-level corporate review; and serve as linchpins of internal communication, interpreting and broadcasting top management's priorities downward and channeling and translating information from the front lines, upward.

As a stereotype, the term *middle manager* connotes mediocrity: unimaginative people defending the status quo, behaving like bureaucrats. But middle managers are closer than top managers to day-to-day operations, customers, and frontline managers and employees—so they know the problems. They also have many creative ideas—often better than their bosses'. Good middle managers provide operating skills and practical problem solving that keep the company working.[60]

Frontline Managers

Frontline managers, or *operational managers*, are lower-level managers who supervise the operations of the organization. These managers often have titles such as supervisor or sales manager. They are directly involved with nonmanagement employees, implementing the specific plans developed with middle managers. This role is critical in the organization, because operational managers are the link between management and nonmanagement personnel. Your first management position probably will fit into this category.

> **frontline managers**
>
> **Lower-level managers who supervise the operational activities of the organization.**

Traditionally, frontline managers have been directed and controlled from above, to make sure that they successfully implement operations in support of company strategy. But in leading companies, the role has expanded. Whereas the operational execution aspect of the role remains vital, in leading companies frontline managers are increasingly called upon to be innovative and entrepreneurial, managing for growth and new business development.

For example, Andy Wong took over a struggling unit at 3M, focused attention on new goals, reenergized a discouraged team of people, introduced new products, and found new markets for old products. His unit became a showcase within 3M—quite an honor in a company known for its innovative and successful business units.[61]

In innovative organizations, outstanding frontline managers are not only *allowed* to initiate new activities but are *expected* to by their top- and middle-level managers. And they are given freedom, incentives, and support to find ways to do so.

Table 1.2 elaborates on the changing aspects of different management levels. You will learn about each of these aspects of management throughout this course.

Working Leaders with Broad Responsibilities

You may have noted that we qualified our descriptions of managerial levels by referring to large organizations. These descriptions represent the traditional model for large organizations. But the trend today is toward less hierarchy and more teamwork. In small

TABLE 1.2
Transformation of Management Roles and Tasks

	Frontline Managers	Middle-Level Managers	Top-Level Managers
Changing roles	• From operational implementers to aggressive entrepreneurs	• From administrative controllers to supportive coaches	• From resource allocators to institutional leaders
Primary value	• Driving business performance by focusing on productivity, innovation and growth within frontline units	• Providing the support and coordination to bring large company advantage to the independent frontline units	• Creating and embedding a sense of direction, commitment and challenge to people throughout the organization
Key activities	• Creating and pursuing new growth opportunities for the business	• Developing individuals and supporting their activities	• Challenging embedded assumptions while establishing a stretching opportunity horizon and performance standards
	• Attracting and developing resources and competencies	• Linking dispersed knowledge, skills, and best practices across units	• Institutionalizing a set of norms and values to support cooperation and trust
	• Managing continuous performance improvement within the unit	• Managing the tension between short-term performance and long-term ambition	• Creating an overarching corporate purpose and ambition

SOURCE: C. Bartlett and S. Goshal, "The Myth of the Generic Manager: New Personal Competencies for New Management Roles," *California Management Review* Vol. 40, No. 1, Fall 1997, pp. 92–116.

firms—and in those large companies that have adapted to the times—managers have strategic, tactical, *and* operational responsibilities. They are *complete* businesspeople; they have knowledge of all business functions, are accountable for results, and focus on serving customers both inside and outside their firms. All of this requires the ability to think strategically, translate strategies into specific objectives, coordinate resources, and do real work with lower-level people.

In short, today's best managers can do it all; they are "working leaders."[62] They focus on relationships with other people and on achieving results. They don't just make decisions, give orders, wait for others to produce, and then evaluate results. They get dirty, do hard work themselves, solve problems, and produce value.

Management Skills

Performing management functions and achieving competitive advantage are the cornerstones of a manager's job. However, understanding this does not ensure success. Managers need a variety of skills to *do* these things *well*. Skills are specific abilities that result from knowledge, information, practice, and aptitude. Although managers need many individual skills, which you will learn about throughout the text, consider three general categories: technical skills, interpersonal and communication skills, and conceptual and decision skills.[63] When the key management functions are performed by managers who have these critical management skills, the result is a high-performance work environment.

A **technical skill** is the ability to perform a specialized task that involves a certain method or process. Most people develop a set of technical skills to complete the activities that are part of their daily work lives. The technical skills you learn in school will provide you with the opportunity to get an entry-level position; they will also help you as a manager. For example, your accounting and finance courses will develop the technical skills you need to understand and manage the financial resources of an organization.

> **technical skill**
>
> **The ability to perform a specialized task involving a particular method or process.**

Conceptual and decision skills involve the manager's ability to identify and resolve problems for the benefit of the organization and everyone concerned. Managers use these skills when they consider the overall objectives and strategy of the firm, the interactions among different parts of the organization, and the role of the business in its external environment. As you acquire greater responsibility, you must exercise your conceptual and decision skills with increasing frequency. You will confront issues that involve all aspects of

> **conceptual and decision skills**
>
> **Skills pertaining to the ability to identify and resolve problems for the benefit of the organization and its members.**

Successful managers, such as Amazon.com CEO Jeffrey Bezos, have the ability to work well with people.

the organization and must consider a larger and more interrelated set of decision factors. Much of this text is devoted to enhancing your conceptual and decision skills, but remember that experience also plays an important part in their development.

interpersonal and communication skills

People skills; the ability to lead, motivate, and communicate effectively with others.

Interpersonal and communication skills influence the manager's ability to work well with people. These skills are often called *people skills*. Managers spend the great majority of their time interacting with people,[64] and they must develop their abilities to lead, motivate, and communicate effectively with those around them.

A *Fortune* article decried the lack of communication and other "people" skills among recent MBAs launching their management careers.[65] It is vital to realize the importance of these skills in getting a job, keeping it, and performing well in it. As one expert commented, "In many, many companies, the reason a manager fails is not because he doesn't have the technical skills. It's because he doesn't have the people skills."[66]

The importance of these skills varies by managerial level. Technical skills are most important early in your career. Conceptual and decision skills become more important than technical skills as you rise higher in the company. But interpersonal skills are important throughout your career, at every level of management. Many high-potential, "fast-track" managers have had their careers "derailed" because of problems in the interpersonal arena.[67]

Managerial Skills, Decisions, and Careers

The managerial skills described above translate into good or bad decisions that affect reputations and careers—managers' own and those of the people whose careers they affect. Here are a few recent examples, prior to the chapter's final section on careers.

- Charles Schwab was honored for the way he handled his company's recent layoffs. Schwab and his co-CEO took a 50 percent pay cut, 750 other execs took cuts, and the firm encouraged employees to take off Fridays without pay. Only when those moves failed did they lay off 3,400 people. They softened the blow with 60 days' notice, stock-option grants, education stipends, and a $7,500 bonus to anyone who returned within 18 months.
- In contrast to the Schwab layoffs, the airlines were securing a $15 billion bailout from Congress when they announced plans to lay off 100,000 people. Three airlines invoked a clause claiming that emergency circumstances allowed them to bypass customary notice, severance, and early-retirement incentives. When this aroused public opinion, they backed off somewhat.
- Several people received special attention from *Fortune* magazine for their career-limiting moves. CEO Linda Wachner of Warnaco, the women's apparel maker, was kicked out without severance pay after 15 years. Warnaco is bankrupt, and its stock, once worth $44, was trading for pennies. A key customer, Calvin Klein, called Wachner a "cancer" on his brand. Wachner considered suing Warnaco for the $44 million golden parachute promised in her employment contract.
- CEO Neal Patterson of Cerner, a health care software company, was furious when he arrived to an empty corporate parking lot at 7:30 one March morning. He sent a blistering email to company managers, threatening to fire loafers. The memo said that "hell will freeze over" before he tolerates a lot that isn't "substantially full . . . You have two weeks. Tick, tock." A week later the email was all over the Web, precipitating a three-day, 22 percent drop in the stock price.
- Also suffering a shortage of decision-making and interpersonal skills, and receiving embarrassing publicity in *Fortune:* An analyst in the Carlyle Group's Seoul office sent friends an email describing his "harem of chickies" and bankers catering to his "every whim." The email made the rounds of the financial community (and some of it hit *The New York Times*). The young analyst was fired.

SOURCES: P. Sellers, "Home Depot's Home Defense," *Fortune*, October 15, 2001, p. 106; J. Kahn and B. O'Keefe, "Best & Worst 2001," *Fortune*, December 24, 2001, pp. 139–44.

You and Your Career

Chances are, you will work for several different organizations during your career.[68] Jobs are no longer as secure for managers as they used to be. But the shortage of talented managers means that companies must develop and retain good people. Although companies no longer "guarantee" jobs permanently, those that provide long-term career benefits like training and profit sharing and some degree of security can improve corporate performance. Employee loyalty and commitment are still important; they improve teamwork, while temporary employment does not generate the high levels of service and quality that create customer satisfaction. Companies offering "employability" to workers, in the form of training and other learning experiences while employees fulfill important responsibilities, tend to be more successful.[69]

What should you do to forge a successful, gratifying career? You are well advised to be both a specialist and a generalist, to be self-reliant and connected, to actively manage your relationship with your organization, and to be fully aware of what is required to not only survive, but also to thrive, in today's world.

Be Both a Specialist and a Generalist

If you think your career will be as a specialist, think again. Chances are, you will not want to stay forever in strictly technical jobs with no managerial responsibilities. Accountants are promoted to accounting department heads and team leaders, sales representatives become sales managers, writers become editors, and nurses become nursing directors. As your responsibilities increase, you must deal with more people, understand more about other aspects of the organization, and make bigger and more complex decisions. Beginning to learn now about these managerial challenges may yield benefits sooner than you think.

So, it will help if you can become both a specialist and a generalist.[70] Seek to become a *specialist:* you must be an expert in something. This will give you specific skills that help you provide concrete, identifiable value to your firm and to customers. And over time, you should learn to be a *generalist*, knowing enough about a variety of business or technical disciplines so that you can understand and work with different perspectives.

Be Self-Reliant

To be self-reliant means to take full responsibility for yourself, your actions, and your career.[71] You cannot count on your boss or your company to take care of you. A useful metaphor is to think of yourself as a business, with you as president and sole employee. Table 1.3 gives some specific advice about what this means in practice.

To make this point in another way: To add value, you must think and act like an entrepreneur.

Find new ways to make your overall performance better. Take responsibility for change; be an innovator.[72] Don't just do your work and wait for orders; look for opportunities to contribute in new ways, to develop new products and processes, and to generate constructive change that strengthens the company and benefits customers and colleagues.

Be Connected

Being *connected* means having many good working relationships and being a team player with strong interpersonal skills.[73] For example, those who want to become partners in professional service organizations like accounting, advertising, and consulting firms strive constantly to build a network of contacts. Their goal is to work not only with lots of clients but also with a half dozen or more senior partners, including several from outside their home offices and some from outside their country.

Playing golf is considered an excellent way to make contacts and build a network. BusinessWeek produced a supplement to the magazine in summer 2002, noting, "Business golf is very much a part of the modern world. Whether you're opening doors or closing deals, whether you're entertaining clients or being entertained, golf probably plays an important role."

TABLE 1.3
Keys to Career Management

Vicky Farrow of Sun Microsystems gave the following advice to help people assume responsibility for their own careers:

1. Think of yourself as a business.
2. Define your product: What is your area of expertise?
3. Know your target market: To whom are you going to sell this?
4. Be clear on why your customer buys from you. What is your "value proposition"— what are you offering that causes him to use you?
5. As in any business, strive for quality and customer satisfaction, even if your customer is just someone else in your organization—like your boss.
6. Know your profession or field and what's going on there.
7. Invest in your own growth and development, the way a company invests in research and development. What new products will you be able to provide?
8. Be willing to consider changing your career.

SOURCE: W. Kiechel III, "A Manager's Career in the New Economy," *Fortune*, April 4, 1994, pp. 68–72. Copyright © 1994 Times, Inc. All rights reserved. Reprinted by permission.

Having a network of "social resources" will enhance your career success because networks give you access to information, to resources, and to people who will help you.[74] Just ask Jay Alix, a successful advisor to and acquirer of troubled companies. Believing that in his competitive business getting hired is not a function of competence alone, but also of whom you know, Mr. Alix prides himself on his networking prowess. He stays in constant touch with hundreds of people, and calls his network of contacts "the daisy chain."[75]

Look at this another way: All business is a function of human relationships.[76] Building competitive advantage depends not only on you but on other people. Management is personal. Commercial dealings are personal. Purchase decisions, repurchase decisions, and contracts all hinge on relationships. Even the biggest business deals— takeovers—are intensely personal and emotional. Without good work relationships, you are an outsider, not a good manager and leader.

Actively Manage Your Relationship with Your Organization

Many of the previous comments suggest the importance of taking responsibility for your own actions and your own career. Unless you are self-employed and your own boss, one way to do this is to think about the nature of the relationship between you and your employer. Figure 1.1 shows two possible relationships—and you have some control over which relationship you will be in.

Relationship #1 is one in which you view yourself as an employee, and passively expect your employer to tell you what to do and give you pay and benefits. Your employer is in charge, and you are a passive recipient of its actions. Your contributions are likely to be minimal—you won't strengthen your organization, and if all organizational members

FIGURE 1.1
Two Relationships: Which Will You Choose?

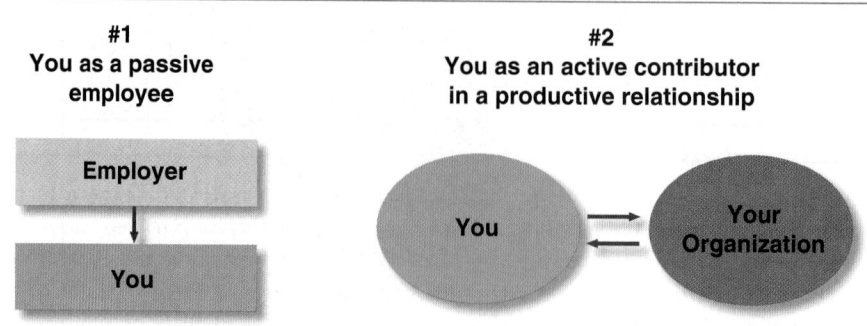

take this perspective, the organization is not likely to be strong for the long run. Personally, you may lose your job, or keep your job in a declining organization, or receive few positive benefits from working there and either quit or become cynical and unhappy in your work.

In contrast, relationship #2 is a two-way relationship in which you and your organization both benefit from one another. The mindset is different: Instead of doing what you are told, you think about how you can contribute—and you act accordingly. To the extent that your organization values your contributions, you are likely to benefit in return by receiving full and fair rewards, support for further personal development, and a more gratifying work environment. If you think in broad terms about how you can help your company, and if others think like this as well, there is likely to be continuous improvement in the company's ability to innovate, cut costs, and deliver quality products quickly to an expanding customer base. As the company's bottom line strengthens, benefits accrue to shareholders as well as to you and other employees.

What is the nature of the contributions you can make? You can do your basic work. But you can, and should, go further. You can also figure out new ways to add value—by thinking of and implementing new ideas that improve processes and results. You can do this by using your technical knowledge and skills, as in developing a better information system, accounting technique, or sales technique.

You also can contribute with your managerial actions (see Figure 1.2). You can execute the essential management functions and deliver competitive advantage. You can deliver strategic value (Part 2 of this book). You can take actions that help build a more dynamic organization (Part 3). You can mobilize people to contribute to their fullest potential (Part 4). And you can learn and change—and help your colleagues and company learn and change—in order to adapt to changing realities and forge a successful future (Part 5).

Survive and Thrive

Table 1.4 shows a resume that might help a person to not just survive, but to thrive, in the 21st century.[77] Don't be discouraged if your resume doesn't match this idealized resume—it's tough to match, especially early in life! But do think about the messages. It indicates the kinds of skills that companies need now more than ever—and therefore

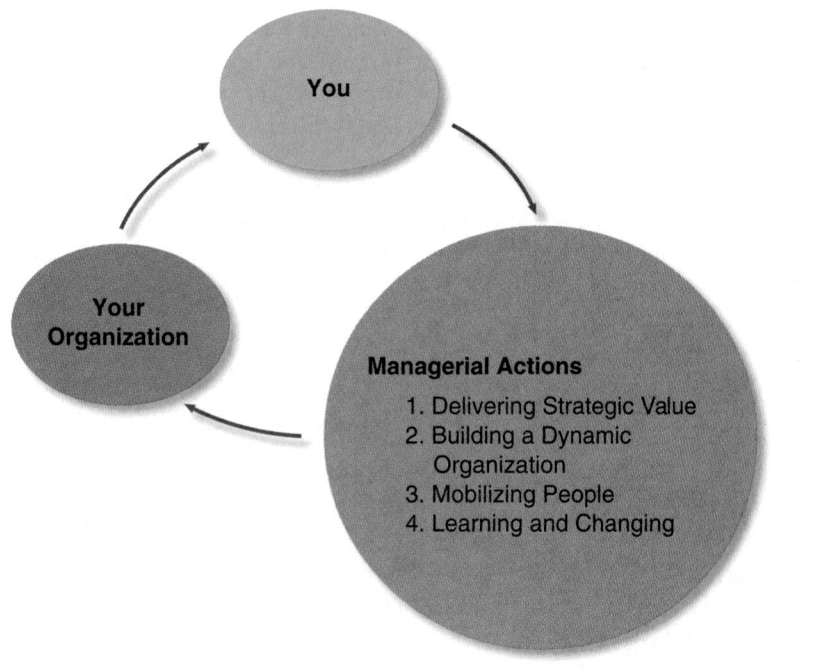

FIGURE 1.2
Managerial action is your opportunity to contribute

TABLE 1.4
A Resume for the
21st Century

Experience

- Multinational Corp—Worked with top-notch mentors in an established company with global operations. Managed a talented and fickle staff and helped tap new markets.
- Foreign Operation LLC—A stint at a subsidiary of a U.S. company, or at a foreign operation in a local market. Exposure to different cultures, conditions, and ways of doing business.
- Startup Inc.—Helped to build a business from the ground up, assisting with everything from product development to market research. Honed entrepreneurial skills.
- Major Competitor Ltd.—Scooped up by the competition and exposed to more than one corporate culture.

Education

- Liberal Arts University—Majored in economics, but took courses in psychology (how to motivate customers and employees), foreign language (the world is a lot bigger than the 50 states), and philosophy (to seek vision and meaning in your work).
- Graduate Studies—The subject almost doesn't matter, so long as you developed your thinking and analytical skills.

Extracurricular

- Debating (where you learned to market ideas and think on your feet).
- Sports (where you learned discipline and team work).
- Volunteer work (where you learned to step outside your own narrow world to help others).
- Travel (where you learned about different cultures).

SOURCE: D. Brady "Wanted: Eclectic Visionary with a Sense of Humor," *Business Week.* August 28, 2000, p. 144.

the skills you should consider working to develop and the experiences you might want to accumulate.

Management consultant and author Tom Peters points out that now—far more than ever—you will be accountable for your actions and for results.[78] In the past, people at many companies could show up, do an OK job, get a decent evaluation, and get a raise equal to the cost of living and maybe higher. Today, managers must do more, better, and it will all be far more visible. Managers will have many teammates, all around the globe, some of whom will know each other personally but many of whom will never meet. You are likely to move from project to project and from team to team. You will be evaluated "pass by pass, at-bat by at-bat—for the quality and uniqueness and timeliness and passion" of your contribution.[79] Peters concludes that the minimal skills you will need to survive and thrive are to be a master at something that the world values (and be able to state succinctly what it is); to develop a strong network of colleagues who can help (and whom you will help) with current and future projects; to have entrepreneurial skills that help you act as if you were running your own business; to love technology; to market yourself (for example, via a personal website); and to be willing to constantly improve and even reinvent yourself.

A study of career success led the author to state, "In the current economic environment, people who fear competition, want security, and demand stability are often sinking like rocks in water."[80] Success requires high standards, self-confidence in competitive situations, and a willingness to keep growing and learning new things.[81] You will need to learn how to think strategically, discern and convey your business vision, make decisions, and work in teams. You will need to deliver competitive advantage and thrive on change. These and other topics, essential to your successful career, provide the focus for the following chapters.

KEY TERMS

Conceptual and decision skills, p. 19

Controlling, p. 16

Cost competitiveness, p. 13

Frontline managers, p. 17

Innovation, p. 11

Interpersonal and communication skills, p. 20

Knowledge management, p. 8

Leading, p. 15

Management, p. 14

Middle-level managers, p. 17

Organizing, p. 15

Planning, p. 15

Quality, p. 12

Speed, p. 13

Technical skills, p. 19

Top-level managers, p. 17

SUMMARY OF LEARNING OBJECTIVES

Now that you have studied Chapter 1, you should know:

The major challenges of managing in the new competitive landscape.

Managers today must deal with dynamic forces that create greater and more constant change than ever before. Among many forces that are creating a need for managers to rethink their approaches, we highlighted four major waves of change: the Internet, globalization, knowledge management, and collaboration across organizational boundaries.

The drivers of competitive advantage for your company.

Because business is a competitive arena, you need to deliver value to customers in ways that are superior to your competitors. The four pillars of competitive advantage are innovation, quality, speed, and cost.

The functions of management and how they are evolving in today's business environment.

Despite massive change, management retains certain foundations that will not disappear. The primary functions of management are planning, organizing, leading, and controlling. Planning is analyzing a situation, determining the goals that will be pursued, and deciding in advance the actions needed to pursue these goals. Organizing is assembling the resources needed to complete the job and coordinating employees and tasks for maximum success. Leading is motivating people and stimulating high performance. Controlling is monitoring the progress of the organization or the work unit to-

ward goals and then taking corrective action if necessary. In today's business environment, these functions more broadly require creating strategic value, building a dynamic organization, mobilizing people, and learning and changing.

The nature of management at different organizational levels.

Top-level, strategic managers are the senior executives and are responsible for the organization's overall management. Middle-level, tactical managers translate general goals and plans into more specific objectives and activities. Frontline, operational managers are lower-level managers who supervise operations.

The skills you need to be an effective manager.

To execute management functions successfully, managers need technical skills, conceptual and decision skills, and interpersonal and communication skills. A technical skill is the ability to perform a specialized task involving a certain method or process. Conceptual and decision skills help the manager recognize complex and dynamic issues, analyze the factors that influence those issues or problems, and make appropriate decisions. Interpersonal and communication skills enable the manager to interact and work well with people.

What to strive for as you manage your career.

To help you succeed in your career, keep in mind several goals: Be both a specialist and a generalist; be self-reliant but also connected; actively manage your relationship with your organization; and continuously improve your skills in order to perform in the ways demanded in the changing work environment.

DISCUSSION QUESTIONS

1. Identify and describe a great manager. What makes him or her stand out from the crowd?

2. Have you ever seen or worked for an ineffective manager? Describe the causes and the consequences of the ineffectiveness.

3. Describe how the Internet and globalization affect your daily life.

4. Identify some examples of how different organizations collaborate "across boundaries."

5. Name a great organization. How do you think management contributes to making it great?

6. Name an ineffective organization. What can management do to improve it?

7. Give examples you have seen of firms that are outstanding and weak on each of the four pillars of competitive advantage. Why do you choose the firms you do?

8. Describe your use of the four management functions in the management of your daily life.

9. Discuss the importance of technical, conceptual, and inter-personal skills at school and in jobs you have held.

10. What are your strengths and weaknesses as you contemplate your career? How do they correlate with the skills and behaviors identified in the chapter?

11. Devise a plan for developing yourself and making yourself attractive to potential employers. How would you go about improving your managerial skills?

Would You Work Here?

Siebel Systems sells complex software packages. Some people love it there and are rewarded handsomely, but others don't survive the place for very long.

People say that the founder and CEO, Tom Siebel, is brilliant. They also say he is the most intense, competitive, driven person they know. "Running a business is a fundamentally rational process" says Siebel (p. 132). "We unemotionally put things on the table, look each other straight in the eye, and state the facts."

Siebel Systems doesn't miss deadlines, like so many other software companies do. It releases new versions of its product every spring, right on schedule. And it is the only enterprise-software company in the United States to zoom past $1 billion in revenues without serious problems along the way. It grew like crazy, but everything is carefully controlled.

Siebel has rules for everything. Offices must have medium-blue carpeting, off-white walls, gray desktops. There is no eating at desks, no cartoons or posters on doors. An occasional photo of family or friends is OK—but not too many. Men must wear suit and tie, and women must wear pant or skirt suits and pantyhose. Siebel says, "I like to think of us as the Tiger Woods of the information technology industry. Tiger Woods does not play the U.S. Open in cutoffs, sneakers, and a Budweiser T-shirt. That's unimaginable. His shirt is pressed. His shoes are shined. And his level of performance—his driving average, his score—has exceeded all other competitors."

Contrasting the work environment of his company with those of the Silicon Valley stereotype, Siebel says, "We go to work to realize our professional aspirations, not to have a good time. We could be having encounter groups and yoga classes, and I could play the guitar in the rock & roll band at the company picnic. Instead we're just trying to create good products, satisfied customers, and loyal employees. I think we're doing that" (p. 133). He also says "There are people who think I'm God's gift to technology, and people who think I'm the world's biggest S.O.B" (p. 140).

Siebel wants all of his people to focus on the customer, and motivates them by systematically and regularly measuring customer satisfaction with specific departments and individuals. These results determine bonuses and commissions. Moreover, to remind his people who matters most, every conference room is named after a Siebel customer. Says Siebel, "The cornerstone of our corporate culture is that we are committed to do whatever it takes to make sure that each and every one of our customers succeeds" (p. 136).

Each quarter, Siebel communicates corporate objectives to the company. Two days later, department managers communicate their departmental objectives. Two weeks later, individual objectives are established. And precisely three months later, each employee receives a formal performance evaluation.

Personal goals are posted on the company intranet. They can be viewed at any time by anybody. Every six months, the bottom 5 percent are asked to leave.

All of Siebel's 1,500 sales agents file weekly progress reports on current deals. They handicap the odds of a "close"—"5 percent, opportunity qualified," "15 percent, proposal presented," up to 100 percent when the contract is signed. The report details dates of contacts, known competitive bidders, and dates when rivals are eliminated.

Every single employee, including secretaries, security guards—everyone—must complete at least five Web-based tutorials on Siebel products each quarter. Each tutorial ends in an exam, with 90 percent or above required to pass. Test results go into digital files and are considered in quarterly performance reviews.

Siebel believes that if he keeps micromanaging, the company will grind to a halt, so he is trying to loosen up a bit and stop over-controlling. Some people say that he is changing. But the character of the company remains: If you want to succeed there, you must be smart, thorough, fastidious about the details, and perhaps a workaholic. You must also be fast; Siebel sometimes calls on a customer on a Friday and promises a proposal by Monday. One employee says, "That's part of the reason we win so many deals. We turn on a dime" (p. 140).

Siebel was one of the first (on February 27, 2001) to warn Wall Street analysts of a possible tech depression. He laid off 800 people; cut off three business units that were losing money;

Thomas Siebel, founder and CEO of Siebel Systems, strives to create good products, satisfied customers, and loyal employees.

cut travel, marketing, and hiring budgets; and cut top executives' pay by 20 percent. He also was one of the first to state that the recession was over and that tech would rebound beginning in the first quarter of 2002, when he started hiring again.

DISCUSSION QUESTIONS

1. On a 10-point scale, in which 1 = not at all and 10 = extremely, how attractive is Siebel as a place to work?

2. What are the strengths and weaknesses of the organization and its leader?

3. Based on this profile, do you think Siebel will do well in the long run? How is it doing now?

4. How would you advise Mr. Siebel?

5. If you were interested in working for Siebel, would it see you as an attractive candidate? Why or why not?

6. If you worked for Siebel, how would you contribute to making the company stronger?

SOURCE: M. Warner, "Confessions of a Control Freak," *Fortune*, September 4, 2000, pp. 130–40; C. Hawn, "The Man Who Sees Around Corners," *Forbes*, January 21, 2002, pp. 72–78; B. Fryer, "High Tech the Old-Fashioned Way: An Interview with Tom Siebel of Siebel Systems," *Harvard Business Review*, March 2001, pp. 118–25.

1.1 Effective Managers

OBJECTIVES

1. To better understand what behaviors contribute to effective management.

2. To conceive a ranking of critical behaviors that you personally believe reflects their importance to your success as a manager.

INSTRUCTIONS

1. Following is a partial list of behaviors in which managers may engage. Rank these items in terms of their importance for effective performance as a manager. Put a 1 next to the item that you think is most important, 2 for the next most important, down to 10 for the least important.

2. Bring your rankings to class. Be prepared to justify your results and rationale. If you can add any behaviors to this list that might lead to success or greater management effectiveness, write them in.

Effective Managers Worksheet

_____ Communicates and interprets policy so that it is understood by the members of the organization.

_____ Makes prompt and clear decisions.

_____ Assigns subordinates to the jobs for which they are best suited.

_____ Encourages associates to submit ideas and plans.

_____ Stimulates subordinates by means of competition among employees.

_____ Seeks means of improving management capabilities and competence.

_____ Fully supports and carries out company policies.

_____ Participates in community activities as opportunities arise.

_____ Is neat in appearance.

_____ Is honest in all matters pertaining to company property or funds.

SOURCE: Excerpted from Lawrence R. Jauch, Arthur G. Bedeian, Sally A. Coltrin, and William F. Glueck, *The Managerial Experience: Cases, Exercises, and Readings,* 5th ed. Copyright © 1989. Reprinted with permission of South-Western, a division of Thomson Learning, www.thomsonrights.com.

1.2 Career Planning

OBJECTIVES

1. To explore your career thinking.

2. To visualize your ideal job in terms as concrete as possible.

3. To summarize the state of your career planning, and to become conscious of the main questions you have about it at this point.

INSTRUCTIONS

Read the instructions for each activity, reflect on them, and then write your response. Be as brief or extensive as you like.

EXPERIENTIAL EXERCISES

Career Planning Worksheet

1. Describe your ideal occupation in terms of responsibilities, skills, and how you would know if you were successful.

_____

_____

_____

_____

_____

_____

_____

_____

2. Identify 10 statements you can make today about your current career planning. Identify 10 questions you need answered for career planning

10 statements	10 questions
1. _____	1. _____
2. _____	2. _____
3. _____	3. _____
4. _____	4. _____
5. _____	5. _____
6. _____	6. _____
7. _____	7. _____
8. _____	8. _____

9. _____   9. _____

_____   _____

_____   _____

10. _____   10. _____

_____   _____

_____   _____

Source: Judith R. Gordon, *Diagnostic Approach to Organizational Behavior*. Copyright © 1983 Pearson Education, Inc. Reprinted by permission of Pearson Education, Inc. Upper Saddle River, NJ.

The Evolution of Management

For thousands of years, managers have wrestled with the same issues and problems confronting executives today. Around 1100 B.C., the Chinese practiced the four management functions—planning, organizing, leading, and controlling—discussed in Chapter 1. Between 350 and 400 B.C., the Greeks recognized management as a separate art and advocated a scientific approach to work. The Romans decentralized the management of their vast empire before the birth of Christ. During medieval times, the Venetians standardized production through the use of an assembly line, building warehouses and using an inventory system to monitor the contents.[1]

But throughout history most managers operated strictly on a trial-and-error basis. The challenges of the industrial revolution changed that. Management emerged as a formal discipline at the turn of the century. The first university programs to offer management and business education, the Wharton School at the University of Pennsylvania and the Amos Tuck School at Dartmouth, were founded in the late 19th century. By 1914, 25 business schools existed.[2]

Thus, the management profession as we know it today is relatively new. This appendix explores the roots of modern management theory. Understanding the origins of management thought will help you grasp the underlying contexts of the ideas and concepts presented in the chapters ahead.

Although this appendix is titled "The Evolution of Management," it might be more appropriately called "The Revolutions of Management," because it documents the wide swings in management approaches over the last 100 years. Out of the great variety of ideas about how to improve management, parts of each approach have survived and been incorporated into modern perspectives on management. Thus, the legacy of past efforts, triumphs, and failures has become our guide to future management practice.

EARLY MANAGEMENT CONCEPTS AND INFLUENCES

Communication and transportation constraints hindered the growth of earlier businesses. Therefore, improvements in management techniques did not substantially improve performance. However, the industrial revolution changed that. As companies grew and became more complex, minor improvements in management tactics produced impressive increases in production quantity and quality.[3]

The emergence of **economies of scale**—reductions in the average cost of a unit of production as the total volume produced

increases—drove managers to strive for further growth. The opportunities for mass production created by the industrial revolution spawned intense and systematic thought about management problems and issues—particularly efficiency, production processes, and cost savings.[4]

Figure A.1 provides a timeline depicting the evolution of management thought through the decades. This historical perspective is divided into two major sections: classical approaches and contemporary approaches. Many of these approaches developed simultaneously, and they often had a significant impact on one another. Some approaches were a direct reaction to the perceived deficiencies of previous approaches. Others developed as the needs and issues confronting managers changed over the years. All the approaches attempted to explain the real issues facing managers and provide them with tools to solve future problems.

Figure A.1 will reinforce your understanding of the key relationships among the approaches and place each perspective in its historical context.

CLASSICAL APPROACHES

The classical period extended from the mid-19th century through the early 1950s. The major approaches that emerged during this period were systematic management, scientific management, administrative management, human relations, and bureaucracy.

Systematic Management During the 19th century, growth in U.S. business centered on manufacturing.[5] Early writers such as Adam Smith believed the management of these firms was chaotic, and their ideas helped to systematize it. Most organizational tasks were subdivided and performed by specialized labor. However, poor coordination among subordinates and different levels of management caused frequent problems and breakdowns of the manufacturing process.

The **systematic management** approach attempted to build specific procedures and processes into operations to ensure coordination of effort. Systematic management emphasized economical operations, adequate staffing, maintenance of inventories to meet consumer demand, and organizational control. These goals were achieved through:

- Careful definition of duties and responsibilities.
- Standardized techniques for performing these duties.

FIGURE A.1
The Evolution of Management Thought

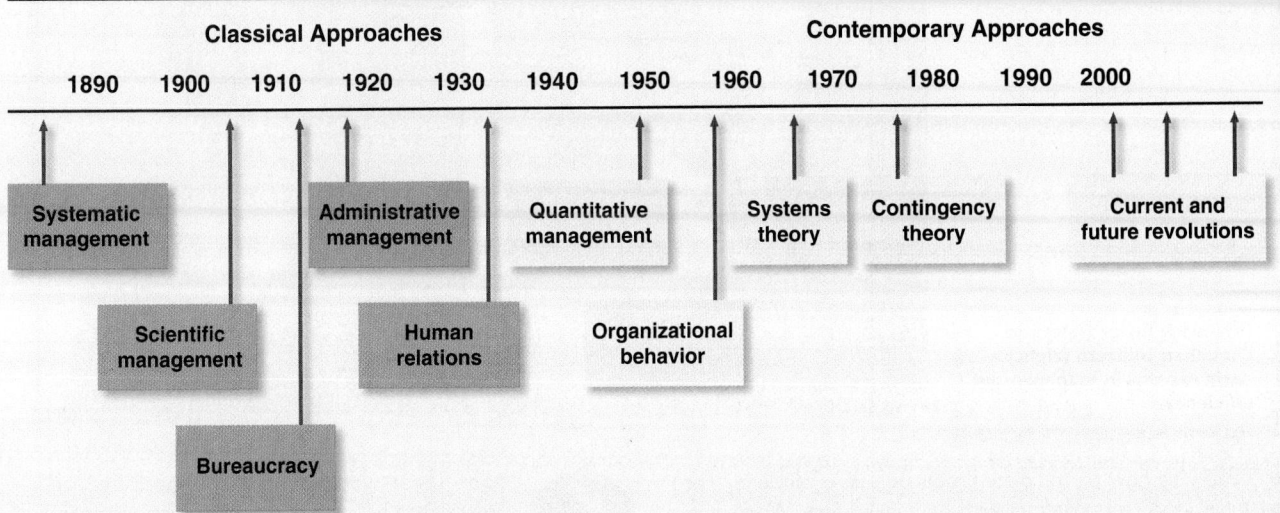

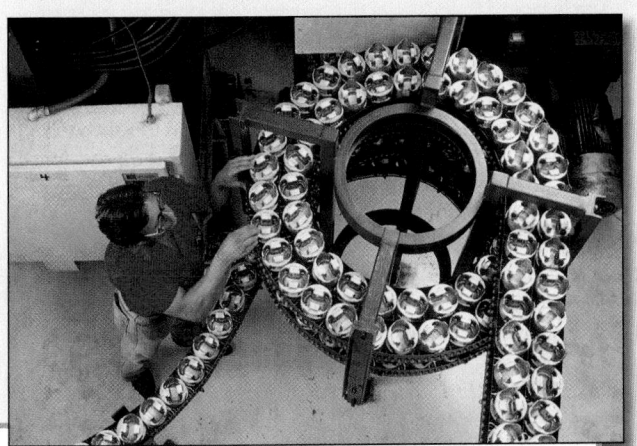

Production costs dropped as mass manufacturing lowered unit costs. Thus economies of scale was born, a concept that persists in the modern manufacturing era.

- Specific means of gathering, handling, transmitting, and analyzing information.
- Cost accounting, wage, and production control systems to facilitate internal coordination and communications.

Systematic management emphasized internal operations because managers were concerned primarily with meeting the explosive growth in demand brought about by the Industrial Revolution. In addition, managers were free to focus on internal issues of efficiency, in part because the government did not constrain business practices significantly. Finally, labor was poorly organized. As a result, many managers were oriented more toward things than toward people.

Table A.1 lists some of the key concepts, contributions, and limitations of systematic management. Although systematic management did not address all the issues 19th-century managers faced, it tried to raise managers' awareness about the most pressing concerns of their job.

Scientific Management Systematic management failed to lead to widespread production efficiency. This shortcoming became apparent to a young engineer named Frederick Taylor who was hired by Midvale Steel Company in 1878. Taylor discovered that production and pay were poor, inefficiency and waste were prevalent, and most companies had tremendous unused potential. He concluded that management decisions were unsystematic and that no research to determine the best means of production existed.

In response, Taylor introduced a second approach to management, known as **scientific management**.[6] This approach advocated the application of scientific methods to analyze work and

TABLE A.1
Systematic Management

Key Concepts
Systematized manufacturing operations.
Coordination of procedures and processes built into internal operations.
Emphasis on economical operations, inventory management, and cost control.
Contributions
Beginning of formal management in the United States.
Promotion of efficient, uninterrupted production.
Limitations
Ignored relationship between an organization and its environment.
Ignored differences in managers' and workers' views.

Frederick Taylor (left) and
Dr. Lillian Gilbreth (right) were
early experts in management
efficiency.

to determine how to complete production tasks efficiently. For example, U.S. Steel's contract with the United Steel Workers of America specified that sand shovelers should move 12.5 shovelfuls per minute; shovelfuls should average 15 pounds of river sand composed of 5.5 percent moisture.[7]

Taylor identified four principles of scientific management:

1. Management should develop a precise, scientific approach for each element of one's work to replace general guidelines.

2. Management should scientifically select, train, teach, and develop each worker so that the right person has the right job.

3. Management should cooperate with workers to ensure that jobs match plans and principles.

4. Management should ensure an appropriate division of work and responsibility between managers and workers.

To implement this approach, Taylor used techniques such as time-and-motion studies. With this technique, a task was divided into its basic movements, and different motions were timed to determine the most efficient way to complete the task.

After the "one best way" to perform the job was identified, Taylor stressed the importance of hiring and training the proper worker to do that job. Taylor advocated the standardization of tools, the use of instruction cards to help workers, and breaks to eliminate fatigue.

 Another key element of Taylor's approach was the use of the differential piecerate system. Taylor assumed workers were motivated by receiving money. Therefore, he implemented a pay system in which workers were paid additional wages when they exceeded a standard level of output for each job. Taylor concluded that both workers and management would benefit from such an approach.

Scientific management principles were widely embraced. Other proponents, including Henry Gantt and Frank and Lillian Gilbreth, introduced many refinements and techniques for applying scientific management on the factory floor. One of the most famous examples of the application of scientific management is the factory Henry Ford built to produce the Model T.

At the turn of the century, automobiles were a luxury that only the wealthy could afford. They were assembled by craftspeople who put an entire car together at one spot on the factory

 floor. These workers were not specialized, and Henry Ford believed they wasted time and energy bringing the needed parts to the car. Ford took a revolutionary approach to automobile manufacturing by using scientific management principles.

After much study, machines and workers in Ford's new factory were placed in sequence so that an automobile could be assembled without interruption along a moving production line. Mechanical energy and a conveyor belt were used to take the work to the workers.

The manufacture of parts likewise was revolutionized. For example, formerly it had taken one worker 20 minutes to assemble a flywheel magneto. By splitting the job into 29 different operations, putting the product on a mechanical conveyor, and changing the height of the conveyor, Ford cut production time to 5 minutes.

By 1914 chassis assembly time had been trimmed from almost 13 hours to $1\frac{1}{2}$ hours. The new methods of production required complete standardization, new machines, and an adaptable labor force. Costs dropped significantly, the Model T became the first car accessible to the majority of Americans, and Ford dominated the industry for many years.[8]

The legacy of Taylor's scientific management approach is broad and pervasive. Most important, productivity and efficiency in manufacturing improved dramatically. The concepts of scientific methods and research were introduced to manufacturing. The piecerate system gained wide acceptance because it more closely aligned effort and reward. Taylor also emphasized the need for cooperation between management and workers. And the concept of a management specialist gained prominence.

Despite these gains, not everyone was convinced that scientific management was the best solution to all business problems. First, critics claimed that Taylor ignored many job-related social and psychological factors by emphasizing only money as a worker incentive. Second, production tasks were reduced to a set of routine, machinelike procedures that led to boredom, apathy, and quality control problems. Third, unions strongly opposed scientific management techniques because they believed management might abuse their power to set the standards and the piecerates, thus exploiting workers and diminishing their importance. Finally, although scientific management resulted in intense scrutiny of the internal efficiency of organizations, it did not help managers deal with broader external issues such as competitors and

TABLE A.2
Scientific Management

Analyzed work using scientific methods to determine the "one best way" to complete production tasks.

Emphasized study of tasks, selection and training of workers, and cooperation between workers and management.

Improved factory productivity and efficiency.

Introduced scientific analysis to the workplace.

Piecerate system equated worker rewards and performance.

Instilled cooperation between management and workers.

Simplistic motivational assumptions.

Workers viewed as parts of a machine.

Potential for exploitation of labor.

Excluded senior management tasks.

Ignored relationship between the organization and its environment.

TABLE A.3
Fayol's 14 Principles of Management

1. *Division of work*—divide work into specialized tasks and assign responsibilities to specific individuals.
2. *Authority*—delegate authority along with responsibility.
3. *Discipline*—make expectations clear and punish violations.
4. *Unity of command*—each employee should be assigned to only one supervisor.
5. *Unity of direction*—employees' efforts should be focused on achieving organizational objectives.
6. *Subordination of individual interest to the general interest*—the general interest must predominate.
7. *Remuneration*—systematically reward efforts that support the organization's direction.
8. *Centralization*—determine the relative importance of superior and subordinate roles.
9. *Scalar chain*—keep communications within the chain of command.
10. *Order*—order jobs and material so they support the organization's direction.
11. *Equity*—fair discipline and order enhance employee commitment.
12. *Stability and tenure of personnel*—promote employee loyalty and longevity.
13. *Initiative*—encourage employees to act on their own in support of the organization's direction.
14. *Esprit de corps*—promote a unity of interests between employees and management.

government regulations, especially at the senior management level. Table A.2 summarizes some of the key concepts, contributions, and limitations of scientific management.

Administrative Management The **administrative management** approach emphasized the perspective of senior managers within the organization, and argued that management was a profession and could be taught.

An explicit and broad framework for administrative management emerged in 1916, when Henri Fayol, a French mining engineer and executive, published a book summarizing his management experiences. Fayol identified five functions and 14 principles of management. The five functions, which are very similar to the four functions discussed in Chapter 1, include planning, organizing, commanding, coordinating, and controlling. Table A.3 lists and defines the 14 principles. Although some critics claim Fayol treated the principles as universal truths for management, he actually wanted them applied flexibly.[9]

A host of other executives contributed to the administrative management literature. These writers discussed a broad spectrum of management topics, including the social responsibilities of management, the philosophy of management, clarification of business terms and concepts, and organizational principles. Chester Barnard's and Mary Parker Follet's contributions have become classic works in this area.[10]

Barnard, former president of New Jersey Bell Telephone Company, published his landmark book *The Functions of the Executive* in 1938. He outlined the role of the senior executive: formulating the purpose of the organization, hiring key individuals, and maintaining organizational communications.[11] Mary Parker Follet's 1942 book *Dynamic Organization* extended Barnard's work by emphasizing the continually changing situations that managers face.[12] Two of her key contributions—the notion that managers desire flexibility and the differences between motivating groups and individuals—laid the groundwork for the modern contingency approach discussed later in the chapter.

All the writings in the administrative management area emphasize management as a profession along with fields such as law and medicine. In addition, these authors offered many recommendations based on their personal experiences, which often included managing large corporations. Although these perspectives and recommendations were considered sound, critics noted that they might not work in all settings. Different types of personnel, industry conditions, and technologies may affect the appropriateness of these principles.

Table A.4 summarizes the administrative management approach.

Human Relations A fourth approach to management, **human relations,** developed during the 1930s. This approach aimed at understanding how psychological and social processes interact with the work situation to influence performance. Human relations was the first major approach to emphasize informal work relationships and worker satisfaction.

This approach owes much to other major schools of thought. For example, many of the ideas of the Gilbreths (scientific management) and Barnard and Follet (administrative management) influenced the development of human relations from 1930 to 1955. In fact, human relations emerged from a research project that began as a scientific management study.

TABLE A.4
Administrative Management

Key Concepts
Fayol's five functions and 14 principles of management.
Executives formulate the organization's purpose, secure employees, and maintain communications.
Managers must respond to changing developments.

Contributions
Viewed management as a profession that can be trained and developed.
Emphasized the broad policy aspects of top-level managers.
Offered universal managerial prescriptions.

Limitation
Universal prescriptions need qualifications for environmental, technological, and personnel factors.

Western Electric Company, a manufacturer of communications equipment, hired a team of Harvard researchers led by Elton Mayo and Fritz Roethlisberger. They were to investigate the influence of physical working conditions on workers' productivity and efficiency in one of the company's factories outside Chicago. This research project, known as the *Hawthorne Studies*, provided some of the most interesting and controversial results in the history of management.[13]

The Hawthorne Studies were a series of experiments conducted from 1924 to 1932. During the first stage of the project (the Illumination Experiments), various working conditions, particularly the lighting in the factory, were altered to determine the effects of those changes on productivity. The researchers found no systematic relationship between the factory lighting and production levels. In some cases, productivity continued to increase even when the illumination was reduced to the level of moonlight. The researchers concluded that the workers performed and reacted differently because the researchers were observing them. This reaction is known as the **Hawthorne Effect.**

This conclusion led the researchers to believe productivity may be affected more by psychological and social factors than by physical or objective influences. With this thought in mind, they initiated the other four stages of the project. During these stages, the researchers performed various work group experiments and had extensive interviews with employees. Mayo and his team eventually concluded that productivity and employee behavior were influenced by the informal work group.

Human relations proponents argued that managers should stress primarily employee welfare, motivation, and communication. They believed social needs had precedence over economic needs. Therefore, management must gain the cooperation of the group and promote job satisfaction and group norms consistent with the goals of the organization.

Another noted contributor to the field of human relations was Abraham Maslow.[14] In 1943, Maslow suggested that humans have five levels of needs. The most basic needs are the physical needs for food, water, and shelter; the most advanced need is for self-actualization, or personal fulfillment. Maslow argued that people try to satisfy their lower-level needs and then progress upward to the higher-level needs. Managers can facilitate this process and achieve organizational goals by removing obstacles and encouraging behaviors that satisfy people's needs and organizational goals simultaneously.

Although the human relations approach generated research into leadership, job attitudes, and group dynamics, it drew heavy criticism.[15] Critics believed that one result of human relations—a belief that a happy worker was a productive worker—was too simplistic. While scientific management overemphasized the economic and formal aspects of the workplace, human relations ignored the more rational side of the worker and the important characteristics of the formal organization. However, human relations was a significant step in the development of management thought, because it prompted managers and researchers to consider the psychological and social factors that influence performance.

Table A.5 summarizes the human relations approach.

Bureaucracy   Max Weber, a German sociologist, lawyer, and social historian, showed how management itself could be more efficient and consistent in his book *The Theory of Social and Economic Organizations*.[16] The ideal model for management, according to Weber, is the **bureaucracy** approach.

Weber believed bureaucratic structures can eliminate the variability that results when managers in the same organization have different skills, experiences, and goals. Weber advocated that the jobs themselves be standardized so that personnel changes would not disrupt the organization. He emphasized a structured, formal network of relationships among specialized positions in an organization. Rules and regulations standardize behavior, and authority resides in positions rather than in individuals. As a result, the organization need not rely on a particular individual, but will realize efficiency and success by following the rules in a routine and unbiased manner.

TABLE A.5
Human Relations

Key Concepts
Productivity and employee behavior are influenced by the informal work group.
Cohesion, status, and group norms determine output. Managers should stress employee welfare, motivation, and communication.
Social needs have precedence over economic needs.

Contributions
Psychological and social processes influence performance.
Maslow's hierarchy of needs.

Limitations
Ignored workers' rational side and the formal organization's contribution to productivity.
Research findings later overturned the simplistic belief that happy workers are always more productive.

TABLE A.6
Bureaucracy

Key Concepts
Structured, formal network of relationships among specialized positions in an organization.
Rules and regulations standardize behavior.
Jobs staffed by trained specialists who follow rules.
Hierarchy defines the relationship among jobs.

Contributions
Promotes efficient performance of routine organizational activities.
Eliminates subjective judgment by employees and management.
Emphasizes position rather than the person.

Limitations
Limited organizational flexibility and slow decision making.
Ignores the importance of people and interpersonal relationships.
Accumulation of power can lead to authoritarian management.
Rules may become ends in themselves.
Difficult to dismantle once established.

According to Weber, bureaucracies are especially important because they allow large organizations to perform the many routine activities necessary for their survival. Also, bureaucratic positions foster specialized skills, eliminating many subjective judgments by managers. In addition, if the rules and controls are established properly, bureaucracies should be unbiased in their treatment of people, both customers and employees.

Many organizations today are bureaucratic. Bureaucracy can be efficient and productive. However, bureaucracy is not the appropriate model for every organization. Organizations or departments that need rapid decision making and flexibility may suffer under a bureaucratic approach. Some people may not perform their best with excessive bureaucratic rules and procedures.

Other shortcomings stem from a faulty execution of bureaucratic principles rather than from the approach itself. Too much authority may be vested in too few people; the procedures may become the ends rather than the means; or managers may ignore appropriate rules and regulations. Finally, one advantage of a bureaucracy—its permanence—can also be a problem. Once a bureaucracy is established, dismantling it is very difficult.

Table A.6 summarizes the key concepts, contributions and limitations of bureaucracy.

CONTEMPORARY APPROACHES

The contemporary approaches to management include quantitative management, organizational behavior, systems theory, and the contingency perspective. The contemporary approaches have developed at various times since World War II, and they continue to represent the cornerstones of modern management thought.

Quantitative Management   Although Taylor introduced the use of science as a management tool early in the 20th century, most organizations did not adopt the use of quantitative techniques for management problems until the 1940s and 1950s.[17] During World War II, military planners began to apply mathematical techniques to defense and logistic problems. After the war, private corporations began assembling teams of quantitative experts to tackle many of the complex issues confronting large organizations. This approach, referred to as **quantitative management,** emphasizes the application of quantitative analysis to management decisions and problems.

Quantitative management helps a manager make a decision by developing formal mathematical models of the problem. Computers have facilitated the development of specific quantitative methods. These include such techniques as statistical decision theory, linear programming, queuing theory, simulation, forecasting, inventory modeling, network modeling, and break-even analysis. Organizations apply these techniques in many areas, including production, quality control, marketing, human resources, finance, distribution, planning, and research and development.

Despite the promise quantitative management holds, managers do not rely on these methods as the primary approach to decision making. Typically they use these techniques as a supplement or tool in the decision process. Many managers will use results that are consistent with their experience, intuition, and judgment, but they will reject results that contradict their beliefs. Also, managers may use the process to compare alternatives and eliminate weaker options.

Several explanations account for the limited use of quantitative management. Many managers have not been trained in using these techniques. Also, many aspects of a management decision cannot be expressed through mathematical symbols and formulas. Finally, many of the decisions managers face are nonroutine and unpredictable.

Table A.7 summarizes the quantitative management approach.

TABLE A.7
Quantitative Management

Key Concept
Application of quantitative analysis to management decisions.

Contributions
Developed specific mathematical methods of problem analysis.
Helped managers select the best alternative among a set.

Limitations
Models neglect nonquantifiable factors.
Managers not trained in these techniques and may not trust or understand the techniques' outcomes.
Not suited for nonroutine or unpredictable management decisions.

Organizational Behavior   During the 1950s, a transition took place in the human relations approach. Scholars began to recognize that worker productivity and organizational success are based on more than the satisfaction of economic or social needs. The revised perspective, known as **organizational behavior,** studies and identifies management activities that promote employee effectiveness through an understanding of the complex nature of individual, group, and organizational processes. Organizational behavior draws from a variety of disciplines, including psychology and sociology, to explain the behavior of people on the job.

During the 1960s, organizational behaviorists heavily influenced the field of management. Douglas McGregor's Theory X and Theory Y marked the transition from human relations.[18] According to McGregor, Theory X managers assume workers are lazy and irresponsible and require constant supervision and external motivation to achieve organizational goals. Theory Y managers assume employees *want* to work and can direct and control themselves. McGregor advocated a Theory Y perspective, suggesting that managers who encourage participation and allow opportunities for individual challenge and initiative would achieve superior performance.

Other major organizational behaviorists include Chris Argyris, who recommended greater autonomy and better jobs for workers,[19] and Rensis Likert, who stressed the value of participative management.[20] Through the years, organizational behavior has consistently emphasized development of the organization's human resources to achieve individual and organizational goals. Like other approaches, it has been criticized for its limited perspective, although more recent contributions have a broader and more situational viewpoint. In the past few years, many of the primary issues addressed by organizational behavior have experienced a rebirth with a greater interest in leadership, employee involvement, and self-management.

Table A.8 summarizes the key concepts, contributions, and limitations of organizational behavior.

Systems Theory   The classical approaches as a whole were criticized because they (1) ignored the relationship between the organization and its external environment, and (2) usually stressed one aspect of the organization or its employees at the expense of other considerations. In response to these criticisms, management scholars during the 1950s stepped back from the details of the organization to attempt to understand it as a whole system. These efforts were based on a general scientific approach called **systems theory.**[21] An organization is a managed system that transforms inputs (raw materials, people, and other resources) into outputs (the goods and services that comprise its products).

Table A.9 summarizes systems theory.

Contingency Perspective   Building on systems theory ideas, the **contingency perspective** refutes universal principles of management by stating that a variety of factors, both internal and external to the firm, may affect the organization's performance.[22] Thus, there is no "one best way" to manage and organize, because circumstances vary. For example, a universal strategy of offering low-cost products would not succeed in a market that is not cost conscious.

Situational characteristics are called **contingencies.** Understanding contingencies helps a manager know which sets of circumstances dictate which management actions. You will learn the recommendations for the major contingencies throughout this text. The contingencies include

1. Circumstances in the organization's external environment.
2. The internal strengths and weaknesses of the organization.
3. The values, goals, skills, and attitudes of managers and workers in the organization.
4. The types of tasks, resources, and technologies the organization uses.

TABLE A.8
Organizational Behavior

Key Concepts
Promotes employee effectiveness through understanding of individual, group, and organizational processes.
Stresses relationships among employees, managers, and the work they perform for the organization.
Assumes employees want to work and can control themselves (Theory Y).
Contributions
Increased participation, greater autonomy, individual challenge and initiative, and enriched jobs may increase performance.
Recognized the importance of developing human resources.
Limitation
Some approaches ignored situational factors, such as the environment and the organization's technology.

TABLE A.9
Systems Theory

Key Concepts
Organization is viewed as a managed system.
Management must interact with the environment to gather inputs and return the outputs of its production.
Organizational objectives must encompass both efficiency and effectiveness.
Organizations contain a series of subsystems.
There are many avenues to the same outcome.
Synergies exist where the whole is greater than the sum of the parts.
Contribution
Recognized the importance of the organization's relationship with the external environment.
Limitation
Does not provide specific guidance on the functions and duties of managers.

TABLE A.10
Contingency Perspective

Key Concepts
Situational contingencies influence the strategies, structures, and processes that result in high performance.
There is more than one way to reach a goal.
Managers may adapt their organizations to the situation.

Contributions
Identified major contingencies.
Argued against universal principles of management.

Limitations
Not all important contingencies have been identified.
Theory may not be applicable to all managerial issues.

With an eye to these contingencies, a manager may categorize the situation and then choose the proper competitive strategy, organization structure, or management process for the circumstances.

Researchers continue to identify key contingency variables and their effects on management issues. As you read the topics covered in each chapter, you will notice similarities and differences among management situations and the appropriate responses. This perspective should represent a cornerstone of your own approach to management. Many of the things you will learn about throughout this course apply a contingency perspective.

Table A.10 summarizes the contingency perspective.

CONTEMPORARY APPROACHES

All of these historical perspectives have left legacies that affect contemporary management thought and practice. Their undercurrents continue to flow, even as the context and the specifics change.

But new approaches to management continue to appear, and contribute to an ever-changing management profession. The remaining chapters report on these dynamic, contemporary perspectives. For example, the 1980s brought a new gospel called *quality management*, new perspectives on competition and on business strategy, a focus on excellence, and a renewed interest in people, including both employees and customers.[23] The 1990s brought theories and practices such as learning organizations, lean manufacturing, knowledge management, and the characteristics of corporate cultures that help to build great, enduring companies.[24] The rest of this book, and perhaps the rest of your career, will be spent enacting the management functions, the drivers of competitive advantage, the enduring aspects of the historical perspectives, and the continually evolving contemporary perspectives on the successful practice of management.

KEY TERMS

administrative management A classical management approach that attempted to identify major principles and functions that managers could use to achieve superior organizational performance, p. 33.

bureaucracy A classical management approach emphasizing a structured, formal network of relationships among specialized positions in the organization, p. 34.

contingencies Factors that determine the appropriateness of managerial actions, p. 36.

contingency perspective An approach to the study of management proposing that the managerial strategies, structures, and processes that result in high performance depend on the characteristics, or important contingencies, or the situation in which they are applied, p. 36.

economies of scale Reductions in the average cost of a unit of production as the total volume produces increases, p. 30.

Hawthorne Effect People's reactions to being observed or studied resulting in superficial rather than meaningful changes in behavior, p. 34.

human relations A classical management approach that attempted to understand and explain how human psychological and social processes interact with the formal aspects of the work situation to influence performance, p. 33.

organizational behavior A contemporary management approach that studies and identifies management activities that promote employee effectiveness by examining the complex and dynamic nature of individual, group, and organizational processes, p. 36.

quantitative management A contemporary management approach that emphasizes the application of quantitative analysis to managerial decisions and problems, p. 35.

scientific management A classical management approach that applied scientific methods to analyze and determine the "one best way" to complete production tasks, p. 31.

systematic management A classical management approach that attempted to build into operations the specific procedures and processes that would ensure coordination of effort to achieve established goals and plans, p. 30.

systems theory A theory stating that an organization is a managed system that changes inputs into outputs, p. 36.

DISCUSSION QUESTIONS

1. How does today's business world compare with the one of 40 years ago? What is different about today, and what is not so different?

2. What is scientific management? How might today's organizations use it?

3. Table A.3 lists Fayol's 14 principles of management, first published in 1916. Are they as useful today as they were then? Why or why not? *When* are they most, and least, useful?

4. What are the advantages and disadvantages of a bureaucratic organization?

5. In what situations are quantitative management concepts and tools applicable?

6. Choose any organization and describe its system of inputs and outputs.

7. Why did the contingency perspective become such an important approach to management? Generate a list of contingencies that might affect the decisions you make in your life or as a manager.

8. For each of the management approaches discussed in the chapter, give examples you have seen. How effective or ineffective were they?

A.1 Approaches to Management

OBJECTIVES

1. To help you conceive a wide variety of management approaches.
2. To clarify the appropriateness of different management approaches in different situations.

INSTRUCTIONS

Your instructor will divide your class randomly into groups of four to six people each. Acting as a team, with everyone offering ideas and one person serving as official recorder, each group will be responsible for writing a one-page memo to your present class. Subject matter of your group's memo will be "My advice for managing people today is . . ." The fun part of this exercise (and its creative element) involves writing the memo from the viewpoint of the person assigned to your group by your instructor.

Among the memo viewpoints your instructor may assign are:

- An ancient Egyptian slave master (building the great pyramids)
- Henri Fayol
- Frederick Taylor
- Mary Parker Follett
- Douglas McGregor

- A contingency management theorist
- A Japanese auto company executive
- The chief executive officer of IBM in the year 2030
- Commander of the Starship Enterprise II in the year 3001
- Others, as assigned by your instructor

Use your imagination, make sure everyone participates, and try to be true to any historical facts you've encountered. Attempt to be as specific and realistic as possible. Remember, the idea is to provide advice about managing people from another point in time (or from a particular point of view at the present time).

Make sure you manage your 20-minute time limit carefully. A recommended approach is to spend 2 to 3 minutes putting the exercise into proper perspective. Next, take about 10 to 12 minutes brainstorming ideas for your memo, with your recorder jotting down key ideas and phrases. Have your recorder use the remaining time to write your group's one-page memo, with constructive comments and help from the others. Pick a spokesperson to read your group's memo to the class.

SOURCE: R. Krietner and A. Kinicki, *Organization Behavior*, 3d ed. (Burr Ridge, IL: Richard D. Irwin, 1994), pp. 30–31.

A.2 The University Grading System Analysis

OBJECTIVES

1. To learn to identify the components of a complex system.
2. To better understand organizations as systems.
3. To visualize how a change in policy affects the functioning of an organization system.

INSTRUCTIONS

1. Assume that your university has decided to institute a pass–fail system of grading instead of the letter-grade system it presently has. Apply the systems perspective learned from this chapter to understanding this decision.
2. Answer the questions on the Grading System Analysis Worksheet individually, or in small groups, as directed by your instructor.

DISCUSSION QUESTIONS

Share your own or your group's responses with the entire class. Then answer the following questions.

1. Did you diagram the system in the same way?
2. Did you identify the same system components?
3. Which subsystems will be affected by the change?
4. How do you explain differences in your responses?

Grading System Analysis Worksheet

DESCRIPTION

1. What subsystems compose the system (the university)? Diagram the system.

_____

_____

_____

2. Identify in this system: inputs, outputs, transformations.

_____

_____

_____

DIAGNOSIS

3. Which of the subsystems will be affected by the change; that is, what changes are likely to occur throughout the system as a result of the policy change?

_____

_____

_____

SOURCE: J. Gordon, A _Diagnostic Approach to Organizational Behavior_ (Englewood Cliffs, NJ: Prentice-Hall, 1983), p. 38. Reprinted with permission of Prentice-Hall, Inc., Englewood Cliffs, NJ.

CHAPTER 2

The External Environment

The essence of a business is outside itself.

—**Peter Drucker**

CHAPTER OUTLINE

A Look Ahead
The Macroenvironment
Law and Regulations
The Economy
Technology
Demographics
Social Issues and the Natural Environment
The Competitive Environment
Competitors
Threat of New Entrants
Threat of Substitutes
Suppliers
Customers
Environmental Analysis
Environmental Scanning
Scenario Development
Forecasting
Benchmarking
Responding to the Environment
Adapting to the Environment: Changing Yourself
Influencing Your Environment
Changing the Environment You Are In
Choosing a Response Approach

LEARNING OBJECTIVES

After studying Chapter 2, you will know:

1. How environmental forces influence organizations, as well as how organizations can influence their environments.

2. How to make a distinction between the macroenvironment and the competitive environment.

3. Why organizations should attend to economic and social developments in the international environment.

4. How to analyze the competitive environment.

5. How organizations respond to environmental uncertainty.

TELECOMS FACE EXTERNAL PRESSURES

While there was plenty of blame to go around after the dot-com meltdown in the early 2000s, from poor strategy to corporate greed, another factor played a role in the failure of many firms: government regulations. A lawyer for Global Crossing, which filed for bankruptcy after falling from its exalted position as one of the top-earning telecom firms, likened the fees demanded by all levels of government to robbery, saying, "They're being held up."

Local, state, and government agencies demanded excessive fees or free services from firms before granting them rights-of-way for cables. Moreover, breaking through the red tape sometimes took years before access was approved as the firms' requests worked their way through bureaucracies and legal hurdles. The results for consumers were delays in service, limited providers, and higher prices when the excessive fees were passed on to them.

For example, although Global Crossing had been told that it needed only a routine permit to finish its trans-Pacific fiber-optic cable over the final 60 miles to Seattle, the federal National Oceanic and Atmospheric Administration (NOAA) then required $5 million from the firm as a fee for laying the cable within a federal marine sanctuary. The permit fees included $3.9 million to monitor the effects of the cable on the sanctuary's starfish, coral, sponges, and other sea life over 10 years and $500,000 to finance a visitors-center exhibit about the ocean floor. A separate $7.2 million easement fee was charged by NOAA for the fair market value of the ocean property easement.

Other telecom participants, such as phone providers, complain that the cable systems receive exclusive franchises while they must compete with each other (as well as with the cable systems). Government agencies are allowed by law to seek only "fair and reasonable compensation" for rights-of-way, which the agencies feel means the equivalent of market rents, while the firms feel they should not have to pay for more than the impact of their work. "If we cut up the street, we believe we should have to restore it, but when we

Staying connected is essential to business, but telecom firms often face high government fees in providing services.

see fees based on my gross operating revenues, I have a problem tying that to the city's costs," says Williams Communications's Rick Wolfe.

Here are some of examples of the barriers faced by telecom firms:

- *High fees*. For the right to run wires in White Plains, New York, to provide fast data services to businesses, AT&T was asked to pay 5 percent not only of the local phone-service revenue but also of long-distance, wireless, and cable-service income from the town. Eugene, Oregon, charges 9 percent of basic phone revenue.

- *Demands for free service*. When Williams wanted to lay 10 miles of cable along Maryland highways, that state's department of transportation required Williams to provide free fiber-optic cable that monitors the temperature of state roads and links computers so that citizens can apply for state licenses online, in addition to $780,000 a year in right-of-way fees.

- *Red tape.* When Qwest installed less than a mile of wire for broadband service for its one business customer, Berkeley, California, the city charged it for excessive information, such as business plans, application fees, and underground maps, which Qwest called "intrusive and a tremendous amount of work." (A court struck down many of the paperwork rules.)
- *Delays.* After 10 months of repeatedly contacting Shreveport, Lovisiana, as it tried to finalize a franchise, Adelphia dropped its plans. Culver City, California, forced Adelphia, Level 3 Communications, and Metromedia Fiber Network to wait nearly two years while it debated a right-of-way ordinance.

Federal Communications Commission Chairman Michael Powell noted his agency's "growing concern about rights-of-way as a barrier." Texas, Florida, Michigan, and Kansas recently limited the fees cities can charge, and a bill has been introduced in Congress to curb the right-of-way fees levied by federal agencies such as NOAA.

Source: Adapted from Paul Davidson, "Cities, Feds Force Firms to Pay for Rights-of-Way," *USA Today,* July 2, 2002.

Besides problems of their own making, telecom firms were beset by government fees and restrictions—factors of the external environment—that affected their ability to compete effectively. This chapter discusses how pressures from outside organizations create the external context in which organizations operate.

As you learned in the first chapter, organizations are open systems that are affected by, and in turn affect, their external environments. By **external environment,** we mean all relevant forces outside the organization's boundaries. By *relevant,* we mean factors to which managers must pay attention to help their organizations compete effectively and survive.

Many of these factors are uncontrollable. Companies large and small are buffeted or battered by recession, government interference, competitors' actions, and so forth. But their lack of control does not mean that managers can ignore such forces, use them as excuses for poor performance, and try to just get by. Managers must stay abreast of external developments and react accordingly. Moreover, as we will discuss later in this chapter, it sometimes is possible to influence components of the external environment. We will examine ways in which organizations can do just that.

Figure 2.1 shows the external environment of a firm. The firm exists in its **competitive environment,** which is composed of the firm and competitors, suppliers, customers, new entrants, and substitutes. At the more general level is the **macroenvironment,** which includes legal, political, economic, technological, demographic, and social and natural factors that generally affect all organizations.

external environment

All relevant forces outside a firm's boundaries, such as competitors, customers, the government, and the economy.

competitive environment

The immediate environment surrounding a firm; includes suppliers, customers, competitors, and the like.

macroenvironment

The most general environment; includes governments, economic conditions, and other fundamental factors that generally affect all organizations.

A Look Ahead

This chapter discusses the basic characteristics of an organization's environment and the importance of that environment for strategic management. Later chapters will elaborate on many of the basic environmental forces introduced here. For example, technology will be discussed again in Chapter 17. The global environment gets a thorough treatment in Chapter 6, which is devoted entirely to international management. Other chapters focus on ethics, social responsibility, and the natural environment. Chapter 18 reiterates the theme that recurs throughout this text: Organizations must change continually because environments change continually.

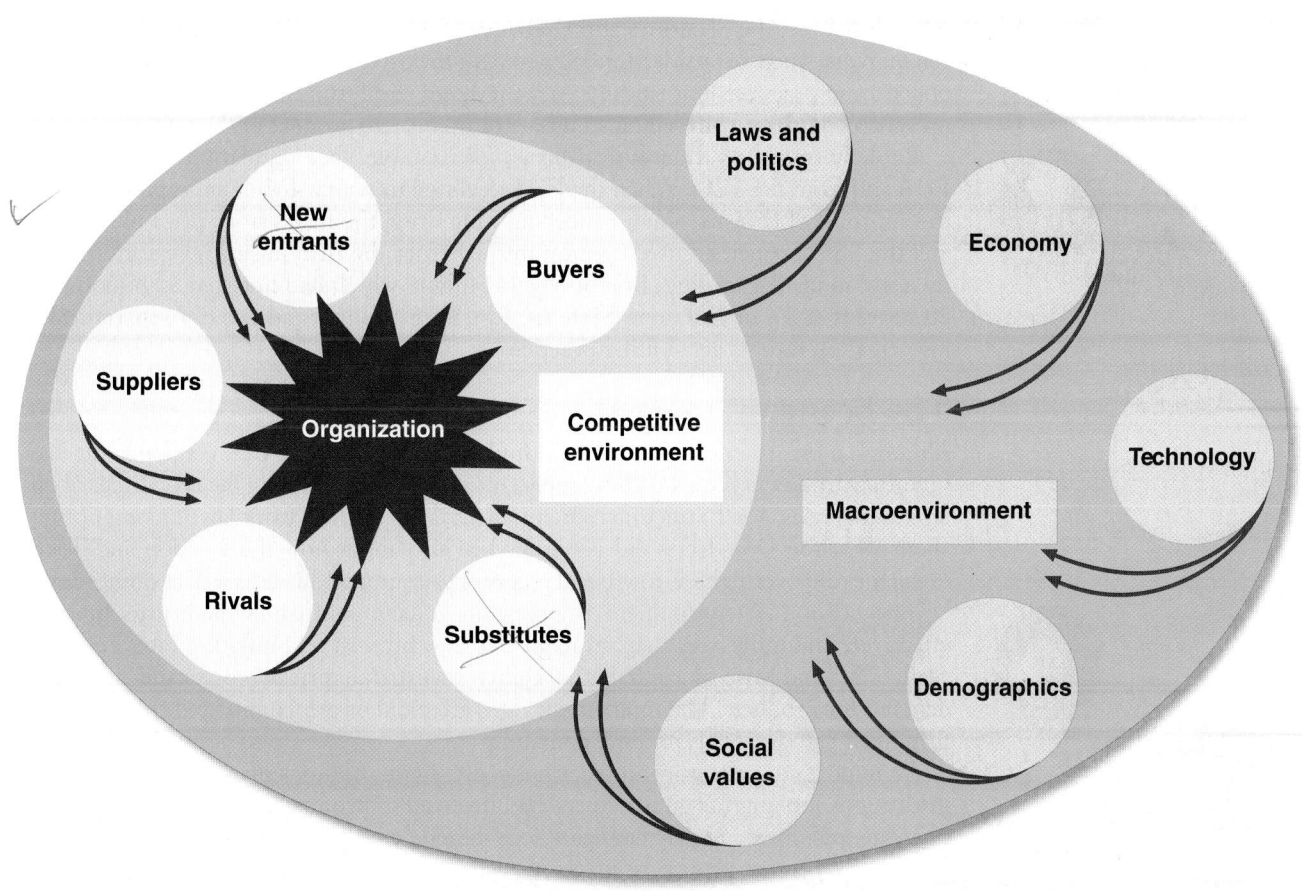

FIGURE 2.1
The External Environment

The Macroenvironment

All organizations operate in a macroenvironment, which is defined by the most general elements in the external environment that potentially can influence strategic decisions. Although a top executive team may have unique internal strengths and ideas about its goals, it must consider external factors before taking action.

Laws and Regulations

U.S. government policies both impose strategic constraints and provide opportunities. The government can affect business opportunities through tax laws, economic policies, and international trade rulings. An example of restraint on business action is the U.S. government's standards regarding bribery. In some countries, bribes and kickbacks are common and expected ways of doing business, but for U.S. firms these are illegal practices. Indeed, some U.S. businesses have been fined for using bribery when competing internationally.

Regulators are specific government organizations in a firm's more immediate task environment. Regulatory agencies such as the Occupational Safety and Health Administration (OSHA), the Interstate Commerce Commission (ICC), the Federal Aviation Administration (FAA), the Equal Employment Opportunity Commission (EEOC), the National Labor Relations Board (NLRB), the Office of Federal Contract Compliance Programs (OFCCP), and the Environmental Protection Agency (EPA) have the power to investigate company practices and take legal action to ensure compliance with the laws.

For example, the Securities and Exchange Commission (SEC) regulates U.S. financial markets; since the insider-trading scandals, the SEC has changed investment houses' policies and practices dramatically. And the Food and Drug Administration (FDA) can prevent a company from selling an unsafe or ineffective product to the public.

Publicly traded pharmaceutical firms, for example, face regulation both from the FDA and from the SEC. When the FDA declined to review IMClone's application for the approval of Erbitux, a new cancer-fighting drug, the firm's stock price plummeted and the SEC opened an investigation into whether the firm misled investors and was involved in insider trading. Bristol-Myers Squibb, which had invested $2 billion for a 20 percent stake in IMClone Systems, lost $875 million and faced a separate SEC investigation into its accounting practices.[1]

The Economy

Although most Americans are used to thinking in terms of the U.S. economy, the economic environment is created by complex interconnections among the economies of different countries. Wall Street investment analysts begin their workday thinking not just about what the Dow Jones did yesterday but also about how the London and Tokyo exchanges did overnight. Growth and recessions occur worldwide as well as domestically.

The economic environment dramatically affects companies' ability to function effectively and influences their strategic choices. Interest and inflation rates affect the availability and cost of capital, the ability to expand, prices, costs, and consumer demand for products. Unemployment rates affect labor availability and the wages the firm must pay, as well as product demand.

An important economic influence has centered on the stock market. Individuals and institutions looking for good returns had invested in promising companies, including start-ups and dot-coms. When technology-based firms during the 1990s provided better than 20 percent returns to investors, more individuals entered the capital markets (Figure 2.2). With the slide in technology stocks and the mistrust of corporate accounting, the returns fell to negative numbers in the early 2000s, although other economic indicators remained strong.[2]

Economic conditions change over time and are difficult to predict. Bull and bear markets come and go. Periods of dramatic growth may be followed by a recession. Every trend undoubtedly will end—but when? Even when times seem good, budget deficits or other considerations create concern about the future.

Technology

Today a company cannot succeed without incorporating into its strategy the astonishing technologies that exist and continue to evolve. Technological advances create new products, advanced production techniques, and better ways of managing and communicating.

FIGURE 2.2

Twelve-Month Comparison of Stock Markets

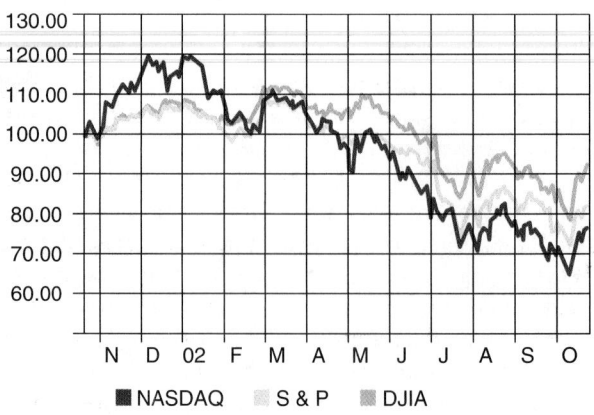

SOURCE: www.nasdaq.com.

In addition, as technology evolves, new industries, markets, and competitive niches develop. For example, the advent of computers created a huge industry. Early entrants in biotechnology are trying to establish dominant positions, while later entrants work on technological advances that will give them a competitive niche.

New technologies also provide new production techniques. In manufacturing, sophisticated robots perform jobs without suffering fatigue, requiring vacations or weekends off, or demanding wage increases. Until the U.S. steel industry began modernizing its plants, its productivity lagged far behind that of the technologically superior Japanese plants.

New technologies also provide new ways to manage and communicate. Computerized management information systems (MIS) make information available when needed. Computers monitor productivity and note performance deficiencies. Telecommunications allow conferences to take place without requiring people to travel to the same location. Consider the following discussion of changes in the field of retail sporting goods. As you can see, technological advances create innovations in business. Strategies developed around the cutting edge of technological advances create a competitive advantage; strategies that ignore or lag behind competitors in considering technology lead to obsolescence and extinction. This issue is so important that we devote an entire chapter (Chapter 17) to the topic.

FROM THE PAGES OF

BusinessWeek

Sports Gear Goes Geek

As Lance Armstrong tackles the French Alps, he's measuring his ascent with the help of an engineering marvel from Nike and the Japanese watchmaker Seiko: an altimeter built into a titanium-coated wristwatch. Armstrong's eyes are protected by sunglasses from Oakley that are precision molded to thousandths of an inch for aerodynamic efficiency and equipped with optical lenses so clear that a laser beam can pass through them without noticeable defraction. Under Armstrong's body floats a superstrong carbon fiber-epoxy bicycle frame built to cut the wind with teardrop-shaped tubing and weighing in at a pixiesque 2.27 pounds.

Mirroring changes in the manufacturing and aerospace industries over the past decade, cycling has experienced a rapid evolution from gut check to geek tech. Computerized engineering and materials science have influenced the design of everything from pedals, to shoes, to gear assemblies. In sports ranging from golf and tennis to sailing and softball, sports-equipment companies increasingly apply space-age techniques they once reserved for the pros to everyday products. It's all part of a mad scramble to win customers and improve margins in a sports-equipment market that totaled $65 billion in 2001 in the United States alone.

As computer power soared and prices sank, three dimensional (3-D) modeling quickly got cheap. A select group of sporting-goods companies took notice. Most were in areas where athletes rely heavily on technology, such as golf, cycling, tennis, and running. As they incorporated 3-D modeling into design and production, those firms found that they were able to tweak designs to unprecedented tolerances. "We're moving a nose piece a hundredth of an inch back and forth to make sure it looks the best. It's pretty obsessive," says Oakley's president, Colin Baden. The Foothill Ranch (California) company produces not only sunglasses but also wristwatches and apparel.

Computerized design also spawned a generation of machines that use digital coordinates to generate precision scale models in light-reactive plastics or wax, and those machines can receive commands from any place around the globe. Engineers could go from concept drawings to prototypes in hours, not days. Sporting-goods companies with serious design shops either own such a device or use one regularly. Oakley's Baden can input design parameters into his prototype machine in the morning, have resin sunglass models by noon, pop in premade lenses, and have mountain bikers and skiers test the models and provide feedback by 5 P.M. Nike's Boyd notes that this quick cycle is particularly important in sports where ergonomic factors are crucial to a product's sales potential.

More powerful computers also have given designers the ability to simulate stress tests virtually. That in turn has encouraged designers to try using newer materials in their products, since they no longer have to worry about overengineering the entire package to compensate for unknown stress patterns. "If we find a material process that might have been used to make taillights for cars but think it would have a great application in a new category like watches, we would be in the forefront of trying to use that no matter what the disastrous consequences might be," says Oakley's Baden.

The design and manufacturing advances boost the companies' bottom lines. While it's hard to quantify the precise savings, most outfits claim that they cut costs with computers by reducing staffing, pushing products to market faster, and eliminating mistakes earlier in the design and concept stages. In the early 1990s Oakley introduced two or three new sunglass frames per year. In 2001 it introduced 11.

Greater product variety has helped generate steadily growing sales (higher by 18 percent in 2001). "If we can apply the latest in technology in our manufacturing efforts, we tend to gain substantially in our margins," says Baden. Boosting margins, as well as stoking demand with innovative products, has become an imperative in the sector, especially in the current rocky economy. According to the sports-market researcher SGMA International, U.S. manufacturers' sales of sports equipment, apparel, footwear, and recreational vehicles, watercraft, and bicycles to wholesalers fell by 1.8 percent in 2001, declining to $65 billion from $66.1 billion in 2000. In certain products, such as cycling, sales declined by double digits. Slackening demand increases the pressure on sporting-goods companies to cut costs further, and this probably means that even more will turn to computer-aided design and manufacturing.

So far the majority of sports outfits, most of which design simple products, remain largely in the Dark Ages when it comes to using advanced computer techniques. "Some of them are older industries. They haven't broken into a lot of the new materials and design processes. We see a lot of opportunities there," says Brian Vogel, president of the Sommerville, Massachusetts, product-design firm Altitude. More businesses could quickly make the switch once the benefits become clearer and as companies start to understand how accessible these new technologies are. Most design software today costs less than $10,000. And Boyd regularly runs his programs on his laptop; he even designed a new sports CD player for Nike on a flight to Hong Kong. All this goes to show that cutting-edge companies such as Nike and Oakley continue to forge ahead faster than Lance Armstrong on his finish-line kick along the Champs Elysées.

SOURCE: Alex Salkever, "Sports Gear Goes Geek," *BusinessWeek*, July 16, 2002.

New technologies have been adapted to new purposes, such as sporting goods. World champion cyclist Lance Armstrong is high-tech from helmet to shoes to bicycle.

Demographics

Demographics are measures of various characteristics of the people comprising groups or other social units. Work groups, organizations, countries, markets, and societies can be described statistically by referring to their members' age, gender, family size, income, education, occupation, and so forth.

Companies must consider workforce demographics in formulating their human resources strategies. Population growth influences the size and composition of the labor force. By 2010, the U.S. civilian labor force, growing at a rate of 1.1 percent annually, is expected to reach

demographics

Measures of various characteristics of the people who comprise groups or other social units.

approximately 158 million. Fluctuations in the birthrate influence population trends somewhat. In past years, the number of younger workers (16 to 24 years of age) has declined, but now that children of the baby-boom generation are entering the workforce, this age group is expected to grow 16.8 percent by 2010. At the same time, baby boomers themselves are reaching retirement age, and so the number of older workers (55 and above) will rise to about 15 percent of the labor force. Eventually, declining participation in work of older persons will largely offset the increase in the number of persons in this population group.

Immigration is also a factor that significantly influences the U.S. population and labor force. Over the last decade immigrants have accounted for approximately 40 percent of the U.S. population growth, a trend that has an important impact on the labor force. Immigrants are frequently of working age but have different educational and occupational backgrounds from the rest of the labor force. By 2010, the labor force will be even more diverse than it is today. White males will constitute approximately 39 percent of the labor force, African-Americans 13 percent, Hispanics 13 percent, and Asians and others 6 percent.

Women continue to join the U.S. labor force in record numbers. In 1970, women made up only about one-third of the labor force. By 2010 women are expected to account for over 51.9 percent, a trend that provides companies with more talent from which to choose.[3]

A more diverse workforce has its advantages, but managers have to make certain they provide equality for women and minorities with respect to employment, advancement opportunities, and compensation. Strategic plans must be made for recruiting, retaining, training, motivating, and effectively utilizing people of diverse demographic backgrounds with the skills needed to achieve the company's mission.

Social Issues and the Natural Environment

Societal trends regarding how people think and behave have major implications for management of the labor force, corporate social actions, and strategic decisions about products and markets.

During the 1980s and 1990s women in the workforce often chose to delay having children as they focused on their careers, but today more working women are having children and then returning to the workforce. As a result, companies have introduced more supportive policies, including family leave, flexible working hours, and child care assistance. Many firms also extend these benefits to all employees or allow them to design their own benefits packages, where they can choose from a menu of available benefits that suit their individual situations. Domestic partners, whether they are in a marital relationship or not, also are covered by many employee benefit programs. Firms provide these benefits as a way of increasing a source of competitive advantage: an experienced workforce.

The new Honda FCX, the first hydrogen-powered fuel cell vehicle, is the first car in the world to be certified as a Zero-Emission Vehicle.

A prominent issue today pertains to natural resources: drilling for oil in formerly protected areas in the United States. Firms in the oil industry face considerable public opinion both in favor of preserving the natural environment, and against the country's dependence on other countries for fuel. Automakers face similar concerns about air quality as they strive to create more fuel-efficient cars.[4] The protection of the natural environment is so important to managerial decision that we devote Appendix C following Chapter 5 to it.

The Competitive Environment

All organizations are affected by the general components of the macroenvironment we have just discussed. Each organization also functions in a closer, more immediate competitive environment. The competitive environment includes the specific organizations with which the organization interacts. As shown in Figure 2.3, the competitive environment includes rivalry among current competitors, threat of new entrants, threat of substitutes, power of suppliers, and power of customers. This model was originally developed by Michael Porter, a Harvard professor and a noted authority on strategic management. According to Porter, successful managers do more than simply react to the environment; they act in ways that actually shape or change the organization's environment. In strategic decision making, Porter's model is an excellent method for analyzing the competitive environment in order to adapt to or influence the nature of competition.

Competitors

Among the various components of the competitive environment, competitors within the industry must first deal with one another. When organizations compete for the same customers and try to win market share at the others' expense, all must react to and anticipate their competitors' actions.

The first question to consider is: Who is the competition? Sometimes answers are obvious. Coca-Cola and PepsiCo are competitors, as are the Big Three automakers: General Motors, Ford, and DaimlerChrysler. But sometimes organizations focus too exclusively on traditional rivalries and miss the emerging ones. Historically, Sears & Roebuck focused on its competition with J.C. Penney. However, Sears' real competitors are Kmart and Wal-Mart at the low end; Target in the middle; Nordstrom at the high end; and a variety of catalogers, such as L.L. Bean, and Eddie Bauer. Similarly, United Airlines, Delta, American, and U.S.Airways have focused their attention on a battle over long haul and international routes. In the process, they all but ignored smaller carriers such as Southwest, Alaska Air, and Jet Blue that have grown and succeeded in regional markets.[5]

Thus, as a first step in understanding their competitive environment, organizations must identify their competitors. Competitors may include (1) small domestic firms, especially their entry into tiny, premium markets; (2) overseas firms, especially their efforts to solidify positions in small niches (a traditional Japanese tactic); (3) big, new domestic companies exploring new markets; (4) strong regional competitors; and (5) unusual entries such as Internet shopping.

FIGURE 2.3

The Competitive Environment

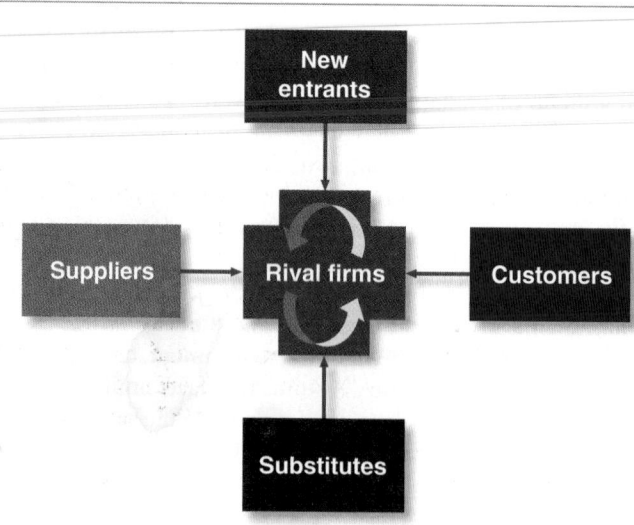

Once competitors have been identified, the next step is to analyze how they compete. Competitors use tactics such as price reductions, new-product introductions, and advertising campaigns to gain advantage over their rivals. It's essential to understand what competitors are doing when you are honing your own strategy. Competition is most intense when there are many direct competitors (including foreign contenders), when industry growth is slow, and when the product or service cannot be differentiated in some way.

New, high-growth industries offer enormous opportunities for profits. When an industry matures and growth slows, profits drop. Then, intense competition causes an industry shakeout: Weaker companies are eliminated, and the strong companies survive.[6]

Threat of New Entrants

New entrants into an industry compete with established companies. If many factors prevent new companies from entering the industry, the threat to established firms is less serious. If there are few such **barriers to entry,** the threat of new entrants is more serious. Some major barriers to entry are government policy, capital requirements, brand identification, cost disadvantages, and distribution channels. The government can limit or prevent entry, as occurs when the FDA forbids a new drug entrant. Some industries, such as trucking and liquor retailing, are regulated; more subtle government controls operate in fields such as mining and ski area development. Patents are also entry barriers. When a patent expires, other companies can then enter the market. For example, when the pharmaceutical firm Eli Lilly and Co.'s patent on its antidepressant drug Prozac expired, it lost its U.S. monopoly on the drug and its sales plunged. Barr Laboratories Inc. won the right to be the exclusive seller of a generic version of Prozac for six months. After that period other copycats flooded the market, eroding Barr's sales of the drug.

barriers to entry

Conditions that prevent new companies from entering an industry.

Other barriers are less formal but can have the same effect. Capital requirements may be so high that companies won't risk or try to raise such large amounts of money. Brand identification forces new entrants to spend heavily to overcome customer loyalty. The cost advantages established companies hold—due to large size, favorable locations, existing assets, and so forth—also can be formidable entry barriers.

Finally, existing competitors may have such tight distribution channels that new entrants have difficulty getting their products or services to customers. For example, established food products already have supermarket shelf space. New entrants must displace existing products with promotions, price breaks, intensive selling, and other tactics.

Threat of Substitutes

Technological advances and economic efficiencies are among the ways that firms can develop substitutes for existing products. For example, although Southwest Airlines has developed strong rivalries with other airlines, it also competes—as a substitute—with bus companies such as Greyhound and rental car companies such as Avis. Southwest has gotten its cost base down to such a low point that it is now cheaper to fly from Los Angeles to Phoenix than it is to take a bus or rent a car. This particular example shows that substitute products or services can limit another industry's revenue potential. Companies in those industries are likely to suffer growth and earnings problems unless they improve quality or launch aggressive marketing campaigns.[7]

In addition to current substitutes, companies need to think about potential substitutes that may be viable in the near future. For example, as alternatives to fossil fuels, experts suggest that nuclear fusion, solar power, and wind energy may prove useful one day. The advantages promised by each of these technologies are many: inexhaustible fuel supplies, electricity "too cheap to meter," zero emissions, universal public acceptance, and so on. Yet while they may look good on paper (and give us a warm, fuzzy feeling inside), they often come up short in terms of economics and/or technical viability. Table 2.1 shows a list of products and potential substitutes.[8]

If the Product Is . . .	The Substitute Might Be . . .
Cotton	Polyester
Coffee	Soft drinks
Fossil fuels	Solar fusion
Movie theater	Home video/DVD
Music CD	Radio/MP3
Automobile	Train, bus, bicycle
Personal computer	Personal Digital Assistant (PDA)
Sugar	Nutrasweet
House	Apartment, condo, mobile home
Bricks	Aluminum siding
Trashy magazine	Internet
Local telephone	Cellular phone, pager

TABLE 2.1
Potential Substitutes
for Products

Suppliers

Recall from our discussion of open systems that organizations must acquire resources from their environment and convert those resources into products or services to sell. Suppliers provide the resources needed for production and may come in the form of people (supplied by trade schools and universities), raw materials (supplied by producers, wholesalers, and distributors), information (supplied by researchers and consulting firms), and financial capital (supplied by banks and other sources). But suppliers are important to an organization for reasons that go beyond the resources they provide. Suppliers can raise their prices or provide poor-quality goods and services. Labor unions can go on strike or demand higher wages. Workers may produce defective work. Powerful suppliers, then, can reduce an organization's profits, particularly if the organization cannot pass on price increases to its customers.

The summer of 2002 saw yet another threat of a baseball strike—the 9th since 1972—by the major league baseball union.

One particularly noteworthy set of suppliers to some industries is the international labor unions. Although unionization in the United States has dropped to about 10 percent of the private labor force, labor unions are still particularly powerful in industries such as steel, autos, and transportation. Even the Screen Actors Guild, the union representing workers in the entertainment industry, exerts considerable power on behalf of its members. For example, Tiger Woods was fined $100,000 for making a nonunion Buick commercial during a strike by the American Federation of Television and Radio Artists. Labor unions represent and protect the interests of their members with respect to hiring, wages, working conditions, job security, and due process appeals. Historically, the relationship between management and labor unions has been adversarial; however, both sides seem to realize that to increase productivity and competitiveness, management and labor must work together in collaborative relationships. Troubled labor relations can create higher costs and productivity declines and eventually lead to layoffs.[9]

FROM THE PAGES OF

Online Auctions: Connecting with Suppliers

Web technology has had a major impact on the way organizations connect with their suppliers. In many industries, firms have established Internet procurement portals for online auctioning. These auctions can be for purchases that range from cleaning supplies to security systems to office furniture—you name it. The portals themselves are set up as Internet firms and typically are established as joint ventures among partners. The belief is that online auctions will streamline business-to-business (B2B) transactions and make the whole purchasing process more efficient. Here is just a sample:

Automotive: The Big Three automakers—DaimlerChrysler, Ford, and General Motors—pooled the $240 billion they spend each year on parts to team up on an online supplies exchange. That marketplace was expected to involve annual transactions totaling more than $300 billion. The new company now has a name, Covisint (go to www. covisint.com to find out what it means), and the initiative has added Nissan, Renault, Commerce One, Oracle, and PSA Peugeot Citroen. Covisint has headquarters in Amsterdam, Tokyo, and Southfield, Michigan, as well as offices in Frankfurt, Paris, and Brazil.

Computers: E2open was formed in 2000 as a platform where computing, networking, and consumer electronics equipment industries can implement new ways to communicate, coordinate, and collaborate in a manner that increases efficiencies and profits for all. The founders included leaders Acer, Hitachi, IBM, LG Electronics, Lucent Technologies, Matsushita Electric (Panasonic), Nortel Networks, Seagate Technology, Solectron, and Toshiba.

Retail: GlobalNetXchange (GNX) is a B2B retail marketplace set up by Sears Roebuck, French retailer Carrefour, Kroger, and several others (including software company Oracle). Since its inception, the members of GNX have conducted over 5500 auctions valued at more than $US 4.1 billion. One competitor is WorldWide Retail Exchange, an online auction established by 22 of the world's largest retailers, such as Royal Ahold and Target. Wal-Mart has its own online marketplace that it uses for supplier auctioning: Wal-Mart buys and sells twice as many goods as Sears and Carrefour combined.

Consumer goods: Transora.com is an online supplier exchange established by 49 consumer-goods makers, including Procter & Gamble, Sara Lee, and Coca-Cola.

Oil: More than 240 companies use Altra Energy Technology's online services to buy, sell, and transport products such as natural gas, fuels, and electricity.

Will it work? There are still some questions that need to be answered. Altra is the first (and only) profitable exchange. Governance remains a prickly issue for many of these exchanges. Can member companies, which usually are competitors, truly cooperate and allow an independent management team to lead the joint venture? Suppliers are often reluctant to participate. Already many of the industry-led marketplaces have retained Big Five consulting firms to help oversee negotiations during the start-up phase. Yet the future looks promising: Unlike some risky Net start-ups, there is good reason to believe these industry exchanges will succeed. AMR Research projects that 29 percent of all commercial transactions, worth some $5.7 trillion, will flow through the Internet by 2004. Founders of these trading exchanges "bring so much transaction volume to the table, they are not going to let it fail," says Rory Jones, a PricewaterhouseCoopers partner in its e-markets practice.

SOURCES: Jennifer Gill, "What Most Big B2B Exchanges Are Missing: A CEO," *Business Week*, July 14, 2000, online; Michael Arndt, "Sears: Can the Old Retail King Win a B2B Throne?" *Business Week*, February 29, 2000, online; David Welch, "Can Covisint Climb Out of a Ditch?" *Business Week*, May 21, 2001; Spencer Ante, "Q&A with Altra CEO Paul Bourke," *Business Week*, May 14, 2001.

Organizations are at a disadvantage if they become overly dependent on any powerful supplier. A supplier is powerful if the buyer has few other sources of supply or if the supplier has many other buyers. For example, if computer companies can go only to Microsoft for software or only to Intel for microchips, those suppliers can exert a great deal of pressure. In many cases, companies build up switching costs. **Switching costs** are fixed costs buyers face if they change suppliers. For example, once a buyer learns how to operate a supplier's equipment, such as computer software, the buyer faces both economic and psychological costs in changing to a new supplier.[10]

> **switching costs**
>
> Fixed costs buyers face when they change suppliers.

Choosing the right supplier is an important strategic decision. Suppliers can affect manufacturing time, product quality, and inventory levels. The relationship between suppliers and the organization is changing in some companies. The close supplier relationship has become a new model for many organizations, such as Ford Motor, that are using a just-in-time manufacturing approach (discussed in Chapters 16 and 17).

Customers

Customers purchase the products or services an organization offers. Without customers, a company won't survive. You are a **final consumer** when you buy a McDonald's hamburger or a pair of jeans from a retailer at the mall. **Intermediate consumers** buy raw materials or wholesale products and then sell to final consumers. Intermediate customers actually make more purchases than individual final consumers do. Examples of intermediate customers include retailers, who buy clothes from wholesalers and manufacturers' representatives before selling them to their customers, and industrial buyers, who buy raw materials (such as chemicals) before converting them into final products.

> **final consumer**
>
> Those who purchase products in their finished form.
>
> **intermediate consumer**
>
> A customer who purchases raw materials or wholesale products before selling them to final customers.

Like suppliers, customers are important to organizations for reasons other than the money they provide for goods and services. Customers can demand lower prices, higher quality, unique product specifications, or better service. They also can play competitors against one another, as occurs when a car customer (or a purchasing agent) collects different offers and negotiates for the best price.

Customer service means giving customers what they want or need, the way they want it, the first time. This usually depends on the speed and dependability with which an organization can deliver its products or services. Actions and attitudes that mean excellent customer service include the following:

> **customer service**
>
> The speed and dependability with which an organization can deliver what customers want.

- Speed of filling and delivering normal orders.
- Willingness to meet emergency needs.
- Merchandise delivered in good condition.
- Readiness to take back defective goods and resupply quickly.

- Availability of installation and repair services and parts.
- Service charges (that is, whether services are "free" or priced separately).[11]

In all businesses—services as well as manufacturing—strategies that emphasize good customer service provide a critical competitive advantage. The organization is at a disadvantage if it depends too heavily on powerful customers. Customers are powerful if they make large purchases or if they can easily find alternative places to buy. If you are the largest customer of a firm and there are other firms from which you can buy, you have power over that firm, and you are likely to be able to negotiate with it successfully. Your firm's biggest customers—especially if they can buy from other sources—will have the greatest negotiating power over you. Customer relationship management is discussed more fully in Chapter 9.

Environmental Analysis

If managers do not understand how the environment affects their organizations or cannot identify opportunities and threats that are likely to be important, their ability to make decisions and execute plans will be severely limited. For example, if little is known about customer likes and dislikes, organizations will have a difficult time designing new products, scheduling production, developing marketing plans, and the like. In short, timely and accurate environmental information is critical for running a business.

But information about the environment is not always readily available. **Environmental uncertainty** means that managers do not have enough information about the environment to understand or predict the future. Uncertainty arises from two related factors: (1) complexity and (2) dynamism. Environmental *complexity* refers to the number of issues to which a manager must attend as well as their interconnectedness. For example, industries that have many different firms that compete in vastly different ways tend to be more complex—and uncertain—than industries with only a few key competitors. Similarly, environmental *dynamism* refers to the degree of discontinuous change that occurs within the industry. For example, high-growth industries with products and technologies that change rapidly tend to be more uncertain than stable industries where change is less dramatic and more predictable.[12]

As environmental uncertainty increases, managers must develop techniques and methods for collecting, sorting through, and interpreting information about the environment. By analyzing environmental forces—in both the macroenvironment and the competitive environment—managers can identify opportunities and threats that might affect the organization.

> **environmental uncertainty**
>
> **Lack of information needed to understand or predict the future.**

Environmental Scanning

Perhaps the first step in coping with uncertainty in the environment is pinning down what might be of importance. It is frequently the case that organizations (and individuals) act out of ignorance, only to regret those actions in the future. IBM, for example, had the opportunity to purchase the technology behind xerography but turned it down. Xerox saw the potential, and the rest is history. However, Xerox researchers later developed the technology for the original computer mouse, but not seeing the potential, the company missed an important market opportunity.

To understand and predict changes, opportunities, and threats, organizations such as Monsanto, Weyerhaeuser, and Union Carbide spend a good deal of time and money monitoring events in the environment. **Environmental scanning** means both searching out information

> **environmental scanning**
>
> **Searching for and sorting through information about the environment.**

that is unavailable to most people and sorting through that information to interpret what is important and what is not. Managers can ask questions such as

- Who are our current competitors?
- Are there few or many entry barriers to our industry?
- What substitutes exist for our product or service?
- Is the company too dependent on powerful suppliers?
- Is the company too dependent on powerful customers?[13]

competitive intelligence

Information that helps managers determine how to compete better.

Answers to these questions help managers develop **competitive intelligence,** the information necessary to decide how best to manage in the competitive environment they have identified. Porter's competitive analysis, discussed earlier, can guide environmental scanning and help managers evaluate the competitive potential of different environments. Table 2.2 describes two extreme environments: an attractive environment, which gives a firm a competitive advantage, and an unattractive environment, which puts a firm at a competitive disadvantage.[14]

Scenario Development

scenario

A narrative that describes a particular set of future conditions.

As managers attempt to determine the effect of environmental forces on their organizations, they frequently develop **scenarios** of the future. Scenarios combine alternative combinations of different factors into a total picture of the environment and the firm. For example, as Congress and the president try to work toward a balanced budget and eventually reduce the federal debt, they have developed several different scenarios about what the economy is likely to do over the next decade or so. Frequently, organizations develop a *best-case scenario* (i.e., if events occur that are favorable to the firm), a *worst-case scenario* (i.e., if events are all unfavorable), and some middle-ground alternatives. The value of scenario development is that it helps managers develop contingency plans for what they might do given different outcomes.[15]

Forecasting

forecasting

Method for predicting how variables will change the future.

Whereas environmental scanning is used to identify important factors and scenario development is used to develop alternative pictures of the future, **forecasting** is used to predict exactly how some variable or variables will change in the future. For example, in making capital investments, firms may try to forecast how interest rates will change. In deciding to expand or downsize a business, firms may try to forecast the demand for goods and services or forecast the supply and demand of labor they probably would

TABLE 2.2
Attractive and Unattractive Environments

Environmental Factor	Unattractive	Attractive
Competitors	Many; low industry growth; equal size; commodity	Few; high industry growth; unequal size differentiated
Threat of entry	High threat; few entry barriers	Low threat; many barriers
Substitutes	Many	Few
Suppliers	Few; high bargaining power	Many; low bargaining power
Customers	Few; high bargaining power	Many; low bargaining power

use. Available publications such as *Business Week's Business Outlook* provide forecasts to businesses both large and small.

Although forecasts are designed to help executives make predictions about the future, their accuracy varies from application to application. Because they extrapolate from the past to project the future, forecasts tend to be most accurate when the future ends up looking a lot like the past. Of course, we don't need sophisticated forecasts in those instances. Forecasts are most useful when the future will look radically different

The National Aeronautics and Space Administration (NASA) leads the world in preparing and launching missions from earth to the frontiers of space. However, an audit for the President's Quality Award suggested that NASA consider benchmarking as a way to progress from incremental improvement to breakthrough improvements.

To improve processes, NASA and its contractors were challenged to begin sharing information, a concept that initially was met with resistance. Because the contractors were essentially competitors and had closely guarded information and performance levels, they hesitated to work in collaborative benchmarking efforts. Over time, however, reluctance to share information was overcome as participants realized that NASA's objective was to provide an opportunity to learn from contractors and help them improve their own processes, rather than to force every participant's process into the same mold. Soon the consortium participants learned to work together as a team to facilitate effective benchmarking, optimize efficiencies, and leverage quality improvements across all participating organizations.

Participants were encouraged to share practices and learn more about how each organization achieved its results. As the various practices were discussed, the team began to identify the processes that contributed to performance that was superior to that of the other organizations. These were identified as best practices; team participants then adapted the best practices to their own organizations. In adapting and implementing these best practices, contractors produced a combined savings of $41,000 and reduced cycle time by 57 percent. These results benefited each participant organization as well as NASA—their common customer.

Consortium benchmarking like that used by NASA can be a cost-effective alternative to conventional benchmarking. When participants join forces, the cost to each participant is generally less than it would be for each contractor to conduct a study individually. Continued informal benchmarking among the consortium process owners has a synergistic benefit by creating a culture that values continual improvement and teamwork to achieve excellence. It builds a foundation for continued benchmarking, formal and/or informal, through the use of common terminology, tools, and techniques.

The approach prevents "industrial tourism," or plant visits simply to see what is out there. Benchmarking can provide a wealth of ideas on which to build significant improvement. The commitment of resources to participate in a benchmarking study is typically well worth the effort involved because of the insights that result from learning from others.

SOURCE: Adapted from Denise DeVito and Sara Morrison, "Benchmarking: A Tool for Sharing and Cooperation," *Journal for Quality and Participation,* Fall 2000, vol. 23 no. 4, pp. 56–61.

Collaborative Benchmarking: A Tool for Sharing and Cooperation

from the past. Unfortunately, that is when forecasts tend not to be so accurate. The more things change, the less confidence we tend to have in our forecasts. The best advice for using forecasts might include the following:

- Use multiple forecasts and perhaps average their predictions.
- Remember that accuracy decreases the farther into the future you are trying to predict.
- Forecasts are no better than the data used to construct them.
- Use simple forecasts (rather than complicated ones) where possible.
- Important events often are surprises and represent a departure from predictions.[16]

Benchmarking

In addition to trying to predict changes in the environment, firms can undertake intensive study of the best practices of various firms to understand their sources of competitive advantage. **Benchmarking** means identifying the best-in-class performance by a company in a given area, say, product development or customer service, and then comparing your processes to theirs. To accomplish this, a benchmarking team would collect information on its own company's operations and those of the other firm in order to determine gaps. These gaps serve as a point of entry to learn the underlying causes of performance differences. Ultimately, the team would map out a set of best practices that lead to world-class performance. We will discuss benchmarking further in Chapter 4.[17]

benchmarking

The process of comparing an organization's practices and technologies with those of other companies.

Responding to the Environment

Organizations have a number of options for responding to the environment. In general, these options can be grouped into three categories: (1) adapting to the environment, (2) influencing the environment, and (3) selecting a new environment.

Adapting to the Environment: Changing Yourself

To cope with environmental uncertainty, organizations frequently make adjustments in their structures and work processes. In the case of uncertainty arising from environmental complexity, we can say that organizations tend to adapt by *decentralizing* decision making. For example, if a company faces a growing number of competitors in various markets, if different customers want different things, if the characteristics of different products keep increasing, and if production facilities are being built in different regions of the world, it may be impossible for the chief executive (or a small group of top executives) to keep abreast of all activities and understand all the operational details of a business. In these cases, the top management team is likely to give authority to lower-level managers to make decisions that benefit the firm. The term **empowerment** is used frequently today to talk about this type of decentralized authority. We will address empowerment and decision making in more detail in Chapters 3 and 9.

empowerment

The process of sharing power with employees, thereby enhancing their confidence in their ability to perform their jobs and their belief that they are influential contributors to the organization.

In response to uncertainty caused by change (dynamism) in the environment, organizations tend to establish more flexible structures. In today's business world, it is commonplace for the term *bureaucracy* to take on a bad connotation. Most of us recognize that bureaucratic organizations tend to be formalized and very stable; frequently they are unable to adjust to change or exceptional circumstances that "don't fit the rules." And while bureaucratic organizations may be efficient and controlled if the environment is stable, they tend to be slow-moving and plodding when products, technologies, customers, competitors, and the like start changing over time. In these cases, more *organic* structures tend to have the flexibility needed to adjust to change. Although we will discuss organic structures in more detail in Chapter 9, suffice it to say here that they are less formal than bureaucratic organizations, and so decisions tend to be made more

	Stable	Dynamic
Complex	Decentralized	Decentralized
	Bureaucratic (standardized skills)	Organic (mutual adjustment)
Simple	Centralized	Centralized
	Bureaucratic (standardized work processes)	Organic (direct supervision)

TABLE 2.3
Four Approaches for Managing Uncertainty

through interaction and mutual adjustment among individuals rather than via a set of predefined rules. Table 2.3 shows four different approaches that organizations can take in adapting to environmental uncertainty.

Adapting at the Boundaries   From the standpoint of an open system, organizations create buffers on both the input and output sides of their boundaries with the environment. **Buffering** is one such approach used for adapting to uncertainty. On the input side, organizations establish relationships with employment agencies to hire part-time and temporary help during rush periods when labor demand is difficult to predict. The growth of contingent workers in the U.S. labor force is a good indication of the popularity of this approach to buffering input uncertainties. On the output side of the system, most organizations use some type of ending inventories that allow them to keep merchandise on hand in case a rush of customers decide to buy their products. Auto dealers are a particularly common example of this use of buffers, but we can see similar use of buffer inventories in fast-food restaurants, bookstores, clothing stores, and even real estate agencies.[18]

> **buffering**
>
> **Creating supplies of excess resources in case of unpredictable needs.**

Auto dealers typically have a buffer inventory of products but then cut prices to increase demand at the end of the model year.

In addition to buffering, organizations may try **smoothing** or leveling normal fluctuations at the boundaries of the environment. For example, during winter months (up north) when automobile sales drop off, it is not uncommon for dealers to cut the price of their in-stock vehicles to increase demand. At the end of each clothing season, retailers discount their merchandise to clear it out in order to make room for incoming inventories. These are each examples of smoothing environmental cycles in order to level off fluctuations in demand.

Adapting at the Core   While buffering and smoothing work to manage uncertainties at the boundaries of the organization, firms also can establish **flexible processes** that allow for adaptation in their technical core. For example, firms increasingly try to customize their products and services to meet the varied and changing demands of customers. Even in manufacturing, where it is difficult to change basic core processes, firms are adopting techniques of mass customization that help them create flexible factories.

Instead of mass-producing large quantities of a "one-size-fits-all" product, with mass customization organizations can produce individually customized products at an equally low cost. Whereas Henry Ford used to claim that "you could have a Model T in any color you wanted, as long as it was black," auto companies now offer a wide array of colors and trim lines, with different options and accessories. The process of mass customization involves the use of a network of independent operating units in which each performs a specific process or task such as making a dashboard assembly on an automobile. When an order comes in, different modules join forces to deliver the product or service as specified by the customer. We will discuss mass customization and flexible factories in more depth in Chapter 9.[19]

Influencing Your Environment

In addition to adapting or reacting to the environment, organizations can develop proactive responses aimed at changing the environment. Two general types of proactive responses are independent action and cooperative action.

Independent Action   A company uses **independent strategies** when it acts on its own to change some aspect of its current environment.[20] Table 2.4 shows the definitions and uses of these strategies. For example, when Southwest Airlines enters a new market, it demonstrates competitive aggression by cutting fares so that other, less-efficient airlines must follow it down. In contrast, Kellogg Company typically promotes the cereal industry as a whole, thereby demonstrating competitive pacification. Weyerhaeuser Company advertises its reforestation efforts (public relations). First Boston forgoes its Christmas party and donates thousands of dollars to the poor (voluntary action). Dow Chemical recently sued General Electric for hiring away some of its engineers (legal action). Dow Corning lobbied and recently won the right to put silicon implants back on the market (political action). Each of these examples shows how organizations—on their own—can have an impact on the environment.

Cooperative Action   In some situations, two or more organizations work together using cooperative strategies to influence the environment.[21] Table 2.5 shows several examples of **cooperative strategies.** An example of contracting occurs when suppliers and customers, or managers and labor unions, sign formal agreements about the terms and conditions of their future relationships. These contracts are explicit attempts to make their future relationship predictable. An example of cooptation might occur when universities invite wealthy alumni to join their boards of directors.

TABLE 2.4 Independent Action

Strategy	Definition	Examples
Competitive aggression	Exploiting a distinctive competence or improving internal efficiency for competitive advantage.	Aggressive pricing, comparative advertising (e.g., Advil)
Competitive pacification	Independent action to improve relations with competitors.	Helping competitors find raw materials
Public relations	Establishing and maintaining favorable images in the minds of those making up the environment.	Sponsoring sporting events
Voluntary action	Voluntary commitment to various interest groups, causes, and social problems.	Ronald McDonald Houses
Legal action	Company engages in private legal battle with competition on antitrust deceptive and advertising or other grounds.	Blue Mountain Art, Inc.'s, lawsuit against Hallmark for allegedly copying its cards
Political action	Efforts to influence elected representatives to create a more favorable business environment or limit competition.	ARCO's corporate constituency programs; issue advertising; lobbying at state and national levels

SOURCE: Reprinted from *Journal of Marketing*, published by the American Marketing Association. C. Zeithaml and V. Zeithaml, "Environmental Management: Revising the Marketing Perspective," Spring 1984.

Finally, an example of *coalition* formation might be when local businesses band together to curb the rise of employee health care costs and when organizations in the same industry form industry associations and special-interest groups. You may have seen cooperative advertising strategies, such as when dairy producers, beef producers, orange growers, and the like, jointly pay for television commercials.

TABLE 2.5 Cooperative Action

Strategy	Definition	Examples
Contraction	Negotiation of an agreement between the organization and another group to exchange goods, services, information, patents, and so on.	Contractual marketing systems
Cooptation	Absorbing new elements into the organization's leadership structure to avert threats to its stability or existence.	Consumer and labor representatives and bankers on boards of directors
Coalition	Two or more groups coalesce and act jointly with respect to some set of issues for some period of time.	Industry associations; political initiatives of the Business Roundtable and the U.S. Chamber of Commerce.

SOURCE: Reprinted from *Journal of Marketing*, published by the American Marketing Association. C. Zeithaml and V. Zeithaml, "Environmental Management: Revising the Marketing Perspective," Spring 1984.

strategic maneuvering

An organization's conscious efforts to change the boundaries of its task environment.

At a more organizational level, organizations establish strategic alliances, partnerships, joint ventures, and mergers with competitors to deal with environmental uncertainties. Cooperative strategies such as these make most sense when (1) taking joint action will reduce the organizations' costs and risks and (2) cooperation will increase their power (that is, their ability to successfully accomplish the changes they desire).

Changing the Environment You Are In

As we noted previously, organizations can cope with environmental uncertainty by changing themselves (environmental adaptation), changing the environment, or changing the environment they are in. We refer to this last category as **strategic maneuvering.** By making a conscious effort to change the boundaries of its competitive environment, firms can maneuver around potential threats and capitalize on arising opportunities.[22] Table 2.6 defines and gives examples of several of these strategies, including domain selection, diversification, merger and acquisition, and divestiture.

prospectors

Companies that continuously change the boundaries for their task environments by seeking new products and markets, diversifying and merging, or acquiring new enterprises.

defenders

Companies that stay within a stable product domain as a strategic maneuver.

Organizations engage in strategic maneuvering when they move into different environments. Some companies, called **prospectors,** are more likely than others to engage in strategic maneuvering.[23] Aggressive companies continuously change the boundaries of their competitive environments by seeking new products and markets, diversifying, and merging or acquiring new enterprises. In these and other ways, corporations put their competitors on the defensive and force them to react. **Defenders,** on the other hand, stay within a more limited, stable product domain.

TABLE 2.6
Strategic Maneuvering

Strategy	Definition	Examples
Domain selection	Entering industries or markets with limited competition or regulation and ample suppliers and customers; entering high-growth markets.	IBM's entry into the personal computer market; Miller's entry into the light-beer market
Diversification	Investing in different types of businesses, manufacturing different types of products, or geographic expansion to reduce dependence on a single market or technology.	General Electric's purchase of RCA and NBC
Merger and acquisition	Combining two or more firms into a single enterprise; gaining possession of an ongoing enterprise.	RJR and Nabisco, Sperry and Burroughs (now Unisys), Boeing and McDonnell Douglas
Divestiture	Selling one or more businesses.	Kodak and Eastman Chemical

SOURCE: Reprinted from *Journal of Marketing,* published by the American Marketing Association. C. Zeithaml and V. Zeithaml, "Environmental Management: Revising the Marketing Perspective," Spring 1984.

Choosing a Response Approach

Three general considerations help guide management's response to the environment. First, organizations should attempt to *change appropriate elements of the environment.* Environmental responses are most useful when aimed at elements of the environment that (1) cause the company problems, (2) provide it with opportunities, and (3) allow the company to change successfully. Thus, automobile companies faced with intense competition from Japanese automakers successfully lobbied (along with labor) for government-imposed ceilings on Japanese imports. And one charcoal producer, hoping to increase consumers' opportunities to use its product, launched a campaign to increase daylight saving time.

Second, organizations should *choose responses that focus on pertinent elements of the environment.* If a company wants to better manage its competitive environment, competitive aggression and pacification are viable options. Political action influences the legal environment, and contracting helps manage customers and suppliers.

Third, companies should *choose responses that offer the most benefit at the lowest cost.* Return-on-investment calculations should incorporate short-term financial considerations as well as long-term impact. Strategic managers who consider these factors carefully will guide their organizations to competitive advantage more effectively.

KEY TERMS

Barriers to entry, p. 49

Benchmarking, p. 56

Buffering, p. 57

Competitive environment, p. 42

Competitive intelligence, p. 54

Cooperative strategies, p. 58

Customer service, p. 52

Defenders, p. 66

Demographics, p. 46

Empowerment, p. 56

Environmental scanning, p. 53

Environmental uncertainty, p. 53

External environment, p. 42

Final consumer, p. 52

Flexible processes, p. 58

Forecasting, p. 54

Independent strategies, p. 58

Intermediate consumer, p. 52

Macroenvironment, p. 42

Prospectors, p. 60

Scenario, p. 54

Smoothing, p. 58

Strategic maneuvering, p. 60

Switching costs, p. 52

SUMMARY OF LEARNING OBJECTIVES

Now that you have studied Chapter 2, you should know:

How environmental forces influence organizations, as well as how organizations can influence their environments.

Organizations are open systems that are affected by, and in turn affect, their external environments. Organizations receive financial, human, material, and information resources from the environment; transform those resources into finished goods and services; and then send those outputs back into the environment.

How to make a distinction between the macroenvironment and the competitive environment.

The macroenvironment is composed of international, legal and political, economic, technological, and social forces that influence strategic decisions. The competitive environment is composed of forces closer to the organization, such as current competitors, threat of new entrants, threat of substitutes, suppliers, and customers. Perhaps the simplest distinction between the macroenvironment and the competitive environment is in the amount of control a firm can exert on external forces. Macroenvironmental forces such as the economy and social trends are much less controllable than are forces in the competitive environment such as suppliers and customers.

Why organizations should attend to economic and social developments in the international environment.

Developments in other countries have a profound effect on the way U.S. companies compete. European unification, for example, is creating a formidable buying and selling bloc. The North American Free Trade Agreement opened up trade among the United States, Canada, and Mexico. Managed well, the European Union and NAFTA represent opportunities for market growth, joint ventures, and the like. Managed poorly, these free trade agreements may give advantage to more competitive firms and nations.

How to analyze the competitive environment.

Environments can range from favorable to unfavorable. To determine how favorable a competitive environment is, managers should consider the nature of the competitors, potential new entrants, threat of substitutes, suppliers, and customers. Analyzing how these five forces influence the organization provides an indication of potential threats and opportunities. Attractive environments tend to be those which have high industry growth, few competitors, products that can be differentiated, few potential entrants, many barriers to entry, few substitutes, many suppliers (none with much power), and many customers. After identifying and analyzing competitive forces, managers must formulate a strategy that minimizes the power external forces have over the organization (a topic discussed more fully in Chapter 5).

How organizations respond to environmental uncertainty.

Responding effectively to the environment often involves devising proactive strategies to change the environment. Strategic maneuvering, for example, involves changing the boundaries of the competitive environment through domain selection, diversification, mergers, and the like. Independent strategies, on the other hand, do not require moving into a new environment but rather changing some aspect of the current environment through competitive aggression, public relations, legal action, and so on. Finally, cooperative strategies, such as contracting, cooptation, and coalition building, involve the working together of two or more organizations.

DISCUSSION QUESTIONS

1. This chapter's opening quote by Peter Drucker said, "The essence of a business is outside itself." What do you think this means? Do you agree?

2. What are the most important forces in the macroenvironment facing companies today?

3. Go back to the telecom example in "Setting the Stage." What other organizations have faced or are facing similar circumstances in their external environments?

4. What are the main differences between the macroenvironment and the competitive environment?

5. What kinds of changes do companies make in response to environmental uncertainty?

6. We outlined several proactive responses that organizations can make to the environment. What examples have you seen recently of an organization's responding effectively to its environment? Did the effectiveness of the response depend on whether the organization was facing a threat or an opportunity?

CONCLUDING CASE

Many New Airlines will Never Grow Old

Thanks to a weak economy and the continuing effects of September 11, 2001, many new entrants are struggling or going out of business. Pro Air Inc., grounded by federal regulators over safety concerns, and tiny AccessAir in Iowa have both filed for bankruptcy protection, as has Vanguard Airlines Inc., hurt by high fuel prices, operational problems, and overly rapid growth.

As start-ups have discovered so often in the cutthroat airline business, it's easy to enter the fray but hard to succeed. Yes, the giants have been accused of crushing the small fry with predatory tactics, fortress hubs, and big frequent-flier programs. But start-ups often make mistakes—from choosing the wrong routes to running sloppy operations. That worries consumer advocates, who want more competition to keep the majors in check. And if consolidation follows on the heels of UAL Corp.'s deal to buy US Airways Group Inc., "you're going to need new entry more than ever," says Kevin P. Mitchell, chairman of the Business Travel Coalition, which represents big corporations.

Certainly, there are success stories. JetBlue Airways, the best-financed start-up in airline history, appears to be off to a phenomenal start since February 2000. The low-fare airline that offers live TV and leather upholstery is filling 72 percent of the seats on its eight new Airbus A320s. It flies to 9 cities, going up to 12 in November 2000. CEO David Neeleman says the airline,

based at New York's John F. Kennedy International Airport, posted a "double-digit" profit margin in August and should be profitable this year. It just raised another $30 million from its investors on top of the $130 million it started with. Neeleman "is the most successful airline entrepreneur of the last 10 years," says Darryl Jenkins, director of the Aviation Institute at George Washington University.

And after a rocky start, six-year-old Frontier Airlines Inc. in Denver seems to be on course. It is benefiting in part from operational and labor woes at UAL's United Airlines. Second-quarter net income doubled to more than $16 million as the airline attracted more business passengers and raised fares. Likewise, 10-year-old Spirit Airlines has proved to be a survivor after shifting its strategy to avoid markets dominated by one major carrier. It even moved its home base last year from Northwest Airline Corp.'s hub in Detroit to Fort Lauderdale.

But for every JetBlue and Frontier, there seems to be a Pro Air. Even before the Federal Aviation Administration revoked Pro Air's operating certificate in 2000—a move Pro Air is contesting—the airline was ailing. Despite winning contracts from major companies such as General Motors Corp., it failed to offer the frequent flights that business passengers demanded and spread itself too thin, with only three aircraft. What's more, it chose to compete head-on in Detroit with Northwest. "They were lucky to fly as long as they did," says Cameron R. Burr, a partner at the Burr Group, an investment firm. Pro Air insists it was about to raise $70 million right before the FAA shut it down.

Some experts see a smoother ride ahead. Led by United and its recent pilot contract, major carriers are expected to see big increases in labor costs. That probably means higher fares for passengers—and a bigger pricing umbrella for the little guys to work under. And even if the economy softens, "that will refocus [customers] on economic value" instead of frequent-flier benefits, says Stanley L. Pace, head of Bain & Co.'s airline practice. But until then, the new guys in the skies have little room for error.

QUESTIONS

1. Which of the five forces of competition seem to be having the greatest impact on the airline industry: buyers, suppliers, rivals, new entrants, or substitutes? How attractive is this industry?

2. Imagine you were running one of these start-up airlines. What response(s) would you suggest given the environmental situation?

3. Do you see any similarities between the airline industry and the telecom industry discussed at the beginning of the chapter in "Setting the Stage"?

SOURCE: Wendy Zellner and Michael Arndt, "Many New Airlines Will Never Grow Old," *Business Week*, October 23, 2000, p. 104.

CHAPTER 3

Managerial Decision Making

The business executive is by profession a decision maker. Uncertainty is his opponent. Overcoming it is his mission.

—John McDonald

CHAPTER OUTLINE

Characteristics of Managerial Decisions
Lack of Structure
Uncertainty and Risk
Conflict
The Stages of Decision Making
Identifying and Diagnosing the Problem
Generating Alternative Solutions
Evaluating Alternatives
Making the Choice
Implementing the Decision
Evaluating the Decision
The Best Decision
Barriers to Effective Decision Making
Psychological Biases
Time Pressures
Social Realities
Decision Making in Groups
Potential Advantages of Using a Group
Potential Problems of Using a Group
Managing Group Decision Making
Leadership Style
Constructive Conflict
Encouraging Creativity
Organizational Decision Making
Constraints on Decision Makers
Models of Organizational Decision Processes
Negotiations and Politics
Decision Making in a Crisis
Emergent Strategies

LEARNING OBJECTIVES

After studying Chapter 3, you will know:

1. The kinds of decisions you will face as a manager.

2. How to make "rational" decisions.

3. The pitfalls you should avoid when making decisions.

4. The pros and cons of using a group to make decisions.

5. The procedures to use in leading a decision-making group.

6. How to encourage creative decisions.

7. The processes by which decisions are made in organizations.

8. How to make decisions in a crisis.

WHAT TO DO? FROM FAST ACTION TO INACTION

Sometimes managers are forced into action, and sometimes this occurs in tragic circumstances. When the World Trade Center was attacked, Merrill Lynch's offices were destroyed and three employees were killed. The firm had plans in place for potential crises such as power loss, loss of water, loss of a building, and loss of voice and data communications. It did not have a plan for all those problems occurring at once.

Management quickly set priorities: make sure people were all right; relocate 9,000 employees; put infrastructure in place; get the firm trading again. It was a tremendous challenge, and as Merrill executive Bob McCann put it, "We were calling audibles from the line of scrimmage. It didn't always go smoothly, but it worked" (p. 134). Amazingly, Merrill Lynch was trading when the U.S. market reopened on September 19.

Fortunately, most managerial decisions are not born of tragedy, and are not so frighteningly newsworthy. Here are a few recent examples of situations that you probably haven't heard about but that are important nonetheless. Consider what you would have done.

Imagine that you get a report that a folding chair that your company sells collapsed, and a customer strained a muscle. What would you do?

Or you manage a different company, one that sells smoke alarms, and a few customers tell you their alarms don't work properly. What actions would you take?

Or you learn that some removable seats on the jogging strollers you sell were not snapped onto the frame. Now what?

Or a hinge on a baby crib's drop gate is defective. What do you do?

In the last case, the Baby's Dream furniture company notified the Consumer Product Safety Commission (CPSC)—but not until nine injuries were reported—and the company was fined $200,000 for not reporting the defect promptly.

For the jogging strollers, Baby Trend's management acted decisively by contacting 120 Babies "R" Us stores, checking 2,250 strollers to make sure the snaps were fastened, and retrieving the strollers already sold.

The error in production seemed small to some, but Baby Trend acted decisively and responsibly.

For the smoke alarms, Harvey Grossblatt of Universal Security Instruments decided to collect more information, contacted an independent laboratory and the CPSC, and learned that neither could find a problem with the alarms. But whereas so many decision makers would consider the episode to be over, Grossblatt said, "Let's have an abundance of caution, and let's deal with it," and recalled 34,000 smoke alarms, at a cost of $150,000.

What about the folding chair incident? Peter Jenkins of Boston Warehouse Trading Corp. had no idea whether it was a freak accident or a flawed chair. He described it as very stressful, because he didn't know whether there really was a problem and didn't know what to do. Fortunately, he conducted tests in the company's warehouse, discovered a screw that was too small and weakened the chairs, notified the CPSC, and recalled 1,800 chairs. "I wouldn't want my mother sitting on [one]," he said.

This chapter is not about product recalls, or the CPSC, or ethics and social responsibility, which are discussed thoroughly in Chapter 5. It is about decision making, the most basic and constant managerial activity. The topics covered include decision making under crisis circumstances.

Whereas the context and specifics of decisions differ, the examples described above reveal some common aspects of most managerial decisions: They are consequential but ambiguous; plans can help, although the realities are often impossible to anticipate; it is not always clear that there is a problem at all or whether a decision is needed; inaction may constitute the wrong decision; different managers apply different criteria in reaching a final choice; and once a decision is made, appropriate action must be taken to implement it.

Sources: D. Rynecki, "The Bull Fights Back," *Fortune*, October 15, 2001, pp. 131–36; B. Kwon, "When Bad Things Happen to Good Companies," *Fortune Small Business*, November 2000, pp. 104–08; J. Mull and N. St. Pierre, "How Will Firestone and Ford Steer Through This Blowout?" *Business Week*, August 28, 2000, p. 54.

The best managers make decisions constantly, and make them well. At CNN, the president makes critical decisions every minute or two, all day long, while standing eye-to-eye with reporters, editors, and others. Executive producers may make a hundred decisions during a live one-hour show. And these instantaneous decisions have lasting impact. It is no task for the indecisive or squeamish. As CNN's vice chairman said, "Nobody is going to tell you what to do. It's up to you to figure out what to do, then do it. Always take the proactive path. Ask for advice, sure, but don't sit on your hands waiting for an order."[1]

Decisions. If you can't make them, you won't be an effective manager. This chapter discusses the kinds of decisions managers face, how they are made, and how they *should* be made.

Characteristics of Managerial Decisions

Managers face problems constantly. Some problems that require a decision are relatively simple; others seem overwhelming. Some demand immediate action, while others take months or even years to unfold.

Actually, managers often ignore problems.[2] For several reasons, they avoid taking action.[3] First, managers can't be sure how much time, energy, or trouble lies ahead once they start working on a problem. Second, getting involved is risky; tackling a problem but failing to solve it successfully can hurt a manager's track record. Third, because problems can be so perplexing, it is easier to procrastinate or to get busy with less demanding activities.

It is important to understand why decision making can be so challenging. Figure 3.1 illustrates several characteristics of managerial decisions that contribute to their difficulty and pressure. Most managerial decisions lack structure and entail risk, uncertainty, and conflict.

Lack of Structure

Lack of structure is the usual state of affairs in managerial decision making.[4] Although some decisions are routine and clear-cut, for most there is no automatic procedure to follow. Problems are novel and unstructured, leaving the decision maker uncertain about how to proceed.

A well-known distinction illustrating this point is between programmed and nonprogrammed decisions. **Programmed decisions** have been encountered and made before. They have objectively correct answers and can be solved by using simple rules, policies, or numerical computations. If you face a programmed decision, there exists a clear procedure or structure for arriving at the right decision. For example, if you are a small-business

programmed decisions

Decisions encountered and made before, having objectively correct answers, and solvable by using simple rules, policies, or numerical computations.

FIGURE 3.1
Characteristics of
Managerial Decisions

owner and must decide the amounts for your employees' paychecks, you can use a formula—and if the amounts are wrong, your employees will prove it to you. Table 3.1 gives some other examples.

If most important decisions were programmed, managerial life would be much easier. But managers typically face **nonprogrammed decisions:** new, novel, complex decisions having no certain outcomes. There are a variety of possible solutions, all of which have merits and drawbacks. The decision maker must create or impose a method for making the decision; there is no predetermined structure on which to rely. As Table 3.1 suggests, important, difficult decisions tend to be nonprogrammed, and they demand creative approaches.

> **nonprogrammed decisions**
>
> **New, novel, complex decisions having no proven answers.**

	Programmed Decisions	**Nonprogrammed Decisions**
Problem	Frequent, repetitive, routine. Much certainty regarding cause and effect relationships.	Novel, unstructured. Much uncertainty regarding cause-and-effect relationships.
Procedure	Dependence on policies, rules, and definite procedures.	Necessity for creativity, intuition, tolerance for ambiguity, creative problem solving.
Examples		
Business firm	Periodic reorders of inventory.	Diversification into new products and markets.
University	Necessary grade-point average for good academic standing.	Construction of new classroom facilities.
Health care	Procedure for admitting patients.	Purchase of experimental equipment.
Government	Merit system for promotion of state employees.	Reorganization of state government agencies.

TABLE 3.1
Comparison of Types
of Decisions

SOURCE: J. Gibson, J. Ivancevich, and J. Donnelly, Jr., *Organizations: Behavior, Structure, Processes*, 10th ed. Copyright ©2000 by The McGraw-Hill Companies. Reproduced with permission of The McGraw-Hill Companies.

Uncertainty and Risk

certainty

The state that exists when decision makers have accurate and comprehensive information.

If you have all the information you need, and can predict precisely the consequences of your actions, you are operating under a condition of **certainty**.[5] Managers are expressing their preference for certainty when they are not satisfied hearing about what *may have* happened or *might* happen, and insist on hearing what *did* or *will* happen.[6] But perfect certainty is rare. For important, nonprogrammed managerial decisions, uncertainty is the rule.

Uncertainty means the manager has insufficient information to know the consequences of different actions. Decision makers may have strong opinions—they may feel sure of themselves—but they are still operating under conditions of uncertainty if they lack pertinent information and cannot estimate accurately the likelihood of different results of their actions.

uncertainty

The state that exists when decision makers have insufficient information.

When you can estimate the likelihood of various consequences, but still do not know with certainty what will happen, you are facing **risk.** Risk exists when the probability of an action being successful is less than 100 percent, and losses may occur. If the decision is the wrong one, you may lose money, time, reputation, or other important assets.

risk

The state that exists when the probability of success is less than 100 percent, and losses may occur.

Risk, like uncertainty, is a fact of life in managerial decision making. But this is not the same as *taking* a risk. Enron was built on risk, with disastrous consequences. Former CEO Jeff Skilling described Enron as "a great marriage of the risk-taking mentality of the oil patch with the risk-taking mentality of the financial markets" (p. B3).[7] Whereas it sometimes seems as though risk takers are admired, and that entrepreneurs and investors thrive on taking risks, the reality is that good decision makers prefer to *manage* risk. This means that while they accept the fact that consequential decisions entail risk, they do everything they can to anticipate the risk, minimize it, and control it.

Managers prefer certainty to uncertainty. For example, Jim Rogers, CEO of Cinergy, an electric and gas supplier, would be happy to have one major regulation about carbon dioxide emissions passed now.[8] That would be better than multiple, unpredictable regulations over the coming years; he prefers certainty now to the uncertainties created by "death by 1,000 cuts," which makes long-term planning impossible.

The weather affects business in many ways, far beyond the obvious examples.

As another example, a company called Surface Systems (SSI) profits by specifying probabilities, thereby reducing (but by no means eliminating) uncertainty for decision makers.[9] SSI forecasts the weather as it pertains to particular business problems. More than $1 trillion of the U.S. economy—including orchards, construction, airline travel, and clothing and ice cream sales—is affected by temperature, precipitation, wind, and humidity. Forty-four state departments of transportation pay SSI to tell them when to salt their highways, because roads require just one-tenth the amount of salt if it's applied just before the snowfall rather than afterward. Amusement parks, if they know the odds of rain during the hours when customers might make detours to movie theaters instead, can save on labor and food costs. Reducing uncertainty isn't merely psychologically comforting; it has real value.

George Conrades, the chairman and CEO of Akamai Technologies, says, "We operate in an environment—the Internet—where there's an enormous amount of uncertainty. You can't be sure what's going to happen tomorrow, never mind next year. The danger is that the uncertainty can lead to paralysis. You spend so much time trying to nail down all the possibilities and risks, you never get around to taking action. And if that happens—if you become indecisive—you're dead" (p. 120).[10]

Conflict

Important decisions are even more difficult because of the conflict managers face. **Conflict,** which exists when the manager must consider opposing pressures from different sources, occurs at two levels.

First, individual decision makers experience psychological conflict when several options are attractive, or when none of the options is attractive. For instance, a manager may have to decide whom to lay off, when she doesn't want to lay off anyone. Or she may have three promising job applicants for one position—but choosing one means she has to reject the other two.

> **conflict**
>
> **Opposing pressures from different sources. Two levels of conflict are psychological conflict and conflict that arises between individuals or groups.**

Second, conflict arises between individuals or groups. The chief financial officer argues in favor of increasing long-term debt to finance an acquisition. The chief executive officer, however, prefers to minimize such debt and find the funds elsewhere. The marketing department wants more product lines to sell to its customers, and the engineers want higher-quality products. But the production people want to lower costs by having longer production runs of fewer products with no changes. Few decisions are without conflict.

FROM THE PAGES OF

BusinessWeek

Pfizer Takes on Risk

Pharmaceutical giant Pfizer spent $116 billion to buy Warner-Lambert. Pfizer got not only a product poised to be the world's best-selling medication, but also the largest research and development organization in the industry. *Business Week* said, "Be careful what you wish for," alluding to the risks associated with the deal, with consequences difficult to forecast.

The acquisition has numerous potential costs and benefits. In the drug industry, bigger research programs are not necessarily better; a study by Boston Consulting Group showed no relationship between R&D budget and productivity. And it is not clear whether anyone can successfully manage a $4.7 billion R&D program, the size of the new operation. John F. Niblack, vice chairman and head of the R&D effort, says, "No one has ever operated at this scale before. There's no manual on how to do this" (p. 217).

Adding to the risk is that this big program is the product of a merger of companies with different management structures. Pfizer has a formal, team-oriented decision process; Warner's was faster and more flexible. Pfizer hopes to combine the financial benefits of a huge corporation with the entrepreneurialism of the smaller biotech company, but blending the two cultures may be difficult. Many Warner executives have left the new company.

On the other hand, according to Pfizer's Henry A. McKinnell, previous mergers have happened because of slow growth, failing research pipelines, and patent problems. This merger, in contrast, is between two of the fastest-growing companies in the industry.

Another risk: Rising costs in the industry could become a political target, and drug prices could fall through the floor. Pfizer will need to maintain growth via a steady stream of new, blockbuster drugs. Such a product portfolio has evaded other giant pharmaceutical companies, and some Wall Street analysts are skeptical.

Perhaps the biggest uncertainty of all, and the most pervasive source of difficulty in forecasting outcomes of the company's efforts, is nature. The diseases that offer the greatest opportunities in the business are the most complex and difficult to tackle, and therefore entail the greatest risks. For example, Pfizer was hopeful about an experimental compound for the treatment of late-stage prostate cancer and an advanced form of lung cancer that was supposed to shut off the blood supply to tumors. But it failed to stop the cancers, and Pfizer had to halt the trials. Other promising compounds had to be abandoned when they led to unexpected side effects in some patients. By nature, nature is unpredictable.

Pfizer hopes to manage the risk and uncertainty through its massive R&D effort, its partnerships, and a highly aggressive approach to marketing its successful products. Warner was attractive to Pfizer because of Lipitor, the world's top selling drug and possibly soon the world's first $10 billion drug. But a serious competitive threat looms in AstraZeneca's powerful new anticholesterol agent, Crestor. The good news for Pfizer is that physicians know Lipitor and already are comfortable with it. Pfizer may be able to convince doctors that they are better off using a drug they know well rather than trying a new drug with the risk of unknown problems.

Thus in the end, the success of Pfizer's decision to acquire Warner and its decisions surrounding product development depend on how well it manages risk and influences another set of decisions beset by risk and uncertainty: those made by physicians in treating their patients.

SOURCES: A. Barrett, "Pfizer; How Big is Too Big?," *Business Week*, August 28, 2000, pp. 216–22; A. Barrett, "Taking Aim at a Pfizer Hit," *Business Week*, January 14, 2002, pp. 112–13.

The Stages of Decision Making

Faced with these challenges, how can you make good decisions? The ideal decision-making process moves through six stages. At companies that have institutionalized the process, these stages are intended to answer the following questions:[11] What do we want to change? What's preventing us from reaching the "desired state"? How *could* we make the change? What's the *best* way to do it? Are we following the plan? and How well did it work out?

More formally, as Figure 3.2 illustrates, decision makers should (1) identify and diagnose the problem, (2) generate alternative solutions, (3) evaluate alternatives, (4) make the choice, (5) implement the decision, and (6) evaluate the decision.

Identifying and Diagnosing the Problem

The first stage in the decision-making process is to recognize that a problem exists and must be solved. Typically, a manager realizes some discrepancy between the current state (the way things are) and a desired state (the way things ought to be). Such discrepancies—say, in organizational or unit performance—may be detected by comparing current performance against (1) *past* performance, (2) the *current* performance of other organizations or units, or (3) *future* expected performance as determined by plans and forecasts.[12]

Recognizing that a problem exists is only the beginning of this stage. The decision maker also must want to do something about it and must believe that the resources and abilities necessary for solving the problem exist.[13] Then the decision maker must dig in deeper and attempt to *diagnose* the true cause of the problem symptoms that surfaced.

For example, a sales manager knows that sales have dropped drastically. If he is leaving the company soon or believes the decreased sales volume is due to the economy (which he can't do anything about), he won't take action. But if he does try to solve the problem, he should not automatically reprimand his sales staff, add new people, or increase the advertising budget. He must analyze *why* sales are down and then develop a solution appropriate to his analysis. Asking why, of yourself and others, is essential to understanding the real problem.

Useful questions to ask and answer in this stage include[14]

- Is there a difference between what is actually happening and what should be happening?
- How can you describe the deviation, as specifically as possible?
- What is/are the cause(s) of the deviation?
- What specific goals should be met?
- Which of these goals are absolutely critical to the success of the decision?

Generating Alternative Solutions

In the second stage, problem diagnosis is linked to the development of alternative courses of action aimed at solving the problem. Managers generate at least some alternative solutions based on past experiences.[15]

Solutions range from ready made to custom made.[16] Decision makers who search for **ready-made solutions** use ideas they have tried before or follow the advice of others who have faced similar problems. **Custom-made solutions,** by contrast, must be designed for specific problems. This technique requires combining ideas into new, creative solutions. For example, the Sony Walkman was created by combining two existing products: earphones and a tape player.[17] Potentially, custom-made solutions can be devised for any challenge. Later in the chapter, we will discuss how to generate creative ideas.

Importantly, there are potentially many more alternatives available than managers may realize. For example, what would you do if one of your competitors reduced prices? An obvious choice would be to reduce your own prices. But when American Airlines, Northwest Airlines, and other carriers engaged in fare wars in the early 1990s, the result was record volume of air travel and record losses for the industry.[18]

Fortunately, cutting prices in response to a competitor's price cuts is not the only alternative available, although sometimes it is assumed to be. If one of your competitors cuts prices, don't automatically respond with the initial, obvious response. Generate multiple options, and thoroughly forecast the consequences of these different options. Options other than price cuts include nonprice responses such as emphasizing consumer risks to low-priced products, building awareness of your products' features and overall quality, and communicating your cost advantage to your competitors so they realize that they can't win a price war. Winn-Dixie used that last strategy to its advantage against Food Lion, and the stores stopped competing on price. If you do decide to cut your price as a last resort, do it fast—if you do it slowly, your competitors will gain sales in the meantime, and it may embolden them to employ the same tactic again in the future.[19]

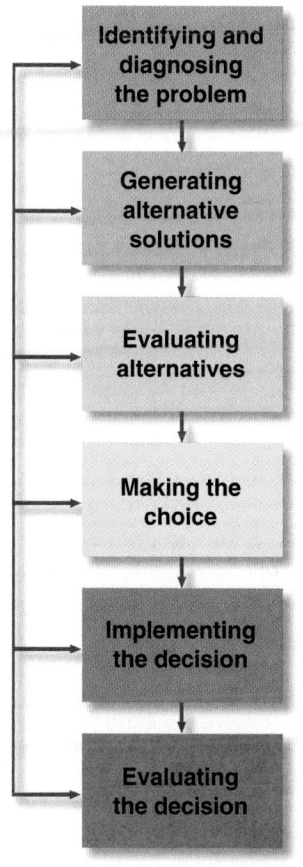

FIGURE 3.2
The Stages of Decision Making

ready-made solutions
Ideas that have been seen or tried before.

custom-made solutions
The combination of ideas into new, creative solutions.

Evaluating Alternatives

The third stage involves determining the value or adequacy of the alternatives that were generated. Which solution will be the best?

Too often, alternatives are evaluated with little thought or logic. After Walter P. Chrysler died, Chrysler's lawyer sometimes contacted the ghost of Walter P. for advice. The lawyer would excuse himself from the meeting, go into Chrysler's office, close the door and drapes, turn off the lights, and conjure up Chrysler's spirit. Then the lawyer would return to the meeting and reveal his findings, which the Chrysler executives would use to make the final decision.[20]

Obviously, alternatives should be evaluated more carefully than this. Fundamental to this process is to predict the consequences that will occur if the various options are put into effect.

Managers should consider several types of consequences. Of course, they must attempt to predict the effects on financial or other performance measures. But there are other, less clear-cut consequences to address.[21] Decisions set a precedent; will this precedent be a help or a hindrance in the future? Also, the success or failure of the decision will go into the track records of those involved in making it.

Refer again to your original goals, defined in the first stage. Which goals does each alternative meet, and fail to meet? Which alternatives are most acceptable to you and to other important stakeholders? If several alternatives may solve the problem, which can be implemented at the lowest cost? If no alternative achieves all your goals, perhaps you can combine two or more of the best ones.

Key questions here are:[22]

- Is our information about alternatives complete and current? If not, can we get more and better information?
- Does the alternative meet our primary objectives?
- What problems could we have if we implement the alternative?

Companies who housed operations in and around the World Trade Center had to rely on contingency plans after 9/11, many of them key players in the financial markets. Those that could, reassured clients and the world that operations would continue. Many took out patriotic, inspirational ads such as this one from Standard & Poor's.

Of course, results cannot be forecast with perfect accuracy. But sometimes decision makers can build in safeguards against an uncertain future by considering the potential consequences of several different scenarios. Then they generate **contingency plans**—alternative courses of action that can be implemented based on how the future unfolds.

contingency plans

Alternative courses of action that can be implemented based on how the future unfolds.

For example, scenario planners making decisions about the future might consider four alternative views of the future state of the U.S. economy:[23] (1) An economic boom with 5 to 6 percent annual growth and the United States much stronger than its global competitors; (2) a moderately strong economy with 2 to 3 percent growth and the United States pulling out of a recession; (3) a pessimistic outlook with no growth, rising unemployment, and recession; or (4) a worse scenario with global depression, massive unemployment, and widespread social unrest.

Some scenarios will seem more likely than others, and some may seem highly improbable. Ultimately, one of the scenarios will prove to be more accurate than the others. The process of considering multiple scenarios raises important "what if?" questions for decision makers and highlights the need for preparedness and contingency plans.

As you read this, what economic scenario is unfolding? What are the important current events and trends? What scenarios could evolve six or eight years from now? How will *you* prepare?

Making the Choice

Once you have considered the possible consequences of your options, it is time to make your decision. Important concepts here are maximizing, satisficing, and optimizing.[24]

Maximizing is making the best possible decision. The maximizing decision realizes the greatest positive consequences and the fewest negative consequences. In other words, maximizing results in the greatest benefit at the lowest cost, with the largest expected total return. Maximizing requires searching thoroughly for a complete range of alternatives, carefully assessing each alternative, comparing one to another, and then choosing or creating the very best.

maximizing

A decision realizing the best possible outcome.

Satisficing is choosing the first option that is minimally acceptable or adequate; the choice appears to meet a targeted goal or criterion. When you satisfice, you compare your choice against your goal, not against other options. Satisficing means that a search for alternatives stops at the first one that is okay. Commonly, people do not expend the time or energy to gather more information. Instead, they make the expedient decision based on readily available information. Satisficing is sometimes a result of laziness; other times, there is no other option because time is short, information is unavailable, or other constraints make it impossible to maximize.

satisficing

Choosing an option that is acceptable, although not necessarily the best or perfect.

Let's say you are purchasing new equipment and your goal is to avoid spending too much money. You would be maximizing if you checked out all your options and their prices, and then bought the cheapest one that met your performance requirements. But you would be satisficing if you bought the first one you found that was within your budget and failed to look for less expensive options.

Optimizing means that you achieve the best possible balance among several goals. Perhaps, in purchasing equipment, you are interested in quality and durability as well as price. So, instead of buying the cheapest piece of equipment that works, you buy the one with the best combination of attributes, even though there may be options that are better on the price criterion and others that are better on the quality and durability criteria.

optimizing

Achieving the best possible balance among several goals.

The same idea applies to achieving business goals: One marketing strategy could maximize sales, while a different strategy might maximize profit. An optimizing strategy is the one that achieves the best balance among multiple goals.

Implementing the Decision

The decision-making process does not end once a choice is made. The chosen alternative must be implemented. Sometimes the people involved in making the choice must put it into effect. At other times, they delegate the responsibility for implementation to others, such as when a top management team changes a policy or operating procedure and has operational managers carry out the change.

Those who implement the decision must *understand* the choice and why it was made. They also must be *committed* to its successful implementation. These needs can be met by involving those people in the early stages of the decision process. At Steelcase, the world's largest manufacturer of office furniture, new product ideas are put through simultaneous design, engineering, and marketing scrutiny.[25] This is in contrast to an approach in which designers design and the concept is later relayed to other departments for implementation. In the latter case, full understanding and total commitment of all departments are less likely.

Managers should plan implementation carefully. Adequate planning requires several steps:[26]

1. Determine how things will look when the decision is fully operational.
2. Chronologically order, perhaps with a flow diagram, the steps necessary to achieve a fully operational decision.
3. List the resources and activities required to implement each step.
4. Estimate the time needed for each step.
5. Assign responsibility for each step to specific individuals.

Decision makers should assume that things will *not* go smoothly during implementation. It is very useful to take a little extra time to *identify potential problems* and *identify potential opportunities.* Then, you can take actions to prevent problems and also be ready to seize on unexpected opportunities. Useful questions are:

- What problems could this action cause?
- What can we do to prevent the problems?
- What unintended benefits or opportunities could arise?
- How can we make sure they happen?
- How can we be ready to act when the opportunities come?

Many of the chapters in this book are concerned with implementation issues: how to implement strategy, allocate resources, organize for results, lead and motivate people, manage change, and so on. View the chapters from that perspective, and learn as much as you can about how to implement properly.

Evaluating the Decision

The final stage in the decision-making process is evaluating the decision. This means collecting information on how well the decision is working. Quantifiable goals—a 20 percent increase in sales, a 95 percent reduction in accidents, 100 percent on-time deliveries—can be set before the solution to the problem is implemented. Then objective data can be gathered to accurately determine the success (or failure) of the decision.

Decision evaluation is useful whether the feedback is positive or negative. Feedback that suggests the decision is working implies that the decision should be continued and perhaps applied elsewhere in the organization. Negative feedback, indicating failure, means that either (1) implementation will require more time, resources, effort, or thought or (2) the decision was a bad one.

If the decision appears inappropriate, it's back to the drawing board. Then the process cycles back to the first stage: (re)definition of the problem. The decision-making process begins anew, preferably with more information, new suggestions, and an approach that attempts to eliminate the mistakes made the first time around.

The Best Decision

How can managers tell whether they have made the best decision? One approach is to wait until the results are in. But what if the decision has been made but not yet implemented? While nothing can guarantee a "best" decision, managers should at least be confident that they followed proper *procedures* that will yield the best possible decision under the circumstances. This means that the decision makers were appropriately vigilant in making the decision. **Vigilance** occurs when the decision makers carefully and conscientiously execute all six stages of decision making, including making provisions for implementation and evaluation.[27]

vigilance

A process in which a decision maker carefully executes all stages of decision making.

Even if managers reflect on these decision-making activities and conclude that they were executed conscientiously, they still will not know whether the decision will work; after all, nothing guarantees a good outcome. But they *will* know that they did their best to make the best possible decision.

Most of the causes of business failures described in the following section are a result of inadequate vigilance. Consider them decision traps; if you own a business and find yourself thinking in the following ways, you may be making poor decisions.

Why do firms fail? What kills companies is poor decisions at the top. Once entrepreneurs decide to start a business, they put their hearts into it but sometimes fail to use their heads. Faulty thought processes include:

- *I need to make the decisions myself.* Early on, you are responsible for everything. But over time, you need to bring in good people and let go a bit. Stay in touch with what's happening, but you have to delegate more, give other people more responsibility, and let them do what they do best.

- *E-commerce is easy and cheap.* It's easy to construct a website that can handle transactions. But most e-commerce efforts have failed, and many big companies have had to try many times before getting it close to right. The strategic, technological, and organizational issues should not be underestimated.

- *We don't need to make a profit.* Yeah, right. Obviously wrong, but the year 2000 was well under way before a lot of people learned the hard way that the new economy didn't mean that all the old rules no longer applied.

- *My forecasts are conservative.* You may think you can make your plan work because you have made cautious predictions. But you'd better have contingency plans in case your forecasts prove wrong. A rule of thumb is that start-ups take twice as long or need three times as much money as their founders predict. Sales projections are almost never met.

- *With this much money to work with, we can't miss.* It's tough to have to pinch pennies. But too much money may make for risky or poorly thought out decisions, and you will lose control of costs.

- *Fortunately, our biggest customer is General Motors (or Nokia, or IBM).* Traditionally, many managers would have loved to be in such a position. Today they'd better be ready in case they lose their biggest customer—it happens all the time.

SOURCES: B. G. Posner, "Why Companies Fail," *Inc.*, June 1993, pp. 102–6; R. Balu (Ed.), "Starting your Startup," *Fast Company*, January–February 2000, pp. 81–114; and A. Segars, "The Seven Myths of E-Commerce," *Financial Times Mastering Management Review*, January 2000, pp. 28–35.

Why Businesses Fail

Barriers to Effective Decision Making

Vigilance and full execution of the six-stage decision-making process are the exception rather than the rule in managerial decision making. But research shows that when managers use such rational processes, better decisions result.[28] Managers who make sure they engage in these processes are more effective.

Why don't people automatically invoke such rational processes? It is easy to neglect or improperly execute these processes. The problem may be improperly defined, or goals misidentified. Not enough solutions may be generated, or they may be evaluated incompletely. A satisficing rather than maximizing choice may be made. Implementation may be poorly planned or executed, or monitoring may be inadequate or nonexistent. And decisions are influenced by subjective psychological biases, time pressures, and social realities.

Psychological Biases

Decision makers are far from objective in the way they gather, evaluate, and apply information toward making their choices. People have biases that interfere with objective rationality. The examples that follow represent only a few of the many documented subjective biases.[29]

illusion of control

People's belief that they can influence events, even when they have no control over what will happen.

The **illusion of control** is a belief that one can influence events even when one has no control over what will happen. Gambling is one example: Some people believe they have the skill to beat the odds even though most people, most of the time, cannot. In business, such overconfidence can lead to failure because decision makers ignore risks and fail to objectively evaluate the odds of success. Relatedly, they may have an unrealistically positive view of themselves or their companies,[30] believe they can do no wrong, or hold a general optimism about the future that can lead them to believe they are immune to risk and failure.[31] For example, overconfidence was one contributor to the fall of Enron. Professor Jeffrey Pfeffer of Stanford described Enron's saga as one of "unmitigated pride and arrogance. My impression is that they thought they knew everything, which always is the fatal flaw" (p. A11).[32]

framing effects

A psychological bias influenced by the way in which a problem or decision alternative is phrased or presented.

Framing effects refer to how problems or decision alternatives are phrased or presented, and how these subjective influences can override objective facts. In one example, managers indicated a desire to invest more money in a course of action that was reported to have a 70 percent chance of profit than in one said to have a 30 percent chance of loss.[33] The choices were equivalent in their chances of success; it was the way the options were framed that determined the managers' choices. Thus, framing can exert an undue, irrational influence on people's decisions.

discounting the future

A bias weighting short-term costs and benefits more heavily than longer-term costs and benefits.

Often decision makers engage in **discounting the future.** That is, in their evaluation of alternatives, they weigh short-term costs and benefits more heavily than longer-term costs and benefits. Consider your own decision about whether to go for a dental checkup. The choice to go poses short-term financial costs, anxiety, and perhaps physical pain. The choice not to go will inflict even greater costs and more severe pain if dental problems worsen. How do you choose? Many people decide to avoid the short-term costs by not going for regular checkups, but end up facing much greater pain in the long run.

The same bias applies to students who don't study, weight watchers who sneak dessert or skip an exercise routine, and working people who take the afternoon off to play golf when they really need to work. It can also affect managers who hesitate to invest funds in research and development programs that may not pay off until far into the future. In all these cases, the avoidance of short-term costs or the seeking of short-term rewards results in negative long-term consequences.

Professional gambling establishments count on people's willingness to try to beat the odds. Their illusion of control is a major contributor to the high profits earned by most casinos.

When U.S. companies sacrifice present value to invest for the future—such as when Weyerhaeuser incurs enormous costs for its reforestation efforts that won't lead to harvest until 60 years in the future—it seems the exception rather than the rule. Discounting the future partly explains governmental budget deficits, environmental destruction, and decaying urban infrastructure.[34]

Individuals differ in their approaches to decision making. One well-known measure that assesses how people differ from one another, the Myers-Briggs Type Indicator (MBTI), has implications for how people make decisions both individually and in groups.

The basis for the MBTI is that people have preferences for one way of doing things over another. This is not about skill or ability, but about what people would do and how they would do it given free choice to exercise their true preferences. If you were to complete the MBTI, your results would indicate your preferences with respect to four basic choices:

1. Which do you prefer: extraversion (E)—attending to the external world of action, people, activities, and things—or introversion (I)—attending to the internal world of reflection, thought, ideas, and concepts?
2. Do you prefer sensing (S)—absorbing detailed, factual information through all the senses, through direct experience—or intuiting (N)—seeing the big picture and learning through reading, discussing, and interpreting?
3. Do you prefer thinking (T)—making decisions based on rational, economic logic and objective, quantitative criteria—or feeling (F)—making decisions also in a logical way but invoking personal values and impact on other people?
4. Do you prefer judging (J)—living a structured, well-planned, organized life, and making decisions quickly in order to reach closure—or perceiving (P)—being flexible and adaptable, going with the flow, and being comfortable with postponing decisions and keeping options open?

Think about your own preferences on these dimensions. What implications do these different types—especially S versus N and T versus F—have for decision making? And what are the implications for a group of people making decisions together? For example, what if everyone at the meeting is an E? Or everyone an I? Everyone a T, or everyone an F?

SOURCES: S. K. Hirsh and J. M. Kummerow, *Introduction to Type in Organizations* (Oxford: Oxford Psychologists Press, 1994); and D. Leonard and S. Straus, "Putting Your Company's Whole Brain to Work," *Harvard Business Review*, July–August 1997, pp. 110–21.

Your Personality Affects Your Decision Making

Time Pressures

In today's rapidly changing business environment, the premium is on acting quickly and keeping pace. The most conscientiously made business decisions can become irrelevant and even disastrous if managers take too long to make them.

How can managers make decisions quickly? Some natural tendencies, at least for North Americans, might be to skimp on analysis (not be too vigilant), suppress conflict, and make decisions on one's own without consulting other managers.[35] These strategies may speed up decision making, but they reduce decision *quality*.

Can managers under time pressure make both timely and high-quality decisions? A recent study of decision-making processes in microcomputer firms—a high-tech, fast-paced industry—showed some important differences between fast-acting and slower-acting firms.[36] The fast-acting firms realized significant competitive advantages without sacrificing the quality of their decisions.

What tactics do such companies use? First, instead of relying on old data, long-range planning, and futuristic forecasts, they focus on *real-time information:* current information obtained with little or no time delay. For example, they constantly monitor daily operating measures like work in process rather than checking periodically the traditional accounting-based indicators such as profitability.

Second, they *involve people more effectively and efficiently* in the decision-making process. They rely heavily on trusted experts, and this yields both good advice and the confidence to act quickly despite uncertainty. They also take a *realistic view of conflict:* They value differing opinions, but they know that if disagreements are not resolved, the top executive must make the final choice in the end. Slow-moving firms, in contrast, are stymied by conflict. Like the fast-moving firms they seek consensus, but when disagreements persist, they fail to come to a decision.

Social Realities

As the description of decision making in the microcomputer industry implies, many decision are made by a group rather than by an individual manager. In slow-moving firms, interpersonal factors decrease decision-making effectiveness. Even the manager acting alone is accountable to the boss and to others and must consider the preferences and reactions of many people. Important managerial decisions are marked by conflict among interested parties. Therefore, many decisions are the result of intensive social interactions, bargaining, and politicking.

The remainder of this chapter focuses on the social context of decisions, including decision making in groups and the realities of decision making in organizations.

Decision Making in Groups

Sometimes a manager finds it necessary to convene a group of people for the purpose of making an important decision. Some advise that in today's complex business environment, significant problems should *always* be tackled by teams.[37] Managers therefore must understand how groups and teams operate and how to use them to improve decision making. You will learn much more about how teams work later in the book.

The basic philosophy behind using a group to make decisions is captured by the adage "two heads are better than one." But is this statement really valid? Yes, it is—potentially.

If enough time is available, groups usually make higher-quality decisions than most individuals acting alone. However, groups often are inferior to the *best* individual.[38] How well the group performs depends on how effectively it capitalizes on the potential advantages and minimizes the potential problems of using a group. Table 3.2 summarizes these issues.

Potential Advantages of Using a Group

If other people have something to contribute, using groups to make a decision offers at least five potential advantages.[39]

1. More *information* is available when several people are making the decision. If one member doesn't have all the facts or the pertinent expertise, another member might.

TABLE 3.2
Pros and Cons of Using a Group to Make Decisions

Potential Advantages	Potential Disadvantages
1. Larger pool of information.	1. One person dominates.
2. More perspectives and approaches.	2. Satisficing.
3. Intellectual stimulation.	3. Groupthink.
4. People understand the decision.	4. Goal displacement.
5. People are committed to the decision.	

2. A greater number of *perspectives* on the issues, or different *approaches* to solving the problem, are available. The problem may be new to one group member but familiar to another. Or the group may need to consider other viewpoints—financial, legal, marketing, human resources, and so on—to achieve an optimal solution.

3. Group discussion provides an opportunity for *intellectual stimulation*. It can get people thinking and unleash their creativity to a far greater extent than would be possible with individual decision making.

These three potential advantages of using a group improve the chance that a more fully informed, higher-quality decision will result. Thus, managers should involve people with different backgrounds, perspectives, and access to information. They should not involve only their cronies who think the same way they do.

4. People who participate in a group discussion are more likely to *understand* why the decision was made. They will have heard the relevant arguments both for the chosen alternative and against the rejected alternatives.

5. Group discussion typically leads to a higher level of *commitment* to the decision. Buying into the proposed solution translates into high motivation to ensure that it is executed effectively.

The last two advantages improve the chances that the decision will be implemented successfully. Therefore, managers should involve the people who will be responsible for implementing the decision as early in the deliberations as possible.

Potential Problems of Using a Group

Things *can* go wrong when groups make decisions. Most of the potential problems concern the process through which group members interact with one another.[40]

1. Sometimes one group member *dominates* the discussion. When this occurs—such as when a strong leader makes his or her preferences clear—the result is the same as it would be if the dominant individual made the decision alone. Individual dominance has two disadvantages. First, the dominant person does not necessarily have the most valid opinions, and may even have the most unsound ideas. Second, even if that person's preference leads to a good decision, convening as a group will have been a waste of everyone else's time.

2. *Satisficing* is more likely with groups. Most people don't like meetings and will do whatever they can to end them. This may include criticizing members who want to continue exploring new and better alternatives. The result is a satisficing rather than an optimizing or maximizing decision.

3. *Pressure to avoid disagreement* can lead to a phenomenon called *groupthink*. **Groupthink** occurs when people choose not to disagree or raise objections because they don't want to break up a positive team spirit. Some groups want to think as one, tolerate no dissension, and strive to remain cordial. Such groups are overconfident, complacent, and perhaps too willing to take risks. Pressure to go along with the group's preferred solution stifles creativity and the other behaviors characteristic of vigilant decision making.

groupthink

A phenomenon that occurs in decision making when group members avoid disagreement as they strive for consensus.

4. *Goal displacement* often occurs in groups. The goal of group members should be to come up with the best possible solution to the problem. But when **goal displacement** occurs, new goals emerge to replace the original ones. It is common for two or more group members to have different opinions and present their conflicting cases. Attempts at rational persuasion become heated disagreement. Winning the argument becomes the new goal. Saving face and defeating the other person's idea become more important than solving the problem.

goal displacement

A condition that occurs when a decision-making group loses sight of its original goal and a new, possibly less important, goal emerges.

Effective managers pay close attention to the group process; they manage it carefully. The following sections and later chapters provide suggestions for the effective management of group meetings.

Managing Group Decision Making

Figure 3.3 illustrates the requirements for effectively managing group decision making: (1) an appropriate leadership style; (2) the constructive use of disagreement and conflict; and (3) the enhancement of creativity.

Leadership Style

The leader of a decision-making body must attempt to minimize process-related problems. The leader should avoid dominating the discussion or allowing another individual to dominate. This means encouraging less vocal group members to air their opinions and suggestions and asking for dissenting viewpoints.

At the same time, the leader should not allow the group to pressure people into conforming. The leader should be alert to the dangers of groupthink and satisficing. Also, she should be attuned to indications that group members are losing sight of the primary objective: to come up with the best possible solution to the problem.

This implies two things. First, don't lose sight of the problem. Second, make a decision! Keep in mind the slow-moving microcomputer firms that were paralyzed when group members couldn't come to an agreement.

Constructive Conflict

Total and consistent agreement among group members can be destructive. It can lead to groupthink, uncreative solutions, and a waste of the knowledge and diverse viewpoints that individuals bring to the group. Thus, a certain amount of *constructive* conflict should exist.[41] Some companies, including Sun Microsystems, Compaq, and

FIGURE 3.3
Managing Group Decision Making

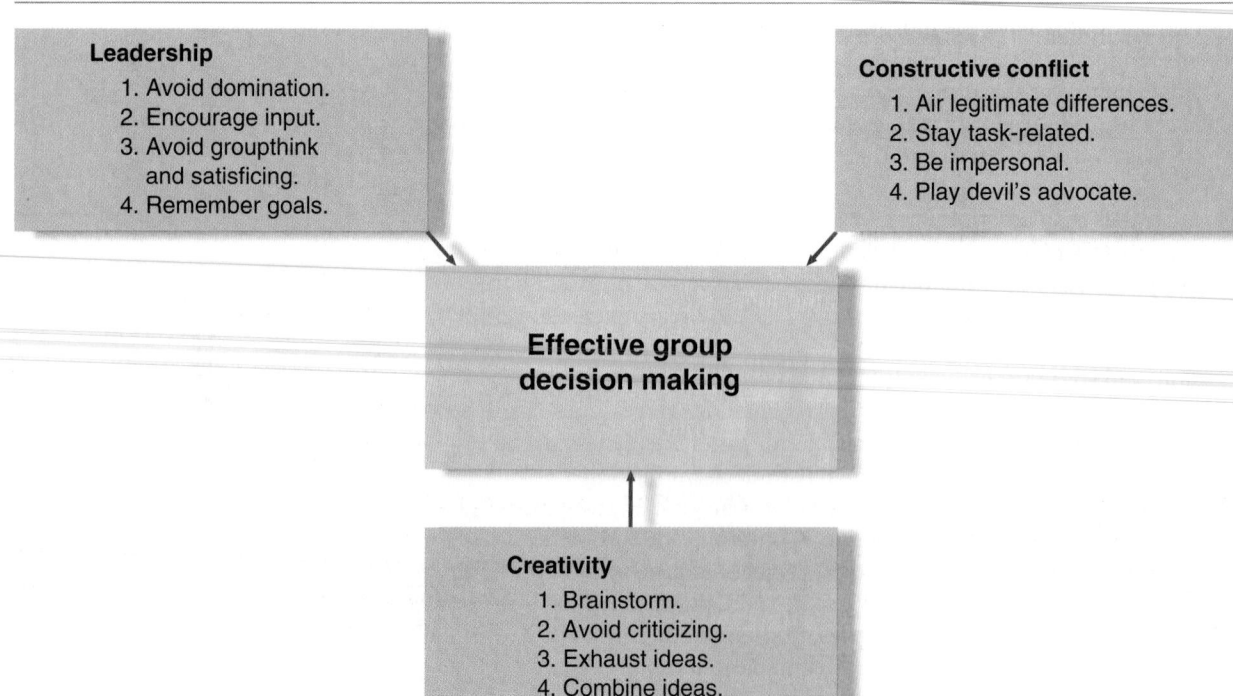

Leadership
1. Avoid domination.
2. Encourage input.
3. Avoid groupthink and satisficing.
4. Remember goals.

Constructive conflict
1. Air legitimate differences.
2. Stay task-related.
3. Be impersonal.
4. Play devil's advocate.

Effective group decision making

Creativity
1. Brainstorm.
2. Avoid criticizing.
3. Exhaust ideas.
4. Combine ideas.

United Parcel Service, take steps to ensure that conflict and debate are generated within their management teams.[42]

The most constructive type of conflict is **cognitive conflict,** or differences in perspectives or judgments about issues. In contrast, **affective conflict** is emotional and directed at other people. Affective conflict is likely to be destructive to the group because it can lead to anger, bitterness, goal displacement, and lower-quality decisions. Cognitive conflict, in contrast, can air legitimate differences of opinion and develop better ideas and problem solutions. Conflict, then, should be task related rather than personal.[43]

> **cognitive conflict**
>
> Issue-based differences in perspectives or judgments.
>
> **affective conflict**
>
> Emotional disagreement directed toward other people.

Managers can increase the likelihood of constructive conflict by assembling teams of different types of people, by creating frequent interactions and active debates, and by encouraging multiple alternatives to be generated from a variety of perspectives.[44] Conflict also can be generated formally through structured processes.[45] Two techniques that purposely program cognitive conflict into the decision-making process are devil's advocacy and the dialectic method.

A **devil's advocate** has the job of criticizing ideas. The group leader can formally assign people to play this role. Requiring people to point out problems can lessen inhibitions about disagreeing and make the conflict less personal and emotional.

An alternative to devil's advocacy is the dialectic. The **dialectic** goes a step beyond devil's advocacy by requiring a structured debate between two conflicting courses of action.[46] The philosophy of the dialectic stems from Plato and Aristotle, who advocated synthesizing the conflicting views of a thesis and an antithesis. Structured debates between plans and counterplans can be useful prior to making a strategic decision. For example, one team might present the case for acquiring a firm while another team advocates not making the acquisition.

> **devil's advocate**
>
> A person who has the job of criticizing ideas to ensure that their downsides are fully explored.
>
> **dialectic**
>
> A structured debate comparing two conflicting courses of action.

Generating constructive conflict does not need to be done on such a formal basis, and is not solely the leader's responsibility. Any team member can introduce cognitive conflict by being honest with opinions; by not being afraid to disagree with others; by pushing the group to action if it is taking too long, or making the group slow down if necessary; and by advocating long-term considerations if the group is too focused on short-term results. Introducing constructive conflict is a legitimate and necessary responsibility of all group members interested in improving the group's decision-making effectiveness.

Encouraging Creativity

As you've already learned, ready-made solutions to a problem can be inadequate or unavailable. In such cases, custom-made solutions are necessary. This means the group must be creative in generating ideas.

Some say we are in the midst of the next great business revolution: the "creative revolution."[47] Said to transcend the agricultural, industrial, and information revolutions, the most fundamental unit of value in the creativity revolution is ideas. Creativity is more than just an option; it is essential to survival. Allowing people to be creative may be one of the manager's most important and challenging responsibilities.

You might be saying to yourself, "I'm not creative." But even if you are not an artist or a musician, you do have potential to be creative in countless other ways. You are being creative if you (1) bring a new thing into being *(creation)*; (2) join two previously unrelated things *(synthesis)*; or (3) improve something or give it a new application *(modification)*. You don't need to be a genius in school, either—Thomas Edison and

Rolf Smith, formerly of the U.S. Air Force, now leads companies on outdoor "Thinking Expeditions."

Albert Einstein were not particularly good students. Nor does something need to change the world to be creative; the "little things" can always be done in new, creative ways that add value to the product and the customer.

How do you "get" creative?[48] Recognize the almost infinite "little" opportunities to be creative. Assume you can be creative if you give it a try. Obtain sufficient resources, including facilities, equipment, information, and funds. Escape from work once in a while. Read widely, and try new experiences. Talk to people, constantly, about the issues and ideas with which you are wrestling. And take a course or find a good book about creative thought processes; there are plenty available.

How do you "get" creativity out of other people?[49] Give creative efforts the credit they are due, and don't punish creative failures. If possible, relax pressure for short-term results. Place bets on innovative ideas without heeding projected returns. Stimulate and challenge people intellectually, and give people some creative freedom. Allow enough time to explore different ideas. Put together teams of people with different styles of thinking and behaving. Get your people in touch with customers, and let them bounce ideas around—but don't pay so much attention to customers that they distract you from novel, high-potential ideas. Protect your people from managers who demand immediate payoffs, who don't understand the importance of creative contributions, or who try to take credit for others' successes. And strive to be creative yourself—you'll set a good example.

A commonly used technique is brainstorming. In **brainstorming**, group members generate as many ideas about a problem as they can. As the ideas are presented, they are posted so that everyone can read them, and people can use the ideas as building blocks. The group is encouraged to say anything that comes to mind, with one exception: No criticism of other people or their ideas is allowed. This rule was violated at the Walt Disney Company when, during a brainstorming session for the design of Euro Disneyland, two architects began shoving each other and almost came to blows.[50]

In the proper brainstorming environment—free of criticism—people are less inhibited and more likely to voice their unusual, creative, or even wild ideas. By the time people have exhausted their ideas, a long list of alternatives has been generated. Only then does the group turn to the evaluation stage. At that point, many different ideas can be considered, modified, or combined into a creative, custom-made solution to the problem.

Although brainstorming is a common practice, some research has shown that face-to-face groups generate fewer independent ideas than the same number of people working alone. This is because in a group: (1) some people, worried about what others might think, are reluctant to express their ideas; (2) people don't always work as hard as if they are alone and accountable for results as individuals; and (3) listening to others takes time that can block people's productivity. But the potential benefits of good brainstorming are clear.[51]

brainstorming

A process in which group members generate as many ideas about a problem as they can; criticism is withheld until all ideas have been proposed

Organizational Decision Making

Individuals and groups make decisions constantly, throughout organizations. To understand decision making in organizations, a manager must consider a number of additional concepts and processes, including (1) the constraints decision makers face, (2) organizational decision processes, (3) negotiations and politics, (4) decision making during a crisis, and (5) emergent strategies.

Rolf Smith, who launched the U.S. Air Force's first Office of Innovation and now leads companies on outdoor "Thinking Expeditions," says that if you truly pay attention to ideas—even the small, seemingly insignificant ones—then you'll create an environment in which people feel comfortable generating and offering them (p. 162). A playful approach is often effective. "Play" is the name of a small but fast-growing marketing agency gaining attention for its playful work environment and its productive brainstorming sessions for companies including Calvin Klein, PricewaterhouseCooper, Oscar Mayer, and Disney. At a typical recent session, a meeting generated more than 70 ideas for a Weather Channel marketing campaign.

The most carefully studied examples of brainstorming come from IDEO, a firm that has contributed to the design of thousands of products in dozens of industries.

A "brainstormer" at IDEO is a scheduled, face-to-face meeting called to generate ideas. The rules of brainstorming are posted on the wall, and enforced. Several benefits of brainstorming accrue to IDEO. First, the company generates more solutions to design products. Second, brainstorming adds variety and fun to the job. Third, it helps designers acquire wisdom, to be both confident and humble, as they learn what they know and also what they don't know. Fourth, it encourages people to respect others and work to gain others' respect, so they go out of their way to contribute and to help one another. Fifth, it impresses clients ("We really wow'em!"). Sixth, it provides income. Clients are billed for the brainstorming sessions. And whereas clients in all industries have complaints about their bills, complaints about these charges are rare because clients see the value.

And the design results? Examples are the original Apple computer mouse, Crest Toothpaste's Neat Squeeze tubes, bike helmets, an electric guitar, Nike sunglasses, part of the Jaminator toy guitar, an angioplasty device, fishing equipment, Smith ski goggles, and a combination beach chair and cooler. IDEO has won more *Business Week* Design Excellence Awards, for several years running, than any other product design firm.

SOURCES: Sutton and A. Hargadon, "Brainstorming Groups in Context: Effectiveness in a Product Design Firm." *Administrative Science Quarterly* 41, (1996), pp. 685–718; B. Nussbaum, "Winners: The Best Product Designs of the Year," *Business Week*, June 2, 1997, pp. 38–41; IDEO was just selected by Scott Adams, creator of Dilbert, to redesign, on behalf of office workers everywhere, the fame of Dilbert's work life: the office cubicle.

Constraints on Decision Makers

Organizations—or, more accurately, the people who make important decisions—cannot do whatever they wish. They face various constraints—financial, legal, market, human, and organizational—that inhibit certain actions. Capital or product markets may make an expensive new venture impossible. Legal restrictions may restrain the kinds of international business activities in which a firm can participate. Labor unions may defeat a contract proposed by management, contracts may prevent certain managerial actions, and managers and investors may block a takeover attempt.

Suppose you have a great idea that will provide a revolutionary service for your bank's customers. You won't be able to put your idea into action immediately. You will have to sell it to the people who can give you the go-ahead and also to those whose help you will need to carry out the project. You might start by convincing your boss of your idea's merit. Next, the two of you may have to hash it out with a vice president. Then maybe the president has to be sold. At each stage, you must listen to these individuals' opinions and suggestions and often incorporate them into your original concept. Ultimately, you will have to derive a proposal acceptable to everyone.

In addition, ethical and legal considerations must be thought out carefully. You will have plenty of opportunity to think about ethical issues in Chapter 5. Decision makers must consider ethics and the preferences of many constituent groups—the realities of life in organizations.

Models of Organizational Decision Processes

bounded rationality

A less-than-perfect form of rationality in which decision makers cannot be perfectly rational because decisions are complex and complete information is unavailable.

Just as with individuals and groups, organizational decision making historically was described with rational models like the one depicted earlier in Figure 3.2. But Nobel laureate Herbert Simon challenged the rational model and proposed an important alternative called *bounded rationality*. According to Simon's **bounded rationality,** decision makers cannot be truly rational because (1) they have imperfect, incomplete information about alternatives and consequences; (2) the problems they face are so complex; (3) human beings simply cannot process all the information to which they are exposed; (4) there is not enough time to process all relevant information fully; and (5) people, including managers within the same firm, have conflicting goals.

When these conditions hold—and they do for most consequential managerial decisions—perfect rationality will give way to more biased, subjective, messier decision processes. For example, the **incremental model** of decision making occurs when decision makers make small decisions, take little steps, move cautiously, and move in piecemeal fashion toward a bigger solution. The classic example is the budget process, which traditionally begins with the budget from the previous period and makes incremental decisions from that starting point.

incremental model

Model of organizational decision making in which major solutions arise through a series of smaller decisions.

coalitional model

Model of organizational decision making in which groups with differing preferences use power and negotiations to influence decisions.

The **coalitional model** of decision making arises when people disagree on goals or compete with one another for resources. The decision process becomes political, as groups of individuals band together and try collectively to influence the decision. Two or more coalitions form, each representing a different preference, and each tries to use power and negotiations to sway the decision.

garbage can model

Model of organizational decision making depicting a chaotic process and seemingly random decisions.

The **garbage can model** of decision making occurs when people aren't sure of their goals, or disagree about the goals, and likewise are unsure of or in disagreement about what to do. This occurs because some problems are so complex that they are not well understood, and also because decision makers move in and out of the decision process because they have so many other things to attend to as well. This model implies that some decisions are chaotic, and almost random. You can see that this is a dramatic departure from rationality in decision making.

Negotiations and Politics

As the coalitional model suggests, decision makers often need to negotiate, bargain, or compromise. Some decisions must be negotiated with parties outside the organization, such as local government, consumer groups, or environmental groups. Even inside the organization, decisions are negotiated among a number of people.

The fact that decisions often must be negotiated implies that they are political; that is, they galvanize the preferences of competing groups and individuals. The decision that is best on objective grounds may lose out because powerful individuals push through their preferred alternatives. Strategic decisions, pay raises, promotions, and budgets, all may be made (and criticized) on the basis of politics.

Organizational politics, in which people try to influence organizational decisions so that their own interests will be served and use power to pursue hidden agendas, can reduce decision-making effectiveness.[52] One of the best ways to reduce such politics, and to make sure that constructive cognitive conflict does not degenerate into affective conflict, is to *create common goals* for members of the team—that is, make the decision-making process a collaborative, rather than a competitive, exercise by establishing a goal around which the group can rally. In one study, top management teams with stated goals like "build the biggest financial war chest" for an upcoming competitive battle, or "create *the* computer firm of the decade," or "build the best damn machine on the market" were less likely to have dysfunctional conflict and politics between members.[53]

Most managers accept political realities and consider them a basic challenge of organizational life.[54] For any important decision that you wish to influence, it is essential that you identify and marshal the support of powerful individuals or interest groups.

Decision Making in a Crisis

In crisis situations, managers must make decisions under a great deal of pressure.[55] You know some of the most famous recent crises: the *Exxon Valdez;* Barings Bank's collapse; airline crashes; the Firestone Tire recall (see the concluding case); and of course the terrorist attacks. Union Carbide's gas leak in Bhopal, India, killed thousands of people; several people were killed in the cyanide poisonings of Johnson & Johnson's Tylenol. As outlined in Table 3.3, the two companies handled their crises in very different ways. To this day, J&J is known for its effective handling of the crisis, as outlined in the table.

Your organization should be prepared for crises in advance. However, many Fortune 1000 firms have no crisis-management plan at all.[56] Table 3.4 lists some common rationalizations that prevent companies from preparing for and managing crises properly. Effective managers do not allow these evasions to prevent them from preparing carefully for crisis.

Although many companies don't concern themselves with crisis management, it is imperative that it be on management's agenda. An effective plan for crisis management (CM) should include the following elements.[57]

1. *Strategic actions* such as integrating CM into strategic planning and official policies.
2. *Technical and structural actions* such as creating a CM team and dedicating a budget to CM.
3. *Evaluation and diagnostic actions* such as conducting audits of threats and liabilities, and establishing tracking systems for early warning signals.
4. *Communication actions* such as providing training for dealing with the media, local communities, and police and government officials.
5. *Psychological and cultural actions* such as showing a strong top management commitment to CM and providing training and psychological support services regarding the human and emotional impacts of crises.

Ultimately, it is imperative that management be able to answer the following questions:[58]

- What kinds of crises could your company face?
- Can your company detect a crisis in its early stages?
- How will it manage a crisis if one occurs?
- How can it benefit from a crisis after it has passed?

The last question makes an important point: A crisis, managed effectively, can have *benefits.* Old as well as new problems can be resolved, new strategies and competitive advantages may appear, and positive change can emerge. And if someone steps in and manages the crisis well, a hero is born.

As a leader during a crisis,[59] don't pretend that nothing happened (as with managers at one firm after a visitor died in the hallway despite employees' efforts to save him). Communicate and reinforce the organization's values. Try to find ways for people to support one another, and remember that people will take cues from your behavior. You should be optimistic but brutally honest. Show emotion, but not fear. "You have

TABLE 3.3
Two Disasters

Union Carbide	Johnson & Johnson
Failed to identify as a crisis the public perception that the company was a negligent, uncaring killer.	Identified the crisis of public perception that Tylenol was unsafe and J&J was not in control.
No planning before reacting:	Planned before reacting:
CEO immediately went to India to inspect damage.	CEO picked one executive to head crisis team.
All executives involved.	Rest of company involved only on a need-to-know basis.
Set no goals.	Set goals to:
	Stop the killings.
	Find reasons for the killings.
	Provide assistance to the victims.
	Restore Tylenol's credibility.
Action: Damage control/stonewalling.	Action: Gave complete information.
Distanced itself.	Worked with authorities.
Misrepresented safety conditions.	Pulled Tylenol from shelves (first-year cost: $150 million).
Did not inform spokespeople.	Used strong marketing program.
Adopted bunker mentality.	Reissued Tylenol with tamper-proof packaging.
Chronic problems continued:	Crisis resolved:
Public confidence low.	Public confidence high.
Costly litigation.	Sales high again.
No formal crisis plan resulted.	Well-documented crisis management plan.

TABLE 3.4
Mistaken Assumptions:
How *Not* to Handle Crisis
Management

We don't have a crisis.
We can handle a crisis.
Crisis management is a luxury we can't afford.
If a major crisis happens, someone else will rescue us.
Accidents are just a cost of doing business.
Most crises are the fault of bad individuals; therefore, there's not much we can do to prevent them.
Only executives need to be aware of our crisis plans; why scare our employees or members of the community?
We are tough enough to react to a crisis in an objective and rational manner.
The most important thing in crisis management is to protect the good image of the organization through public relations and advertising campaigns.

SOURCE: From C. M. Pearson and I. I. Mitroff. "From Crisis Prone to Crisis Prepared: A Framework for Crisis Management," *The Executive*, February 1993, pp. 48–59. Reprinted by permission of the Academy of Management.

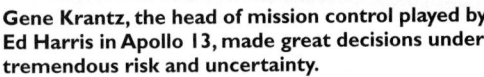
Gene Krantz, the head of mission control played by Ed Harris in Apollo 13, made great decisions under tremendous risk and uncertainty.

to be cooler than cool," says Gene Krantz of Apollo 13 ground control fame. But don't ignore the problems, or downplay them and reassure too much; don't create false hopes. Give people the bad news straight—you'll gain credibility, and when the good news comes, it will really mean something.[60]

Emergent Strategies

Soon you will learn more about how managers formulate strategies for their firms to pursue. Again, a rational model can describe this process in its ideal form. But once again, the reality of organizational decision making often differs. **Emergent strategy** is the strategy that the organization "ends up" pursuing, based not solely on what was originally planned and attempted, but also on what actually evolves from all the activities engaged in by people throughout the organization.

> **emergent strategy**
>
> **The strategy that evolves from all the activities engaged in by people throughout the organization.**

As shown in Figure 3.4, decision making and strategy emergence are dynamic processes through which people engage in discovery; make decisions; carry out those choices in sometimes tentative, trial-and-error ways; and discover new things and new ways by chance. Discovery is the process of systematically gathering facts and analyzing them. This forms the basis for decision making, which includes generating and selecting goals and courses of action. Action, then, is implementation and evaluation. Discovery continues unabated.

Thus, emergent strategies may start with planning from the top executives, but may also involve trial-and-error, experimenting, learning from mistakes, seizing unexpected

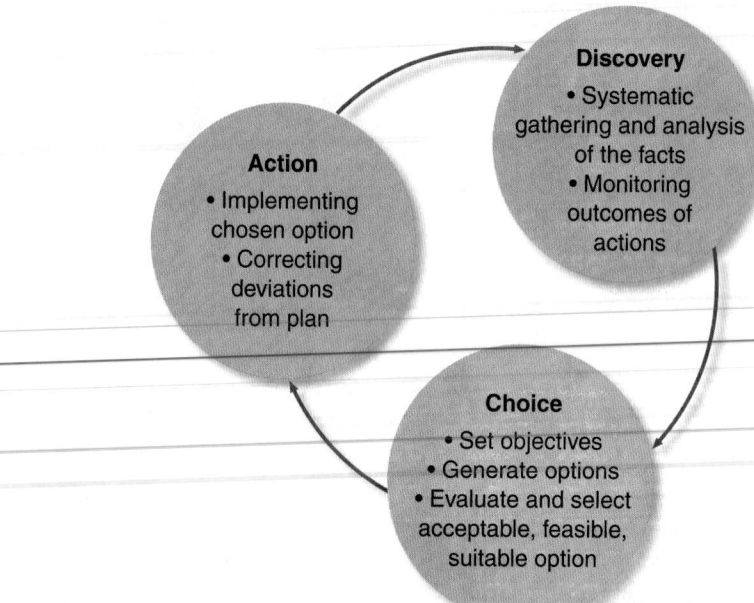

FIGURE 3.4
Emergent Strategies

SOURCE: Adapted from Ralph D. Stacey. *Strategic Management and Organizational Dynamics.* London: Pittman Publishing; 1993, p. 27.

opportunities, and so on. And these activities can occur at any organizational level, in any unit, at any location.

In fact, some decisions are made not by thorough analysis, but by trying several things and seeing what works. Sometimes it's worth taking action before doing a thorough analysis, in order to learn. Such an approach—compared to companies that take too much time overanalyzing—can offer a competitive edge in uncertain times.[61]

KEY TERMS

Affective conflict, p. 81

Bounded rationality, p. 84

Brainstorming, p. 82

Certainty, p. 68

Coalitional model, p. 84

Cognitive conflict, p. 81

Conflict, p. 69

Contingency plans, p. 72

Custom-made solutions, p. 71

Devil's advocate, p. 81

Dialectic, p. 81

Discounting the future, p. 76

Emergent strategy, p. 87

Framing effects, p. 76

Garbage can model, p. 84

Goal displacement, p. 79

Groupthink, p. 79

Illusion of control, p. 76

Incremental model, p. 84

Maximizing, p. 73

Nonprogrammed decisions, p. 67

Optimizing, p. 73

Programmed decisions, p. 66

Ready-made solutions, p. 71

Risk, p. 68

Satisficing, p. 73

Uncertainty, p. 68

Vigilance, p. 74

SUMMARY OF LEARNING OBJECTIVES

Now that you have studied Chapter 3, you should know:

The kinds of decisions you will face as a manager.

Most important managerial decisions are ill structured and characterized by uncertainty, risk, and conflict. Yet managers are expected to make rational decisions in the face of these challenges.

How to make "rational" decisions.

The ideal decision-making process involves six stages. The first, identifying and diagnosing the problem, requires recognizing a discrepancy between the current state and a desired state and then delving below surface symptoms to uncover the underlying causes of the problem. The second stage, generating alternative solutions, requires adopting ready-made or designing custom-made solutions. The third, evaluating alternatives, means predicting the consequences of different alternatives, sometimes through building scenarios of the future. Fourth, a solution is chosen; the solution might maximize, satisfice, or optimize. Fifth, people implement the decision; this stage requires more careful planning than it often receives. Finally, managers should evaluate how well the decision is working. This means gathering objective, valid information about the impact the decision is having. If the evidence suggests the problem is not getting solved, either a better decision or a better implementation plan must be developed.

The pitfalls you should avoid when making decisions.

Situational and human limitations lead most decision makers to satisfice rather than maximize. Psychological biases, time pressures, and the social realities of organizational life may prevent rational execution of the six decision-making stages. But vigilance and an understanding of how to manage decision-making groups and organizational constraints will improve the process and result in better decisions.

The pros and cons of using a group to make decisions.

Advantages include more information, perspectives, and approaches brought to bear on problem solving; intellectual stimulation; greater understanding by all of the final decision; and higher commitment to the decision once it is made. Potential dangers or disadvantages of using groups include individual domination of discussions, satisficing, groupthink, and goal displacement.

The procedures to use in leading a decision-making team.

Effective leaders in decision-making teams or groups avoid dominating the discussion; encourage people's input; avoid groupthink and satisficing; and stay focused on the group's goals. They encourage constructive conflict via devil's advocacy and the dialectic, posing opposite sides of an issue or solutions to a problem. They also encourage creativity through a variety of techniques.

How to encourage creative decisions.

When creative ideas are needed, leaders should set a good example by being creative themselves. They should recognize the almost infinite "little" opportunities for creativity and have confidence in their own creative abilities. They can inspire creativity in others by pushing for creative freedom, rewarding creativity, and not punishing creative failures. They should encourage interaction with customers, stimulate discussion, and protect people from managers who might squelch the creative processes. Brainstorming is one of the most popular techniques for generating creative ideas.

The processes by which decisions are made in organizations.

Decision making in organizations is often a highly complex process. Individuals and groups are constrained by a variety of factors and constituencies. In practice, decision makers are boundedly rational rather than purely rational. Some decisions are made on an incremental basis. Coalitions form to represent different preferences. The process is often chaotic, as depicted in the garbage can model. Politics enter the process, decisions are negotiated, crises arise, and strategies emerge and evolve.

How to make decisions in a crisis.

Crisis conditions make sound, effective decision making more difficult. However, it is possible for crises to be managed well. A strategy for crisis management can be developed beforehand, and the mechanisms put into readiness, so that if crises do arise, decision makers are prepared.

DISCUSSION QUESTIONS

1. Refer back to "Setting the Stage." If you didn't know the conclusions to those incidents, what would you have done? What do you think of the decisions those managers made?

2. Identify some risky decisions you have made. Why did you take the risks? How did they work out? Looking back, what did you learn?

3. Identify a decision you made that had important unexpected consequences. Were the consequences good, bad, or both? Should you, and could you, have done anything differently in making the decision?

4. What do you think is your Myers-Briggs type? What are the personal implications?

5. Recall a recent decision that you had difficulty making. Describe it in terms of the characteristics of managerial decisions.

6. What do you think are some advantages and disadvantages to using computer technology in decision making?

7. Do you think that when managers make decisions they follow the decision-making steps as presented in this chapter? Which steps are apt to be overlooked or given inadequate

attention? What can people do to make sure they do a more thorough job?

8. Discuss the potential advantages and disadvantages of using a group to make decisions. Give examples from your experience.

9. Suppose you are the CEO of a major corporation and one of your company's oil tanks has erupted, spilling thousands of gallons of oil into a river that empties into the ocean. What do you need to do to handle the crisis?

10. Look at the mistaken assumptions described in Table 3.4. Why do such assumptions arise, and what can be done to overcome these biases?

11. Identify some problems you want to solve. Brainstorm with others a variety of creative solutions.

Trying to Move on after a Crisis

Put yourself in the shoes of Jac Nasser, CEO of Ford. A crisis strikes from out of the blue. How you handle the crisis will determine whether you keep your job, and will affect your reputation forever.

Nasser became CEO in late 1998. By now you probably are aware of the subsequent tragedy: Reports of fatal accidents due to faulty tires on Ford Explorer sport utilities and Ranger pickup trucks began appearing, and eventually more than 100 deaths were attributed to the tires peeling off under pressure. Ford acknowledged that it knew about tire failures in Venezuela in 1998. When Ford first notified Firestone of a potential problem, Firestone failed to act.

Nasser did not cause the problems. But as CEO, they became his responsibility.

What to do? Nasser was briefed about the tire failures in early July 2000, and created a war room (actually, several rooms) on the 11th floor of Ford's world headquarters in Dearborn, Michigan. Daily task force meetings included manufacturing, engineering, finance, public affairs, and legal and regulatory executives. The public-affairs unit monitored media coverage, and reviewed developments each morning in a global conference call. Work on the crisis went on night and day, every day, and involved 500 people directly and thousands more indirectly.

Adding greatly to the decision-making and public relations challenges was that Ford had to coordinate its actions with Bridgestone/Firestone, the producer of the defective tires. Bridgestone/Firestone is a Japanese-owned company with very different cultural norms, including norms about not making information available to the public. Communications between Ford and Firestone were difficult. Ford did not want to get into a public dispute with its supplier, but did want to distance itself from the tire defects. Ford communicated with everyone—customers, dealers, the media, the government, other suppliers—about what it was doing. But it tried to avoid quibbling about whose fault it was and who would have to pay for it. Rather, the concern was to get a handle on the problem as quickly as possible.

Ford was in an awkward position. Car manufacturers warrant all components—except tires. Therefore, they don't collect tire data. Ford immediately started gathering as much valid data as it could, and made the data publicly available.

The company engaged in an exhaustive effort to gather, analyze, and disseminate relevant information from four continents. It then recalled 6.5 million Firestone tires. This was a huge logistical challenge. Ford had to obtain replacement tires from competing manufacturers, and find enough service bays to change all those tires.

Nasser closed three assembly plants and used their 70,000 new tires as replacements for consumers. Think about the repercussions of that decision. These plants are the mainstay of the auto industry. Closing one plant is extremely tough, both financially and operationally. The company had to mothball machinery, secure partially assembled cars, and stop the supply of parts. And whereas lost production means lost revenues, costs didn't decrease much because workers received most of their base pay. One company official

Many think that Jac Nasser's "decision making" led to his replacement by now CEO, William Clay Ford, great-grandson of Henry Ford.

called Nasser's decision to close the plants "the most courageous decision I've seen since I've been at Ford"(p. 124).

Ford's public relations challenge was enormous. Historically, auto companies often tried to hide problems from the public, and Ford's handling of the exploding Pintos in the 1970s was a notorious example. But when Nasser met with the lead technical person in charge of light trucks, he advised him to be completely open, share any and all data and incidents, and hold back no information whatsoever. Nasser also advised him not to be constrained by product-liability concerns. "If you are mesmerized by that, you will not ultimately do what's right for the customer"(p. 126).

Nasser did many things well, but criticisms and tough questions ensued. Why didn't the company act sooner to identify the defects? Why wasn't Chairman Bill Ford, Jr., used as a spokesman during the crisis? Why didn't he go directly to the scene of the crisis and personally demonstrate his concern for the people involved? Why were there temporary shortages of replacement tires? And how would Nasser perform during the investigations and lawsuits?

In October 2000, John Lampe was named the new chairman of Bridgestone/Firestone. He kept busy tackling what he called "challenges" and "opportunities" rather than problems. He and the company were dedicated to keeping the Firestone name, which he said has a tremendous heritage and loyal following. When a reporter asked if he would agree to a "customer satisfaction" campaign to replace any tires not named in the recall if customers asked for replacements, he replied "No, ma'am" (p. E10). But he committed to recalling all problem tires specified in the recall, ahead of schedule. And both he and Nasser appeared in commercials, separately, attempting to restore credibility and repair their companies' reputations.

Much remained unresolved. Each company blamed the other. Each claimed the other withheld important information. Each felt betrayed after a business relationship that lasted nearly a century. Consumer confidence—in the entire Firestone brand, not just the recalled tires—fell to an all-time low. Class-action litigation heated up, and congressional hearings may continue. Ford reported its first annual loss in 10 years, and announced a series of plant closings, layoffs, and production slowdowns.

Japan's Bridgestone started pouring money into bringing Bridgestone tires into the U.S. middle market traditionally held by Firestone. Whereas some observers had speculated that Bridgestone might phase out the Firestone name, executives maintained

that the new campaign was not triggered by the crisis. The company was eager to give Bridgestone a bigger presence in North America, but also insisted it wants to restore Firestone's image and business. Although Bridgestone broke off its relationship with Ford, some executives signaled their interest in resuming the relationship. But meanwhile, Bridgestone started building a stronger relationship with General Motors.

One other big development: When Nasser returned to Detroit, exhausted, from a brutal congressional hearing, his top 20 executives chanted "We back Jac" while wearing masks bearing his likeness, bulletproof vests, and buttons proclaiming "We'll take a bullet for Jac." But Chairman William Clay Ford, Jr., great-grandson of Henry Ford, fired Nasser and made himself CEO.

Some say Nasser was so busy with the Firestone crisis that he left William Clay Ford out of the decision-making loop, a political blunder. Some say Firestone so distracted him that he couldn't devote time to other company needs, and results suffered. And some say that with the crisis, other product recalls, and a souring economy, Ford and Nasser were hit by the perfect storm.

QUESTIONS

1. What do you think of how Nasser and Ford handled the crisis? What could they have done differently?

2. Could Nasser have saved his job? If not, why not? If so, how?

3. How damaged is the Firestone brand? The Explorer brand? The Ford brand?

4. What should Bridgestone/Firestone and Ford do now?

SOURCES: A. Taylor, III., "Jac Nasser's Biggest Test," *Fortune,* September 18, 2000, pp. 123–28, C.E. Mayer, "Hot Situation, Cool Head: Firestone's New Chief Undaunted by Recall," *The Washington Post,* November 17, 2000, pp. E1, E10; J. Muller and J. Green, with N. St. Pierre and P. Moore, "Firestone and Ford: The Ride Gets Bumpier," *Business Week,* September 11, 2000, p. 42; J. Palmer, "Will a Major Restructuring Revive the No. 2 Automaker?" *Barron's,* January 14, 2002, p. 10; "Jacques A. Nasser," *Business Week,* January 14, 2002, p. 78; L. Chappell, "Bridgestone Gets a Big Boost," *Advertising Age,* November 26, 2001, p. 31; K. Naughton, "Ford's 'Perfect Storm,'" *Newsweek,* September 17, 2001, pp. 48–50; J. O'Rourke, "Bridgestone/Firestone, Inc. and Ford Motor Company: How a Product Safety Crisis Ended a Hundred-Year Relationship," *Corporate Reputation Review,* Autumn 2001, pp. 255–64.

3.1   Competitive Escalation: The Dollar Auction

OBJECTIVE

To explore the effects of competition on decision making.

INSTRUCTIONS

Step 1: 5 Minutes.   The instructor will play the role of auctioneer. In this auction, the instructor will auction off $1 bills (the instructor will inform you whether this money is real or imaginary). All members of the class may participate in the auction at the same time.

The rules for this auction are slightly different from those of a normal auction. In this version, *both the highest bidder and the next highest bidder will play their last bids* even though the dollar is awarded only to the highest bidder. For example, if Bidder A bids 15 cents for the dollar and Bidder B bids 10 cents, and there is no further bidding, then A pays 15 cents for the dollar and receives the dollar, while B pays 10 cents and receives nothing. The auctioneer will lose 75 cents on the dollar just sold.

Bids must be made in multiples of 5 cents. The dollar will be sold when there is no further bidding. If two individuals bid the

EXPERIENTIAL EXERCISES

same amount at the same time, ties are resolved in favor of the bidder located physically closest to the auctioneer. *During each round, there is to be no talking except for making bids.*

Step 2: 15 Minutes.   The instructor (auctioneer) will auction off five individual dollars to the class. Any student may bid in an effort to win the dollar. A record sheet of the bidding and winners can be kept in the worksheet that follows.

DISCUSSION QUESTIONS

1. Who made the most money in this exercise—one of the bidders or the auctioneer? Why?

2. As the auction proceeded, did bidders become more competitive or more cooperative? Why?

3. Did two bidders ever pay more for the money being auctioned than the value of the money itself? Explain how and why this happened.

4. Did you become involved in the bidding? Why?

    a. If you became involved, what were your motivations? Did you accomplish your objectives?

    b. If not, why didn't you become involved? What did you think were the goals and objectives of those who did become involved?

5. Did people say things to one another during the bidding to influence their actions? What was said, and how was it influential?

Dollar Auction Worksheet

	Amount paid by winning bidder	Amount paid by second bidder	Total paid for this dollar
First dollar			
Second dollar			
Third dollar			
Fourth dollar			
Fifth dollar			

SOURCE: Excerpted from R. Lewicki, *Experiences in Management and Organizational Behavior,* 3rd ed. Copyright © 1991 John Wiley & Sons, Inc. This material is used by permission of John Wiley and Sons, Inc.

3.2   Group Problem-Solving Meeting at the Community Agency

OBJECTIVE
To understand the interactions in group decision making through role playing a meeting between a chairman and his subordinates.

INSTRUCTIONS

1. Gather role sheets for each character and instructions for observers.

2. Set up a table in front of the room with five chairs around it arranged in such a way that participants can talk comfortably and have their faces visible to observers.

3. Read the introduction and cast of characters.

4. Five members from the class are selected to role play the five characters. All other members act as observers. The participants study the roles. All should play their roles without referring to the role sheets.

5. The observers read the instructions for observers.

6. When everyone is ready, John Cabot enters his office, joins the others at the table, and the scene begins. Allow 20 minutes to complete the meeting. The meeting is carried to the point of completion unless an argument develops and no progress is evident after 10 or 15 minutes of conflict.

DISCUSSION QUESTIONS

1. Describe the group's behavior. What did each member say? Do?

2. Evaluate the effectiveness of the group's decision making.

3. Did any problems exist in leadership, power, motivation, communication, or perception?

4. How could the group's effectiveness be increased?

INTRODUCTION

The Community Agency is a role-play exercise of a meeting between the chairman of the board of a social service agency and four of his subordinates. Each character's role is designed to recreate the reality of a business meeting. Each character comes to the meeting with a unique perspective on a major problem facing the agency as well as some personal impressions of the other characters developed over several years of business and social associations.

THE CAST OF CHARACTERS
John Cabot, the Chairman, was the principal force behind the formation of the Community Agency, a multiservice agency. The agency employs 50 people, and during its 19 years of operations has

enjoyed better client relations, a better service record, and a better reputation than other local agencies because of a reputation for high-quality service at a moderate cost to funding agencies. Recently, however, competitors have begun to overtake the Community Agency, resulting in declining contracts. John Cabot is expending every possible effort to keep his agency comfortably at the top.

Ron Smith, Director of the agency, reports directly to Cabot. He has held this position since he helped Cabot establish the agency 19 years ago.

Joan Sweet, Head of Client Services, reports to Smith. She has been with the agency 12 years, having worked before that for HEW as a contracting officer.

Tom Lynch, Head Community Liaison, reports to Joan Sweet. He came to the Community Agency at Sweet's request, having worked with Sweet previously at HEW.

Jane Cox, Head Case Worker, also works for Joan Sweet. Cox was promoted to this position two years ago. Prior to that time,

Jane had gone through a year's training program after receiving an MSW from a large urban university.

TODAY'S MEETING

John Cabot has called the meeting with these four managers in order to solve some problems that have developed in meeting service schedules and contract requirements. Cabot must catch a plane to Washington in half an hour; he has an appointment to negotiate a key contract that means a great deal to the future of the Community Agency. He has only 20 minutes to meet with his managers and still catch the plane. Cabot feels that getting the Washington contract is absolutely crucial to the future of the agency.

SOURCE: Judith R. Gordon, *A Diagnostic Approach to Organizational Behavior.* Copyright © 1983 Pearson Education, Inc. Reprinted by permission of Pearson Education, Inc., Upper Saddle River, NJ.

SSS Software In-Basket Exercise

One way to assess your own strengths and weaknesses in management skills is to engage in an actual managerial work experience. The following exercise gives you a realistic glimpse of the tasks faced regularly by practicing managers. Complete the exercise, and then compare your own decisions and actions with those of classmates.

SSS Software designs and develops customized software for businesses. It also integrates this software with the customer's existing systems and provides system maintenance. SSS Software has customers in the following industries: airlines, automotive, finance/banking, health/hospital, consumer products, electronics, and government. The company has also begun to generate important international clients. These include the European Airbus consortium and a consortium of banks and financial firms based in Kenya.

SSS Software has grown rapidly since its inception just over a decade ago. Its revenue, net income, and earnings per share have all been above the industry average for the past several years. However, competition in this technologically sophisticated field has grown very rapidly. Recently, it has become more difficult to compete for major contracts. Moreover, although SSS Software's revenue and net income continue to grow, the rate of growth declined during the last fiscal year.

SSS Software's 250 employees are divided into several operating divisions with employees at four levels: nonmanagement, technical/professional, managerial, and executive. Nonmanagement employees take care of the clerical and facilities support functions. The technical/professional staff perform the core technical work for the firm. Most managerial employees are group managers who supervise a team of technical/professional employees working on a project for a particular customer. Staff who work in specialized areas such as finance, accounting, human resources, nursing, and law are also considered managerial employees. The executive level includes the 12 highest-ranking employees at SSS Software. There is an organization chart in Figure A that illustrates SSS Software's structure. There is also an Employee Classification Report that lists the number of employees at each level of the organization.

In this exercise, you will play the role of Chris Perillo, Vice President of Operations for Health and Financial Services. You learned last Wednesday, October 13, that your predecessor,

Michael Grant, has resigned and gone to Universal Business Solutions, Inc. You were offered his former job, and you accepted it. Previously, you were the Group Manager for a team of 15 software developers assigned to work on the Airbus consortium project in the Airline Services Division. You spent all of Thursday and Friday and most of the weekend finishing up parts of the project, briefing your successor, and preparing for an interim report you will deliver in Paris on October 21.

It is now 7 A.M. Monday, and you are in your new office. You have arrived at work early so you can spend the next two hours reviewing material in your in-basket (including some memos and messages to Michael Grant), as well as your voice mail and email. Your daily planning book indicates that you have no appointments today or tomorrow but will have to catch a plane for Paris early Wednesday morning. You have a full schedule for the remainder of the week and all of next week.

ASSIGNMENT

During the next two hours, review all the material in your in-basket, as well as your voice mail and email. Take only two hours. Using the following response form as a model, indicate how you want to respond to each item (that is, via letter/memo, email, phone/voice mail, or personal meeting). If you decide not to respond to an item, check "no response" on the response form. All of your responses must be written on the response forms. Write your precise, detailed response (do not merely jot down a few notes). For example, you might draft a memo or write out a message that you will deliver via phone/voice mail. You may also decide to meet with an individual (or individuals) during the limited time available on your calendar today or tomorrow. If so, prepare an agenda for a personal meeting and list your goals for the meeting. As you read through the items, you may occasionally observe some information that you think is relevant and want to remember (or attend to in the future) but that you decide not to include in any of your responses to employees. Write down such information on a sheet of paper titled "note to self."

SOURCE: D. Whetten and K. Cameron, *Developing Management Skills,* 3rd ed. (New York: Harper Collins, 1995).

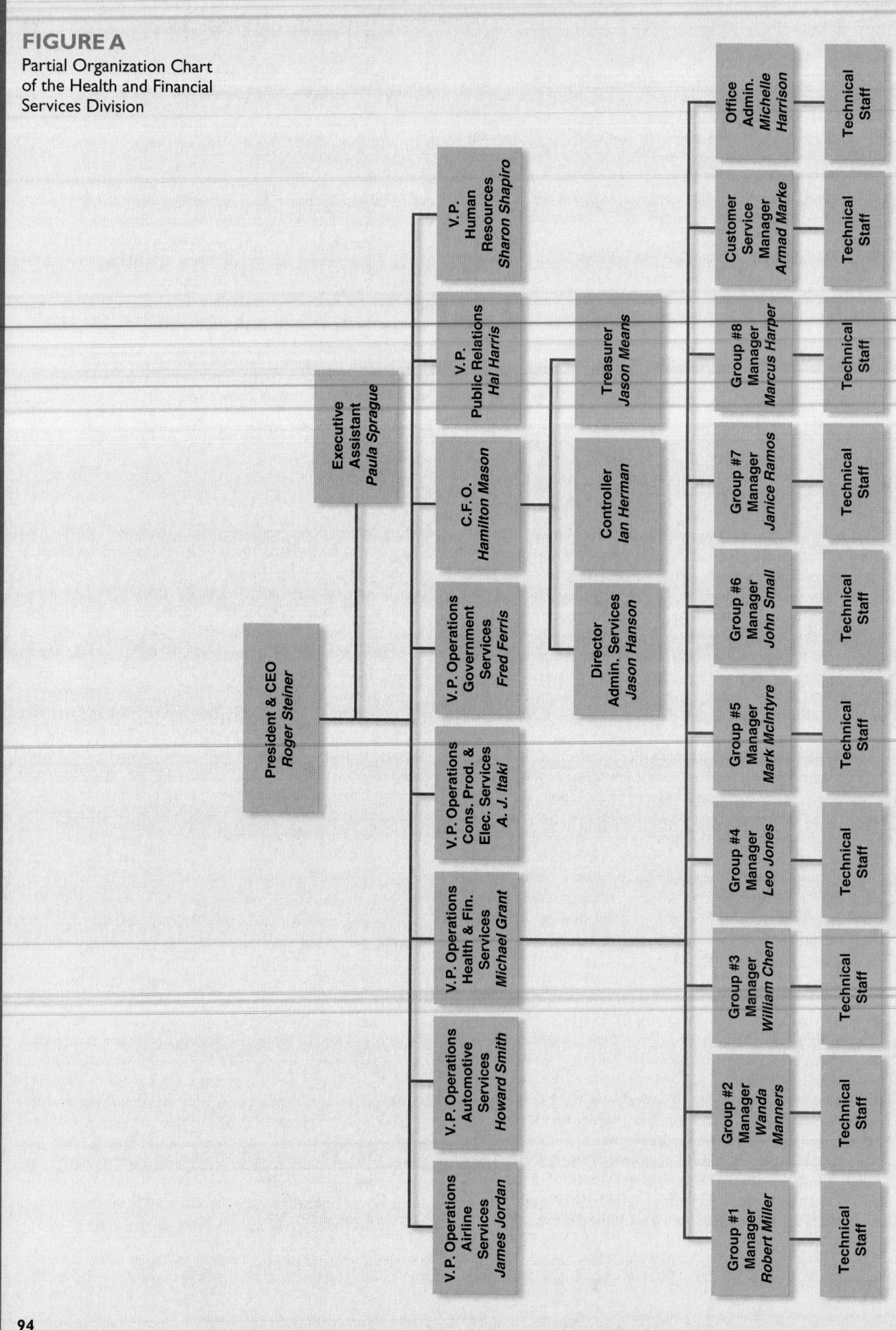

SAMPLE RESPONSE FORM

Relates To:

Memo # _____   Email # _____   Voice mail # _____

Response form:

_____ Letter/Memo   _____ Meet with person (when, where)

_____ Email   _____ Note to self

_____ Phone call/Voice mail _____ No response

ITEM 1 MEMO

TO: All Employees

FROM: Roger Steiner, Chief Executive Officer

DATE: October 15

I am pleased to announce that Chris Perillo has been appointed as Vice President of Operations for Health and Financial Services. Chris will immediately assume responsibility for all operations previously managed by Michael Grant. Chris will have end-to-end responsibility for the design, development, integration, and maintenance of custom software for the health and finance/banking industries. This responsibility includes all technical, financial, and staffing issues. Chris will also manage our program of software support and integration for the recently announced merger of three large health maintenance organizations (HMOs). Chris will be responsible for our recently announced project with a consortium of banks and financial firms operating in Kenya. This project represents an exciting opportunity for us, and Chris's background seems ideally suited to the task.

   Chris comes to this position with an undergraduate degree in Computer Science from the California Institute of Technology and an M.B.A. from the University of Virginia. Chris began as a member of our technical/professional staff six years ago and has most recently served for three years as a Group Manager supporting domestic and international projects for our airlines industry group, including our recent work for the European Airbus consortium.

   I am sure you all join me in offering congratulations to Chris for this promotion.

ITEM 2 MEMO

TO: All Managers

FROM: Hal Harris, Vice President, Community and Public Relations

DATE: October 15

For your information, the following article appeared on the front page of the business section of Thursday's *Los Angeles Times*.

   In a move that may create problems for SSS Software, Michael Grant and Janice Ramos have left SSS Software and moved to Universal Business Solutions Inc. Industry analysts see the move as another victory for Universal Business Solutions Inc. in their battle with SSS Software for share of the growing software development and integration business. Both Grant and Ramos had been with SSS Software for over 7 years. Grant was most recently Vice President of Operations for all SSS Software's work in two industries: health and hospitals, and finance and banking. Ramos brings to Universal Business Solutions Inc. her special expertise in the growing area of international software development and integration.

   Hillary Collins, an industry analyst with Merrill Lynch, said "the loss of key staff to a competitor can often create serious problems for a firm such as SSS Software. Grant and Ramos have an insider's understanding of SSS Software's strategic and technical limitations. It will be interesting to see if they can exploit this knowledge to the advantage of Universal Business Solutions Inc."

ITEM 3 MEMO

TO: Chris Perillo
FROM: Paula Sprague, Executive Assistant to Roger Steiner
DATE: October 15
Chris, I know that in your former position as a Group Manager in the Airline Services Division, you probably have met most of the group managers in the Health and Financial Services Division, but I thought you might like some more personal information about them. These people will be your direct reports on the management team.
Group #1: Bob Miller, 55-year-old white male, married (Anne) with two children and three grandchildren. Active in local Republican politics. Well regarded as a "hands-off" manager heading a high-performing team. Plays golf regularly with Mark McIntyre, John Small, and a couple of V.P.s from other divisions.
Group #2: Wanda Manners, 38-year-old white female, single with one school-age child. A fitness "nut," has run in several marathons. Some experience in Germany and Japan. Considered a hard-driving manager with a constant focus on the task at hand. Will be the first person to show up every morning.
Group #3: William Chen, 31-year-old male of Chinese descent, married (Harriet), two young children from his first marriage. Enjoys tennis and is quite good at it. A rising star in the company, he is highly respected by his peers as a "man of action" and a good friend.
Group #4: Leo Jones, 36-year-old white male, married (Janet), with an infant daughter. Recently returned from paternity leave. Has traveled extensively on projects, since he speaks three languages. Has liked hockey ever since the time he spent in Montreal. Considered a strong manager who gets the most out of his people.
Group #5: Mark McIntyre, 45-year-old white male, married (Mary Theresa) to an executive in the banking industry. No children. A lot of experience in Germany and Eastern Europe. Has been writing a mystery novel. Has always been a good "team player," but several members of his technical staff are not well respected and he hasn't addressed the problem.
Group #6: John Small, 38-year-old white male, recently divorced. Three children living with his wife. A gregarious individual who likes sports. He spent a lot of time in Mexico and Central America before he came to SSS Software. Recently has been doing mostly contract work with the federal government. An average manager, has had some trouble keeping his people on schedule.
Group #7: This position vacant since Janice Ramos left. Roger thinks we ought to fill this position quickly. Get in touch with me if you want information on any in-house candidates for any position.
Group #8: Marcus Harper, 42-year-old black male, married (Tamara) with two teenage children. Recently won an award in a local photography contest. Considered a strong manager who gets along with peers and works long hours.
Customer Services: Armand Marke, 38-year-old Armenian male, divorced. A basketball fan. Originally from Armenia. Previously a Group Manager. Worked hard to establish the Technical Services Phone Line, but now has pretty much left it alone.
Office Administrator: Michelle Harrison, 41-year-old white female, single. Grew up on a ranch and still rides horses whenever she can. A strict administrator.
There are a number of good folks here, but they don't function well as a management team. I think Michael played favorites, especially with Janice and Leo. There are a few cliques in this group and I'm not sure how effectively Michael dealt with them. I expect you will find it a challenge to build a cohesive team.

ITEM 4 MEMO

> TO: Chris Perillo
>
> FROM: Wanda Manners, Group 2 Manager
>
> DATE: October 15, 1998
>
> CONFIDENTIAL AND RESTRICTED
>
> Although I know you are new to your job, I feel it is important that I let you know about some information I just obtained concerning the development work we recently completed for First National Investment. Our project involved the development of asset management software for managing their international funds. This was a very complex project due to the volatile exchange rates and the forecasting tools we needed to develop.
>
> As part of this project, we had to integrate the software and reports with all their existing systems and reporting mechanisms. To do this we were given access to all of their existing software (much of which was developed by Universal Business Solutions Inc.). Of course, we signed an agreement acknowledging that the software to which we were given access was proprietary and that our access was solely for the purpose of our system integration work associated with the project.
>
> Unfortunately, I have learned that some parts of the software we developed actually "borrow" heavily from complex application programs developed for First National Investment by Universal Business Solutions Inc. It seems obvious to me that one or more of the software developers from Group 5 (that is, Mark McIntyre's group) inappropriately "borrowed" algorithms developed by Universal Business Solutions Inc. I am sure that doing so saved us significant development time on some aspects of the project. It seems very unlikely that First National Investment or Universal Business Solutions Inc. will ever become aware of this issue.
>
> Finally, First National Investment is successfully using the software we developed and is thrilled with the work we did. We brought the project in on time and under budget. You probably know that they have invited us to bid on several other substantial projects.
>
> I'm sorry to bring this delicate matter to your attention, but I thought you should know about it.

ITEM 5A MEMO

> TO: Chris Perillo
>
> FROM: Paula Sprague, Executive Assistant to Roger Steiner
>
> DATE: October 15
>
> RE: Letter from C.A.R.E. Services (copies attached)
>
> Roger asked me to work on this C.A.R.E. project and obviously wants some fast action. A lot of the staff are already booked solid for the next couple of weeks. I knew that Elise Soto and Chu Hung Woo have the expertise to do this system, and when I checked with them, they were relatively free. I had them pencil in the next two weeks and wanted to let you know. Hopefully, it will take a "hot potato" out of your hands.

ITEM 5B COPY OF FAX

C.A.R.E.
Child and Adolescent Rehabilitative and Educational Services
A United Way Member Agency
200 Main Street
Los Angeles, California 90230

DATE: October 11

Mr. Roger Steiner, CEO
SSS Software
13 Miller Way
Los Angeles, California 90224

Dear Roger,

This letter is a follow-up to our conversation after last night's board meeting. I appreciated your comments during the board meeting about the need for sophisticated computer systems in nonprofit organizations and I especially appreciate your generous offer of assistance to have SSS Software provide assistance to deal with the immediate problem with our accounting system. Since the board voted to fire the computer consultant, I am very worried about getting our reports done in time to meet the state funding cycle.

Thanks again for your offer of help during this crisis.

Sincerely yours,

Janice Polocizwic

Janice Polocizwic
Executive Director

ITEM 5C COPY OF LETTER

SSS SOFTWARE
13 Miller Way
Los Angeles, CA 90224
213-635-2000

DATE: October 12

Janice Polocizwic
Executive Director, C.A.R.E. Services
200 Main Street
Los Angeles, California 90230

Dear Janice,

I received your fax of October 11. I have asked Paula Sprague, my executive assistant, to line up people to work on your accounting system as soon as possible. You can expect to hear from her shortly.

Sincerely,

Roger Steiner

Roger Steiner

cc: Paula Sprague, Executive Assistant

ITEM 6 MEMO

TO:	Michael Grant
FROM:	Harry Withers, Group 6 Technical Staff
DATE:	October 12

PERSONAL AND CONFIDENTIAL

Our team is having difficulty meeting the submission deadline of November 5 for the Halstrom project. Kim, Fred, Peter, Kyoto, Susan, Mala, and I have been working on the project for several weeks, but are experiencing some problems and may need additional time. I hesitate to write this letter, but the main problem is that our group manager, John Small, is involved in a relationship with Mala. Mala gets John's support for her ideas and brings them to the team as required components of the project. Needless to say, this has posed some problems for the group. Mala's background is especially valuable for this project, but Kim and Fred, who have both worked very hard on the project, do not want to work with her. In addition, one member of the team has been unavailable recently because of child-care needs. Commitment to the project and team morale have plummeted. However, we'll do our best to get the project finished as soon as possible. Mala will be on vacation the next two weeks, so I'm expecting that some of us can complete it in her absence.

ITEM 7 VOICE MAIL

Hello, Michael. This is Jim Bishop of United Hospitals. I wanted to talk with you about the quality assurance project that you are working on for us. When José Martinez first started talking with us, I was impressed with his friendliness and expertise. But recently, he doesn't seem to be getting much accomplished and has seemed distant and on-edge in conversations. Today, I asked him about the schedule and he seemed very defensive and not entirely in control of his emotions. I am quite concerned about our project. Please give me a call at 213-951-1234.

ITEM 8 VOICE MAIL

Hi, Michael. This is Armand. I wanted to talk with you about some issues with the Technical Services Phone Line. I've recently received some complaint letters from Phone Line customers whose complaints have included: long delays while waiting for a technician to answer the phone; technicians who are not knowledgeable enough to solve problems; and, on occasion, rude service. Needless to say, I'm quite concerned about these complaints.

I believe that the overall quality of the phone line staff is very good, but we continue to be understaffed, even with the recent hires. The new technicians look strong, but are working on the help line before being fully trained. Antolina, our best tech, often brings her child to work, which is adding to the craziness around here.

I think you should know that we're feeling a lot of stress here. I'll talk to you soon.

ITEM 9 VOICE MAIL

Hi Chris, it's Pat. Congratulations on your promotion. They definitely picked the right person. It's great news—for me, too. You've been a terrific mentor so far, so I'm expecting to learn a lot from you in your new position. How about lunch next week?

ITEM 10 VOICE MAIL

Chris, this is Bob Miller. Just thought you'd like to know that John's joke during our planning meeting has disturbed a few of the women in my group. Frankly, I think the thing's being blown out of proportion, especially since we all know this is a good place for both men and women to work. Give me a call if you want to chat about this.

ITEM 11 VOICE MAIL

Hello. This is Lorraine Adams from Westside Hospital. I read in today's Los Angeles Times that you will be taking over from Michael Grant. We haven't met yet, but your division has recently finished two large million-dollar projects for Westside. Michael Grant and I had some discussion about a small conversion of a piece of existing software to be compatible with the new systems. The original vendor had said that they would do the work but has been stalling, and I need to move quickly. Can you see if Harris Wilson, Chu Hung Woo, and Elise Soto are available to do this work as soon as possible? They were on the original project and work well with our people. You can call me at 213-555-3456.

Um . . . (long pause) I guess I should tell you that I got a call from Michael offering to do this work. But I think I should stick with SSS Software. Give me a call.

ITEM 12 VOICE MAIL

Hi, Chris. This is Roosevelt Moore calling. I'm a member of your technical/professional staff. I used to report to Janice Ramos, but since she left the firm, I thought I'd bring my concerns directly to you. I'd like to arrange some time to talk with you about my experience since returning from six weeks of paternity leave. Some of my major responsibilities have been turned over to others. I seem to be out of the loop and wonder if my career is at risk. Also, I am afraid that I won't be supported or seriously considered for the opening created by Janice's departure. Frankly, I feel I'm being screwed for taking my leave. I'd like to talk with you this week.

ITEM 13 EMAIL

To:	Michael Grant
From:	José Martinez, Group 1 Technical Staff
Date:	October 12

I would like to set up a meeting with you as soon as possible. I suspect that you will get a call from Jim Bishop of United Hospitals and want to be sure that you hear my side of the story first. I have been working on a customized system design for quality assurance for them using a variation of the J-3 product we developed several years ago. They had a number of special requirements and some quirks in their accounting systems, so I have had to put in especially long hours. I've worked hard to meet their demands, but they keep changing the ground rules. I keep thinking, this is just another J-3 I'm working on, but they have been interfering with an elegant design I have developed. It seems I'm not getting anywhere on this project. Then Mr. Bishop asked me if the system was running yet. I was worn out from dealing with the Controller, and I made a sarcastic comment to Mr. Bishop. He gave me a funny look and just walked out of the room.

I would like to talk with you about this situation at your earliest convenience.

ITEM 14 EMAIL

TO: Chris Perillo

FROM: John Small, Group 6 Manager

DATE: October 15

Welcome aboard, Chris. I look forward to meeting with you. I just wanted to put a bug in your ear about finding a replacement for Janice Ramos. One of my technical staff, Mala Abendano, has the ability and drive to make an excellent group manager. I have encouraged her to apply for the position. I'd be happy to talk with you further about this, at your convenience.

ITEM 15 EMAIL

TO: Chris Perillo

FROM: Paula Sprague, Executive Assistant to Roger Steiner

DATE: October 15

Roger asked me to let you know about the large contract we have gotten in Kenya. It means that a team of four managers will be making a short trip to determine current needs. They will assign their technical staff the task of developing a system and software here over the next six months, and then the managers and possibly some team members will be spending about 10 months on site in Kenya to handle the implementation. Roger would appreciate an email of your thoughts about the issues to be discussed at this meeting, additional considerations about sending people to Kenya, and about how you will put together an effective team to work on this project. The October 15 memo I sent to you will provide you with some information you'll need to start making these decisions.

ITEM 16 EMAIL

TO: Chris Perillo

FROM: Sharon Shapiro, V. P. of Human Resources

DATE: October 15

RE: Upcoming meeting

I want to update you on the rippling effect of John Small's sexual joke at last week's planning meeting. Quite a few women have been very upset and have met informally to talk about it. They have decided to call a meeting of all the people concerned about this kind of behavior throughout the firm. I plan to attend, so I'll keep you posted.

ITEM 17 EMAIL

TO: All SSS-Software Managers
FROM: Sharon Shapiro, Vice President, Human Resources
DATE: October 14
RE: Promotions and External Hires

Year-to-date (January through September) promotions and external hires

Level	Race					Sex		Total
	White	Black	Asian	Hispanic	Native American	M	F	
Hires into Executive Level	0 (0%)	0 (0%)	0 (0%)	0 (0%)	0 (0%)	0 (0%)	0 (0%)	0
Promotions to Executive Level	0 (0%)	0 (0%)	0 (0%)	0 (0%)	0 (0%)	0 (0%)	0 (0%)	0
Hires into Management Level	2 (67%)	1 (33%)	0 (0%)	0 (0%)	0 (0%)	2 (67%)	1 (33%)	3
Promotions to Management Level	7 (88%)	0 (0%)	1 (12%)	0 (0%)	0 (0%)	7 (88%)	1 (12%)	8
Hires into Technical/ Professional Level	10 (36%)	6 (21%)	10 (36%)	2 (7%)	0 (0%)	14 (50%)	14 (50%)	28
Promotions to Technical/ Professional Level	0 (0%)	0 (0%)	0 (0%)	0 (0%)	0 (0%)	0 (0%)	0 (0%)	0
Hires into Non-Management Level	4 (20%)	10 (50%)	2 (10%)	4 (20%)	0 (0%)	6 (30%)	14 (70%)	20
Promotions to Non-Management Level	NA	NA	NA	NA	NA	NA	NA	NA

SSS Software employee (EEO) classification report as of June 30

Level	Race					Sex		Total
	White	Black	Asian	Hispanic	Native American	M	F	
Executive Level	11 (92%)	0 (0%)	1 (8%)	0 (0%)	0 (0%)	11 (92%)	1 (8%)	12
Management Level	43 (90%)	2 (4%)	2 (4%)	1 (2%)	0 (0%)	38 (79%)	10 (21%)	48
Technical/ Professional Level	58 (45%)	20 (15%)	37 (28%)	14 (11%)	1 (1%)	80 (62%)	50 (38%)	130
Non-Management Level	29 (48%)	22 (37%)	4 (7%)	4 (7%)	1 (2%)	12 (20%)	48 (80%)	60
Total	141 (56%)	44 (18%)	44 (18%)	19 (8%)	2 (1%)	141 (56%)	109 (44%)	250

Employee Raiding

Litson Cotton Yarn Manufacturing Company, located in Murray, New Jersey, decided as a result of increasing labor costs to relocate its plant in Fairlee, a southern community of 4,200. Plant construction was started, and a human resources office was opened in the state employment office, located in Fairlee.

Because of ineffective HR practices in the other three textile mills located within a 50-mile radius of Fairlee, Litson was receiving applications from some of the most highly skilled and trained textile operators in the state. After receiving applications from approximately 500 people, employment was offered to 260 male and female applicants. These employees would be placed immediately on the payroll with instructions to await final installation of machinery, which was expected within the following six weeks.

The managers of the three other textile companies, faced with resignations from their most efficient and best-trained employees, approached the Litson managers with the complaint that their labor force was being "raided." They registered a strong protest to cease such practices and demanded an immediate cancellation of the employment of the 260 people hired by Litson.

Litson managers discussed the ethical and moral considerations involved in offering employment to the 260 people. Litson

clearly faced a tight labor market in Fairlee, and management thought that if the 260 employees were discharged, the company would face cancellation of its plans and large construction losses. Litson management also felt obligated to the 260 employees who had resigned from their previous employment in favor of Litson.

The dilemma was compounded when the manager of one community plant reminded Litson that his plant was part of a nationwide chain supplied with cotton yarn from Litson. He implied that Litson's attempts to continue operations in Fairlee could result in cancellation of orders and the possible loss of approximately 18 percent market share. It was also suggested to Litson managers that actions taken by the nationwide textile chain could result in cancellation of orders from other textile companies. Litson's president held an urgent meeting of his top subordinates to (1) decide what to do about the situation in Fairlee, (2) formulate a written policy statement indicating Litson's position regarding employee raiding, and (3) develop a plan for implementing the policy.

SOURCE: J. Champion and J. James, *Critical Incidents in Management: Decision and Policy Issues,* 6th ed. (Burr Ridge, IL: Richard D. Irwin, 1989).

Effective Management

Dr. Sam Perkins, a graduate of the Harvard University College of Medicine, had a private practice in internal medicine for 12 years. Fourteen months ago, he was persuaded by the Massachusetts governor to give up private practice to be director of the State Division of Human Services.

After one year as director, Perkins recognized he had made little progress in reducing the considerable inefficiency in the division. Employee morale and effectiveness seemed even lower than when he had assumed the position. He realized his past training and experiences were of a clinical nature with little exposure to effective management techniques. Perkins decided to research literature on the subject of management available to him at a local university.

Perkins soon realized that management scholars are divided on the question of what constitutes effective management. Some believe people are born with certain identifiable personality traits that make them effective managers. Others believe a manager can learn to be effective by treating subordinates with a personal and considerate approach and by giving particular attention to their need for favorable working conditions. Still others emphasize the importance of developing a management style characterized by either authoritarian, democratic, or laissez-faire approaches. Perkins was further confused when he learned that a growing number of scholars advocate that effective management is contingent on the situation.

Since a state university was located nearby, Perkins contacted the dean of its college of business administration. The dean referred him to the director of the college's management center, Professor Joel McCann. Discussions between Perkins and McCann resulted in a tentative agreement that the management center would organize a series of management training sessions for the State Division of Human Services. Before agreeing on the price tag for the management conference, Perkins asked McCann to prepare a proposal reflecting his thoughts on the following questions:

1. How will the question of what constitutes effective management be answered during the conference?

2. What will be the specific subject content of the conference?

3. Who will the instructors be?

4. What will be the conference's duration?

5. How can the conference's effectiveness be evaluated?

6. What policies should the State Division of Human Services adopt regarding who the conference participants should be and how they should be selected? How can these policies be best implemented?

SOURCE: J. Champion and J. James, *Critical Incidents in Management: Decision and Policy Issues,* 6th ed. (Burr Ridge, IL: Richard D. Irwin, 1989).

Foundations of Management
- Managing
- The External Environment
- Managerial Decision Making

Planning:
Delivery Strategic Value
- Planning and Strategic Management
- Ethics and Corporate Responsibility
- International Management
- New Ventures

Strategy Implementation

Organizing: Building a Dynamic Organization
- Organization Structure
- The Responsive Organization
- Human Resources Management
- Managing the Diverse Workforce

Leading:
Mobilizing People
- Leadership
- Motivating for Performance
- Managing Teams
- Communicating

Controlling:
Learning and Changing
- Managerial Control
- Managing Technology and Innovation
- Creating and Managing Change

Planning and Strategy

Part Two introduces key concepts of planning and strategy. The topics emphasize the decisions made by top managers and their implications for the entire organization. Chapter 4 presents a summary of the planning process and an overview of how senior executives manage strategically. The next three chapters treat subjects that have emerged recently as vital considerations for modern managers. Chapter 5 examines the impact of ethical concerns and social and political factors on major decisions. Chapter 6 addresses the pressing reality of managing in a global competitive environment. Finally, Chapter 7 describes entrepreneurs and the new ventures they create. These chapters will provide the reader with a clear understanding of the strategic directions that effective organizations pursue.

CHAPTER 4

Planning and Strategic Management

Manage your destiny, or someone else will.
—Jack Welch, Former CEO, General Electric

CHAPTER OUTLINE

An Overview of Planning Fundamentals
  The Basic Planning Process
Levels of Planning
  Strategic Planning
  Tactical and Operational Planning
  Linking Tactical, Operational, and
  Strategic Planning
Strategic Planning
  Step 1: Establishment of Mission, Vision,
  and Goals
  Step 2: Analysis of External Opportunities
  and Threats
  Step 3: Analysis of Internal Strengths
  and Weaknesses
  Step 4: SWOT Analysis and Strategy
  Formulation
  Step 5: Strategy Implementation
  Step 6: Strategic Control

LEARNING OBJECTIVES

After studying Chapter 4, you will know:

1. How to proceed through the basic steps in any planning process.

2. How strategic planning integrates with tactical and operational planning.

3. Why it is important to analyze both the external environment and the internal resources of the firm before formulating a strategy.

4. The choices available for corporate strategy.

5. How companies can achieve competitive advantage through business strategy.

6. How core competencies provide the foundation for business strategy.

7. The keys to effective strategy implementation.

GETTING INTO THE GROOVE AT HARD ROCK CAFÉ

Hard Rock Café unplugged? Not anymore. To pump up the volume, the Orlando-based company—which oversees 141 locations in 108 countries—developed a "three-part, music-centric strategy to reinvent the 30-year-old brand" for its restaurants, hotels, and casinos. In spite of the weak economy and the fallout from September 11, 2001, that hurt other entertainment and travel firms, the firm's business remained strong through 2002. By focusing its strategy on its mission and values statement—"to spread the spirit of rock 'n'

The Hard Rock Café carries its strategy—to be identified with rock 'n' roll—through to its hotel signs.

roll by delivering an exceptional entertainment and dining experience. We are committed to being an important, contributing member of our community, and offering the Hard Rock family a fun, healthy, and nurturing work environment while ensuring our long-term success."—Hard Rock seems to have succeeded where others in the theme restaurant industry have faltered.

To get its groove back in the niche it invented, Hard Rock focused more on today's music than on nostalgia. In addition, the company diversified a bit and partnered a lot. The risk it takes with this strategy is losing its focus on the food and restaurant business; the publisher of *Restaurant Business*

noted, "Hard Rock has built an extraordinary brand, but I'm not sure how well they will do as music entrepreneurs. One is a business of selling food and T-shirts, and the other is one of entertaining people with hip content." Hard Rock seems to have been successful at both.

In addition to expanding and redesigning its restaurants, Hard Rock offered more late-night musical acts both at the restaurants and at its hotels, and it offered the music live to its other venues via the Web—one aspect of the firm's Internet strategy. According to the firm's chief financial officer and head of strategic planning, Hard Rock plans to "use the Web to create a forum for up-and-coming artists and to bring national bands that play our large concert venues into the smaller location." (The firm also uses the Internet to offer merchandise on its hardrock.com website and to maintain the Hard Rock 'n' Shop store within the eBay website.) Hard Rock worked with Microsoft to build a state-of-the-art network for e-commerce and digital streaming of live events in real time.

Hard Rock's refocused strategy came after nearly a decade of waning growth and revenues in the theme restaurant, which suffered from overly rapid expansion. Firms such as Planet Hollywood and Fashion Café faltered in the overcrowded industry, and sales plummeted. Hard Rock Hotels, four-star urban hotels/resorts in the most sought-after tourist destinations, are music-based as well. Its casinos in Las Vegas and London also feature live music venues. By following a strategy of providing music within and beyond its theme business, Hard Rock has a sound basis for planning.

Source: Stefani Eads, "Hard Rock Café Lays Down a New Groove," *Business Week*, September 20, 2000; "Investor Relations," http://www.rank.com.

Setting the Stage

Hard Rock Café, as do other successful organizations, determined its strategy as part of its planning process. Although few firms make their planning decisions known, a few key ideas are fundamental to the planning process. This chapter examines, the most important concepts and processes involved in planning and strategic management. By learning these concepts, and reviewing the steps outlined, you will be on your way to understanding the current approaches to the strategic management of today's organizations.

An Overview of Planning Fundamentals

The importance of formal planning in organizations has grown dramatically. Until the mid-1900s, most planning was unstructured and fragmented, and formal planning was restricted to a few large corporations. Although management pioneers such as Alfred Sloan of General Motors instituted formal planning processes, planning became a widespread management function only during the last 35 years. While larger organizations adopted formal planning initially, even small firms operated by aggressive, opportunistic entrepreneurs now engage in formal planning.[1]

Planning is the conscious, systematic process of making decisions about goals and activities that an individual, group, work unit, or organization will pursue in the future. Planning is not an informal or haphazard response to a crisis; it is a purposeful effort that is directed and controlled by managers and often draws on the knowledge and experience of employees throughout the organization. Planning provides individuals and work units with a clear map to follow in their future activities; at the same time this map may allow for individual circumstances and changing conditions.

The Basic Planning Process

Because planning is a decision process, the important steps followed during formal planning are similar to the basic decision-making steps discussed in Chapter 3. Figure 4.1 shows these formal planning steps and their decision process counterparts, as discussed in Chapter 3.

Step 1: Situational Analysis   As the contingency approach advocates, planning begins with a **situational analysis.** Within their time and resource constraints, planners should gather, interpret, and summarize all information relevant to the planning issue in question. A thorough situational analysis studies past events, examines current conditions, and attempts to forecast future trends. It focuses on the internal forces at work in the organization or work unit and, consistent with the open-systems approach, examines influences from the external environment. The outcome of this step is the identification and diagnosis of planning assumptions, issues, and problems.

> **situational analysis**
>
> A process planners use, within time and resource constraints, to gather, interpret and summarize all information relevant to the planning issue under consideration.

A thorough situational analysis will point toward the planning decisions you will need to make. For example, one major medical center took 10 months to collect and analyze historical information and other data from consumers, government agencies, and insurance firms, among other groups. The resulting situational analysis document was 250 pages long, but thanks to the thoroughness of this stage, what needed to be done was clear. The remaining steps took only three months, and the center's final document was only 50 pages long.

Step 2: Alternative Goals and Plans   Based on the situational analysis, the planning process should generate alternative goals that may be pursued in the future and the alternative plans that may be used to achieve those goals. This step in the process should stress creativity and encourage managers and employees to assume a broad perspective on their jobs. Evaluation of the merits of these alternative goals and plans should be delayed until a range of alternatives has been developed.

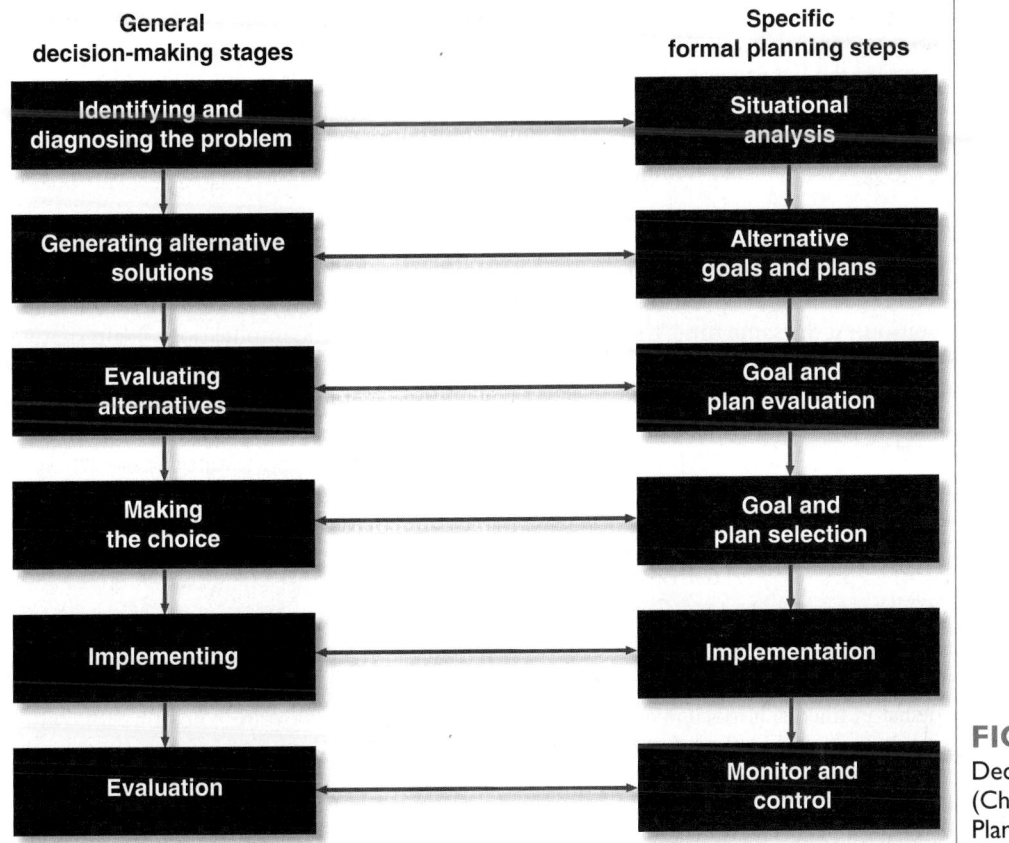

General decision-making stages | Specific formal planning steps

General decision-making stages	Specific formal planning steps
Identifying and diagnosing the problem	Situational analysis
Generating alternative solutions	Alternative goals and plans
Evaluating alternatives	Goal and plan evaluation
Making the choice	Goal and plan selection
Implementing	Implementation
Evaluation	Monitor and control

FIGURE 4.1

Decision-Making Stages (Chapter 3) and Formal Planning Steps (Chapter 4)

Goals are the targets or ends the manager wants to reach. Goals should be specific, challenging, and realistic. For example, General Electric's goal of being first or at least second in all its markets is specific and challenging. When appropriate, goals also should be quantified and linked to a time frame. They should be acceptable to the managers and employees charged with achieving them, and they should be consistent both within and among work units.

goal

A target or end that management desires to reach.

Plans are the actions or means the manager intends to use to achieve goals. At a minimum, this step should outline alternative actions that may lead to the attainment of each goal, the resources required to reach the goal through those means, and the obstacles that may develop. Aramark's plan to become the premier provider of corporate services outlines the company's activities designed to expand business in catering, food services, and uniform services, as well as health and education. This plan is focused on the company's goals of 10 percent annual growth in sales and profitability.[2]

plans

The actions or means managers intend to use to achieve organizational goals.

In this chapter we will talk about various types of plans. Some plans, called *single-use plans*, are designed to achieve a set of goals that are not likely to be repeated in the future. For example, city planners might prepare for an upcoming sesquicentennial celebration by putting in place a plan for parades, festivities, speeches, and the like. Other plans, called *standing plans*, focus on ongoing activities designed to achieve an enduring set of goals. For example, many companies have standing plans for their efforts to recruit minority group members and women. Frequently, standing plans become more permanent policies and rules for running the organization. Finally, *contingency plans* might be referred to as "what if" plans. They include sets of actions to be taken when a company's initial plans have not worked well or if events in the external environment require a sudden change. For example, companies worked feverishly at the end of 1999 to prevent Y2K problems. At the same time, they made preparations—contingency plans—for how they would continue if the systems failed. This planning paid off at the Veterans Affairs Medical Center in

Miami, Florida. On the night of November 23, 1999, a power surge caused a short in the hospital's main electrical panel. Power was lost to all passenger elevators in the main building, and the lights were out in most places. Meanwhile, doctors were in the middle of an open-heart surgery procedure. Luckily, an emergency plan had been rehearsed through months of preparation for potential Y2K-related disasters. Surgeons finished the open-heart procedure using flashlights (and the patient's prognosis was bright).[3]

Step 3: Goal and Plan Evaluation   Next, decision makers must evaluate the advantages, disadvantages, and potential effects of each alternative goal and plan. Decision makers must prioritize those goals or even eliminate some from further consideration. At the same time, the manager needs to consider the implications of alternative plans designed to meet high-priority goals.

In some companies, special teams of managers with diverse backgrounds conduct this evaluation. During major planning efforts at Atlantic Richfield Company (ARCO), senior executives meet with planning groups from strategic planning, public and government affairs, operations, marketing, and other areas. Often the different perspectives and ideas such groups generate lead to a more balanced and comprehensive review of company goals and plans. This approach often identifies new alternatives or refines existing ones.

Step 4: Goal and Plan Selection   The planner is now in a position to select the most appropriate and feasible goals and plans. The evaluation process should identify the priorities and trade-offs among goals and plans and leave the final choice to the decision maker. Experienced judgment always plays an important role. The following example of Sysco illustrates the goals set by that firm. However, as you will discover later in the chapter, relying on judgment alone may not be the best way to proceed.

Typically, a formal planning process leads to a written set of goals and plans that are appropriate and feasible within a predicted set of circumstances. In some organizations, the alternative generation, evaluation, and selection steps generate planning **scenarios,** as discussed in Chapter 2. A different contingency plan is attached to each scenario. The manager pursues the goals and implements the plans associated with the most likely scenario. However, the work unit is prepared to switch to another set of plans if the situational contingencies change and another scenario becomes relevant. This approach helps a firm avoid crises and allows greater flexibility and responsiveness.

scenario

A narrative that describes a particular set of future conditions.

FROM THE PAGES OF

Why Sysco Looks Appetizing

FROM THE PAGES OF

BusinessWeek

Lean times aren't crimping the ambitions of Houston-based Sysco, the biggest U.S. food distributor, which plans to double sales over the next six years. The firm, which distributes food and other items to restaurants, hospitals, schools, and hotels, wants to more than double its total annual sales to $50 billion in just six years. To put the goal in perspective, it took Sysco some 32 years to reach its current $23.4 billion in annual sales from the $115 million-a-year level it had when the company went public in 1970. The Chief executive officer (CEO) and chairman, Charles Cotros, says that achieving its lofty growth target can be done by using straightforward tactics.

Indeed, Sysco is a model of consistency, having posted sales and profit increases for 26 years in a row. "It's a very solid company in a not-so-solid economy," says a Standard & Poor's (S&P) equity analyst in New York. "It's in a very good industry in which it's the market share leader. It's going to outperform in these times." Sysco clearly is benefiting from the trend among consumers to eat more meals in restaurants. Despite lean economic times, the average person still eats out an average of 4.2 times every week.

Sysco also benefits whether consumers stick to the basics or splurge on a fancy meal. It generates nearly two-thirds of its sales by acting as a grocery store to restaurants, selling them everything from basic items such as lettuce and paper napkins to beluga caviar, Brie, and other upscale gourmet fare. "They have the staff and the size to get the best quality at good prices. And the thing they have that is important for customers is reliability," said another analyst.

Sysco also has plenty of room to increase its market share in that customers now get only about one-third of what they need through Sysco. The company also is improving its position in supplying independent restaurants. Sysco also can provide specialized services, such as help with inventory control, to these independent outlets. Other profit boosters include selling the company's own brands, which provide fatter margins than do third-party ones. Sysco also is continuing to expand sales of nonfood items, partly by acquiring equipment and paper-supply companies.

Of course, there are still reasons for caution. For one thing, Cotros is set to hand over the reins to Richard Schnieders, currently president and chief operations officer, on January 1, 2003. Though Schnieders has been with the company for two decades, there's always the risk that the transition won't go off as easily as predicted. A recession could slow the company's momentum, which could result in a pronounced downturn.

Cotros contends that the management change should go off without a hitch. "This has been in the planning stages for years," he notes. And even the slowing economy isn't a huge worry, he says: "We think we could certainly continue to grow even in times when things might be slowing down."

SOURCE: Eric Wahlgren, "Why Sysco Looks Appetizing," *Business Week*, August 15, 2002.

Step 5: Implementation Once managers have selected the goals and plans, they must implement the plans designed to achieve the goals. The best plans are useless unless they are implemented properly. Managers and employees must understand the plan, have the resources necessary to implement it, and be motivated to do so. If both managers and employees have participated in the previous steps of the planning process, the implementation phase probably will be more effective and efficient. Employees usually are better informed, more committed, and more highly motivated when a goal or plan is one that they helped develop.

Finally, successful implementation requires that the plan be linked to other systems in the organization, particularly the budget and reward systems. If the budget does not provide the manager with sufficient financial resources to execute the plan, the plan is probably doomed. Similarly, goal achievement must be linked to the organization's reward system. Many organizations use incentive programs to encourage employees to achieve goals and to implement plans properly. Commissions, salaries, promotions, bonuses, and other rewards are based on successful performance.

Step 6: Monitor and Control Although it sometimes is ignored, the final step in the formal planning process—monitor and control—is essential. Because planning is an ongoing, repetitive process, managers must continually monitor the actual performance of their work units according to the unit's goals and plans. Also, they must develop control systems that allow the organization to take corrective action when the plans are implemented improperly or when the situation changes. You will study control systems in greater detail later in this chapter and in Chapter 16.

Levels of Planning

In Chapter 1 you learned about the three major types of managers: top-level (*strategic* managers), middle-level (*tactical* managers), and frontline (*operational* managers). Because planning is an important management function, managers at all three levels use it. However, the scope and activities of the planning process at each level of the organization often differ.

Strategic Planning

Strategic planning involves making decisions about the organization's long-term goals and strategies. Strategic plans have a strong external orientation and cover major portions of the organization. Senior executives are responsible for the development and execution of the strategic plan, although they usually do not formulate or implement the entire plan personally.

Strategic goals are major targets or end results that relate to the long-term survival, value, and growth of the organization. Strategic managers—top-level managers—usually establish goals that reflect both effectiveness (providing appropriate outputs) and efficiency (a high ratio of outputs to inputs). Typical strategic goals include various measures of return to shareholders, profitability, quantity and quality of outputs, market share, productivity, and contribution to society.

A **strategy** is a pattern of actions and resource allocations designed to achieve the goals of the organization. The strategy an organization implements is an attempt to match the skills and resources of the organization to the opportunities found in the external environment; that is, every organization has certain strengths and weaknesses. The actions, or strategies, the organization implements should be directed toward building strengths in areas that satisfy the wants and needs of consumers and other key factors in the organization's external environment. Also, some organizations may implement strategies that change or influence the external environment, as discussed in Chapter 2.

Tactical and Operational Planning

Once the organization's strategic goals and plans are identified, they become the basis of planning done by middle-level and frontline managers. Goals and plans become more specific and involve shorter periods of time as planning moves from the strategic level to the operational level. **Tactical planning** translates broad strategic goals and plans into specific goals and

---

strategic planning

A set of procedures for making decisions about the organization's long-term goals and strategies.

strategic goals

Major targets or end results relating to the organization's long-term survival, value, and growth.

strategy

A pattern of actions and resource allocations designed to achieve the organization's goals.

tactical planning

A set of procedures for translating broad strategic goals and plans into specific goals and plans that are relevant to a distinct portion of the organization, such as a functional area like marketing.

Whole Foods' operational goals focus on providing products that satisfy its customers.

plans that are relevant to a definite portion of the organization, often a functional area like marketing or human resources, as discussed in Chapter 10. Tactical plans focus on the major actions a unit must take to fulfill its part of the strategic plan.

Operational planning identifies the specific procedures and processes required at lower levels of the organization. Frontline managers usually develop plans for very short periods of time and focus on routine tasks such as production runs, delivery schedules, and human resources requirements, as we discuss in Chapter 16 and 17.

> **operational planning**
>
> The process of identifying the specific procedures and processes required at lower levels of the organization.

Linking Tactical, Operational, and Strategic Planning

The organization's strategic, tactical, and operational goals and plans must be consistent and mutually supportive. Whole Foods Market, for example, links its tactical and operational planning directly to its strategic planning. The firm describes itself on its website as a mission-driven company that aims to set the standards for excellence for food retailers. The firm measures its success in fulfilling its vision by "customer satisfaction, Team Member excellence and happiness, return on capital investment, improvement in the state of the environment, and local and larger community support."

Whole Foods' strategic goal is to sell the highest-quality products that also offer high value for our customers. Its operational goals focus on ingredients, freshness, taste, nutritive value, safety, and appearance that meet or exceed its customers' expectations, including guaranteeing product satisfaction. Tactical goals include store environments that are "inviting, fun, unique, informal, comfortable, attractive, nurturing and educational" and safe and inviting work environments for its employees.

Starbucks, has built its strategy of growth and profitability around the notion of excellent service and ambience. No longer is coffee just a morning ritual; it has evolved into something with a far more existential quality. "We are trying to create a '*third place*' for our customers," says Chairman Howard Shultz. "A '*third place*' is a place between home and work where people can come to get their own personal time out, their respite, meet with friends, have a sense of gathering."

A key tactical planning issue for Starbucks is linking its obsession with service and quality to a healthy bottom line. Excellent service attracts new customers and keeps loyal customers coming back. Excellent service and quality depend on highly efficient processes for brewing coffee and terrific customer relations. These processes in turn are carried out by a dedicated and well-trained workforce. According to Schultz, "We've never viewed coffee as a commodity. And we've never viewed our people as commodities. I think the foundation of our success is the passionate commitment we have to the quality of coffee that we buy and roast, and making sure that the people in our company are not simply a line item. We view our people as business partners." The company's "Bean Stock" program gives all employees the opportunity to own stock in the company, and the company's commitment to training and benefits has established Starbucks as the employer of choice in the industry (its turnover rate is one-fifth that of others in the industry).

One method for linking strategic and operational planning at Starbucks is the balanced scorecard. Figure 4.2 shows how the balanced scorecard works. There are four primary cells: financial, customer, process, and people/learning. In each cell, Starbucks would identify the key drivers that help translate strategic goals to operational issues. Each of those goals would also have a set of metrics. For example, under customer metrics, Starbucks might look at percentage of repeat customers, number of new customers, growth rate, and the like. Under people/learning, managers might measure the number of suggestions provided by employees, participation in the Bean Stock program, employee turnover, training hours spent, and the like.

Each of these cells links vertically. People management issues such as rewards, training, suggestions, and the like, can be linked to efficient processes (brewing the perfect

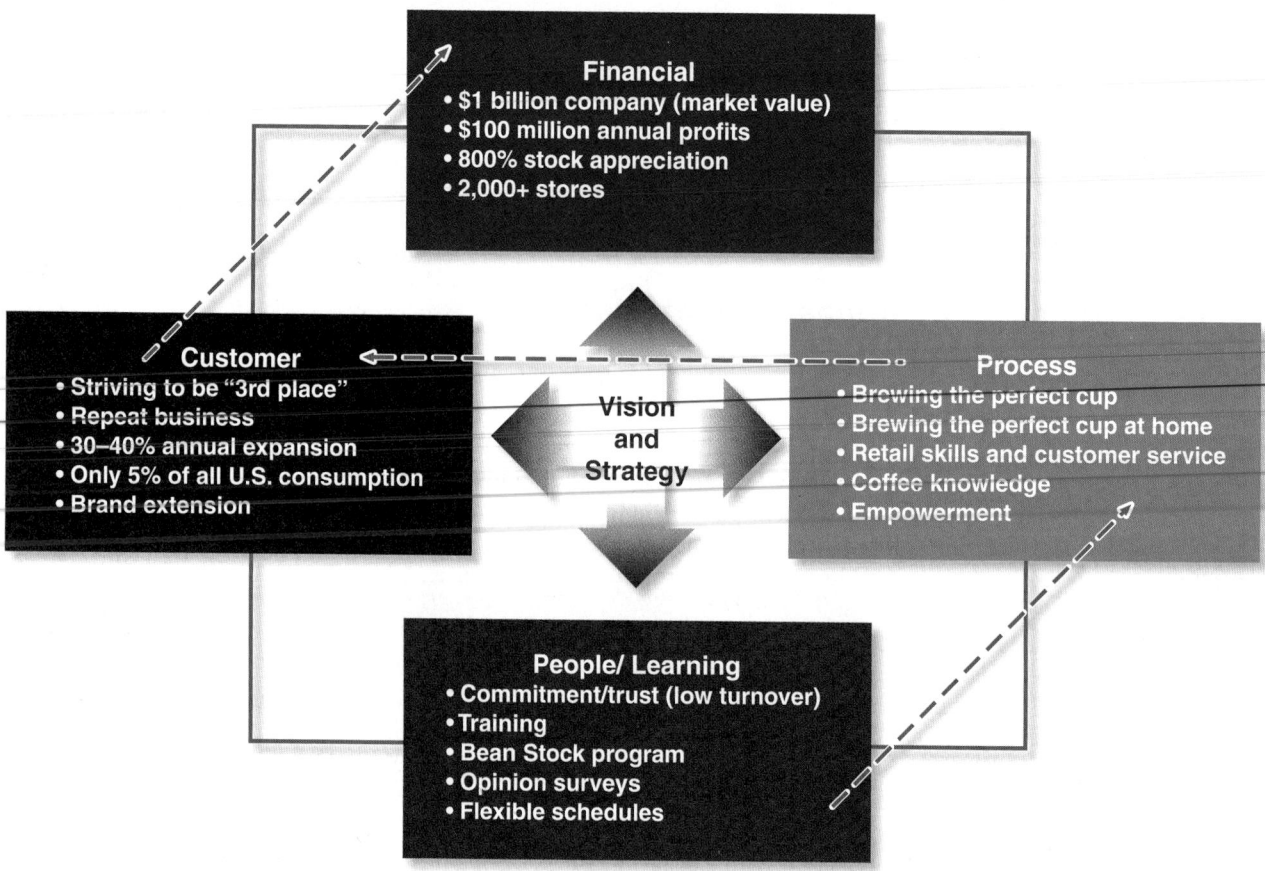

FIGURE 4.2
Applying the Balanced
Scorecard for Starbucks

cup, customer service, etc.). These processes then lead to better customer loyalty and growth. Growth and customer loyalty in turn lead to higher profitability and market value. As shown in Table 4.1, the balanced scorecard can be used to develop measures and standards for each of these operational areas. And when implemented in this way, it helps translate strategic and tactical issues into operational criteria.[4]

TABLE 4.1
Using the Balanced
Scorecard for Planning

1. *Clarify the vision:* Executive team and middle managers use the balanced scorecard to translate a generic vision into a strategy that is understood and communicated.

2. *Develop business unit scorecards:* Each business unit develops its own scorecard that translates strategic goals into tactical and operational goals.

3. *Review business unit scorecards:* The CEO and this executive team review the business unit scorecards. This review identifies cross-business issues that are used to revise the strategic plan.

4. *Communicate the scorecard to the entire company:* Managers and employees develop individual scorecards that link strategic and tactical plans to operational issues relevant to them. Individual objectives and rewards are linked to these scorecards.

5. *Conduct annual strategy reviews:* The previous year's performance is reviewed, and strategies are updated. Each business unit is asked to develop a position on each issue as a prelude to strategic planning.

SOURCE: Adapted from R. S. Kaplan and D. Norton, "Using the Balanced Scorecard as a Strategic Management System," *Harvard Business Review,* January–February 1996, pp. 75–85.

Strategic Planning

Strategic decision making is one of the most exciting and controversial topics in management today. In fact, many organizations currently are changing the ways they develop and execute their strategic plans.

Traditionally, strategic planning emphasized a top-down approach—senior executives and specialized planning units developed goals and plans for the entire organization. Tactical and operational managers received those goals and plans, and their own planning activities were limited to specific procedures and budgets for the units.

Over the years, managers and consulting firms innovated a variety of analytical techniques and planning approaches, many of which have been critical for analyzing complex business situations and competitive issues. In many instances, however, senior executives spent too much time with their planning specialists to the exclusion of line managers in the rest of the organization. As a result, a gap often developed between strategic managers and tactical and operational managers, and managers and employees throughout the organization became alienated and uncommitted to the organization's success.[5]

Today, however, senior executives increasingly are involving managers throughout the organization in the strategy formation process.[6] The problems just described and the rapidly changing environment of the last 25 years have forced executives to look to all levels of the organization for ideas and innovations to make their firms more competitive. Although the CEO and other top managers continue to furnish the strategic direction, or "vision," of the organization, tactical and even operational managers often provide valuable inputs to the organization's strategic plan. In some cases, these managers also have substantial autonomy to formulate or change their own plans. This increases flexibility and responsiveness, critical requirements for success in the modern organization.

Because of this trend, a new term for the strategic planning process has emerged: *strategic management*. **Strategic management** involves managers from all parts of the organization in the formulation and implementation of strategic goals and strategies. It integrates strategic

strategic management

A process that involves managers from all parts of the organization in the formulation and implementation of strategic goals and strategies.

Tactical planning at the Gap, including marketing, was important in reinforcing the firm's strategy of commitment to basic fashion for its core group of customers.

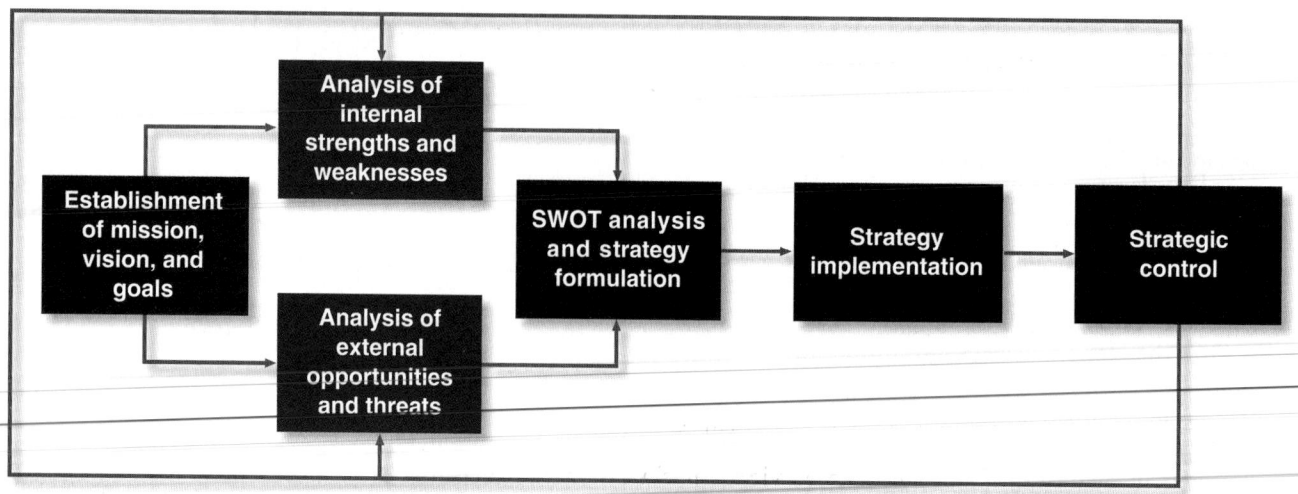

FIGURE 4.3
The Strategic Management Process

planning and management into a single process. Strategic planning becomes an ongoing activity in which all managers are encouraged to think strategically and focus on long-term, externally oriented issues as well as short-term tactical and operational issues.

Figure 4.3 shows the six major components of the strategic management process: (1) establishment of mission, vision, and goals; (2) analysis of external opportunities and threats; (3) analysis of internal strengths and weaknesses; (4) SWOT (strengths, weaknesses, opportunities, and threats) analysis and strategy formulations; (5) strategy implementation; and (6) strategic control. Because this process is a planning and decision process, it is similar to the planning framework discussed earlier. Although organizations may use different terms or emphasize different parts of the process, the components and concepts described in this section are found either explicitly or implicitly in every organization.

Step 1: Establishment of Mission, Vision, and Goals

mission

An organization's basic purpose and scope of operations.

The first step in strategic planning is establishing a mission, vision, and goals for the organization. The **mission** is the basic purpose and values of the organization, as well as its scope of operations. It is a statement of the organization's reason for existing. The mission often is written in terms of the general clients it serves. Depending on the scope of the organization, the mission may be broad or narrow. For example, the mission of Kellogg Company is to be the world's leading producer of ready-to-eat cereal products and to manufacture frozen pies and waffles, toaster pastries, soups, and other convenience foods. In contrast, the local bar found next to most campuses has the implicit mission of selling large quantities of inexpensive beer to college students.

strategic vision

The long-term direction and strategic intent of a company.

The **strategic vision** moves beyond the mission statement to provide a perspective on where the company is headed and what the organization can become. Although the terms *mission* and *vision* often are used interchangeably, the vision statement ideally clarifies the long-term direction of the company and its *strategic intent.*

Strategic goals evolve from the mission and vision of the organization. The chief executive officer of the organization, with the input and approval of the board of directors, establishes the mission, vision, and major strategic goals. The concepts and information within the mission statement, vision statement, and strategic goals statement may not be identified as such, but they should be communicated to everyone who

has contact with the organization. Large firms, for example, generally provide public formal statements of their missions, visions, and goals. Here is the *Washington Post*'s statement of goals from its website:

- To produce the best newspapers, magazines, television programs, and other products we can.
- To run an outstanding business, measured by the increase in intrinsic shareholder value over time.
- To be not just a good, but an exceptional place for people to work, and a leader in the hiring and promotion of minorities and women.
- To be a company that provides outstanding customer service.
- To be creative, adaptive, flexible, and intelligent enough to adapt to the changes in our business environment.
- To be a respected part of the communities where we do business.

Barnes & Noble.com 's Internet firm provides a business strategy statement on its website:

Barnes & Noble.com's objective is to build a profitable e-commerce business by focusing on information, entertainment, and education products and services that can be delivered either physically or digitally. We seek to become the leading online retailer for consumers who want to purchase books and complementary information-based products. Central to achieving this objective, Barnes & Noble.com's operating strategy is focused on rapidly extending its brand and increasing its customer base by:

- Continually enhancing the user experience of our online stores
- Offering a large product selection and fast delivery
- Continuing to expand the product offering within our online stores
- Pursuing advertising as well as cross-marketing/promotional activities with Barnes & Noble and Bertelsmann properties
- Leveraging the strong Barnes & Noble brand name, retail network, and expertise as well as Bertelsmann's direct marketing strength and content assets
- Strengthening and expanding our strategic alliances with third-party websites and content providers
- Pursuing acquisitions, joint ventures, and other similar strategic investments and relationships with complementary businesses and companies
- Continuing to increase the number of websites in our Affiliate Network
- Continuing to invest in technology to further develop state-of-the-art products, services, and logistics platforms

Although neither statement is called a mission statement, each includes the firm's mission, vision, and goals.[7]

Step 2: Analysis of External Opportunities and Threats

The mission and vision drive the second component of the strategic management process: analysis of the external environment. Successful strategic management depends on an accurate and thorough evaluation of the environment. The various components of the environment were introduced in Chapter 2.

Table 4.2 lists some of the important activities in an environmental analysis. The analysis begins with an examination of the industry. Next, organizational stakeholders are examined. **Stakeholders** are groups and individuals who affect and are affected by the achievement of the organization's mission, goals, and strategies. They include buyers, suppliers, competitors, government and regulatory agencies, unions and employee groups, the financial community, owners and shareholders, and trade associations. The environmental analysis provides a map of these stakeholders and the ways they influence the organization.[8]

stakeholders

Groups and individuals who affect and are affected by the achievement of the organization's mission, goals, and strategies.

Industry and Market Analysis
• *Industry profile:* major product lines and significant market segments in the industry.
• *Industry growth:* growth rates for the entire industry, growth rates for key market segments, projected changes in patterns of growth, and the determinants of growth.
• *Industry forces:* threat of new industry entrants, threat of substitutes, economic power of buyers, economic power of suppliers, and internal industry rivalry (recall Chapter 2).
Competitor Analysis
• *Competitor profile:* major competitors and their market shares.
• *Competitor analysis:* goals, strategies, strengths, and weaknesses of each major competitor.
• *Competitor advantages:* the degree to which industry competitors have differentiated their products or services or achieved cost leadership.
Political and Regulatory Analysis
• *Legislation and regulatory activities* and their effects on the industry.
• *Political activity*: the level of political activity that organizations and associations within the industry undertake (see Chapter 5).
Social Analysis
• *Social issues:* current and potential social issues and their effects on the industry.
• *Social interest groups:* consumer, environmental, and similar activist groups that attempt to influence the industry (see Chapters 5 and 6).
Human Resources Analysis
• *Labor issues:* key labor needs, shortages, opportunities, and problems confronting the industry (see Chapters 10 and 11).
Macroeconomic Analysis
• *Macroeconomic conditions:* economic factors that affect supply, demand, growth, competition, and profitability within the industry.
Technological Analysis
• *Technological factors:* scientific or technical methods that affect the industry, particularly recent and potential innovations (see Chapter 17).

TABLE 4.2
Environmental Analysis

The environmental analysis also should examine other forces in the environment, such as macroeconomic conditions and technological factors. One critical task in environmental analysis is forecasting future trends. As noted in Chapter 2, forecasting techniques range from simple judgment to complex mathematical models that examine systematic relationships among many variables. Even simple quantitative techniques outperform the intuitive assessments of experts. Judgment is susceptible to bias, and managers have a limited ability to process information. Managers should use subjective judgments as inputs to quantitative models or when they confront new situations.

The following material on Toys 'R' Us shows the power of understanding the external environment, and correctly forecasting future trends in the industry.

The Toys 'R' Us example illustrates how organizations must develop a clear sense of market opportunities by analyzing the external environment. In the same way, executives can identify potential threats as well.

John H. Eyler, Jr., is the latest chief executive of long-troubled Toys 'R' Us, Inc. He's made a lot of changes in order to bring a bit of the magic back to the company. The hope is that by showing shoppers a friendlier, more helpful face and lining shelves with great toys not available elsewhere, Toys 'R' Us can break out of the low-price supermarket approach that hyperefficient Wal-Mart does much better. In 1998, Wal-Mart overtook toys 'R' Us as the number one U.S. toy seller.

Eyler is the third Toys 'R' Us CEO since founder Charles Lazarus retired in 1994, and his store overhaul is the company's third since 1996. Toys 'R' Us has found that offering the widest selection 12 months a year just isn't enough to keep customers happy. "When I started, if you had good selection and good prices, that was the key," says Lazarus, now 77 and still a member of the board of directors. "Today, our competition is very good, and we have to be better." Eyler is in the process of revamping his stores to create more of a shopping experience and a forum to launch new brands, including more exclusive in-store offerings. After watching competitors such as Kmart declare bankruptcy and closing a slew of stores himself, Eyler knows too well that consumers are a tough lot to please in this environment. "The ferocity and price competition has never been stiffer than during this past holiday season," said Eyler in 2002, he estimates that 15 percent of all toy sales are now controlled by retailers that won't exist in five years.

The chain struggled so hard trying to figure out how to beat the latest challenge—online toy stores—that it finally joined them instead, linking up with Amazon.com to create a joint website. The move made the Toys 'R' Us site profitable more quickly than it would have been on its own. Overall, retailers seem more sanguine about a shift to online sales, partly because online toy sales are not expected to exceed 10 percent to 15 percent of the industry total in the long term. After several sites closed down, it now seems less likely that the Internet will be the threat to toy stores that it may be to musicsellers and booksellers.

If customers respond to the changes at Toys 'R' Us, Eyler will have gone a long way toward proving that he has figured out how to make a 1980s-style, big-box retailer attractive to today's shopper. But he faces stiff headwinds. Retailers have already begun wringing their hands, worried about the gloomy shadow that a jittery stock market, higher gas prices, and a slowing economy might cast upon consumers. Normally consistent specialty merchants such as Gap, Inc., and Home Depot, Inc., have been performing less well recently.

But competitors are only part of the challenge. Eyler wants to begin mending fences with Hasbro (maker of Tonka trucks) and Mattel (home of Barbie) so that he has a steady supply of inventory when it is needed. His answer: more systematic stocking of the top 1,500 toys that make up two-thirds of the chain's sales. Toys 'R' Us, like every other retailer, knows it can't be sure it won't run out of the hot toys—the Pokemons and Tickle Me Elmos—the week before Christmas. But it can ensure that standbys such as Monopoly will be in stores 90 percent of the time. Eyler says that a one-season wonder might make $75 million in a year—sizable, but still only 1 percent of U.S. sales. "We can't make a consistently profitable business on the back of a hot toy," he insists.

But if Toys 'R' Us cannot reestablish relations with suppliers, it will take a lot longer to bring customers around. Their animosity goes much deeper than not finding enough of the right toys. A recent Sanford C. Bernstein study of U.S. shoppers' opinions of 15 big retailers found that Toys 'R' Us ranked near the bottom of the list on measures such as service—only Kmart, Inc., ranked lower—and value for the dollar. Overall, shoppers ranked the chain 10th out of the 15 retailers.

Eyler is making progress. Wall Street analyst Donald I. Trott hears at least once a week from an investor who has been pleasantly surprised after visiting one of the new stores. "A lot of these investors are finding personally that they're having a very different experience at the store," says Trott. With stiff competition from Wal-Mart, Target Corp., and others, there's little room for mistakes. "What Toys 'R' Us has lost is their uniqueness, and that they will not be able to recapture," says retail consultant Kurt Barnard. Eyler's out to prove the naysayers wrong. But this isn't child's play.

Source: Condensed from Nanette Byrnes, "Can CEO John Eyler Fix the Chain?" *Business Week*, December 4, 2000, 3710, no. 128, online; Diane Brady, "What's the Toy Story?" *Business Week*, February 8, 2002; Nanette Byrnes, "Toys 'R' Us May Be More Fun Next Year," *Business Week*, December 18, 2001

Frequently, the difference between an opportunity and a threat depends on how a company positions itself strategically. For example, Southwest Airlines' original base of operations at Love Field (outside of Dallas, Texas) was seen as a problem for the company. Other major competitors were permitted to fly into the larger and state-of-the-art Dallas–Fort Worth Airport, but Southwest was not. However, given this apparent threat, Southwest built its strategy around point-to-point flights into smaller airports that catered to business travelers. Other airlines soon found that they could not compete with Southwest in its niche. What was originally seen as a threat turned into an opportunity for Southwest.[9]

Step 3: Analysis of Internal Strengths and Weaknesses

At the same time external analysis is conducted, the strengths and weaknesses of major functional areas within the organization are assessed. Internal analysis provides strategic decision makers with an inventory of the organization's skills and resources as well as its overall and functional performance levels. Many of your other business courses will prepare you to conduct internal analysis. Table 4.3 lists some of the major components of the internal resource analysis.

TABLE 4.3
Internal Resource Analysis

Financial Analysis
Examines financial strengths and weaknesses through financial statements such as a balance sheet and an income statement and compares trends to historical and industry figures (see Chapter 18).
Human Resources Assessment
Examines strengths and weaknesses of all levels of management and employees and focuses on key human resources activities, including recruitment, selection, placement, training, labor (union) relationships, compensation, promotion, appraisal, quality of work life, and human resources planning (see Chapters 10 and 11).
Marketing Audit
Examines strengths and weaknesses of major marketing activities and identifies markets, key market segments, and the competitive position (market share) of the organization within key markets.
Operations Analysis
Examines the strengths and weaknesses of the manufacturing, production, or service delivery activities of the organization (see Chapters 9, 16, and 17).
Other Internal Resource Analyses
Examine, as necessary and appropriate, the strengths and weaknesses of other organizational activities, such as research and development (product and process), management information systems, engineering, and purchasing.

Resources and Core Competencies Without question, strategic planning has been strongly influenced in recent years by a focus on internal resources. **Resources** are inputs to production (recall systems theory) that can be accumulated over time to enhance the performance of a firm. Resources can take many forms, but tend to fall into two broad categories: (1) *tangible assets* such as real estate, production facilities, raw materials, and so on, and (2) *intangible assets* such as company reputation, culture, technical knowledge, and patents, as well as accumulated learning and experience. The Walt Disney Company, for example, has developed its strategic plan on combinations of tangible assets (e.g., hotels and theme parks) as well as intangible assets (brand recognition, talented craftspeople, culture focused on customer service).[10]

resources

Inputs to a system that can enhance performance.

Effective internal analysis provides a clearer understanding of how a company can compete through its resources. Resources are a source of competitive advantage only under certain circumstances. First, if the resource is instrumental for creating customer *value*—that is, if it increases the benefits customers derive from a product or service relative to the costs they incur—the resource can lead to a competitive advantage. For example, Wal-Mart's computerized inventory control system helps make certain that products are on the shelves and that inventory costs are minimized. In this case, Wal-Mart's information technology is clearly a valuable resource.

Second, resources are a source of advantage if they are *rare* and not equally available to all competitors. Even for extremely valuable resources, if all competitors have equal access, the resource cannot provide a source of competitive advantage. For example, when long-distance telephone service was deregulated, AT&T no longer had exclusive use of its telecommunications infrastructure. For companies such as Merck, DuPont, Dow Chemical, and others, patented formulas represent important resources that are both rare and valuable.

Third, if resources are *difficult to imitate*, they provide a source of competitive advantage. Xerox, for example, believed for many years that no one could duplicate its reprographic capabilities. Kodak and Canon soon proved Xerox wrong. McDonald's brand name recognition, in contrast, has been extremely difficult for competitors such as Burger King, Wendy's, and others to duplicate.[11]

Finally, resources can enhance a firm's competitive advantage when they are well *organized*. For example, AT & T has an aggressive program to manage its resources. Called Real-Time Quality, the program is a data-driven approach to maximizing the effectiveness and efficiency of its operations. The program emphasizes

* Rigorous monitoring of in-process measures and process results
* Ongoing problem solving and corrective action
* Anticipation and prevention of future problems
* Immediate and continuous improvement in performance and cost of systems and processes

With systems such as the Real-Time Quality program, AT & T's resources enhance the firm's competitive advantage.[12]

As shown in Figure 4.4, when resources are valuable, rare, inimitable, and organized, they can be viewed as a company's core competencies. Simply stated, a **core competence** is something a company does especially well relative to its competitors. Honda, for example, has a core competence in small engine design and manufacturing; Sony has a core competence in miniaturization; Federal Express has a core competence in logistics and customer service. Typically, a core competence refers to a set of skills or expertise in some activity, rather than physical or financial assets. For example, among U.S. automobile manufacturers, General Motors has traditionally been viewed as having a core competence in marketing, while Ford has established quality as its number one strength. Recently Chrysler redefined its core competence around design and engineering.

core competencies

The unique skills and/or knowledge an organization possesses that give it an edge over competitors.

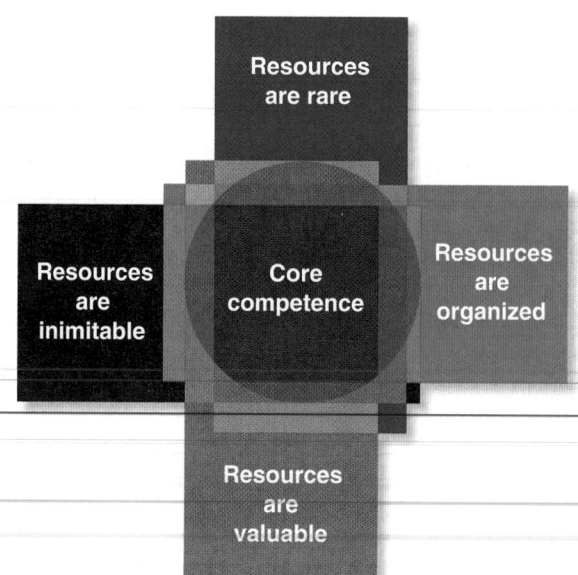

FIGURE 4.4
Resources and Core
Competence

Benchmarking   Benchmarking is the process of assessing how well one company's basic functions and skills compare to those of some other company or set of companies. The goal of benchmarking is to thoroughly understand the "best practices" of other firms, and to undertake actions to achieve both better performance and lower costs. For example, Xerox Corporation, a pioneer in benchmarking, established a program to study 67 of its key work processes against "world-class" companies. Many of these companies were not in the copier business. For example, in an effort to improve its order fulfillment process, Xerox studied L. L. Bean, the clothing mail-order company. Benchmarking programs have helped Xerox and a myriad of other companies, such as Ford, Corning, Hewlett-Packard, and Anheuser-Busch, make great strides in eliminating inefficiencies and improving competitiveness. Perhaps the only downside of benchmarking is that it only helps a company perform as well as its competitors; strategic management ultimately is about surpassing those companies.[13]

Step 4: SWOT Analysis and Strategy Formulation

SWOT analysis

A comparison of strengths, weaknesses, opportunities, and threats that helps executives formulate strategy.

After analyzing the external environment and internal resources, strategic decision makers have the information they need to formulate corporate, business, and functional strategies of the organization. A comparison of strengths, weaknesses, opportunities, and threats normally is referred to as a **SWOT analysis.** SWOT analysis helps executives summarize the major facts and forecasts derived from the external and internal analyses. From this, executives can derive a series of statements that identify the primary and secondary strategic issues confronting the organization. Strategy formulation builds on SWOT analysis to utilize the strengths of the organization in order to capitalize on opportunities, counteract threats, and alleviate internal weaknesses. In short, strategy formulation moves from simply analysis to devising a coherent course of action.

corporate strategy

The set of businesses, markets, or industries in which an organization competes and the distribution of resources among those entities.

Corporate Strategy   **Corporate strategy** identifies the set of businesses, markets, or industries in which the organization competes and the distribution of resources among those businesses. Figure 4.5 shows four basic corporate strategy alternatives, ranging from very specialized to highly diverse. A **concentration** strategy focuses on a single business competing in a single industry. In the food-retailing industry, Kroger, Safeway, and A&P all pursue concentration strategies. Frequently companies pursue concentra-

concentration

A strategy employed for an organization that operates a single business and competes in a single industry.

Supply chain — Vertical integration — Concentration — Vertical integration — Distribution channels

Concentric diversification

Primary industry

Unrelated industry

Conglomerate diversification

tion strategies to gain entry into an industry, when industry growth is good, or when the company has a narrow range of competencies.

A **vertical integration** strategy involves expanding the domain of the organization into supply channels or to distributors. At one time, Henry Ford had fully integrated his company from the ore mines needed to make steel all the way to the showrooms where his cars were sold. Vertical integration generally is used to eliminate uncertainties and reduce costs associated with suppliers or distributors. A strategy of **concentric diversification** involves moving into new businesses that are related to the company's original core business. William Marriott expanded his original restaurant business outside Washington, D.C., by moving into airline catering, hotels, and fast food. Each of these businesses within the hospitality industry is related in terms of the services it provides, the skills necessary for success, and the customers it attracts. Often companies such as Marriott pursue a strategy of concentric diversification to take advantage of their strengths in one business to gain advantage in another. Because the businesses are related, the products, markets, technologies, or capabilities used in one business can be transferred to another.

In contrast to concentric diversification, **conglomerate diversification** is a corporate strategy that involves expansion into unrelated businesses. Union Pacific Corporation has diversified from its original base in railroads to such wide-ranging industries as oil and gas exploration, mining, microwave and fiber-optic systems, hazardous waste disposal, trucking, and real estate. Typically, companies pursue a conglomerate diversification strategy to minimize risks due to market fluctuations in one industry. The corporate strategy of an organization is sometimes called its business portfolio. One of the most popular techniques for analyzing and communicating corporate strategy has been the BCG matrix.

Trends in Corporate Strategy   In recent years, corporate America has been swept by a wave of mergers and acquisitions such as Hewlett-Packard and Compaq, Chrysler and Mercedes Benz, and Bell Atlantic and GTE (to create Verizon). Such mergers and acquisitions often influence the organization's corporate strategy either by concentrating in one industry or by diversifying its portfolio.

vertical integration

The acquisition or development of new businesses that produce parts or components of the organization's product.

concentric diversification

A strategy used to add new businesses that produce related products or are involved in related markets and activities.

conglomerate diversification

A strategy used to add new businesses that produce unrelated products or are involved in unrelated markets and activities.

In response to senior executives' needs to understand and manage complex, modern organizations, the Boston Consulting Group (BCG) introduced the growth/share matrix. The BCG matrix is shown in Figure 4.6. Each business in the corporation is plotted on the matrix on the basis of the growth rate of its market and the relative strength of its competitive position in that market (market share). The business is represented by a circle whose size depends on the business's contribution to corporate revenues.

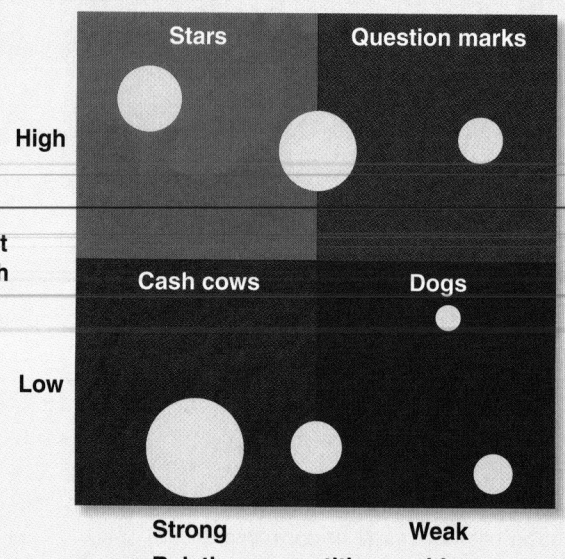

FIGURE 4.6
Resources and Core Competence.

High-growth, weak-competitive-position businesses are called *question marks*. They require substantial investment to improve their position; otherwise, divestiture is recommended. High-growth, strong-competitive-position businesses are called *stars*. These businesses require heavy investment, but their strong position allows them to generate the needed revenues. Low-growth, strong-competitive-position businesses are called *cash cows*. These businesses generate revenues in excess of their investment needs and therefore fund other businesses. Finally, low-growth, weak-competitive-position businesses are called *dogs*. The remaining revenues from these businesses are realized, and then the businesses are divested.

The BCG matrix and similar tools can help both the corporation and the businesses if they are used as vehicles for discussion rather than as bases for major strategic decisions. The matrix should be applied with other techniques, and strategic managers must emphasize the development of long-term competitive advantages for all businesses. No single technique is a substitute for creativity, insight, or leadership.

SOURCES: P. Haspeslagh, "Portfolio Planning: Uses and Limits," *Harvard Business Review* 60, no. 1 (1982). pp. 58–67; R. Hamermesh, *Making Strategy Work* (New York: John Wiley & Sons, 1986); and R.A. Proctor. "Toward a New Model for Product Portfolio Analysis," *Management Decision* 28, no. 3 (1990), pp. 14–17.

The value of implementing a diversified corporate strategy depends on individual circumstances. Many critics have argued that unrelated diversification hurts a company more often than it helps it. In recent years, a number of diversified companies have sold their peripheral businesses so that they could concentrate on a more focused portfolio. For example, Merck & Company sold its consumer products business to focus on the application of biotechnology in the pharmaceutical industry. Sears sold Allstate Insurance to concentrate more on the core business of retail merchandising. Kodak sold off Eastman Chemical to boost profitability and concentrate more on its imaging business.[14]

In contrast, the diversification efforts of an organization competing in a slow-growth, mature, or threatened industry often are applauded. Many recent bank mergers, such as the creation of Citigroup from Travelers and Citicorp, were designed to yield greater efficiencies and increased market share in the banking industry.

Although the merits of diversification are an issue for continued study, most observers agree that organizations usually perform better if they implement a more concentric diversification strategy in which businesses are somehow related or similar to one another. Disney, for example, spent $19 billion to merge with ABC/Cap Cities. While the two companies are somewhat different, their businesses are complementary. Disney's success in movies and videos is matched by ABC's network TV as well as its production capabilities in Cap Cities. Though Disney has a cable channel (the Disney Channel), its ability to reach millions of viewers has been enhanced by ABC's presence in network television.[15]

Business Strategy   After the top management team and board make the corporate strategic decisions, executives must determine how they will compete in each business area. **Business strategy** defines the major actions by which an organization builds and strengthens its competitive position in the marketplace. A competitive advantage typically results from one of two generic business strategies introduced here and elaborated in Chapter 7.[16]

> **business strategy**
>
> **The major actions by which a business competes in a particular industry or market.**

First, organizations such as Wal-Mart and Southwest Airlines (mentioned earlier) pursue competitive advantage through **low-cost strategies.** Businesses using a low-cost strategy attempt to be efficient and offer a standard, no-frills product. They often are large and try to take advantage of economies of scale in production or distribution. In many cases, the large size allows them to sell their products and services at a lower price, which leads to higher market share, volume, and, ultimately, profits. To succeed, an organization using this strategy often must be the cost leader in its industry or market segment. However, even a cost leader must offer a product that is acceptable to customers compared to competitors' products. As Gordon Bethune, CEO of Continental Airlines, has said, "You can make a pizza so cheap that no-one will buy it." In the end, organizations need to use a cost strategy to increase value to customers, rather than take it away.[17]

> **low-cost strategy**
>
> **A strategy an organization uses to build competitive advantage by being efficient and offering a standard, no-frills product.**

Second, an organization may pursue a **differentiation strategy.** With a differentiation strategy, a company attempts to be unique in its industry or market segment along some dimensions that customers value. This unique or differentiated position within the industry often is based on high product quality, excellent marketing and distribution, or superior service. Nordstrom's commitment to quality and customer service in the retail apparel industry is an excellent example of a differentiation strategy. While it perhaps is not as fancy as competitors such as Saks Fifth Avenue and Neiman Marcus, Nordstrom focuses on providing a full assortment of clothing and accessories to customers and ensuring that they get personal attention. The company's personal shopper program has become a hit in all of the company's 83 full-line stores. Customers can come in and enjoy a refreshing beverage in a private room while a tireless assistant brings them endless wardrobe options. Nordstrom's personal shoppers reinforce efficiency, speed, and individual service. Better still for the customer, there is absolutely no charge for the service. In an otherwise impersonal and at times overwhelming department store, Nordstrom's differentiates itself by returning to the days when service was more genteel and individualized.[18]

> **differentiation strategy**
>
> **A strategy an organization uses to build competitive advantage by being unique in its industry or market segment along one or more dimensions.**

Functional Strategy   The final step in strategy formulation is to establish the major functional strategies. **Functional strategies** are implemented by each functional area of the organization to support the

> **functional strategies**
>
> **Strategies implemented by each functional area of the organization to support the organization's business strategy.**

Nordstrom differentiates itself from its competitors with superior customer service and selection of fashion.

business strategy. The typical functional areas include production, human resources, marketing, research and development, finance, and distribution. For example, Cirque du Soleil's expansion plan includes focusing on functional strategies, including training and other activities related to the creative process.

Functional strategies typically are put together by functional area executives with the input and approval of the executives responsible for business strategy. Senior strategic decision makers review the functional strategies to ensure that each major department is operating in a manner consistent with the business strategies of the organization.

FROM THE PAGES OF

Cirque du Soleil's Expanding Big Top

BusinessWeek

In a huge, hangar-style training studio at the circus company's Montreal headquarters, gymnast Cletus Okpoh is perched on a trapeze some 45 feet off the ground. A coach yells instructions at him, and Okpoh, clad only in Lycra shorts, periodically drops from the trapeze and plunges toward the floor. After bungee cords catch him and send him flying back up, he tries to grab the bar, usually misses, and ends up bouncing up and down on the elastic cords. "Focus is the key," the coach yells at one point. "And don't forget to squeeze your bum together."

Here's hoping that executives at Cirque don't miss the bar when they embark on an ambitious expansion plan that the company hopes will one day make it nearly as ubiquitous and multifaceted as Disney. Already, Cirque du Soleil is a fascinating company. In addition to five unique traveling big-top shows, it now has three that are performed in permanent arenas: one at Walt Disney World in Orlando, Florida, and two in Las Vegas, at the Bellagio and Treasure Island hotels. All told, the Cirque employs 2,400 people and will have revenues of an astonishing $500 million Canadian (about $325 million U.S.) in 2001, 90 percent of it generated by its whimsical circus shows.

The group was founded by a troupe of street performers 18 years ago, and its guiding genius is CEO Guy Lalibert, age 42, a one time fire-eater and street musician who ran away from home as a teenager. Early on he charmed the Quebec government into giving the troupe more than $1 million to buy equipment. In 2000 Lalibert bought out the company's cofounder, who had wanted to take Cirque public.

Cirque du Soleil's top execs have laid out a new five-year plan. The company's strategy will continue to be different from that of Disney, MGM, and other entertainment rivals. Cirque du Soleil styles itself as a pure content provider whose main business is harnessing the creativity of performers, producers, and other artists, not owning and operating hotels and other properties. Instead, it focuses its attention and finances on training and other activities related to the creative process. For instance, Cirque makes all its own costumes, and to ensure that its artists are well fed, it hires gourmet chefs to accompany the traveling shows.

Daniel Lamarre, president of shows and new ventures, predicts that Cirque du Soleil will expand at a rate of about 25 percent annually over the next five years, which would boost its annual revenues to roughly $1 billion (U.S.) by 2007. In mid-June it announced plans to open two more permanent productions in Las Vegas in partnership with MGM Mirage, and the companies are exploring other joint ventures around the world. Meanwhile, Cirque is talking with potential partners about opening new permanent shows in other cities, including London, Tokyo, and New York.

Around 2005 it expects to also start generating substantial growth from a panoply of new initiatives, including Cirque du Soleil hotel/spas with a circus ambience. The facilities also will be "heavily multimedia," which might mean everything from airing films of Cirque performances to having computer-generated virtual characters strolling the halls. As early as 2005, Cirque du Soleil hopes to have finished a prototype hotel/spa in Montreal that will be used as a "laboratory" to develop and try out its ideas.

Meanwhile, Cirque du Soleil is rapidly expanding its film, television, and recording operations. It already has deals with a number of big partners, including the major Canadian TV networks, Bravo in the United States, Fuji in Japan, and Televisa in Mexico. An example of the kind of programming it hopes to do is a 13-part TV series (to be aired by Canadian networks and in the United States by Bravo) that will follow some of its performers as they prepare for a show. Cirque also has plans to shoot a new TV variety series, is working on an animated children's television show, and has hired experienced record producers to expand its music operation.

Unlike most circuses, Cirque du Soleil has a target audience that consists of adults, not children, with tickets going for around $100 per person. The company believes each individual show can be kept going for up to 15 years before it has to be retired. It has grown so rapidly because its productions—which combine circus acrobatics with the narrative of theater—fill a deep human need to gather together and experience something marvelous. It's refreshing to see a company succeed so well by betting everything on its ability to astonish and amaze its customers.

SOURCE: Thane Peterson, "Cirque du Soleil's Expanding Big Top," *Business Week*, June 25, 2002.

Step 5: Strategy Implementation

As with any plan, formulating the appropriate strategy is not enough. Strategic managers also must ensure that the new strategies are implemented effectively and efficiently. Recently corporations and strategy consultants have been paying more attention to implementation. They realize that clever techniques and a good plan do not guarantee success. This greater appreciation is reflected in two major trends.

First, organizations are adopting a more comprehensive view of implementation. The strategy must be supported by decisions regarding the appropriate organization structure, technology, human resources, reward systems, information systems, organization culture, and leadership style. Just as the strategy of the organization must be matched to the external environment, it must fit the multiple factors responsible for its implementation. The remainder of this section discusses these factors and the ways in which they can be used to implement strategy.

Second, many organizations are extending the more participative strategic management process to implementation. Managers at all levels are involved with strategy formulation and the identification and execution of the means to implement the new strategies. Senior executives still may orchestrate the overall implementation process,

Change starts with the leader

The Silent Killers	Principles for Engaging and Changing the Silent Killers
Top-down or laissez-faire senior management style	With the top team and lower levels, the CEO/general manager creates a partnership built around the development of a compelling business direction, the creation of an enabling organizational context, and the delegation of authority to clearly accountable individuals and teams.
Unclear strategy and conflicting priorities	The top team, as a group, develops a statement of strategy, and priorities that members are willing to stand behind are developed.
An ineffective senior management team	The top team, as a group, is involved in all steps in the change process so that its effectiveness is tested and developed.
Poor vertical communication	An honest, fact-based dialogue is established with lower levels about the new strategy and the barriers to implementing it.
Poor coordination across functions, businesses, or borders	A set of businesswide initiatives and new organizational roles and responsibilities are defined that require "the right people to work together on the right things in the right way" to implement the strategy.
Inadequate down-the-line leadership skills and development	Lower-level managers develop skills through newly created opportunities to lead change and drive key business initiatives. They are supported with just-in-time coaching, training, and targeted recruitment. Those who still are not able to make the grade must be replaced.

FIGURE 4.7

Attacking the Six Barriers to Strategy Implementation

SOURCE: Reprinted from M. Beer and R. A Eisenstat, "The Silent Killers of Strategy Implementation and Learning," *MIT Sloan Management Review* (Summer 2000), 4 (4), pp. 29–40, by permission of the publisher. Copyright © 2000 by MIT. All rights reserved.

but they place much greater responsibility and authority in the hands of others in the organization. In general, strategy implementation involves four related steps:

- *Step 1: Define strategic tasks.*   Articulate in simple language what must be done in a particular business to create or sustain a competitive advantage. Define strategic tasks to help employees understand how they contribute to the organization. This also can redefine relationships among the parts of the organization.
- *Step 2: Assess organization capabilities.*   Evaluate the organization's ability to implement the strategic tasks. A task force (typically) interviews employees and managers to identify specific issues that help or hinder effective implementation. Results are summarized for top management.
- *Step 3: Develop implementation agenda:*   Management decides how it will change its management pattern, how critical interdependencies will be managed, what skills and individuals are needed in key roles, and what structures, measures, information, and rewards might ultimately support specified behavior. A philosophy statement, communicated in value terms, is the natural outcome of this process.
- *Step 4: Implementation plan:*   The top management team, the employee task force, and others develop the implementation plan. The top management team monitors progress. The employee task force is charged with providing feedback about how others in the organization are responding to the changes.

This process, though straightforward, does not always go smoothly. Figure 4.7 shows six different barriers to strategy implementation and provides a description of some key principles for overcoming these "silent killers." By paying closer attention to the processes by which strategies are implemented, executives, managers, and employees can play an important role in making sure that strategic plans are actually carried out.[19]

Step 6: Strategic Control

The final component of the strategic management process is strategic control. A **strategic control system** is designed to support managers in evaluating the organization's progress with its strategy and, when discrepancies exist, taking corrective action. The system must encourage efficient operations that are consistent with the plan while allowing the flexibility to adapt to changing conditions. As with all control systems, the organization must develop performance indicators, an information system, and specific mechanisms to monitor progress.

> **strategic control system**
>
> **A system designed to support managers in evaluating the organization's progress regarding its strategy and, when discrepancies exist, taking corrective action.**

Most strategic control systems include some type of budget to monitor and control major financial expenditures. The dual responsibilities of a control system—efficiency and flexibility—often seem contradictory with respect to budgets. The budget usually establishes limits on spending, but changing conditions or innovation may require different financial commitments during the budgetary period. To solve this dilemma, some companies have responded with two separate budgets: strategic and operational. For example, managers at Texas Instruments Incorporated control two budgets under the OST (objectives-strategies-tactics) system. The strategic budget is used to create and maintain long-term effectiveness, and the operational budget is tightly monitored to achieve short-term efficiency. The topic of control in general, and budgets in particular, will be discussed in more detail in Chapter 16.

KEY TERMS

Business strategy, p. 125	Low-cost strategy, p. 125	Strategic goals, p. 112
Concentration, p. 122	Mission, p. 116	Strategic management, p. 115
Concentric diversification, p. 123	Operational planning, p. 113	Strategic planning, p. 112
Conglomerate diversification, p. 123	Plans, p. 109	Strategic vision, p. 116
Core competencies, p. 121	Resources, p. 121	Strategy, p. 112
Corporate strategy, p. 122	Scenario, p. 110	SWOT analysis, p. 122
Differentiation strategy, p. 125	Situational analysis, p. 108	Tactical planning, p. 112
Functional strategies, p. 125	Stakeholders, p. 117	Vertical integration, p. 123
Goal, p. 109	Strategic control system, p. 129	

SUMMARY OF LEARNING OBJECTIVES

Now that you have studied Chapter 4, you should know:

How to proceed through the basic steps in any planning process.

The planning process begins with a situation analysis of the external and internal forces affecting the organization. This will help identify and diagnose issues and problems and may bring to the surface alternative goals and plans for the firm. Next, the advantages and disadvantages of these goals and plans should be evaluated against one another. Once a set of goals and a plan have been selected, implementation involves communicating the plan to employees, allocating resources, and making certain that other systems such as rewards and budgets are supporting the plan. Finally, planning requires that control systems be put in place to monitor progress toward the goals.

How strategic planning integrates with tactical and operational planning.

Strategic planning is different from operational planning in that it involves making long-term decisions about the entire organization. Tactical planning translates broad goals and strategies into specific actions to be taken within parts of the organization. Operational planning identifies the specific short-term procedures and processes required at lower levels of the organization.

Why it is important to analyze both the external environment and the internal resources of the firm before formulating a strategy.

Strategic planning is designed to leverage the strengths of a firm while minimizing the effects of its weaknesses. It is difficult to know the potential advantage a firm may have unless external analysis is done well. For example, a company may have a talented marketing department or an efficient production system. However, there is no way to determine whether these internal characteristics are sources of competitive advantage until something is known about how well the competitors stack up in these areas.

The choices available for corporate strategy.

Corporate strategy identifies the breadth of a firm's competitive domain. Corporate strategy can be kept narrow, as in a concentration strategy, or can move to suppliers and buyers via vertical integration. Corporate strategy also can broaden a firm's domain via concentric (related) diversification or conglomerate (unrelated) diversification.

How companies can achieve competitive advantage through business strategy.

Companies gain competitive advantage in two primary ways. They can attempt to be unique in some way by pursuing a differentiation strategy, or they can focus on efficiency and price by pursuing a low-cost strategy.

How core competencies provide the foundation for business strategy.

A core competence is something a company does especially well relative to its competitors. When this competence, say, in engineering or marketing, is in some area important to market success, it becomes the foundation for developing a competitive advantage.

The keys to effective strategy implementation.

Many good plans are doomed to failure because they are not implemented correctly. Strategy must be supported by structure, technology, human resources, rewards, information systems, culture, leadership, and so on. Ultimately, the success of a plan depends on how well employees at low levels are able and willing to implement it. Participative management is one of the more popular approaches used by executives to gain employees' input and ensure their commitment to strategy implementation.

DISCUSSION QUESTIONS

1. This chapter opened with a quote from former CEO of GE Jack Welch: "Manage your destiny, or someone else will." What does this mean for strategic management? What does it mean when Welch adds," or someone else will"?

2. How do strategic, operational, and tactical planning differ? How might the three levels complement one another in an organization?

3. What accounts for the shift from strategic planning to strategic management? In which industries would you be most likely to observe these trends?

4. In your opinion, what are the core competencies of companies in the auto industry such as General Motors, Ford, and Chrysler? How do these competencies help them compete against foreign competitors such as Honda, Toyota, Nissan, Mercedes Benz, BMW, and others?

5. What are the key challenges in strategy implementation? What barriers might prevent strategy implementation?

CONCLUDING CASE

What Lies Ahead

What if you could predict today which industries are fated to flourish or fail in the 21st century? What if, a decade past, you could have imagined the impact of the Internet? And what if, five years ago, you had foreseen today's labor market or soaring health care costs? Then maybe you could hang out your shingle as a futurist and charge corporate clients or the federal government big bucks to help them prepare for the vagaries that lie ahead.

Even armed with statistics and other historical data, however, you would not have been able to predict the terrorist attacks of September 11, 2001, and the ensuing economic effects on both domestic and economic business. Although the following predictions do not take the effect of the attacks into account, they represent the kind of forward-looking thinking that strategic planners employ. Following the predictions is an afterword about the attacks.

PREDICTION 1: LABOR

Forecast: If you're waiting for a rising unemployment rate to ease your labor woes, you'll be waiting a long time. You've got a few more years of a tight labor supply, predicts Roger E. Herman, a futurist who looks at the workplace. And don't get your hopes up too high after that, cautions Edie Weiner, president of Weiner, Edrich, Brown, Inc., in Manhattan. Entry-level talent will become more plentiful in the next few years with the maturing of Generation Y, but the shortage of senior managers won't let up for years. There are 76 million baby boomers moving through the labor market, but only 44 million Gen-Xers, the first of whom will turn 40 in 2004.

Implications: Recruitment and retention efforts will become more important than ever, particularly with senior managers. "If you don't have a stable workforce, you are at a competitive disadvantage," warns Herman. You might take some comfort in the fact that your rivals will be just as hard-pressed, although that means they'll be gunning for your employees. You'll want to keep your successful strategies close to the vest. Your rivals certainly will.

PREDICTION 2: REAL ESTATE

Forecast: Small companies will relocate in record numbers during the next decade as they get squeezed by two powerful forces—a tight labor market and rising rents—according to real estate futurist Roulac. Employees in their twenties and thirties, who will be in short supply over the next five years, move around at twice the rate of older people.

To attract these mobile workers, small companies will be forced to create strong images for themselves and spend more time and money marketing themselves. The right location will be crucial, says Roulac, who conducts an analysis he calls a "geostrategy" of cultural, economic, and other factors that help companies determine the best locale for their business.

Implications: You'll want to choose the kind of hometown base your target employees want, one with a high quality of life, strong education, public transportation, and recreation and entertainment amenities. "If you're not in a place where people choose to be, you may not be able to attract employees," says Roulac. As more companies seek new homes and demand keeps pushing commercial rents skyward, more companies will seek to buy their own office space. Alternatively, they will scale down their current space and move some employees to less expensive outlying areas that are accessible by public transportation, says Christopher Ireland, CEO of Cheskin Research, a Redwood Shores (California) forecasting firm. (In fact, she did just that with her own company.) That means small companies may lose the classic advantage of having a flexible, cohesive workforce all under one roof. They will increasingly be faced with managing employees in multiple locations. That will require more logistical coordination and technology so that everyone will stay on the same page. Ireland says she now manages employees at five different locations, making communications and office culture issues more important than ever.

PREDICTION 3: CUSTOMER RELATIONS

Forecast: The current pace of corporate mergers and acquisitions will continue over the coming decade, and so small businesses are in for a rough ride as their trusty major accounts vanish, predicts Jennifer Jarratt, futurist at Coates & Jarratt, Inc., based in Washington, D.C. "You just don't have the continuity that you had several years ago," says Weiner.

Implications: To cope with customer churn, more small companies will be forced to step up their marketing and rethink their business strategies. Rather than focus so heavily on big corporate clients, they will pursue more stable small to midsize ones, predicts Jarratt. Companies also will attempt to cope by narrowing their focus to serve a more select group of customers and give them superior service. That strategy potentially could help small businesses retain their clients that merge or are acquired.

While some small companies with desirable businesses will undoubtedly get gobbled up as mergers escalate, Weiner doesn't foresee a future without small business. To the contrary, as giant mergers take place, big corporations will abandon some market niches, leaving new opportunities for smaller businesses, she says. "As merged companies try to find efficiencies, they create demand for outsourcing, which spurs growth in medium and smaller businesses," says Weiner.

PREDICTION 4: WEALTH TRANSACTIONS

Forecast: In what is expected to be one of the largest wealth transfers in history, baby boomers will inherit thousands of family businesses and billions of dollars from their parents over the next two decades, says futurist Johnson.

Implications: Some small businesses will profit from an infusion of new blood and leadership that will help them grow. Others will be acquired, leaving heirs with money to invest in other ventures. Baby boomers, who will begin to face age discrimination in the workplace, will also use their inheritances to start new businesses or buy existing businesses that are coming up for sale, says futurist Weiner.

As small-business growth is spurred, business consulting opportunities will abound to provide these newly minted entrepreneurs with everything from succession planning to financial services, says Weiner. For example, Weiner has studied the trend and sees a future for her own company. She says she is already planning to expand her future consulting services to serve more small companies. Other businesses may want to consider a similar move.

PREDICTION 5: TECHNOLOGY

Forecast: The next 50 years will see the evolution of what David Smith of Technology Futures, Inc., calls the Age of Bio. Biological science will be applied to manufacturing, information processing, and other fields. As computing power surpasses the abilities of the human mind by 2040, artificial intelligence will become a reality.

Implications: The field of "bioinformatics" will explode. Someday you may trade in your computer monitor for a "retinal display" or use a DNA computer. "Instead of having to dig in the ground for specialty chemicals we'll be able to grow them," says Smith. These changes will breed new business opportunities. All this new technology will require more energy resources. But rising prices for oil and diminishing natural resources will trigger the growth of so-called green industries that use alternative energy, says Jarratt. Running your business could get easier, too. Artificial intelligence might let you turn over to computers an ever-growing array of tasks, says Smith. But since computers still don't have feelings, more consultants will be needed to handle the human issues that arise in the workplace.

WHEN BUSINESS IS SCARED STAGNANT

The new millennium really began on September 11, 2001. True, the economies of the United States and the rest of the globe were showing worrying signs of distress in the weeks and months before terrorists crashed three passenger planes into the World Trade Center and the Pentagon. But by striking down a key pillar of America's leadership—its unbridled faith in its own security—the catastrophe has plunged the world into an uncertain new era. A decade ago, when the Cold War was history and nations rushed to embrace free markets, the world seemed united by shared opportunity. It now seems united by a dread of risk.

After living through the past year, Americans have some legitimate reasons to be scared. We have learned that there are terrorists who want to destroy this country. People can be killed by opening envelopes containing anthrax. In the business world some respected executives have turned out to be brazen cheaters. And the stock market has become far less reliable than most people used to think. The bear market is both a symptom of the fears and a cause of them. But there is a chance that the pendulum is swinging too far, right past prudence and into the realm of unreasoning fear. There is a danger that America could scare itself into stagnation, retreating so much that economic growth stalls.

This time around, a retreat of investors from risk taking could have a broader impact. Start with infrastructure. Cut off from access to capital, phone and cable companies are being forced to scale back the deployment of broadband communications networks, which potentially could have enormous payoffs. Many new products will never get their shot at success as companies struggle to find the capital necessary to roll them out on a large scale. An aversion to risk taking could force companies to skimp on research and development, delaying the introduction of as-yet-unimagined products in a variety of fields ranging from software, to biotechnology, to fuel cells.

It's not just about money. Innovative companies are having a harder time getting and retaining workers. "Three years ago we had people standing in line wanting to go to early-stage companies because they thought there would be a windfall," says Steve Maxwell, an executive recruiter in Boston for Russell Reynolds Associates. Now seasoned managers would rather sit tight. "There is more risk aversion than at any time during the past several years," says James W. Breyer, managing partner of venture capitalist Accel Partners in Palo Alto, California.

One of the less recognized advances of the boom years was financial innovation, and now that's under assault. Investment banks had engineered new ways for companies to hedge or speculate. Today, understandably, many CEOs don't want the words *creative* and *finance* to appear within five miles of each other. But clamping down on the legitimate use of financial tools could make companies less efficient and more unstable.

It would be especially troubling if *risk* became a dirty word. The trick is to have a clear-eyed view of the trade-offs between risks and rewards. A sensible level of confidence—neither the euphoria of the 1990s nor the fear of the 2000s—would benefit just about everyone.

SOURCE: Alison Stein Wellner, "What Comes Next," *Business Week*, December 4, 2000, 3710, p. F24; Peter Coy, "When Business Is Scared Stagnant," *Business Week*, August 26, 2002.

QUESTIONS

1. How would these forecasts affect the planning process in organizations?

2. Is the impact different for small firms versus large firms?

3. What other forecasts might you have made if you had had a "crystal ball" and could have predicted September 11?

4.1   Strategic Planning

OBJECTIVE

To study the strategic planning of a corporation recently in the news.

INSTRUCTIONS

Business Week magazine frequently has articles on the strategies of various corporations. Find a recent article on a corporation in an industry of interest to you. Read the article and answer the following questions.

Strategic Planning Worksheet

1. Has the firm clearly identified what business it is in and how it is different from its competitors? Explain.

_____

_____

_____

_____

_____

_____

2. What are the key assumptions about the future that have shaped the firm's new strategy?

_____

_____

_____

_____

_____

_____

3. What key strengths and weaknesses of the firm influenced the selection of the new strategy?

_____
_____
_____
_____
_____
_____

4. What specific objectives has the firm set in conjunction with the new strategy?

_____
_____
_____
_____
_____
_____

SOURCE: R. R. McGrath, Jr., _Exercises in Management Fundamentals_, p. 15. Copyright © 1984. Reprinted by permission of Pearson Education, Inc., Upper Saddle River, NJ.

4.2   Formulating Business Strategy

OBJECTIVES

1. To illustrate the complex interrelationships central to the formulation of business strategy.
2. To demonstrate the use of SWOT (strengths, weaknesses, opportunities, and threats) analysis in a business situation.

INSTRUCTIONS

1. Your instructor will divide the class into small groups and assign each group a well-known organization for analysis.
2. Each group will
   a. Study the SWOT Introduction and the SWOT Worksheet to understand the work needed to complete the assignment.
   b. Obtain the needed information about the organization under study through library research, interviews, and so on.
   c. Complete the SWOT Worksheet.
   d. Prepare group responses to the discussion questions
3. After the class reconvenes, group spokespersons will present group findings.

DISCUSSION QUESTIONS

1. Why would most organizations not develop strategies for matches between opportunities and strengths?
2. Why would most organizations not develop strategies for matches between opportunities and weaknesses?
3. Why do most organizations want to deal from strength?

SWOT INTRODUCTION

One of the more commonly used strategy tools is SWOT (strengths, weaknesses, opportunities, and threats) analysis, which is accomplished in four steps:

Step 1: Analyze the organization's internal environment, identifying its strengths and weaknesses.

Step 2: Analyze the organization's external environment, identifying its opportunities and threats.

Step 3: Match (1) strengths with opportunities, (2) weaknesses with threats, (3) strengths with threats, and (4) weaknesses with opportunities.

Step 4: Develop strategies for those matches which appear to be of greatest importance to the organization. Most organizations give top priority to strategies that involve the matching of strengths with opportunities and second priority to strategies that involve the matching of weaknesses with threats. The key is to exploit opportunities in areas where the organization has a strength and to defend against threats in areas where the organization has a weakness.

SWOT Worksheet

Organization being analyzed: _____

Internal Analysis	External Analysis

Strengths

_____
_____
_____
_____
_____
_____

Opportunities

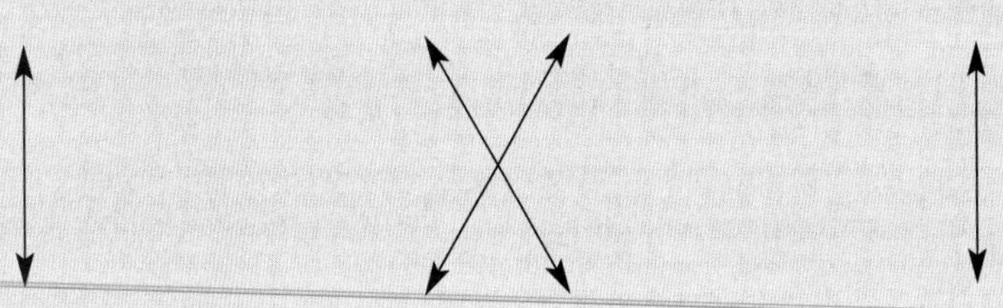

_____
_____
_____
_____
_____
_____
_____
_____
_____
_____
_____

Weaknesses

_____
_____
_____
_____
_____
_____
_____

Threats

_____
_____
_____
_____
_____
_____
_____

Strategies that match strengths with opportunities	Strategies that match weaknesses with threats
_____	_____
_____	_____
_____	_____
_____	_____
_____	_____
_____	_____
_____	_____
_____	_____
_____	_____
_____	_____
_____	_____
_____	_____
_____	_____
_____	_____

Strategies that match strengths with threats	Strategies that match weaknesses with opportunities
_____	_____
_____	_____
_____	_____
_____	_____
_____	_____
_____	_____
_____	_____
_____	_____
_____	_____
_____	_____
_____	_____
_____	_____
_____	_____

CHAPTER 5

Ethics and Corporate Responsibility

It is truly enough said that a corporation has no conscience; but a corporation of conscientious men is a corporation with a conscience.

—Henry David Thoreau

CHAPTER OUTLINE

Ethics
  Ethical Systems
  Business Ethics
  The Ethics Environment
  Ethical Decision Making
Corporate Social Responsibility
  Contrasting Views
  Reconciliation
  Corporate Social Responsiveness
The Political Environment
  Competitive Advantage
  Corporate Legitimacy
  Strategies for Influencing the Political
    Environment
The Natural Environment
  A Risk Society
  Ecocentric Management
  Environmental Agenda for the Future

LEARNING OBJECTIVES

After studying Chapter 5, you will know:

1. How different ethical perspectives guide decision making.

2. How companies influence the ethics environment.

3. The options you have when confronting ethical issues.

4. The important issues surrounding corporate social responsibility.

5. How the political and social environment affects your firm's competitive position and legitimacy.

6. The strategies corporations use to manage the political and social environment.

7. The role of managers in our natural environment.

CORPORATE AMERICA: HOW'S IT DOING?

In a recent survey in the United States, nearly three-quarters of the respondents believe that business is too powerful, and controls too many aspects of their lives. Slightly less than half think that what's good for business is good for most Americans. And two-thirds think that big profits are more important to big companies than safe, reliable products.

What explains the discontent? This chapter discusses some recent incidents and issues in business news. But to set the context for later specifics, consider some broader explanations:

- Many people are feeling overworked but not getting their fair share of the rewards. Relatedly, most people perceive a growing gap between society's "haves and have-nots," both in the United States and globally.

- Big business is not as accountable as it was in the past. Big government and unions have lost clout, and the power imbalance causes resentment. As *Business Week* put it, "For two decades market deregulation has fostered competition and lowered many prices. But the pendulum may have swung too far for many citizens, who now take the gains for granted and want to dampen the extremes that can come with unfettered capitalism" (p. 146).

- Americans gave credit to corporate America for the prosperity of the 90s; by 2002, they were outraged and resentful.

- A generation ago, antibusiness attitudes were found mostly among young people. Today, they cut across generations, geography, and income levels. Moreover, the Net makes negative information and commentaries more readily available, and provides, to those who care about the issues, additional power to have an impact.

- Customers are frustrated by uncaring HMOs, poor service from airlines and telephone companies, and high drug prices. A small minority believe that large companies are ethical, that they are straightforward and honest in dealing with consumers and employees.

Pollster Daniel Yankelovich states that, "There's an increased readiness to believe negative things about corporations today, which makes it a dangerous time for companies. Executives haven't had to worry about social issues for a generation, but there's a yellow light flashing now, and they better pay attention" (p. 147).

The news gets worse. Those results and quotes came from a poll conducted in August 2000—*before* the Enron, Arthur Andersen, WorldCom, and other scandals created even more cynicism. Enron, at that time the biggest (and fastest) corporate bankruptcy in U.S. history, further rocked people's perceptions of corporate ethics, accounting practices, and financial markets. By early 2002, only 16 percent of Americans reported "a great deal of confidence" in people running major companies; those reporting "hardly any" confidence went to 24 percent from 13 percent in 1999.

Disenchantment with corporate America is widespread, and a real problem.

Two-thirds of Americans gave corporate America credit for the prosperity of the 90s. But three-quarters believe that it's too powerful, and controls too many aspects of their lives.

Sources: A. Bernstein, "Too Much Corporate Power?," *Business Week*, September 11, 2000, pp. 145–58; "*BusinessWeek*/Harris Poll: "A Growing Sense of Anger," *Business Week*, February 4, 2002, p. 35; A. Bernstein, with B. Grow, D. Little, S. Holmes, and D. Brady, "Bracing for a Backlash," *Business Week*, February 4, 2002, pp. 34–36; L. Walczak, R. Dunham, and P. Dwer. Let the Reforms Begin. *Business Week*, July 22, 2002, pp. 26–31.

In the wake of their bankruptcies, Enron and WorldCom became shorthand for corporate scandal. The sagas engulfed company executives, Wall Street accountants, politicians and regulators, and shareholders and employees.[1] One cause: a culture of greed and arrogance that bred excessive secrecy.

A culture of misformation and secrecy is typical of some other public companies that have given in to the pressure to inflate stock prices by all possible means.[2] The failure has undermined the public's trust in the integrity of the public markets. Stated one CEO: "Credibility and trust is everything. And because of the recession, because of Enron, that trust has evaporated."[3]

The Enron, WorldCom, and related cases raised a lot of issues, and continue to have repercussions. What companies should do in the wake of the scandals seems simple:[4] Make sure your own accounting and financial-reporting practices are solid; explain how you report your results; double-check the independence of your auditors; speak clearly about your approach to business, and how you make your profits; talk candidly about what is and isn't acceptable behavior. But do you know what the problem is with using Enron and companies like it as examples of lax company ethics? It's too easy. It's perfectly clear that there are "bad guys" in these cases, and many of the ethical lapses are now obvious. It becomes too easy to say, "I would never do things like that."

Many of the decisions you will face will pose ethical dilemmas, and the "right thing to do" is not nearly as evident as it is in recent big-news business scandals.

This chapter discusses ethics, and the social responsibilities of business.

Ethics

The aim of ethics is to identify both the rules that should govern people's behavior and the "goods" that are worth seeking. Ethical decisions are guided by the underlying values of the individual. Values are principles of conduct such as caring, honesty, keeping of promises, pursuit of excellence, loyalty, fairness, integrity, respect for others, and responsible citizenship.[5]

ethics

The system of rules governing the ordering of values.

Most people would agree that all of these values are admirable guidelines for behavior. However, ethics becomes a more complicated issue when a situation dictates that one value overrule others. **Ethics** is the system of rules that governs the ordering of values.

ethical issue

Situation, problem, or opportunity in which an individual must choose among several actions that must be evaluated as right or wrong.

An **ethical issue** is a situation, problem, or opportunity in which an individual must choose among several actions that must be evaluated as right or wrong.[6] Ethical issues arise in every facet of life; we concern ourselves here with business ethics in particular. **Business ethics** comprises the moral principles and standards that guide behavior in the world of business.[7]

business ethics

The moral principles and standards that guide behavior in the world of business.

Ethical Systems

Moral philosophy refers to the principles, rules, and values people use in deciding what is right or wrong. This is a simple definition in the abstract, but often terribly complex and difficult when facing real choices. How do you decide what is right and wrong? Do you know what criteria you apply, and how you apply them?

moral philosophy

Principles, rules, and values people use in deciding what is right or wrong.

Ethics scholars point to various major ethical systems as guides.[8] The first ethical system, **universalism,** states that individuals should uphold certain values, such as honesty, regardless of the immediate result. The important values are those that society needs to function. For instance, people should always be honest because otherwise communication would break down.

universalism

The ethical system upholding certain values regardless of immediate result.

But rarely are things so simple. Before we describe other ethical systems, consider the following example, and think about how you or others would resolve it. Remember, what you would do is not necessarily what others would do. And what people say, hope, or think they would do is often different from what they *really* would do, faced with the demands and pressures of the real situation.

Suppose that Sam Colt, a sales representative, is preparing a sales presentation for his firm, Midwest Hardware, which manufactures nuts and bolts. Colt hopes to obtain a large sale from a construction firm that is building a bridge across the Missouri River near St. Louis. The bolts manufactured by Midwest Hardware have a 3 percent defect rate, which, although acceptable in the industry, makes them unsuitable for use in certain types of projects, such as those that might be subject to sudden, severe stress. The new bridge will be located near the New Madrid Fault line, the source of the United States' greatest earthquake in 1811. The epicenter of that earthquake, which caused extensive damage and altered the flow of the Missouri, is about 190 miles from the new bridge site.

Bridge construction in the area is not regulated by earthquake codes. If Colt wins the sale, he will earn a commission of $25,000 on top of his regular salary. But if he tells the contractors about the defect rate, Midwest may lose the sale to a competitor whose bolts are slightly more reliable. Thus, Colt's ethical issue is whether to point out to the bridge contractor that in the event of an earthquake, some Midwest bolts could fail.

SOURCE: O. C. Farrell and J. Fraedrich, *Business Ethics: Ethical Decision Making and Cases*, 3rd ed. Copyright © 1997 by Houghton Mifflin Company. Used with permission.

Not everyone would behave the same in this scenario. Different individuals would apply different moral philosophies. Consider each of the following moral philosophies and the actions to which they might lead in the bridge example.[9]

Teleology **Teleology** considers an act to be morally right or acceptable if it produces a desired result. The result can be anything desired by the person, including pleasure, personal growth, money, knowledge, or other self-interest. The key criterion is the consequences of the act, so teleology is sometimes referred to as consequentialism.

> **teleology**
>
> Considers an act to be morally right or acceptable if it produces a desired result.

Two types of teleology are *egoism* and *utilitarianism*. **Egoism** defines acceptable behavior as that which maximizes consequences for the individual. "Doing the right thing," the focus of moral philosophy, is defined by egoism as "do the act that promotes the greatest good for oneself." If everyone follows this system, according to its proponents, the well-being of society as a whole should increase. This notion is similar to Adam Smith's concept of the invisible hand in business. Smith argued that if every organization follows its own economic self-interest, the total wealth of society will be maximized.

> **egoism**
>
> An ethical system defining acceptable behavior as that which maximizes consequences for the individual.

Utilitarianism is also concerned with consequences, and as such is a teleological philosophy. But unlike egoism, utilitarianism seeks the greatest good for the greatest number of people. A utilitarian approach seeks to maximize total utility, achieving the greatest benefit for people affected by a decision.

> **utilitarianism**
>
> An ethical system stating that the greatest good for the greatest number should be the overriding concern of decision makers.

Deontology **Deontology** focuses on the rights of individuals. Attention to individual rights ensures that equal respect is given to all persons. In this way, actions that maximize utility for many parties will be rejected if they do serious injustice to just one party. In contrast, utilitarianism might allow such an action in the spirit of maximizing overall consequences. Utilitarianism concentrates more on ends, and deontology more on means.

> **deontology**
>
> Focuses on rights of individuals.

What criteria do *you* use? You may or may not be able at this point to choose the perspective that you use or would use in making tough decisions. But it should be clear that ethical issues can be evaluated from many different perspectives, that each perspective has a different basis for deciding right and wrong, and that people will disagree because they are assessing ethics by different ethical standards.

Relativism   Perhaps it seems clear that the individual makes ethical choices on a personal basis, applying personal perspectives. But this is not necessarily the case. **Relativism** defines ethical behavior based on the opinions and behaviors of relevant other people. This perspective acknowledges the existence of different ethical viewpoints, and turns to other people for advice, input, and opinions. Professional bodies provide guidelines to follow, and decision makers can convene a group to share perspectives and derive conclusions. Group consensus is sought; a positive consensus signifies that an action is right, ethical, and acceptable.

relativism

Bases ethical behavior on the opinions and behaviors of relevant other people.

virtue ethics

A perspective that what is moral comes from what a mature person with "good" moral character would deem right.

Virtue ethics   The moral philosophies just described apply different types of rules and reasoning. **Virtue ethics** is a perspective that goes beyond the conventional rules of society by suggesting that what is moral must also come from what a mature person with "good" moral character would deem right. Society's rules provide a moral minimum, and then moral individuals can transcend rules by applying their personal virtues such as faith, honesty, and integrity.

Individuals differ in this regard. **Kohlberg's model of cognitive moral development** classifies people into one of three categories based on their level of moral judgment.[10] People in the *preconventional* stage make decisions based on concrete rewards and punishments and immediate self-interest. People in the *conventional* stage conform to the expectations of ethical behavior held by groups or institutions such as society, family, or

Kohlberg's model of cognitive moral development

Classifies people based on their level of moral judgment.

peers. People in the *principled* stage take a broader perspective in which they see beyond authority, laws, and norms and follow their self-chosen ethical principles.[11] Some people forever reside in the preconventional stage, some move into the conventional stage, and some develop further yet into the principled stage. Over time, and through education and experience, people may change their values and ethical behavior.

Returning to the bolts-in-the-bridge example, *egoism* would result in keeping quiet about the bolts' defect rate. *Utilitarianism* would dictate a more thorough cost-benefit analysis and possibly the conclusion that the probability of a bridge collapse is so low compared to the utility of jobs, economic growth, and company growth that the defect rate is not worth mentioning. *Deontology* would likely create an obligation to tell because of the potential danger. The *relativist* perspective might prompt the salesperson to look at company policy and general industry practice, and to seek opinions from colleagues and perhaps trade journals and ethics codes. Whatever is then perceived to

The average CEO earned $13.1 million in 2001, according to the results of Business Week's 51st annual Executive Pay Scoreboard, compiled with Standard & Poor's Institutional Market Services. Steve Jobs, of Apple Computer Inc., landed the mother of all bonuses after three years of working for free: his own $90 million jet, a Gulfstream V. Outrageous, some would say. Perfectly ethical, say others.

be a consensus or normal practice would dictate action. And finally, *virtue ethics*, applied by people in the principled stage of moral development, would likely lead to full disclosure about the product and risks, and perhaps suggestions for alternatives that would reduce the risk.[12]

These major ethical systems underlie personal moral choices and ethical decisions in business.

Business Ethics

Insider trading, illegal campaign contributions, bribery, famous court cases, and other scandals have created a perception that business leaders use illegal means to gain competitive advantage, increase profits, or improve their personal positions. Until the Enron/Andersen scandal, shareholders tended to ignore fraudulent financial reporting, as long as profits and market share didn't suffer.[13] In a recent survey of 200 professionals, 35 percent admitted lying to customers and colleagues. By the way, you might find it interesting that surveys suggest that males are more likely to behave unethically than females.[14]

Neither young managers[15] nor consumers[16] believe top executives are doing a good job of establishing high ethical standards. Some even joke that *business ethics* has become a contradiction in terms.

Most business leaders believe they uphold ethical standards in business practices.[17] But many managers and their organizations must deal frequently with ethical dilemmas, and the issues are becoming increasingly complex. For example, many people seek spiritual renewal in the workplace, in part reflecting a broader religious awakening in America, while others argue that this trend violates religious freedom and the separation of church and boardroom.[18] Tables 5.1 and 5.2 show some important examples of ethical dilemmas in business.

Think about this: Just how ethical are businesspeople? Opinions differ.

Are businesspeople ethical? The following statements are taken from a recent article in *Across the Board*, an influential magazine for American executives:

- Business "is a game with different rules from those that apply to the rest of society." (p. 17)
- "Most large firms ... suffer from a surfeit of ethics. They have their high ethics ... ethics as it is preached. Then they also have an ethics as it is practiced." (p. 18)
- MBA students "won't necessarily cheat or lie more than other people, but they ... are more willing to accept the unethicalness of others, because they expect it as normal." (p. 18)
- "Is there something about large business organizations in particular that leads people astray? The answer seems to be: just about everything." (p. 18)
- "The essence of business is competition, making business still a game where winning matters more than how the game is played." (p. 21)
- "In most of the infamous cases of corporate wrongdoing—the exploding Pinto is a famous example—it was not just one person who did wrong but sometimes dozens." (p. 21)
- "Everyone agrees that lying is unethical, but misrepresentation during a purchase negotiation is widely considered not to be lying, because if all parties know that everyone is lying there is no deception and thus no sin." (p. 22)

On the other hand, this article generated outrage from many readers, who wrote in a subsequent issue of the magazine:

- "[I and others] would strongly debate the notion that business ethics is different from everyday ethics." (p. 48)
- "For every unethical or amoral manager, there is at least another manager trying to do the right thing for the right reasons." (p. 48)
- "People can make the difference. They can set the tone of ethical behavior ... it's imperative. It will make the difference for the future. Because a sale is nice, but the future is the future." (p. 49)
- "There are certainly many companies—even hierarchical ones operating in highly competitive environments with enormous sums of money at stake—whose managers do behave responsibly, indeed sometimes even courageously." (p. 49)
- "Business will (must) act in such a way that its market approves. Thank goodness that today's societal market demands accountability and checks ethical behavior." (p. 50)
- "At the heart of business success ... is customer or client trust and loyalty. This trust and loyalty is [sic] built by product or service credibility, reliability, and performance,

Differences of Opinion

which is [sic] reinforced by ethical standards and behavior. Attempting to define business interests and ethical interests as separate, or antithetical, ignores this fundamental fact of how business survives and prospers." (p. 50)

SOURCES: J. Krohe Jr., "Ethics Are Nice, but Business Is Business," *Across the Board*, April 1997, pp. 16–22; and D. Driscoll, M. Rion, M. Roth, D. Vogel, L. Pincus, and D. Orlov, "Who Says Ethics Are 'Nice'?" *Across the Board*, June 1997, pp. 47–50. Reprinted with permission of the Conference Board.

TABLE 5.1
Some Current Ethical Issues

ARTISTIC CONTROL Rock musicians, independent filmmakers, and other artists are rebelling against control by big media and retail companies.
BRANDS In-your-face marketing campaigns have sparked antibrand attitudes among students.
CEO PAY Nearly three-fourths of Americans see executive pay packages as excessive.
COMMERCIALISM IN SCHOOLS Parent groups have mounted battles in hundreds of communities against advertising in the public schools.
CONSUMERISM Anger and frustration are mounting over high gasoline and drug prices, poor airline service, and HMOs that override doctors' decisions.
FRANKENFOODS Europeans' skepticism about genetically modified food is taking hold in the United States, making targets of companies such as Monsanto.
GLOBALIZATION Environmentalists, students, and unionists charge that global trade and economic bodies operate in the interests of multinational companies.
POLITICS Public revulsion over the corporate bankrolling of politicians has energized campaign-finance reform activists.
SWEATSHOPS Anti-sweatshop groups have sprung up on college campuses; they routinely picket clothing manufacturers, toymakers, and retailers.
URBAN SPRAWL Groups in more than 100 cities have blocked big-box superstores by Wal-Mart and other chains.
WAGES Some 56 percent of workers feel they are underpaid, especially as wages since 1992 have topped inflation by 7.6 percent, while productivity is up 17.9 percent.

SOURCE: A. Bernstein, "Too Much Corporate Power?" *Business Week*, September 11, 2000, pp. 146–47.

The Ethics Environment

Ethics are not shaped only by society and by individual development and virtue. They also may be influenced by the company's work environment. The **ethical climate** of an organization refers to the processes by which decisions are evaluated and made on the basis of right and wrong.[19]

ethical climate

In an organization it refers to the processes by which decisions are evaluated and made on the basis of right and wrong.

When people make decisions that are judged by ethical criteria, these questions always seem to get asked: Why did she do it? Good motives or bad ones? His responsibility or someone else's? Who gets the credit, or the blame? So often, responsibility for unethical acts is placed squarely on the individual who commits them. But the work environment has a profound influence, as well.

Consider the question of responsibility in the case of illegal, unethical actions at Sears, Roebuck. Sears, Roebuck did not set out to defraud its automotive service customers in the early 1990s. Nor did employees necessarily intend to cheat consumers. But when the company instituted high-pressure, unrealistic quotas and incentives, people's judg-

TABLE 5.2
Ethical Decision Making in
the International Context

What would you do in each of these true-life situations, and why?

- You are a sales representative for a construction company in the Middle East. Your company wants very much to land a particular project. The cousin of the minister who will award the contract informs you that the minister wants $20,000 in addition to the standard fees. If you do not make this payment, your competition certainly will—and will get the contract.

- You are international vice president of a multinational chemical corporation. Your company is the sole producer of an insecticide that will effectively combat a recent infestation of West African crops. The minister of agriculture in a small, developing African country has put in a large order for your product. Your insecticide is highly toxic and is banned in the United States. You inform the minister of the risks of using your product, but he insists on using it and claims it will be used "intelligently." The president of your company believes you should fill the order, but the decision ultimately is yours.

- You are a new marketing manager for a large automobile tire manufacturer. Your company's advertising agency has just presented plans for introducing a new tire into the Southeast Asia market. Your tire is a truly good product, but the proposed advertising is deceptive. For example, the "reduced price" was reduced from a hypothetical amount that was established only so it could be "reduced," and claims that the tire was tested under the "most adverse" conditions ignore the fact that it was not tested in prolonged tropical heat and humidity. Your superiors are not concerned about deceptive advertising, and they are counting on you to see that the tire does extremely well in the new market. Will you approve the ad plan?

SOURCE: N. Adler, *International Dimensions of Organizational Behavior*, 2nd ed. (Boston: Kent, 1997).

ment was affected. Management did not make clear the distinction between unnecessary service and legitimate preventive maintenance. Moreover, customers were often ignorant or oblivious. A vast gray area of repair options was exaggerated, overinterpreted, and misrepresented. The company may not have intended to deceive customers, but the result of the work environment was that consumers and attorneys general in more than 40 states accused the company of fraud. The total cost of the settlement was an estimated $60 million.[20]

As illustrated by the Sears example, unethical corporate behavior may be the responsibility of an unethical individual; but it often also reveals a company culture that is ethically lax.[21]

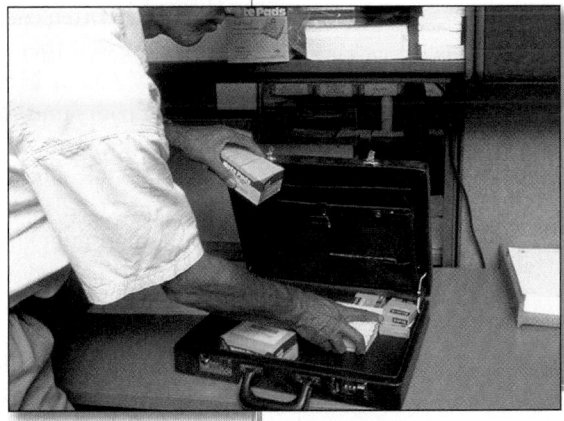

Employees sometimes feel that "borrowing" a few office supplies from their company helps conpensate for any perceived inequities in pay or other benefits.

Danger Signs   In organizations, it is an ongoing challenge to maintain consistent ethical behavior by all employees. What are some danger signs that an organization may be allowing or even encouraging unethical behavior among its people? Many factors create a climate conducive to unethical behavior, including (1) excessive emphasis on short-term revenues over longer-term considerations; (2) failure to establish a written code of ethics; (3) a desire for simple, "quick fix" solutions to ethical problems; (4) an unwillingness to take an ethical stand that may impose financial costs; (5) consideration of ethics solely as a legal issue or a public relations tool; (6) lack of clear procedures for handling ethical problems; and (7) responding to the demands of shareholders at the expense of other constituencies.[22]

Corporate Ethical Standards   People often give in to what they perceive to be the pressures or preferences of powerful others. States Professor Arthur Brief of Tulane University, "If the boss says, 'Achieve a specific sales or profit target, period,'

I think people will do their very best to achieve those directions even if it means sacrificing their own values. They may not like it, but they define it as part of the job."[23]

Although it's easy to find excuses for unethical behavior, the excuses are often bogus.[24] "I was told to do it" implies no thought and blind obedience. "Everybody's doing it" often really means that someone is doing it, but it's rarely everybody; regardless, conventional doesn't mean correct. "Might equals right" is a rationalization. "It's not my problem" is sometimes a wise perspective, if it's a battle you can't win, but sometimes it's just a cop-out. "I didn't mean for that to happen, it just felt right at the time" can be prevented with more forethought and analysis.

IBM uses a guideline for business conduct that asks employees to determine whether under the full glare of examination by associates, friends, and family, they would remain comfortable with their decisions. One suggestion is to imagine how you would feel if you saw your decision and its consequences on the front page of the newspaper.[25] This "light of day" or "sunshine" ethical framework is extremely powerful.[26]

Such fear of exposure compels people more strongly in some cultures than in others. In Asia, anxiety about losing face often makes executives resign immediately if they are caught in ethical transgressions, or if their companies are embarrassed by revelations in the press. By contrast, in the United States, exposed executives might respond with indignation, intransigence, pleading the 5th amendment, stonewalling, an everyone-else-does-it self-defense, or by not admitting wrongdoing and giving no sign that resignation ever crossed their minds. Partly because of legal tradition, the attitude often is: Never explain, never apologize, don't admit the mistake, do not resign, even if the entire world knows exactly what happened.[27]

Ethics Codes   One visible sign of possible corporate commitment to ethical behavior is a written code of ethics. Often, the statements are just for show, but when implemented well they can change a company's ethical climate for the better and truly encourage ethical behavior.

Ethics codes must be carefully written and tailored to individual companies' philosophies. Aetna Life & Casualty believes that tending to the broader needs of society is essential to fulfilling its economic role. Johnson & Johnson has one of the most famous ethics codes (see Table 5.3). J&J consistently receives high rankings for community and social responsibility in *Fortune*'s annual survey of corporate reputations.

Most ethics codes address subjects such as employee conduct, community and environment, shareholders, customers, suppliers and contractors, political activity, and technology. Often the codes are drawn up by the organizations' legal departments and begin with research into other companies' codes. The Ethics Resource Center in Washington assists companies interested in establishing a corporate code of ethics.[28]

To make an ethics code effective, do the following:[29] (1) involve those who have to live with it in writing the statement; (2) have a corporate statement, but also allow separate statements by different units throughout the organization; (3) keep it short and therefore easily understood and remembered; (4) don't make it too corny—make it something important that people really believe in; and (5) set the tone at the top, having executives talk about and live up to the statement. When reality differs from the statement—as when a motto says people are our most precious asset or a product is the finest in the world, but in fact people are treated poorly or product quality is weak—the statement becomes a joke to employees rather than a guiding light.[30]

Ethics Programs   Corporate ethics programs commonly include formal ethics codes articulating the company's expectations regarding ethics; ethics committees that develop policies, evaluate actions, and investigate violations; ethics communication

> *We believe our first responsibility is to the doctors, nurses, and patients, to mothers and all others who use our products and services.* In meeting their needs everything we do must be of high quality. We must constantly strive to reduce our costs in order to maintain reasonable prices. Customers' orders must be serviced promptly and accurately. Our suppliers and distributors must have an opportunity to make a fair profit.
>
> *We are responsible to our employees:* the men and women who work with us throughout the world. Everyone must be considered as an individual. We must respect their dignity and recognize their merit. They must have a sense of security in their jobs. Compensation must be fair and adequate, and working conditions clean, orderly, and safe. Employees must feel free to make suggestions and complaints. There must be equal opportunity for employment, development, and advancement for those qualified. We must provide competent management, and their actions must be just and ethical.
>
> *We are responsible to the communities in which we live and work and to the world community as well.*
>
> *We must be good citizens*—support good works and charities and bear our fair share of taxes. We must encourage civic improvements and better health and education.
>
> *We must maintain in good order the property we are privileged to use, protecting the environment and natural resources.*
>
> *Our final responsibility is to our stockholders.* Business must make a sound profit. We must experiment with new ideas. Research must be carried on, innovative programs developed, and mistakes paid for. New equipment must be purchased, new facilities provided, and new products launched. Reserves must be created to provide for adverse times.
>
> When we operate according to these principles, the stockholders should realize a fair return.

TABLE 5.3
Johnson & Johnson's Ethics Code

SOURCE: Reprinted with permission of Johnson & Johnson.

systems giving employees a means of reporting problems or getting guidance; ethics officers or ombudspersons who investigate allegations and provide education; ethics training programs; and disciplinary processes for addressing unethical behavior.[31]

Ethics programs can range from compliance-based to integrity-based.[32] **Compliance-based ethics programs** are designed by corporate counsel to prevent, detect, and punish legal violations. Compliance-based programs increase surveillance and controls on people and impose punishments on wrongdoers. Program elements include establishing and communicating legal standards and procedures, assigning high-level managers to oversee compliance, auditing and monitoring compliance, reporting criminal misconduct, punishing wrongdoers, and taking steps to prevent offenses in the future.

Such programs should reduce illegal behavior and help the company stay out of court. But they do not create a moral commitment to ethical conduct; they merely ensure moral mediocrity. As Richard Breeden, former chairman of the SEC, said, "It is not an adequate ethical standard to aspire to get through the day without being indicted."[33]

Integrity-based ethics programs go beyond the mere avoidance of illegality; they are concerned with the law but also with instilling in people a personal responsibility for ethical behavior. With such a program, companies and people govern themselves through a set of guiding principles that they embrace.

> **compliance-based ethics programs**
>
> Company mechanisms typically designed by corporate counsel to prevent, detect, and punish legal violations.

> **integrity-based ethics programs**
>
> Company mechanisms designed to instill in people a personal responsibility for ethical behavior.

This ad from the National Organization on Disabilities is a public service message that promotes the value of people with disabilities. Its intent is to break down the stereotypes that often cause companies to overlook or not hire disabled workers.

For example, the Americans with Disabilities Act (ADA) requires companies to change the physical work environment so it will allow people with disabilities to function on the job. Mere compliance would involve making the necessary changes to avoid legal problems. Integrity-based programs would go further by training people to understand and perhaps change attitudes toward people with disabilities, and sending clear signals that people with disabilities also have valued abilities. This goes far beyond taking action to stay out of trouble with the law.

When top management has more personal commitment to responsible ethical behavior, programs tend to be better integrated into operations, thinking, and behavior. For example,[34] at a meeting of about 25 middle managers at a major financial services firm, every one of them told the company's general counsel that they had never seen or heard of the company's ethics policy document. The policies existed but were not a part of the everyday thinking of managers. In contrast, one health care products company bases one-third of managers' annual pay raises on how well they carry out the company's ethical ideals. Their ethical behavior is assessed by superiors, peers, and subordinates—making ethics a thoroughly integrated aspect of the way the company and its people do business.

Companies with strong integrity-based programs include Martin Marietta, NovaCare (a provider of rehabilitation services to hospitals and nursing homes), and Wetherill Associates (a supplier of electrical parts to the automotive market). These companies believe that their programs contribute to competitiveness, higher morale, and sustainable relationships with key stakeholders.[35]

Ethical Decision Making

Good people sometimes commit unethical acts because they do not carefully think through the consequences and implications of their actions.[36] Corporate policies can help ensure ethical decision making. And you may be able to buy some time, analyze the subtleties, and let your moral instincts emerge.[37] In addition, some guidelines for decision making may help you avoid inadvertent ethical breaches.[38]

First, *define the issue clearly*. What is the context of the issue? Who are the affected stakeholders? Talk to various stakeholders to ensure that all the facts are considered. Often a decision maker omits this step, assuming he already understands the problem without stopping to consider all of its components.

Second, *identify the relevant values in the situation*. Any ethical dilemma involves multiple values: the various consequences of your choices, what you care about the most, and what others care about the most. Clearly stating these values focuses attention on the ethical component of the decision.

Third, *weigh the conflicting values and choose an option that balances them*, with greatest emphasis on the most important values. At this stage, the decision maker must decide which values are more important than others. Companies that have clearly defined their values through a code of ethics and other actions already have clarified the value priorities. In organizations in which values are unclear or inconsistent, balancing the values is a more difficult challenge.

Fourth, *implement the decision*. This step may require justifying your actions. Because the short- and long-term ethical consequences already have been assessed, you can more effectively defend the decision to stakeholders.

What can you do if you see managers in your company behaving in ways that go against your ethical principles? Sherron Watkins warned Enron's then-chairman, Kenneth Lay, of major irregularities in the company's accounting practices months before the corporation collapsed.[39] "I am incredibly nervous that we will implode in a wave of accounting scandals," she wrote directly to Lay after her first, anonymous memo was ignored. Ultimately she became something of a hero, but the road for whistleblowers—people who tell others, inside or outside the organization, of the wrongdoing they observe—is a very tough one. Most regret having blown the whistle.[40] Your other options include the following, among others:[41] (1) Don't think about it; (2) go along with it to avoid conflict; (3) object, verbally or via memo; (4) quit; or (5) negotiate and build a consensus for changing the unethical behavior. What are the advantages and disadvantages of each of these options? What other options can you think of? What do you think determines which option a person chooses?

Corporate Social Responsibility

Should business be responsible for social concerns lying beyond its own economic well-being? Do social concerns affect a corporation's financial performance? The extent of business's responsibility for noneconomic concerns has been hotly debated. In the 1960s and 1970s, the political and social environment became more important to U.S. corporations as society turned its attention to issues like equal opportunity, pollution control, energy and natural resource conservation, and consumer and worker protection.[42] Public debate addressed these issues and how business should respond to them. This controversy focused on the concept of corporate social responsibility.

Corporate social responsibility is the obligation toward society assumed by business. The socially responsible business maximizes its positive effects on society and minimizes its negative effects.[43]

Social responsibilities can be categorized more specifically,[44] as shown in Figure 5.1. The **economic responsibilities** of business are to produce goods and services that society wants at a price that perpetuates the business and satisfies its obligations to investors.

Legal responsibilities are to obey local, state, federal, and relevant international laws. **Ethical responsibilities** include meeting other societal expectations, not written as law. As such, ethics is one dimension of social responsibility. Finally, **voluntary responsibilities** are additional behaviors and activities that society finds desirable and that the values of the business support. Examples include supporting community projects and making charitable contributions.

Although criteria and standards for determining these responsibilities vary among organizations and countries, some efforts have been made to establish sets of global or universal ethical principles. For example, it is widely agreed that all people are morally obligated to adhere to core principles such as avoid harm to others, respect the autonomy of others, avoid lying, and honor agreements.[45] Appendix B shows the international ethics code created by the Caux Roundtable in Switzerland, collaborating with business leaders from Europe, Japan, and the United States.

corporate social responsibility

Obligation toward society assumed by business.

economic responsibilities

To produce goods and services that society wants at a price that perpetuates the business and satisfies its obligations to investors.

legal responsibilities

To obey local, state, federal, and relevant international laws.

ethical responsibilities

Meeting other social expectations, not written as law.

voluntary responsibilities

Additional behaviors and activities that society finds desirable and that the values of the business support.

Contrasting Views

Two basic and contrasting views about which principles should guide managerial responsibility are common. The first holds that managers act as agents for shareholders and, as such, are obligated to maximize the present value of the firm. This tenet of capitalism is widely associated with the early writings of Adam Smith in *The Wealth of Nations*, and more recently with Milton Friedman, the Nobel Prize–winning economist of the University of Chicago. With his now-famous dictum "The social responsibility of

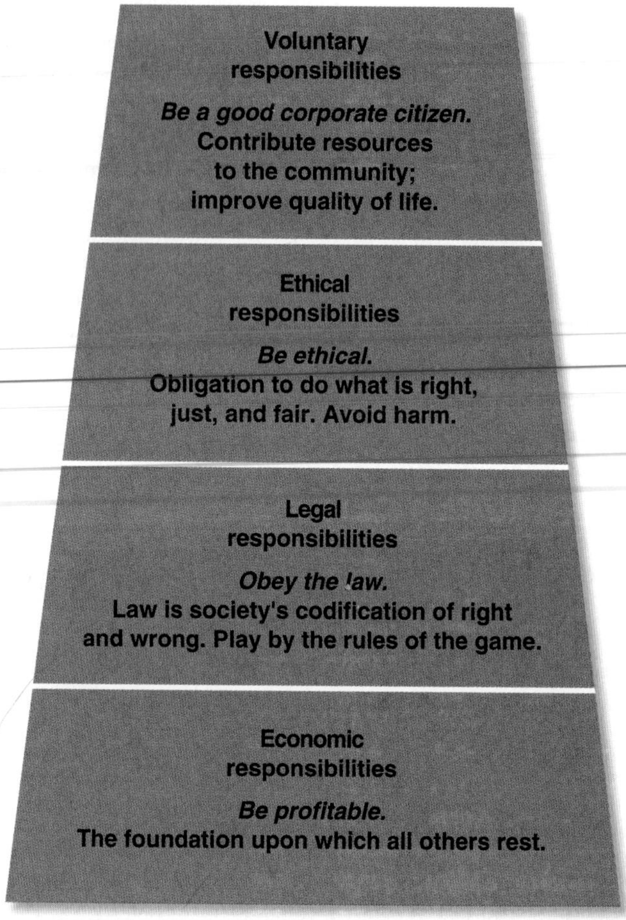

Voluntary
responsibilities

Be a good corporate citizen.
Contribute resources
to the community;
improve quality of life.

Ethical
responsibilities

Be ethical.
Obligation to do what is right,
just, and fair. Avoid harm.

Legal
responsibilities

Obey the law.
Law is society's codification of right
and wrong. Play by the rules of the game.

Economic
responsibilities

Be profitable.
The foundation upon which all others rest.

FIGURE 5.1
The Pyramid of Corporate
Social Responsibility

SOURCE: Archie B.Carroll, "The Pyramid of Corporate Responsibility: Toward the Moral Management of Organization Stake-holders." adaptation of Figure 3, p. 42. Reprinted from *Business Horizon.* July/August 1991. Copyright 1991 by the Trustees at Indiana University, Kelley School of Business.

business is to increase profits," Friedman contended that organizations may help improve the quality of life as long as such actions are directed at increasing profits.

Some considered Friedman to be "the enemy of business ethics," but his position was ethical: He believed that it was unethical for unelected business leaders to decide what was best for society, and unethical for them to spend shareholders' money on projects unconnected to key business interests.[46]

This is the second perspective, different from the profit maximization perspective: that managers should be motivated by principled moral reasoning. Followers of Friedman and *The Wealth of Nations* might sneer at such soft-headed propaganda. But Adam Smith wrote about a world different from the one we are in now, driven in the 18th century by the self-interest of small owner-operated farms and craft shops trying to generate a living income for themselves and their families. This self-interest was quite different from that of top executives of modern corporations.[47] It is interesting to note that Adam Smith also wrote *A Theory of Moral Sentiments*, in which he argued that "sympathy," defined as a proper regard for others, is the basis of a civilized society.[48]

Advocates of corporate social responsibility argue that organizations have a wider range of responsibilities that extend beyond the production of goods and services at a profit. As members of society, organizations should actively and responsibly participate in the community and in the larger environment.

How would these perspectives apply to the following example?

Some people argue that U.S. tobacco companies should not promote tobacco abroad. The tobacco companies disagree. The Chinese already manufacture and consume well over 1 trillion cigarettes annually (90 percent of Chinese males and 63 percent of Japanese males smoke), and the U.S. tobacco industry wants part of that market. U.S. tobacco companies argue that Asians complain about the menace of American cigarette conglomerates but do little in terms of requiring warning labels, prohibiting sales to minors, or banning smoking. Taiwan has a cigarette brand called "Long Life," and Japan's tepid health warning reads, "Please don't smoke too much."

Fewer than 10 percent of Asian women and adolescents smoke, and U.S. companies have promised not to court those markets. Nevertheless, a Taiwanese official complained that U.S. manufacturers handed out cigarettes to 12-year-olds at amusement parks. Critics claim that saturation marketing, depicting smoking as glamorous, rugged, and very Western, is designed to entice the enormous, untapped market of Asian women and teens.

Antismoking activists maintain that an unbridled pursuit of profit is fueling an anti-American backlash and hostility toward other U.S. exports. They are now mounting a global campaign, enlisting the World Health Organization in sanctioning a global treaty, the Framework Convention on Tobacco Control (FCTC). The treaty would make it easier for governments to implement tobacco controls and create a system to monitor compliance.

But the global market is vast: $300 billion in sales, roughly half of which goes to taxes. Public health officials will be pleased if 20 years from now the number of smokers has held steady at 1.25 billion. However, predictive models indicate that far more people will be smoking by then, and the World Bank predicts that 10 million people per year will have tobacco-related deaths by 2030, more than by any other killer. But tobacco interests counter that taxes on their products go directly into the coffers of poor countries that need the money. As the industry sees it, the economic future lies in the developing world.

SOURCES: S. Mallaby, "Trade and Trade-Offs on Tobacco," *The Washington Post*, January 14, 2002, p. A17; E. Brown, "The World Health Organization Takes on Big Tobacco," *Fortune*, September 17, 2001, pp. 117–124; M. Levin, "U.S. Tobacco Firms Push Eagerly into the Asian Market," *Marketing News*, January 21, 1991, pp. 2. 14; P. Schmeiser, "Pushing Cigarettes Overseas," *New York Times Magazine*, July 10, 1988, pp. 16 ff; and A. Bernstein, "Too Much Corporate Power?" *Business Week*, September 11, 2000, pp. 145–58.

Reconciliation

It used to be that profit maximization and corporate social responsibility were regarded as antagonistic, leading to opposing policies. But now, in a more "ethicized" business climate, the two views can converge.[49] As the contemporary British economist and management scholar Charles Handy put it, "Markets, for wealth and efficiency, need to be balanced by sympathy [as Adam Smith defined it], for civilization."[50] The argument that ethical behavior is both right and more profitable is more common today than in the "greed decade" of the 1980s.[51]

Earlier attention to corporate social responsibility focused on alleged wrongdoing and how to control it. More recently, attention has been on the possible competitive advantage of socially responsible actions. For example, a recent study showed that corporate social responsibility enhances company reputations, which in turn makes them more attractive employers, and they attract more applicants.[52] Thus corporate social responsibility can provide competitive advantage by helping to attract and perhaps retain superior employees.

Socially responsible actions can have other long-term advantages for organizations. Companies can avoid unnecessary and costly regulation if they are socially responsible. Honesty and fairness—including admitting mistakes; apologizing genuinely, quickly, and sincerely; and making up for mistakes—may pay great dividends to the conscience, to the personal reputation, to the public image of the company, and in the market response.[53] In addition, society's problems can offer business opportunities, and profits can be made from systematic and vigorous efforts to solve these problems. In other words, it can pay to be good.[54]

Merck, for example, states in its internal management guide, "We are in the business of improving human life. All of our actions must be measured by our success in achieving this goal." Merck got in trouble in 2002 over its financial reporting practices, but historically the company has shown its commitment to improving human life. For example, Merck developed a drug called Mectizan to cure "river blindness," a disease that infected over a million people. That's a big potential market, except that the victims could not afford the product. Merck hoped that someone else would help pay for the cure, but the company gave the drug away for free, and invested in costly distribution efforts to make sure the people who needed it were able to get it.[55]

Asked why Merck did this, then-CEO Roy Vagelos said to not do so would have been to violate the reason the company was in business and would demoralize its scientists. He also cited an earlier example: After World War II, Merck brought streptomycin to Japan to cure tuberculosis, which was devastating Japan. Merck made no money but did tremendous good. And today Merck has a tremendous reputation and presence in Japan.[56]

Corporate Social Responsiveness

How companies respond to the corporate social responsibility debate is called **corporate social responsiveness.**[57] The two are sometimes distinguished by the acronyms CSR1 and CSR2. Whereas CSR1 (corporate social responsibility) refers to principles, philosophies, and beliefs, CSR2 (corporate social responsiveness) refers to the processes companies follow and the actions they take. These processes and strategies are reactive, defensive, accommodative, and proactive. Table 5.4 summarizes these responses.

> **corporate social responsiveness**
>
> **The process companies follow and the actions they take in the domain of corporate social responsibility.**

Corporate social responsibility and responsiveness have their critics, in both academia and business.[58] Critics say these ideas came from outside the business world and are value laden, poorly defined, and vague. To many, they are not as meaningful as stakeholder management. Managers do not manage relationships with society, they say, but with multiple stakeholders. As such, stakeholder management is much more directly relevant, real, and manageable.

Stakeholder management considers key stakeholders and the specific issues relevant to each.[59] For any manager, stakeholders would include the company, employees, shareholders, customers, suppliers, and public stakeholders.[60] *Company issues* include economic performance, organizational mission or purpose, the competitive environment, and corporate codes. *Employee issues* include compensation and rewards, health and assistance programs, leaves of absence, dismissals and appeals, terminations and layoffs, discrimination, family accommodation, safety, career planning, and others. *Shareholder issues* include shareholder rights, advocacy, communications, and complaints. *Customer issues* include communications, complaints, product safety,

TABLE 5.4
Approaches to Corporate Social Responsiveness

Approach	Posture or Strategy	Performance
1. Reactive	Deny responsibility	Do less than required
2. Defensive	Admit responsibility but fight it	Do the least that is required
3. Accommodative	Accept responsibility	Do all that is required
4. Proactive	Anticipate responsibility	Do more than required

SOURCE: M. B. E. Clarkson, "A Stakeholder Framework for Analyzing and Evaluating Corporate Social Performance," *Academy of Management Review* 20, pp. 92–117. Copyright © 1995. Reproduced with permission of Academy of Management via Copyright Clearance Center.

Hanna Anderson has received awards for its community commitment, including a program called Hanna-downs that donates customers' outgrown clothing to local charities and disaster relief.

services, and others. *Supplier issues* include relative power, treatment, and other issues. *Public issues* include public health and safety, energy conservation, public policy, environmental issues, involvement in public policy, social donations, and community relations.

Many of these managerially relevant issues are discussed in other parts of this book. After describing some ethical and social issues surrounding the Internet, we will turn our attention to two issues in particular: the political environment and the natural environment.

The Political Environment

Through regulation, government decision makers exert control over key areas of managerial decision making—areas where managers often do not want to lose control. While managers use public policy to define their social responsibilities, they also may recognize the need to influence the laws and regulations that constitute public policy. Therefore, organizations attempt to influence the political environment to achieve two principal goals within their ethical structures: competitive advantage and corporate legitimacy.

Competitive Advantage

In many cases, the corporate community sees government as an adversary. However, many progressive organizations realize that government may be the source of competitive advantages for an individual company or an entire industry.[61] For example, public policy may prevent or limit entry into an industry by new foreign or domestic competitors. Government may subsidize failing companies or provide tax breaks to some. Federal patents are used to protect innovative products or production process technologies. Legislation may be passed to support industry prices, thereby guaranteeing profits or survival. Finally, regulation may favor competitors in one region of the country.

Specific examples of public policy beneficial to business are numerous. Government loan guarantees saved Chrysler Corporation from probable bankruptcy and gave it the opportunity to become a viable, profitable corporation. The utility industry entered into the nuclear power business only after the government provided

Recall "Setting the Stage," about the power of corporations and the perception that they hold too much control over people's lives. Some say that corporations can gain complete control over individuals via the Internet. The issues include intellectual capital, free speech, and privacy.

Regarding *intellectual capital,* some view the Internet as a copying machine run amok, in which anyone can make perfect copies of anything, regardless of copyright. Many believe that this is a dire threat to the entertainment and publishing industries. But the opposite threat may be more serious, as copyright holders may eventually be able to monitor and charge users for every single use. Intellectual property rights traditionally are intended to balance the interests of producers with those of society; with the Net, it remains to be seen whether and how such a balance will emerge.

Regarding *free speech,* cyberspace can promote free and open communications, or it may control our lives in ways unimaginable and undesired. Right now it is not clear in which direction we're headed. Design decisions can permit or prohibit anonymity on the Net, and include or exclude certain types of speech. Some fear that the government or commercial forces will censor Internet content. Blocking or filtering can be done upstream by Internet service providers, portals, or employers, and users may be unaware. Others think that censorship is unlikely, and that Internet surfers or parents will make their own choices and block what they don't like. Many prefer that organizations be required to disclose their filtering policies, believing that this will make censorship less likely.

Privacy needs to be a concern of every company that does business on the Net. Some fear that cyberspace may eliminate all of our privacy, as vendors gain access to people's Internet shopping and buying patterns. DoubleClick sells clickstream data, E-Loan is struggling to keep customers' highly confidential financial data completely secure, and people are beginning to worry that employers will purchase such data on job applicants. Think about it: How would you feel if anyone could purchase data showing everything you read, every website you visited, every file you downloaded, every message you sent or received, and every purchase you made?

SOURCE: C. Shapiro, "Will E-Commerce Erode Liberty?" *Harvard Business Review,* May–June 2000, pp. 189–99; and L. Lessig, *Code and Other Laws of Cyberspace* (New York: Basic Books, 2000).

insurance through the Price-Anderson Act. Since the Great Depression, farmers have been the beneficiaries of government aid and subsidies. Several airlines received help from the government or employed various regulatory and legal maneuvers in order to survive.

Corporate Legitimacy

corporate legitimacy

A motive for organizational involvement in the public policy process. The assumption is that organizations are legitimate to the extent that their goals, purposes, and methods are consistent with those of society.

domain defense

Activities intended to counter challenges to the organization's legitimacy.

The second motive for corporate involvement in the public process is to increase **corporate legitimacy.**[62] Corporations are legitimate to the extent that their goals, purposes, and methods are consistent with those of society. Because the broader social system is the source of corporate support and allows organizations to pursue their goals, corporations must be sensitive to the expectations and values society establishes. These expectations, in the form of social norms, laws, and regulations, act as controls on the company's behavior. Gross or frequent violations of these expectations will cause the corporation to lose its support and will limit its discretion.

Corporations sometimes face threats that challenge the legitimacy of their existence or their actions. They may be criticized for their efforts to gain competitive advantage, or questions regarding their social responsibility or ethical behavior may be raised. Activity intended to counter challenges to the organization's legitimacy is called **domain defense.**[63] It is designed to strengthen the corporation's right to exist and to operate freely. Domain defense occurs when organizations, acting in their own self-interest, use socially responsible and ethical behavior to maintain and enhance their legitimacy.

Strategies for Influencing the Political Environment

Managers have an array of strategic options for dealing with the political environment. Many corporations have specialized units for managing these activities. The **public affairs department** of a corporation monitors key events and trends in the political and social environment, analyzes their effects on the organization, recommends the appropriate corporate responses, and implements political strategies. A successful public affairs program enhances an organization's credibility, facilitates a timely and appropriate response to issues, and has a positive financial impact (although this impact may be difficult to measure accurately).[64]

Depending on the needs of an industry or of an individual company, the public affairs department performs a variety of important activities.[65]

> **public affairs department**
>
> **A department that monitors key events and trends in the organization's political and social environments, analyzes their effects on the organization, recommends organizational responses, and implements political strategies.**

- *Issues management.* It identifies important social, political, economic, and technological developments and integrates this information into strategic planning.
- *Government relations (federal, state, and local).* It monitors legislative and regulatory developments, assesses their implications, and tries to affect the course of public policy.
- *Public relations.* It communicates information about the organization to the media.
- *International relations.* It promotes company interests in foreign capitals and in international forums.
- *Investor and stockholder relations.* It is often in charge of company communications with investors, brokerage houses, and other financial institutions.
- *Corporate contributions.* It frequently coordinates company contributions to the community.
- *Institutional advertising.* To heighten public awareness, it often engages in image building through nonproduct advertising.

Corporations use a variety of specific strategies and vehicles to manage the political environment.[66]

Lobbying, the most traditional form of influencing the political environment, involves efforts by political professionals or company executives to establish communication channels with regulatory bodies, legislators, and their staffs. It is designed to convey the company's sentiments and attempt to influence the decisions of legislators and key advisers. Enron brought a modern-day twist to the age-old practice of lobbying by creating "the matrix"—a computer program that calculated how much a proposed regulatory change would cost the company.[67] Executives then decided whether it was worth mobilizing lobbyists and other components of its influence machinery to fight the change.

> **lobbying**
>
> **Efforts to influence regulatory bodies, legislators, and their staff.**

Political action committees (PACs) make donations to candidates for political office. The PAC system has received much criticism; some opponents complain that it gives large donors an unfair advantage both in an election and when their interests are brought before the elected legislator.

For example, Arthur Andersen's PAC donated $630,000 to Republicans and $360,000 to Democrats between 2000 and January 2002.[68] There is nothing unusual about this, but these facts came under scrutiny after its performance as Enron's auditor. Even if Anderson had done nothing illegal, it faced a public relations disaster that drove clients away.

> **political action committees (PACs)**
>
> **Political action groups that represent an organization and make donations to candidates for political office.**

corporate constituency programs

Organizational efforts to identify, educate, and motivate individuals to take political action that could benefit the organization.

coalition building

Working with other organizations or groups of voters that share political interests on a particular legislative issue.

stonewalling

The use of public relations, legal action, and administrative processes to prevent or delay the introduction of legislation and regulation that may have an adverse impact on the organization.

strategic retreat

Efforts to adapt products and processes to changes in the political and social environments while minimizing the negative effects of those changes.

Corporate constituency programs encourage interested stakeholders to engage in grassroots political activity on behalf of the corporation.[69] These actions may include writing a letter to a congressperson or local politician, signing a petition, marching in a demonstration, or expressing an opinion on a television or radio talk show. **Coalition building** involves efforts to find other organizations or groups of voters who share interest in a particular legislative issue and attempt to influence the environment through combined effort and power.

The final two political strategies—stonewalling and strategic retreat—are less proactive than the strategies just discussed. **Stonewalling** is the use of public relations, legal action, and administrative processes to delay legislation and regulation that may have an adverse impact on the organization. However, stonewalling often consumes considerable time and money that could be spent on activities leading to long-term positive outcomes. In fact, it often boomerangs, generating more criticism, damaging brand images and sales, and hurting the stock price.[70]

Strategic retreat involves an organization's efforts to adapt its products and processes to changes in the political and social environment while minimizing the negative effects of those changes. Senior managers may realize that the new law or regulation has support in most segments of society. Political action or stonewalling to oppose the change could have more negative consequences for the company, particularly in the long term, than would adapting to the environment or implementing more proactive strategies.[71]

What strategies do you see in the following example?

Global Warming as a Business Issue

Global climate change is a controversial business issue. How convincing is the evidence on global warming? Some believe the future of the Winter Olympics is endangered, because winter itself is in danger. Others believe that the doom and gloom talk about the state of the planet is bogus and exaggerated.

ExxonMobil is one company that maintains that the global warming evidence is inconclusive. If the company can postpone regulation of carbon dioxide emissions, it can protect short-term asset values. It may even be able to convince the public that global warming is a smaller threat than government regulation. But the number of companies with this perspective is dwindling. Most (not all) scientists fear serious consequences of global warming. And consider this: According to business leaders at the World Economic Forum in Davos, Switzerland, global warming is the most pressing issue facing the business world today.

Shifts in global climate present risks and also business opportunity. Managers who care will work to influence regulations, make efforts to reduce the problems associated with climate change, and inform the public about those efforts.

Many industries and companies are directly affected by the weather; planning now for the potential consequences of climate change is essential. For example, insurance companies need to adapt their predictive models regarding financial losses. Realtors need to learn flood patterns. The tourism industry should anticipate how new storm patterns will change demand for different vacation locations, including depressed demand for affected tropical areas and ski resorts. Agricultural companies may need to abandon investments in regions that become too warm, and invest heavily in new areas where farming becomes more viable. Timber operations may need to spend more money on fire management.

Environmental shifts create business opportunities as well. Seed sellers can develop crops that deliver higher yields in drier conditions. ABB and Honeywell are investing in sophisticated thermostats and other products whose value will increase as energy costs increase. Ford and GM view global warming as an opportunity to gain advantage over rivals that are less advanced technologically. Both are investing in cars that do not produce carbon dioxide (a greenhouse gas), and may be able to dominate a new market.

BP Amoco has been a real leader in working to reduce global warming. In 1997, CEO Sir John Brown became the first oilman to declare the serious possibility of global warming, and clashed with others in the industry. He pledged voluntary reductions of carbon dioxide emissions, and he has led the industry to adopt more pro-environmental attitudes on other issues, including wastewater disposal.

SOURCES: K. O'Neill Packard and F. Reinhardt, "What Every Executive Needs to Know about Global Warming," *Harvard Business Review*, July–August 2000, pp. 129–35; "A Big-Oil Man Gets Religion," *Fortune*, March 6, 2000, pp. F87–F89; "Defending Science," *The Economist*, February 2, 2002, pp. 15–16; R. C. Anderson and B. McKibben, "Winterless Olympics?" *The Washington Post*, February 8, 2002, p. A31.

The Natural Environment

Most large corporations developed in an era of abundant raw materials, cheap energy, and unconstrained waste disposal.[72] Many of the technologies developed during this era are contributing to the destruction of ecosystems. Industrial-age systems follow a linear flow of extract, produce, sell, use, and discard—what some call a "take-make-waste" approach.[73] But perhaps no time in history has offered greater possibilities for a change in business thinking.

Business used to look at environmental issues as a no-win situation: You either help the environment and hurt your business, or help your business only at a cost to the environment. But now a paradigm shift is taking place in corporate environmental management: the deliberate incorporation of environmental values into competitive strategies and into the design and manufacturing of products.[74] Why? In addition to philosophical reasons, companies "go green" to satisfy consumer demand, to react to a competitor's greening actions, to meet requests from customers or suppliers, to comply with guidelines, and to create competitive advantage. According to Chad Holliday, chairman and CEO of DuPont, focusing on environmental sustainability provides a comprehensive way of doing business that helps develop new products, markets, partnerships, and intellectual property that create growth.

A Risk Society

We live in a risk society. That is, the creation and distribution of wealth generate by-products that can cause injury, loss, or danger to people and the environment. The fundamental sources of risk in modern society are the excessive production of hazards and ecologically unsustainable consumption of natural resources.[75] Risk has proliferated through population explosion, industrial pollution, and environmental degradation.[76]

Industrial pollution risks include air pollution, smog, global warming, ozone depletion, acid rain, toxic waste sites, nuclear hazards, obsolete weapons arsenals, industrial accidents, and hazardous products. Over 30,000 uncontrolled toxic waste sites have been documented in the United States alone, and the number is increasing by perhaps 2,500 per year. The situation is far worse in other parts of the world. The pattern, for toxic waste and many other risks, is one of accumulating risks and inadequate remedies.

The institutions that create environmental and technological risk (corporations and government agencies) also are responsible for controlling and managing the risks.[77] For example, in December 2001, GE was ordered by the EPA to spend $460 million to dredge PCBs it had dumped into the Hudson River in earlier decades. It fought bitterly against the decision because of the cost and because the actions had been taken decades earlier, when they were legal. In 2002, Monsanto faced the same problem from a facility in Mississippi that had dumped PCBs, legally, from the 1930s to the 1970s.[78]

Ecocentric Management

Ecocentric management has as its goal the creation of sustainable economic development and improvement of quality of life worldwide for all organizational stakeholders.[79] Management decisions seek to minimize negative environmental impact through all aspects of the organization. Ecocentric management encourages low energy use, smaller resource quantities, environmentally appropriate production technologies, and products with eco-friendly packaging and recyclable materials. It minimizes waste and pollution and tries to renew natural resources.[80] You can read more specifics about this approach in Appendix C at the end of this chapter.

With ecocentric management, each business function operates with the ecology in mind. An important example is **design for environment (DFE)**, a tool for creating products that are easier to recover, reuse, or recycle. All environmental effects of a product are examined during the design phase. The analysis is cradle-to-grave: full assessment of all inputs, through a detailed analysis of how customers use and dispose of it.

Profitability need not suffer and may in time be positively affected by ecocentric philosophies and practices. Some, but not all, research has indicated a positive relationship between corporate environmental performance and profitability.[81]

In Sweden, an organization called The Natural Step works with business leaders to create operational strategies with both environmental and economic benefits.[82] The Natural Step works with scientists to create sustainability guidelines and has a board of governors that includes nine business leaders. Its methods are collaborative rather than adversarial. Swedish companies that have worked with The Natural Step include IKEA International, Scandic Hotels, and Electrolux International.

OUR PROCESS TO REDUCE SULFUR IN GASOLINE HELPS THOSE WHO DON'T EVEN DRIVE.

Sulfur is a naturally occurring element in gasoline and contributes to air pollution. But until recently, the methods used to remove sulfur from gasoline weren't very efficient. So Phillips is developing a new process that removes more than 90% of the sulfur in standard gasoline without significant loss of octane or volume. It's an innovation that will help us reduce harmful emissions from cars, improve air quality and meet proposed sulfur regulations for years to come. And it's just one of the many ways we live up to the name The Performance Company.

PHILLIPS PETROLEUM COMPANY 66

For a copy of our annual report, call 918-661-3700, write to: Phillips Annual Report, B-41, Adams Bldg., Bartlesville, OK 74004, or visit us at www.phillips66.com.

Phillips Petroleum lauds their environmental achievements in this ad by highlighting their development of a new process to reduce sulfur in gasoline without reducing performance. By showing their concern for the environment, Phillips can create a competitive advantage over other oil companies, especially in the minds of environmentally conscious consumers.

At least 20 U.S.-based organizations are now working with The Natural Step. Ray Anderson, CEO of Interface, a $1 billion carpet manufacturer based in Atlanta that works with The Natural Step principles, said his realization of the importance of sustainability came "as a spear in the chest for me, and I determined almost in an instant to change my company . . . it began in the heart . . . that's where the next industrial revolution has to begin—in the hearts of people—to do the right thing" (p. 72).

The most admired company in Britain, British Petroleum, ranks No. 1 in that country in environmental responsibility. For example, BP spent about $80 million adding environmental safeguards to a facility in Scotland. CEO John Browne said, "Unlike in the U.S., there was no regulatory pressure at all to do that in Scotland, but we did it voluntarily. It's our way of saying to people, we're here to stay." [83]

> **ecocentric management**
>
> Its goal is the creation of sustainable economic development and improvement of quality of life worldwide for all organizational stakeholders.
>
> **design for environment (DFE)**
>
> A tool for creating products that are easy to recover, reuse, or recycle.

Environmental Agenda for the Future

In the past, companies were oblivious to their negative environmental impact. More recently, many began striving for low impact. Now, some strive for positive impact, and to sell solutions to the world's problems.

Webs of companies with a common ecological vision can combine their efforts into high-leverage, impactful action.[84] In Kalundborg, Denmark, such a collaborative alliance exists among an electric power generating plant, an oil refiner, a biotech production plant, a plasterboard factory, cement producers, heating utilities, a sulfuric acid producer, and local agriculture and horticulture. Chemicals, energy (for both heating and cooling), water, and organic materials flow among companies. Resources are conserved, "waste" materials generate revenues, and water, air, and ground pollution all are reduced.

Companies not only have the *ability* to solve environmental problems; they are coming to see and acquire the *motivation* as well. Many industries are now turning their attention to pursuing what some see as one of the biggest opportunities in the history of commerce—solving environmental problems.[85]

KEY TERMS

Business ethics, p. 138

Coalition building, p. 154

Compliance-based ethics programs, p. 145

Corporate constituency programs, p. 154

Corporate legitimacy, p. 152

Corporate social responsibility, p. 147

Corporate social responsiveness, p. 150

Deontology, p. 139

Design for environment (DFE), p. 156

Domain defense, p. 152

Ecocentric management, p. 156

Economic responsibilities, p. 147

Egoism, p. 139

Ethical climate, p. 142

Ethical issue, p. 138

Ethical responsibilities, p. 147

Ethics, p. 138

Integrity-based ethics programs, p. 145

Kohlberg's model of cognitive moral development, p. 140

Legal responsibilities, p. 147

Lobbying, p. 153

Moral philosophy, p. 138

Political action committees (PACs), p. 153

Public affairs department, p. 153

Relativism, p. 140

Stonewalling, p. 154

Strategic retreat, p. 154

Teleology, p. 139

Universalism, p. 138

Utilitarianism, p. 139

Virtue ethics, p. 140

Voluntary responsibilities, p. 147

SUMMARY OF LEARNING OBJECTIVES

Now that you have studied Chapter 5, you should know:

How different ethical perspectives guide decision making.

The purpose of ethics is to identify the rules that govern human behavior and the "goods" that are worth seeking. Ethical decisions are guided by the individual's values, or principles of conduct such as honesty, fairness, integrity, respect for others, and responsible citizenship. Different ethical systems include universalism; teleology, including egoism and utilitarianism; deontology; relativism; and virtue ethics. These philosophical systems, as practiced by different individuals according to their level of cognitive moral development and other factors, underlie the ethical stances of individuals and organizations.

How companies influence the ethics environment.

Different organizations apply different ethical perspectives and standards. Ethical codes sometimes are helpful, although they must be implemented properly. Ethics programs can range from compliance-based to integrity-based. An increasing number of organizations are adopting ethics codes. Such codes address employee conduct, community and environment, shareholders, customers, suppliers and contractors, political activity, and technology.

The options you have when confronting ethical issues.

Individuals have a variety of options when they witness unethical behavior. Their choice of action will depend on both their beliefs about the action's likely outcomes and their own moral judgment. When faced with ethical dilemmas, you should define the issue clearly, identify relevant values, weigh conflicting values, choose an appropriate option, and implement your decision.

The important issues surrounding corporate social responsibility.

Corporate social responsibility is the extension of the corporate role beyond economic pursuits. It includes not only economic but also legal, ethical, and voluntary responsibilities. Advocates believe managers should consider societal and human needs in their business decisions because corporations are members of society and carry a wide range of responsibilities. Critics of corporate responsibility believe managers' first responsibility is to increase profits for the shareholders who own the corporation. The two perspectives are potentially reconcilable. Whereas corporate social responsibility (CSR1) refers to principles, philosophies, and beliefs surrounding these issues, corporate social responsiveness (CSR2) is the processes companies actually use and the actions they take.

How the political and social environment affects your firm's competitive position and legitimacy.

Corporations have two goals within their ethical structures: competitive advantage and corporate legitimacy. Progressive organizations realize that the government can be an ally and a source of competitive advantage rather than just an adversary. Corporate legitimacy comes from goals, purposes, and methods that are consistent with those of society. Thus, organizations must be sensitive to the expectations and values of society.

The strategies corporations use to manage the political and social environment.

The public affairs department monitors the political and social environment, analyzes its impact on the organization, and implements political strategies. Strategies include lobbying, political action committees, corporate constituency programs, coalition building, stonewalling, and strategic retreat. Generally, strategies that adapt to or change the environment are most effective in the long run.

The role of managers in our natural environment.

Organizations have contributed risk to society and have some responsibility for reducing risk to the environment. They also have the capability to help solve environmental problems. Ecocentric management attempts to minimize negative environmental impact, create sustainable economic development, and improve the quality of life worldwide. Some companies now are moving beyond pollution prevention programs and zero-impact efforts to interorganizational alliances and strategic initiatives that pursue positive opportunities to solve environmental problems.

DISCUSSION QUESTIONS

1. Assess the possible explanations for people's cynicism toward business outlined in "Setting the Stage." Do you agree that people are as negative as the *Business Week*/Harris Poll survey suggests? Support your arguments.

2. Consider the various ethical systems described early in the chapter. Identify concrete examples from your own past decisions or the decisions of others you have seen or read about.

3. Choose one or more topics from Table 5.1 and discuss the ethical issues surrounding them.

4. What would you do in each of the scenarios described in Table 5.2, "Ethical Decision Making in the International Context"?

5. Identify and discuss illegal, unethical, and socially responsible business actions in the current news.

6. Does your school have a code of ethics? If so, what does it say? Is it effective? Why or why not?

7. You have a job you like at which you work 40 to 45 hours per week. How much off-the-job volunteer work would you do? What kinds of volunteer work? How will you react if your boss makes it clear he or she wants you to cut back on the outside activities and devote more hours to your job?

8. What are the arguments for and against the concept of corporate social responsibility? Where do you stand, and why? Give your opinions, specifically, with respect to the text discussions of American cigarettes, Enron, and the Internet.

9. How can the political and social environment both constrain and help the corporation in its pursuit of competitive advantage? Give examples.

10. Under what conditions might stonewalling and strategic retreat be the most appropriate political strategies? Have you seen these tactics work?

11. A company in England slaughters 70,000 baby ostrich chicks each year for their meat. It told a teen magazine that it would stop if it received enough complaints. Analyze this policy, practice, and public statement using the concepts discussed in the chapter.

12. A Nike ad in the U.S. magazine *Seventeen* shows a picture of a girl, aged perhaps 8 or 9. The ad reads,

    If you let me play . . .
    I will like myself more.
    I will have more self-confidence.

    I will suffer less depression.
    I will be 60 percent less likely to get breast cancer.
    I will be more likely to leave a man who beats me.
    I will be less likely to get pregnant before I want to.
    I will learn what it means to be strong.
    If you let me play sports.

    Assess this ad in terms of chapter concepts surrounding ethics and social responsibility. What questions would you ask in doing this analysis?

13. Should companies like GE and Monsanto be held accountable for actions of decades past, then legal but since made illegal as their harmful effects became known?

Nike Controversies

"A company that ignores its social responsibility is playing with fire," stated one critic of Nike. Another condemned Nike for glorifying violence and bad taste, and for doing "nothing to promote values, especially among impressionable youngsters." International soccer barons fumed that Nike is infecting futbol with the American disease of money-will-get-you-everything. Human rights groups accused Nike contractors of operating their factories like prison camps, hiring 13-year-old children and treating workers "little better than slaves." Nike denied such charges, but also is changing its ways.

Nike has always prided itself on its radical, rebellious, anti-establishment image. Its brashness has paid off big-time in the United States. But Nike believes that its future lies in the international arena. The company wants to generate more than half of its revenues overseas. But as its marketing efforts expanded into international markets, many of the company's decisions were decried as irresponsible.

For example, a Nike ad in *Soccer America* magazine crowed, "Europe, Asia, and Latin America: Barricade your stadiums. Hide your trophies. Invest in some deodorant. As Asia and Latin America have been crushed, so shall Europe . . . the world has been

warned." The deodorant line did not amuse, and Nike was seen by many as the ugly American trashing hallowed traditions.

A TV commercial featured a Manchester United player explaining how spitting at a fan and insulting a coach won him a Nike contract. A Nike advertising campaign at the Atlanta Olympic Games employed the slogan, "You don't win silver, you lose gold." Olympic committees from several countries were incensed; The slogan was said to denigrate the Olympic spirit of competition, and belittled all the athletes who failed to win gold.

Several years ago it was reported that in Vietnam, Nike paid its workers a daily wage less than the cost of three meals of rice, vegetables, and tofu. American businessman Thuyen Nguyen interviewed 35 Vietnamese workers and concluded that 32 had lost weight, and that they were subjected to humiliations, including having stiffly enforced limits of two drinks of water and one bathroom break in an eight-hour shift; being hit over the head for poor workmanship; being forced to kneel with their hands in the air for up to 25 minutes; having their mouths taped for talking; and being "sun-dried"—forced to stand in the hot sun for lengthy periods writing their mistakes over and over. Nike was criticized in *Doonesbury* for the factory conditions in Vietnam, although even Nike critics concede that Nike is not the only, or the worst, corporate offender.

Many people consider the Vietnam factory conditions as highly unethical. But the Nicaraguan foreign minister said that anti-sweatshop activities could cost jobs and investment in Latin America's poorest country, where unemployment is near 50 percent. "By causing firms to leave they are going to leave our workers in the lurch . . . We are on the first rung of the ladder. It is important we are not knocked off" (p. 16). In a *Fortune* article titled "The Case for Sweatshops," David R. Henderson of the Hoover Institution and the Naval Postgraduate School argues that critics must not lose sight of what happens when low-wage child laborers lose their jobs. "They are worse off," Henderson writes. "You don't make someone better off by taking away the best of their bad options . . . sweatshops, in short, are a path from poverty to greater wealth"(p. 22).

People like Mao Genhe agree—they believe that they and their families are much better off since Nike came to China. Mr. Genhe earns $150 a month working in a factory that supplies makers of Nike and Adidas shoes. He sends most of it to his family, bought a new plow for his parents' rice fields, built his parents a new house (adding a 21-inch color TV), and is saving money to

Nike had designs on untapped market share in the international arena, but had to overcome controversies such as the accusation by human rights groups that their factories were like prison camps.

open a store with his wife. Thanks primarily to foreign investment and exports, urban per capita income in China has grown tenfold since 1978. Much of the income growth has come from thousands of shoe, garment, toy, and electronics factories.

In late 1997, Nike announced at its shareholder meeting that it would sever ties with four Indonesian factories for violating labor standards. Such violations are exceptions, though, said the chairman. But in mid-1998, Nike chairman Phil Knight publicly acknowledged how much damage the criticism had done to his company's image, and announced that it would raise the minimum wage for its workers and impose American air quality standards on its overseas plants.

Nike now states that it wants consumers to hold it accountable for the conditions in the factories where Nike products are made. Nike invited 16 students to monitor 32 of its partner factories, and published their uncensored findings on its website, www.nikebiz.com. It is releasing other auditing reports as well. Others in the industry have refused to make such audits public, and Nike's announcement that it was doing so was both a coup for anti-sweatshop activists and probably a spur to other companies in the industry to do the same.

QUESTIONS

1. Nike's success in the United States is inarguable. What about its strategies and tactics? What do you think of the actions described above? Are they just business decisions that generated some criticism? Or are they also irresponsible, unethical?

2. If some of Nike's decisions are unethical, which are the most unethical, and which the least? How did you reach these judgments?

3. What do you think of the Nike response to the criticism?

4. What else, if anything, should Nike do about the issues raised in the case?

SOURCES: "Nike Sanctions 3 Firms for Labor Abuses," *International Herald Tribune*, September 24, 1997, p. 19; B. Herbert, "Making Billions on the Backs of Hungry Women," *International Herald Tribune*, April 1, 1997, p. 9; R. Thurow, "In Global Push, Nike Finds Its Brash Ways Don't Always Pay Off," *The Wall Street Journal*, May 6, 1997, pp. 1, 6; D. R. Henderson, "The Case for Sweatshops," *Fortune*, October 28, 1996, pp. 20, 22; E. J. Dionne, Jr. "Swoosh! Shaming Net Results," *International Herald Tribune*, May 15, 1998, p. 11; A. Bernstein, "Too Much Corporate Power?" *Business Week*, September 11, 2000, pp. 145–58; L. Lee and A. Bernstein, "Commentary: Who Says Student Protests Don't Matter?" *Business Week*, June 12, 2000, pp. 94–96; M. L. Clifford and P. Engardio with E. Malkin, D. Roberts, and W. Echikson, "Up the Ladder, Global Trade: Can All Nations Benefit?" *Business Week*, November 6, 2000, pp. 78–84; I. G. Osorio, "How the Anti-Sweatshop Movement Hurts the People It Claims to Help," *Review—Institute of Public Affairs*, December 2001, pp. 15–16.

5.1   Measuring Your Ethical Work Behavior

OBJECTIVES

1. To explore a range of ethically perplexing situations.

2. To understand your own ethical attitudes.

INSTRUCTIONS

Make decisions in the situations described in the Ethical Behavior Worksheet. You will not have all the background information on each situation, and, instead, you should make whatever assumptions you feel you would make if you were actually confronted with the decision choices described. Select the decision choice that most closely represents the decision you feel you would make personally. You should choose decision options even though you can envision other creative solutions that were not included in the exercise.

Ethical Behavior Worksheet

Situation 1.   You are taking a very difficult chemistry course, which you must pass to maintain your scholarship and to avoid damaging your application for graduate school. Chemistry is not your strong suit, and, because of a just-below-failing average in the course, you will have to receive a grade of 90 or better on the final exam, which is two days away. A janitor, who is aware of your plight, informs you that he found the master for the chemistry final in a trash barrel and has saved it. He will make it available to you for a price, which is high but which you could afford. What would you do?

_____ (a) I would tell the janitor thanks, but no thanks.

_____ (b) I would report the janitor to the proper officials.

_____ (c) I would buy the exam and keep it to myself.

_____ (d) I would not buy the exam myself, but I would let some of my friends, who are also flunking the course, know that it is available.

Situation 2.   You have been working on some financial projections manually for two days now. It seems that each time you think you have them completed your boss shows up with a new assumption or another "what-if" question. If you only had a copy of a spreadsheet software program for your personal computer, you could plug in the new assumptions and revise the estimates with ease. Then, a colleague offers to let you make a copy of some software that is copyrighted. What would you do?

_____ (a) I would accept my friend's generous offer and make a copy of the software.

_____ (b) I would decline to copy it and plug away manually on the numbers.

_____ (c) I would decide to go buy a copy of the software myself, for $300, and hope I would be reimbursed by the company in a month or two.

_____ (d) I would request another extension on an already overdue project date.

Situation 3.   Your small manufacturing company is in serious financial difficulty. A large order of your products is ready to be delivered to a key customer when you discover that the product is simply not right. It will not meet all performance specifications, will cause problems for your customer, and will require rework in the field; however, this, you know, will not become evident until after the customer has received and paid for the order. If you do not ship the order and receive the payment as expected, your business may be forced into bankruptcy. And if you delay the shipment or inform the customer of these problems, you may lose the order and also go bankrupt. What would you do?

_____ (a) I would not ship the order and place my firm in voluntary bankruptcy.

_____ (b) I would inform the customer and declare voluntary bankruptcy.

_____ (c) I would ship the order and inform the customer, after I received payment.

_____ (d) I would ship the order and not inform the customer.

Situation 4.   You are the cofounder and president of a new venture, manufacturing products for the recreational market. Five months after launching the business, one of your suppliers informs you it can no longer supply you with a critical raw material since you are not a large-quantity user. Without the raw material, the business cannot continue. What would you do?

_____ (a) I would grossly overstate my requirements to another supplier to make the supplier think I am a much larger potential customer in order to secure the raw material from that supplier, even though this would mean the supplier will no longer be able to supply another, noncompeting small manufacturer who may thus be forced out of business.

_____ (b) I would steal raw material from another firm (noncompeting) where I am aware of a sizable stockpile.

_____ (c) I would pay off the supplier, since I have reason to believe that the supplier could be "persuaded" to meet my needs with a sizable "under the table" payoff that my company could afford.

_____ (d) I would declare voluntary bankruptcy.

Situation 5.   You are on a marketing trip for your new venture for the purpose of calling on the purchasing agent of a major prospective client. Your company is manufacturing an electronic system that you hope the purchasing agent will buy. During the course of your conversation, you notice on the cluttered desk of the purchasing agent several copies of a cost proposal for a system from one of your direct competitors. This purchasing agent has previously reported mislaying several of your own company's proposals and has asked for additional copies. The purchasing agent leaves the room momentarily to get you a cup of coffee, leaving you alone with your competitor's proposals less than an arm's length away. What would you do?

_____ (a) I would do nothing but await the man's return.

_____ (b) I would sneak a quick peek at the proposal, looking for bottom-line numbers.

_____ (c) I would put the copy of the proposal in my briefcase.

_____ (d) I would wait until the man returns and ask his permission to see the copy.

SOURCE: Jeffry A. Timmons, *New Venture Creation*, 3rd ed. pp. 285–86. Copyright © 1994 by Jeffry A. Timmons. Reproduced with permission of the author.

5.2   Social Responsibility

OBJECTIVES

1. To have a look at a socially responsible undertaking of a firm.

2. To examine the pros and cons of firms taking on the role of trying to solve social ills.

INSTRUCTIONS

There are many arguments for and against firms taking a role in trying to alleviate community or social ills. Find an example of a business acting in a manner that is clearly socially responsible, such as providing job training programs for the unemployed or providing financial support for urban renewal. You may be able to find your own example of this locally, or in articles in business periodicals.

Ethical Behavior Worksheet

1. Briefly describe the firm and its program(s). _____

_____

_____

2. What is the rationale the firm uses to support this program? _____

_____

_____

3. What is the response from those affected by the program? _____

_____

_____

4. What is the response, if any, from those who oppose the program? _____

_____

_____

5. Do you think the company is benefiting from the program to the extent of the program's cost? _____

_____

_____

SOURCE: R. R. McGrath Jr., *Exercises in Management Fundamentals*, p. 192. Copyright ©1985 Pearson Education, Inc. Reprinted by permission of Pearson Education, Inc., Upper Saddle River, NJ.

5.3   Strategy for Dealing with Toxic Waste in the River

OBJECTIVES

1. To examine your attitude toward managing in our natural environment.
2. To explore new strategies for dealing with a natural-environment challenge.

INSTRUCTIONS

1. Read the following scenario about discovery of a toxic effluent by a firm's chemist.
2. You are the manager and must decide how to respond to the discovery of the unsuspected toxic by-product.

Discovery of a Toxic By-Product

You are the plant manager of a small chemical plant north of St. Louis. For years your firm dumped its untreated effluents into the Mississippi as a matter of everyday business. Recently, Environmental Protection Agency standards have required you to install a treatment system to minimize the level of several specific contaminants. Your firm has abided by the ruling; only treated sewage is being dumped into the river. However, you have just received a report from your head chemist, who has discovered that a by-product of a new chemical being produced by the firm is highly toxic. Moreover, the present filtration system utterly fails to filter out the toxic substance. It is all headed downstream toward St. Louis.

Strategy Worksheet

Now that you have this report, what do you plan to do? Consider your alternatives and develop a strategy. If part of your strategy is to get in touch with your boss at company headquarters in Chicago, state what recommendation you intend to make.

_____

_____

_____

_____

_____

_____

_____

_____

_____

_____

_____

_____

_____

5.4   An Environmental Protection Code of Ethics

OBJECTIVES

1. To further clarify the role business plays in environmental pollution.

2. To identify codes of ethics that businesses adopt to minimize the potential adverse impact of their activities on the environment.

INSTRUCTIONS

1. Your instructor will divide the class into small groups and assign each group one or more environmental problems to investigate.

2. For each environmental problem assigned, the groups will complete the Environmental Code of Ethics Worksheet by investigating the things business does that affect the environment and developing "code of ethics" statements by which businesses can deal with the problems in a positive, socially responsible manner.

3. After the class reconvenes, group spokespersons present group findings.

4. The class may proceed to the development of an overall Environmental Code of Ethics for businesses.

The Environmental Code of Ethics Worksheet

In the space provided, identify business activities that contribute to the environmental problem(s) assigned by your instructor and develop code of ethics statements that can be adopted to deal with the problem(s).

Environmental Pollution Problem: _____

Business Activity	Corresponding Code of Ethics Statement
_____	_____
_____	_____
_____	_____
_____	_____
_____	_____
_____	_____
_____	_____
_____	_____
_____	_____
_____	_____
_____	_____

The Caux Round Table Business Principles of Ethics

PRINCIPLE 1. THE RESPONSIBILITIES OF BUSINESSES: BEYOND SHAREHOLDERS TOWARD STAKEHOLDERS

The value of a business to society is the wealth and employment it creates and the marketable products and services it provides to consumers at a reasonable price commensurate with quality. To create such value, a business must maintain its own economic health and viability, but survival is not a sufficient goal.

Businesses have a role to play in improving the lives of all their customers, employees, and shareholders by sharing with them the wealth they have created. Suppliers and competitors as well should expect businesses to honor their obligations in a spirit of honesty and fairness. As responsible citizens of the local, national, regional, and global communities in which they operate, businesses share a part in shaping the future of those communities.

PRINCIPLE 2. THE ECONOMIC AND SOCIAL IMPACT OF BUSINESS: TOWARD INNOVATION, JUSTICE, AND WORLD COMMUNITY

Businesses established in foreign countries to develop, produce, or sell should also contribute to the social advancement of those countries by creating productive employment and helping to raise the purchasing power of their citizens. Businesses also should contribute to human rights, education, welfare, and vitalization of the countries in which they operate.

Businesses should contribute to economic and social development not only in the countries in which they operate, but also in the world community at large, through effective and prudent use of resources, free and fair competition, and emphasis upon innovation in technology, production, methods, marketing, and communications.

PRINCIPLE 3. BUSINESS BEHAVIOR: BEYOND THE LETTER OF LAW TOWARD A SPIRIT OF TRUST

While accepting the legitimacy of trade secrets, businesses should recognize that sincerity, candor, truthfulness, the keeping of promises, and transparency contribute not only to their own credibility and stability but also to the smoothness and efficiency of business transactions, particularly on the international level.

PRINCIPLE 4. RESPECT FOR RULES

To avoid trade friction and to promote freer trade, equal conditions for competition, and fair and equitable treatment for all participants, businesses should respect international and domestic rules. In addition, they should recognize that some behavior, although legal, may still have adverse consequences.

PRINCIPLE 5. SUPPORT FOR MULTILATERAL TRADE

Businesses should support the multilateral trade systems of GATT/World Trade Organization and similar international agreements. They should cooperate in efforts to promote the progressive and judicious liberalization of trade, and to relax those domestic measures that unreasonably hinder global commerce, while giving due respect to national policy objectives.

PRINCIPLE 6. RESPECT FOR THE ENVIRONMENT

A business should protect and, where possible, improve the environment, promote sustainable development, and prevent the wasteful use of natural resources.

PRINCIPLE 7. AVOIDANCE OF ILLICIT OPERATIONS

A business should not participate in or condone bribery, money laundering, or other corrupt practices; indeed, it should seek cooperation with others to eliminate them. It should not trade in arms or other materials used for terrorist activities, drug traffic, or other organized crime.

PRINCIPLE 8. CUSTOMERS

We believe in treating all customers with dignity, irrespective of whether they purchase our products and services directly from us or otherwise acquire them in the market. We therefore have a responsibility to:

- provide our customers with the highest quality products and services consistent with their requirements;
- treat our customers fairly in all respects of our business transactions, including a high level of service and remedies for their dissatisfaction;

- make every effort to ensure that the health and safety of our customers, as well as the quality of their environment, will be sustained or enhanced by our products and services;
- assure respect for human dignity in products offered, marketing, and advertising; and respect the integrity of the culture of our customers.

PRINCIPLE 9. EMPLOYEES

We believe in the dignity of every employee and in taking employee interests seriously. We therefore have a responsibility to:

- provide jobs and compensation that improve workers' living conditions;
- provide work conditions that respect each employee's health and dignity;
- be honest in communications with employees and open in sharing information, limited only by legal and competitive restraint;
- listen to and, where possible, act on employee suggestions, ideas, requests, and complaints;
- engage in good faith negotiations when conflict arises;
- avoid discriminatory practices and guarantee equal treatment and opportunity in areas such as gender, age, race, and religion;
- promote in the business itself the employment of differently abled people in places of work where they can be genuinely useful;
- protect employees from avoidable injury and illness in the workplace;
- encourage and assist employees in developing relevant and transferable skills and knowledge; and
- be sensitive to serious unemployment problems frequently associated with business decisions, and work with the government, employee groups, other agencies and each other in addressing these dislocations.

PRINCIPLE 10. OWNERS/INVESTORS

We believe in honoring the trust our investors place in us. We therefore have a responsibility to:

- apply professional and diligent management in order to secure a fair and competitive return on our owners' investment;
- disclose relevant information to owners/investors subject only to legal requirements and competitive constraints;
- conserve, protect, and increase the owners/investors' assets; and
- respect owners/investors' requests, suggestions, complaints, and formal resolutions.

PRINCIPLE 11. SUPPLIERS

Our relationship with suppliers and subcontractors must be based on mutual respect. We therefore have a responsibility to:

- seek fairness and truthfulness in all of our activities, including pricing, licensing, and rights to sell;
- ensure that business activities are free from coercion and unnecessary litigation;
- foster long-term stability in the supplier relationship in return for value, quality, competitiveness, and liability;
- share information with suppliers and integrate them into our planning processes;
- pay suppliers on time and in accordance with agreed terms of trade; and
- seek, encourage, and prefer suppliers and subcontractors whose employment practices respect human dignity.

PRINCIPLE 12. COMPETITORS

We believe that fair economic competition is one of the basic requirements for increasing the wealth of the nations and, ultimately, for making possible the just distribution of goods and services. We therefore have a responsibility to:

- foster open markets for trade and investments;
- promote competitive behavior that is socially and environmentally beneficial and demonstrates mutual respect among competitors;
- refrain from either seeking or participating in questionable payments of favors to secure competitive advantages;
- respect both tangible and intellectual property rights; and
- refuse to acquire commercial information by dishonest or unethical means, such as industrial espionage.

PRINCIPLE 13. COMMUNITIES

We believe that as global corporate citizens, we can contribute to such forces of reform and human rights as are at work in the communities in which we operate. We therefore have a responsibility in those communities to:

- respect human rights and democratic institutions, and promote them wherever practicable;
- recognize government's legitimate obligation to the society at large and support public policies and practices that promote human development through harmonious relations between business and other segments;
- collaborate with those forces in the community dedicated to raising standards of health, education, workplace safety, and economic well-being;
- promote and stimulate sustainable development and play a leading role in preserving and enhancing the physical environment and conserving the earth's resources;
- support peace, security, diversity, and social integration;
- respect the integrity of local cultures; and
- be a good corporate citizen through charitable donations, educational and cultural contributions, and employee participation in community and civic affairs.

SOURCE: Caux Round Table in Switzerland, "Principles for Business," special advertising supplement contributed as a public service by Canon, *Business Ethics*, May–June 1995, p. 35.

Managing in Our Natural Environment

BUSINESS AND THE ENVIRONMENT: CONFLICTING VIEWS

Some people believe everyone wins when business tackles environmental issues.[1] Others disagree.

The Win-Win Mentality

Business used to look at environmental issues as a no-win situation: You either help the environment and hurt your business, or help your business only at a cost to the environment. Fortunately, things have changed. "When Americans first demanded a cleanup of the environment during the early 1970s, corporations threw a tantrum. Their response ran the psychological gamut from denial to hostility, defiance, obstinacy, and fear. But today, when it comes to green issues, many U.S. companies have turned from rebellious underachievers to active problem solvers."[2] Table C.1 gives just a few examples of things U.S. corporations are doing to help solve environmental problems.

The Earth Summit in Rio in 1992 helped increase awareness of environmental issues. This led to the Kyoto Protocol, an international effort to control global warming that included an unsuccessful meeting in the Hague in November 2000.[3] "There has been an evolution of most groups—whether industry, governments, or nongovernmental organizations—toward a recognition that everyone plays a part in reaching a solution."[4]

Being "green" is potentially a catalyst for innovation, new market opportunities, and wealth creation. Advocates believe that this is truly a win-win situation; actions can be taken that benefit both business and the environment. For example, Procter & Gamble in a span of five years reduced disposable wastes by over 50 percent while increasing sales by 25 percent.[5] Win-win companies will come out ahead of those companies that have an us-versus-them, we-can't-afford-to-protect-the-environment mentality.

Is the easy part over?[6] Companies have found a lot of easy-to-harvest, "low-hanging fruit"—that is, overly costly practices that were made environmentally friendlier and that saved money at the same time. Many big companies have made these easy changes, and reaped benefits from them. Many small companies still have such low-hanging fruit to harvest,[7] and plenty remains to be done.

The Dissenting View

The critics of environmentalism in business are vocal. Some economists maintain that not a single empirical analysis supports the "free lunch view" that spending money on environmental problems provides full payback to the firm.[8] Skepticism should continue, they say; the belief that everyone will come out a winner is naive.

What really upsets many businesspeople is the financial cost of complying with environmental regulations.[9] Consider a few examples:

- GM spent $1.3 billion to comply with California requirements that 10 percent of the cars sold there be emission-free. European automakers spent $7 billion to install pollution-control equipment in all new cars during a five-year period.
- At Bayer, 20 percent of manufacturing costs are for the environment. This is approximately the same amount spent for labor.
- The Clean Air Act alone was expected to cost U.S. petroleum refiners $37 billion, more than the book value of the entire industry.
- California's tough laws are a major reason why manufacturers moved to Arkansas or Nevada.

In industries like chemicals and petroleum, environmental regulations were once considered a threat to their very survival.[10]

Balance

A more balanced view is that business must weigh the environmental benefits of an action against value destruction. The advice here is: Don't obstruct progress, but pick your environmental initiatives carefully. Compliance and remediation efforts will protect, but not increase, shareholder value.[11] And it is shareholder value, rather than compliance, emissions, or costs, that should be the focus of objective cost-benefit analyses. Such an approach is environmentally sound but also hard-headed in a business sense, and is the one approach that is truly sustainable over the long term.

Johan Piet maintains, "Only win-win companies will survive, but that does not mean that all win-win ideas will be successful."[12] In other words, rigorous analysis is essential. Thus, some companies maintain continuous improvement in environmental performance, but fund only projects that meet financial objectives.

Most people understand that business has the resources and the competence to bring about constructive change, and that this creates great opportunity—if well managed—for both business and the environment.

TABLE C.1
What Companies Are Doing to Enhance the Environment

- Toyota established an "ecotechnologies" division both for regulatory compliance and to shape corporate direction, including the development of hybrid electric-combustion automobiles.
- Interface Corporation's new Shanghai carpet factory circulates liquid through a standard pumping loop like those used in most industries. But simply by using fatter pipes and short, straight pipes instead of long and crooked pipes, it cut the power requirements by 92 percent.
- Xerox used "zero-waste-to-landfill" engineering to develop a new remanufacturable copier. AT&T cut paper costs by 15 percent by setting defaults on copiers and printers to double-sided mode.
- Electrolux uses more environmentally friendly water-based and powder paints instead of solvent-based paints, and introduced the first refrigerators and freezers free of chloroflourocarbons.
- Many chemical and pharmaceutical companies, including Novo Nordisk and Empresas La Moderna, are exploring "green chemistry" and seeking biological substitutes for synthetic materials.
- Anheuser-Busch just saved 21 million pounds of metal a year by reducing its beer-can rims by 1/8 of an inch (without reducing its contents).
- Nissan enlisted a group of ecologists, energy experts, and science writers to brainstorm about how an environmentally responsible car company might behave. Among the ideas: to produce automobiles that snap together into electrically powered trains for long trips and then detach for the dispersion to final destinations.

SOURCES: P. M. Senge and G. Carstedt, "Innovating Our Way to the Next Industrial Revolution," *Sloan Management Review*, Winter 2001, pp. 24–38; M. P. Polonsky and P. J. Rosenberger III, "Reevaluating Green Marketing: A Strategic Approach," *Business Horizons*, September–October, 2001, pp. 21–30; C. Garfield, *Second to None: How Our Smartest Companies Put People First* (Burr Ridge, IL; Business One-Irwin, 1992); H. Bradbury and J. A. Clair, "Promoting Sustainable Organizations with Sweden's Natural Step," *Academy of Management Executive*, November 1999, pp. 63–74; A. Loving, L. Hunter Lovins, and P. Hawken, "A Road Map for Natural Capitalism, " *Harvard Business Review*, May–June 1999, pp. 145–58; P. Hawken, A. Lovings, and L. Hunter Lovins, *Natural Capitalism* (Boston: Little Brown, 1999); S. L. Hart and M. B. Milstein, "Global Sustainability and the Creatine Destruction of Industries," *Sloan Management Review*, Fall 1999, pp. 23–32

WHY MANAGE WITH THE ENVIRONMENT IN MIND?

Business is turning its full attention to environmental issues for many reasons, including legal compliance, cost effectiveness, competitive advantage, public opinion, and long-term thinking.

Legal Compliance   Table C.2 shows just some of the most important U.S. environmental laws. Government regulations and

TABLE C.2
Some U.S Environmental Laws

Superfund [Comprehensive Environmental Response, Compensation, and Liability Act (CERCLA)]: Establishes potential liability for any person or organization responsible for creating an environmental health hazard. Individuals may be prosecuted, fined, or taxed to fund cleanup.

Clean Water Act [Federal Water Pollution Control Act]: Regulates all discharges into surface waters, and affects the construction and performance of sewer systems. The Safe Drinking Water Act similarly protects ground-waters.

Clean Air Act: Regulates the emission into the air of any substance that affects air quality, including nitrous oxides, sulfur dioxide, and carbon dioxide.

Community Response and Right-to-Know Act: Mandates that all facilities producing, transporting, storing, using, or releasing hazardous substances provide full information to local and state authorities and maintain emergency-action plans.

Federal Hazardous Substances Act: Regulates hazards to health and safety associated with consumer products. The Consumer Product Safety Commission has the right to recall hazardous products.

Hazardous Materials Transportation Act: Regulates the packaging, marketing, and labeling of shipments of flammable, toxic, and radioactive materials.

Resource Conservation and Recovery Act: Extends to small-quantity generators the laws regulating generation, treatment, and disposal of solid and hazardous wastes.

Surface Mining Control and Reclamation Act: Establishes environmental standards for all surface-mining operations.

Toxic Substances Control Act: Addresses the manufacture, processing, distribution, use, and disposal of dangerous chemical substances and mixtures.

SOURCE: Dennis C. Kinlaw, *Competitive and Green: Sustainable Performance in the Environmental Age* (Amsterdam: Pfeiffer & Co., 1993). Reprinted by permission of the author.

liability for damages provide strong economic incentives to comply with environmental guidelines. Most industries already have made environmental protection regulation and liability an integral part of their business planning.[13] The U.S. Justice Department has handed out tough prison sentences to executives whose companies violate hazardous-waste requirements.

Many businesspeople consider the regulations to be too rigid, inflexible, and unfair. In response to this concern, regulatory reform may become more creative. The Aspen Institute Series on the Environment in the Twenty-First Century is trying to increase the cost-effectiveness of compliance measures through more flexibility in meeting standards and relying on market-based incentives. Such mechanisms, including tradable permits, pollution charges, and deposit refund systems, provide positive financial incentives for good environmental performance.[14]

Cost Effectiveness   Environmentally conscious strategies can be cost-effective.[15] In the short run, company after company is realizing cost savings from repackaging, recycling, and other approaches. Union Carbide, for instance, faced costs of $30 a ton for disposal of solid wastes and $2,000 a ton for disposal of hazardous wastes. By recycling, reclaiming, or selling its waste, it avoided $8.5 million in costs *and* generated $3.5 million in income during a six-month period. Dow Chemical launched a 10-year program to improve its environmental, health, and safety performance worldwide. Dow projects that the environmental improvements will save $1.8 billion over the 10-year period.[16]

Environmentally conscious strategies offer long-run cost advantages as well. Companies that are functioning barely within legal limits today may incur big costs—being forced to pay damages or upgrade technologies and practices—when laws change down the road.

A few of the other cost savings include fines, cleanups, and litigation; lower raw materials costs; reduced energy use; less expensive waste handling and disposal; lower insurance rates; and possibly higher interest rates.

Competitive Advantage   Corporations gain a competitive advantage by channeling their environmental concerns into entrepreneurial opportunities and by producing higher-quality products that meet consumer demand. Business opportunities abound in pollution protection equipment and processes, waste cleanup, low-water-use plumbing, new lightbulb technology, and marketing of environmentally safe products like biodegradable plastics. With new pools of venture capital, government funding, and specialized investment funds available, environmental technology has become a major sector of the venture-capital industry.[17]

In addition, companies that fail to innovate in this area will be at a competitive *disadvantage*. Environmental protection is not only a universal need; it is also a major export industry. U.S. trade has suffered as other countries—notably Germany—have taken the lead in patenting and exporting anti–air pollution and other environmental technologies. If the United States does not produce innovative, competitive new technologies, it will forsake a growth industry and see most of its domestic spending for environmental protection go to imports.[18]

In short, competitive advantage can be gained by maintaining market share with old customers, and by creating new products for new market opportunities. And if you are an environmental leader, you may set the standards for future regulations—regulations that you are prepared to meet, while your competitors are not.

Public Opinion   The majority of the U.S. population believes business must clean up; few people think it is doing its job well. Gallup surveys show that more than 80 percent of U.S. consumers consider environmentalism in making purchases. An international survey of 22 countries found that majorities in 20 countries gave priority to environmental protection even at the risk of slowing economic growth. Consumers seem to have reached the point of routinely expecting companies to come up with environmentally friendly alternatives to current products and practices.[19]

Companies also receive pressure from local communities and from their own employees. Sometimes the pressure is informal and low key, but much pressure is exerted by environmental organizations, aroused citizen groups, societies and associations, international codes of conduct, and environmentally conscious investors.[20]

Another important reason for paying attention to environmental impact is TRI, the Toxic Release Inventory.[21] Starting in 1986, the EPA required all the plants of approximately 10,000 U.S. manufacturers to report annual releases of 317 toxic chemicals into the air, ground, and water. The substances include freon, PCBs, asbestos, and lead compounds. Hundreds of others have been added to the list. The releases are not necessarily illegal, but they provide the public with an annual environmental benchmark. TRI provides a powerful incentive to reduce emissions.

Finally, it is useful to remember that companies recover very slowly in public opinion from the impact of an environmental disaster. Adverse public opinion may affect sales as well as the firm's ability to attract and retain talented people. You can see why companies like P&G consider concern for the environment a consumer need, making it a basic and critical business issue.

Long-Term Thinking   Long-term thinking about resources helps business leaders understand the nature of their responsibilities with regard to environmental concerns. Economic arguments, sustainable growth, and the tragedy of the commons highlight the need for long-term thinking.

Economic Arguments   In Chapter 3, we discussed long-term versus short-term decision making. We stated that it is common for managers to succumb to short-term pressure for profits and to avoid spending now when the potential payoff is years down the road. In addition, some economists maintain that it is the responsibility of management to maximize returns for shareholders, implying the preeminence of the short-term profit goal.

But other economists argue that such a strategy caters to immediate profit maximization for stock speculators and neglects serious investors who are with the company for the long haul. Attention to environmental issues enhances the organization's long-term viability because the goal is the long-term creation of wealth for the patient, serious investors in the company[22]—not to mention the future state of our planet and the new generations who will inhabit it.

Sustainable Growth   Today many companies are moving beyond the law to be truly environmentalist in their philosophies and practices. Their aim is to jointly achieve the goals of economic growth and environmental quality in the long run by striving for sustainable growth. **Sustainable growth** is economic growth and development that meets the organization's present needs without harming the ability of future generations to meet their needs.[23] Sustainability is fully compatible with the natural ecosystems that generate and preserve life.

Some believe that the concept of sustainable growth offers[24] (1) a framework for organizations to use in communicating to all stakeholders, (2) a planning and strategy guide, and (3) a tool for evaluating and improving the ability to compete. The principle can begin at the highest organizational levels and be made explicit in performance appraisals and reward systems.

The Tragedy of the Commons   In a classic article in *Science*, Garrett Hardin described a situation that applies to all business decisions and social concerns regarding scarce resources like clean water, air, and land.[25] Throughout human history, a commons was a tract of land shared by communities of people on which they grazed their animals. A commons has limited **carrying capacity,** or the ability to sustain a population, because it is a finite resource. For individual herders, short-term interest lies in adding as many animals to the commons as they can. But problems develop as more herders add more animals to graze the commons. This leads to tragedy: As each herder acts in his short-term interest, the long-run impact is the destruction of the commons. The solution is to make choices according to long-run rather than short-run consequences.

In many ways, we are witnessing this **tragedy of the commons.** Carrying capacities are shrinking as precious resources, water chief among them, become scarcer. Inevitably, conflict arises—and solutions are urgently needed.

The Environmental Movement   The 1990s were labeled the "earth decade" when a "new environmentalism" with new features emerged.[26] For example, proponents of the new environmentalism asked companies to reduce their wastes, use resources prudently, market safe products, and take responsibility for past damages. These requests were formalized in the CERES principles (see Table C.3).

The new environmentalism combined many diverse viewpoints, but initially it did not blend easily with traditional business values. Some of the key aspects of this philosophy are noted in the following discussion of the history of the movement.[27]

Conservation and Environmentalism   A strand of environmental philosophy that is not at odds with business management is **conservation.** The conservation movement is anthropocentric (human centered), technologically optimistic, and concerned chiefly with the efficient use of resources. The movement seeks to avoid waste, promote the rational and efficient use of natural resources, and maximize long-term yields, especially of renewable resources.

The **environmental movement,** in contrast, historically has posed dilemmas for business management. Following the lead of early thinkers like George Perkins Marsh (1801–1882), it has shown that the unintended negative effects of human economic activities on the environment often are greater than the benefits. For example, there are links between forest cutting and soil ero-

TABLE C.3
The CERES Principles

- **Protection of the biosphere:** Minimize the release of pollutants that may cause environmental damage.
- **Sustainable use of natural resources:** Conserve nonrenewable resources through efficient use and careful planning.
- **Reduction and disposal of waste:** Minimize the creation of waste, especially hazardous waste, and dispose of such materials in a safe, responsible manner.
- **Wise use of energy:** Make every effort to use environmentally safe and sustainable energy sources to meet operating requirements.
- **Risk reduction:** Diminish environmental, health, and safety risks to employees.
- **Marketing of safe products and services:** Sell products that minimize adverse environmental impact and are safe for consumers.
- **Damage compensation:** Accept responsibility for any harm the company causes the environment; conduct bioremediation; and compensate affected parties.
- **Disclosure of environmental incidents:** Public dissemination of accidents relating to operations that harm the environment or pose health or safety risks.
- **Environmental directors:** Appoint at least one board member who is qualified to represent environmental interests; create a position of vice president for environmental affairs.
- **Assessment and annual audit:** Produce and publicize each year a self-evaluation of progress toward implementing the principles and meeting all applicable laws and regulations worldwide. Environmental audits will also be produced annually and distributed to the public.

SOURCES: *Chemical Week*, September 20, 1989, copyright permission granted by *Chemical Week* magazine. *CERES Coalition Handbook*.

sion and between the draining of marshes and lakes and the decline of animal life.

Other early environmentalists, such as John Muir (1838–1914) and Aldo Leopold (1886–1948), argued that humans are not above nature but a part of it. Nature is not for humans to subdue but is sacred and should be preserved not simply for economic use but for its own sake—and for what people can learn from it.

Science and the Environment   Rachel Carson's 1962 best-selling book *The Silent Spring* helped ignite the modern environmental movement by alerting the public to the dangers of unrestricted pesticide use.[28] Carson brought together the findings of toxicology, ecology, and epidemiology in a form accessible to the public. Blending scientific, moral, and political arguments, she connected environmental politics and values with scientific knowledge.

Barry Commoner's *Science and Survival* (1963) continued in this vein. Commoner expanded the scope of ecology to include everything in the physical, chemical, biological, social, political, economic, and philosophical worlds.[29] He argued that all of these elements fit together, and have to be understood as a whole. According to Commoner, the symptoms of environmental problems are in the biological world, but their source lies in economic and political organizations.

Economics and the Environment

Economists promote growth for many reasons: to restore the balance of payments, to make nations more competitive, to create jobs, to reduce the deficit, to provide for the elderly and the sick, and to reduce poverty. Environmentalists criticize economics for its notions of efficiency and its emphasis on economic growth.[30] For example, environmentalists argue that economists do not adequately consider the unintended side effects of efficiency. Environmentalists hold that economists need to supplement estimates of the economic costs and benefits of growth with estimates of other factors that historically were not measured in economic terms.[31]

Economists and public policy analysts argue that the benefits of eliminating risk to the environment and to people must be balanced against the costs. Reducing risk involves determining how effective the proposed methods of reduction are likely to be and how much they will cost. There are many ways to consider cost factors. Analysts can perform cost-effectiveness analyses, in which they attempt to figure out how to achieve a given goal with limited resources, or they can conduct more formal risk-benefit and cost-benefit analyses, in which they quantify both the benefits and the costs of risk reduction.[32]

Qualitative Judgments in Cost-Benefit Analysis

Formal, quantitative approaches to balancing costs and benefits do not eliminate the need for qualitative judgments. For example, how does one assess the value of a magnificent vista obscured by air pollution? What is the loss to society if a particular genetic strain of grass or animal species becomes extinct? How does one assess the lost opportunity costs of spending vast amounts of money on air pollution that could have been spent on productivity enhancement and global competitiveness?

Fairness cannot be ignored when doing cost-benefit analysis.[33] For example, the costs of air pollution reduction may have to be borne disproportionately by the poor in the form of higher gasoline and automobile prices. Intergenerational fairness also plays a role.[34] Future generations have no representatives in the current market and political processes. To what extent should the current generation hold back on its own consumption for the sake of posterity? This question is particularly poignant because few people in the world today are well off. To ask the poor to reduce their life's chances for the sake of a generation yet to come is asking for a great sacrifice.

International Perspectives

Environmental problems present a different face in various countries and regions of the world. The United States and Great Britain lag behind Germany and Japan in mandated emissions standards.[35] In Europe, the Dutch, the Germans, and the Danes are among the most environmentally conscious. Italy, Ireland, Spain, Portugal, and Greece are in the early stages of developing environmental policies. Poland, Hungary, the Czech Republic, and former East Germany are the most polluted of the world's industrialized nations.[36]

U.S. companies need to realize that there is a large growth market in Western Europe for environmentally "friendly" products. U.S. managers also need to be fully aware of the environmental movement in Western Europe. Environmentalists in Europe have been successful in halting many projects.[37] China has been paying a high ecological price for its rapid economic growth. But the government has begun recognizing the problem and is creating some antipollution laws.[38]

Industries that pollute or make polluting products will have to adjust to the new reality, and companies selling products in certain parts of the world must take into account a growing consumer consciousness about environmental protection. Manufacturers may even be legally required to take products and packaging back from customers after use, to recycle or dispose

The environmental movement is a worldwide phenomenon. The "Greens," pictured here demonstrating in LePuy, France, are a growing European political party.

of. In order to meet these requirements in Germany, and be prepared for similar demands in other countries, Hewlett-Packard redesigned its office-machine packaging worldwide.

WHAT MANAGERS CAN DO

To be truly "green"—that is, a cutting-edge company with respect to environmental concerns—legal compliance is not enough. Progressive companies stay abreast *and* ahead of the laws by going beyond marginal compliance and anticipating future requirements and needs.[39] But companies can go further still by experimenting continually with innovations that protect the environment. McDonald's, for example, conducted tests and pilot projects in composting food scraps and in offering refillable coffee mugs and starch-based (biodegradable) cutlery.[40]

Systems Thinking   The first thing managers can do to better understand environmental issues in their companies is to engage in systems thinking. Environmental considerations relate to the organization's inputs, processes, and outputs.[41] *Inputs* include raw materials and energy. Environmental pressures are causing prices of some raw materials, such as metals, to rise. This greatly increases the costs of production. Higher energy costs are causing firms to switch to more fuel-efficient sources.

Firms are considering new *processes* or methods of production that will reduce water pollution, air pollution, noise and vibration, and waste. They are incorporating technologies that sample and monitor (control) these by-products of business processes. Some chemical plants have a computerized system that flashes warnings when a maximum allowable pollution level is soon to be reached. Many companies keep only minimal stocks of hazardous materials, making serious accidents less likely.

Outputs have environmental impact, whether the products themselves or the waste or by-products of processes. To reduce the impact of its outputs, Herman Miller recycles or reuses nearly all waste from the manufacturing process. It sells fabric scraps to the auto industry, leather trim to luggage makers, and vinyl to stereo and auto manufacturers. It buys back its old furniture, refurbishes it, and resells it. Its corporatewide goal is to send zero waste to landfills. Environmental manager Paul Murray says, "There is never an acceptable level of waste at Miller. There are always new things we can learn."[42]

Strategic Integration   Systems thinking reveals that environmental issues permeate the firm, and therefore should be addressed in a comprehensive, integrative fashion. Perhaps the first step is to create the proper mindset. Does your firm see environmental concerns merely in terms of a business versus environment trade-off, or does it see in it a potential source of competitive advantage and an important part of a strategy for long-term survival and effectiveness? The latter attitude, of course, is more likely to set the stage for the following strategic actions.

These ideas help to strategically integrate environmental considerations into the firm's ongoing activities:[43]

1. *Develop a mission statement and strong values supporting environmental advocacy.* Table C.4 shows Procter & Gamble's environmental quality policy.

TABLE C.4
Procter & Gamble's Environmental Quality Policy

Procter & Gamble is committed to providing products of superior quality and value that best fill the needs of the world's consumers. As part of this, Procter & Gamble continually strives to improve the environmental quality of its products, packaging, and operations around the world. To carry out this commitment, it is Procter & Gamble's policy to:

- Ensure our products, packaging, and operations are safe for our employees, consumers, and the environment.

- Reduce or prevent the environmental impact of our products and packaging in their design, manufacture, distribution, use, and disposal whenever possible.

- Meet or exceed the requirements of all environmental laws and regulations.

- Continually assess our environmental technology and programs, and monitor programs toward environmental goals.

- Provide our consumers, customers, employees, communities, public interest groups, and others with relevant and appropriate factual information about the environmental quality of P&G products, packaging, and operations.

- Ensure every employee understands and is responsible and accountable for incorporating environmental quality considerations in daily business activities.

- Have operating policies, programs, and resources in place to implement our environmental quality policy.

SOURCE: K. Dechant and B. Altman, "Environmental Leadership: From Compliance to Competitive Advantage," *The Academy of Management Executive,* August 1994, p. 10. Reprinted by permission.

2. *Establish a framework for managing environmental initiatives.* Some industries have created voluntary codes of environmental practice, for example, the chemical industry's Responsible Care Initiative. Not all standard practices are adopted by all companies, however.[44] At J&J,[45] Environmental Regulatory Affairs uses external audit teams to conduct environmental audits. The Community Environmental Responsibility Program includes strategy and planning, and the development of products and processes with neutral environmental impact.

3. *Engage in "green" process and product design.* The German furniture maker Wilkhahn uses an integrated strategic approach that minimizes the use of virgin resources and uses recycled materials in an environmentally designed plant.[46]

4. *Establish environmentally focused stakeholder relationships.* Many firms work closely with the FDA and receive technical assistance to help convert to more energy-efficient facilities. And to defray costs as well as develop new ideas, small companies like WHYCO Chromium Company establish environmental management partnerships with firms like IBM and GM.[47]

5. *Provide internal and external education.* Engage employees in environmental actions. Dow's WRAP program has cut millions of pounds of hazardous and solid waste and emissions, and achieved annual cost savings of over $10 million, all through employee suggestions.[48] At the same time, inform the public of your firm's environmental initiatives. For example, eco-labeling can urge consumers to recycle and communicate the environmental friendliness of your product. And BP/Amoco redesigned its logo (BP's logo has always been green) as a sun-based emblem, reflecting its strategic vision of a hydrogen/solar-based energy future.[49]

Life Cycle Analysis

Increasingly, firms are paying attention to the pollution caused by their manufacturing processes in the context of the total environmental impact throughout the life cycle of their products.[50] **Life-cycle analysis (LCA)** is a process of analyzing all inputs and outputs to determine the total environmental impact of the production and use of a product. LCA quantifies the total use of resources, and the releases into the air, water, and land. For example, Xerox is using product life-cycle analysis in its design-for-environment tool kit in its efforts to make research and technology investment decisions to improve environmental performance.[51]

Green design considers the extraction of raw materials, product packaging, transportation, and disposal. Consider packaging alone. Goods make the journey from manufacturer to wholesaler to retailer to customer, and are then recycled back to the manufacturer. They may be packaged and repackaged several times, from bulk transport, to large crates, to cardboard boxes, to individual consumer sizes. Repackaging not only creates waste—it costs *time*. The design of initial packaging in sizes and formats adaptable to the final customer can minimize the need for repackaging, cut waste, and realize financial benefits.

Implementation

How can companies implement "greening" strategies? A fundamental requirement for effective environmentalism is a commitment by top management. Specific actions could include commissioning an environmental audit in which an outside company checks for environmental hazards, drafting (or reviewing) the organization's environmental policy, communicating the policy and making it highly visible throughout the organization, having environmental professionals within the company report directly to the president or CEO, allocating sufficient resources to support the environmental effort, and building bridges between the organization and other companies, governments, environmentalists, and local communities.

Ultimately, it is essential to make employees accountable for any of their actions that have environmental impact.[52] Texaco, Du Pont, and other companies evaluate managers on their ideas for minimizing pollution and for new, environment-friendly products. Kodak ties some managers' compensation to the prevention of chemical spills; the company attributes to this policy a dramatic reduction in accidents.[53]

Companies can employ all areas of the organization to meet the challenges posed by pollution and environmental challenges. A variety of companies have responded creatively to these challenges[54] and may serve as models for other organizations. The following sections describe more specific actions companies can take to address environmental issues.

Strategy   Actions companies can take in the area of strategy include the following:

1. *Cut back on environmentally unsafe businesses.* Du Pont, the leading producer of CFCs, announced it would voluntarily pull out of this $750 million business.[55]

2. *Carry out R&D on environmentally safe activities.* Du Pont claimed it spents up to $1 billion on the best replacements for CFCs. Shell is investing in solar and renewable energy.[56]

3. *Develop and expand environmental cleanup services.* Building on the expertise gained in cleaning up its own plants, Du Pont formed a safety and environmental resources division to help industrial customers clean up their toxic wastes.[57]

4. *Compensate for environmentally risky projects.* AES has a long-standing policy of planting trees to offset its power plants' carbon emission.[58]

5. *Make your company accountable to others.* Royal Dutch Shell and Bristol-Myers Squibb are trendsetters in green reporting.[59] Danish health care and enzymes company Novo Nordisk purposely asked for feedback from environmentalists, regulators, and other interested bodies from around Europe. Its reputation has been enhanced, its people have learned a lot, and new market opportunities have been identified.[60]

6. *Make every new product environmentally better than the last.* This is IBM's goal. IBM aims to use recyclable materials, reduce hazardous materials, reduce emissions, and use natural energy and resources in packaging.[61]

Public Affairs   In the area of public affairs, companies can take a variety of actions:

1. *Attempt to gain environmental legitimacy and credibility.* The cosponsors of Earth Day included Apple Computer, Hewlett-Packard, and the Chemical Manufacturers Association. McDonald's has tried to become a corporate environmental "educator." Ethel M. Chocolates, in public tours of its Las Vegas factory, showcases effective handling of its industrial wastes.[62]

2. *Try to avoid losses caused by insensitivity to environmental issues.* As a result of Exxon's apparent lack of concern after the *Valdez* oil spill, 41 percent of Americans polled said they would consider boycotting the company.[63] MacMillan Bloedel lost a big chunk of sales almost overnight when it was targeted publicly as a clear-cutter and chlorine user.[64]

3. *Collaborate with environmentalists.* Executives at Pacific Gas & Electric seek discussions and joint projects with any willing environmental group, and ARCO has prominent environmentalists on its board of directors.

The Legal Area   Actions companies can take in the legal area include the following:

1. *Try to avoid confrontation with state or federal pollution control agencies.* W. R. Grace faced expensive and time-consuming

lawsuits as a result of its toxic dumps. Browning-Ferris, Waste Management Inc., and Louisiana-Pacific were charged with pollution control violations, damaging their reputations.

2. *Comply early.* Because compliance costs only increase over time, the first companies to act will have lower costs. This will enable them to increase their market share and profits and win competitive advantage. 3M's goal was to meet government requirements to replace or improve underground storage tanks five years ahead of the legally mandated year.

3. *Take advantage of innovative compliance programs.* Instead of source-by-source reduction, the EPA's bubble policy allows factories to reduce pollution at different sources by different amounts, provided the overall result is equivalent. Therefore, 3M installed equipment on only certain production lines at its tape-manufacturing facility in Pennsylvania, thereby lowering its compliance costs.[65] Today, there is greater use of economic instruments like tradable pollution permits, charges, and taxes to encourage improvements.[66] *Joint implementation* involves companies in industrialized nations working with businesses in developing countries to help them reduce greenhouse gas emissions. The company lending a hand then receives credit toward fulfilling its environmental obligations at home. The developing country receives investment, technology, and jobs; the company giving a lending hand receives environmental credits; and the world gets cleaner air.[67]

4. *Don't deal with fly-by-night subcontractors for waste disposal.* They are more likely to cut corners, break laws, and do a poor job. Moreover, the result for you could be bad publicity and legal problems.[68]

Operations   The actions companies can take in the area of operations include the following:

1. *Promote new manufacturing technologies.* Louisville Gas and Electric took the lead in installing smokestack scrubbers, Consolidated Natural Gas pioneered the use of clean-burning technologies, and Nucor developed state-of-the-art steel mills.

2. *Practice reverse logistics.* Firms move packaging and other used goods from the consumer back up the distribution channel to the firm. Make them not just costs, but a source of revenue—inputs to production. Fuji Australia believes that remanufacturing has generated returns in the tens of millions of dollars.[69]

3. *Encourage technological advances that reduce pollution from products and manufacturing processes.* 3M's "Pollution Prevention Pays" program is based on the premise that it is too costly for companies to employ add-on technology; instead, they should attempt to eliminate pollution at the source.[70] Pollution prevention, more than pollution control, is related to both better environmental performance and better manufacturing performance, including cost and speed.[71]

4. *Develop new product formulations.* Weyerhaeuser, recognizing the decreasing supply of timber and growing demand, is working to produce high-quality wood on fewer, continuously

regenerated acres.[72] Electrolux has developed a sun-powered lawn mower and a chainsaw that runs on vegetable oil.[73] Many companies are developing green pesticides.

5. *Eliminate manufacturing wastes.* 3M replaced volatile solvents with water-based ones, thereby eliminating the need for costly air pollution control equipment. BPAmoco implemented a similar program.

6. *Find alternative uses for wastes.* When DuPont halted ocean dumping of acid iron salts, it discovered that the salts could be sold to water treatment plants at a profit. A Queensland sugarcane facility powers production via sugarcane waste.[74]

7. *Insist that your suppliers have strong environmental performance.* Chiquita Banana had a spotty environmental record, but now its plantations are certified by the Rainforest Alliance, and Wal-Mart has named Chiquita its most environmentally conscious supplier.[75] Scott Paper discovered that many of its environmental problems were "imported" through the supply chain. Initially focusing on pulp suppliers, the company sent questionnaires asking for figures on air, water, and land releases, energy consumption, and energy sources. Scott was astonished at the variance. For example, carbon dioxide emissions varied by a factor of 17 among different suppliers. Scott dropped the worst performers and announced that the best performers would in the future receive preference in its purchasing decisions.[76]

8. *Assemble products with the environment in mind.* Make them easy to snap apart, sort, and recycle, and avoid glues and screws.

Marketing   Companies can also take action in the marketing area:

1. *Cast products in an environment-friendly light.* Most Americans believe a company's environmental reputation influences what they buy.[77] Companies such as Procter & Gamble, Colgate-Palmolive, Lever Brothers, 3M, and Sunoco try to act on the basis of this finding. Wal-Mart has made efforts to provide customers with recycled or recyclable products.

2. *Avoid attacks by environmentalists for unsubstantiated or inappropriate claims.* When Hefty marketed "biodegradable" garbage bags, that claim was technically true, but it turned out that landfill conditions didn't allow decomposition to occur.[78] The extensive public backlash affected not only Hefty bags but also other Hefty products. Hefty didn't lie, but it did exaggerate. Its tactics overshadowed well-intentioned greening actions.

3. *Differentiate your product via environmental services.* ICI takes back and disposes of customers' waste as a customer service. Disposal is costly, but the service differentiates the firm's products. Teach customers how to use and dispose of products; for instance, farmers inadvertently abuse pesticides. Make education a part of a firm's after-sales service.

4. *Take advantage of the Net.* The EcoMall (www.ecomall.com/biz/) promotes a number of environmentally oriented firms in 68 product categories. Firms using the Net target green consumers globally, effectively, and efficiently.[79]

Accounting   Actions companies can take in the accounting area include the following:

1. *Collect useful data.* The best current reporters of environmental information include Dow Europe, Danish Steel Works, BSO/Origin, 3M, and Monsanto. BSO/Origin has begun to explore a system for corporate environmental accounting.[80]

2. *Make polluters pay.* CIBA-GEIGY has a "polluter pays principle" throughout the firm, so managers have the incentive to combat pollution at the sources they can influence.[81]

3. *Demonstrate that antipollution programs pay off.* 3M's Pollution Prevention Pays program is based on the premise that only if the program pays will there be the motivation to carry it out. Every company needs to be cost-effective in its pollution reduction efforts.

4. *Use an advanced waste accounting system.* Do this in addition to standard management accounting, which can hinder investment in new technologies. Waste accounting makes sure all costs are identified and better decisions can be made.

5. *Adopt full cost accounting.* This approach, called for by Frank Popoff, Dow's chairman, ensures that the price of a product reflects its full environmental cost.[82]

6. *Show the overall impact of the pollution reduction program.* Companies have an obligation to account for the costs and benefits of their pollution reduction programs. 3M claims half a *billion* dollars in savings from pollution prevention efforts.[83]

Finance   In the area of finance, companies can do the following:

1. *Gain the respect of the socially responsible investment community.* Many investment funds in the United States and Europe take environmental criteria into account. A study by ICF Kaiser concluded that environmental improvements could lead to significant reduction in the perceived risk of a firm, with a possible 5 percent increase in the stock price.[84] Socially responsible rating services and investment funds try to help people invest with a "clean conscience."[85]

2. *Recognize true liability.* Investment houses often employ environmental analysts who search for companies' true environmental liability in evaluating their potential performance. Bankers look at environmental risks and environmental market opportunities when evaluating a company's credit rating.[86] The Securities and Exchange Commission in New York requires some companies to report certain environmental costs. The Swiss Bank Corp. has specialized Environmental Performance Rating Units to include environmental criteria in order to improve the quality of financial analysis.[87]

3. *Fund and then assist green companies.* Ann Winblad of Hummer Winblad Venture Partners was one of the first venture capitalists to coach green entrepreneurs to increase their business skills and chances of success.[88]

4. *Recognize financial opportunities.* Worldwide, one of these great opportunities is water. Water must be purified and delivered reliably to everyone worldwide. Three billion people lack sanitary sewage facilities, and 1 billion have poor access to drinking water. Infrastructures in big cities, including those in the United States, are seriously deteriorating. Supplying clean water to people and companies is a $400 billion-a-year industry—one-third larger than the global pharmaceutical industry. Companies like Thames, Suez, and Vivendi are aggressively pursuing this market. They are betting that water in the 21st century will be like oil in the 20th century. A Bear Stearns analyst calls water the best sector for the next century.[89]

KEY TERMS

carrying capacity   The ability of a finite resource to sustain a population. p. 169

conservation   An environmental philosophy that seeks to avoid waste, promote the rational and efficient use of natural resources, and maximize long-term yields, especially of renewable resources. p. 169

environmental movement   An environmental philosophy postulating that the unintended negative effects of human economic activities on the environment are often greater than the benefits, and that nature should be preserved. p. 169

life-cycle analysis (LCA)   A process of evaluating all inputs and outputs to determine the total environmental impact of the production and use of a product. p. 172

sustainable growth   Economic growth and development that meet the organization's present needs without harming the ability of future generations to meet their needs. p. 169

tragedy of the commons   The environmental destruction that results as individuals and businesses consume finite resources (the "commons") to serve their short-term interests without regard for the long-term consequences. p. 169

DISCUSSION QUESTIONS

1. To what extent can and should we rely on government to solve environmental problems? What are some of government's limitations? Take a stand on the role and usefulness of government regulations on business activities.

2. To what extent should managers today be responsible for cleaning up mistakes from years past that have hurt the environment?

3. How would you characterize the environmental movement in Western Europe? How does it differ from the U.S. movement? What difference will this make to a multinational company that wants to produce and market goods in many countries?

4. What business opportunities can you see in meeting environmental challenges? Be specific.

5. You are appointed environmental manager of XYZ Company. Describe some actions you will take to address environmental challenges. Discuss obstacles you are likely to encounter in the company and how you will manage them.

6. Interview a businessperson about environmental regulations and report your findings to the class. How would you characterize his or her attitude? How constructive is his or her attitude?

7. Interview a businessperson about actions he or she has taken that have helped the environment. Report your findings to the class and discuss.

8. Identify and discuss some examples of the tragedy of the commons. How can the tragedies be avoided?

9. Discuss the status of recycling efforts in your community or school, your perspectives on it as a consumer, and what business opportunities could be available.

10. What companies currently come to mind as having the best and worst reputations with respect to the environment? Why do they have these reputations?

11. Choose one product and discuss its environmental impact through its entire life cycle.

12. What are you, your college or university, and your community doing about the environment? What would you recommend doing?

CHAPTER 6

International Management

It was once said that the sun never sets on the British Empire. Today, the sun does set on the British Empire, but not on the scores of global empires, including those of IBM, Unilever, Volkswagen, and Hitachi.

—Lester Brown

CHAPTER OUTLINE

The Global Environment
  European Unification
  The Pacific Rim
  North America
  The Rest of the World
Consequences of a Global Economy
Global Strategy
  Pressures for Global Integration
  Pressures for Local Responsiveness
  Choosing a Global Strategy
Entry Mode
  Exporting
  Licensing
  Franchising
  Joint Ventures
  Wholly Owned Subsidiaries
Management across Borders
  Skills of the Global Manager
  Understanding Cultural Issues
  Ethical Issues in International Management

LEARNING OBJECTIVES

After studying Chapter 6, you will know:

1. Why the world economy is becoming more integrated than ever before.

2. What integration of the global economy means for individual companies and their managers.

3. The strategies organizations use to compete in the global marketplace.

4. The various entry modes organizations use to enter overseas markets.

5. How companies can approach the task of staffing overseas operations.

6. The skills and knowledge managers need to manage globally.

7. Why cultural differences across countries influence management.

A BUMPY RIDE AT DAIMLERCHRYSLER

FROM THE PAGES OF

BusinessWeek

It was the deal heard 'round the world. In May 1998, a stunning $36 billion merger was announced by Daimler Benz and Chrysler Corporation. The marriage promised to rock the global auto industry and provide a blueprint for international consolidation on an epic scale. But the union didn't turn out to be a merger made in heaven. Daimler chief Jurgen E. Schrempp grabbed the wheel of DaimlerChrysler (DCX). His cochairman from Chrysler, Robert J. Eaton, took a backseat. And Thomas T. Stallkamp, Chrysler's president, got caught in between.

At the first meeting of the global management team, the officers ate, drank, mixed, and matched for two days; Germans joined Americans in discussion groups, with a member of the board of management—the company's top executives—heading up each table. After the breakout sessions and dinner, the hotel turned into a giant, free-form cocktail party. A Chrysler finance exec, Thomas F. Gilman, began playing piano in the bar, and Americans and Germans alike joined in to sing. Schrempp and the group bellowed song after song until the wee hours. The German cochairman led one final chorus of "Bye, Bye, Miss American Pie." Then, with a wild gleam in his eye, Schrempp grabbed his ever-present assistant, Lydia Deininger, picked her up, and threw her over his shoulder. Schrempp snatched a bottle of champagne in his free hand, raised it in the air, and yelled out with a grin: "See you later, boys!" "It's odd," Stallkamp said. "Some people say it's Continental, but it's not appropriate business behavior."

It was only the tip of the cultural iceberg. The Germans smoked, drank wine with lunch, and worked late hours, sending out for pizza and beer at their desks. The old Chrysler banned smoking and alcohol in its facilities. The Americans worked around the clock on deadlines but didn't stay late as a routine. The yawning gap in pay scales fueled an undercurrent of tension. The Americans earned two, three, and in some cases four times as much as their German counterparts. But the expenses of U.S. workers were tightly controlled compared with those of the German system. Daimler-side employees thought nothing of flying to Paris or New York for a half-day meeting, then capping the visit with a fancy dinner and a night in an expensive hotel. The Americans blanched at the extravagance.

The Germans and Americans simply did business differently. The six-hour time difference didn't help. By the time the Americans started their day, the Germans had already had lunch. Stuttgart always seemed to have a head start on Auburn Hills. German management-board members had executive assistants who prepared detailed position papers on any number of issues. The Americans didn't have assigned aides and formulated their decisions by talking directly to engineers or other specialists. A German decision worked its way through the bureaucracy for final approval at the top. Then it was set in stone. The

Juergen Schrempp, CEO and chairman of DaimlerChrysler AG.

Setting the Stage

Americans allowed midlevel employees to proceed on their own initiative, sometimes without waiting for executive-level approval.

Eaton slowly but surely withdrew, grew detached, and didn't contribute. Schrempp didn't exactly intimidate Eaton. He overwhelmed him. For his part, Eaton saw himself as a team builder: "I think my legacy is the cultural change and building the strong team. It wouldn't have happened if I wasn't there." But some of his own execs could not get past the barriers Eaton had erected. Stallkamp had hoped the Chrysler side could use Eaton as a "silver bullet" to be fired at crucial times to tip an issue its way. But that couldn't happen if Eaton wasn't up for it.

The public view of DaimlerChrysler as a "merger of equals" had begun to crack. U.S. investors fled from the stock because the company wasn't incorporated in America. High-profile defections of Chrysler execs fed the image of German control. Two vice presidents quit to join Ford Motor Co. The management board shrank from 17 members to 13, with 8 Germans and 5 Americans. A new business structure was put in place, with three equal automotive pillars: Mercedes-Benz cars, Chrysler, and heavy trucks.

At the end of 2000, Schrempp told German media that it could take two to four years to turn the tide at Chrysler. He replaced Eaton's short-lived successor, James P. Holden, with Dieter Zetsche, age 47, a veteran Daimler executive, and named Wolfgang Bernhard, who had handled the launch of Mercedes's flagship S-Class sedans, chief operating officer. For the rest of the team he is relying on Chrysler veterans who have been plucked from relative obscurity after a rash of high-ranking defections. At least these Americans won't have to wait for scary transatlantic phone calls to find out what the Germans are thinking. The presence of so many Americans points to something else: a tacit acknowledgment by the Germans that they have a lot to learn about the workings of a mass-market giant like Chrysler.

While Zetsche shares information openly with the management team, once he makes a decision, it's final. "He can be extremely personable one minute," said one Chrysler executive. "And the next minute, you wish to God you were somewhere else." At the moment, this odd blend of saviors and survivors—ironically, the first true German-American management team at DaimlerChrysler—offers Chrysler's best shot at renewal.

On July 18, 2002, DaimlerChrysler reported a big improvement in second quarter profits, a signal that its recovery may be shifting into gear. "We're on the right path," Schrempp said. It was good news for Schrempp too. The second quarter results were all the more remarkable given the tough business climate. With 2002 vehicle sales down slightly in Europe and also in the United States, where automakers are locked in a profit-eroding price war, DaimlerChrysler has been under pressure in its two biggest markets.

Source: Bill Vlasic and Bradley A. Stertz, "Taken for a Ride," *Business Week Online*, June 5, 2000; Joann Muller, Jeff Green, and Christine Tierney, "Chrysler's Rescue Team: Can It Stop the Bleeding?" *Businessweek Online*, January 15, 2001; Christine N. Tierney "DaimlerChrysler Steps on the Gas," *Business Week*, July 19, 2002.

As the DaimlerChrysler story shows, today's manager constantly must make decisions about whether and how to pursue global opportunities. Of course, these opportunities need to be evaluated carefully, not just from a competitive or financial standpoint but from a cultural and managerial standpoint as well. It is often the case that global opportunities look good on paper but don't pan out if managers are unable to work in a different international context.

This chapter reviews the reasons for the globalization of competition, examines why international management differs from domestic management, considers how companies expand globally, and sees how companies can develop individuals to manage across borders.

The Global Environment

The global economy is becoming more integrated than ever before. For example, in January 1995, the World Trade Organization (WTO) was formed and now has 144 member countries, including China. (the International Monetary Fund, set up by the United Nations in 1945, serves a similar purpose and includes 184 countries). WTO rules apply to over 90 percent of international trade. Recently the WTO has become controversial, as its role has expanded from reducing tariffs to eliminating nontariff barriers. The controversy stems from the fact that the WTO can be used to challenge environmental, health, and other regulations. These regulations often serve legitimate social goals but may be regarded as impediments to international trade. You can see the importance—and stickiness—of this issue at http://www.wto.org/.

In addition to the WTO, there are other economic influences that operate on a global scale. Three areas, typically referred to as the triad of North America, Europe, and Asia, are the most dominant. However, other developing countries and regions represent important areas for economic growth as well. Figure 6.1 shows a map of the major international trade areas.

European Unification

Europe is integrating economically to form the biggest market in the world. The euro, adopted in 2001, created a common currency. In concept, the European Union (EU) will allow goods, services, capital, and human resources to flow freely across national borders. The goal of unification is to strengthen Europe's position as the third economic superpower, with the United States and Japan.[1]

Under the Maastricht Treaty, member countries have agreed to adopt a common European currency called the euro. However, the pace of unification has been slower

FIGURE 6.1 Major International Trade Areas

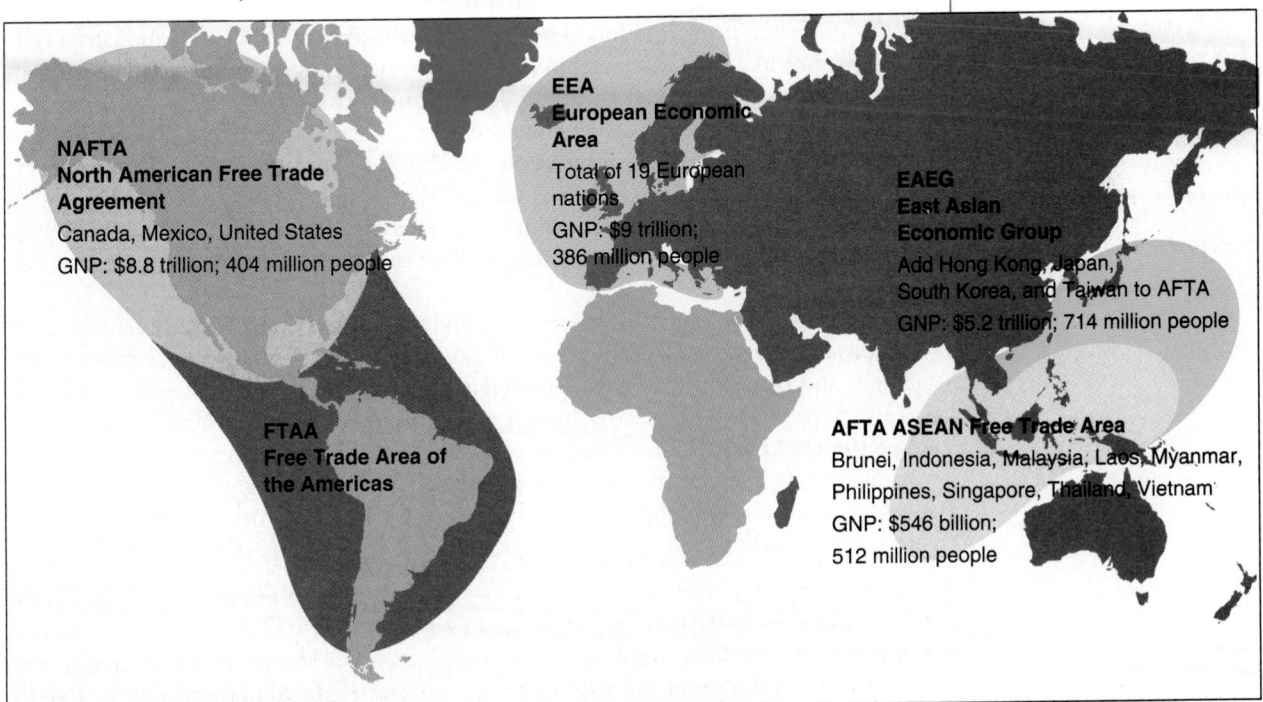

SOURCE: Michael Czinkota and Ilkka Ronkainen, *International Marketing*, 6th ed. Copyright © 2001. Reprinted with permission of South-Western, a division of Thomson Learning, www.thomsonrights.com.

Exchange rates in early 2002
in Prague, Czech Republic.

than anticipated. There are structural issues within Europe that need to be corrected for the EU to function effectively. In particular, Western Europeans on average work fewer hours, earn more pay, take longer vacations, and enjoy far more social entitlements than do their counterparts in North America and Asia. To be competitive in a global economy, Europeans must increase their level of productivity. In the past, powerful trade unions fiercely defended social benefits, and local governments regulated the labor markets. Both of these actions have encouraged companies such as Siemens and ABB Asea Brown Boveri Ltd. to move operations abroad. Now it appears that labor markets are being deregulated and that there are more incentives to create jobs.[2]

Unification will create a more competitive Europe. The EU's share of the world's top 100 industrial firms is rising. The community is pursuing an active industrial policy to enhance its competitiveness in information technology. It is making fast gains in semiconductors and is restructuring in defense and aerospace.

The impact is hard to predict, but there are many possibilities. U.S. exports to Europe could be replaced by the goods of European producers; European exports could replace U.S. products in other markets; U.S. capital could flow into Europe to the detriment of capital formation and productivity growth in the United States. Another possibility is a "Fortress Europe" that restricts trade with countries outside EU walls.

The consensus among U.S. observers is that the United States must remain vigilant to ensure that a Fortress Europe does not close itself to U.S. goods and services. Management and labor must work cooperatively to achieve high levels of quality that will make U.S. products and services attractive to consumers in Europe and other markets across the world. The United States needs not only managers who will stay on top of worldwide developments and manage high-quality, efficient organizations but a well-educated, well-trained, and continually *retrained* labor force to remain competitive with the Europeans, the Japanese, and other formidable competitors.[3]

The Pacific Rim

Among the Pacific Rim countries, Japan dominated world attention during much of the last decade. But Japan is hardly the only important global player from the Pacific region. China is developing and becoming more prosperous. Even Japan is concerned about the countries known as the "four tigers" or the "four dragons": South Korea, Taiwan, Singapore, and Hong Kong. Korea is foremost among them; its immediate goal is to become one of the world's 10 most technologically advanced nations. Already the four dragons, along with other Asian growth nations like Thailand, Malaysia, and the Philippines, account for more trade with the United States than Japan does.[4]

For the last several years, the 21 member countries of the Asia-Pacific Economic Cooperation (APEC) have been working to reduce trade barriers and establish general rules for investment and policies that encourage international commerce. Recent volatility in global financial markets has been linked directly to economic uncertainties in the Pacific Rim. The U.S. government has been working with APEC countries to stabilize the economic environment and facilitate more open-trade agreements. Although the United States has been trading with member countries such as Australia, Singapore, Malaysia, Japan, Indonesia, China, and South Korea, APEC holds much the same promise as NAFTA and the EU in facilitating and strengthening international business relationships. Member countries represent 40 percent of the world's population and 50 percent of the world's economic output.[5]

North America

The **North American Free Trade Agreement (NAFTA)** combined the economies of the United States, Canada, and Mexico into the world's largest trading bloc with more than 370 million customers and approximately $6.5 trillion in total gross national product (GNP). Within the next 10 years, virtually all U.S. industrial exports into Mexico and Canada will be duty-free. Although the United States has had a longer-standing agreement with Canada, Mexico has quickly emerged as the United States' third-largest trading partner as a result of NAFTA. U.S. industries that have benefited in the short run include capital-goods suppliers, manufacturers of consumer durables, grain producers and distributors, construction equipment manufacturers, the auto industry, and the financial industry, which now has privileged access into a previously protected market.

> **North American Free Trade Agreement (NAFTA)**
>
> An economic pact that combined the economies of the United States, Canada, and Mexico into the world's largest trading bloc.

Despite the potential benefits of NAFTA, Mexico will need to bolster its infrastructure and take care of troubling environmental issues to support its economic growth. Mexico recently established a comprehensive statute for environmental regulation to address issues such as air pollution, hazardous waste, water pollution, and noise pollution. Surprisingly, Mexico has very strict laws protecting natural resources, many of which were fashioned after U.S. laws. However, there has not been sufficient enforcement of those laws. Mexico has some way to go in developing a strong environmental services industry to handle environmental protection and cleanup. Both the United States and Mexico are committing up to $8 billion for environmental protection.[6]

The Border Environment Cooperation Commission (BECC) is working with 68 communities throughout the Mexico–U.S. border region to address their environmental concerns. To date, the BECC has certified 60 water, wastewater, and municipal solid waste infrastructure projects. These projects will represent a total estimated investment of $1.15 billion (see http://www.nadbank.org/).

The Rest of the World

We can't begin to fully discuss all the important developments, markets, and competitors shaping the global environment. But we can convey the immense potential for other major developments and new competitive threats and opportunities. For example, globalization so far has left out three huge, high-potential regions of the world: the Middle East, Africa, and Latin America.[7] The following box about a free-trade agreement for North and South America discusses one possible group. Together these regions account for a major share of the world's natural resources and are among the fastest-growing economies. Their potential has not begun to be realized.[8]

FROM THE PAGES OF

BusinessWeek

It's one of the biggest and boldest ideas ever proposed in the realm of commerce: the Free Trade Area of the Americas (FTAA). Stretching from the Bering Strait to Cape Horn, with a population of 800 million and a combined gross domestic product of more than $11 trillion, the FTAA would be the largest free-trade zone on the planet, a vast market marked by nonexistent or very low tariffs, streamlined customs regulations, and the gradual disappearance of quotas, subsidies, and other impediments to trade.

To date, this vast commercial bloc exists only on paper. Officials from 34 countries have been working on the details of a pact for nearly seven years. Recently, hopes for the FTAA seemed dim as nations struggled to reach agreement on a host of complicated issues. But a powerful new advocate for the idea has now emerged. President George W. Bush has placed the FTAA firmly at the top of his ambitious trade agenda. The former Texas governor has seen firsthand the benefits of cross-border commerce with Mexico through NAFTA.

Many negotiators from the Americas maintain that the FTAA will become a reality in some form or another. Policymakers already have mapped out a comprehensive agenda spanning everything from intellectual property-rights protection to guarantees for cross-border investments. Procedures to speed goods through customs—a notorious source of bureaucratic hassle—have been drafted and are being put into practice.

That's not to say that a deal is a sure thing. Many civil groups are demanding that their concerns be heard. U.S. unions fear that FTAA would prompt manufacturers to move en masse to low-wage locations in Latin America. But beyond all the maneuvering, there's another reason the FTAA probably will move forward, even with the inevitable wrangles and delays. For Latin nations, the opportunity for preferential access to the largest market in the world—the United States—is too good to pass up. And in the United States business executives are increasingly alarmed that the rest of the world is banding together into trade blocs—blocs that are also seeking treaties with the major countries of Latin America. The European Union, currently the world's largest trading club, signed a free-trade agreement with Mexico in 2001. Now it's pursuing a pact with Mercosur, the customs union made up of Brazil, Argentina, Uruguay, and Paraguay.

Prospects for an FTAA got a boost in August 2001 when the Senate gave President Bush final approval to negotiate market-opening trade deals that Congress can approve or reject but not amend. Unfortunately, the resentment generated by the perception of the United States' benign neglect of the region's economic hardship has temporarily cooled enthusiasm among Latin American leaders to embrace a pact that many criticized as one-sided from the outset. Although most nations still support an agreement, rising poverty and unemployment are testing the public's tolerance for policies that require sacrifice up-front, and so reaching a final deal won't be easy.

SOURCES: Geri Smith, "Betting on Free Trade," *Business Week,* April 23, 2001; Joshua Goodman, "O'Neill, Free Speech, and Free Trade," *Business Week,* August 5, 2002.

Consequences of a Global Economy

The increasing integration of the global economy has had many consequences. First, over the last decade the volume of world trade has grown at a faster rate than has the volume of world output. Over the last few decades, world output has grown by approximately 30 percent while world trade has grown by over 50 percent.[9] Years of emphasis on international commerce by major industrial countries, as well as recent liberalized trading brought about by NAFTA, EU, and APEC, have resulted in lowering the barriers to the free flow of goods, services, and capital among nation-states. The impact of these trends is staggering. The dollar value of international trade (merchandise exports and commercial services) is approximately $6.82 trillion. Most experts expect competition to increase as trade is liberalized, and as is often the case,

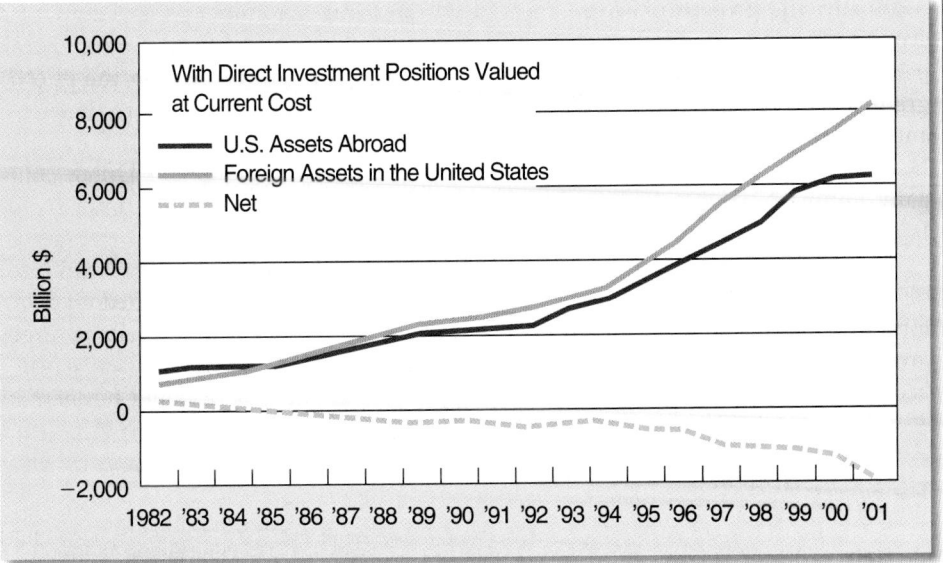

FIGURE 6.2
Direct Investment Positions on a Historical-Cost Basis, 1982–2001

SOURCE: Elena L. Nguyen, "The International Investment Position of the United States at Yearend 2001," *Survey of Current Business*, July 2002, pp. 10–11.

the more efficient players will survive. To succeed in this industrial climate, managers need to study opportunities in existing markets, as well as work to enhance the competitiveness of their firms. Second, *foreign direct investment (FDI)* is playing an ever-increasing role in the global economy as companies of all sizes invest in overseas operations (see Figure 6.2). As shown in Table 6.1, foreign direct investments are matched closely on a regional basis by U.S. investments abroad. The major investments have been among the United States, Europe, and Japan. These figures support the idea of the economic triad mentioned earlier.[10]

A third consequence of an increasingly integrated global economy is that imports are penetrating deeper into the world's largest economies. For the first time, manufactured goods rather than raw materials account for more than half of Japan's imports.[11] The growth of imports is a natural by-product of the growth of world trade and the trend toward the manufacture of component parts, or even entire products, overseas before shipping them back home for final sale.

	U.S. Investment Abroad	Foreign Direct Investment in the United States
All countries	$1,381,674	$1,321,063
Canada	139,031	108,600
Europe	725,793	946,758
Latin America and other Western Hemisphere	269,556	58,881
Africa	15,872	3,264
Middle East	12,643	6,039
Asia and Pacific	216,501	197,522

TABLE 6.1
U.S. and Foreign Direct Investments, in Millions of Dollars, 2001

SOURCE: Maria Borga and Daniel R. Yorgason, "Direct Investment Positions for 2001: Country and Industry Detail," *Survey of International Business*, July 2002, pp. 25–35.

Finally, the growth of world trade, FDI, and imports implies that companies around the globe are finding their home markets under attack from foreign competitors. This is true in Japan, where Kodak has taken market share in the photographic film industry away from Fuji; in the United States, where Japanese automakers have captured market share from General Motors (GM), Ford, and DaimlerChrysler; and in Western Europe, where the once-dominant Dutch company Philips N. V. has lost market share in the consumer electronics industry to Japan's JVC, Matsushita, and Sony.

What does all this mean for the manager? Compared with only a few years ago, *opportunities are greater* because the movement toward free trade has opened up many formerly protected national markets. The potential for export, and for making direct investments overseas, is greater today than ever before. *The environment is more complex* because today's manager often has to deal with the challenges of doing business in

TABLE 6.2   The *Business Week* Global 1000

Rank 2002	Rank 2001	Firm	Country	Market Value, Billions of U.S.$
1	1	General Electric	U.S.	309.46
2	2	Microsoft	U.S.	275.70
3	3	Exxon Mobil	U.S.	271.23
4	6	Wal-Mart Stores	U.S.	240.91
5	5	Citigroup	U.S.	223.04
6	4	Pfizer	U.S.	216.78
7	8	Royal Dutch/Shell Group	Neth./Britain	194.55
8	9	BP	Britain	192.12
9	21	Johnson & Johnson	U.S.	186.94
10	13	Intel	U.S.	184.67
11	12	American International Group	U.S.	174.99
12	23	Coca-Cola	U.S.	138.00
13	10	International Business Machines	U.S.	137.72
14	11	Ntt DoCoMo	Japan	135.86
15	16	Merck	U.S.	129.68
16	15	GlaxoSmithKline	Britain	126.27
17	27	Novartis	Switzerland	123.93
18	26	Philip Morris	U.S.	122.93
19	36	Bank of America	U.S.	117.09
20	17	Verizon Communications	U.S.	116.84
21	39	Procter & Gamble	U.S.	116.38
22	24	Hsbc Holdings	Britain	116.34
23	19	Systems	U.S.	115.53
24	18	SBC Communications	U.S.	114.53
25	30	Berkshire Hathaway	U.S.	114.36

main competitive weapon and competition is intense (for example, hand-held calculators and semiconductor chips). It is also important in industries in which key international competitors are based in countries with low factor costs (e.g., low labor and energy costs).

The presence of competitors engaged in *global strategic coordination* is another factor that creates pressure for global integration. Reacting to global competitive threats calls for global strategic coordination, which creates pressure to centralize decisions regarding the competitive strategies of different national subsidiaries at corporate headquarters. Thus, once one multinational company in an industry adopts global strategic coordination, its competitors may be forced to respond in kind.

Pressures for Local Responsiveness

In some circumstances, companies must be able to adapt to different needs in different locations. Strong pressures for local responsiveness emerge when *consumer tastes and preferences differ significantly* among countries. In such cases, product and/or marketing messages have to be customized.

In the automobile industry, for example, demand by U.S. consumers for pickup trucks is strong. This is particularly true in the South and West, where many families have a pickup truck as a second or third vehicle. In contrast, in Europe pickup trucks are viewed as utility vehicles and are purchased primarily by companies rather than by individuals. As a result, automakers must tailor their marketing messages to the differences in consumer demand.

Pressures for local responsiveness also emerge when there are *differences in traditional practices* among countries. For example, in Great Britain people drive on the left side of the road, creating a demand for right-hand-drive cars, whereas in neighboring France people drive on the right side of the road. Obviously, automobiles must be customized to accommodate this difference in traditional practices.

Differences in distribution channels and sales practices among countries also may create pressures for local responsiveness. In the pharmaceutical industry, the Japanese distribution system differs radically from the U.S. system. Japanese doctors will respond unfavorably to an American-style, high-pressure sales force. Thus, pharmaceutical companies have to adopt different marketing practices in Japan (soft versus hard sell).

Finally, *economic and political demands* imposed by host country governments may necessitate a degree of local responsiveness. Most important, threats of protectionism, economic nationalism, and local content rules (rules requiring that a certain percentage of a product be manufactured locally) dictate that international companies manufacture locally.

Choosing a Global Strategy

Figure 6.3 shows the integration – responsiveness grid, implying the existence of four approaches to international competition: the international model, the multinational model, the global model, and the transnational model. Each of these types of organizations differs in terms of its approach to strategy as well as the structure and systems that drive operations.

The International Model The **international organization model** is designed to help companies exploit their existing core capabilities to expand into foreign markets. The international model uses subsidiaries in each country in which the company does business, with ultimate control exercised by the parent company. In particular, while subsidiaries may have some latitude to adapt products to local conditions, core functions such as research and development tend to be centralized in the parent company.

> **international organization model**
>
> An organization model that is composed of a company's overseas subsidiaries and characterized by greater control by the parent company over the research function and local product and marketing strategies than is the case in the multinational model.

Consequently, subsidiary dependence on the parent company for new products, processes, and ideas requires a great deal of coordination and control by the parent company.

The advantage of this model is that it facilitates the transfer of skills and know-how from the parent company to subsidiaries around the globe. For example, IBM, Xerox, and Kodak all profited from the transfer of their core skills in technology and R&D overseas. The overseas successes of Kellogg, Coca-Cola, Heinz, and Procter & Gamble are based more on marketing know-how than on technological expertise. During the late 1900s, many Japanese companies, including Toyota and Honda, successfully penetrated U.S. markets with their core competencies in manufacturing relative to local competitors. Still others have based their competitive advantage on general management skills. These factors explain the growth of international hotel chains such as Hilton International, Intercontinental, and Sheraton.

One disadvantage of the international model is that it does not provide maximum latitude for responding to local conditions. In addition, it frequently does not provide the opportunity to achieve a low-cost position via scale economics.

muitinational organization model

An organization model that consists of the subsidiaries in each country in which a company does business, with ultimate control exercised by the parent company.

The Multinational Model In contrast to the international model, the **multinational organization model** uses subsidiaries (i.e., independent companies) in each country in which the company does business and provides a great deal of discretion to those subsidiaries to respond to local conditions. Each local subsidiary is a self-contained unit with all the functions required for operating in the host market. Thus, each subsidiary has its own manufacturing, marketing, research, and human resources functions. Because of this autonomy, each multinational subsidiary can customize its products and strategies according to the tastes and preferences of local consumers; the competitive conditions; and political, legal, and social structures.

The multinational model was widespread among many of the early European corporations, such as Unilever and Royal Dutch Shell. One advantage of allowing local responsiveness is that there is less need for coordination and direction from corporate headquarters. Since each subsidiary is a self-contained unit, few transfers of goods and services occur among subsidiaries, thus alleviating problems with transfer pricing and the like.

A major disadvantage of the multinational form is higher manufacturing costs and duplication of effort. Although a multinational can transfer core skills among its international operations, it cannot realize scale economies from centralizing manufacturing facilities and offering a standardized product to the global marketplace. Moreover, because a multinational approach tends to decentralize strategy decisions (discussed further in Chapters 8 and 9), it is difficult to launch coordinated global attacks against competitors. This can be a significant disadvantage when competitors have this ability.

A Procter & Gamble ad that appeared in a popular Japanese woman's magazine in August 2002.

The Global Model The **global organization model** is designed to enable a company to market a standardized product in the global marketplace and to manufacture that product in a limited number of locations where the mix of costs and skills is most favorable. The global model has been adopted by companies that view the world as one market and assume that there are no tangible differences among countries with regard to consumer tastes and preferences. Procter & Gamble, for example, has been successful in Europe against Unilever because it has approached the entire continent as a unified whole.

Companies that adopt the global model tend to become the low-cost players in any industry. These companies construct global-scale manufacturing facilities in a few selected low-cost locations so that they can realize scale economies. These scale economies come from spreading the fixed costs of investments in new-product development, plant and equipment, and the like, over worldwide sales. By using centralized manufacturing facilities and global marketing strategies, Sony was able to push down its unit costs to the point where it became the low-cost player in the global television market. This enabled Sony to take market share away from Philips, RCA, and Zenith, all of which used traditionally based manufacturing operations in each major national market (a characteristic of the multinational approach). Because operations are centralized, subsidiaries usually are limited to marketing and service functions.

On the downside, because a company pursuing a purely global approach tries to standardize its products and services, it may be less responsive to consumer tastes and demands in different countries. Attempts to lower costs through global product standardization may result in a product that fails to satisfy anyone. For example, while Procter & Gamble has been quite successful using a global approach, the company experienced problems when it tried to market Cheer laundry detergent in Japan. Unfortunately for P&G, the product did not "suds up" as promoted in Japan because the Japanese use a great deal of fabric softener, which suppresses suds. Moreover, the claim that Cheer worked in all water temperatures was irrelevant in Japan, where most washing is done in cold water.

Companies pursuing a pure global approach to strategy require increased coordination and paperwork and additional staff. Moreover, such companies must decide how to price transfers of goods and services among parts of the company based in different countries. Transfer-pricing problems are difficult enough to resolve within just one country; in a global company, transfer pricing can be further complicated by volatile exchange rates.

The Transnational Model

In today's global economy, achieving a competitive advantage often requires the *simultaneous* pursuit of gains from local responsiveness, transfer of know-how, and cost economies.[13] This raises the question of whether it is possible to design an organization that enables a company to reap all the benefits of global expansion simultaneously. Recently a number of companies, including Sony, Unilever, Caterpillar, and Philips, have been experimenting with a new organization model—the transnational organization model—that is designed to do just that.

In companies that adopt the **transnational organization model,** certain functions, particularly research, tend to be centralized at home. Other functions also are centralized, but not necessarily in the home country. To achieve cost economies, companies may base global-scale production plants for labor-intensive products in low-wage countries such as Mexico and Singapore and locate production plants that require a skilled workforce in high-skill countries such as Germany and Japan.

Other functions, particularly marketing, service, and final-assembly functions, tend to be based in the national subsidiaries to facilitate greater local responsiveness. Thus, major components may be manufactured in centralized production plants to realize scale economies and then shipped to local plants, where the final product is assembled and customized to fit local needs.

global organization model

An organization model consisting of a company's overseas subsidiaries and characterized by centralized decision making and tight control by the parent company over most aspects of worldwide operations. Typically adopted by organizations that base their global competitive strategy on low cost.

transnational organization model

An organization model characterized by centralization of certain functions in locations that best achieve cost economies; basing of other functions in the company's national subsidiaries to facilitate greater local responsiveness; and fostering of communication among subsidiaries to permit transfer of technological expertise and skills.

Sony Corporation knew from the popularity of its original PlayStation system that PlayStation 2 would be a blockbuster, and the firm tailored its efforts to build up the demand for the product as well as its supplies. PlayStation 2 is the successor to Sony's best-selling game system, which in 1999 contributed 40 percent of the company's operating profit, selling more than 73 million units since its debut in 1994. Sony's PS2, with a year's head start in stores, leads with about 14 million systems sold in North America since its launch in October 2000. The PS2 launch easily amounted to $200 million in sales, the fastest-selling consumer electronics product in history.

When PlayStation 2 was set to go on sale in Japan in 2000, Ken Kutaragi, chief of Sony Corp.'s video-game operations, picked the hip Tokyo flagship store Tsutaya, the country's largest purveyor of movies, recorded music, and games to stage the countdown to the launch. To release the computer entertainment system in the North American market, Sony Computer Entertainment America Inc. announced the biggest consumer electronics launch in history, including extensive advertising efforts, promotions, sponsorships, television advertising during *The Simpsons,* a hands-on trial at Super Bowl XXXV events, "underground" sponsorships such as the Raveworld tour, and even an in-theater trailer featuring the PlayStation 2 launch library that was projected to reach more than 48 million moviegoers.

The machine became the must-have Chistmas item. For its North American debut on October 26, 2000, the company shipped 500,000 units of the PlayStation 2 computer entertainment system, followed by shipments of approximately 100,000 units per week through the holiday season. Just two months after its launch, the company estimated that a total of 1.3 million units was shipped into the North American market. With an unprecedented library of software and backed by an extensive marketing campaign, the company shipped 3 million units in the United States by March 31, 2001, of the total worldwide production estimate of 10 million units for the product, within the same time period. "PlayStation has become a part of American and worldwide culture," said Matt Gravett of the Reston, Virginia–based PC Data.

To meet the overwhelming demand for the PlayStation 2 computer entertainment system worldwide, Sony Computer Entertainment Inc. ramped up production capacity from 400,000 units a month to more than 1 million units a month in the fall, with a further increase to 1.4 million units by the end of 2000, a historic milestone for the industry. Sony

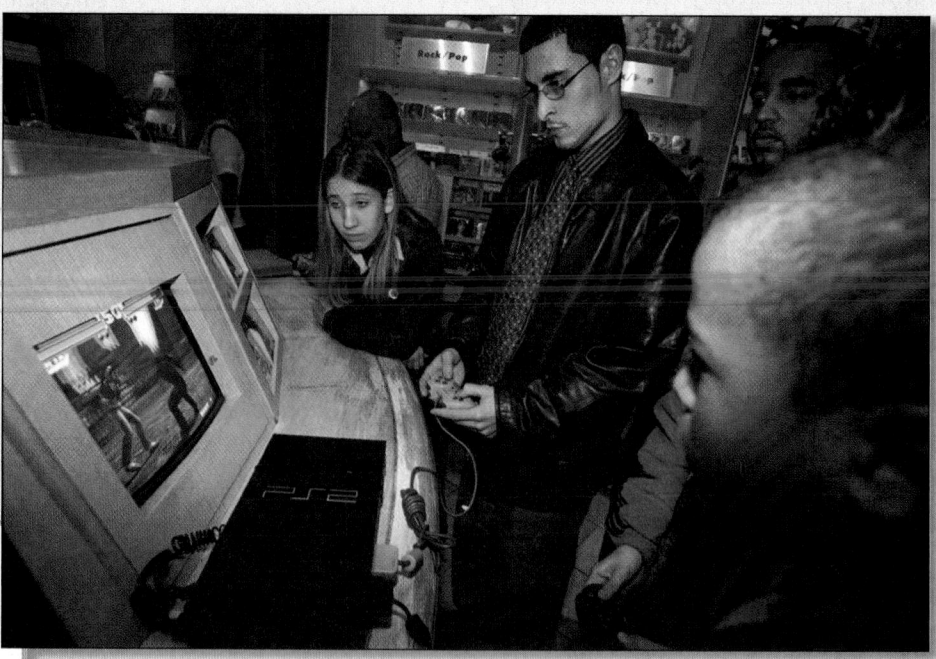

Customers gathered at the Sony store on Madison Avenue to try out the new PlayStation 2 system on its introduction in late 2000.

doubled its production of the unit after parts shortages left many consumers empty-handed following the introduction of the video game console in Europe and the United States.

Sony's goal was to ship about 500,000 PlayStation 2s to the United Kingdom, about 400,000 to France, and 350,000 to Germany by the end of March, said Fleur Breteau, a Sony Europe spokeswoman. The same PlayStation 2 that retails for $299 in the United States was priced, before the euro, at 299 pounds ($425) in Britain, 2,990 francs ($385) in France, and 869 marks ($375) in Germany. Each unit was also subject to a duty of 2.2 percent, or roughly $9, when imported for sale in to the European Union. Sony absorbed the cost of the tariffs rather than passing it on to European consumers, who already pay a hefty premium over what U.S. video game addicts pay.

Although the company loses money on each of the 128-bit game machines it produces, revenue from high-margin game software is a major source of earnings for Sony, maker of the Grand Turismo series of racing games. Short supply hurt the Japanese video-game software developer Konami, whose video game software sales fell to 25.3 billion yen in the six months that ended in September from 35.1 billion yen in the same period a year earlier when foreign game players delayed purchases as they awaited PlayStation 2's debut, the developer said. The shortage also hurt European and U.S. game publishers, whose sales fell as customers waited for PlayStation 2. After the shipment of more consoles, Electronic Boutique of the United Kingdom said sales at stores open longer than a year surged 15 percent in December after PlayStation 2 consoles became available.

The PlayStation 2 Network Adaptor, introduced in summer 2002, even lets players battle via the Net. Online games generated about $700 million in 2002 and will account for a fraction of the expected $11 billion-plus U.S. video game industry in 2003. As Sony and competitors draw more non-personal-computer video gamers online, within four years the audience worldwide could grow to 23 million players from fewer than 3 million today, says David Cole, an analyst with DFC Intelligence, a market research firm in San Diego. Through PlayStation.com, gamers in North America, Europe, Japan, and Australasia (including Australia and New Zealand) also can access region-specific websites for the system.

Sony's efforts at creating and supplying a worldwide demand for its game system have paid off: If not for PS2, Sony would have fallen into the red in fiscal 2001.

SOURCES: Irene M. Kunii, "How Do You Say 'Cool' in Japanese? Tsutaya," *Business Week*, May 13, 2002; Mike Snider, "Eager Buyers Scramble for PlayStation 2s," *USA Today*, October 27, 2000; "PlayStation 2 Caught in EU Tariff Game," *Associated Press*, November 22, 2000; Mike Snider, "Video Games Jump Online," *USA Today*, August 27, 2002; "Sony to Double PlayStation 2 Production," *Bloomberg*, January 16, 2001; Cristina Lindblad, "The *Business Week* Global 1000," *Business Week*, July 15, 2002.

Caterpillar Tractor is a transnational company.[14] The need to compete with low-cost competitors such as Komatsu has forced Caterpillar to look for greater cost economies by centralizing global production at locations where the factor cost/skill mix is most favorable. At the same time, variations in construction practices and government regulations across countries mean that Caterpillar must be responsive to local needs. On the integration–responsiveness grid in Figure 6.3, therefore, Caterpillar is situated toward the top right-hand corner.

To deal with these simultaneous demands, Caterpillar has designed its products to use many identical components and has invested in a few large-scale component-manufacturing facilities to fill global demand and realize scale economies. But while the company manufactures components centrally, it has assembly plants in each of its major markets. At these plants Caterpillar adds local product features, tailoring the finished product to local needs. Thus, Caterpillar is able to realize many of the benefits of global manufacturing while managing pressure for local responsiveness by differentiating its product among national markets.

Perhaps the most important distinguishing characteristic of the transnational organization is the fostering of communications among subsidiaries. National subsidiaries communicate better with one another so that they can transfer technological expertise and skills among themselves to their mutual benefit. At the same time, centralized manufacturing plants coordinate their production with local assembly plants, facilitating the smooth operation of an integrated, worldwide production system.

Achieving such communications across subsidiaries requires elaborate formal mechanisms, such as transnational committees staffed by people from the various subsidiaries who are responsible for monitoring coordination among subsidiaries. Equally important is to transfer managers among subsidiaries on a regular basis. This enables international managers to establish a global network of personal contacts in different subsidiaries with whom they can share information as the need arises. Finally, achieving coordination among subsidiaries requires that the head office play a proactive role in coordinating their activities.

Entry Mode

When considering global expansion, international managers must decide on the best means of entering an overseas market. There are five basic ways to expand overseas: exporting, licensing, franchising, entering into a joint venture with a host country company, and setting up a wholly owned subsidiary in the host country.[15] Table 6.3 compares the entry modes.

TABLE 6.3 Comparison of Entry Modes

Exporting	Licensing	Franchising	Joint Venture	Wholly Owned Subsidiary
Advantages				
Scale economies	Lower development costs	Lower development costs	Local knowledge	Maintains control over technology
Consistent with pure global strategy	Lower political risk	Lower political risk	Shared costs and risk	Maintains control over operations
			May be the only option	
Disadvantages				
No low-cost sites	Loss of control over technology	Loss of control over quality	Loss of control over technology	High cost
High transportation costs			Conflict between partners	High risk
Tariff barriers				

Exporting

Most manufacturing companies begin global expansion as exporters and later switch to one of the other modes for serving an overseas market. The advantages of exporting are that it (1) provides scale economies by avoiding the costs of manufacturing in other countries and (2) is consistent with a pure global strategy. By manufacturing the product in a centralized location and then exporting it to other national markets, the company may be able to realize substantial scale economies from its global sales volume.

However, exporting has a number of drawbacks. First, exporting from the company's home base may be inappropriate if other countries offer lower-cost locations for manufacturing the product. An alternative is to manufacture in a location where the mix of factor costs and skills is most favorable and then export from that location to other markets to achieve scale economies. Several U.S. electronics companies have moved some manufacturing operations to the Far East, where low-cost, high-skill labor is available, and export from that location to other countries, including the United States.

A second drawback of exporting is that high transportation costs can make it uneconomical, particularly in the case of bulk products. Chemical companies get around this by manufacturing their products on a regional basis, serving several countries in a region from one facility.

A third drawback is that host countries can impose (or threaten to impose) tariff barriers. As was noted earlier, Japanese automakers reduced this risk by setting up manufacturing plants in the United States.

Licensing

International licensing is an arrangement by which a licensee in another country buys the rights to manufacture a company's product in its own country for a negotiated fee (typically, royalty payments on the number of units sold). The licensee then puts up most of the capital necessary to get the overseas operation going. The advantage of licensing is that the company need not bear the costs and risks of opening up an overseas market.

However, a problem arises when a company licenses its technological expertise to overseas companies. Technological know-how is the basis of the competitive advantage of many multinational companies. But RCA Corporation lost control over its color TV technology by licensing it to a number of Japanese companies. The Japanese companies quickly assimilated RCA's technology and then used it to enter the U.S. market. Now the Japanese have a bigger share of the U.S. market than the RCA brand does.

Franchising

In many respects, franchising is similar to licensing. However, whereas licensing is a strategy pursued primarily by manufacturing companies, franchising is used primarily by service companies. McDonald's, Hilton International, and many other companies have expanded overseas by franchising.

In franchising, the company sells limited rights to use its brand name to franchisees in return for a lump-sum payment and a share of the franchisee's profits. However, unlike most licensing agreements, the franchisee has to agree to abide by strict rules as to how it does business. Thus, when McDonald's enters into a franchising agreement with an overseas company, it expects the franchisee to run its restaurants in a manner identical that is used under the McDonald's name elsewhere in the world.

The advantages of franchising as an entry mode are similar to those of licensing. The most significant disadvantage concerns quality control. The company's brand name guarantees consistency in the company's product. Thus, a business traveler booking into a Hilton International hotel in Hong Kong can reasonably expect the same quality of room, food, and service that he or she would receive in New York. But if overseas franchisees are less concerned about quality than they should be, the impact can go beyond lost sales in the local market to a decline in the company's reputation worldwide. If a business traveler has an unpleasant experience at the Hilton in Hong Kong, she or he may decide never to go to another Hilton hotel—and urge colleagues to do likewise. To make matters worse, the geographic distance between the franchisor and its overseas franchisees makes poor quality difficult to detect.

Joint Ventures

Establishing a joint venture (a formal business agreement discussed in more detail in Chapter 11) with a company in another country has long been a popular means for entering a new market. Joint ventures benefit a company through (1) the local partner's knowledge of the host country's competitive conditions, culture, language, political systems, and business systems and (2) the sharing of development costs and/or risks with the local partner. In addition, many countries' political considerations make joint ventures the only feasible entry mode.

Prior to China opening its borders to trade, many U.S. companies like Eastman Kodak, AT&T, Ford, and GM did business in the country via joint ventures. But, as attractive as they sound, joint ventures have their problems. First, as in the case of licensing, a company runs the risk of losing control over its technology to its venture partner. Second, companies may find themselves at odds with one another. For example, one joint-venture partner may want to move production to a country where demand is growing, while the other would prefer to keep its factories at home running at full capacity. Conflict over who controls what within a joint venture is a primary reason many fail. Indeed, in recent years, the number of global joint ventures has actually declined.[16]

Despite the advantages of joint ventures such as these, those ventures have two possible disadvantages. First, as in the case of licensing, a company runs the risk of losing control over its technology to its venture partner. Second, because control is shared with the partner, the company may lose control over its subsidiaries. Indeed, conflict over who controls what within a joint venture is a primary reason many joint ventures fail.

Wholly Owned Subsidiaries

Establishing a wholly owned subsidiary, that is, an independent company owned by the parent corporation, is the most costly method of serving an overseas market. Companies that use this approach must bear the full costs and risks associated with setting up overseas operations (as opposed to joint ventures, in which the costs and risks are shared, or licensing, in which the licensee bears most of the costs and risks).

Nevertheless, setting up a wholly owned subsidiary offers two clear advantages. First, when a company's competitive advantage is based on technology, a wholly owned subsidiary normally is the preferred entry mode because it reduces the risk of losing control over the technology. This was the case for 3M, which was the first to set up a wholly owned subsidiary in China.[17] The number of wholly owned subsidiaries is at a record high; it is the preferred mode of entry in the semiconductor, electronics, and pharmaceutical industries, for example.

Second, a wholly owned subsidiary gives a company tight control over operations in other countries, which is necessary if it chooses to pursue a global strategy. Establishing a global manufacturing system requires world headquarters to have a high degree of control over the operations of national affiliates. Unlike licensees or joint venture partners, wholly owned subsidiaries usually accept centrally determined decisions about how to produce, how much to produce, and how to price output for transfer among operations.

Managing Across Borders

When establishing operations overseas, headquarter executives have a choice among sending **expatriates** (individuals from the parent country), using **host-country nationals** (natives of the host country), and deploying **third-country nationals** (natives of a country other than the home country or the host country). While most corporations use some combination of all three types of employees, there are advantages and disadvantages of each. Colgate-Palmolive, for example, uses expatriates in an effort to shorten the delivery time of products to market, while AT&T uses expatriates to help transfer the company's culture. In contrast, companies such as Chevron and Texas Instruments make more limited use of expatriates. Chevron typically sends a management team to review the skills of local employees, and sends expatriates only if their technical skills are needed. If expatriates are sent, it is expected that operational control will be passed to local employees. Texas Instruments uses very few expatriates, but relies on phone, fax, and computers to facilitate communication. However, TI frequently sends people on extended travel so they meet their cohorts around the world.[18]

| **expatriates** |
| Parent-company nationals who are sent to work at a foreign subsidiary. |
| **host-country nationals** |
| Natives of the country where an overseas subsidiary is located. |
| **third-country nationals** |
| Natives of a country other than the home country or the host country of an overseas subsidiary. |

Working internationally can be very stressful, even for experienced "globalites." Table 6.4 shows some of the primary stressors for expatriates at different stages of their assignments. It also shows ways for executives to cope with stress as well as some of the things that companies can do to help with the adjustment.

Developing a valuable pool of expatriates is important. However, local employees are more available, tend to have familiarity with the culture and language, and usually cost less because they do not have to be displaced. In addition, local governments often provide incentives to companies that create good jobs for their citizens (or they may place restrictions on the use of expatriates). For these reasons, executives at Allen Bradley, a division of Rockwell International, believe that building a strong local workforce is critical to their success overseas, and they transport key host-country nationals to the United States for skills training. The trend away from using expatriates in top management positions is especially apparent in companies that truly want to create a multinational culture. In Honeywell's European division, for example, many of the top executive positions are held by non-Americans.[19]

Over the years, U.S.-based companies in particular have tended to use more third-country nationals to work in a country different from their own, and different from the parent company's. When Eastman Kodak assembled a management team to devise a launch strategy for its Photo-CD line in Europe, the team members were based in London, but the leader was from Belgium. Because third-country nationals can soften the political tensions between the parent country and the host country, they often represent a convenient compromise.[20]

Skills of the Global Manager

It is estimated that nearly 15 percent of all employee transfers are to an international location. However, a recent survey of 1,500 senior executives showed that there is a critical shortage of U.S. managers equipped to run global businesses.[21] Indicative of

TABLE 6.4   Stressors and Coping Responses in the Developmental Stages of Expatriate Executives

Stage	Primary Stressors	Executive Coping Response	Employer Coping Response
Expatriate selection	Cross-cultural unreadiness.	Engage in self-evaluation.	Encourage expatriate's self- and family evaluation. Perform an assessment of potential and interests.
Assignment acceptance	Unrealistic evaluation of stressors to come. Hurried time frame.	Think of assignment as a growth opportunity rather than an instrument to vertical promotion.	Do not make hard-to-keep promises. Clarify expectations.
Pre- and postarrival training	Ignorance of cultural differences.	Do not make unwarranted assumptions of cultural competence and cultural rules.	Provide pre-, during, and. postassignment training. Encourage support-seeking behavior
Arrival	Cultural shock. Stressor re-evaluation. Feelings of lack of fit and differential treatment.	Do not construe identification with the host and parent cultures as mutually exclusive. Seek social support.	Provide postarrival training. Facilitate integration in expatriate network.
Novice	Cultural blunders or inadequacy of coping responses. Ambiguity owing to inability to decipher meaning of situations.	Observe and study functional value of coping responses among locals. Do not simply replicate responses that worked at home.	Provide follow-up training. Seek advice from locals and expatriate network.
Transitional	Rejection of host or parent culture.	Form and maintain attachments with both cultures.	Promote culturally sensitive policies in host country. Provide Internet access to family and friends at home. Maintain constant communication and periodic visits to parent organization.
Mastery	Frustration with inability to perform boundary-spanning role. Bothered by living with a cultural paradox.	Internalize and enjoy identification with both cultures and walking between two cultures.	Reinforce rather than punish dual identification by defining common goals.
Repatriation	Disappointment with unfulfilled expectations. Sense of isolation. Loss of autonomy.	Realistically reevaluate assignment as a personal and professional growth opportunity.	Arrange prerepatriation briefings and interviews. Schedule postrepatriation support meetings.

SOURCE: J. Sanchez, P. Spector, and C. Cooper, *Academy of Management Executive,* 14 no. 2, pp. 96–106. Copyright © 2000 by Academy of Management. Reproduced with permission of Academy of Management via Copyright Clearance Center.

failure rate

The number of expatriate managers of an overseas operation who come home early.

this fact is the **failure rate** among expatriates (defined as those who come home early), which has been estimated to range from 25 to 50 percent. The average cost of each of these failed assignments ranges from $40,000 to $250,000.[22] Typically, the causes for failure overseas extend beyond technical capability, and include personal and social issues as well. Interestingly, one of the biggest problems is a spouse's inability to adjust to his or her new surroundings. For both the expatriate and the spouse, adjustment requires flexibility, emotional stability, empathy for the culture, communication skills, resourcefulness, initiative, and diplomatic skills.[23]

Interestingly, while many U.S. companies have hesitated to send women abroad—believing that women either do not want international assignments or that other cultures would not welcome women—their success rate has been estimated at 97 percent (far greater than that for their male counterparts).[24] Ironically, for a country that had been viewed as not welcoming foreign women, in Japan U.S. women are first viewed as foreigners (*gaijin* in Japanese) and only second as women. And because it is unusual for women to be sent on foreign assignments, their distinctiveness and visibility tend to increase their chances for success.[25]

Companies such as Levi-Strauss, Bechtel, Monsanto, Whirlpool, and Dow Chemical have worked to identify the characteristics of individuals that will predict their success abroad. Figure 6.4 shows skills that can be used to identify candidates who are likely to succeed in a global environment. Interestingly, in addition to such things as cultural sensitivity, technical expertise, and business knowledge, an individual's success abroad may depend greatly on his or her ability to learn from experience.[26]

FIGURE 6.4
Identifying International Executives

End-State Dimensions	Sample Items
1. Sensitivity to cultural differences	When working with people from other cultures, works hard to understand their perspective.
2. Business knowledge	Has a solid understanding of the company's products and services.
3. Courage to take a stand	Is willing to take a stand on issues.
4. Brings out the best in people	Has a special talent for dealing with people.
5. Acts with integrity	Can be depended on to tell the truth regardless of circumstances.
6. Is insightful	Is good at identifying the most important part of a complex problem.
7. Is committed to success	Clearly demonstrates commitment to seeing the organization succeed.
8. Takes risks	Takes personal as well as business risks.

Learning-Oriented Dimensions	Sample Items
1. Uses feedback	Has changed as a result of feedback.
2. Is culturally adventurous	Enjoys the challenge of working in countries other than his or her own.
3. Seeks opportunities to learn	Takes advantage of opportunities to do new things.
4. Is open to criticism	Appears brittle—as if criticism might cause him or her to break.
5. Seeks feedback	Pursues feedback even when others are reluctant to give it.
6. Is flexible	Doesn't get so invested in things that he or she cannot change when something doesn't work.

SOURCE: Gretchen M. Sprietzer, Morgan W. McCall, and Joan D. Mahoney, "Early Identification of International Executive Potential," *Journal of Applied Psychology* 82, no. 1 (1997), pp. 6–29.

Structure assignments clearly: Develop clear reporting relationships and job responsibilities.

Create clear job objectives.

Develop performance measurements based on objectives.

Use effective, validated selection and screening criteria (both personal and technical attributes).

Prepare expatriates and families for assignments (briefings, training, support).

Create a vehicle for ongoing communication with expatriates.

Anticipate repatriation to facilitate reentry when they come back home.

Consider developing a mentor program that will help monitor and intervene in case of trouble.

TABLE 6.5
How to Prevent Failed Global Assignments

Companies such as Amoco, Mercedes Benz, Hyatt, British Petroleum, and others with large international staffs have extensive training programs to prepare employees for international assignments. Table 6.5 suggests ways to improve their likelihood of success. Other organizations, such as Coca-Cola, Motorola, Chevron, and Mattel, have extended this training to include employees who may be located in the United States but who nevertheless deal in international markets. These programs focus on areas such as language, culture, and career development.

Understanding Cultural Issues

In many ways, cultural issues represent the most elusive aspect of international business. In an era when modern transportation and communication technologies have created a "global village," it is easy to forget how deep and enduring the differences among nations can be. The fact that people everywhere drink Coke, wear blue jeans, and drive Toyotas doesn't mean we are all becoming alike. Each country is unique for reasons rooted in history, culture, language, geography, social conditions, race, and religion. These differences complicate any international activities, and represent the fundamental issues that inform and guide how a company should conduct business across borders.

Ironically, while most of us would guess that the trick to working abroad is learning about the foreign culture, in reality our problems often stem from our being oblivious to our own cultural conditioning. Most of us pay no attention to how culture influences our everyday behavior, and because of this we tend to adapt poorly to situations that are unique or foreign to us. This is one reason why people traveling abroad frequently experience **culture shock**—the disorientation and stress associated with being in a foreign environment. Managers who ignore culture put their organizations at a great disadvantage in the global marketplace. Because each culture has its own norms, customs, and expectations for behavior, success in an international environment depends on one's ability to understand one's own culture and the other culture and to recognize that abrupt changes will be met with resistance.[27]

culture shock

The disorientation and stress associated with being in a foreign environment.

A wealth of cross-cultural research has been conducted on the differences and similarities among various countries. Geert Hofstede, for example, has identified four dimensions along which managers in multinational corporations tend to view cultural differences:

- *Power distance:* the extent to which a society accepts the fact that power in organizations is distributed unequally.

- *Individualism/collectivism:* the extent to which people act on their own or as a part of a group.
- *Uncertainty avoidance:* the extent to which people in a society feel threatened by uncertain and ambiguous situations.
- *Masculinity/femininity:* the extent to which a society values quantity of life (e.g., accomplishment, money) over quality of life (e.g., compassion, beauty).

Figure 6.5 offers a graphic depiction of how 40 different nations differ on the dimensions of individualism/collectivism and power distance. Clearly, cultures such as the United States that emphasize "rugged individualism" differ significantly from collectivistic

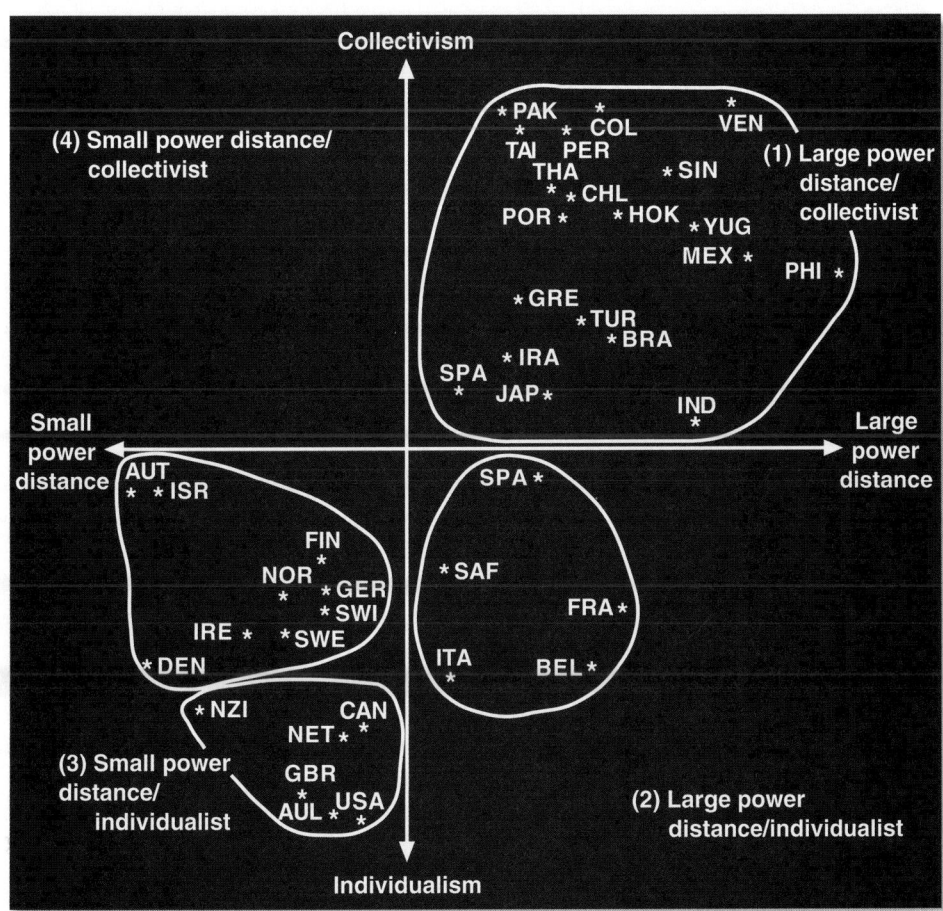

FIGURE 6.5

The Position of the 40 Countries on the Power Distance and Individualism Scales

The 40 Countries
(Showing Abbreviations used above)

ARG Argentina	FRA France	JAP Japan	SIN Singapore
AUL Australia	GBR Great Britain	MEX Mexico	SPA Spain
AUT Austria	GER Germany (West)	NET Netherlands	SWE Sweden
BEL Belgium	GRE Greece	NOR Norway	SWI Switzerland
BRA Brazil	HOK Hong Kong	NZL New Zealand	TAI Taiwan
CAN Canada	IND India	PAK Pakistan	THA Thailand
CHL Chile	IRA Iran	PER Peru	TUR Turkey
COL Colombia	IRE Ireland	PHI Philippines	USA United States
DEN Denmark	ISR Israel	POR Portugal	VEN Venezuela
FIN Finland	ITA Italy	SAF SouthAfrica	YUG Yugoslavia

SOURCE: Geert Hofstede, "Motivation, Leadership, and Organization: Do American Theories Apply Abroad?" *Organizational Dynamics* 9, no. 1 (Summer 1980), pp. 42–63. Reprinted by permission.

cultures such as those of Pakistan, Taiwan, and Colombia. To be effective in cultures that exhibit a greater power distance, managers often must behave more autocratically, perhaps being less participative in decision making. Conversely, in Scandinavian cultures, in Sweden, for instance, where power distance is low, the very idea that management has the prerogative to make decisions on its own may be called into question. Here, managers tend to work more toward creating processes that reflect an "industrial democracy."

Cross-cultural management extends beyond U.S. employees going abroad. As the following case exemplifies, international workers also have a difficult time adjusting to the United States.

Coming to America

Although 78 percent of the companies surveyed by Relocation Resources International (RRI) transferred employees to the United States, only 50 percent of those companies offered unique relocation policies for "inpatriates," or "inpats," as they're called. They're often plunked into a strange land without even the support of an expatriate community that Americans often have to soften the cross-cultural landing. "There's an American on practically every corner in Paris," says Laura Herring, president and CEO of The IMPACT Group. "There is not someone from Dusseldorf on every corner in Clayton, Missouri." Adjusting to life in the United States is not a snap, as the following examples show:

- A commercial marketing specialist for a pharmaceutical company had a particularly challenging family situation. The woman was relocating to the East Coast from Switzerland and needed help finding the right day care for her four-year-old daughter, who spoke Chinese and German but no English. The employer's relocation consultants helped the employee find a family day care setting that would be a good fit for her daughter. The company also arranged for English instruction for the mother and the daughter. Since arriving in the United States at the end of March, the little girl has become more comfortable with day care and is quickly picking up English phrases, including "OK" and "I love you." "She sings a lot of love songs," her mother says.

- In many foreign countries, families have access to low-cost domestic help, and lots of it. A Brazilian chemist was used to having three domestic workers. In the United States, she discovered that the three domestics she could afford were "me, myself, and I."

- A Spanish woman who was relocated with her husband wound up doing laundry and dishes by hand because she didn't know how to use the washing machine and the dishwasher wasn't functioning. Her husband forbade her to call his company for help. She didn't know whom to call, and her husband's promises that he would take care of it went unmet.

- An inpatriated Chinese employee and his wife were relocated from Los Angeles, which has a huge Chinese population, to corporate headquarters in Dallas. It made little difference to the employee, who spent 75 percent of his time traveling to China on sales calls. But his wife, who spoke no English, found herself stranded in suburban Plano without other Chinese speakers, markets, or friends. She was miserable, and after several months the executive pleaded for a return to Los Angeles. Management's first answer was no, Herring says, because the Los Angeles–to–Dallas move had cost $57,000. The company wasn't willing to spend that amount again, but since the executive produced sales of $2 million a month during his overseas trips, was fluent in five Chinese dialects, and was willing to spend 75 percent of his time traveling, losing him would have meant a loss of $36 million in revenue, Herring says.

SOURCE: Carroll Lachnit, "Low-Cost Tips for Successful Inpatriation," *Workforce*, August 2001, pp. 42–47.

Cultural differences can often affect management expectations and styles.

This example shows that culture shock works both ways. But despite the difficulties, there are a number of things that can be done to ease the adjustment of international workers coming to the United States. A few basic categories include the following:

- *Meetings:* Americans may dislike meetings, but they tend to have a fairly specific view of the purpose for them and how much time can be wasted. International workers, by contrast, may have different preconceptions about how time is supposed to be spent in meetings and whether it is being wasted.
- *Work(aholic) schedules:* Workers from other countries can work long hours but may be puzzled about how U.S. workers can survive with only two or three weeks of vacation. Europeans in particular may balk at the idea of working on weekends.
- *Email:* Most of the world has not embraced email and voice mail the way U.S. workers have. Most others would prefer to communicate face to face.
- *Fast-trackers:* Although U.S. companies may take a young MBA student and put him or her on the fast track to management, most other cultures (Germany and Japan in particular) still see no substitute for the wisdom gained through experience.
- *Feedback:* A manager's use of excessive positive feedback tends to be less prevalent in other cultures than in the United States.[28]

Ethical Issues in International Management

If managers are to function effectively in a foreign setting, they must understand how culture influences both how they are perceived and how others behave. One of the most sensitive issues in this regard is understanding how culture plays out in terms of ethical behavior.[29] Issues of right and wrong get blurred as we move from one culture to another, and actions that may be normal and customary in one setting may be unethical—even illegal—in another. The use of bribes, for example, is an accepted part of commercial transactions in many Asian, African, Latin American, and Middle Eastern cultures. In the United States, of course, such behavior is illegal, but what should a U.S. businessperson do when working abroad? Estimates are that bribery and corruption cost U.S. firms over $64 billion in lost business each year.[30]

Though most Americans prefer to conduct business in a manner consistent with prevailing U.S. laws, many people feel that we should not impose our cultural values on others. As a consequence, opinions differ widely on what is acceptable behavior when one is confronted with certain ethical dilemmas. Figure 6.6 shows the results of a survey that asked managers about the ethicality of payments to foreign officials. Surprisingly, less than half of the respondents said that the bribes were never acceptable, and in many cases managers suggested that such behavior would be acceptable if it was the local custom. In reality, these particular views are somewhat naive—while giving and receiving business gifts may be acceptable, the Foreign Corrupt Practices Act (1977) strictly prohibits U.S. employees from providing payments to foreign officials. While small "grease payments" to lower-level figures are permissible under the act, if the dollar amount of the payments is significant and would influence the outcome of negotiations, the transaction is illegal.

Without an understanding of local customs, ethical standards, and applicable laws, an expatriate may be woefully unprepared to work internationally. To safeguard against

FIGURE 6.6
Is This Ethical?

Ethical dilemma: A company paid a $350,000 "consulting" fee to an official of a foreign country. In return, the official promised assistance in obtaining a contract that should produce a $10 million profit for the contracting company.

Percentage of respondents who said the payments were:

49.0%   "never acceptable"
32.5%   "sometimes acceptable"
18.5%   "always acceptable"

SOURCE: J. G. Longenecker, J. A. McKinney, and C. W. Moore, "The Ethical Issues of International Bribery: A Study of Attitudes among U.S. Business Professionals," *Journal of Business Ethics* 7 (1988), pp. 341–46. Reprinted with kind permission from Kluwer Academic Publishers.

these and other ethical problems, companies such as Caterpillar Tractor, General Dynamics, and United Technologies have established codes of conduct for international business. The codes lay out precisely what kinds of actions are permissible and provide procedures and support systems that individuals can use in ambiguous situations. Four steps for establishing and reinforcing these codes might include the following:

- *Clearly articulate the company's values.* For example, Compaq's Corporate Code of Conduct contains 18 pages of practices the company expects employees to use, including conflicts of interest and reporting violations.
- *Train employees to apply the values.* Levi-Strauss has a three-day ethics course (called the Principled Reasoning Approach) that teaches employees how to evaluate situations logically and figure out how ethical values translate into behavior.
- *Let business partners know the standards.* Levi-Strauss has established a set of global sourcing and operating guidelines that address workplace issues for all of its partners. The terms of engagement detail everything from environmental requirements to health and safety issues.
- *Translate ethics into performance appraisal.* H. B. Fuller ties compensation to performance evaluation (which includes an ethical component). It also conducts audits of key people who are in positions that could be subjected to difficult moral decisions.[31]

Interestingly, despite some obvious differences across cultures, research suggests that there are actually a set of five core values that most people embrace regardless of nationality or religion: *compassion, fairness, honesty, responsibility,* and *respect for others.* These values lie at the heart of human rights issues and seem to transcend more superficial differences among Americans, Europeans, and Asians. Finding shared values such as these allows companies to build more effective partnerships and alliances, especially across cultures. It may be the case that as long as people understand that there is a set of core values, they can permit all kinds of differences in strategy and tactics.[32]

To a large extent, the challenge of managing across borders comes down to the philosophies and systems used to manage people. In moving from domestic to international management, managers need to develop a wide portfolio of behaviors along with the capacity to adjust their behavior for a particular situation. This adjustment, however, should not compromise the values, integrity, and strengths of their home country. When managers can transcend national borders, and move among different cultures, they will be in a position to leverage the strategic capabilities of the organization and take advantage of the opportunities that our global economy has to offer.

KEY TERMS

Culture shock, p. 200

Expatriates, p. 197

Failure rate, p. 198

Global organization model, p. 191

Host-country nationals, p. 197

International organization model, p. 189

Multinational organization model, p. 190

North American Free Trade Agreement (NAFTA), p. 181

Third-country nationals, p. 197

Transnational organization model, p. 191

SUMMARY OF LEARNING OBJECTIVES

Now that you have studied Chapter 6, you should know:

Why the world economy is becoming more integrated than ever before.

The gradual lowering of barriers to free trade is making the world economy more integrated. This means that the modern manager operates in an environment that offers more opportunities but is also more complex and competitive than that faced by the manager of a generation ago.

What integration of the global economy means for individual companies and for their managers.

In recent years, rapid growth in world trade, foreign direct investment, and imports has occurred. One consequence is that companies around the globe are now finding their home markets under attack from international competitors. The global competitive environment is becoming a much tougher place in which to do business. However, companies now have access to markets that previously were denied to them.

The strategies organizations use to compete in the global marketplace.

The international corporation builds on its existing core capabilities in R&D, marketing, manufacturing, and so on, to penetrate overseas markets. A multinational is a more complex form that usually has fully autonomous units operating in multiple countries. Subsidiaries are given latitude to address local issues such as consumer preferences, political pressures, and economic trends in different regions of the world. The global organization pulls control of overseas operations back into the headquarters and tends to approach the world market as a "unified whole" by combining activities in each country to maximize efficiency on a global scale. A transnational attempts to achieve both local responsiveness and global integration by utilizing a network structure that coordinates specialized facilities positioned around the world.

The various entry modes organizations use to enter overseas markets.

There are five ways to enter an overseas market: exporting, licensing, franchising, entering into a joint venture, and setting up a wholly owned subsidiary. Each mode has advantages and disadvantages.

How companies can approach the task of staffing overseas operations.

Most executives use a combination of expatriates, host-country nationals, and third-country nationals. Expatriates sometimes are used to quickly establish new country operations, transfer the company's culture, and bring in a specific technical skill. Host-country nationals have the advantages that they are familiar with local customs and culture, may cost less, and are viewed more favorably by local governments. Third-country nationals often are used as a compromise in politically touchy situations or when home-country expatriates are not available.

The skills and knowledge managers need to manage globally.

The causes for failure overseas extend beyond technical capability, and include personal and social issues as well. Success depends on a manager's core skills, such as having a multidimensional perspective; having proficiency in line management and decision making; and having resourcefulness, cultural adaptability, sensitivity, team-building skills, and mental maturity. In addition, helpful augmented skills include computer literacy, negotiating skills, strategic vision, and the ability to delegate.

Why cultural differences across countries influence management.

Culture influences our actions and perceptions as well as the actions and perceptions of others. Unfortunately, we are often unaware of how culture influences us, and this can cause problems. Today managers must be able to change their behavior to match the needs and customs of local cultures. For example, in various cultures, employees expect a manager to be either more or less autocratic or participative. By recognizing their cultural differences, people can find it easier to work together collaboratively and benefit from the exchange.

DISCUSSION QUESTIONS

1. Why is the world economy becoming more integrated? What are the implications of this integration for international managers?

2. Imagine you were the CEO of a major company. What approach to global competition would you choose for your firm: international, multinational, global, or transnational? Why?

3. Why have franchises been so popular as a method of international expansion in the fast-food industry? Contrast this with high-tech manufacturing, where joint ventures and partnerships have been more popular. What accounts for the differences across industries?

4. What are the pros and cons of using expatriates, host-country nationals, and third-country nationals to run overseas operations? If you were expanding your business, what approach would you use?

5. If you had entered into a joint venture with a foreign company but knew that women were not treated fairly in that culture, would you consider sending a female expatriate to handle the start-up? Why or why not?

6. What are the biggest cultural obstacles that we must overcome if we are to work effectively in Mexico? Are there different obstacles in France? Japan?

Wal-Mart and Megastore Wars in Mexico

Crowds in droves turned out for a recent ribbon cutting at a Soriana hypermarket store in Hermosillo, Mexico: A Catholic priest strode through the aisles, splashing holy water about. A mariachi band struck up when the doors swung open, letting in families from this working-class town. Is this a happy scene from an increasingly prosperous Mexico? Well, yes, but that's not all it is. The celebration is evidence of the latest dual between Soriana, a local Mexican retailer, and Wal-Mart de Mexico, the biggest foreign division of the largest retailer in the U.S.

So far Wal-Mart is doing a good job of trouncing the competition south of the border. Just a decade after entering the country, it owns half of the market. "Wal-Mart is formidable, but we aren't afraid of the challenge," says Soriana Ricardo Martin Bringas. The company is investing $250 million this year to open 12 new stores in the northern part of Mexico.

Meanwhile, Mexico's No. 2 and 3 supermarkets, Comerci and Grupo Gigante, are hurting. Comerci has fought back by launching its own version of "everyday low prices" on staples, computers, and electronics, while discarding the sales and contests it once held to lure in shoppers. The problem is that Comerci has far less pricing clout with suppliers than Wal-Mart. Chief Financial Officer Francisco Martinez de la Vega admits the switch will hammer Comerci's profits, but he sees no other way. "Consumers have bought the idea of low everyday prices. Now we have to convince them that our prices are competitive to Wal-Mart's," he says.

The best thing that could happen to Comerci or Gigante would be to link up with a deep-pocketed foreign partner. "If we don't have a partner with a lot of resources . . . Walmex will be 8 to 10 times bigger than us in five years," frets Martinez de la Vega. Most international retailers, though, are wary of investing in Latin American right now.

But Wal-Mart is now being perceived as the bully in the barrio. Mexico's Federal Competition Commission recently conducted a probe into reports that Wal-Mart exerts undue pressure on suppliers to lower their prices and punishes them by removing products from stores shelves if they participate in promotions organized by its rivals. Suppliers are afraid to lodge public complaints. One of them, who declined to be named, says that Wal-Mart buyers in Mexico pulled his product off shelves for several months when he objected to a deep price cut that would have wiped out his profits.

The accusations are reaching a feverish pitch. When a Wal-Mart store in Monterrey was fined by Mexico's Federal Consumer Protection Agency because a shelf price didn't ring up the same at the checkout counter, Soriana's Martin took out full-page ads in national newspapers thanking authorities for sanctioning "foreign supermarkets" for misleading consumers. He also produced a Soriana receipt that he said Wal-Mart wrongly altered and displayed in its store advertising that its own prices were lower. "We're lodging an official complaint," he says. This probably won't be the last of the skirmishes, though. More likely than not, the war among Mexico's megastores will be a fight to the finish.

SOURCE: Condensed from Gerri Smith, "Mexico's War of the Megastores," *Business Week Online*, September 16, 2002.

QUESTIONS

1. What are some of the ethical and cultural issues that Wal-Mart faces in Mexico?

2. Should Wal-Mart rethink its strategy in Mexico in light of criticism? Or should it stay the course?

3. How might Mexico's local supermarkets benefit from international partnerships with other companies?

6.1 Understanding Multinational Corporations

OBJECTIVE

To gain a more thorough picture of how a multinational corporation operates.

INSTRUCTIONS

Perhaps the best way to gain an understanding of multinational corporations is to study a specific organization and how it operates throughout the world. Select a multinational corporation, find several articles on that company, and answer the questions on the Multinational Worksheet.

Multinational Worksheet

1. What is the primary business of this organization?

2. To what extent does the company engage in multinational operations? For example, does it only market its products and/or services in other countries or does it have manufacturing facilities? What portion of the firm's operating income comes from overseas operations?

_____

_____

_____

3. What percentage of the managers in international activities are American (or from the country the corporation considers home)? Are these managers given any special training before their international assignment?

_____

_____

_____

4. What characteristics of the organization have contributed to its success or lack of success in the international marketplace?

_____

_____

_____

SOURCE: R. R. McGrath, Jr., *Exercises in Management Fundamentals* (Englewood Cliffs, NJ: Prentice-Hall, 1985), p. 177. Reprinted by permission of Prentice-Hall, Inc.

6.2   Expatriates versus Locals

OBJECTIVES

1. To help you understand the various advantages and disadvantages of using expatriates and locals as managers and professional staffers.

2. To broaden your understanding of the difficult human resources management problems the multinational enterprise faces.

INSTRUCTIONS

1. Working alone, read the Expatriates versus Locals Situation.

2. Go to the library and research the pros and cons of using expatriates versus locals.

3. Complete the Expatriates versus Locals Worksheet.

4. When the class reconvenes, your instructor can organize a debate on the expatriates versus locals issue.

EXPATRIATES VERSUS LOCALS SITUATION

Your company is planning to open a number of manufacturing and distribution centers in other countries to become a true multinational enterprise. There has been considerable controversy among top management as to how to staff the overseas operations. It's agreed that for nonmanagerial and nonprofessional staff positions, locals should be hired and trained whenever possible. However, for managerial and professional staff positions, there is considerable and sometimes emotional disagreement. You are to investigate the various advantages and disadvantages of using expatriates versus locals in overseas operations.

Expatriates Versus Locals Worksheet

Advantages of Using Expatriates	Advantages of Using Locals

CHAPTER 7

New Ventures

A man is known by the company he organizes.

—**Ambrose Bierce**

CHAPTER OUTLINE

Independent Entrepreneurs
   Why Become an Independent Entrepreneur?
   The Role of the Economic Environment
   What Business Should You Start?
   What Does It Take to Be Successful?
   Planning
   Entrepreneurial Hazards
   Global Start-Ups
Intrapreneurship
   Building Support for Your Idea
   Building Intrapreneurship
   Organizing New Corporate Ventures
   Hazards in Intrapreneurship
   Entrepreneurial Orientation
   3M—A Prototype

LEARNING OBJECTIVES

After studying Chapter 7, you will know:

1. The activities of entrepreneurship.

2. How to find and evaluate ideas for new business ventures.

3. What it takes to be a successful entrepreneur.

4. How to write a great business plan.

5. The important management skills, resources, and strategies needed to avoid failure and achieve success.

6. Key criteria for deciding whether your start-up should be global from the outset.

7. How to foster intrapreneurship and an entrepreneurial orientation in large companies.

HUMBLE BEGINNINGS AND TOP HONORS

Many people begin their entrepreneurial careers with virtually nothing. And some enter the *Inc.* 500 or become *Business Week* "entrepreneurs of the year." Examples include the following:

- Ron Vos started with $125 and couldn't pay people to work for him in his efforts to market alternative rock for major labels. But he recruited unpaid interns on college campuses across the country. In return for experience in the industry, contacts, free CDs, and backstage passes, students handed out free samples on campus and persuaded local radio stations and clubs to play Vos's clients' songs. Today, Hi Frequency Marketing clients include Everclear, Radiohead, and Squirrel Nut Zippers.

- Jason Olim was a student at Brown University when he got his entrepreneurial idea: selling hard-to-find CDs. He didn't have the money to open a real store, so he opened his on the Internet. He and his parents invested $20,000 for a Macintosh, a Unix server, software licenses, engineers to help with programming problems, graphic designers, print advertisements, and a public relations contract. In its first month, his company brought in $387 in revenues. A modest start before things got rolling for CDnow.

- Jeffrey Sprecher recently founded Intercontinental Exchange, Inc., an electronic trading exchange through which energy and trading firms trade commodities. Enron's bankruptcy helped his business grow, as energy traders turned to alternative exchanges. Says Sprecher, "This is one B-to-B exchange that's generating profits and cash—and using Internet technology correctly" (p. 75).

- In 2000, his bosses fired 67-year-old Clive Davis from the helm of the company he founded in 1974, Arista Records. They wanted someone younger. Davis responded not by retiring but by launching J Records. In 18 months, Davis filled J's roster with some of the best new artists in the industry, including Alicia Keys, whose debut album *Songs in A Minor* quickly sold 6 million copies and was nominated for four American Music Awards.

- While other telecom companies founded in the late 1990s took on mountains of debt, Royce Holland started Allegiance Telecom and played it much more safely, borrowing little and expanding slowly. When the shakeout began in 2001, the start-ups with huge interest payments and no profits collapsed. "It's a lot like playing *Survivor*. It seems like somebody is voted off the island every week" (p. 76). So far, Allegiance is still a player.

Arista Records fired Clive Davis, who turned around and launched J records by signing a number of new young artists, including Alicia Keys.

Sources: E. Barker, "Great Companies Started for $1000 or Less," *Inc.*, July, 2000, pp. 56–71; "The List," *Inc. 500 Special Issue*, July 2000, pp. 121–61; J. Akasie, "Imaging, No Inventory," *Forbes*, November 17, 1997, pp. 144–46; "The Top Entrepreneurs," *Business Week*, January 14, 2002, pp. 74–76.

Setting the Stage

entrepreneurship

The pursuit of lucrative opportunities by enterprising individuals.

small business

A business having fewer than 100 employees, independently owned and operated, not dominant in its field, and not characterized by many innovative practices.

Great opportunity is available to those who develop a vitally important skill: entrepreneurship. **Entrepreneurship** occurs when an enterprising individual pursues a lucrative opportunity.[1] To be an entrepreneur is to initiate and build an organization, rather than being only a passive part of one.[2] It involves creating *new* systems, resources, or processes to produce *new* goods or services and/or serve *new* markets.[3]

Entrepreneurship differs from management generally and from small business management in particular. An entrepreneur *is* a manager, but engages in additional activities that not all managers do.[4] Whereas managers operate in a more formal management hierarchy, with more clearly defined authority and responsibility, entrepreneurs use networks of contacts more than formal authority. And whereas managers usually prefer to own assets, entrepreneurs often rent or use assets on a temporary basis. Some say that managers often are slower to act and tend to avoid risk, whereas entrepreneurs are quicker to act and actively manage risk.

How does entrepreneurship differ from managing a small business?[5] A **small business** is often defined as having fewer than 100 employees, being independently owned and operated, not dominant in its field, and not characterized by many innovative practices. Small business owners

TABLE 7.1 Some Myths about Entrepreneurs

Myth 1—Anyone can start a business.

Reality—The easiest part is starting up. What is hardest is surviving, sustaining, and building a venture so its founders can realize a harvest. Perhaps only one in 10 to 20 new businesses that survive five years or more results in a capital gain for the founders.

Myth 2—Entrepreneurs are gamblers.

Reality—Successful entrepreneurs take very careful, calculated risks. They try to influence the odds, often by getting others to share risk with them and by avoiding or minimizing risks if they have the choice. They do not deliberately seek to take more risk or to take unnecessary risk, nor do they shy away from unavoidable risk.

Myth 3—Entrepreneurs want the whole show to themselves.

Reality—It is extremely difficult to grow a higher potential venture by working single-handedly. Higher potential entrepreneurs build a team, an organization, and a company. Besides, 100 percent of nothing is nothing, so rather than taking a large piece of the pie, they work to make the pie bigger.

Myth 4—Entrepreneurs are their own bosses and completely independent.

Reality—Entrepreneurs are far from independent and have to serve many masters and constituencies, including partners, investors, customers, suppliers, creditors, employees, families, and those involved in social and community obligations.

Myth 5—Entrepreneurs work longer and harder than managers in big companies.

Reality—There is no evidence that all entrepreneurs work more than their corporate counterparts. Some do, some do not. Some actually report that they work less.

Myth 6—Entrepreneurs experience a great deal of stress and pay a high price.

Reality—No doubt about it: Being an entrepreneur is stressful and demanding. But there is no evidence that it is any more stressful than numerous other highly demanding professional roles, and entrepreneurs find their jobs very satisfying. They have a high sense of accomplishment, are healthier, and are much less likely to retire than those who work for others. Three times as many entrepreneurs as corporate managers say they plan to never retire.

Myth 7—Starting a business is risky and often ends in failure.

Reality—Talented and experienced entrepreneurs—because they pursue attractive opportunities and are able to attract the right people and necessary financial and other resources to make the venture work—often head successful ventures.

tend not to manage particularly aggressively, and they expect normal, moderate sales, profits, and growth. In contrast, an **entrepreneurial venture** has growth and high profitability as primary objectives. Entrepreneurs manage aggressively and develop innovative strategies, practices, and products. They and their financial backers usually seek rapid growth, immediate and high profits, and sometimes a quick sellout with large capital gains.

> **entrepreneurial venture**
>
> A new business having growth and high profitability as primary objectives.

Simply put, entrepreneurs generate new ideas and turn them into business ventures.[6] But entrepreneurship is not simple, and it is frequently misunderstood. Read Table 7.1 to start you thinking about the myths and realities of this important career option.

Here is another myth, not in the table: Being an entrepreneur is great because you can "get rich quick" and enjoy a lot of leisure time while your employees run the company. But the reality is much more difficult. As described by Tom Peters,[7] "You must have incredible mental toughness to survive—let alone thrive." During the start-up period, you are likely to have a lot of bad days. It's exhausting. Even if you don't have employees, you should expect "communications breakdowns" and other "people problems" with agents, vendors, distributors, family, subcontractors, lenders, whomever. Dan Bricklin, the founder of VisiCalc, advises that the most important thing to remember is this: "You are not your business. On those darkest days when things aren't going so

---

Myth 8—Entrepreneurs are motivated solely by the quest for the almighty dollar.

Reality—Entrepreneurs seeking high potential ventures are more driven by building enterprises and realizing long-term capital gains than by instant gratification through high salaries and perks. A sense of personal achievement and accomplishment, feeling in control of their own destinies, and realizing their vision and dreams are also powerful motivators. Money is viewed as a tool and a way of keeping score.

Myth 9—Entrepreneurs seek power and control over others.

Reality—Successful entrepreneurs are driven by the quest for responsibility, achievement, and results, rather than for power for its own sake. They thrive on a sense of accomplishment and of outperforming the competition, rather than a personal need for power expressed by dominating and controlling others. By virtue of their accomplishments, they may be powerful and influential, but these are more the by-products of the entrepreneurial process than a driving force behind it.

Myth 10—If an entrepreneur is talented, success will happen in a year or two.

Reality—An old maxim among venture capitalists says it all: The lemons ripen in two and a half years, but the pearls take seven or eight. Rarely is a new business established solidly in less than three or four years.

Myth 11—Any entrepreneur with a good idea can raise venture capital.

Reality—Of the ventures of entrepreneurs with good ideas who seek out venture capital, only 1 to 3 out of 100 are funded.

Myth 12—If an entrepreneur has enough start-up capital, he or she can't miss.

Reality—The opposite is often true; that is, too much money at the outset often creates euphoria and a spoiled-child syndrome. The accompanying lack of discipline and impulsive spending usually lead to serious problems and failure.

Myth 13—Entrepreneurs are lone wolves and cannot work with others.

Reality—The most successful entrepreneurs are leaders who build great teams and effective relationships working with peers, directors, investors, key customers, key suppliers, and the like.

Myth 14—Unless you attained 600+ on your SATs or GMATs you'll never be a successful entrepreneur.

Reality—Entrepreneurial IQ is a unique combination of creativity, motivation, integrity, leadership, team building, analytical ability and ability to deal with ambiguity and adversity.

| **independent entrepreneur** |
| An individual who establishes a new organization without the benefit of corporate sponsorship. |
| **intrapreneurs** |
| New venture creators working in big corporations. |

well—and trust me, you will have them—try to remember that your company's failures don't make you an awful person. Likewise, your company's successes don't make you a genius or superhuman"[8] (p. 58).

As you read this chapter, you will learn about two primary sources of new venture creation: independent entrepreneurship and intrapreneurship. **Independent entrepreneurship** occurs when an individual establishes a new organization without the benefit of corporate support. **Intrapreneurs** are new venture creators working in big corporations; they are corporate entrepreneurs.[9]

Independent Entrepreneurs

Our discussion of independent entrepreneurs will answer questions about why people start their own businesses, the role of the economic environment, what kind of business a person should start, what it takes to be successful, planning and decision making, and the hazards of entrepreneurship.

Why Become an Independent Entrepreneur?

Bill Gross has started dozens of companies.[10] When he was a boy, he devised homemade electric games and sold candy for a profit to friends. In college, he built and sold plans for a solar heating device, started a stereo equipment company, and sold a software product to Lotus. In 1991, he sold his educational software company for almost $100 million. And in 1996, he started Idealab!, which hatched dozens of start-ups on the Internet.

Why do Bill Gross and other entrepreneurs do what they do? Entrepreneurs start their own firms because of the challenge, the profit potential, and the enormous satisfaction they hope lies ahead.[11] People starting their own businesses are seeking a better quality of life than they might have at big companies. They seek independence and a feeling of being part of the action. They feel tremendous satisfaction in building something from nothing, seeing it succeed, and watching the market embrace their ideas and products.

In addition, people start their own companies when they see their progress blocked at big corporations. When people are laid off, they often try to start businesses of their own. And when employed people believe there is no promotion in their future, or are frustrated by bureaucracy or other features of corporate life, they may quit and become entrepreneurs.

New immigrants may find existing paths to economic success closed to them.[12] Blocked from conventional means of advancement, these newcomers turn to the alternative paths entrepreneurship provides. For example, the Cuban community in Miami has produced many entrepreneurs, as has the Vietnamese community throughout the United States.

The Role of the Economic Environment

Money is a critical resource for all new businesses. Increases in the money supply and the supply of bank loans, real economic growth, and improved stock market performance lead to both improved prospects and increased sources of capital. In turn, the prospects and the capital increase the rate of business formation. Under favorable conditions, many aspiring entrepreneurs find early success. But economic cycles dictate that favorable conditions will change. To succeed, entrepreneurs must have the foresight and talent to survive when the environment becomes more hostile.

For example, the Internet was called a gold rush and a land grab, with space claimed by whoever got there first.[13] Profits were irrelevant. But traditional bricks-and-mortar companies got serious about the Net and started making the transition to bricks-and-clicks companies that took on the upstarts. In 2000, the money for dot-coms dried up, performance pressures rose, and many high-flying dot-coms failed. Strategy, cost, and profit—more generally, good management—are paramount once again.

Although good economic times may make it easier to start a company and to survive, bad times can offer an opportunity to expand.[14] Steve Jobs loves to innovate and introduce new products while competitors cut back. When Howard Schulz had 17 Starbucks stores, he aggressively expanded when the economy started slowing; when the economy came back, his brand was everywhere. It's also easier to recruit talent during down times.

Sometimes areas with weak economies but potential for growth are overlooked by entrepreneurs. But those who understand the potential can achieve business success. The inner city is an example.

Entrepreneurship in the Inner City

Today's inner cities hold tremendous business opportunity. Many retailers fled the cities and located in the suburbs, forcing inner-city residents to travel long distances for many of their shopping needs. But many entrepreneurs are again locating in the city and reenergizing the urban economy. This trend reversal may restore vital links between businesses and their communities.

Harlem, long a symbol of poverty and urban decay, is undergoing a commercial renaissance—not its first, but its second. Low-cost government loans are contributing to a revitalization. But this renaissance is controversial because it is dominated by corporate projects rather than by local entrepreneurial projects. The new Harlem USA mall dominates the main commercial strip, and includes such chains and superstores as Disney and Old Navy.

Fortunately, local entrepreneurs are keeping the spirit alive. For example, Alvin Reed has refurbished an old club housing one of New York's few original art-deco interiors. His vision harkens to Harlem's first renaissance, from the 1920s and 1930s, when Harlem was renowned for its jazz and club scene, and was to African-American culture what Paris is to the French.

Perhaps Peggy Dodson will broaden this cultural impact. Dodson started Urban Broadcasting Company, Inc., in Harlem. UBC is a hybrid entertainment-telecom firm with rapidly expanding revenues. Dodson and UBC recently launched a national cable network targeting the urban multicultural market, and forged alliances with Sony, Motown Records, and OlympuSat.

SOURCES: J. Kotkin, "Here Comes the Neighborhood," *Inc.,* July 2000, pp. 113–23; G. Gendron, "Making Connections," *Inc.,* July 2000, pp. 17–18; P. Keegan, "Who Owns Harlem?," *Inc.,* August 2000, pp. 56–69; and J. Huey, "Finding New Heros for a New Era," *Fortune,* January 25, 1993, pp. 62–69; B. McCrea, "Powerful Forces," *Black Enterprise,* January 2002, pp. 69–71.

Business Incubators The need to provide a nurturing environment for fledgling enterprises has led to the creation of business incubators. **Business incubators,** often located in industrial parks or abandoned factories, are protected environments for new, small businesses. Incubators offer benefits such as low rents and shared costs. Shared staff costs, such as for receptionists and secretaries, avoid the expense of a full-time employee but still provide convenient access to services. The staff manager is usually an experienced businessperson or consultant who advises the new business owners. Incubators often are associated with universities, which provide technical and business services for the new companies.

business incubators

Protected environments for new, small businesses.

The most amazing region for start-ups is Silicon Valley, a 50-mile-long corridor in California where 20 percent of the world's 100 biggest electronics and software companies were born.[15] Local universities (particularly Stanford), great talent, pioneering successes, and then venture capitalists and a complete tech infrastructure characterized by a risk-taking culture have made the Valley an exceptional environment for incubating ideas and companies. Other regions, including Boston, North Carolina's Research Triangle Park, and Austin, have tried to emulate the Valley's success. None has matched it, although Seattle is coming on strong.[16]

Howard Schulz, chairman and chief executive officer of Starbucks Coffee Co., headquartered in Seattle, WA., waves after cutting the ribbon to inaugurate its store in Toyko's Ginza shopping district. This store is Starbucks' first store outside North America.

Other regions in the world followed suit.[17] Government money and tax breaks helped Taiwan's Hsinchu Science–based industrial park flourish. In the Malaysian jungles, populated by rubber and palm-oil plantations, the Multimedia Supercorridor was planned to become Southeast Asia's Silicon Valley. Cyberjaya is the "intelligent city" at the center of the supercorridor. To entice corporations, the Malaysian government dedicated a 15 × 50 kilometer zone, promised to leave two-thirds of it undeveloped, gave tax exemptions, offered unlimited duty-free importation of multimedia equipment, allowed unrestricted numbers of foreign "knowledge workers" to enter the country, and promised not to censor the Internet. Sun Microsystems, Oracle, Microsoft, and Nippon Telegraph & Telephone Corp. were among the first to sign on. However, after the government invested several billion in the project, the economic crisis came and undermined the park. Now there are few foreign companies and only a few dozen homegrown companies, and the project hasn't come close to achieving its vision.[18]

What Business Should You Start?

You need a good idea, and you need to find or create a good opportunity.

The Idea   Many entrepreneurs and observers say that in contemplating your business, you must start with a great idea. A great product, an untapped market, and good timing are essential ingredients in any recipe for success.

Many great organizations have been built based on a different kind of idea: the founder's desire to build a great organization, rather than to offer a particular product.[19] Bill Hewlett and David Packard decided to start a company, and then figured out what to make. J. Willard Marriott knew he wanted to be in business for himself but didn't have a product in mind until he opened an A&W root beer stand. Masaru Ibuka had no specific product idea when he founded Sony in 1945. Sony's first product attempt, a rice cooker, didn't work, and its first product (a tape recorder) didn't sell. The company stayed alive by making and selling crude heating pads.

Many now-great companies had early failures. But the founders persisted; they believed in themselves, and in their dreams of building great organizations. Whereas

The new magazine *Fortune Small Business (FSB)* started its Small Business Hall of Fame in November 2000. Among the new inductees are:

Michael Dell, who revolutionized the way computers were sold and mounted a competitive assault on IBM. He started in his freshman dorm room.

Earl Graves, who in 1970 started a magazine meant to inspire African-Americans to get into business and teach them to thrive. The average income of his initial target population was $20,000. He needed advertisers, but a mostly white Madison Avenue had no interest. But he persevered. Today there are almost 1 million black-owned businesses in the United States, and Graves's is one of the biggest.

Paul Orfalea, who was a severe dyslexic and failed second and ninth grades. Out of his high school graduating class of 1,500, his class rank was 1,492. But he knew that business was his calling and that he could hire someone to do his reading and writing. In college he rented a small garage behind a taco stand and sold school supplies and copies. His nickname, which he put over the door, was Kinko. Today Kinko's has hundreds of stores that have become like second homes to millions of small business owners and fledgling entrepreneurs.

Louise Raggio's legal victories in Texas paved the way for women in all states to gain equal access to credit.

Louise Raggio, who went to law school at night for five years while raising three sons. When she graduated in 1952, law firms in Dallas wouldn't hire her. Attempting to start her own practice, she discovered that without her husband's signature, she couldn't legally get a bank loan. It became clear that women could not be in business on their own. Over a period of decades, Raggio won legal victories in Texas that paved the way for women in all states to gain equal access to credit and to start their own businesses. Today there are more than 9 million women-owned businesses.

Scott Cook, who was sitting at the kitchen table while his wife, Signe, was writing checks and had the entrepreneur's classic "Eureka!" moment: People need software to handle household finances. His first product, Quicken, was the foundation for his company, Intuit. The small-business accounting software program QuickBooks followed, revolutionizing the industry and chasing Microsoft out of the market.

Russell Simmons, the "godfather of hip-hop," who for the past two decades has been creating trends in rap, comedy, street art, and clothing. His start-ups include Phat Farm and Def Comedy Jam.

SOURCES: P. B. Gray and D. Devlin, "Heroes of Small Business," *Fortune Small Business,* November 2000, pp. 51–64; E. Brown, "From Rap to Retail: Wiring the Hip-Hop Nation," *Fortune,* April 17, 2000, fortune.com; J. Hyatt, "Heroes of Small Business," *Fortune Small Business,* October 2001, pp. 30–32; J. Solomon, "The Secrets of His Success," *Fortune Small Business,* October 2001, pp. 34–38.

---

conventional logic is to see the company as a vehicle for your products, this perspective sees the products as a vehicle for your company. Be prepared to kill or revise an idea, but never give up on your company—this has been a prescription for success for many great entrepreneurs and business leaders.

Think about Sony, Disney, Hewlett-Packard, Procter & Gamble, IBM, and Wal-Mart: Their founders' greatest achievements—their greatest ideas—are their organizations.[20]

The Opportunity Entrepreneurs spot, create, and exploit opportunities in a variety of ways.[21] Jaye Muller spotted an opportunity while touring Europe on a concert tour. The German rock musician missed some important faxes while moving from hotel to hotel. He put his recording career on hold (he still records periodically) and hired some programmers to develop software that can compress faxes into files and send them to Internet email addresses. The company took off.[22]

Shlomo Touboul foresaw the possibility that hackers would try to exploit Java's weaknesses. So he developed a product to protect the programs.

Java, the Internet programming language, was designed to be safe, and was widely perceived to be safe when it first appeared. But Shlomo Touboul saw it differently. When he talked about his plans to market a Java security product, people scoffed. Alone, he worked to develop a product that would protect companies from hostile programs embedded in the Java code. When some Princeton scientists subsequently found ways in which hackers could exploit Java's weak spots, Touboul was ready and far ahead of any would-be competitors.[23]

To spot opportunities, think carefully about events and trends as they unfold. Consider, for example:[24]

- *Technological discoveries.* Start-ups in biotechnology, microcomputers, and nanotechnology followed.
- *Demographic changes.* All kinds of health care organizations have sprung up to serve an aging population.
- *Lifestyle and taste changes.* Start-ups have capitalized on new clothing and music trends, desire for fast food, and growing interest in sports.
- *Economic dislocations,* such as booms or failures. The oil boycott spawned new drilling firms. The steel industry collapse was accompanied by minimill start-ups.
- *Calamities* such as wars and natural disasters. Mt. St. Helen's eruption spawned new tourism companies. Andrew Higgins's business expanded from wooden boats for the Louisiana swamps to the design and mass production of the landing vehicles that carried infantry ashore in World War II. Visionics really took off in late 2001; the company makes biometrics software that matches video images to a database of facial measurements in order to identify anyone from runaways to shoplifters to terrorists.[25]
- *Rule changes by government.* Environmental legislation created opportunities for new consulting firms and cleanup machinery firms. The Small Business Innovation Research Program underwrote new product innovation firms. Deregulation spawned new airlines and trucking companies.

The Next Frontiers

The next frontiers for entrepreneurship—where do they lie? Throughout history, aspiring entrepreneurs have asked this question. Currently, Gary Hoover believes, "Four of the industries that I think look most exciting over the next 20 to 30 years are financial services, health services and health-related things, travel, and education. And all four are really based on the continuing aging of the baby boomers. I keep a list of new business ideas. Right now there are about 70 ideas on it"[26] (p. 72). Add biotech, Eastern Europe, nanotechnology, oceanography . . . make your own list.

One fascinating opportunity for entrepreneurs is outer space.[27] Historically, the space market was driven by the government, and was dominated by big players like Boeing and Lockheed Martin. But now, with huge demand for satellite launches and potential profits skyrocketing, smaller entrepreneurs are entering the field.

George Mueller, CEO of Kistler Aerospace, was a leader in the space shuttle concept.

For example, Kistler Aerospace is going head-to-head against Boeing and Lockheed Martin, with no technological or financial help from NASA, to build a reusable launch vehicle that would take satellites into space at a fraction of the current cost.[28] The senior design team includes the former chief engineers for the Apollo spacecraft, the B-2 bomber, the space shuttle, and the space station.

The CEO is George Mueller, who ran the Apollo program and was a leader in the space shuttle concept and the Gemini, Saturn, and Skylab programs.

Other new ventures in space include satellites for automobile navigation, tracking trucking fleets, and monitoring flow rates and leaks in pipelines; testing designer drugs in the near-zero-gravity environment; and using remote sensing to monitor global warming, spot fish concentrations, and detect crop stress for precision farming. And think about this: Instead of the government funding, managing, and implementing Mars travel, one possibility is that it will offer a $20 billion prize to the winner of a private-company race to the red planet.[29]

The obstacles for entrepreneurs in the space industry are huge. Space start-ups require hundreds of millions of dollars to ramp up, they are highly unlikely to be profitable, most investors steer clear of them, and most will fail miserably. But the entrepreneurs believe that the challenges are merely financial rather than technical, and that whoever pulls it off will change the world.[30]

Side streets There also exists a useful role for trial and error. Some entrepreneurs start their enterprises and then let the market decide whether it likes their ideas or not. This is risky, of course, and should be done only if you can afford the risks. But even if the original idea doesn't work, you may be able to capitalize on the **side street effect.**[31] As you head down a road, you come to unknown places, and unexpected opportunities begin to appear.

And, while you are looking, *prepare* so you are able to act quickly and effectively on the opportunity when it does present itself.

> **side street effect**
>
> **As you head down a road, unexpected opportunities begin to appear.**

What Does It Take to Be Successful?

Many people assume there exists an "entrepreneurial personality."[32] There is no single personality type that predicts entrepreneurial success, but you are more likely to succeed as an entrepreneur if you exhibit certain characteristics. The following characteristics contribute to entrepreneurs' success:[33]

Trial and error can give rise to the side street effect where, like Dorothy in *The Wizard of Oz*, you head down a road and the unexpected begins to appear.

1. *Commitment and determination:* Successful entrepreneurs are decisive, tenacious, disciplined, willing to sacrifice, and able to immerse themselves totally in their enterprises. "You have to have a true passion for what you're doing"[34] (p. 54) says Dan Bricklin, the founder of VisiCalc.
2. *Leadership:* They are self-starters, team builders, superior learners, and teachers.
3. *Opportunity obsession:* They have an intimate knowledge of customers' needs, are market driven, and are obsessed with value creation and enhancement.
4. *Tolerance of risk, ambiguity, and uncertainty:* They are calculated risk takers and risk managers, tolerant of stress, and able to resolve problems.
5. *Creativity, self-reliance, and ability to adapt:* They are open-minded, restless with the status quo, able to learn quickly, highly adaptable, creative, skilled at conceptualizing, and attentive to details.

6. *Motivation to excel:* They have a clear results orientation, set high but realistic goals, have a strong drive to achieve, know their own weaknesses and strengths, and focus on what can be done rather than on the reasons things can't be done.

Making Good Choices   Success is a function not only of personal characteristics, but also of making good choices about the business you start. Figure 7.1 presents a model for conceptualizing entrepreneurial ventures and making the best possible choices. It depicts ventures along two dimensions: innovation and risk. The new venture may involve high or low levels of *innovation*, or the creation of something new and different. It can also be characterized by low or high *risk*. Risk refers primarily to the probability of major financial loss. But it also is more than that; it is psychological risk as perceived by the entrepreneur, including risk to reputation and ego.[35]

The upper-left quadrant, high innovation/low risk, depicts ventures of truly novel ideas with little risk. As examples, the inventors of Lego building blocks and Velcro fasteners could build their products by hand, at little expense. Even some early electronics companies started in this situation. A pioneering product idea from Procter & Gamble might fit here if there are no current competitors and because, for a company of that size, the financial risks of new product investments can seem relatively small.

In the upper-right quadrant, high innovation/high risk, novel product ideas are accompanied by high risk because the financial investments are high and the competition is great. A new drug or a new automobile would likely fall in this category.

Most small business ventures are in the low innovation/high risk cell (lower right). These are fairly conventional entries in well-established fields. New restaurants, retail shops, and commercial outfits involve high investment for the small business entrepreneur and face direct competition from other similar businesses. Finally, the low innovation/low risk category includes ventures that require minimal investment and/or face minimal competition for strong market demand. Examples are some service businesses having low start-up costs and those involving entry into small towns if there is no competitor and demand is adequate.

FIGURE 7.1
Entrepreneurial Strategy Matrix

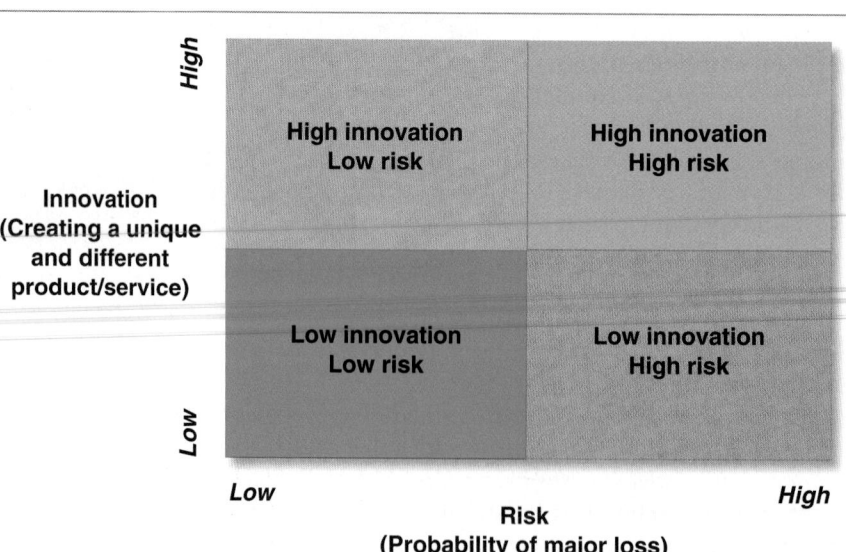

How is this matrix useful? It helps entrepreneurs think about their ventures and decide whether they suit their particular objectives. It also helps identify effective and ineffective strategies. An entrepreneur might find one cell more appealing than others. The lower-left cell is likely to have relatively low payoffs but to provide more security. The higher risk/return trade-offs are in other cells, especially the upper right. So an entrepreneur might place the new venture idea in the appropriate cell and determine whether that cell is the one in which he or she would prefer to operate. If it is, the venture is one that perhaps should be pursued, pending fuller analysis. If it is not, one can reject the idea or take action to move it toward a different cell.

The matrix also can help entrepreneurs remember a useful point: Successful companies do not always require a cutting-edge technology or an exciting new product. Even companies offering the most mundane products—the type that might reside in the lower-left cell—can gain competitive advantage by doing basic things differently from and better than competitors, as the following examples show.

Every year, *Inc.* magazine publishes its list of the 500 fastest-growing companies in the United States. Eddi Speir, one entrepreneur in the *Inc.* 500 list, started his career as a kid selling lollipops in grade school. He made his own mixture out of corn syrup and flavoring, and sold 50 to 75 pops a day at 50 cents each. Per-pop profit was 46 cents—not a bad margin!

Many companies on recent lists are high-tech enterprises. But they also include a bakery, a candlemaker, an auto repair service, a chain of tobacco and cigar stores, and Wetzel's Pretzels.

These are not hot growth industries. But they are industries. And knowing a lot about business and management, in any industry, provides a competitive edge. So your company can grow, even if your industry is not growing.

Larry Harmon of Demar Plumbing, Heating & Air-Conditioning strives to do business like Mary Kay, Walt Disney, Nordstrom's, and Federal Express. The way he sees it, people are not too enamored of plumbing—but would love a plumber who provides world-class customer service. He gives same-day service, trains his staff in customer relations, and makes his customers want to come back to him year after year.

Jim Jeffrey of Pest Control Technologies creates a professional image with white trucks and white uniforms for his employees, while his competitors work in blue jeans and T-shirts. Bear Barnes, a house painter, offers two-year guarantees and maintains a detailed database to target his market, track bids, and record every shade of paint on every house his company services.

Forbes's list of the richest people in America included pig farmer Wendell Murphy, who started with one pen and turned it into the biggest hog-farming business in the country. He became a billionaire. He applied computer technology to manage climate control and manure removal, and help make decisions surrounding when the sows should mate, how to breed, how to feed, and when to sell.

Others on recent *Forbes* lists include people who made their fortunes from a nondairy topping, plumbing fixtures, Beany Babies, classified ads, soft-drink bottling, and self-storage.

In other words, many highly successful entrepreneurs are masters of the ordinary. They are in ordinary, dull (on the face of it) businesses, but they manage them extraordinarily well compared to their competitors.

SOURCES: A. Murphy, "Masters of the Ordinary," *Inc.*, October 1993, pp. 70–71; M. Conlin, "Riding the Revolution," *Forbes*, October 13, 1997, pp. 99–104; "The *Inc.* 500 List 2001," *Inc.*, October 30, 2001, pp. 87–117; A. Greenwood, "The Lollipop Kid," *Inc.*, October 30, 2001, p. 103.

Ordinary Industries, Extraordinary Success

Planning

So you think you have spotted a business opportunity. And you have the personal potential to make it a success. Now what? Should you act on your idea? Where should you begin?

The Business Plan Your excitement and intuition may convince you that you are on to something. But they might not convince anyone else. You will need more thorough planning and analysis. This will help convince other people to get on board, and help you avoid costly mistakes.

The first formal planning step is to do an opportunity analysis. An **opportunity analysis** includes a description of the product or service, an assessment of the opportunity, an assessment of the entrepreneur (you), a specification of activities and resources needed to translate your idea into a viable business, and your source(s) of capital.[36] Table 7.2 shows the questions you should answer in an opportunity analysis.

The opportunity analysis, or opportunity assessment plan, focuses on the opportunity, not the entire venture. It provides the basis for making a decision on whether to act. Then, the **business plan** describes all the elements involved in starting the new venture.[37] The business plan describes the venture and its market, strategies, and future directions. It often has functional plans for marketing, finance, manufacturing, and human resources.

Table 7.3 shows an outline for a typical business plan. The business plan (1) helps determine the viability of your enterprise; (2) guides you as you plan and organize; and (3) helps you obtain financing. It is read by potential investors, suppliers, customers, and others. Get help in writing up a sound plan!

opportunity analysis

A description of the product or service, an assessment of the opportunity, an assessment of the entrepreneur, specification of activities and resources needed to translate your idea into a viable business, and your source(s) of capital.

business plan

A formal planning step that focuses on the entire venture and describes all the elements involved in starting it.

Key Planning Elements Most business plans devote so much attention to financial projections that they neglect other important information—information that matters greatly to astute investors. In fact, financial projections tend to be overly optimistic; investors know this and discount the figures.[38] In addition to the numbers, the best plans convey—and make certain that the entrepreneurs have carefully thought through—five key factors: the people, the opportunity, the competition, the context, and risk and reward.[39]

The *people* should be energetic and have skills and expertise directly relevant to the venture. For many astute investors, the people are the most important variable, more important even than the idea. Venture capital firms often receive 2,000 business plans

TABLE 7.2
Opportunity Analysis

What market need does my idea fill?
What personal observations have I experienced or recorded with regard to that market need?
What social condition underlies this market need?
What market research data can be marshaled to describe this market need?
What patents might be available to fulfill this need?
What competition exists in this market? How would I describe the behavior of this competition?
What does the international market look like?
What does the international competition look like?
Where is the money to be made in this activity?

SOURCE: R. Hisrich and M. Peters, *Entrepreneurship: Starting, Developing, and Managing a New Enterprise*, p. 41 Copyright © 1998 by The McGraw-Hill Companies. Reproduced with permission of The McGraw-Hill Companies.

TABLE 7.3 Outline of a Business Plan

Table of Contents

I. EXECUTIVE SUMMARY
   A. Description of the Business Concept and the Business.
   B. The Opportunity and Strategy.
   C. The Target Market and Projections.
   D. The Competitive Advantages.
   E. The Economics, Profitability, and Harvest Potential.
   F. The Team.
   G. The Offering.

II. THE INDUSTRY AND THE COMPANY AND ITS PRODUCT(S) OR SERVICE(S)
   A. The Industry.
   B. The Company and the Concept.
   C. The Product(s) or Service(s).
   D. Entry and Growth Strategy.

III. MARKET RESEARCH AND ANALYSIS
   A. Customers.
   B. Market Size and Trends.
   C. Competition and Competitive Edges.
   D. Estimated Market Share and Sales.
   E. Ongoing Market Evaluation.

IV. THE ECONOMICS OF THE BUSINESS
   A. Gross and Operating Margins.
   B. Profit Potential and Durability.
   C. Fixed, Variable, and Semivariable Costs.
   D. Months to Breakeven.
   E. Months to Reach Positive Cash Flow.

V. MARKETING PLAN
   A. Overall Marketing Strategy.
   B. Pricing.
   C. Sales Tactics.
   D. Service and Warranty Policies.
   E. Advertising and Promotion.
   F. Distribution.

VI. DESIGN AND DEVELOPMENT PLANS
   A. Development Status and Tasks.
   B. Difficulties and Risks.
   C. Product Improvement and New Products.
   D. Costs.
   E. Proprietary Issues.

VII. MANUFACTURING AND OPERATIONS PLAN
   A. Operating Cycle.
   B. Geographical Location.
   C. Facilities and Improvements.
   D. Strategy and Plans.
   E. Regulatory and Legal Issues.

VIII. MANAGEMENT TEAM
   A. Organization.
   B. Key Management Personnel.
   C. Management Compensation and Ownership.
   D. Other Investors.
   E. Employment and Other Agreements and Stock Option and Bonus Plans.
   F. Board of Directors.
   G. Other Shareholders, Rights, and Restrictions.
   H. Supporting Professional Advisors and Services.

IX. OVERALL SCHEDULE

X. CRITICAL RISKS, PROBLEMS, AND ASSUMPTIONS

XI. THE FINANCIAL PLAN
   A. Actual Income Statements and Balance Sheets.
   B. Pro Forma Income Statements.
   C. Pro Forma Balance Sheets.
   D. Pro Forma Cash Flow Analysis.
   E. Breakeven Chart and Calculation.
   F. Cost Control.
   G. Highlights.

XII. PROPOSED COMPANY OFFERING
   A. Desired Financing.
   B. Offering.
   C. Capitalization.
   D. Use of Funds.
   E. Investor's Return.

XIII. APPENDICES

SOURCE: J. A. Timmons, *New Venture Creation*, 5th ed., p. 374. Copyright © 1999 by Jeffry A. Timmons. Reproduced with permission of the author.

per year; many believe that ideas are a dime a dozen and what counts is the ability to execute. Arthur Rock, a legendary venture capitalist who helped start Intel, Teledyne, and Apple, stated, "I invest in people, not ideas. If you can find good people, if they're wrong about the product, they'll make a switch."[40]

The *opportunity* should provide a competitive advantage that can be defended. Customers are the focus here: Who is the customer? How does the customer make decisions? How will the product be priced? How will the venture reach all customer segments? How much does it cost to acquire and support a customer, and to produce and deliver the product? How easy or difficult is it to retain a customer?

It is also essential to fully consider the *competition*. The plan must identify current competitors and their strengths and weaknesses, predict how they will respond to the new venture, indicate how the new venture will respond to the competitors' responses, identify future potential competitors, and consider how to collaborate with actual or potential competitors. Thus, for example, Andrew Busey created ichat, which became the leading provider of software for chat rooms. But then America Online and Microsoft started competing directly with the young entrepreneur. Busey responded by collaborating with IBM; the Lotus division bundled ichat's software with its Internet-ready version of Notes.[41]

The environmental *context* should be a favorable one from regulatory and economic perspectives. Such factors as tax policies, rules about raising capital, interest rates, inflation, and exchange rates will affect the viability of the new venture. The context can make it easier or harder to get backing and to succeed. Importantly, the plan should make clear that you know that the context inevitably will change, how the changes will affect the business, and how you will deal with the changes.

The *risk* must be understood and addressed as fully as possible. The future is always uncertain, and the elements described in the plan will change over time. Although you cannot predict the future, you must contemplate head-on the possibilities of key people leaving, interest rates changing, a key customer leaving, or a powerful competitor responding ferociously. Then describe what you will do to prevent, avoid, or cope with such possibilities. You should also speak to the end of the process: how to get money out of the business eventually. Will you go public? Will you sell or liquidate? What are the various possibilities for investors to realize their ultimate gains?[42]

Selling the Plan   Once you have written your plan, your goal is to get investors to agree. The elements of a great plan, as just described, are essential. Also important is whom you decide to try to convince to back your plan.

Many entrepreneurs want passive investors who will give them money and let them do what they want. Doctors and dentists generally fit this image. Professional venture capitalists do not, as they demand more control and more of the returns. But when business goes wrong—and chances are, it will—nonprofessional investors are less helpful, and less likely to advance more (needed) money. Sophisticated investors have seen sinking ships before and know how to help. They are more likely to solve problems, provide more money, and also navigate financial and legal waters such as going public.[43]

View the plan as a way for you to figure out how to reduce risk and maximize reward, and to convince others that you understand the entire new venture process. Don't put together a plan built on naïveté or overconfidence or one that cleverly hides major flaws. You might not fool others, and you certainly would be fooling yourself.[44]

Nonfinancial Resources   Also crucial to the success of a new business are nonfinancial resources—particularly other people.

Networks   The entrepreneur is aided greatly by having a *network* of people. *Social capital*—being part of a social network, and having a good reputation—helps entrepreneurs gain access to useful information, gain trust and cooperation from others, recruit employees, form successful business alliances, receive funding from venture capitalists, and become more successful.[45] Networks are so important that Regis McKenna of the McKenna Group says that how well connected your investors are is more important than how much they invest.[46] Similarly, Andrea Williams of E*Offering Group advises that you sign up with investors with the best track records, because they can open doors for you.[47]

Top Management Teams   The top management team is another crucial resource. The board of directors improves the company's image, develops longer-term plans for expansion, supports day-to-day activities, and develops a network of information sources. Michael Dell, founder of Dell Computer at age 19, knows the importance of surrounding himself with talent. He hired managers who were far more experienced than he, and prominent and powerful board members. By 1995, at age 30, Michael Dell held the longest tenure of any chief executive in the industry.[48]

Advisory Boards   Anita Brattina thought after two or three years of running her own marketing firm she would have lots of cash, no debt, and time to enjoy her independence.[49] Eight years later, she still worked 50 to 60 hours a week and was not making much money. So she got an advisory board. Board members taught her how to do cash-flow analysis, suggested some strategic changes, and encouraged her to cultivate relationships with a banker, an accountant, and an attorney. In addition, they helped her interview salespeople, develop a long-term marketing strategy, and reorganize operations. They also vetoed a number of her ideas. Sales went up, after one year of listening to the board and implementing its ideas.

Partners   Often, two people go into business together as partners. Partners can help one another access capital, spread the workload, share the risk, and furnish expertise.

Despite the potential advantages of finding a compatible partner, partnerships are not always marriages made in heaven.

"Mark" talked three of his friends into joining him in starting his own telecommunications company because he didn't want to try it alone. He learned quickly that while he wanted to put money into growing the business, his three partners wanted the company to pay for their cars and meetings in the Bahamas. The company collapsed. "I never thought a business relationship could overpower friendship, but this one did. Where money's involved, people change."

To be successful, partners need to acknowledge one another's talents, let each other do what he or she does best, communicate honestly, and listen to one another. And they must learn to trust each other by making and keeping agreements. If they must break an agreement, it is crucial that they give early notice and clean up after their mistakes.

The image of the family business is one of a business started by one founder and then passed down from generation to generation. Now a different model is appearing: parents and children starting new companies as partners.[50] Linda Oldham quit her job to join her son Todd's business. Todd Oldham is a fashion designer who appeared on MTV's *House of Style*. In similar fashion, Gregg Levin designed a plastic product called the Curve, which bends the visors of baseball caps into perfect curves. His father Barry quit his solo law practice to become his son's partner. Perfect Curve Inc. soon had 250 accounts with 350 stores.

Americans under the age of 30 are more likely than any other age group to start or buy businesses. The children have ideas and stamina. The parents have experience and money. And for some parents, it offers a second career after becoming downsized corporate executives.

Entrepreneurial Hazards

Not all companies get off to a great start. Some die a quick death. Others, a slow, agonizing one. Even those that make honored lists, like the *Forbes* best small companies or *Inc.*'s hottest growth companies, don't always remain on the fast track. Some flame out. Of course, many dot-coms have followed this pattern.

In *Forbes*'s annual list of the 200 best small companies in America, in a 10-year period 42 percent continued to grow impressively, but 56 percent hit trouble and went into negative growth. A common cause is growth into new products, or new geographic areas, that are poorly understood. Success can cause management to become overconfident or complacent. And growth can be so fast that the company goes out of control and isn't managed properly, resulting in lower-quality goods and services. Only 2 percent hit the "middle ground" of continuing to grow, but slowly.[51]

The hazards of entrepreneurship are many. First, you may start your own company and find out that you don't enjoy it. One person who quit a large company to start his own small one stated, "As an executive in a large company, the issues are strategic. You're implementing programs that affect thousands of people. In a small business, the issues are less complex . . . you worry about inventory every day, because you may not be in business next week if you have negative cash flow." His most unpleasant surprise: "How much you have to sell. You're always out selling . . . I didn't want to be a salesman. I wanted to be an executive."[52]

And survival is difficult. As *Fortune* put it, "Misjudgments are punished ruthlessly. When competition gets tougher, small businesses feel it first. Financing is hard to find, sometimes impossible . . . 'In small business there are no small mistakes'—it's a phrase that comes up time and again when you talk to the owners."[53] But, says *Fortune*, most are proud of this description of entrepreneurial hazards.

Failure can be devastating. "I remember thinking I was very comfortable financially, and the crystal chandelier hit the floor . . . I remember trying to find enough money to buy groceries. You never forget that."[54] So stated David Pomije, CEO and founder of Funco, a chain that buys and resells used and new Nintendo and Sega videogames. Fortunately, he has turned the corner; he now operates over 100 stores with sales of $50 million.

Failure can be traced to several hazards; the most common are mortality, the inability to delegate, misuse of funds, and poor planning and controls.

Mortality

One long-term measure of an entrepreneur's success is the fate of the venture after the founder's death. The organization can outlive the entrepreneur under one of two conditions: (1) if the company has gone public, or (2) if the entrepreneur has planned an orderly succession, usually to a family member. Both conditions are relatively rare.

Entrepreneurs often fail to seek public capital if equity capital is scarce and expensive or because they want to maintain control. An entrepreneur who is funded with public equity risks losing the business if stockholders are not satisfied. To avoid this risk, the entrepreneur maintains private control over the business. But founding entrepreneurs often fail to plan for succession. When death occurs, estate tax problems and/or the lack of a skilled replacement for the founder can lead to business failure.

Management guru Peter Drucker offers the following advice to help family-managed businesses survive and prosper.[55] Family members working in the business must be at least as capable and hard-working as other employees; at least one key position should be filled by a nonfamily member; and someone outside the family and the business should help plan succession. Family members who are mediocre performers are resented by others; outsiders can be more objective and contribute expertise the family might not have; and issues of management succession are often the most difficult of all, causing serious conflict and possible breakup of the firm.

Inadequate Delegation

Although mortality contributes to some new venture failures, the founder's death usually cannot be blamed. Most new businesses collapse before their owners do. In these cases, the cause of the demise often can be traced to the entrepreneur's desire to personally control every aspect of the business.

Just as entrepreneurs resist loss of control of the company to either public investors or heirs, they often hesitate to delegate work to people within the business. Active leadership deteriorates into micromanagement, in which managers monitor too strictly, to the minutest detail. For example, during the Internet craze many company founders with great technical knowledge but little experience became "instant experts" in every phase of business, including branding and advertising.[56] Turns out, they didn't know as much as they thought.

Misuse of Funds Many unsuccessful entrepreneurs blame their failure on inadequate financial resources. Yet failure due to a lack of financial resources doesn't necessarily indicate a real lack of money; it could mean a failure to properly use the money available. Entrepreneurs who fail to use their resources wisely usually make one of two mistakes: They apply financial resources to the wrong uses, or they maintain inadequate control over their resources.

One aspiring entrepreneur borrowed $100,000 and used $25,000 of that money to buy a dating service. He then used the remaining $75,000 to buy radio advertising for the business. A few months later, bankrupt and bitter, he blamed his failure on a lack of financial resources. But a more objective view might reveal that he did not use his resources wisely. In this case, he could have entered the business at a lower cost by starting his own operation. In addition, he should not have spent $75,000 on advertising without specific knowledge about how that advertising would affect his business. This entrepreneur failed because he applied his financial resources to the wrong uses.

Poor Planning and Controls Entrepreneurs, in part because they are very busy, often fail to use formal planning and control systems. Planning takes time from activities that entrepreneurs may find more enjoyable, such as selling, producing, and buying. Many entrepreneurs fail because they don't anticipate problems such as cash flow shortages and the loss of key customers.

One common entrepreneurial malady is an aversion to record keeping. Expenses mount, but records do not keep pace. Pricing decisions are based on intuition without adequate reference to costs. As a result, the company earns inadequate margins to support growth.

Internet start-ups' ability to burn through cash was stunning; their managers seemed to have a disdain for traditional management control.[57] True, implementing their business models was expensive, but the seemingly limitless availability of funds and the lack of pressure for profits created a lack of discipline.

For example, Respond.com spent more than $200,000 on a promotional party (free sushi, circus performers, $50 bottles of champagne as party favors). Pixelon.com spent $10 million for a megaconcert at the MGM Grand Hotel in Las Vegas featuring the Who, Sugar Ray, Tony Bennett, and Natalie Cole. The managers of Boo.com (and their entourages) stayed at the best hotels, set up six luxurious offices in six different cities, and operated with few financial controls. They also tried to build the Mercedes Benz of websites, but it wasn't long before they declared bankruptcy.[58]

Even in high-growth companies, great numbers can mask brewing problems. Blinded by the light of growing sales, many entrepreneurs fail to maintain vigilance over other aspects of the business. In the absence of controls, the business veers out of control. As the chief financial officer of FTP Software put it, "Success is the worst thing that can happen to a company. You start believing your own headlines. You get sloppy."[59]

Michael Dell observes that people who are too intent on spending money "forget what the fundamentals are in terms of customers and creating value and being disciplined with capital, and you get pretty horrific results"[60] (p. 71). So don't get overconfident; keep asking critical questions. Is our success based on just one big customer? Is our product just a fad that can fade away? Can other companies easily enter our domain and hurt our business? Are we losing a technology lead? Do we really understand the numbers, know where they come from, and have any hidden causes for concern?

Global Start-Ups

Most people, particularly Americans, have an image of new ventures beginning domestically and then slowly, over time, evolving toward international operations. But another model is the **global start-up**,[61] a new venture that is international from the very beginning.[62]

If you are contemplating a start-up, you should ask the following questions to determine whether you should begin with a domestic or a global outlook:[63] First, where are the best people? The United States has great software designers; Italy is known for fine leathers; Japan, for its manufacturing quality. Are the world-class people you need to make the venture a great success located in the neighborhood, or on the other side of the world?

Second, where is the financing easiest and most suitable? Some entrepreneurs maintain that courting European investors is more productive than approaching U.S. venture capitalists, who have made the investment process less intuitive and more institutionalized and bureaucratic. Third, where are the targeted customers? If a big percentage is abroad, it may be illogical to limit operations domestically.

Fourth, when global operators learn about your venture, will they go head-to-head with you? If so, how quickly? Instead of having to defend your domestic markets, you might be better served by going on the offensive internationally. Fifth, if you postpone going international, will your domestic inertia cripple your longer-term prospects? Strategies and tactics that succeed domestically will not necessarily work internationally, and can interfere when you try to adopt new approaches. Why not learn now about going global, rather than later when you could be too slow and too late?

So, you've decided to begin globally rather than just domestically? You'd better know the critical success factors for global start-ups.[64] You should think globally from day one, and be able to communicate your global vision to everyone else associated with the venture. Your top management team should have international experience, and with your staff you should develop deep cross-cultural understanding.[65] You and your team should have in place a network of trusted financiers, suppliers, distributors, and other business associates. You must have a product (good or service) that provides a clear advantage to customers, in order to overcome the advantages already held by indigenous competitors. It also helps to have other, more intangible assets, such as unique knowledge that competitors lack. You should continue innovating, extending your product line over time in order to maintain or build your lead over competitors. And you should coordinate closely every aspect of the organization worldwide via teamwork, extensive travel, personal communications, a sophisticated communications infrastructure, and constant transfer of knowledge among widely dispersed locations.[66]

Intrapreneurship

Today's large corporations are more than passive bystanders in the entrepreneurial explosion. Even established companies try to find and pursue new and profitable ideas—and they need intrapreneurs to do so. If you work in a company, and are considering preparing a new business venture, Table 7.4 can help you decide whether the new idea is worth pursuing.

Building Support for Your Idea

A manager who has a new idea to capitalize on a market opportunity will need to get others in the organization to buy in or sign on. In other words, you need to build a network of allies who support and will help implement the idea.

If you need to build support for a project idea, the first step involves *clearing the investment* with your immediate boss or bosses.[67] At this stage, you explain the idea and seek approval to look for wider support.

Higher executives often want evidence that the project is backed by your peers before committing to it. This involves *making cheerleaders*—people who will support

TABLE 7.4
Checklist for Choosing Ideas

Fit with Your Skills and Expertise
Do you believe in the product or service?
Does the need it fits mean something to you personally?
Do you like and understand the potential customers?
Do you have experience in this type of business?
Do the basic success factors of this business fit your skills?
Are the tasks of the enterprise ones you could enjoy doing yourself?
Are the people the enterprise will employ ones you will enjoy working with and supervising?
Has the idea begun to take over your imagination and spare time?

Fit with the Market
Is there a real customer need?
Can you get a price that gives you good margins?
Would customers believe in the product coming from your company?
Does the product or service you propose produce a clearly perceivable customer benefit that is significantly better than that offered by competing ways to satisfy the same basic need?
Is there a cost-effective way to get the message and the product to the customers?

Fit with the Company
Is there a reason to believe your company could be very good at the business?
Does it fit the company culture?
Does it look profitable?
Will it lead to larger markets and growth?

What to Do When Your Idea Is Rejected

As an intrapreneur, you will frequently find that your idea has been rejected. There are a few things you can do.
 	
1. Give up and select a new idea.
2. Listen carefully, understand what is wrong, improve your idea and your presentation, and try again.
3. Find someone else to whom you can present your idea by considering:
   a. Who will benefit most if it works? Can they be a sponsor?
   b. Who are potential customers? Will they demand the product?
   c. How can you get to the people who really care about intrapreneurial ideas?

SOURCE: G. Pinchot III, *Intrapreneuring*, Copyright © 1985 by John Wiley & Sons, Inc. Reprinted by permission of the author, www.pinchot.com.

the manager before formal approval from higher levels. Managers at General Electric refer to this strategy as "loading the gun"—lining up ammunition in support of your idea.

Next, *horse trading* begins. You can offer promises of payoffs from the project in return for support, time, money, and other resources that peers and others contribute.

Finally, you should *get the blessing* of relevant higher-level officials. This usually involves a formal presentation. You will need to guarantee the project's technical and political feasibility. Higher management's endorsement of the project and promises of resources help convert potential supporters into an enthusiastic team. At this point, you can go back to your boss and make specific plans for going ahead with the project.

Along the way, expect resistance and frustration—and use passion and persistence, as well as business logic, to persuade others to get on board.[68]

Building Intrapreneurship

Building an entrepreneurial culture is the heart of the corporate strategy at Acordia, a highly successful health care management company.[69] Acordia's success in fostering a culture in which intrapreneurs flourish came from making an intentional decision to foster entrepreneurial thinking and behavior, creating new-venture teams, and changing the compensation system so that it encourages, supports, and rewards creative and innovative behaviors. In other words, building intrapreneurship derives from careful and deliberate planning.

Two common approaches used to stimulate intrapreneurial activity are skunkworks and bootlegging. **Skunkworks** are project teams designated to produce a new product. A team is formed with a specific goal within a specified time frame. A respected person is chosen to be manager of the skunkworks. In this approach to corporate innovation, risk takers are not punished for taking risks and failing—their former jobs are held for them. The risk takers also have the opportunity to earn large rewards.

Bootlegging refers to informal efforts by managers and employees to create new products and new processes. "Informal" can mean "secretive," such as when a bootlegger believes the company will frown on those activities. But the intrapreneurial organization should tolerate and even encourage bootlegging.

Merck, desiring entrepreneurial thinking and behavior in R&D, explicitly rejects budgets for planning and control. New product teams don't *get* a budget. They must persuade people to join the team and commit *their* resources. This creates a survival-of-the-fittest process, mirroring the competition in the real world.[70]

skunkworks

A project team designated to produce a new, innovative product.

bootlegging

Informal efforts by managers and employees to create new products and new processes.

Organizing New Corporate Ventures

For large-scale innovation, strategic alliances—cooperation among different organizations—can be a useful route.

For example, all leading television networks engage in Web-based entrepreneurial efforts, such as CNN's partnership with WebMD to become a health-information portal. NBC Internet, which coordinates NBC's Web activities, led the way beyond conventional television broadcasting with a portfolio of entrepreneurial experiments, including MSNBC.com and NBCi.com, which was intended to supplant Yahoo when broadband becomes dominant on the Web.[71] MSNBC.com has survived, but NBCi.com has not.

These days, large companies often outsource for innovation, providing entrepreneurial opportunities for small firms. But Carly Fiorina, Hewlett-Packard's CEO, figures she has to reinvigorate HP from *within* the company.[72] She told Nick Earle to start as many new Internet businesses inside the company as possible. Mr. Earle established the e-services. solutions group, one of only two groups that cut across all of HP's operating units.

Earle wants all of HP's businesses to operate entrepreneurially. One aspect of this is to work in innovative ways with other companies to create Web services, and to build a *keiretsu*, or ecosystem, of Internet companies around HP. The expanding entrepreneurial ecosystem includes Sprint and Swatch (creating an Internet-ready watch). CEO Fiorina wanted HP to do one such deal every week, with the goal of getting everyone at HP to think along such entrepreneurial lines.[73]

Hazards in Intrapreneurship

Organizations that encourage intrapreneurship face an obvious risk: The effort can fail. One author noted, "There is considerable history of internal venture development by large firms, and it does not encourage optimism."[74] However, this risk can be managed. In fact, failing to foster intrapreneurship may represent a subtler but greater risk than encouraging it. The organization that resists intrapreneurial initiative may lose its ability to adapt when conditions dictate change.

The most dangerous risk in intrapreneurship is the risk of overreliance on a single project. Many companies fail while awaiting the completion of one large, innovative project.[75] The successful intrapreneurial organization avoids overcommitment to a single project and relies on its entrepreneurial spirit to produce at least one winner from among several projects.

Organizations also court failure when they spread their intrapreneurial efforts over too many projects.[76] If there are many intrapreneurial projects, each effort may be too small in scale. Managers will consider the projects unattractive because of their small size. Or, those recruited to manage the projects may have difficulty building power and status within the organization.

The hazards in intrapreneurship, then, are related to scale. One large project is a threat, as are too many underfunded projects. But a carefully managed approach to this strategically important process will upgrade an organization's chances for long-term survival and success.

Entrepreneurial Orientation

Earlier in this chapter, we described the characteristics of individual entrepreneurs. Now we do the same for companies: We describe how companies that are highly entrepreneurial differ from those that are not.

Entrepreneurial orientation is the tendency of an organization to engage in activities designed to identify and capitalize successfully on opportunities to launch new ventures by entering new or established markets with new or existing goods or services.[77] Entrepreneurial orientation is determined by five tendencies: to allow independent action, innovate, take risks, be proactive, and be competitively aggressive.

To *allow independent action* is to grant to individuals and teams the freedom to exercise their creativity, champion promising ideas, and carry them through to completion. *Innovativeness* requires the firm to support new ideas, experimentation, and creative processes that can lead to new products or processes; it requires a willingness to depart from existing practices and venture beyond the status quo. *Risk taking* comes from a willingness to commit significant resources, and perhaps borrow heavily, to venture into the unknown. The tendency to take risks can be assessed by considering whether people are bold or cautious, whether they require high levels of certainty before taking or allowing action, and whether they tend to follow tried-and-true paths.

To be *proactive* is to act in anticipation of future problems and opportunities. A proactive firm shapes the environment and changes the competitive landscape; other firms merely react. Proactive firms are forward thinking and fast to act, and are leaders rather than followers. Similarly, some individuals are more likely to be proactive, to shape and create their own environments, than others who more passively cope with the situations in which they find themselves.[78] Proactive firms encourage and allow individuals and teams to *be* proactive.

Finally, *competitive aggressiveness* is the tendency of the firm to challenge competitors directly and intensely in order to achieve entry or improve its position. In other words, it is a competitive tendency to outperform one's rivals in the marketplace. This might take the form of striking fast to beat competitors to the punch, to tackle them head-to-head, and to analyze and target competitors' weaknesses. Michael Dell provides a good example: He can state clearly how each of his competitors—IBM, Apple, Gateway, Compaq—is vulnerable and poised to fail.[79]

What makes a firm "entrepreneurial" is its engagement in an effective combination of independent action, innovativeness, risk taking, proactiveness, and competitive aggressiveness.[80] The relationship between these factors and the performance of the firm is a complicated one that depends on many things. Nevertheless you can imagine how the opposite profile—too many constraints on action, business as usual, extreme caution, passivity, and a lack of competitive fire—will undermine entrepreneurial activities. And without entrepreneurship, how would firms survive and thrive in a constantly-changing competitive environment?

entrepreneurial orientation

The tendency of an organization to identify and capitalize successfully on opportunities to launch new ventures by entering new or established markets with new or existing goods or services.

3M—A Prototype

3M is a prototype of an entrepreneurial organization. It manages more than 50,000 products. The company respects doers and innovators more than hierarchy and autocratic bosses. People say and do what they believe is right. Management teams in all businesses have substantial freedom, and they pass freedom along to others. In 1949, Chairman William McKnight exhorted his managers to delegate responsibility, encourage people to exercise their own initiative, and be tolerant of mistakes. McKnight's phrases became well known:[81]

- "Listen to anyone with an original idea, no matter how absurd it might sound at first."
- "Encourage, don't nitpick. Let people run with an idea."
- "Hire good people, and leave them alone."
- "Encourage experimental doodling."
- "Give it a try—and quick!"

This carpet has made it through countless birthday parties, two graduation parties, and a keg party you never knew about.

There's protection. Then there's Scotchgard™ protection. The kind that helps keep your carpet looking its best longer by making it easier to clean. So ask for the Scotchgard brand and rest easy knowing the leading name in protection has you covered. Visit us at www.scotchgard.com

SCOTCHGARD
For Carpet

Protection for life's possibilities™

Innovation

3M is one of the best at encouraging experimentation and innovation.

3M competes fiercely in the marketplace, and allows and even encourages its divisions to compete against one another. Within limits, scientists can work on projects of their own choosing and initiative. Lots of resources are available for the development of prototypes and market tests. People talk constantly about ideas for new technologies and new products.

3M has a new chairman and CEO, W. James McNerney, Jr. The first outsider to take the helm, McNerney boldly predicted that he will double 3M's record-breaking revenues of 2000 within 10 years (the 2000 numbers were twice those of 15 years before). He actually is pulling in the reins a bit on the freedom that 3M's business units enjoyed in the past because he thinks money sometimes was spent unwisely. The impact of this change remains to be seen, but McNerney says he understands the challenge: "If I end up killing [the] entrepreneurial spirit, I will have failed"[82] (p. 50).

Management can create environments that foster more entrepreneurship. If your bosses are not doing this, consider trying some entrepreneurial experiments on your own.[83] Seek out others with an entrepreneurial bent. What can you learn from them, and what can you teach others? Sometimes it takes individuals and teams of experimenters to show the possibilities to those at the top. Ask yourself, and ask others: Between the bureaucrats and the entrepreneurs, who is having a more positive impact? And who is having more fun?

KEY TERMS

Bootlegging, p. 230

Business incubators, p. 215

Business plan, p. 222

Entrepreneurial orientation, p.231

Entrepreneurial venture, p. 213

Entrepreneurship, p. 212

Global start-up, p. 228

Independent entrepreneurship, p. 214

Intrapreneurs, p. 214

Opportunity analysis, p. 222

Side street effect, p. 219

Skunkworks, p. 230

Small business, p. 212

SUMMARY OF LEARNING OBJECTIVES

Now that you have studied Chapter 7, you should know:

The activities of entrepreneurship.

Entrepreneurship occurs when enterprising individuals pursue profitable opportunities. The independent entrepreneur is the individual who establishes a new organization. Intrapreneurs are new venture creators who work within the boundaries of their established companies.

How to find and evaluate ideas for new business ventures.

You should always be on the lookout for new ideas, talking to other people and monitoring current products, the business environment, and other indicators of opportunity. Trial and error and preparation play important roles. Ideas should be carefully assessed via opportunity analysis and a thorough business plan.

What it takes to be a successful entrepreneur.

Successful entrepreneurs are determined, effective leaders; obsessed with the opportunity; tolerant of risk, ambiguity, and uncertainty; creative; self-reliant; adaptable; and motivated to excel.

How to write a great business plan.

The business plan helps you determine the viability of your enterprise and convince others to provide financing. It describes the venture and its future, provides financial projections, and includes plans for marketing, manufacturing, and other business functions. The plan should describe at length the people involved in the venture, a full assessment of the opportunity (including customers and competitors), the environmental context (including regulatory and economic perspectives), and the risk (including future risks and how you intend to deal with them).

The important management skills, resources, and strategies needed to avoid failure and achieve success.

Successful entrepreneurs also understand how to plan the new venture, obtain financial resources, and develop a network of other people, including suppliers, customers, partners, and boards of directors. Through effective use of their skills, resources, and appropriate strategy, they avoid major causes of failure, including failure to plan for succession, inadequate delegation, poor financial controls, and inappropriate allocation of financial resources.

Key criteria for deciding whether your start-up should be global from the outset.

Traditionally, new ventures start on a small scale and then expand, occasionally internationally. Now a new model is appearing: the global start-up, which is international from the very beginning. Whether to begin domestically or globally is an important question, answered by determining where the best people are located, where financing is available and most suitable, where the targeted customers are, and how global competitors will react to you.

How to foster intrapreneurship and an entrepreneurial orientation in large companies.

Intrapreneurs work within established companies to develop new goods or services that allow the corporation to reap the benefits of innovation. To facilitate intrapreneurship, organizations use skunkworks—special project teams designated to develop a new product—and allow bootlegging—informal efforts to create new products and processes. Businesses also may work together through strategic alliances to create new ventures. Whatever the approach, the organization must select its projects carefully and fund them appropriately. Ultimately, a true entrepreneurial orientation in a firm comes from encouraging independent action, innovativeness, risk taking, proactive behavior, and competitive aggressiveness.

DISCUSSION QUESTIONS

1. On a 1 to 10 scale, what is your level of personal interest in becoming an independent entrepreneur? Why did you rate yourself as you did?

2. How would you assess your capability of being a successful entrepreneur? What are your strengths and weaknesses? How would you increase your capability?

3. Most entrepreneurs learn the most important skills they need after age 21. How does this affect your outlook and plans?

4. Identify and discuss new ventures that fit each of the four cells in the entrepreneurial strategy matrix.

5. Brainstorm a list of ideas for new business ventures. From where did the ideas come? Which ones are most and least viable, and why?

6. Identify some businesses that have recently opened in your area. What are their chances of survival, and why? How would you advise the owners or managers of those businesses to enhance their success?

7. Assume you are writing a story about what it's really like to be an entrepreneur. To whom would you talk, and what questions would you ask?

8. Conduct interviews with two entrepreneurs, asking whatever questions most interest you. Share your findings with the class. How do the interviews differ from one another, and what do they have in common?

9. Read Table 7.1, "Some Myths about Entrepreneurs." Which myths did you believe? Do you still? Why or why not? Interview two entrepreneurs by asking each myth as a true-or-false question. Then ask them to elaborate on their answers. What did they say? What do you conclude?

10. With your classmates, form small teams of skunkworks. Your charge is to identify an innovation that you think would benefit your school, college, or university, and to outline an action plan for bringing your idea to reality.

11. Identify some bootlegging activities in which you have engaged or have seen others engage. What resulted from the activities? Were the efforts successful? Why or why not?

12. Identify a business that recently folded. What were the causes of the failure? What could have been done differently to prevent the failure?

Enter the Competition

Harvard Business School has an annual business plan competition in which student teams submit ideas and plans for new companies. A panel of business professionals, entrepreneurs, and venture capitalists judges the plans, and the winning teams receive cash prizes and services to help them develop their ideas further.

Harvard offered the country's first business school course in entrepreneurship in 1947. Nonetheless, until recently it was highly unusual for graduates to start their own businesses right out of the program. But today more students are doing it. In 1999, a faculty member said that if the students feared failure, that fear was "vastly outweighed by the fear that timing is everything—that if they don't do it now, this fabulous window of opportunity is going to close. It would be a form of failure not to try."

The winner in 2001 was in the pharmaceutical industry, and in 2002, it was a firm called FishLogic (what do you suppose that is?). Back in 2000, the great majority of submissions were dot-com ventures. The winning submission was Bang Networks, which would provide "leading Internet companies with a first-of-its-kind infrastructure network that will revolutionize the Web," Kristin Rhyne's proposed company, Polished, was the only non-Internet company to become a semifinalist. Polished will provide express spa services at airports, serving tired travelers, flight crews, and other airport personnel.

But of course, things have changed since 2000, since the dot-com bust. So, is a technology start-up a bad idea? Gary Hoover said, "I'm deliberately not mentioning technology as an opportunity area. The thing about technology is that, by definition, advancements will die off. Yesterday's high-tech center is today's industrial graveyard" (p. 72). But Paul Saffo maintains that "the dot-com bubble burst, but the Internet is definitely not over.

Consumers are using the Internet as much as ever. The bottom line on the bubble is that everybody got the magnitude of the revolution right, but they got the time wrong" (p. 75).

Jon Burgstone and Asif Satchu, cofounders of Suppliermarket.com (a runner-up), focused on creating a great company before they chose their business concept. Satchu said, "Our objective, first and foremost, was to create a long-term, sustainable company that values integrity, respect, honesty, commitment, teamwork, and loyalty. In addition, we wanted to have fun and remain friends throughout the journey . . . The reason behind our success is that we focused on the long haul: investing in culture, maintaining values, and creating a stellar team." They further advise, "Build the right management team and partner with the right investors. Choose a business model you can be passionate about 24/7, then focus on the product and listen to the customer."

QUESTIONS

1. How many ideas for new businesses can you and your classmates generate?

2. Which are the best ideas? How did you assess their value?

3. Choose one or more ideas and develop the outline of a business plan.

4. What do you think of the philosophy at Suppliermarket.com? How does it relate to this chapter? What will be the underpinnings of your business?

SOURCES: "The HBS Business Plan Contest; A Mini-cure for the Weary Traveler: Polished; Built to Last: Suppliermarket.com; T. Singer, "What Business Would You Start?" *Inc.*, March 2002, pp. 68–76.

7.1 Take an Entrepreneur to Dinner

OBJECTIVES

1. To get to know what an entrepreneur does, how she or he got started, and what it took to succeed.

2. To interview a particular entrepreneur in depth about his or her career and experiences.

3. To acquire a feeling for whether you might find an entrepreneurial career rewarding.

INSTRUCTIONS

1. Identify an entrepreneur in your area you would like to interview.

2. Contact the person you have selected and make an appointment. Be sure to explain why you want the appointment and to give a realistic estimate of how much time you will need.

3. Identify specific questions you would like to have answered and the general areas about which you would like information. (See the following suggested interview.) Using a com-

bination of open-ended questions, such as general questions about how the entrepreneur got started, what happened next, and so forth, and closed-ended questions, such as specific questions about what his or her goals were, if he or she had to find partners, and so forth, will help keep the interview focused yet allow for unexpected comments and insights.

4. Conduct the interview. If *both* you and the person you are interviewing are comfortable, using a small tape recorder during the interview can be of great help to you later. Remember, too, that you most likely will learn more if you are an "interested listener."

5. Evaluate what you have learned. Write down the information you have gathered in some form that will be helpful to you later on. Be as specific as you can. Jotting down direct quotes is more effective than statements such as "highly motivated individual." And be sure to make a note of what you did not find out.

6. Write a thank-you note. This is more than a courtesy; it will also help the entrepreneur remember you favorably should you want to follow up on the interview.

Suggested Interview

QUESTIONS FOR GATHERING INFORMATION

- *Would you tell me about yourself before you started your first venture?*

  Were your parents, relatives, or close friends entrepreneurial? How so?

  Did you have any other role models?

  What was your education/military experience? In hindsight, was it helpful? In what specific ways?

  What was your previous work experience? Was it helpful? What particular "chunks of experience" were especially valuable or relevant?

  In particular, did you have any sales or marketing experience? How important was it or a lack of it in starting your company?

- *How did you start your venture?*

  How did you spot the opportunity? How did it surface?

  What were your goals? What were your lifestyle or other personal requirements? How did you fit these factors together?

  How did you evaluate the opportunity in terms of the critical elements for success? The competition? The market?

  Did you find or have partners? What kind of planning did you do? What kind of financing did you have?

  Did you have a start-up business plan of any kind? Please tell me about it.

  How much time did it take from conception to the first day of business? How many hours a day did you spend working on it?

  How much capital did it take? How long did it take to reach a positive cash flow and break-even sales volume? If you did not have enough money at the time, what were some ways in which you "bootstrapped" the venture (i.e., bartering, borrowing, and the like)? Tell me about the pressures and crises during that early survival period.

  What outside help did you get? Did you have experienced advisors? Lawyers? Accountants? Tax experts? Patent experts? How did you develop these networks and how long did it take?

  What was your family situation at the time?

  What did you perceive to be your own strengths? Weaknesses?

  What did you perceive to be the strengths of your venture? Weaknesses?

  What was your most triumphant moment? Your worst moment?

  Did you want to have partners or do it solo? Why?

- *Once you got going, then:*

  What were the most difficult gaps to fill and problems to solve as you began to grow rapidly?

  When you looked for key people as partners, advisors, or managers, were there any personal attributes or attitudes you were especially seeking because you knew they would fit with you and were important to success? How did you find them?

  Are there any attributes among partners and advisors that you would definitely try to avoid?

  Have things become more predictable? Or less?

  Do you spend more/same/less time with your business now than in the early years?

  Do you feel more managerial and less entrepreneurial now?

  In terms of the future, do you plan to harvest? To maintain? To expand?

  Do you plan ever to retire? Would you explain?

  Have your goals changed? Have you met them?

  Has your family situation changed?

QUESTIONS FOR CONCLUDING (CHOOSE ONE)

- What do you consider your most valuable asset—the thing that enabled you to "make it"?
- If you had it to do over again, would you do it again, in the same way?
- Looking back, what do you feel are the most critical concepts, skills, attitudes, and know-how you needed to get your company started and grown to where it is today? What will be needed for the next five years? To what extent can any of these be learned?
- Some people say there is a lot of stress being an entrepreneur. What have you experienced? How would you say it compares with other "hot seat" jobs, such as the head of a big company or a partner in a large law, consulting, or accounting firm?
- What are the things that you find personally rewarding and satisfying as an entrepreneur? What have been the rewards, risks, and trade-offs?
- Who should try to be an entrepreneur? Can you give me any ideas there?
- What advice would you give an aspiring entrepreneur? Could you suggest the three most important "lessons" you have learned? How can I learn them while minimizing the tuition?

SOURCE: Jeffry A. Timmons. *New Venture Creation,* 3rd ed. Copyright © 1994 by Jeffry A. Timmons. Reproduced with permission of the author.

7.2 Starting a New Business

OBJECTIVES

1. To introduce you to the complexities of going into business for yourself.
2. To provide hands-on experience in making new business decisions.

INSTRUCTIONS

1. Your instructor will divide the class into teams and assign each team the task of investigating the start-up of one of the following businesses:
   a. Submarine sandwich shop

b. Day care service
c. Bookstore
d. Gasoline service station
e. Other

2. Each team should research the information necessary to complete the New-Business Start-Up Worksheet. The following agencies or organizations might be of assistance:
   a. Small Business Administration
   b. Local county/city administration agencies
   c. Local chamber of commerce
   d. Local small-business development corporation
   e. U.S. Department of Commerce
   f. Farmer's Home Administration
   g. Local realtors
   h. Local businesspeople in the same or a similar business
   i. Banks and S&Ls

3. Each team presents its findings to the class.

New-Business Start-Up Worksheet

1. *Product* _____

   What customer need will we satisfy? _____

   How can our product be unique? _____

2. *Customer* _____

   Who are our customers? What are their profiles? _____

   Where do they live/work/play? _____

   What are their buying habits? _____

   What are their needs? _____

3. *Competition* _____

   Who/where is the competition? _____

   What are their strengths and weaknesses? _____

   How might they respond to us? _____

4. *Suppliers* _____

   Who/where are our suppliers? _____

   What are their business practices? _____

   What relationships can we expect? _____

5. *Location* _____

   Where are our customers/competitors/suppliers? _____

   What are the location costs? _____

   What are the legal limitations to location? _____

6. *Physical Facilities/Equipment* _____

   Rent/own/build/refurbish facilities? _____

   Rent/lease/purchase equipment? _____

   Maintenance? _____

7. *Human Resources* _____

   Availability? _____

   Training? _____

   Costs? _____

8. *Legal/Regulatory Environment* _____

Licenses/permits/certifications? _____

Government agencies? _____

Liability? _____

9. *Cultural/Social Environment* _____

Cultural issues? _____

Social issues? _____

10. *International Environment* _____

International issues? _____

11. *Other* _____

Information for Entrepreneurs

If you are interested in starting or managing a small business, you have access to many sources of information.

PUBLISHED SOURCES

The first step is a complete search of materials in libraries and on the Internet. You can find a huge amount of published information, databases, and other sources about industry, market, competitor, and personnel information. Listed below are additional sources that should help get you started.

Guides and Company Information   Valuable information is available in special issues of *Forbes, Inc., The Economist, Fast Company,* and *Fortune* and in the following:

- Compact D/SEC
- Compustat
- Thomas Register
- Directory of Corporate Affiliations
- Standard & Poor's Register of Corporations, Directors, and Executives
- Standard & Poor's Corporation Records
- Dun & Bradstreet Million Dollar Directory
- Dunn's Million Dollar Disc Plus
- Moody's Manuals
- World Almanac
- Worldscope

Valuable Sites on the Internet

- Entreworld *(http://www.entreworld.org)*—the website of the Kauffman Center for Entrepreneurial Leadership, Ewing Marion Kauffman Foundation.
- Fast Company *(http://www.fastcompany.com)*
- Securities Data *(http://www.securitiesdata.com)*
- Ernst & Young *(http://www.ey.com)*
- Global Access—SEC documents through a subscription-based website. *http://www.disclosure/com*
- INC online *(http://www.inc.com)*
- Success online *(http://www.successmagazine.com)*

Journal Articles via Computerized Indexes

- Dow Jones News
- FirstSearch
- Ethnic News Watch

- LEXIS/NEXIS
- New York Times Index
- Reuters Business Briefings
- Searchbank
- Uncover (http://uncweb.carl.org)
- ABI/Inform
- Wall Street Journal Index

Statistics

- Profiles in Business and Management
- USA Countries
- Zip Code Business Patterns
- Stat-USA (http://www.stat-usa.gov)
- http://www.census.gov (This is the URL for the U.S. Census Bureau that is listed in statistics and financial and operating issues.)
- http://www.census.gov/stat-abstract (This is the URL for the Statistical Abstract of the United States that is listed in statistics and financial and operating issues section.)
- Knight Ridder . . . CRB Commodity Year Book
- Manufacturing USA
- Economic Census
- Economic Statistics Briefing Room (http://www.whitehouse.gov/fsbr/esbr.html)
- Federal Reserve Bulletin
- Survey of Current Business
- Labstat (http://stats.bls.gov/labstat.htm)
- DRI (aka Citibase)
- International Financial Statistics
- Reuterlink PC
- Bloomberg Database

Projections and Forecasts

- Proquest Direct
- Computer Industry Forecasts
- Guide to Special Issues and Indexes to Periodicals
- Value Line Investment Survey

Market Studies

- LifeStyle Market Analyst

Consumer Expenditures
- The Official Guide to American Incomes
- Consumer Expenditure Survey

Other Sources
- Wall Street Transcript
- CIRR: Company & Industry Research Reports
- Brokerage House reports
- Company annual reports

OTHER INTELLIGENCE
Everything entrepreneurs need to know will not be found in libraries, since this information needs to be "highly specific" and "current." This information is most likely available from people—industry experts, suppliers, and the like.

Summarized below are some useful sources of intelligence.

- **Trade associations.**   Trade associations, especially the editors of their publications and information officers, are good sources of information. Especially, trade shows and conferences are prime places to discover the latest activities of competitors.
- **Employees.**   Employees who have left a competitor's company often can provide information about the competitor, especially if the employee departed on bad terms. Also, a firm can hire people away from a competitor. While consideration of ethics in this situation is important, certainly the number of experienced people in any industry is limited, and competitors must prove that a company hired a person intentionally to get specific trade secrets in order to challenge any hiring legally. Students who have worked for competitors are another source of information.
- **Consulting firms.**   Consulting firms frequently conduct industry studies and then make this information available. Frequently, in such fields as computers or software, competitors use the same design consultants, and these consultants can be sources of information.
- **Market research firms.**   Firms doing the market studies, such as those listed under published sources above, can be sources of intelligence.
- **Key customers, manufacturers, suppliers, distributors, and buyers.**   These groups are often a prime source of information.

SOURCE: J. A Timmons. *New Venture Creation,* 5th ed., pp. 98–99. Copyright © 1999 by Jeffry A. Timmons. Reproduced with permission of the author.

Foundation of Management
- Managing
- The External Environment
- Managerial Decision Making

Planning:
Delivery Strategic Value
- Planning and Strategic Management
- Ethics and Corporate Responsibility
- International Management
- New Ventures

Strategy Implementation

Organizing: Building a Dynamic Organization
- Organization Structure
- The Responsive Organization
- Human Resources Management
- Managing The Diverse Workforce

Leading:
Mobilizing People
- Leadership
- Motivating for Performance
- Managing Teams
- Communicating

Controlling:
Learning and Changing
- Managerial Control
- Managing Technology and Innovation
- Creating and Managing Change

Organizing: Building a Dynamic Organization

Now that you know about planning and strategy, the remaining three parts correspond to the other three functions of management: organizing, leading, and controlling. Parts Three, Four, and Five discuss issues pertaining to *implementing* strategic plans. In Part Three, we describe how to organize and staff for maximum effectiveness. Chapter 8 introduces you to different organization structures and explains how to group and delegate tasks. Chapter 9 builds on those basic concepts by describing more complex organization designs. This chapter discusses how firms can adapt quickly to rapidly changing environments and how "corporate America" is restructuring. Chapter 10 addresses the management of human resources. Its focus is on staffing the firm with capable employees and the issues surrounding employee reward systems. Finally, Chapter 11 discusses the challenge of managing today's workforce, one composed of diverse groups of people. Chapters 12 and 13 set the stage for Part Four, which further elaborates on how to manage people.

241

Organization Structure

Take my assets—but leave me my organization and in five years I'll have it all back.

—Alfred P. Sloan, Jr.

CHAPTER OUTLINE

Fundamentals of Organizing
  Differentiation
  Integration
The Vertical Structure
  Authority in Organizations
  Hierarchical Levels
  Span of Control
  Delegation
  Decentralization
The Horizontal Structure
  The Functional Organization
  The Divisional Organization
  The Matrix Organization
Organizational Integration
  Coordination by Standardization
  Coordination by Plan
  Coordination by Mutual Adjustment
  Coordination and Communication
Looking Ahead

LEARNING OBJECTIVES

After studying Chapter 8, you will know:

1. How differentiation and integration influence an organization's structure.

2. How authority operates.

3. The roles of the board of directors and the chief executive officer.

4. How span of control affects structure and managerial effectiveness.

5. How to delegate work effectively.

6. The difference between centralized and decentralized organizations.

7. How to allocate jobs to work units.

8. How to manage the unique challenges of the matrix organization.

9. The nature of important integrative mechanisms.

ADIDAS ENTERS A THREE-LEGGED RACE

Faced with sagging sales in North America as well as tough competition in Europe, Adidas has been reevaluating its game plan and getting its structure in shape. By trimming the fat of duplicated functions and integrating its U.S. organization into the company's global structure, Adidas is expected to return to the industry's "A-team."

The company has a redesigned, three-divisional approach that veers from the traditional "footwear and apparel" structure of most other sporting goods companies. Each of the three divisions will produce its own footwear and apparel lines in order

Adidas recently reintroduced its 1976 Copenhagen shoe, one of its early brands.

to address the needs of consumers in a targeted way:

- The Forever Sport division—which currently accounts for 90 percent of Adidas's overall business—features performance products that also will appeal to the lifestyle sector. It will use the Adidas Performance logo and focus on the training, running, tennis, soccer, and basketball categories.
- The Originals division leverages the company's sports heritage by offering sport-inspired leisure products under the classic Trefoil logo. Its mission is to compete against traditional athletic brands as well as such fashion labels as Polo Sport, Abercrombie & Fitch, and the Gap. In the long term, this division should account for 25 to 30 percent

of the total business and will log double-digit annual growth beginning in 2001.

- The Adidas Equipment division focuses on multifunctional products and is the bridge between the Forever Sport and Original lines. The category uses the new Adidas Equipment logo and eventually will account for 5 to 10 percent of the overall business.

Herbert Hainer, Adidas-Salomon CEO and chairman of the board, concluded, "Our new . . . organizational structure will revolutionize the way Adidas does business. It will provide us with the dynamic framework that we need to aggressively expand our business and will enable us to deliver significant growth rates in the coming years."

The onetime professional soccer player is making a major push for the $7.8 billion U.S. market, which accounts for nearly half of global athletic footwear sales. Things seem to be going Hainer's way; he won high marks for nuts-and-bolts stuff like shortening the product-development cycle and speeding product delivery. Adidas was the best-performing stock on Germany's DAX in 2001, rising 26.5 percent even as the index slumped 19.8 percent. Hainer also kept his promise to deliver 15 percent growth in profits for 2001: $182 million on sales of $5.3 billion. But with the U.S. athletic shoe market flat, it will be hard for Adidas's boss to move closer to his goal of wringing 40 to 50 percent of revenues out of the United States, up from 30 percent now.

Adidas, the world's number two sporting goods maker after Nike Inc., didn't have to pay for the use of its trademark three-stripe apparel in the movie *The Royal Tenenbaums*. Hainer could use a few more breaks like that.

Source: Jeffrey Lacap, "Adidas Embraces New Global Strategy," *Sporting Goods Business*, November 10, 2000, 33, no. 16, p. 8; Judy Leand, "The SGB Interview: Ross McMullin," *Sporting Goods Business*, November 10, 2000, 33, no. 16, p. 44; Roxanna Guilford, "Adidas-Salomon: Apparel, Taxes and Domestic Sales Slow Adidas-Salomon Growth," *Apparel Industry Magazine*, June 2000, 61, no. 6, p. 64; Jack Ewing, "Will Adidas Play Better in Peoria?" *Business Week*, February 25, 2002.

Adidas is a company that pretty much all of us know, but the material in "Setting the Stage" gives us some insight into its struggles and plans for the future. Although a quick story such as this doesn't provide all the details about Adidas's strategy and structure, it does highlight a few important issues that we want to cover in this chapter. Make no mistake: How a company organizes itself is as important as—if not more important than—its strategy. And Adidas, like many other companies, is working hard to make certain that its strategy and structure are aligned with each other.

This chapter focuses on the vertical and horizontal dimensions of organization structure. We begin by covering basic principles of *differentiation* and *integration*. Next, we discuss the vertical structure, which includes issues of *authority*, hierarchy, delegation, and decentralization. We continue on to describe the horizontal structure, which includes functional, divisional, and matrix forms. Finally, we illustrate the ways in which organizations can integrate their structures: coordination by standardization, coordination by plan, and coordination by mutual adjustment.

In the next chapter, we continue with the topic of organization structure but take a different perspective. In that chapter we will focus on the flexibility and responsiveness of an organization, that is, how capable it is of changing its form and adapting to strategy, technology, the environment, and so on.

Fundamentals of Organizing

organization chart

The reporting structure and division of labor in an organization.

To get going, let's start simple. We often begin to describe a firm's structure by looking at its organization chart. The **organization chart** depicts the positions in the firm and how they are arranged. The chart provides a picture of the reporting structure (who reports to whom) and the various activities that are carried out by different individuals. Most companies have official organizational charts drawn up to give people this information.

Figure 8.1 shows the traditional organization chart. Note the various kinds of information that are conveyed in a very simple way:

1. The boxes represent different work.
2. The titles in the boxes show the work performed by each unit.
3. Reporting and authority relationships are indicated by solid lines showing superior-subordinate connections.
4. Levels of management are indicated by the number of horizontal layers in the chart. All persons or units that are of the same rank and report to the same person are on one level.

differentiation

An aspect of the organization's internal environment created by job specialization and the division of labor.

integration

The degree to which differentiated work units work together and coordinate their efforts.

Although the organization chart presents some clearly important structural features, there are other design issues related to structure that—while not so obvious—are no less important. Two fundamental concepts around which organizations are structured are differentiation and integration. **Differentiation** means that the organization is composed of many different units that work on different kinds of tasks, using different skills and work methods. **Integration** means that these differentiated units are put back together so that work is coordinated into an overall product.[1]

Differentiation

division of labor

The assignment of different tasks to different people or groups.

Several related concepts underlie the idea of structural differentiation. For example, differentiation is created through division of labor and job specialization. **Division of labor** means that the work of the organization is subdivided into smaller tasks. Various individuals and units throughout the

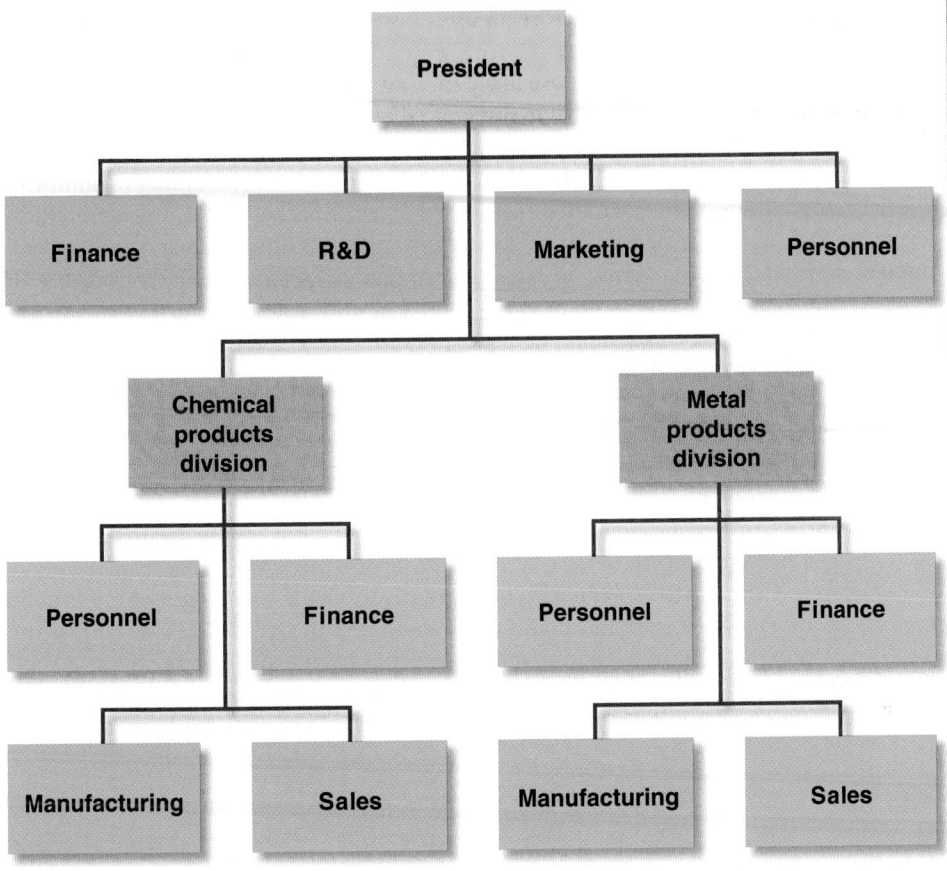

FIGURE 8.1
A Conventional
Organization Chart

organization perform different tasks. **Specialization,** in turn, refers to the fact that different people or groups often perform specific parts of the entire task. The two concepts are, of course, closely related. Secretaries and accountants specialize in, and perform, different jobs; similarly, marketing, finance, and human resources tasks are divided among the respective departments. The numerous tasks that must be carried out in an organization make specialization and division of labor necessities. Otherwise the complexity of the overall work of the organization would be too much for any individual.[2]

> **specialization**
>
> **A process in which different individuals and units perform different tasks.**

Differentiation is high when there are many subunits and many kinds of specialists who think differently. Harvard professors Lawrence and Lorsch found that organizations in complex, dynamic environments (plastics firms in their study) developed a high degree of differentiation in order to cope with the complex challenges. Companies in simple, stable environments (container companies) had low levels of differentiation. Companies in intermediate environments (food companies) had intermediate differentiation.[3]

Integration

As organizations differentiate their structures, managers must simultaneously consider issues of integration. All the specialized tasks in an organization cannot be performed completely independently. Because the different units are part of the larger organization, some degree of communication and cooperation must exist among them. Integration and its related concept, **coordination,** refer to the procedures that link the various parts of the organization to achieve the organization's overall mission.

Integration is achieved through structural mechanisms that enhance collaboration and coordination. Any job activity that links different work units performs an integrative function. Remember, the more highly differentiated

> **coordination**
>
> **The procedures that link the various parts of an organization for the purpose of achieving the organization's overall mission.**

your firm, the greater the need for integration among the different units. Lawrence and Lorsch found that highly differentiated firms were successful if they also had high levels of integration. Organizations are more likely to fail if they exist in complex environments and are highly differentiated, but fail to integrate their activities adequately.[4]

These concepts permeate the rest of the chapter. First, we will discuss *vertical differentiation* within organization structure. This includes issues pertaining to authority within an organization, the board of directors, the chief executive officer, and hierarchical levels, as well as issues pertaining to delegation and decentralization. Next, we will discuss *horizontal differentiation* in an organization's structure including issues of departmentalization that create functional, divisional, and matrix organizations. Finally, we will discuss issues pertaining to structural integration, including coordination, organizational roles, interdependence, and boundary spanning.

The Vertical Structure

corporate governance

The role of a corporation's executive staff and board of directors in ensuring that the firm's activities meet the goals of the firm's stakeholders.

In order to understand issues such as reporting relationships, authority, responsibility, and the like, we need to begin with the vertical dimension of a firm's structure.

Corporate governance is a term describing the oversight of the firm by its executive staff and board of directors. As the following case shows, the public's trust in corporate governance has been eroding recently; legal and internal changes are being made to ensure that corporate governance is vigilant, objective, and working for the long-term interests of the shareholders.

FROM THE PAGES OF

A disenchanted investor vows to vote in favor of every shareholder resolution he can find. An angry employee says she feels betrayed by bosses who have grown rich on stock options while putting the squeeze on health benefits and salaries. A deal maker trying to close a sale hears yet another buyer grouse: "Who's to say this guy isn't lying about the numbers like everyone else?" The latest wave of skepticism may have started with Enron Corp.'s ugly demise, but with each revelation of corporate excess or wrongdoing, the goodwill built up by business during the boom of the last decade has eroded a little more, giving way to widespread suspicion and mistrust. An unrelenting barrage of headlines that tell of Securities and Exchange Commission investigations, indictments, guilty pleas, government settlements, financial restatements, and fines has lent greater credence to the belief that the system is inherently unfair.

The sight of Enron employees tearfully testifying before Congress was a watershed moment in American capitalism. Enron added to the sense that no matter how serious their failure or how imperiled the corporation, those in charge always seem to walk away vastly enriched, while employees and shareholders are left to suffer the consequences of the top managers' ineptitude or malfeasance. When IBM used $290 million from the sale of a business three days before the end of the fourth quarter of 2001 to help it beat Wall Street's profit forecast, it did what was perfectly legal—yet entirely misleading. Such distortions have become commonplace as companies strive to hit a target even at the cost of clarity and fairness.

The inevitable result is growing outrage among corporate stakeholders. Unchecked, that rising bitterness and distrust could prove costly to business and to society. The loss of trust threatens our ability to create new jobs and reignite the economy. It also leaves a taint on the majority of executives and corporations that act with integrity. Directors who fail to direct and CEOs who fail at moral leadership are arguably the most serious challenge facing corporate America today.

More than a half century ago, the Columbia University professors Adolf A. Berle and Gardiner C. Means made clear the divergence between the owners of a corporation and the professional managers hired to run it. After years of lavish stock-option rewards meant to remedy the problem, this divergence is more extreme than ever. The senior executives of public corporations today are often among the largest individual owners of those enterprises, and board members are far more likely to have major equity stakes as well, whether through actual stock ownership or through option grants. In theory, this ownership was supposed to align the interests of management and directors with those of shareholders. However, executives and directors realized that their personal wealth was so closely tied to the price of the company stock that maintaining the share price became the highest corporate value.

As the market overheated, it became less and less tolerant of even the slightest whiff of bad news, rumors of which could wipe out hundreds of millions of dollars of market value at a stroke. Anita M. McGahan, a Boston University business professor, says, "The stakes in admitting problems were very high, both because the market overvalued their stock and because of executive pay." A study by J. Richard Finlay, chairman of Canada's Center for Corporate and Public Governance, showed that many boards devote far more time and energy to compensation than to assuring the integrity of the company's financial reporting systems. At Oracle Corp., where CEO Laurence J. Ellison's exercise of stock options just before the company issued an earnings warning led to a record $706.1 million payout in 2001, the full board met on only five occasions and acted by written consent three times. The compensation committee, by contrast, acted 24 times in formal session or by written consent.

In a report filed by William C. Powers, Jr., an Enron board member, he and his colleagues found an almost total collapse in board oversight. The Powers report concluded that the board's controls were inadequate, that its committees carried out reviews "only in a cursory way," and that the board failed to appreciate "the significance of some of the specific information that came before it."

It's not just the corporation that is at fault. Many of the corporation's outside professionals fell prey to greed and self-interest as well, from Wall Street analysts and investment bankers to auditors and lawyers and even regulators and lawmakers. These players, who are supposed to provide the crucial checks and balances in a system that favors unfettered capitalism, have in many cases been compromised.

- Many analysts urged investors to buy shares in companies solely because their investment banker colleagues could reap big fees for handling underwriting and merger business.
- Far too many auditors responsible for certifying the accuracy of a company's accounts looked the other way so that their firms could rake in millions from audit fees and millions more from higher-margin consulting work.
- Some outside lawyers invented justifications for less than pristine practices to win a bigger cut of the legal fees.
- Far too often, CEOs found that they could buy all the influence they wanted or needed.

SOURCE: John A. Byrne, "How to Fix Corporate Governance," *Business Week*, May 6, 2002.

Authority in Organizations

Authority, the legitimate right to make decisions and to tell other people what to do, is fundamental to the functioning of every organization. For example, a boss has the authority to give an order to a subordinate.

Authority resides in *positions* rather than in people. Thus, the job of vice president of a particular division has authority over that division, regardless of how many people come and go in that position and who currently holds it.

In private business enterprises, the owners have ultimate authority. In most small, simply structured companies, the owner also acts as manager. Sometimes the owner hires another person to manage the business and its employees. The owner gives this

authority

The legitimate right to make decisions and to tell other people what to do.

manager some authority to oversee the operations, but the manager is accountable to—that is, reports and defers to—the owner. Thus, the owner still has the ultimate authority.

Traditionally, authority has been the primary means of running an organization. An order that a boss gives to a lower-level employee usually is carried out. As this occurs throughout the organization day after day, the organization can move forward toward achieving its goals.[5]

We will discuss the authority structure of organizations from the top down, beginning with the board of directors.

The Board of Directors   In corporations, the owners are the stockholders. But because there are numerous stockholders and these individuals generally lack timely information, few are directly involved in managing the organization. Stockholders elect a board of directors to oversee the organization. The board, led by the chair, makes major decisions affecting the organization, subject to corporate charter and bylaw provisions. Boards perform at least three major sets of duties: (1) selecting, assessing, rewarding, and perhaps replacing the CEO; (2) determining the firm's strategic direction and reviewing financial performance; and (3) assuring ethical, socially responsible, and legal conduct.[6]

Some top executives are likely to sit on the board (they are called *inside directors*). Outside members of the board tend to be executives at other companies. The trend in recent years has been toward reducing the number of insiders and increasing the number of outsiders. Today most companies have a majority of outside directors. Boards made up of strong, independent outsiders are more likely to provide different information and perspectives and to prevent big mistakes. Successful boards tend to be those which are active, critical participants in determining company strategies. Campbell Soup's board, for example, took control over selecting a new CEO and routinely conducts performance evaluations of board members to make certain they are active contributors.[7]

The Chief Executive Officer   The authority officially vested in the board of directors is assigned to a chief executive officer (CEO), who occupies the top of the organizational pyramid. The CEO is personally accountable to the board and to the owners for the organization's performance.

It is estimated that in 15 percent of Fortune 500 corporations, one person holds all three positions of CEO, chair of the board of directors, and president.[8] More commonly, however, one person holds two of those positions, with the CEO serving also

Retail managers typically meet informally with employees before and after the business day, as at this Staples store.

as either the chair of the board or the president of the organization. When the CEO is president, the chair may be honorary and may do little more than conduct meetings. In other cases, the chair may be the CEO and the president is second in command.

The Top Management Team   Increasingly, CEOs share their authority with other key members of the top management team. Top management teams typically are composed of the CEO, president, chief operating officer, chief financial officer, and other key executives. Rather than make critical decisions on their own, CEOs at companies such as Shell, Honeywell, and Merck regularly meet with their top management teams to make decisions as a unit.[9]

Hierarchical Levels

In Chapter 1, we discussed the three broad levels of the organizational pyramid, commonly called the **hierarchy.** The CEO occupies the top position and is the senior member of top management. The top managerial level also includes presidents and vice presidents. These are the strategic managers in charge of the entire organization. The second broad level is middle management. At this level, managers are in charge of plants or departments. The lowest level is made up of lower management and workers. It includes office managers, sales managers, supervisors, and other first-line managers, as well as the employees who report directly to them. This level is also called the *operational level* of the organization.

> **hierarchy**
> The authority levels of the organizational pyramid.

An authority structure is the glue that holds these levels together. Generally (but not always), people at higher levels have the authority to make decisions and tell lower-level people what to do. For example, middle managers can give orders to first-line supervisors; first-line supervisors, in turn, direct operative-level workers.

A powerful trend for U.S. businesses over the past few decades has been to reduce the number of hierarchical layers. General Electric used to have 29 levels; today, after a major reorganization, it has only 5. Most executives today believe that fewer layers create a more efficient, fast-acting, and cost-effective organization. This also holds true for the **subunits** of major corporations. A study of 234 branches of a financial services company found that branches with fewer layers tended to have higher operating efficiency than did branches with more layers.[10]

> **subunits**
> Subdivisions of an organization.

Span of Control

The number of people under a manager is an important feature of an organization's structure. The number of subordinates who report directly to an executive or supervisor is called the **span of control.** The implications of differences in the span of control for the shape of an organization are straightforward. Holding size constant, narrow spans build a *tall* organization that has many reporting levels. Wide spans create a *flat* organization with fewer reporting levels. The span of control can be too narrow or too wide. The optimal span of control maximizes effectiveness because it is (1) narrow enough to permit managers to maintain control over subordinates but (2) not so narrow that it leads to overcontrol and an excessive number of managers who oversee a small number of subordinates.

> **span of control**
> The number of subordinates who report directly to an executive or supervisor.

What is the optimal number of subordinates? Five, according to Napoleon.[11] Some managers today still consider five a good number. At one Japanese bank, in contrast, several hundred branch managers report to the same boss.

Actually, the optimal span of control depends on a number of factors. The span should be wider when (1) the work is clearly defined and unambiguous, (2) subordinates are highly trained and have access to information, (3) the manager is highly capable and supportive, (4) jobs are similar and performance measures are comparable, and (5) subordinates prefer autonomy to close supervisory control. If the opposite conditions exist, a narrow span of control may be more appropriate.[12]

Delegation

delegation

The assignment of new or additional responsibilities to a subordinate.

As we look at organizations, and recognize that authority is spread out over various levels and spans of control, the issue of delegation becomes paramount. Specifically, **delegation** is the assignment of authority and responsibility to a subordinate at a lower level. It requires that the subordinate report back to his or her boss in regard to how effectively the assignment was carried out. Delegation is perhaps the most fundamental feature of management, because it entails getting work done through others. Thus, delegation is important at all hierarchical levels. The process can occur between any two individuals in any type of structure with regard to any task.

Some managers are comfortable delegating to subordinates; others are not. Consider the differences between these two office managers and the ways they gave out the same assignment in the following example.

Are Both of These Examples of Delegation?

Manager A: "Call Tom Burton at Nittany Office Equipment. Ask him to give you the price list on an upgrade for our personal computers. I want to move up to a Pentium III with 256 megs of RAM and at least a 40-gigabyte hard drive. Ask them to give you a demonstration of Windows 2000 and Office 2000. I want to be able to establish a LAN for the entire group. Invite Cochran and Snow to the demonstration and let them try it out. Have them write up a summary of their needs and the potential applications they see for the new systems. Then prepare me a report with the costs and specifications of the upgrade for the entire department. Oh, yes, be sure to ask for information on service costs."

Manager B: "I'd like to do something about our personal computer system. I've been getting some complaints that the current systems are too slow, can't run current software, and don't allow for networking. Could you evaluate our options and give me a recommendation on what we should do? Our budget is probably around $3,500 per person, but I'd like to stay under that if we can. Feel free to talk to some of the managers to get their input, but we need to have this done as soon as possible."

Responsibility, Authority, and Accountability   When delegating work, it is helpful to keep in mind the important distinctions among the concepts of authority, responsibility, and accountability.

responsibility

The assignment of a task that an employee is supposed to carry out.

Responsibility means that a person is assigned a task that he or she is supposed to carry out. When delegating work responsibilities, the manager also should delegate to the subordinate enough authority to get the job done. *Authority*, recall, means that the person has the power and the right to make decisions, give orders, draw upon resources, and do whatever else is necessary to fulfill the responsibility. Ironically, it is quite common for people to have more responsibility than authority; they must perform as best they can through informal influence tactics instead of relying purely on authority. More will be said about informal power and how to use it in Chapter 12.

As the manager delegates responsibilities, subordinates are held accountable for achieving results. **Accountability** means that the subordinate's manager has the right to expect the subordinate to perform the job, and the right to take corrective action if the subordinate fails to do so. The subordinate must report upward on the status and quality of his or her performance of the task.

accountability

The expectation that employees will perform a job, take corrective action when necessary, and report upward on the status and quality of their performance.

However, the ultimate responsibility—accountability to higher-ups—lies with the manager doing the delegating. Managers remain responsible and accountable not only for their own actions but for the actions of their subordinates. Thus, managers should not resort to delegation to others as a means of escaping their own responsibilities. In many cases, however, managers refuse to accept responsibility for subordinates' actions. Managers often "pass the buck" or take other evasive action to ensure they are not held accountable for mistakes.[13]

Advantages of Delegation Delegating work offers important advantages. The manager saves time by giving some of his or her own responsibilities to someone else. Then the manager is free to devote energy to important, higher-level activities such as planning, setting objectives, and monitoring performance.

Delegation essentially gives the subordinate a more important job. The subordinate acquires an opportunity to develop new skills and to demonstrate potential for additional responsibilities and perhaps promotion. In essence, the subordinate receives a vital form of on-the-job training that could pay off in the future.

The organization also receives payoffs. Allowing managers to devote more time to important managerial functions while lower-level employees carry out assignments means that jobs are done in a more efficient and cost-effective manner.

How Should Managers Delegate? To achieve the advantages just discussed, delegation must be done properly. As Figure 8.2 shows, effective delegation proceeds through several steps.[14]

The first step in the delegation process, defining the goal, requires that the manager have a clear understanding of the outcome he or she wants. Then the manager should select a person who is capable of performing the task.

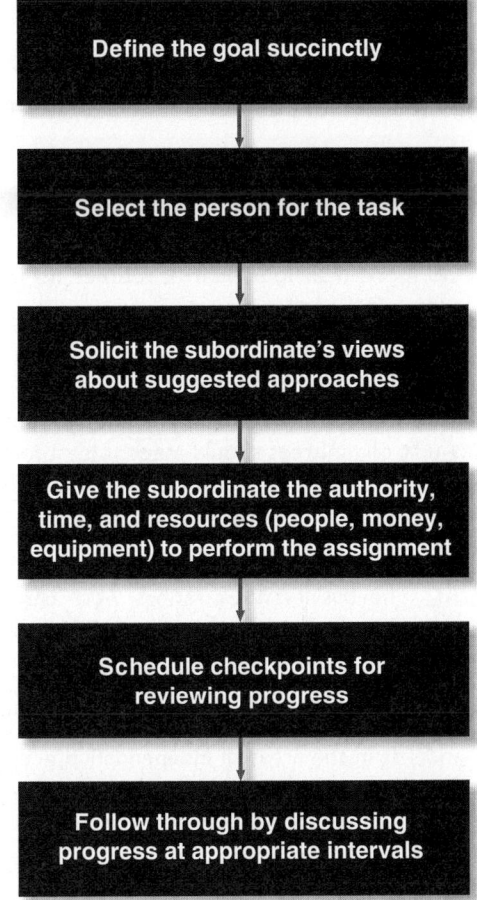

FIGURE 8.2
The Steps in Effective Delegation

The person who gets the assignment should be given the authority, time, and resources needed to carry out the task successfully. Throughout the delegation process, the manager and the subordinate must work together and communicate about the project. The manager should know the subordinate's ideas at the beginning and inquire about progress or problems at periodic meetings and review sessions. Thus, even though the subordinate performs the assignment, the manager is available and aware of its current status.

Some tasks, such as disciplining subordinates and conducting performance reviews, should not be delegated. But when managers err, it usually is because they delegated too little rather than too much. The manager who wants to learn how to delegate more effectively should remember this distinction: If you are not delegating, you are merely *doing* things; but the more you delegate, the more you are truly *building* and *managing* an organization.[15]

FROM THE PAGES OF

BusinessWeek

Here's what we look for in evaluating boards:

INDEPENDENCE

No more than two directors should be current or former company executives, and none should do business with the company or accept consulting or legal fees from it. The audit, compensation, and nominating committees should be made up solely of independent directors.

STOCK OWNERSHIP

Each director should own an equity stake in the company worth at least $150,000, excluding stock options. The only exception: new board members who haven't had time to build a large stake.

DIRECTOR QUALITY

Boards should include at least one independent director with experience in the company's core business and one who is the CEO of an equivalent-size company. Fully employed directors should sit on no more than four boards, retirees no more than seven. Each director should attend at least 75% of all meetings.

BOARD ACTIVISM

Boards should meet regularly without management present and should evaluate their own performance every year. Audit committees should meet at least four times a year. Boards should be frugal on executive pay, decisive when planning a CEO succession, diligent in oversight responsibilities, and quick to act when trouble strikes.

How We Rated Them: The *BusinessWeek* ratings were based on a survey of 51 governance experts conducted for *BusinessWeek* by Harris Interactive, a proxy analysis by *BusinessWeek* of companies identified by survey respondents as having the "most effective" and "least effective" boards, and an analysis of overall board performance by *BusinessWeek* editors. The proxy analysis grades each company on the extent to which it meets 16 governance standards in the areas of independence, accountability, and quality. Performance measures include the board's handling of strategy, oversight, and executive pay. Data were provided by the Investor Responsibility Research Center, the Corporate Library, and Institutional Shareholder Services.

BEST BOARDS

3M   With just one insider on its nine-member board, the company gets high marks for independence. Outside directors include the CEOs of Lockheed-Martin, Allstate, and Amgen. Audit-committee chairman is the former CFO at Sears. No directors have business ties to the company.

APRIA HEALTHCARE   A favorite among governance experts, the board includes three top shareholder activists and features a separate chairman and CEO, a rarity. It moved quickly to accept the resignation of a former CEO when directors discovered that his wife had been hired for a company job.

COLGATE-PALMOLIVE   Directors are well-invested in the company and sit on few additional boards. The compensation committee has awarded premium-priced options to CEO Reuben Mark, which pay off only if stock appreciates by 10% to 70%. A new section on governance has been added to the latest proxy.

GENERAL ELECTRIC   This talent-packed board, with an unrivaled record of creating shareholder value, remains a favorite with governance experts, although there have been recent revelations of lavish retirement perks for former CEO Jack Welch. The company is improving board independence; it recently added Ralph Larsen, former CEO of Johnson & Johnson (*JNJ*) and a longtime champion of good governance. The board recently moved to expense options.

HOME DEPOT   With the departure of co-founder Bernard Marcus, the 12-member board now has only two insiders. Independent directors meet regularly without management. Directors are required to visit 20 stores a year.

INTEL   One of the few boards that have a lead director. No insiders sit on the audit, compensation, or nominating committees. The board conducts an annual self-evaluation. Directors have big stakes in the company.

JOHNSON & JOHNSON   The high-powered board includes Delta Air Lines (*DAL*) CEO Leo Mullin, Lucent Technologies Chairman Henry Schacht, and CSX CEO John Snow. The outside board members own plenty of J&J stock. Only one director sits on more than four boards.

MEDTRONIC   Governance gurus applaud the board's practice of holding regular meetings without the CEO and its performance evaluations for directors. Members are graded on willingness to "hold management accountable" and "meaningful participation" at meetings.

PFIZER   The board was second only to GE in overall approval by governance experts. Independent directors meet without the CEO. No Pfizer executives sit on the audit, nominating, or compensation committees. Stock transactions for directors and executives are posted on the company Web site.

TEXAS INSTRUMENTS   Making its third appearance on *BusinessWeek's* Best Boards list, this highly independent board boasts a roster of well-invested outside directors, including the chief executives of Norfolk Southern, Kimberly-Clark, and Eastman Kodak (*EK*).

WORST BOARDS

APPLE   Founder Steve Jobs owns just two shares in the company. Recently departed director Larry Ellison had none and had missed more than 25% of meetings in the past five years. The CEO of Micro Warehouse, which accounted for nearly 2.9% of Apple's net sales in 2001, sits on the compensation committee. Since 2000, the board has awarded Jobs 27.5 million stock options and a $90 million jet. There is an interlocking directorship—with Gap CEO Mickey Drexler and Jobs sitting on each other's boards.

CONSECO In 2000, the company spent a hefty $45 million to recruit CEO Gary Wendt from GE Capital. Despite the company's recent slide, in July—with the stock hovering at $1—the board awarded Wendt an $8 million bonus. In August, the shares were delisted from the Big Board and now trade at 7 cents. None is a CEO. The board doesn't meet without the CEO at present.

DILLARD'S Before his death in February, Chairman William Dillard presided over a board that included seven directors with ties to the company, including four of his children. No nominating committee—allowing the CEO to hand-pick directors. With two-thirds of board elected by holders of privately held Class B shares, Dillard's is exempt from NYSE governance rules.

GAP Self-dealing includes contracts with the chairman's brother to build and re-model stores and a consulting deal with the chairman's wife. Slow to replace outgoing CEO Mickey Drexler as performance declined. Interlocking directorship with Drexler sitting on the Apple board, while Apple's Steve Jobs sits on Gap's. Two other directors sit on the Charles Schwab board, while Chuck Schwab sits on Gap's.

KMART The board's woes include multiple investigations of company accounting, a $501 million profit restatement, and a federal grand jury probe into pay practices. The board was passive as the company's performance deteriorated before a bankruptcy filing in January. Meanwhile, the board approved $28 million in retention loans to 25 top executives.

QWEST Founder Philip Anschutz has extensive dealings with the company and sits on compensation and nominating committees. The SEC is probing whether Qwest used "swap" transactions to boost revenue. The compensation committee—described as "comatose" by one expert—awarded ex-CEO Joseph Nacchio an $88 million pay package in 2001, one of the worst years in the company's history. No outside director has operating experience in the company's core business.

TYSON FOODS Out of 15 board members, 10 have ties to the company, including seven who have extensive business dealings. CEO John Tyson got a $2.1 million bonus for negotiating the acquisition of meatpacker IBP—which Tyson Foods tried unsuccessfully to back out of—in a year when net income fell 42%. Feds say the company for years conspired to smuggle workers from Mexico for its U.S. poultry-processing plants, a charge Tyson denies.

XEROX The bungled succession of Paul Allaire, accusations of funny accounting, billions in shareholder wealth up in smoke, and a decades-long failure to keep up with changing technology add up to an ineffectual board. With departures of Allaire and CFO Barry Romeril, the board is far more independent. But too many directors sit on too many boards. Director Vernon Jordan's law firm provides legal services. Two audit committee members had attendance problems last year.

HALL OF SHAME

ADELPHIA COMMUNICATIONS Epic self-dealing by members of the Rigas family went undetected. Board has ousted worst offenders, withheld $4.2 million in severance for founder John Rigas. But for Adelphia shareholders, it's too little too late.

ENRON Biggest governance failure in modern corporate history. The board twice waived its ethics guidelines to allow the CFO to participate in off-balance-sheet deals. Ignored warnings from auditors concerning "high-risk" accounting. Failed to follow up on allegations from whistle-blower Sherron Watkins. Directors disavowed responsibility for company failure under oath before Congress.

GLOBAL CROSSING Three of seven directors are insiders. Audit committee lacks anyone with hands-on finance or accounting experience. Company is in bankruptcy. Accounting is under investigation. But chairman Gary Winnick is sitting pretty: He sold $735 million in stock before company's collapse.

METROMEDIA FIBER NETWORK Before a bankruptcy filing in May, three of board's eight members had ties to Metromedia or affiliated companies. The SEC is investigating accounting problems. The company has announced it will write down $4 billion in assets and restate financials for three quarters in 2001. Several directors sold more than $150 million in stock before the company's problems became widely known.

TYCO Disgraced CEO Dennis Kozlowski and others are alleged to have illegally siphoned off more than $100 million in corporate assets. An internal probe revealed that at least three directors or their companies for years received undisclosed Tyco payments for aircraft leases and legal services. To its credit, the board booted out director Frank Walsh after he refused to return $20 million he received for facilitating the CIT Group merger. Tyco is suing Kozlowski to recover five years of income and severance. All nine Kozlowski-era directors are leaving next year.

WARNACO Retail downturn plus massive debt and restructuring charges drove Linda Wachner's once-mighty underwear empire into bankruptcy last year—while the board snoozed. It didn't ask for Wachner's resignation until five months after the bankruptcy filing. Meanwhile, accounting errors forced the board to restate three years of financials. The SEC is considering enforcement action against the company. Two steps in the right direction: recruiting a former American Express CFO for board and fighting Wachner's demand for $25 million in severance.

WORLDCOM The board signed off on financials that had overstated profits by $7.1 billion since 2000. Clifford Alexander Jr., who left the board in January after missing half the meetings in 2001, is chairman of Moody's Investors Service, which didn't downgrade World-Com bonds until April. Chairman Bert Roberts owns a company that was paid $405,000 by WorldCom to provide air-transportation services. Since the bankruptcy filing in July, the board has added three independent directors and initiated a search for a permanent CEO.

SOURCE: Louis Lavelle, "Best and Worst Boards," *Business Week* (October 7, 2002).

Decentralization

The delegation of responsibility and authority *decentralizes* decision making. In a **centralized organization,** important decisions usually are made at the top. In **decentralized organizations,** more decisions are made at lower levels. Ideally, decision making occurs at the level of the people who are most directly affected and have the most intimate knowledge about the problem. This is particularly important when the business environment is fast-changing and decisions must be made quickly and well. Consider the changes at Harley-Davidson.

Most American executives today understand the advantages of pushing decision-making authority down to the point of the action. The level that deals directly with problems and opportunities has the most relevant information and can best foresee the consequences of decisions. Executives also see how the decentralized approach allows people to take more timely action.[16]

At AES, the world's largest global power company (with revenues in excess of $3 billion), all decisions are pushed down to the lowest levels in the organization. Teams in plants have total responsibility for operations and maintenance. According to Cofounder Dennis Bakke and Chairman Roger Sant, giving people the power and responsibility to make important decisions has multiple benefits. It leads to better and faster decisions because decisions are made where the action is. Also, it gives employees a chance to learn and get engaged in the business, turning them into "mini-CEOs." An extreme example of this decentralized approach occurred when the plant executives let the maintenance staff take a stab at investing the $12 million cash reserve held at the plant. By three months into the process, the team was actually beating the returns of the people in the home office who were investing money for the company's treasury![17]

centralized organization

An organization in which high-level executives make most decisions and pass them down to lower levels for implementation.

decentralized organization

An organization in which lower-level managers make important decisions.

In the 1980s, Harley-Davidson faced tough competition from Honda, Suzuki, and Yamaha. The company was able to survive under the direction of a very strong hierarchical, centralized leadership group. The key structural concerns at that time were reining in control, getting a firm grasp on manufacturing costs, and producing a quality product at a reasonable price.

Today, that approach alone probably won't work. The days of controlling leaders and dependent followers are long gone. Harley-Davidson made the transition to a flatter, more empowered organization that decentralizes decision making. In order to support individual growth and excellence, Harley-Davidson replaced hierarchy with collaborative leadership. The changes are built on a philosophy that includes employee empowerment and accountability, mutual trust and respect through education and training, open communications, commitment, and problem solving through consensus. As a consequence of pushing down authority, managers are finding that trust replaces fear-based power. Ultimately the goal is to establish a much more innovative organization that taps into the creativity and resourcefulness of its employees. This is believed to be the type of organization needed to address today's complex business challenges.

Re-creating itself was a success for Harley-Davidson. The firm celebrates its hundredth birthday in 2003, after 16 consecutive years of earnings increases.

SOURCES: Clyde Fessler, "Rotating Leadership at Harley-Davidson: From Hierarchy to Interdependence," *Strategy & Leadership* 25, no. 4 (July/August 1997), pp. 42–43; and Jeffrey Young and Kenneth L. Murrell, "Harley-Davidson Motor Company Organizational Design: The Road to High Performance," *Organization Development Journal*, Spring 1998, 16, no. 1, p. 65.

The Horizontal Structure

Up to this point, we've talked primarily about vertical aspects of organization structure. Issues of authority, span of control, delegation, and decentralization are important in that they give us an idea of how managers and employees relate to one another at different levels. At the same time, separating vertical differentiation from horizontal differentiation is a bit artificial because the elements work simultaneously.

As the tasks of organizations become increasingly complex, the organization inevitably must be subdivided—that is, *departmentalized*—into smaller units or departments. One of the first places this can be seen is in the distinction between line and staff departments. **Line departments** are those which have responsibility for the principal activities of the firm. Line units deal directly with the organization's primary goods or services; they make things, sell things, or provide customer service. At General Motors, for example, line departments include product design, fabrication, assembly, distribution, and the like. Line managers typically have much authority and power in the organization. They have the ultimate responsibility for making major operating decisions. They also are accountable for the "bottom-line" results of their decisions.

Staff departments are those which provide specialized or professional skills that support line departments. These would include research, legal, accounting, public relations, and human resources departments. Each of these specialized units often has its own vice president, and some are vested with a great deal of authority, as when accounting or finance groups approve and monitor budgetary activities. But while staff units formerly focused on

line departments

Units that deal directly with the organization's primary goods and services.

staff departments

Units that support line departments.

monitoring and controlling performance, today most staff units are moving toward a new role focused on strategic support and expert advice.[18]

As organizations divide work into different units, we can detect patterns in the way departments are clustered and arranged. The three basic approaches to **departmentalization** are functional, divisional, and matrix. We will talk about each and highlight some of their similarities and differences.

The Functional Organization

In a **functional organization,** jobs (and departments) are specialized and grouped according to *business functions* and the skills they require: production, marketing, human resources, research and development, finance, accounting, and so forth. At perhaps the most basic level, we can think about a functional structure being organized around a firm's value chain. A **value chain** depicts the relationships among separate activities that are performed to create a product or service. Figure 8.3 *(a)* shows a generic value chain, and Figure 8.3 *(b)* shows how it might be translated into an organization's functional structure.[19]

Functional departmentalization is common in both large and small organizations. Large companies may organize along several different functional groupings, including groupings unique to their businesses. For example, Carmike Cinema, which operates 2,275 screens in 312 theaters in 35 states, has vice presidents of finance, real estate, operations, advertising, information systems, technical, and concessions and a vice president who is the head film buyer.

The traditional functional approach to departmentalization has a number of potential advantages for an organization:[20]

1. *Economies of scale can be realized.* When people with similar skills are grouped, more efficient equipment can be purchased, and discounts for large purchases can be used.
2. *Monitoring of the environment* is more effective. Each functional group is more closely attuned to developments in its own field and therefore can adapt more readily.
3. *Performance standards* are better maintained. People with similar training and interests may develop a shared concern for performance in their jobs.
4. People have greater opportunity for *specialized training* and *in-depth skill development.*
5. Technical specialists are relatively *free of administrative work.*
6. *Decision making* and *lines of communication* are simple and clearly understood.

The functional form has disadvantages as well as advantages. People may care more about their own function than about the company as a whole, and their attention to functional tasks may make them lose focus on overall product quality and customer satisfaction. Managers develop functional expertise but do not acquire knowledge of the other areas of the business; they become specialists, but not generalists. Between functions, conflicts arise, and communication and coordination fall off. In short, while functional differentiation may exist, *functional integration* may not.

As a consequence, the functional structure may be most appropriate in rather simple, stable environments. If the organization becomes fragmented (or *disintegrated*), it may be difficult to develop and bring new products to market and difficult to respond quickly to customer demands and other changes. Particularly when companies are growing and business environments are changing, the need arises to integrate work areas more effectively so that the organization can be more flexible and responsive. Other forms of departmentalization can be more flexible and responsive than the functional structure.

departmentalization

Subdividing an organization into smaller subunits.

functional organization

Departmentalization around specialized activities such as production, marketing, and human resources.

value chain

Sequence of activities that flow from raw materials to the delivery of a product or service.

a. Generic value chain

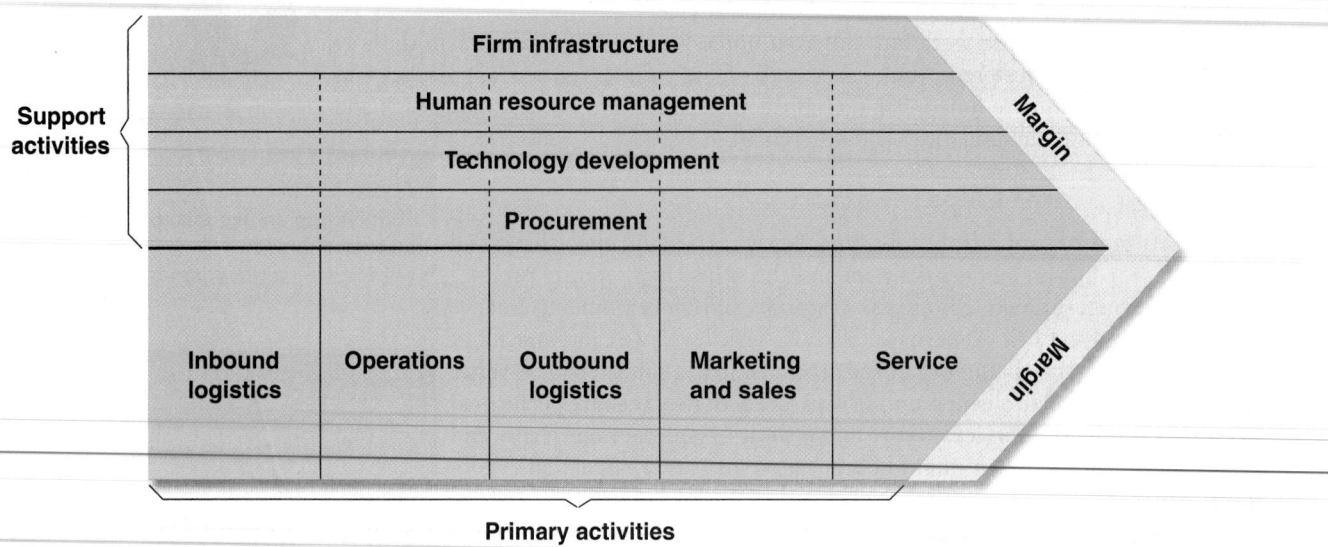

SOURCE: Michael Porter, *Competitive Advantage: Creating and Sustaining Superior Performance* (New York: Free Press, 1985).

b. Functional Structure

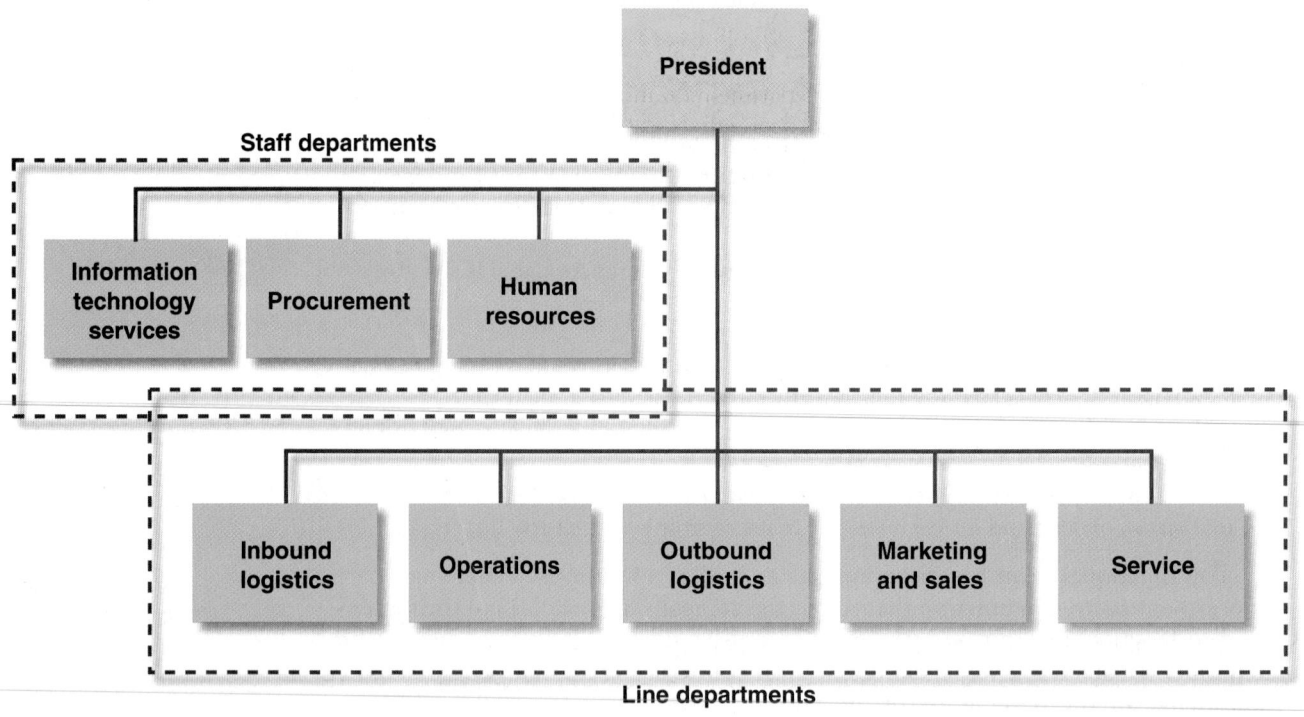

FIGURE 8.3

Generic Value Chain and Functional Structure

Demands for total quality, customer service, innovation, and speed have made clear the shortcomings of the functional form for some firms. Functional organizations are highly differentiated and create barriers to coordination across functions. Cross-functional coordination is essential for total quality, customer service, innovations, and speed. The functional organization will not disappear, in part because functional specialists will always be needed, but functional managers will make fewer decisions. The more important units will be cross-functional teams that have integrative responsibilities for products, processes, or customers.[21]

The Divisional Organization

The discussion of a functional structure's weaknesses leads us to the **divisional organization.** As organizations grow and become increasingly diversified, they find that functional departments have difficulty managing a wide variety of products, customers, and geographic regions. In this case, organizations may restructure in order to group all functions into a single division, and duplicate each of the functions across all the divisions. Division A has its own operations and marketing department, Division B has its own operations and marketing department, and so on. In this regard, separate divisions may act almost as separate businesses or profit centers and work autonomously to accomplish the goals of the entire enterprise. Table 8.1 presents examples of how the same tasks would be organized under functional and divisional structures.

> **divisional organization**
> Departmentalization that groups units around products, customers, or geographic regions.

There are several ways to create a divisional structure. It can be created around products, customers, or geographic regions. Each of these is described in the following sections.

Product Divisions   In the product organization, all functions that contribute to a given product are organized under one manager. In the product organization, managers in charge of functions for a particular product report to a product manager. Johnson & Johnson is one example of this form. J&J has 168 independent divisions in 33 groups, each responsible for a handful of products worldwide.

The product approach to departmentalization offers a number of advantages:[22]

1. *Information needs are managed more easily.* Less information is required, because people work closely on one product and need not worry about other products.
2. *People have a full-time commitment to a particular product line.* They develop a greater awareness of how their jobs fit into the broader scheme.
3. *Task responsibilities are clear.* When things go wrong in a functional organization, functional managers can "pass the buck" ("That other department is messing up, making it harder for us to do our jobs"). In a product structure, managers are more independent and accountable because they usually have the resources they need to perform their tasks. Also, the performances of different divisions can be compared by contrasting their profits and other measures.
4. *People receive broader training.* General managers develop a wide variety of skills, and they learn to be judged by results. Many top executives received crucial early experience in product structures.

Functional Organization	Divisional Organization
A central purchasing department.	Each division has its own purchasing unit.
Separate companywide marketing, production, design, and engineering departments.	Each product group has experts in marketing, design, production, and engineering.
A central-city health department.	The school district and the prison have their own health units.
Plantwide inspection, maintenance, and supply departments.	Production Team Y does its own inspection, maintenance, and supply.
A university statistics department teaches statistics for the entire university.	Each department hires statisticians to teach its own students.

TABLE 8.1
Examples of Functional and Divisional Organization

SOURCE: George Strauss and Leonard R. Sayles, *Strauss and Sayles's Behavioral Strategies for Managers,* © 1980, p. 221. Reprinted by permission of Prentice-Hall, Inc., Englewood Cliffs, New Jersey.

Because the product structure is more flexible than the functional structure, it is best suited for unstable environments, when an ability to adapt rapidly to change is important. But the product structure also has disadvantages. It is difficult to coordinate across product lines and divisions. And although managers learn to become generalists, they may not acquire the depth of functional expertise that develops in the functional structure.

Furthermore, functions are not centralized at headquarters, where they can be done for all product lines or divisions. Such duplication of effort is expensive. Also, decision making is decentralized in this structure, and so top management can lose some control over decisions made in the divisions. Proper management of all the issues surrounding decentralization and delegation, as discussed earlier, is essential for this structure to be effective.[23]

Customer and Geographic Divisions   Some companies build divisions around groups of customers or around geographic distinctions. Adidas, mentioned in "Setting the Stage," is organized into *customer* divisions. Similarly, a hospital may organize its services around child, adult, psychiatric, and emergency cases. Bank loan departments commonly allocate assignments on the basis of whether customers are requesting consumer, mortgage, small-business, corporate, or agricultural loans.

In contrast to customers, divisions can be structured around geographic regions. Sears, for example, was a pioneer in creating *geographic divisions*. Geographic distinctions include district, territory, region, and country. In companies like the industrial wholesaler diagrammed in Figure 8.4, different managers are in charge of the Southwest, Pacific, Midwest, Northeast, and Southeast regions. Seagram International is one of many companies that assign managers to Europe, the Far East, and Latin America.

The primary advantage of both the product and customer/regional approaches to departmentalization is the ability to focus on customer needs and provide faster, better service. But again, duplication of activities across many customer groups and geographic areas is expensive.

The Matrix Organization

A **matrix organization** is a hybrid form of organization in which functional and divisional forms overlap. Managers and staff personnel report to two bosses—a functional manager

FIGURE 8.4
Geographic Divisions

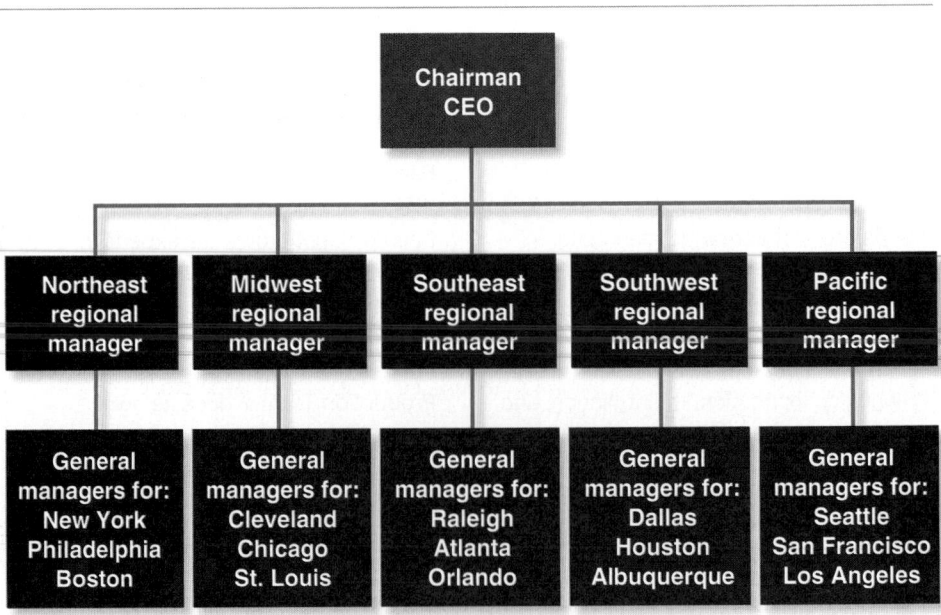

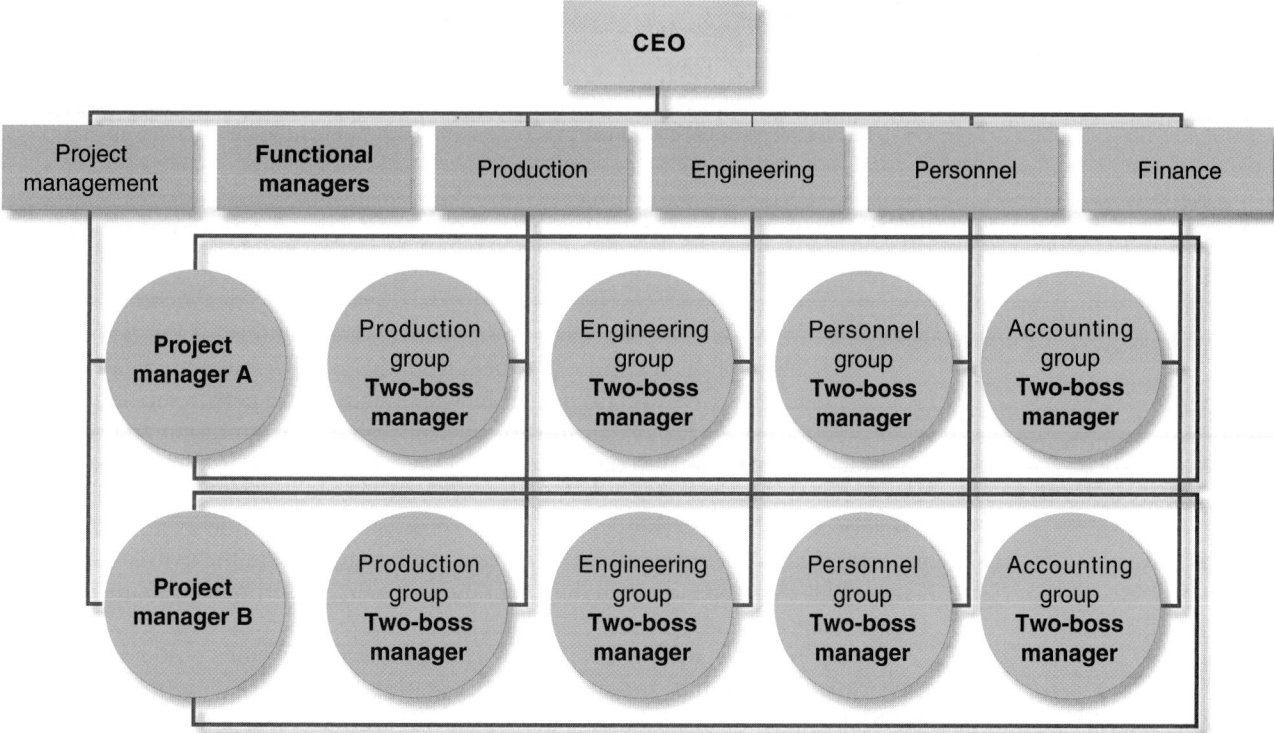

SOURCE: D. Robey and C. Sales, *Designing Organizations*, 4th ed. (1994), p. 222. Copyright © 1994 by The McGraw-Hill Companies. Reprinted by permission of The McGraw-Hill Companies.

and a divisional manager. Thus, matrix organizations have a dual rather than a single line of command. Figure 8.5 illustrates the basic matrix structure.

The matrix form originated in the aerospace industry, first with TRW in 1959 and then with NASA. Applications now occur in hospitals and health care agencies, entrepreneurial organizations, government laboratories, financial institutions, and multinational corporations.[24] Companies that have used or currently use the matrix form include IBM, Boeing, General Electric, Dow Chemical, Xerox, Shell Oil, Texas Instruments, Bechtel, Phillips Petroleum, and Dow Corning.

FIGURE 8.5
Matrix Organizational Structure

matrix organization

An organization composed of dual reporting relationships in which some managers report to two superiors—a functional manager and a divisional manager.

Pros and Cons of the Matrix Form   Like other organization structures, matrix has both strengths and weaknesses. Table 8.2 summarizes the advantages of using a matrix structure. The major potential advantage is a higher degree of flexibility and adaptability.

TABLE 8.2
Advantages of the Matrix Design

- Decision making is decentralized to a level where information is processed properly and relevant knowledge is applied.
- Extensive communications networks help process large amounts of information.
- With decisions delegated to appropriate levels, higher management levels are not overloaded with operational decisions.
- Resource utilization is efficient because key resources are shared across several important programs or products at the same time.
- Employees learn the collaborative skills needed to function in an environment characterized by frequent meetings and more informal interactions.
- Dual career ladders are elaborated as more career options become available on both sides of the organization.

SOURCE: H. Kolodny, "Managing in a Matrix," *Business Horizons*, March–April 1981, pp. 17–24.

- Confusion can arise because people do not have a single superior to whom they feel primary responsibility.
- The design encourages managers who share subordinates to jockey for power.
- The mistaken belief can arise that matrix management is the same thing as group decision making—in other words, everyone must be consulted for every decision.
- Too much democracy can lead to not enough action.

TABLE 8.3
Disadvantages of the Matrix Design

SOURCE: H. Kolodny, "Managing in a Matrix," *Business Horizons*, March–April 1981, pp. 17–24.

unity-of-command principle

A structure in which each worker reports to one boss, who in turn reports to one boss.

Table 8.3 summarizes the potential shortcomings of the matrix form. Many of the disadvantages stem from the matrix's inherent violation of the **unity-of-command principle,** which states that a person should have only one boss. Reporting to two superiors can create confusion and a difficult interpersonal situation.

Matrix Survival Skills   To a large degree, problems can be avoided if the key managers in the matrix learn the behavioral skills demanded in the matrix structure.[25] These skills vary depending on the job in the four-person diamond structure shown in Figure 8.6.

The *top executive*, who heads the matrix, must learn to balance power and emphasis between the product and functional orientations. *Product or division managers* and *functional managers* must learn to collaborate and manage their conflicts constructively. Finally, the *two-boss managers* or employees at the bottom of the diamond must learn how to be responsible to two superiors. This means prioritizing multiple demands and sometimes even reconciling conflicting orders. Some people function poorly under this ambiguous, conflictual circumstance; sometimes this signals the end of their careers with the company. Others learn to be proactive, communicate effectively with both superiors, rise above the difficulties, and manage these work relationships constructively.

The Matrix Form Today   The popularity of the matrix form waned during the end of the 1980s, when many companies had difficulty implementing it. But lately, it

FIGURE 8.6
The Matrix Diamond

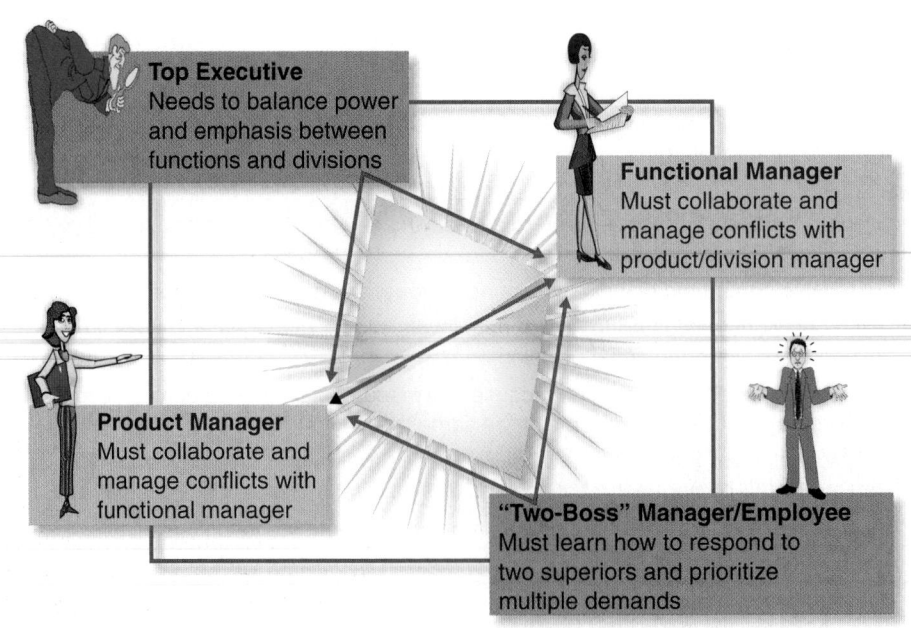

Top Executive
Needs to balance power and emphasis between functions and divisions

Functional Manager
Must collaborate and manage conflicts with product/division manager

Product Manager
Must collaborate and manage conflicts with functional manager

"Two-Boss" Manager/Employee
Must learn how to respond to two superiors and prioritize multiple demands

has come back strong. Reasons for this resurgence include pressures to consolidate costs and be faster to market, creating a need for better coordination across functions in the business units, and a need for coordination across countries for firms with global business strategies. Many of the challenges created by the matrix are particularly acute in an international context.[26]

The structure of the matrix hasn't changed, but our understanding of it has. The key to managing today's matrix is not the formal structure itself but the realization that the matrix is a *process*. Companies that have had trouble adopting the matrix form may have been correct in creating such a multidimensional structure to cope with environmental complexity, but they needed to go further than trying to construct a flexible organization simply by changing the structure. The formal structure is merely the organization's anatomy. Executives must also attend to its physiology—the relationships that allow information to flow through the organization—and its psychology—the norms, values, and attitudes that shape how people think and behave.[27] We will address these issues in the next chapter and in Part 4 of the text, which focuses on how to lead and manage people. The issues also arise again in Chapter 16 on control and culture.

Organizations with highly specialized staff, such as NASA astronaut Susan J. Helms (left), shown here with Russian cosmonaut Yury V. Usachev in the International Space Station, typically use a matrix structure.

Organizational Integration

Although we have covered both the vertical and the horizontal dimensions of organizational structure, we really have only focused on structural *differentiation*. At the outset we noted that as organizations differentiate their structures, they also need to be concerned about *integration* and *coordination*. Because of specialization and the division of labor, different groups of managers and employees develop different orientations. Depending on whether employees are in a functional department or a divisional group, are line or staff, and so on, they will think and act in ways that are geared toward their particular work units. In short, people working in separate functions, divisions, and business units literally tend to forget about one another. When this happens, it is difficult for managers to combine all their activities into an integrated whole.

There are a variety of approaches available to managers to help them make certain that interdependent units and individuals will work together to achieve a common purpose. Coordination methods include standardization, plans, and mutual adjustment.[28]

Coordination by Standardization

When organizations coordinate activities by establishing routines and standard operating procedures that remain in place over time, we say that work has been standardized. **Standardization** constrains actions and integrates various units by regulating what people do. People often know how to act—and know how to interact—because there are standard operating procedures that spell out what they should do. Employee manuals and policies, for example, may explain what actions a manager should take to discipline an employee or deal with an unhappy customer.

> **standardization**
>
> Establishing common rules and procedures that apply uniformly to everyone.

Organizations also may rely on rules and regulations to govern how people interact (we call this *formalization*). Simple policies regarding attendance, dress, and decorum, for example, may help eliminate a good deal of uncertainty at work. But an important assumption underlying both standardization and formalization is that the rules and procedures should apply to most (if not all) situations. These approaches, therefore, are most appropriate in situations that are relatively stable and unchanging. In some cases, when the work environment requires flexibility, coordination by standardization may not be very effective. Who hasn't experienced a time when rules and

Banks are among the most standardized of organizations, from operating procedures through dress codes, reinforcing to their customers and employees that the organization and their dealings with it are stable and reliable.

procedures—frequently associated with a slow bureaucracy—prevented timely action to address a problem? In these instances, we often refer to rules and regulations as "red tape."[29]

Coordination by Plan

If it is difficult to lay out the exact rules and procedures by which work should be integrated, organizations may provide more latitude by establishing goals and schedules for interdependent units. **Coordination by plan** does not require the same high degree of stability and routinization required for coordination by standardization. Interdependent units are free to modify and adapt their actions as long as they meet the deadlines and targets required for working with others.

> **coordination by plan**
>
> Interdependent units are required to meet deadlines and objectives that contribute to a common goal.

In writing this textbook, for example, we (the authors) sat down with a publication team that included the editors, the marketing staff, the production group, and support staff. Together we ironed out a schedule for developing this book that covered approximately a two-year period. That development plan included dates and "deliverables" that specified what was to be accomplished and forwarded to the others in the organization. The plan allowed for a good deal of flexibility on each subunit's part, and the overall approach allowed us to work together effectively.

Coordination by Mutual Adjustment

Ironically, the simplest and most flexible approach to coordination may just be to have interdependent parties talk to one another. **Coordination by mutual adjustment** involves feedback and discussions to jointly figure out how to approach problems and devise solutions that are agreeable to everyone. The popularity of teams today is in part due to the fact that they allow for flexible coordination; teams can operate under the principle of mutual adjustment.

> **coordination by mutual adjustment**
>
> Units interact with one another to make accommodations in order to achieve flexible coordination.

But the flexibility of mutual adjustment as a coordination device does not come without some cost. "Hashing out" every issue takes a good deal of time and may not be the most expedient approach for organizing work. Imagine how long it would take to accomplish even the most basic tasks if subunits had to talk through every situation. At the same time, mutual adjustment can be very effective when problems are novel and cannot be programmed in advance with rules, procedures, or plans. Particularly in crisis situations in which rules and procedures don't apply, mutual adjustment is likely to be the most effective approach to coordination.

Coordination and Communication

Today's environments tend to be complex, dynamic, and (therefore) uncertain. Huge amounts of information flow from the external environment to the organization and back to the environment. To cope, organizations must acquire, process, and respond to that information. Doing so has direct implications for how firms organize. To function effectively, organizations need to develop structures for processing information.

Figure 8.7 shows two general strategies that can help managers cope with high uncertainty and heavy information demands. First, management can act to reduce the need for information. Second, it can increase its capacity to handle more information.[30]

Option 1: Reducing the Need for Information   Managers can reduce the need for information in two ways: (a) creating slack resources and (b) creating self-contained tasks. *Slack resources* are simply extra resources on which organizations can rely "in a pinch" so that if they get caught off guard, they can still adjust. Inventory, for example, is a type of slack resource that provides extra stock on hand in case it is needed. With extra inventory, an organization does not have to have as much information about sales demand, lead time, and the like. Employees also can be a type of slack resource. For example, Walden Kayaks, a manufacturer of kayaks, has only eight full-time employees. However, the company has contacts with a crew of 14 part-time employees who come aboard during busy seasons. These part-timers represent a type of slack resource for Walden Paddlers in that the company does not have to perfectly forecast sales peaks, but can rely on supplementary workers to handle irregularities.[31]

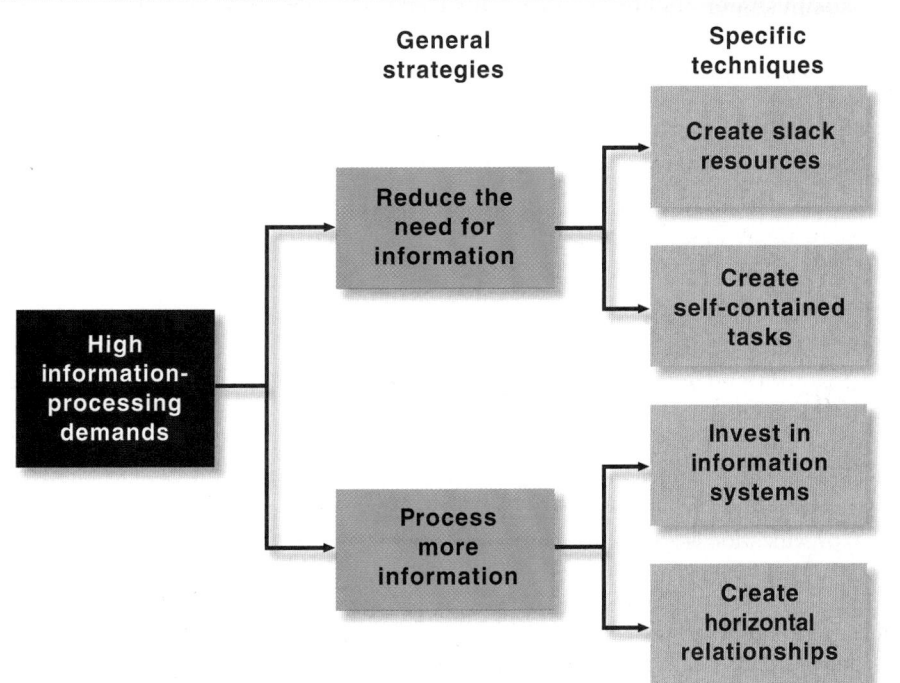

General strategies

Specific techniques

High information-processing demands

Reduce the need for information

Create slack resources

Create self-contained tasks

Process more information

Invest in information systems

Create horizontal relationships

FIGURE 8.7

Managing High Information-Processing Demands

Like slack resources, creating *self-contained tasks* allows organizations to reduce the need for some information. *Creating self-contained tasks* refers to changing from a functional organization to a product or project organization and giving each unit the resources it needs to perform its task. Information-processing problems are reduced because each unit has its own full complement of specialties instead of functional specialties that have to share their expertise among a number of different product teams. Communications then flow within each team rather than among a complex array of interdependent groups.

Option 2: Increasing Information-Processing Capability   Instead of reducing the need for information, an organization may take the approach of increasing its information-processing capability. It can *invest in information systems*, which usually means employing or expanding computer systems. And it can create horizontal relationships to foster coordination across different units. Such horizontal relationships are effective because they increase integration, which Lawrence and Lorsch suggest is necessary for managing complex environments. As uncertainty increases, the following horizontal processes may be used, ranging from the simplest to the most complex.[32]

1. *Direct contact (mutual adjustment)* among managers who share a problem. In a university, for example, a residence hall adviser might call a meeting to resolve differences between two feuding students who live in adjacent rooms.
2. *Liaison roles,* or specialized jobs to handle communications between two departments. A fraternity representative is a liaison between the fraternity and the interfraternity council, the university, or the local community.
3. *Task forces,* or groups of representatives from different departments, brought together temporarily to solve a common problem. For example, students, faculty, and administrators may be members of a task force charged with bringing distinguished speakers to campus for a current-events seminar.
4. *Teams,* or permanent interdepartmental decision-making groups. An executive council made up of department heads might meet regularly to make decisions affecting a college of engineering or liberal arts.
5. *Product, program, or project managers* who direct interdisciplinary groups with a common task to perform. In a college of business administration, a faculty administrator might head an executive education program of professors from several disciplines.
6. *Matrix organizations,* composed of dual relationships in which some managers report to two superiors. Your instructors, for example, may report to department heads in their respective disciplines and also to a director of undergraduate or graduate programs.

Several of these processes are discussed further in Chapter 14, where we examine managing teams and intergroup relations.

Looking Ahead

The organization chart, differentiation, integration, authority, delegation, coordination, and the like, convey fundamental information about an organization's structure. However, the information so far has provided only a snapshot. The real organization is more like a motion picture—it moves! More flexible and innovative—even virtual—forms of organizations are evolving.

No organization is merely a set of static work relationships. Because organizations are composed of people, they are hotbeds of social relationships. Networks of individuals cutting across departmental boundaries interact with one another. Various friendship groups or cliques band together to form *coalitions*—members of the organization who jointly support a particular issue and try to ensure that their viewpoints determine the outcome of policy decisions.[33]

In the corporate world, the word "reorganization" can be chilling. "Did something go wrong?" people ask, "Did somebody lose or win?" Corporate reorganizations may be prompted by failures, but often they are essential elements of success. Done properly, reorganization can move people into new areas where they can be more creative and effective. People often hit plateaus, get too comfortable in their jobs, and no longer come up with new approaches. A realignment presents them with fresh challenges. Great results can happen when people who have worked in product areas get closer to customers, and when people who have been working with customers join the product-development cycle. This mixing helps customer-driven companies conceive and deliver better products.

Whatever the impetus, reorganizations are a lot of work, and they carry risks. For example, if you elect to broaden the experience of an executive by moving him or her from one important job to another, you run the risk that neither job will be performed as well as it was. The new structure may not work as well as the old one. Still, a company unwilling to ever reorganize is rather calcified in terms of how it responds to the marketplace. That is a risk, too. Today any company can find itself driven out of business if it is not adaptive. Sometimes it takes several years for a company to recognize it should have changed, and by then it may be too late.

About every two years, Microsoft undertakes a major reorganization. Even though reorganizations are expected, they still create anxiety for almost everyone, including me. My concern is always whether or not we are making the right decisions, and whether key employees will be enthusiastic about their new roles. I gain confidence about a reorganization when I see that it makes clear what every group is to do, minimizes the dependencies and overlap between groups, and offers developing employees larger responsibilities.

Bill Gates, founder, chairman, and chief software engineer for Microsoft, believes corporate reorganizations are essential elements to success.

Employees worry about how their careers will be shaped by the new corporate structure. Managers become overly concerned about how their titles or the number of people reporting to them will change. At Microsoft we try to keep titles from carrying too much meaning, simply because descriptive titles encourage inflexibility among people during reorganizations. For example, many people here have the title "product manager." We give these people significant marketing responsibilities, but some report to others who have the same title. Some of our best people don't have anyone working for them. Some run large groups, but others are asked to take on a small but important project or even work alone. You must have great people in every corner.

In designing a new structure, you must strike a balance between keeping it logical and keeping executives happy and effective by giving them assignments they want and will handle well. During our most recent change, we asked: What are our goals? How can we move them into practice? What does this imply for our structure? Will our people be excited about their new roles? Over two months our thinking evolved.

How you communicate the news of a reorganization is significant. I'm a big believer in electronic mail, but describing the details of a reorganization to employees is more effective in person. We gathered thousands of employees together, put key executives on stage, and allocated one hour for questions and answers. We welcomed tough questions, and wanted employees to see first-hand how we responded. We wanted to know what employees were thinking.

In any reorganization, some people distinguish themselves by making it succeed. Other people show inflexibility and inability to rise above their views and interests. A few managers choose not to fit into the new structure or actually don't fit in. It's okay to lose some managers, but high turnover is damaging. The company must show managers a long-term career plan. Employees who don't understand how the company values their skills or where those skills can take them, are bound to be restless. And that can mean an unhappy, ineffective organization—whether reorganized or not.

SOURCE: Excerpt from Bill Gates, "Reorganization: A Necessary Art," *Executive Excellence,* December 2000, 17, no. 12, p. 3. Reprinted with permission.

Thus, the formal organization structure does not describe everything about how the company really works. Even if you know departments and authority relationships, there is still much to understand. How do things really get done? Who influences whom, and how? Which managers are the most powerful? How effective is the top leadership? Which groups are most and which are least effective? What is the nature of communication patterns throughout the organization? These issues are discussed throughout the rest of the book.

Now you are familiar with the basic organizing concepts discussed in this chapter. In the next chapter, we will discuss the current challenges of designing the modern organization with which the modern executive constantly grapples.

KEY TERMS

Accountability, p. 250

Authority, p. 247

Centralized organization, p. 255

Coordination, p. 245

Coordination by mutual adjustment, p. 264

Coordination by plan, p. 264

Corporate governance, p. 246

Decentralized organization, p. 255

Delegation, p. 250

Departmentalization, p. 257

Differentiation, p. 244

Division of labor, p. 244

Divisional organization, p. 259

Functional organization, p. 257

Hierarchy, p. 249

Integration, p. 244

Line departments, p. 256

Matrix organization, p. 261

Organization chart, p. 244

Responsibility, p. 250

Span of control, p. 249

Specialization, p. 245

Staff departments, p. 256

Standardization, p. 263

Subunits, p. 249

Unity-of-command principle, p. 262

Value chain, p. 257

SUMMARY OF LEARNING OBJECTIVES

Now that you have studied Chapter 8, you should know:

How differentiation and integration influence an organization's structure.

Differentiation means that organizations have many parts. Specialization means that various individuals and units throughout the organization perform different tasks. The assignment of tasks to different people or groups often is referred to as the division of labor. But the specialized tasks in an organization cannot all be performed independently of one another. Coordination links the various tasks in order to achieve the organization's overall mission. When there are many different specialized tasks and work units, the organization is highly differentiated; the more differentiated the organization is, the more integration or coordination is required.

How authority operates.

Authority is the legitimate right to make decisions and tell other people what to do. Authority is exercised throughout the hierarchy, as bosses have the authority to give orders to subordinates. Through the day-to-day operation of authority, the organization proceeds toward achieving its goals. Owners or stockholders have ultimate authority.

The roles of the board of directors and the chief executive officer.

Boards of directors report to stockholders. The board of directors controls or advises management, considers the firm's legal and other interests, and protects stockholders' rights. The chief executive officer reports to the board and is accountable for the organization's performance.

How span of control affects structure and managerial effectiveness.

Span of control is the number of people who report directly to a manager. Narrow spans create tall organizations, and wide spans create flat ones. No single span of control is always appropriate; the optimal span is determined by characteristics of the work, the subordinates, the manager, and the organization.

How to delegate work effectively.

Delegation is the assignment of tasks and responsibilities. Delegation has many potential advantages for the manager, the subordinate, and the organization. But to be effective, the process must be managed carefully. The manager should define the goal, select the person, solicit opinions, provide resources, schedule checkpoints, and discuss progress periodically.

The difference between centralized and decentralized organizations.

In centralized organizations, most important decisions are made by top managers. In decentralized organizations, many decisions are delegated to lower levels.

How to allocate jobs to work units.

Jobs can be departmentalized on the basis of function, product, customers, or geography. Most organizations use several different types of departmentalization.

How to manage the unique challenges of the matrix organization.

The matrix is a complex structure with a dual authority structure. A well-managed matrix enables organizations to adapt to change. But it can also create confusion and interpersonal diffi-

culties. People in all positions in the matrix—top executives, product and function managers, and two-boss managers—must acquire unique survival skills.

The nature of important integrating mechanisms.

Managers can coordinate interdependent units through standardization, plans, and mutual adjustment. Standardization occurs when routines and standard operating procedures are put in place. They typically are accompanied by formalized rules. Coordination by plan is more flexible and allows more freedom in how tasks are carried out but keeps interdependent units focused on schedules and joint goals. Mutual adjustment involves feedback and discussions among related parties to accommodate each other's needs. It is at once the most flexible and simple to administer, but it is time-consuming.

DISCUSSION QUESTIONS

1. Using the concepts in the chapter, discuss the advantages and disadvantages of the organization structure approach described in "Setting the Stage."

2. What are some advantages and disadvantages of being in the CEO position?

3. Would you like to sit on a board of directors? Why or why not? If you did serve on a board, what kind of organization would you prefer? As a board member, in what kinds of activities do you think you would most actively engage?

4. Interview a member of a board of directors and discuss that member's perspectives on his or her role.

5. Pick a job you have held and describe it in terms of span of control, delegation, responsibility, authority, and accountability.

6. Why do you think managers have difficulty delegating? What can be done to overcome these difficulties?

7. Consider an organization in which you have worked, draw its organization chart, and describe it by using terms in this chapter. How did you like working there, and why?

8. Would you rather work in a functional or divisional organization? Why?

9. If you learned that a company had a matrix structure, would you be more or less interested in working there? Explain your answer. How would you prepare yourself to work effectively in a matrix?

10. Brainstorm a list of methods for integrating interdependent work units. Discuss the activities that need to be undertaken and the pros and cons of each approach.

Lucent: Clean Break, Clean Slate?

The company that could seemingly do no wrong in the first three years after it was spun off from AT&T in 1996 seriously lost its way in 2000. Worst of all, it has been completely bested by archrival Nortel Networks Corp. in the key market for optical-fiber telephone switches (see Chapter 2, "At the Speed of Light").

The contrast with Nortel is what stings Lucent execs the most. It was only a few years ago that Nortel was the industry dog. But today, Nortel has 45 percent of the exploding optical-transmission-switch market. That compares with just 15 percent for Lucent, which decided in 1996 to develop a slower switch precisely because its customers weren't asking for anything faster. Lucent now rues the decision to settle for less transmission speed. And Chairman Henry Schacht is quick to acknowledge that

he is as much at fault as former CEO Richard McGinn. Schacht says he is planning one-on-one meetings with Lucent's customers and is reviewing all the processes now in place with an eye to streamlining Lucent's cumbersome structure.

Under McGinn, Lucent embarked on an organizational overhaul in September 2000. To head key divisions, it has appointed some aggressive new outsiders who are not mired in the company's bureaucratic mindset. One of those, CFO Deborah C. Hopkins, is putting in place a companywide standard for evaluating a product's profitability, replacing the piecemeal, business-by-business standard used before. The company is also chopping away at management layers, more closely tying compensation to performance, and trying to better integrate its vaunted Bell Labs with product-development teams. But the world's largest telecom-equipment maker actually has a more cosmic task: It must remake itself into a company that can be quick to respond to needs, quick to deliver new technology, and far less bureaucratic. And it has to do all of this while suffering from a 20 percent turnover rate that is siphoning off top talent.

Granted, such an overhaul has been prescribed for just about every lumbering old economy behemoth. Lucent is determined to pull itself apace with that market. And it may have a secret weapon: In September, Lucent named Jeong Kim to head its optical-networks business. Clearly different from the Lucent lifers around him, Kim has reorganized the group into 17 small divisions based on product lines, with managers closely matched to customers and compensation tied to performance. His goal: to improve time to delivery by 30 percent. "I have a 100-day plan," he says.

Kim's entrepreneurial spirit is sorely needed at Lucent, and he is convinced he already has had a positive effect on morale. He recently visited a Lucent plant in North Andover, Massachusetts, and found general managers there very involved in suggesting ways the operation could be improved. "They were really taking ownership of their operation. And morale was running really high. I was very encouraged."

Lucent also must start regaining the trust of its employees if it wants to stem the flood of talent that started rushing out the door as soon as executives' pre-IPO options vested on October 1, 1999. And it hasn't done any better at hanging on to the employees who came on board with its many acquisitions. Adopted employees who have headed for the doors regularly complain that they found themselves stifled by Lucent's many-layered management. "There are a lot of top-level people trying to get out of Lucent right now," one Silicon Valley headhunter says.

Lucent's executives are making all the right turnaround noises. William T. O'Shea, vice president for corporate strategy and business development, is in charge of a massive effort that kicked off in summer 2000 to streamline Lucent's businesses. The goal: to encourage entrepreneurship. "We are putting new people in charge and organizing groups to focus their energy in small teams," he says, rather than structuring the company in large, often uncommunicative divisions. And the company is including Bell Lab researchers in these teams, to make sure that their inventions are properly promoted. "We are bringing a much broader collection of people to the table internally to make strategic decisions," he says.

New chief executive Patricia Russo also is pushing hard to get Lucent back on track. She was named CEO in November 2001 after an eight-month stint as chief operating officer at Eastman Kodak Co. And she has turnaround experience: Before taking her current post, Russo was best known at Lucent for improving the fortunes of the unit that sold communications gear to corporations, now an independent company known as Avaya Inc. "As someone who was with the company and left and came back, I can tell you this is a very different place. Terrific progress has been made," she says.

There's no debate there. Staff cuts under former CEO Henry Schacht have eliminated $2 billion in operating expenses. Capital expenses were slashed from $1.9 billion in fiscal 2000 to $1.4 billion in 2001 and were expected to hit a maximum of $750 million in 2002. The company reduced its working capital by $3 billion, beating its target of $2 billion. Schacht also launched new products, which led to the recapture of lost optical share.

Russo says the turnaround will continue even if the markets for telecom equipment don't rebound much. "There's a lot more we can do that will have huge leverage on the bottom line," she says. Russo, D'Amelio, and Robert C. Holder, executive vice president for product organizations, are meeting with Lucent's other managers to size up prospects for the business through 2003. Based on that review, scheduled to conclude within weeks, they are expected to cut up to 5,000 more jobs, lower capital spending and operating expenses, and possibly sell more assets. They believe those steps will boost margins to about 35 percent.

QUESTIONS

1. How would you characterize the changes in Lucent's vertical and horizontal structures?

2. What are the strategic reasons behind these changes in strategy?

3. What other management issues do you see in this case? How do they combine with issues of structure?

SOURCE: Condensed from Catherine Arnst, Roger O. Crockett, Andy Reinhardt, and John Shinal, "Lucent: Clean Break, Clean Slate?" *Business Week Online*, October 26, 2000; Steve Rosenbush, "Lucent: One Step Forward, Two Steps Back," *Business Week*, April 8, 2002.

8.1   The Business School Organization Chart

OBJECTIVES

1. To clarify the factors that determine organization structure.

2. To provide insight into the workings of an organization.

3. To examine the working relationships within an organization.

INSTRUCTIONS

1. Draw an organization chart for your school of business. Be sure to identify all the staff and line positions in the school.

Specify the chain of command and the levels of administration. Note the different spans of control. Are there any advisory groups, task forces, or committees to consider?

2. Review the chapter material on organization structure to help identify both strong and weak points in your school's organization. Now draw another organization chart for the school, incorporating any changes you believe would improve the quality of the school. Support the second chart with a list of recommended changes and reasons for their inclusion.

DISCUSSION QUESTIONS

1. Is your business school well organized? Why or why not?

2. Is your school's organization organic or mechanistic? In what ways?

3. In what ways is the school's structure designed to suit the needs of students, faculty, staff, the administration, and the business community?

8.2 Mechanistic and Organic Structures

OBJECTIVES

1. To think about your own preferences when it comes to working in a particular organizational structure.

2. To examine aspects of organizations by using as an example this class you are a member of.

INSTRUCTIONS

1. Complete the Mechanistic and Organic Worksheet below.

2. Meet in groups of four to six persons. Share your data from the worksheet. Discuss the reasons for your responses, and analyze the factors that probably encouraged your instructor to choose the type of structure that now exists.

Mechanistic and Organic Worksheet

1. Indicate your general preference for working in one of these two organizational structures by circling the appropriate response:

Mechanistic	1	2	3	4	5	6	7	8	9	10	**Organic**

2. Indicate your perception of the form of organization that is used in this class by circling the appropriate response for each item:

A. **Task-role definition Rigid**	1	2	3	4	5	6	7	8	9	10	**Flexible**
B. **Communication Vertical**	1	2	3	4	5	6	7	8	9	10	**Multidirectional**
C. **Decision making Centralized**	1	2	3	4	5	6	7	8	9	10	**Decentralized**
D. **Sensitivity to the environment Closed**	1	2	3	4	5	6	7	8	9	10	**Open**

SOURCE: Keith Davis and John W. Newstrom, *Human Behavior at Work,* 9th ed., p. 358. Copyright © 1993 by The McGraw-Hill Companies. Reprinted by permission of The McGraw-Hill Companies.

CHAPTER 9

The Responsive Organization

Bureaucracy defends the status quo long past the time when the quo has lost its status.

—Laurence J. Peter

CHAPTER OUTLINE

Today's Imperatives
Organizing for Optimal Size
   The Case for Big
   The Case for Small
   Being Big and Small
Organizing for Environmental Response
   Organizing for Customer Responsiveness
Organizing for Technological Response
   Types of Technology Configurations
   Organizing for Flexible Manufacturing
   Organizing for Speed: Time-Based Competition
Organizing for Strategic Response
   Organizing around Core Competencies
   The Network Organization
   Strategic Alliances
   The Learning Organization
   The High-Involvement Organization
Final Thoughts about Responsive Organizations

LEARNING OBJECTIVES

After studying Chapter 9, you will know:

1. The market imperatives a firm must meet to survive.

2. The potential advantages of creating an organic form of organization.

3. How a firm can "be" both small and big.

4. How to manage information-processing demands.

5. How firms organize to meet customer requirements.

6. How firms organize around different types of technology.

7. The new types of dynamic organizational concepts and forms that are being used for strategic responsiveness.

KEEPING FLEXTRONICS FLEXIBLE

Flextronics Corp. may not be a household name, but it turns heads in telecommunications circles. Flextronics is an electronic manufacturing services (EMS) business. EMS companies relieve their corporate customers of the gritty business of making things so that the customers can focus on product development instead. For example, Hewlett-Packard, the world's leading brand of personal printers, doesn't make a single printer. Microsoft's Xbox game machines aren't manufactured by Microsoft; they're manufactured by Flextronics, as are Palm Pilots and Direct TV boxes. If you can "dream it," Flextronics can not only make it but design it, too.

Under the leadership of CEO Michael Marks, Flextronics, which is now headquartered in Singapore, grew monstrously in the last decade. Revenues rocketed from $193 million in 1993 to over $13 billion in 2002. The company gobbled up competitor after competitor and purchased the manufacturing facilities of cash-strapped tech companies at an astonishing pace.

If you ask Marks about his company's corporate structure and strategy, he probably will refer you to the Flextronics *International Corporate Policy Manual*, which has 80 pages—all of them blank. He sometimes lets subordinates purchase multi-million-dollar companies without showing him the paperwork. He disdains staff meetings, and he refuses to draw up an organization chart delineating managers' responsibilities over the firm's 70,000 employees.

Marks believes that global contract manufacturing is all about speed and flexibility. The time it takes to get a prototype into mass production and onto retail shelves can determine whether a digital gadget is a wild success or a miserable failure. "It's not the big who eat the small. It's the fast who eat the slow," says Marks.

Flextronics was the first in its industry to go global. It now has production faculties in over 28 countries. Labor-intensive manufacturing is conducted in countries with lower labor costs, while jobs requiring greater expertise, such as design and testing, are handled in countries where the skill base is deeper. The firm's suppliers are colocated alongside manufacturing facilities, giving Flextronics maximum flexibility to meet demand.

The basketball hoop hanging in Marks's modest, if somewhat disheveled, office seems to sum up his personal and business style. He is an ardent player of the game. Moreover, he is convinced that Flextronics can retain the agility of a start-up while dominating the big leagues.

Sources: Frank Bigney, Jr., "You Name It, We'll Make It," *Time*, August 25, 2001, pp. 6–9; Pete Engardio, "Flextronics: Few Rules, Fast Response," *Business Week*, October 23, 2000, p. 148F.

Flextronics makes various electronic and computer items for other companies who then put their brand name on the item. The company is not a household name, but produces products for companies that are household names. Pictured here is Michael Marks, Chairman and CEO.

As you can guess from reading Setting the Stage, successful companies may be "breaking the rules" about how organizations should be run. Or at least they are *changing* the rules—opening up their game, to use an analogy from sports.

Chapter 8 described the formal structure of organizations. The ideas we discussed there are traditional and basic and are fundamental to understanding organizations. But a firm's formal structure is only part of the story. There are other subtle aspects of organizing that really distinguish how firms operate for maximum effectiveness. Organizations are not static structures but complex systems in which many people do many different things at the same time. The overall behavior of organizations does not just pop out of a chart but emerges out of other processes, systems, and relationships among interrelated parties. In today's modern firm, new approaches to organizing are emerging. The emphasis in this chapter is not on the formal organization but on organizing for *action*.

Today's Imperatives

The formal structure is put in place to *control* people, decisions, and actions. But in today's fast-changing business environment, *responsiveness*—quickness, agility, the ability to adapt to changing demands—is more vital than ever to a firm's survival.[1]

Progressive companies place a premium on being able to act, and act fast. They want to act in accordance with customer needs and other outside pressures. They want to take actions to correct past mistakes and also to prepare for an uncertain future. They want to be able to respond to threats and opportunities. To do these things, they try to operate organically, manage size effectively, process huge amounts of information, and adopt new forms of organization.

Many years after Max Weber wrote about the concept of bureaucracy, two British management scholars (Burns and Stalker) described what they called the **mechanistic organization**.[2] The common mechanistic structure they described was similar to Weber's bureaucracy, but they went on to suggest that in the modern corporation, the

mechanistic organization

A form of organization that seeks to maximize internal efficiency.

organic structure

An organizational form that emphasizes flexibility.

mechanistic structure is not the only option. The **organic structure** stands in stark contrast to the mechanistic organization. It is much less rigid and, in fact, emphasizes flexibility. The organic structure can be described as follows:

1. Jobholders have broader responsibilities that change as the need arises.
2. Communication occurs through advice and information rather than through orders and instructions.
3. Decision making and influence are more decentralized and informal.
4. Expertise is highly valued.
5. Jobholders rely more heavily on judgment than on rules.
6. Obedience to authority is less important than commitment to the organization's goals.
7. Employees depend more on one another and relate more informally and personally.

Figure 9.1 contrasts the formal structure of an organization—epitomized by the organization chart—to the informal structure, which is much more organic. Astute managers are keenly aware of the network of interactions among the organization's members, and structure around this network to increase agility. People in organic organizations work more as teammates than as subordinates who take orders from the boss, thus breaking away from the traditional bureaucratic form.[3]

We rely on the ideas underlying the organic structure and networks as a foundation for discussing the newer forms of organization described in this chapter. The more organic a firm is, the more responsive it will be to changing competitive demands and market realities. For the remainder of this chapter, we summarize some of the most important issues that require organizations to adopt either organic or mechanistic structures. These include organizing for optimal size, organizing for environmental response, organizing for technological response, and organizing for strategic response.

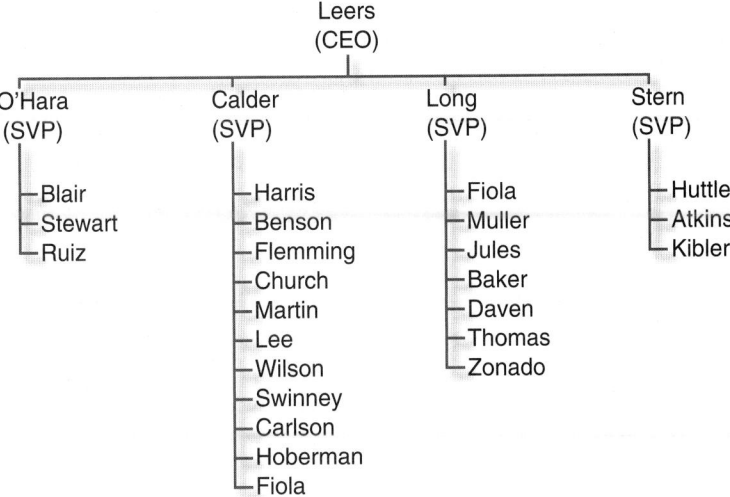

FIGURE 9.1(*a*)
Organization Chart Shows
Who's on Top

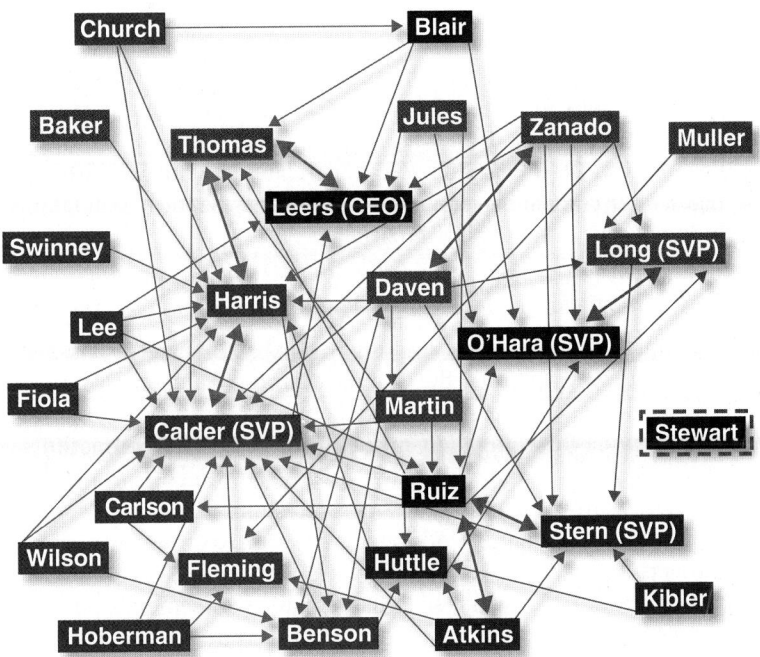

FIGURE 9.1(*b*)
Advice Network Reveals
Knowledge Flow

Organizing for Optimal Size

One of the most important characteristics of an organization is its size. Large organizations are typically less organic and more bureaucratic. For example, at Hewlett-Packard, before the reduction of its stifling bureaucracy, it took over 90 people on nine committees more than seven months to decide what to name some new software.[4]

In large organizations, jobs become more specialized. More distinct groups of specialists get created because large organizations can add a new specialty at lower proportional expense. The complexity these numerous specialties create makes the

organization harder to control. Therefore, in the past management added more levels to keep spans of control from becoming too large. To cope with complexity, large companies tend to become more bureaucratic. Rules, procedures, and paperwork are introduced.

Thus, with size comes greater complexity, and complexity brings a need for increased control. In response, organizations adopt bureaucratic strategies of control. The conventional wisdom is that bureaucratization increases efficiency but decreases a company's ability to innovate. So is large size a good thing or a bad thing? Let's see.

The Case for Big

Bigger was better after World War II, when foreign competition was limited and growth seemed limitless. To meet high demand for its products, U.S. industry embraced high-volume, low-cost manufacturing methods. IBM, General Motors (GM), and Sears all grew into behemoths during those decades.

Alfred Chandler, a pioneer in strategic management, noted that big companies were the engine of economic growth throughout the 20th century.[5] Size creates *scale economies*, that is, lower costs per unit of production. And size can offer specific advantages such as lower operating costs, greater purchasing power, and easier access to capital. For example, Microsoft spends nearly $4 billion each year on research and development, far more than its rivals can afford.[6] Similarly, Wal-Mart, now the largest company in America, has the purchasing power to buy merchandise in larger volumes and sell it at lower prices than its competitors can. Size also creates **economies of scope;** materials and processes employed in one product can be used to make other, related products. With such advantages, huge companies with lots of money may be the best at taking on large foreign rivals in huge global markets.

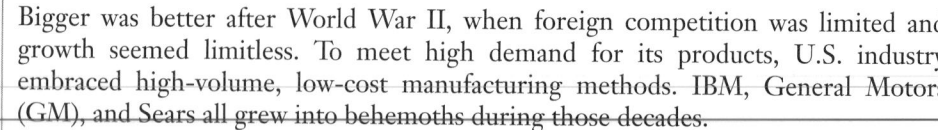

> **economies of scope**
>
> **Economies in which materials and processes employed in one product can be used to make other, related products.**

The Case for Small

But a huge, complex organization can find it hard to manage relationships with customers and among its own units. Bureaucracy can run rampant. Too much success can breed complacency, and the resulting inertia hinders change. Experts suggest that this is a surefire formula for being "left in the dust" by hungry competitors. As consumers demand a more diverse array of high-quality, customized products supported by excellent service, giant companies have begun to stumble. There is some evidence, for example, that as firms get larger and their market share grows, customers begin to view their products as having lower quality. Larger companies are more difficult to coordinate and control. Thus, while size may enhance efficiency by spreading fixed costs out over more units, it also may create administrative difficulties that inhibit efficient performance. A new term has entered the business vocabulary: *diseconomies of scale*, or the costs of being too big. "Small is beautiful" has become a favorite phrase of entrepreneurial business managers.[7]

Smaller companies can move fast, can provide quality goods and services to targeted market niches, and can inspire greater involvement from their people. Nimble, small firms frequently outmaneuver big bureaucracies. They introduce new and better products, and they steal market share. The premium now is on flexibility and responsiveness—the unique potential strengths of the small firm. For example, in 2000 a group of engineers at Lucent Technologies uncovered a superior technology that delivered wireless data faster and cheaper. But Lucent, fearing that it would cannibalize its own product line, wedded itself to the existing technology. In response, the engineers started their own small, successful competing firm, Flarion Technologies. "The fact that we could come up with our best work and still not have it go anywhere was a clear sign that big company structure was not right for us," says Rajiv Laroia, one of the founding engineers.[8]

Being Big and Small

Small *is* beautiful for unleashing energy and speed. But in buying and selling, size offers market power. The challenge, then, is to be both big and small to capitalize on the advantages of each.

The investment bank Edward D. Jones is known as the Wal-Mart of Wall Street. Its vast network of 7,000 independent brokers extends into rural and suburban communities all over the United States. The company, which refused to jump on the dot-com bandwagon, provides sound, personalized investing advice to "mom and pop" investors and delivers superior returns. In essence, Edward D. Jones is trying to combine the best of both worlds—personalized local service and a national reach.[9]

From a different angle, companies such as Southwest Airlines, AES (mentioned in Chapter 8), Starbucks, and Motorola are large companies that work hard to act small. Each is considered among the best-managed companies in the world. To avoid problems of growth and size, they decentralize decision making and organize around small, adaptive, team-based work units.

Agilent Technologies CEO, Ned Barnholt, describes downsizing as a balancing act. Agilent is trying—through downsizing—to make good decisions for the company's future.

Downsizing   As large companies attempt to regain the responsiveness of small, they often face the dilemma of downsizing. **Downsizing** (or **rightsizing**) is the planned elimination of positions or jobs. Common approaches to downsizing include eliminating functions, hierarchical levels, or units.[10] It is hard to pick up a newspaper without seeing announcements of another company downsizing; likewise, it is hard to name a major corporation that has not downsized in recent years. The list includes IBM, Citicorp, AT&T, Kodak, Goodyear, Exxon, Xerox, TRW, and GM.

Historically, layoffs tended to affect manufacturing firms, and operative-level workers in particular. But given that the most recent cycle of downsizing has focused on delayering and eliminating bureaucratic structures, "white-collar" middle managers have been those chiefly affected.

What can be done to manage downsizing effectively, to help make it a more effective "rightsizing"? First of all, firms should avoid excessive (cyclical) hiring to help reduce the need to engage in major or multiple downsizings. But beyond that, firms must avoid common mistakes such as making slow, small, frequent layoffs; implementing voluntary early retirement programs that entice the best people to leave; and laying off so many people that the company's work can no longer be performed. Instead, firms can engage in a number of positive practices to ease the pain of downsizing:

- Choose positions to be eliminated by engaging in careful analysis and strategic thinking.
- Train people to cope with the new situation.
- Identify and protect talented people.
- Give special attention and help to those who have lost their jobs.
- Communicate constantly with people about the process.
- Emphasize a positive future and people's new roles in attaining it.[11]

Interestingly, the people who lose their jobs because of downsizing are not the only ones deeply affected. Those who survive the process—who keep their jobs—tend to exhibit what has become known as **survivor's syndrome**.[12] They struggle with heavier workloads, wonder who will be next to go, try to figure out how to survive, lose commitment to the company and faith in their bosses, and become narrow-minded, self-absorbed, and risk-averse. As a consequence, morale and productivity usually drop.

You will learn more about some of these ideas in later chapters on human resources management, leadership, motivation, communication, and managing change.

downsizing

The planned elimination of positions or jobs.

rightsizing

A successful effort to achieve an appropriate size at which the company performs most effectively.

survivor's syndrome

Loss of productivity and morale in employees who remain after a downsizing.

The following story shows how smaller competitors—even in an industry as complex as banking—can offer superior service, excellent performance, and financial strength for their customers.

FROM THE PAGES OF

For Small Banks, It's a Wonderful Life

BusinessWeek

Michael Berk, chief executive of H&S Yacht Sales in San Diego, has had more bankers than southern California has sunny days. Each time his bank merged with another, he says, service got worse. "The big joke was if we wanted to find out something about our accounts, it was, 'Call the 800 number in Fargo,'" says Berk, whose company sells $60 million in luxury boats a year. He moved all his business to the Beverly Hills, California–based City National Bank, which has just $10 billion in assets. In four days, Berk got the line of credit he had waited three months for at his old bank. City National reps even call Berk regularly to check in on him.

Small banks are back on the map. A few years ago they seemed headed for extinction as retail banks consolidated into a few national players and then expanded into everything from insurance to investment banking. Hell-bent on cutting costs, the megabanks closed tens of thousands of branches, raised account minimums, and slapped on ATM fees. It was a big miscalculation. "Retail has been an undervalued business," says Gordon J. Goetzmann, managing vice president at the First Manhattan Consulting Group, which specializes in financial services. "Big banks just don't get it."

Scorned customers have become a ripe market for community banks. Small banks specialize in the royal treatment. Some serve Starbucks coffee. Others offer free baby-sitting and investment advice. They all cater to markets that big banks have given short shrift, including small businesses, minority groups, and rural areas. "The big guys abandoned small towns where their roots don't run deep, and we've taken the market," says J. W. Davis, president of the 15-branch MountainBank Financial Corp. of Henderson, North Carolina.

The battle isn't just for fringe markets. Vernon W. Hill, chairman of Commerce Bancorp Inc. in Cherry Hill, New Jersey, is moving into New York, home turf of the nation's largest players: Citigroup (C) and J. P. Morgan Chase (JPM). Thousands flocked to the opening of Commerce's Midtown Manhattan branch last fall for free sandwiches, shoe shines, and caricatures. Lured by free checking, no minimum balances, extended hours, and even free toasters, customers deposited $1 million in the first week.

"Small banks can make money in almost any environment," says John Lyons, president and bank stock portfolio manager for New York's Keefe Managers Inc. Small banks have been mostly immune to the static economy. Unlike those of the big banks, their customers tend to be local businesses with less exposure to broad economic cycles. Besides, falling interest rates have cut the small banks' cost of funds, boosted their already higher margins, and fueled record mortgage refinancings. Even when interest rates rise, service fees for existing mortgages will continue to feed profits.

Some of the best small banks are thriving because many of their executives once worked at megabanks. They add tight financial management to the small banks' warm and fuzzy service. Joseph M. Grant, chairman of upstart Texas Capital Bank, was chief financial officer at Electronic Data Systems and CEO of Texas American Bancshares, the sixth largest bank holding company in Texas during his tenure in the late 1980s. Others are importing different kinds of expertise. For example, Keefe helped Bay View Capital Corp. in San Mateo, California, hire Robert B. Goldstein, a veteran of small-bank turnarounds, as CEO in 2001. Goldstein has slashed Bay View's bad loans to $83 million from $800 million.

The attention to bread-and-butter customers is the same formula that, along with shrewd acquisitions, propelled Seattle's tiny Washington Mutual Inc. to become a $275 billion national bank in a decade. Khaki-clad tellers still roam the floor asking customers what they need. The answer, obviously, has been more TLC and less ATM.

SOURCE: Mara Der Hovanesian and Heather Timmons, "For Small Banks, It's a Wonderful Life," *BusinessWeek Online*, May 6, 2002, www.businessweek.com.

Organizing for Environmental Response

Apart from organizing for optimal size, organizations have to adapt to external environments. In a sense, this is the crux of creating a responsive organization. In Chapter 2, we introduced various approaches organizations might take to respond to the environment. They included *adapting* to the environment, *influencing* the environment, and *selecting* a new environment. In this section, we want to delve more deeply into how organizations organize for environmental response.

Organizing for Customer Responsiveness

Although it is valuable to discuss environmental uncertainty in general, at this point we hope to move to a more concrete set of circumstances. From Chapter 2 recall that the environment is composed of many different parts (government, suppliers, competitors, and the like). Perhaps no other aspect of the environment has had a more profound impact on organizing in recent years than a focus on *customers*. Dr. Kenichi Ohmae points out that any business unit must take into account three key players: the *company* itself, the *competition*, and the *customer*. These components form what Ohmae refers to as the *strategic triangle*, as shown in Figure 9.2. Managers need to balance the strategic triangle, and successful organizations use their strengths to create value by meeting customer requirements better than competitors do.

Customer Relationship Management (CRM)   **Customer relationship management** is a multifaceted process, typically mediated by a set of information technologies, that focuses on creating two-way exchanges with customers so that firms have an intimate knowledge of their needs, wants, and buying patterns. In this way, CRM helps companies understand, as well as anticipate, the needs of current and potential customers. And in that way, it is part of a business strategy for managing customers to maximize their long-term value to an enterprise.[13]

> **customer relationship management**
>
> A multifaceted process focusing on creating two-way exchanges with customers to foster intimate knowledge of their needs, wants, and buying patterns.

As discussed throughout this book, customers want quality goods and service, low cost, innovative products, and speed. Traditional thinking considered these basic customer wants as a set of potential trade-offs. For instance, customers wanted high quality or low costs passed along in the form of low prices. But world-class companies today know that the "trade-off" mentality no longer applies. Customers want it *all*, and they are learning that somewhere an organization exists that will provide it all.

But if all companies seek to satisfy customers, how can a company realize a competitive advantage? World-class companies have learned that almost any advantage is temporary, for competitors will strive to catch up. Simply stated—though obviously

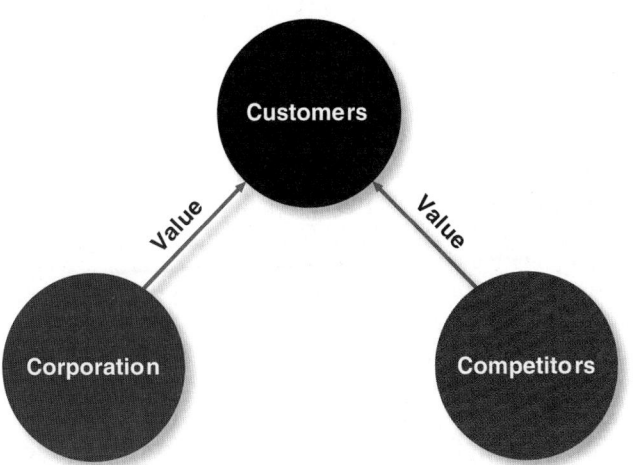

FIGURE 9.2
The Strategic Triangle

not simply done—a company attains and retains competitive advantage by continuing to improve. This concept—*kaizen*, or continuous improvement—is an integral part of Japanese operations strategy. Motorola, a winner of the Malcolm Baldrige National Quality Award, operates with the philosophy that "the company that is satisfied with its progress will soon find that its customers are not."

As organizations focus on responding to customer needs, they soon find that traditional meaning of a customer expands to include "internal customers." The word *customer* now refers to the *next process*, or *wherever the work goes next*.[14] This highlights the idea of interdependence among related functions and means that all functions of the organization—not just marketing people—have to be concerned with customer satisfaction. All recipients of a person's work, whether co-worker, boss, subordinate, or external party, come to be viewed as the customer.

Total quality management (TQM)   **Total quality management** is a way of managing in which everyone is committed to continuous improvement of his or her part of the operation. In business, success depends on having quality products. As described in Chapter 1 and throughout the book, TQM is a comprehensive approach to improving product quality and thereby customer satisfaction. It is characterized by a strong orientation toward customers (external and internal) and has become an umbrella theme for organizing work. TQM reorients managers toward involving people across departments in improving all aspects of the business. Continuous improvement requires integrative mechanisms that facilitate group problem solving, information sharing, and cooperation across business functions. As a consequence, the walls that separate stages and functions of work tend to come down, and the organization operates more in a team-oriented manner.[15]

total quality management

An integrative approach to management that supports the attainment of customer satisfaction through a wide variety of tools and techniques that result in high-quality goods and services.

W. Edwards Deming was one of the founders of the quality management movement. His "14 points" of quality emphasized a holistic approach to management that demands intimate understanding of the process—the delicate interaction of materials, machines, and people that determines productivity, quality, and competitive advantage:

1. Create constancy of purpose—strive for long-term improvement rather than short-term profit.
2. Adopt the new philosophy—don't tolerate delays and mistakes.
3. Cease dependence on mass inspection—build quality into the process on the front end.
4. End the practice of awarding business on price tag alone—build long-term relationships.
5. Improve constantly and forever the system of production and service—at each stage.
6. Institute training and retraining—continual updating of methods and thinking.
7. Institute leadership—provide the resources needed for effectiveness.
8. Drive out fear—people must believe it is safe to report problems or ask for help.
9. Break down barriers among departments—promote teamwork.
10. Eliminate slogans, exhortations, and arbitrary targets—supply methods, not buzzwords.
11. Eliminate numerical quotas—they are contrary to the idea of continuous improvement.
12. Remove barriers to pride in workmanship—allow autonomy and spontaneity.
13. Institute a vigorous program of education and retraining—people are assets, not commodities.
14. Take action to accomplish the transformation—provide a structure that enables quality.

The Baldrige Criteria and TQM in the United States
As you know, the Baldrige Award is the prestigious award given to U.S. companies that achieve quality excellence. The award is granted on the basis of the seven following criteria. Included are brief descriptions of the strengths of companies that have applied for the Baldrige Award and some guidelines for further improvement:

Clarke American Checks won the 2001 Malcolm Baldrige award for quality.

1. *Leadership.* Senior managers in the best companies are committed to quality, have communicated quality values throughout their companies, and have instilled a strong customer orientation. They need to make certain that they balance financial performance with operational issues as well.
2. *Information and analysis.* The very best TQM companies have excellent information systems. Companies need to make certain that information is well organized to support quality management.
3. *Strategic quality planning.* The best TQM companies have written quality plans and quality goals (often stretch goals). In addition, companies need to make certain that they communicate those plans to people so that everyone knows how his or her activities and objectives relate to the overall plans.
4. *Human resource development and management.* Teams focus on quality improvement projects, all employees receive basic quality training, and plenty of resources are devoted to safety. Beyond this, companies have to make certain that teams are managed effectively and that management truly empowers these teams to make decisions. The performance evaluation system should be aligned with the quality management system.
5. *Management of process quality.* Most companies use statistical process control, have quality programs in conjunction with their suppliers, have greatly improved the development of new goods and services, and have developed measures of the service production process. Areas for improvement include limited new-product development activity (particularly services), slow and inadequate feedback from customers, and the lack of quality systems audits.
6. *Quality and operational results.* The best Baldrige companies demonstrate the quality of their products and their sustained year-to-year improvement with objective data.
7. *Customer focus and satisfaction.* The better Baldrige companies use surveys and focus groups to assess customer satisfaction, train their customer service representatives well, establish service standards, give more authority to service representatives to solve customer problems, and work hard to provide easy access and quick response times to customers. In addition, companies have to understand customer needs and expectations clearly. Customer data need to be used in new-product development, and companies need to pay attention to lost customers, new customers, and competitors' customers.[16]

As you can see, total quality requires a thorough, extensive, integrated approach to organizing. Looking carefully at the strengths and improvement needs of good U.S. companies on the Baldrige criteria, you can see that quality comes from the issues and practices discussed throughout this course.

ISO 9000 The influence of TQM on the organizing process has become even more acute with the emergence of ISO 9000. **ISO 9000** is a series of quality standards developed by a committee working under the International Organization for Standardization. The purpose of the standards is to improve total quality in all businesses for the benefit of producers and

ISO 9000

A series of quality standards developed by a committee working under the International Organization for Standardization to improve total quality in all businesses for the benefit of both producers and consumers.

consumers alike. ISO 9000 originally was designed for manufacturing; however, most of the standards also can be applied readily to services operations.

U.S. companies first became interested in ISO 9000 because overseas customers, particularly the European Community (EC), embraced it. Companies that comply with the quality guidelines of ISO 9000 can apply for official certification; some countries and companies demand certification as an acknowledgment of compliance before they will do business. Now, some U.S. customers as well are making the same demand.[17]

Reengineering   Extending from TQM and a focus on organizing around customer needs, organizations also have embraced the notion of reengineering (introduced in Chapter 1). The principal idea of reengineering is to revolutionize key organizational systems and processes to answer the question: "If you were the customer, how would you like us to operate?" The answer to this question forms a vision for how the organization should run, and then decisions are made and actions are taken to make the organization operate like the vision. Processes such as product development, order fulfillment, customer service, inventory management, billing, and production are redesigned from scratch just as if the organization were brand new and just starting out.

For example: Procter & Gamble learned that the average family buying its products rather than private-label or low-price brands pays an extra $725 per year. That figure, P&G realized, was far too high, and a signal that the company's high prices could drive the company to extinction. Other data also signaled the need for P&G to change. Market shares of famous brands such as Comet, Mr. Clean, and Ivory had been dropping for 25 years. P&G was making 55 price changes *daily* on about 80 brands, and inaccurate billings were common. Its plants were inefficient, and the company had the highest overhead in the business. It was clear that it had to cut prices, and to do that it had to cut costs.

In response, P&G reengineered. The company tore down and rebuilt nearly every activity that contributed to its high costs. It redesigned the way it develops, manufactures, distributes, prices, markets, and sells products. The reengineering was difficult, time-consuming, and expensive. But now, after the changes, price changes are rare, factories are far more efficient, inventory is way down, and sales and profits are up. And P&G brands are now priced comparably to store brands. P&G may have reinvented itself as a leader in the industry once again, and created for itself a long-term competitive advantage that others are scrambling to match.[18]

As you can see, reengineering is not about making minor organizational changes here and there. It is about completely overhauling the operation, in revolutionary ways, in order to achieve the greatest possible benefits to the customer and to the organization.

Organizing for Technological Response

technology

The systematic application of scientific knowledge to a new product, process, or service.

Broadly speaking, **technology** can be viewed as the methods, processes, systems, and skills used to transform resources (inputs) into products (outputs). Although we will discuss technology—and innovation—more fully in Chapter 17, in this chapter we want to highlight some of the important influences technology has on organizational design.

Types of Technology Configurations

Research by Joan Woodward laid the foundation for understanding technology and structure. According to Woodward, there are three basic technologies that characterize how work is done: small batch, large batch, and continuous process technologies. These three classifications are equally useful for describing either service or manufacturing technologies. Each differs in terms of volume produced and variety of products/services offered. Each also has a different influence on organizing.[19]

Small Batch Technologies When goods or services are provided in very low volume or **small batches,** a company that does such work is called a *job shop.* An example is John Thomas, a specialty printer in Lansing, Michigan, that manufactures printed material for the florist and garden industry. A service example is the doctor's office, which provides a high variety of low-volume, customized services.

small batches

Technologies that produce goods and services in low volume.

In a small batch organization, structure tends to be very organic. There tend not to be a lot of rules and formal procedures, and decision making tends to be decentralized. The emphasis is on mutual adjustment among people.

Large Batch Technologies As volume increases, product variety usually decreases. Companies with higher volumes and lower varieties than a job shop tend to be characterized as **large batch,** or mass production technologies. Examples of large batch technologies include the auto assembly operations of General Motors, Ford, and Chrysler. In the service sector, McDonald's and Burger King are good examples. Their production runs tend to be more standardized, and all customers receive similar (if not identical) products. Machines tend to replace people in the physical execution of work. People run the machines.

large batch

Technologies that produce goods and services in high volume.

With a large batch technology, structure tends to be more mechanistic. There tend not to be many more rules and formal procedures, and decision making tends to be centralized with higher spans of control. Communication tends to be more formal in companies where hierarchical authority is more prominent.

Continuous Process Technologies At the very-high-volume end of the scale are companies that use **continuous process** technologies, technologies that do not stop and start. Domino Sugar and Shell Chemical, for example, use continuous process technologies where there are a very limited number of products to be produced. People are completely removed from the work itself. It is done entirely by machines and/or computers. In some cases, it may be that people run the computers that run the machines.

continuous process

A process that is highly automated and has a continuous production flow.

Ironically, with continuous process technology, structure can return to a more organic form because less monitoring and supervision are needed. Communication tends to be more informal in companies where fewer rules and regulations are established.

Organizing for Flexible Manufacturing

Although issues of volume and variety often have been seen as trade-offs in a technological sense, today organizations are trying to produce both high-volume and high-variety products at the same time. This is referred to as **mass customization.**[20] Automobiles, clothes, computers, and other products are increasingly being manufactured to match each customer's taste, specifications, and budget. While this seemed only a fantasy a few years ago, mass customization is quickly becoming more prevalent among leading firms. You can now buy clothes cut to your proportions, supplements with the exact blend of the vitamins and minerals you like, CDs with the music tracks you choose, and textbooks whose chapters are picked out by your professor.[21]

mass customization

The production of varied, individually customized products at the low cost of standardized, mass-produced products.

How do companies organize to pull off this kind of customization at such low cost? As shown in Table 9.1, they organize around a dynamic network of relatively independent operating units.[22] Each unit performs a specific process or task—called a *module*—such as making a component, performing a credit check, or performing a particular welding method. Some modules may be performed by outside suppliers or vendors.

Mass Customization	
Products	High variety and customization
Product design	Collaborative design; significant input from customers
	Short product development cycles
	Constant innovation
Operations and processes	Flexible processes
	Business process reengineering (BPR)
	Use of modules
	Continuous improvement (CI)
	Reduced setup and changeover times
	Reduced lead times
	JIT delivery and processing of materials and components
	Production to order
	Shorter cycle times
	Use of information technology (IT)
Quality management	Quality measured in customer delight
	Defects treated as capability failures
Organizational structure	Dynamic network of relatively autonomous operating units
	Learning relationships
	Integration of the value chain
	Team-based structure
Workforce management	Empowerment of employees
	High value on knowledge, information, and diversity of employee capabilities
	New product teams
	Broad job descriptions
Emphasis	Low-cost production of high-quality, customized products

TABLE 9.1
Key Features in Mass
Customization

SOURCE: Reprinted with permission of APICS—The Educational Society for Resource Management, *Production and Inventory Management,* Volume 41, Number 1, 2000, pp. 56–65.

Different modules join forces to make the good or provide a service. How and when the various modules interact with one another are dictated by the unique requests of each customer. The manager's responsibility is to make it easier and less costly for modules to come together, complete their tasks, and then recombine to meet the next customer demand. The ultimate goal of mass customization is a never-ending campaign to expand the number of ways a company can satisfy customers. The Internet has also made it easy for customers to choose their product preferences online and for companies to take an order straight to the manufacturing floor.

computer-integrated manufacturing

The use of computer-aided design and computer-aided manufacturing to sequence and optimize a number of production processes.

Computer-Integrated Manufacturing   **Computer-integrated manufacturing (CIM)** encompasses a host of computerized production efforts linked together. Two examples are computer-aided design and computer-aided manufacturing, which offer the ultimate in computerized process technologies. For example, a manufacturer's engineering function may contain a large variety of software applications used in both electronic and mechanical design. Using CIM, different design

team members can work on the network from remote sites, often their homes. These systems provide maximum process flexibility with the lowest costs of production. They produce high-variety and high-volume products at the same time.[23]

CIM potentially affords greater control and predictability of production processes, reduced waste, faster throughput times, and higher quality. But a company cannot "buy" its way out of competitive trouble simply by investing in superior hardware (technology) alone. It also must ensure that it has strategic and "people" strengths and a well-designed plan for implementing the technological changes.

Flexible Factories   As the name implies, **flexible factories** provide more production options and a greater variety of products. They differ from traditional factories in three primary ways: lot size, flow patterns, and scheduling.[24]

First, the traditional factory has long production runs, generating high volumes of a standardized product. Flexible factories have much shorter production runs, with many different products. Second, traditional factories move parts down the line from one location in the production sequence to the next. Flexible factories are organized around products, in work cells or teams, so that people work closely together and parts move shorter distances with shorter or no delays. Third, traditional factories use centralized scheduling, which is time-consuming, inaccurate, and slow to adapt to changes. Flexible factories use local or decentralized scheduling, in which decisions are made on the shop floor by the people doing the work.

> **flexible factories**
>
> **Manufacturing plants that have short production runs, are organized around products, and use decentralized scheduling.**

Lean Manufacturing   **Lean manufacturing** means an operation that is both efficient and effective; it strives to achieve the highest possible productivity and total quality, cost-effectively, by eliminating unnecessary steps in the production process and continually striving for improvement. Rejects are unacceptable, and staff, overhead, and inventory are considered wasteful. In a lean operation, the emphasis is on quality, speed, and flexibility more than on cost, efficiency, and hierarchy. But with a well-managed lean production process—like the operations at Toyota, Nissan, and Chrysler—a company can develop, produce, and distribute products with half or less of the human effort, space, tools, time, and overall cost.[25]

> **lean manufacturing**
>
> **An operation that strives to achieve the highest possible productivity and total quality, cost-effectively, by eliminating unnecessary steps in the production process and continually strives for improvement.**

For the lean approach to result in more effective operations, the following conditions must be met:[26]

- People are broadly trained rather than specialized.
- Communication is informal and horizontal among line workers.
- Equipment is general purpose.
- Work is organized in teams, or cells, that produce a group of similar products.
- Supplier relationships are long-term and cooperative.
- Product development is concurrent, not sequential, and is done by cross-functional teams.

In recent years, many companies have tried to become more lean by cutting overhead costs, laying off operative-level workers, eliminating layers of management, and utilizing capital equipment more efficiently. But if the move to lean manufacturing is simply a harsh, haphazard cost-cutting approach, the result will be chaos, overworked people, and low morale.

Organizing for Speed: Time-Based Competition

Companies worldwide have devoted so much energy to improving product quality that high quality is now the standard attained by all top competitors. Competition has driven quality to such heights that quality products no longer are enough to distinguish one company from another. *Time* is emerging as the key competitive advantage that can separate market leaders from also-rans.[27]

Companies today must learn what the customer needs and meet those needs as quickly as possible. **Time-based competition (TBC)** refers to strategies aimed at reducing the total time it takes to deliver the product or service. There are several key organizational elements to TBC: logistics, just-in-time (JIT), and simultaneous engineering. JIT production systems reduce the time it takes to manufacture products. Logistics speeds the delivery of products to customers. Both are essential steps toward bringing products to customers in the shortest time possible. In today's world, speed is essential.

time-based competition (TBC)

Strategies aimed at reducing the total time it takes to deliver a product or service.

Logistics

Logistics is the movement of resources into the organization (inbound) and products from the organization to its customers (outbound). As an extension of the organization's technology configuration, the organization of the logistics function is often critical to an organization's responsiveness and competitive advantage.

logistics

The movement of the right goods in the right amount to the right place at the right time.

Logistics is a great mass of parts, materials, and products moving via trucks, trains, planes, and ships. An average box of breakfast cereal spends 104 days getting from the factory to the supermarket, moving through the warehouses of wholesalers, distributors, brokers, and others! If the grocery industry streamlined logistics, it could save an estimated $30 billion annually.[28] Depending on the product, the duplication and inefficiency in distribution can cost far more than making the product itself.

By contrast, Saturn's distribution system is world class. GM has contracted with both Ryder System and Penske Global Automotive to perform inbound logistics and distribution management for Saturn. Suppliers, factories, and dealers are linked so tightly and efficiently that Saturn barely has any parts inventory.[29]

Just-in-Time Operations

An additional element of TBC involves **just-in-time (JIT)** operations. JIT calls for subassemblies and components to be manufactured in very small lots and delivered to the next stage in the process precisely at the time needed, or "just in time." A customer order triggers a factory order and the production process. The supplying work centers do not produce the next lot of product until the consuming work center requires it. Even external suppliers deliver to the company just in time.

just-in-time (JIT)

A system that calls for subassemblies and components to be manufactured in very small lots and delivered to the next stage of the production process just as they are needed.

Just-in-time is a companywide philosophy oriented toward eliminating waste throughout all operations and improving materials throughout. In this way, excess inventory is eliminated and costs are reduced. The ultimate goal of JIT is to better serve the customer by providing higher levels of quality and service.[30]

JIT represents a number of key production concepts. The system, which originated in Japan's Toyota Motor Corporation, includes the following concepts:

- *Elimination of waste.* Eliminate all waste from the production process, including waste of time, people, machinery, space, and materials.
- *Perfect quality.* Produce perfect parts even when lot sizes are reduced, and produce the product exactly when it is needed in the exact quantities that are needed.
- *Reduced cycle times.* Accomplish the entire manufacturing process more rapidly. Reduce setup times for equipment, move parts only short distances (machinery is placed in closer proximity), and eliminate all delays. The goal is to reduce action to the time spent working on the parts. For most manufacturers today, the percentage of time parts are worked on is about 5 percent of the total production time. JIT seeks to eliminate the other 95 percent, that is, to reduce to zero the time spent not working on the parts.

- *Employee involvement.* In JIT, employee involvement is central to success. The workers are responsible for production decisions. Managers and supervisors are coaches. Top management pledges that there will never be layoffs due to improved productivity.
- *Value-added manufacturing.* Do only those things (actions, work, etc.) that add value to the finished product. If it doesn't add value, don't do it. For example, inspection does not add value to the finished product, so make the product correctly the first time and inspection will not be necessary.
- *Discovery of problems and prevention of recurrence.* Foolproofing, or failsafing, is a key component of JIT. To prevent problems from arising, their cause(s) must be known and acted on. Thus, in JIT operations, people try to find the "weak link in the chain" by forcing problem areas to the surface so that preventive measures may be determined and implemented.

Many believe that only a fraction of JIT's potential has been realized and that its impact will grow as it is applied to other processes, such as service, distribution, and new-product development.[31]

Simultaneous Engineering JIT is a vital component of TBC, but JIT concentrates on reducing time in only one function: manufacturing. TBC attempts to deliver speed in *all* functions—product development, manufacturing, logistics, and customer service. Customers will not be impressed if you manufacture quickly but it takes weeks for them to receive their products or get a problem solved.

Many companies are turning to simultaneous engineering as the cornerstone of their TBC strategy. **Simultaneous engineering**—also an important component of total quality management—is a major departure from the old development process in which tasks were assigned to various functions in sequence. When R&D completed its part of the project, the work was "passed over the wall" to engineering, which completed its task and passed it over the wall to manufacturing, and so on. This process was highly inefficient, and errors took a long time to correct.

simultaneous engineering

A design approach in which all relevant functions cooperate jointly and continually in a maximum effort aimed at producing high-quality products that meet customers' needs.

Ernest Bastien of Toyota points to a RAV4 electric vehicle during the first day of the Electric Vehicle Association of Americas Conference in Sacramento, Calif. Toyota continues to make improvements to its line of cars, trucks, and SUVs.

In contrast, simultaneous engineering incorporates the issues and perspectives of all the functions—and customers and suppliers—from the beginning of the process. This team-based approach results in a higher-quality product that is designed for efficient manufacturing *and* customer needs.[32]

Some managers resist the idea of simultaneous engineering. Why should marketing, product planning and design, and R&D "allow" manufacturing to get involved in "their" work? The answer is: because the decisions made during the early, product-concept stage determine most of the manufacturing cost and quality. Furthermore, manufacturing can offer ideas about the product because of its experience with the prior generation of the product and with direct customer feedback. Also, the other functions must know early on what manufacturing can and cannot do. Finally, when manufacturing is in from the start, it is a full and true partner and will be more committed to decisions it helped make.

Not Your Father's Factory

FROM THE PAGES OF

BusinessWeek

Detroit automakers have an estimated cost disadvantage of $1,600 per vehicle versus the Japanese, according to a Deutsche Banc Alex. Brown Inc. analysis. It is flexibility, not wages, that gives these nonunion transplants a productivity edge, most experts agree. Japanese-owned factories typically build two or more models on a single assembly line. That's especially helpful as automakers turn out more low-volume niche models. If sales of one model start to wane, they can quickly crank up the production of another model. But Big Three factories were designed to build large volumes of a single model. All the Detroit companies are racing to make their plants more flexible.

To be sure, U.S. automakers already have taken big steps to improve productivity. In 1979, it took GM an average of 41 hours to assemble a vehicle; by 2001, that was down to 26.1 hours. In fact, GM's Oshawa, Ontario, factory, which makes Chevrolet Impalas and Monte Carlos, was North America's most efficient in 2001, says manufacturing consultant Harbour & Associates Inc. in Troy, Michigan. But overall, U.S. carmakers still lag behind Toyota, Honda, and Nissan in productivity.

Strict labor pacts sometimes have been a hindrance. In 1999, GM was stymied by United Auto Workers (UAW) objections when it tried to open a more efficient factory near Cleveland—Project Yellowstone—that would have relied on outside suppliers for more subassembly work. Only recently did it win the UAW's cooperation in building a superefficient modular factory in Lansing, Michigan. The plant has a flexible body shop where robots can be reprogrammed quickly to weld together vehicles ranging from cars to SUVs. It can produce the new Cadillac CTS in just 17 hours—as fast as Nissan's U.S.-best plant in Smyrna, Tennessee.

Modular manufacturing techniques are commonplace in the transplant factories, and that can be a big competitive advantage. A cockpit module—the portion of the interior the driver sees and touches, including the instrument panel and steering wheel—that is preassembled by a nearby supplier and then installed as a single component at the assembly plant can shave as much as 25 percent off the cost of producing that system. That preassembly work is providing growth opportunities for U.S.-based suppliers such as Delphi Corp., a GM spin-off. Delphi built a factory five miles away from Mercedes's Tuscaloosa, Alabama, plant to supply cockpit modules for the German automaker's first SUV, the M-Class. Every 2 1/2 minutes, Delphi workers get an electronic signal from the Mercedes factory telling them precisely what color dashboard panel to build next and what features to include, such as a CD player or navigation system. The finished modules are sent in small batches to the Mercedes plant, where they can be installed quickly.

With profits practically nonexistent for domestic automakers, the pressure to do more with less is changing the way companies develop vehicles. They've squeezed suppliers about as far as they can. Now they're sharing more platforms and components across brands. And they're focusing on how to wring out waste and eliminate defects long before a vehicle hits manufacturing. Not only does this reduce production costs, it improves quality. That, in turn, means further savings of hundreds of dollars per vehicle because of fewer warranty claims and incentives. "We've got to be efficient while we're innovative," says Ford's chief financial officer, Allan Gilmour. "American companies haven't done a very good job of that."

Cars keep getting cheaper. Prices have been falling since 1998, yet consumers are getting more for their money. Sophisticated safety features such as antilock brakes, side air bags, traction control, and stability-control systems are now more widely available. Quality is better, too. This is great news for consumers but expensive for automakers, which are being pressured to keep product lines fresh even as margins shrink. "Essentially, the customer is deciding who's going to thrive and who's not," says Ron Harbour, president of Harbour & Associates.

All the turmoil is a golden opportunity for Detroit, says Delphi CEO J. T. Battenberg III: "The industry is reinventing itself at a time when competition is going to get fierce. But fortunately, it's occurring in an era where there will be a lot more affluent buyers." Detroit probably will have to settle for a shrinking piece of the pie. The industry that emerges will look very different but may well be stronger. And that will be a good thing for everybody.

SOURCE: Joann Muller, "Autos: A New Industry," *Business Week*, July 15, 2002, pp. *(FILL)*

Organizing for Strategic Response

As our discussions thus far have focused on organizing in ways that improve responsiveness, they have been, in a sense, about competitive advantage and strategy. Organizational size, environmental adaptation, technology decisions, and the like, are all elements of strategic management, as you know. And they all influence the design of organizations.

At the same time, there are issues directly pertaining to other aspects of strategy that influence how an organization is structured and managed. These issues include core competencies, network organizations, strategic alliances, learning organizations, and high-involvement organizations.

Organizing around Core Competencies

A recent, different, and important perspective on strategy, organization, and competition hinges on the concept of *core competence*.[33] Companies compete not just with their products but also on the basis of their core strengths and expertise.

As you learned in Chapter 4, a core competence is the capability—knowledge, expertise, skill—that underlies a company's ability to be a leader in providing a range of specific goods or services. A core competence gives value to customers, makes the company's products different from (and better than) those of competitors, and can be used in creating new products. Think of core competencies as the roots of competitiveness, and products as the fruits.

What are some concrete examples of core competencies? And how can they be used to make firms more responsive and competitive?

Successfully developing a world-class core competence opens the door to a variety of future opportunities; failure means being foreclosed from many markets. Thus, a well-understood, well-developed core competence can enhance a company's responsiveness and competitiveness. Strategically, this means that companies should commit to excellence and leadership in competencies before they commit to winning market share for specific products. Organizationally, this means that the corporation should be viewed as a portfolio of competencies, not just a portfolio of specific businesses. Companies should strive for core competence leadership, not just product leadership.

Managers who want to strengthen their firms' competitiveness via core competencies need to focus on several related issues:

- Identify existing core competencies.
- Acquire or build core competencies that will be important for the future.
- Keep investing in competencies so that the firm remains world-class and better than competitors.
- Extend competencies to find new applications and opportunities for the markets of tomorrow.[34]

Sharp and Toshiba committed years ago to being the world's best creators of flat-screen displays. They wanted to monopolize the markets for flat screens, although they didn't yet know all the potential product applications. A business case could not be made for each application; in fact, all applications couldn't even be envisioned. But the companies knew that this would be an important technology of the future.

The applications began with calculators. Over time, flat-screen displays were needed in pocket diaries, laptop computers, miniature televisions, LCD projection televisions, and video telephones. By committing early to a *competence,* these companies were ready for new and future *products* and *markets.*

As another example, SKF is the world's largest manufacturer of roller bearings. Are roller bearings its core competence? No, this would limit its products and market access. SKF's core competencies are antifriction, precision engineering, and making perfectly spherical devices. Perhaps it could manufacture other products, for example, the round, high-precision rolling heads that go inside a VCR or the tiny balls in roller-ball pens.

Some other examples of companies with special competencies, which feed many specific products, are Hewlett-Packard (measurement computing, communications); Sony (miniaturization); Rubbermaid (low-tech plastics); Lotus (enterprise computing or "groupware"); 3M (adhesives and advanced materials); EDS (systems integration); and Motorola (wireless communications).

SOURCES: G. Hamel and C. K. Prahalad, *Competing for the Future* (Boston: Harvard Business School Press, 1994); M. Loeb, "How to Grow a New Product Every Day," *Fortune,* November 14, 1994, pp. 269–70; L. Hays, S. Lipin, and W. Bulkeley, "Software Landscape Shifts as IBM Makes Hostile Bid for Lotus," *The Wall Street Journal,* June 6, 1995, pp. A1, A10.

The Network Organization

The notion of core competencies takes us right into a discussion of network organizations. In contrast to the traditional, hierarchical firm performing all the business functions, the network organization is a collection of independent, mostly single-function firms. As depicted in Figure 9.3, the **network organization** describes not one organization but the web of interrelationships among many firms. Network organizations are flexible arrangements among designers, suppliers, producers, distributors, and customers where each firm is able to pursue its own distinctive competence. The network as a whole,

network organization

A collection of independent, mostly single-function firms.

FIGURE 9.3
A Dynamic Network

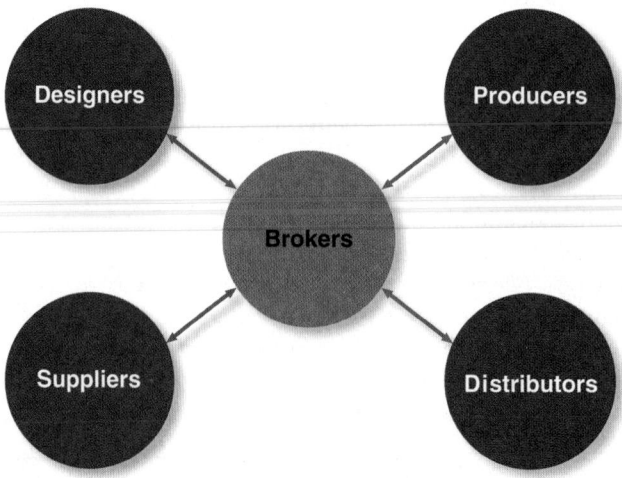

SOURCE: R. Miles and C. Snow, "Organizations: New Concepts for New Forms," *California Management Review,* Spring 1986, p. 65. Copyright © 1986 by The Regents of the University of California. Reprinted from the *California Management Review,* Vol. 28, No. 3 by permission of The Regents.

then, can display the technical specialization of the functional structure, the market responsiveness of the product structure, and the balance and flexibility of the matrix.[35]

The **dynamic network**—also called the *modular* or *virtual* corporation—is composed of temporary arrangements among members that can be assembled and reassembled to meet a changing competitive environment. The members of the network are held together by contracts that stipulate results expected (market mechanisms) rather than by hierarchy and authority. Poorly performing firms can be removed and replaced.

> **dynamic network**
>
> **Temporary arrangements among partners that can be assembled and reassembled to adapt to the environment.**

Such arrangements are common in the electronics, toy, and apparel industries, each of which creates and sells trendy products at a fast pace. For example, Reebok owns no plants; it designs and markets but does not produce. Nike owns only one small factory that makes sneaker parts. Other examples include the Bombay Company, Louis Galoob Toys, Brooks Brothers, and the Registry (which markets the services of independent software engineers, programmers, and technical writers). In biotechnology, smaller firms do research and manufacture, and the drug giants market the products.[36]

Successful networks potentially offer flexibility, innovation, quick responses to threats and opportunities, and reduced costs and risk. But for these arrangements to be successful, several things must occur:

- The firm must choose the right specialty. This must be something (product or service) that the market needs and for which the firm is better at providing than other firms.
- The firm must choose collaborators that also are excellent at what they do and that provide complementary strengths.
- The firm must make certain that all parties fully understand the strategic goals of the partnership.
- Each party must be able to trust all the others with strategic information and also trust that each collaborator will deliver quality products even if the business grows quickly and makes heavy demands.

The role of managers shifts in a network from that of command and control to more like that of a **broker.** Broker/managers serve several important boundary roles that aid network integration and coordination:

> **broker**
>
> **A person who assembles and coordinates participants in a network.**

- *Designer role.* The broker serves as a network architect who envisions a set of groups or firms whose collective expertise could be focused on a particular product or service.
- *Process engineering role.* The broker serves as a *network co-operator* who takes the initiative to lay out the flow of resources and relationships and makes certain that everyone shares the same goals, standards, payments, and the like.
- *Nurturing role.* The broker serves as a network developer that nurtures and enhances the network (like team building) to make certain the relationships are healthy and mutually beneficial.[37]

Strategic Alliances

As discussed earlier, the modern organization has a variety of links with other organizations. These links are more complex than the standard relationships with traditional stake-holders such as suppliers and clients. Today even fierce *competitors* are working together at unprecedented levels to achieve their strategic goals. To combat Microsoft's

FedEx drop boxes are now positioned next to United States Postal Service mailboxes.

online user ID platform, called Passport, a number of companies have joined forces to promote a different software standard. GM, Ford, and DaimlerChrysler have been doing joint research and development, and Federal Express now has drop-off boxes at U.S. Postal Service facilities.[38]

A **strategic alliance** is a formal relationship created with the purpose of joint pursuit of mutual goals. In a strategic alliance, individual organizations share administrative authority, form social links, and accept joint ownership. Such alliances are blurring firms' boundaries. They occur between companies and their competitors, governments, and universities. Such partnering often crosses national and cultural boundaries. Companies form strategic alliances to develop new technologies, enter new markets, and reduce manufacturing costs. Alliances are often the fastest, most efficient way to achieve objectives. Moreover, strategic alliances can pay off not only through the immediate deal, but through creating additional, unforeseen opportunities and opening new doors to the future.[39]

Managers typically devote plenty of time to screening potential partners in financial terms. But for the alliance to work, managers also must foster and develop the human relationships in the partnership. Asian companies seem to be the most comfortable with the nonfinancial, "people" side of alliances; European companies the next so; and U.S. companies the least. Thus, U.S. companies may need to pay extra attention to the human side of alliances. Table 9.2 shows some recommendations for how to do this. In fact, most of the ideas apply not only to strategic alliances but to any type of relationship.[40]

strategic alliance

A formal relationship created among independent organizations with the purpose of joint pursuit of mutual goals.

The Learning Organization

Being responsive requires continually changing and learning new ways to act. Some experts have stated that the only sustainable advantage is learning faster than the competition. This has led to a new term that is now part of the vocabulary of most managers: the learning organization.[41] A **learning organization** is "an organization skilled at creating, acquiring, and transferring knowledge, and at modifying its behavior to reflect new knowledge and insights."[42]

learning organization

An organization skilled at creating, acquiring, and transferring knowledge, and at modifying its behavior to reflect new knowledge and insights.

TABLE 9.2
How I's Can Become We's

The best alliances are true partnerships that meet these criteria:

1. *Individual excellence:* Both partners add value, and their motives are positive (pursue opportunity) rather than negative (mask weaknesses).

2. *Importance:* Both partners want the relationship to work because it helps them meet long-term strategic objectives.

3. *Interdependence:* The partners need each other; each helps the other reach its goal.

4. *Investment:* The partners devote financial and other resources to the relationship.

5. *Information:* The partners communicate openly about goals, technical data, problems, and changing situations.

6. *Integration:* The partners develop shared ways of operating; they teach each other and learn from each other.

7. *Institutionalization:* The relationship has formal status with clear responsibilities.

8. *Integrity:* Both partners are trustworthy and honorable.

SOURCE: Adapted and reprinted by permission of *Harvard Business Review.* From R. M. Kanter, "Collaborative Advantage: The Art of Alliances," July–August 1994, pp. 96–108. Copyright © 1994 by the Harvard Business School Publishing Corporation; all rights reserved.

GE, Corning, and Honda are good examples of learning organizations. Such organizations are skilled at solving problems, experimenting with new approaches, learning from their own experiences, learning from other organizations, and spreading knowledge quickly and efficiently.

How do firms become true learning organizations? There are a few important ingredients.[43]

1. Their people engage in disciplined thinking and attention to details, making decisions based on data and evidence rather than guesswork and assumptions.
2. They search constantly for new knowledge, looking for expanding horizons and opportunities rather than quick fixes to current problems.
3. They carefully review both successes and failures, looking for lessons and deeper understanding.
4. Learning organizations benchmark—they identify and implement the best business practices of other organizations, stealing ideas shamelessly.
5. They share ideas throughout the organization via reports, information systems, informal discussions, site visits, education, and training.

The High-Involvement Organization

Participative management is becoming increasingly popular as a way to create a competitive advantage. Particularly in high-technology companies facing stiff international competition, such as Microsystems and Compaq Computer, the aim is to generate high levels of commitment and involvement as employees and managers work together to achieve organizational goals.

In a **high-involvement organization,** top management ensures that there is a consensus about the direction in which the business is heading. The leader seeks input from his or her top management team and from lower levels of the company. Task forces, study groups, and other techniques are used to foster participation in decisions that affect the entire organization. Also fundamental to the high-involvement organization is continual feedback to participants regarding how they are doing compared to the competition and how effectively they are meeting the strategic agenda.

high-involvement organization

A type of organization in which top management ensures that there is consensus about the direction in which the business is heading.

Structurally, this usually means that even lower-level employees have a direct relationship with a customer or supplier and thus receive feedback and are held accountable for a product or service delivery. The organizational form is a flat, decentralized structure built around a customer, product, or service. Employee involvement is particularly powerful when the environment changes rapidly, work is creative, complex activities require coordination, and firms need major breakthroughs in innovation and speed—in other words, when companies need to be more responsive.[44]

Final Thoughts about Responsive Organizations

As organizations strive to maximize responsiveness, they have to balance their needs for efficiency and effectiveness. We have pointed out throughout this chapter (and the one before) that *any* approach to organizing has its strengths and limitations. And we have noted that advantages gained by a firm through innovative structures and systems are likely to be short-lived. Competitors catch up.

Today's advantages are tomorrow's "table stakes": requirements that need to be met if a firm expects to be a major player in an industry. Increasingly we hear executives embrace the ideals of GE's Jack Welch, who say that his goal is to create a *boundaryless organization* capable of doing anything, anytime, anywhere around the world. This is, of course, a lofty goal and one that requires organizations to transcend the limits of their existing structures, technologies, and systems.[45]

KEY TERMS

Broker, p. 291

Computer-integrated manufacturing (CIM), p. 284

Continuous process, p. 283

Customer relationship management, p. 279

Downsizing, p. 277

Dynamic network, p. 291

Economies of scope, p. 276

Flexible factories, p. 285

High-involvement organization, p. 293

ISO 9000, p. 281

Just-in-time (JIT), p. 286

Large batch, p. 283

Lean manufacturing, p. 286

Learning organization, p. 292

Logistics, p. 286

Mass customization, p. 283

Mechanistic organization, p. 274

Network organization, p. 290

Organic structure, p. 274

Rightsizing, p. 277

Simultaneous engineering, p. 287

Small batches, p. 283

Strategic alliance, p. 292

Survivor's syndrome, p. 277

Technology, p. 282

Time-based competition (TBC), p. 286

Total quality management, p. 280

SUMMARY OF LEARNING OBJECTIVES

Now that you have studied Chapter 9, you should know:

The market imperatives a firm must meet to survive.

Organizations have a formal structure to help control what goes on within them. But to survive today, firms need more than control—they need responsiveness. They must act quickly and adapt to fast-changing demands.

The potential advantages of creating an organic form of organization.

The organic form emphasizes flexibility. Organic organizations are decentralized, informal, and dependent on the judgment and expertise of people with broad responsibilities. The organic form is not a single formal structure but a concept that underlies all the new forms discussed in this chapter.

How a firm can 'be' both small and big.

Historically, large organizations have had important advantages over small. Today, small size has advantages, including the ability to act quickly, respond to customer demands, and serve small niches. The ideal firm today combines the advantages of both. It creates many small, flexible units, while the corporate levels add value by taking advantage of its size and power.

How to manage information-processing demands.

Integrative mechanisms help coordinate the efforts of differentiated subunits. Slack resources and self-contained tasks reduce the need to process information. Information systems and horizontal relationships help the organization process information.

How firms organize to meet customer requirements.

Firms have embraced principles of continuous improvement and total quality management to respond to customer needs. Baldrige criteria and ISO 9000 standards help firms organize to meet better quality specifications. Extending these, reengineering efforts are directed at completely overhauling processes to provide world-class customer service.

How firms organize around different types of technology.

Organizations tend to move from organic structures to mechanistic structures and back to organic structures as they transition from small batch to large batch and continuous process technologies. To organize for flexible manufacturing, organizations pursue mass customization via computer-integrated manufacturing and lean manufacturing. To organize for time-based competition, firms emphasize their logistics operations, just-in-time operations, and simultaneous engineering.

The new types of dynamic organizational concepts and forms that are being used for strategic responsiveness.

New and emerging organizational concepts and forms include core competencies, network organizations, strategic alliances learning organizations, and high-involvement organizations.

DISCUSSION QUESTIONS

1. Discuss evidence you have seen of the imperatives for change, flexibility, and responsiveness faced by today's firms.

2. Describe large, bureaucratic organizations with which you have had contact that have not responded flexibly to customer demands. Also describe examples of satisfactory responsiveness. What do you think accounts for the differences between the responsive and nonresponsive organizations?

3. Considering the potential advantages of large and small size, would you describe the "feel" of your college or university

as big, small, or small within big? Why? What might make it feel different?

4. What is a core competence? Generate some examples of companies with distinctive competencies, identifying what those competencies are. Brainstorm some creative new products and markets to which these competencies could be applied.

5. If you were going into business for yourself, what would be your core competencies? What competencies do you have now, and what competencies are you going to develop? Describe what your role would be in a network organiza-

tion, and the competencies and roles of other firms you would want in your network.

6. Identify some recently formed alliances between competitors. What are the goals of the alliance? What brought them together? What have they done to ensure success? How are they doing now?

7. What skills will you need to work effectively in (1) a network organization, (2) a learning organization, and (3) a high-involvement organization? Be specific, generating long lists. Would you enjoy working in these environments? Why or why not? What can you do to prepare yourself for these eventualities?

The Biggest Grocery Store You've Never Heard Of: Grabbing "Ahold" of the Virtual Market

It's not likely that other online grocers will repeat the mistakes made by Webvan. The Foster City, California, company originally relied on technology and a high-cost warehouse to fulfill orders. Before going out of business Webvan did an about-face: It spent $2 billion in an effort to re-create a regular supermarket's distribution service.

"This is an industry that already has a pretty efficient distribution system," says Mary Brett Whitfield, a director of e-retail intelligence systems for Pricewaterhouse Coopers. "Grocery stores are literally at every major intersection in most metropolitan markets."

Chicago-based Peapod was actually the first grocer to couple home delivery with electronic ordering by having customers install its proprietary software in their home computers. Peapod delivered out of stores before it fell under Webvan's influence. It subsequently converted to a central warehouse distribution like Webvan's, which was also unsuccessful.

Online grocers soon figured out that retail chains with existing infrastructure held a big advantage and began forming alliances with them. For example, GroceryWorks.com is now a part of Safeway. Peapod was rescued by the Dutch giant Ahold. Ahold went on a global buying spree in the 1990s, grabbing a large chunk of the U.S. market along the way. Its chief competitor is now Wal-mart, which is striking fear into the hearts of grocery executives everywhere.

Ahold owns over 9,000 stores. None of them, however, are named Ahold. "What makes Ahold unique is that we are perceived by our customers as the local guy," says the company's CEO, Cees van der Hoeven.

Van der Hoeven says he envisions a day when his cut-price stores in Guatemala offer tips on discounting to its colleagues in America and when lighting for every Ahold supermarket from Bangkok to Boston will be ordered from the same supplier. Ahold's back office will squeeze suppliers into offering rock-bottom prices to all stores.

All this will take place in the "virtual Internet world" and will be invisible to the 40 million customers who shop at Ahold stores every week. The dream is a long way off, though. Currently, only about 5 percent of Ahold's products are even ordered cross-continentally.

"E-retailers need more than just technological bells and whistles to create a sustainable business model," says Geof Wissman, principal consultant, Pricewaterhouse Coopers. "The basic problem with technology is that it is often thought of as a strategy, not as a strategic tool." For example, technology alone is not a compelling enough reason for consumers to shop online, he says.

Retailing changes come slowly if consumers are required to change their behavior, agrees Whitfield. The online grocery craze may be limited to people with time-related or mobility-related needs.

Storage areas at Ahold's stores will be converted into "fast pick" fulfillment centers to handle the orders of Peapod customers.

Mike Spindler, president of MyWebGrocer, remains confident in online selling. According to Spindler, about 500 supermarkets are Web-enabled for picking orders. He predicts that that number will be 1,500 in a year.

Despite their unhappy fates, online grocers such as Webvan had a glimpse into the future. They saw that they could give people back their discretionary time. Technology, superior distribution systems, and size can give companies like Ahold a competitive leg up, but ultimately the game still revolves around the consumer's needs.

QUESTIONS

1. How was Webvan structured differently from Peapod? Which company's structure was superior?

2. How did size and organization play a role in the merger of online grocers with "brick-and-mortar" stores?

3. How can large grocers like Ahold organize themselves for customer responsiveness?

SOURCES: Elaine Pollack, "Supermarkets: A Challenge Ahead," *Chain Store Age Executive,* August 2002, 78, pp. 30–31; Michael Garry, "Selling Online: A Work in Progress," *Supermarket News,* July 22, 2002, p. 77; Richard Tomlinson, "The Biggest Grocer You've Never Heard Of," *Fortune International,* July 8, 2002, 146, p. 72; Dan Alaimo, "Stores May Succeed Where Webvan Failed," *Supermarket News,* October 8, 2001, p. 24.

9.1   Decentralization: Pros and Cons

OBJECTIVE

To explore the reasons for, as well as the pros and cons of, decentralizing.

INSTRUCTIONS

The following Decentralization Worksheet contains some observations on decentralization. As you review each of the statements, provide an example that illustrates why this statement is important and related problems and benefits of the situation or condition indicated in the statement.

Decentralization Worksheet

A large number of factors determine the extent to which a manager should decentralize. Clearly, anything that increases a manager's workload creates pressure for decentralization because only a finite level of work can be accomplished by a single person. As with many facets of management, there are advantages and disadvantages to decentralization.

1. The greater the diversity of products, the greater the decentralization.

2. The larger the size of the organization, the more the decentralization.

3. The more rapidly changing the organization's environment, the more decentralization.

4. Developing adequate, timely controls is the essence of decentralizing.

_____

_____

_____

_____

5. Managers should delegate decisions that involve large amounts of time but minimal erosions of their power and control.

_____

_____

_____

_____

6. Decentralizing involves delegating authority, and therefore, the principles of delegation apply to decentralization. (List the principles of delegation before you start your discussion.)

_____

_____

_____

_____

SOURCE: R. R. McGrath, Jr., _Exercises in Management Fundamentals_ (Englewood Cliffs, NJ: Prentice-Hall, 1985) pp. 59–60. Reprinted by permission of Prentice-Hall, Inc.

9.2   The University Culture

OBJECTIVES

1. To measure the culture at your university.
2. To study the nature of organization culture.
3. To understand how a culture can be changed.

INSTRUCTIONS

1. Working alone, complete and score the University Culture Survey.
2. In small groups, exchange survey scores and develop responses to the discussion questions.
3. Group spokespersons report group findings to the class.

DISCUSSION QUESTIONS

1. In what respects did students agree or disagree on survey test items?
2. What might account for differences in students' experiences and attitudes with respect to the university culture?
3. How can the survey results be put to constructive use?

CHAPTER 10

Human Resources Management

You can get capital and erect buildings, but it takes people to build a business.

—Thomas J. Watson, Founder, IBM.

CHAPTER OUTLINE

Strategic Human Resources Management
  The HR Planning Process
Staffing the Organization
  Recruitment
  Selection
  Workforce Reductions
Developing the Workforce
  Training and Development
Performance Appraisal
  What Do You Appraise?
  Who Should Do the Appraisal?
  How Do You Give Employees Feedback?
Designing Reward Systems
  Pay Decisions
  Incentive Systems and Variable Pay
  Employee Benefits
  Legal Issues in Compensation and Benefits
  Health and Safety
Labor Relations
  Labor Laws
  Unionization
  Collective Bargaining
  What Does the Future Hold?

LEARNING OBJECTIVES

After studying Chapter 10, you will know:

1. How companies use human resources management to gain competitive advantage.

2. Why companies recruit both internally and externally for new hires.

3. The various methods available for selecting new employees.

4. Why companies spend so much on training and development.

5. How to determine who should appraise an employee's performance.

6. How to analyze the fundamental aspects of a reward system.

7. How unions influence human resources management.

8. How the legal system influences human resources management.

THE ONLINE DASH FOR TALENT

In 1996 Steven Rothberg was publishing an employment magazine called *College Recruiter.* Employers paid to advertise in the magazine, which was distributed free to on-campus career centers. A director at one of those centers mentioned to Rothberg that she didn't know what the Internet was and didn't have email "but that a lot of her students had told her they were doing their career search on the Internet," Rothberg says. They were researching companies that recruited on-campus and applying to jobs out of town.

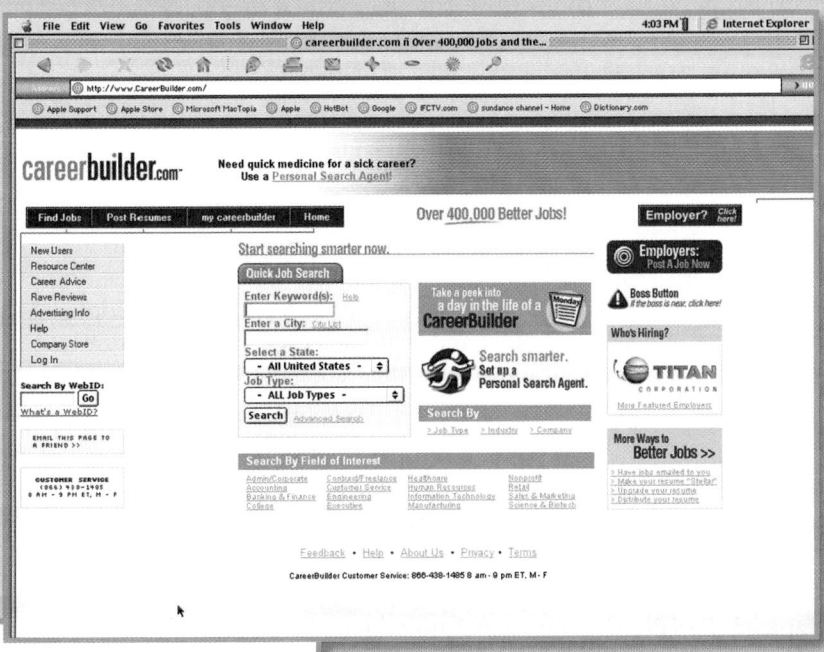

With more than 130 leading local newspapers, along with USA Today, Careerbuilder.com gives top employers the mechanism to find top candidates.

Subsequent to that conversation, Rothberg got his own website: He paid a high school $3,000 to get CollegeRecruiter.com up and running. Within three months, the site was turning a profit. Three years later, he stopped publishing the print magazine altogether because the website was earning the bulk of the company's revenues and all of its profits.

Besides CollegeRecruiter.com, other online job sites have sprouted up in abundance. Monster.com is, of course, the biggest online job site on the Web. Yahoo recently purchased HotJobs.com, putting it in a strong second place. CareerBuilder.com has allied itself with the largest job recruiting force in the country—newspapers. The company was purchased by the media giants Knight-Ridder and Tribune Co., whose papers now post their ads on the site.

Seventy-three percent of all companies currently use the Internet for recruiting. If a corporation is looking to attract top talent globally or a job seeker wants to check opportunities outside his or her local area, the Internet is the only way to go. Online recruiting tends to be not only cheaper but faster, too. The total recruiting time for a candidate hired through the Internet is 21 days, whereas traditional recruiting generally takes up to 90 days.

New technology called *wrapping* has made it easier than ever for companies to post their jobs on Monster and its competitors. "I call it 'do-nothing recruiting,'" says Gerry Crispin, coauthor of *CareerXroads,* a best-selling online recruiting reference book. "Rather than you pushing your jobs onto [online sites], they will automatically come to your website and see which jobs are new, copy them, and bring them to their traffic site. You do nothing but keep your organization's website up-to-date."

Online recruiting seems like a great new tool, but don't be fooled. "There are still more people reading newspapers than are going to Monster or HotJobs by a long shot," says Barton Crockett, a publishing industry analyst at J. P. Morgan. Still, if employers are going to beat their competitors to the punch in the future, they are going to have to get online. Studies show that virtually 100 percent of college students use the Web and that the vast majority turn to it first when looking for opportunities.

Sources: Bill Leonard, "Wrapping Up Online Recruiting Efforts in One Package," *HRMagazine,* August 2002, p. 23; "Hiring College Students This Summer? Then Go Online," *HR Briefing,* May 15, pp. 6–7; Alex Daniels, "An Online Job War," *Newbytes,* February 6, 2002; "Monster.com Continues Leadership Position in Career Category," *Business Wire,* October 15, 2001, p. 70.

Human resources management (HRM), historically known as personnel management, deals with formal systems for managing people at work. We begin this chapter by describing HRM as it relates to strategic management. The quote by Thomas Watson, founder of IBM, summarizes our view of the importance of people to any organization. We also discuss more of the "nuts and bolts" of HRM: staffing, training, performance appraisal, rewards, and labor relations. Throughout the chapter, we discuss legal issues that influence each aspect of HRM. In the next chapter, we expand this focus to address related issues of managing a diverse workforce.

---

human resources management (HRM)

Formal systems for the management of people within an organization.

Strategic Human Resources Management

HRM has assumed a vital strategic role in recent years as organizations attempt to compete through people. Recall from Chapter 4, "Planning and Strategic Management," that firms can create a competitive advantage when they possess or develop resources that are valuable, rare, inimitable, and organized. We can use the same criteria to talk about the strategic impact of human resources:

1. **Creates value.** People can increase value through their efforts to decrease costs or provide something unique to customers or some combination of the two. Empowerment programs, total quality initiatives, and continuous improvement efforts at companies such as Corning, Xerox, and Saturn are intentionally designed to increase the value that employees place on the bottom line.

2. **Is rare.** People are a source of competitive advantage when their skills, knowledge, and abilities are not equally available to all competitors. Top companies invest a great deal to hire and train the best and the brightest employees in order to gain advantage over their competitors. Recently, Dow Chemical went to court to stop General Electric from hiring away its engineers. This case shows that some companies recognize both the value and the rareness of certain employees.

3. **Is difficult to imitate.** People are a source of competitive advantage when their capabilities and contributions cannot be copied by others. Disney, Southwest Airlines, and Mirage Resorts are known for creating unique cultures that get the most from employees (through teamwork) and are difficult to imitate.

4. **Is organized.** People are a source of competitive advantage when their talents can be combined together and deployed rapidly to work on new assignments at a moment's notice. Teamwork and cooperation are two pervasive methods for ensuring an organized workforce. But companies such as Spyglass (a software company) and AT&T have invested in information technology to help allocate and track employee assignments to temporary projects.

These four criteria highlight the importance of people and show the closeness of HRM to strategic management. In a recent survey by *USA Today* and Deloitte & Touche, nearly 80 percent of corporate executives said the importance of HRM in their firms has grown substantially over the last 10 years, and two-thirds said that HR expenditures are now viewed as a strategic investment rather than simply a cost to be minimized.[1] Because employee skills, knowledge, and abilities are among the most distinctive and renewable resources on which a company can draw, their strategic management is more important than ever. Increasingly, organizations are recognizing that their success depends on what people know, that is, their knowledge and skills. The term **human capital** (or, more broadly, *intellectual capital*) often is used today to describe the strategic value of employee skills and knowledge.

But while concepts such as sustainable competitive advantage and human capital are certainly important, they remain only ideas for action. On a day-to-day basis, HR managers have many concerns regarding their workers and

---

human capital

The knowledge, skills, and abilities of employees that have economic value.

the entire personnel puzzle. These concerns include managing layoffs; addressing employee loyalty issues; managing diversity; creating a well-trained, highly motivated workforce; and containing health care costs. Balancing these issues is a difficult task, and the best approach is likely to vary depending on the circumstances of the organization. A steel producer facing a cutback in business may need human resources activities to assist with layoffs, whereas a semiconductor company may need more staff to produce enough microchips to meet the demands of the burgeoning personal computer market. The emphasis on different HR activities depends on whether the organization is growing, declining, or standing still. This leads to the practical issues involved in HR planning.

The HR Planning Process

"Get me the right kind and the right number of people at the right time." It sounds simple enough, but meeting an organization's staffing needs requires strategic human resources planning: an activity with a strategic purpose derived from the organization's plans.

The HR planning process occurs in three stages: planning, programming, and evaluating. First, HR managers need to know the organization's business plans to ensure that the right number and types of people are available—where the company is headed, in what businesses it plans to be, what future growth is expected, and so forth. Few things are more damaging to morale than having to lay off recently hired college graduates because of inadequate planning for future needs. Second, the organization conducts programming of specific human resources activities, such as recruitment, training, and layoffs. In this stage, the company's plans are implemented. Third, human resources activities are evaluated to determine whether they are producing the results needed to contribute to the organization's business plans. Figure 10.1 illustrates the components of the human resources planning process. In this chapter, we focus on human resources planning and programming. Many of the other factors listed in Figure 10.1 are discussed in later chapters.

Demand Forecasts   Perhaps the most difficult part of human resources planning is conducting *demand* forecasts, that is, determining how many and what type of people are needed. Demand forecasts for people needs are derived from organizational

FIGURE 10.1

An Overview of the HR Planning Process

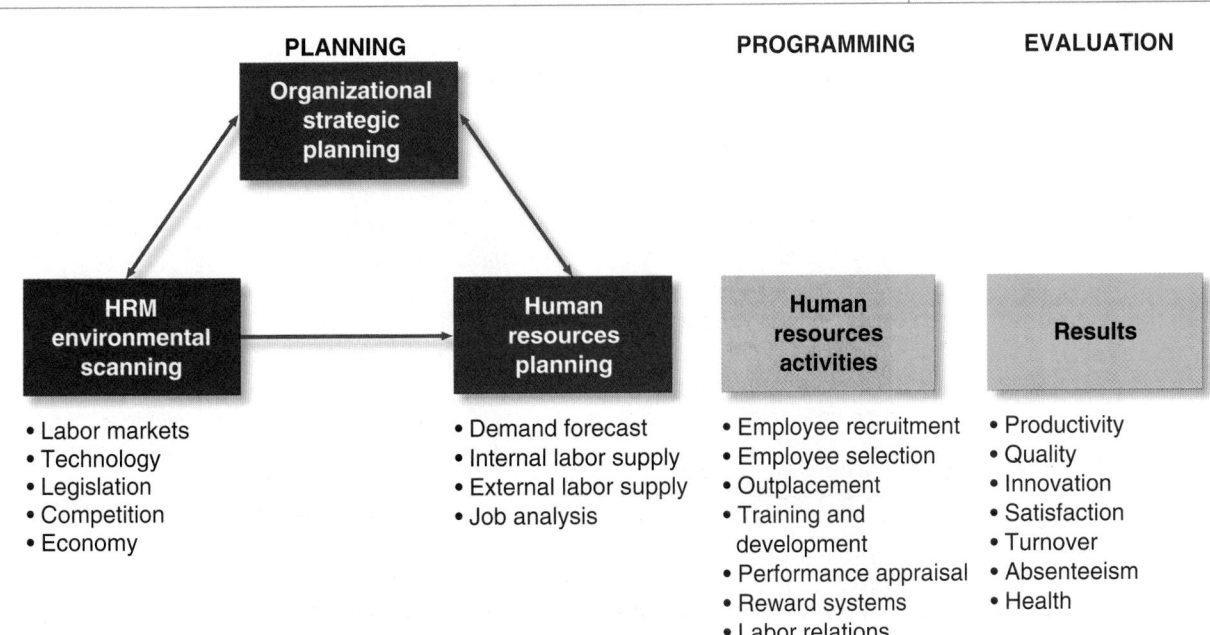

PLANNING		PROGRAMMING	EVALUATION
Organizational strategic planning			
HRM environmental scanning	Human resources planning	Human resources activities	Results
• Labor markets • Technology • Legislation • Competition • Economy	• Demand forecast • Internal labor supply • External labor supply • Job analysis	• Employee recruitment • Employee selection • Outplacement • Training and development • Performance appraisal • Reward systems • Labor relations	• Productivity • Quality • Innovation • Satisfaction • Turnover • Absenteeism • Health

plans. For example, when the pharmaceutical company Merck developed Propecia, a new drug to cure baldness, managers had to estimate the future size of this market based on demographic projections. Based on current sales and projected future sales growth, managers estimate the plant capacity needed to meet future demand, the sales force required, the support staff needed, and so forth. At this point, the number of labor-hours required to operate a plant, sell the product, distribute it, service customers, and so forth, can be calculated. These estimates are used to determine the demand for different types of workers.

Labor Supply Forecasts   In concert with demand forecasts, the *supply of labor* must be forecast, that is, estimates of how many and what types of employees the organization actually will have. In performing a supply analysis, the organization estimates the number and quality of its current employees as well as the available external supply of workers. To estimate internal supply, the company typically relies on past experiences with turnover, terminations, retirements, or promotions and transfers. A computerized human resources information system assists greatly in supply forecasting.

Externally, organizations have to look at workforce trends to make projections. Worldwide, there is a growing gap between the world's supply of labor and the demand for labor.[2] Most of the well-paid jobs are generated in the cities of the industrialized world, but many skilled and unskilled human resources are in the developing nations. This gap is leading to massive relocation (including immigrants, temporary workers, and retirees) and a reduction of protectionist immigration policies (as countries come to rely on and compete for foreign workers).

Forecasts of a diverse workforce have become fact. The business world is no longer the exclusive domain of white males. Minorities, women, immigrants, older and disabled workers, and other groups have made the management of diversity a fundamental activity of the modern manager. Because of the importance of managing the "new workforce," the next chapter is devoted entirely to this topic.

Reconciling Supply and Demand   Once managers have a good idea of both the supply of and the demand for various types of employees, they can start developing approaches for reconciling the two. In some cases, organizations find that they need

Predictions of a diverse workforce have become fact in today's business world.

more people than they currently have (i.e., a labor deficit). In such cases, organizations can hire new employees, promote current employees to new positions, or "outsource" work to contractors. In other cases, organizations may find that they have more people than they need (i.e., a labor surplus). If this is detected far enough in advance, organizations can use attrition—the normal turnover of employees—to reduce the surplus. In other instances, the organization may lay off employees or transfer them to other areas. The give and take of supply and demand is now playing out on the Internet, as discussed next.

FROM THE PAGES OF

BusinessWeek

And Now, the Just-in-Time Employee

"Stop thinking of yourself as an employee and start thinking of yourself as a 'service provider,'" advises journalist Naomi Klein, who writes about current corporate trends such as outsourcing and downsizing. According to Klein, 83 percent of the fastest-growing American companies are now outsourcing work they once hired people to perform.

Contractors constitute a nimble group of service providers that can grow and shrink according to the demands of the global marketplace. Geography doesn't matter as long as a person is hooked onto the end of a computer terminal. Think of it as a human capital exchange similar to the stock market. The legions of contractors who keep their résumés permanently posted on Monster.com are growing evidence of a new labor economy where workers day-trade their talents. More and more companies such as elance.com are popping up on the Web, creating an auction where everyone from screenwriters to scientists can sell his or her talents.

Andy Abramson, a sports market consultant, figures he makes 7 percent more as a gun for hire than he can make as a manager in a firm. The constant influx of new projects keeps the work interesting and flexible. But there is a dark side to "free agency." Contractors generally are not paid health or other benefits, and some get weary of having to search for every new gig.

Still, the ranks of free agents are growing. By 2010, 41 percent of the workforce will be employed on a contract basis, according to a poll by the Lansing, Michigan, market research firm EPIC/MRA. Career experts believe that like actors or athletes, talented business superstars will have agents. Groups of workers will come together to tackle projects jointly only to disband when the projects are finished, a model that's already common in Silicon Valley and Hollywood.

Increasingly, companies will keep their most prized employees on site and outsource everything else. For example, when the computer-display unit of Nokia entered the U.S. market, it did so with only five key employees. Sales, marketing, logistics, and technical support functions were farmed out. Microsoft has outsourced many of its tasks, although downsizing employees and subsequently outsourcing work to them have caused the company some legal problems.

And just because an employee is on staff doesn't mean she or he isn't thinking like a free agent. A typical 32-year-old, for example, has already held nine jobs, according to the U.S. Department of Labor. Experts predict that younger workers will hold as many as 20 different positions in their lifetimes.

According to Bruce Tulgan, the author of *Winning the Talent Wars,* getting top talent on your corporate team is critical no matter who the players are. Tulgan says corporations must abandon traditional ideas about the old-fashioned employee. He even envisions a day when companies no longer see employees who have left for other jobs as "traitors" but as "alumni" who are reemployable and are welcomed back.

SOURCES: Betty Caplan, "What Happened to Good Old Work?" *Africa News Service,* May 22, 2002 p.1008142u9658; condensed from Michelle Conlin, "And Now, the Just-in-Time Employee," *Business Week Online,* August 28, 2000.

Job Analysis   While issues of supply and demand are fairly "macro" activities that are conducted at an organizational level, HR planning also has a "micro" side called *job analysis*. **Job analysis** does two things.[3] First, it tells the HR manager about the job itself: the essential tasks, duties, and responsibilities involved in performing the job. This information is called a *job description*. Second, job analysis describes the skills, knowledge, abilities, and other characteristics needed to perform the job. This is called the *job specification*.

> **job analysis**
>
> A tool for determining what is done on a given job and what should be done on that job.

Job analysis provides the information that virtually every human resources activity requires. It assists with the essential HR programs: recruitment, training, selection, appraisal, and reward systems. For example, a thorough job analysis helps organizations defend themselves in lawsuits involving employment practices.[4] Ultimately, job analysis helps increase the value added by employees to the organization because it clarifies what is really required to perform effectively.

Staffing the Organization

Once HR planning is completed, managers can focus on staffing the organization. The staffing function consists of three related activities: recruitment, selection, and outplacement.

Recruitment

> **recruitment**
>
> The development of a pool of applicants for jobs in an organization.

Recruitment activities help increase the pool of candidates that might be selected for a job. Recruitment may be internal to the organization (considering current employees for promotions and transfers) or external. Each approach has advantages and disadvantages.[5]

Internal Recruiting   The advantages of internal recruiting are that employers know their employees, and employees know their organization. External candidates who are unfamiliar with the organization may find they don't like working there. Also, the opportunity to move up within the organization may encourage employees to remain with the company, work hard, and succeed. Recruiting from outside the company can be demoralizing to employees. Many companies, such as Sears Roebuck and Eli Lilly, prefer internal to external recruiting for these reasons.

Internal staffing has some drawbacks. If existing employees lack skills or talent, internal recruitment yields a limited applicant pool, leading to poor selection decisions. Also, an internal recruitment policy can inhibit a company that wants to change the nature or goals of the business by bringing in outside candidates. In changing from a rapidly growing, entrepreneurial organization to a mature business with more stable growth, Dell Computer went outside the organization to hire managers who better fit those needs.

Many companies that rely heavily on internal recruiting use a job-posting system. A *job-posting system* is a mechanism for advertising open positions, typically on a bulletin board. Texas Instruments uses job posting. Employees complete a request form indicating interest in a posted job. The posted job description includes a list of duties and the minimum skills and experience required.

External Recruiting   External recruiting brings in "new blood" to a company and can inspire innovation. Among the most frequently used sources of outside applicants are Internet job boards, newspaper advertisements, employee referrals, and college campus recruiting.

Newspaper advertising remains the most popular recruiting source. However, readership bases are declining as more job searchers turn to the Web. Employee referrals are another frequently used source of applicants.[6] Some companies actively encourage employees to refer their friends by offering cash rewards. The advantages of campus recruiting include a large pool of people from which to draw, applicants with up-to-date training, and a source of innovative ideas.[7]

The average rating for nine recruitment sources on a 5-point scale
(1 = not good, 3 = average, 5 = extremely good):

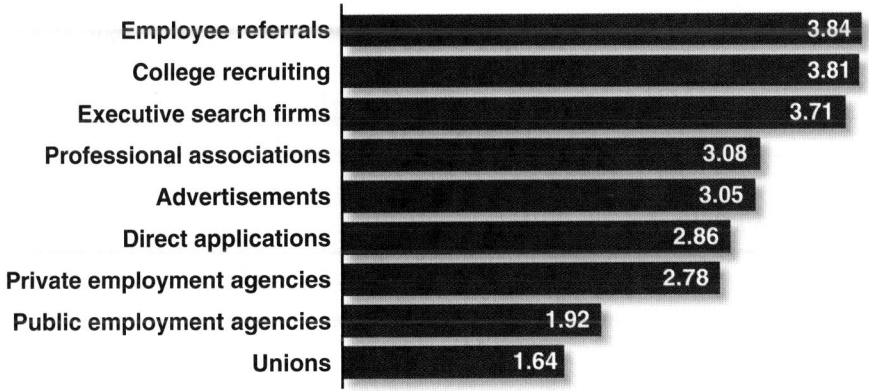

Employee referrals	3.84
College recruiting	3.81
Executive search firms	3.71
Professional associations	3.08
Advertisements	3.05
Direct applications	2.86
Private employment agencies	2.78
Public employment agencies	1.92
Unions	1.64

SOURCE: David E. Terpstra, "The Search for Effective Methods," *HRFocus*, May 1996, pp. 16–17. Reprinted by permission. Copyright © HRFocus, September 1996, www.ioma.com.

FIGURE 10.2
Effectiveness of
Recruitment Sources

The popularity of various recruiting methods notwithstanding, Figure 10.2 shows how 201 HR executives rated the effectiveness of nine different recruiting sources.

Selection

Selection builds on recruiting and involves decisions about whom to hire. As important as these decisions are, they are—unfortunately—at times made in very careless or cavalier ways. In this section we describe a number of selection instruments to which you may soon be exposed in your own careers.

> **selection**
>
> Choosing from among qualified applicants to hire into an organization.

Applications and Résumés Application blanks and résumés provide basic information to prospective employers. In order to make a first cut through candidates, employers review the profiles and backgrounds of various job applicants. Applications and résumés typically include information about the applicant's name, educational background, citizenship, work experiences, certifications, and the like. While providing important information, applications and résumés tend not to be extremely useful for making final selection decisions.

Interviews *Interviews* are the most popular selection tool, and every company uses some type of interview. However, employment interviewers must be careful about what they ask and how they ask it. Questions that are not job-related are prohibited. In an unstructured (or nondirective) interview, the interviewer asks different interviewees different questions. The interviewer may also use probes, that is, ask follow-up questions to learn more about the candidate.[8]

In a **structured interview,** the interviewer conducts the same interview with each applicant. There are two basic types of structured interview. The first approach—called the *situational interview*—focuses on hypothetical situations. Zale Corporation, a major jewelry chain, uses this type of structured interview to select sales clerks. A sample question is: "A customer comes into the store to pick up a watch he had left for repair. The watch is not back yet from the repair shop, and the customer becomes angry. How would you handle the situation?" The second approach—called the *behavioral description interview*—explores what candidates have actually done in the past. In selecting college students for an officer training program, the U.S. Army asks the following

> **structured interview**
>
> Selection technique that involves asking all applicants the same questions and comparing their responses to a standardized set of answers.

question to assess a candidate's ability to influence others: "What was the best idea you ever sold to a supervisor, teacher, peer, or subordinate?"

Reference Checks   *Reference checks* are another commonly used screening device. Virtually all organizations use either a reference or an employment and education record check. Although reference checking makes sense, reference information is becoming increasingly difficult to obtain as a result of several highly publicized lawsuits. In one case, an applicant sued a former boss on the grounds that the boss told prospective employers the applicant was a "thief and a crook." The jury awarded the applicant $80,000.[9]

Personality Tests   *Personality tests* are less popular for employee selection, largely because they are hard to defend in court.[10] However, they are regaining popularity, and chances are that at some point in your career you will complete some personality tests. A number of well-known paper-and-pencil inventories measure personality traits such as sociability, adjustment, and energy. Typical questions are "Do you like to socialize with people?" and "Do you enjoy working hard?"

Drug Testing   *Drug testing* is now a frequently used screening instrument. Since the passage of the Drug-Free Workplace Act of 1988, applicants and employees of federal contractors and Department of Defense contractors and those under Department of Transportation regulations have been subject to testing for illegal drugs. According to a survey by the American Management Association, 80 percent of U.S. firms test their employees and 94 percent rescind job offers to applicants who test positive.

Genetic testing tries to identify the likelihood of contracting a disease (such as emphysema) on the basis of a person's genetic makeup. It is far less common than drug testing and remains controversial.[11]

Cognitive Ability Tests   *Cognitive ability tests* are among the oldest employment selection devices. These tests measure a range of intellectual abilities, including verbal comprehension (vocabulary, reading) and numerical aptitude (mathematical calculations). About 20 percent of U.S. companies use cognitive ability tests for selection purposes.[12] Figure 10.3 shows some examples of cognitive ability test questions.

Performance Tests   *Performance tests* are procedures in which the test taker performs a sample of the job. Most companies use some type of performance test, typically for secretarial and clerical positions. The most widely used performance test is the typing test. However, performance tests have been developed for almost every occupation, including managerial positions. Assessment centers are the most notable offshoot of the managerial performance test.[13]

assessment center

A managerial performance test in which candidates participate in a variety of exercises and situations.

Assessment centers originated during World War II. A typical **assessment center** consists of 10 to 12 candidates who participate in a variety of exercises or situations; some of the exercises involve group interactions, and others are performed individually. Each exercise taps a number of critical managerial dimensions, such as leadership, decision-making skills, and communication ability. Assessors, generally line managers from the organization, observe and record information about the candidates' performance in each exercise. AT&T was the first organization to use assessment centers. Since then, a number of large organizations have used or currently are using the assessment center technique, including Bristol-Myers, the FBI, and Sears.

Integrity Tests   *Integrity tests* are used to assess a job candidate's honesty. Two forms of integrity tests are polygraphs and paper-and-pencil honesty tests. Polygraphs, or lie detector tests, have been banned for most employment purposes.[14] Paper-and-pencil honesty tests are more recent instruments for measuring integrity.

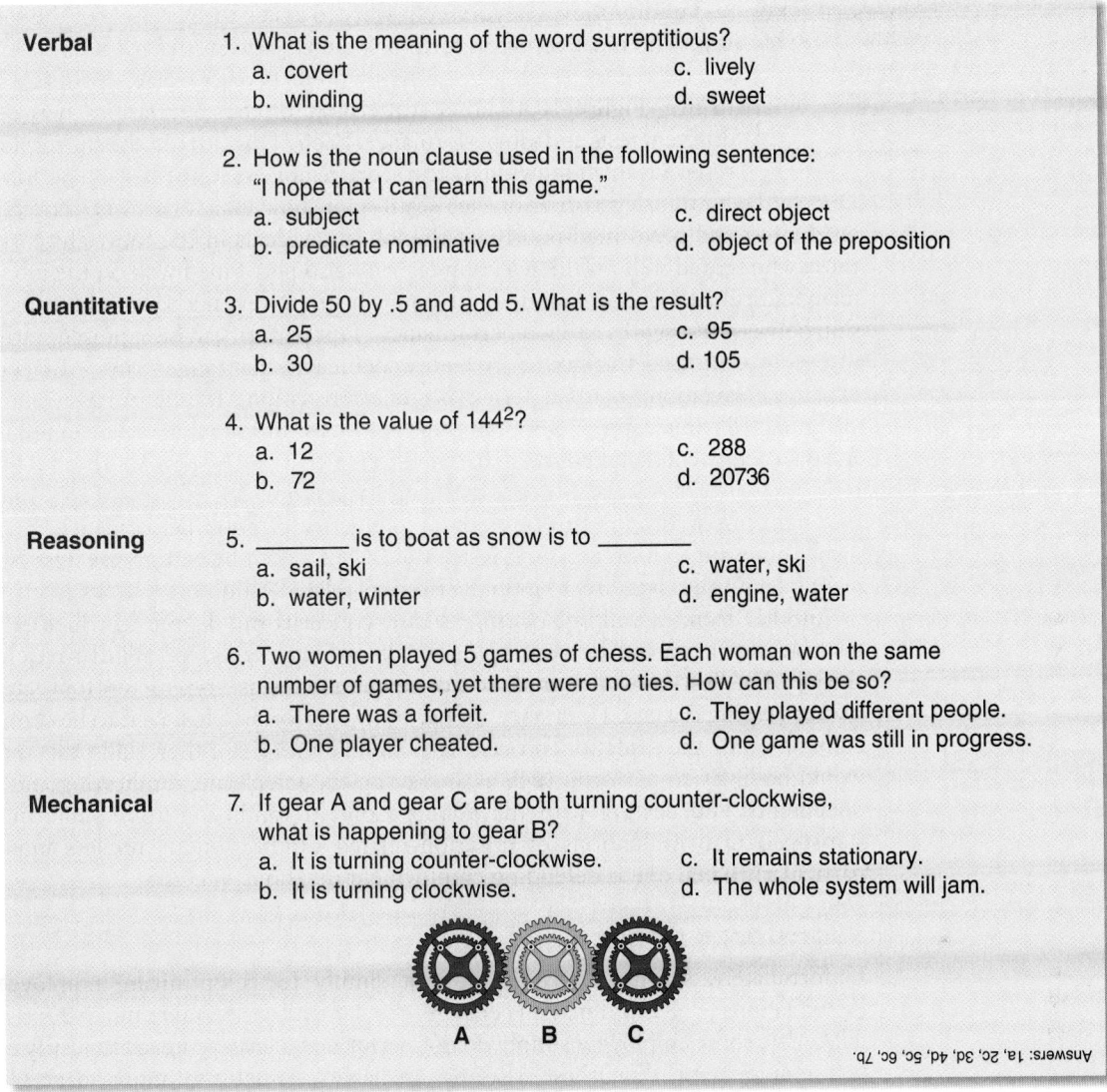

Verbal	1. What is the meaning of the word surreptitious?

Verbal

1. What is the meaning of the word surreptitious?
   a. covert   c. lively
   b. winding   d. sweet

2. How is the noun clause used in the following sentence:
   "I hope that I can learn this game."
   a. subject   c. direct object
   b. predicate nominative   d. object of the preposition

Quantitative

3. Divide 50 by .5 and add 5. What is the result?
   a. 25   c. 95
   b. 30   d. 105

4. What is the value of 144^2?
   a. 12   c. 288
   b. 72   d. 20736

Reasoning

5. _____ is to boat as snow is to _____
   a. sail, ski   c. water, ski
   b. water, winter   d. engine, water

6. Two women played 5 games of chess. Each woman won the same
   number of games, yet there were no ties. How can this be so?
   a. There was a forfeit.   c. They played different people.
   b. One player cheated.   d. One game was still in progress.

Mechanical

7. If gear A and gear C are both turning counter-clockwise,
   what is happening to gear B?
   a. It is turning counter-clockwise.   c. It remains stationary.
   b. It is turning clockwise.   d. The whole system will jam.

A   B   C

Answers: 1a, 2c, 3d, 4d, 5c, 6c, 7b.

SOURCE: George Bohlander, Scott Snell, and Arthur Sherman, *Managing Human Resources*, 12th ed. Copyright © 2001.
Reprinted by permission of South-Western, a division of Thomson Learning, www.thomsonrights.com.

FIGURE 10.3
Sample Measures of Cognitive Ability

These tests include questions such as whether a person has ever thought about steal-ing and whether he or she believes other people steal ("What percentage of people take more than $1 from their employer?"). Payless ShoeSource, based in Topeka, Kansas, has used an honesty test to reduce employee theft. Within only a year of implementing the program, inventory losses dropped by 20 percent, to less than 1 percent of sales. Despite compelling evidence such as this, the accuracy of these tests is still debatable.[15]

Reliability and Validity   Regardless of the method used to select employees, two crucial issues that need to be addressed are a test's reliability and its valid-ity. **Reliability** refers to the consistency of test scores over time and across alternative measurements. For example, if three different interviewers talked to the same job candidate but drew very different conclusions about the candidate's abilities, we might suspect that there were problems with the reliability of one or more of the selection tests or interview procedures.

reliability

The consistency of test scores over time and across alternative measurements.

validity

The degree to which a selection test predicts or correlates with job performance.

Validity moves beyond reliability to assess the accuracy of the selection test. The most common form of validity, *criterion-related validity*, refers to the degree to which a test actually predicts or correlates with job performance. Figure 10.4 shows scatterplots of the correlations between two different tests and job performance. Each of the dots on the scatterplots corresponds to an individual's test score relative to his or her job performance. Dots in the bottom-left corner of each scatterplot show individuals who scored poorly on the test and performed poorly on the job. Individuals in the top-right corner are those who scored well on the selection test and also performed well on the job. When many individual scores are plotted, the points begin to reveal a pattern in the relationship between test scores and job performance. This pattern can be captured statistically with a correlation coefficient (i.e., a validity coefficient) that ranges from -1.0 (a perfect negative correlation) to 1.0 (a perfect positive correlation). In reality, most validity coefficients fall somewhere in between these extremes. In Figure 10.4, for example, Test A has a validity coefficient of zero (0.0), indicating that there is no relationship between test scores and job success. Test B, however, has a validity coefficient of $.75$, indicating that high test scores tend to be strongly predictive of good performance. Managers would not want to use Test A—it is not valid—but would be wise to use Test B for selecting employees because it has high criterion-related validity.

Another form of validity, *content validity*, concerns the degree to which selection tests measure a representative sample of the knowledge, skills, and abilities required for the job. The best-known example of a content-valid test is a typing test for secretaries, because typing is a task a secretary almost always performs. However, to be completely content-valid, the selection process also should measure other skills the secretary would be likely to perform, such as answering the telephone, duplicating and faxing documents, and dealing with the public. Content validity is more subjective (less statistical) than evaluations of criterion-related validity, but is no less important, particularly when one is defending employment decisions in court.

Workforce Reductions

Unfortunately, staffing decisions do not simply focus on hiring employees. As organizations evolve and markets change, the demand for certain employees rises and falls. Also, some employees simply do not perform at a level required to justify continued employment. For these reasons, managers sometimes must make difficult decisions to terminate their employment.

Layoffs   As a result of the massive restructuring of American industry brought about by mergers and acquisitions, divestiture, and increased competition, organizations

FIGURE 10.4
Correlation Scatterplots

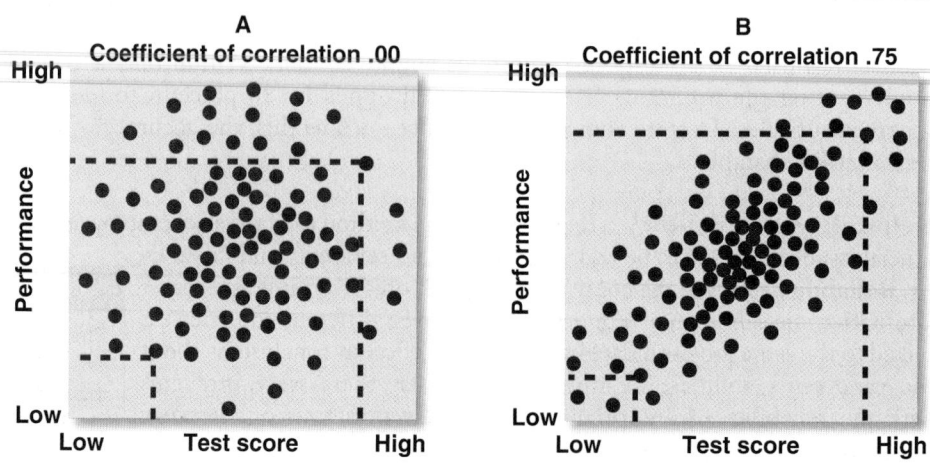

have been *downsizing*—laying off large numbers of managerial and other employees. Dismissing any employee is tough, but when a company lays off a substantial portion of its workforce, the results can rock the foundations of the organization.[16] The victims of restructuring face all the difficulties of being let go—loss of self-esteem, demoralizing job searches, and the stigma of being out of work. **Outplacement** is the process of helping people who have been dismissed from the company to regain employment elsewhere. This can help to some extent, but the impact of layoffs goes further than the employees who leave. For many of the employees who remain with the company, disenchantment, distrust, and lethargy overshadow the comfort of still having a job. In many respects, how management deals with dismissals will affect the productivity and satisfaction of those who remain. A well-thought-out dismissal process eases tensions and helps remaining employees adjust to the new work situation.

> **outplacement**
>
> **The process of helping people who have been dismissed from the company to regain employment elsewhere.**

Organizations with strong performance evaluation systems benefit because the survivors are less likely to believe the decision was arbitrary. Further, if care is taken during the actual layoff process—that is, if workers are offered severance pay and help in finding a new job—remaining workers will be comforted. Companies also should avoid stringing out layoffs, that is, dismissing a few workers at a time.

Termination   People sometimes "get fired" for poor performance or other reasons. Should an employer have the right to fire a worker? In 1884, a Tennessee court ruled: "All may dismiss their employee(s) at will for good cause, for no cause, or even for cause morally wrong." The concept that an employee may be fired for any reason is known as *employment-at-will* or *termination-at-will* and was upheld in a 1908 Supreme Court ruling.[17] The logic is that if the employee may quit at any time, the employer is free to dismiss at any time.

Since the mid-1970s, courts in most states have made exceptions to this doctrine. For example, public policy is a policy or ruling designed to protect the public from harm. One exception to the employment-at-will concept under public policy is employee whistle-blowing. For example, if a worker reports an environmental violation to the regulatory agency and the company fires him or her, the courts may argue that the firing was unfair because the employee acted for the good of the community. Another example is that employees may not be fired for serving on a jury.

Employers can avoid the pitfalls associated with dismissal by developing progressive and positive disciplinary procedures.[18] By *progressive*, we mean that a manager takes graduated steps in attempting to correct a workplace behavior. For example, an employee who has been absent receives a verbal reprimand for the first offense. A second offense invokes a written reprimand. A third offense results in employee counseling and probation, and a fourth results in a paid-leave day to think over the consequences of future rule infractions. The employer is signaling to the employee that this is the "last straw." Arbitrators are more likely to side with an employer that fires someone when they believe the company has made sincere efforts to help the person correct his or her behavior.

The **termination interview,** in which the manager discusses the company's position with the employee, is a stressful situation for both parties. Most experts believe that the immediate superior should be the one to deliver the bad news to employees. However, it is often good to have a third party, such as the HR manager, present to serve as a witness, to provide support for an anxious manager, or to diffuse anger by pulling the employee's attention away from the manager. In addition, some suggest that the best time to let someone go is Friday afternoon. However, the research evidence does not support this completely. Finally, it may be a good idea to conduct the termination interview in a neutral location, such as a conference room, so that the manager and employee can exit gracefully afterward. Table 10.1 provides some other guidelines for conducting a termination interview.[19]

> **termination interview**
>
> **A discussion between a manager and an employee about the employee's dismissal.**

Do's	Don'ts
• Give as much warning as possible for mass layoffs.	• Don't leave room for confusion when firing. Tell the individual in the first sentence that he or she is terminated.
• Sit down one on one with the individual, in a private office.	
• Complete a termination session within 15 minutes.	• Don't allow time for debate during a termination session.
• Provide written explanations of severance benefits.	• Don't make personal comments when firing someone; keep the conversation professional.
• Provide outplacement services away from company headquarters.	• Don't rush a fired employee offsite unless security is an issue.
• Be sure the employee hears about his or her termination from a manager, not a colleague.	• Don't fire people on significant dates, like the 25th anniversary of their employment or the day their mother died.
• Express appreciation for what the employee has contributed, if appropriate.	• Don't fire employees when they are on vacation or have just returned.

TABLE 10.1
Advice on Termination

SOURCE: S. Alexander, "Firms Get Plenty of Practice at Layoffs, but They Often Bungle the Firing Process," *The Wall Street Journal,* November 14, 1991, p. 31. Copyright © 1991 Dow Jones & Co., Inc. Reproduced with permission of Dow Jones & Co., Inc. via Copyright Clearance Center.

Legal Issues and Equal Employment Opportunity   In 1964, Congress passed the *Civil Rights Act*, which prohibits discrimination in employment based on race, sex, color, national origin, and religion. Title VII of the act specifically forbids discrimination in employment decisions such as recruitment, hiring, discharge, layoff, discipline, promotion, compensation, and access to training.[20] In 1972, the act was amended to allow the Equal Employment Opportunity Commission (EEOC) to take employers to court. The amendments also expanded the scope of the act to cover private and public employers with 15 or more employees, labor organizations, and public and private employment agencies.

Nevertheless, employment discrimination remains a controversial and costly issue for both organizations and individuals. Opponents of the 1991 *Civil Rights Act* argued that the act would force companies to hire on the basis of mandated quotas rather than choosing the most qualified candidates. But the new bill provides protection for many groups. The 1991 *Civil Rights Act* also provides for punitive damages to workers who sue under the *Americans with Disabilities Act*. The latter act, passed in 1990, prohibits employment discrimination against people with disabilities. Recovering alcoholics or drug abusers, cancer patients in remission, and AIDS victims are covered by this legislation.

Thousands of court cases have challenged employment decisions and practices. Today, one common reason why employers are sued is *adverse impact*, in which an apparently neutral employment practice adversely affects a *group* of individuals protected by the *Civil Rights Act*.[21] Discrimination issues provide a means for both minority groups and individuals to seek Title VII protection from employment discrimination. Today, the "Uniform Guidelines on Employee Selection Procedures" deal specifically with how to develop employment practices that comply with the law.[22]

Many other important staffing laws affect employment practices. The *Rehabilitation Act* of 1973 and the *Americans with Disabilities Act* of 1990 prohibit discrimination against persons with physical and mental disabilities. The *Age Discrimination in Employment Act (ADEA)* of 1967 and amendments in 1978 and 1986 prohibit discrimination against people age 40 and over. The *Immigration Act* of 1990 was designed to allow immigrants into the country based on what they can contribute to the economy.

This legislation nearly tripled the cap on immigrant visas to 140,000 but limited nonimmigrant or temporary visas to 90,000 (the latter category previously had been unrestricted). This new law complicates the hiring process for non-U.S. professionals under temporary visas such as investment bankers, scientists, and engineers. Finally, the *Worker Adjustment and Retraining Notification Act* of 1989, commonly known as the *WARN Act* or *Plant Closing Bill*, requires covered employers to give affected employees 60 days' written notice of plant closings or mass layoffs. Table 10.2 summarizes many of these major equal employment laws.

U.S. Equal Employment Laws   **TABLE 10.2**

Act	Major Provisions	Enforcement and Remedies
Equal Pay Act (1963)	Prohibits gender-based pay discrimination between two jobs substantially similar in skill, effort, responsibility, and working conditions.	Fines up to $10,000, imprisonment up to 6 months, or both; enforced by Equal Employment Opportunity Commission (EEOC); private actions for double damages up to 3 years' wages, liquidated damages, reinstatement, or promotion.
Title VII of Civil Rights Act (1964)	Prohibits discrimination based on race, sex, color, religion, or national origin in employment decisions: hiring, pay, working conditions, promotion, discipline, or discharge.	Enforced by EEOC; private actions, back pay, front pay, reinstatement, restoration of seniority and pension benefits, attorneys' fees and costs.
Executive Orders 11246 and 11375 (1965)	Requires equal opportunity clauses in federal contracts; prohibits employment discrimination by federal contractors based on race, color, religion, sex, or national origin.	Established Office of Federal Contract Compliance Programs (OFCCP) to investigate violations; empowered to terminate violater's federal contracts.
Age Discrimination in Employment Act (1967)	Prohibits employment discrimination based on age for persons over 40 years; restricts mandatory retirement.	EEOC enforcement; private actions for reinstatement, back pay, front pay, restoration of seniority and pension benefits; double unpaid wages for willful violations; attorneys' fees and costs.
Vocational Rehabilitation Act (1973)	Requires affirmative action by all federal contractors for persons with disabilities; defines disabilities as physical or mental impairments that substantially limit life activities.	Federal contractors must consider hiring disabled persons capable of performance after reasonable accommodations.
Americans with Disabilities Act (1990)	Extends affirmative action provisions of Vocational Rehabilitation Act to private employers; requires workplace modifications to facilitate disabled employees; prohibits discrimination against disabled.	EEOC enforcement; private actions for Title VII remedies.
Civil Rights Act (1991)	Clarifies Title VII requirements: disparate treatment impact suits, business necessity, job relatedness; shifts burden of proof to employer; permits punitive damages and jury trials.	Punitive damages limited to sliding scale only in intentional discrimination based on sex, religion, and disabilities.
Family and Medical Leave Act (1991)	Requires 12 weeks' unpaid leave for medical or family needs: paternity, family member illness.	Private actions for lost wages and other expenses, reinstatement.

Developing the Workforce

The skills and performance of employees and managers must be upgraded continually. Meeting this requirement involves training and development activities and appraising performance for the purposes of giving feedback and motivating people to perform at their best.

Training and Development

Large corporations spend an average of $63 million each on formal training annually. Add in informal education and development exercises and the total amount corporations spend exceeds $200 billion; that's slightly more than spending on public and private elementary and secondary education combined.[23]

Fortune 500 companies such as General Electric and General Motors have invested heavily in training. IBM's annual training costs have at times exceeded Harvard University's annual operating expenses. But the economic downturn after September 11, 2001, has taken a toll on training budgets. Many companies are now relying on cheaper methods of training such as e-learning and Web-based simulations to train large numbers of employees.

Cutting training programs presents its own dangers. The American Society for Training and Development argues that as a percentage of total payroll, the average organizational investment in training is too small.[24] This is of great concern in light of the fact that today's jobs require more education but that the education level of U.S. workers has not kept pace. What's more, companies need to ensure that employees who have survived layoffs can lead their organizations through tough times.

Overview of the Training Process   Although we use the general term *training* here, training sometimes is distinguished from development. **Training** usually refers to teaching lower-level employees how to perform their present jobs, while **development** involves teaching managers and professional employees broader skills needed for their present and future jobs. *Phase one* of training should include a **needs assessment.** An analysis should be conducted to identify the jobs, people, and departments for which training is necessary. Job analysis and performance measurements are useful for this purpose.

Phase two involves the design of training programs. Based on needs assessment, training objectives and content can be established. *Phase three* involves decisions about the training methods to be used (see Figure 10.5). A basic decision for selecting a training method is whether to provide on-the-job or off-the-job training. Examples of training methods include lectures, role playing, programmed learning, case discussion, business simulation, behavior modeling (watching a videotape and imitating what is observed), assigned readings, conferences, job rotation, vestibule training (practice in a simulated job environment), and apprenticeship training. Finally, *phase four* of training should evaluate the program's effectiveness in terms of employee reactions, learning, behavior transferred to the job, and bottom-line results.

Types of Training   Companies invest in training to enhance individual performance and organizational productivity. The most popular areas include computer applications, management skills/development and supervisory skills, technical skills, and communication skills. In addition to these, several topics are particularly noteworthy.

Orientation training typically is used to familiarize new employees with their new jobs, work units, and the organization in general. Done well, orientation training has a number of reputed benefits, including lower

training

Teaching lower-level employees how to perform their present jobs.

development

Teaching managers and professional employees broad skills needed for their present and future jobs.

needs assessment

An analysis identifying the jobs, people, and departments for which training is necessary.

orientation training

Training designed to introduce new employees to the company and familiarize them with policies, procedures, culture, and the like.

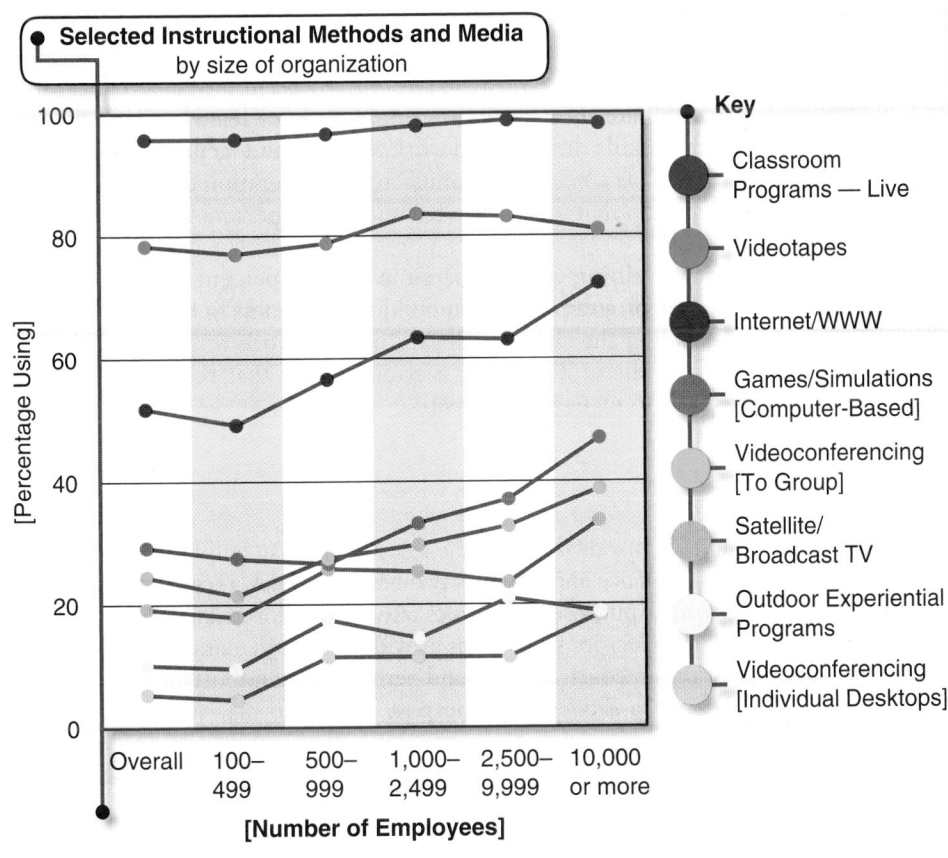

Selected Instructional Methods and Media
by size of organization

[Percentage Using]

Key

Classroom Programs — Live

Videotapes

Internet/WWW

Games/Simulations [Computer-Based]

Videoconferencing [To Group]

Satellite/ Broadcast TV

Outdoor Experiential Programs

Videoconferencing [Individual Desktops]

Overall | 100–499 | 500–999 | 1,000–2,499 | 2,500–9,999 | 10,000 or more

[Number of Employees]

SOURCE: "The Human Side of Business," From *Training* magazine, Copyright © 2000 by VNU Business Publications USA. Reproduced with permission of VNU Business Publications USA via Copyright Clearance Center.

FIGURE 10.5
Instructional Methods

When the U.S. Army called on Hollywood for help, it got it. The Army wanted better military training simulators for a variety of reasons, including cost. For example, the price tag for a live-fire exercise involving a single Bradley fighting vehicle is just under $5,000. Compare that to $11 for a combat exercise in a simulator. However, it wasn't just computer wizardry that the Army wanted to tap into but also compelling human stories similar to Hollywood dramas, says Jim Blake, senior scientist at the Army Simulation, Training and Instrumentation Command in Orlando, Florida. Blake and the rest of the brass believe that living, breathing scenarios better simulate the true emotional feel of combat, resulting in better decision making when bullets really do fly.

To lead the charge, the Army elisted the Institute of Creative Technologies (ICT) at the University of Southern California. ICT in turn signed on an A-team of Hollywood directors, writers, and special effects creators from films such as *Apollo 13, Star Wars,* and *Titanic* to work on the project. Sony was hired to adapt its PlayStation game console for virtual training, and Paramount Pictures was brought in to deliver Internet simulations to recruits. Other projects under way at ICT include simulations to help soldiers practice negotiation, learn new cultures, and deal with hostage situations.

Of course, military pilots regularly spend long hours on simulators to hone their skills in an environment where crashing has no consequences, and the U.S. Marines have used a modified version of the computer game *Doom* to train their troops for firefights. "The military would like to see a training experience achieve the highest level of fidelity," says Blake. So far the ICT simulations have been a big hit with the troops. After all, they sure beat boot camp.

SOURCES: Bruce Wiebusch, "War Game Boys," *Design News,* January 7, 2002, 57, p. 23; Dennis Blank, "Can Tinseltown's War Games Train G.I. Joe?" *Business Week Online,* January 3, 2001.

G.I. Joe Goes Hollywood

team training

Training that provides employees with the skills and perspectives they need to work in collaboration with others.

diversity training

Programs that focus on identifying and reducing hidden biases against people with differences and developing the skills needed to manage a diversified workforce.

employee turnover, increased morale, better productivity, and lower recruiting and training costs.

Team training has taken on more importance as organizations reorganize to facilitate individuals working together. Team training teaches employees the skills they need to work together and facilitates their interaction. Coca-Cola's Fountain Manufacturing Operation developed a team training program that focused on technical, interpersonal, and team interaction skills.[25]

Diversity training is now offered in over 50 percent of all U.S. organizations. The programs focus on building awareness of diversity issues as well as providing the skills employees need to work with others who are different from them. This topic is so important that the next chapter is devoted solely to managing diversity.

Performance Appraisal

performance appraisal (PA)

Assessment of an employee's job performance.

Performance appraisal (PA) is the assessment of an employee's job performance. Performance appraisal has two basic purposes. First, appraisal serves an *administrative* purpose. It provides information for making salary, promotion, and layoff decisions, as well as providing documentation that can justify these decisions in court. Second, and perhaps more important, performance appraisal serves a *developmental* purpose. The information can be used to diagnose training needs, career planning, and the like. Feedback and coaching based on appraisal information provide the basis for improving day-to-day performance.

What Do You Appraise?

Performance measures fall into one of three basic categories: traits, behaviors, and results. *Trait appraisals* involve subjective judgments about employee performance. They contain dimensions such as initiative, leadership, and attitude, and ask raters to indicate how much of each trait an employee possesses. Because trait scales tend to be ambiguous (as well as subjective), they often lead to personal bias and may not be suitable for obtaining useful feedback. Therefore, while this approach is extremely common—trait scales are easy to develop and implement—these scales unfortunately are often not valid.

Behavioral appraisals, while still subjective, focus more on observable aspects of performance. They were developed in response to the problems of trait appraisals. These scales focus on specific, prescribed behaviors which can help ensure that all parties understand what the ratings are really measuring. Because they are less ambiguous, they also can help provide useful feedback. Figure 10.6 contains an example of a behaviorally anchored rating scale (BARS) for evaluating quality.

Results appraisals tend to be more objective and can focus on production data such as sales volume (for a salesperson), units produced (for a line worker), or profits (for a

management by objectives (MBO)

A process in which objectives set by a subordinate and a supervisor must be coached within a given time period.

manager). One approach to results appraisals—called **management by objectives (MBO)**—involves a subordinate and a supervisor agreeing on specific performance goals (objectives). They then develop a plan that describes the time frame and criteria for determining whether the objectives have been reached. The aim is to agree on a set of objectives that are clear, specific, and reachable. For example, an objective for a salesperson might be to increase sales 25 percent during the following year. An objective for a computer programmer might be to complete two projects within the next six months. MBO has several advantages and can be useful when managers want to empower employees to adapt their behavior as they deem necessary in order to achieve desired results. Although MBO helps focus employees on reaching specific goals and encourages planning and development, it often focuses too much on short-term achievement and ignores long-term goals.

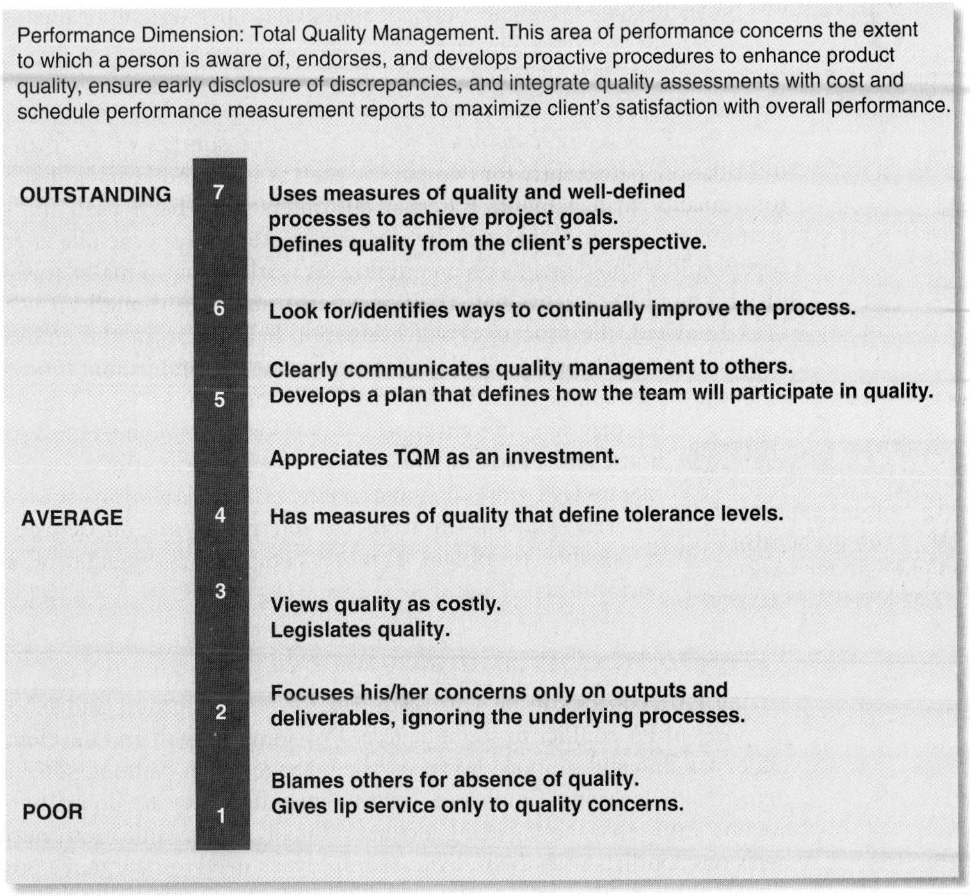

Performance Dimension: Total Quality Management. This area of performance concerns the extent to which a person is aware of, endorses, and develops proactive procedures to enhance product quality, ensure early disclosure of discrepancies, and integrate quality assessments with cost and schedule performance measurement reports to maximize client's satisfaction with overall performance.

OUTSTANDING	7	**Uses measures of quality and well-defined processes to achieve project goals. Defines quality from the client's perspective.**
	6	**Look for/identifies ways to continually improve the process.**
	5	**Clearly communicates quality management to others. Develops a plan that defines how the team will participate in quality.**
		Appreciates TQM as an investment.
AVERAGE	4	**Has measures of quality that define tolerance levels.**
	3	
		Views quality as costly. Legislates quality.
	2	**Focuses his/her concerns only on outputs and deliverables, ignoring the underlying processes.**
		Blames others for absence of quality.
POOR	1	**Gives lip service only to quality concerns.**

SOURCE: Landy, Jacobs, and Associates. Used with permission.

FIGURE 10.6
Example of BARS Used for Evaluating Quality

None of these performance appraisal systems is easy to conduct properly, and all have drawbacks that must be guarded against. In choosing an appraisal method, the following guidelines may prove helpful:

1. Always take legal considerations into account.
2. Base performance standards on job analysis.
3. Communicate performance standards to employees.
4. Evaluate employees on specific performance-related behaviors rather than on a single global or overall measure.
5. Document the PA process carefully.
6. If possible, use more than one rater (discussed in the next section).
7. Develop a formal appeal process.[26]

Who Should Do the Appraisal?

Just as there are multiple methods for gathering performance appraisal information, there are several different sources who can provide PA information. *Managers* and *supervisors* are the traditional source of appraisal information because they are often in the best position to observe an employee's performance. However, companies such as Coors, General Foods, and Digital are turning to peers and team members to provide input to the performance appraisal. *Peers* and *team member*s often see different dimensions of performance, and are often best at identifying leadership potential and interpersonal skills.

One increasingly popular source of appraisal is a person's subordinates. Appraisal by *subordinates* has been used by companies such as Xerox and IBM to give superiors feedback on how their employees view them. However, because this process gives employees power over their bosses, it normally is used only for developmental purposes.

Internal and external customers also are used as sources of performance appraisal information, particularly for companies, such as Ford and Honda, that are focused on total quality management. External customers have been used for some time to appraise restaurant employees, but internal customers can include anyone inside the organization who depends on an employee's work output. Finally, it is usually a good idea for employees to evaluate their own performance. Although *self-appraisals* may be biased upward, the process of self-evaluation helps increase the employee's involvement in the review process and is a starting point for establishing future goals.

Because each source of PA information has some limitations, and since different people may see different aspects of performance, companies such as Westinghouse and Eastman Kodak have taken to using multiple-rater approaches that involve more than one source for appraisal information. By combining different sources—in a process referred to as **360 degree appraisal**—it is possible to obtain a more complete assessment of an employee's performance.

---

360 degree appraisal

Process of using multiple sources of appraisal to gain a comprehensive perspective on one's performance.

How Do You Give Employees Feedback?

Giving PA feedback can be a stressful task for both managers and subordinates. The purposes of PA conflict to some degree. Providing growth and development requires understanding and support; however, the manager must be impersonal and be able to make tough decisions. Employees want to know how they are doing, but typically they are uncomfortable about getting feedback. Finally, the organization's need to make HR decisions conflicts with the individual employee's need to maintain a positive image.[27] These conflicts often make a PA interview difficult; therefore, managers should conduct such interviews thoughtfully.

There is no one "best" way to do a PA interview. The most difficult interviews are those with employees who are performing poorly. Here is a useful PA interview format to use when an employee is performing below acceptable standards:

1. Summarize the employee's specific performance. Describe the performance in behavioral or outcome terms, such as sales or absenteeism. Don't say the employee has a poor attitude; rather, explain which employee behaviors indicate a poor attitude.
2. Describe the expectations and standards, and be specific.
3. Determine the causes for the low performance; get the employee's input.
4. Discuss solutions to the problem, and have the employee play a major role in the process.
5. Agree to a solution. As a supervisor, you have input into the solution. Raise issues and questions, but also provide support.
6. Agree to a timetable for improvement.
7. Document the meeting.

Follow-up meetings may be needed. Here are some guidelines for giving feedback to an average employee:

1. Summarize the employee's performance, and be specific.
2. Explain why the employee's work is important to the organization.
3. Thank the employee for doing the job.
4. Raise any relevant issues, such as areas for improvement.
5. Express confidence in the employee's future good performance.

Designing Reward Systems

Reward systems are another major set of HRM activities. Most of this section will be devoted to monetary rewards such as pay and fringe benefits. Although traditionally pay has been of primary interest, benefits have received increased attention in recent years. Benefits currently make up a far greater percentage of the total payroll than they did in past decades.[28] The typical employer today pays nearly 40 percent of payroll costs in benefits. Accordingly, employers are trying to find ways to reduce these costs. Another reason for the growing interest in benefits is increased complexity. Many new types of benefits are now available, and tax laws affect myriad fringe benefits, such as health insurance and pension plans.

Pay Decisions

Reward systems can serve the strategic purposes of attracting, motivating, and retaining people. The wages paid to employees are based on a complex set of forces. Beyond the body of laws governing compensation, a number of basic decisions must be made in choosing the appropriate pay plan. Figure 10.7 illustrates some of the factors that influence the wage mix.

Three types of decisions are crucial for designing an effective pay plan: pay level, pay structure, and individual pay.

Pay level refers to the choice of whether to be a high-, average-, or low-paying company. Compensation is a major cost for any organization, and so low wages can be justified on a short-term financial basis. But being the high-wage employer—the highest-paying company in the region—ensures that the company will attract many applicants. Being a wage leader may be important during times of low unemployment or intense competition.

The *pay structure* decision is the choice of how to price different jobs within the organization. Jobs that are similar in worth usually are grouped together into job families. A pay grade, with a floor and a ceiling, is established for each job family. Figure 10.8 illustrates a hypothetical pay structure.

Finally, *individual pay decisions* concern different pay rates for jobs of similar worth within the same family. Differences in pay within job families are decided in two ways. First, some jobs are occupied by individuals with more seniority than others. Second, some people may be better performers who are therefore deserving of a higher level of pay.

FIGURE 10.7

Factors Affecting the Wage Mix

SOURCE: George Bohlander, Scott Snell, and Arthur Sherman, *Managing Human Resources,* 12th ed. Copyright © 2001. Reprinted by permission of South-Western, a division of Thomson Learning, www.thomsonrights.com.

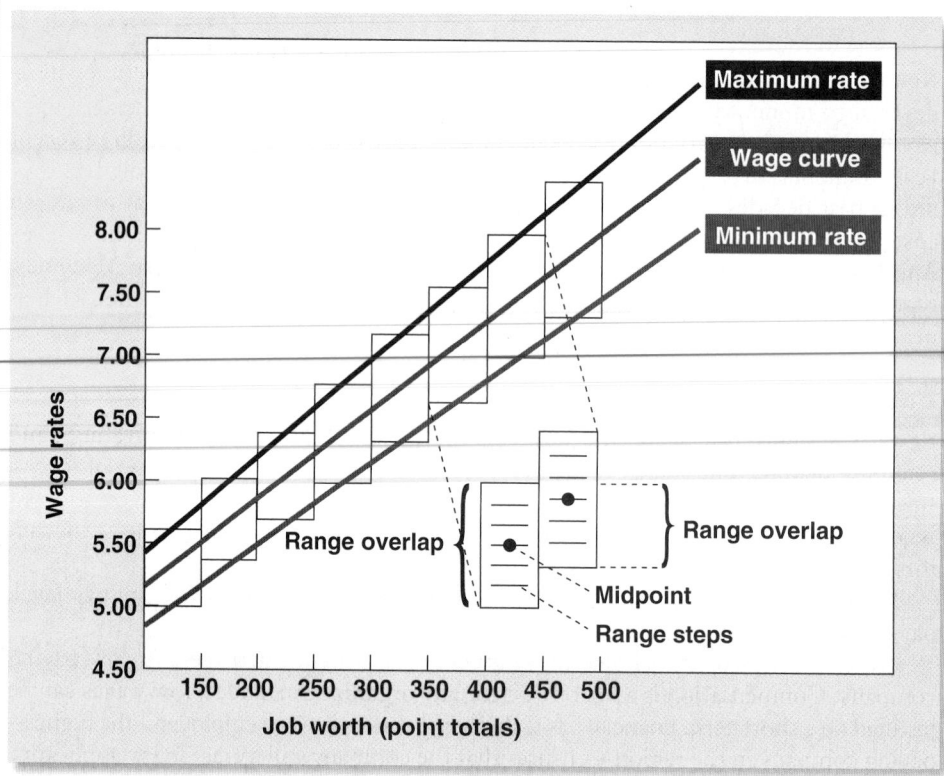

FIGURE 10.8
Pay Structure

SOURCE: From *Managing Human Resources*, 11th ed., by Sherman/Bohlander/Snell. Copyright © 1998. Reprinted with permission of South-Western, a division of Thomson Learning, www.thomsonrights.com.

Incentive Systems and Variable Pay

A number of incentive systems have been devised to encourage and motivate employees to be more productive.[29] (See Chapter 13 for more discussion of rewarding performance.) *Individual incentive plans* are the most common type of incentive plan. An individual incentive system consists of an objective standard against which a worker's performance is compared. Pay is determined by the employee's performance. Individual incentive plans are used frequently in sales jobs. If effectively designed, individual incentive plans can be highly motivating.

There are several types of group incentive plans in which pay is based on group performance. *Gainsharing plans* concentrate on saving money.[30] The best known is the Scanlon plan, which is based on a function of the ratio between labor costs and the sales value of production. An additional feature of the Scanlon plan is the use of employee committees to evaluate workers' suggestions for improving productivity.

Profit-sharing plans give employee incentives based on unit, department, plant, or company productivity. Nucor Steel, one of the nation's most profitable steel companies, relies heavily on a group-oriented profit-sharing plan. The entire company—4,000 employees—is broken down into bonus groups. For instance, each mill consists of groups of 25 to 35 employees who perform a complete task (e.g., melting and casting the steel or rolling the steel). Each group has a production standard and is paid for the amount of production over the specified level.[31]

When objective performance measures are not available but the company still wants to base pay on performance, it uses a *merit pay system*. Individuals' pay raises and bonuses are based on the judgmental merit rating they receive from their boss. Over the years, Lincoln Electric Company has been noted as having a particularly effective merit pay plan.[32]

Employee Benefits

Like pay systems, employee benefit plans are subject to regulation. Employee benefits are divided into those required by law and those optional for an employer.

The three basic required benefits are workers' compensation, social security, and unemployment insurance. *Workers' compensation* provides financial support to employees suffering a work-related injury or illness. *Social security*, as established in the Social Security Act of 1935, provides financial support to retirees; in subsequent amendments, the act was expanded to cover disabled employees. The funds come from payments made by employers, employees, and self-employed workers. *Unemployment insurance* provides financial support to employees who are laid off for reasons they cannot control. Companies that have terminated fewer employees pay less into the unemployment insurance fund; thus, organizations have an incentive to keep terminations at a minimum.

A large number of benefits are not required to be employer-provided. The most common are pension plans and medical and hospital insurance. Other optional employee benefits include dental insurance, life insurance, and vacation time. Because of the wide variety of possible benefits and the considerable differences in employee preferences and needs, companies often use **cafeteria** or **flexible benefit programs.** In this type of program, employees are given credits that they "spend" on benefits they desire. FinPac Corporation, a small computer software company, provides each employee with a required amount of life and disability insurance. Then employees use their credits toward individualized packages of additional benefits, including medical and dental insurance, dependent care, extra life insurance, and cash.

> **cafeteria benefit program**
>
> An employee benefit program in which employees choose from a menu of options to create a benefit package tailored to their needs

> **flexible benefit programs**
>
> Benefit programs in which employees are given credits to spend on benefits that fit their unique needs.

Legal Issues in Compensation and Benefits

A number of laws affect employee compensation and benefits. *The Fair Labor Standards Act (FLSA)* of 1938 set minimum wages, maximum hours, child labor standards, and overtime pay provisions. The Department of Labor monitors and enforces the FLSA. *Nonexempt* employees are entitled to premium pay for overtime (e.g., time and one-half). *Exempt* employees (e.g., executives, administrators, and professionals) are not subject to the overtime and minimum wage provisions.[33]

The *Equal Pay Act (EPA)* of 1963, now enforced by the EEOC, prohibits unequal pay for men and women who perform equal work. Equal work means jobs that require equal skill, effort, and responsibility and are performed under similar working conditions. The law does permit exceptions where the difference in pay is due to a seniority system, a merit system, an incentive system based on quantity or quality of production, or any other factor other than sex, such as market demand. Although equal pay for equal work may sound like common sense, many employers have fallen victim to this law by rationalizing that men, traditionally the "breadwinners," deserve more pay than women or by giving equal jobs different titles (senior assistant versus office manager) as the sole basis for pay differences.

One controversy concerns male and female pay differences within the same company. **Comparable worth** doctrine implies that women who perform *different* jobs of *equal* worth as those performed by men should be paid the same wage.[34] In contrast to the equal-pay-for-equal-work notion, comparable worth suggests that the jobs need *not* be the same to require the same pay. For example, nurses (predominantly female) were found to be paid considerably less than skilled craftworkers (predominantly male), even though the two jobs were found to be of equal value or worth.[35] Under the Equal Pay Act, this would not constitute pay discrimination because the jobs are very different. But under the comparable-worth concept, these findings would indicate discrimination because the jobs are of equal worth.

> **comparable worth**
>
> Principle of equal pay for different jobs of equal worth.

Miners rescued after being trapped 240-feet underground at the Black Wolf Coal Companies' Quecreek Mine in Somerset, Pennsylvania.

To date, no federal law requires comparable worth, and the Supreme Court has made no decisive rulings about it. However, some states have considered developing comparable-worth laws, and others already have implemented comparable-worth changes, raising the wages of female-dominated jobs. For example, Minnesota passed a comparable-worth law for public-sector employees after finding that women on average were paid 25 percent less than men. Several other states have comparable-worth laws for public-sector employees, including Iowa, Idaho, New Mexico, Washington, and South Dakota.[36]

Some laws influence mostly benefit practices. The *Pregnancy Discrimination Act* of 1978 states that pregnancy is a disability and qualifies a woman to receive the same benefits that she would with any other disability. The *Employee Retirement Income Security Act (ERISA)* of 1974 protects private pension programs from mismanagement. ERISA requires that retirement benefits be paid to those who vest or earn a right to draw benefits and ensures retirement benefits for employees whose companies go bankrupt or who otherwise cannot meet their pension obligations.

Health and Safety

The *Occupational Safety and Health Act (OSHA)* of 1970 requires employers to pursue workplace safety. Employers must maintain records of injuries and deaths caused by workplace accidents and submit to on-site inspections. Large-scale industrial accidents and nuclear power plant disasters worldwide have focused attention on the importance of workplace safety.

Coal mining is one of many industries that benefit from safety laws. Mining is one of the five most dangerous jobs to perform, according to the U.S. Bureau of Labor Statistics. Nearly every coal miner can name a friend or family member who has been killed, maimed, or stricken with black lung disease. "You die quick or you die slow," reports one mine worker. However, according to the Mine Safety and Health Administration, mines have become safer. In 1991, 61 miners died in the United States and 14,668 were injured, compared with 61 miners killed and 6,099 injured a decade later.[37]

Labor Relations

labor relations

The system of relations between workers and management.

Labor relations is the system of relations between workers and management. Labor unions recruit members, collect dues, and ensure that employees are treated fairly with respect to wages, working conditions, and other issues. When workers organize for the purpose of negotiating with management to improve their wages, hours, or working conditions, two processes are involved: unionization and collective bargaining. These processes have evolved over a 50-year period in the United States to provide important employee rights.[38]

Labor Laws

Try to imagine what life would be like with unemployment at 25 percent. Pretty grim, you would say. Legislators in 1935 felt that way too. Therefore, organized labor received its Magna Carta with the passage of the National Labor Relations Act.

The *National Labor Relations Act* (also called the *Wagner Act* after its legislative sponsor) ushered in an era of rapid unionization by (1) declaring labor organizations legal, (2) establishing five unfair employer labor practices, and (3) creating the National Labor Relations Board (NLRB). Today, the NLRB conducts unionization elections, hears unfair labor practices complaints, and issues injunctions against offending employers. The Wagner Act greatly assisted the growth of unions by enabling workers to use the law and the courts to organize and collectively bargain for better wages, hours, and working conditions.

Public policy began on the side of organized labor in 1935, but over the next 25 years the pendulum swung toward the side of management. The *Labor-Management Relations Act*, or *Taft-Hartley Act* (1947), protected employers' free-speech rights, defined unfair labor practices by unions, and permitted workers to decertify (reject) a union as their representative.

Finally, the *Labor-Management Reporting and Disclosure Act*, or *Landrum-Griffin Act* (1959), swung the public policy pendulum midway between organized labor and management. By declaring a bill of rights for union members, establishing control over union dues increases, and imposing reporting requirements for unions, Landrum-Griffin was designed to curb abuses by union leadership and rid unions of corruption.

Unionization

How do workers join unions? Through a union organizer or local union representative, workers learn what benefits they may receive by joining.[39] The union representative distributes authorization cards that permit workers to indicate whether they want an election to be held to certify the union to represent them. The National Labor Relations Board will conduct a certification election if at least 30 percent of the employees sign authorization cards. Management has several choices at this stage: to recognize the union without an election, to consent to an election, or to contest the number of cards signed and resist an election.

If an election is warranted, an NLRB representative will conduct the election by secret ballot. A simple majority of those voting determines the winner. Thus, apathetic workers who do not show up to vote in effect support the union. If the union wins the election, it is certified as the bargaining unit representative.

During the campaign preceding the election, efforts are made by both management and the union to persuade the workers how to vote. Most workers, though, are somewhat resistant to campaign efforts, having made up their minds well before the NLRB appears on the scene. If the union wins the election, management and the union are legally required to bargain in good faith to obtain a collective bargaining agreement or contract.

Why do workers vote for a union? Four factors play a significant role (see Figure 10.9).[40] First, economic factors are important, especially for workers in low-paying jobs; unions attempt to raise the average wage rate for their members. Second, job dissatisfaction encourages workers to seek out a union. Poor supervisory practices, favoritism, lack of communication, and perceived unfair or arbitrary discipline and discharge are specific triggers of job dissatisfaction. Third, the belief that the union can obtain desired benefits can generate a pro-union vote. Finally, the image of the union can determine whether a dissatisfied worker will seek out the union. Headline stories of union corruption and dishonesty can discourage workers from unionization.

Collective Bargaining

In the United States, management and unions engage in a periodic ritual (typically every three years) of negotiating an agreement over wages, hours, and working conditions. Two types of disputes can arise during this process. First, before an agreement is reached, the workers may go on strike to compel agreement on their terms. Such an action is known as an *economic strike* and is permitted by law. Once the agreement is signed, however, management and the union can still disagree over *interpretation* of the agreement. Usually they settle their disputes through arbitration. **Arbitration** is the use of a neutral third party, typically jointly selected, to resolve the dispute. The United States uses arbitration while an agreement is in effect to avoid *wildcat strikes* (in which workers walk off the job in violation of the contract) or unplanned work stoppages.

arbitration

The use of a neutral third party to resolve a labor dispute.

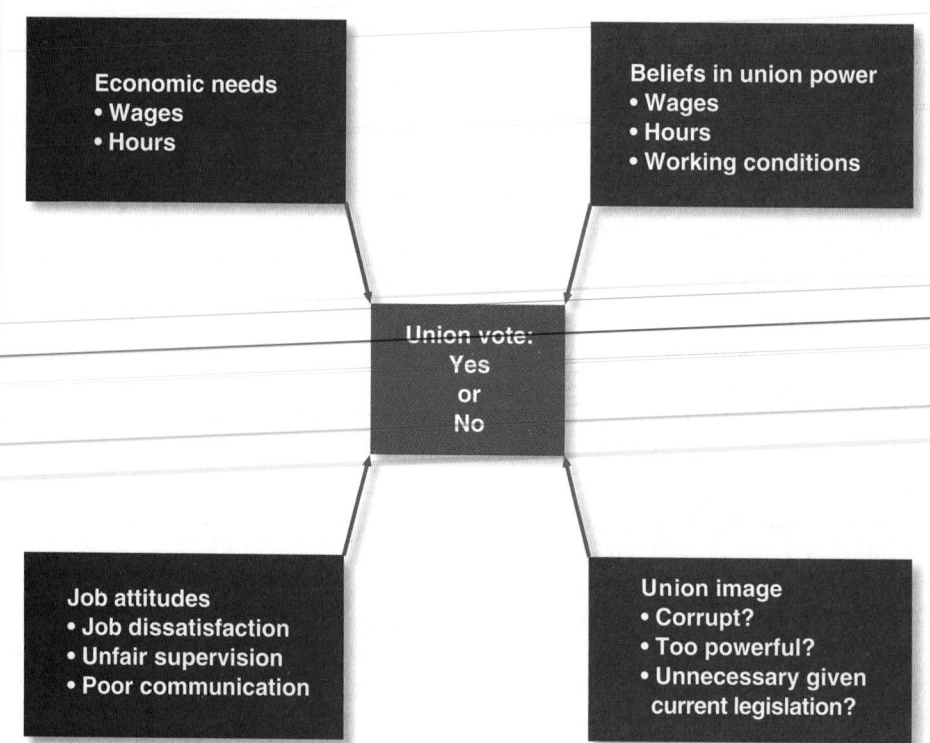

FIGURE 10.9
Determinants of Union
Voting Behavior

union shop

An organization with a union and a union security clause specifying that workers must join the union after a set period of time.

right-to-work

Legislation that allows employees to work without having to join a union.

What does a collective bargaining agreement contain? In a **union shop**, a union security clause specifies that workers must join the union after a set period of time. **Right-to-work** states, through restrictive legislation, do not permit union shops; that is, workers have the right to work without being forced to join a union. The southern United States has many right-to-work states. The wage component of the contract spells out rates of pay, including premium pay for overtime and paid holidays. Individual rights usually are specified in terms of the use of seniority to determine pay increases, job bidding, and the order of layoffs.

A feature of any contract is the grievance procedure. Unions perform a vital service for their membership in this regard by giving workers a voice in what goes on during both contract negotiations and administration through the grievance procedure.[41] In about 50 percent of discharge cases that go to arbitration, the arbitrator overturns management's decision and reinstates the worker.[42] Unions have a legal duty of fair representation, which means they must represent all workers in the bargaining unit and ensure that workers' rights are protected.

What Does the Future Hold?

In recent years, union membership has declined to less than 12 percent of the U.S. labor force as a consequence of changing laws concerning employee rights, global competition, decreased demand for the products of traditionally unionized industries, the rise of the service economy (which is difficult to unionize), and changing expectations of the new workforce. Some people applaud unions' apparent decline. Others hope for an eventual reemergence based on the potential power of management–union cooperation to help U.S. businesses in the global economy. Unions may play a different role in the future, one that is less adversarial and more cooperative with management. Unions are adapting to changing workforce demographics; they are paying more attention to women, older workers, and people who work at home. Elimination of inefficient work rules, the introduction of profit sharing, and a guarantee of no layoffs

Buzz Hargrove (L), President of the Canadian Auto Workers union, shakes hands with Tim Hartmann, Vice President of human resources for the Ford Motor Company of Canada.

were seen as a big step toward a fundamentally different, cooperative long-term relationship. What seems clear is that when companies recognize that their success depends on the talents and energies of employees, the interests of unions and managers begin to converge. Rather than one side exploiting the other, unions and managers find common ground based on developing, valuing, and involving employees. Particularly in knowledge-based companies, the balance of power is shifting toward employees. Individuals, not companies, own their own human capital. And these employees are free, within limits, to leave the organization, taking their human capital with them. This leaves organizations in a particularly vulnerable position if they manage poorly. To establish competitive capability, organizations are searching for ways to obtain, retain, and engage their most valuable resources: human resources.

KEY TERMS

360 degree appraisal, p. 316

Arbitration, p. 321

Assessment center, p. 306

Cafeteria benefit programs, p. 319

Comparable worth, p. 319

Development, p. 312

Diversity training, p. 314

Flexible benefit programs, p. 319

Human capital, p. 300

Human resources management (HRM), p. 300

Job analysis, p. 304

Labor relations, p. 320

Management by objectives (MBO), p. 314

Needs assessment, p. 312

Orientation training, p. 312

Outplacement, p. 309

Performance appraisal (PA), p. 314

Recruitment, p. 304

Reliability, p. 307

Right-to-work, p. 322

Selection, p. 305

Structured interview, p. 305

Team training, p. 314

Termination interview, p. 309

Training, p. 312

Union shop, p. 322

Validity, p. 308

SUMMARY OF LEARNING OBJECTIVES

Now that you have studied Chapter 10, you should know:

How companies use human resources management to gain competitive advantage.

To succeed, companies must align their human resources to their strategies. Effective planning is necessary to make certain that the right number and kind of employees are available to implement a company's strategic plan. It is clear that hiring the most competent people is a very involved process. Companies that compete on cost, quality, service, and so on also should use their staffing, training, appraisal, and reward systems to elicit and reinforce the kinds of behaviors that underlie their strategies.

Why companies recruit both internally and externally for new hires.

Some companies prefer to recruit internally to make certain that employees are familiar with organizational policies and values. AT&T's Resource Link is an example of a company trying very hard to make certain that available work goes to internal candidates before looking externally. In other instances, companies prefer to recruit externally to find individuals with new ideas and fresh perspectives.

The various methods available for selecting new employees.

There are a myriad of selection techniques from which to choose. Interviews and reference checks are the most common. Personality tests and cognitive ability tests measure an individual's aptitude and potential to do well on the job. Other selection techniques include assessment centers and integrity tests. Regardless of the approach used, any test should be able to demonstrate reliability (consistency across time and different interview situations) and validity (accuracy in predicting job performance).

Why companies spend so much on training and development.

People cannot depend on a set of skills for all of their working lives. In today's changing, competitive world, old skills quickly become obsolete and new ones become essential for success. Refreshing or updating an individual's skills requires a great deal of continuous training. Companies understand that gaining a competitive edge in quality of service depends on having the most talented, flexible workers in the industry.

How to determine who should appraise an employee's performance.

Many companies are using multiple sources of appraisal because different people see different sides of an employee's performance. Typically, a superior is expected to evaluate an employee, but peers and team members are often in a good position to see aspects of performance that a superior misses. Even an employee's subordinates are being asked more often today to give their input in order to get yet another perspective on the evaluation. Particularly in companies concerned about quality, internal and external customers also are surveyed. Finally, employees should evaluate their own performance, if only to get them thinking about their own performance, as well as to engage them in the appraisal process.

How to analyze the fundamental aspects of a reward system.

Reward systems are broken down into three basic components: pay level, pay structure, and individual pay determination. To achieve an advantage over competitors, executives may want to generally pay a higher wage to their company's employees, but this decision must be weighed against the need to control costs (pay-level decisions often are tied to strategic concerns such as these). To achieve internal equity (paying people what they are worth relative to their peers within the company), managers must look at the pay structure, making certain that pay differentials are based on knowledge, effort, responsibility, working conditions, seniority, and so on. Individual pay determination often is based on merit or the different contributions of individuals. In these cases it is important to make certain that men and women receive equal pay for equal work, and managers may wish to base pay decisions on the idea of comparable worth (equal pay for an equal contribution).

How unions influence human resources management.

Labor relations involve the interactions between workers and management. One mechanism by which this relationship is conducted is unions. Unions seek to present a collective voice for workers, to make their needs and wishes known to management. Unions negotiate agreements with management regarding a range of issues such as wages, hours, working conditions, job security, and health care. One important tool that unions can use is the grievance procedure established through collective bargaining. This gives employees a way to seek redress for wrongful action on the part of management. In this way, unions make certain that the rights of all employees are protected.

How the legal system influences human resources management.

The legal system influences managers by placing constraints on the ways potential and actual employees are treated. Equal opportunity laws ensure that companies do not discriminate in their hiring and training practices. The Fair Labor Standards Act and the Equal Pay Act ensure that people earn fair compensation for the contribution they make to the organization. The Occupational Safety and Health Act ensures that employees have a safe and healthy work environment. Labor laws seek to protect the rights of both employees and managers so that their relationship can be productive and agreeable.

DISCUSSION QUESTIONS

1. How will changes in the labor force affect HRM practices for year 2010?

2. Describe the major regulations governing HRM practices.

3. Define job analysis. Why is job analysis relevant to each of the six key HRM activities discussed in the chapter (i.e., planning, staffing, training, performance appraisal, reward systems, labor relations)?

4. What are the various methods for recruiting employees? Why are some better than others? In what sense are they better?

5. What is a "test"? Give some examples of tests used by employers.

6. What purpose does performance appraisal serve? Why are there so many different methods of appraisal?

7. What are some key ideas to remember when conducting a performance interview?

8. How would you define an effective reward system? What role do benefits serve in a reward system?

9. Why do workers join unions? What implications would this have for an organization that wishes to remain nonunion?

10. Discuss the advantages and disadvantages of collective bargaining for the employer and the employee.

Boomerang Hiring: Maybe You *Can* Go Back

Many workers fantasize about finding other jobs and saying "so long" to their current employers. What most people don't realize, though, is that about 30 percent of those who do move on really would like to hear from their old bosses. A growing number are even asking to return to their former jobs.

"Bomerang" employees—workers who have left their jobs for another position, say, at a dot-com, only to return later—are becoming more prevalent. It's not unusual for workers to find themselves missing their old jobs. Employees are "far less picky about where they work—as long as they can get work now," says Michael Fidrych, senior vice president at a Boston placement agency called The Communications Collaborative. And former bosses are frequently all too happy to welcome them back. "More than ever, our clients are asking us for individuals we have placed with them in the past," says Fidrych.

Some employees who leave voluntarily are lured back by higher salaries. Other employees who were good performers but were let go during tough economic times also make good candidates. "The clients are aware that [the employee's] prior experience ensures good quality and less 'ramp-up' time," says Fidrych. "Put simply, calling them back saves time and money."

Such is the case with Sara McCann, an account manager at South of Boston Media Group. "I wasn't actively searching for new employment," says McCann. However, an old co-worker contacted her about an opening after she had been at her new job for over a year. She says her prior experience definitely helped her land a new position in a new division at South of Boston: "It allowed me to have an insider's view on the company's missions and procedures. I was already familiar with the product."

Responding to the boomerang trend, many companies are reviewing and revamping their rehiring policies. Things that need to be considered in such a review include who is eligible to return, rehiring precedents that have already been set, legal issues surrounding 401(k)s and pensions, and what to do about tenure when it comes to vacation time and bonuses.

Bruce Meyer, a marketing specialist in human capital practices, advises employers and employees to be realistic with regard to

their expectations. "The reason [employees] return in times of trouble and uncertainty is that we all tend to look back at things we know and things we're comfortable with," Meyer says. In many instances, though, that sense of security can't be re-created because circumstances change after a departure. Still, employers and employees with realistic expectations have a very good chance of forging a new, successful relationship, he says. Companies can improve their chances of successfully hiring boomerang employees if they do the following:

- Examine their policies, keeping in mind that some employees may return to the company after having left.
- Reject handling each rehire on a case-by-case basis. Develop policies on how returning employees are going to be treated, but make sure they're flexible.
- Examine whether rehiring policies actually create an incentive for employees to leave and return later.
- Examine the history of the person you are considering rehiring. What was the reason he or she left in the first place?
- Hire the best person for the job regardless of rehiring policies.
- Differentiate between employees who leave to take other jobs and those who are on protected absences such as military, family, or medical leave.

QUESTIONS

1. Why is boomerang hiring becoming more prevalent?

2. What are some of the benefits and costs of rehiring former employees?

3. Does rehiring help or hurt a company in the long run?

SOURCES: Chelsea Lower, "You Can Go Back Again: Return Workers a Viable Option—'Boomerang' Employees Allow Firms to Forego Searches and Training," *Boston Business Journal*, December 14, 2001, pp. 33–34; Barbara Jorgensen, "Deja Vu," *Electronic Business*, July 2000, p. 58.

10.1 The "Legal" Interview

OBJECTIVES

1. To introduce you to the complexities of employment law.
2. To identify interview practices that might lead to discrimination in employment.

INSTRUCTIONS

1. Working alone, review the text material on interviewing and discrimination in employment.
2. In small groups, complete the "Legal" Interview Worksheet.
3. After the class reconvenes, group spokespersons present group findings.

"Legal" Interview Worksheet

The employment interview is one of the most critical steps in the employment selection process. It also may be an occasion for discriminating against individual employment candidates. The following represents questions that interviewers often ask job applicants. Identify the legality of each question by circling L (legal) or I (illegal) and briefly explain your decision.

Interview Question	Legality	Explanation
1. Could you provide us with a photo for our files?	L I	_____
2. Have you ever used another name (previous married name or alias)?	L I	_____
3. What was your maiden name?	L I	_____
4. What was your wife's maiden name?	L I	_____
5. What was your mother's maiden name?	L I	_____
6. What is your current address?	L I	_____
7. What was your previous address?	L I	_____
8. What is your social security number?	L I	_____
9. Where was your place of birth?	L I	_____
10. Where were your parents born?	L I	_____
11. What is your national origin?	L I	_____
12. Are you a naturalized citizen?	L I	_____
13. What languages do you speak?	L I	_____
14. What is your religious/church affiliation?	L I	_____
15. What is your racial classification?	L I	_____
16. How many dependents do you have?	L I	_____
17. What are the ages of your dependent children?	L I	_____
18. What is your marital status?	L I	_____
19. How old are you?	L I	_____
20. Do you have proof of your age (birth certificate or baptismal record)?	L I	_____
21. Whom do we notify in case of an emergency?	L I	_____
22. What is your height and weight?	L I	_____
23. Have you ever been arrested?	L I	_____
24. Do you own your own car?	L I	_____
25. Do you own your own house?	L I	_____

26. Do you have any charge accounts?	L I	_____
27. Have you ever had your salary garnished?	L I	_____
28. To what organizations do you belong?	L I	_____
29. Are you available to work on Saturdays and Sundays?	L I	_____
30. Do you have any form of disability?	L I	_____

10.2 The Pay Raise

OBJECTIVES

1. To further your understanding of salary administration.
2. To examine the many facets of performance criteria, performance criteria weighting, performance evaluation, and rewards.

INSTRUCTIONS

1. Working in small groups, complete the Pay Raise Worksheet.
2. After the class reconvenes, group spokespersons present group findings.

Pay Raise Worksheet

April Knepper is the new supervisor of an assembly team. It is time for her to make pay raise allocations for her subordinates. She has been budgeted $30,000 to allocate among her seven subordinates as pay raises. There have been some ugly grievances in other work teams over past allocations, and so April has been advised to base the allocations on objective criteria that can be quantified, weighted, and computed in numerical terms. After she makes her allocations, April must be prepared to justify her decisions. All of the evaluative criteria available to April are summarized as follows:

Employee	EEO status	Seniority	Output Rating*	Absent Rate	Supervisory Ratings			
					Skills	Initiative	Attitude	Personal
David Bruce	Caucasian Male	15 yrs.	0.58	0.5%	Good	Poor	Poor	Nearing retirement. Wife just passed away. Having adjustment problems.
Eric Cattalini	Caucasian Male	12 yrs.	0.86	2.0	Excellent	Good	Excellent	Going to night school to finish his BA degree.
Chua Li	Asian Male	7 yrs.	0.80	3.5	Good	Excellent	Excellent	Legally deaf.
Marilee Miller	Black Female	1 yr.	0.50	10.0	Poor	Poor	Poor	Single parent with three children.
Victor Munoz	Hispanic Male	3 yrs.	0.62	2.5	Poor	Average	Good	Has six dependents. Speaks little English.
Derek Thompson	Caucasian Male	11 yrs.	0.64	8.0	Excellent	Average	Average	Married to rich wife. Personal problems.
Sarah Vickers	Caucasian Female	8 yrs.	0.76	7.0	Good	Poor	Poor	Women's activist. Wants to create a union.

*Output rating determined by production rate less errors and quality problem.

CHAPTER 11

Managing the Diverse Workforce

"e pluribus unum"

CHAPTER OUTLINE

Diversity: A Brief History

Diversity Today

    The Size of the Workforce

    The Workers of the Future

    The Age of the Workforce

Managing Diversity versus Affirmative Action

    Competitive Advantage through Diversity

    Challenges of a Diverse Workforce

Multicultural Organizations

How Organizations Can Cultivate a Diverse Workforce

    Top Management Leadership and Commitment

    Organizational Assessment

    Attracting Employees

    Diversity Training

    Retaining Employees

LEARNING OBJECTIVES

After studying Chapter 11, you will know:

1. How changes in the U.S. workforce make diversity a critical organizational and managerial issue.

2. The distinction between affirmative action and managing diversity.

3. How companies can gain a competitive edge by managing diversity effectively.

4. What challenges a company is likely to encounter with a diverse workforce.

5. How an organization can take steps to cultivate diversity.

SEEING THE BENEFITS OF HIRING THE BLIND

For the blind, finding a job is likely to involve a lot of search effort. Even the simplest things, such as filling out a job application, can pose problems; not very many applications come in a Braille version.

Barry Honig heads the executive-placement firm Riskon in New York City. Honig takes a special interest in helping people with disabilities find jobs, especially the blind. Why? Because he is blind. He says clients want to hire people with disabilities but often are confused about the steps they need to take and the accommodations they need to make.

Technology solutions allow the visually impaired to operate computers, making the workplace more diverse.

In recent years, assistive technology has been the key to putting many visually impaired people into the marketplace by allowing them to do things such as operate computers. Low-tech and high-tech solutions both exist. Low-tech solutions include something as simple as putting silicon on a knob to let blind employees know if an operating switch is on or off or putting Braille labels on vending machines in break rooms. High-tech devices enlarge type on computers, produce a synthesized voice that reads the content aloud, and translate the output into Braille. "Window-Eyes," a Windows 2000–based screen reader, is a top-selling enlargement product. JAWS (Job Access with Speech) for Windows speaks the letters on the keyboard as a blind person types them. Enlargement and voice-output devices vary in price from about $500 to $2,000. Braille scanners and printers can run from $500 for basic models to $15,000 for top-of-the-line machines.

But the issue isn't just about companies having the right technology and the money to spend on it—it's about having the right mindset for hiring the blind. Honig says that during the first meeting with a candidate, an interviewer should ask if the blind person needs help—but not insist on giving it. He or she also should realize that visually impaired persons won't be familiar with the layout of the office and should ask them if extending an arm for guidance would help. And, of course, don't pet or distract seeing-eye dogs. As for applicants, Honig advises: "Be up-front and be comfortable about your disability. Ask the question, 'How am I going to do my job?' And be very honest with the answer."

Honig, who worked on Wall Street for several years, says that the financial services industry is a good hunting ground for the blind: "It's rough and tumble, especially on Wall Street, but people have no problem hiring the disabled as long as they can make them money." Technology industries are also good because people working in that field are used to thinking of technology as a "barrier-breaking tool."

The tech industry is where Margaret Redman and her husband, David, work. Both are visually impaired and are employed by Earthlink in technology support. David was the first visually impaired person in the company. "My husband and I showed them that a blind person could be a [tech assistant] on the phones, so they hired more blind people, who we both trained," Margaret Redman explains.

Honig says that companies want to do the right thing but sometimes need a little push to understand the benefits of hiring the blind. "I know having a disability is a life of being told what your limits are by employers and co-workers," says Margaret Redman. "But my husband and I have been working to push the limits people and companies think of."

Source: Suzanne Robitaille, "Bringing the Blind into the Workplace," *Business Week Online*, January 23, 2002.

Setting the Stage

managing diversity

Managing a culturally diverse workforce by recognizing the characteristics common to specific groups of employees while dealing with such employees as individuals and supporting, nurturing, and utilizing their differences to the organization's advantage.

As the case in "Setting the Stage" illustrates, building a more diverse workforce is one of corporate America's biggest challenges. **Managing diversity** involves such things as recruiting, training, promoting, and utilizing to full advantage individuals with different backgrounds, beliefs, capabilities, and cultures. Managing diversity is more than just hiring minorities and women. It means understanding and appreciating employee differences to build a more effective and profitable organization.

This chapter examines the meaning of diversity and the management skills and organizational processes involved in managing the diverse workforce effectively. We also explore the social and demographic changes and economic and employment shifts that are creating this changing U.S. workforce.

Diversity: A Brief History

Managing diversity is not a new or futuristic management issue. From the late 1800s to the early 1900s, most of the groups that immigrated to the United States were from Italy, Poland, Ireland, and Russia. Members of those groups were considered outsiders because they did not speak English and had different customs and work styles. They struggled, often violently, to gain acceptance in industries such as steel, coal, automobile manufacturing, insurance, and finance. In the 1800s, it was considered poor business practice for white Protestant–dominated insurance companies to hire Irish, Italians, Catholics, or Jews.

By the 1960s, the struggle for acceptance by the various white ethnic and religious groups had succeeded. Once the white male members of the various ethnic and religious groups were assimilated successfully into the workforce, the stage was set for the next "outsiders": cultural and racial minorities and women. Today more than half the U.S. workforce consists of people other than white, U.S.-born males, and this trend is expected to continue. Two-thirds of all global migration is into the United States.

The traditional American image of diversity has been one of assimilation. The United States was considered the "melting pot" of the world, a country in which ethnic and racial differences were blended into an American purée. In real life, many ethnic and most racial groups retained their identities, but they did not express them at work. Employees often abandoned most of their ethnic and cultural distinctions while at work to keep their jobs and get ahead. Many Europeans came to the United States, Americanized their names, perfected their English, and tried to enter the mainstream as quickly as possible.

Today's immigrants are willing to be part of an integrated team, but they no longer are willing to sacrifice their cultural identities to get ahead. Nor will they have to do so. Companies are finding that they should be more accommodating of differences, and that doing so pays off in business. Companies also are beginning to realize that their customers have become increasingly diverse and that retaining a diversified workforce can provide a competitive advantage in the marketplace.

Diversity Today

Today *diversity* refers to far more than skin color and gender. It is a broad term used to refer to all kinds of differences, as summarized in Figure 11.1. These differences include religious affiliation, age, disability status, military experience, sexual orientation, economic class, educational level, and lifestyle in addition to gender, race, ethnicity, and nationality.

Although members of different groups (white males, people born during the Depression, homosexuals, Vietnam veterans, Hispanics, Asians, women, blacks, etc.) share within their groups many common values, attitudes, and perceptions, there is also much diversity within each of these categories. Every group is made up of individuals who are unique in personality, education, and life experiences. There may be more differences among, say, three Asians from Thailand, Hong Kong, and Korea than among a white, an African-American, and an Asian all born in Chicago. And not all white males share the same personal or professional goals and values or behave alike.

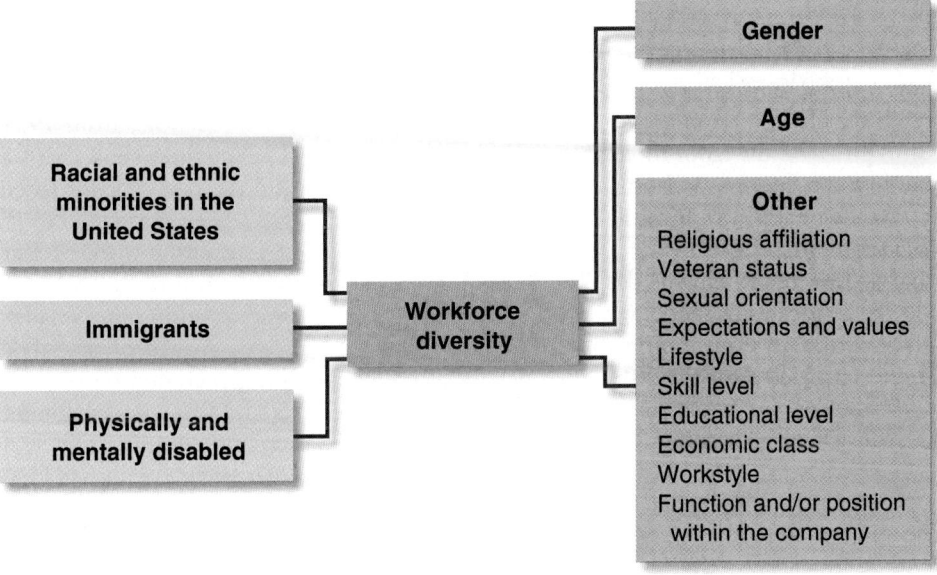

FIGURE 11.1
Components of a
Diversified Workforce

Thus, managing diversity may seem a contradiction within itself. It means being acutely aware of characteristics *common* to a group of employees, while also managing these employees as *individuals*. Managing diversity means not just tolerating or accommodating all sorts of differences, but supporting, nurturing, and utilizing these differences to the organization's advantage. U.S. businesses will not have a choice of whether to have a diverse workforce; if they want to survive, they must learn to manage a diverse workforce sooner or better than their competitors do.

Diversity programs, which began popping up in the early 1980s, are everywhere. A Society for Human Resource Management (SHRM) study found that three of four Fortune 500 firms and more than a third (36 percent) of respondents from firms of all sizes offer them. Another issue altogether, however, is their effectiveness. Figure 11.2 shows the results of a SHRM study of the perceived benefit of these diversity programs.

FIGURE 11.2
How Effective Is Your
Diversity Program?

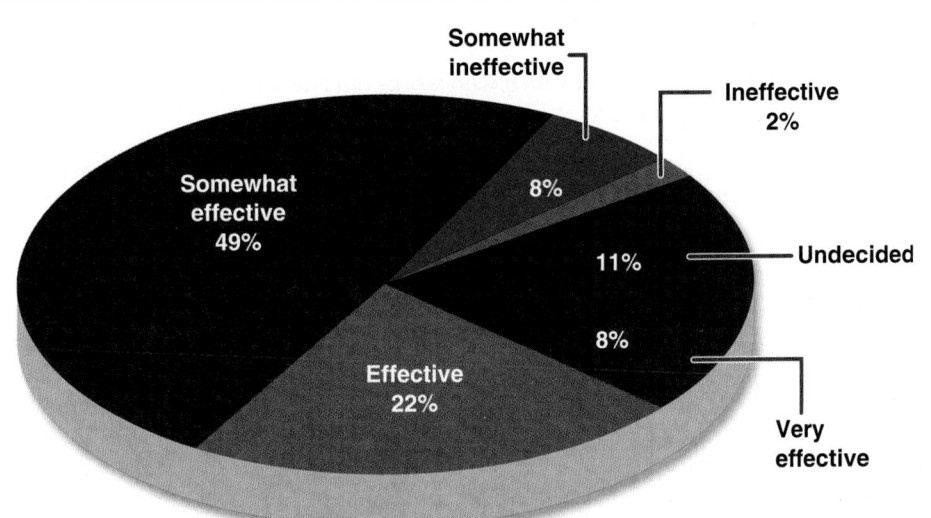

SOURCE: Helen Lippman, "Harnessing the Power of Diversity," *Business and Health,* June 1999, 17, no. 6, p. 40. Reprinted with permission from *Business & Health,* Medical Economics Co., Montvale, NJ.

The Size of the Workforce

The U.S. civilian labor force is expected to reach 158 million by 2010, up from 125 million in 1990. Though a 21 percent growth rate over 20 years may seem high, it is actually much lower than was the case in previous decades. For example, from 1975 through 1990, the labor force grew at a rate of 33 percent. The numbers show a slowing in both the number of people joining the labor force and the rate of labor force growth, which is now projected at 1.2 percent per year.[1]

During most of its history, the United States experienced a surplus of workers. But that is expected to change despite the economic recession at the turn of this century. Lower birthrates in the U.S. and other developed countries are resulting in a smaller labor force. An even more substantial slowdown in the pace of growth of the labor force is projected for the 2015–2025 period, as the baby-boom generation retires.[2]

Employers are likely to outsource some work to factories and firms in developing nations where birthrates are high and the labor supply is more plentiful. But they will have to compete for the best candidates from a relatively smaller and more diverse U.S. labor pool. Employers will need to know who these new workers are—and must be prepared to meet their needs.

The Workers of the Future

Until recently, white American-born males dominated the U.S. workforce. Businesses catered to their needs. However, while this group still constitutes the largest percentage of workers—at about 38 percent of the workforce—it accounts for only 15 percent of the net growth (those entering minus those leaving). The remaining 85 percent of workforce growth is accounted for by U.S.-born white females, immigrants, and minorities.

Gender Issues   One of the most important developments in the U.S. labor market has been the growing number of women working outside the home. Social changes during the 1960s and 1970s coupled with financial necessity caused women to enter the workforce and redefine their roles. Consider this:

- Women make up about 47 percent of the workforce.
- Ninety-nine of 100 women will work for pay at some point in their lives.
- The overall labor force participation rate of women continues to increase while the participation rate of men declines.
- The long-term increase in the female labor force largely reflects the greater frequency of paid work among mothers.
- In 1973, 20 percent of multiple job holders were women. Today, a full 40 percent of women hold multiple jobs.
- One of every five married women who works outside the home earns more than her husband does.[3]

For many women, as well as their spouses, balancing work life with family responsibilities and parenting presents an enormous challenge. Although men's roles in our society have been changing, women still adopt the bulk of family responsibilities, including homemaking, child care, and care of elderly parents. Employers who make it easier for their workers to balance work and family commitments are better able to recruit and retain women. To attract top talent, some companies are offering benefits such as on-site child care and physical therapy, in-home care for the disabled and elderly family members, and surveys to determine how satisfied employees are with their work-life balance.

However, the average full-time working female still earns much less than does the average working male—only about 75 percent as much as men in the same job (recall the discussion in Chapter 10 about equal pay and comparable worth). Fortunately, the median earnings of young women (ages 16 to 24) are 95 percent of those of young men. At the level of vice president, the average female earns over 40 percent less than a male in the same job. However, this situation is getting somewhat better. Over the last decade, the average total compensation of women executives has more than doubled, but it still falls significantly short of that of men. At the very top, the disparities are even greater: The 20 highest-paid male executives in the United States in 2001 averaged $138.5 million in total compensation (including salary, stock options, and so forth), while the 20 best-paid women earned only $11.2 million each.[4]

Some of the discrepancy in compensation is the consequence of both the level and types of jobs women receive. As women—along with minorities—move up the corporate ladder, they encounter a "glass ceiling." The **glass ceiling** is an invisible barrier that makes it difficult for women and minorities to move beyond a certain level in the corporate hierarchy. In 1981, for example, only 1 percent of executives in *Fortune 500* companies were women, and by 1991 this number had increased to only 3 percent. But the situation is improving, albeit too slowly. Today, the percentage of women who hold the title of executive vice president has jumped to almost 13 percent. Across all management levels, the picture is even more encouraging. Since 1981, the percentage of women managers has nearly doubled. Women also hold about 12 percent of all board seats in Fortune 500 companies. Nonetheless, evidence persists that women who climb the corporate ladder are faced with making choices between their careers and their families. According to the General Accounting Office, nearly 60 percent of male managers have children at home, compared with 40 percent of female managers.[5] Table 11.1. lists top women executives and the companies for which they work. Table 11.2 shows the best companies for women according to the National Association of Female Executives.

glass ceiling
An invisible barrier that makes it difficult for certain groups, such as minorities and women, to move beyond a certain level in the organizational hierarchy.

One persistent concern for both men and women is the problem of **sexual harassment.** Sexual harassment falls into two different categories. The first, *quid pro quo harassment*, occurs when "submission to or rejection of sexual conduct is used as a basis for employment decisions." The second type of harassment, *hostile environment*, occurs when unwelcome sexual conduct "has the purpose or effect of unreasonably interfering with job performance or creating an intimidating, hostile, or offensive working environment." Table 11.3 shows the basic components of an effective sexual harassment policy. Companies such as Avon, Corning, and Metro-Goldwyn-Mayer have found that a strong commitment to diversity leads to fewer problems with sexual harassment.[6]

sexual harassment
Conduct of a sexual nature that has negative consequences for employment.

Before moving on, it is important to note that gender issues and the changing nature of work do not apply just to women. In some ways, the changing status of women has given men the opportunity to redefine their roles, expectations, and lifestyles. Some men are deciding that there is more to life than corporate success and are choosing to scale back work hours and commitments in order to spend time with their families. Worker values are shifting toward personal time, quality of life, self-fulfillment, and family. Workers today, both men and women, are looking to achieve a balance between career and family.

Minorities and Immigrants In addition to gender issues, the importance and scope of diversity are evident in the growth of racial minorities and immigrants in the workforce. Consider these facts:

- Minorities and immigrants hold approximately one of every four jobs in the United States.
- Nonwhites make up only about one-third of the growth rate in the workforce. Asian and Hispanics workforces are growing the fastest, followed by the African-American workforce.

Women like Anne M. Mulcahy, President and CEO of Xerox, are taking their place on the top rung of the corporate ladder.

TABLE 11.1   The A-List: Top Women Executives

Rank	Name	Company	Title
1	Carly Fiorina	Hewlett-Packard	Chairman and CEO
2	Betsy Holden	Kraft Foods	Co-CEO
3	Meg Whitman	eBay	President and CEO
4	Indra Nooyi	PepsiCo	President and CFO
5	Andrea Jung	Avon Products	Chairman and CEO
6	Anne Mulcahy	Xerox	Chairman and CEO
7	Karen Katen	Pfizer	EVP; President, Pharmaceuticals Group
8	Pat Woertz	ChevronTexaco	EVP, Downstream
9	Abigail Johnson	Fidelity Management & Research	President
10	Oprah Winfrey	Harpo Entertainment Group	Chairman
11	Ann Moore	AOL Time Warner	Chairman and CEO, Time Inc.
12	Judy McGrath	Viacom	President, MTV Networks Music Group
13	Colleen Barrett	Southwest Airlines	President and COO
14	Shelly Lazarus	Ogilvy & Mather Worldwide Lucent	Chairman and CEO
15	Pat Russo	Lucent Technologies	President and CEO
16	Betsy Bernard	AT&T	President and CEO, AT&T Consumer
17	Amy Brinkley	Bank of America	Chief Risk Officer
18	Lois Juliber	Colgate-Palmolive	COO
19	Sherry Lansing	Viacom	Chairman, Motion Picture Group, Paramount
20	Stacey Snider	Vivendi Universal	Chairman, Universal Pictures
21	Judy Lewent	Merck	EVP and CFO
22	Marjorie Magner	Citigroup	COO, Global Consumer Group
23	Ann Livermore	Hewlett-Packard	President, HP Services
24	Cathleen Black	Hearst Magazines	President
25	Doreen Toben	Verizon	EVP and CFO

- Ethnic Americans now constitute nearly 25 percent of the total population.
- By 2020, most of California's entry-level workers will be Hispanic.
- English has become the second language for much of the population in California, Texas, and Florida.
- The number of foreign-born U.S. residents is at the highest level in U.S. history, representing 1 in 10 U.S. residents.
- The younger Americans are, the more likely they are to be persons of color.
- At least 6.8 million people in the United States identify themselves as multiracial.[7]

These numbers indicate that the term *minority*, as it is used typically, may soon become outdated. Particularly in urban areas where white males do not predominate, managing diversity means more than eliminating discrimination; it means capitalizing on the wide variety of skills available in the labor market. Organizations that do not take full advantage of the skills and capabilities of minorities and immigrants are severely limiting their potential talent pool and their ability to understand and capture minority markets.

Even so, the evidence shows some troubling disparities in employment. Compared to white males who in 2001 had an unemployment rate of 3.7 percent, the unemployment rate for African-American males over 20 years old was 8.0 percent. In the same year, the weekly earnings of white males was around $694 compared to $518 for

Rank	Name	Company	Title
26	Amy Pascal	Sony	Chairman, Columbia Pictures
27	Vivian Banta	Prudential Financial	Vice Chairman, Insurance
28	Janet Robinson	New York Times Co.	SVP, Newspaper Operations
29	Pam Strobel	Exelon	EVP; CEO Exelon Energy Delivery
30	Dina Dublon	J.P. Morgan Chase	EVP and CFO
31	Nancy Peretsman	Allen & Co.	EVP and Managing Director
32	Susan Arnold	Procter & Gamble	Beauty & Feminine Care
33	Mary Kay Haben	Kraft Foods	Group VP, Kraft Foods North America
34	Deb Henretta	Procter & Gamble	President, Global Baby Care
35	Carole Black	Lifetime Entertainment Services	President and CEO
36	Jamie Gorelick	Fannie Mae	Vice Chair
37	Marce Fuller	Mirant	President and CEO
38	Kathi Seifert	Kimberly-Clark	EVP
39	Anne Sweeney	Walt Disney	President, ABC Cable Networks
40	Marilyn Carlson Nelson	Carlson Cos.	Chairman and CEO
41	Anne Stevens	Ford Motor	VP, North America Vehicle Operations
42	Sallie Krawcheck	Sanford C. Bernstein	Chairman and CEO
43	Carol Tomé	Home Depot	EVP and CFO
44	Marion Sandler	Golden West Financial	Co-Chairman and Co-CEO
45	Louise Francesconi	Raytheon	VP; President, Missile Systems
46	Vanessa Castagna	J.C. Penney	EVP; CEO, J.C. Penney Stores
47	Larree Renda	Safeway	EVP, Retail Operations
48	Dawn Lepore	Charles Schwab	Vice Chair
49	Fran Keeth	Royal Dutch Petroleum	President and CEO, Shell Chemical LP
50	Heidi Miller	Bank One	EVP and CFO

SOURCE: "Most Powerful Women in Business," *Fortune*, October 14, 2002. Reprinted with permission.

African-Americans and $438 for Hispanics.[8] Additionally, the Bureau of Labor Statistics has found that there are fewer executive, administrative, and managerial people of color employed throughout the nation. White people hold 17.8 million executive, administrative, and managerial positions compared to 1.6 million African-American people and 1.1 million people of Hispanic origin.

To address these problems, many organizations are working to do a better job of providing opportunities to minorities. Dunn and Bradstreet, for example, sponsors summer internship programs for minority MBA students. Lockheed Martin has partnered the American Management Association's Operation Enterprise to establish two-week paid summer internship programs for high school and college students. These internship programs help students and organizations learn about one another and, ideally, turn into full-time employment opportunities. Table 11.4 shows the top 10 companies for diversity recruitment and retention according to DiversityInc. com.

Mentally and Physically Disabled   The largest unemployed minority population in the United States is people with disabilities. It is composed of people of all ethnic backgrounds, cultures, and ages. According to the U.S. Census Bureau, in the last decade the number of Americans with disabilities increased 25 percent, outpacing any other subgroup of the U.S. population. Of the nearly 70 million families in the United

TABLE 11.2 Best Companies for Women

Rank	Company	Rank in 2000	Total Employees	Women Employees	Women Department/ Division Heads	Women on Board of Directors	Women Among Top 5 Earnings
1	Avon	1	7,188	5,332	47%	6 (55%)	2
2	Scholastic	3	7,430	5,120	249 (52%)	4 (31%)	3
3	Liz Claiborne	7	6,745	4,923	123 (63%)	3 (30%)	1
4	Aetna	6	36,148	28,469	19 (36%)	4 (33%)	None
5	Washington Mutual Inc.	4	42,049	29,073	880 (49%)	4 (24%)	1
6	Prudential Financial Group	15	31,899	17,709	1,489 (39%)	3 (14%)	1
7	TIAA-CREF	–	6,044	3,312	121 (35%)	9 (30%)	None
8	Hewlett-Packard	5	41,000	15,000	82 (23%)	2 (22%)	3
9	The New York Times Company	–	14,000	5,861	57 (29%)	3 (21%)	1
10	WellPoint Health Networks Inc.	9	14,020	10,699	242 (46%)	3 (38%)	1
11	Lincoln Financial Group	25	6,536	4,218	227 (30%)	3 (27%)	None
12	SBC Communications Inc.	13	199,029	95,534	79 (29%)	6 (29%)	None
13	Advantica Restaurant Group	12	42,856	22,182	39 (39%)	2 (20%)	1
14	Fannie Mae	22	4,499	2,396	237 (45%)	4 (31%)	1
15	CIGNA	–	39,574	30,460	867 (41%)	2 (18%)	None
16	Merck & Co., Inc.	10	43,896	24,132	1,308 (33%)	3 (23%)	1
17	Principal Financial Group	–	13,861	9,846	296 (35%)	4 (29%)	None
18	USA Education, Inc. ("Sallie Mae")	Honor Roll	5,695	3,909	45 (41%)	2 (13%)	None
19	State Street	11	15,628	7,468	551 (34%)	3 (17%)	1
20	The Phoenix Companies, Inc.	Honor Roll	1,461	823	32 (40%)	2 (13%)	1
21	Sears, Roebuck and Co.	Honor Roll	122,332	60,714	59 (26%)	2 (20%)	1
22	Con Edison	17	12,655	1,937	30 (23%)	3 (23%)	1
23	Federated Department Stores Inc.	Honor Roll	150,009	113,311	4 (18%)	2 (18%)	1
24	The Allstate Corporation	24	39,384	23,769	512 (31%)	2 (17%)	None
25	IBM	23	147,862	46,043	521 (22%)	2 (13%)	None

SOURCE: Reprinted with permission from February 2002 *Executive Female Magazine*, the publication of the National Association for Female Executives (www.nafe.com).

1. Develop a comprehensive organizationwide policy on sexual harassment and present it to all current and new employees. Stress that sexual harassment will not be tolerated under any circumstances. Emphasis is best achieved when the policy is publicized and supported by top management.

2. Hold training sessions with supervisors to explain Title VII requirements, their role in providing an environment free of sexual harassment, and proper investigative procedures when charges occur.

3. Establish a formal complaint procedure in which employees can discuss problems without fear of retaliation. The complaint procedure should spell out how charges will be investigated and resolved.

4. Act immediately when employees complain of sexual harassment. Communicate widely that investigations will be conducted objectively and with appreciation for the sensitivity of the issue.

5. When an investigation supports employee charges, discipline the offender at once. For extremely serious offenses, discipline should include penalties up to and including discharge. Discipline should be applied consistently across similar cases and among managers and hourly employees alike.

6. Follow up on all cases to ensure a satisfactory resolution of the problem.

TABLE 11.3
Basic Components of an Effective Sexual Harassment Policy

SOURCE: George Bohlander, Scott Snell, and Arthur Sherman, *Managing Human Resources*, 12th ed. Copyright © 2001. Reprinted by permission of South-Western, a division of Thomson Learning, www.thomsonrights.com.

States, more than 20 million have at least one member with a disability. Over the last decade, only about 10 percent of severely disabled adults have been employed. Meanwhile, fully two-thirds of disabled adults without jobs say they want to work.[9]

The Americans with Disabilities Act (ADA), introduced in Chapter 10, defines a disability as a physical or mental impairment that substantially limits one or more major life activities. Examples of such physical or mental impairments include those resulting from conditions such as orthopedic, visual, speech, and hearing impairments; cerebral palsy; epilepsy; muscular dystrophy; multiple sclerosis; HIV infections; cancer; heart disease; diabetes; mental retardation; emotional illness; specific learning disabilities; drug abuse; and alcoholism.[10]

The strengths and weaknesses of the ADA can be demonstrated in two ways. There has been a dramatic increase in accessibility to public facilities since its passage. But the unemployment rate for disabled persons remains virtually unchanged since the ADA was passed in 1990. As Fred Grandy, president and CEO of Goodwill Industries International, says, "The Americans with Disabilities Act, on balance, has created a more favorable environment" for people with disabilities, but it has not actually

1. JPMorgan Chase
2. Procter & Gamble
3. Pitney Bowes
4. Verizon
5. FleetBoston
6. Sempra
7. American Airlines
8. Eastman Kodak
9. Deloitte & Touche
10. Wells Fargo

TABLE 11.4
Top 10 Companies for Diversity Recruitment and Retention

SOURCE: Copyright © 2002, DiversityInc.com. Reproduced with permission.

improved their employment fortunes. For that segment of the U.S. population, unemployment typically is about 70 percent. And in that figure lies the debate.[11]

Individuals with disabilities have found themselves isolated from job opportunities largely because they have lacked access to educational and workplace environments. In addition, the attitudes of many employers and those of the disabled themselves have been barriers to employment. Today laws and technology are providing access to education and jobs. For most businesses, the mentally and physically disabled represent a largely unexplored labor market. Frequently, employers have found disabled employees are more dependable than typical employees, miss fewer days of work, and exhibit lower turnover.

One high-profile test of the limits of the ADA's applicability is Casey Martin's lawsuit against the Professional Golf Association (PGA). Because he has a degenerative condition of the muscle and bone in his right leg, Martin cannot walk an entire round of golf (which is required under PGA rules). In order that he might compete, Martin sued the PGA under the ADA for the right to use a golf cart in tournaments and won.

The Age of the Workforce

The baby-boom generation (born between 1946 and 1964) is aging, which will cause the average age of the workforce to increase to around 41 by the year 2008. The number of people age 50 to 65 will increase at more than twice the rate of the overall population, and by 2008 over 16 percent of the workforce will be 55 years of age or older. At the same time, the number of younger workers (ages 16 to 24) is expected to drop to 16 percent in 2008.[12]

As a result of these trends, the Bureau of Labor Statistics projects that entry-level workers will be in short supply and that fewer new workers will enter the labor force than will be lost through retirement.[13] Many older employees are opting for early retirement even though there is no longer a mandatory retirement age and life expectancies have increased. Companies therefore need to retain and hire older, experienced workers.

Retirement-age workers can be encouraged to remain in or reenter the workforce on a flexible or part-time basis, whether for economic reasons, desire for social interaction, or the need to be productive. Table 11.5 shows how creative companies are rethinking their retirement policies and solving their skilled-labor shortage by finding ways to attract and retain people over 55. These companies save on turnover and training costs and capitalize on the experience of their older employees.

TABLE 11.5

Top Five Approaches for More Fully Utilizing Older Employees

Approaches to More Fully Utilizing Older Employees	Approaches Considered Very or Moderately Effective	Businesses that Have Implemented the Approach
Benefit packages targeted toward older employees	68%	18%
Part-time work arrangements with continuation of benefits	64	30
Educating managers about ways to utilize older employees	60	25
Increased availability of part-time work for older employees (regardless of benefits)	55	36
Skill training for older employees	55	44

SOURCE: "American Business and Older Employees: A Survey of Findings," American Association of Retired Persons (AARP). Copyright © 2002 AARP (www.aarp.org). Reprinted with permission.

Four of five baby boomers say they'll be showing up for work at least part-time for years to come. In *Beyond 50: A Report to the Nation on Economic Security,* the American Association of Retired Persons (AARP) takes a look at the economic and social well-being of this fast-growing age group. Government data from the Bureau of Labor Statistics already show an uptick in the number of older workers punching in. In 2001, 32.3 percent of people age 55 and over were in the labor force, the highest participation rate for this group since 1980.

Business Week Online reporter Jennifer Gill spoke with John Rother, the AARP's director of legislation and public policy, about recent labor-force trends and the 50-plus worker. Here are edited excerpts of their conversation:

Q: John, do you think corporate America is doing enough to both attract and keep 50-plus workers?
A: We're in a very tight labor market. And it's certainly less expensive to hold on to a good employee who's already trained and loyal to the company than it is to go out and recruit. Nonetheless, we don't see very many employers who are doing the kinds of things that would specifically be targeted to older workers—to keep them on the job or to hire new ones. It's disappointing.

We did a survey in 2000 of employers, and [they] rated older workers very highly. And yet, they didn't have phased retirement programs or part-time work arrangements with continuing benefits. So they seem to appreciate the need and the skills, but they haven't yet figured out what to do to attract and retain older employees.

We know that most older workers want job flexibility. They want the opportunity to work fewer hours, to work part-year, or take more extended time off to be with grandchildren. Flexible benefits are part of that as well so that people who cut back their hours aren't in a position of losing their health insurance or pensions.

Q: Why haven't more companies implemented phased retirement programs?
A: I think a lot of it is simply not having a model that they can copy or not being sure that the effort that it takes to get something up and running is going to pay off. The academic studies are in place, and there's the experience of companies that use these programs [to prove] that [phased retirement programs] are very effective. But for many human resources departments, it's not at the top of their list of things to focus on.

Q: If I'm a 50-plus job seeker, how can I figure out if a potential employer is serious about hiring older workers?
A: Again, every company and every job classification has differences. But what speaks most strongly to the sincerity of the interest in hiring older workers is hiring older workers. If there are other people who have been brought into the company at an older age, that certainly is [a] powerful [message].

It's not just age, though. One issue that I think people should take seriously is keeping their skills up to date. Some companies really disadvantage their older workers by not giving them the same training opportunities that they give to younger workers.

Q: If I'm looking for a part-time position or a flexible work arrangement, should I bring that up during the interview?
A: In a tight labor market, if the person feels that he or she has skills that would be helpful to the company, then it's certainly better to be clear up-front about what you're willing to do. But it's a question of how accurately you can assess your relative bargaining power.

Q: The *Beyond 50* report finds that labor-force participation for people 65 and over appears to be bouncing back a bit. Why?
A: That's one of the key findings from our report. The trend to early retirement has taken a turn. In about 1985 [the number of people working beyond age 65] bottomed out, and there has been an increase since then.

Primarily it's [because of] opportunities in the labor force, but on top of that there are two trends driving this, and they're at different ends of the labor spectrum. Unfortunately, at the low end, with more and more people arriving at retirement without pensions or without much in the way of savings, there's going to be a very large number of people who are really going to have to work.

On the other end of the labor spectrum, people who are highly skilled and highly educated want to continue working because they have interesting jobs, and they see their job as part of their self-expression. For both of those reasons, we think that the number of people working beyond age 65, at least part-time, will probably increase in the future.

Q: How do you think baby boomers will approach retirement?
A: Baby boomers are at a point in their lives where their careers are very important to them. For many boomers, work is the key to their identity. Are they going to want to continue having some [working] relationship? Yes. But will they continue to want to work the hours that they're working, or necessarily just stay in the same job? I doubt that.

Q: Do you think we'll see more people working beyond 70 or even 75?
A: People who work in that age group are few and far between, and mostly they're one extreme or the other—[either] they are trying to supplement a very inadequate level of income, or they're unique in their ability to make contributions. Or they are people who just love what they do. You know, like many people in Congress, for example.

SOURCE: *Jennifer Gill, "As the Workforce Ages . . ." Business Week Online,* June 28, 2001.

That's what it says on William Payson's bumper sticker. Payson, who is nearly 80, eschewed retirement at age 65 and instead moved to Campbell, California, to push his skills as a marketing consultant in Silicon Valley. Many retired baby boomers say they're bored, and more of them want to go back to work, according to a new survey. But they're not interested in the same jobs they had in the past. Almost half of the newly retired are thinking about starting a business or forging a different career, according to the survey of 350 seniors by Dell Webb Corp., a retirement community developer.

Payson says that the reception Silicon Valley recruiters gave him was cool, to say the least. "As soon as they saw my gray hair, I could see their jaws drop," he recalls. But Payson didn't get mad: He started his own business. It's based on the conviction that a lot of other seniors aren't ready for the rocking chair yet but also do not want full-time jobs. Rather, they'd prefer to work on short-term assignments that give them maximum flexibility.

Payson's company, Senior Staff Job Information Exchange, seeks to match employers with those restless seniors. He maintains a database of 20,000 computer professionals nationwide from "novices to gurus" and 5,000 nontech employees, who are mostly clerical workers from northern California

It's a matter of how they define leisure, according to Robert Becker, a professor at Clemson University. "To boomers, leisure may mean starting the business of their dreams. To their elders it might mean kicking back and playing an occasional game of horseshoes."

Twenty-six percent of the boomers surveyed who had already retired said they're interested in working because they need the money. Many boomers' stock market–based retirement plans were affected by the dismal economy in 2001. But a fourth of boomer retirees said they miss their friends at work. An additional 24 percent said they wanted something to do.

Two years ago, Mike Leavene, then 50, retired after 22 years with the Missouri Highway Patrol and moved to Sun City Grand, Arizona. He also retired from the Army Reserves. "I got bored after two months," Leavene says. "I was looking for something different but a job that would fit in with my law enforcement background." He eventually found a job as an investigator for the Arizona Registrar of Contractors.

One key to why boomers don't want to quit work may be why they left in the first place. One-fourth planned to retire when they did, but an equal number say they were forced out of their companies or elected to take early retirement. Only 6 percent said they retired because they were burned out.

Meeting the needs of the new retirees who want to work is creating new challenges to developers such as Del Webb Corp. More homes now have home offices, and developments are being built closer to places where people can work. They also are bringing college classes to retirees so that they can receive the education they need for new careers.

"Retire? Hell, No. I'm Not Even Tired Yet!"

Payson waxes enthusiastic about the graying of America, which he believes will change how employers view seniors: "The over-50 set is the fastest-growing segment in the United States. It will take time for employers to come around, but they're going to realize there's no place else for them to go. The world is running out of kids."

SOURCES: Maureen West, "Retired Boomers Wanting to Work," *Arizona Republic*, February 2, 2002; Stephanie B. Goldberg, "Finding Slots for Senior Programmers in Silicon Valley," *Business Week Online*, August 4, 2000.

U.S. Department of Labor data indicate that the United States is becoming a predominantly service-oriented economy. Manufacturing represents only 12 percent of all jobs. People without high school diplomas are at a distinct disadvantage, because their employment opportunities are becoming confined to the lowest-paying service jobs. Even the lower-skilled occupations of the future will require workers who can communicate well and read and comprehend instructions and who have a working knowledge of basic mathematics. For example, the job of assembly-line worker traditionally was considered a low-skill occupation. Today many of these workers are learning statistical process control techniques, which require a solid foundation in mathematics.

There is a growing gap between the knowledge and skills jobs require and those many employees and applicants possess. Skill deficiencies are particularly acute among minority workers and many immigrant populations. Illiteracy is often the underlying problem. More than a third of job applicants tested in reading and mathematics lacked the basic skills necessary to perform the jobs they sought, according to the American Management Association's (AMA) annual survey on workplace testing.

FIGURE 11.3
Model of Diversity Management Strategy

Valuing Diversity in the Workplace

Culture

Organizationwide Image
- Organization fosters mutual respect
- Organization fosters sense of belonging
- Differences are accepted
- Corporatewide diversity-training program

Concern for Equality
- Equal respect for minority and majority group
- Equal performance expectations for minority and majority group
- Equal rewards for minority and majority group
- Equal pay and income
- Valuing diversity

Opportunity

Career Development
- Promotion of multicultural employees
- Opportunity for development of new skills
- Preference to minorities in promotion
- Access to top-management positions

Hiring Practices
- Active recruitment and hiring of multicultural employees
- Equal opportunities for minorities
- Affirmative action program

Leadership

Management Practices
- Take all employees seriously
- Recognize the capabilities of all employees
- Support all employees
- Communicate effectively with all employees
- Value a diverse work group
- Respect the cultural beliefs and needs of employees
- Accept non–English-speaking employees

SOURCE: Kathleen Iverson, "Managing for effective workforce diversity," *Cornell Hotel and Restaurant Administration Quarterly;* (April 2000) 41 No 2: 31–38.

Eighty-five percent of companies said they do not hire skills-deficient applicants, but nearly 75 percent hire them and offer remedial training. An additional 8 percent offer "other" actions that include retesting at a later date.[14] Figure 11.3 shows some of the methods used for remedial training.

Employers are combating this basic-skills gap in a number of ways. One approach is in-house basic-skills training programs. Ford, for example, offers reading courses at 25 of its plants. Domino's uses a videodisc program to teach reading and math. Other strategies include partnerships with public schools; community colleges; and local, state, and federal agencies. Many companies, including Esprit de Corp. and Hasbro, Inc., teach their employees English as a second language or offer second-language training to managers and employees to communicate the idea that languages other than English are valued. Hasbro invites employees' families and friends to the classes to help reinforce learning off the job.[15]

Managing Diversity versus Affirmative Action

Affirmative action (discussed in Chapter 10) was instituted to curb discrimination and correct the past exclusion of women and minorities from U.S. organizations. While a good deal of progress has been made in hiring women and minorities, Table 11.6 reveals that in most industries, these groups continue to be clustered disproportionately at the bottom of corporate hierarchies (recall our earlier discussion of the *glass ceiling*).

In reality, a legislated approach tends to result in fragmented efforts that do not achieve the integrative goals of managing diversity. Employment discrimination still persists in organizations, and even after nearly three decades of government legislation, equal employment opportunity (EEO) and affirmative action laws have not adequately improved the upward mobility of women and minorities.

In fact, critics argue that the laws result in *de facto* employment quotas, and those companies that conscientiously pursue affirmative action have had claims of

TABLE 11.6
Where Women and Minorities Are Now

Percentage of managers who are women		Percentage of managers who are minorities	
Industry	Percentage	Industry	Percentage
Finance insurance, real estate	41.4%	Retail trade	13.0%
Services	38.9	Transportation, communications, and public utilities	12.0
Retail trade	38.5	Services	11.0
Transportation, communications, and public utilities	25.6	Finance, insurance, and real estate	11.0
Wholesale trade	20.9	Agriculture	1.3
Manufacturing	15.9	Wholesale trade	0.9
Agriculture	14.5	Manufacturing	0.8
Construction	10.4	Mining	0.7
Mining	9.8	Construction	0.6

SOURCE: Federal Glass Ceiling Commission.

preferential treatment and reverse discrimination leveled against them. Reverse discrimination exists when qualified white males are passed over for employment opportunities in favor of members of protected classes. For these reasons, several members of Congress have argued that the EEO and affirmative action laws should be changed dramatically or eliminated altogether.

In contrast to EEO and affirmative action programs, managing diversity means moving beyond legislated mandates to embrace a proactive business philosophy that values differences. Managing diversity involves organizations making changes in their systems, structures, and management practices in order to eliminate barriers that may keep people from reaching their full potential. The goal is not to treat all people the same but to treat people as individuals, recognizing that each employee has different needs and will need different things to succeed. This approach implies that different people in the workplace sometimes should be treated equally but differently.

Competitive Advantage through Diversity

For many organizations, the original impetus to diversify their workforces was social responsibility and legal necessity (recall Chapters 5 and 10). Morally, ethically, and legally, it is simply the right thing to do. Today many organizations are approaching diversity from a more practical, business-oriented perspective. Increasingly, diversity can be a powerful tool for building competitive advantage. A study by the Department of Labor's Glass Ceiling Institute showed that the stock performance of firms that were high performers on diversity-related goals were over twice as high as that of other firms. Conversely, announcements of damage awards from discrimination lawsuits frequently has had a negative effect on stock returns.[16] There are many advantages—and some obvious challenges—to managing a diverse workforce. Some of these are summarized in Table 11.7 and discussed in the following section.

Ability to Attract and Retain Motivated Employees   For companies facing changing demographics and business needs, diversity makes good sense. Companies with a reputation for providing opportunities for diverse employees will have a competitive advantage in the labor market and will be sought out by the most qualified employees. In addition, when employees believe their differences are not merely tolerated but valued, they may become more loyal, productive, and committed.

Better Perspective on a Differentiated Market   Companies such as Avon, Prudential, Eastman Kodak, and Toys "R" Us are committed to diversity because as the composition of the American workforce changes, so does the customer base of these companies. Just as women and minorities may prefer to work for an employer that values diversity, they may prefer to patronize such organizations.

Many Asian-Americans, African-Americans, Mexican-Americans, and women have entered the middle class and now control consumer dollars. A multicultural workforce can provide a company with greater knowledge of the preferences and consuming habits of this diversified marketplace. This knowledge can assist companies in designing products and developing marketing campaigns to meet those consumers' needs. In addition, for at least some products and services, a multicultural sales force may help

Advantages	Challenges
• Fulfills social responsibility	• Lower cohesiveness
• Helps attract, retain, and motivate employees	• Communication problems
• Gains greater knowledge of diversified marketplace	• Mistrust and tension
• Promotes creativity, innovation, and problem solving	• Stereotyping
• Enhances organizational flexibility	

TABLE 11.7
The Diverse Workforce: Advantages and Challenges

an organization sell to diverse groups. A diverse workforce also can give a company a competitive edge in a global economy by facilitating understanding of other customs, cultures, and marketplace needs.

Ability to Leverage Creativity and Innovation in Problem Solving
Work team diversity promotes creativity and innovation, because people from different backgrounds hold different perspectives on issues. Diverse groups have a broader base of experience from which to approach a problem; when effectively managed, they invent more options and create more solutions than homogeneous groups do. In addition, diverse work groups are freer to deviate from traditional approaches and practices. The presence of diversity also can help minimize "groupthink" (recall Chapter 3).[17]

Enhancement of Organizational Flexibility
A diverse workforce can enhance organizational flexibility, because managing diversity successfully requires a corporate culture that tolerates many different styles and approaches. Less restrictive policies and procedures and less standardized operating methods enable organizations to become more flexible and thus better able to respond quickly to environmental changes (recall Chapters 2 and 9). Executives at PepsiCo, Verizon, Kodak, and Prudential are so convinced of the competitive potential of a diverse workforce that they tie a portion of management compensation to success in recruiting and promoting minorities and women.[18]

Challenges of a Diverse Workforce
A diverse workforce also poses many challenges. Many of these challenges, summarized in Table 11.7, can be turned into advantages if the workforce is managed effectively.

Lower Cohesiveness   Diversity can create a lack of cohesiveness. Cohesiveness refers to how tightly knit the group is and the degree to which group members perceive, interpret, and act on their environment in similar or mutually agreed-upon ways. Because of their lack of similarity in language, culture, and/or experience, diverse groups typically are less cohesive than homogeneous groups. Often mistrust, miscommunication, stress, and attitudinal differences reduce cohesiveness, which in turn can diminish productivity. Group cohesiveness will be discussed in greater detail in Chapter 14.

Communication Problems   Perhaps the most common negative effect of diversity is communication problems. These difficulties include misunderstandings, inaccuracies, inefficiencies, and slowness. Speed is lost when not all group members are fluent in the same language or when additional time is required to explain things.

Diversity also increases errors and misunderstandings. Group members may assume they interpret things similarly when in fact they do not, or they may disagree because of their different frames of reference.[19]

Mistrust and Tension   People prefer to associate with others who are like themselves. This tendency often leads to mistrust and misunderstanding of those who are different because of a lack of contact and low familiarity. It also causes stress and tension, and reaching agreement on problems can be difficult.

Stereotyping   We learn to see the world in a certain way on the basis of our backgrounds and experiences. Our interests, values, and cultures act as filters and distort, block, and select what we see and hear. We see and hear what we expect to see and hear.

Group members often inappropriately stereotype their "different" colleagues rather than accurately perceiving and evaluating those individuals' contributions, capabilities, aspirations, and motivations.

Such stereotypes in turn affect how people are treated. Employees stereotyped as unmotivated or emotional will be given less-stress-provoking (and perhaps less important) jobs than their co-workers. Those job assignments will create frustrated employees, perhaps resulting in lower commitment, higher turnover, and underused skills.[20]

Multicultural Organizations

To capitalize on the benefits and minimize the costs of a diverse workforce, organizations need to examine their assumptions about people and cultures. At a basic level, it is possible to categorize organizations according to their prevailing assumptions. Table 11.8 shows some of the most fundamental assumptions and describes how they influence management. Based on these assumptions, we can classify organizations as one of three types.

Some organizations are **monolithic.** This type of organization has very little *cultural integration;* in other words, it employs few women, minorities, or any other groups that differ from the majority. The organization is highly homogeneous in terms of its employee population. In monolithic organizations, if groups other than the norm are employed, they are found primarily in low-status jobs. Minority group members must adopt the norms of the majority to survive. This fact, coupled with small numbers, keeps conflicts among groups low. Discrimination and prejudice typically prevail, informal integration is almost nonexistent, and minority group members do not identify strongly with the company.

Most large U.S. organizations made the transition from monolithic to *plural* organizations in the 1960s and 1970s because of changing demographics as well as societal forces such as the civil rights and women's movements. **Plural organizations** have a more diverse employee population and

monolithic organization

An organization that has a low degree of structural integration—employing few women, minorities, or other groups that differ from the majority—and thus has a highly homogeneous employee population.

plural organization

An organization that has a relatively diverse employee population and makes an effort to involve employees from different gender, racial, or cultural backgrounds.

Diversity Assumptions and Their Implications for Management | **TABLE 11.8**

Common and misleading assumptions		Less common and more appropriate assumptions	
Homogeneity	*Melting pot myth:* We are all the same.	Heterogeneity	*Image of cultural pluralism:* We are not all the same; groups within society differ across cultures.
Similarity	*Similarity myth:* "They" are all just like me.	Similarity and difference	*They are not just like me:* Many people differ from me culturally. Most people exhibit both cultural similarities and differences when compared to me.
Parochialism	*Only-one-way myth:* Our way is the only way. We do not recognize any other way of living or working.	Equifinality	*Our way is not the only way:* There are many culturally distinct ways of reaching the same goal, of working, and of living one's life.
Ethnocentrism	*One-best-way myth:* Our way is the best way. All other approaches are inferior versions of our way.	Culture contingency	*Our way is one possible way:* There are many different and equally good ways to reach the same goal. The best way depends on the culture of the people involved.

SOURCE: From "Diversity Assumptions and Their Implications for Management" by Nancy J. Adler, *Handbook of Organization,* 1996. Reprinted courtesy of Marcel Dekker, Inc. NY.

The U.S. military has, for years, made a deliberate effort to diversify throughout its ranks.

take steps to involve persons from different gender, racial, or cultural backgrounds. These organizations use an affirmative action approach to managing diversity: They actively try to hire and train a diverse workforce and to ensure against any discrimination against minority group members. They typically have much more integration than do monolithic organizations, but like monolithic organizations, they often have minority group members clustered at certain levels or in particular functions within the organization.

Because of greater cultural integration, affirmative action programs, and training programs, the plural organization has some acceptance of minority group members into the informal network, much less discrimination, and less prejudice. Improved employment opportunities create greater identification with the organization among minority group members. Often the resentment of majority group members, coupled with the increased number of women and minorities, creates more conflict than exists in the monolithic organization.

multicultural organization

An organization that values cultural diversity and seeks to utilize and encourage it.

The plural organization fails to address the cultural aspects of integration. In contrast, in **multicultural organizations** diversity not only exists but is valued. These organizations fully integrate gender, racial, and minority group members both formally and informally. The multicultural organization is marked by an absence of prejudice and discrimination and by low levels of intergroup conflict. Such an organization creates a *synergistic* environment in which all members contribute to their maximum potential and the advantages of diversity can be fully realized.[21]

How Organizations Can Cultivate a Diverse Workforce

An organization's plans for becoming multicultural and making the most of its diverse workforce should include (1) securing top management leadership and commitment, (2) assessing the workforce, (3) attracting employees, (4) developing employees, and (5) retaining employees.

Top Management Leadership and Commitment

Obtaining top management leadership and commitment is critical for diversity programs to succeed. One way to communicate this commitment to all employees—as well as to the external environment—is to incorporate the organization's attitudes toward diversity into the corporate mission statement and into strategic plans and objectives. Managerial compensation can be linked directly to accomplishing diversity objectives. Adequate funding must be allocated to the diversity effort to ensure its success. Also, top management can set an example for other organization members by participating in diversity programs and making participation mandatory for all managers.

Some organizations have established corporate offices or committees to coordinate the companywide diversity effort and provide feedback to top management. Digital Equipment Corporation has a "director of valuing differences," Honeywell has a "director of workforce diversity," and Avon has a "director of multicultural planning and design." Other companies prefer to incorporate diversity management into the function of director of affirmative action or EEO.

The work of managing diversity cannot be done by top management or diversity directors alone. Many companies rely on minority advisory groups or task forces to monitor organizational policies, practices, and attitudes; assess their impact on the diverse groups within the organization; and provide feedback and suggestions to top management.

For example, Digital Equipment Corporation uses Core Groups, in which employees from different backgrounds form small groups to address stereotypes and other relevant issues. At Equitable Life Assurance Society, Business Resource Groups meet regularly with the CEO to discuss issues pertaining to women, African-Americans, and Hispanics and make recommendations for improvement. U.S. West has a Pluralism Council that advises senior management on how to manage and utilize the company's diverse workforce more effectively. At Honeywell, disabled employees formed a council to discuss their needs. They proposed and accepted an accessibility program that went beyond federal regulations for accommodations of disabilities.

As you can see, progressive companies are moving from asking managers what they think minority employees need to asking the employees themselves what they need.

Organizational Assessment

The next step in managing diversity is to establish an ongoing assessment of the organization's workforce, culture, policies, and practices in areas such as recruitment, promotions, benefits, and compensation. In addition, the demographics of the labor pool and the customer base should be evaluated. The objective is to identify problem areas and make recommendations where changes are needed.

For example, many women and Asians are at a disadvantage when aggressiveness is a valued part of the organization's culture. After analysis, management might decide that the organizational values need to be changed so that other styles of interacting are equally acceptable. Corporate values and norms should be identified and critically evaluated regarding their necessity and their impact on the diverse workforce.

Attracting Employees

Companies can attract a diverse, qualified workforce by using effective recruiting practices, accommodating employees' work and family needs, and offering alternative work arrangements.

Recruitment   A company's image can be a strong recruiting tool. Companies with reputations for hiring and promoting all types of people have a competitive advantage. Xerox gives prospective minority employees reprints of an article that rates the company as one of the best places for African-Americans to work. Hewlett-Packard ensures that its female candidates are familiar with its high rating by *Working Woman* magazine.

Pictured here is Anja Mansfield, corporate recruiter with Howard Industries. Smart companies strive to beat their competitors by hiring a more diverse workforce, believing the move will ultimately result in broader market share.

Many employers are implementing policies to attract more women, ensure that women's talents are used to full advantage, and avoid losing their most capable female employees.

Many minorities and economically disadvantaged people are physically isolated from job opportunities. Companies can bring information about job opportunities to the source of labor, or they can transport the labor to the jobs. Polycast Technology in Stamford, Connecticut, contracts with a private van company to transport workers from the Bronx in New York City to jobs in Stamford. Days Inn recruits homeless workers in Atlanta and houses them in a motel within walking distance of their jobs. Burger King has done a lot to recruit and hire immigrants in its fast-food restaurants. Following are guidelines for diversity planning.

Steps in Diversity Planning

Like affirmative action plans, voluntary workforce diversity plans often are based on numerical standards for the employment of minorities and women. Numerical standards are a critical element in planning, because they give managers something to strive for and benchmarks for measuring success. To be successful, the standards must be both realistic—tailored to the company's essential qualifications for filling jobs—and based on sound figures indicating the availability of qualified candidates in the labor markets.

CALCULATING REALISTIC AND OBTAINABLE STANDARDS

Step 1: Set general qualifications. In order to understand the workforce and the general qualifications applicants must have to fill a position, HR managers must address four important questions:

- How much experience do people in this position generally have?
- What education ordinarily is needed for this job?
- What salary ordinarily is paid for this job?
- From what geographic regions are workers ordinarily recruited?

Step 2: Match positions to U.S. census categories. The U.S. Bureau of the Census reports the percentage of workers in each race and sex group for 501 occupational categories. Match each position in the company to one of the 501 categories. Job description information helps make this matching easier.

Step 3: Identify qualified workers. Qualified workers are those with the education, location, experience, and current salary level who fall within the range required for each position. Since the objective is to maximize diversity, the pool of workers should not be overly restrictive here.

Step 4: Calculate percentages. For each position, calculate the percentage of workers in the qualified pool who are minorities and women. Compare this number with the percentages in the census categories.

Step 5: Set numerical standards. Using these data, calculate hiring standards for jobs, groups of jobs, and the overall business unit. Long-term diversity goals then can be determined by evaluating where the company should be at some future date.

SOURCE: Adapted from David S. Evans and Miriam Y. Oh, "Diversity Planning," *HRMagazine*, June 1996, pp. 127–34.

Accommodating Work and Family Needs   More job seekers are putting family needs first. Corporate work and family policies are now one of the most important recruiting tools.

Employers that have become involved in child care report decreased turnover and absenteeism and improved morale. In addition to providing child care, many companies now assist with care for elderly dependents, offer time off to care for sick family members, provide parental leaves of absence, and offer a variety of benefits that can be tailored to individual family needs. Some companies are accommodating the needs and concerns of dual-career couples by limiting relocation requirements or providing job search assistance to relocated spouses.

Alternative Work Arrangements   Another way companies accommodate diversity is to offer flexible work schedules and arrangements. When the New Haven region of People's Bank based in Bridgeport, Connecticut, was having difficulty recruiting part-time tellers, the region's employee relations specialist initiated the Working Parent Program. The program allowed part-timers to schedule their hours to coincide with their children's: home by 3 P.M., with summers and school holidays off. Staffing problems were solved by being flexible, using part-timers to cover peak hours, and hiring college students to fill in during holidays and summers.[22]

Other creative work arrangements include compressed workweeks (for example, four 10-hour days) and job sharing, in which two part-time workers share one full-time job. Another option to accommodate working mothers and the disabled is teleworking (working from home) or telecommuting (working from home via computer hookup to the main work site). This option has been slow to catch on, but the organizations that have tried it report favorable results.

Diversity Training

As you learned in Chapter 10, employees can be developed in a variety of ways. *Diversity training programs* attempt to identify and reduce hidden biases and develop the skills needed to manage a diversified workforce effectively. Traditionally, most management training has been based on the assumption that "managing" means managing a homogeneous, often white-male, full-time workforce. But gender, race, culture, and other differences create an additional layer of complexity.[23]

More than 50 percent of all U.S. organizations sponsor some sort of diversity training. Typically, diversity training has two components: awareness building and skill building.

Awareness Building   *Awareness building* is designed to increase awareness of the meaning and importance of valuing diversity.[24] Its aim is not to teach specific skills but to sensitize employees to the assumptions they make about others and how those assumptions affect their behaviors, decisions, and judgment.

To build awareness, people are taught to become familiar with myths, stereotypes, and cultural differences as well as the organizational barriers that inhibit the full contributions of all employees. They develop a better understanding of corporate culture, requirements for success, and career choices that affect opportunities for advancement.

In most companies, the "rules" for success are ambiguous, unwritten, and perhaps inconsistent with written policy. A common problem for women and minorities is that they are unaware of many of the rules that are obvious to people in the mainstream. Valuing diversity means teaching the unwritten "rules" or cultural values to those who need to know them and changing the rules when necessary to benefit employees and hence the organization. It also requires inviting "outsiders" in and giving them access to information and meaningful relationships with people in power.

Skill Building   *Skill building* is designed to allow all employees and managers to develop the skills they need to deal effectively with one another and with customers in a diverse environment. Most of the skills taught are interpersonal, such as active listening, coaching, and giving feedback. Hewlett-Packard and Wisconsin Power and

Light provide both awareness and skill building. These companies attempt to transfer the training to the job by asking managers to develop personal action plans before they leave the program. For example, a manager may recognize from training that his record of retaining African-American sales representatives is poor and plans to spend more time coaching these salespeople.[25]

Experiential exercises and videotapes often are used in the training programs to help expose stereotypes and encourage employees to discuss fears, biases, and problems. One widely used training tool is a series of seven 30-minute videotapes titled *Valuing Diversity*, produced by Copeland-Griggs with funding from 50 corporations, including Hewlett-Packard, Xerox, U.S. West, and Procter & Gamble. Table 11.9 provides a set of guidelines for designing effective diversity training.

Retaining Employees

As replacing qualified and experienced workers becomes more difficult and costly, retaining good workers will become much more important. Aetna estimates its annual turnover expense at more than $100 million—largely money spent on training new employees and the costs of their lower productivity during the learning period. When Deloitte & Touche had problems retaining minorities and women, top executives moved quickly. The firm not only ameliorated its problems, it created a more positive environment for all employees. A number of policies and strategies, like the following, can be used to increase retention of all employees, especially those who are "different" from the norm.[26]

Support Groups   Companies can help form minority networks and other support groups to promote information exchange and social support. Support groups provide

TABLE 11.9
Guidelines for Diversity Training

1. **Position training in your broad diversity strategy.** Training is one important element of managing diversity, but on its own it will probably fail. Culture change means altering underlying assumptions and systems that guide organizational behavior. Training programs must be internally consistent with, and complement, other initiatives focused on culture change.

2. **Do a thorough needs analysis.** Do not start training prematurely. As with any training program, eagerness to "do something" may backfire unless you have assessed what specific aspects of diversity need attention first. Focus groups help identify what employees view as priority issues.

3. **Distinguish between education and training.** Education helps build awareness and understanding but does not teach usable skills. Training involves activities that enhance skills in areas such as coaching, conducting performance appraisals, and adapting communications styles. Education and training are both important but they're not the same.

4. **Use a participative design process.** Tap a multitude of parties to ensure that the content and tone of the program are suitable to everyone involved. Outsider consultants often provide fresh perspectives, and have credibility. Insiders have specific company knowledge, sensitivity to local issues, and long-standing relationships with company members. Balance these various sources.

5. **Test the training thoroughly before rollout.** Given the sensitivity, even volatility, of diversity issues, use diversity councils and advocacy groups to pilot the programs. Build in ample feedback time to allow these groups to address sensitive concerns, and refine the training.

6. **Incorporate diversity programs into the core training curriculum.** One-time programs do not have a lasting impact. Blend the program's content into other training programs such as performance appraisal, coaching, and so on.

SOURCE: From *Training: The Human Side of Business*. Copyright © 1993 by VNU Business Publications USA. Reproduced with permission of VNU Business Publications USA via Copyright Clearance Center.

emotional and career support for members who traditionally have not been included in the majority's informal groups. They also can help diverse employees understand work norms and the corporate culture.

At Apple headquarters in Cupertino, California, support groups include a Jewish cultural group, a gay/lesbian group, an African-American group, and a technical women's group. Avon encourages employees to organize into African-American, Hispanic, and Asian networks by granting them official recognition and assigning a senior manager to provide advice. These groups help new employees adjust and provide direct feedback to management on problems that concern the groups. Avon once had a women's network, but that group disbanded years ago. With women holding a large majority percent of management positions, female employees at Avon believed the group was no longer necessary.

Mentoring   Many people have been puzzled at the inability of women and minorities to move up beyond a certain point on the corporate ladder (the glass ceiling). To help these groups enter the informal network that provides exposure to top management and access to information about organizational politics, many companies have implemented formal mentoring programs. **Mentors** are higher-level managers who help ensure that high-potential people are introduced to top management and socialized into the norms and values of the organization.

> **mentors**
>
> **Higher level managers who help ensure that high-potential people are introduced to top management and socialized into the norms and values of the organization.**

Procter & Gamble's "Mentor Up" program has been working very successfully. The number of women at the general manager/vice-president level has more than tripled in the last decade. General Electric has formed a 10,000-strong women's network whose goal is to foster professional development and facilitate women's advancement.[27]

Career Development and Promotions   Because they are hitting a glass ceiling, many of the most talented women and minority group members are leaving their organizations in search of better opportunities elsewhere. In response, companies such as Mobil Oil and Honeywell have established teams to evaluate the career progress of women, minorities, and employees with disabilities and to devise ways to move them up through the ranks.

Fannie Mae employee mentor program in action. Having mentors helps entry-level employees from different backgrounds make headway within organizations.

Systems Accommodation   Organizations can support diversity by recognizing cultural and religious holidays, differing modes of dress, and dietary restrictions, as well as accommodating the needs of individuals with disabilities. One important disabling condition is AIDS. Under the ADA, organizations must accommodate AIDS sufferers as they would persons with any other disability, permitting and even encouraging them to continue working for as long as they are able and, if warranted, allowing flexible scheduling.

Accountability   For diversity efforts to succeed, managers must be held accountable for workforce development. Organizations must ensure that their performance appraisal and reward systems reinforce the importance of effective diversity management. Baxter Health Care, Coca-Cola, and Merck (as well as Prudential and Kodak, mentioned earlier) all tie compensation to managers' performance in diversity efforts.[28]

For 25 years, U.S. corporations were striving to integrate their workforces because of regulatory and social responsibility pressures. Today globalization, changing demographics, and the expansion of ethnic markets at home have made managing a diverse workforce a bottom-line issue. Companies now realize that to remain competitive in the coming years, they will have to make managing diversity a strategic priority to attract top talent.

KEY TERMS

Glass ceiling, p. 333

Managing diversity, p. 330

Mentors, p. 351

Monolithic organization, p. 345

Multicultural organization, p. 346

Plural organization, p. 345

Sexual harassment, p. 333

SUMMARY OF LEARNING OBJECTIVES

Now that you have studied Chapter 11, you should know:

How changes in the U.S. workforce are making diversity a critical organizational and managerial issue.

The labor force is getting older and more ethnic, with a higher proportion of women. And while the absolute number of workers is increasing, the growth in jobs is outpacing the numerical growth of workers. In addition, the jobs that are being created frequently require higher skills than the typical worker can provide; thus, we are seeing a growing skills gap. To be competitive, organizations can no longer take the traditional approach of depending on white males to form the core of the workforce. Today, managers must look broadly to make use of talent wherever it can be found. As the labor market changes, organizations that can recruit, develop, motivate, and retain a diverse workforce will have a competitive advantage.

The distinction between affirmative action and managing diversity.

Affirmative action is designed to correct past exclusion of women and minorities from U.S. organizations. But despite the accomplishments of affirmative action, it has not eliminated barriers that prevent individuals from reaching their full potential. Managing diversity goes beyond hiring people who are different from the norm and seeks to support, nurture, and use employee difference to the organization's advantage.

How companies can gain a competitive edge by managing diversity effectively.

Managing diversity is a bottom-line issue. If managers are effective at managing diversity, they will have an easier time attracting, retaining, and motivating the best employees. They will be more effective at marketing to diverse consumer groups in the United States and globally. They will have a workforce that is more creative, more innovative, and better able to solve problems. In addition, they are likely to increase the flexibility and responsiveness of the organization to environmental change.

What challenges a company is likely to encounter with a diverse workforce.

The challenges for managers created by a diverse workforce include decreased group cohesiveness, communication problems, mistrust and tension, and stereotyping. These challenges can be turned into advantages by means of training and effective management.

How an organization can take steps to cultivate diversity.
To be successful, organizational efforts to manage diversity must have top management support and commitment. Organizations should first undertake a thorough assessment of their cultures, policies, and practices, as well as the demographics of their labor pools and customer bases. Only after this diagnosis has been completed is a company in position to initiate programs designed to attract, develop, motivate, and retain a diverse workforce.

DISCUSSION QUESTIONS

1. What opportunities do you see as a result of changes in our nation's workforce?

2. Is prejudice declining in our society? In our organizations? Why or why not?

3. What distinctions can you make between affirmative action and managing diversity?

4. How can we overcome obstacles to diversity such as mistrust and tension, stereotyping, and communication problems?

5. How can organizations meet the special needs of different groups (e.g., work and family issues) without appearing to show favoritism to those particular sets of employees?

6. How can diversity give a company a competitive edge? Can diversity really make a difference in the bottom line? How?

Diversity Is in Good Hands at Allstate

In today's competitive environment, companies continue to look for ways to improve their performance and achieve corporate objectives. The task is not easy, but the team of human resources (HR) executives at Allstate Corp. has found that its diversity strategy has become one of the company's most potent competitive weapons. It has long been Allstate's position that diversity is about neither political mandates nor legal obligation. Rather, the company's vision is: "Diversity is Allstate's strategy for leveraging differences in order to create a competitive advantage." This strategy has two major points: one internally focused and the other externally focused. According to Joan Crockett, VP of human resources, the internal diversity focus is about "unlocking the potential for excellence in all workers by providing them the tools, resources, and opportunities to succeed." The external focus of diversity is about making certain that the workforce matches the experiences, backgrounds, and sensitivities of the markets it serves. In this context, Allstate managers view diversity not as a goal but as a process that is integrated into the daily life of the company.

Allstate launched its first affirmative action program back in 1969. In the early days, its commitment to diversity didn't always link recruitment, development, and retention strategies to business performance. The company focused more on affirmative action and diversity awareness through education and training. And while these initiatives were considered innovative in their day, they had no articulated business outcome. Carlton Yearwood, director of diversity management, notes that the key question has become: "How do you take this workforce of differences and bring them together in a more powerful way so that it can impact business results?" Allstate has taken four specific steps:

Step One: Succession Planning. A diverse slate of candidates is identified and developed for each key position. Allstate's integrated process enables it to track and measure key drivers of career development and career opportunities, ensuring that the company's future workforce will be diverse at all levels. Allstate's succession planning has made a difference that is easy to measure.

Employment of women and minorities has grown at a rate far surpassing national averages. Today, 40 percent of Allstate's executives and managers are women and 20 percent are minorities.

Step Two: Development. Through the company's employee development process, all employees receive an assessment of their current job skills and a road map for developing the critical skills necessary for advancement. Options include education, coaching and mentoring, and classroom training. Leaders are provided employee feedback on which they can base future development plans. In addition, all of Allstate's nonagent employees with service of more than one year have completed diversity training courses.

Step Three: Measurement. Twice a year the company takes a snapshot of all 40,000 employees through a survey called the Diversity Index. As part of a larger online employee survey and feedback process called the Quarterly Leadership Measurement System (QLMS), the Diversity Index taps the following questions:

1. To what extent does our company deliver quality service to customers regardless of their ethnic background, gender, age, and so on?

2. To what extent are you treated with respect and dignity at work? To what extent does your immediate manager/team leader seek out and utilize the different backgrounds and perspectives of all employees in your work group?

3. How often do you observe insensitive behavior at work, for example, inappropriate comments or jokes about ethnic background, gender, age, and so on?

4. To what extent do you work in an environment of trust where employees/agents are free to offer different opinions?

Management communicates the results of this survey and actively solicits feedback from employees on creating action plans to solve problems and improve work processes.

Step Four: Accountability and Reward. To link compensation to the company's diversity goals, 25 percent of each manager's merit pay is based on the diversity index and the QLMS. Karleen Zuzich, assistant vice president of HR, says that this sharpens the focus on the initiative. "What you measure is what people focus on. This really sends a clear signal that management of people and doing that well is really important."

To help employees maintain a balance between work and personal life, Allstate has a number of programs in place. For example, it has an on-site child care center at its headquarters and three near-site child care centers, all of which offer parents discount programs. It also has on-site dry cleaning, oil change, and postal and catering services and allows for flexible work arrangements for its employees. The Allstate Center for Assistive Technology (ACAT) helps employees with disabilities that include carpal tunnel syndrome, mobility impairments, and multiple sclerosis. For example, when one information technology employee began experiencing hearing problems, the ACAT team was deployed to fit him with a special home phone for use when he was on night call.

However, when Allstate announced that it would reorganize its 15,000 agents under a single independent contractor program in 1999, 300 current and former agents filed a complaint with the Equal Employment Opportunity Commission. It alleged that Allstate's requirement that they sign a discrimination release in order to receive the benefits that went along with becoming an independent contractor was retaliatory. The company disagreed.

The action does not seem to have affected Allstate's ability to continue to garner awards for its diversity efforts. In 2002, it again was named one of the "50 Best Companies for Minorities" by *Fortune*. It made the top 10 in the "100 Best Companies for Working Mothers" survey compiled by *Working Mother* magazine.

A. Magazine counted it among "Five Model Companies for Asians," and *Minority MBA* magazine has named it a top-10 company.

The accolades are nice, but they still represent an opportunity for further improvement, says Crockett. "In the process of applying for awards and citations like these, we gain the feedback needed to continually improve our results," she notes. "We are convinced that the outstanding results Allstate employees deliver every day for shareholders and policy holders are in part the fruits of our diversity strategy. And we expect the steps we have taken to embrace diversity as a business strategy to continue paying off in the years to come."

QUESTIONS

1. What competitive advantages is Allstate likely to gain from a diversity strategy?

2. Should competitiveness be the major issue, or is social responsibility more important?

3. What other diversity initiatives would you suggest the company undertake?

SOURCES: "American's 50 Best Companies for Minorities," *Fortune*, July 28, 2002; "Allstate Works to Help Its People Succeed," *Diversity in Action*, February/March 2002; Joan Crockett, "Diversity: Winning Competitive Advantage through a Diverse Workforce," *HR Focus*, 76, no. 5 (May 1999), pp. 9–10; Joan Crockett, "Diversity as a Business Strategy," *Management Review*, 88, no. 5 (May 1999), p. 62; Louisa Wah, "Diversity at Allstate: A Competitive Weapon," *Management Review*, 88, no. 7 (July–August 1999), pp. 24–30.

11.1 Being Different

OBJECTIVES

1. To increase your awareness of the feeling of "being different."

2. To better understand the context of "being different."

INSTRUCTIONS

1. Working alone, complete the Being Different Worksheet.

2. In small groups, compare worksheets and prepare answers to the discussion questions.

3. After the class reconvenes, group spokespersons present group findings.

DISCUSSION QUESTIONS

1. Were there students who experienced being different in situations that surprised you?

2. How would you define "being different"?

3. How can this exercise be used to good advantage?

Being Different Worksheet

Think back to a recent situation in which you experienced "being different" and answer the following questions:

1. Describe the situation in which you experienced "being different."

_____

_____

2. Explain how you felt.

_____

_____

3. What did you do as a result of "being different"? (That is, in what way was your behavior changed by the feeling of "being different"?)

_____

_____

4. What did others in the situation do? How do you think they felt about the situation?

_____

_____

5. How did the situation turn out in the end?

_____

_____

6. As a result of that event, how will you probably behave differently in the future? In what way has the situation changed you?

_____

_____

11.2   He Works, She Works

INSTRUCTIONS

1. Complete the He Works, She Works Worksheet. In the appropriate spaces, write what you think the stereotyped responses would be. Do not spend too much time considering any one item. Rather, respond quickly and let your first impression or thought guide your answer.

2. Compare your individual responses with those of other class members or participants. It is interesting to identify and discuss the most frequently used stereotypes.

He Works, She Works Worksheet

The family picture is on _his_ desk: _He's a solid, responsible family man._
   His desk is cluttered: _____

_____

   _He's_ talking with co-workers: _____

_____

   _He's_ not at his desk: _____

_____

   _He's_ not in the office: _____

_____

The family picture is on _her_ desk: _Her family will come before her career._
   Her desk is cluttered: _____

_____

   She's talking with co-workers: _____

_____

   She's not at her desk: _____

_____

   She's not in the office: _____

_____

The family picture is on *his* desk: *He's a solid, responsible family man.*

He's having lunch with the boss: _____

_____

The boss criticized *him:* _____

_____

He got an unfair deal: _____

_____

He's getting married: _____

_____

He's going on a business trip: _____

_____

He's leaving for a better job: _____

_____

The family picture is on *her* desk: *Her family will come before her career.*

She's having lunch with the boss: _____

_____

The boss criticized *her:* _____

_____

She got an unfair deal: _____

_____

She's getting married: _____

_____

She's going on a business trip: _____

_____

She's leaving for a better job: _____

_____

SOURCE: F. Luthans, *Organizational Behavior.* Copyright © 1989 by The McGraw-Hill Companies. Reproduced with the permission of The McGraw-Hill Companies.

The Merger of Federal Express and the Flying Tigers Line

It was January 1990. Thomas R. Oliver, senior vice president of International Operations for Federal Express Corporation, was on his way to meet with the members of his "Tigerclaws" Committee. The operational merger of Flying Tigers with Federal Express was supposed to have been concluded last August. Yet anticipated and unanticipated problems kept surfacing. International operations were draining financial resources, and there were other problems that had to be immediately resolved.

Several days ago, Mr. Oliver had met with Mr. Fred Smith, the company founder and CEO, and had been assigned the job of heading a special task force whose purpose was to direct the Flying Tigers' merger efforts and resolve the resulting problems. Mr. Oliver requested, and got, representatives of senior execu-

tives from every department of the company to form what he named the Tigerclaws Committee (see exhibit "The Tigerclaws Committee"). This committee had the power to cut across departmental bureaucratic lines. It had the resources of all the departments behind it to reach fast-track solutions to any problems in existence. Even with such commitments, Mr. Oliver realized what a formidable task he and his committee were facing.

EXPRESS AND FREIGHT FORWARDING INDUSTRIES

In 1990, sending documents or packages by priority mail was viewed as a necessary convenience, rather than a luxury. The

The Tigerclaws Committee

Departments that are represented
Memphis SuperHub
Business Application
Airfreight Systems
Q.A. Audits
Planning and Administration
International Clearance
Communications
Ramp Plans/Program
Hub Operations
Personnel Services
International Operations
Central Support Services
Customer Support
COSMOS/Pulsar System Division
COO/Quality Improvement

domestic market was led by Federal Express Corporation with 53 percent of the market, followed by United Parcel Service at 19 percent. The U.S. Postal Service had 3 to 4 percent of the market.[1] The overnight letter traffic was characterized by slow growth because of the increased use of facsimile machines.

The increasing competition between express delivery services and the traditional air freight industry was changing the face of international cargo transportation. Many independent freight carriers complained that big couriers and integrated carriers were poaching on their market niches. Others ignored the competition, believing that the more personalized relationships provided by the traditional air freight companies would keep clients coming back. Still, such companies as Federal Express were having a big effect on the air freight industry. Express couriers were building their nondocument business by 25 to 30 percent a year.

EXPRESS SERVICES IN THE UNITED STATES

Federal Express, United Parcel Service (UPS), Airborne Express, and the U.S. Postal Service were quickly introducing services that promised to translate the fundamentals of speed and information into a powerful competitive edge. They were stressing good service at lower costs. For example, UPS had started offering discounts to its bigger customers and shippers that shipped over 250 pieces weekly. In addition, UPS was building an $80 million computer and telecommunications center to provide support for all operations worldwide. Airborne's chief advantage was that it operated its own airport and had begun operating a "commerce park" around its hub in Wilmington, Ohio.

EUROPE

The international document and parcel express delivery business was one of the fastest-growing sectors in Europe. Although the express business would become more important in the single European market, none of the four principal players in Europe was European. DHL, Federal Express, and UPS were United States companies while TNT was Australian. Europe was not expected to produce a challenger because the "Big Four" were buying smaller rivals at such a fast pace that the odds seemed to be heavily against a comparable competitor emerging.[2]

PACIFIC RIM

The Asia-Pacific air express market was expanding by 20 percent to 30 percent annually, and the world's major air express and air freight companies had launched massive infrastructure buildups to take advantage of this growth. Industry leader DHL strengthened its access to air service by agreeing to eventually sell 57.5 percent of the equity of its international operation to Japan Air Lines, Lufthansa, and Nissho Iwai trading company. TNT Skypak's strength was in providing niche services, and its ability to tap into the emerging Asian–East European route with its European air hub. Two new U.S. entrants, Federal Express and UPS, were engaged in an undeclared price war. Willing to lose millions of dollars annually to carve out a greater market share, Federal Express already had captured about 10 percent of Pacific express business and 15 percent of freight. UPS's strategy was to control costs and to offer no-frills service at low rates. All four companies were seeking to expand the proportion of parcels, which would yield about twice the profits of the express documents business.[3]

MAJOR AIRLINES

Since the common adaptation of wide-body jets, major international airlines had extra cargo space in their planes. Japan Air Lines and Lufthansa were two of the worldwide players, with most national airlines providing regional services.

Airlines were expanding and automating their cargo services to meet the challenges presented by fast-growing integrated carriers. Two strategies were being employed: (1) the development of new products to fill the gap between the demand for next-day service and traditional air cargo service and (2) computerization of internal passenger and cargo operations.[4]

THE MERGING ORGANIZATIONS: FEDERAL EXPRESS CORPORATION

Frederick W. Smith, founder of Federal Express Corporation, went to Yale University, where he was awarded a now infamous "C" on an economics paper that outlined his idea for an overnight delivery service.[5] After college and military service, Smith began selling corporate jets in Little Rock, Arkansas. In 1973, he tapped his $4 million inheritance, rounded up $70 million in venture capital, and launched Federal Express, testing his college paper's thesis. The company turned profitable after three years.

Federal Express always had taken pride in its people-oriented approach and its emphasis on service to its customers. Mr. Smith believed that, in the service industry, it is the employees that make the business.[6] The philosophy of Smith and his managing staff was manifested in many ways, including: (1) extensive orientation programs, (2) training and communications programs, (3) promotion of employees from within, and (4) a tuition reimbursement program.

Federal Express's "open door policy" for the expression of employee concerns also illustrated the commitment of top management to resolve problems.[7]

As to services, Federal Express stressed the importance of on-time delivery and established a 100 percent on-time delivery goal. It has achieved a record 95 percent on-time delivery. In 1990, Federal Express was one of the five U.S. firms to win the Malcolm Baldrige National Quality Award. This award was given by the U.S. government to promote quality awareness and to recognize the quality achievements of U.S. companies.

Frederick W. Smith had a vision for the overnight express delivery business. Although Federal Express was the No. 1 express firm in the United States, Mr. Smith firmly believed that globalization was the future for the express business.[8] From 1986 to 1988, Federal Express struggled to become a major player in international deliveries. The company ran head-on into entrenched overseas rivals, such as DHL, and onerous foreign regulations.[9]

Frustrated with the legal processes in negotiating for landing rights that were restricted by bilateral aviation treaties,[10] Mr. Smith reversed his promise to build only from within and started on a series of acquisitions. From 1987 to 1988, Federal purchased 15 minor delivery companies, mostly in Europe. In December 1988, Mr. Smith announced the merger of Tiger International, Inc., best known for its Flying Tigers airfreight service. On paper, the merger of Federal Express and Tiger International seemed to be a marriage made in heaven. As one Federal Express executive pointed out: "If we lay a route map of Flying Tigers over that of Federal Express, there is almost a perfect match. There are only one or two minor overlaps. The Flying Tigers' routes are all over the world, with highest concentration in the Pacific Rim countries, while Federal Express's routes are mostly in domestic U.S.A." As a result of the merger, Federal Express's world routes were completed. For example, the acquisition of Flying Tigers brought with it the unrestricted cargo landing rights at three Japanese airports that Federal Express had been unsuccessful in acquiring for the last three years.[11]

One high-level Federal Express employee commented that the merger brought other benefits besides routes. He said: "We got a level of expertise with the people we brought in and a number of years of experiences in the company in handling air freight . . . You have to look at this acquisition also as a defensive move. If we hadn't bought Flying Tigers, UPS might have bought Flying Tigers."

THE MERGING ORGANIZATIONS: TIGER INTERNATIONAL, INC.

Tiger International, Inc., better known for The Flying Tigers Line, Inc., freight service, or Flying Tigers, was founded 40 years ago by Robert Prescott. Over the years, the company became modestly profitable. But in 1977, Smith won his crusade for air-cargo deregulation over the strident objection of Prescott. Heightened competition, troubled acquisitions, and steep labor costs led to big losses at Tigers. In 1986, Stephen M. Wolf, the former chairman of Republic Airline Inc., came on board at Tigers and managed to get all employees, including those represented by unions, to accept wage cuts. As Tigers rebounded financially, it was ripe to be taken over by one of the major delivery service companies. In 1988, Federal Express announced the acquisition of Tigers to the pleasure of some and dismay of others. At the announcement, some

Tigers' employees shouted, "TGIF—Thank God It's Federal" or "It's purple [Federal Express] not brown [UPS]—thank goodness." In contrast, Robert Sigafoos, who wrote a corporate history of Federal Express, commented, "Prescott must be turning over in his grave."[12]

Flying Tigers always had a distinctive culture, one that partly developed from the military image of its founders. Tigers' employees stressed "Tiger Spirit" or teamwork. Since Mr. Wolf took over as the chairman and CEO at an extremely difficult time, the general orientation of Flying Tigers was to keep the company flying.

THE MERGER

Federal Express announced the acquisition of Flying Tigers in December 1988. However, because of government regulations, the actual operational merging of the two companies did not occur until August 1989.

One top-level Federal Express executive, with considerable expertise in mergers, described the process in the following way: "I think that after any merger you go through three phases. You come in and you have euphoria. Everybody's happy. The second phase is the transition phase. In that phase, the primary qualification that every employee must have is sadomasochistic tendencies, because you kill yourself going through it . . . And then you start coming out of that into the regeneration and regrowth phase, where you clean up all this hazy area without knowing exactly what you are going to do or thinking this works and trying it out . . . In the meantime, going through all that turmoil creates a number of problems . . . People's morale starts to dip. People start to question all the leadership. You start to see the company reorganizing, you know, trying to figure out, well, what's the best thing to do here or there or whatever and, all of a sudden, all of the confidence that ever existed in the whole world starts to diminish."

Although the two companies were supposed to now become one, problems from the merger kept surfacing. Some of these problems were to be anticipated with the merger of two companies of these sizes. However, many problems were not anticipated and had become very costly to the company.

HUMAN RESOURCES MANAGEMENT PROBLEMS

There were union questions. Federal Express traditionally had been a nonunion shop, while the Flying Tigers' employees were predominately unionized. During the merger, the National Mediation Board could not determine a majority among the pilots at Federal Express and Flying Tigers. The board requires a majority to decide the union status at any firm. Because a majority could not be determined, the mediation board decided to allow the temporary mix of union and nonunion employees until the fall of 1989, when elections would determine if there would be union representation. The ruling had created ambiguities in employee status and raised some important financial and legal issues for Federal Express, unions, and employees.[13]

An executive in the international division described Federal Express's feelings on unions: "They [Flying Tigers] had a lot of unions. Tigers was a traditional company . . . and we [Federal Express] don't dislike unions . . . Our feelings about unions is [sic]

that if you get a union, you deserve it, because you have not managed your business well. We would like to think that we could keep that old family [feeling]. We realize that we can't keep the old family. It's very difficult to keep the family spirit corporatewide [after a merger]."

Tiger people had a variety of attitudes to job offers after the merger. The employees of Federal Express believed that Federal Express was a great place to work, mainly because of its people-oriented policies. Because of this belief, most of the managers thought that the Flying Tigers' employees would "welcome the merger with open arms." A communications official said: "We tried to position Federal Express as a great place to work, a wonderful place to be—cutting edge technology, a great aircraft fleet, a great employee group, good management—all those types of things."

Flying Tigers had a rich and long history. Tiger employees prided themselves on their team spirit and their willingness to take pay cuts for the good of The Flying Tiger Line, Inc., during the lean years. Employees proudly displayed items with the Tiger logo on them.

A long-time Tiger employee and member of one of the pre-merger Tiger committees remarked on the job offers: "For the employees, it [the merger] was a spectrum, we've got all of them on a line. Up in front, we've got those employees for whom the merger was the best thing that ever happened to them. In the back, you've got the employees where it was the worst thing that ever happened—because of personal things, they decided to leave the company. And then there's the group of employees in the middle, which really composed the majority of Flying Tigers' employees, that it really didn't matter one way or the other since they never moved. All they did was change their uniforms from Friday to Monday. They're basically doing the same jobs in the same locations." A member of his family and many friends refused to accept a job with Federal Express. He explained their refusal, by saying: "Because [Federal Express was] taking the name away. You were taking the history of the Flying Tiger line away . . . because we were a small company, we were like a close-knit family." Another middle-level former Tiger said, "Although a lot of merger information was provided to people at headquarters in L.A., people at other locations, like Boston, received less information." She said that some Tigers refused the job offer for the following reason: "They left, I think, just because of the attitude that . . . you're taking Flying Tigers away and I don't want to go with you." Some Tigers hoped that Federal Express would permit them to keep the Flying Tiger name or change the company name to Federal Tigers.

There were cultural differences. A Federal Express executive on the Tigerclaws Committee commented on cultural differences by saying: "The difference was astounding. Absolutely astounding. Federal Express's employees, typically, they seem to be younger, we're all in uniforms, enthusiastic about the company. You can walk around Federal Express and everybody can tell you what the corporate philosophy is . . . I remember standing in the Los Angeles airport facility . . . it's typical Federal Express. And you go over to the Tiger facility and here are all of these much older guys standing around. None of them in any type of uniform, clothes were all over the mat, there was [sic] no apparent standards, whatsoever. You know, kicking some of the packages, tossing them, or throwing

them. It was just . . . just terrible. I couldn't believe it. But that was part of the way they did business. They referred to a lot of the cargo that they carried as big, ugly freight. And to us . . . we go around thinking every customer's package is the most important thing we carry."

A former Tiger employee shared her perspective on the differences: "Most of the employees that you dealt with you had known for a lot of years. We used to work together side by side very closely for 20 years. And this company, Federal Express, isn't even 20 years old. You walk into a meeting or classroom or something . . . Federal Express people are introducing themselves to other Federal Express people. Tiger people found that really hard to believe—that you didn't know everybody at Federal Express."

During the announcement of the merger, Mr. Smith made a job offer to all the employees of Flying Tigers. Almost 90 percent of the 6,600 former Tiger employees took the offer. In a two-week period, from July 15 to 31, over 4,000 new jobs were to be created and Tiger employees transferred to these jobs. Many employees had to be relocated, because the old Tiger hub in Columbus, Ohio, was phased out, and primarily only freight and maintenance personnel were kept at the hub in Los Angeles. Some job placements were troublesome, because the human resources department had difficulty obtaining job descriptions and pay scales from Flying Tigers. During the haste, there were quite a number of mismatches of jobs and employees.

One of Federal Express's personnel officers remarked: "I was concerned about being able to meet employee's expectations. A lot of times people coming in from outside of Federal Express have this—I mean it's a great place, but they have this picture that it's a fairy tale place, and that there aren't any real problems and that everybody gets his own way. So I was concerned about the expectations that people brought, both positive and negative. How are we going to make people feel real good about the company?"

To help former Flying Tigers' employees determine whether to accept Federal Express's job offers, Federal Express provided the employees with detailed information about the company. Videotapes introducing Federal Express and explaining the benefits of working for the company were mailed to the homes of Tiger employees. Additionally, many Tiger employees were flown into Federal Express's headquarters in Memphis and given the "grand tour." "Express Teams," groups of four to five employees, visited Flying Tigers' locations and gave them previews of what it was like to work for Federal Express.

Regarding expectations, one long-time Tiger remarked: "There's still a lot of unhappy people in Memphis that came out of L.A., because I think they expected an awful lot. They had the option of saying no to a job and being out on the street looking for something else, or they could come to Memphis and have Federal Express be their employer. And there are a lot of people that still take offense at the fact that Federal Express bought Flying Tigers. But those people have an attitude that they have to deal with." Another former Tiger remarked: "And I honestly thought that by going from a small company to a large company, I was just going to be another number. But . . . it's also their attention to people. All of the hype and promotion they did before T-day [merger day] to Flying Tiger people that they were people oriented . . . we really didn't [know] what that meant and what it would mean to us individually until we became employees."

SUMMARY

Since 1985, Federal Express's international business had lost approximately $74 million and given company executives a lifetime supply of headaches.[14] To improve Federal Express's competitive position with its overseas rivals and overcome the foreign regulations regarding landing rights, Frederick Smith announced in December 1988 the acquisition of Tiger International, Inc. Although the combined companies would have $2.1 billion in debt, Flying Tigers was expected to provide Federal Express with desperately needed international delivery routes. The Tiger acquisition would allow Federal Express to use its own planes for overseas package delivery where Federal Express used to contract other carriers. In addition, Tigers' sizable long-range fleet could be used to achieve dominance in the international heavy-freight business that Federal Express had yet to crack.

Suppose you had been in Thomas Oliver's shoes and were the head of the Tigerclaws Committee. What were the major problems and opportunities facing Federal Express? What should be the priorities of the Tigerclaws Committee? How would you solve or reduce the problems and exploit the opportunities?

SOURCE: A case study by Howard S. Tu, Fogelman College of Business and Economics, Memphis State University; and Sherry E. Sullivan, Bowling Green State University.

Questionable Purchasing Practices

Motton Electronics was widely respected in the industry as being fair, dependable, and progressive. Cy Bennett, founder of the company, was chair of the board and majority stockholder. One of the company's progressive practices was to employ professional managers as members of top management. Each carefully selected manager received an excellent salary for performing his or her job. None of the top management group served on the board.

One month ago, Bennett reported to the board that he had facts proving that the director of purchasing for the company, Russell Hale, was giving preferential treatment to certain vendors and, in turn, was receiving merchandise and money. After the chair presented the evidence, the board formally condemned such purchasing practices by unanimous vote.

Immediately following this action, a vocal board member asserted that he believed the chief executive officer was responsible for all employee behavior on the job, that such administrative negligence should not be tolerated, and that the board needed a policy on the issue. This statement triggered an extensive discussion among the directors on topics such as shared responsibility for subordinates' actions, relevant duties of the board of directors, and related policy implications.

The meeting ended with a motion, unanimously supported, that Bennett (1) decide on appropriate measures regarding the errant director of purchasing and (2) develop and implement a policy on shared responsibility.

Bennett believed his prompt action on these matters would be critical to managerial performance, to the firm's profitability, and to the value of his majority block of company stock.

SOURCE: J. Champion and J. Hames, *Critical Incidents in Management: Decision and Policy Issues,* 6th ed. (Burr Ridge, IL: Richard D. Irwin, 1989).

Workforce Reduction Policy

Five years ago Wireweave, Inc., moved to a rural area 25 miles outside a large southern city. The company, formerly situated in a midwestern industrial city, chose this location primarily because of the lower wage rates paid in the community, a nonunion tradition in the region, and a favorable tax situation.

Wireweave, a manufacturer of wire products, has two major high-volume product lines: aluminum wire screen and dish racks. The dish racks are supplied to several appliance manufacturers for use in automatic dishwashers.

Because of intense industry competition, Wireweave's management realized several years ago that if Wireweave was to continue manufacturing aluminum wire screen and dish racks—and even stay in business—it would have to procure up-to-date equipment, become more automated and computerized, and even use robots for some of the hottest and dustiest jobs. After a two-year evalua-tion of production needs and an analysis of technologically advanced manufacturing equipment (including robots), Wireweave purchased equipment that would modernize production and replace 65 employees, representing about 33 percent of the total labor force. Significant labor costs would be saved by this employment reduction. As a result, Steve Jackson, president of Wireweave, expected the company to regain its competitiveness and profitability.

The following spring, shortly after installing the new equipment, Jackson called in Muriel Fincher, human resources director, and told her that the company could no longer afford to employ the unneeded workers. He requested that she decide on an acceptable plan for reducing company employment by 65 persons, and the sooner the better in terms of company profitability. Jackson also asked that she recommend a specific operating policy covering future workforce reductions.

Fincher had successfully handled some tough challenges as human resources director, but the latest assignments from Jackson were the most difficult ones she had faced. As Fincher considered relevant options and constraints, her deliberations were dominated by three factors: (1) the company's economic and ethical responsibilities to terminated employees, (2) the

potential morale problems for employees who would be retained, and (3) the pressure from Jackson for a prompt decision and action.

SOURCE: J. Champion and J. James, *Critical Incidents in Management: Decision and Policy Issues,* 6th ed. (Burr Ridge, IL: Richard D. Irwin. 1989).

Foundations of Management
- Managing
- The External Environment
- Managerial Decision Making

Planning:
Delivering Strategic Value
- Planning and Strategic Management
- Ethics and Corporate Responsibility
- International Management
- New Ventures

Strategy Implementation

Organizing: Building a Dynamic Organization
- Organization Structure
- The Responsive Organization
- Human Resources Management
- Managing the Diverse Workforce

Leading:
Mobilizing People
- Leadership
- Motivating for Performance
- Managing Teams
- Communicating

Controlling:
Learning and Changing
- Managerial Control
- Managing Technology and Innovation
- Creating and Managing Change

Leading: Mobilizing People

Now that you know about organizing and staffing, Part Four elaborates on managing people by discussing the third function of management: leading. Effective managers know how to lead others toward unit and organizational success. Chapter 12 explores the essential components of leadership, including the use of power in the organization. Chapter 13 focuses on motivating people, with implications for enhancing performance. Chapter 14 examines work teams, including the management of relationships between groups. Finally, Chapter 15 addresses a vital management activity: communication. Here, you will learn how to maximize your effectiveness in communicating with other people throughout the organization.

CHAPTER 12

Leadership

Every soldier has a right to competent command.

—Julius Caesar

CHAPTER OUTLINE

Vision
Leading and Managing
Leading and Following
Power and Leadership
  Sources of Power
Traditional Approaches to
  Understanding Leadership
  Leader Traits
  Leader Behaviors
  Situational Approaches to Leadership
Contemporary Perspectives on Leadership
  Charismatic Leadership
  Transformational Leadership
  Post-Heroic Leadership
  A Note on Courage
Developing Your Leadership Skills

LEARNING OBJECTIVES

After studying Chapter 12, you will know:

1. What it means to be a leader.

2. How a good vision helps you be a better leader.

3. How to understand and use power.

4. The personal traits and skills of effective leaders.

5. The behaviors that will make you a better leader.

6. What it means to be a charismatic and transformational leader.

7. How to further your own leadership development.

SOME PROMINENT LEADERS

- Andrea Jung has been one of the most successful CEOs of a U.S. corporation in recent years. She has overhauled everything Avon does. After becoming CEO, Jung sold Avon products door to door, and in the process learned about the customers and the challenges of her sales force. Once she knew Avon's shortcomings, she established a turnaround plan. Jung announced the need for new product lines, blockbuster products, selling Avon in retail stores (which Avon had

Andrea Jung, CEO of Avon Products Inc., the world's leading direct seller of beauty products. Jung is helping rewrite Avon's business rules by launching its first retail brand, "beComing".

never done in its long history), and cutting millions in costs. The plan was highly ambitious, and most people thought she couldn't pull it off. One Paine Webber analyst reported that the plan had "a high probability of disappointment." Jung proved the critics wrong. "The results are strikingly different than they have been under any other CEO," says a Merrill Lynch analyst. Avon's board members recently named her chairman, a title they had been withholding until they saw how she performed.

- E*Trades' CEO Christos Costakos wants to move the company from a basic online brokerage to a financial services supermarket, with checking accounts, car loans, mortgages, insurance, and credit cards. Critics worry that the firm's client base is low-end and won't use the full array of services, especially during a bear market. And its total assets are small potatoes compared to Charles Schwab and Fidelity. When asked if his five-year-old company can get that big, Costakos says, "I just get so crazy when you guys ask that. [The big companies] have been in business for 40 years . . . they were in our position at age five" (p. 90).

- David S. Potrruck transformed Charles Schwab, the traditional financial services company, into a prototype of how a huge company could move quickly and compete successfully with the small, new players in the Internet age. He began by transforming himself into an executive who listens "to hear rather than to answer." He says, "The more I am known by those I want to follow me, and the more I can know them, the greater will be our ability to do great things together."

- Francis Collins, director of the National Institute of Health's National Human Genome Research Institute, and J. Craig Venter, former CEO of Celera Genomics, were direct competitors. They don't like each other. But they shared a vision. In 2000 they jointly announced that their organizations had deciphered the biochemical "letters" of human DNA. Knowing the genetic codes will transform medicine and lead to a revolution in the diagnosis and treatment of diseases. The joint announcement by these two visionaries marked the beginning of the genomic era.

Sources: K. Brooker, "It Took a Lady to Save Avon," *Fortune*, October 15, 2001, pp. 202–8; J. Helyar, "At E*Trade, Growing Up Is Hard to Do," *Fortune*, March 18, 2002, pp. 88–90. F. Andrews, "Hard Lessons Learned at Schwab," *The New York Times*, April 30, 2000, Section 3, p. 7; F. Golden and M. D. Lemonick, "The Race is Over," *Time*, July 3, 2000, pp. 18–25.

People get excited about the topic of leadership. They want to know: What makes a great leader? Executives at all levels in all industries are interested in this question. They believe the answer will bring improved organizational performance and personal career success. They hope to acquire the skills that will transform an "average" manager into a true leader like the ones described in "Setting the Stage."

Fortunately, leadership can be taught—and learned. According to one source, "Leadership seems to be the marshaling of skills possessed by a majority but used by a minority. But it's something that can be learned by anyone, taught to everyone, denied to no one."[1]

What is leadership? To start, a leader is one who influences others to attain goals. The greater the number of followers, the greater the influence. And the more successful the attainment of worthy goals, the more evident the leadership. But we must explore beyond this bare definition to capture the excitement and intrigue that devoted followers and students of leadership feel when they see a great leader in action, and to understand what organizational leaders really do and what it really takes to gain entry into *Fortune*'s Hall of Fame for U.S. Business Leadership.

Outstanding leaders combine good strategic substance and effective interpersonal processes to formulate and implement strategies that produce results and sustainable competitive advantage.[2] They may launch enterprises, build organization cultures, win wars, or otherwise change the course of events.[3] They are strategists who seize opportunities others overlook, but "they are also passionately concerned with detail—all the small, fundamental realities that can make or mar the grandest of plans."[4]

Vision

"The leader's job is to create a vision," stated Robert L. Swiggett, former chair of Kollmorgen Corporation.[5] Until a few years ago, *vision* was not a word one heard managers utter. But today, having a vision for the future and communicating that vision to others are known to be essential components of great leadership. "If there is no vision, there is no business," maintains entrepreneur Mark Leslie.[6] Joe Nevin, an MIS director, described leaders as "painters of the vision and architects of the journey."[7] Practicing businesspeople are not alone in this belief; academic research shows that a clear vision and communication of that vision lead to higher venture growth in entrepreneurial firms.[8]

vision

A mental image of a possible and desirable future state of the organization.

A **vision** is a mental image of a possible and desirable future state of the organization. It expresses the leader's ambitions for the organization.[9] The best visions are both ideal and unique.[10] If a vision conveys an *ideal*, it communicates a standard of excellence and a clear choice of positive values. If the vision is also *unique*, it communicates and inspires pride in being different from other organizations. The choice of language is important; the words should imply a combination of realism and optimism, an action orientation, and resolution and confidence that the vision will be attained.[11]

Great leaders imagine an ideal future for their organizations that goes beyond the ordinary and beyond what others may have thought possible. They strive to realize significant achievements that others have not. In short, as the following examples show, leaders must be forward looking and clarify the directions in which they want their organizations, and even entire industries, to move.

Here are some examples of business leaders and their visions:

• John Malone of Liberty Media wants to create the world's largest cable company. His goal is an international cable empire, including millions of subscribers in Europe, Latin America, Japan, and Australia. He wants people not only subscribing to his service but also buying lots of his content. Malone would feed them programming through Liberty Media's holdings in content companies, including Rupert Murdoch's News Corp. and Discovery Communications. While some people believe that Malone is downplaying the difficulties of operating in a world that is both global and local, and the possibility that international cable will become a black hole, Malone's bet is that he can feed the world a constant stream of phone service, Internet access, and pay TV.

- Vern Raburn's vision would do for air travel what the PC did for computing. He intends to build a six-seater jet that goes just as far, almost as fast, and burns much less fuel at a fraction of the cost of competing jets. The plan is to open up private air travel to far more people than can now afford it. He'll go after business travelers and wealthy individuals, and also create air-limo services that will compete with major airlines' first- and business-class fares. The editor of *Flying* magazine calls the idea "mind-boggling. It would be unprecedented in the history of aviation" (p. 136). Critics think it will be impossible. But as the designer of the jet's revolutionary engine says, "They think we can't do it because *they* can't. It's the 'if it doesn't exist, it can't exist' theorem" (p. 136).

AOL Chairman and CEO Steve Case's vision of "ruling the Internet" involves an interactive future where software takes a backseat.

- Phil Turner was facilities manager at Raychem Corporation, fixing toilets and air conditioners. But rather than believing that the workers in the facilities were performing menial jobs and making only trivial contributions to the organization, Turner viewed their work as a mission—to make people feel good, "to lift people's spirits through beauty, cleanliness, and functionality, enthusiasm, good cheer, and excellence."

SOURCES: J. Kouzes and B. Posner, *The Leadership Challenge* (San Francisco: Jossey-Bass, 1995); E. Schonfeld, "The Little (Jet) Engine That Could," *Fortune*, July 24, 2000, pp. 132–42; J. Guyon, "Malone's Global Grab," *Fortune*, February 18, 2002, pp. 98–100.

As you can see, visions can be small or large and can exist throughout all organizational levels as well as at the very top. The important points are that (1) a vision is necessary for effective leadership; (2) a person or team can develop a vision for any job, work unit, or organization; and (3) many people, including managers who do not develop into strong leaders, do not develop a clear vision—instead, they focus on performing or surviving on a day-by-day basis.

Put another way, leaders must know what they want.[12] And other people must understand what that is. The leader must be able to articulate the vision, clearly and often. Other people throughout the organization should understand the vision and be able to state it clearly themselves. That's a start. But the vision means nothing until the leader and followers take action to turn the vision into reality.[13]

Two metaphors reinforce the important concept of vision.[14] The first is the jigsaw puzzle. It is much easier to put a puzzle together if you have the picture on the box cover in front of you. Without the picture, or vision, the lack of direction is likely to result in frustration and failure. The second metaphor is the slide projector. Imagine a projector that is out of focus. If you had to watch blurred images for a long period of time, you would get confused, impatient, and disoriented. You would stop following the presentation and lose respect for the presenter. It is the leader's job to focus the projector. That is what communicating a vision is all about: making it clear where you are heading.

Imagine trying to complete a challenging jigsaw puzzle without the "vision" of what you're working toward.

Not just any vision will do. Visions can be inappropriate, and even fail, for a variety of reasons.[15] First, an inappropriate vision may reflect merely the leader's personal needs. Such a vision can be unethical, or may fail because of lack of acceptance by the market or by those who must implement it.

Second (and related to the first), an inappropriate vision may ignore stakeholder needs. Third, the leader must stay abreast of environmental changes. Although effective leaders maintain confidence and persevere despite obstacles, the time may come when the facts dictate that the vision must change. You will learn more about change and how to manage it later in the text.

Leading and Managing

Effective managers are not necessarily true leaders. Many administrators, supervisors, and even top executives execute their responsibilities successfully without being great leaders. But these positions afford opportunity for leadership. The ability to lead effectively, then, will set the excellent managers apart from the average ones.

Whereas management must deal with the ongoing, day-to-day complexities of organizations, true leadership includes effectively orchestrating important change.[16] While managing requires planning and budgeting routines, leading includes setting the direction (creating a vision) for the firm. Management requires structuring the organization, staffing it with capable people, and monitoring activities; leadership goes beyond these functions by inspiring people to attain the vision. Great leaders keep people focused on moving the organization toward its ideal future, motivating them to overcome whatever obstacles lie in the way.

Many observers decry the rarity of strong leadership.[17] While many managers focus on superficial activities and worry about short-term profits and stock prices, too few have emerged as leaders who foster innovation and the attainment of long-term goals. And whereas many managers are overly concerned with "fitting in" and not rocking the boat, those who emerge as leaders are more concerned with making important decisions that may break with tradition but are humane, moral, and right. The leader puts a premium on substance rather than on style.

It is important to be clear here about several things. First, management and leadership are both vitally important. To highlight the need for more leadership is not to minimize the importance of management or managers. It is to say that leadership involves unique processes that are distinguishable from basic management processes.[18] Moreover, just because they involve different processes does not mean that they require different, separate people. The same individual can exemplify effective managerial processes, leadership processes, both, or neither.

Some people still will dislike the idea of distinguishing between management and leadership, maintaining it is artificial or derogatory toward the managers and management processes that make orgnizations run. Perhaps a better or more useful distinction is between supervisory and strategic leadership.[19] **Supervisory leadership** is behavior that provides guidance, support, and corrective feedback for the day-to-day activities of work unit members. **Strategic leadership** gives purpose and meaning to organizations. Strategic leadership involves anticipating and envisioning a viable future for the organization, and working with others to intitate changes that create such a future.[20]

supervisory leadership

Behavior that provides guidance, support, and corrective feedback for the day-to-day activities of work unit members.

strategic leadership

Behavior that gives purpose and meaning to organizations, envisioning and creating a positive future.

Leading and Following

Organizations succeed or fail not only because of how well they are led but because of how well followers follow. Just as managers are not necessarily good leaders, people are not always good followers. The most effective followers are capable of independent thinking and at the same time are actively committed to organizational goals.[21] Robert Townsend, who led a legendary turnaround at Avis, says that the most important characteristic of a follower may be the willingness to tell the truth.[22] Great leaders do the same.[23]

As a manager, you will be asked to play the roles of both leader and follower. As you lead the people who report to you, you will report to your boss. You will be a member of some teams and committees, and you may chair others. While the leadership roles get the glamour and therefore are the roles that many people covet, followers must perform their responsibilities conscientiously as well.

Effective followers are distinguished from ineffective ones by their enthusiasm and commitment to the organization and to a person or purpose—an idea, a product—other than themselves or their own interests. They master skills that are useful to their organizations, and they hold to performance standards that are higher than required. Effective followers may not get the glory, but they know their contributions to the organization are valuable. And as they make those contributions, they study leaders in preparation for their own leadership roles.[24]

Power and Leadership

Central to effective leadership is **power**—the ability to influence other people. In organizations, this often means the ability to get things done or accomplish one's goals despite resistance from others.

power

The ability to influence others.

Sources of Power

One of the earliest and still most useful approaches to understanding power suggests that leaders have five important potential sources of power in organizations.[25] Figure 12.1 shows those power sources.

Legitimate Power The leader with *legitimate power* has the right, or the authority, to tell others what to do; employees are obligated to comply with legitimate orders. For example, a supervisor tells an employee to remove a safety hazard, and the employee removes the hazard because he has to obey the authority of his boss. In contrast, when a staff person lacks the authority to give an order to a line manager, the staff person has no legitimate power over the manager. As you might guess, managers have more legitimate power over their direct reports than they do over their peers, bosses, and others inside or outside their organizations.[26]

Reward Power The leader who has *reward power* influences others because she controls valued rewards; people comply with the leader's wishes in order to receive those rewards. For example, a manager works hard to achieve her performance goals to get a positive performance review and a big pay raise from her boss. On the other hand, if company policy dictates that everyone receive the same salary increase, a leader's reward power decreases because he or she is unable to give higher raises.

Coercive Power The leader with *coercive power* has control over punishments; people comply to avoid those punishments. For instance, a manager implements an absenteeism policy that administers disciplinary actions to offending employees. A manager has less coercive power if, say, a union contract limits her ability to punish. In general, lower-level managers have less legitimate, coercive, and reward power than do middle- and higher-level managers.[27]

Referent Power The leader with *referent power* has personal characteristics that appeal to others; people comply because of admiration, a desire for approval, personal liking, or a desire to be like the leader. For example, young, ambitious managers emulate the work habits and personal style of a successful, charismatic

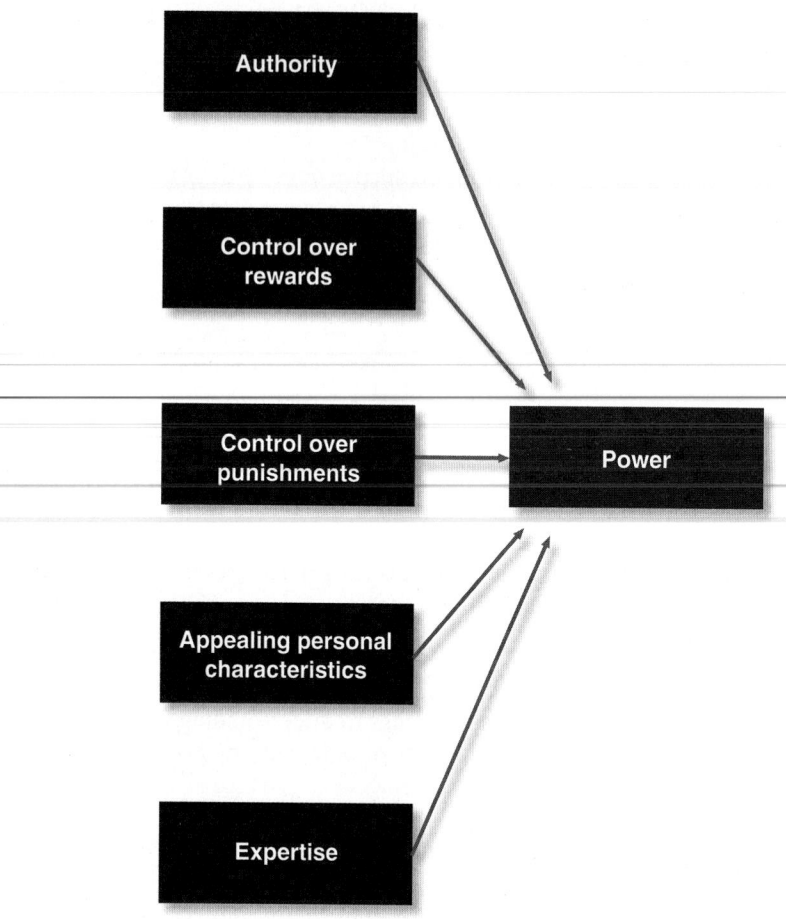

FIGURE 12.1
Sources of Power

SOURCE: Adapted from J. R. P. French and B. Raven, "The Bases of Social Power," in *Studies in Social Power,* ed. D. Cartwright (Ann Arbor, MI: Institute for Social Research, 1959).

executive. An executive who is incompetent, disliked, and commands little respect has little referent power.

Expert Power   The leader who has *expert power* has certain expertise or knowledge; people comply because they believe in, can learn from, or can otherwise gain from that expertise. For example, a sales manager gives her salespeople some tips on closing a deal. The salespeople then alter their sales techniques because they respect the manager's expertise. On the other hand, this manager may lack expert power in other areas, such as finance; thus, her salespeople may ignore her advice concerning financial matters.

People who are in a position that gives them the right to tell others what to do, who can reward and punish, who are well liked and admired, and who have expertise on which other people can draw will be powerful members of the organization. All of these sources of power are potentially important. Although it is easy to assume that the most powerful bosses are those who have high legitimate power and control major rewards and punishments, it is important not to underestimate the more "personal" sources like expert and referent power. These personal sources of power are the ones most closely related to people's motivation to perform to their managers' expectations.[28]

Traditional Approaches to Understanding Leadership

Three traditional approaches to studying leadership are the trait approach, the behavioral approach, and the situational approach.

Leader Traits

The **trait approach** is the oldest leadership perspective and was dominant for several decades. This approach seems logical for studying leadership: It focuses on individual leaders and attempts to determine the personal characteristics (traits) that great leaders share. What set Winston Churchill, Alexander the Great, Gandhi, Napoleon, and Martin Luther King apart from the crowd? The trait approach assumes the existence of a leadership personality and assumes that leaders are born, not made.

> **trait approach**
>
> A leadership perspective that focuses on individual leaders and attempts to determine the personal characteristics that great leaders share.

From 1904 to 1948, over 100 leadership trait studies were conducted.[29] At the end of that period, management scholars concluded that no particular set of traits is necessary for a person to become a successful leader. Enthusiasm for the trait approach diminished, but some research on traits continued. By the mid-1970s, a more balanced view emerged: Although no traits ensure leadership success, certain characteristics are potentially useful. The current perspective is that some personality characteristics—many of which a person need not be born with but can strive to acquire—do distinguish effective leaders from other people.[30]

1. **Drive.** *Drive* refers to a set of characteristics that reflect a high level of effort. Drive includes high need for achievement, constant striving for improvement, ambition, energy, tenacity (persistence in the face of obstacles), and initiative. In several countries, the achievement needs of top executives have been shown to be related to the growth rates of their organizations.[31] But the need to achieve can be a drawback if leaders focus on personal achievement and get so personally involved with the work that they do not delegate enough authority and responsibility. And whereas need for achievement has been shown to predict organizational effectiveness in entrepreneurial firms, it does not predict success for division heads in larger and more bureaucratic firms.[32]

2. **Leadership motivation.** Great leaders not only have drive; they *want to lead*. They have a high need for power, preferring to be in leadership rather than follower positions. A high power need induces people to attempt to influence others, and sustains interest and satisfaction in the process of leadership. When the power need is exercised in moral and socially constructive ways, rather than to the detriment of others, leaders inspire more trust, respect, and commitment to their vision.

3. **Integrity.** *Integrity* is the correspondence between actions and words. Honesty and credibility, in addition to being desirable characteristics in their own right, are especially important for leaders because these traits inspire trust in others.

4. **Self-confidence.** *Self-confidence* is important for a number of reasons. The leadership role is challenging, and setbacks are inevitable. Self-confidence allows a leader to overcome obstacles, make decisions despite uncertainty, and instill confidence in others.

5. **Knowledge of the business.** Effective leaders have a high level of *knowledge* about their industries, companies, and technical matters. Leaders must have the intelligence to interpret vast quantities of information. Advanced degrees are useful in a career, but ultimately less important than acquired expertise in matters relevant to the organization.[33]

To many, Colin Powell is an example of a powerful and charismatic leader.

FROM THE PAGES OF

BusinessWeek

Andrea Jung is CEO of Avon Products, and tackled what may have been the toughest turnaround challenge in consumer products. Avon was at a crucial turning point in its history. Founded in 1886, it pioneered door-to-door selling and hit its peak when the mothers of most of today's women tried their first lipstick. The direct sales model, tremendously successful when most women didn't work, is now antiquated. It was up to Jung to make sure this old company with an old model survives in the modern era.

Jung had very little operating experience when she took over in 1999. Suddenly she was running a company with 3 million independent sales reps and operations in 137 countries. She vowed to make Avon as big in the women's beauty business as Disney is in entertainment. She wants Avon to be the "ultimate relationship marketer of products and services for women."

Jung needs to rebuild the company from the ground up. Much more than selling cosmetics door-to-door, Avon will be the source for anything and everything a woman wants to buy. Possible products include vitamins and nutritional supplements, in-store spa facials and massages, and financial services and legal advice targeted toward women. Each customer will have three choices for how to buy: through an Avon rep, in a store, or online.

High hopes lie with the Web. The biggest challenge: figuring out how the Avon reps will fit in. The reps produce 98 percent of the company's revenues, and they have been the backbone of the company, and of its brand image, forever. Jung says, "If we don't include them in everything we do, then we're just another retail brand, just another Internet site, and I don't see the world needing more of those" (p. 140). Jung surveyed the reps about the website and created incentives for them to get involved. She is involving both the computer-savvy and the computer-illiterate in the process. Among other things, the site asks customers if they want a personal eRepresentative in their Zip code. "What we do is about relationships, affiliations, being with other people. That is never going to go out" (p. 140).

Jung needs the support of those millions of independent sales reps and employees to get today's women to buy an old brand. Addressing 13,000 reps at a sales convention, she stated, "Avon is first and foremost about you. I stand here before you and promise you that that will never change" (p. 138). To women in a Chinese factory, she said "We will change the future of women around the world!" (p. 138).

The performance pressure is huge. Jung is one of the most-watched CEOs in the United States. So far, the sales reps are responding enthusiastically, and few observers are betting against her.

SOURCE: N. Byrnes, "Avon: The New Calling," *Business Week*, September 18, 2000, pp. 137–48.

Finally, there is one personal skill that may be the most important: the ability to perceive the needs and goals of others and to adjust one's personal leadership approach accordingly.[34] Effective leaders do not rely on one leadership style; rather, they are capable of using different styles as the situation warrants.[35] This quality is the cornerstone of the situational approaches to leadership, which we will discuss shortly.

Leader Behaviors

behavioral approach

A leadership perspective that attempts to identify what good leaders do—that is, what behaviors they exhibit.

The **behavioral approach** to leadership attemps to identify what good leaders do. Should leaders focus on getting the job done or on keeping their followers happy? Should they make decisions autocratically or democratically? In the behavioral approach, personal characteristics are considered less important than the actual behaviors leaders exhibit.

Three general categories of leadership behavior have received particular attention: behaviors related to task performance, group maintenance, and employee participation in decision making.

Task Performance Leadership requires getting the job done. **Task performance behaviors** are the leader's efforts to ensure that the work unit or organization reaches its goals. This dimension is variously referred to as *concern for production*, *directive leadership*, *initiating structure*, or *closeness of supervision*. It includes a focus on work speed, quality and accuracy, quantity of output, and following the rules.[36]

> **task performance behaviors**
>
> Actions taken to ensure that the work group or organization reaches its goals.

Group Maintenance In exhibiting **group maintenance behaviors,** leaders take action to ensure the satisfaction of group members, develop and maintain harmonious work relationships, and preserve the social stability of the group. This dimension is sometimes referred to as *concern for people*, *supportive leadership*, or *consideration*. It includes a focus on people's feelings and comfort, appreciation of them, and stress reduction.[37]

> **group maintenance behaviors**
>
> Actions taken to ensure the satisfaction of group members, develop and maintain harmonious work relationships, and preserve the social stability of the group.

What *specific* behaviors do performance- and maintenance-oriented leadership imply? To help answer this question, assume you are asked to rate your boss on these two dimensions. If a leadership study were conducted in your organization, you would be asked to fill out a questionnaire similar to the one in Table 12.1. The behaviors indicated in the first set of questions represent performance-oriented leadership; those indicated in the second set represent maintenance-oriented leadership.

Questions Assessing Task Performance and Group Maintenance Leadership **TABLE 12.1**

Task Performance Leadership

1. Is your superior strict about observing regulations?
2. To what extent does your superior give you instructions and orders?
3. Is your superior strict about the amount of work you do?
4. Does your superior urge you to complete your work by a specified time?
5. Does your superior try to make you work to your maximum capacity?
6. When you do an inadequate job, does your superior focus on the inadequate way the job is done?
7. Does your superior ask you for reports about the progress of your work?
8. How precisely does your superior work out plans for goal achievement each month?

Group Maintenance Leadership

1. Can you talk freely with your superior about your work?
2. Does your superior generally support you?
3. Is your superior concerned about your personal problems?
4. Do you think your superior trusts you?
5. Does your superior give you recognition when you do your job well?
6. When a problem arises in your workplace, does your superior ask your opinion about how to solve it?
7. Is your superior concerned about your future benefits, such as promotions and pay raises?
8. Does your superior treat you fairly?

SOURCE: Reprinted from J. Misumi and M. Peterson, "The Performance-Maintenance (PM) Theory of Leadership: Review of a Japanese Research Program," *Administrative Science Quarterly* 30, no. 2 (June 1985), by permission of *Administrative Science Quarterly*, © 1985 by Johnson Graduate School of Management, Cornell University.

Leader-Member Exchange (LMX) theory

Highlights the importance of leader behaviors not just toward the group as a whole but toward individuals on a personal basis.

participation in decision making

Leader behaviors that managers perform in involving their employees in making decisions.

autocratic leadership

A form of leadership in which the leader makes decisions on his or her own and then announces those decisions to the group.

democratic leadership

A form of leadership in which the leader solicits input from subordinates.

laissez-faire

A leadership philosophy characterized by an absence of managerial decision making.

One theory of leadership, **Leader-Member Exchange (LMX) theory**,[38] highlights the importance of leader behaviors not just toward the group as a whole but toward individuals on a personal basis. The focus is primarily on the leader behaviors historically considered group maintenance.[39] According to LMX theory, and as supported by research evidence, maintenance behaviors such as trust, open communication, mutual respect, mutual obligation, and mutual loyalty form the cornerstone of relationships that are satisfying and perhaps more productive.[40]

Remember, though, the potential for cross-cultural differences. Maintenance behaviors are important everywhere, but the specific behaviors can differ from one culture to another. For example, in the United States, maintenance behaviors include dealing with people face-to-face; in Japan, written memos are preferred over giving directions face-to-face, thus avoiding confrontation and permitting face-saving in the event of disagreement.[41]

Participation in Decision Making How should a leader make decisions? More specifically, to what extent should leaders involve their people in making decisions?[42] The **participation-in-decision-making** dimension of leadership behavior can range from autocratic to democratic. **Autocratic leadership** makes decisions and then announces them to the group. **Democratic leadership** solicits input from others. Democratic leadership seeks information, opinions, and preferences, sometimes to the point of meeting with the group, leading discussions, and using consensus or majority vote to make the final choice.

The Effects of Leader Behavior How the leader behaves influences people's attitudes and performance. Studies of these effects focus on autocratic versus democratic decision styles or on performance- versus maintenance-oriented behaviors.

Decision Styles The classic study comparing autocratic and democratic styles found that a democratic approach resulted in the most positive attitudes, whereas an autocratic approach resulted in somewhat higher performance.[43] A **laissez-faire** style, in which the leader essentially made no decisions, led to more negative attitudes and lower performance. These results seem logical and probably represent the prevalent beliefs among managers about the general effects of these decision-making approaches.

Democratic styles, appealing though they may seem, are not always the most appropriate. When speed is of the essence, democratic decision making may be too slow, or people may demand decisiveness from the leader.[44] Whether a decision should be made autocratically or democratically depends on the characteristics of the leader, the followers, and the situation.[45] Thus, a situational approach to leader decision styles, discussed later in the chapter, is appropriate.

Performance and Maintenance Behaviors The performance and maintenance dimensions of leadership are independent of each other. In other words, a leader can behave in ways that emphasize one, both, or neither of these dimensions. Some research indicates that the ideal combination is to engage in both types of leader behaviors.

In the well-known Ohio State studies, a team of Ohio State University researchers investigated the effects of leader behaviors in a truck manufacturing plant of International Harvester.[46] Generally, supervisors who were high on *main-*

On the average, men and women are equally effective as leaders. However, the situation may make a difference: Male leaders tend to be more effective in military settings, and women are usually more effective in educational, social service, and government organizations. Why this is so is not completely clear.

Think about it for a moment: Do women and men behave differently in leadership roles? Is there a "male" leadership style, and if so, does it differ from the "female" style? Some think so, but Carly Fiorina, one of the most visible and powerful female executives in the United States, is described as gutsy, bold, and unflinching—words typically reserved for male CEOs taking big gambles.

According to an article in *Harvard Business Review*, the first female executives had to behave like men to get to the top. But women are moving into top management by drawing on unique skills and attitudes that men are less likely to possess. Men, says author Judy Rosener, are more likely to rely on their formal authority and on rewards and punishments (legitimate, reward, and coercive powers), whereas women tend to use their charisma, interpersonal skills, hard work, and personal contacts. In Rosener's study, women leaders claimed to encourage participation, share power and information, and enhance other people's self-worth. Additional academic research confirms that women managers tend to be more participative than males.

Admiral Louise Wilmot was the highest-ranking woman in the U.S. Navy when she retired.

Admiral Louise Wilmot was the highest-ranking woman in the U.S. Navy when she retired. Her leadership style emphasized teamwork and interpersonal relationships. When asked if her style arose because she is a woman, she replied that as a leader you should "preserve your person and preserve whatever you are that is good and wholesome and makes you interesting and different from everyone else. There is no reason in the world to surrender your soul, your person, or your spirit" (p. 89).

Cisco's John Chambers is one Silicon valley male who sees tremendous strengths in women leaders. He believes that great female leadership talent is waiting to be tapped, and is about to explode onto the Silicon Valley scene. Support for this comes from Harvard's Rosabeth Moss Kanter's comment, "Women get high ratings on exactly those skills needed to succeed in the global Information Age, where teamwork and partnering are so important" (p. 76).

SOURCE: J. B. Rosener, "Ways Women Lead," *Harvard Business Review* 68 (May–June 1990), pp. 103–11; A. Eagly, S. Karom, and M. Makhijani, "Gender and the Effectiveness of Leaders: A Meta-Analysis," *Psychological Bulletin*, 1995, pp. 125–45; V. H. Vroom, "Leadership and the Decision-Making Process," *Organizational Dynamics*, Spring 2000, pp. 82–93; P. Sellers, "The 50 Most Powerful Women in Business," *Fortune*, October 16, 2000, pp. 131–16, E. Fagenson-Eland and P. J. Kidder, "A Conversation with Rear Admiral Louise Wilmot: Taking the Lead and Leading the Way," *Organizational Dynamics*, Winter 2000, pp. 80–91; R. Sharpe, "As Leaders, Women Rule," *Business Week*, November 20, 2000, pp 74–84; A. Stanley, "For Women, to Soar Is Rare, to Fall Is Human," *The New York Times*, January 13, 2002, sec. 3, pp. 1, 10.

tenance behaviors (which the researchers termed *consideration*) had fewer grievances and less turnover in their work units than supervisors who were low on this dimension. The opposite held for *task performance behaviors* (which the team called *initiating structure*). Supervisors high on this dimension had more grievances and higher turnover rates.

When maintenance and performance leadership behaviors were considered together, the results were more complex. But one conclusion was clear: When a leader must be high on performance-oriented behaviors, he or she should *also* be maintenance oriented. Otherwise the leader will have employees with high rates of turnover and grievances.

At about the same time the Ohio State studies were being conducted, an equally famous research program at the University of Michigan was studying the impact of the same leader behaviors on groups' job performance.[47] Among other things, the researchers concluded that the most effective managers engaged in what they called *task-oriented behavior:* planning, scheduling, coordinating, providing resources, and setting performance goals. Effective managers also exhibited more *relationship-*

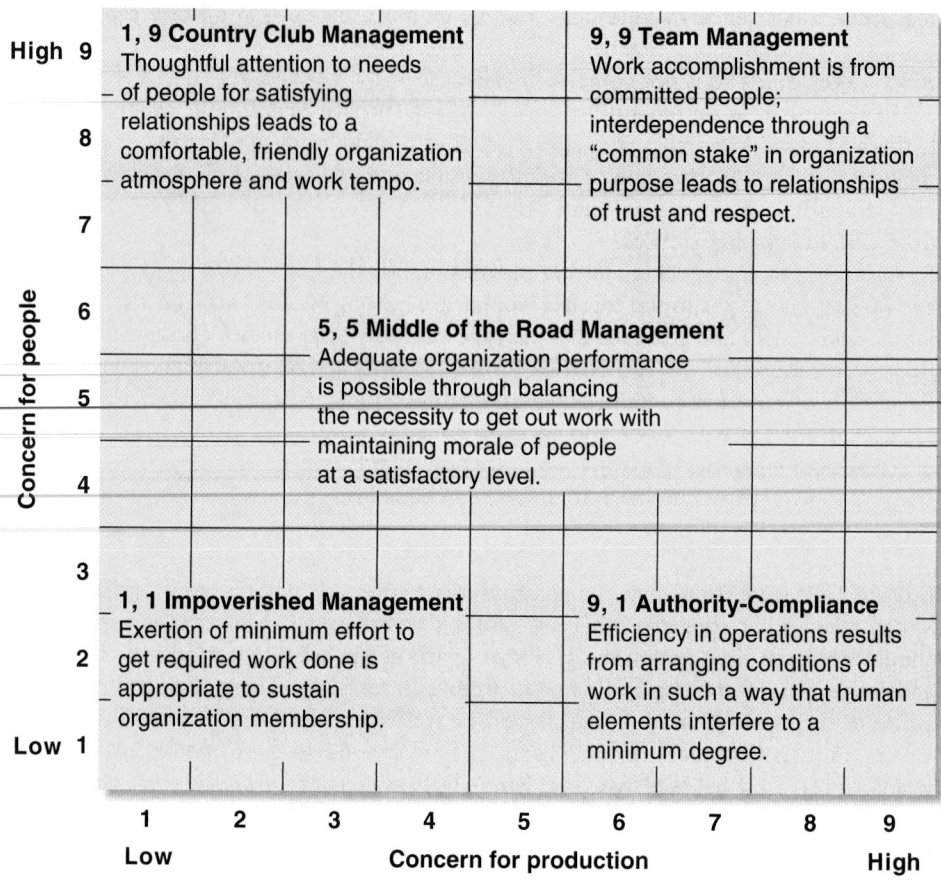

FIGURE 12.2
The Leadership Grid®

SOURCE: The Leadership Grid® Figure from *Leadership Dilemmas—Grid Solutions*, p. 29, by Robert R. Blake and Anne Adams McCanse. Copyright © 1991, by Robert R. Blake and the Estate of Jane S. Mouton. Used with permission. All rights reserved.

oriented behavior: demonstrating trust and confidence, being friendly and considerate, showing appreciation, keeping people informed, and so on. As you can see, these dimensions of leader behavior are essentially the task performance and group maintenance dimensions.

After the Ohio State and Michigan findings were published, it became popular to talk about the ideal leader as one who is always both performance and maintenance oriented. The best-known leadership training model to follow this style is Blake and Mouton's Leadership Grid.®[48] In grid training, managers are rated on their performance-oriented behavior (called *concern for production*) and maintenance-oriented behavior (*concern for people*). Then their scores are plotted on the grid shown in Figure 12.2. The highest score is a 9 on both dimensions.

As the figure shows, joint scores can fall at any point on the grid. Managers who did not score a 9,9—for example, those who were high on concern for people but low on concern for production—would then receive training on how to become a 9,9 leader.

For a long time, grid training was warmly received by U.S. business and industry. Later, however, it was criticized for embracing a simplistic, one-best-way style of leadership and ignoring the possibility that 9,9 is not best under all circumstances. For example, even 1,1 can be appropriate if employees know their jobs (and therefore don't need to receive directions). Also, they may enjoy their jobs and their co-workers enough that whether the boss shows personal concern for them is not very important. Nonetheless, if the manager is uncertain how to behave, it probably is best to exhibit behaviors that are related to both task performance and group maintenance.[49]

In fact, a wide range of effective leadership styles exists. Organizations that understand the need for diverse leadership styles will have a competitive advantage in the modern business environment over those that believe there is only "one best way."

Situational Approaches to Leadership

According to proponents of the **situational approach** to leadership, universally important traits and behaviors don't exist. They believe effective leader behaviors vary from situation to situation. *The leader should first analyze the situation and then decide what to do.* In other words, look before you lead.

> **situational approach**
>
> **Leadership perspective proposing that universally important traits and behaviors do not exist, and that effective leadership behavior varies from situation to situation.**

A head nurse in a hospital described her leadership style:

My leadership style is a mix of all styles. In this environment I normally let people participate...

But in a code blue situation where a patient is dying I automatically become very autocratic: "You do this; you do that; you, out of the room; you all better be quiet; you, get Dr Mansfield." The staff tell me that's the only time they see me like that. In an emergency like that, you don't have time to vote, talk a lot, or yell at each other. It's time for someone to set up the order.

I remember one time, one person saying, "Wait a minute, I want to do this." He wanted to do the mouth-to-mouth resuscitation. I knew the person behind him did it better, so I said, "No, he does it." This fellow told me later that I hurt him so badly to yell that in front of all the staff and doctors. It was like he wasn't good enough. So I explained it to him: that's the way it is. A life was on the line. I couldn't give you warm fuzzies. I couldn't make you look good because you didn't have the skills to give the very best to that patient who wasn't breathing anymore.

A similar business example comes from a division manager in a food and beverage company. When she was appointed to her position, the division was performing poorly, morale was terrible, and her charge was to turn the division around. The manager started participatively, with one-on-one conversations to get to know people and hear their opinions. She then held a three-day off-site meeting so people could offer solutions for various problems. After consensus emerged about the problems, priorities, and action plans, she shifted into a more autocratic style. She assigned specific managers to be responsible and accountable for each action step. Then, during the first few weeks of implementation, she continually reminded people of the new vision, the urgency, and the serious consequences if people failed to meet their responsibilities. "I had to be brutal about this follow-up and make sure this stuff happened. It was going to take discipline and focus" (p. 89). Seven months after the manager entered the crisis situation and started the turnaround efforts, the division exceeded its profit target by $5 million.

SOURCE: J. Wall, *Bosses* (Lexington, MA: Lexington Books, 1986), pp. 103–4; and D. Goleman, "Leadership That Gets Results," *Harvard Business Review*, March–April 2000, pp. 78–90.

Democracy and Autocracy

The leaders described above have their own intuitive situational approach to leadership. They know the potential advantages of the participatory approach to decision making, but they also know that in some circumstances they must make decisions on their own.

The first situational model of leadership was proposed in 1958 by Tannenbaum and Schmidt. In their classic *Harvard Business Review* article, these authors described how managers should consider three factors before deciding how to lead: forces in the

Situational Factors for Problem Analysis	
Decision significance:	The significance of the decision to the success of the project or organization.
Importance of commitment:	The importance of team members' commitment to the decision.
Leader's expertise:	Your knowledge or expertise in relation to this problem.
Likelihood of commitment:	The likelihood that the team would commit itself to a decision that you might make on your own.
Group support for objectives:	The degree to which the team supports the organization's objectives at stake in this problem.
Group expertise:	Team members' knowledge or expertise in relation to this problem.
Team competence:	The ability of team members to work together in solving problems.

TABLE 12.2
Situational Factors for
Problem Analysis

SOURCE: V. Vroom, "Leadership and the Decision-Making Process," *Organizational Dynamics*, Spring 2000, pp. 82–94. Copyright © 2000 with permission from Elsevier Science.

manager, forces in the subordinate, and forces in the situation.[50] Forces in the manager include the manager's personal values, inclinations, feelings of security, and confidence in subordinates. Forces in the subordinate include the employee's knowledge and experience, readiness to assume responsibility for decision making, interest in the task or problem, and understanding and acceptance of the organization's goals. Forces in the situation include the type of leadership style the organization values, the degree to which the group works effectively as a unit, the problem itself and the type of information needed to solve it, and the amount of time the leader has to make the decision.

Consider which of these forces makes an autocratic style most appropriate and which dictates a democratic, participative style. By engaging in this exercise, you are constructing a situational theory of leadership.

Although the Tannenbaum and Schmidt article was published almost a half century ago, most of its arguments remain valid. Since that time, other situational models have emerged. We will focus here on two of them: the Vroom model for decision making and path-goal theory. Others are summarized in the appendix to this chapter.

The Vroom Model of Leadership   This situational model follows in the tradition of Tannenbaum and Schmidt. The **Vroom model** emphasizes the participative dimension of leadership: how leaders go about making decisions. The model uses the basic situational approach of assessing the situation before determining the best leadership style.[51]

Vroom model

A situational model that focuses on the participative dimension of leadership.

Table 12.2 shows the situational factors used to analyze problems. Each is based on an important attribute of the problem the leader faces and should be assessed as either high or low.

The Vroom model, shown in Figure 12.3, operates like a funnel. You answer the questions one at a time, choosing high or low for each, sometimes skipping some questions as you follow the appropriate path. Eventually, you reach one of 14 possible endpoints.

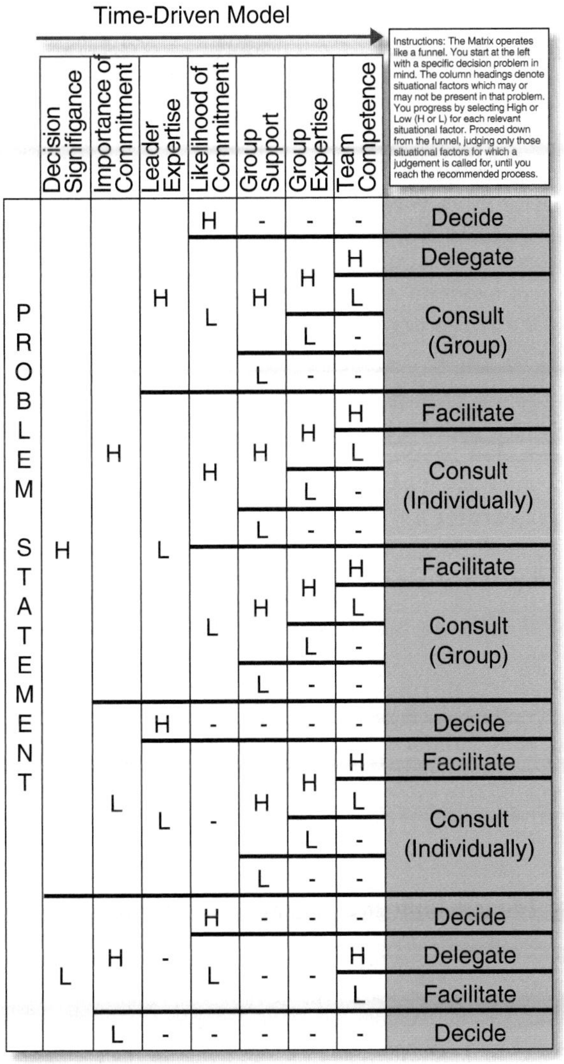

Time-Driven Model

Decision Significance	Importance of Commitment	Leader Expertise	Likelihood of Commitment	Group Support	Group Expertise	Team Competence	
H	H	H	H	–	–	–	Decide
		L	L	H	H	H	Delegate
						L	Consult (Group)
					L	–	Consult (Group)
				L	–	–	Consult (Group)
	H	H	H	H	H	H	Facilitate
						L	Consult (Individually)
					L	–	Consult (Individually)
				L	–	–	Consult (Individually)
		L	L	H	H	H	Facilitate
						L	Consult (Group)
					L	–	Consult (Group)
				L	–	–	Consult (Group)
	L	H	–	–	–	–	Decide
		L	–	H	H	H	Facilitate
						L	Consult (Individually)
					L	–	Consult (Individually)
				L	–	–	Consult (Individually)
L	H	–	H	–	–	–	Decide
			L	–	–	H	Delegate
						L	Facilitate
L	–	–	–	–	–	–	Decide

Instructions: The Matrix operates like a funnel. You start at the left with a specific decision problem in mind. The column headings denote situational factors which may or may not be present in that problem. You progress by selecting High or Low (H or L) for each relevant situational factor. Proceed down from the funnel, judging only those situational factors for which a judgement is called for, until you reach the recommended process.

FIGURE 12.3
Vroom's Model of Leadership Style

SOURCE: V. Vroom, "Leadership and the Decision-Making Process," *Organizational Dynamics*, Spring 2000, pp. 82–94. Copyright © 2000 with permission from Elsevier Science.

For each endpoint, the model states which of five decision styles is most appropriate. Several different decision styles may work, but the style recommended is the one that takes the least amount of time.

Figure 12.4 defines the five leader decision styles. The five styles indicate that there are several shades of participation, not just autocratic or democratic.

The boxed example on page 380 presents a managerial decision for you to work through using the model.

Of course, not every managerial decision warrants this complicated analysis. But the model becomes less complex after you work through it a couple of times. Also, using the model for major decisions ensures that you consider the important situational factors and alerts you to the most appropriate style to use.

Path-Goal Theory   Perhaps the most generally useful situational model of leadership effectiveness is path-goal theory. Developed by Robert House, **path-goal theory** gets its name from its concern with

path-goal theory

A theory that concerns how leaders influence subordinates' perceptions of their work goals and the paths they follow toward attainment of those goals.

Setting: Banking

Your Position: President & Chief Executive Officer

The bank examiners have just left, insisting that many of your commercial real estate loans be written off, thereby depleting already low capital. Along with many other banks in your region, your bank is in serious danger of being closed by the regulators. As the financial problems surfaced, many of the top executives left to pursue other interests, but fortunately, you were able to replace them with three highly competent younger managers. While they had no prior acquaintance with one another, each is a product of a fine training program with one of the money center banks in which they rotated through positions in each of the banking functions.

Your extensive experience in the industry leads you to the inevitable conclusion that the only hope is a two-pronged approach involving reduction of all but the most critical expenses and the sale of assets to other banks. The task must be accomplished quickly since further deterioration of the quality of the loan portfolio could result in a negative capital position, forcing regulators to close the bank.

The strategy is clear to you, but you have many details that will need to be worked out. You believe that you know what information will be needed to get the bank on a course for future prosperity. You are fortunate in having three young executives to help you. While they have had little experience in working together, you know that each is dedicated to the survival of the bank. Like you, they know what needs to be done and how to do it.

SOURCE: V. Vroom, "Leadership and the Decision-Making Process," *Organizational Dynamics*, Spring 2000, pp. 82–94.

FIGURE 12.4

Vroom's Leader Decision Styles

Adaptation of Tannenbaum and Schmidt's Taxonomy

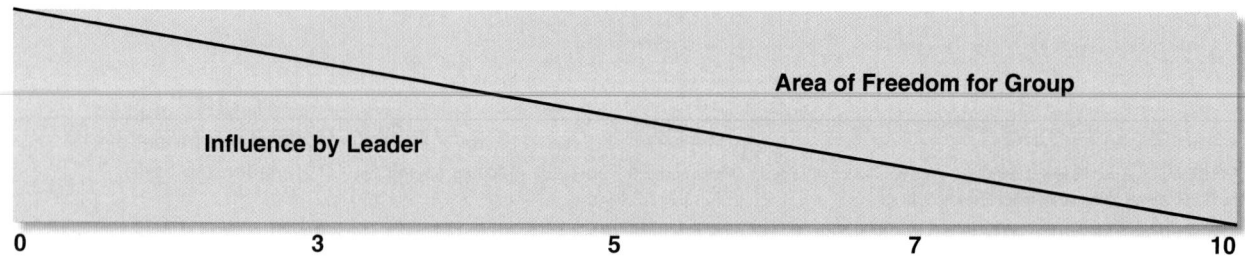

Decide	Consult Individually	Consult Group	Facilitate	Delegate
You make the decision alone and either announce or "sell" it to the group. You may use your expertise in collecting information that you deem relevant to the problem from the group or others.	You present the problem to the group members individually, get their suggestions, and then make the decision.	You present the problem to the group members in a meeting, get their suggestions, and then make the decision.	You present the problem to the group in a meeting. You act as a facilitator, defining the problem to be solved and the boundaries within which the decision must be made. Your objective is to get concurrence on a decision. Above all, you take care to ensure that your ideas are not given any greater weight than those of others simply because of your position.	You permit the group to make the decision within prescribed limits. The group undertakes the identification and diagnosis of the problem, developing alternative procedures for solving it, and deciding on one or more alternative solutions. While you play no direct role in the group's deliberations unless explicitly asked, your role is an important one behind the scenes, providing needed resources and encouragement.

SOURCE: V. Vroom, "Leadership and the Decision-Making Process," *Organizational Dynamics*, Spring 2000, pp. 82–94. Copyright © 2000 with permission from Elsevier Science.

how leaders influence followers' perceptions of their work goals and the paths they follow toward goal attainment.[52]

answer to the boxed Vroom banker problem:

Answers are H H H L H H L. The preferred decision style is to consult your group.

The key situational factors in path-goal theory are (1) personal characteristics of followers and (2) environmental pressures and demands with which followers must cope to attain their work goals. These factors determine which leadership behaviors are most appropriate.

The four pertinent leadership behaviors are (1) *directive leadership*, a form of task performance-oriented behavior; (2) *supportive leadership*, a form of group maintenance-oriented behavior; (3) *participative leadership*, or decision style; and (4) *achievement-oriented leadership*, or behaviors geared toward motivating people, such as setting challenging goals and rewarding good performance.

These situational factors and leader behaviors are merged in Figure 12.5. As you can see, appropriate leader behaviors—as determined by characteristics of followers and the work environment—lead to effective performance.

The theory also specifies *which* follower and environmental characteristics are important. There are three key follower characteristics. *Authoritarianism* is the degree to which individuals respect, admire, and defer to authority. *Locus of control* is the extent to which individuals see the environment as responsive to their own behavior. People with an *internal* locus of control believe that what happens to them is their own doing; people with an *external* locus of control believe that it is just luck or fate. Finally, *ability* is people's beliefs about their own abilities to do their assigned jobs.

Path-goal theory states that these personal characteristics determine the appropriateness of various leadership styles. For example, the theory makes the following propositions:

* A directive leadership style is more appropriate for highly authoritarian people, because such people respect authority.
* A participative leadership style is more appropriate for people who have an internal locus of control, because these individuals prefer to have more influence over their own lives.
* A directive style is more appropriate when subordinates' ability is low. The directive style helps people understand what has to be done.

Appropriate leadership style is also determined by three important environmental factors: people's tasks, the formal authority system of the organization, and the primary work group.

* Directive leadership is inappropriate if tasks already are well structured.
* If the task and the authority or rule system are dissatisfying, directive leadership will create greater dissatisfaction.
* If the task or authority system is dissatisfying, supportive leadership is especially appropriate, because it offers one positive source of gratification in an otherwise negative situation.
* If the primary work group provides social support to its members, supportive leadership is less important.

Path-goal theory offers many more propositions. In general, the theory suggests that the functions of the leader are to (1) make the path to work goals easier to travel by providing coaching and direction; (2) reduce frustrating barriers to goal attainment; and (3) increase opportunities for personal satisfaction by increasing payoffs to people for achieving performance goals.

How best to do these things depends on your people and on the work situation. Again: Analyze, then adapt your style accordingly.

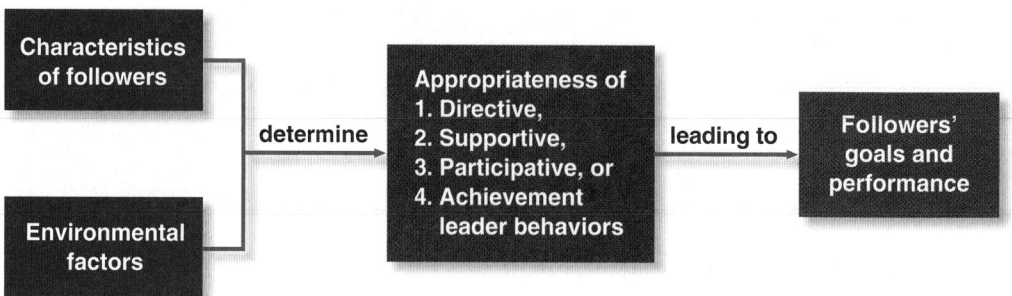

FIGURE 12.5
The Path-Goal Framework

Substitutes for Leadership   Sometimes leaders don't have to lead, or situations constrain their ability to lead effectively. The situation may be one in which leadership is unnecessary or has little impact. **Substitutes for leadership** can provide the same influence on people that leaders otherwise would have.

substitutes for leadership

Factors in the workplace that can exert the same influence on employees that leaders would provide.

Certain follower, task, and organizational factors are substitutes for task performance-oriented and group maintenance-oriented leader behaviors.[53] For example, group maintenance behaviors are less important and have less impact if people already have a closely knit group, they have a professional orientation, the job is intrinsically satisfying, or there is great physical distance between leader and followers. Physicians who are strongly concerned with professional conduct, enjoy their work, and work independently do not need social support from hospital administrators.

Task performance leadership is less important and will have less of a positive effect if people have a lot of experience and ability, feedback is supplied to them directly from the task or by computer, or the rules and procedures are rigid. If these factors are operating, the leader does not have to tell people what to do or how well they are performing.

The concept of substitutes for leadership does more than indicate when a leader's attempts at influence will and will not work. It provides useful and practical prescriptions for how to manage more efficiently.[54] If the manager can develop the work situation to the point where a number of these substitutes for leadership are operating, less time will need to be spent in direct attempts to influence people. The leader will be free to spend more time on other important activities.

Contemporary Perspectives on Leadership

So far, you have learned the major classic approaches to understanding leadership. Now we will discuss a number of new developments that are revolutionizing our understanding of this important aspect of management. These developments include charismatic leadership, transformational leadership, and post-heroic leadership.

Charismatic Leadership

Like many great leaders, Ronald Reagan had charisma. Lee Iacocca, Thomas Watson, Alfred Sloan, and Steve Jobs are good examples of charismatic leaders in industry. Herb Kelleher of Southwest Airlines is a highly charismatic leader whose departure from the company has people seriously worried about whether anyone can succeed in his place.[55]

Charisma is a rather evasive concept; it is easy to spot but hard to define. When executive recruiter Korn/Ferry International advised CEO wannabes to "develop charisma," *Business Week* responded sarcastically, "What's next? Grow a third eye? Master telekinesis?" (p. 86).[56]

What *is* charisma, and how does one acquire it? According to one definition, "Charisma packs an emotional wallop for followers above and beyond ordinary esteem, affection, admiration, and trust . . . The charismatic is an idolized hero, a messiah and a savior . . . "[57] As you can see from this quotation, many people, particularly North Americans, value charisma in their leaders. But some people don't like the term charisma;[58] it can be associated with the negative charisma of evil leaders whom people follow blindly.[59]

Charismatic leaders are dominant and exceptionally self-confident and have a strong conviction in the moral righteousness of their beliefs.[60] They strive to create an aura of competence and success and communicate high expectations for and confidence in followers.

The charismatic leader articulates ideological goals and makes sacrifices in pursuit of those goals.[61] Martin Luther King had a dream for a better world, and John F. Kennedy spoke of landing a human on the moon. In other words, such leaders have a compelling vision. The charismatic leader also arouses a sense of excitement and adventure. He or she is an eloquent speaker who exhibits superior verbal skills, which helps communicate the vision and motivate followers. Walt Disney mesmerized people with his storytelling, had enormous creative talent, and instilled in his organization strong values of good taste, risk taking, and innovation.[62]

Leaders who possess these characteristics or do these things inspire in their followers trust, confidence, acceptance, obedience, emotional involvement, affection, admiration, and higher performance.[63] Evidence for the positive effects of charismatic leadership has been found in a wide variety of groups, organizations, and management levels, and in countries including India, Singapore, the Netherlands, China, Japan, and Canada.[64]

Charisma has been shown to improve corporate financial performance, particularly under conditions of uncertainty[65]—that is, in risky circumstances when people have difficulty understanding what they should do when environments are changing. Uncertainty is stressful, and makes organizations more receptive to the ideas and actions of charismatic leaders.

charismatic leader

A person who is dominant, self-confident, convinced of the moral righteousness of his or her beliefs, and able to arouse a sense of excitement and adventure in followers.

Martin Luther King was a brilliant, charismatic leader who had a compelling vision, a dream for a better world.

Transformational Leadership

Charisma contributes to transformational leadership. **Transformational leaders**[66] get people to transcend their personal interests for the sake of the larger community.[67] They generate excitement and revitalize organizations. At Hewlett-Packard, the ability to generate excitement is an explicit criterion for selecting managers. In the United Kingdom, Richard Branson of Virgin Group is a transformational leader. Branson built a global business empire, and is regularly cited as a role model by young people who seek successful business careers without compromising personal ethics and a balanced life.[68]

The transformational process moves beyond the more traditional *transactional* approach to leadership. **Transactional leaders** view management as a series of transactions in which they use their legitimate, reward, and coercive powers to give commands and exchange rewards for services rendered. Unlike transformational leadership, transactional leadership is dispassionate;

transformational leader

A leader who transforms a vision into reality and motivates people to transcend their personal interests for the good of the group.

transactional leaders

Leaders who manage through transactions, using their legitimate, reward, and coercive powers to give commands and exchange rewards for services rendered.

Great leaders clear the path toward performance goals.

it does not excite, transform, empower, or inspire people to focus on the interests of the group or organization. However, transactional approaches may be more effective for individualists than for collectivists[69] (recall Chapter 6).

Generating Excitement   Transformational leaders generate excitement in three primary ways.[70] First, they are *charismatic*, as described earlier. Second, they give their followers *individualized attention*. Transformational leaders delegate challenging work to deserving people, keep lines of communication open, and provide one-on-one mentoring to develop their people. They do not treat everyone alike, because not everyone *is* alike.

Third, transformational leaders are *intellectually stimulating*. They arouse in their followers an awareness of problems and potential solutions. They articulate the organization's opportunities, threats, strengths, and weaknesses. They stir the imagination and generate insights. Therefore, problems are recognized and high-quality solutions are identified and implemented with the full commitment of followers.

Skills and Strategies   At least four skills or strategies contribute to transformational leadership.[71] First, transformational leaders *have a vision*—a goal, an agenda, or a results-orientation that grabs people's attention. Second, they *communicate their vision*; through words, manner, or symbolism, they relate a compelling image of the ultimate goal. Third, transformational leaders *build trust* by being consistent, dependable, and persistent. They position themselves clearly by choosing a direction and staying with it, thus projecting integrity. Finally, they have a *positive self-regard*. They do not feel self-important or complacent; rather, they recognize their personal strengths, compensate for their weaknesses, nurture and continually develop their talents, and know how to learn from failure. They strive for success rather than merely try to avoid failure.

Transformational leadership has been identified in industry, the military, and politics.[72] Examples of transformational leaders include Henry Ford, General George Patton, Lee Iacocca, and Jan Carlzon.[73] As with studies of charisma, transformational leadership and its positive impact on follower satisfaction and performance[74] have been demonstrated in countries the world over, including Egypt, Germany, China, England, and Japan.[75]

Transforming Leaders Importantly, transformational leadership is not the exclusive domain of presidents and chief executives. Ford Motor Company, in collaboration with the University of Michigan School of Business, put thousands of middle managers through a program designed to stimulate transformational leadership.[76] The training included analysis of the changing business environment, company strategy, and personal reflection and discussion about the need to change. Participants assessed their own leadership styles and developed a specific change initiative to implement after the training—a change that would make a needed and lasting difference for the company.

Over the next six months, the managers implemented change on the job. Almost half of the initiatives resulted in transformational changes in the organization or work unit; the rest of the changes were smaller, more incremental, or more personal. Whether managers made small or transformational changes depended on their attitude going into the training, their level of self-esteem, and the amount of support they received from others on the job for their efforts. Thus, some managers did not respond as hoped. But almost half embraced the training, became more transformational in orientation, and tackled significant transformational changes for the company.[77]

Post-Heroic Leadership

A common view of leaders is that they are heroes. Phenomenally talented, they step forward in difficult times and save the day. But in these complex times, it is foolhardy to assume that a great top executive can solve all problems by himself or herself.[78] Arnold Schwarzenegger isn't going to intervene and make things right.

Effective leadership must permeate the organization, not reside in one or two superstars at the top. The leader's job becomes one of spreading leadership abilities throughout the firm.[79] Make people responsible for their own performance. Create an environment in which each person can figure out what needs to be done and then do it well. Point the way and clear the path so that people can succeed. Give them the credit they deserve. Make heroes out of *them*.

Thus, what is now required of leaders is less the efficient management of resources, and more the effective unleashing of intellectual capital and human resources. In other words, you should *capitalize on all the brains and talent in your organization*.

Key roles personifying post-heroic leadership in the 21st century include:

1. *Using vision to motivate and inspire.* A recent survey showed that executives consider this to be the most important skill for future global leaders. According to Percy Barnevik, "It is important that people in an organization have something to be proud of . . . Our employees . . . like to see a purpose that goes beyond numbers. It is important that a company can be perceived as changing the world in a positive way" (pp. 19–20).[80]
2. *Empowering employees at all levels.* Ken Melrose, CEO of Toro, said "You best lead by serving the needs of your people. You don't do their jobs for them; you enable them to learn and progress on the job" (p. 22).[81] Most people want to expand their own knowledge, feel involved in their organization, and contribute to its success.

3. *Accumulating and sharing internal knowledge.* At PeopleSoft, everyone from the CEO to the newest recruit gets the same top-of-the line laptop with lots of performance enhancements. The purpose is to break down hierarchical status differences and support the global communications network. The laptop isn't a device for personal productivity; it's the entry point for a worldwide information infrastructure.[82]

4. *Challenging the status quo and enabling creativity.* The philosophy of encouraging risk taking in the pursuit of innovation prompts Wood Dickinson, CEO of the Dickinson movie theatre chain, to tell his managers to try new things and not worry about having "intelligent failures in the pursuit of service excellence" (p. 31).[83] The new competitive landscape is swarming with opportunities that are best addressed via innovation and creativity.

A Note on Courage

To be a good leader, you need the courage to create a vision of greatness for your unit; identify and manage allies, adversaries, and fencesitters; and execute your vision, often against opposition. This does not mean you should commit career suicide by alienating too many powerful people; it does mean taking reasonable risks, with the good of the firm at heart, in order to produce constructive change.

Specifically, some acts of courage required to fulfill your vision will include:[84] (1) seeing things as they are and facing them head-on, making no excuses and harboring no wishful illusions; (2) saying what needs to be said to those who need to hear it; and (3) persisting despite resistance, criticism, abuse, and setbacks. Courage includes stating the realities, even when they are harsh, and publicly stating what you will do to help and what you want from others. This means laying the cards on the table honestly: Here is what I want from you . . . What do you want from me?[85]

Developing Your Leadership Skills

As with other things, you must work at *developing* your leadership abilities. Great musicians and great athletes don't become great on natural gifts alone. They also pay their dues by practicing, learning, and sacrificing. Leaders in a variety of fields, when asked how they became the best leader possible, offered the following comments:[86]

- "I've observed methods and skills of my bosses that I respected."
- "By taking risks, trying, and learning from my mistakes."
- "Reading autobiographies of leaders I admire to try to understand how they think."
- "Lots of practice."
- "By making mistakes myself and trying a different approach."
- "By purposely engaging with others to get things done."
- "By being put in positions of responsibility that other people counted on."

How do you go about developing your leadership abilities? Start by thinking about your potential employer. Look for how it develops leadership talent. Best practices include paying close executive-level attention to the development of people, providing assignments that stretch the abilities of up-and-coming talent, creating individualized development plans, and providing multirater feedback.[87] Companies best at leadership development include Johnson & Johnson, Hewlett-Packard, Shell International, General Electric, and the World Bank.[88]

More generally, get out of your "comfort zone." That is, don't seek out and remain in easy, nonchallenging situations; enter, create, and face situations that require you to adapt and change. This is the best way to learn, and it is the way great executives learn.[89]

More specifically, here are some developmental experiences you should seek:[90]

- *Assignments:* Building something from nothing; fixing or turning around a failing operation; taking on project or task force responsibilities; accepting international assignments.
- *Other people:* Having exposure to positive role models; increasing visibility to others; working with people of diverse backgrounds.
- *Hardships:* Overcoming ideas that fail and deals that collapse; confronting others' performance problems; breaking out of a career rut.
- *Other events:* Formal courses; challenging job experiences; supervision of others; experiences outside work.

These experiences do not guarantee that you will develop into an effective leader. But without them, your development will surely be constrained. Seek these experiences; expect mistakes and don't beat yourself up over them; and take time to learn from your experiences.

KEY TERMS

Autocratic leadership, p. 374

Behavioral approach. p. 372

Charismatic leader, p. 383

Democratic leadership, p. 374

Group maintenance behaviors, p. 373

Laissez-faire, p. 374

Leader-Member Exchange (LMX) theory, p. 374

Participation in decision making, p. 374

Path-goal theory, p. 379

Power, p. 369

Situational approach, p. 377

Strategic leadership, p. 368

Substitutes for leadership, p. 382

Supervisory leadership, p. 368

Task performance behaviors, p. 373

Trait approach, p. 371

Transactional leaders, p. 383

Transformational leader, p. 383

Vision, p. 366

Vroom model, p. 378

SUMMARY OF LEARNING OBJECTIVES

Now that you have studied Chapter 12, you should know:

What it means to be a leader.

A leader is one who influences others to attain goals. Leaders orchestrate change, set direction, and motivate people to overcome obstacles and move the organization toward its ideal future.

How a good vision helps you be a better leader.

Outstanding leaders have vision. A vision is a mental image that goes beyond the ordinary and perhaps beyond what others thought possible. The vision provides the direction in which the leader wants the organization to move.

How to understand and use power.

Having power and using it appropriately are essential attributes of an effective leader. Managers have five potential sources of power: legitimate, reward, coercive, referent, and expert. These power sources are potentially available to managers at all organizational levels and should be used appropriately.

The personal traits and skills of effective leaders.

The old idea that leaders have certain traits or skills fell into disfavor but lately has been resurrected. Important leader characteristics include drive, leadership motivation, integrity, self-confidence, and knowledge of the business. Perhaps the most important skill is the ability to accurately perceive the situation and then change behavior accordingly.

The behaviors that will make you a better leader.

Important leader behaviors include task performance, group maintenance, and participation in decision making. Exhibiting more rather than fewer of these behaviors will enhance your effectiveness in the long run. The Vroom model helps a leader decide how much participation to use in making decisions. Path-goal theory assesses characteristics of the followers, the leader, and the situation; it then indicates the appropriateness of directive, supportive, participative, or achievement-oriented leadership behaviors.

What it means to be a charismatic and transformational leader.

To have charisma is to be dominant and self-confident, to have a strong conviction of the righteousness of your beliefs, to create an aura of competence and success, and to communicate high expectations for and confidence in your followers. Charisma is one component of transformational leadership. Transformational leaders translate a vision into reality by getting

people to transcend their individual interests for the good of the larger community. They do this through charisma, individualized attention to followers, intellectual stimulation, formation and communication of their vision, building of trust, and positive self-regard.

How to further your own leadership development.

You can develop your own leadership skills not only by understanding what effective leadership is all about, but also by seeking challenging developmental experiences. Such important life experiences come from taking challenging assignments, through exposure in working with other people, by overcoming hardships and failures, by taking formal courses, and by other actions.

DISCUSSION QUESTIONS

1. What elements from the chapter do you see in the leaders described in "Setting the Stage"?

2. Is there a difference between effective management and effective leadership? Explain your views and learn from others' views.

3. Identify someone you think is an effective leader. What traits and skills does this person possess that make him or her effective?

4. Do you think most managers can be transformational leaders? Why or why not?

5. In your own words, define courage. What is the role of courage in leadership? Give examples of acts of leadership you consider courageous.

6. Do you think men and women differ in their leadership styles? If so, how? Do men and/or women prefer different styles in their bosses? What evidence do you have for your answers?

7. Who are your heroes? Try to identify some traditional heroes and also some that are "post-heroic." What makes them heroes, and what can you learn from them?

8. Assess yourself as a leader based on what you have read in this chapter. What are your strengths and weaknesses?

9. Identify the developmental experiences you have had that may have strengthened your ability to lead. What did those experiences teach you? Also identify some developmental experiences you need to acquire, and how you will seek them. Be specific.

10. Consider a couple of decisions you are facing that could involve other people. Use the Vroom model to decide what approach to use to make the decisions.

11. Consider a job you hold or held in the past. Consider how your boss managed you. How would you describe him or her as a leader? What substitutes for leadership would you have enjoyed seeing put into place?

12. Consider an organization of which you are a leader or a member. What could great transformational leadership accomplish in the organization?

CONCLUDING CASE

Following a Legend

Jeffrey Immelt is following a legend. He is succeeding GE's CEO Jack Welch, who created more shareholder value—almost $500 billion—than anyone in history. *Business Week* describes Welch as the epitome of the "CEO as maximum leader for all seasons—a human dynamo who through sheer force of personality and brilliance of vision can transform any company, no matter how big or how complicated, into an engine of perpetual outperformance" (p. 88). During his 20-year reign at GE, Welch's face graced countless book and magazine covers; he was one of the most famous business-people on the planet; and he was the most admired executive in the United States. He is widely considered the best CEO in America, and some consider him the best manager of the century.

Even Welch made mistakes early in his tenure. Obviously, he survived those mistakes. But today's environment, faced by Immelt, is more unforgiving. Times are tough, characterized by more turbulence in executive suites than in the past. Honeymoons are short. Impatience runs high when the investment community isn't quickly made happy. Two-thirds of all companies worldwide have replaced their CEO at least once between 1995 and 2002. More than 1,000 U.S. CEOs left office in 2000 alone. And *Business Week* speculates about an even bigger epidemic of CEO firings yet to come.

Immelt's college classmates call him a natural leader; Welch says simply, "People follow him." He has been successful at inspiring

As if following a legend wasn't enough, GE's CEO Jefferey Immelt also faces today's impatient investment community.

GE is a highly complex conglomerate in many different industries. Some suspect that only someone of Welch's skills and stature could hold it together. With Wall Street's preference for companies to focus on fewer industries than GE does, and high expectations for profitability, Immelt could face enormous pressure to break up GE. But not many corporations can buy GE's businesses, because those businesses are so valuable and expensive. Maybe, though, some corporations can trade their businesses for GE's.

GE was named *Fortune*'s most admired company in 2002, for the fifth year in a row. Its businesses generate almost a billion dollars monthly, and GE has a AAA credit rating. Yet in the wake of the recent business scandals, analysts wonder more skeptically than in the past about GE's uncanny ability to match almost perfectly its estimates, as earnings go higher and higher. Are the numbers legitimate? Immelt finds himself having to tell interviewers that no, he is not an earnings cheat. In fact, the company has rightly refused to play the game of whispering low earnings estimates so it can then reveal positive earnings "surprises" that are better than the estimates.

But circumstances are putting Immelt on the defensive. Even with brilliant leadership, it will be almost impossible to keep the stock price climbing as it did under Welch. Immelt is immensely talented and capable, but his position may be shaky if he doesn't deliver results.

innovation. A major customer is impressed with Immelt's decisiveness. The customer had a long-standing request that he couldn't convince others at GE to act on. "The first time I met Jeff . . . he made the decision in a minute. He told me, 'That makes total sense. We'll do it'" (p. 97).

Welch had four big ideas and initiatives: globalization, services, digitization, and the quality program Six Sigma. Immelt does not plan to add a fifth, just to do those four more broadly and deeply. He says he is very comfortable with the way GE is run. But he has experience in only 3 of 10 GE divisions, most of it in GE's highly entrepreneurial Plastics Division. And he has never worked overseas. Nonetheless, Immelt sees great opportunities in global expansion and weaving the Internet into everything GE does.

GE's Appliances Division is struggling, and NBC (owned by GE) is facing daunting competition. Recent disasters at NBC include the XFL, the closure of the Internet spinout NBCi, and *Survivor* competing successfully with NBC's Thursday night lineup. Also embarrassingly, GE's announced acquisition of Honeywell fell through. But in some ways this was a relief, because Honeywell's numbers had dropped and integrating the two companies would have been very difficult.

QUESTIONS

1. Imagine that you are in Jeffrey Immelt's position. Assume that you are more experienced than you are now, and that you legitimately earned your way into the position. What would you feel emotionally?

2. Immelt has huge responsibilities and faces major challenges. How would you advise him to proceed? What should he do as leader?

3. What has Immelt been doing lately, and how is GE faring?

4. What skills and knowledge do you have now that would be useful in an important business leadership position? What skills and knowledge do you need to acquire? What is your plan to develop as a leader?

SOURCES: Bianco and L. Lavell, "The CEO Trap," *Business Week,* December 11, 2000, pp. 86–92; P. Moore with N. Byrnes, "The Man Who Would Be Welch," *Business Week,* December 11, 2000, pp. 94–97; J. Useem, "It's All Yours, Jeff: Now What?" *Fortune,* September 17, 2001, pp. 64–68; J. Fox, "What's So Great about GE?" *Fortune,* March 4, 2002, pp. 64–67.

12.1   Power and Influence

OBJECTIVE

To explore the nature of power and influence, and your attitudes toward different kinds of power and influence.

INSTRUCTIONS

Read the introductions, "A. Power" and "B. Influence," to the Power and Influence Worksheet, and complete those sections of the worksheet. Then read and complete "C. Power and influence."

Power and Influence Worksheet

A. Power

A number of people have made statements about power and winning (e.g., P.T. Barnum, Mao Tse-tung, Leo Durocher, Lord Acton, Vince Lombardi). Some of these statements are listed in the table that follows. Indicate how you feel about each of the statements by circling number 1 if you strongly disagree, number 5 if you strongly agree, and so on.

	Strongly Disagree	Disagree	Neutral	Agree	Strongly Agree
Winning is everything.	1	2	3	4	5
Nice guys finish last.	1	2	3	4	5
There can only be one winner.	1	2	3	4	5
There's a sucker born every minute.	1	2	3	4	5
You can't completely trust anyone.	1	2	3	4	5
All power rests at the end of the gun.	1	2	3	4	5
Power seekers are greedy and can't be trusted.	1	2	3	4	5
Power corrupts; absolute power corrupts absolutely.	1	2	3	4	5
You get as much power as you pay for.	1	2	3	4	5

B. Influence

During the past week or so you have come in contact with many people. Some have influenced you positively, some negatively. Try to recall recent experiences with employers, peers, teachers, parents, clergy, and the like who may have influenced you in some way. Then try to think about how and why they influenced you as they did.

1. On the following table, list the names of all those who influenced you during the past week or so according to the kind of power that person used. The same person's name may appear under more than one type of power if that person used multiple power bases. Also, indicate whether the influence was positive (+) or negative (−).

Power Base	Names and Whether (+) or (−)
Legitimate authority	
Reward	
Coercive	
Referent	
Expert	

2. After examining your list, check (✓) the following questions.

	Yes	No
a. Was there one person who had + marks appearing under several power bases?	_____	_____
b. Was there one person who had − marks appearing under several power bases?	_____	_____
c. Did you find that most of the people with + marks tended to fall under the same power bases?	_____	_____
d. Did you find that most of the people with − marks tended to fall under the same power bases?	_____	_____

3. From your answers to the last two questions, list which power bases you found to be positive (+) and which you found to be negative (−).

+	−
_____	_____
_____	_____
_____	_____
_____	_____
_____	_____

Do you think you personally prefer to use those power bases you listed under + when you try to influence people? Do you actually use them?

C. Power and influence
From the table in Part B, find the one person whom you think had the strongest positive influence on you (Person 1), and the one who had the strongest negative influence (Person 2). These are most likely the persons whose names appear most frequently.

In the following table, place a 1 on the line for each statement that best indicates how you think Person 1 would respond to that statement. Put a 2 on the line for each statement that reflects how you think Person 2 would respond to that item.

	Strongly Disagree	Disagree	Neutral	Agree	Strongly Agree
Winning is everything.	_____	_____	_____	_____	_____
Nice guys finish last.	_____	_____	_____	_____	_____
There can only be one winner.	_____	_____	_____	_____	_____
There's a sucker born every minute.	_____	_____	_____	_____	_____
You can't completely trust anyone.	_____	_____	_____	_____	_____
All power rests at the end of the gun.	_____	_____	_____	_____	_____
Power seekers are greedy and can't be trusted.	_____	_____	_____	_____	_____
Power corrupts; absolute power corrupts absolutely.	_____	_____	_____	_____	_____
You get as much power as you pay for.	_____	_____	_____	_____	_____

Now compare your responses in Part A to those in Part C. Do you more closely resemble Person 1 or Person 2? Do you prefer to use the kinds of power that person uses? Which kinds of power do you use most frequently? Which do you use least frequently? When do you feel you have the greatest power? When do you have the least power? How do these answers compare to what you found in Part B3?

SOURCE: Excerpted from Lawrence R. Jauch, Arthur G. Bedeian, Sally A. Coltin, and William F. Glueck, *The Managerial Experience: Cases, Exercises, and Readings*, 5th ed. Copyright © 1989. Reprinted with permission of South-Western, a division of Thomson Learning, www.thomsonrights.com.

12.2   Evaluating Your Leadership Style

OBJECTIVES

1. To examine your personal style of leadership.
2. To study the nature of the leadership process.
3. To identify ways to improve or modify your leadership style.

INSTRUCTIONS

1. Working alone, complete and score the Leadership Style Survey.
2. In small groups, exchange scores, compute average scores, and develop responses to the discussion questions.
3. After the class reconvenes, group spokespersons present group findings.

DISCUSSION QUESTIONS

1. In what ways did your experience or lack of experience influence your responses to the survey?
2. In what ways did student scores and student responses to survey test items agree? In what ways did they disagree?
3. What do you think accounts for differences in student leadership attitudes?
4. How can students make constructive use of the survey results?

Leadership Style Survey

This survey describes various aspects of leadership behavior. To measure your leadership style, respond to each statement according to the way you would act (or think you would act) if you were a work group leader.

	Always	Frequently	Occasionally	Seldom	Never
1. I would allow team members the freedom to do their jobs in their own way.	5	4	3	2	1
2. I would make important decisions on my own initiative without consulting the workers.	5	4	3	2	1
3. I would allow the team members to make their own decisions.	5	4	3	2	1
4. I would not try to socialize with the workers.	5	4	3	2	1
5. I would allow team members to do their jobs as they see fit.	5	4	3	2	1
6. I would consider myself to be the group's spokesperson.	5	4	3	2	1
7. I would be warm, friendly, and approachable.	5	4	3	2	1
8. I would be sure that the workers understand and follow all the rules and regulations.	5	4	3	2	1
9. I would demonstrate a real concern for the workers' welfare.	5	4	3	2	1
10. I would be the one to decide what is to be done and how it is to be done.	5	4	3	2	1
11. I would delegate authority to the workers.	5	4	3	2	1
12. I would urge the workers to meet production quotas.	5	4	3	2	1
13. I would trust the workers to use good judgment in decision making.	5	4	3	2	1
14. I would assign specific tasks to specific people.	5	4	3	2	1
15. I would let the workers establish their own work pace.	5	4	3	2	1

	Always	Frequently	Occasionally	Seldom	Never
16. I would not feel that I have to explain my decisions to workers.	5	4	3	2	1
17. I would try to make each worker feel that his or her contribution is important.	5	4	3	2	1
18. I would establish the work schedules.	5	4	3	2	1
19. I would encourage workers to get involved in setting work goals.	5	4	3	2	1
20. I would be action oriented and results oriented.	5	4	3	2	1
21. I would get the workers involved in making decisions.	5	4	3	2	1
22. I would outline needed changes and monitor action closely.	5	4	3	2	1
23. I would help the group achieve consensus on important changes.	5	4	3	2	1
24. I would supervise closely to ensure that standards are met.	5	4	3	2	1
25. I would consistently reinforce good work.	5	4	3	2	1
26. I would nip problems in the bud.	5	4	3	2	1
27. I would consult the group before making decisions.	5	4	3	2	1

Classic Contingency Models of Leadership

The chapter described some situational or contingency models of leadership; here are two more, presented here in the interest of conserving chapter space.

FIEDLER'S CONTINGENCY MODEL

Fiedler's contingency model of leadership effectiveness states that effectiveness depends on two factors: the personal style of the leader and the degree to which the situation gives the leader power, control, and influence over the situation.[1] Figure E.1 illustrates the contingency model. The upper half of the figure shows the situational analysis, and the lower half indicates the appropriate style. In the upper portion, three questions are used to analyze the situation:

1. Are leader–member relations good or poor? (To what extent is the leader accepted and supported by group members?)

2. Is the task structured or unstructured? (To what extent do group members know what their goals are and how to accomplish them?)

3. Is the leader's position power strong or weak (high or low)? (To what extent does the leader have the authority to reward and punish?)

These three sequential questions create a decision tree in which a situation is classified into one of eight categories. The lower the category number, the more favorable the situation is for the leader; the higher the number, the less favorable the situation. Originally, Fiedler called this variable "situational favorableness" but now calls it "situational control." Situation 1 is the best: Relations are good, task structure is high, and power is high. In the least favorable situation (8), in which the leader has very little situational control, relations are poor, tasks lack structure, and the leader's power is weak.

Different situations dictate different leadership styles. Fiedler measured leadership styles with an instrument assessing the leader's *least preferred coworker* (LPC); that is, the attitude toward the follower the leader liked the least. This was considered an

FIGURE E.1

Fiedler's Analysis of Situations in Which the Task- or Relationship-Motivated Leader is More Effective

Leader–member relations	Good				Poor			
Task structure	Structured		Unstructured		Structured		Unstructured	
Leader position power	High	Low	High	Low	High	Low	High	Low
	1	2	3	4	5	6	7	8

Favorable for leader →→→→→→→→→→→→→→ Unfavorable for leader

| Type of leader most effective in the situation | Task-motivated | Task-motivated | Task-motivated | Relationship-motivated | Relationship-motivated | Relationship-motivated | Relationship-motivated | Task-motivated |

SOURCE: D. Organ and T. Bateman, *Organizational Behavior*, 4th ed. Copyright © 1990 by The McGraw-Hill Companies. Reproduced with permission of The McGraw-Hill Companies.

indication more generally of leaders' attitudes toward people. If a leader can single out the person she likes the least, but her attitude is not all that negative, she received a high score on the LPC scale. Leaders with more negative attitudes toward others would receive low LPC scores.

Based on the LPC score, Fiedler considered two leadership styles. **Task-motivated leadership** places primary emphasis on completing the task and is more likely exhibited by leaders with low LPC scores. **Relationship-motivated leadership** emphasizes maintaining good interpersonal relationships and is more likely from high-LPC leaders. These leadership styles correspond to task performance and group maintenance leader behaviors, respectively.

The lower part of Figure E.1 indicates which style is situationally appropriate. For situations 1, 2, 3, and 8, a task-motivated leadership style is more effective. For situations 4 through 7, relationship-motivated leadership is more appropriate.

Fiedler's theory was not always supported by research. It is better supported if three broad rather than eight specific levels of situational control are assumed: low, medium, and high. It was quite controversial in academic circles; among other arguable things, it assumed that leaders cannot change their styles but must be assigned to situations that suit their styles. However, the model has withstood the test of time and still receives attention. Most important, it initiated and continues to emphasize the importance of finding a fit between the situation and the leader's style.

HERSEY AND BLANCHARD'S SITUATIONAL THEORY

Hersey and Blanchard developed an important situational model that added another factor the leader should take into account before deciding whether task performance or maintenance behaviors are more important. Originally called the *life cycle theory of leadership,* their **situational theory** highlights the maturity of the followers as the key situational factor.[2] **Job maturity** is the level of the follower's skills and technical knowledge relative to the task being performed; **psychological maturity** is the follower's self-confidence and self-respect. High-maturity followers have both the ability and the confidence to do a good job.

The theory proposes a negative linear relationship between a follower's maturity and the degree of task performance behaviors

a leader should use. The more mature the followers, the less the leader needs to organize and explain tasks. The required amount of maintenance behaviors is a bit more complex. The relationship is curvilinear: Maintenance behaviors are not important with followers of low or high levels of maturity but are important for followers of moderate maturity. For low-maturity followers, the emphasis should be on performance-related leadership; for moderate-maturity followers, performance leadership is somewhat less important and maintenance behaviors become more important; and for high-maturity followers, neither dimension of leadership behavior is important.

Little academic research has been done on this situational theory, but the model is extremely popular in management training seminars. Regardless of its scientific validity, Hersey and Blanchard's model provides a reminder that it is important to treat different people differently. Moreover, it suggests the importance of treating the same individual differently from time to time as he or she changes jobs or acquires more maturity in her or his particular job.[3]

APPENDIX KEY TERMS

Fiedler's contingency model of leadership effectiveness A situational approach to leadership postulating that effectiveness depends on the personal style of the leader and the degree to which the situation gives the leader power, control, and influence over the situation, p. 394

Hersey and Blanchard's situational theory A life cycle theory of leadership developed by Hersey and Blanchard postulating that a manager should consider an employee's psychological and job maturity before deciding whether task performance or maintenance behaviors are more important, p. 395

job maturity The level of the employee's skills and technical knowledge relative to the task being performed, p. 395

psychological maturity An employee's self-confidence and self-respect, p. 395

Relationship-motivated leadership Leadership that places primary emphasis on maintaining good interpersonal relationships, p. 395

task-motivated leadership Leadership that places primary emphasis on completing a task, p. 395

CHAPTER 13

Motivating for Performance

The worst mistake a boss can make is not to say well done.
—John Ashcroft, Business Executive
The reward of a thing well done is to have done it.
—Ralph Waldo Emerson

CHAPTER OUTLINE

Motivating for Performance
Setting Goals
  Goals That Motivate
  Limitations of Goal Setting
Reinforcing Performance
Performance-Related Beliefs
  The Effort-to-Performance Link
  The Performance-to-Outcome Link
  Impact on Motivation
  Managerial Implications of Expectancy Theory
Understanding People's Needs
  Maslow's Need Hierarchy
  ERG Theory
  McClelland's Needs
  Need Theories: International Perspectives
Designing Motivating Jobs
  Job Rotation, Enlargement, and Enrichment
  Herzberg's Two-Factor Theory
  The Hackman and Oldham Model of Job Design
  Empowerment
Achieving Fairness
  Assessing Equity
  Restoring Equity
  Fair Process
Job Satisfaction
  Quality of Work Life
  Psychological Contracts

LEARNING OBJECTIVES

After studying Chapter 13, you will know:

1. The kinds of behaviors managers need to motivate in people.

2. How to set challenging, motivating goals.

3. How to reward good performance.

4. The key beliefs that affect people's motivation.

5. The ways in which people's individual needs affect their behavior.

6. How to create a motivating, empowering job.

7. How people assess fairness and how to achieve fairness.

8. The causes and consequences of a satisfied workforce.

TWO CONTRASTING APPROACHES TO MOTIVATION

Harvard Business School publishes 35,000 cases worldwide. The case purchased most often is about Lincoln Electric Company of Cleveland. Lincoln Electric produces industrial electric motors and is the world's largest manufacturer of arc welding products.

The attraction of the case is Lincoln's success at motivating workers by tying pay to performance. All of its people—most of whom are factory workers, and many without college degrees—participate in the company's incentive plan. All but two share in the annual bonus—the president and the

Lincoln Electric Company's merit pay plan allows most workers to double their base salary via their annual bonus.

chair. The two top executives are paid based on a percentage of sales; if sales go down, they take the first pay cut.

Lincoln also has a piecework rate, with which workers earn money based on how much they produce. All jobs in the company have pay ranges (hourly or salary) so that individuals who perform at their highest capability can move up to the top of the range for their particular job.

Every six months, the CEO personally reviews all merit ratings. Everyone is rated in four performance categories: output, quality, dependability (ability to work without supervision), and cooperation and ideas. Over the 50-plus years in which

the system has been in place, the average year-end bonus has been 95.5 percent of base. In other words, employees commonly double their annual income by virtue of the annual bonus.

Lincoln has been number one in its business worldwide for the entire life of the incentive system. Most people's performance is outstanding—and they don't require much supervision. The foreman-to-worker ratio is 1:100. Typically it's 1:25, even 1:10 in some plants. The cost savings help pay the bonus.

Lincoln Electric has outlasted giants like Westinghouse to dominate a fiercely competitive industry. Managers attribute their company's success to a philosophy: a strong belief in the power of unfettered capitalism. Through this approach, Lincoln has some of the highest paid factory workers in the world. Some call Lincoln a dressed-up sweatshop, while others call it good business.

AES Corporation espouses a very different philosophy about motivating people. AES develops, acquires, builds, owns, and operates independent power projects worldwide, and in early 2002 was the biggest such company in the world.

Chairman Roger Sant and CEO Dennis Bakke built their company around the principles of fairness, integrity, social responsibility, and fun. The employees are truly "empowered." That is, frontline employees make and execute important decisions without interference from above.

Sant speaks about one of the key principles: "The word *fun* can be misleading. AES is fun because the people who work here are fully engaged. They have total responsibility for decisions. They are accountable for results. What they do every day matters to the company, and it matters to the communities we operate in. We do celebrate a lot—because lots of great things are happening. We just did a billion-dollar deal, for instance, and that called for a party. But it's what happens before the celebrations that's really fun" (p. 112).

Adds Bakke, "The struggle before the deal, for instance, the challenge and the creativity required to make it work, taking risks, even the sleepless nights. Believe it or not, those things are really fun because they engage people—heart, mind, and soul. And that was the kind of company we set out to create, one in which people could have engaging experiences on a daily basis" (p. 112).

Sources: R. M. Hodgetts, "A Conversation with Donald F. Hastings of The Lincoln Electric Company," *Organizational Dynamics*, Winter 1997, pp. 68–74; D. F. Hastings, "Lincoln Electric's Harsh Lessons from International Expansion," *Harvard Business Review*, May–June 1999, pp. 162–78; S. Wetlaufer, "Organizing for Empowerment: An Interview with AES's Roger Sant and Dennis Bakke," *Harvard Business Review*, January–February 1999, pp. 110–23; D. Eisenberg, "Where People Are Never Let Go," *Time*, June 18, 2001, pp. 40–41; "Fewer and Bigger Power Owners Dominate the Global Marketplace," *Engineering News Record*, December 3, 2002, pp. PC56–81.

Lincoln Electric and AES have come up with powerful solutions to the age-old question tackled in this chapter: How can a manager motivate people to work hard and perform at their best levels?

A sales manager in another company had a different approach to this question. Each month, the person with the worst sales performance took home a live goat for the weekend. The manager hoped the goat-of-month employee would be so embarrassed that he or she would work harder the next month to increase sales.[1]

This sales manager may get high marks for creativity. But if he is graded by results, as he grades his salespeople, he will fail. He may succeed in motivating a few of his people to increase sales, but some good people will be motivated to quit the company.

Motivating for Performance

Understanding why people do the things they do on the job is not an easy task for the manager. *Predicting* their response to management's latest productivity program is harder yet. Fortunately, enough is known about motivation to give the thoughtful manager practical, effective techniques for increasing people's effort and performance.

motivation

Forces that energize, direct, and sustain a person's efforts.

Motivation refers to forces that energize, direct, and sustain a person's efforts. All behavior, except involuntary reflexes like eye blinks (which have little to do with management), is motivated. A highly motivated person will work hard toward achieving performance goals. With adequate ability and understanding of the job, such a person will be highly productive.

To be effective motivators, managers must know what behaviors they want to motivate people to exhibit. Although productive people appear to do a seemingly limitless number of things, most of the important activities can be grouped into five general categories.[2] The company must motivate people to (1) *join the organization*; (2) *remain in the organization*; and (3) *come to work regularly*. On these points, you should reject the common recent notion that loyalty is dead, and accept the challenge of creating an environment that will attract and energize people so that they commit to the organization.[3]

Of course, companies also want people to (4) *perform*—that is, once employees are at work, they should work hard to achieve high *output* (productivity) and high *quality*. Finally, managers want employees to (5) *exhibit good citizenship*. Good citizens of the organization are committed, satisfied employees who perform above and beyond the call of duty by doing extra things that can help the company. The importance of citizenship behaviors may be less obvious than productivity, but these behaviors help the organization function smoothly. They also make managers' lives easier.

Many ideas have been proposed to help managers motivate people to engage in these constructive behaviors. The most useful of these ideas are described in the following pages. We start with the most fundamental *processes* that influence the motivation of all people. These processes—described by goal-setting, reinforcement, and expectancy theories—suggest basic and powerful actions for managers to take.

Then we discuss the *content* of what people want and need from work, how individuals differ from one another, and how understanding people's needs leads to powerful prescriptions about designing motivating jobs and empowering people to perform at the highest possible levels. Finally, we discuss the most important beliefs and perceptions about fairness that people hold toward work, and the implications for managers.

Setting Goals

Providing work-related goals for people is an extremely effective way to stimulate motivation. In fact, it is perhaps the most important, valid, and useful single approach to motivating performance. Therefore, we discuss it first.

Goal-setting theory states that people have conscious goals that energize them and direct their thoughts and behaviors toward a particular end.[4] With the principle that goals matter in mind, managers set goals for employees. For example, a cable-TV company might set goals for increasing the number of new subscribers, or the number of current subscribers who pay for premium channels, or the timeliness of responses to customer inquiries.[5]

> **goal-setting theory**
>
> **A motivation theory stating that people have conscious goals that energize them and direct their thoughts and behaviors toward a particular end.**

Goals That Motivate

What kinds of goals most effectively motivate people? How can managers set motivating goals for the people who report to them?

First, goals should be *acceptable* to employees. This means, among other things, that they should not conflict with people's personal values and that people have reasons to pursue the goals. Allowing people to participate in setting their work goals—as opposed to having the boss set goals for them—is often a great way to generate goals that people accept and pursue willingly.

Second, acceptable, maximally motivating goals are *challenging but attainable*. In other words, they should be high enough to inspire better performance but not so high that people can never reach them. One team of consultants to an international corporation created more than 40 programs aimed at increasing quality. The company announced it did not expect significant quality improvement until the *fourth year* of the program. Such a goal is not nearly demanding enough.[6]

Third, goals should be *specific*, *quantifiable*, and *measurable*. Ideal goals do not merely exhort employees to improve performance, start doing their best, increase productivity, or decrease the length of time customers must wait to receive service. Goals should be more like Caterpillar Tractor's guaranteed parts delivery within 24 hours. Such deadlines, and measurable performance goals, are specific, quantifiable goals that employees are motivated to achieve.

Limitations of Goal Setting

Goal setting is an extraordinarily powerful management technique. But like anything else, even specific, challenging, attainable goals work better under some conditions than others. Individual performance goals can be dysfunctional if people work in a group and cooperation among team members is essential to team performance.[7] Individualized goals can create competition and reduce cooperation. If cooperation is important, performance goals should be established *for the team*.

It is important *not* to establish a single productivity goal if there are other important dimensions of performance.[8] For instance, productivity goals will likely enhance productivity, but they may also cause employees to neglect other things like tackling new projects or developing creative solutions to job-related problems. The manager who wants to motivate creativity should establish creativity goals along with productivity goals. Even the prestigious Baldrige award for quality has been criticized for generating such zealous pursuit that companies focus single-mindedly on winning the award at the expense of other key elements of business success.[9]

Top firms today set "stretch goals"—targets that are exceptionally demanding, and that some people would never even think of. But impossible though they may seem to some, they are in fact attainable. Stretch goals generate a major shift away from mediocrity and toward tremendous achievement.

Medtronic, the leader in the medical-device industry, has an annual goal of generating 70 percent of its sales from products introduced within the past two years. Schwab people don't view their company as the leader in discount brokerage; they view it as having captured only 1 percent of the savings of investors in the United States. In other words, they aim at landing the available 99 percent.

Boeing's stretch goals were to cut the cost of manufacturing an airplane 25 percent, and then it reduced the time needed to build one from 18 months to 8 months. States Boeing's CEO, "We're doing things we didn't think were possible."

Some legendary business leaders drove themselves and their people via stretch goals. In the 1950s, when the label "Made in Japan" conveyed to Americans that the product was cheap junk, Sony's Akio Morita set out to change the world's perception of Japanese quality. At the time, he had fewer than 1,000 employees, with no significant overseas presence. Yet he succeeded. And in the United States, Sam Walton started out in 1945 by wanting to make his store in Newport the best variety store in Arkansas. Later, in 1977, he declared that Wal-Mart would double in size and become a $1 billion company within four years. Even in 1990, when Wal-Mart seemed to be everywhere and sales had reached $30 billion, he set targets of doubling the number of stores and achieving sales volume of $125 billion.

But as the text suggests, goals have limitations. For example, continually "raising the bar" for growth in stock values created "ever-higher expectations [that] could not be met without financial and accounting practices that were the equivalent of steroids" (p. A23). Make sure your stretch goals are tempered by accountability for the behavior used to attain them.

Sony's Akio Morita's goal to change the world's perception of Japanese quality was achieved with products like the Sony "boom box," VCR, and the Walkman. Most people think high quality when they think of a Sony TV, and are willing to pay the higher price Sony is able to charge for one.

SOURCES: J. Collins and J. Porras, *Built to Last* (London: Century Business, 1996); S. Tully, "Why to Go for Stretch Targets," *Fortune,* November 4, 1994, pp. 145–58; K. Thompson, W. Hochwarter, and N. Mathys, "Stretch Targets: What Makes Them Effective?" *Academy of Management Executive* 11 (1997), pp. 48–60; G. Hamel, "Reinvent Your Company, *Fortune,* June 12, 2000, pp. 98–118; G. F. Will, "The Arrogance of the Executives," *The Washington Post,* January 17, 2002, p. A23.

Reinforcing Performance

Goals are universal motivators. So are the processes of reinforcement described in this section. In 1911, psychologist Edward Thorndike formulated the **law of effect:** Behavior that is followed by positive consequences probably will be repeated.[10] This powerful law of behavior laid the foundation for countless investigations into the effects of the positive consequences, called **reinforcers,** that motivate behavior. **Organizational behavior modification** attempts to influence people's behavior, and improve performance,[11] by systematically managing work conditions and the consequences of people's actions.

Four key consequences of behavior either encourage or discourage people's behavior (see Figure 13.1):

1. **Positive reinforcement**—applying a consequence that increases the likelihood that the person will repeat the behavior that led to it. Examples of positive reinforcers include compliments, letters of commendation, favorable performance evaluations, and pay raises.

law of effect

A law formulated by Edward Thorndike in 1911 stating that behavior that is followed by positive consequences will likely be repeated.

reinforcers

Positive consequences that motivate behavior.

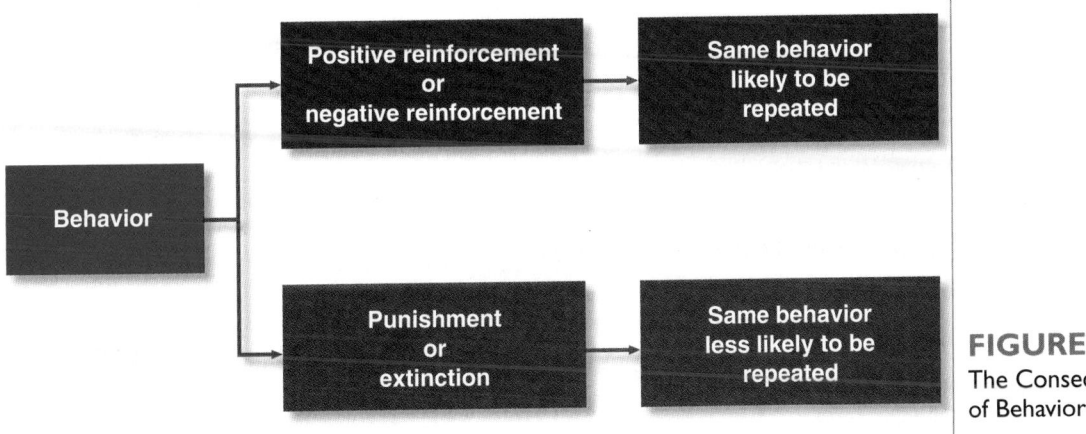

FIGURE 13.1
The Consequences of Behavior

North American Tool & Die provided monthly cash awards for creativity.[12] At Immunex, employees received on-the-spot Applause Awards worth from $250 to $2,500.[13] But it is important to remember that feedback and social reinforcers, including recognition for a job well done, are as powerful as monetary reinforcers.[14]

2. **Negative reinforcement**—removing or withholding an undesirable consequence. For example, a manager takes an employee (or a school takes a student) off probation because of improved performance. A few years ago, Nordstrom, a prominent retailer, received a great deal of negative publicity about its overreliance on negative reinforcement as a motivational tool. Frequent threatening memos admonished people to achieve every one of their many performance goals: "If any of these areas are not met to our expectations, you will be terminated." Another memo reminded employees that calling in sick once every three months is "a lot" and enough to "question your dedication."[15] Negative reinforcement in these examples occurs when people perform well and avoid punishment.

3. **Punishment**—administering an aversive consequence. Examples include criticizing or shouting at an employee, assigning an unappealing task, and sending a worker home without pay. Negative reinforcement can involve the *threat* of punishment, but not delivering it when employees perform satisfactorily. Punishment is the actual delivery of the aversive consequence. Managers use punishment when they think it is warranted or when they believe others expect them to, and they usually concern themselves with following company policy and procedure.[16]

4. **Extinction**—withdrawing or failing to provide a reinforcing consequence. When this occurs, motivation is reduced and the behavior is *extinguished*, or eliminated. Examples include not giving a compliment for a job well done, forgetting to say thanks for a favor, and setting impossible performance goals so that the person never experiences success.

The first two consequences, positive and negative reinforcement, are positive for the person receiving them—the person either gains something or avoids something negative. Therefore, the person who experiences these consequences will be motivated to behave in the ways that led to the reinforcement. The last two consequences, punishment and extinction, are negative outcomes for the person receiving them: Motivation to repeat the behavior that led to the undesirable results will be reduced.

organizational behavior modification (OB Mod)

The application of reinforcement theory in organizational settings.

positive reinforcement

Applying consequences that increase the likelihood that a person will repeat the behavior that led to it.

negative reinforcement

Removing or withholding an undesirable consequence.

punishment

Administering an aversive consequence.

extinction

Withdrawing or failing to provide a reinforcing consequence.

"The things that get rewarded get done" is what one author called The Greatest Management Principle in the World. With this in mind, Michael LeBoeuf offered prescriptions for effectively motivating high performance. Companies, and individual managers, should reward the following:

1. *Solid solutions* instead of quick fixes.
2. *Risk taking* instead of risk avoiding.
3. *Applied creativity* instead of mindless conformity.
4. *Decisive action* instead of paralysis by analysis.
5. *Smart work* instead of busywork.
6. *Simplification* instead of needless complication.
7. *Quietly effective behavior* instead of squeaky wheels.
8. *Quality work* instead of fast work.
9. *Loyalty* instead of turnover.
10. *Working together* instead of working against.

TABLE 13.1

The Greatest Management Principle in the World

SOURCE: From *The Greatest Management Principle in the World* by Michael LeBoeuf. Copyright © 1985 by Michael LeBoeuf. Used by permission of Berkeley Publishing Group, a division of Penguin Putnam, Inc.

Sometimes organizations and managers reinforce the wrong behaviors.[17] Whereas executive stock options were intended to motivate executives to care more about the company's stock price, they have motivated executives to engage in inappropriate behaviors to manipulate the stock price rather than create real value.[18] The company that bases performance reviews on short-term results is reinforcing a short-run perspective in decision making. At the same time, it is discouraging behaviors that will pay off in the long run. Programs that punish employees for absenteeism beyond a certain limit may actually encourage them to be absent. People may use up all their allowable absences and fail to come to work regularly until they reach the point where their next absence will result in punishment.

Managers must identify which kinds of behaviors they reinforce and which they discourage (see Table 13.1). The reward system has to support the firm's strategic intent, defining performance in terms of the pursuit of strategic objectives.[19] Reward employees for developing themselves in strategically important ways—for building new skills that are critical to strengthening core competencies and creating value.

Managers should be creative in their use of reinforcers.[20] Some companies awarded Palm Pilots to employees who recruited good, new talent. Nortel offered free housecleaning or spa weekends to employees who provided referrals.[21] Innovative managers use nonmonetary rewards, including intellectual challenge, greater responsibility, autonomy, recognition, flexible benefits, and greater influence over decisions. These and other rewards for high-performing employees, when creatively devised and applied, can continue to motivate when pay and promotions are scarce.[22]

Performance-Related Beliefs

expectancy theory

A theory proposing that people will behave based on their perceived likelihood that their effort will lead to a certain outcome and on how highly they value that outcome.

Reinforcement theory describes the processes by which factors in the work environment affect people's behavior. Expectancy theory adds to that some of the cognitive processes that go on in people's heads. According to **expectancy theory**, the person's work *efforts* lead to some level of *performance*.[23] Then performance results in one or more *outcomes* for the person (see Figure 13.2). People develop two important beliefs linking these three events: expectancy, which links effort to performance, and instrumentality, which links performance to outcomes.

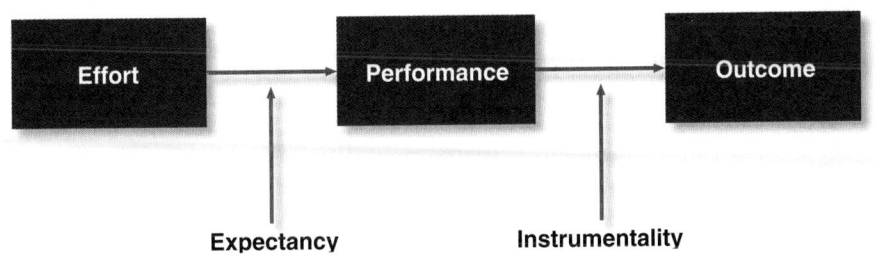

FIGURE 13.2
Basic Concepts of
Expectancy Theory

The Effort-to-Performance Link

The first belief, **expectancy,** is people's perceived likelihood that their efforts will enable them to attain their performance goals. An expectancy can be high (up to 100 percent), such as when a student is confident that if she studies hard she can get a good grade on the final. An expectancy can also be low (down to a 0 percent likelihood), such as when a suitor is convinced that his dream date will never go out with him.

> **expectancy**
>
> Employees' perception of the likelihood that their efforts will enable them to attain their performance goals.

All else equal, high expectancies create higher motivation than do low expectancies. In the preceding examples, the student is more likely to study for the exam than the suitor is to pursue the dream date, even though both want their respective outcomes.

Expectancies can vary among individuals, even in the same situation. For example, a sales manager might initiate a competition in which the top salesperson wins a free trip to Hawaii. In such cases, the few top people, who have performed well in the past, will be more motivated by the contest than will the historically average and below-average performers. The top people will have higher expectancies—stronger beliefs that their efforts can help them turn in the top performance.

The Performance-to-Outcome Link

The example about the sales contest illustrates how performance results in some kind of **outcome,** or consequence, for the person. Actually, it often results in several outcomes. For example, turning in the best sales performance could lead to (1) a competitive victory, (2) the free trip to Hawaii, (3) feelings of achievement, (4) recognition from the boss, (5) prestige throughout the company, and (6) resentment from other salespeople.

> **outcome**
>
> A consequence a person receives for his or her performance.

Winning a competition for a free trip to Hawaii would be great, but what about the losers?

---

instrumentality

The perceived likelihood that performance will be followed by a particular outcome.

valence

The value an outcome holds for the person contemplating it.

But how certain is it that performance will result in all of those outcomes? Will winning the contest really lead to resentment? For that matter, will it really lead to increased prestige?

These questions address the second key belief described by expectancy theory: instrumentality.[24] **Instrumentality** is the perceived likelihood that performance will be followed by a particular outcome. Like expectancies, instrumentalities can be high (up to 100 percent) or low (approaching 0 percent).

Also, each outcome has an associated valence. **Valence** is the value the outcome holds for the person contemplating it. Valences can be positive (up to 1.0, in the theory's mathematical formulation), like the Hawaiian vacation, or negative (down to -1.0), like the other salespeople's resentment.

Impact on Motivation

For motivation to be high, expectancy, instrumentalities, and total valence of all outcomes must all be high. A person will not be highly motivated if any of the following conditions exist:

1. He believes he can't perform well enough to achieve the positive outcomes that he knows the company provides to good performers (high valence and high instrumentality but low expectancy).
2. He knows he can do the job, and is fairly certain what the ultimate outcomes will be (say, a promotion and a transfer). However, he doesn't want those outcomes or believes other, negative outcomes outweigh the positive (high expectancy and high instrumentality but low valence).
3. He knows he can do the job, and wants several important outcomes (a favorable performance review, a raise, and a promotion). But he believes that no matter how well he performs, the outcomes will not be forthcoming (high expectancy and positive valences but low instrumentality).

Managerial Implications of Expectancy Theory

Expectancy theory helps the manager zero in on key leverage points for influencing motivation. Three implications are crucial:

1. *Increase expectancies.* Provide a work environment that facilitates good performance, and set realistically attainable performance goals. Provide training, support, and encouragement so that people are confident they can perform at the levels expected of them. Recall from Chapter 12 that charismatic leaders excel at boosting their followers' confidence.
2. *Identify positively valent outcomes.* Understand what people want to get out of work. Think about what their jobs provide them and what is not, but could be, provided. Consider how people may differ in the valences they assign to outcomes. Know the need theories of motivation, described in the next section, and their implications for identifying important outcomes.
3. *Make performance instrumental toward positive outcomes.* Make sure that good performance is followed by personal recognition and praise, favorable performance reviews, pay increases, and other positive results. Also, make sure that working hard and doing things well will have as few negative results as possible. It is useful to realize, too, that bosses usually provide (or withhold) rewards, but others do so as well, including peers, direct reports, customers, and others.[25] A division of Wells Fargo distributed Monopoly money to employees, and told them to award it to helpful colleagues. The recipients then converted the play money to real money. Similarly, Northwest Airlines distributed cash-convertible certificates to frequent flyers and invited them to award the certificates to Northwest employees who deserved them.

Understanding People's Needs

So far we have focused on processes underlying motivation. The manager who appropriately applies goal-setting, reinforcement, and expectancy theories is creating essential motivating elements in the work environment. But characteristics of the person also affect motivation. The following *content theories* indicate the kinds of needs that people want to satisfy. People have different needs energizing and motivating them toward different goals and reinforcers. The extent to which and the ways in which a person's needs are met or not met at work affect his or her behavior on the job.

The most important content theories describing people's needs are Maslow's need hierarchy, ERG theory, and McClelland's needs.

Maslow's Need Hierarchy

Abraham Maslow organized five major types of human needs into a hierarchy, as shown in Figure 13.3.[26] The **need hierarchy** illustrates Maslow's conception of people satisfying their needs in a specified order, from bottom to top. The needs, in ascending order, are:

> **need hierarchy**
>
> **A conception of human needs organizing needs into a hierarchy of five major types.**

1. *Physiological* (food, water, sex, and shelter).
2. *Safety or security* (protection against threat and deprivation).
3. *Social* (friendship, affection, belonging, and love).
4. *Ego* (independence, achievement, freedom, status, recognition, and self-esteem).
5. *Self-actualization* (realizing one's full potential, becoming everything one is capable of being).

According to Maslow, people are motivated to satisfy the lower needs before they try to satisfy the higher needs. Also, once a need is satisfied, it is no longer a powerful motivator. For example, labor unions negotiate for higher wages, benefits, safety standards, and job security. These bargaining issues relate directly to the satisfaction of Maslow's lower-level needs. Only after the physiological and safety needs are reasonably satisfied do the higher-level needs—social, ego, and self-actualization—become dominant concerns.

FIGURE 13.3
Maslow's Need Hierarchy

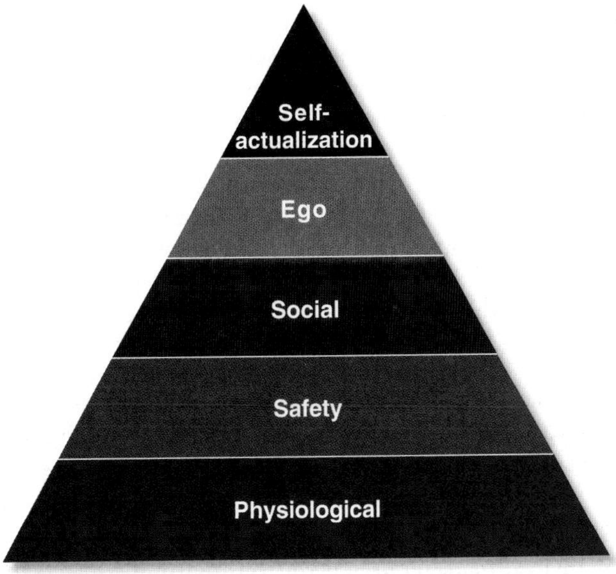

SOURCE: D. Organ and T. Bateman, *Organizational Behavior* 4th ed. Copyright © 1990 by The McGraw-Hill Companies. Reproduced with permission of The McGraw-Hill Companies.

Federal Express treats employees not as a cost to be controlled but as an asset to be developed.

Maslow's hierarchy, however, is a simplistic and not altogether accurate theory of human motivation.[27] For example, not everyone progresses through the five needs in hierarchical order. But Maslow made three important contributions. First, he identified important need categories, which can help managers create effective positive reinforcers. Second, it is helpful to think of two general levels of needs, in which lower-level needs must be satisfied before higher-level needs become important. Third, Maslow alerted managers to the importance of personal growth and self-actualization.

Self-actualization is the best-known concept arising from this theory. According to Maslow, the average person is only 10 percent self-actualized. In other words, most of us are living our lives and working at our jobs with a large untapped reservoir of potential. The implication is clear: Create a work environment that provides training, resources, autonomy, responsibilities, and challenging assignments. This type of environment gives people a chance to use their skills and abilities in creative ways and allows them to achieve more of their full potential.

So treat people not merely as a cost to be controlled but an asset to be developed. Many companies, including AT&T, Procter & Gamble, Du Pont, General Electric, Levi Strauss, and Coast Gas of Watsonville, California, are embarking on programs that provide personal growth experiences for their people.[28] An employee at Federal Express said, "The best I can be is what I can be here. Federal Express . . . gave me the confidence and self-esteem to become the person I had the potential to become" (p. 63).[29]

Organizations gain by making full use of their human resources. Employees also gain by capitalizing on opportunities to meet their higher-order needs on the job. At Du Pont, managers set personal growth goals along with performance goals. "In the past," says one executive, "[people asked] what job am I getting next? Now, it's more, how can I be developed as a person?"[30]

ERG Theory

A theory of human needs that is more advanced than Maslow's is Alderfer's ERG theory.[31] Maslow's theory has general applicability, but Alderfer aims his theory expressly at understanding people's needs at work.

ERG theory postulates three sets of needs: existence, relatedness, and growth. *Existence* needs are all material and physiological desires. *Relatedness* needs involve relationships with other people and are satisfied through the process of mutually sharing thoughts and feelings. *Growth* needs motivate people to productively or creatively change themselves or their environment. Satisfaction of the growth needs comes from fully utilizing personal capacities and developing new capacities.

ERG theory

A human needs theory developed by Alderfer postulating that people have three basic sets of needs which can operate simultaneously.

What similarities do you see between Alderfer's and Maslow's needs? Roughly speaking, existence needs subsume physiological and security needs, relatedness needs are similar to social and esteem needs, and growth needs correspond to self-actualization.

ERG theory proposes that several different needs can be operating at once. Thus, whereas Maslow would say that self-actualization is important to people only after other sets of needs are satisfied, Alderfer maintains that people—particularly working people in our postindustrial society—can be motivated to satisfy both existence and growth needs at the same time.

Maslow's theory is better known to American managers than Alderfer's, but ERG theory has more scientific support.[32] Both have practical value in that they remind managers of the types of reinforcers or rewards that can be used to motivate people. Regardless of whether the manager prefers the Maslow or the Alderfer theory of needs, he or she can motivate people by helping them satisfy their needs, and particularly by offering opportunities for self-actualization and growth.

McClelland's Needs

David McClelland also identified a number of basic needs that guide people. The most important needs for managers, according to McClelland, are the needs for achievement, affiliation, and power.[33]

The need for *achievement* is characterized by a strong orientation toward accomplishment and an obsession with success and goal attainment. Most managers and entrepreneurs in the United States have high levels of this need and like to see it in their employees.

The need for *affiliation* reflects a strong desire to be liked by other people. Individuals who have high levels of this need are oriented toward getting along with others and may be less concerned with performing at high levels.

The need for *power* is a desire to influence or control other people. This need can be a negative force—termed *personalized power*—if it is expressed through the aggressive manipulation and exploitation of others. People high on the personalized-power need want power purely for the pursuit of their own goals. But the need for power also can be a positive motive—called *socialized power*—because it can be channeled toward the constructive improvement of organizations and societies.

Low need for affiliation and moderate to high need for power are associated with managerial success for both higher- and lower-level managers.[34] Recall from Chapter 12 that high power and achievement needs are traits that relate to effective leadership. One reason the need for affiliation is not important for management and leadership success is that people high on this need have difficulty making tough but necessary decisions that will make some people unhappy.

Need Theories: International Perspectives

How do the need theories apply abroad?[35] Whereas managers in the United States care most strongly about achievement, esteem, and self-actualization, managers in Greece and Japan are motivated more by security. Social needs are most important in Sweden, Norway, and Denmark. "Doing your own thing"—the phrase from the 1960s that describes an American culture oriented toward self-actualization—is not even translatable into Chinese. "Achievement" too is difficult to translate into most other languages. Researchers in France, Japan, and Sweden would have been unlikely to even conceive of McClelland's achievement motive, because people of those countries are more group-oriented than individually oriented.

Clearly, achievement, growth, and self-actualization are profoundly important in the United States (and in other Anglo-American countries like Canada and Great Britain). But these needs are not universally important. Every manager must remember that need importance varies from country to country and that people may not be motivated by the same needs. Generally, no single way is best, and managers can customize their approaches by considering how individuals differ.[36]

Designing Motivating Jobs

Here's an example of a company that gave a "reward" that didn't motivate. One of Mary Kay Ash's former employers gave her a sales award: a flounder fishing light. Unfortunately, she doesn't fish. Fortunately, she later was able to design her own organization around both *intrinsic* as well as *extrinsic* motivators that *mattered* to her people.[37] **Extrinsic reinforcers** are rewards given to high-performing people by the boss, the company, or some other person. An **intrinsic reward** is reward the person derives directly from performing the job itself. An interesting project, an intriguing subject that is fun to study, a completed sale, and the discovery of the perfect solution to a difficult problem all can give people the feeling that they have done something well. This is the essence of the motivation that comes from intrinsic rewards.

extrinsic reinforcers

Reinforcers given to a person by the boss, the company, or some other person.

intrinsic reward

Reward a worker derives directly from performing the job itself.

Intrinsic rewards are essential to the motivation underlying creativity.[38] A challenging problem, a chance to create something new, and work that is exciting in and of itself can provide intrinsic motivation that inspires people to devote time and energy to the task. So do managers who allow people some freedom to pursue the tasks that interest them most. The opposite situations result in routine, habitual behaviors which interfere with creativity.[39] A study in manufacturing facilities found that employees initiated more applications for patents, made more novel and useful suggestions, and were rated by their managers as more creative when their jobs were challenging and their managers did not control their activities closely.[40] On the other hand, some jobs and organizations create environments that quash creativity and motivation.[41]

The classic example of a demotivating job is the highly specialized assembly line job; each worker performs one boring operation before passing the work along to the next worker. Such specialization, or the "mechanistic" approach to job design, was the prevailing practice through most of the 20th century.[42]

But jobs that are too simple and routine result in employee dissatisfaction, absenteeism, and turnover. Moreover, people at many successful firms have become millionaires, leading to turnover problems. The only way to keep such employees is to let them design their own jobs so that their work is more interesting than it would be elsewhere.[43] Increasingly, jobs are being designed in the following ways to increase intrinsic rewards and therefore motivation.

Job Rotation, Enlargement, and Enrichment

job rotation

Changing from one routine task to another to alleviate boredom.

With **job rotation,** workers who spend all their time in one routine task can instead move from one job to another. Rather than dishing out the pasta in a cafeteria line all day, a person might work the pasta, then the salads, and then the vegetables, drinks, or desserts. Job rotation is intended to alleviate boredom by giving people different things to do.

As you may guess, however, the person may just be changing from one boring job to another. But job rotation can benefit everyone when done properly, with people's input and career interests in mind. At G.S.I. Transcomm Data Systems of Pittsburgh, people often voice their preferences and rotate laterally to new assignments. Examples include an operations manager who moved into sales management, a programmer who moved into service for longtime customers, and a receptionist who moved into sales.[44] The result of the rotation policy often is a reenergized worker who stays with the company.

Job enlargement is similar to job rotation in that people are given different tasks to do. But whereas job rotation involves doing one set of tasks at one time and leaving those tasks for a different set at a different time, job enlargement means that the worker is given additional tasks at the same time. Thus, an assembly worker's job is enlarged if he or she is given two tasks rather than one to perform. In a study of job enlargement in a financial services organization, enlarged jobs led to higher job satisfaction, better error detection by clerks, and improved customer service.[45]

job enlargement

Giving people additional tasks at the same time to alleviate boredom.

With job enlargement, the person's additional tasks are at the same level of responsibility. More profound changes occur when jobs are enriched. **Job enrichment** means that jobs are restructured or redesigned by adding higher levels of responsibility. This includes giving people not only more tasks but higher-level ones, such as when decisions are delegated downward and authority is decentralized. Efforts to redesign jobs by enriching them are now common in American industry. Herzberg's two-factor theory was the first approach to job enrichment, followed by the Hackman and Oldham model.

job enrichment

Changing a task to make it inherently more rewarding, motivating, and satisfying.

Herzberg's Two-Factor Theory

Frederick Herzberg's **two-factor theory** distinguished between two broad categories of factors that affect people working on their jobs.[46] The first category, **hygiene factors,** are *characteristics of the workplace:* company policies, working conditions, pay, co-workers, supervision, and so forth. These factors can make people unhappy if they are poorly managed. If they are well managed, and viewed as positive by employees, the employees will no longer be dissatisfied. However, no matter how good these factors are, they will not make people truly satisfied or motivated to do a good job.

According to Herzberg, the key to true job satisfaction and motivation to perform lies in the second category: the motivators. The **motivators** describe the *job itself*, that is, what people *do* at work. Motivators are the nature of the work itself, the actual job responsibilities, opportunity for personal growth and recognition, and the feelings of achievement the job provides. When these factors are present, jobs are presumed to be both satisfying and motivating for most people.

Herzberg's theory has been criticized by many scholars, and for that reason we will not go into more detail about his original theory. But Herzberg was a pioneer in the area of job design and still is a respected name among American managers. Furthermore, even if the specifics of his theory do not hold up to scientific scrutiny, he made several very important contributions. First, Herzberg's theory highlights the important distinction between extrinsic rewards (from hygiene factors) and intrinsic rewards (from motivators). Second, it reminds managers not to count solely on extrinsic rewards to motivate workers but to focus on intrinsic rewards as well. Third, it set the stage for later theories, such as the Hackman and Oldham model, that explain more precisely how managers can enrich people's jobs.

two-factor theory

Herzberg's theory describing two factors affecting people's work motivation and satisfaction.

hygiene factors

Characteristics of the workplace, such as company policies, working conditions, pay, and supervision, that can make people dissatisfied.

motivators

Factors that make a job more motivating, such as additional job responsibilities, opportunities for personal growth and recognition, and feelings of achievement.

In the early 1900s, cigar makers paid people to read stories to employees working boring jobs. In the textile industry during the same period, managers allowed kittens to play on the floor, also to help workers fight boredom.

Now, bored employees wear Walkmans. People who wear them say doing so helps them get through a dull work day by keeping their minds off stress factors and making the time go faster. They also say the music—or the soaps—are not a distraction and have no effect on their job performance.

Some employers prohibit the Walkmans, maintaining they interfere with concentration and communication. But others see benefits. A Banc One executive sees people developing rhythmic work patterns, and believes the Walkmans improve concentration and quality. A study of assembly-line workers in a medical-equipment factory found that headphones had no impact on job performance, and that people wearing them reported higher job satisfaction.

Other people bored at work spend time in chatrooms, engage in other non-work-related Internet activities, and play computer games. At a nuclear power plant, employees became hooked to the multiuser game Doom. The information technology manager claimed that safety wasn't compromised directly, but the Doom files are huge and can slow down the PC network. The manager, interviewed for a magazine article, requested anonymity.

Some employees do these things during work, some during lunch, some while on the telephone. One company believed that perhaps 60 percent to 70 percent of website visits by its employees are unrelated to business. Many companies are cracking down. Kraft Foods installed a system preventing employees from visiting websites unrelated to their jobs, with the chief information officer saying, "We're here for business purposes, not for individual entertainment." Meanwhile, employees everywhere are finding ways to resist management's attempts to monitor and control. Don's Boss Page on the Web featured "Stealth Surfing: secret tips and tricks from the pros on how to look busy at work while you're cruising the Internet."

Wearing a walkman while working— how does this affect motivation?

Motivator, Hygiene, or Distractor?

Some managers claim that these activities rob the company of productivity, others claim no effect, and still others maintain that people need a break once in a while. Many executives engage in the same activities, whereas some executives insist on firing anyone caught doing these things when he or she is supposed to be working.

What do you think? What do these activities have to do with job design, motivation, and job satisfaction? If you were a manager, how would you handle policy on this issue, and what would you do with people engaging in these activities?

SOURCE: C. Powell, "When Workers Wear Walkmans on the Job," *The Wall Street Journal*, July 11, 1994, pp. B1, B8; J. Stuller, "Games Workers Play," *Across the Board,* July–August 1997, pp. 16–22; and C. Harmon, "Goofing Off at Work: First You Log On," *International Herald Tribune,* September 23, 1997, pp. 1, 10.

The Hackman and Oldham Model of Job Design

Following Herzberg's work, Hackman and Oldham proposed a more complete model of job design.[47] Figure 13.4 illustrates their model. As you can see, well-designed jobs lead to high motivation, high-quality performance, high satisfaction, and low absenteeism and turnover. These outcomes occur when people experience three critical psychological states: (1) They believe they are doing something meaningful because their work is important to other people; (2) they feel personally responsible for how the work turns out; and (3) they learn how well they performed their jobs.

These psychological states occur when people are working on enriched jobs, that is, jobs that offer the following five core job dimensions:

1. *Skill variety*—different job activities involving several skills and talents. For example, at Ashton Photo in Salem, Oregon, employees decide what skills they need and grade themselves on their performance. Rewards are also based on the ability to teach others new skills.[48]

FIGURE 13.4
The Hackman and Oldham Model of Job Enrichment

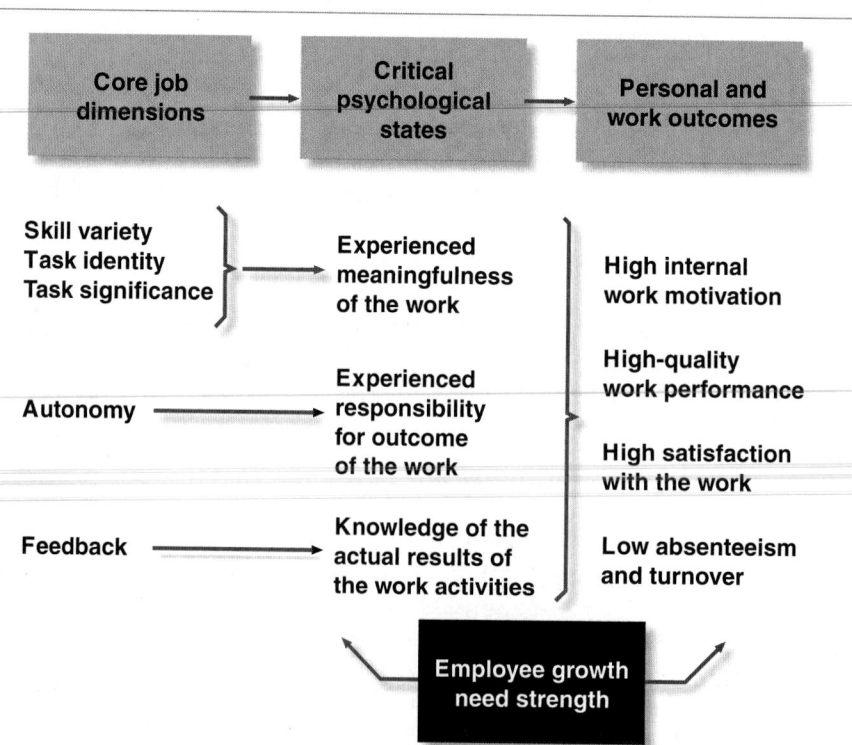

lems, solutions, and opportunities for innovation on which they are "empowered" to act.

What actions can leaders take to empower their people and generate these positive outcomes? Empowering people means allowing them to participate in decision making, expressing confidence in their ability to perform at high levels, designing their jobs so they have greater freedom, setting meaningful and challenging goals, applauding outstanding perfomance, and encouraging people to take personal responsibility for their work. It also means providing people access to information and to other resources, and providing social and sometimes emotional support.[68]

It is essential to give people clear strategic direction, but to leave some room for flexibility and calculated risk taking. For example, Southwest Airlines' strategic principle of "meet customers' short-haul travel needs at fares competitive with the cost of automobile travel" helps employees keep strategic objectives in mind and use their discretion in making complicated decisions about service offerings, route selection, cabin design, ticketing procedures, and pricing.[69] More specific actions include increasing signature authority at all levels; reducing the number of rules and approval steps; assigning nonroutine jobs; allowing independent judgment, flexibility, and creativity; defining jobs more broadly as projects rather than tasks; and providing more freedom of access to resources and people throughout the organization (and outside the organization!).[70]

Significantly, empowerment does not mean allowing people to decide trivial things like what color to paint the lunchroom. For empowerment to make a difference, people must have an impact on things about which they care, such as quality and productivity.[71] Companies including Lord Corporation in Dayton, Ohio (which produces engine mounts for aircraft), Herman Miller (the Michigan-based furniture manufacturer), Johnsonville Foods, and Goodyear all were highly successful and received great acclaim for their empowerment programs.[72]

You should not be surprised when empowerment causes some problems, at least in the short term. This is the case with virtually any change, including changes for the better. People may make mistakes at first, especially until they have had adequate training. And because more training is needed, costs are higher. Also, because people acquire new skills and make greater contributions, they may demand higher wages. But if they are well-trained and truly empowered, they will deserve them—and both they and the company will benefit.

Achieving Fairness

Ultimately, one of the most important issues in motivation surrounds how people view their contributions to the organization and what they receive from the organization. Ideally, they will view their relationship with their employer as a well-balanced, mutually beneficial exchange. As people work and realize the outcomes or consequences of their actions, they develop beliefs about how appropriate those outcomes are. Basically, they assess how fairly the organization treats them.

The starting point for understanding how people interpret their contributions and outcomes is equity theory.[73] **Equity theory** proposes that when people assess how fairly they are treated, they consider two key factors: outcomes and inputs. *Outcomes*, as in expectancy theory, refer to the various things the person receives on the job: recognition, pay, benefits, satisfaction, security, job assignments, punishments, and so forth. *Inputs* refer to the contributions the person makes to the organization: effort, time, talent, performance, extra commitment, good citizenship, and so forth. People have a general expectation that the outcomes they receive will reflect, or be proportionate to, the inputs they provide—a fair day's pay (and other outcomes) for a fair day's work (broadly defined by how people view all their contributions).

> **equity theory**
>
> A theory stating that people assess how fairly they have been treated according to two key factors: outcomes and inputs.

But this comparison of outcomes to inputs is not the whole story. People also pay attention to the outcomes and inputs others receive. At salary review time, for example, most people—from executives on down—try to pick up clues that will tell them who got the high raises. As described in the following section, they compare ratios, restore equity if necessary, and derive more or less satisfaction based on how fairly they believe they have been treated.

Assessing Equity

Equity theory suggests that people compare the ratio of their own outcomes to inputs against the outcome-to-input ratio of some comparison person. The comparison person can be a fellow student, a co-worker, a boss, or an average industry pay scale. Stated more succinctly, people compare:

$$\text{Their own } \frac{\text{Outcomes}}{\text{Inputs}} \text{ versus Others' } \frac{\text{Outcomes}}{\text{Inputs}}$$

If the ratios are equivalent, people believe the relationship is equitable, or fair. Equity causes people to be satisfied with their treatment. But the person who believes his or her ratio is lower than another's will feel inequitably treated. Inequity causes dissatisfaction and leads to an attempt to restore balance to the relationship.

There are many examples of inequity and the negative feelings it creates. For example, some CEOs receive astronomical pay despite poor company performance. According to *Fortune*, "The American public isn't angered by big pay. It's angered by perceived injustice" (p. 70).[74] As a student, perhaps you have been in the following situation. You stay up all night and get a C on the exam. Meanwhile another student studies a couple of hours, goes out for the rest of the evening, gets a good night's sleep, and gets a B on the exam. You perceive your inputs (time spent studying) as much greater than the other student's, but your outcomes are lower. You are displeased at the unfairness of the situation.

In business, the same thing happens with pay raises. One manager puts in 60-hour weeks, has a degree from a prestigious university, and believes she is destined for the top. When her archrival—whom she perceives as less deserving ("she never comes into the office on weekends, and all she does when she is here is butter up the boss")—gets the higher raise or the promotion, she experiences severe feelings of inequity. Perceived pay inequities may be the reason major league baseball teams that have great differences in their player salaries tend to win fewer games.[75]

Assessments of equity are not made objectively. They are subjective perceptions or beliefs. In the preceding example, the person who got the higher raise probably felt she deserved it. Even if she admits she doesn't put in long workweeks, she may convince herself she doesn't need to because she's so talented. The student who got the higher grade may believe it was a fair, equitable result because (1) she kept up all semester, while the other student did not, and (2) she's smart (ability and experience, not just effort, can be seen as inputs).

Restoring Equity

People who feel inequitably treated and dissatisfied are motivated to do something to restore equity. They have a number of options that they carry out by actually doing something to change the ratios, or by reevaluating the situation and deciding it is equitable after all.

The equity equation shown earlier indicates a person's options for restoring equity. People who feel inequitably treated can *reduce their inputs* by giving less effort, performing at lower levels, retaliating in ways that hurt other people and the organization,[76] or quitting ("Well, if that's the way things work around here, there's no way I'm going to work that hard [or stick around]"). Or they can attempt to *increase their outcomes* ("My boss [or teacher] is going to hear about this. I deserve more; there must be some way I can get more").

Other ways of restoring equity focus on changing the other person's ratio. A person can *decrease others' outcomes*. For example, an employee may sabotage work to create problems for his company or his boss. A person can also change her perceptions of inputs or outcomes ("That promotion isn't as great a deal as he thinks. The pay is not that much better, and the headaches will be unbelievable"). It is also possible to *increase others' inputs*, particularly by changing perceptions ("The more I think about it, the more he deserved it. He's worked hard all year, he's competent, and it's about time he got a break").

Thus, a person can restore equity in a number of ways by behaviorally or perceptually changing inputs and outcomes.

Fair Process

Inevitably, managers make decisions that have outcomes more favorable for some than for others. Those with favorable outcomes will be pleased; those with worse outcomes, all else equal, will be more displeased. But managers desiring to put salve on the wounds—say, of people they like or respect or want to keep and motivate—still can take actions to reduce the dissatisfaction. The key is for people to believe that managers provide **procedural justice**—using fair process in decision making and helping others know that the process was as fair as possible. When people perceive procedural fairness, they are more likely to support decisions, decision makers, and organizations.[77]

> **procedural justice**
>
> **Using fair process in decision making and making sure others know that the process was as fair as possible.**

Even if people believe that their *outcome* was inequitable and unfair, they are more likely to view justice as having been served if the *process* was fair. For example, someone receiving a low pay raise, or someone overlooked for promotion or for a juicy assignment, might question the fairness of the decision. If the manager explains how she went about making the decision, and the logic behind the decision, and if the decision was made in an unbiased way, it is more likely to be understood and accepted. If it is not fully accepted, at least the employee will have had a fair hearing, a chance to voice complaints, ask questions, and receive in return the time and good faith effort from the boss. Most compelling of all, if employees make decisions together with the manager, and attention is paid to fair process, in the end an individual may not get that for which he or she hoped, but will at least understand that the procedures used were as fair as possible.

For example, at an elevator plant in the United States, an army of consultants arrived one day, unexplained and annoying.[78] The rumor mill kicked in; employees thought that the plant was to be shut down, or that some of them would be laid off. Three months later, management unveiled its new plan, involving a new method of manufacturing based on teams. When employees sat in silence, management and the consultants (who finally were introduced to employees at this meeting) were pleased at the presumably positive reaction. But as the changes were implemented, management did not adequately answer questions about the purpose of the changes, employees resisted, conflicts arose, and the formerly popular plant manager lost the trust of his people. Costs skyrocketed, and quality plummeted.

Concerned, management conducted an employee survey. Employees were skeptical that the survey results would lead to any positive changes and were worried that management would be angry that people had voiced their honest opinions. But management reacted by saying, "We were wrong, we screwed up, we didn't use the right

process." They went on to share with employees critical business information, the limited options available, and the dire consequences if the company didn't change. Employees saw the dilemma, and came to view the business problem as theirs as well as management's, but were scared that some of them would lose their jobs. Management retained the right to lay people off if business conditions grew worse, but also made several promises: no layoffs as a result of changes made; cross-training programs for employees; no replacements of departing people until conditions improved; a chance for employees to serve in new roles, as consultants on quality issues; and sharing of sales and cost data on a regular basis.

The news was bad, but people understood it and began to share responsibility with management. This was the beginning of the restoration of trust and commitment, and of steady improvements in performance.[79]

Motivation at Charles Schwab

Charles Schwab is one of the world's most successful financial services companies. It also was one of the first big traditional companies that "got it"—that figured out how to successfully make the move to the Internet world. In the parlance, Schwab was a bricks-and-mortar company that became an outstanding bricks-and-clicks company. An excellent book chronicling the change, and written by the executives who made it happen, is called *Clicks and Mortar: Passion Driven Growth in an Internet Driven World*.

Charles Schwab "got it." His bricks-and-mortar company became an outstanding bricks-and-clicks company.

In explaining the title, the authors stated that "Clicks" refers to the Internet, "where the world of information is a click away. But we are not driven or inspired by mere digital purity ... we are inspired by our passion for providing meaning from it, by creating something from the chaos that makes a difference to others ... It is passion and conviction that hold people and their companies and customers together in the Internet world. The passion that created the business, the passion that drives employees and that creates the loyal customers—that is the 'Mortar.'"

What does this mean in reality? What does Schwab measure and reward? Schwab does everything it can to motivate people to do the things it wants people to commit to, be passionate about, and continue developing. In assessing people for recruiting and increased responsibility, it looks for people who:

- *Demonstrate a passion for service.*
- *Demonstrate results orientation.*
- *Create vision and think strategically.*
- *Inspire trust.*
- *Build organizational relationships.*
- *Encourage and manage differences.*
- *Manage resources effectively.*
- *Inspire and develop others.*
- *Communicate effectively.*
- *Manage technology.*
- *Lead change and innovation.*
- *Seek self-development.*

These behaviors are a far cry from just working harder or faster or doing analyses, or increasing market share by 2 percent, or achieving a certain ROI. Schwab decided these were the things it needed people to do, and—remembering that the things that get rewarded get done—it set up systems that motivate people to do them. To do these things is to enrich work, for oneself and for others. And according to Schwab, these are the things needed to succeed in the new era.

SOURCE: D. S. Pottruck and T. Pearce, "*Clicks and Mortar: Passion Driven Growth in an Internet Driven World.* Copyright © 2000. This material is used by permission of Jossey-Bass, Inc., a subsidiary of John Wiley & Sons, Inc.

Job Satisfaction

If people feel fairly treated from the outcomes they receive, or the processes used, they will be satisfied. A satisfied worker is not necessarily more productive than a dissatisfied one; sometimes people are happy with their jobs because they don't have to work hard! But job dissatisfaction, aggregated across many individuals, creates a workforce that is more likely to exhibit (1) higher turnover; (2) higher absenteeism; (3) lower corporate citizenship; (4) more grievances and lawsuits; (5) strikes; (6) stealing, sabotage, and vandalism; (7) poorer mental and physical health (which can mean higher job stress, higher insurance costs, and more lawsuits;[80] and (8) poor customer service.[81] All of these consequences of dissatisfaction, either directly or indirectly, are costly to organizations.

Quality of Work Life

Quality of work life (QWL) programs create a workplace that enhances employee well-being and satisfaction. The general goal of QWL programs is to satisfy the full range of employee needs. People's needs apparently are well met at the Container Store: It was rated number one in the 100 Best Companies to Work For, in part because 97 percent of employees surveyed say that "people care about each other here").[82] Another company on the list is Medtronic, which takes pride in Medtronic's reputation as a "human" place to work. "If it's not, we've failed totally" (p. 118).[83]

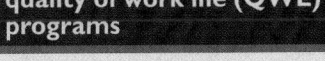

quality of work life (QWL) programs

Programs designed to create a workplace that enhances employee well being.

QWL has eight categories:[84]

1. Adequate and fair compensation.
2. A safe and healthy environment.
3. Jobs that develop human capacities.
4. A chance for personal growth and security.
5. A social environment that fosters personal identity, freedom from prejudice, a sense of community, and upward mobility.
6. Constitutionalism, or the rights of personal privacy, dissent, and due process.
7. A work role that minimizes infringement on personal leisure and family needs.
8. Socially responsible organizational actions.

Organizations differ drastically in their attention to QWL. Critics claim that QWL programs don't necessarily inspire employees to work harder if the company does not tie rewards directly to individual performance. Advocates of QWL claim that it improves organizational effectiveness and productivity. The term *productivity*, as applied by QWL programs, means much more than each person's quantity of work output.[85] It also includes turnover, absenteeism, accidents, theft, sabotage, creativity, innovation, and especially the quality of work.

Psychological Contracts

The relationship between individuals and employing organizations typically is formalized by a written contract. But in employees' minds there also exists a **psychological contract**—a set of perceptions of what they owe their employers, and what their employers owe them.[86] This contract, whether it is seen as being upheld or violated—and whether the parties trust one another or not—has important implications for employee satisfaction and motivation and the effectiveness of the organization.

Wal-Mart, under the legendary Sam Walton, offered a psychological contract to its people: We'll pay less-than-top wages, but we'll care about you and be fair with you, and you'll work hard for us in return. Fairness included many small but important things: "an open door" policy in which workers could share concerns with managers at any level, a real chance for hourly workers to earn promotions into salaried management positions, scheduling work hours with family needs in mind, and other acts of personal consideration. Unfortunately, some say that this "contact" is now frayed, in large part because of Wal-Mart's incredible growth, mammoth size, 24/7 store hours, and a narrower focus on the bottom line. The psychological contract that generated committed employees and a culture that provided a real competitive advantage is, say some, in danger of becoming merely an extinct legend.[87]

In today's world, the relationship between employer and employee is not the stable, secure one of decades past. It is more accurately described as "no guarantees." People who perceive their psychological contract as secure and comfortable are likely to be surprised and angered when business conditions change. Extending the equity theory ratio, people compare:[88]

$$\frac{\text{Benefits provided by the organization}}{\text{Benefits promised by the organization}} \text{ versus } \frac{\text{Contributions provided by the employee}}{\text{Contributions promised by the employee}}$$

Historically, in many companies this relationship has been stable and predictable. Now, mergers and layoffs and other disruptions have thrown asunder the "old deal."[89] As a McGraw-Hill executive put it, "The 'used-to-be's' must give way to the realities of 'What is and what will be.'"[90] The fundamental "used-to-be" of traditionally managed organizations was that employees were expected to be loyal and employers would provide secure employment. Today, the implicit contract goes something like this:[91] If people stay, do their own job plus someone else's (who has been downsized), and do additional things like participating in task forces, the company will try to provide a job (if it can), provide gestures that it cares, and keep providing more or less the same pay (with periodic small increases). The likely result of this not-very-satisfying arrangement: uninspired people and a business trying to survive.

But a better deal is possible, for both employers and employees.[92] Ideally, your employer will provide continuous skill updating and an invigorating work environment in which you can use your skills and are motivated to stay even though you may have other job options.[93] You could work for a company that provides the following deal: If you develop the skills we need, apply them in ways that help the company succeed, and behave consistently with our values, we will provide for you a challenging work environment, support for your development, and full, fair rewards for your contributions. The result of such a "contract" is much more likely to be a mutually beneficial, high-performing, successful organization.

KEY TERMS

Empowerment, p. 411

Equity theory, p. 413

ERG theory, p. 406

Expectancy, p. 403

Expectancy theory, p. 402

Extinction, p. 401

Extrinsic reinforcers, p. 407

Goal-setting theory, p. 399

Growth need strength, p. 411

Hygiene factors, p. 409

Instrumentality, p. 404

Intrinsic reward, p. 407

Job enlargement, p. 408

Job enrichment, p. 408

Job rotation, p. 408

Law of effect, p. 400

Motivation, p. 398

Motivators, p. 409

Need hierarchy, p. 405

Negative reinforcement, p. 401

Organizational behavior modification (OB Mod), p. 401

Outcome, p. 403

Positive reinforcement, p. 401

Procedural justice, p. 415

Psychological contract, p. 418

Punishment, p. 401

Quality of work life (QWL) programs, p. 417

Reinforcers, p. 400

Two-factor theory, p. 409

Valence, p. 404

SUMMARY OF LEARNING OBJECTIVES

Now that you have studied Chapter 13, you should know:

The kinds of behaviors managers need to motivate in people.

All important work behaviors are motivated. Managers need to motivate employees to join and remain in the organization and to exhibit high attendance, job performance, and citizenship.

How to set challenging, motivating goals.

Goal setting is a powerful motivator. Specific, quantifiable, and challenging but attainable goals motivate high effort and performance. Goal setting can be used for teams as well as for individuals. Care should be taken that single goals are not set to the exclusion of other important dimensions of performance.

How to reward good performance.

Organizational behavior modification programs influence behavior at work by arranging consequences for people's actions. Most programs use positive reinforcement as a consequence, but other important consequences are negative reinforcement, punishment, and extinction. Care must be taken to reinforce appropriate, not inappropriate, behavior. Innovative managers use a wide variety of rewards for good performance.

The key beliefs that affect people's motivation.

Expectancy theory describes three important work-related beliefs. That is, motivation is a function of people's (1) expectancies, or effort-performance links; (2) instrumentalities, or performance-outcome links; and (3) the valences people attach to the outcomes of performance. Equity theory also addresses important beliefs about fairness.

The ways in which people's individual needs affect their behavior.

Maslow's five most important needs are physiological, safety, social, ego, and self-actualization. Alderfer's ERG theory describes three sets of needs: existence, relatedness, and growth. McClelland emphasizes three different needs: achievement, affiliation, and power. Because people are inclined to satisfy their various needs, these theories help to suggest to managers the kinds of rewards that motivate people.

How to create a motivating, empowering job.

One approach to satisfying needs and motivating people is to create intrinsic motivation through the improved design of jobs. Jobs can be enriched by building in more skill variety, task identity, task significance, autonomy, and feedback. Empowerment is the most recent development in the creation of motivating jobs. Empowerment includes the perceptions of meaning, competence, self-determination, and impact, and comes from an environment in which people have necessary information, knowledge, power, and rewards.

How people assess fairness, and how to achieve fairness.

Equity theory states that people compare their inputs and outcomes to the inputs and outcomes of others. Perceptions of equity (fair treatment) are satisfying; feelings of inequity (unfairness) are dissatisfying and motivate people to change their behavior or their perceptions to restore equity. In addition to fairness of outcomes, as described in equity theory, fairness is also appraised and managed through procedural justice.

The causes and consequences of a satisfied workforce.

A satisfied workforce has many advantages for the firm, including lower absenteeism and turnover; fewer grievances, lawsuits, and strikes; lower health costs; and higher-quality work. One general approach to generating higher satisfaction for people is to implement a quality of work life program. QWL seeks to provide a safe and healthy environment, opportunity for personal growth, a positive social environment, fair treatment, and other improvements in people's work life. These and other benefits from the organization, exchanged for contributions from employees, create a psychological contract. Over time, how the psychological contract is upheld or violated, and changed unfairly or fairly, will influence people's satisfaction and motivation.

DISCUSSION QUESTIONS

1. Referring to "Setting the Stage," how would you like to work in systems like those at Lincoln Electric and AES, and why?

2. Why do you think it is so difficult for managers to empower their people?

3. Think of a job you hold currently or held in the past. How would you describe the psychological contract? How does (did) this affect your attitudes and behaviors on the job?

4. If a famous executive or sports figure were to give a passionate motivational speech, trying to persuade people to work harder, what do you think the impact would be? Why?

5. Give some examples of situations in which you wanted to do a great job but were prevented from doing so. What was the impact on you, and what would this suggest to you in your efforts to motivate other people to perform?

6. Discuss the similarities and differences between setting goals for other people and setting goals for yourself. When does goal setting fail, and when does it succeed?

7. Identify four examples of people inadvertently reinforcing the wrong behaviors, or punishing or extinguishing good behaviors.

8. Assess yourself on McClelland's three needs. On which need are you highest, and on which are you lowest? What are the implications for you as a manager?

9. Identify a job you have worked and appraise it on Hackman and Oldham's five core job dimensions. Also describe the degree to which it made you feel empowered. As a class, choose one job and discuss together how it could be changed to be more motivating and empowering.

10. Using expectancy theory, analyze how you have made and will make personal choices, such as a major area of study, a career to pursue, or job interviews to seek.

11. Describe a time when you felt unfairly treated and explain why. How did you respond to the inequity? What other options might you have had?

12. Provide examples of how outcomes perceived as unfair can decrease motivation. Then discuss how procedural justice, or fair process, can help overcome the negative effects.

13. What are the implications for your career of, and how will you prepare for, the psychological contracts described at the end of the chapter?

In Need of Motivation at Toys 'R' Us

FROM THE PAGES OF

BusinessWeek

In 1998, Toys 'R' Us was the number one U.S. toy seller. In 2000, Wal-Mart was number one. Toys 'R' Us was in the middle of a string of sales and earnings disappointments, wrestling with management problems, and described as "long-troubled" and the store of "unhelpful sales clerks, warehouse-length aisles done in dismal gray and blue, and Christmas-eve frustration" (p. 129). CEO John H. Eyler, Jr., wants to change all that.

To beat the challenge of online toy stores, Toys 'R' Us linked with Amazon.com to create a joint website. This was a promising move, but the economy was weakening. And there was no "must-have" toy for Christmas that would automatically bring in extra crowds. Moreover, the slow economy in 2001 and 2002 forced retailers, including Toys 'R' Us, to close stores. Even as the economy started to recover, retailers were concerned that consumption patterns would not return to prerecession levels.

Eyler's analysis showed inventory and delivery problems that the company worked to remedy. But another huge challenge was the opinion of U.S. shoppers. Many customers griped about unhelpful sales staff. One woman, trying to buy an infant bathtub, couldn't find one and finally went to the customer-service booth for help. She was told that if the store had one, it was on the floor, and if it didn't have one, she was out of luck. When she convinced the clerk to check by computer, they found five bathtubs in stock. The clerk said it would be several hours before someone could take one down for the customer, who then left without the bathtub. This was no isolated incident. A study of 15 big retailers ranked Toys 'R' Us 14th in customer service.

One advantage Toys 'R' Us has is its wide assortment of products. But customers have wide selections online and at some other stores as well, and Toys 'R' Us does not have the same cost advantage that it used to enjoy. Moreover, all that product in-store means that a lot of space is required, customers may have questions or not know about all of their options, and employees need

Striving to get customers to return, Toys 'R' Us must perform as well or better than the competition.

when so many U.S. consumers complain about the sorry state of customer service in many industries, maybe Toys 'R' Us can figure out a way to generate the quality of service that customers will appreciate and tell their friends about. And maybe customers will start coming back to the store for more. As CEO John Eyler worked to turn the giant toy company around, *Business Week* named him a "Manager to Watch" in 2002. The retail environment in 2002 was brutal, and he needed strong results.

QUESTIONS

1. In a store like Toys 'R' Us, what constitutes good customer service?

2. Now be specific: As a customer or Toys 'R' Us manager, precisely what dimensions of customer service would you like employees to provide? Give concrete examples of poor and great service you have seen.

product knowledge and the willingness to share that knowledge with customers.

So, like so many companies, Toys 'R' Us must do a lot of things as well as its competitors, and also find its distinctive competitive advantage. Strategically, the company no longer wants to battle discounters like Wal-Mart on their turf, preferring to narrow its product assortments and add more exclusive items. Perhaps, too, it can create a unique shopping environment. And perhaps it can somehow motivate its staff to provide great service. At a time

3. As a manager, how would you motivate those behaviors? Be as specific as possible in making concrete action recommendations to motivate the highest possible levels of customer service.

SOURCE: N. Byrnes, "Toy 'R' Us: Can CEO John Eyler Fix The Chain?" *Business Week*, December 4, 2000, pp. 128–40; L. Braham and R. Berner, "The Wrong Time for REITs?" *Business Week Online*, p. 88 March 11, 2002; R. Berner and G. Khermouch, "Retail Reckoning," *Business Week Online*, December 10, 2001, pp. 72–77; "Managers to Watch 2002," *Business Week Online*, January 14, 2002, pp. 52–72.

13.1 Job Satisfaction and Job Performance: A Debate Exercise

OBJECTIVE

The objective of this exercise is to explore the relationship between job satisfaction and job performance.

INSTRUCTIONS

This in-class exercise takes the form of a nontraditional four-way debate. Students will be divided by the instructor into four debating teams, each having four or five members. The remaining students will then be divided into judging teams consisting of three to six members each. The debate itself will focus on the relationship between job satisfaction and job performance.

DEBATING POSITIONS

Each debating team will be assigned one of the following four positions:

1. There is a direct positive relationship between job satisfaction and job performance. The higher an employee's job satisfaction, the higher will be her or his job performance and vice versa.

2. Job satisfaction is related to job performance in only the following way: A slight amount of job dissatisfaction is a pre-

requisite to high job performance. Thus, employees who are somewhat dissatisfied with their jobs will have higher productivity than those who are very dissatisfied or those who are completely satisfied with their jobs.

3. Job performance ultimately causes an employee's job satisfaction (high or low). If employees achieve high job performance, they will receive high rewards and this, in turn, will result in high job satisfaction. If employees perform poorly on their jobs, resulting rewards will be low as will the employees' job satisfaction.

4. This position will be provided by the instructor.

The debate consists of two rounds. In round one each team first states its position and then tries to convince the judges, through the use of examples and other evidence, that its position is fully legitimate. During round two of the debate, each debating team counters the position of the other teams, that is, team one criticizes teams two, three, and four; team two criticizes teams one, three, and four, and so on. The group being countered may not rebut the criticisms made by the other teams during the debate unless specifically told to do so by the instructor. Group members just listen.

Round two, the last round of the debate, ends when team four has finished criticizing the positions of the other three teams. All debaters will be given a 10-minute recess between rounds one and two in order to finalize their criticisms of the other teams.

The judging teams' role during the debate is to "search for the truth," not select a "winner." They are to listen to all of the different arguments presented during the debate and, after it has ended, discuss the different positions among themselves until a consensus is reached regarding the "true" relationship between job satisfaction and job performance. There are no

constraints placed on the judges; they are free to disagree with all of the positions presented, to agree with parts of two or more of them, and so forth. After their deliberations are complete (usually about 10 minutes), each judging team presents its conclusions to the class. Judges should hold preliminary discussions of the four positions during the intermission between rounds one and two.

SOURCE: R. Bruce McAfee and Paul J. Champagne, *Organizational Behavior: A Manager's View.* Copyright © 1987. Reprinted with permission of South-Western College Publishing, a division of Thomson Learning.

13.2 What Do Students Want from Their Jobs?

OBJECTIVES
1. To demonstrate individual differences in job expectations.
2. To illustrate individual differences in need and motivational structures.
3. To examine and compare intrinsic rewards.

INSTRUCTIONS
1. Working alone, complete the "What I Want from My Job" survey.
2. In small groups, compare and analyze differences in the survey results and prepare group responses to the discussion questions.

3. After the class reconvenes, group spokespersons present group findings.

DISCUSSION QUESTIONS
1. Which job rewards are extrinsic, and which are intrinsic?
2. Were more response differences found in intrinsic or in extrinsic rewards?
3. In what ways do you think blue-collar workers' responses would differ from those of college students?

What I Want from My Job Survey

Determine what you want from a job by circling the level of importance of each of the following job rewards.

	Very Important	Moderately Important	Indifferent	Moderately Unimportant	Very Unimportant
1. Advancement opportunities	5	4	3	2	1
2. Appropriate company policies	5	4	3	2	1
3. Authority	5	4	3	2	1
4. Autonomy and freedom on the job	5	4	3	2	1
5. Challenging work	5	4	3	2	1
6. Company reputation	5	4	3	2	1
7. Fringe benefits	5	4	3	2	1
8. Geographic location	5	4	3	2	1
9. Good co-workers	5	4	3	2	1
10. Good supervision	5	4	3	2	1
11. Job security	5	4	3	2	1
12. Money	5	4	3	2	1
13. Opportunity for self-development	5	4	3	2	1
14. Pleasant office and working conditions	5	4	3	2	1
15. Performance feedback	5	4	3	2	1
16. Prestigious job title	5	4	3	2	1
17. Recognition for doing a good job	5	4	3	2	1
18. Responsibility	5	4	3	2	1
19. Sense of achievement	5	4	3	2	1
20. Training programs	5	4	3	2	1
21. Type of work	5	4	3	2	1
22. Working with people	5	4	3	2	1

CHAPTER 14

Managing
Teams

No one can whistle a symphony. It takes an orchestra to play it.

—Halford E. Luccock

CHAPTER OUTLINE

The Contributions of Teams
Benefits of Groups
The New Team Environment
  Types of Teams
  Self-Managed Teams
How Groups Become Teams
  Group Activities
  The Passage of Time
  A Developmental Sequence: From Group
    to Team
  Why Groups Sometimes Fail
Building Effective Teams
  A Performance Focus
  Motivating Teamwork
  Member Contributions
  Norms
  Roles
  Cohesiveness
  Building Cohesiveness and High
    Performance Norms
Managing Lateral Relationships
  Managing Outward
  Lateral Role Relationships
  Intergroup Conflict
  Managing Conflict
  Conflict Styles

LEARNING OBJECTIVES

After studying Chapter 14, you will know:

1. How teams contribute to your organization's effectiveness.

2. What makes the new team environment different from the old.

3. How groups become teams.

4. Why groups sometimes fail.

5. How to build an effective team.

6. How to manage your team's relationships with other teams.

7. How to manage conflict.

TWO HIGH-IMPACT TEAMS

"The Internet is going to have as much of an impact on the automobile industry as Henry Ford's mass-merchandising and production methods did in the 1920s" (p. 120), stated Lee Sage, global leader of Ernst & Young's automotive-industry consulting practice. At Ford and Toyota, two work teams are trying to make that happen.

At Ford, Thor Ibsen led the unit that set out to change the entire company by using the Internet to give consumers total choice in finding or creating exactly the vehicle they want. One of

Thor Ibsen's eConsumer Group wants to make Ford the first automaker to offer customers a build-to-order service option.

Ibsen's teams was the eConsumer Group, which wanted to make Ford the first automaker modeled after Dell's build-to-order business model. Lead times for autos are too long to offer build-to-order service for every

customer, but the team did want it to be an option if a specific car or truck wasn't already somewhere in the channel from factory to dealer.

In the beginning, senior executives often didn't reply to Thor's email messages. But thanks to the efforts and talents of Ibsen's team, Jim Schroer, Ford's VP for global marketing, now says the Internet team generated a momentum that was impossible to ignore. "We have an enormous opportunity as the industry shifts to e-business . . . we intend to lead the industry in e-business" (p. 124). And, he said, "Getting a team to come together and execute . . . ideas is probably the most important piece of it all."

At Toyota, Peter Dames led the electronic-commerce strategy team that wanted to "convince the rest of the company that those things have an impact on everything else—our budget, our strategy, our margins. Half the work we do here is evangelizing" (p. 120).

Toyota is history-rich, very profitable, and proud. Dames's goal was to show the rest of the company that playing by old rules, revering tradition, and sticking to familiar processes didn't cut it.

His team members didn't adhere to the unwritten shirt-and-tie dress code; they wore jeans and sneakers. They designed their own business cards with images of a spaceman and a toy robot—very different from Toyota's standard cards. Dames wanted his team to be rebellious, and to be highly visible within Toyota.

One team member said, "We've been involved with every major Internet initiative at the company, and technology has never been the problem." Another picked up the theme: "It's always been about getting people to work differently and redefining business processes. That's the toughest nut to crack" (p. 136).

Source: S. Kirsner, "Collision Course," *Fast Company*, January–February 2000, pp. 118–44; A. Layne, "Thor Ibsen: How to Create on Internet Time," *Fast Company*, May 2000. www.fastcompany.com/online/resources/

The Ford and Toyota teams described in "Setting the Stage" are unique, but in many ways are like most work teams. Such teams are created because of a perceived need or opportunity, have a mission and a task to perform, must meet the expectations of others, often face initial skepticism, and have to wrestle with "group dynamics." Sometimes they "work," and sometimes they don't. At Ford and Toyota, optimism ran high as these teams gained momentum, but then the business environment changed as the Internet revealed its fallibility. Who knows how these teams will be doing by the time you read this? The Ford and Toyota teams may have achieved tremendous success, or may still be working at it but struggling, or may have failed altogether. The team members may have used these teams as career launching pads, or may be identified with failures. The goal of this chapter is to help make sure that your work teams succeed rather than fail.

The Ford and Toyota teams, and other teams dedicated to other causes,[1] are transforming the ways in which companies do business. Almost all companies now use teams to produce goods and services, to manage projects, and to make decisions and run the company.[2] Stated the CEO of Texas Instruments, "No matter what your business, these teams are the wave of the future."[3]

For you, this has two vital implications. First, you *will* be working in and perhaps managing teams. Second, the *ability* to work in and lead teams is valuable to your employer and important to your career.

The Contributions of Teams

It is no wonder that team-based approaches to work have generated such excitement. Used appropriately, teams can be powerfully effective as a:

- *Building block for organization structure.* Organizations like Semco and Kollmorgen, manufacturer of printed circuits and electro-optic devices, are structured entirely around teams. A team-oriented structure is also in place at Kyocera Corporation, which was voted the best-managed company in Japan.
- *Force for productivity.* Shenandoah Life Insurance Company credited its new team organization with a 50 percent increase in the handling of applications and customer service requests, with fewer people.[4]
- *Force for quality.* Quality rose 50 percent in a Nortel facility, and Federal Express reduced billing errors and lost packages by 13 percent. Boeing's engineering teams built its new 777 passenger jet with far fewer design errors than occurred in earlier programs,[5] and Boeing received the fastest flight certification ever for a new commercial aircraft.[6]

- *Force for cost reduction.* Honeywell's teams saved over $11 million after reducing production times and shipping over 99 percent of orders on time.[7] Boeing management claims that it could not have developed the 777 without cross-functional teams; it would have been prohibitively expensive.[8]

- *Force for speed.* 3M, Daimler Chrysler, and many other companies are using teams to create new products faster. Lenders cut home mortgage approval times from weeks to hours, and life insurance companies cut time to issue new policies from six weeks to one day.[9]
- *Force for change.* Some companies have become more entrepreneurial in part through the creation of client service groups.[10] At KPMG Netherlands, a strategic integration team of 12 partners, with 100 other professionals divided into 14 task forces, led strategic and cultural changes by studying future trends and scenarios, defining core competencies, and dealing with organizational challenges.[11]

- *Force for innovation.* The auto industry relies on project teams to develop new vehicles, including Ford's great success with its Taurus project.[12] At 3M, work teams turned around one division by tripling the number of new products.[13]

3M's innovative success stories are numerous and legendary, emerging through the use of teams that are small entrepreneurial businesses within the larger corporation.

Benefits of Groups

Before discussing how to develop such high-performance teams, let us talk briefly about groups more generally. Groups form because they are useful. In organizations, groups serve numerous functions. Some of these functions benefit the organization directly; others benefit primarily the group's members.[14]

The organization benefits because groups have greater *total resources* (skills, talents, information, energy) than individuals do. Therefore, they can perform jobs that can't be done by individuals working alone. They also have a greater *diversity of resources*, which enables groups to perform complex tasks. Groups can aid decision making, as you learned in Chapter 3. When group members exchange knowledge and ideas, it is an important catalyst for creativity and innovation.[15] Groups also help socialize new members, control individuals' behavior, and facilitate organizational performance, innovation, and change.

Groups also provide many benefits for their members. The group is a very useful learning mechanism. Members learn about the company and themselves, and they acquire new skills and performance strategies. The group can satisfy important personal needs, such as affiliation and esteem. Other needs are met as group members receive tangible organizational rewards that they could not have achieved working alone.

Group members can provide one another with feedback; identify opportunities for growth and development; and train, coach, and mentor.[16] A marketing representative can learn about financial modeling from a colleague on a new product development team, and the financial expert can learn about consumer marketing. Experience working together in a group, and developing strong team problem-solving capabilities, is a vital supplement to specific job skills or functional expertise. And the skills are transferable to new positions.

The New Team Environment

The words *group* and *team* often are used interchangeably.[17] Modern managers sometimes use the word *teams* to the point that it has become cliche; they talk about teams while skeptics perceive no real teamwork. Thus, making a distinction between groups and teams can be useful. A *working group* is a collection of people who work in the same area or have been drawn together to undertake a task but do not necessarily come together as a unit and achieve significant performance improvements. A real **team** is formed of people (usually a small number) with complementary skills who trust one another and are committed to a common purpose, common performance goals, and a common approach for which they hold themselves mutually accountable.[18] A real team is committed to working together successfully to achieve high performance.

> **team**
>
> A small number of people with complementary skills who are committed to a common purpose, set of performance goals, and approach for which they hold themselves mutually accountable.

Organizations have been using groups for a long time, but things are different today.[19] Real teams are being more fully integrated into the organizational structure, and their authority is increasing. Managers realize more than ever that teams can provide competitive advantage and greatly improve organizational performance. They know the potential for the whole is far greater than the sum of its individual parts.

Thus, teams today are used in many different ways, and to far greater effect, than in the past. Table 14.1 highlights just a few of the differences between the traditional work environment and the way true teams work today. Ideally, people are far more involved, they are better trained, cooperation is higher, and the culture is one of learning as well as producing.

Traditional Environment	Team Environment
Managers determine and plan the work.	Managers and team members jointly determine and plan the work.
Jobs are narrowly defined.	Jobs require broad skills and knowledge.
Cross-training is viewed as inefficient.	Cross-training is the norm.
Most information is "management property."	Most information is freely shared at all levels.
Training for nonmanagers focuses on technical skills.	Continuous learning requires interpersonal, administrative, and technical training for all.
Risk taking is discouraged and punished.	Measured risk taking is encouraged and supported.
People work alone.	People work together.
Rewards are based on individual performance.	Rewards are based on individual performance and contributions to team performance.
Managers determine "best methods."	Everyone works to continously improve methods and processes.

TABLE 14.1
The New Team
Environment

SOURCE: From *Leading Teams* by J. Zenger and Associates. Reprinted by permission.

Types of Teams

work teams

Teams that make or do things like manufacture, assemble, sell, or provide service.

project and development teams

Teams that work on long-term projects but disband once the work is completed.

parallel teams

Teams that operate separately from the regular work structure, and exist temporarily.

management teams

Teams that coordinate and provide direction to the subunits under their jurisdiction and integrate work among subunits.

There may be hundreds of groups and teams in your organization. Very generally, teams can be divided into four primary types.[20] **Work teams** make or do things such as manufacture, assemble, sell, or provide service. These typically are well defined, a clear part of the formal organizational structure, and composed of a full-time, stable membership. These are what most people think of when they think of teams in organizations.[21]

Project and development teams work on long-term projects, often over a period of years. They have specific assignments, such as research or new-product development, and members usually must contribute expert knowledge and judgment. These teams work toward a one-time product, disbanding once their work is completed. Then new teams are formed for new projects.

Parallel teams operate separately from the regular work structure of the firm on a temporary basis. Members often come from different units or jobs and are asked to do work that is not normally done by the standard structure. Their charge is to recommend solutions to specific problems. They usually do not have authority to act, however. Examples include task forces and quality or safety teams formed to study a particular problem that has come up.

Management teams coordinate and provide direction to the subunits under their jurisdiction and integrate work among subunits.[22] The management team is based on authority stemming from hierarchical rank and is responsible for the overall performance of the business unit. Managers responsible for different subunits form a team together, and at the top of the organization resides the executive management team that establishes strategic direction and manages the firm's overall performance.

Some of the all-time great work teams include the Walt Disney studio in the 1930s, the Apple Macintosh team, the Manhattan Project, the engineering teams at Xerox's legendary Palo Alto Research Center (PARC), and the elite corps of aeronautical engineers and fabricators who built radically new planes at Lockheed's top-secret Skunk Works. A team now working at Lockheed Martin may achieve similar legendary status.

Tom Burbage's Joint Strike Fighter (JSF) team was charged with winning a five-year battle with Boeing in the most lucrative competition in Pentagon history. The company that won the contract—potentially worth $200 billion— would develop a radar-evading, sound-barrier-busting aircraft that would serve as the combat jet of the future for the U.S. Air Force, Navy, and Marines and the United Kingdom's Royal Air Force and Royal Navy.

To meet the expectations of the U.S. armed services, Burbage's team had to solve seemingly impossible technical problems. The plane needed to be able to take off in tight places and make vertical landings on aircraft carriers and lighter ships. Think about that: Among so many other challenges, they needed to defy gravity by generating enough thrust to vertically lift a 30,000-pound plane. Guess what? They pulled it off. After 10 years of work, the Marine version of the aircraft took its first-ever vertical flight in the high desert of California. And Lockheed won the contract.

Now the JSF team must coordinate the efforts of hundreds of U.S. and foreign subcontractors and numerous U.S. and U.K. government agencies, and meet a daunting deadline: The Air Force expects the JSF aircraft to be in full service by October 2005. The team may not yet be a legend, but its next results may make it so.

Source: W. Bennis and P. Ward Biederman, *Organizing Genius: The Secrets of Creative Collaboration* (Reading, MA: Addison-Wesley, 1997); B. Breen, "High Stakes, High Bets," *Fast Company*, April 2002, pp. 66–78; B. Breen, "From Postmortems to Premortems," *Fast Company*, April 2002, p. 76.

Self-Managed Teams

Today there exist many different types of work teams with many different labels. The terms can be confusing, and sometimes are used interchangeably out of a lack of awareness of actual differences. Figure 14.1 shows the different types according to how much autonomy they have.[23] To the left, teams are more traditional with little decision-making authority, being under the control of direct supervision. To the right there is more autonomy, decision-making power, and self-direction.

Pictured here is Tom Burbage, who assembled a team at Lockheed Martin to build the Joint Strike Fighter for the government. It was the largest aviation contract in U.S. history. Maybe this project team will achieve legendary status.

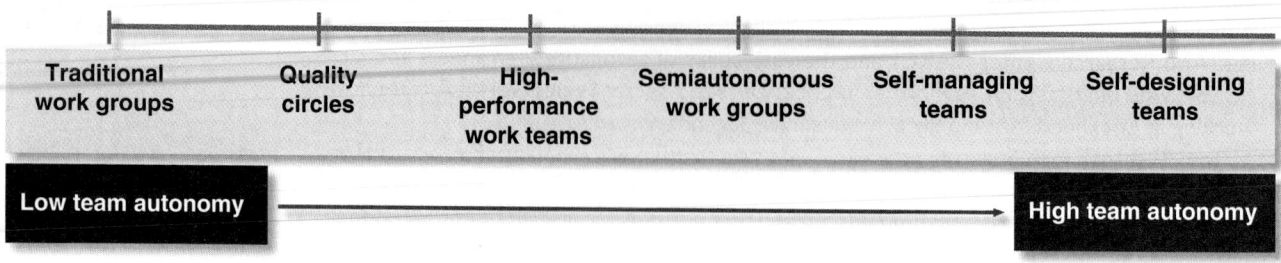

SOURCE: R. Banker, J. Field, R. Schroeder, and K. Sinha, "Impact of Work Teams on Manufacturing Performance: A Longitudinal Field Study," *Academy of Management Journal.* Copyright © 1996 by Academy of Management. Reproduced with permission of Academy of Management via Copyright Clearance Center.

FIGURE 14.1
Team Autonomy Continuum

self-managed teams

Autonomous work groups in which workers are trained to do all or most of the jobs in a unit, have no immediate supervisor, and make decisions previously made by first-line supervisors.

traditional work groups

Groups that have no managerial responsibilities.

quality circles

Voluntary groups of people drawn from various production teams who make suggestions about quality.

semiautonomous work groups

Groups that make decisions about managing and carrying out major production activities, but still get outside support for quality control and maintenance.

autonomous work groups

Groups that control decisions about and execution of a complete range of tasks.

self-designing teams

Teams with control over the design of the team, as well as the responsibilities of autonomous work groups.

The trend today is toward **self-managed teams,** in which workers are trained to do all or most of the jobs in the unit, they have no immediate supervisor, and they make decisions previously made by first-line supervisors.[24] Self-managed teams are most frequently found in manufacturing. People often resist self-managed work teams,[25] in part because they don't want so much responsibility and the change is difficult. But compared to traditionally managed teams, self-managed teams appear to be more productive, have lower costs, provide better customer service, provide higher quality, have better safety records, and are more satisfying for members.

Referring to Figure 14.1, **traditional work groups** have no managerial responsibilities. The first-line manager plans, organizes, staffs, directs, and controls them, and other groups provide support activities, including quality control and maintenance. **Quality circles** are voluntary groups of people drawn from various production teams who make suggestions about quality but have no authority to make decisions or execute. **Semiautonomous work groups** make decisions about managing and carrying out major production activities, but still get outside support for quality control and maintenance. **Autonomous work groups,** or *self-managing teams,* control decisions about and execution of a complete range of tasks—acquiring raw materials and performing operations, quality control, maintenance, and shipping. They are fully responsible for an entire product or an entire part of a production process. **Self-designing teams** do all of that and go one step further—they also have control over the design of the team. They decide themselves whom to hire, whom to fire, and what tasks the team will perform.

Movement from left to right on the continuum corresponds with more and more worker participation. Toward the right, the participation is not trivial and not merely advisory. It has real substance, including not just suggestions but action and impact. When companies have introduced teams that reach the point of being truly self-managed, results have included lower costs and greater levels of team productivity, quality, and customer satisfaction.[26] Overall, semiautonomous and autonomous teams are known to improve the organization's financial and overall performance, at least in North America.[27]

Such results are inspiring U.S.-based multinational firms to use self-managed teams in their foreign facilities. For example, Goodyear Tire & Rubber has initiated self-managed work teams in Europe, Latin America, and Asia; Sara Lee in Puerto Rico and Mexico; and Texas Instruments in Malaysia. These companies are learning—and other companies should be forewarned—of the different ways different cultures might respond to self-managed teams, and to customize implementation according to cultural values.[28]

How Groups Become Teams

As a manager, you will want your group to become an effective team. To accomplish this, it will help you to understand how groups can become true teams, and why groups sometimes fail to become teams. Groups become true teams via basic group activities, the passage of time, and team development activities.

Group Activities

Assume you are the leader of a newly formed group. What will you face as you attempt to develop your group into a high-performing team? If groups are to develop successfully, they will engage in various activities, including:[29]

- *Forming*—group members attempt to lay the ground rules for what types of behavior are acceptable.
- *Storming*—hostilities and conflict arise, and people jockey for positions of power and status.
- *Norming*—group members agree on their shared goals, and norms and closer relationships develop.
- *Performing*—the group channels its energies into performing its tasks.

Groups that deteriorate move to a *declining* stage, and temporary groups add an *adjourning* or terminating stage. Groups terminate when they complete their task or when they disband due to failure or loss of interest.

A recent study investigated the group development activities of **transnational teams,** defined as work groups composed of multinational members whose activities span multiple countries.[30] Such teams differ from other work teams not only by being multicultural, but also by often being geographically dispersed, being psychologically distant, and working on highly complex projects having considerable impact on company objectives. In the beginning, such teams need to use *advocacy skills*—building the team's legitimacy, linking the team's mission to the corporate strategy, networking to obtain resources, and "bureaucracy busting" to eliminate old routines and facilitate experimentation. As the teams evolve, they use more *catalytic skills*, including working with external constituents, differentiating individual roles and responsibilities, building commitment, and rewarding members for their contributions.

> **transnational teams**
>
> **Work groups composed of multinational members whose activities span multiple countries.**

> Self-managed teams can have a positive effect on productivity. But people often resist self-managed teams in part because they don't want so much responsibility and the change is difficult.

Eventually, mature teams invoke *integrative skills* such as emphasizing accomplishment and excellence, coordinating and problem solving, and measuring progress and results.

The Passage of Time

A key aspect of development is the passage of time. Groups pass through critical periods, or times when they are particularly open to formative experiences.[31] The first such critical period is in the forming stage, at the first meeting, when rules, norms, and roles are established that set long-lasting precedents. A second critical period is the midway point between the initial meeting and a deadline (e.g., completing a project or making a presentation). At this point, the group has enough experience to understand its work; it comes to realize that time is becoming a scarce resource and it must "get on with it;" and there is enough time left to change its approach if necessary.

In the initial meeting, the group should establish desired norms, roles, and other determinants of effectiveness considered throughout this chapter. At the second critical period (the midpoint), groups should renew or open lines of communication with outside constituencies. The group can use fresh information from its external environment to revise its approach to performing its task and ensure that it meets the needs of customers and clients. Without these activities, groups may get off on the wrong foot from the beginning, and members may never revise their behavior in the appropriate direction.[32]

A Developmental Sequence: From Group to Team

As a manager or group member, you should expect the group to engage in all the activities just discussed at various times. But groups are not always successful. They do not always engage in the developmental activities that turn them into effective, high-performing teams.

A useful developmental sequence is depicted in Figure 14.2. The figure shows the various activities as the leadership of the group moves from traditional supervision, through a more participative approach, to true team leadership.[33]

It is important to understand a couple of things about this model. Groups do not necessarily keep progressing from one "stage" to the next; they may remain permanently in the supervisory level, or become more participative but never make it to true team leadership. Therefore, progress on these dimensions must be a conscious goal of the leader and the members, and all should strive to meet these goals. Your group can meet these goals, and become a true team, by engaging in the activities in the figure.

Why Groups Sometimes Fail

Team building does not necessarily progress smoothly through such a sequence, culminating in a well-oiled team and superb performance.[34] Some groups never do work out. Such groups can be frustrating for managers and members, who may feel they are a waste of time, and that the difficulties outweigh the benefits. Says a top consultant: "Teams are the Ferraris of work design. They're high performance but high maintenance and expensive."[35]

It is not easy to build high-performance teams. *Teams* is often just a word used by management to describe merely putting people into groups. "Teams" sometimes are launched with little or no training or support systems. For example, managers as well as group members need new skills to make the group work. These skills include learning the art of diplomacy, tackling "people issues" head on, and walking the fine line between encouraging autonomy and rewarding team innovations without letting the team get too independent and out of control.[36] Giving up some control is very difficult

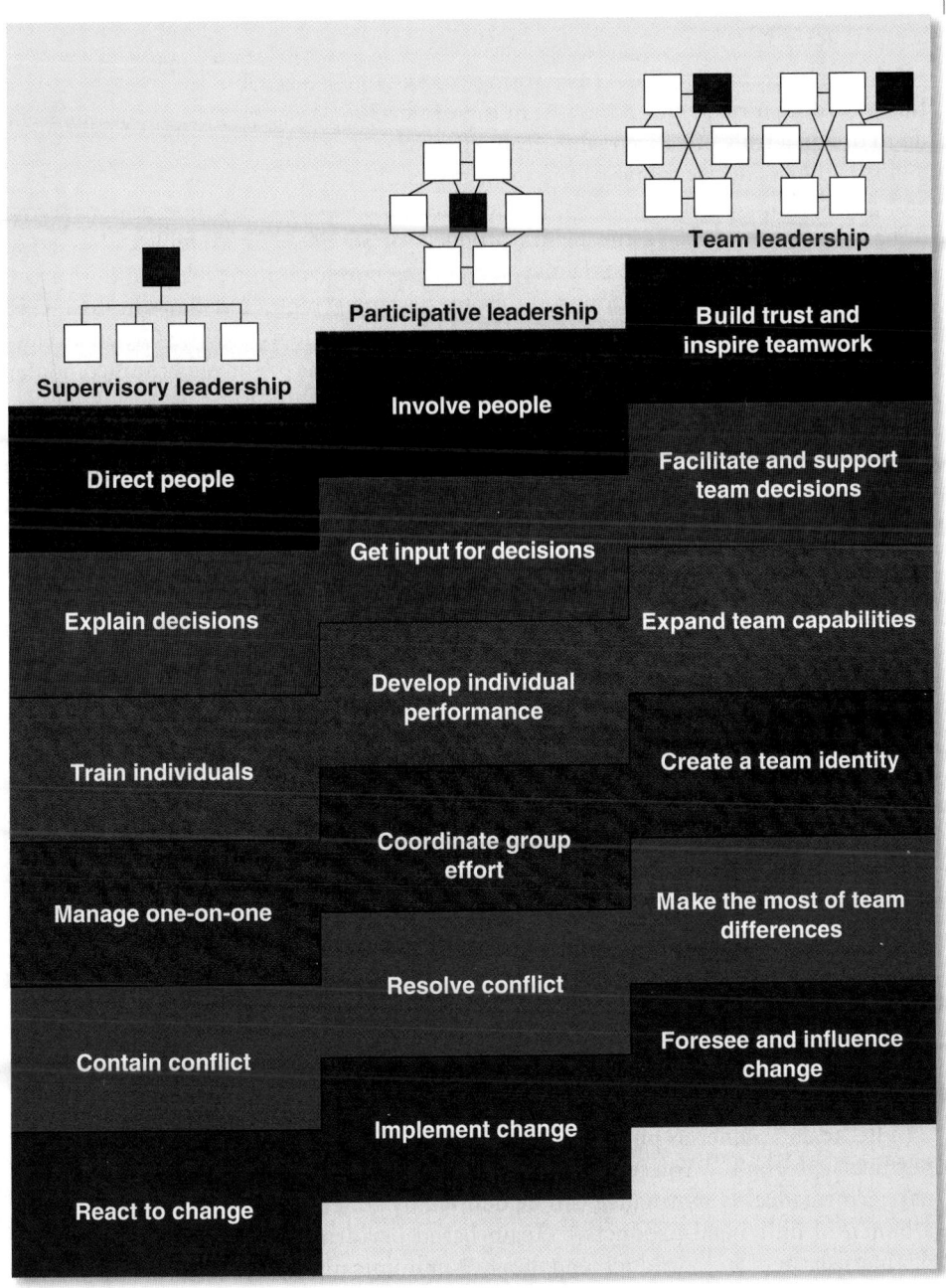

Supervisory leadership

Direct people

Explain decisions

Train individuals

Manage one-on-one

Contain conflict

React to change

Participative leadership

Involve people

Get input for decisions

Develop individual performance

Coordinate group effort

Resolve conflict

Implement change

Team leadership

Build trust and inspire teamwork

Facilitate and support team decisions

Expand team capabilities

Create a team identity

Make the most of team differences

Foresee and influence change

FIGURE 14.2
Stepping up to Team Leadership

SOURCE: From *Leading Teams* by J. Zenger and Associates. Reprinted by permission.

for managers from traditional systems; they have to realize they will gain control in the long run by virtue of creating stronger, better-performing units.

Teams should be truly empowered, as discussed in Chapter 13. The benefits of teams are reduced when they are not allowed to make important decisions—in other words, when management doesn't trust them with important responsibilities. If teams must acquire permission for every innovative idea, they will revert to making safe, traditional decisions.[37] Thus, management must truly support teams by giving them some freedom and rewarding their contributions.

Failure lies in not knowing and doing what makes teams successful. To be successful you must apply clear thinking and appropriate practices.[38] That is what the rest of the chapter is about.

Building Effective Teams

All the considerations just described form the building blocks of an effective work team. But what does it really mean for a team to be effective? What precisely, can a manager do to design a truly effective team? Team effectiveness is defined by three criteria.[39]

First, the *productive output* of the team meets or exceeds the standards of quantity and quality; the team's output is acceptable to those customers, inside or outside the organization, who receive the team's products or services. As examples, Procter & Gamble's business teams are effective at reducing costs and at developing new products.[40] Clarence L. "Kelly" Johnson's group designed, built, and flew the first U.S. tactical jet fighter, XP80, in 143 days.[41] Tom West's legendary Eclipse Group at Data General worked overtime for a year and a half to create the 32-bit superminicomputer that heralded the next generation of minicomputers.[42]

Second, team members realize *satisfaction* of their personal needs. P&G's team members enjoy the opportunity to participate creatively. Johnson and West gave their teams the freedom to innovate and stretch their skills. Team members were enthusiastic and realized great pride and satisfaction in their work.

Third, team members remain *committed* to working together again; that is, the group doesn't burn out and disintegrate after a grueling project. Looking back, the members are glad they were involved. In other words, effective teams remain viable and have good prospects for repeated success in the future.[43]

A Performance Focus

The key element of effective teamwork is commitment to a common purpose.[44] The best teams are ones that have been given an important performance challenge by management, and then come to a common understanding and appreciation of their purpose. Without such understanding and commitment, a group will be just a bunch of individuals.

The best teams also work hard at developing a common understanding of how they will work together to achieve their purpose.[45] They discuss and agree upon such things as how tasks and roles will be allocated and how they will make decisions. The team should develop norms for examining its performance strategies and be amenable to changing when appropriate. With a clear, strong, motivating purpose, and effective performance strategies, people will pull together into a powerful force that has a chance to achieve extraordinary things.

The team's general purpose should be translated into specific, measurable performance goals.[46] You learned in Chapter 13 about how goals motivate individual performance. Performance can be defined by collective end products instead of a bunch of individual products.[47] Team-based performance goals help define and distinguish the team's product, encourage communication within the team, energize and motivate team members, provide feedback on progress, signal team victories (and defeats), and ensure that the team focuses clearly on results. Recent research demonstrates that teams with both difficult goals and incentives to attain them achieve the highest performance levels.[48]

The best team-based measurement systems will inform top management of the team's performance and help the team understand its own processes and gauge its own progress. Ideally, the team will play the lead role in designing its own measurement system. This is a great indicator of whether the team is truly empowered.[49]

Teams, like individuals, need feedback on their performance. Feedback from customers is critical. Some customers for the team's products are inside the organization. Teams should be responsible for satisfying them, and should be given or should seek performance feedback. Better yet, wherever possible, teams should interact directly with external customers who make the ultimate buy decisions about their products and services. This will be the most honest, and most crucial and useful, performance feedback of all.[50]

Motivating Teamwork

Sometimes individuals work less hard and are less productive when they are members of a group. Such **social loafing** occurs when individuals believe that their contributions are not important, others will do the work for them, their lack of effort will go undetected, or they will be the lone sucker if they work hard but others don't. On the other hand, sometimes individuals work harder when they are members of a group than when they are working alone. This **social facilitation effect** occurs because individuals usually are more motivated when others are present, they are concerned with what others think of them, and they want to maintain a positive self-image.

social loafing
Working less hard and being less productive when in a group.
social facilitation effect
Working harder when in a group than when working alone.

A social facilitation effect is maintained, and a social loafing effect can be avoided, when group members know each other, they can observe and communicate with one another, clear performance goals exist, the task is meaningful to the people working on it, they believe that their efforts matter and others will not take advantage of them, and the culture supports teamwork.[51] Thus, ideally it will be clear that everyone works hard, contributes in concrete ways to the team's work, and is accountable to other team members. Accountability to one another, rather than just to "the boss," is an essential aspect of good teamwork. Accountability inspires mutual commitment and trust.[52] Trust in your teammates—and their trust in you—may be the ultimate key to effectiveness.

Team effort is also generated by designing the team's task to be motivating. Techniques for creating motivating tasks appear in the guidelines for job enrichment discussed in Chapter 13. Tasks are motivating when they use a variety of member skills and provide high task variety, identity, significance, autonomy, and performance feedback.

Ultimately, teamwork is best motivated by tying rewards to team performance.[53] Team-based incentives are particularly powerful in smaller groups and smaller firms.[54] If team performance can be measured validly, team-based rewards can be given accordingly. It is not easy to move from a system of rewards based on individual performance to one based on team performance. Importantly, it also may not be appropriate, unless people are truly interdependent and must collaborate to attain true team goals.[55] Sometimes team-based rewards can be added to existing rewards already based on individual performance. In the case of a financial services firm, year 1 of a new team system included pay increases based 15 percent on team performance, increasing to 50 percent by year 3.[56]

If team performance is difficult to measure validly, then desired behaviors, activities, and processes that indicate good teamwork can be rewarded. Individuals within teams can be given differential rewards based on teamwork indicated by active participation, cooperation, leadership, and other contributions to the team.

If team members are to be rewarded differentially, such decisions are better *not* left to the boss.[57] They should be made by the team itself, via peer ratings or multirater evaluation systems. Team members are in a better position to observe, know, and make valid reward allocations. Finally, the more teams the organization has, and the more of a full team orientation that exists, the more valid and effective it will be to distribute rewards via gainsharing and other organizationwide incentives.

Member Contributions

Team members should be selected and trained so they become effective contributors to the team. Teams often hire their new members.[58] Miller Brewing Company and Eastman Chemical teams select members on the basis of tests designed to predict how well they will contribute to team success in an empowered environment. At Hannaford Brothers Company, a retail supermarket and food distributor in New York, new employees become "team certified" and then join their teams. At Texas Instruments, Human Resources screens applicants; then team members interview them and make selection decisions.

Many teams often undergo training exercises to learn team-building techniques. This group of people is learning the basic rule of trusting fellow colleagues. The blindfolded person falls backwards, trusting that his teammates will catch him and not let him fall. Trust must be earned, not demanded.

Some companies have computer systems combining PC networks with databases and videoconferencing to help teams identify and find the right new people. Generally, the skills required by the team include technical or functional expertise, problem-solving and decision-making skills, and interpersonal skills. Some managers and teams mistakenly overemphasize some skills, particularly technical or functional, and underemphasize the others. It is vitally important that all three types of skills be represented, and developed, among team members.

Development Dimensions International provides people with 300 hours of training, mostly about how to work in teams, but also technical cross-training. K Shoes, Ltd., trains team members in teamwork, overall business knowledge, supplier partnership development, and retail management. Kodak provides 150 hours of first-year training on team effectiveness, including teaching people to cross-train others, and 120 more hours subsequently on the same team skills plus business and financial skills.[59]

Norms

norms

Shared beliefs about how people should think and behave.

Norms are shared beliefs about how people should think and behave. From the organization's standpoint, norms can be positive or negative. In some teams, everyone works hard; in other groups, employees are antimanagement and do as little work as possible. Some groups develop norms of taking risks, others of being conservative.[60] A norm could dictate that employees speak either favorably or critically of the company. Team members may show concern about poor safety practices, drug and alcohol abuse, and employee theft, or they may not care about these issues (or may even condone such practices). Health consciousness is the norm among executives at some companies, but smoking is the norm at tobacco companies. Some groups have norms of distrust and of being closed toward one another, but as you might guess, norms of trust and open discussion about conflict can improve group performance.[61]

A professor described his consulting experiences at two companies that exhibited different norms in their management teams.[62] At Federal Express Corporation, a young manager interrupted the professor's talk by proclaiming that a recent decision by top management ran counter to the professor's point about corporate planning. He was challenging top management to defend its decision. A hot debate ensued, and after an hour everyone went to lunch without a trace of hard feelings. But at another corporation, the professor opened a meeting by asking a group of top managers to describe the company's culture. There was silence. He asked again. More silence. Then someone passed him an unsigned note that read, "Dummy, can't you see that we can't speak our minds? Ask for the input anonymously, in writing." As you can see, norms are important, and can vary greatly from one group to another.

Roles

Roles are different sets of expectations for how different individuals should behave. Whereas norms apply generally to all team members, different roles exist for different members within the norm structure.

Two important sets of roles must be performed.[63] **Task specialist** roles are filled by individuals who have particular job-related skills and abilities. These employees keep the team moving toward task accomplishment. **Team maintenance specialists** develop and maintain harmony within the team. They boost morale, give support, provide humor, soothe hurt feelings, and generally exhibit a concern with members' well-being.

roles
Different sets of expectations for how different individuals should behave.
task specialist
An individual who has more advanced job-related skills and abilities than other group members possess.
team maintenance specialist
Individual who develops and maintains team harmony.

Note the similarity between these roles and the important task performance and group maintenance leadership behaviors you learned about in Chapter 12. As suggested in that chapter, some of these roles will be more important than others at different times and under different circumstances. But these behaviors need not be carried out only by one or two leaders; any member of the team can carry out these roles at any time. Over time, both types of roles can be performed by different individuals to maintain an effectively functioning work team.

If the team has a formal leader, the leader's role is to keep the team's purpose, goals, and approach relevant and meaningful; build commitment and confidence; strengthen the mix and level of team members' skills; manage relationships with outsiders; remove obstacles to the team's performance; create opportunities for the team and its members; and do real work, not just supervise.[64]

Self-managed teams report to a management representative who sometimes is called the coach. For example, at Wilson Sporting Goods Company, coaches facilitate and provide support and direction to teams, and hourly associates share leadership responsibilities with the coaches.[65] In true self-managed teams, the coach is not a true member of the team.[66] This is because the group is supposed to make its own decisions, and because the relative power of the management representative can have a dampening effect on the team's openness and autonomy.

The role of the coach, then, is to help the team understand its role in the organization, and to act as a resource for the team. The coach can provide information, resources, and opinions that team members do not or cannot acquire on their own. And the coach should be an advocate for the team in the rest of organization.

Cohesiveness

One of the most important properties of a work team is cohesiveness.[67] **Cohesiveness** refers to how attractive the team is to its members, how motivated members are to remain in the team, and the degree to which team members influence one another. In general, it refers to how tightly knit the team is.

cohesiveness
The degree to which a group is attractive to its members, members are motivated to remain in the group, and members influence one another.

The Importance of Cohesiveness Cohesiveness is important for two primary reasons. First, it contributes to *member satisfaction*. In a cohesive team, members communicate and get along well with one another. They feel good about being a part of the team. Even if their jobs are unfulfilling or the organization is oppressive, people gain some satisfaction from enjoying their co-workers.

Second, cohesiveness has a major impact on *performance*. A recent study of the creation of manufacturing teams led to a conclusion that performance improvements in both quality and productivity occurred in the most cohesive unit, whereas conflict within another team prevented any quality or productivity improvements.[68] Sports fans read about this all the time. When teams are winning, players talk about the team being close, getting along well, and knowing one another's games. In contrast, losing is attributed to infighting and divisiveness. Generally, cohesiveness clearly can and does have a positive effect on performance.[69]

But this interpretation is simplistic; exceptions to this intuitive relationship occur. Tightly knit work groups can be disruptive to the organization, such as when they sabotage the assembly line, get their boss fired, or enforce low performance norms.

When does high cohesiveness lead to good performance, and when does it result in poor performance? This depends on (1) the task, and (2) whether the group has high or low performance norms.

The Task   If the task is to make a decision or solve a problem, cohesiveness can lead to poor performance. Groupthink (discussed in Chapter 3) occurs when a tightly knit group is so cooperative that agreeing with one another's opinions and refraining from criticizing others' ideas become norms. The following example illustrates this tendency.

The Abilene Paradox

The July afternoon in Coleman, Texas (population 5,607), was particularly hot—104 degrees as measured by the Walgreen's Rexall Ex-Lax temperature gauge. In addition, the wind was blowing fine-grained West Texas topsoil through the house. But the afternoon was still tolerable—even potentially enjoyable. There was a fan going on the back porch; there was cold lemonade; and finally, there was entertainment. Dominoes. Perfect for the conditions. The game required little more physical exertion than an occasional mumbled comment, "Shuffle 'em," and an unhurried movement of the arm to place the spots in the appropriate perspective on the table. All in all, it had the makings of an agreeable Sunday afternoon in Coleman—that is, it was until my father-in-law suddenly said, "Let's get in the car and go to Abilene and have dinner at the cafeteria."

I thought, "What, go to Abilene? Fifty-three miles? In this dust storm and heat? And in an unairconditioned 1958 Buick?"

But my wife chimed in with, "Sounds like a great idea. I'd like to go. How about you, Jerry?" Since my own preferences were obviously out of step with the rest, I replied, "Sounds good to me," and added, "I just hope your mother wants to go."

"Of course I want to go," said my mother-in-law. "I haven't been to Abilene in a long time."

So into the car and off to Abilene we went. My predictions were fulfilled. The heat was brutal. We were coated with a fine layer of dust that was cemented with perspiration by the time we arrived. The food in the cafeteria provided first-rate testimonial material for antacid commercials.

Some four hours and 106 miles later we returned to Coleman, hot and exhausted. We sat in front of the fan for a long time in silence. Then, both to be sociable and to break the silence, I said, "It was a great trip, wasn't it?"

No one spoke.

Finally, my mother-in-law said, with some irritation, "Well, to tell the truth, I really didn't enjoy it much and would rather have stayed here. I just went along because the three of you were so enthusiastic about going. I wouldn't have gone if you all hadn't pressured me into it."

I couldn't believe it. "What do you mean 'you all'?" I said. "Don't put me in the 'you all' group. I was delighted to be doing what we were doing. I didn't want to go. I only went to satisfy the rest of you. You're the culprits."

My wife looked shocked. "Don't call me a culprit. You and Daddy and Mama were the ones who wanted to go. I just went along to be sociable and keep you happy. I would have had to be crazy to want to go out in heat like that."

Her father entered the conversation abruptly. "Hell!" he said.

He proceeded to expand on what was already absolutely clear. "Listen, I never wanted to go to Abilene. I just thought you might be bored. You visit so seldom I wanted to be sure you enjoyed it. I would have preferred to play another game of dominoes and eat the leftovers in the icebox."

After the outburst of recrimination, we all sat back in silence. Here we were, four reasonably sensible people who, of our own volition, had just taken a 106-mile trip across a godforsaken desert in furnacelike temperatures through a cloudlike dust storm to eat unpalatable food at a hole-in-the-wall cafeteria in Abilene, when none of us had really wanted to go. In fact, to be more accurate, we'd done just the opposite of what we wanted to do. The whole situation simply didn't make sense.

SOURCE: Reprinted from *Organizational Dynamics,* Jerry B. Harvey, "The Abilene Paradox." Summer 1974. Copyright © 1974 with permission from Elsevier Science.

In the Abilene example, the group was exhibiting groupthink. Disagreement, which is more likely to occur in noncohesive groups, could have led to a better decision: to stay in Coleman. For a cohesive group to make good decisions, it should establish a norm of constructive disagreement. This is important for groups up to the level of boards of directors;[70] in top management teams it has been shown to improve the financial performance of companies.[71]

Cohesiveness can enhance performance, particularly if the task is to produce some tangible output. In day-to-day work groups for which decision making is not the primary task, the effect of cohesiveness on performance can be positive. But that depends on the group's performance norms.[72]

Performance Norms   Some groups are better than others at ensuring that their members behave the way the group prefers. Cohesive groups are more effective than noncohesive groups at norm enforcement. But the next question is: Do they have norms of high or low performance?

As Figure 14.3 shows, the highest performance occurs when a cohesive team has high performance norms. But if a highly cohesive group has low performance norms, that group will have the worst performance. In the group's eyes, however, it will have succeeded in achieving its goal of poor performance. Noncohesive groups with high performance norms can be effective from the company's standpoint. However, they won't be as productive as they would be if they were more cohesive. Noncohesive groups with low performance norms perform poorly, but they will not ruin things for management as effectively as can cohesive groups with low performance norms.

Building Cohesiveness and High Performance Norms

As Figure 14.3 suggests, managers should build teams that are cohesive and have high performance norms. The following actions can help create such teams:[73]

1. *Recruit members with similar attitudes, values, and backgrounds.* Similar individuals are more likely to get along with one another. Don't do this,

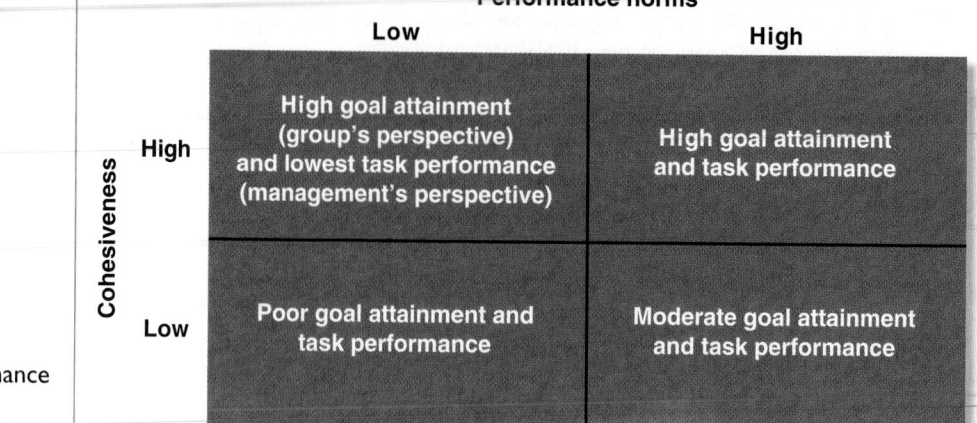

FIGURE 14.3
Cohesiveness, Performance
Norms, and Group
Performance

though, if the team's task requires heterogeneous skills and inputs. For
example, a homogeneous committee or board might make relatively poor
decisions, because it will lack different information and viewpoints and may
succumb to groupthink.

2. *Maintain high entrance and socialization standards.* Teams and organizations that
are difficult to get into have more prestige. Individuals who survive a difficult
interview, selection, or training process will be proud of their accomplishment
and feel more attachment to the team.

3. *Keep the team small* (but large enough to get the job done). The larger the
group, the less important members may feel. Small teams make individuals feel
like large contributors.

4. *Help the team succeed, and publicize its successes.* You read about empowerment
in the last chapter; you can empower teams as well as individuals.[74] Be a
path-goal leader who facilitates success; the experience of winning brings
teams closer together. Then, if you inform superiors of your team's successes,
members will believe they are part of an important, prestigious unit. Teams
that get into a good performance track continue to perform well as time
goes on; groups that don't often enter a downward spiral in which problems
compound over time.[75]

5. *Be a participative leader.* Participation in decisions gets team members more
involved with one another and striving toward goal accomplishment. Too
much autocratic decision making from above can alienate the group from
management.

6. *Present a challenge from outside the team.* Competition with other groups makes
team members band together to defeat the enemy (witness what happens to
school spirit before the big game against an archrival). Some of the greatest
teams in business and in science have been completely focused on winning a
competition.[76] But don't *you* become the outside threat. If team members
dislike you as a boss, they will become more cohesive—but their performance
norms will be against you, not with you.

7. *Tie rewards to team performance.* To a large degree, teams are motivated
just as individuals are—they do the things that are rewarded. Make sure
that high-performing teams get the rewards they deserve and that poorly
performing groups get relatively few rewards. You read about this earlier.
Bear in mind that not just monetary rewards but also recognition for

good work are powerful motivators. Recognize and celebrate team accomplishments. The team will become more cohesive and perform better to reap more rewards. Performance goals will be high, the organization will benefit from higher team motivation and productivity, and the individual needs of team members will be better satisfied. Ideally, being a member of a high-performing team, recognized as such throughout the organization, will become a badge of honor.[77]

But keep in mind that strong cohesiveness encouraging "agreeableness" can be dysfunctional. For problem solving and decision making, the team should establish norms promoting an open, constructive atmosphere including honest disagreement over issues without personal conflict and animosity.[78] Thus, the team can avoid groupthink and a trip to Abilene.

Managing Lateral Relationships

Teams do not function in a vacuum; they are interdependent with other teams. For example, at Miller Brewing Company, major team responsibilities include coordinating with other teams and policy groups. At Texas Instruments, teams are responsible for interfacing with other teams to eliminate production bottlenecks and implement new processes, and also for working with suppliers on quality issues.[79] Thus, some activities crucial to the team are those that entail dealing with people *outside* the group.

Managing Outward

Several vital roles link teams to their external environments, that is, to other individuals and groups both inside and outside the organization. A specific type of role that spans team boundaries is the gatekeeper, a team member who stays abreast of current information in scientific and other fields and informs the group of important developments. Information useful to the group can also include information about resources, trends, and political support throughout the corporation or the industry.[80]

The team's strategy dictates the team's mix of internally versus externally focused roles and how the mix changes over time. General team strategies include informing, parading, and probing.[81] The **informing** strategy entails concentrating first on the internal team process to achieve a state of performance readiness. Then the team informs outsiders of its intentions. **Parading** means the team's strategy is to simultaneously emphasize internal team building and achieve external visibility. **Probing** involves a focus on external relations. This strategy requires team members to interact frequently with outsiders; diagnose the needs of customers, clients, and higher-ups; and experiment with solutions.

The appropriate balance between an internal and external strategic focus and between internal and external roles depends on how much the team needs information, support, and resources from outside. When teams have a high degree of dependence on outsiders, probing is the best strategy. Parading teams perform at an intermediate level, and informing teams are likely to fail. They are too isolated from the outside groups on which they depend.

Informing or parading strategies may be more effective for teams that are less dependent on outside groups, for example, established teams working

informing

A team strategy that entails concentrating first on the internal team process to achieve a state of performance readiness, then informing outsiders of its intentions.

parading

A team strategy that entails simultaneously emphasizing internal team building and achieving external visibility.

probing

A team strategy that requires team members to interact frequently with outsiders, diagnose their needs, and experiment with solutions.

on routine tasks in stable external environments. But for most important work teams of the future—task forces, new-product teams, and strategic decision-making teams tackling unstructured problems in a rapidly changing external environment—effective performance in roles that involve interfacing with the outside will be vital.

Lateral Role Relationships

Managing relationships with managers of other groups and teams means engaging in a dynamic give-and-take that ensures proper coordination throughout the management system. To many managers, this process often seems like a chaotic free-for-all. It is useful to identify the different types of lateral role relationships and take a strategic approach to building constructive relationships.

Different teams, like different individuals, have roles to perform. As teams carry out their roles, several distinct patterns of working relationships develop.[82]

1. *Work-flow relationships* emerge as materials are passed from one group to another. A group commonly receives work from one unit, processes it, and sends it to the next unit in the process. Your group, then, will come before some groups and after others in the process.
2. *Service relationships* exist when top management centralizes an activity to which a large number of other units must gain access. Common examples are technology services, libraries, and clerical staff. Such units must service other people's requests.
3. *Advisory relationships* are created when teams with problems call on centralized sources of expert knowledge. For example, staff members in the human resources or legal department advise work teams.
4. *Audit relationships* develop when people not directly in the chain of command evaluate the methods and performances of other teams. Financial auditors check the books, and technical auditors assess the methods and technical quality of the work.
5. *Stabilization relationships* involve auditing before the fact. In other words, teams sometimes must obtain clearance from others—for example, for large purchases—before they take action.
6. *Liaison relationships* involve intermediaries between teams. Managers often are called upon to mediate conflict between two organizational units. Public relations people, sales managers, purchasing agents, and others who work across organizational boundaries serve in liaison roles as they maintain communications between the organization and the outside world.

By assessing each working relationship with another unit ("From whom do we receive, and to whom do we send work? What permissions do we control, and to whom must we go for authorizations?"), teams can better understand whom to contact and when, where, why, and how to do so. Coordination throughout the working system improves, problems are avoided or short-circuited before they get too serious, and performance improves.[83]

Intergroup Conflict

The complex maze of interdependencies throughout organizations provides boundless opportunity for conflict to arise among groups and teams. Some conflict is constructive for the organization, as we discussed in Chapter 3. Michael Eisner, CEO and chairman of Disney, says that the key to ideas and innovation is to create an environment of supportive conflict, or what he calls "appropriate friction."[84] But many things cause great potential for destructive conflict: the sheer number and variety of contacts; ambiguities in jurisdiction and responsibility; differences in goals; intergroup competition for scarce resources; different perspectives held by members of different units; varying time horizons in which some units attend to long-term considerations and others focus on short-term needs; and other factors.

Tensions and anxieties are likely to arise in demographically diverse teams, or teams from different parts of the organization, or teams composed of contrasting personalities. Both demographic[85] and cross-functional[86] heterogeneity initially lead to problems such as stress, lower cooperation, and lower cohesiveness at first. But over time and with communication, diverse groups tend to become more cooperative and perform better than do homogeneous groups. Norms of cooperation can improve performance,[87] as does the fact that cross-functional teams engage in more external communication with more areas of the organization.[88]

Managing Conflict

Teams inevitably face conflicts and must decide how to manage them. The aim should be to make the conflict productive, that is, to make those involved believe they have benefited rather than lost from the conflict.[89] People believe they have benefited from a conflict when (1) a new solution is implemented, the problem is solved, and it is unlikely to emerge again, and (2) work relationships have been strengthened and people believe they can work together productively in the future.

How can conflict be managed? A recent study of human resource (HR) managers and the conflicts with which they deal provides some insight.[90] HR managers deal with every type of conflict imaginable: interpersonal difficulties from minor irritations to jealousy to fights; operations issues, including union issues, work assignments, overtime, and sick leave; discipline over infractions ranging from drug use and theft to sleeping on the job; sexual harassment and racial bias; pay and promotion issues; and feuds or strategic conflicts among divisions or individuals at the highest organizational levels.

In the study, the HR managers successfully settled most of the disputes. These managers typically follow a four-stage strategy. They *investigate* by interviewing the disputants and others and gathering more information. They *decide* how to resolve the dispute, often in conjunction with the disputants' bosses. They *take action* by explaining their decisions and the reasoning, and advise or train the disputants to avoid future incidents. And they *follow up* by documenting the conflict and the resolution, and monitoring the results by checking back with the disputants and their bosses. Throughout, the objectives of the HR people are to be fully informed so they understand the conflict; to be active and assertive in trying to resolve it; to be as objective, neutral, and impartial as humanly possible; and to be flexible by modifying their approaches according to the situation.[91]

Here are some other recommendations for more effective conflict management.[92] Don't allow dysfunctional conflict to build, or hope or assume that it will go away. Address it before it escalates. Try to resolve it, and if the first efforts don't

Conflicts can arise for any team—the trick is to make them productive. This ad promotes the American Arbitration Association's mission to train professionals on how to effectively minimize and manage conflict— "before the mud starts flying."

work, try others. And remember the earlier discussion (Chapter 13) of procedural justice. Even if disputants are not happy with your decisions, there are benefits to providing fair treatment, making a good faith effort, giving them a voice in the proceedings, and so on. Remember, too, that you may be able to ask HR specialists to help with difficult conflicts.

avoidance

A reaction to conflict that involves ignoring the problem by doing nothing at all, or deemphasizing the disagreement.

accommodation

A style of dealing with conflict involving cooperation on behalf of the other party but not being assertive about one's own interests.

compromise

A style of dealing with conflict involving moderate attention to both parties' concerns.

competing

A style of dealing with conflict involving strong focus on one's own goals, and little or no concern for the other person's goals.

collaboration

A style of dealing with conflict emphasizing both cooperation and assertiveness in order to maximize both parties' satisfaction.

Conflict Styles

How people manage conflict depends in part on their country's cultural norms. For example, Chinese people are more concerned with collective than with individual interests, and are more likely than managers in the United States to turn to higher authorities to make decisions rather than resolve conflicts themselves.[93] But culture aside, any team or individual has several options regarding approaches to use in conflicts with others.[94] These personal styles of dealing with conflict, shown in Figure 14.4, are distinguished based on how much people strive to satisfy their own concerns (the assertiveness dimension) and to what degree they focus on satisfying the other party's concerns (the cooperation dimension). For example, a common reaction to conflict is **avoidance.** In this situation, people do nothing to satisfy themselves or others. They either ignore the problem by doing nothing at all or address it by merely smoothing over or deemphasizing the disagreement. This, of course, fails to solve the problem or clear the air.

Accommodation means cooperating on behalf of the other party but not being assertive about one's own interests. **Compromise** involves moderate attention to both parties' concerns, being neither highly cooperative nor highly assertive. This style results in satisficing but not optimizing solutions. **Competing** is a highly competitive response in which people focus strictly on their own wishes and are unwilling to recognize the other person's concerns. Finally, **collaboration** emphasizes both cooperation and assertiveness. The goal is to maximize satisfaction for both parties.

Different approaches are necessary at different times.[95] For example, competing can be healthy if it promotes positive motivation, and even necessary when cutting costs or dealing with other scarce resources.

FIGURE 14.4
Conflict Management strategies

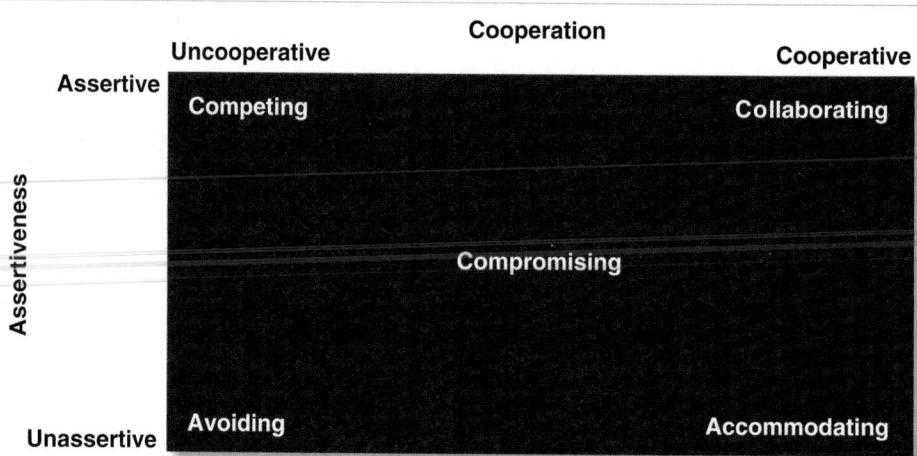

SOURCE: K. Thomas, "Conflict and Conflict Management." In *Handbook of Industrial and Organizational Psychology,* ed. M. D. Dunnette. Copyright © 1976. Reprinted by permission of the editor.

Compromise may be useful when people are under time pressure, when they need to achieve a temporary solution, or when collaboration fails. People should accommodate when they learn they are wrong or to minimize loss when they are outmatched. Even avoiding may be appropriate if the issue is trivial or resolving the conflict should be someone else's responsibility.

But when the conflict concerns important issues, when both sets of concerns are valid and important, when a creative solution is needed, and when commitment to the solution is vital to implementation, collaboration is the ideal approach. Collaboration can be achieved by airing feelings and opinions, addressing all concerns, and avoiding goal displacement by not letting personal attacks interfere with problem solving. An important technique is to invoke **superordinate goals**—higher-level organizational goals toward which all teams should be striving and that ultimately need to take precedence over personal or unit preferences.[96] Collaboration offers the best chance of reaching mutually satisfactory solutions based on the ideas and interests of all parties, and of maintaining and strengthening work relationships.

superordinate goals

Higher-level goals taking priority over specific individual or group goals.

KEY TERMS

Accommodation, p. 444

Autonomous work groups, p. 430

Avoidance, p. 444

Cohesiveness, p. 437

Collaboration, p. 444

Competing, p. 444

Compromise, p. 444

Informing, p. 441

Management teams, p. 428

Norms, p. 436

Parading, p. 441

Parallel teams, p. 428

Probing, p. 441

Project and development teams, p. 428

Quality circles, p. 430

Roles, p. 437

Self-designing teams, p. 430

Self-managed teams, p. 430

Semiautonomous work groups, p. 430

Social facilitation effect, p. 435

Social loafing, p. 435

Superordinate goals, p. 445

Task specialist, p. 437

Team, p. 427

Team maintenance specialist, p. 437

Traditional work groups, p. 430

Transnational teams, p. 431

Work teams, p. 428

SUMMARY OF LEARNING OBJECTIVES

Now that you have studied Chapter 14, you should know:

How teams can contribute to your organization's effectiveness.

Teams are building blocks for organization structure and forces for productivity, quality, cost savings, speed, change, and innovation. They have the potential to provide many benefits for both the organization and individual members.

What makes the new team environment different from the old.

Compared to traditional work groups that were closely supervised, today's teams have more authority and often are self-managed. Teams now are used in many more ways, for many more

purposes, than in the past. Generally, types of teams include work teams, project and development teams, parallel teams, and management teams. More specifically, types of work teams range from traditional groups with low autonomy to self-designing teams with high autonomy.

How groups become teams.

Groups carry on a variety of important developmental activities, including forming, storming, norming, and performing. For a group to become a team, it should move beyond traditional supervisory leadership, become more participative, and ultimately enjoy team leadership. A true team has members who complement one another; who are committed to a common purpose, performance goals, and approach; and who hold themselves accountable to one another.

Why groups sometimes fail.

Teams do not always work well. Some companies underestimate the difficulties of moving to a team-based approach. Teams require training, empowerment, and a well-managed transition to make them work. Groups may fail to become effective teams unless managers and team members commit to the idea, understand what makes teams work, and implement appropriate practices.

How to build an effective team.

Create a team with a high-performance focus by establishing a common purpose; by translating the purpose into measurable team goals; by designing the team's task so it is intrinsically motivating; by designing a team-based performance measurement system; and by providing team rewards.

Work to develop a common understanding of how the team will perform its task. Make it clear that everyone has to work hard and contribute in concrete ways. Establish mutual accountability and build trust among members. Examine the team's strategies periodically and be willing to adapt.

Make sure members contribute fully by selecting them appropriately, training them, and checking that all important roles are carried out. Take a variety of steps to establish team cohesiveness and high performance norms.

And don't just manage inwardly. Manage the team's relations with outsiders, too.

How to manage your team's relationships with other teams.

Perform important roles such as gatekeeping, informing, parading, and probing. Identify the types of lateral role relationships you have with outsiders. This can help coordinate efforts throughout the work system.

How to manage conflict.

Conflict arises because of the sheer number of contacts, ambiguities, goal differences, competition for scarce resources, and different perspectives and time horizons. Depending on the situation, five basic interpersonal approaches to managing conflict can be used: avoidance, accommodation, compromise, competition, and collaboration. Superordinate goals offer a focus on higher-level organizational goals that can help generate a collaborative relationship.

DISCUSSION QUESTIONS

1. Why do you think some people resist the idea of working in teams? How would you deal with their resistance?
2. Consider a job you have held, and review Table 14.1 about the traditional and new team environment. Which environment best describes your job? Assess your job on each of the dimensions described in the table.
3. Assess your job as in question 2, using Figure 14.2, "Stepping Up to Team Leadership." Which leadership "stage" characterized your job environment?
4. Identify some things from a previous job that could have been done differently to move your work group closer toward the "team leadership" depicted in Figure 14.2.
5. Experts say that teams are a means, not an end. What do you think they mean? What do you think happens in a company that creates teams just for the sake of having teams because it's a fad or just because it sounds good? How can this pitfall be avoided?
6. Choose a sports team with which you are familiar. Assess its effectiveness and discuss the factors that contribute to its level of effectiveness.
7. Assess the effectiveness, as in question 6, of a student group with which you have been affiliated. Could anything have been done to make it more effective?
8. Consider the various roles members have to perform for a team to be effective. Which roles would play to your strengths, and which to your weaknesses? How can you become a better team member?
9. Can you think of any personal examples of the Abilene Paradox? Explain what happened and why.
10. What do you think are your own most commonly used approaches to handling conflict? Least common? What can you do to expand your repertoire and become more effective at conflict management?
11. Generate real examples of how superordinate goals have helped resolve a conflict. Identify some current conflicts and provide some specific ideas for how superordinate goals could be used to help.
12. Have you ever been part of a group that was "self-managed"? What was good about it, and what not so good? Why do many managers resist this idea? Why do some people love the idea of being a member of such a team, while others don't?
13. How might self-managed teams operate differently in different cultures? What are the advantages, disadvantages, and implications of homogeneous versus highly diverse self-managed teams?

Group Meetings: Love 'em or Hate 'em

A lot of people hate meetings. A lot of companies are overrun by too many unproductive, morale-sapping meetings. But some meetings are just too good to miss. Here are a few, as described by the people who love them:

- MaMaMedia.com holds weekly meetings called Thought Provoking sessions that provide a creative refuge from the daily work. Rebecca Randall never misses them because "it's a great way for me to step outside of the day-to-day routine and come up with new approaches to doing my job." The company provides Web-based "playful learning" for kids 12 and under, and the meetings "approximate the way children learn through exploration, fun, surprise, and imagination." Each week, a different work team plans and hosts the meeting.

- At Kaufman and Broad Home Corp., one of the top home builders in the United States, the monthly After 5 meeting of the marketing and communications staff is usually held in the Marketing War Room, although one was held in a bus doing 65 miles per hour. The meetings are brainstorming sessions aimed a taking the company's brand image into fun new territory. One meeting led to a major promotional campaign that used a full-scale replica of Marge and Homer Simpson's home. The norm at the meetings is that anything goes: "Think The McLaughlin Group, only nicer. The best ideas sound absolutely insane at first, so we don't want people to be editing their thoughts. The unspoken rule: If you think it, say it."

- Nortel's Caribbean and Latin American division airs its Virtual Leadership Academy live and once a month. Using teleconferencing technologies, the Leadership Academy educates geographically dispersed employees about important strategic issues. Emma Carrasco never misses it because the networked meetings "let us tap into leadership ability and expertise throughout the company . . . We leverage and showcase Nortel's technology as well as its culture . . . and reinforce a core cultural tenet: that groundbreaking technology is about elevating, not replacing, human interaction."

- Terry Pope, Operations Manager for Motorola, never misses the daily morning production meeting with 30-plus managers, engineers, and technicians. The purpose is to communicate the last 24 hours' problems that need to be addressed during the next 24 hours. If a problem is identified, the person responsible says, "Here's what's wrong, and here's what we're doing now to make sure that it doesn't happen again." He never misses the meeting because it "sets the pace for the entire factory and defines its culture. It's a daily demonstration of our ability to perform."

- Peter Kirwan has regular "Fireside Chats" with his engineers, programmers, and technical writers. The norms of the meetings are relaxed honesty and constructive criticism. "This is a chance to discuss tough issues in a friendly, informal setting . . . Business issues are always changing, and so are personal and organizational issues." He starts the meeting by opening a homemade cardboard "fireplace" and pulling up chairs. It's silly, on purpose. It loosens people up, and they talk. He learns, and helps them to learn.

- Entrepreneur Craig Forman never misses Sunday nights with his family. "This 'meeting' brings us together and gives us the motivation to attack the week. It's an anchor for all three of us." He wants to make sure his family's priorities don't get lost in the frenzy of Silicon Valley's start-up culture.

QUESTIONS

1. Can you identify common themes among, and differences between, these group gatherings?

2. People who attend these regular meetings don't want to miss them. Why do you think this is the case?

3. What do you think these meetings do for morale, cohesiveness, and team productivity? How and why do they have these effects?

4. What meetings do you have that you would rather avoid, and why? Do you have any that you really look forward to, and why?

5. When you are a manager, what regular meetings will you have, and how will you (a) avoid having people dread them, and (b) get people to "not want to miss" them? What else will you do to create a strong "team"?

SOURCES: C. Olofson, "Play Hard, Think Big," *Fast Company Online*, January 2001, p. 64; C. Olofson, "Can We Talk? Put Another Log on the Fire," *Fast Company Online*, October 1999, p. 86; A. Wilson, "All in the Family," *Fast Company Online*, March 2000, p. 72; M. Goldberg, "At Motorola, the Meeting Is the Network," *Fast Company Online*, October 1997, p. 70; C. Olofson, "Global Reach, Virtual Leadership," *Fast Company Online*, September 1999, p. 80; C. Olofson, "Open Minds after Closing Time," *Fast Company Online*, June 1999, p. 72.

14.1 Prisoners' Dilemma: An Intergroup Competition

INSTRUCTIONS

1. The instructor explains what will take place in this exercise and assigns people to groups. Two types of teams are formed and named Red and Blue (with no more than eight per group) and are not to communicate with the other team in any way, verbally or nonverbally, except when told to do so by the instructor. Groups are given time to study the Prisoner's Dilemma Tally Sheet.

2. (3 min.) Round 1. Each team has three minutes to make a team decision. Write your decisions when the instructor says time is up.

3. (2 min.) The choices of the teams are announced for Round 1. The scores are entered on the Tally Sheet.

4. (4–5 min.) Round 2 is conducted in the same manner as Round 1.

5. (6 min.) Round 3 is announced as a special round, for which the payoff points are doubled. Each team is instructed to send one representative to chairs in the center of the room. After representatives have conferred for three minutes, they return

to their teams. Teams then have three minutes, as before, in which to make their decisions. When recording their scores, they should be reminded that points indicated by the payoff schedule are doubled for this round only.

6. (8–10 min.) Rounds 4, 5, and 6 are conducted in the same manner as the first three rounds.

7. (6 min.) Round 7 is announced as a special round, in which the payoff points are "squared" (multiplied by themselves: e.g., a score of 4 would be $4^2 = 16$). A minus sign would be retained: e.g., $-(3)^2 = -9$. Team representatives meet for three minutes; then the teams meet for three minutes. At the instructor's signal, the teams write their choices; then the two choices are announced.

8. (6 min.) Round 8 is handled exactly as Round 7 was. Payoff points are squared.

9. (10–20 min.) The point total for each team is announced, and the sum of the two team totals is calculated and compared to the maximum positive or negative outcomes ($+108$ or -108 points). A discussion on win–lose situations, competition, and so on will be conducted.

Prisoners' Dilemma Tally Sheet

Instructions: For 10 successive rounds, the Red team will choose either an A or a B and the Blue team will choose either an X or a Y. The score each team receives in a round is determined by the pattern made by the choices of both teams, according to the schedule below.

Payoff Schedule:

AX—Both teams win 3 points.

AY—Red team loses 6 points; Blue team wins 6 points.

BX—Red team wins 6 points; Blue team loses 6 points.

BY—Both teams lose 3 points.

Scorecard:

Round	Minutes	Choice		Cumulative points	
		Red Team	Blue Team	Red Team	Blue Team
1	3				
2	3				
3*	3 (reps.) 3 (teams)				
4	3				
5	3				
6*	3 (reps.) 3 (teams)				
7**	3 (reps.) 3 (teams)				
8**	3 (reps.) 3 (teams)				

*Payoff points are doubled for this round. **Payoff points are squared for this round. (Retain the minus sign.)

SOURCE: Dorothy Hai, "Prisoner's Dilemma," in *Organizational Behavior: Experiences and Cases.* Copyright © 1986. Reprinted with permission of South-Western College Publishing, a division of Thomson Learning.

14.2   The Traveler's Check Scam Group Exercise

INSTRUCTIONS

1. (3 min.) Group selects an observer. The observer remains silent during the group problem-solving process, recording the activities of the group on the Observer's Report Form.

2. (15 min.) Group members read the following problem and proceed to solve it.

3. (2 min.) When the group has a solution to the problem upon which all members agree, it will be written on a note and handed to the instructor.

4. (5 min.) The observer briefs the group on the problem-solving processes observed during the exercise.

5. (25 min.) The small group discusses the following topics:

    a. Did the group decide on a problem solution process before it attempted to solve the problem? If so, what was it?

    b. Was the solution of the problem hindered in any way by the lack of an appropriate agreed-upon group problem-solving process? Explain.

    c. Who were the leaders of the group during the exercise? What did they do? Critique their leadership activities.

    d. What communications patterns were used by the group during the exercise? Who participated the most? Who participated the least? Describe individual behaviors.

    e. Did the group solve the problem? How many members of the group discovered the correct answer on their own?

    f. Was using the group to solve this problem better than assigning the problem to one person? Explain the rationale for your answer.

THE CASE OF MICKEY THE DIP

Mickey the Dip, an expert pickpocket and forger, liked to work the Los Angeles International Airport on busy days. His technique was to pick the pockets of prosperous-looking victims just before they boarded planes to the East Coast. This gave Mickey five hours to use stolen credit cards before the owners could report their losses.

One morning Mickey snatched a fat wallet from a traveler and left the airport to examine his loot. To his surprise he found no credit cards but instead $500 in traveler's checks. After 20 minutes of practice, Mickey could sign a perfect imitation of the victim's signature. He then proceeded to a large department store where all suits were being sold for 75 percent of the regular price. Mickey purchased a suit for $225 and paid for it with $300 in stolen traveler's checks. After the clerk who served him went to lunch, he bought another suit for $150 and paid for it with the remaining $200 of stolen traveler's checks. Later, Mickey switched the labels on the two suits and, using the receipt from the $225 suit, returned the $150 suit at a centralized return desk for a refund. The refund clerk took the suit and gave Mickey eleven $20 bills, which he stuffed into his pocket and disappeared.

When the department store deposited the traveler's checks, they were returned as forgeries. Assuming the store normally sold suits at twice their wholesale price and used 10 percent of sales as an overhead cost figure, what was the cash value of the loss suffered by the store as a result of Mickey's caper? Do not consider taxes in your computations.

THE TRAVELER'S CHECK SCAM EXERCISE OBSERVER'S REPORT

1. What happened during the first few minutes the group met after members finished reading the problem? (List behaviors of specific group members.)

2. Identify the group role played by each group member during the exercise. Give examples of the behavior of each.

3. Were there any conflicts within or among group members during the exercise? Explain the nature of the conflicts and the behavior of the individual(s) involved.

4. How were decisions made in the group? Give specific examples.

5. How could the group improve its problem-solving skills?

SOURCE: Peter P. Dawson, *Fundamentals of Organizational Behavior.* Copyright © 1985 Pearson Education, Inc. Reprinted by permission of Pearson Education, Inc., Upper Saddle River, NJ.

CHAPTER 15

Communicating

Electronic engineers have yet to devise a better interoffice communications system than the water cooler.

—Leo Ellis

CHAPTER OUTLINE

Interpersonal Communication
One-Way versus Two-Way Communication
Communication Pitfalls
Mixed Signals and Misperception
Oral and Written Channels
Electronic Media
Communications Networks
Media Richness
Improving Communication Skills
Improving Sender Skills
Nonverbal Skills
Improving Receiver Skills
Effective Supervision
Organizational Communication
Downward Communication
Upward Communication
Horizontal Communication
Informal Communication
Boundarylessness

LEARNING OBJECTIVES

After studying Chapter 15, you will know:

1. The important advantages of two-way communication.

2. Communication problems to avoid.

3. When and how to use the various communication channels.

4. Ways to become a better "sender" and "receiver" of information.

5. How to improve downward, upward, and horizontal communication.

6. How to work with the company grapevine.

7. The advantages and characteristics of the boundaryless organization.

THE POWER OF DIALOGUE

A steel mill in the Midwest had endured 30 years of labor–management animosity. People called each other names, threw chairs, stormed out of meetings, and staged work slowdowns. Neither management nor labor trusted the other, and both sides doubted that reconciliation was possible. But tough competition from minimills forced them to try to cooperate. So they agreed to try a participative total quality improvement process, and formed joint problem-solving committees.

In the initial meetings, consultants helped the groups communicate more constructively. Instead of placing blame and resurrecting old conflicts, people tried to step away from the past and really think about the present and the future. They began talking honestly about concerns, and openly considered other viewpoints.

The process was not an easy one; it took time, effort, and courage. But eventually, for the first time, both managers and union personnel began to talk about the business as theirs. They came to recognize that they all were part of the same organization, and they began to think together rather than separately.

According to the union president, the old antagonism became a thing of the past. "That's gone. Now we're looking at the future." The CEO described it this way: "The process became a

method of exchanging thoughts and realizing that none of us have the answer, but together we might have a better answer."

Dialogue is a powerful tool with people outside the firm as well. States Tom Rapsas, "In business, a dialogue is the give and take of information between a customer and a company. Mailing a piece of communication or persuading a customer to visit a website does not constitute a dialogue. It must be a two-way flow of information in which you get the information a customer has given you and respond with value-added information . . . The aim of dialogue is simple: By having an ongoing conversation with customers, you can build a relationship with them. As that relationship grows in time, you gain that customer's trust."

While some companies ignore customers, others engage them in active dialogue in order to strengthen both products and customer relationships. At Cisco, customers have open access to Cisco's information, knowledge base, and user community via an online service, and they engage in dialogue, solving each other's problems. Some companies have extensive conversations with customers and potential customers about product features. Likewise, Ford's suppliers collaborate in developing new vehicles.

Thus, in progressive companies, customers and other "outsiders" step out of their traditional roles and become cocreators of value. The best conversations are a dialogue of equals. Done right, customers and others outside the firm become a source of competitive advantage. Effective dialogue is the source of that source.

Source: Used with permission of the publisher, from Organizational Dynamics, Autumn 1993, copyright © 1993. American Management Association, New York. All rights reserved. Also, N. M. Dixon, "The Hallways of Learning," Organizational Dynamics, Spring 1997, pp. 23–34; R. Heifetz and D. Laurie, "The Work of Leadership," Harvard Business Review, January–February 1996, pp. 124–34; C. K. Prahalad and V. Ramaswamy, "Co-opting Customer Competence," Harvard Business Review, January–February 2000, pp. 79–87; T. Raspas, "Make Your Creative Work Smarter by Using Dialogue & Data," Target Marketing, March 2002, pp. 81–82; L.K. Geller, "Find Out What Customers and Prospects Really Want!" Target Marketing, March 2002, pp. 32–34.

Although it took time, eventually managers and union personnel began to think together rather than separately.

Setting the Stage

Two types of discourse work together to help a group become a team and an organization become a more effective organization. The two types—and their impact—are illustrated in "Setting the Stage." **Discussion** is like a ping-pong match, with people hitting the ball back and forth.[1] Each person is trying to win a debate, in the sense of having his or her view accepted by the group. Discussions can be polite, and useful, but they can also work at cross-purposes and become destructive.

Dialogue, in contrast, has the goal of going beyond one person's understanding. The goal is not to "win," but for the team to come to a common, deep understanding. Dialogue explores complex issues from many viewpoints.[2] It requires a commitment to the truth, honesty about people's own beliefs, true listening, and open-mindedness toward others' beliefs. Free exploration of ideas helps people think and learn together.[3]

Every group and organization should have both. But common danger is plenty of discussion and argument, but not much in the way of real dialogue.

Discussion and dialogue are examples of how people communicate. Effective communication is a fundamental aspect of job performance and managerial effectiveness.[4] In this chapter, we will present important communication concepts and some practical guidelines for improving your effectiveness. We will discuss both interpersonal and organizational communication.

discussion

A type of discourse in which each person attempts to win a debate by having his or her view accepted by others.

dialogue

A discourse in which members explore complex issues from many viewpoints in order to come to a common, deeper understanding.

Interpersonal Communication

communication

The transmission of information and meaning from one party to another through the use of shared symbols.

Communication is the transmission of information and meaning from one party to another through the use of shared symbols. Figure 15.1 shows a general model of the communication process.

The *sender* initiates the process by conveying information to the *receiver*—the person for whom the message is intended. The sender has a *meaning* he or she wishes to communicate and *encodes* the meaning into symbols (e.g., the words chosen for the message). Then the sender *transmits*, or sends, the message through some *channel*, such as a verbal or written medium.

The receiver *decodes* the message (e.g., reads it) and attempts to *interpret* the sender's meaning. The receiver may provide *feedback* to the sender by encoding a message in response to the sender's message.

The communication process often is hampered by *noise*, or interference in the system, that blocks perfect understanding. Noise could be anything that interferes with accurate communication: ringing telephones, thoughts about other things, or simple fatigue or stress.

FIGURE 15.1
A Model of the Communication Process

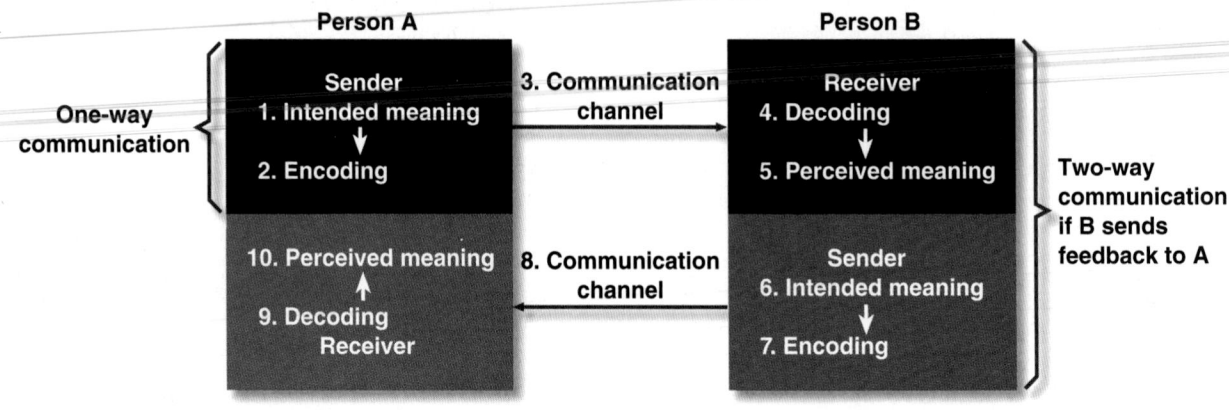

CHAPTER 14

Managing Teams

No one can whistle a symphony. It takes an orchestra to play it.

—Halford E. Luccock

CHAPTER OUTLINE

The Contributions of Teams
Benefits of Groups
The New Team Environment
　Types of Teams
　Self-Managed Teams
How Groups Become Teams
　Group Activities
　The Passage of Time
　A Developmental Sequence: From Group
　　to Team
　Why Groups Sometimes Fail
Building Effective Teams
　A Performance Focus
　Motivating Teamwork
　Member Contributions
　Norms
　Roles
　Cohesiveness
　Building Cohesiveness and High
　　Performance Norms
Managing Lateral Relationships
　Managing Outward
　Lateral Role Relationships
　Intergroup Conflict
　Managing Conflict
　Conflict Styles

LEARNING OBJECTIVES

After studying Chapter 14, you will know:

1. How teams contribute to your organization's effectiveness.

2. What makes the new team environment different from the old.

3. How groups become teams.

4. Why groups sometimes fail.

5. How to build an effective team.

6. How to manage your team's relationships with other teams.

7. How to manage conflict.

---

tical treatment of the communica-
communications can break down.
A manager who is alert to potential
are more effective communication.
een one-way and two-way commu-
, and the various communication

munication

of the model in Figure 15.1
ection—from the sender to
sends a memo to a subordi-
es an order over the phone.
he room.

completing the Figure 15.1
ed. One-way communication
ome two-way if the manager
asks the receiver if he has any
to alternative suggestions for
down and listens to his son's

only that the receiver provides feedback
feedback. In these constructive exchanges,
rather than delivered from one person to

common than it should be because it is
executive finds it easier to dash off a memo
ate. Also, he doesn't have to deal with ques-
isagrees.

cult and time-consuming than one-way com-
e; fewer mistakes occur, and fewer problems
estions, share concerns, and make suggestions
erstand more precisely what is being commu-
e information.[5]

not always "get across" to the receiver. You are
there is a perfect correlation between what you

e communication process. In the encoding stage,
ts typed in the wrong places, facts left out, or
ransmission stage, a memo gets lost on a cluttered
parency are too small to read from the back of the
biguous inflections.

the receiver doesn't listen carefully or reads too
. And, of course, receivers can misinterpret the
ong conclusion from an unclear memo, a listener
ss too personally, or a sideways glance is taken the

tual and filtering processes create misin-
rocess of receiving and interpreting infor-
sses are not perfectly objective. They are
ed motives and attitudes toward the sender
iased interpretations. People often assume

one-way communication

A process in which information flows in only one direction—from the sender to the receiver, with no feedback loop.

two-way communication

A process in which information flows in two directions—the receiver provides feedback, and the sender is receptive to the feedback.

perception

The process of receiving and interpreting information.

that others share their views, and naturally pay more attention to their own views than to those of others.[7] But perceptual differences get in the way of shared consensus. It helps to see others' viewpoints as legitimate, and incorporate others' perspectives into your interpretation of issues.[8] Generally, adopting another person's viewpoint is fundamental to working collaboratively. And at a more personal level, your ability to take others' perspectives—say, to really understand the viewpoints of customers or suppliers—can lead to higher assessments of your performance.[9]

filtering

The process of withholding, ignoring, or distorting information.

Filtering is the process of withholding, ignoring, or distorting information. Senders do this, for example, when they tell the boss what they think the boss wants to hear, or give unwarranted compliments rather than honest criticism. Receivers also filter information; they may fail to recognize an important message, or attend to some aspects of the message but not others.

Filtering and subjective perception pervade one interesting aspect of the communications dynamic: how men and women differ in their communicating styles. A manager at a magazine who tended to phrase the assignments she gave her reporters as questions—"How would you like to do the X project with Y?" and "I was thinking of putting you on the X project; is that okay?"—was criticized by her male boss, who told her she did not assume the proper demeanor with her staff.[10] Another, the owner of a retail operation, told one of her store managers to do something by saying, "The bookkeeper needs help with the billing. How would you feel about helping her out?" He said fine, but didn't do it. Whereas the boss thought he meant he would do it, he said he meant he would think about how he would feel about helping. He decided he had better things to do.[11]

Because of such filtering and perceptual differences, you cannot assume the other person means what you think he means, or understands the meanings you intend. Managers need to excel at reading interactions, and adjusting their communication styles and perceptions to the people with whom they interact.[12] The very human tendencies to filter and perceive subjectively underlie much of the ineffective communication, and the need for more effective communication practices, that you will read about in the rest of this chapter.

Mixed Signals and Misperception

A common thread underlying the discussion so far is that people's perceptions can undermine attempts to communicate. People do not pay attention to everything going on around them. They inadvertently send mixed signals that can

Any interpersonal situation holds potential for perceptual errors, filtering, and other communication breakdowns.

...ey
... of importance of each of the following job rewards.

Moderately Important	Indifferent	Moderately Unimportant	Very Unimportant
		2	1
4	3		1
		2	1
4	3	2	
4	3		1
	3	2	1
4	3	2	1
4	3	2	1
4	3	2	1
4	3	2	1
4	3	2	1
4	3	2	1
4	3		1
4	3	2	
4	3		1
5		2	1
5	4	3	2	1
5	4	3	2	1
5	4	3	2	1
5	4	3	2	1
5	4	3	2	1
5	4	3	2	1
5	4	3	2	1
5	4	3	2	1
5	4			

undermine the intended messages. Different people attend to different things, and people interpret the same thing in different ways. All of this creates problems in communication.

If the communication is between people from different cultures, these problems are magnified.[13]Communication "breakdowns" often occur when business transactions take place between people from different countries. Chapter 6 introduced you to the importance of these cultural issues. Table 15.1 offers suggestions for communicating effectively with someone who speaks a different language.

TABLE 15.1
What Do I Do If They Do Not Speak My Language?

Verbal Behavior
• *Clear, slow speech*. Enunciate each word. Do not use colloquial expressions.
• *Repetition*. Repeat each important idea using different words to explain the same concept.
• *Simple sentences*. Avoid compound, long sentences.
• *Active verbs*. Avoid passive verbs.

Nonverbal Behavior
• *Visual restatements*. Use as many visual restatements as possible, such as pictures, graphs, tables, and slides.
• *Gestures*. Use more facial and appropriate hand gestures to emphasize the meaning of words.
• *Demonstrations*. Act out as many themes as possible.
• *Pauses*. Pause more frequently.
• *Summaries*. Hand out written summaries of your verbal presentation.

Accurate Interpretation
• *Silence*. When there is a silence, wait. Do not jump in to fill the silence. The other person is probably just thinking more slowly in the nonnative language or translating.
• *Intelligence*. Do not equate poor grammar and mispronunciation with lack of intelligence; it is usually a sign of nonnative language use.
• *Differences*. If unsure, assume difference, not similarity.

Comprehension
• *Understanding*. Do not just assume that they understand; assume that they do not understand.
• *Checking comprehension*. Have colleagues repeat their understanding of the material back to you. Do not simply ask if they understand or not. Let them explain what they understand to you.

Design
• *Breaks*. Take more frequent breaks. Second language comprehension is exhausting.
• *Small modules*. Divide the material to be presented into smaller modules.
• *Longer time frame*. Allocate more time for each module than you usually need for presenting the same material to native speakers of your language.

Motivation
• *Encouragement*. Verbally and nonverbally encourage and reinforce speaking by nonnative language participants.
• *Drawing out*. Explicitly draw out marginal and passive participants.
• *Reinforcement*. Do not embarrass novice speakers.

SOURCE: N. Adler, *International Dimensions of Organizational Behavior.* Copyright © 1986. Reprinted with permission of South-Western College Publishing, a division of Thomson Learning.

The following example further highlights the operation of mixed signals and misperceptions. A bank CEO knew that to be competitive he had to downsize his organization, and the employees who remained would have to commit to customer service, become more empowered, and really *earn* customer loyalty.[14] Knowing that his employees would have doubts and concerns about the coming reorganization, he decided to make a promise to them that he would do his best to guarantee employment, growth, and training.

What signals did the CEO communicate to his people by his promises? One positive signal was that he cared about his people. But he also signaled that *he* would take care of *them*, thus undermining his goal of giving them more responsibility and empowering them. The employees wanted management to take responsibility for the market challenge that *they* needed to face—to handle things for them when *they* needed to learn the new ways of doing business. Inadvertently, the CEO spoke to their backward-looking need for security when he had meant to make them see that the bank's future depended on *their* efforts.

Consider how many problems could be avoided—and how much more effective communication could be—if people took the time to (1) ensure that the receivers attend to the message they are sending; (2) consider the other party's frame of reference and attempt to convey the message from that perceptual viewpoint; (3) take concrete steps to minimize perceptual errors and improper signals in both sending and receiving; and (4) send *consistent* messages. You should make an effort to predict people's interpretations of your messages and think in terms of how they could *misinterpret* your messages. It helps to say not only what you mean but also what you *don't* mean. Every time you say, "I am not saying *X*, I am saying *Y*," you eliminate a possible misinterpretation.[15]

Oral and Written Channels

Communication can be sent through a variety of channels (steps 3 and 8 in the Figure 15.1 model), including oral, written, and electronic. Each channel has advantages and disadvantages.

Oral communication includes face-to-face discussion, telephone conversations, and formal presentations and speeches. Advantages are that questions can be asked and answered; feedback is immediate and direct; the receiver(s) can sense the sender's sincerity (or lack thereof); and oral communication is more persuasive and sometimes less expensive than written. However, oral communication also has disadvantages: It can lead to spontaneous, ill-considered statements (and regret), and there is no permanent record of it (unless an effort is made to record it).

Written communication includes memos, letters, reports, computer files, and other written documents. Advantages to using written messages are that the message can be revised several times, it is a permanent record that can be saved, the message stays the same even if relayed through many people, and the receiver has more time to analyze the message. Disadvantages are that the sender has no control over where, when, or if the message is read; the sender does not receive immediate feedback; the receiver may not understand parts of the message; and the message must be longer to contain enough information to answer anticipated questions.[16]

You should weigh these considerations when deciding whether to communicate orally or in writing. Also, sometimes use both channels, such as following up a meeting with a confirming memo or writing a letter to prepare someone for your phone call.

Electronic Media

A vital category of communication channels is electronic media. Managers use computers not only to gather and distribute quantitative data but to "talk" with others electronically. In electronic decision rooms, software supports simultaneous access to shared files, and allows people to share views and do work collectively.[17] Other means of electronic communication include *teleconferencing*, in which groups of people in different locations interact over telephone lines (*audioconferencing*) and perhaps also see one another on television monitors as they participate in group discussions (*videoconferencing*).

Advantages   *Advantages* of electronic communication are numerous and dramatic. Within firms, the advantages include the sharing of more information, and speed and efficiency in delivering routine messages to large numbers of people across vast geographic areas. It can reduce time spent traveling, talking, and photocopying. It's also cheap. Alcoa reduced its cost base by over $1 billion by installing a system that enables it to manage in real time—that is, making decisions immediately, on the basis of accurate information communicated "live," as it happens.[18]

Some companies, including Boeing, use brainstorming software that allows anonymous contributions, presuming this will add more honesty to internal discussions. Some research indicates more data sharing and critical argumentation, and higher-quality decisions, with a group decision support system than is found in face-to-face meetings.[19] But anonymity also offers great potential for lies, gossip, insults, threats, harassment, and the release of confidential information.[20]

Disadvantages   *Disadvantages* of electronic communication include the difficulty of solving complex problems, which require more extended, face-to-face interaction,

---

FROM THE PAGES OF **BusinessWeek**

Dialogue with Computers

Speech may be the ultimate bridge between people and machines; Bill Gates calls speech "not just the future of Windows, but the future of computing itself." In 2002, IBM launched its Super Human Speech Recognition Project to improve technical capability and create systems capable of not just linguistic identification but true contextual understanding and the ability to reply to open-ended questions.

Speech-recognition software programs will do for you (rather, with you) such things as get airline reservations, trade stocks, and retrieve voicemail, email, and faxes from a unified mailbox. Voice-controlled Web-browsing programs will mean that you won't have to click for hours on end. You will be able to surf the Net without using a keyboard, by giving oral commands on the phone. And Tellme Networks wants to offer you a single toll-free number that would be the last one you ever need to dial, on which you can simply say "Connect me with the nearest muffler shop" or "Call my mother." You won't get a dial tone, but a personal virtual assistant that will call your friend or anyone you want at your command.

Says Sunil Soares of IBM, "Voice today is where the Web was in 1994. There are a lot of different applications for voice, many of which are still being discovered." *Business Week* stated, "We can't guess what kinds of dialogs will evolve among humans and machines in the next century. But it's certain we'll all soon be spending a lot more time chatting with computers." For example, a Toyota team is attempting to use the Internet to put two-way communication into the automobile. My Car Universe is a prototype 3-D website created in partnership with Intel, HP, Compaq, and design agency Spike Australia. The computer and driver both convey and receive information, asking questions and taking desired action. The computer informs when the brake pads are low, and asks if the driver wants to book an appointment with the local Toyota dealership. The car tells the user that concert tickets for a certain favorite band are going on sale, and offers to plan a route to buy tickets. It states when gas is needed, and tells the driver where she can get some en route. It can send security messages to a pager or Palm Pilot, notifying the owner if someone is struggling to get into the car. Real-time traffic data and an MP3 jukebox aren't far off.

SOURCE: N. Gross, P. Judge, O. Port, and S. Wildstrom, "Let's Talk!" *Business Week*, February 23, 1998, pp. 45–53; E. Nee, "Who Wants to Talk to the Web?" *Fortune*, November 13, 2000, pp. 317–24; S. Kirsner, "Collision Course," *Fast Company*, January–February 2000, pp. 118–44; P. McDougall, "Innovation: Speech Recognition's Next Iteration," *Information Week*, January 7, 2002, p. 20; K. Merritt, "Giving Voice to Mobile Workers," *Frontline Solutions*, February 2002, pp. 8–9.

and the inability to pick up subtle, nonverbal, or inflectional clues about what the communicator is thinking or conveying. Although organizations rely heavily on computer-aided communication for group decision making, face-to-face groups generally take less time, make higher-quality decisions, and are more satisfying for members.[21] Email is most appropriate, then, for routine messages that do not require the exchange of large quantities of complex information. It is less suitable for confidential information, resolving conflicts, or negotiating.[22]

One inevitable consequence of electronic mail is "flaming": hurling insults, sending "nastygrams," venting frustration, snitching on co-workers to the boss, and otherwise breaching bureaucratic protocol.[23] Email liberates people to send things they would not say to a person's face. The lack of nonverbal cues can result in "kidding" remarks being taken seriously, causing resentment and regret. It is not unheard of for confidential messages, including details about people's personal lives and insulting, embarrassing remarks, to become public knowledge through electronic leaks.

Other downsides to electronic mail are important to know.[24] Different people and sometimes different working units latch onto different channels as their medium of choice. For example, an engineering division might use email most, but a design group might rely primarily on voice mail or printed faxes, and neglect email.[25] Another disadvantage is that email messages sometimes are monitored or seen inadvertently by those for whom they are not intended. Deleting messages does not destroy them; they are saved elsewhere. Recipients can forward them to others, unbeknownst to the original sender. And they can be used in court cases to indict individuals or companies. Email messages are private property—but the private property of the system's owner, not of the sender.[26]

The Virtual Office Many entrepreneurs conduct business via open "offices" on the Internet, working off their computers from wherever they happen to be. Similarly, major companies like IBM, AT&T, GE, and Chiat/Day are slashing office space and giving people laptops or powerful notebook computers, telecommunications software, voice mail, and other communications technologies so they can work virtually anywhere, anytime.[27] Based on the philosophy that management's focus should be on what people do, not where they are, the **virtual office** is a mobile office in which people can work anywhere—their home, car, airport, customers' offices—as long as they have the tools to communicate with customers and colleagues.[28] One observer calls the virtual office "the most radical redefinition of the workplace since the Industrial Revolution."[29]

Spacious corner office, redefined.

SIEMENS
Global network of innovation

The virtual office nowadays can be as close as the deck on the back of your lake house. This Siemens ad promotes their ability to help with information exchange solutions from cellular phones to optical networks. What problems do you think might occur with virtual offices, besides the lack of in-office interaction?

In the short run, at least, the benefits appear substantial. Compaq Computer reduced sales costs and administrative expenses from 22 percent of revenue to 12 percent. Perkin-Elmer, which makes scientific equipment, was able to close 35 branch offices. AT&T says mobile offices allow salespeople to spend 15 to 20 percent more time with customers.[30] And most people like the flexibility it gives them.

But what will be the longer-term impact on productivity and morale? We may be in danger of losing too many "human moments," those authentic encounters that happen only when two people are physically together.[31] Some people hate being forced to work at home. Some valuable people have quit. Some send faxes, email, and voice mail in the middle of the night—and others receive them. Some work around the clock and still feel they are not doing enough. The long hours of being constantly close to the technical tools of work can cause burnout. And some companies are learning that direct supervision at the office is necessary to maintain the quality of work, especially when employees are inexperienced and need guidance. One company president says, "As soon as I separate my supervisors from the people they're supposed to be developing, I make it difficult for effective coaching to occur.[32]

The "virtual office" proved its value in 2001 through its ability to keep businesses going despite the terrorist attacks. But the virtual office requires changes in human beings as well as presenting technical challenges.[33] The virtual office is much hyped and useful, but it will not replace real offices and face-to-face work.

U.S. workers believe that between 33 percent and 50 percent of their email messages are irrelevant.

Managing the Electronic Load   Electronic communication media seem essential these days, and people wonder how they ever worked without them. At the same time, the sheer volume of communication can be overwhelming.[34]

Fortunately, a few rules of thumb can help you in your electronic communications.[35] Use a medium that you know your audience uses. For messages delivered to many people, use a medium everyone understands is priority. Better yet, use multiple channels. If the message is important, make its importance clear. If you are requesting action, make that clear as well. Don't overrely on electronic media; other channels, including old-fashioned face-to-face conversation, are better for some purposes.

For the problem of information overload, the challenge is to separate the truly important from the routine. Effective managers find time to think about bigger business issues, and don't get too bogged down in responding to every message that seems urgent but may be trivial. Essential here is to think strategically about your goals, identify the things that are most important, and prioritize your time around those goals. This is easier said than done, of course, but it is essential, and it helps. And then, by the way, you can apply technological solutions: software that, based on the most important information needs you identify for yourself, can help protect you from the electronic information quagmire.[36]

Some companies are recognizing the downsides of electronic media overuse. They discourage people from sending too many unnecessary emails. Smith Kline Beecham, the Philadelphia-based pharmaceutical firm, charges business units fees based on the number and length of email messages. Computer Associates shuts down the email system every day for two hours. Many firms, and individuals and teams, set aside time every day, free from emails and phones, to work on their primary tasks. They often report this to be the most productive part of the day.[37]

Communications Networks

The volume of communication an individual receives depends in part on his or her position in decision-making structures (see Figure 15.2).[38] Independent, decentralized decision makers have the lowest communication needs. Local store managers or local banks may make their own decisions without conferring with other stores, branches, or headquarters. More centralized decision makers need and receive greater volumes of relevant information from different sites and from people both inside and outside the firm. Having such a central location in a network helps your job performance—unless the network is made up of people who don't like each other and hinder each other's careers![39] Some decentralized decision makers are so interconnected that they require even more information than centralized ones. They make independent decisions, but their decisions must be based on vast amounts of information from remote sites available through electronic or other networks. As

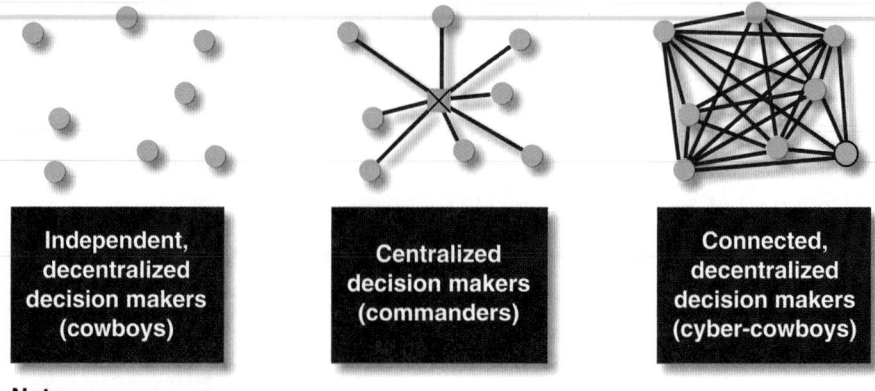

Note

🔵 = Places where actions are taken and information is generated

✖ = Centralized decision maker

FIGURE 15.2
Three Communication
Networks

shown in Figure 15.2, information needs to be brought to all the decentralized decision makers, not just a single centralized one.

Such complex networks of communications are exaggerated even further when we consider interorganization collaborations, discussed in previous chapters (and illustrated in Figure 15.3).[40] Firms today commonly are in a number of external networks, simultaneously and in succession. Even greater attention must be paid not only to the strategic decisions surrounding the partnerships, but also to having an adequate information technology infrastructure through which people communicate and cooperate effectively.

FIGURE 15.3
Levels of Complexity in
Technology Collaboration
and Networks

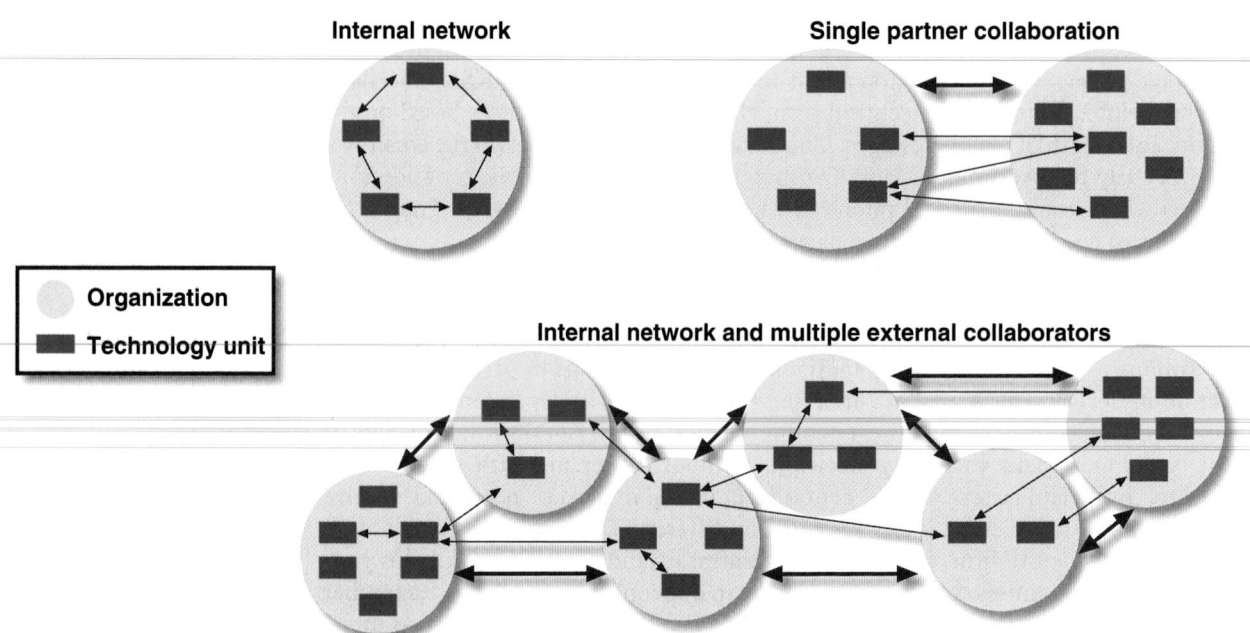

TABLE 15.2
Sample Situations of Media
Choice

Situation 1: A midsize construction firm wants to announce a new employee benefit program.

Poor choice: Memo   **Better choice:** Small group meetings

Rationale: The memo does not offer the feedback potential necessary to explain what may be seen as obscure information. Moreover, with these employees there is a possibility of literacy problems. A group meeting will allow for an oral explanation after which participants can more easily ask questions about any of the complex materials.

Situation 2: A manager wishes to confirm a meeting time with 10 employees.

Poor choice: Phone   **Better choice:** Voice mail or email

Rationale: For a simple message like this, there is no need to use a rich medium when a lean one will do the job.

Situation 3: Increase enthusiasm in midsize insurance company for a program that asks employees from different departments to work on the same project team.

Poor choice: Email, voice mail   **Better choice:** Face-to-face, telephone

Rationale: In situations requiring persuasion the sender must be able to quickly adapt the message to the receiver in order to counter objections. This is not a feature of either email or v-mail. Face-to-face communication offers the sender the greatest flexibility. The phone is the next best alternative.

Situation 4: A group of engineers who are geographically dispersed want to exchange design ideas with one another.

Poor choice: Teleconference   **Better choice:** Fax, computer conference

Rationale: A teleconference is apt to overly accentuate the status and personality differences among the engineers. Fax or computer conferencing would allow the quality of the ideas to be the central focus of interaction. Moreover, quick feedback is still possible with these media.

Situation 5: Describe a straightforward but somewhat detailed and updated version of a voice mail system to 1,000 employees who are geographically dispersed.

Poor choice: Newsletter   **Better choice:** Videotape

Rationale: If employees are already persuaded of the updated system's merit, you can probably use the newsletter. But a videotape graphically conveys information that requires demonstration, and will educate people about procedures.

SOURCE: From *Communicating for Managerial Effectiveness* by P.G. Clampitt. Copyright © 1991 by Sage Publications, Inc. Reprinted by permission of Sage Publications, Inc.

As complex as communication networks can be, you can take steps to simplify them. For example, a global customer-account-management team established two ground rules: (1) whenever a member had any meeting with a customer, the member was to send a briefing to all team members; and (2) they designated a primary contact on the team for each customer, with no one else on the team authorized to discuss or decide strategies or policies with the customer. If contacted by a customer, team members would direct the customer to the appropriate contact person. These steps simplified communication channels and greatly reduced contradictory and confusing messages.[41]

Media Richness

Some communication channels convey more information than others. The amount of information a medium conveys is called **media richness.**[42] The more information or cues a medium sends to the receiver, the "richer" the

media richness

The degree to which a communication channel conveys information.

medium is.[43] The richest media are more personal than technological, provide quick feedback, allow lots of descriptive language, and send different types of cues. Thus, face-to-face communication is the richest medium because it offers a variety of cues in addition to words: tone of voice, facial expression, body language, and other nonverbal signals. It also allows more descriptive language than, say, a memo does. In addition, it affords more opportunity for the receiver to give feedback to and ask questions of the sender, turning one-way into two-way communication.

The telephone is less rich than face-to-face communication, electronic mail is less rich yet, and memos are the least rich medium. In general, you should send difficult and unusual messages through richer media, transmit simple and routine messages through less rich media like memos, and use multiple media for important messages that you want to ensure people attend to and understand.[44] You should also consider factors such as which medium your receiver prefers, the preferred communication style in your organization, and cost.[45] Table 15.2 gives some sample situations for choosing channels based on the message and the audience.

Improving Communication Skills

In recent years, employers have been dismayed by college graduates' poor communication skills. A demonstrated ability to communicate effectively makes a job candidate more attractive and distinguishes him or her from others. You can do many things to improve your communication skills, both as a sender and as a receiver.

Improving Sender Skills

Senders can improve their skills in making persuasive presentations, writing, language use, and sending nonverbal messages.

Presentation and Persuasion Skills   As a manager, you will be called on frequently to "state your case" on a variety of issues. You will have information and perhaps an opinion or proposal to present to others. Typically, your goal will be to "sell" your idea. In other words, your challenge will be to persuade others to go along with your personal recommendation. As a leader, some of your toughest challenges will arise when people do not want to do what has to be done. Leaders have to be persuasive to get people "on board."[46]

In some organizations, as often in life, how you say things may count for more than what you say. If this is the case in your organization, you might strive for style and entertainment in your presentations. But as a manager, you should establish a communication culture that emphasizes accuracy, integrity, fairness, and objectivity rather than mere showmanship and image projection.[47]

Your attitude is very important here. Persuasion is not what a lot of people think it is: merely selling an idea or convincing others to see things your way. Don't assume that it takes a John Wayne approach, with a one-shot effort to make an up-front hard sell, and resisting compromise.[48] It usually is more constructive to consider it a process of learning from each other and negotiating a shared solution. It requires credibility, which comes from expertise and relationships in which people know you are trustworthy. Effective persuasion is an attempt to find an emotional connection with the other person and a common ground on which mutual interests meet.[49]

In conveying an important message, it is useful to be *redundant*. This is not to say that you should stand in front of your audience and repeat yourself over and over again. It means you should state your viewpoint in a variety of ways and at different times with different audiences. Great leaders convey their visions by seizing every opportunity to talk about them and communicate them tirelessly until their followers "buy into" the message.

The most powerful and persuasive messages are simple and informative, are told with stories and anecdotes, and convey excitement.[50] GE's Jack Welch had tremendous success with his simple message to all employees of speed, simplicity, and self-confidence. Lawrence Bossidy of AlliedSignal took a similar approach by talking frequently about the three P's: performance (meeting the numbers), portfolio (getting the right product mix), and people (attracting and motivating employees).[51] And the credible communicator backs up the message with actions consistent with the words.

Writing Skills   Effective writing is more than correct spelling, punctuation, and grammar (although these help!). Good writing above all requires clear, logical thinking.[52] The act of writing can be a powerful aid to thinking, because you have to think about what you really want to say and what the logic is behind your message.[53]

You want people to find your memos and reports readable and interesting. Strive for clarity, organization, readability, and brevity.[54] Brevity is much appreciated by readers who are overloaded with documents, including wordy memos. Use a dictionary and a thesaurus, and avoid fancy words. Charles Krauthammer, the newspaper columnist, praises brevity in a column titled "Make it Snappy."[55] He notes that Ian Wilmut, the scientist who cloned the sheep Dolly, announced his findings to the scientific community in a three-page journal article. Two of the greatest speeches in American history fit on part of one wall at the Lincoln memorial. The Truman doctrine, which set the course of American foreign policy for half a century, took only 18 minutes to deliver. Watson and Crick's article announcing the discovery of the structure of DNA was just over one page.

Your first draft rarely is as good as it could be. If you have time, revise it. Take the reader into consideration. Go through your entire letter, memo, or report and delete all unnecessary words, sentences, and paragraphs. Use specific, concrete words rather than abstract phrases. Instead of saying, "A period of unfavorable weather set in," say, "It rained every day for a week."

Be critical of your own writing. If you want to improve, start by reading *The Elements of Style* by William Strunk and E. B. White and the most recent edition of *The Little, Brown Handbook*.[56]

Language   Word choice can enhance or interfere with communication effectiveness. For example, jargon is actually a form of shorthand and can make communication more effective when both the sender and the receiver know the buzzwords. But when the receiver is unfamiliar with the jargon, misunderstandings result. When people from different functional areas or disciplines communicate with one another, misunderstandings often occur because of "language" barriers. As in writing, simplicity usually helps.

Therefore, whether speaking or writing, you should consider the receiver's background and adjust your language accordingly. When you are receiving, don't assume that your understanding is the same as the speaker's intentions. Japanese people use the simple word *hai* (yes) to convey that they understand what is being said; it does not necessarily mean that they agree. Asian businesspeople rarely use the direct "no," using more subtle or tangential ways of disagreeing.[57]

Global teams fail when members have difficulties communicating because of language, cultural, and geographic barriers. Heterogeneity harms team functioning at first. But when they develop ways to interact and communicate, teams develop a common identity and perform well.[58]

When conducting business overseas, try to learn something about the other country's language and customs. Americans are less likely to do this than people from some other cultures; most Americans do not consider a foreign language necessary for doing business abroad, and a significant majority of U.S. firms do not require employees sent abroad to know the local language.[59] But those who do will have a big edge over their competitors who do not.[60] Making the effort to learn the local language builds rapport, sets a proper tone for doing business, aids in adjustment to culture shock, and especially can help you "get inside" the other culture.[61] You will learn more about how people think, feel, and behave, both in their lives and in their business dealings.

The challenges of language differences in communication are not merely a matter of convenience, preference, or customers. In extreme cases, they can be a matter of life and death. Airline pilots, copilots, and first officers sometimes speak different languages and have only a rudimentary knowledge of their partners' languages. In Korea, few ground controllers speak English, so American pilots are required by law to be paired with a Korean first officer. But what if a crisis arises, and the American and the Korean have trouble understanding each other? The problem goes beyond language to cultural norms. Korea's rigid hierarchical, authoritarian culture means that those of lower rank or younger age hesitate to volunteer information, ask questions, or make suggestions.

Lewis and Clark needed Charbonneau and Sacagawea to help them communicate with the Indian tribes they encountered on their expedition. Lewis spoke English to Charbonneau's partner, who translated into French, which Charbonneau then translated into Hidatsu, the language spoken throughout the Upper Midwest. But when they reached the Pacific, the Indians there spoke only Walla Walla, a language not known to any of them. Fortunately, years before they had captured a Shoshone warrior who spoke both Hidatsu and Walla Walla. Without this chain of translators, Lewis and Clark may not have rewritten American history.

And consider the war in Afghanistan: The United States and its partners were trying to defeat an Arabic-speaking force (Osama bin Laden and his collaborators); defeat a Pashto-speaking faction (the Taliban); strengthen the Northern Alliance, whose members speak Uzbek, Tajik, and Dari; manage a coalition whose members speak those languages and several others; and rebuild a country capable of getting along with its neighbors, who speak Chinese and Farsi.

English appears to be accepted everywhere and to be spoken by almost everyone. But English is the mother tongue of only 5 percent of the world's population, and people much prefer to speak their own languages. Many businesspeople from other countries are tired of native English speakers assuming it is their responsibility to make the extra effort and speak English. They will respond better to those who don't insist on English. As the examples above should make clear, sometimes knowing other languages and having skilled interpreters are nothing short of essential.

SOURCES: S. Glain, "Language Barrier Proves Dangerous in Korea's Skies," *The Wall Street Journal*, October 4, 1994, pp. B1, B16; M. Posner, "Beating the Language Barrier," *Credit Management*, October 2001, p. 16; J. Freivalds, *Communication World*, December/January 2001/2002, pp. 8–11.

Nonverbal Skills

As you know, people send and interpret signals other than those that are spoken or written. Nonverbal messages can support or undermine the stated message. Often, nonverbal cues make a greater impact than other signals. In employees' eyes, managers' actions often speak louder than the words managers choose.

In conversation, except when you intend to convey a negative message, you should give nonverbal signals that express warmth, respect, concern, a feeling of equality, and a willingness to listen. Negative nonverbal signals show coolness, disrespect, lack of interest, and a feeling of superiority.[62] The following suggestions can help you send positive nonverbal signals.

First, use *time* appropriately. Avoid keeping your employees waiting to see you. Devote sufficient time to your meetings with them, and communicate frequently with them to signal your interest in their concerns. Second, make your *office arrangement* conducive to open communication. A seating arrangement that avoids separation of people helps establish a warm, cooperative atmosphere (in contrast, an arrangement in which you sit behind your desk and your subordinate sits before you creates a more intimidating, authoritative environment).[63] Third, remember your *body language*. Research indicates that facial expression and tone of voice can account for 90 percent of the communication between two people.[64] Several nonverbal body signals convey a positive attitude toward the other person: assuming a position close to the person;

gesturing frequently; maintaining eye contact; smiling; having an open body orientation, such as facing the other person directly; uncrossing the arms; and leaning forward to convey interest in what the other person is saying.

Silence is an interesting nonverbal situation. The average American is said to spend about twice as many hours per day in conversation as the average Japanese.[65] North Americans tend to talk to fill silences. Japanese allow long silences to develop, believing they can get to know people better. Japanese believe that two people with good rapport will know each other's thoughts. The need to use words implies a lack of understanding.

Nonverbal Signals in Different Countries   Here are just a few nonverbal mistakes that Americans might make in other countries.[66] Nodding the head up and down in Bulgaria means no. The American thumb-and-first-finger circular A-OK gesture is vulgar in Brazil, Singapore, Russia, and Paraguay. The head is sacred in Buddhist cultures, so you must never touch someone's head. In Muslim cultures, never touch or eat with the left hand, which is thought unclean. Crossing your ankle over your knee is rude in Indonesia, Thailand, and Syria. Don't point your finger toward yourself in Germany or Switzerland—it insults the other person.

You also need to correctly interpret the nonverbal signals of others. Chinese scratch their ears and cheeks to show happiness. Greeks puff air after they receive a compliment. Hondurans touch their fingers below their eyes to show disbelief or caution. Japanese indicate embarrassment or "no" by sucking in air and hissing through their teeth. Vietnamese look to the ground with their heads down to show respect. Compared to Americans, Russians use fewer facial expressions, and Scandinavians fewer hand gestures, whereas people in Mediterranean and Latin cultures may gesture and touch more. Brazilians are more likely than Americans to interrupt, Arabs to speak loudly, and Asians to respect silence.

Use these examples not to stereotype but to remember that people have different styles and to aid in communication accuracy.

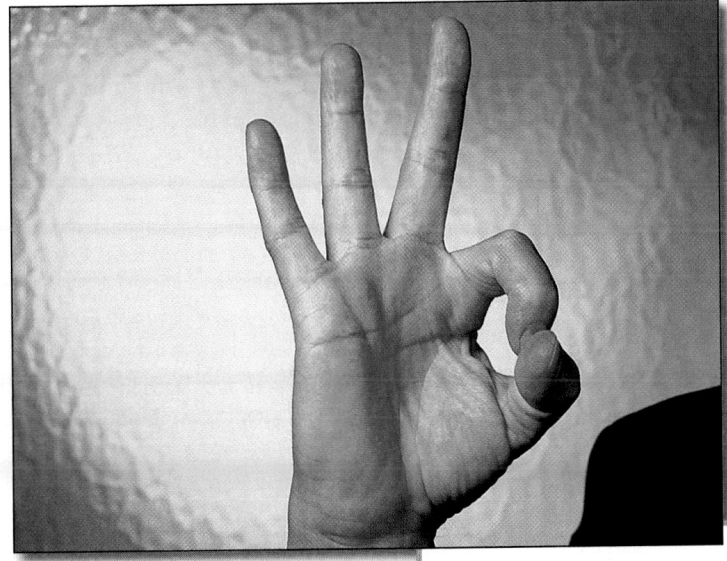

The American thumb-and-first-finger circular "OK" gesture is vulgar in Brazil, Singapore, Russia, and Paraguay.

Improving Receiver Skills

Once you become effective at sending oral, written, and nonverbal messages, you are halfway home toward becoming a complete communicator. However, you must also develop adequate receiving capabilities. Receivers need good listening, reading, and observational skills.

Listening   In today's demanding work environment, managers need better listening skills.[67] Although it is easy to assume that good listening is easy and natural, in fact it is difficult and not nearly as common as needed.

A basic technique called *reflection* will help a manager listen effectively.[68] **Reflection** is a process by which a person states what he or she believes the other person is saying. This technique places a greater emphasis on listening than on talking. When both parties actively engage in reflection, they get into each other's frame of reference rather than listening and responding from their own. The result is more accurate two-way communication.

reflection
Process by which a person states what he or she believes the other person is saying.

The best-known corporate effort to heighten managers' listening skills was based on an advertising theme—"We understand how important it is to listen"—that reflected a basic philosophy and way of doing business.[69] The company's senior management development specialists created listening training seminars for company personnel, drawing from a study of the 100 best and 100 worst listeners in the freshman class at the University of Minnesota. Table 15.3 summarizes these effective listening techniques.

Listening begins with personal contact. Staying in the office, keeping the door closed, and eating lunch at the desk are sometimes necessary to get pressing work done, but that is no way to stay on top of what's going on. Better to walk the halls, initiate conversations and go to lunch even with people outside your area, have coffee in a popular gathering place, and maybe even move your desk onto the factory floor.[70]

When a manager takes time to really listen to and get to know people, they think, "She's showing an interest in me" or "He's letting me know that I matter" or "She values my ideas and contributions." Trust develops. Listening and learning from others are even more important for innovation than for routine work. Successful change and innovation come through lots of human contact.

Reading   Illiteracy is a significant problem in the United States. Even if illiteracy is not a problem in your organization, reading mistakes are common and costly. As a receiver, for your own benefit, read memos as soon as possible, before it's too late to respond. You may skim most of your reading materials, but read important memos, documents, and passages slowly and carefully. Note important points for later referral.

TABLE 15.3
Ten Keys to Effective Listening

1. *Find an area of interest.* Even if you decide the topic is dull, ask yourself, "What is the speaker saying that I can use?"

2. *Judge content, not delivery.* Don't get caught up in the speaker's personality, mannerisms, speaking voice, or clothing. Instead, try to learn what the speaker knows.

3. *Hold your fire.* Rather than getting immediately excited by what the speaker seems to be saying, withhold evaluation until you understand the speaker's message.

4. *Listen for ideas.* Don't get bogged down in all the facts and details; focus on central ideas.

5. *Be flexible.* Have several systems for note taking, and use the system best suited to the speaker's style. Don't take too many notes or try to force everything said by a disorganized speaker into a formal outline.

6. *Resist distraction.* Close the door, shut off the radio, move closer to the person talking, or ask him or her to speak louder. Don't look out the window or at papers on your desk.

7. *Exercise your mind.* Some people tune out when the material gets difficult. Develop an appetite for a good mental challenge.

8. *Keep your mind open.* Many people get overly emotional when they hear words referring to their most deeply held convictions, for example, *union, subsidy, import, Republican* or *Democrat,* and *big business.* Try not to let your emotions interfere with comprehension.

9. *Capitalize on thought speed.* Take advantage of the fact that most people talk at a rate of about 125 words per minute, but most of us think at about four times that rate. Use those extra 400 words per minute to think about what the speaker is saying rather than turning your thoughts to something else.

10. *Work at listening.* Spend some energy. Don't just pretend you're paying attention. Show interest. Good listening is hard work, but the benefits outweigh the costs.

SOURCE: Ralph G. Nichols, "Listening Is a 10-Part Skill," *Nation's Business* 45 (July 1957), pp. 56–60. Cited in R. C. Huseman, C. M. Logue, and D. L. Freshley, eds., *Readings in Interpersonal and Organizational Communication* (Boston: Allyn & Bacon, 1977).

Consider taking courses to increase your reading speed and comprehension skills. Finally, don't limit your reading to items about your particular job skill or technical expertise; read materials that fall outside your immediate concerns. You never know when a creative idea that will help you in your work will be inspired by a novel, a biography, a sports story, or an article about a problem in another business or industry.

Observing   Effective communicators are also capable of observing and interpreting nonverbal communications. (As Yogi Berra said, "You can observe a lot by watching.") For example, by reading nonverbal cues a presenter can determine how her talk is going and adjust her approach if necessary. Some companies train their sales forces to interpret the nonverbal signals of potential customers. People can also decode nonverbal signals to determine whether a sender is being truthful or deceitful. Deceitful communicators maintain less eye contact, make either more or fewer body movements than usual, and smile either too much or too little. Verbally, they offer fewer specifics than do truthful senders.[71]

A vital source of useful observations comes from personally visiting plants and other locations to get a firsthand view of operations.[72] Many corporate executives rely heavily on reports from the field and don't travel to remote locations to observe firsthand what is going on. Even great reports are no substitute for actually seeing things happen in practice. Frequent visits to the field, and careful observation, can help a manager develop deep understanding of current operations, future prospects, and ideas for how to fully exploit capabilities.[73]

States Michael Eisner of Disney, "Sometimes you just have to be there with your people. You have to be in the same room with them, look them in the eyes, hear their voices. I'll tell you one thing. Most of the bad decisions I've made I've made while teleconferencing. In creative companies, you have to be able to read body language—see the look in people's eyes when an idea is launched, see whether they fall asleep" (p. 122).[74]

Of course, you must *accurately interpret* what you observe. A Canadian conducting business with a high-ranking official in Kuwait was surprised that the meeting was held in an open office and was interrupted constantly.[75] He interpreted the lack of a big, private office and secretary to mean that the Kuwaiti was of low rank and uninterested in doing business, and he lost interest in the deal. The Canadian observed the facts accurately, but his perceptual biases and lack of awareness regarding how norms differ across cultures caused him to misinterpret what he saw.

The Japanese are particularly skilled at interpreting every nuance of voice and gesture, putting most Westerners at a disadvantage.[76] When one is conducting business in Asian or other countries, local guides can be invaluable not only to interpret language but to "decode" behavior at meetings, subtle hints and nonverbal cues, who the key people are, and how the decision-making process operates.

Effective Supervision

Many studies have compared good and poor supervisors' communications skills.[77] Supervisors who receive higher evaluations exhibit several key characteristics. First, they *communicate more information*. For example, they give advance notice of impending changes, explain the reasons behind policies and regulations, and enjoy conversing with their subordinates. Second, effective supervisors *prefer asking and persuading* to telling and demanding (but are capable of using both styles if necessary). Third, they are *sensitive to people's feelings and needs*. For example, they are careful to reprimand privately rather than publicly. Finally, they are *willing, empathic listeners*. They respond with understanding to all questions from employees and give fair consideration to, and are willing to take appropriate action on, complaints and suggestions.

Thus, effective managers are more "communication minded" than are ineffective managers. People who lack confidence in their communication skills, both oral and written, tend to avoid communication situations altogether. This tendency would be a severe handicap for any manager.[78]

Organizational Communication

Being a skilled communicator is essential to being a good manager and team leader. But communication must also be managed throughout the organization. Every minute of every day, countless bits of information are transmitted through an organization. We will discuss downward, upward, horizontal, and informal communication in organizations.

Downward Communication

downward communication

Information that flows from higher to lower levels in the organization's hierarchy.

Downward communication refers to the flow of information from higher to lower levels in the organization's hierarchy. Examples include a manager giving an assignment to a secretary, a supervisor making an announcement to his subordinates, and a company president delivering a talk to her management team. Downward communication that provides relevant information enhances employee identification with the company, supportive attitudes, and decisions consistent with the organization's objectives.[79]

People must receive the information they need to perform their jobs and become (and remain) loyal members of the organization. But they often lack adequate information.[80] One problem is *information overload:* They are bombarded with so much information that they fail to absorb everything. Much of the information is not very important, but its volume causes a lot of relevant information to be lost.

A second problem is a *lack of openness* between managers and employees. Managers may believe "No news is good news," "I don't have time to keep them informed of everything they want to know," or "It's none of their business, anyway." Some managers withhold information even if sharing it would be useful.

A third problem is *filtering,* introduced earlier in the chapter. When messages are passed from one person to another, some information is left out. When a message passes through many people, each transmission may cause further information losses. The message can also be distorted as people add their own words or interpretations.

Filtering poses serious problems in organizations. As messages are communicated downward through many organizational levels, much information is lost. The data in Figure 15.4 suggest that by the time messages reach the people for whom they are intended, the receivers may get very little useful information.

The fewer the number of authority levels through which communications must pass, the less information will be lost or distorted. Recall from earlier chapters that

FIGURE 15.4
Information Loss in Downward Communication

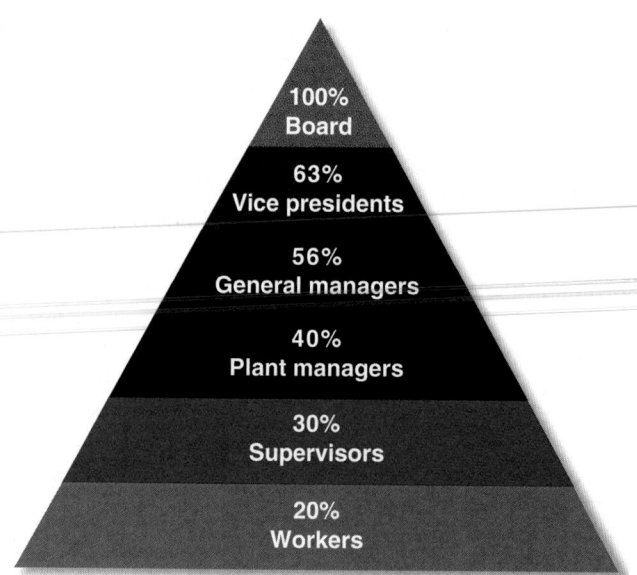

100%
Board

63%
Vice presidents

56%
General managers

40%
Plant managers

30%
Supervisors

20%
Workers

companies are reducing the number of hierarchical layers. You can now see that the flatter organization offers another advantage: fewer problems caused by filtering of information as it cascades through many layers.

Coaching   Some of the most important downward communications occur when managers give performance feedback to their direct reports. We discussed earlier the importance of giving feedback and positive reinforcement when it is deserved. It is also important to explicitly discuss poor performance and areas that can be improved.

Coaching is dialogue with a goal of helping another be more effective and achieve his or her full potential on the job.[81] When done properly, coaching develops executives and enhances performance.[82] When people have performance problems, or exhibit behaviors that need to be changed, coaching is often the best way to help a person change and succeed. And coaching is not just for poor performers; as even the greatest athletes know, it is for anyone who is good and aspires to excellence. Although coaches for executives sometimes are hired from the outside,[83] it often is incumbent upon managers to be coaches themselves.

> **coaching**
>
> Dialogue with a goal of helping another be more effective and achieve his or her full potential on the job.

Companies such as Coca-Cola use coaching as an essential part of their executive development process. When done well, coaching is true dialogue between two committed people engaged in joint problem solving. Thus, it is far more than an occasion for highlighting poor performance, delivering reprimands, or giving advice. Good coaching requires achieving real understanding of the problem, the person, and the situation; jointly generating ideas for what to do; and encouraging the person to improve. Good coaches ask a lot of questions, listen well, provide input, and also encourage others to think for themselves. Effective coaching requires honesty, calmness, and supportiveness—all aided by a sincere desire to help. The ultimate and longest-lasting form of help is to help people think through and solve their own problems.

Downward Communication in Difficult Times   Adequate downward communication can be particularly valuable during difficult times. During corporate mergers and acquisitions, employees are anxious as they wonder how the changes will affect them. Ideally—and ethically—top management communicates with employees about the change as early as possible.

But some argue against that approach, maintaining that informing employees about the reorganization might cause them to quit too early. Then too, top management often cloisters itself, prompting rumors and anxiety. CEOs and other senior execs are surrounded by lawyers, investment bankers, and so on—people who are paid merely to make the deal happen, not to make it work. Yet with the people who are affected by the deal, you must increase, not decrease, communication.[84]

In a merger of two Fortune 500 companies, two plants received very different information.[85] All employees at both plants received the initial letter from the CEO announcing the merger. But after that, one plant was kept in the dark while the other was continually filled in on what was happening. Top management gave employees information about layoffs, transfers, promotions and demotions, and changes in pay, jobs, and benefits.

Which plant do you think fared better as the difficult transitional months unfolded? In both plants, the merger decreased employees' job satisfaction and commitment to the organization and increased their belief that the company was untrustworthy, dishonest, and uncaring. In the plant whose employees got little information, these problems persisted for a long time. But in the plant where employees received complete information, the situation stabilized and attitudes improved toward their normal levels. Full communication not only helped employees survive an anxious period; it served a symbolic value by signaling care and concern for employees. Without such communications, employee reactions to a merger or acquisition may be so negative as to undermine the corporate strategy.

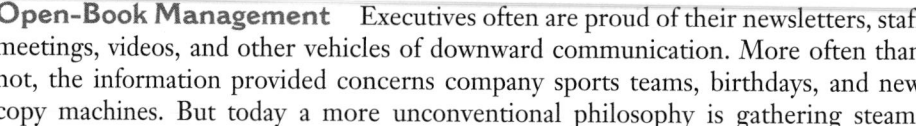

Open-Book Management   Executives often are proud of their newsletters, staff meetings, videos, and other vehicles of downward communication. More often than not, the information provided concerns company sports teams, birthdays, and new copy machines. But today a more unconventional philosophy is gathering steam.

open-book management

Practice of sharing with employees at all levels of the organization vital information previously meant for management's eyes only.

Open-book management is the practice of sharing with employees at all levels of the organization vital information previously meant for management's eyes only. This includes financial goals, income statements, budgets, sales, forecasts, and other relevant data about company performance and prospects.

These practices are controversial, as many managers prefer to keep such information to themselves. Sharing strategic plans and financial information with employees could lead to leaks to competitors or to employee dissatisfaction with compensation. But the companies that share this information claim a favorable impact on motivation and productivity. Cecil Ursprung, president and CEO of Reflexite Corporation in New Britain, Connecticut, said, "Why would you tell 5 percent of the team what the score was and not the other 95 percent?"[86]

Father of scientific management Frederick Taylor early in the 20th century would have considered opening the books to all employees "idiotic."[87] Almost everyone else would have also, including top executives, middle managers, union leaders, and employees. But then Springfield ReManufacturing Corporation, which was on the brink of collapse, tried it.[88] The company turned around dramatically, achieving profitability and a small measure of fame as it publicized its success in *Inc.* magazine and elsewhere. Other small companies joined the movement. Now, bigger companies like Amoco Canada, R. R. Donnelley, Wabash National, Baxter Healthcare, and AES Corporation are doing it as well. AES, a global power producer listed on the New York Stock Exchange, shares so much financial data with its employees that every one of them has been declared an insider for stock-trading purposes.

Opening the books, done properly, is a complete communications system that makes sense to people on the shop floor just as it does to the top executives. The basic steps toward open-book management include:[89] (1) provide the information; (2) teach basic finance and the basics of the business; (3) empower people to make decisions based on what they know; and (4) make sure everyone shares directly in the company's success (and risks), such as through stock ownership and bonuses. Table 15.4 provides more detail.

This is dramatically different from the traditional closed-book approach in which people may or may not have a clue about how the company is doing, may or may not believe the things that management tells them, and may or may not believe that their personal performance makes a difference. You can see, then, the potential impact on motivation of communication that helps people understand why it is important for

TABLE 15.4
Principles of Open-Book Management

1. Turn the management of a business into a game that employees can win.
2. Open the books and share financial and operating information with employees.
3. Teach employees to understand the financial statements of the company.
4. Show employees how their work influences financial results.
5. Link nonfinancial measures to financial results.
6. Target priority areas and empower employees to make improvements.
7. Review results together and keep employees accountable.
8. Post results and celebrate successes.
9. Distribute bonus awards based on employee contributions to financial outcomes.
10. Share the ownership of the company with employees.

SOURCE: T. R. V. Davis, "Open-Book Management: Its Promise and Pitfalls," *Organizational Dynamics*, Winter 1997, pp. 7–20. Copyright © 1997, with permission from Elsevier Science.

them, and everyone, to care about business results. It can motivate people to figure out how they can contribute in different ways, to learn new skills, and to work harder and smarter to improve performance.

Upward Communication

Upward communication travels from lower to higher ranks in the hierarchy. Adequate upward communication is important for several reasons.[90] First, managers learn what's going on. Management gains a more accurate picture of subordinates' work, accomplishments, problems, plans, attitudes, and ideas. Second, employees gain from the opportunity to communicate upward. People can relieve some of their frustrations, achieve a stronger sense of participation in the enterprise, and improve morale. Third, effective upward communication facilitates downward communication as good listening becomes a two-way street.

> **upward communication**
> Information that flows from lower to higher levels in the organization's hierarchy.

Boeing's engineers went on strike in 2000 with nearly disastrous consequences for the company. At Boeing, the emphasis had been on downward communication, without much upward communication.[91] But even the downward communications were inadequate, failing to include explanations about major changes, or plans for the future. Upper management failed to listen to or respond to the perceptions, needs, and suggestions of the company's engineers. The lack of attention to upward communication meant that management didn't know about the engineers' low morale, and then was blindsided by the strike. Of course, strikes usually have multiple causes, but poor communications were critical. After the strike, Boeing's new president, Phil Condit, said, "All of us have a greater understanding of what is meant by the issue of "respect." One day I hope we can all look back on this as a turning point, a time when we more clearly recognized the importance of listening to and seeking to understand one another."[92]

The problems common in upward communication are similar to those for downward communication. Managers, like their subordinates, are bombarded with information and may neglect or miss information from below. Furthermore, some employees are not always open with their bosses; in other words, filtering occurs upward as well as downward. People tend to share only good news with their bosses and suppress bad news, because they (1) want to appear competent; (2) mistrust their boss and fear that if he or she finds out about something they have done they will be punished; (3) fear the boss will punish the messenger, even if the reported problem is not that person's fault; or (4) believe they are helping their boss if they shield him or her from problems. For these and other reasons, managers may not learn about important problems.

Managing Upward Communication Generating useful information from below requires doing two things. First, managers should *facilitate* upward communication. For example, they could have an open-door policy and encourage people to use it, have lunch or coffee with employees, pass out surveys that ask specific questions of people, or institute a program for productivity suggestions. These mechanisms are just a few possibilities that will make upward communication easier.

But managers must also *motivate* people to provide valid information. Useful upward communication must be reinforced and not punished. The person who tries to talk to the manager about a problem must not be brushed off consistently. An announced open-door policy must truly be open-door. Also, people must trust their supervisor and know that the manager will not hold a grudge if they deliver negative information.

The manager interested in improving upward communications can ask for employee advice, make informal visits to plants, really think about and respond to employee suggestions, and distribute summaries of new ideas and practices inspired by employee suggestions and actions.[93] For example, many executives practice MBWA (management by wandering around). That term, coined by Ed Carlson of United Airlines, refers simply

BusinessWeek

Upward Communications Are Valuable, but Often Ignored

Sherron Watkins, an Enron vice president, wrote a letter to CEO Kenneth Lay warning that the company might "implode in a wave of accounting scandals." Watkins's letter was triggered by CEO Jeffrey Skilling's sudden resignation. As everyone now knows, her worst fears were realized.

Watkins's letter clearly identified what was wrong: top executives who closed their eyes to (or perhaps encouraged) questionable accounting maneuvers; leaders who ignored ordinary investors and basic principles of accounting; outside auditors and lawyers who were caught in conflicts of interest that led them to fail to question what was going on. Watkins's letter said, "Employees question our accounting propriety consistently and constantly."

Lay talked to Watkins about it for an hour, and ordered an outside investigation. But against Watkins's advice, he appointed the company's longtime Houston law firm, which had worked on many of the suspect partnerships, to investigate. Moreover, Enron and the law firm agreed they would not second-guess Arthur Andersen's audits. The only purpose of the inquiry was to learn if there was any new information that might warrant a broader investigation. The law firm concluded that there was no need for further investigation, although it did warn of a "serious risk of adverse publicity and litigation."

Lay never fully disclosed the partnerships or explained how they would affect investors, but claimed there were no accounting irregularities and no other bad news to come.

Five days after Watkins wrote to Lay, she took her concerns to an Andersen audit partner. He conveyed her concerns to senior Andersen management on the Enron account. As of this writing, it was not clear if they took any action at that time.

Perhaps Skilling and Andersen executives shouldn't have needed a letter and a phone call from Watkins to know that things were amiss. Skilling later claimed in front of the Senate Banking, Housing, and Urban Affairs Committee that he had no idea about the problems. Several senators, said *Business Week*, found it "odd, indeed incomprehensible, that Skilling never caught a whiff that something was rotten at Enron." He blamed his subordinates and his accountants, over and over, for not alerting him to Enron's troubles. A member of Congress said that Skilling seemed "awfully clueless."

SOURCES: L. Woellert, "Skilling's Sequel: Clueless," *Business Week*, February 27, 2002, http://www.businessweek.com/index.html.; W. Zellner, S. F. Anderson, and L. Cohn, "A Hero—and a Smoking-Gun Letter," *Business Week*, January 28, 2002, pp. 34–35.

Enron's Jeff Skilling testifying, but not saying much, to Congress.

to getting out of the office, walking around, and talking frequently and informally with employees.[94]

Horizontal Communication

Much information needs to be shared among people on the same hierarchical level. Such **horizontal communication** can take place among people in the same work team. Other important communication must occur between people in different departments. For example, a purchasing agent discusses a problem with a production engineer and a task force of department heads meets to discuss a particular concern. Communicating with others outside the firm, including Wall Street,[95] is another vital type of horizontal communication.

> **horizontal communication**
> **Information shared among people on the same hierarchical level.**

Horizontal communication has several important functions.[96] First, it allows sharing of information, coordination, and problem solving among units. Second, it helps solve conflicts. Third, by allowing interaction among peers, it provides social and emotional support to people. All these factors contribute to morale and effectiveness.

Managing Horizontal Communication The need for horizontal communication is similar to the need for integration, discussed in Chapter 8. Particularly in complex environments, in which decisions in one unit affect another, information must be shared horizontally. As examples of good horizontal communication, Motorola holds an annual conference for sharing best learnings across functional and business groups throughout the company. NASA colocates scientists from different disciplines. Hewlett-Packard uses common databases for different product groups to share information and ideas.[97]

GE offers a great example of how to use productive horizontal communication as a competitive weapon.[98] GE's businesses could operate completely independently, but each is supposed to help the others. They transfer technical resources, people, information, ideas, and money among themselves. GE accomplishes this high level of communication and cooperation through easy access between divisions and to the CEO; a culture of openness, honesty, trust, and mutual obligation; and quarterly meetings in which all the top executives get together informally to share information and ideas. The same kinds of things are done at lower levels as well.

Informal Communication

Organizational communications differ in formality. *Formal communications* are official, organization-sanctioned episodes of information transmission. They can move upward, downward, or horizontally and often are prearranged and necessary for performing some task.

Informal communication is more unofficial. People gossip;[99] employees complain about their boss; people talk about their favorite sports teams; work teams tell newcomers how to get by.

The **grapevine** is the social network of informal communications that helps people interpret the organization, translates management's formal messages into "employee language," and conveys information that the formal system leaves unsaid. However, the grapevine can be destructive when irrelevant or erroneous gossip and rumors proliferate and harm operations.[100]

> **grapevine**
> **Informal communication network.**

Managing Informal Communication Most of the suggestions for improving personal skills and organizational communication—writing, speaking, listening, facilitating and reinforcing upward communication, and so on—typically are applied to improving formal communication. But they can help improve informal communication as well. Additional considerations apply to managing informal communication effectively.

Rumors start over any number of topics, including who's leaving, who's getting a promotion, salaries, job security, and costly mistakes. Rumors can destroy people's faith and trust in the company—and in each other. But the grapevine cannot be eliminated. Therefore, managers need to *work with* the grapevine.

The grapevine can be managed in several ways.[101] First, if the manager hears a story that could get out of hand, he or she should *talk to the key people* involved to get the facts and their perspectives.

Second, suggestions for *preventing* rumors from starting include: explain things that are important but have not been explained; dispel uncertainties by providing facts; and work to establish open communications and trust over time.[102]

Third, *neutralize* rumors once they have started: disregard the rumor if it is ridiculous (has no credence with others); openly confirm any parts that are true; make public comments (no comment is seen as a confirmation of the rumor); deny the rumor, if the denial is based in truth (don't make false denials); make sure communications about the issue are consistent; select a spokesperson of appropriate rank and knowledge; and hold town meetings if needed.[103]

Boundarylessness

Many executives and management scholars today consider free access to information in all directions to be an organizational imperative. Jack Welch of GE coined the term *boundarylessness*. A **boundaryless organization** is one in which there are no barriers to information flow. Instead of boundaries separating people, jobs, processes, and places, ideas, information, decisions, and actions move to where they are most needed.[104] This does not imply a random free-for-all of unlimited communication and information overload. It implies information available *as needed* moving quickly and easily enough so that the organization functions far better as a whole than as separate parts.[105]

boundaryless organization

Organization in which there are no barriers to information flow.

As GE's chief learning officer, Steve Kerr said to managers, "I bet every one of you goes home at night with stuff in your head that would help the company . . . and you don't tell your boss" because "it's awkward or risky. Imagine if you could just unleash the power of the collective knowledge right in this room; imagine the good it would do."[106] Kerr uses the metaphor of the organization as a house having three kinds of boundaries: the floors and ceilings, the walls that separate the rooms, and the outside walls. These barriers[107] correspond in organizations to the boundaries

GE's successful Workout program shows the benefits of open dialogue across boundaries.

between different organizational levels, different units and departments, and the organization and its external stakeholders—for example, suppliers and customers. GE adds a fourth wall: global boundaries separating domestic from global operations.

GE's famous Workout program is a series of meetings for business members across multiple hierarchical levels, characterized by extremely frank, tough discussions that break down vertical boundaries. Workout has involved over 222,000 GE people; in any given week over 20,000 are participating in a Workout program.[108] Workout is also done with customers and suppliers, breaking down outside boundaries.

GE uses plenty of other techniques to break down boundaries, as well. It relentlessly benchmarks competitors and companies in other industries to learn best practices all over the world. GE places different functions together physically, such as engineering and manufacturing. It shares services across units. And it sometimes shares physical locations with its customers.

At the beginning of the chapter, we talked about the importance of open dialogue. Boundaryless organizations intentionally create dialogue across boundaries, turning barriers into permeable membranes. As the GE people put it, people from different parts of the organization need to learn "how to talk."[109] They must also learn "how to walk." That is, dialogue is essential, but must be followed by commensurate action.

KEY TERMS

Boundaryless organization, p. 474

Coaching, p. 469

Communication, p. 452

Dialogue, p. 452

Discussion, p. 452

Downward communication, p. 468

Filtering, p. 454

Grapevine, p. 473

Horizontal communication, p. 473

Media richness, p. 461

One-way communication, p. 453

Open-book management, p. 470

Perception, p. 453

Reflection, p. 465

Two-way communication, p. 453

Upward communication, p. 471

Virtual office, p. 458

SUMMARY OF LEARNING OBJECTIVES

Now that you have studied Chapter 15, you should know:

The important advantages of two-way communication.

One-way communication flows from the sender to the receiver, with no feedback loop. In two-way communication, each person is both a sender and a receiver as both parties provide and react to information. One-way communication is faster and easier but less accurate than two-way; two-way communication is slower and more difficult, but is more accurate and results in better performance.

Communication problems to avoid.

The communication process involves a sender who conveys information to a receiver. Problems in communication can occur in all stages: encoding, transmission, decoding, and interpreting. Noise in the system further complicates communication, creating more distortion. Moreover, feedback may be unavailable or misleading. Subjective perceptions and filtering add to the possibility of error.

When and how to use the various communications channels.

Communications are sent through oral, written, and electronic channels. All have important advantages and disadvantages that should be considered before choosing a channel. Electronic media have a huge impact on interpersonal and organizational communications and make possible the virtual office. Key advantages of electronic media are speed, cost, and efficiency, but the downsides are also significant, including information overload. Media richness, or how much and what sort of information a channel conveys, is one factor to consider as you decide which channels to use and how to use them both efficiently and effectively.

Ways to become a better "sender" and "receiver" of information.

Practice writing, be critical of your work, and revise. Train yourself as a speaker. Use language carefully and well, and work to overcome cross-cultural language differences. Be alert to the nonverbal signals that you send, including your use of time as perceived by other people. Know the common bad listening habits, and work to overcome them. Read widely, and engage in careful, firsthand observation and interpretation.

How to improve downward, upward, and horizontal communication.

Actively manage communications in all directions. Implement the guidelines discussed in the first part of the chapter, practice dialogue more than discussion, and engage in two-way communication more than one-way. Make information available to others. Useful approaches to downward communication include coaching, special communications during difficult periods, and open-book management. You should also both facilitate and motivate people to communicate upward. Many mechanisms exist for enhancing horizontal communications.

How to work with the company grapevine.

The informal flow of information can contribute as much as formal communication can to organizational effectiveness and morale. Managers must understand that the grapevine cannot be eliminated, and should be managed actively. Many of the suggestions for managing formal communications apply also to managing the grapevine. Moreover, managers can take steps to prevent rumors or neutralize the ones that do arise.

The advantages and characteristics of the boundaryless organization.

Boundaries—psychological if not physical—exist between different organizational levels, units, and organizations and external stakeholders. The ideal boundaryless organization is one in which there are no barriers to information flow. Ideas, information, decisions, and actions move to where they are most needed. Information is available as needed, freely accessible, so the organization as a whole functions far better than as separate parts.

DISCUSSION QUESTIONS

1. Think of an occasion when you faced a miscommunication problem. What do you think caused the problem? How do you think it should have been handled better?

2. Have you ever *not* given someone information or opinions that perhaps you should have? Why? Was it the right thing to do? Why or why not? What would cause you to be glad that you provided (or withheld) negative or difficult information? What would cause you to regret providing/withholding it?

3. Think back to "discussions" and "dialogues" you have heard. Talk about the differences between a discussion and a dialogue. How can a discussion be turned into a constructive dialogue?

4. Share with the class some of your experiences—both good and bad—with electronic media.

5. Report examples of "mixed signals" you have received (or sent). How can you reduce the potential for misunderstanding and misperception as you communicate with others?

6. What makes you want to say to someone, "You're not listening!"?

7. What do you think about the practice of open-book management? What would you think about it if you were running your own company?

8. Discuss organizational rumors you have heard: what they were about, how they got started, how accurate they were,

and how people reacted to them. What lessons can you learn from these episodes?

9. Refer to the section on "The Virtual Office." What do you think will be the long-term impact of the mobile office on job satisfaction and performance? If you were a manager, how would you maximize the benefits and minimize the drawbacks? If you worked in this environment, how would you manage yourself to maximize your performance and avoid burnout?

10. Have you ever made or seen mistakes due to people not speaking a common language well? How do you or will you deal with others who do not speak the same language as you?

11. Have you ever tried to coach someone? What did you do well, and what mistakes did you make? How can you become a better coach?

12. Have you ever been coached by someone? What did he or she do well, and what mistakes were made? How was it for you to be on the receiving end of the coaching, and how did you respond? What is required to be successful as the "receiver" of someone else's coaching attempts?

13. Think about how companies communicate with Wall Street and the media, and how analysts on TV communicate with viewers. What concepts from the chapter apply, and how can you become a more astute "consumer" of such information?

Would You Really Do It?

Imagine that you own and manage a small or midsize company. You pick the industry; you pick the location. Imagine that the firm is all yours.

You read in *Inc.* or *Fast Company* or *Harvard Business Review* about the latest management innovation: open-book management. You read about the original success story: Jack Stack bought Springfield ReManufacturing from International Harvester in 1983. It was collapsing after being rocked by a highly leveraged buyout. It had a first-year operating loss of about $60,000, over 100 employees who needed to be paid, and a debt-to-equity ratio of 89:1. Jack Stack opened the books, trained his people, and persuaded them to view the business as a game they could learn to play and win. The company returned to profitability, and is now written up in magazines and books as a brilliant model of how to do it.

You learn also of a number of companies that realized great results through opening the books, and understand the reasons why from taking a management course. And then you learn that Springfield ReManufacturing now holds seminars to teach other companies how to practice open-book management. You go to one, and you participate in exercises, simulations, and games to learn more about it. You are impressed, and are inclined to give it a try.

But there are downsides, as you learn when you get home and read another article. Your company has been around for a while, and the operating norms are pretty well established. How will people respond to this idea of opening the books? Will they understand? What will they think of the numbers? Will they want higher pay? Do they want a more active role in the company affairs? Do they really want to know the numbers?

Importantly, you will need to train them. You will need to commit to a lengthy, time-consuming learning period. Some of your managers and accountants, who had been privy to the confidential information, might not like the idea. They might fear they will lose power and status, or they might not trust the workers with the information. Possibly some confidential information will leak to competitors.

There are a few other issues as well. Changes in accounting and financial systems and statements will be required, performance measures will need to be linked with financial statements, and a system of rewards linked to performance must be established. The system must be understood by everyone and, above all, be seen as fair.

An intriguing issue here is pay. Pay is just about the only thing kept secret at AES, where financial and market data, and even the details of potential acquisition decisions, are widely circulated even though some people worry that information will be leaked to competitors. However, even the topic of pay secrecy may be open for debate. CEO Dennis Bakke says, "Personal compensation issues are confidential, but we're not even sure why that has to be the case" (p. 117).

You are not naive about the potential downsides of opening your books, or the implementation challenges. Not everyone will like the idea—including your friends, who own *their* own companies. Their concerns are yours as well: Can my managers really

After saving Springfield ReManufacturing, Jack Stack started offering seminars to teach other companies how to practice open-book management.

share the financial information? Can they really delegate decisions they used to make? What if outsiders learn our costs and other data? (Customers and suppliers would renegotiate prices; competitors might gain advantage.) How much information is enough, or too much? Is open-book management suitable for only certain kinds of businesses?

QUESTIONS

1. You have the sole authority to make this decision for your company. Yes or no: Would you implement an open-book system?

2. If the answer is no, what would you do and say if some of your people came to you and proposed it?

3. If you are undecided, would you convene a meeting to discuss the idea? If so, how would you handle the meeting?

4. If your answer is yes, how would you proceed?

5. What do you think about the issue of pay secrecy? What is your opinion—both as an employee and as company president? If you were president, what would you do about it?

SOURCES: J. Case, "Opening the Books," *Harvard Business Review*, March–April 1997, pp. 118–27; R. T. V. Davis, "Open-Book Management: Its Promise and Pitfalls," *Organizational Dynamics*, Winter 1997, pp. 7–20; S. Wetlaufer, "Organizing for Empowerment: An Interview with AES's Roger Sant and Dennis Bakke," *Harvard Business Review*, January–February 1999, pp. 110–23; R. Aggarwal and B. Simkins, "Open Book Management: Optimizing Human Capital," *Business Horizons* 44 (2001), pp. 5–13.

15.1   Nonverbal Communication

OBJECTIVE

To become more conscious of nonverbal messages.

INSTRUCTIONS

Following is a list of nonverbal communication "methods." Pick a day on which you will attempt to keep track of these methods.

Think back at the end of the day to three people with whom you communicated in some way. Record how you responded to these people in terms of their nonverbal communication methods. Identify those that had the greatest and least effect on your behavior.

Nonverbal Communication Worksheet

Medium	What Was the Message?	How Did You Respond?	Which Affected Your Behavior Most and Least?
How they shook hands			
Their posture			
Their facial expressions			
Their appearance			
Their voice tones			
Their smiles			
The expressions in their eyes			
Their confidence			
The way they moved			
The way they stood			
How close they stood to you			
How they smelled			
Symbols or gestures they used			
How loudly they spoke			

SOURCE: Excerpted from Lawrence R. Jauch, Arthur G. Bedian, Sally A. Coltrin, and William F. Glueck, *The Managerial Experience* 5th ed. Copyright © 1989. Reprinted with permission of South-Western, a division of Thomson Learning, www.thomsonrights.com.

15.2   Listening Skills Survey

OBJECTIVES

1. To measure your skills as a listener.

2. To gain insight into the factors that determine good listening habits.

3. To demonstrate how you can become a better listener.

INSTRUCTIONS

1. Working alone, complete the Listening Skills Survey.

2. In small groups, compare scores, discuss survey test items, and prepare responses to the discussion questions.

3. After the class reconvenes, group spokespersons present group findings.

DISCUSSION QUESTIONS

1. In what ways did students' responses on the survey agree or disagree?

2. What do you think accounts for the differences?

3. How can the results of this survey be put to practical use?

LISTENING SKILLS SURVEY

To measure your listening skills, complete the following survey by circling the degree to which you agree with each statement.

	Strongly Agree	Agree	Neither Agree nor Disagree	Disagree	Strongly Disagree
1. I tend to be patient with the speaker, making sure she or he is finished speaking before I respond in any fashion.	5	4	3	2	1
2. When listening I don't doodle or fiddle with papers and things that might distract me from the speaker.	5	4	3	2	1
3. I attempt to understand the speaker's point of view.	5	4	3	2	1
4. I try not to put the speaker on the defensive by arguing or criticizing.	5	4	3	2	1
5. When I listen, I focus on the speaker's feelings.	5	4	3	2	1
6. I let a speaker's annoying mannerisms distract me.	5	4	3	2	1
7. While the speaker is talking, I watch carefully for facial expressions and other types of body language.	5	4	3	2	1
8. I never talk when the other person is trying to say something.	5	4	3	2	1
9. During a conversation, a period of silence seems awkward to me.	5	4	3	2	1
10. I want people to just give me the facts and allow me to make up my own mind.	5	4	3	2	1
11. When the speaker is finished, I respond to his or her feelings.	5	4	3	2	1
12. I don't evaluate the speaker's words until she or he is finished talking.	5	4	3	2	1
13. I formulate my response while the speaker is still talking.	5	4	3	2	1
14. I never pretend that I'm listening when I'm not.	5	4	3	2	1
15. I can focus on message content even if the delivery is poor.	5	4	3	2	1
16. I encourage the speaker with frequent nods, smiles, and other forms of body language.	5	4	3	2	1
17. Sometimes I can predict what someone is going to say before she or he says it.	5	4	3	2	1
18. Even if a speaker makes me angry, I hold my temper.	5	4	3	2	1
19. I maintain good eye contact with the speaker.	5	4	3	2	1
20. I try to focus on the speaker's message, not his or her delivery.	5	4	3	2	1
21. If I am confused by a statement someone makes, I never respond until I have asked for and received adequate clarification.	5	4	3	2	1

Frank Perriman's Appointment

Indefatigable Mutual Insurance is a large, national company with more than 10,000 employees in the 50 states and Canada. Its basic organization has been as shown in the organization chart. Each divisional vice president has access to the president if so desired, but most communications between the field and the home office are with the functional vice presidents, who set policy and monitor performance in their respective functional areas. Two senior vice presidents have acted as staff to the president in their areas of expertise—one in actuarial and statistical matters and the other in investments and finance. In general, Indefatigable has been a highly centralized, regionally dispersed organization.

Frank Perriman has had exceptional success at Indefatigable. After experience primarily in sales, Frank was appointed vice president of the Middle Division at age 35—the youngest such appointment in the company's history. One annual report contained an individual picture of Perriman (the only divisional vice president so honored) with a caption describing him as an example of what could happen to young people at Indefatigable. However, most executives were old.

After eight years as division vice president, Perriman was promoted to senior vice president (thus making three senior vice presidents) and transferred to the home office. The president sent the bulletins shown on page 481.

At the time Perriman thought he had no problem. After all, he had been given a significant promotion. Nonetheless, he was concerned because he feared resentment from others and was unclear about what the president wanted. Perriman had recently attended an executive program in which they had discussed a case titled "The Dashman Company," which told about

a new vice president who failed to exert any impact on the organization (see the Dashman Company case on page 481). Accordingly, he decided to see Professor Eagleson, who had conducted various management training programs for the company.

During the conversation, Eagleson pointed out that there was a disparity in the managerial styles of the various division vice presidents. For example, when conducting a training program for managers in the Northern Division, he had the divisional functional managers draw an organization chart (illustrated on page 482). When sitting in the Northern Division's vice president's office one day, a divisional functional manager had come in with a problem about how to treat a certain policyholder. The vice president had asked the manager to read the relevant home office regulation on the matter and then directed the functional manager to adhere exactly to the home office rule.

By chance, Professor Eagleson had once been sitting in Perriman's office when a similar event occurred. After listening to the divisional manager and reading the home office regulation, Perriman had advised the manager that the regulation didn't exactly apply, so they were free to handle the matter as they deemed best. If headquarters would later complain to the manager, Perriman promised to say the action was his responsibility. When the Middle Division divisional managers had drawn the organization chart in their training session, it was as pictured on page 483. In general, Eagleson felt that the Northern Division's vice president's behavior was more typical of the division vice presidents than Perriman's.

Organizational chart

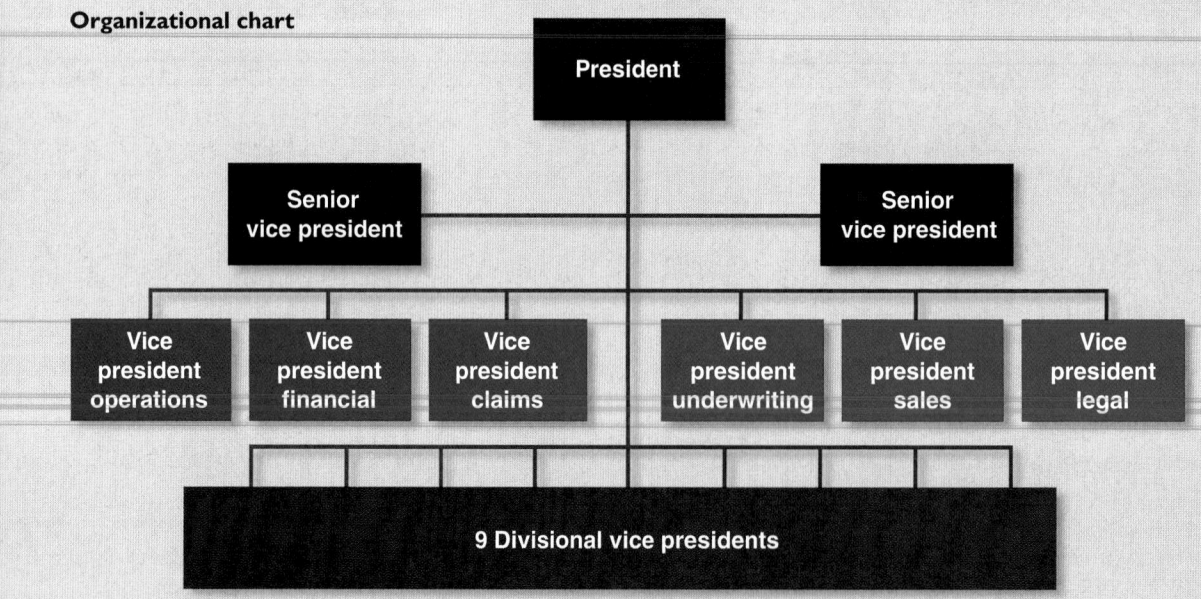

HOME OFFICE ADMINISTRATION
June 29

ORGANIZATIONAL BULLETIN—GENERAL No. 349
Effective August 1, Mr. Frank Perriman, Vice President and Division Manager, Middle Division, will transfer to the President's staff at the home office.

Perriman will be responsible to the President for achieving division performance in accordance with company policies and objectives.

Mr. Perriman will assist Division Managers in obtaining well-coordinated efforts by all departments and will establish and use measurements of results for each Division.

Divisional Vice Presidents will report to and be responsible to Mr. Perriman.

Thomas Achison
President

HOME OFFICE ADMINISTRATION
July 14

ORGANIZATIONAL BULLETIN—GENERAL No. 351
Effective July 14, the Board of Directors made the following election: Mr. Frank Perriman—Senior Vice President

Thomas Achison
President

Dashman Company

The Dashman Company was a large concern making many types of equipment for the armed forces of the United States. It had over 20 plants, located in the central part of the country, whose purchasing procedures had never been completely coordinated. In fact, the head office of the company had encouraged each of the plant managers to operate with their staffs as separate independent units in most matters. Late in 1940, when it began to appear that the company would face increasing difficulty in securing certain essential raw materials, Mr. Manson, the company's president, appointed an experienced purchasing executive, Mr. Post, as vice president in charge of purchasing, a position especially created for him. Mr. Manson gave Mr. Post wide latitude in organizing his job, and he assigned Mr. Larson as Mr. Post's assistant. Mr. Larson had served the company in a variety of capacities for many years and knew most of the plant executives personally. Mr. Post's appointment was announced through the formal channels usual in the company, including a notice in the house organ published by the company.

One of Mr. Post's first decisions was to begin immediately to centralize the company's purchasing procedure. As a first step he decided that he would require each of the executives who handled purchasing in the individual plants to clear with the head office all purchase contracts which they made in excess of $10,000. He felt that if the head office was to do any coordinating in a way that would be helpful to each plant and to the company as a whole, he must be notified that the contracts were being prepared at least a week before they were to be signed. He talked his proposal over with Mr. Manson, who presented it to his board of directors. They approved the plan.

Although the company made purchases throughout the year, the beginning of its peak buying season was only three weeks away at the time this new plan was adopted. Mr. Post prepared a letter to be sent to the 20 purchasing executives of the company. The letter follows:

Dear: _____

The board of directors of our company has recently authorized a change in our purchasing procedures. Hereafter, each of the purchasing executives in the several plants of the company will notify the vice president in charge of purchasing of all contracts in excess of $10,000 they are negotiating at least a week in advance of the date on which they are to be signed. I am sure that you will understand that this step is necessary to coordinate the purchasing requirements of the company in these times when we are facing increasing difficulty in securing essential supplies. This procedure should give us in the central office the information we need to see that each plant secures the optimum supply of materials. In this way the interests of each plant and of the company as a whole will best be served.

Yours very truly,

Mr. Post showed the letter to Mr. Larson and invited his comments. Mr. Larson thought the letter an excellent one but suggested that, since Mr. Post had not met more than a few of the purchasing executives, he might like to visit all of them and take the matter up with each of them personally. Mr. Post dismissed the idea at once because, as he said, he had so many things to do at the head office that he could not get away for a trip. Consequently he had the letters sent out over his signature.

During the two following weeks replies came in from all except a few plants. Although a few executives wrote at greater length, the following reply was typical:

Dear Mr. Post:

Your recent communication in regard to notifying the head office a week in advance of our intention to sign contracts has been received. This suggestion seems a most practical one. We want to assure you that you can count on our cooperation.

Yours very truly,

During the next six weeks the head office received no notices from any plant that contracts were being negotiated. Executives in other departments who made frequent trips to the plants reported that the plants were busy, and the usual routines for that time of year were being followed.

Partial organizational chart as drawn by Northern Division divisional functional managers

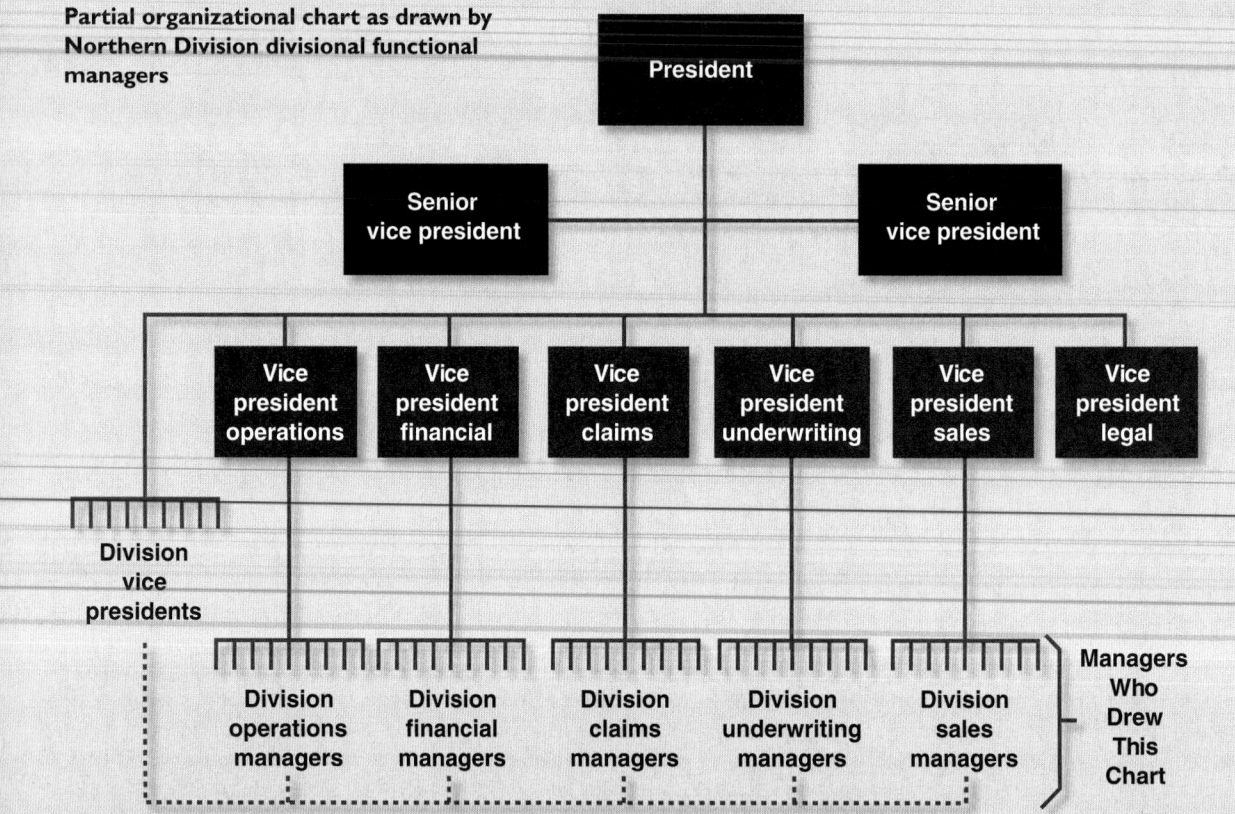

When Perriman asked Eagleson what he thought the president expected of the new position, the professor said he wasn't sure. Nonetheless, he mentioned that when he recently had seen the president about the company training programs, the executive had expressed concern about his age, next year's 100th anniversary celebration of the firm, and the company's expense position. He had remarked on the way to lunch that the only thing wrong with the company was that the field personnel "just didn't follow home office rules." The president indicated that the company was losing money on automobile insurance policies, especially because sales was selling to less desirable risks—contrary to the company's long-standing strategy of preferred risks. Perhaps, the president concluded, the field staff should be reduced and sales curtailed.

Pondering these points, Perriman wondered if one of his first steps as a senior vice president should be to pick a fight with one of the home office functional vice presidents to impress the division vice presidents with his willingness to battle on their behalf.

QUESTIONS

1. Discuss any problems Perriman might have in establishing authority and influence in his new post.

2. What factors should aid Perriman?

3. How do you think the divisional vice presidents will react to this appointment? Why?

4. How do you think the functional vice presidents will react to this appointment? Why?

5. How do you think Achison should have proceeded?

6. How do you interpret the differences in the organization charts as drawn by the division functional managers in the Northern Division compared with the Middle Division?

7. What do the president's remarks to Professor Eagleson suggest about his intentions for Perriman as the new senior vice president?

8. What recommendations would you offer Perriman now? Why?

Partial organizational chart as drawn by Middle Division divisional functional managers

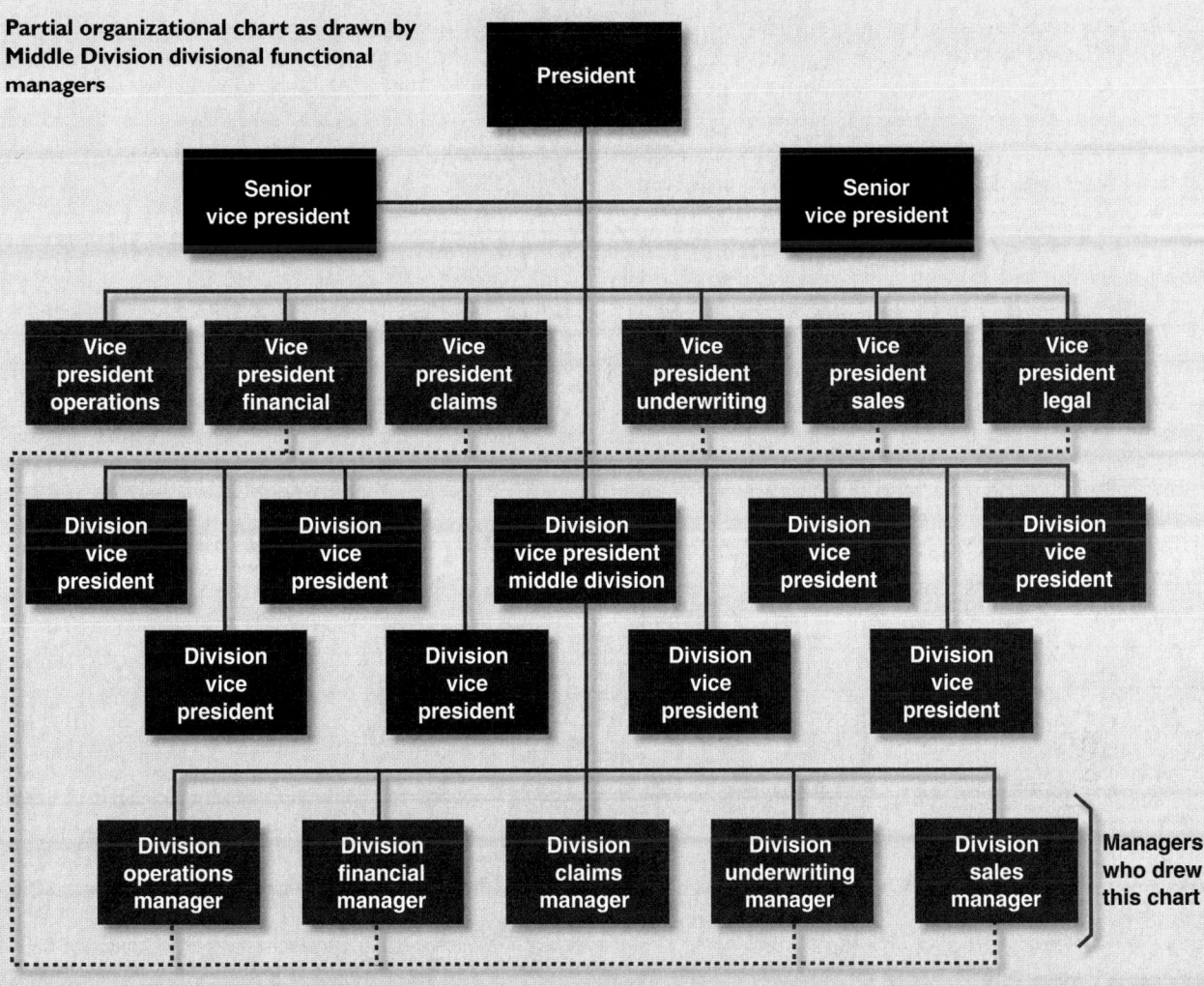

Suggestion System Policy

OFFICE OF THE PRESIDENT
Memorandum
Date: Friday, November 18
From: Bob Adams, president
To: John Sullens, vice president for human resources

Employee suggestion systems have been around for a long time. The positive financial impact of suggestion systems is significant in some organizations, according to my reading. For example, the National Association of Suggestions Systems estimates that 80 percent of the 500 largest U.S. corporations have such programs and that employee suggestions save the nation's companies more than $500 million a year.

The negative aspect of the suggestion system is that employees may become disgruntled about how the company runs the system. You may recall that two United Airlines employees charged in court that United stole their suggestion for a reduced-fare plan for employees of all airlines, that United successfully implemented the plan, and that United cheated them out of hundreds of thousands of dollars that they had coming under the company's suggestion

system. They cited a provision of United Airlines' suggestion system rules that stated, "An employee is entitled to 10 percent of a typical year's profits resulting from an idea submitted through the suggestion system and successfully implemented."

During the trial, expert witnesses testified that in a typical year of operations under the reduced-fare plan, United earned $3 million attributable to the plan, of which 10 percent, or $300,000, rightfully belongs to the two employees who submitted the suggestion. The jury found that the company acted in bad faith by failing to pay off under the suggestion system and assessed $1.8 million in damages against the airline, which a judge later reduced to $368,000.

We can't afford to risk such financial peril! It's crucial, therefore, that you promptly review our suggestion system rules and policies and that you give me recommendations on the following issues. Include advantages and disadvantages associated with your policy recommendations.

1. *Calculation of award amount.* Should we offer a flat amount of money for each accepted suggestion, or should the award be

based on a percentage of the savings (earnings) during some period? What percentage? What period?

2. *Maximum award.* Should we have a maximum limit on the pay-off for any single suggestion (perhaps $10,000), or should it be open-ended?

3. *Time of award payment.* Should we pay the award in full when the suggestion is accepted or as the savings (earnings) are realized annually?

4. *Joint award allocation.* When two or more employees combine on a suggestion, how should we allocate the award among them?

5. *Originality.* Should we pay off for suggestions that help us, even if they aren't original with the employee(s) making the suggestion?

6. *Impetus award.* Are you in favor of an "impetus award" in the range of $100 to $500 to recognize a suggestion that hastens an action initiated by the company before receipt of the suggestion?

7. *Written rules.* Do you think we need to spell out in writing every aspect of our suggestion system, or will an informal approach be more conducive to employee participation?

8. *Proof of knowledge.* Should we require all employees to sign a form stating that they have read and understand the suggestion system's rules (if we decide to write them up)?

9. *Another limitation.* Should an employee be limited to suggestions relating only to his or her area of the organization?

10. *An exclusion.* Should our marketing function and financial policy (including product and service pricing) be excluded from the suggestion system?

11. *Evaluation.* Do you have any suggestions on a procedure for evaluating suggestions?

12. *Abandonment.* Maybe dropping the suggestion system would be easier. What do you think?

We are reviewing all aspects of our suggestion system policy. Our attorney recommends abandonment. Let me hear from you as soon as possible. Treat this as a priority item.

SOURCE: J. M. Champion and J. H. James, *Critical Incidents in Management: Decision and Policy Issues*, 6th ed., McGraw-Hill Companies, Inc., 1989.

Quality Circle Consequence

John Stevens, plant manager of the Fairlead Plant of Lockstead Corporation, which manufactures structural components for aircraft wings and bodies, became interested in using quality circles to improve performance in his plant. *Quality circles* was the name used to describe joint labor-supervision participation teams operating at the shop-floor level at Lockstead. Other companies called quality circles by names such as "productivity groups," "people involvement programs," and "departmental teams." Whatever the name, the purpose of quality circles was to improve the quality of manufacturing performance.

The subject of quality circles was a hot topic in the press. Stevens had seen books on Japanese management and productivity successes, which featured the use of quality circles. All these books featured the slogan "None of us is as smart as all of us."

Other books related quality circles to productivity gains. Articles on quality circles appeared often in trade journals and in business magazines, including *Business Week*.

Stevens also had a pamphlet from a management consulting firm announcing a "new and improved" training course for quality circle leaders, scheduled consecutively in Birmingham, Alabama; Williamsburg, Virginia; and Orlando, Florida. Another consultant offered "a program that will teach your managers and supervisors how to increase productivity and efficiency without making costly investments . . . by focusing on techniques germane to the quality circle process." Stevens was impressed enough to attend an advanced management seminar at a large midwestern university. A large part of the program concentrated on quality circles.

Professor Albert Mennon particularly impressed Stevens with his lectures on group discussion, team problem solving, and group decision making. Mennon convinced Stevens that employees

meeting in quality circle teams with adequate leaders could effectively consider problems and formulate quality decisions that would be acceptable to employees. The staff conducting this state-of-the-art seminar covered five areas: (1) how to train quality circle members in the six-step problem sequence; (2) a description of what leaders and facilitators should do during the quality circle sessions; (3) planning and writing a policy guide; (4) developing an implementation plan; and (5) measuring quality circle progress and success.

Both the company and its employees were expected to benefit from a successfully implemented quality circle program. The list of payoffs included increased job satisfaction, productivity improvement, efficiency gains, and improved performance and labor relations. Moreover, it was expected that a reduction would occur in areas such as grievance loads, absenteeism, and costs.

Returning to his plant after the seminar, Stevens decided to practice some of the principles he had learned. He called together the 25 employees of Department B and told them that production standards established several years ago were too low in view of the recent installation of automated equipment. He gave the workers the opportunity to discuss the mitigating circumstances and to decide among themselves, as a group, what their standards should be. On leaving the room, he believed that the workers would establish much higher standards than he would have dared propose.

After an hour of discussion, the group summoned Stevens and notified him that, contrary to his opinion, they had decided the standards already were too high and, since they had been given the authority to establish their own standards, they were making a reduction of 10 percent. Stevens knew these standards were far too low to provide a fair profit on the owner's investment. Yet he believed his refusal to accept the group decision would be disastrous. Stevens thought of telephoning Professor Mennon for consultation on the quality circle dilemma, but he chose to act on his own.

Several options filled Steven's mind: (1) He could accept the blame for the quality circle experiment having gone awry and tell them to begin anew; (2) he could establish incentive pay adjustment linkages between the quality circle's decisions and productivity improvement; (3) he might even operate at a loss for a short while to prove that the original quality circle decision had been unacceptable; or (4) he might abandon the participative team program. Stevens needed a decision, an operational policy for the quality circle program, and an implementation plan.

SOURCE: J. H. Champion and J. H. James, *Critical Incidents in Management: Decision and Policy Issues*, 6th ed, McGraw-Hill Companies, Inc., 1989.

PART FIVE

Foundations of Management
- Managing
- The External Environment
- Managerial Decision Making

**Planning:
Delivering Strategic Value**
- Planning and Strategic Management
- Ethics and Corporate Responsibility
- International Management
- New Ventures

Strategy Implementation

Organizing: Building a Dynamic Organization
- Organization Structure
- The Responsive Organization
- Human Resources Management
- Managing the Diverse Workforce

**Leading:
Mobilizing People**
- Leadership
- Motivating for Performance
- Managing Teams
- Communicating

**Controlling:
Learning and Changing**
- Managerial Control
- Managing Technology and Innovation
- Creating and Managing Change

Controlling: Learning and Changing

In Parts One through Four, you learned about the foundations of management, planning and strategy and how to implement plans by organizing, staffing, and leading. Part Five concludes with three chapters about controlling and changing what the organization and its people are doing. Chapter 16 describes managerial control, including issues related to culture as well as techniques for ensuring that intended activities are carried out and goals are accomplished.

The last two chapters focus on change and renewal. Chapter 17 discusses technology and innovation, including a strategic approach to new technologies and the creation of a culture for innovation. Chapter 18 examines an ongoing challenge for the modern executive: becoming world-class through the management of change. In that chapter, we describe the nature of this challenge and how managers can deal with it. Some of the topics you learned about in earlier chapters play central roles in the change process; Chapter 18 should remind you how your understanding of them will benefit your managerial career.

CHAPTER 16

Managerial Control

More than at any time in the past, companies will not be able to hold themselves together with the traditional methods of control: hierarchy, systems, budgets, and the like . . . The bonding glue will increasingly become ideological.

—Collins & Porras[1]

Use your good judgment in all situations. There will be no additional rules.

—Nordstrom's employee manual

CHAPTER OUTLINE

Bureaucratic Control Systems
    The Control Cycle
    Approach to Bureaucratic Control
    Management Audits
    Budgetary Controls
    Financial Controls
    The Downside of Bureaucratic Control
    Designing Effective Control Systems
The Other Controls: Markets and Clans
    Market Control
    Clan Control: The Role of Empowerment and Culture

LEARNING OBJECTIVES

After studying Chapter 16, you will know:

1. Why companies develop control systems for employees.

2. How to design a basic bureaucratic control system.

3. The purposes for using budgets as a control device.

4. How to interpret financial ratios and other financial controls.

5. The procedures for implementing effective control systems.

6. The different ways in which market control mechanisms are used by organizations.

7. How clan control can be approached in an empowered organization.

CHRYSLER STOPS THE SKID

When Jurgen Schrempp merged Germany's Daimler-Benz with Chrysler Corp. in 1998, all of Detroit feared that he and his lieutenants would march in and trample the American manufacturer. Perhaps they should have. As it turned out, Schrempp and his German team probably gave U.S. managers too much rein. In fact, after the merger, the Daimler-Chrysler empire looked pretty shaky: Sales plummeted from over $8 billion to just $1.2 billion. "Chrysler has always been the canary in the mine shaft," says researcher Sean McAlinden, who

was a big improvement over the $148 million loss the American branch had suffered the year before.

In addition to instituting tighter cost controls, DaimlerChrysler focused on quality. Warranty repair costs per vehicle dropped a dramatic 20 percent, and Chrysler led Detroit automakers in *Consumer Reports'* annual product reliability survey in 2001. The company also jumped from 18th to 12th place in J.D. Power and Associates' quality study. "The gains were among the most rapid jumps in the study's history," says Joe Ivers of J.D. Powers.

"We're pleased and encouraged, but we're never satisfied," remarked a Chrysler spokesman about the improvements. Indeed, Zetsche says his plan is to beat the quality industry leader, Toyota, within five years. To do that, his company will have to stick to its agenda of preempting problems with new models, correcting glitches in current models (such as the hugely popular PT Cruiser, which recently was recalled), and servicing owners' vehicles fast and accurately the first time they bring them into

DaimlerChrysler aims to improve quality by eliminating bugs in popular models such as the PT Cruiser before they reach consumers.

pointed out that economic slowdown in the United States had made for grim times industrywide. Chrysler just felt the pain first.

But Schrempp never doubted his strategy, although just about everyone else did. "We're on the right track," he proudly reported in 2002, when the company began to make a turnaround. Case in point: Dieter Zetsche, Chrysler's new German CEO, managed to wring out $1.2 billion in savings and generate $788 million in earnings in 2001. That

the dealerships. To reassure consumers who have long doubted the reliability of Chrysler models, the company also began offering a seven-year, 100,000-mile warranty on engines and transmissions. The company's effort to step on the gas appears to be working. In addition to increasing profits, DaimlerChrysler's share price has surged.

Sources: Christine N. Tierney, "DaimlerChrysler Steps on the Gas," *Business Week Online*, July 19, 2002; Susan Carney, "Quality Control Pays Off at DaimlerChrysler," *The Detroit News*, June 28, 2002; Christine Tierney and Jeff Green, "Can Schrempp Stop the Careening at Chrysler?" *Business Week*, December 4, 2002.

Setting the Stage

How does a respected company like DaimlerChrysler get out of control? Left on their own, people may knowingly or unknowingly act in ways that they perceive to be beneficial to them individually but that may work to the detriment of the organization as a whole. This is what happened at Chrysler. Without some means of regulating what people do, an organization can literally fall apart. In this regard, control is one of the fundamental forces that keep the organization together.[2]

control

Any process that directs the activities of individuals toward the achievement of organizational goals.

Control typically is defined as any process that directs the activities of individuals toward the achievement of organizational goals. Some managers don't want to admit it (see Table 16.1), but control problems—the lack of controls or the wrong kinds of controls—frequently cause irreparable damage to organizations. Ineffective control systems result in problems ranging from employee theft to peeling tire tread problems to escalating fuel prices in California. Employees simply wasting time cost U.S. employers billions of dollars each year![3]

Control has been called one of the Siamese twins of management. The other twin is planning. Some means of control are necessary because once managers form plans and strategies, they must ensure that the plans are carried out. This means making sure that other people are doing what needs to be done and not doing inappropriate things. If plans are not carried out properly, management must take steps to correct the problem. This is the primary control function of management. Ensuring creativity, enhancing quality, reducing costs—managers must figure out ways to control what occurs in their organizations.

Not surprisingly, effective planning facilitates control, and control facilitates planning. Planning lays out a framework for the future and, in this sense, provides a blueprint for control. Control systems, in turn, regulate the allocation and utilization of resources and, in so doing, facilitate the process of planning. In today's complex organizational environment, both functions have become more difficult to implement at the same time that they have become more important in every department of the organization. Managers today must control their people, inventories, quality, and costs, to mention just a few of their responsibilities.

According to William Ouchi of the University of California at Los Angeles, managers can apply three broad strategies for achieving organizational control: bureaucratic control, market control, and clan control.[4]

bureaucratic control

The use of rules, regulations, and authority to guide performance.

Bureaucratic control is the use of rules, regulations, and formal authority to guide performance. It includes such things as budgets, statistical reports, and performance appraisals to regulate behavior and results.

TABLE 16.1   The Leadership Symptoms of an Out-of-Control Company

David Ferrari, president of Argus Management Corporation, maintains that many businesses are in big trouble without the CEO even knowing it. The symptoms:

- **Misplaced confidence**—believing that everything they do is right and they cannot make mistakes.
- **Blame deflection**—if they admit they are in trouble, they blame everything but themselves.
- **Avoidance**—doing "busy work" that is easy to handle rather than tackling the big, companywide issues.
- **An eye to the past**—justifying current practices by saying, "We've always done it that way."
- **Blind optimism**—refusing to believe bad numbers and believing that things will take care of themselves.
- **Setting a poor example**—spending lavishly on perks for themselves rather than living up to the same stringent standards expected of others.
- **Isolation**—other people—subordinates, directors, outsiders—don't send warning signals or stand up to the CEO to convince him or her that things are perilously out of control.

System Control	Features and Requirements
Bureaucratic control	Uses formal rules, standards, hierarchy, and legitimate authority. Works best where tasks are certain and workers are independent.
Market control	Uses prices, competition, profit centers, and exchange relationships. Works best where tangible output can be identified and market can be established between parties.
Clan control	Involves culture, shared values, beliefs, expectations, and trust. Works best where there is "no one best way" to do a job and employees are empowered to make decisions.

SOURCES: W. G. Ouchi, "A Conceptual Framework for the Design of Organizational Control Mechanisms," *Management Science* 25 (1979), pp. 833–48; W. G. Ouchi, "Markets, Bureaucracies, and Clans," *Administrative Science Quarterly* 25 (1980), pp. 129–41; and Richard D. Robey and C. A. Sales, *Designing Organizations* (Burr Ridge, IL: Richard D. Irwin, 1994).

TABLE 16.2
Characteristics of Controls

Market control involves the use of pricing mechanisms to regulate activities in organizations as though they were economic transactions. Business units may be treated as profit centers and trade resources (services or products) with one another via such mechanisms. Managers who run these units may be evaluated on the basis of profit and loss. **Clan control,** unlike the first two types, does not assume that the interests of the organization and individuals naturally diverge. Instead, clan control is based on the idea that employees may share the values, expectations, and goals of the organization and act in accordance with them. When members of an organization have common values and goals—and trust one another—formal controls may be less necessary. Clan control is based on many of the interpersonal processes described in Chapter 12 on leadership and Chapter 14 on groups and teams (e.g., group norms and cohesiveness).

Table 16.2 summarizes the main features of bureaucratic, market, and culture controls. We use this framework as a foundation for our discussions throughout the chapter.

> **market control**
>
> Control based on the use of pricing mechanisms and economic information to regulate activities within organizations.

> **clan control**
>
> Control based on the norms, values, shared goals, and trust among group members.

Bureaucratic Control Systems

Bureaucratic (or formal) control systems are designed to measure progress toward planned performance and, if necessary, to apply corrective measures to ensure that performance is in line with managers' objectives. Control systems detect and correct significant variations, or discrepancies, in the results obtained from planned activities.

The Control Cycle

Figure 16.1 shows a typical control system with four major steps: (1) setting performance standards, (2) measuring performance, (3) comparing performance against the standards and determining deviations, and (4) taking corrective action.

Step 1: Setting Performance Standards Every organization has goals: profitability, innovation, satisfaction of constituencies, and so on. A **standard** is the level of expected performance for a given goal. Standards are performance targets that establish desired performance levels, motivate performance, and serve as benchmarks against which to assess actual performance. Standards can be set for any activity—financial activities, operating activities, legal compliance, charitable contributions, and so on.[5]

> **standard**
>
> Expected performance for a given goal: a target that establishes a desired performance level, motivates performance, and serves as a benchmark against which actual performance is assessed.

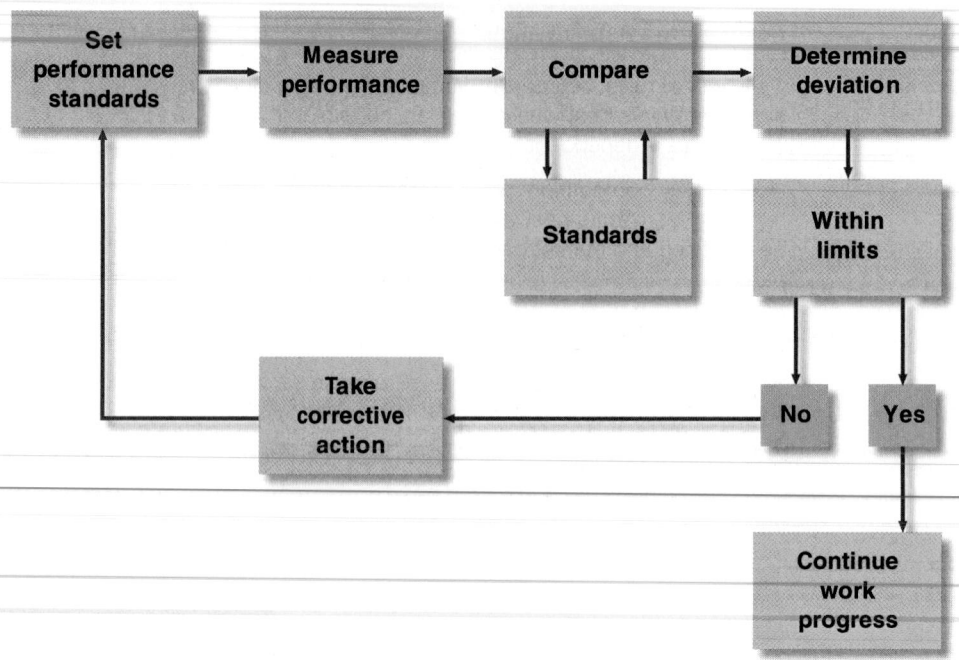

FIGURE 16.1
The Control Process

We have discussed setting performance standards in other parts of the text. For example, employee goal setting for motivation is built around the concept of specific, measurable performance standards. Such standards should be challenging and typically should aim for improvement over past performance. Typically, performance standards are derived from job requirements. Examples might include increasing market share by 10 percent, reducing costs 20 percent, and answering customer complaints within 24 hours. But performance standards don't apply just to people in isolation—they frequently reflect the integration of human and system performance. BAE Systems, for example, makes control systems for aircraft engines (these controls are essentially computers mounted on the engines to monitor performance, control speed, and optimize fuel efficiency). These controls have to withstand extreme temperatures and vibration. And because they're used on a wide variety of military and commercial aircraft, they must be highly reliable. "Every four seconds, one of our engine controls takes off," notes Dave Herr, director of operations. "At this instant there are a quarter of a million people flying somewhere, trusting our engine control." In producing these controls, workers in BAE's plant set very stringent performance standards for quality and reliability. The failure rate (termed a "shutdown rate") of the engine controls is just 0.7 incident per million hours. That means you'd have to fly 24 hours a day, every day for a century, to experience one in-flight engine shutdown. That's a pretty incredible standard.[6]

Performance standards can be set with respect to (1) quantity, (2) quality, (3) time used, and (4) cost. For example, production activities include volume of output (quantity), defects (quality), on-time availability of finished goods (time use), and dollar expenditures for raw materials and direct labor (cost). Many important aspects of performance, such as customer service, can be measured by the same standards—adequate supply and availability of products, quality of service, speed of delivery, and so forth.

One word of caution: The downside of establishing performance targets and standards is that they may not be supported by other elements of the control system. Each piece of the system is important and dependent on the others. Otherwise the system can get terribly out of balance. Let's look at some of the other pieces.

Step 2: Measuring Performance   The second step in the control process is to measure performance levels. For example, managers can count units produced, days absent, papers filed, samples distributed, and dollars earned. Performance data commonly are obtained from three sources: written reports, oral reports, and personal observations.

Written reports include computer printouts. Thanks to computers' increasing capabilities and decreasing costs, both large and small companies can gather huge amounts of performance data.

One common example of *oral reports* occurs when a salesperson contacts his or her immediate manager at the close of each business day to report the accomplishments, problems, or customers' reactions during the day. The manager can ask questions to gain additional information or clear up any misunderstandings. When necessary, tentative corrective actions can be worked out during the discussion.

Personal observation involves going to the area of activities and watching what is occurring. The manager can observe work methods, employees' nonverbal signals, and the general operation. Personal observation gives an intimate picture of what is going on, but it also has some disadvantages. It does not provide accurate quantitative data; the information usually is general and subjective. Also, employees can misconstrue personal observation as mistrust or lack of confidence. Nevertheless, many managers believe there is no good substitute for firsthand observation. As you learned in earlier chapters, personal contact can increase leadership visibility and upward communication. It also provides valuable information about performance to supplement written and oral reports.

Step 3: Comparing Performance with the Standard

The third step in the control process is comparing performance with the standard. In this process, the manager evaluates the performance. For some activities relatively small deviations from the standard are acceptable, while in others a slight deviation may be serious. Managers who perform the controlling work therefore must analyze and evaluate the results carefully.

The managerial **principle of exception** states that control is enhanced by concentrating on the exceptions, or significant deviations, from the expected result or standard. In comparing performance with the standard, managers need to direct their attention to the exception. For example, controlling the quality of components produced on an assembly line might show that only 5 pieces per 1,000 fall out of line. These five components are the exceptions and should be investigated further.[7]

> **principle of exception**
>
> A managerial principle stating that control is enhanced by concentrating on the exceptions or significant deviations from the expected result or standard.

With the principle of exception, only exceptional cases require corrective action. The manager should not be concerned with performance that equals or closely approximates the expected results. This principle is important in controlling. Managers can save much time and effort if they apply the principle of exception.

Step 4: Taking Corrective Action

The last step in the control process is to take action to correct significant deviations. This step ensures that operations are adjusted where necessary to achieve the initially planned results. Where significant variances are discovered, the manager should take immediate and vigorous action. Effective control cannot tolerate needless delays, excuses, or exceptions.

An alternative approach is for the corrective action to be taken not by higher-ups but by the operator at the point of the problem. In computer-controlled production technology, two basic types of control are feasible: specialist control and operator control. With *specialist control*, operators of computer-numerical-control (CNC) machines must notify engineering specialists of malfunctions. With this traditional division of labor, the specialist takes corrective action. With *operator control*, multiskilled operators can rectify their own problems as they occur. At companies such as Harley-Davidson, not only is this strategy more efficient (because deviations are controlled closer to their source), operators benefit by virtue of a more enriched job.[8]

The appropriate corrective action depends on the nature of the problem. The corrective action may involve a change in a procedure or method, a disciplinary action, a new way to check the accuracy of manufactured parts, or a major organizational modification. Or it may simply be an inexpensive investment in employee training. At Corning, the source of major quality and production problems was traced to minute drafting errors by the engineering group. One of the solutions was quite simple: An engineer was sent to a proofreading class.[9]

Approaches to Bureaucratic Control

feedforward control

The control process used before operations begin, including policies, procedures, and rules designed to ensure that planned activities are carried out properly.

The three approaches to bureaucratic control are feedforward, concurrent, and feedback. **Feedforward control** takes place before operations begin and includes policies, procedures, and rules designed to ensure that planned activities are carried out properly. Examples include inspection of raw materials and proper selection and training of employees. **Concurrent control** takes place while plans are being carried out. It includes directing, monitoring, and fine-tuning activities as they occur. **Feedback control** focuses on the use of information about results to correct deviations from the acceptable standard after they arise.

Feedforward Control Feedforward control (sometimes called *preliminary control*) is future-oriented; its aim is to prevent problems before they arise. Instead of waiting for results and comparing them with goals, a manager can exert control by limiting activities in advance. For example, companies have policies defining the scope within which decisions are made. A company may dictate that managers adhere to clear ethical and legal guidelines when making decisions. Formal rules and procedures also prescribe people's actions before they occur. Stating that a financial officer must approve expenditures over $1,000 or that only components that pass all safety tests can be used in a product specifies in advance which actions can and cannot be taken. To prevent loan defaults, banks may require extensive loan documentation, reviews, and approvals by bank officers before authorizing a loan.[10]

concurrent control

The control process used while plans are being carried out, including directing, monitoring, and fine-tuning activities as they are performed.

Concurrent Control Concurrent control, which takes place while plans are carried out, is the heart of any control system. On the production floor, all efforts are directed toward producing the correct quantity and quality of the right products in the specified amount of time. In an airline terminal, the baggage must get to the right airplanes before flights depart. In factories, materials must be available when and where needed, and breakdowns in the production process must be repaired immediately. Concurrent control also is in operation when supervisors watch employees to ensure they work efficiently and avoid mistakes. Advances in information technology have created powerful concurrent controls. Computerized systems give managers immediate access to data from the most remote corners of their companies. For example, managers can update budgets continuously based on an ongoing flow of performance data. In production facilities, monitoring systems that track errors per hour, machine speeds, and other measures allow managers to correct small production problems continuously before they become disasters.

feedback control

Control that focuses on the use of information about previous results to correct deviations from the acceptable standard.

Feedback Control Feedback control implies that performance data were gathered and analyzed and the results were returned to someone (or something) in the process to make corrections. When supervisors monitor behavior, they are exercising concurrent control. When they point out and correct improper performance, they are using feedback as a means of control.

Timing is an important aspect of feedback control. Long time lags often occur between performance and feedback, such as when actual spending is compared with the quarterly budget or when some aspect of performance is compared to the projection made a year earlier. If feedback on performance is not timely, managers cannot quickly identify and eliminate the problem and prevent more serious harm.[11]

Some feedback processes are under real-time (concurrent) control, such as a computer-controlled robot on an assembly line. Such units have sensing units that continually determine whether they are in the correct position to perform their functions. If they are not, a built-in control device makes immediate corrections.

Six Sigma Isn't Just for Widgets Anymore

In the mid-1980s, Motorola was being beaten consistently in the competitive marketplace by foreign firms that were able to produce higher-quality products at a lower cost. Bob Galvin, Motorola's then-CEO, started the company on a quality path now known as "six sigma." Sigma is the Greek letter used in statistics to designate the estimated standard deviation or variation in a process. The lower the "sigma level," the more variation or defects in the process. The higher the sigma level, the fewer the defects.

"Sigma level" often is used as a shorthand notation for indicating the number of defects per million opportunities (DPMO) involved in a process. For example, a "two sigma level" process has 308,537 DPMO (not a very controlled process). As shown in Table 16.3, if a process has a "three sigma level," it has 6,210 DPMO. So, what is six sigma? Six sigma means operating at less than 3.4 DPMO. That's essentially being defect-free 99.99966 percent of the time. The six sigma program at Motorola provided an intense management focus on preventing defects in products, processes, and services; reducing cycle times; and controlling costs in order to generate value to the customer.

The results were dramatic. Motorola became the market leader and won the Malcolm Baldrige National Quality Award in 1988. Six sigma has since been embraced by many other companies, most notably General Electric (GE), Honeywell, Merck, and Dow Chemical. This process has led to significant cost reductions, increased market share, and superior financial performance.

GE spent $600 million on six sigma projects in 2002, mostly on salaries for 4,000 full-time six sigma experts and basic training for an additional 100,000 employees. But it has been worth it: The company estimates that it has saved $8 billion so far and that another $2.5 billion in savings is possible. In fact, GE believes in six sigma so much that it ties a full 40 percent of managers' salaries to six sigma activities. Dow estimates that six sigma methods helped it reduce assembly line defects by as much as 70 percent, which ultimately will save that company $1.5 billion.

"Six Sigma might be the maturation of everything we've learned over the last 100 years about quality," says Gregory H. Watson, a consultant and past president of the American Society for Quality.

TABLE 16.3
Relationship between Sigma Level and Defects per Million Opportunities

Sigma Level	DPMO	Is Four Sigma Good Enough?
2σ	308,537	Consider these everyday examples of four sigma quality . . .
3σ	66,807	• 20,000 lost articles of mail per hour
4σ	**6,210**	• Unsafe drinking water 15 minutes per day
5σ	233	• 5,000 incorrect surgical operations per week
6σ	3.4	• 200,000 wrong prescriptions each year
		• No electricity for 7 hours each month

SOURCE: Tom Rancour and Mike McCracken, "Applying 6 Sigma Methods for Breakthrough Safety Performance," *Professional Safety*, October 2000, 45, no. 10, 29–32. Reprinted with permission.

The methodology isn't just for the factory floor, either. At Wellmark, Inc., a Des Moines, Iowa, managed-care company, it used to take 65 days or more to add a new doctor to its insurance plan. Six sigma methodology allowed the company to determine where the paperwork was being held up and fix the problem. Today, the company can add a doctor in 30 days, even though it has fewer employees. Hospitals that use six sigma report that the methodology has allowed them to standardize intraveneous drug practices, lowering the incidence of patients mistakenly given the wrong medications. The time needed to process lab results also has been cut.

SOURCES: Michael Arndt, "Where Precision Is Life or Death," *Business Week Online*, July 22, 2002; "Quality Isn't Just for Widgets," *Business Week Online*, July 22, 2002; "The Nuts and Bolts of Six Sigma," *Business Week Online*, July 22, 2002; George Eckes, "Making Six Sigma Last," *Ivey Business Journal*, January–February 2002, p. 77; Tom Rancour and Mike McCracken, "Applying Six Sigma Methods for Breakthrough Safety Performance," *Professional Safety*, October 2000, 45, no. 10, pp. 29–32.

Management Audits

management audits

An evaluation of the effectiveness and efficiency of various systems within an organization.

Over the years, **management audits** have developed as a means for evaluating the effectiveness and efficiency of various systems within an organization, from social responsibility to accounting control. Management audits may be external or internal. Managers conduct external audits of other companies and internal audits of their own companies. Some of the same tools and approaches are used for both types of audits.[12]

External Audits An **external audit** occurs when one organization evaluates another organization. Typically an external body such as a CPA firm conducts financial audits of an organization (accounting audits are discussed later). But any company can conduct external audits of competitors or other companies for its own strategic decision-making purposes. This type of analysis (1) investigates other organizations for possible merger or acquisition, (2) determines the soundness of a company that will be used as a major supplier, or (3) discovers the strengths and weaknesses of a competitor to maintain or better exploit the competitive advantage of the investigating organization. Publicly available data usually are used for these evaluations.[13]

external audit

An evaluation conducted by one organization, such as a CPA firm, on another.

External audits were used in feedback control in the discovery and investigation of the savings and loan scandals. They also are useful for preliminary control because they can prevent problems from occurring. If a company gathers adequate, accurate information about acquisition candidates, it is more likely to acquire the most appropriate companies and avoid unsound acquisitions.

Internal Audits **Internal audits** assess (1) what the company has done for itself and (2) what it has done for its customers or other recipients of its goods or services. The company can be evaluated on a number of factors, including financial stability, production efficiency, sales effectiveness, human resources development, earnings growth, public relations, civic responsibility, and other criteria of organizational effectiveness. The audit reviews the company's past, present, and future.[14]

internal audit

A periodic assessment of a company's own planning, organizing, leading, and controlling processes.

To perform a management audit, a list of desired qualifications is drawn up and weights are attached to each qualification. Among the more common undesirable practices uncovered by a management audit are the performance of unnecessary work, duplication of work, poor inventory control, uneconomical use of equipment and machines, procedures that are more costly than necessary, and wasted resources. Square D, the electrical equipment manufacturer, discovered it could throw away four manuals with 760 rules and regulations in favor of 11 policy statements. At Heinz, a quality program aimed mostly at eliminating waste and rework is predicted to save $250 million over three years.[15]

Budgetary Controls

Budgetary control is one of the most widely recognized and commonly used methods of managerial control. It ties together feedforward control, concurrent control, and feedback control, depending on the point at which it is applied. *Budgetary control* is the process of finding out what's being done and comparing the results with the corresponding budget data to verify accomplishments or remedy differences. Budgetary control commonly is called **budgeting.**

Fundamental Budgetary Considerations In private industry, budgetary control begins with an estimate of sales and expected income. Table 16.4 shows a budget with estimates for sales and expenses for the first three months of the year. There is space to enter the actual accomplishments to expedite a comparison between expected and actual results. Note that the total expenses plus estimated gross profit equal the total sales expectancy.

> **budgeting**
> The process of investigating what is being done and comparing the results with the corresponding budget data to verify accomplishments or remedy differences. Also called budgetary controlling.

Budgeting information is supplied to the entire enterprise or to any of its units; it is not confined to financial matters. Units other than dollars typically can be used. For example, industry uses budgeting of production in physical units and of labor by different skills.

A primary consideration of budgeting is the length of the budget period. All budgets are prepared for a definite time period. Many budgets are for one, three, or six months or for one year. The length of time selected depends on the primary purpose of the budgeting. The period chosen should include the enterprise's complete normal cycle of activity. For example, seasonal variations should be included both for production and for sales. The budget period commonly coincides with other control devices, such as managerial reports, balance sheets, and statements of profit and loss. In addition, the extent to which reasonable forecasts can be made should be considered in selecting the length of the budget period.

Budgetary control proceeds through several stages. *Establishing expectancies* starts with the broad plan for the company and the estimate of sales, and it ends with budget approval and publication. The *budgetary operations* stage, then, deals with finding out what is being accomplished and comparing the results with expectancies. The last stage, as in any control process, involves taking corrective action when necessary.

A Sales-Expense Budget **TABLE 16.4**

	January Expectancy	Actual	February Expectancy	Actual	March Expectancy	Actual
Sales	$1,200,000		$1,350,000		$1,400,000	
Expenses						
General overhead	310,000		310,000		310,000	
Selling	242,000		275,000		288,000	
Producing	327,000		430,500		456,800	
Research	118,400		118,400		115,000	
Office	90,000		91,200		91,500	
Advertising	32,500		27,000		25,800	
Estimated gross profit	80,100		97,900		112,900	

Although practices differ widely, a member of top management often serves as the chief coordinator for formulating and using the budget. Usually the treasurer, controller, or chief accountant has these duties. He or she needs to be less concerned with the details than with resolving conflicting interests, recommending adjustments when needed, and giving official sanction to the budgetary procedures.

Types of Budgets

There are many types of budgets. Some of the more common types are as follows:

- *Sales budget.* Usually data for the sales budget are prepared by month, sales area, and product.
- *Production budget.* The production budget commonly is expressed in physical units. Required information for preparing this budget includes types and capacities of machines, economic quantities to produce, and availability of materials.
- *Cost production budget.* The information in the cost production budget sometimes is included in production budgets. Comparing production cost with sales price shows whether profit margins are adequate.
- *Cash budget.* The cash budget is essential to every business. It should be prepared after all other budget estimates are completed. The cash budget shows the anticipated receipts and expenditures, the amount of working capital available, the extent to which outside financing may be required, and the periods and amounts of cash available.
- *Master budget.* The master budget includes all the major activities of the business. It brings together and coordinates all the activities of the other budgets and can be thought of as a "budget of budgets."

Who's Auditing the Auditors?

Auditing used to be the main event for CPA firms such as the now-defunct Andersen Consulting. But that changed with the rise of "management consulting" in the 1990s. In an effort to land lucrative consulting contracts, the auditing function at Big Five firms was sidelined and even sold at bargain rates to corporate clients such as Enron. In fact, in 1999, Enron paid Andersen more for consulting than it did for auditing its books. But it wasn't just

A senior managing partner of Arthur Andersen, C. E. Andrews (left), speaks in Houston as defense attorney Rusty Hardin (right) listens, after Andersen was convicted of obstructing justice by shredding Enron-related documents.

Andersen that got caught up in the consulting frenzy. According to *The Accounting Review,* by the end of the 1990s, the total consulting revenues of the major accounting firms were three times more than the auditing revenues.

Did the prospect of big bucks cause Andersen to look the other way when auditing Enron's balance sheet? Probably. Andersen's CEO, Joe Berardino, claims that he never was told the most basic details about the Enron controversy until it erupted into headlines.

"Quality wasn't discussed. Content wasn't discussed. Everything was measured in terms of the buck," says Barbara Ley Toffler, an Andersen partner from 1995 to 1999. "Joe was blind to the conflict. He was the most aggressive pursuer of revenue that I ever met."

Berardino tried to straighten out the Enron mess by hiring former Federal Reserve Board chairman Paul Volker. The plan was to spin off Andersen's consulting arm and remake the firm into an entity that did only auditing. But those efforts failed when the U.S. Justice Department indicted and convicted the firm for numerous violations, including shredding Enron's documents. "The culture of the company changed because it got deeply involved in the consulting business," laments Volker. That left the remaining "Big Four" and Congress wondering whether stricter regulations and separating CPA firms by function might make for better checks and balances.

SOURCE: John A. Byrne, "Joe Berardino's Fall from Grace," *Business Week Online,* August 12, 2002.

Accounting records must be inspected periodically to ensure they were properly prepared and are correct. **Accounting audits,** which are designed to verify accounting reports and statements, are essential to the control process. This audit is performed by members of an outside firm of public accountants. Knowing that accounting records are accurate, true, and in keeping with generally accepted accounting practices (GAAP) creates confidence that a reliable base exists for sound overall controlling purposes.[16]

> **accounting audits**
>
> Procedures used to verify accounting reports and statements.

Activity-Based Costing It is widely recognized that traditional methods of cost accounting may be inappropriate in today's business environment because they are based on outdated methods of rigid hierarchical organization. Instead of assuming that organizations are bureaucratic "machines" that can be separated into component functions such as human resources, purchasing, and maintenance, companies such as Chrysler, Hewlett-Packard, and GE have begun using **activity-based costing (ABC)** to allocate costs across business processes.

ABC starts with the assumption that organizations are collections of people performing many different but related activities to satisfy customer needs. The ABC system is designed to identify those streams of activity and then to allocate costs across particular business processes. The basic procedure works as follows (see Figure 16.2): First, employees are asked to break down what they do each day in order to define their *basic activities.* For example, employees in Dana Corporation's material control department engage in a number of activities that range from processing sales orders and sourcing parts to requesting engineering changes and solving problems. These activities form the basis for ABC. Second, managers look at total expenses computed by traditional accounting— fixed costs, supplies, salaries, fringe benefits, and so on—and spread total amounts over the activities according to the amount of time spent on each activity. At Dana, customer service employees spend nearly 25 percent of their time processing sales orders and only about 3 percent scheduling parts. Thus, 25 percent of the total cost ($144,846) goes to order processing and 3 percent ($15,390) goes to scheduling parts. As can be seen in Figure 16.2, both the traditional and ABC systems reach the same bottom line. However, because the ABC method allocates costs across business processes, it provides a more accurate picture of how costs should be charged to products and services.[17]

> **activity-based costing (ABC)**
>
> A method of cost accounting designed to identify streams of activity and then to allocate costs across particular business processes according to the amount of time employees devote to particular activities.

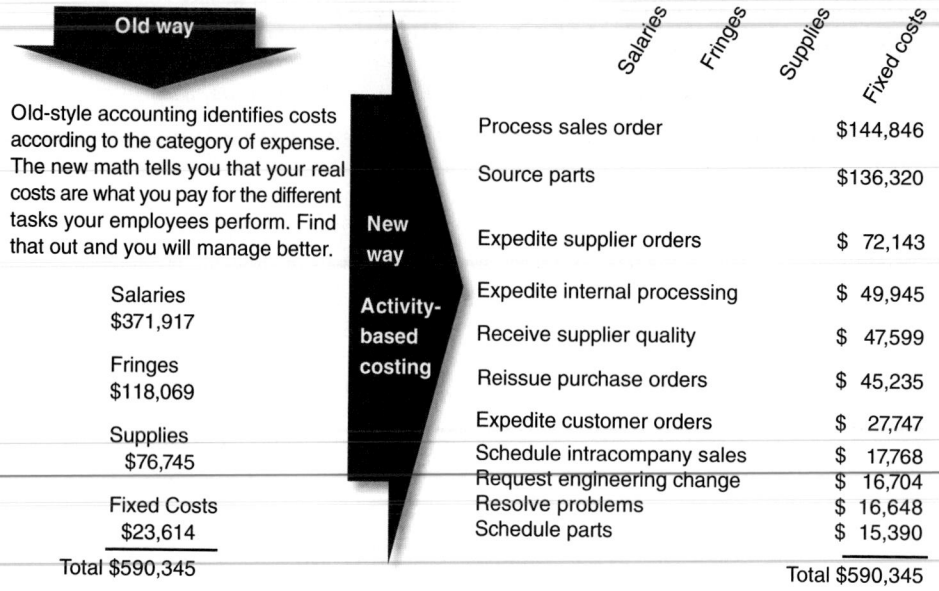

	Salaries	Fringes	Supplies	Fixed costs
Process sales order				$144,846
Source parts				$136,320
Expedite supplier orders				$ 72,143
Expedite internal processing				$ 49,945
Receive supplier quality				$ 47,599
Reissue purchase orders				$ 45,235
Expedite customer orders				$ 27,747
Schedule intracompany sales				$ 17,768
Request engineering change				$ 16,704
Resolve problems				$ 16,648
Schedule parts				$ 15,390
				Total $590,345

Old way

Old-style accounting identifies costs according to the category of expense. The new math tells you that your real costs are what you pay for the different tasks your employees perform. Find that out and you will manage better.

Salaries $371,917

Fringes $118,069

Supplies $76,745

Fixed Costs $23,614

Total $590,345

New way

Activity-based costing

SOURCE: Courtesy Dana Corporation.

FIGURE 16.2
How Dana Discovers What Its True Costs Are

Perhaps more important than the accuracy of ABC, the system highlights where wasted activities are occurring or if activities cost too much relative to the benefits they provide to customers. By providing this type of information, ABC has become a valuable method for streamlining business processes.

Financial Controls

In addition to budgets, businesses commonly use other statements for financial control. Two financial statements that help control overall organizational performance are the balance sheet and the profit and loss statement.

The Balance Sheet   The **balance sheet** shows the financial picture of a company at a given time. This statement itemizes three elements: (1) assets, (2) liabilities, and (3) stockholders' equity. **Assets** are the values of the various items the corporation owns. **Liabilities** are the amounts the corporation owes to various creditors. **Stockholders' equity** is the amount accruing to the corporation's owners. The relationship among these three elements is as follows:

Assets = Liabilities + Stockholders' equity

Table 16.5 shows an example of a balance sheet. During the year, the company grew because it enlarged its building and acquired more machinery and equipment by means of long-term debt in the form of a first mortgage. Additional stock was sold to help finance the expansion. At the same time, accounts receivable were increased and work in process was reduced. Observe that Total assets ($3,053,367) = Total liabilities ($677,204 + $618,600) + Stockholders' equity ($700,000 + $981,943 + $75,620).

Summarizing balance sheet items over a long period of time uncovers important trends and gives a manager further insight into overall performance and areas in which adjustments need to be made.

balance sheet

A report that shows the financial picture of a company at a given time and itemizes assets, liabilities, and stockholders' equity.

assets

The values of the various items the corporation owns.

liabilities

The amounts a corporation owes to various creditors.

stockholders' equity

The amount accruing to the corporation's owners.

The Profit and Loss Statement   The **profit and loss statement** is an itemized financial statement of the income and expenses of a company's operations. Table 16.6 shows a comparative statement of profit and loss for two consecutive years. In this illustration, the operating revenue of the enterprise has increased. Expense also has increased, but at

Comparative Balance Sheet for the Years Ending December 31	This Year	Last Year
Assets		
Current assets:		
Cash	$161,870	$119,200
U.S. Treasury bills	250,400	30,760
Accounts receivable	825,595	458,762
Inventories:		
Work in process and finished products	429,250	770,800
Raw materials and supplies	251,340	231,010
Total current assets	1,918,455	1,610,532
Other assets:		
Land	157,570	155,250
Building	740,135	91,784
Machinery and equipment	172,688	63,673
Furniture and fixtures	132,494	57,110
Total other assets before depreciation	1,202,887	367,817
Less: Accumulated depreciation and amortization	67,975	63,786
Total other assets	1,134,912	304,031
Total assets	$3,053,367	$1,914,563
Liabilities and stockholders' equity		
Current liabilities:		
Accounts payable	$287,564	$441,685
Payrolls and withholdings from employees	44,055	49,580
Commissions and sundry accruals	83,260	41,362
Federal taxes on income	176,340	50,770
Current installment on long-term debt	85,985	38,624
Total current liabilities	667,204	622,021
Long-term liabilities:		
15-year, 9 percent loan, payable in each of the years 2002–2015	210,000	225,000
5 percent first mortgage	408,600	
Registered 9 percent notes payable		275,000
Total long-term liabilities	618,600	500,000
Stockholders' equity:		
Common stock: authorized 1,000,000 shares, outstanding last year 492,000 shares, outstanding this year 700,000 shares at $1 par value	700,000	492,000
Capital surplus	981,943	248,836
Earned surplus	75,620	51,706
Total liabilities and stockholders' equity	$3,053,367	$1,914,563

TABLE 16.5
A Comparative Balance Sheet

a lower rate, resulting in a higher net income. Some managers draw up tentative profit and loss statements and use them as goals. Then performance is measured against these goals or standards. From comparative statements of this type, a manager can identify trouble areas and correct them.

profit and loss statement

An itemized financial statement of the income and expenses of a company's operations.

Comparative Statement of Profit and Loss for the Years Ending June 30			
	This Year	**Last Year**	**Increase or Decrease**
Income:			
Net sales	$ 253,218	$ 257,636	$ 4,418*
Dividends from investments	480	430	50
Other	1,741	1,773	32
Total	255,439	259,839	4,400*
Deductions:			
Cost of goods sold	180,481	178,866	1,615
Selling and administrative expenses	39,218	34,019	5,199
Interest expense	2,483	2,604	121*
Other	1,941	1,139	802
Total	224,123	216,628	7,495
Income before taxes	31,316	43,211	11,895*
Provision for taxes	3,300	9,500	6,200*
Net income	$28,016	$33,711	$5,695*

TABLE 16.6
A Comparative Statement of Profit and Loss

*Decrease.

Controlling by profit and loss is most commonly used for the entire enterprise and, in the case of a diversified corporation, its divisions. However, if controlling is by departments, as in a decentralized organization in which department managers have control over both revenue and expense, a profit and loss statement is used for each department. Each department's output is measured, and a cost, including overhead, is

Carving Up GE Capital

GE chairman Jeffrey R. Immelt didn't stick his head in the sand when a wave of accounting scandals rolled over corporate America in 2001–2002. One such scandal even involved perks for GE's former CEO, Jack Welch, who is considered a corporate legend. Immelt was determined to set the accounting record straight. He promised his company's cooperation in the investigation of Welch. He supported congressional and New York Stock Exchange reforms. He pledged to appoint only independent directors to his board. He also took a carving knife to GE's massive financial unit, GE Capital.

GE Capital is a provider of financial products ranging from mortgage insurance to equipment management. Its revenues account for a full 40 percent of GE's profits. In recent years, GE Capital has grown into a behemoth, encompassing more than two dozen businesses. It had become something of a mystery to investors. Many of them couldn't figure out how the division made its money or whether profits were the result of growth or acquisitions.

By breaking GE Capital into four pieces—equipment management, commercial finance, insurance, and consumer finance units—Immelt made the business easier to understand. For example, all the insurance elements were brought under one roof called GE Insurance. That made it easier to contrast GE's insurance operations with those of competitors such as Allstate and Prudential. It also created more competition and accountability within each division—no more hiding under the giant GE Capital umbrella.

That can be good and bad. For example, the insurance losses after September 11, 2001, were a drain. But isolating the bad news to a single division made the performance of the other three easier to gauge. "I love it." exclaims GE Vice Chairman Dennis D. Dammerman about the breakup, noting that it should give the public more familiarity with each group's day-to-day operations: "It's not a great big blob anymore." Shareholders should now be able to figure out for themselves how to asses each unit's bottom-line results.

SOURCE: Diane Brady, "GE Capital in Four Easy Pieces," *Business Week Online*, August 2, 2002.

charged to each department's operation. Expected net income is the standard for measuring a department's performance.

Financial Ratios   An effective approach for checking on the overall performance of an enterprise is to use key financial ratios. Ratios help indicate possible strengths and weaknesses in a company's operations. Key ratios are calculated from selected items on the profit and loss statement and the balance sheet. We will briefly discuss three categories of financial ratios: liquidity, leverage, and profitability.

- **Liquidity ratios.** *Liquidity ratios* indicate a company's ability to pay short-term debts. The most common liquidity ratio is *current assets to current liabilities*, called the **current ratio** or *net working capital ratio*. This ratio indicates the extent to which current assets can decline and still be adequate to pay current liabilities. Some analysts set a ratio of 2 to 1, or 2.00, as the desirable minimum.
- **Leverage ratios.** *Leverage ratios* show the relative amount of funds in the business supplied by creditors and shareholders. An important example is the **debt-equity ratio,** which indicates the company's ability to meet its long-term financial obligations. If this ratio is less than 1.5, the amount of debt is not considered excessive.
- **Profitability ratios.** *Profitability ratios* indicate management's ability to generate a financial return on sales or investment. For example, **return on investment (ROI)** is a ratio of profit to capital used, or a rate of return from capital.

> **current ratio**
>
> A liquidity ratio which indicates the extent to which short-term assets can decline and still be adequate to pay short-term liabilities.

> **debt-equity ratio**
>
> A leverage ratio which indicates the company's ability to meet its long term financial obligations.

> **return on investment (ROI)**
>
> A ratio of profit to capital used, or a rate of return from capital.

Using Financial Ratios   Although ratios provide both performance standards and indicators of what has occurred, exclusive reliance on financial ratios can have negative consequences. Because ratios usually are expressed in compressed time horizons (monthly, quarterly, or yearly), they often cause **management myopia**—managers focus on short-term earnings and profits at the expense of their longer-term strategic obligations.[18] Control systems using long-term (e.g., three- to six-year) performance targets can reduce management myopia and focus attention farther into the future.

> **management myopia**
>
> Focusing on short-term earnings and profits at the expense of longer-term strategic obligations.

A second negative outcome of ratios is that they relegate other important considerations to a secondary position. Research and development, management development, progressive human resources practices, and other considerations may receive insufficient attention. Therefore, the use of ratios should be supplemented with other control measures. Organizations can hold managers accountable for market share, number of patents granted, sales of new products, human resources development, and other performance indicators.

The Downside of Bureaucratic Control

So far you have learned about control from a mechanical viewpoint. But organizations are not strictly mechanical; they are composed of people. While control systems are used to constrain people's behavior and make their future behavior predictable, people are not machines that automatically fall into line as the designers of control systems intend. In fact, control systems can lead to dysfunctional behavior. A control system cannot be effective without consideration of how people will react to it. For effective control of employee behavior, managers should consider three types of potential responses to control: rigid bureaucratic behavior, tactical behavior, and resistance.[19]

Rigid Bureaucratic Behavior   Often people act in ways that will help them look good on the control system's measures. This tendency can be useful, because it causes people to focus on the behaviors management requires. But it can result in rigid, inflexible behavior geared toward doing *only* what the system requires.

Rigid bureaucratic behavior occurs when control systems prompt employees to stay out of trouble by following the rules. Unfortunately, such systems often lead to poor customer service and make the entire organization slow to act (recall the discussion of bureaucracy in Chapter 10).

We have all been victimized at some time by rigid bureaucratic behavior. Reflect for a moment on this now classic story of a "nightmare" at a hospital:

> At midnight, a patient with eye pains enters an emergency room at a hospital. At the reception area, he is classified as a nonemergency case and referred to the hospital's eye clinic. Trouble is, the eye clinic doesn't open until the next morning. When he arrives at the clinic, the nurse asks for his referral slip, but the emergency room doctor had forgotten to give it to him. The patient has to return to the emergency room and wait for another physician to screen him. The physician refers him back to the eye clinic and to a social worker to arrange payment. Finally, a third doctor looks into his eye, sees a small piece of metal, and removes it—a 30-second procedure.[20]

Stories such as these have, of course, given bureaucracy a bad name. Some managers will not even use the term *bureaucratic control* because of its potentially negative connotation. That is unfortunate because the control system itself is not the problem. The problems occur when the systems are no longer viewed as tools for running the business, but as rules for dictating rigid behavior.

Tactical Behavior   Control systems will be ineffective if employees engage in tactics aimed at "beating the system." The most common type of tactical behavior is to manipulate information or report false performance data. People may produce two kinds of invalid data: about what *has* been done and about what *can* be done. False reporting about the past is less common, because it is easier to identify someone who misreports what happened than someone who gives an erroneous prediction or estimate of what might happen. Still, managers sometimes change their accounting systems to "smooth out" the numbers. That's what happened at MCI Worldcom. By mischaracterizing expenses, managers were able to distort the bottom line by $4 billion. Also, people may intentionally feed false information into a management information system to cover up errors or poor performance.[21]

More commonly, people falsify their predictions or requests for the future. When asked to give budgetary estimates, employees usually ask for larger amounts than they need. On the other hand, they sometimes submit unrealistically *low* estimates when they believe a low estimate will help them get a budget or a project approved. Budget-setting sessions can become tugs-of-war between subordinates trying to get slack in the budget and superiors attempting to minimize slack. Similar tactics are exhibited when managers negotiate unrealistically low performance standards so that subordinates will have little trouble meeting them; when salespeople project low forecasts so they will look good by exceeding them; and when workers slow down the work pace when time-study analysts are setting work pace standards. In these and other cases, people are concerned only with their own performance figures rather than with the overall performance of their departments or companies.[22]

Resistance to Control   Often people strongly resist control systems. This occurs for several reasons. First, comprehensive control systems increase the accuracy of performance data and make employees more accountable for their actions. Control systems uncover mistakes, threaten people's job security and status, and decrease people's autonomy.

Second, control systems can change expertise and power structures. For example, management information systems can make the costing, purchasing, and production decisions previously made by managers. Thus, individuals fear a loss of expertise, power, and decision-making authority.

Third, control systems can change the social structure of an organization. They can create competition and disrupt social groups and friendships. People may end up competing against those with whom they formerly had comfortable, cooperative relationships. Because people's social needs are so important, they will resist control systems that reduce social need satisfaction.

Fourth, control systems may be seen as an invasion of privacy, lead to lawsuits, and cause low morale.

If you want a job in corporate America, you're probably going to have to take a drug test. What was once a controversial practice has become commonplace. In 1996, employee drug testing reached an all-time high. Eighty-one percent of major companies reported that they were doing it. However, the numbers are starting to decline. Fewer workers are testing positive, too. In 1998, 13.6 percent of corporate drug-screening tests came back positive, compared with just 5 percent today.

Some employers have halted drug testing altogether. Agilent Technology stopped testing applicants a couple of years ago because of the tight labor market. Requiring applicants to take a urine test and then waiting for the results slowed the hiring process when candidates were receiving multiple offers. Even with the softening of the job market, Agilent has no plans to resume testing in the near term. Part of the reason companies are forgoing testing is the cost. A drug test can cost between $15 to $50, and accountants at corporations are beginning to wonder whether the expense is really worth it.

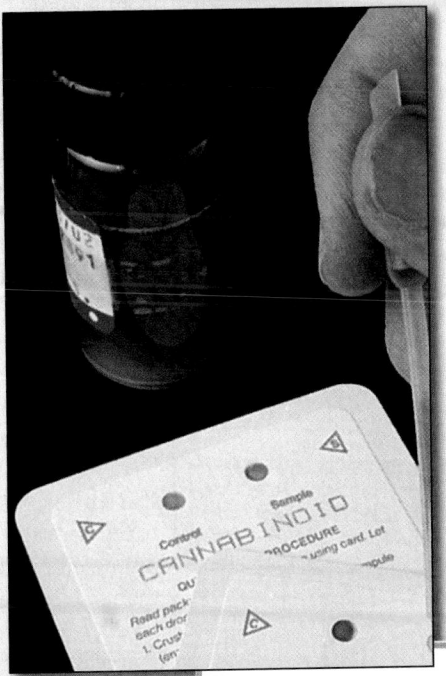

However, more companies are electronically monitoring their employees than ever before. Eighty-two percent of major U.S. firms review employee communications, such as email and phone calls, or videotape their employees, according to a recent survey by the American Management Association (AMA). "Privacy in today's workplace is largely illusory," says Ellen Bayer, who is with the association. "In this era of open space cubicles, shared desk space, networked computers and teleworkers, it is hard to realistically hold on to a belief in private space."

Moreover, it has been estimated that cyberloafing accounts for 30 percent to 40 percent of lost worker productivity. Losses amount to $54 billion annually for U.S. companies, some experts think. Twenty-five percent of employees say they use the Internet for personal purposes during office hours. Thirteen percent say they spend more than two hours a day surfing. "The dirty little secret of e-commerce is that it's being done from nine to five," says Andrew Meyeer, marketing vice president of Websense, Inc., a San Diego–based maker of monitoring software. In fact, nearly two of three companies have disciplined employees for Internet misuse, and one of three has terminated an employee. Xerox, the New York Times, Edward Jones, and First Union Bank are among them. Chevron and Microsoft both settled sexual harassment lawsuits that resulted from emails that circulated through those companies.

> Drug testing is one of the ways organizations monitor employees. Some people favor the control measure, but change their minds when personally asked to submit a urine specimen.

WHY MONITOR EMPLOYEES?

There are few laws that regulate what or whom companies can monitor. "Work is carried out on equipment belonging to employers who have a legal right to the work product of the employees using it," Bayer says. Employers who answered a recent AMA survey listed the following reasons for monitoring their employees:

- *Legal compliance.* In regulated industries, taping telemarketing activities gives both the company and the consumer some degree of legal protection.
- *Legal liability.* Employees who are unwittingly exposed to offensive material on colleagues' computer screens may contend that they are being subjected to a hostile work environment.
- *Performance evaluation.* Taping customer service and consumer relations employees helps employers evaluate and improve job performance.

- *Productivity measures.* Monitoring workers allows employers to gauge to the extent to which employees are being productive.
- *Security/proprietary concerns.* Companies have an interest in protecting corporate information that could fall into the hands of a competitor.

Ninety percent of companies that monitor their employees notify them about it before doing so, though. And most say they monitor employees randomly and at intervals—not continuously. Nonetheless, journalist Bob Rosner offers some sage advice when it comes to electronic communications: "Write every email as if your boss will eventually read it."

SOURCES: Jennifer Gill, "Going on Ecstasy Alert," *Business Week Online*, August 14, 2001; John Reh, "Your Boss Is Watching You," *About Inc.*, June 25, 2001; Michelle Conlin, "Workers: Surf at Your Own Risk," *Business Week Online*, June 12, 2000.

Designing Effective Control Systems

Effective control systems maximize potential benefits and minimize dysfunctional behaviors. To achieve this, management needs to design control systems that (1) are based on valid performance standards, (2) communicate adequate information to employees, (3) are acceptable to employees, (4) use multiple approaches, and (5) recognize the relationship between empowerment and control.

Establish Valid Performance Standards An effective control system must be based on valid and accurate performance standards. The most effective standards, as discussed earlier, tend to be expressed in quantitative terms; they are objective rather than subjective. Also, the measures should not be capable of being easily sabotaged or faked. Moreover, the system must incorporate all important aspects of performance. As you learned earlier, unmeasured behaviors are neglected. But management also must defend against another problem: too many measures that create overcontrol and employee resistance. To make many controls tolerable, managers can devote attention to a few key areas while setting "satisfactory" performance standards in others. Or they can establish simple priorities. The purchasing agent may have to meet targets in the following sequence: quality, availability, cost, inventory level. Finally, managers can set tolerance ranges. For example, in financial budgeting optimistic, expected, and minimum levels sometimes are specified.

Many companies' budgets set cost targets only. This causes managers to control spending, but also to neglect earnings. At Emerson Electric, profit rather than cost is the key measure. If an unanticipated opportunity to increase market share arises, managers can spend what they need to go after it. The phrase "it's not in the budget" is less likely to stifle people at Emerson than it is at most other companies.

This principle applies to nonfinancial aspects of performance as well. At Motorola, the recruiting department used to be measured by how much money it spent for each new hire. Now it is measured by how well its recruits subsequently perform.[23]

Provide Adequate Information Management must communicate to employees the importance and nature of the control system. Then people must receive feedback about their performance. Feedback motivates people and provides information that enables them to correct their own deviations from performance standards. Allowing people to initiate their own corrective action encourages self-control and reduces the need for outside supervision.

Information should be as accessible as possible, particularly when people must make decisions quickly and frequently. For example, a national food company with its own truck fleet had a difficult problem. The company wanted drivers to go through customer sales records every night, insert new prices from headquarters every morning, and still make their rounds—an impossible set of demands. To solve this control problem, the company installed personal computers (PCs) in more than 1,000 delivery trucks. Now drivers use their PCs for constant communication with headquarters. Each night drivers send information about the stores, and each morning headquarters sends prices and recommended stock mixes.

In general, a manager designing a control system should evaluate the information system in terms of the following questions:

1. Does it provide people with data relevant to the decisions they need to make?
2. Does it provide the right amount of information to decision makers throughout the organization?
3. Does it provide enough information to each part of the organization about how other, related parts of the organization are functioning?[24]

Ensure Acceptability to Employees   Employees are less likely to resist a control system and exhibit dysfunctional behaviors if they accept the system. They are more likely to accept systems that have useful performance standards but are not over-controlling. One Food Lion (a supermarket chain) store manager said to a *Fortune* reporter about standards he considered unreasonable, "I put in more and more and more time—a hundred hours a week—but no matter . . . I could never satisfy the supervisors . . . They wanted 100 percent conditions, seven days a week, 24 hours a day. And there's no . . . way you could do it."[25] Employees will find systems more acceptable if they believe the standards are possible to achieve.

The control system should emphasize positive behavior rather than focusing on controlling negative behavior alone. As noted earlier, companies such as Emerson look at profits rather than costs. Jean-Marie Descarpentries of Franco-British CMB Packaging clearly prefers to highlight the positive: He has the heads of 94 profit centers project their best possible performance if everything goes perfectly. He wants his managers to "dream the impossible dream." Then he avoids penalizing people who just miss their lofty goals by assessing them based on how they performed this year versus last year and against the performances of the best managers in the industry.[26]

One of the best ways to establish reasonable standards and thus gain employee acceptance of the control system is to set standards participatively. As we discussed in Chapter 4, participation in decision making secures people's understanding and acceptance and results in better decisions. Allowing employees to participate in control system decisions that affect their jobs directly will help overcome resistance and foster acceptance of the system.

Use Multiple Approaches   Multiple controls are necessary. For example, casinos exercise control over card dealers by (1) requiring them to have a card dealer's license before being hired; (2) using various forms of direct scrutiny, including up to three levels of direct supervision, closed-circuit cameras, and observation through one-way mirrors; and (3) requiring detailed paperwork to audit transfers of cash and cash equivalents.[27] As you learned earlier in this chapter, control systems generally should include both financial and nonfinancial performance targets and incorporate aspects of preliminary, concurrent, and feedback control.

The Other Controls: Markets and Clans

Although the concept of control has always been a central feature of organizations, the principles and philosophies underlying its use are changing. In the past, control was focused almost exclusively on bureaucratic (and market) mechanisms. Generations of managers were taught that they could maximize productivity by regulating what employees did on the job—through standard operating procedures, rules, regulations, and close supervision. To increase output on an assembly line, for example, managers in the past tried to identify the "one best way" to approach the work and then to monitor employees' activities to make certain that they followed standard operating procedures. In short, they controlled work by dividing and simplifying tasks, a process we referred to in Chapter 1 as *scientific management*.

Although formal bureaucratic control systems are perhaps the most pervasive in organizations (and the most talked about in management textbooks), they are not always the most effective. *Market controls* and *clan controls* may both represent more flexible, though no less potent, approaches to regulating performance.

Market Control

In contrast to bureaucratic controls, market controls involve the use of economic forces—and the pricing mechanisms that accompany them—to regulate performance. The system works like this: In cases where output from an individual, department, or business unit has value to other people, a price can be negotiated for its exchange. As a market for these transactions becomes established, two effects occur:

- Price becomes an indicator of the value of the product or service.
- Price competition has the effect of controlling productivity and performance.

The basic principles that underlie market controls can operate at the corporate level, the business unit (or department) level, and the individual level. Figure 16.3 shows a few different ways in which market controls are used in an organization.

Market Controls at the Corporate Level In large, diversified companies, market controls often are used to regulate independent business units. Particularly in large conglomerate firms that act as holding companies, business units typically are treated as profit centers that compete with one another. Top executives may place very few bureaucratic controls on business unit managers but use profit and loss data for evaluating performance. While decision making and power are decentralized to the business units, market controls ensure that business unit performance is in line with corporate objective.

FIGURE 16.3

Examples of Market Control

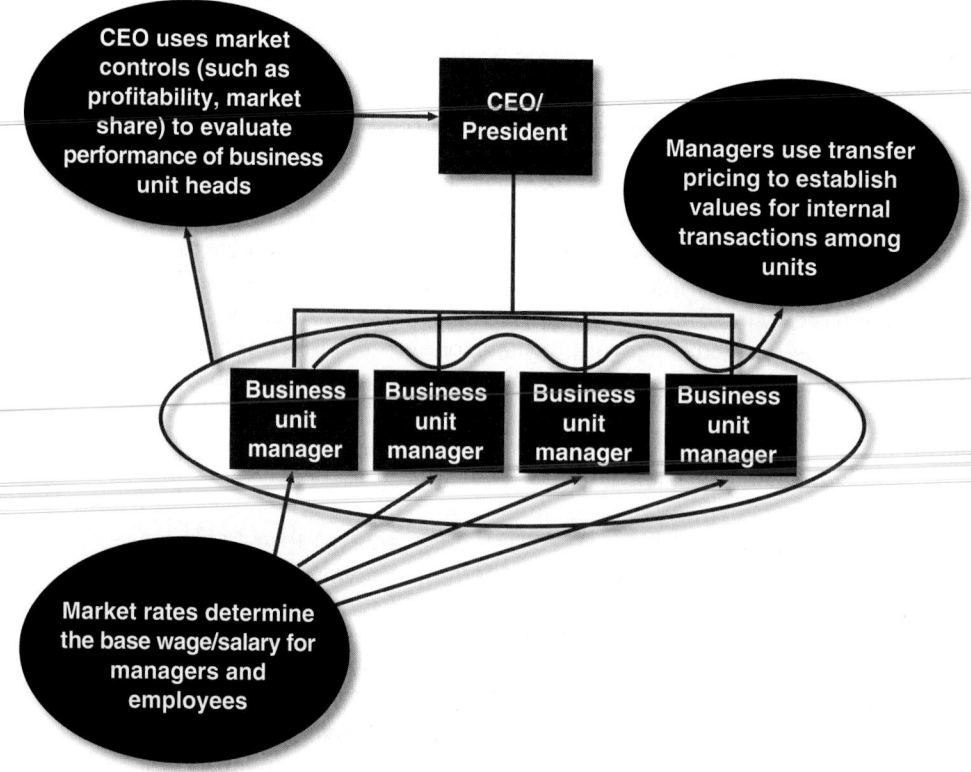

Use of market control mechanisms in this way has been criticized by those who insist that economic measures do not reflect the complete value of an organization adequately. Employees often suffer as diversified companies are repeatedly bought and sold based on market controls.

Market Controls at the Business Unit Level Market control also can be used within business units to regulate exchanges among departments and functions. Transfer pricing is one method that organizations use to try to reflect market forces for internal transactions. A **transfer price** is the charged by one unit in the organization for a product or service that it supplies to another unit of the same organization. For example, in automobile manufacturing, a transfer price may be affixed to components and subassemblies before they are shipped to subsequent business units for final assembly. Ideally, the transfer price reflects the price that the receiving business unit would have to pay for that product or serivice in the marketplace.

transfer price

Price charged by one unit for a product or service provided to another unit within the organization.

As organizations have more options to outsource products and services to external partners, market controls such as transfer prices provide natural incentives to keep costs down and quality up. Consider the situation in which training and development activities can be done internally by the human resources department or outsourced to a consulting firm. If the human resources department cannot supply quality traning at a reasonable price, there may be no reason for that department to exist inside the firm. Organizations such as Continental Airlines, IBM, and Corning have placed strict market controls on their human resources functions in order to manage costs and performance.[28]

Market Controls at the Individual Level Market controls also are used at the individual level. For example, in situations where organizations are trying to hire employees, the supply and demand for particular skills influence the wages employees can expect to receive and the rate organizations are likely to pay. Employees or job candidates who have more valuable skills tend to be paid a higher wage. Of course, wages don't always reflect market rates—sometimes they are based (perhaps arbitrarily) on internal resource considerations—but the market rate is often the best indicator of an employee's potential worth to a firm.

Market-based controls such as these are important in that they provide a natural incentive for employees to enhance their skills and offer them to potential firms. Even after individuals gain employment, market-based wages are important as controls in that persons with higher economic value may be promoted faster to higher positions in the organization.

Market controls often are used by boards of directors to manage CEOs of major corporations. Ironically, CEOs usually are seen as the ones controlling everyone else in the company, but the fact is that the CEO is accountable to the board of directors, and the board must devise ways to ensure that the CEO acts in its interest. Believe it or not, CEOs often do not want to accept the associated risk required to achieve higher profits for the owners and consequently may act in ways that make them look good personally (such as making the company bigger or more diversified) but that don't translate into higher profits for the firm.

To attach some strings to the actions of CEOs, boards typically use at least two types of incentives on top of base salary: First, some type of bonus is tied to short-term profit targets, such as return on equity. In large U.S. companies, most of the pay of CEOs is now at risk, meaning it's variable depending on the performance of the company. In addition to short-term incentives, boards use some type of long-term incentives linked to the firm's share price, usually through stock options. Options are viewed as a way to turn managers into owners who will keep one eye on the stock price. By having options tied to their pay, CEOs have an incentive to deliver superior performance over time. Once a minor perk, options now account for 80 percent of the executive-compensation pie.[29]

Clan Control: The Role of Empowerment and Culture

Increasingly, managers are discovering that control systems based solely on bureaucratic and market mechanisms are insufficient for directing today's workforce. There are several reasons for this.

- *Employees' jobs have changed.* The nature of work is evolving. Employees working with computers, for example, have more variability in their jobs, and much of their work is intellectual and therefore invisible. Because of this, there is no one best way to perform a task, and programming or standardizing jobs becomes extremely difficult. Close supervision is also unrealistic since it is nearly impossible to supervise activities such as reasoning and problem solving.
- *The nature of management has changed.* The role of managers is evolving, too. It used to be the case that managers knew more about the job than employees did. Today, it is typical for employees to know more about their jobs than anyone else does. We refer to this as the shift from touch labor to knowledge work. When real expertise in organizations exists at the very lowest levels, hierarchical control becomes impractical.[30]
- *The employment relationship has changed.* The social contract at work is being renegotiated. It used to be that employees were most concerned about issues such as pay, job security, and the hours of work. Today, however, more and more employees want to be more fully engaged in their work, taking part in decision making, devising solutions to unique problems, and receiving assignments that are challenging and involving. They want to use their brains.

For these three reasons, the concept of *empowerment* not only has become more popular in organizations, it has become a necessary aspect of a manager's repertoire of control. With no "one best way" to approach a job and no way to scrutinize what employees do every day, managers must empower employees to make decisions and trust that they will act in the best interests of the firm. But this does not mean giving up control. Instead, it means that managers need to make better use of clan control, as opposed to authoritarian control.[31] As we noted at the beginning of this chapter, *clan control* involves creating relationships built on mutual respect and encouraging each individual to take responsibility for his or her actions. Employees work within a guiding framework of values, and they are expected to use good judgment. At Nordstrom, the fashion retailer, for example, instead of a thick manual laying out company policies, employees are simply given a five- by eight-inch card that reads: "Use good judgment in all situations. There will be no additional rules." The emphasis in an empowered organization is on satisfying customers, not on pleasing the boss. Mistakes are tolerated as the unavoidable by-product of dealing with change and uncertainty and are viewed as opportunities to learn. And team members learn together. Table 16.7 provides a set of guidelines for managing in an empowered world.

Understanding Culture's Role in Control   Organization culture is the foundation of clan control. **Organization culture** is the set of important assumptions about the organization and its goals and practices that members of the company share. It is a system of shared values about what is important and beliefs about how the world works. In this way, a company's culture provides a framework that organizes and directs people's behavior on the job. That's the essence of control.[32]

organization culture

The set of important assumptions about the organization and its goals and practices that members of the company share.

Cultures can be strong or weak; strong cultures can have great influence on how people think and behave. A strong culture is one in which everyone understands and believes in the firm's goals, priorities, and practices. A strong culture can be a real advantage to the organization if the behaviors it encourages and facilitates are appropriate ones. At several points in this textbook, we have alluded to strong cultures at companies such as Southwest Airlines, Starbuck's Coffee, and the Walt Disney Company that encourage extraordinary devotion to customer service. Employees in

1. *Put control where the operation is*. Layers of hierarchy, close supervision, and checks and balances are quickly disappearing and being replaced with self-guided teams. For centuries even the British Empire—as large as it was—never had more than six levels of management including the Queen.

2. *Use "real time" rather than after-the-fact controls*. Issues and problems must be solved at the source by the people doing the actual work. Managers become a resource to help out the team.

3. *Rebuild the assumptions underlying management control to build on trust rather than distrust*. Today's "high-flex" organizations are based on empowerment, not obedience. Information must facilitate decision making, not police it.

4. *Move to control based on peer norms*. Clan control is a powerful thing. Workers in Japan, for example, have been known to commit suicide rather than disappoint or lose face within their team. Although this is extreme, it underlines the power of peer influence. The Japanese have a far more homogeneous culture and set of values than we do. In North America, we must build peer norms systematically and put much less emphasis on managing by the numbers.

5. *Rebuild the incentive systems to reinforce responsiveness and teamwork*. The twin goals of adding value to the customer and team performance must become the dominant raison d'être of the measurement systems.

TABLE 16.7
Management Control in an Empowered Setting

SOURCE: Gerald H. B. Ross, "Revolution in Management Control," *Management Accounting*, November 1990, pp. 23–27. Reprinted by permission.

these companies don't need rule books to dictate how they act; their actions are rooted in their companies' cultures.

However, a strong culture that encourages the wrong behaviors can severely hinder the company's efforts to bring about appropriate changes. IBM, for example, frequently is discussed as an organization that had a very strong culture that served it well for several decades. But the uniformity and conformity established by IBM's culture were ill suited for creating the more dynamic and flexible organization needed today. One of Lou Gerstner's first tasks after taking over as CEO was to transform the culture to focus on creativity, innovation, and radical thinking. One symbolic gesture in that regard was relaxing IBM's traditional dress code of white shirts and blue pin-striped suits. The dress code itself was not important, but it represented the stodgy old IBM that Gerstner wanted to change.

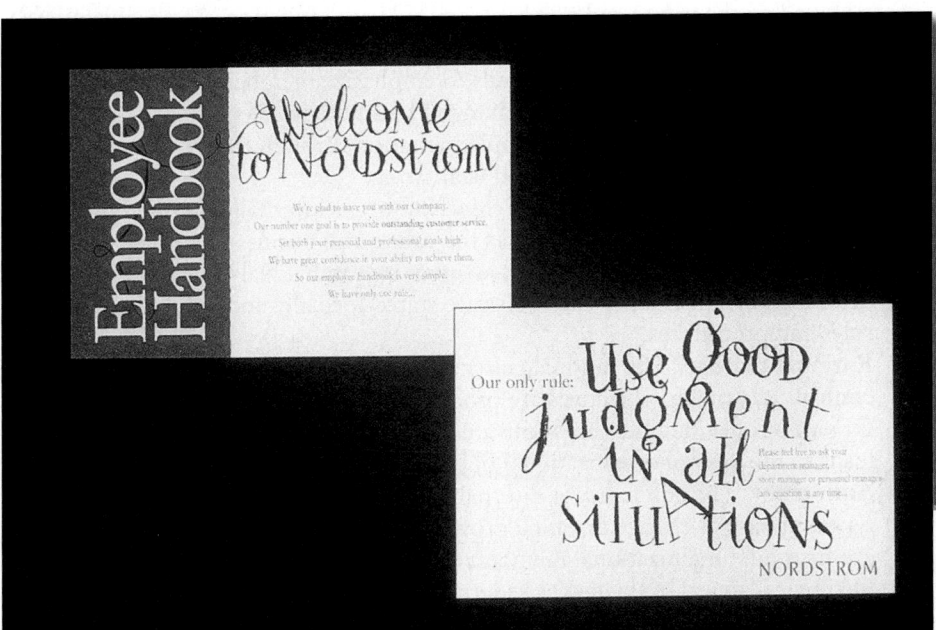

At Nordstrom, the fashion retailer, employees are simply given a five-by-eight-inch card with one rule on it.

In contrast to strong cultures, weak cultures have the following characteristics: Different people hold different values, there is confusion about corporate goals, and it is not clear from one day to the next what principles should guide decisions. As you can guess, such a culture fosters confusion, conflict, and poor performance. Most managers would agree that they want to create a strong culture that encourages and supports goals and useful behaviors that will make the company more effective.[33]

Diagnosing Culture Let's say you want to understand a company's culture. Perhaps you are thinking about working there and you want a good "fit," or perhaps you are working there right now and want to expand your repertoire of clan control. How would you go about making the diagnosis? A variety of things will give you useful clues about culture:

- *Corporate mission statements and official goals* are a starting point, as they will tell you the firm's desired public image. But you still need to figure out whether the public statements truly reflect how the firm conducts business.
- *Business practices* can be observed. How a company responds to problems, makes strategic decisions, and treats employees and customers tells a lot about what top management really values.
- *Symbols, rites, and ceremonies* give further clues about culture. For instance, status symbols can give you a feel for how rigid the hierarchy is and for the nature of relationships between lower and higher levels. Who is hired and fired—and why—and the activities that are rewarded indicate the firm's real values.
- *The stories people tell* carry a lot of information about the company's culture. Every company has its myths, legends, and true stories about important past decisions and actions that convey the company's main values. Traditionally, Frito-Lay tells service stories, Johnson & Johnson tells quality stories, and 3M tells innovation stories. The stories often feature the company's heroes: persons once or still active who possessed the qualities and characteristics that the culture especially values and who act as models for others about how to behave.

In general, cultures can be categorized according to whether they emphasize flexibility versus control and whether their focus is internal or external to the organization. By juxtaposing these two dimensions, we can describe four types of organizational cultures (see Figure 16.4):

- **Group culture.** A group culture is internally oriented and flexible. It tends to be based on the values and norms associated with affiliation. An organizational member's compliance with organizational directives flows from trust, tradition, and long-term commitment. It tends to emphasize member development and values participation in decision making. The strategic orientation associated with this cultural type is one of implementation through consensus building. Leaders tend to act as mentors and facilitators.
- **Hierarchical culture.** The hierarchical culture is internally oriented by more focus on control and stability. It has the values and norms associated with a bureaucracy. It values stability and assumes that individuals will comply with organizational mandates when roles are stated formally and enforced through rules and procedures.
- **Rational culture.** The rational culture is externally oriented and focused on control. Its primary objectives are productivity, planning, and efficiency. Organizational members are motivated by the belief that performance that leads to the desired organizational objectives will be rewarded.
- **Adhocracy.** The adhocracy is externally oriented and flexible. This culture type emphasizes change in which growth, resource acquisition, and innovation are stressed. Organizational members are motivated by the importance or ideological appeal of the task. Leaders tend to be entrepreneurial and risk takers. Other members tend to have these characteristics as well.[34]

**Flexible
Processes**

Type: Group
Dominant Attribute:
 Cohesiveness, participation,
 teamwork, sense of family
Leadership Style: Mentor,
 facilitator, parent figure
Bonding: Loyalty, tradition,
 interpersonal cohesion
Strategic Emphasis: Toward
 developing human resources,
 commitment, and morale

Type: Adhocracy
Dominant Attribute:
 Entrepreneurship, creativity,
 adaptability, dynamism
Leadership Style: Innovator,
 entrepreneur, risk taker
Bonding: Flexibility, risk,
 entrepreneur
Strategic Emphasis: Toward
 innovation, growth, new
 resources

**Internal
Maintenance**

**External
Positioning**

Type: Hierarchy
Dominant Attribute: Order, rules
 and regulations, uniformity,
 efficiency
Leadership Style: Coordinator,
 organizer, administrator
Bonding: Rules, policies and
 procedures, clear expectations
Strategic Emphasis: Toward
 stability, predictability, smooth

Type: Rational
Dominant Attribute: Goal
 achievement, environment
 exchange, competitiveness
Leadership Style: Production–
 & achievement–oriented,
 decisive
Bonding: Goal orientation,
 production, competition
Strategic Emphasis: Toward
 competitive advantage and
 market superiority

**Control–Oriented
Processes**

SOURCE: Kim S. Cameron and Robert E. Quinn, *Diagnosing and Changing Organizational Culture* (Englewood Cliffs, NJ: Addison-Wesley, 1988).

FIGURE 16.4
Competing Values Model of Culture

Managing Culture to Reinforce Clan Control Most companies today know that improving quality, adopting a customer orientation, and other moves necessary to being competitive are so essential that they require deep-rooted cultural changes.[35]

Top management can take several approaches to managing culture. First, corporate leadership should espouse lofty ideals and visions for the company that will inspire the organization's members. (We first spoke of vision in Chapter 4 on strategy, and we discussed it more fully in Chapter 12 on leadership.) The vision—whether it concerns quality, integrity, innovation, or whatever—should be articulated over and over until it becomes a tangible presence throughout the organization.

Second, executives must give constant attention to the mundane details of daily affairs such as communicating regularly, being visible and active throughout the company, and setting examples. The CEO not only should talk about the vision, he or she should embody it day in and day out. This makes the CEO's pronouncements credible, creates a personal example others can emulate, and builds trust that the organization's progress toward the vision will continue over the long run.

Important here are the moments of truth when hard choices must be made. Imagine top management trumpeting a culture that emphasizes quality and then discovering that a part used in a batch of assembled products is defective. The decision whether to replace the part at great expense in the interest of quality or to ship the defective part just to save time and money will go a long way toward reinforcing or destroying a quality-oriented culture.

All along, it is essential that the CEO and other executives celebrate and reward those who exemplify the new values. Another key to managing culture involves hiring, socializing newcomers, and promoting on the basis of the new corporate values. In this way, the new culture will begin to permeate the organization. While this may seem a time-consuming approach to building a new culture, executives must recognize that it can take years to replace a long-term culture of traditional values with one that embodies the competitive values needed in the future.

The resiliency and time investment of clan control are a "double-edged sword." Clan control takes a long time to develop and an even longer time to change. This gives an organization stability and direction during periods of upheaval in the environment or the organization (e.g., during changes in the top management). Yet if managers want to establish a new culture—a new form of clan control—they must help employees unlearn the old values and embrace the new. We will talk about this transition process more in the final chapter of this book (Chapter 18, "Creating and Managing Change").

KEY TERMS

Accounting audits, p. 499

Activity-based costing (ABC), p. 499

Assets, p. 500

Balance sheet, p. 500

Budgeting, p. 497

Bureaucratic control, p. 490

Clan control, p. 491

Concurrent control, p. 494

Control, p. 490

Current ratio, p. 503

Debt-equity ratio, p. 503

External audit, p. 496

Feedback control, p. 494

Feedforward control, p. 494

Internal audit, p. 496

Liabilities, p. 500

Management audit, p. 496

Management myopia, p. 503

Market control, p. 491

Organization culture, p. 510

Principle of exception, p. 493

Profit and loss statement, p. 501

Return on investment (ROI), p. 503

Standard, p. 491

Stockholders' equity, p. 500

Transfer price, p. 509

SUMMARY OF LEARNING OBJECTIVES

Now that you have studied Chapter 16, you should know:

Why companies develop control systems for employees.

Left to their own devices, employees may act in ways that do not benefit the organization. Control systems are designed to eliminate idiosyncratic behavior and keep employees directed toward achieving the goals of the firm. Control systems are a steering mechanism for guiding resources, for helping each individual act in behalf of the organization.

How to design a basic bureaucratic control system.

The design of a basic control system involves four steps: (1) setting performance standards, (2) measuring performance, (3) comparing performance with the standards, and (4) eliminating unfavorable deviations by taking corrective action. Performance standards should be valid, and should cover issues such as quantity, quality, time, and cost. Once performance is compared with the standards, the principle of exception suggests that the manager needs to direct attention to the exceptional cases that have significant deviations. Then the manager takes the action most likely to solve the problem.

The purposes for using budgets as a control device.

Budgets combine the benefits of feedforward, concurrent, and feedback controls. They are used as an initial guide for allocating resources, a reference point for using funds, and a feedback mechanism for comparing actual levels of sales and expenses to their expected levels. Recently, companies have modified their budgeting processes to allocate costs over basic processes (such as customer service) rather than to functions or departments. By changing the way they prepare budgets, many companies have discovered ways to eliminate waste and improve business processes.

How to interpret financial ratios and other financial controls.

The basic financial statements are the balance sheet and the profit and loss statement. The balance sheet compares the value of company assets to the obligations the company owes to owners and creditors. The profit and loss statement shows company income relative to costs incurred. In addition to these statements, companies look at liquidity ratios (whether the company can pay its short-term debts), leverage ratios (the extent to which the company is funding operations by going into debt), and profitability ratios (profit relative to investment). These ratios provide a goal for managers as well as a standard against which to evaluate performance.

The procedures for implementing effective control systems.

To maximize the effectiveness of controls, managers should (1) design control systems based on valid performance standards, (2) ensure that employees are provided with adequate information about their performance, (3) encourage employees to participate in the control system's design, (4) see that multiple approaches are used (such as bureaucratic, market, and clan control), and (5) recognize the relationship between empowerment and control.

The different ways in which market control mechanisms are used by organizations.

Market controls can be used at the level of the corporation, the business unit or department, or the individual. At the corporate level, business units are evaluated against one another based on profitability. At times less profitable businesses are sold while more profitable businesses receive more resources. Within business units, transfer pricing may be used to approximate market mechanisms to control transactions among departments. At the individual level, market mechanisms control the wage rate of employees and can be used to evaluate the performance of individual managers.

How clan control can be approached in an empowered organization.

Increasingly, it is not practical to approach control from a centralized, mechanistic viewpoint. In today's organizations, it is difficult to program "one best way" to approach work, and it is often difficult to monitor performance. To be responsive to customers, companies must harness the expertise of employees and give them the freedom to act on their own initiative. To maintain control while empowering employees, companies should (1) use self-guided teams, (2) allow decision making at the source of the problems, (3) build trust and mutual respect, (4) base control on a guiding framework of norms, and (5) use incentive systems that encourage teamwork.

DISCUSSION QUESTIONS

1. Can you think of an instance in which an organization did not use some form of control? What happened?

2. How are leadership and control different? How are planning and control different? How are structure and control different?

3. Of the four steps in the control process, which is the most important?

4. What are the pros and cons of bureaucratic controls such as rules, procedures, and supervision?

5. How effective is organizational culture as a control mechanism? What are its strengths? Its limitations? When would a manager rely on clan control the most?

6. Does empowerment imply the loss of control? Why or why not?

Procter & Gamble Lets Go of the Reins and Goes for a Spin

When Durk Jager became the CEO of Procter & Gamble, he announced changes that would enable the consumer-products behemoth to move more quickly to match the pace of the marketplace. Jager was attempting to remake the 160-year-old culture of the consumer-products manufacturer, which has long been shrouded in secrecy and steeped in strict discipline. P&G employees, who had been required to wear dresses or blue suits, started going casual. Rewriting memos 20 times went by the wayside. Disgruntled workers were encouraged to complain anonymously on the company intranet and visit the "Ask Durk" site to request a direct answer from Jager.

But P&G's makeover turned out to be only skin-deep. Costs soared when Jager went on a new-product development binge. Managers blamed one another, and morale sank. After missing three consecutive quarter targets, Jager found himself ousted from his position as CEO after only 18 months.

Many people, such as Alecia Swasy, the author of *Soap Opera: The Inside Story of Procter & Gamble*, were skeptical from the get-go. "This is a company that monitors every move they make, reporters' phone calls, employees' health records—everything," says Swasy. While Swasy was reporting for *The Wall Street Journal*, P&G even tried unsuccessfully to shut down her sources at the company by asking a court for her phone records.

In June 2000, Procter & Gamble turned the reins over to CEO Alan Lafley, who is less autocratic and somewhat looser. "Too much time was being spent inside Procter & Gamble and not enough outside," Lafley contends. To get a feel for what products consumers use, the CEO has even been known to make "house calls" incognito. "I once colored hair with a couple of English folks," he says. "I was amazed at how complicated it is. Women have to give up half a day and have their best friend along. I'm sure that we can improve on that."

The rollout of P&G's very successful SpinBrush toothbrush would suggest that Lafley's leadership style is working. At a trial test, consumers were so excited about the gadget that they begged to take it home. Better yet, while other electronic toothbrushes sold for $50, they would be able to buy SpinBrush for just $5.

SpinBrush marked a radical departure from the old ways of P&G. For once it didn't insist on controlling every step of product development, probably in part because it didn't conceive of SpinBrush in the first place. Four Cleveland-area entrepreneurs invented it and then sold it to P&G. Three of them even went on P&G's payroll to shepherd it through the system. "My job was to not allow P&G to screw it up," says John Osher, the lead entrepreneur behind SpinBrush.

Even though Lafley cut the Cleveland entrepreneurs a lot of slack when it came to bending P&G's rules, the culture change was not an easy one for the insular company. Some P&G employees were worried that brush's packaging, which allowed consumers to make the brush spin in the store, would run down its batteries.

CONCLUDING CASE

Procter & Gamble CEO, Alan Lafley.

Other employees wanted to delay the product's rollout until the company had retooled factories and built up inventory.

Despite the slowdowns, SpinBrush rolled on into the marketplace, taking its place on store shelves in 35 countries. It turned out to be P&G's quickest product launch ever. Consumers got cleaner teeth, and Wall Street smiled. After Lafley's takeover, P&G's share price got a 60 percent boost to 25 times expected earnings.

QUESTIONS

1. How can large companies such as P&G maintain control and still foster innovation within their organizations?

2. In your opinion, is organizational culture only "skip-deep"? Do you think clan control translates to improved performance?

SOURCES: Robert Berner, "Why P&G's Smile Is So Bright," *Business Week*, August 12, 2002; Luisa Kroll, "A Fresh Face," *Forbes.com*, July 8, 2002; Peter Glaauszka, "Is P&G's Makeover Only Skin Deep?" *Business Week*, November 15, 1999, 3655, p. 52.

16.1   Safety Program

OBJECTIVE

To understand some of the specific activities that fall under the management functions *planning, organizing, controlling and staffing*, and *directing*.

INSTRUCTIONS

After reading the following case, briefly describe the kinds of steps you would take as production manager in trying to solve your safety problem. Be sure to relate your answer specifically to the activities of *planning, organizing, controlling and staffing*, and *directing*.

MANAGING THE VAMP CO. SAFETY PROGRAM

If there are specific things that a manager does, how are they done? What does it "look like" when one manages? The following describes a typical situation in which a manager performs managerial functions:

As production manager of the Vamp Stamping Company, you've become quite concerned over the metal stamping shop's safety record. Accidents that resulted in operators' missing time on the job have increased quite rapidly in the past year. These

more serious accidents have jumped from 3 percent of all accidents reported to a current level of 10 percent.

Because you're concerned about your workers' safety as well as the company's ability to meet its customers' orders, you want to reduce this downtime accident rate to its previous level or lower within the next six months.

You call the accident trend to the attention of your production supervisors, pointing out the seriousness of the situation and their continuing responsibility to enforce the gloves and safety goggles rules. Effective immediately, every supervisor will review his or her accident reports for the past year, file a report summarizing these accidents with you, and state their intended actions to correct recurring causes of the accidents. They will make out weekly safety reports as well as meet with you every Friday to discuss what is being done and any problems they are running into.

You request the union steward's cooperation in helping the safety supervisor set up a short program on shop safety practices.

Because the machine operators are having the accidents, you encourage your supervisors to talk to their workers and find out what they think can be done to reduce the downtime accident rate to its previous level.

While the program is going on, you review the weekly reports, looking for patterns that will tell you how effective the program is and where the trouble spots are. If a supervisor's operators are not decreasing their accident rate, you discuss the matter in considerable detail with the supervisor and his or her key workers.

SOURCE: From Theodore T. Herbert, *The New Management: Study Guide*, 4th ed., p. 41. Copyright © 1983 Pearson Education. Reprinted by permission of Pearson Education, Inc., Upper Saddle River, NJ.

16.2 Preliminary, Concurrent, and Feedback Control

OBJECTIVES

1. To demonstrate the need for control procedures.

2. To gain experience in determining when to use preliminary, concurrent, and feedback controls.

INSTRUCTIONS

1. Read the text materials on preliminary, concurrent, and feedback control.

2. Read the Control Problem Situation and be prepared to resolve those control problems in a group setting.

3. Your instructor will divide the class into small groups. Each group completes the Preliminary, Concurrent, and Feedback Control Worksheet by achieving consensus on the types of control that should be applied in each situation. The group also develops responses to the discussion questions.

4. After the class reconvenes, group spokespersons present group findings.

DISCUSSION QUESTIONS

1. For which control(s) was it easier to determine application? For which was it harder?

2. Would this exercise be better assigned to groups or to individuals?

CONTROL PROBLEM SITUATION

Your management consulting team has just been hired by Technocron International, a rapidly growing producer of electronic surveillance devices that are sold to commercial and government end users. Some sales are made through direct selling, and some through industrial resellers. Direct-sale profits are being hurt by what seem to be exorbitant expenses paid to a few of the salespeople, especially those who fly all over the world in patterns that suggest little planning and control. There is trouble among the resellers because standard contracts have not been established and each reseller has an entirely different contractual relationship. Repayment schedules vary widely from customer to customer. Also, profits are reduced by the need to specialize most orders, making mass production almost impossible. However, no effort has been made to create interchangeable components. There are also tremendous inventory problems. Some raw materials and parts are bought in such small quantities that new orders are being placed almost daily. Other orders are so large that there is hardly room to store everything. Many of these purchased components are later found to be defective and unusable, causing production delays. Engineering changes are made that make large numbers of old components still in storage obsolete. Some delays result from designs that are very difficult to assemble, and assemblers complain that their corrective suggestions are ignored by engineering. To save money, untrained workers are hired and assigned to experienced "worker-buddies" who are expected to train them on the job. However, many of the new people are too poorly educated to understand their assignments, and their worker-buddies wind up doing a great deal of their work. This, along with the low pay and lack of consideration from engineering, is causing a great deal of worker unrest and talk of forming a union. Last week alone there were nine new worker grievances filed, and the U.S. Equal Employment Opportunity Commission has just announced intentions to investigate two charges of discrimination on the part of the company. There is also a serious cash-flow problem, as a number of long-term debts are coming due at the same time. The cash-flow problem could be relieved somewhat if some of the accounts payable could be collected.

The CEO manages corporate matters through five functional divisions: operations, engineering, marketing, finance, and human resources management and general administration.

Preliminary, Concurrent, and Feedback Control Worksheet

Technocron International is in need of a variety of controls. Complete the following matrix by noting the preliminary, concurrent, and feedback controls that are needed in each of the five functional divisions.

Divisions	Preliminary Controls	Concurrent Controls	Feedback Controls
HRM and general administration	_____	_____	_____
Operations	_____	_____	_____
Engineering	_____	_____	_____
Marketing	_____	_____	_____
Finance	_____	_____	_____

CHAPTER 17

Managing Technology and Innovation

A wise man will make more opportunities than he finds.
—Francis Bacon

I've got vision, and the rest of the world wears bifocals.
—Paul Newman, in Butch Cassidy and the Sundance Kid

CHAPTER OUTLINE

Technology and Innovation
  The Technology Life Cycle
  The Diffusion of Technological Innovations
Technological Innovation in a Competitive Environment
  Technology Leadership
  Technology Followership
Assessing Technology Needs
  Measuring Current Technologies
  Assessing External Technological Trends
Framing Decisions about Technological Innovation
  Anticipated Market Receptiveness
  Technological Feasibility
  Economic Viability
  Anticipated Competency Development
  Organizational Suitability
Sourcing and Acquiring New Technologies
  Internal Development
  Purchase
  Contracted Development
  Licensing
  Technology Trading
  Research Partnerships and Joint Venture
  Acquisition of an Owner of the Technology
Technology and Managerial Roles
Organizing for Innovation
  Unleashing Creativity
  Bureaucracy Busting
  Implementing Development Projects
  Technology, Job Design, and Human Resources

LEARNING OBJECTIVES

After studying Chapter 17, you will know:

1. The processes involved in the development of new technologies.

2. How technologies proceed through a life cycle.

3. How to manage technology for competitive advantage.

4. How to assess technology needs.

5. Where new technologies originate and the best strategies for acquiring them.

6. How people play a role in managing technology.

7. How to develop an innovative organization.

8. The key characteristics of successful development projects.

NATIVE AMERICANS STAKE A HIGH-TECH CLAIM

Years ago, tribal elders of the Cheyenne River Sioux paid to have high-speed data cable laid in their South Dakota reservation. At that time, some thought the Indians were putting the horse before the cart, but that didn't stop tribe chairman Greg Bourland from taking Web and computer-assembly classes. He also created the tribe's first Web page, www.sioux.org.

High tech is giving tribes across the country new hope. Like the Cheyenne River Sioux, the Northern Utes laid cable in the Uinta and Ouray reser-

Monette Serawop works in the Uinta River Technology Center run by the Ute Tribe at Fort Duchesne. The technology center is one source for jobs on the reservation. The tribe also owns cattle feed lots, an oil field services company, a grocery store and a bottled water company.

vations, which are about 150 miles east of Salt Lake City. Subsequent to having the cable laid and with the help of federal settlement money from a water-rights dispute, the tribe founded Uinta River Technology (URT), a data-entry start-up.

URT quickly picked up a contract with Utah's Hill Air Force Base to scan 100,000 old engineering drawings onto CD-ROMs. Today the company has several contracts doing data processing for Affiliated Computer Services (ACS), one of the world's largest data-processing concerns. It also is digitizing Immigration and Naturalization Service documents and information for the Illinois Department of Motor Vehicles and has formed an alliance with Oracle Corp.

"We never thought technology would make it here," says Sonny Van, who works for URT. Before URT began hiring, Van would have been lucky to find a job at a service station or a Wal-Mart 25 miles away. Today he makes $9 an hour as a technical-support specialist maintaining URT's computers.

That may not sound like a fortune, but it's a boon to tribe members, who traditionally have had 50 percent unemployment rates. In a 1995 census, 53 percent of American Indian homes lacked even a telephone. Very few had computers.

Initially, it appeared that not very many people on the reservation would have the skills needed to work at a tech firm. But the tribe's business community realized that with a little bit of training, the reservation had plenty of talent that could be put to use quickly.

With government support and help from corporations such as ACS and Oracle, URT was able to train its people and get the operation up and running in March 2001. The number of employees needed to do the work soon doubled, and sales are expected to explode in the near term—in spite of the slowdown in the tech industry and the U.S. economy in general.

Like the Northern Utes, the Cheyenne River Sioux have launched their own data-entry firm, called Lakota Technologies. So far, customers of both tribes seem happy with the work. "Tribal IT outsourcing has been a well-kept secret," says Howard Lackow, director of outsourcing services at the Outsourcing Institute. As tribe members' skills increase, Lackow thinks the companies will move quickly to expand their core business beyond data entry to systems integration or software coding. "It's just a matter of time," he says. For the tribes, time may finally be on their side.

Sources: Olga Kharif, "Native Americans State a High-Tech Claim," *Business Week Online*, November 26, 2001; Steven Oberbeck, "Hedging Their Bets: Utes Diversify Economy on Reservation in Uinta Basin," *Salt Lake Tribune*, April 7, 2002.

Setting the Stage

Technological innovation is daunting in its complexity and pace of change. And as you have no doubt figured out, it is therefore vital for a firm's competitive advantage. Not long ago, new products took years to plan and develop, were standardized and mass produced, and were pushed onto the market through extensive selling and promotional campaigns. With sales lives for these products measured in decades, production processes used equipment dedicated to making only those standardized products and achieved savings through economies of scale. But today's customers often demand products that have yet to be designed. Product development is now a race to become the first to introduce innovative products—products whose lives often are measured in months as they are quickly replaced by other, even more technologically sophisticated products.

Managing today's technology requires that managers understand how technologies emerge, develop, and affect the ways organizations compete and the ways people work. This chapter discusses how technology can affect an organization's competitiveness and how to integrate technology into the organization's competitive strategy. Then we assess the technological needs of the organization and the means by which these needs can be met.

Technology and Innovation

technology

The systematic application of scientific knowledge to a new product, process, or service.

innovation

A change in technology; a departure from previous ways of doing things.

In Chapter 9 ("The Responsive Organization") we defined **technology** as the methods, processes, systems, and skills used to transform resources into products. More broadly speaking, we can think of technology as the commercialization of science, the systematic application of scientific knowledge to a new product, process, or service. In this sense, technology is embedded in every product, service, and procedure used or produced.[1]

If we find a better product, process, or procedure to accomplish our task, we have an innovation. **Innovation** is a change in technology—a departure from previous ways of doing things. Two fundamental types of innovation are product and process innovation. *Process innovations* are changes that affect the methods of producing outputs. In Chapter 9 we discussed flexible manufacturing practices such as just-in-time, massed customization, and simultaneous engineering. Each of these innovations has changed the way products are manufactured and distributed. In contrast, *product innovations* are changes in the actual outputs (products and services) themselves.[2]

There are definable and predictable patterns in the way technologies emerge, develop, and are replaced. Critical forces converge to create new technologies, which then follow well-defined life-cycle patterns. Understanding the forces driving technological development and the patterns they follow can help a manager anticipate, monitor, and manage technologies more effectively.

- First, there must be a *need*, or *demand*, for the technology. Without this need driving the process, there is no reason for technological innovation to occur.
- Second, meeting the need must be theoretically possible, and the *knowledge* to do so must be available from basic science.
- Third, we must be able to *convert* the scientific knowledge into practice in both engineering and economic terms. If we can theoretically do something but doing it is economically impractical, the technology cannot be expected to emerge.
- Fourth, the *funding, skilled labor, time, space,* and *other resources* needed to develop the technology must be available.
- Finally, *entrepreneurial initiative* is needed to identify and pull all the necessary elements together.

The Technology Life Cycle

Technological innovations typically follow a relatively predictable pattern called the **technology life cycle.** Figure 17.1 depicts the pattern. The cycle begins with the recognition of a need and a perception of a means by which the need can be satisfied through applied science or knowledge. The knowledge and ideas are brought together and developed, culminating in a new technological innovation. Early progress can be slow in these formative years as competitors experiment a great deal with product design and operational characteristics to meet consumer needs. This is where the rate of product innovation tends to be highest. For example, during the early years of the auto industry, companies tried a wide range of machines, including electric and steam-driven cars, to determine which product would be most effective. Eventually the internal combustion engine emerged as the dominant design, and the number of product innovations leveled off.

> **technology life cycle**
>
> A predictable pattern followed by a technological innovation, from its inception and development to market saturation and replacement.

Once early problems are resolved and a dominant design emerges, improvements come more from process innovations to refine the technology. It is at this point that companies can gain an advantage by pursuing process efficiencies and cost competitiveness. In the auto example, as companies settled on a product standard, they began leveraging the benefits of mass production and vertical integration to improve productivity. These process innovations were instrumental in lowering production costs and bringing the price of automobiles in line with consumer budgets.[3]

Eventually the new technology begins to reach the upper limits of both its performance capabilities and the spread of its usage. Development slows and becomes increasingly costly, and the market becomes saturated (i.e., there are few new customers). The technology can remain in this mature stage for some time—as in the case of autos—or can be replaced quickly by another technology offering superior performance or economic advantage. The evolution of life cycles can take decades or even centuries, as in the case of iron and steelmaking technologies. A dramatic example of technology evolution can be found in spatial auditory devices for the blind.

As the example of KASPA shows, a technology life cycle can be made up of many individual *product* life cycles. Each of these products is an incremental improvement over its predecessors. In this way, technological development involves significant

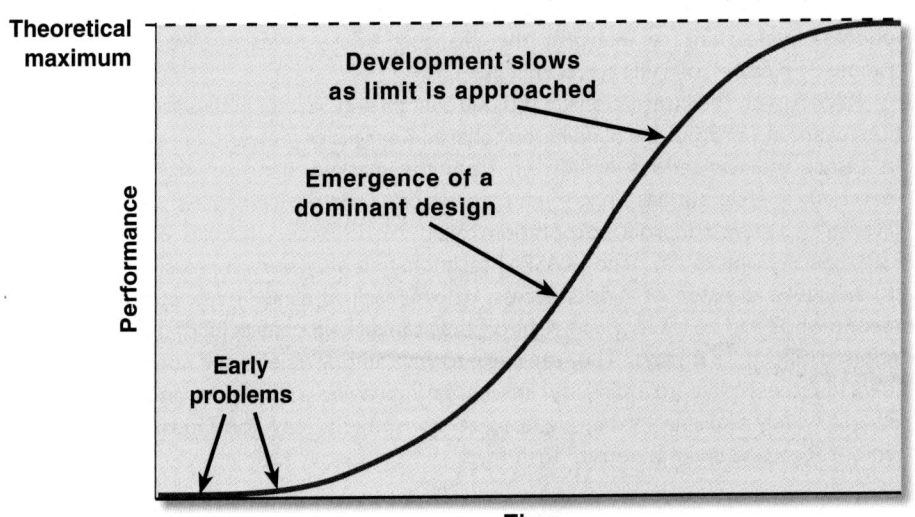

FIGURE 17.1
The Technology Life Cycle

innovations, often representing entirely new technologies, followed by a large number of small, incremental innovations. Ongoing development of a technology increases the benefits gained through its use, makes the technology easier to use, and allows more applications. In the process, the use of the technology expands to new adopters.

A Man with Vision

FROM THE PAGES OF

BusinessWeek

Bats and dolphins find their way around with natural sonar systems that enable them to perceive the dimensions of their world with reflected sound. So why not humans? It's an idea that Leslie Kay, an expert in submarine sonar from New Zealand, has devoted nearly 40 years to researching. He's developing sonar systems to help the visually impaired navigate their darkened world.

As a result of radical improvements in his technology, Kay's latest device may be on the verge of becoming accepted by the blind as an essential mobility tool alongside the venerable cane and seeing-eye dog. Dubbed KASPA, for Kay's Auditory Spatial Perception Aid, the device is worn like a headband. It emits frequency-modulated ultrasound signals similar to those made by some animals. Embedded a few inches apart in the band are two receptors that produce stereophonic sounds in earphones, just as the distance between our eyes produces stereovisual images, permitting depth perception. The sounds change in pitch to reflect the distance and dimension of objects around the KASPA wearer. In tests, blind children have used KASPA to ride bikes through obstacle courses, and one blind child even batted a softball. Kay has high hopes that KASPA will give the blind the previously unimaginable ability to accurately perceive and visualize their physical surroundings, as bats and dolphins do. "The stage has been reached when blind persons can walk about like sighted persons do in a busy shopping area, going in and out of shops. They'll be able to recognize their location relative to the many landmarks on the way," Kay says.

Small improvements to Leslie Kay's KASPA might breathe new life into the product and give greater mobility to the blind.

Kay, who is nearing 80, developed his first sonar device for the blind in the 1970s. Called the SonicGuide, it looked like a pair of eyeglasses. Similar to KASPA, a module over the nosepiece radiated pulses of high-frequency ultrasound. Two matching receivers captured the reflected signals and transmitted them as audible sound to a pair of earphones. By learning to interpret the changing echoes, wearers would develop an "acoustic picture" of their surroundings.

KASPA won the international $100,000 Saatchi and Saatchi Innovation in Communication Award in 1998, but the blind haven't shared Kay's vision. Fewer than 1,000 units were sold before the device was withdrawn from the market that year. Kay continued his research for a while but has since given up promoting the device himself.

However, a new nonprofit corporation called World Access for the Blind might help KASPA see the light of day. "The [KASPA] technology is very, very impressive," says Daniel Kish, executive director of World Access, who himself is blind. "I can put a KASPA on someone who's had no training, and, right off, they can pick up objects [and] understand their relation to objects," Kish says. "They can begin to walk among objects and not run into them."

World Access plans to refine the device by improving its comfort and range before making it widely available. "What we hope to do is take a very good idea, really quite an ingenious idea, and make it better," Kish says.

SOURCE: Robert Preidt, "Seeing with Sound," *HealthScout News*, April 22, 2001; Alan Hall, "Sonar Sight for the Blind," *Business Week Online*, December 11, 2000.

The Diffusion of Technological Innovations

The spread in the use of a new technology over time follows an S-shaped pattern (see Figure 17.2). This pattern, first observed in 1903, has been verified with many new technologies and ideas in a wide variety of industries and settings.[4] The adopters of a new technology fall into five groups.

The first group, representing approximately 2.5 percent of adopters, consists of the *innovators*. Typically innovators are adventurous, but some might consider them headstrong or even extreme.

The next 13.5 percent of adopters are *early adopters*. This group is critical to the success of a new technology, because its members include well-respected opinion leaders. Early adopters often are the people or organizations to which others look for leadership, ideas, and up-to-date technological information. The next group, representing 34 percent of adopters, is the *early majority*. These adopters are more deliberate and take longer to decide to use something new. Often they are important members of a community or industry, but typically not the leaders.

Representing the next 34 percent are the late *majority*. Members of this group are more skeptical of technological change and approach innovation with great caution, often adopting only out of economic necessity or increasing social pressure.

The final 16 percent are *laggards*. Often isolated and highly conservative in their views, laggards are extremely suspicious of innovation and change.

The speed with which an innovation spreads depends largely on five attributes. An innovation will spread quickly if it:

1. Has a great advantage over its predecessor.
2. Is compatible with existing systems, procedures, infrastructures, and ways of thinking.
3. Has less rather than greater complexity.
4. Can be tried or tested easily without significant cost or commitment.
5. Can be observed and copied easily.

Designing products with these technological considerations in mind can make a critical difference in their success.

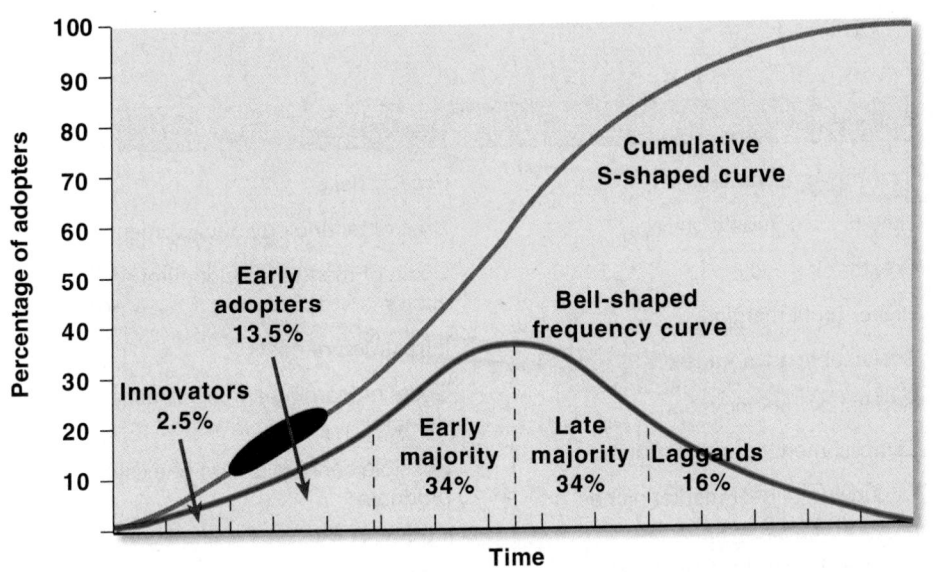

FIGURE 17.2
Technology Dissemination Pattern and Adopter Categories

Technological Innovation in a Competitive Environment

Discussions about technology life cycles and diffusion patterns may imply that technological change occurs naturally or automatically. Just the opposite; change is neither easy nor natural in organizations (we discuss change more fully in the next chapter). Decisions about technology and innovation are very strategic and need to be approached in a systematic way.

In Chapter 4, we discussed two generic strategies a company can use to position itself in the market: low cost and differentiation. With *low-cost* leadership, the company maintains an advantage because it has a lower cost than its competitors. With a *differentiation* strategy, the advantage comes from having a unique product or service for which customers are willing to pay a premium price.[5] Technological innovations can support either of these strategies: They can be used to gain cost advantage through pioneering lower-cost product designs and creating low-cost ways to perform needed operations, or they can support differentiation by pioneering unique products or services that increase buyer value and thus command premium prices.

In some cases, a new technology can completely change the rules of competition within an industry.[6] Leading companies that respond ineffectively to technological opportunities can falter while new companies emerge as the dominant competitors. The stories of how Microsoft and Intel grew from the opportunities provided by IBM are well known.

But industries seldom are transformed overnight. Typically, signals of a new technology's impact are visible well in advance, leaving time for companies and people to respond. For example, almost any competitor in the telecommunications industry fully understands the potential value of cellular technology. Often the key issue is not *whether* to adopt a new technology but *when* to adopt it and how to integrate the change with the organization's operating practices and strategies.

Technology Leadership

The adage "timing is everything" is applied to many things, ranging from financial investments to telling jokes. It also applies to the development and exploitation of new technologies. Industry leaders such as Xerox, 3M, Hewlett-Packard, and Merck built and now maintain their competitive positions through early development and application of new technologies. However, technology leadership imposes costs and risks, and it is not the best approach for every organization (see Table 17.1).[7]

TABLE 17.1
Advantages and Disadvantages of Technology Leadership

Advantages	Disadvantages
First-mover advantage	Greater risks
Little or no competition	Cost of technology development
Greater efficiency	Costs of market development and customer education
Higher profit margins	
Sustainable advantage	Infrastructure costs
Reputation for innovation	Costs of learning and eliminating defects
Establishment of entry barriers	Possible cannibalization of existing products
Occupying of best market niches	
Opportunities to learn	

Advantages of Technology Leadership What makes innovators and technology leadership attractive is the potential for high profits and first-mover advantages. Being the first to market with new technologies can provide significant competitive advantage. If technology leadership increases an organization's efficiency relative to competitors, it achieves a cost advantage. The organization can use the advantage to reap greater profits than competitors or attract more customers by charging lower prices. Similarly, if a company is first to market with a new technology, it may be able to charge a premium price because it faces no competition. Higher prices and greater profits can defray the costs of developing new technologies.

This one-time advantage of being the technology leader can be turned into a sustainable advantage. Sustainability of a lead depends on competitors' ability to duplicate the technology and the organization's ability to keep building on the lead quickly enough to outpace competitors. It can do this in several ways. The reputation for being an innovator can create an ongoing advantage and even spill over to the company's other products. For example, 3M's reputation for innovation and quality differentiates some of its standard products, such as adhesive tape, and allows a product to command a premium price. A competitor may be able to copy the product but not the reputation. Patents and other institutional barriers also can be used to block competitors and maintain leadership. Polaroid successfully kept industry giant Kodak out of the instant-photography market for years through a series of patents and new products such as JoyCam and i-Zone until digital photography changed the market entirely.[8]

The first mover also can preempt competitors by occupying the best market niches. If it can establish high switching costs (recall Chapter 2) for repeat customers, these positions can be difficult for competitors to capture. Microsoft has dominated the software market for computers with its Windows operating system because of the large library of software that is packaged with it. Although other companies can offer more advanced software, their products are not as attractive because they are not bundled as the Windows-based systems are (Ironically, this advantage was so intractable that it was viewed as monopolistic in court.)[9]

Technology leadership can provide a significant learning advantage. While competitors may be able to copy or adopt a new technology, ongoing learning by the technology leader can keep a company ahead by generating minor improvements that are difficult to imitate. Many Japanese manufacturers use several small, incremental improvements generated with their *kaizen* programs (recall Chapter 9) to upgrade the quality of their products and processes continuously. All these minor improvements cannot be copied easily by competitors, and collectively they can provide a significant advantage.[10]

Disadvantages of Technology Leadership However, being the first to develop or adopt a new technology does not always lead to immediate advantage and high profits. While such potential may exist, technology leadership imposes high costs and risks that followers are not required to bear. Being the leader thus can be more costly than being the follower. These costs include educating buyers unfamiliar with the new technology, building an infrastructure to support the technology, and developing complementary products to achieve the technology's full potential. Also, regulatory approval may be needed. For example, the cost of producing a new drug, including testing and the expense of obtaining FDA approval, is estimated at around $200 million. While followers do not get the benefits of being first to market, they can copy the drug for a fraction of this cost once the original patents expire.[11]

Being a pioneer carries other risks. If raw materials and equipment are new or have unique specifications, a ready supply at a reasonable cost may not be available. Or the technology may not be fully developed and may have problems yet to be resolved. In addition, the unproved market for the technology creates uncertainty in demand. Finally, the new technology may have an adverse impact on existing structures or business. It may cannibalize current products or make existing investments obsolete.

Technology Followership

Not all organizations are equally prepared to be technology leaders, nor would leadership benefit each organization equally. Much of the difference in choosing to be a technology leader or follower depends on how a company positions itself to compete, the benefits gained through the use of a technology, and the characteristics of the organization.

Interestingly, technology followership also can be used to support both low-cost and differentiation strategies. If the follower learns from the leader's experience, it can avoid the costs and risks of technology leadership, thereby establishing a low-cost position. Personal computer (PC) manufacturers have been successful with this type of followership strategy. IBM's personal computer market share within the United States has never matched that of its mainframes largely because of low-cost technology followers such as Dell and Gateway. Followership also can support differentiation. By learning from the leader, the follower can adapt the products or delivery systems to fit buyers' needs more closely.

Adoption timing is dependent on the organization's strategic needs and technology skills as well as the potential benefits of the new technology. As discussed earlier, technologies do not emerge in their final state; rather, they undergo *development over time* (see Figure 17.3). Development makes the technology easier to use and more adaptable to various strategies. At the same time, *complementary products and technologies* may be developed and introduced that make the main technology more useful. For example, software and printer technologies traditionally lag computer hardware technology, limiting the usefulness of hardware technology breakthroughs.

These complementary products and technologies combine with the *gradual diffusion* of the technology to form a shifting competitive impact from the technology. The appropriate time for an organization to adopt technological innovations is when the costs and risks of switching to the technology are outweighed by the benefits. This point differs among organizations and depends largely on a company's characteristics and strategies.[12]

FIGURE 17.3
Dynamic Forces of a Technology's Competitive Impact

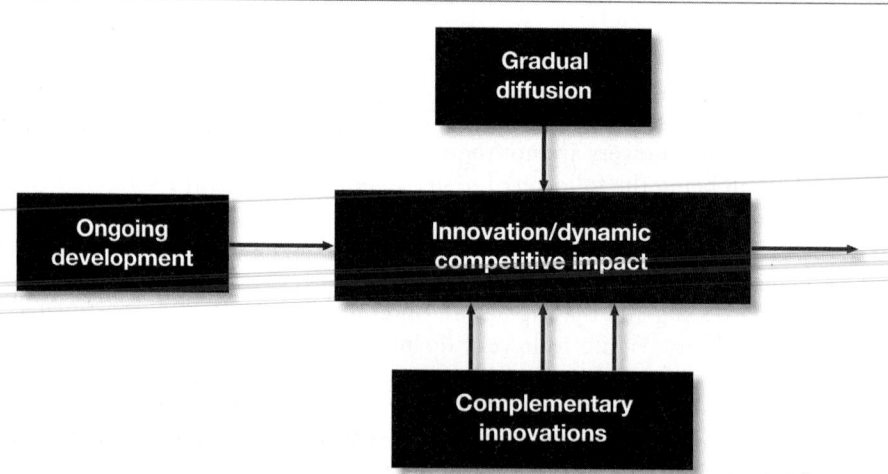

SOURCE: D. M. Schroeder, "A Dynamic Perspective on the Impact of Process Innovation upon Competitive Strategies," *Strategic Management Journal* 11 (January 1990), pp. 25–42.

Assessing Technology Needs

A decade ago, the major U.S. steel companies suffered from significant cost disadvantages relative to non-U.S. producers. Those high costs were due largely to poor productivity resulting from aging plants and obsolete equipment. U.S. companies lagged their European and Japanese counterparts in adopting new, productivity-enhancing process technologies such as the basic oxygen furnace and the continuous-casting process. If the U.S. companies had accurately assessed and adopted these technologies in a timely manner, the massive layoffs (about 60 percent) of the industry's workforce could have been avoided.

Assessing the technology needs of the organization involves measuring current technologies as well as external trends affecting the industry.

Measuring Current Technologies

Before organizations can devise strategies for developing and exploiting technological innovation, they must gain a clear understanding of their current technology base. A **technology audit** helps clarify the key technologies on which an organization depends. The most important dimension of a new technology is its competitive value. One technique for measuring competitive value categorizes technologies as emerging, pacing, key, and base.[13]

technology audit

Process of clarifying the key technologies on which an organization depends.

- *Emerging technologies* are still under development and thus are unproved. They may, however, significantly alter the rules of competition in the more distant future.
- *Pacing technologies* have yet to prove their full value but have the potential to alter the rules of competition by providing significant advantage.
- *Key technologies* have proved effective, but they also provide a strategic advantage because not everyone uses them. Knowledge and dissemination of these technologies are limited, and they continue to provide some first-mover advantages.
- *Base technologies* are those that are commonplace in the industry; everyone must have them to be able to operate. Thus, they provide little competitive advantage.

Technologies can evolve rapidly through these categories. For example, electronic word processing was considered an emerging technology in the late 1970s. By the early 1980s, it could have been considered pacing. While promising advantages, the technology's cost and capabilities restricted its usefulness to a limited number of applications. With continued improvements and more powerful computer chips, electronic word processing quickly became a key technology. Its costs dropped, its usage spread, and it demonstrated the capacity to enhance productivity. By the late 1980s, it was considered a base technology in most applications. Word processing technology is now used so widely that it is viewed as a routine activity in almost every office.

Assessing External Technological Trends

Just as with any planning, decisions about technology must balance internal capabilities (strengths and weaknesses) with external opportunities and threats. There are several techniques that organizations use to better understand how technology is changing within an industry.

Benchmarking   As mentioned in Chapter 4, benchmarking is the process of comparing the organization's practices and technologies with those of other companies. The ability to benchmark technologies against those of competitors can vary among industries. While competitors understandably are reluctant to share their secrets, information trading for benchmarking is not uncommon and can prove highly

valuable. For example, Harley-Davidson's recovery of its reputation for manufacturing quality motorcycles began only after company executives toured Honda's plant and witnessed firsthand the weaknesses of Harley's manufacturing technologies and the vast potential for improvement. In fact, Japanese companies often are willing to show U.S. competitors their operations because they believe the U.S. companies won't use the information!

It is important to benchmark against potential competitors in other nations. There may be key or pacing technologies in use that can be imported easily and offer significant advantage. Also, overseas firms may be more willing to share their knowledge if they are not direct competitors and if they are eager to exchange information for the benefit of both companies.

Scanning   Whereas benchmarking focuses on what is being done currently, scanning focuses on what can be done and what is being developed. In other words, benchmarking examines key and perhaps some pacing technologies, while scanning seeks out pacing and emerging technologies—those just being introduced and still in development.

Scanning typically involves a number of tactics, many of them the same as those used in benchmarking. However, scanning places greater emphasis on identifying and monitoring the sources of new technologies for an industry. It also may dictate that executives read more cutting-edge research journals and attend research conferences and seminars. The extent to which scanning is done depends largely on how close to the cutting edge of technology an organization needs to operate.

Framing Decisions about Technological Innovation

Once an organization has done a thorough job of analyzing its current technological position, it can begin to make decisions about how to proceed into the future to either develop or exploit emerging technological innovations. Decisions about technological innovations must balance many interrelated factors. The most effective approach to technology depends not only on the technology's potential to support the organization's strategic needs but also on the organization's skills and capabilities to exploit the technology successfully. The organization's competitive strategy, the technical abilities of its employees to deal with the new technology, the fit of the technology with the company's operations, and the company's ability to deal with the risks and ambiguities of adopting a new technology all must be timed to coincide with the dynamic forces of a developing technology. This does not always mean waiting for the technology to develop. Often it requires changing the capabilities and strategies of the organization to match the needs of the technology. This could include hiring new people, training existing employees, changing internal policies and procedures, and changing strategies. These considerations are discussed next.

Anticipated Market Receptiveness

The first consideration that needs to be addressed in developing a strategy around technological innovation is market potential. In many cases, innovations are stimulated by external demand for new products and services. For example, current work to develop low earth-orbiting satellites (LEOs) for wireless Internet access is motivated by a clear understanding of its worldwide market potential. Telecommunications companies such as AT&T, Motorola, TRW, and Loral are working diligently to develop innovative technologies in this arena.[14]

In assessing market receptiveness, executives need to make two determinations. In the short run, there should be an immediate application that demonstrates the value of the new technology. In the long run, there needs to be a set of applications that show the technology is the proven means to satisfy a market need. For example, despite the recent dominant use of audio compact discs (CDs), the shift to technologies such as MP3 may result in CDs becoming less attractive. LPs, cassettes, and eight-tracks (does anyone remember them?) are virtually nonexistent today.

The handwriting is on the chalkboard. Apple is losing its long-held dominance in schools. More Macs are still in place than PCs, but that lead is eroding like a sand castle in the rain. Apple's sales are falling farther behind as schools increasingly choose PCs over Macs.

Dell is now the runaway schoolhouse leader, representing nearly 35 percent of all new sales compared to Apple's 15.2 percent. Consumers still get more processing power and storage in a PC for the price than with a Mac, but study after study has shown that Macs are less expensive to run and maintain—and schools tend to keep computers for years. Some are still running their original Macs.

Apple also offers a great package: easy-to-use software called PowerSchool that lets teachers track attendance, update grades, and post homework assignments online. Yet despite all these advantages, the Mac's standing continues to fall in schools.

What's the explanation? The answer has more to do with sociology than with pricing. Apple is getting trampled by a herd mentality, and Dell is the beneficiary—patiently riding in back, not leading the charge. Parents of schoolchildren are asking, "Why should my child work on a Mac when we have PCs at home and in the office?" That's a powerful argument. While teachers may favor Macs, they frequently are caught between parents and administrators. In most schools, teachers don't have much of a say in budgetary or technology decisions. Administrators who spend little time in classrooms decide which computers the teachers will use. If they consult anyone, it's typically info-tech specialists, who largely are trained on PCs.

What, if anything, can Apple do? For starters, it must ensure that Macs work seamlessly with PCs. In that regard, it has made huge strides. Students can now flourish as Mac renegades in a PC school, thanks to the new Mac networking features. No one need ever know that the students are working from a Mac. But even though Apple dominated schools throughout most of the 1990s, the experience didn't breed hordes of Mac users. Most kids grew up and quietly went to work in the PC world, making the switch without any trouble.

Despite the setback, Apple isn't throwing in the towel. With the newly styled line, Mac is healthier than ever, and Apple is continuing to develop new trend-setting products. Its tiny, award-winning digital music player, iPod, for example, is one such product that has sprouted roots in the marketplace.

SOURCE: Condensed from Charles Haddad, "Apple, the Saddest School Dropout," *Business Week Online*, September 18, 2002.

Technological Feasibility

In addition to market receptiveness, organizations must consider the feasibility of technological innovations. Visions can stay unrealized for a long time. Technical obstacles may represent barriers to progress. Companies such as Intel and Cyrix face continual hurdles in developing newer and faster computer chips.

Since Intel brought the first microprocessor to market in 1971, chip makers have made dramatic advances in computing. The number of transistors on a chip, and its resulting performance, has doubled nearly every 18 to 24 months, upholding what has become known as Moore's Law (Gordon Moore is the cofounder of Intel).

But the frontier of microprocessor technology is being restricted by the combined forces of physics and economics. The wires that run between transistors right now are 400 times thinner than a human hair. Can they be made skinnier yet? Yes, but the task of continually doubling the speed of electrons passing wires of near-zero width will be tricky—and maybe impossible—at some point. Even if it's technically feasible, can companies afford the massive investments needed to do this?[15]

Other industries face similar technological hurdles. In the oil industry, for example, technological barriers prevent exploration and drilling in the deepest parts of the ocean. In medicine, scientists and doctors work continuously to identify the causes of and cures for diseases such as cancer and AIDS. In aviation and aeronautics, researchers are working to refine technologies that allow pilots to "see" through clouds. Each of these potentially valuable innovations is slowed by the technical limits of currently available technologies.[16]

Economic Viability

Closely related to technological feasibility is economic viability. Apart from whether a firm can "pull off" a technological innovation, executives must consider whether there is a good financial incentive for doing so. For example, the use of solar fusion to generate electricity has been technically feasible for years. However, its cost remains prohibitively higher than the cost of fossil fuels. Similarly, the use of fuel-cell technology for automobiles is almost technically feasible, but its costs are still too high.

The issue of economic viability takes us back to our earlier discussion of adoption timing. Earlier adopters may have first-mover advantages, but there are costs associated with this strategic approach. The development costs of a particular technological innovation may be quite high, such as in pharmaceuticals, chemicals, and software. Patents and copyrights often help organizations recoup the costs of their investments in technological innovations. Without such protection, the investments in research and development might not be justifiable.

An exception to the "economic viability" rule might be the now-classic story of Merck and the drug Mectizan. Mectizan is the commercial name for a drug called *ivermectin* developed by Merck scientists to cure river blindness (onchocerciasis). The success rate of the drug has been astoundingly high, but governments in the third-world countries where it is needed cannot afford it. Seeing no economic viability, Merck executives decided to commercialize the drug anyway and donate it to those who need it. Merck has gotten help from organizations including the World Health Organization (WHO), the United Nations Development Programme, and the Carter Center. Millions of people in Africa, the Middle East, and Latin America have gotten treatment.[17]

Handheld computers continue to grow more powerful and spawn a host of peripherals.

Anticipated Competency Development

It has been stated repeatedly in this text that organizations should (and do) build their strategies based on core competencies. This advice applies to technology and innovation strategies as well. Frequently, we can view technological innovations that are the tangible product of intangible—or tacit—knowledge and capabilities that make up a firm's core competence. The Merck and Intel examples illustrate instances in which core competencies in research and development lead to new technological innovations.

By contrast, firms that are not technology-oriented must develop new competencies in order to survive. For example, when Amazon.com changed the face of e-retailing in the 1990s, traditional brick-and-mortar bookstores had to adapt quickly. To regain competitiveness, they had to bolster their information technology competencies, which wasn't always an easy thing to do.

The upshot of this is that while certain technologies may have tremendous market applicability, firms must have (or develop) the internal competencies needed to execute their technology strategies. Without the skills needed to implement an innovation, even promising technological advances may prove disastrous.

Organizational Suitability

The final issues that tend to be addressed in deciding on technological innovations have to do with the culture of the organization, the interests of managers, and the expectations of stakeholders. Companies such as 3M and Sony that are seen as proactive "technology-push" innovators tend to have cultures that are more outward-looking and opportunistic. Executives accord considerable priority to developing and exploiting technological expertise, and decision makers tend to have bold intuitive visions of the future. Typically there are technology champions who articulate competitively aggressive, first-mover technological strategies. In many cases, executives are more concerned about the opportunity costs of not taking action than they are about the potential to fail.

By contrast, *defender* firms such as Rolls Royce tend to adopt a more circumspect posture toward innovation. Their strategies are focused more on deepening their capability base through complementary technologies that extend rather than replace their current ones. Strategic decisions are likely to be based on careful analysis and experience in the industry setting. A hybrid *analyzer* firm such as Matsushita (see the Concluding Case) tends to allow others to demonstrate solid demand in new arenas before it responds. As we noted earlier, these types of firms tend to adopt an early-follower strategy to grab a dominant position more from their strengths in marketing and manufacturing than through technological innovation.[18]

Every company has different capabilities to deal with new technology. As discussed previously, early adopters have characteristics different from those of late adopters. Early adopters of new technologies tend to be larger, more profitable, and more specialized. Therefore, they are in an economic position to absorb the risks associated with early adoption while profiting more from its advantages. In addition, the people involved in early adoption are more highly educated, have a greater ability to deal with abstraction, can cope with uncertainty more effectively, and have strong problem-solving capabilities. Thus, early adopters can more effectively manage the difficulties and uncertainty of a less fully developed technology.[19]

As shown in Table 17.2, these five considerations (market receptiveness, technological feasibility, economic viability, competency development, and organizational suitability) all jointly influence decisions about technology innovations. Even one of these can derail an otherwise promising project.

TABLE 17.2

Framing Decisions about Technological Innovation

Considerations	Examples
Market Receptiveness—Assess external demand for the technology (short/long run).	Cell phones, MP3, personal digital assistants (PDAs), HDTV, etc.
Technological Feasibility—Evaluate technical barriers to progress.	Deep-sea oil exploration, physical size of PC microprocessors
Economic Viability—Examine any cost considerations and forecast profitability.	Solar fusion, fuel cells for automobiles, missile defense system
Competency Development—Determine if current competencies are sufficient.	Information technology in hospitals, digital technology in cameras
Organizational Suitability—Assess the fit with culture and managerial systems.	Steel companies focusing on creativity and innovation

BusinessWeek

When Steve Jobs unveiled Apple Computer's digital music player, the iPod, in 2001, he predicted that the slick metallic device—the smallest of its kind on the market—would be one of the hottest products of the season. He was right.

Over the next few months, Apple sold about 120,000 iPods, grabbing a good chunk of the digital music market. Not bad for a company that until then had had no presence in that business.

But industry giants weren't about to let Apple muscle in easily. Toshiba followed with the introduction of a new player, Mobilphile, which is larger and more expensive but has a removable hard drive. iPod owners who want more capacity have to buy a new model, whereas a Mobilphile user can simply buy a more capacious hard drive and slide it into the old device. Mobilphile also downloads songs from the computer to the player slightly faster than iPod does.

Already, "the response [to Mobilphile] has been incredible," claims Craig Eggeris, director of merchandising for DVD and digital products at Toshiba America Consumer Products in New Jersey. "We seem to have hit the correct nerve."

Apple continues to develop leading-edge products, like iPOD. The MP3 player, which weighed in at a mere 184 grams, was the first to hold 1,000 songs.

Besides Toshiba, Apple has to look out for competitors, such as California-based Sonic Blue, that are coming out with players even smaller than iPod. The old CD market is still a threat, too. CD players are much less expensive than MP3 players, making them a more attractive option for many budget-conscious consumers.

But Apple says it can stay ahead of the competition. "We continue to innovate," says Apple product manager Stan Ng. The company recently added calendar and address-book capabilities to the iPod, and photo and video viewing could be coming next. It also rolled out a Windows-based version of the device and is developing a version that syncs wirelessly with consumers' computers.

Even if iPod hits a rough patch, Apple probably won't turn and run from the market as it did in 1998, when it discontinued its Newton personal digital assistant. The market forecast for MP3s is simply too good. Experts are predicting that demand should grow ninefold by 2006, from 1 million to 9 million units. With numbers like that, Apple should still be able to get a good bite.

SOURCE: Olga Kharif, "iPod: A Seed for Growth?" *Business Week Online*, August 27, 2002.

Sourcing and Acquiring New Technologies

Developing new technology may conjure up visions of scientists and product developers working in research and development (R&D) laboratories like that of Bell Labs. However, new technology also can come from many other sources, including suppliers, manufacturers, users, other industries, universities, the government, and overseas companies. While every source of innovation should be explored, each industry usually has specific sources for most of its new technologies. For example, because of the limited size of most farming operations, innovations in farming most often come from manufacturers, suppliers, and government extension services. Seed manufacturers develop and market new, superior hybrids; chemical producers improve pesticides and herbicides; and equipment manufacturers design improved farm equipment. Land-grant universities develop new farming techniques, and extension agents spread their usage.

In many industries, however, the primary sources of new technology are the organizations that use the technology. For instance, over three-fourths of scientific innovations are developed by the users of the scientific instruments being improved and subsequently may be licensed or sold to manufacturers or suppliers.[20]

Essentially, the question of how to acquire new technology is a **make-or-buy decision.** In other words, should the organization develop the technology itself or acquire it from an outside source? However, the decision is not that simple. There are many alternatives, and each has advantages and disadvantages. Some of the more common options are discussed in the following sections.

> **make-or-buy decision**
>
> **The question an organization asks itself about whether to acquire new technology from an outside source or develop it itself.**

Internal Development

Developing a new technology within the company has the potential advantage of keeping the technology proprietary (exclusive to the organization). This provides an important advantage over competitors.

Purchase

Most technology already is available in products or processes that can be purchased openly. For example, a bank that needs sophisticated information-processing equipment need not develop the technology itself. It can simply purchase the technology from manufacturers or suppliers. In most situations, this is the simplest, easiest, and most cost-effective way to acquire new technology.

Contracted Development

If the technology is not available and a company lacks the resources or time to develop it internally, it may choose to contract the development from outside sources. Possible contractors include other companies, independent research laboratories, and university and government institutions.

Licensing

Certain technologies that are not easily purchased as part of a product can be licensed for a fee. Pioneers of the VHS format for videocassette recorders held the critical patents, but they freely licensed the technology and the right to use it to competing manufacturers of video equipment. This practice helped make VHS the dominant format (over Beta) by providing other manufacturers with easy access to the technology, thereby creating an industry standard.

Technology Trading

Technology trading is another way to gain access to new technologies. Ironically, this tactic sometimes is used between rival companies. For example, U.S. steel producers that use the minimill concept freely trade a great deal of know-how among one another. In some cases, this activity extends to training (without charge) a competitor's employees in new process improvements. While not all industries are amenable to technology sharing, trading is becoming increasingly common because of the high cost of developing advanced technologies independently.[21]

Research Partnerships and Joint Ventures

Research partnerships are arrangements designed to jointly pursue specific new-technology development. Typically, each member enters the partnership with different skills or resources needed for successful new-technology development. An effective combination is an established company and a start-up. Joint ventures are similar in most respects to research partnerships, but they tend to have greater permanence and their outcomes result in entirely new companies.[22]

Acquisition of an Owner of the Technology

If a company lacks the needed technology but wishes to acquire proprietary ownership of it, one option is to purchase the company that owns the technology. This transaction can take a number of forms, ranging from an outright purchase of the entire company to a minority interest sufficient to gain access to the technology. Sun Microsystems' CEO, Scott McNealy, readily acknowledges that part of his firm's strategy is to acquire companies with emerging technologies. In the fast-paced world of Internet computing, there is no way one firm can do it all itself.[23]

Choosing among these alternatives can be simplified by asking the following basic questions:

1. Is it important (and possible) in terms of competitive advantage that the technology remain proprietary?
2. Are the time, skills, and resources for internal development available?
3. Is the technology readily available outside the company?

As Figure 17.4 illustrates, the answers to these questions guide the manager to the most appropriate technology acquisition option.

FIGURE 17.4
Technology Acquisition Options

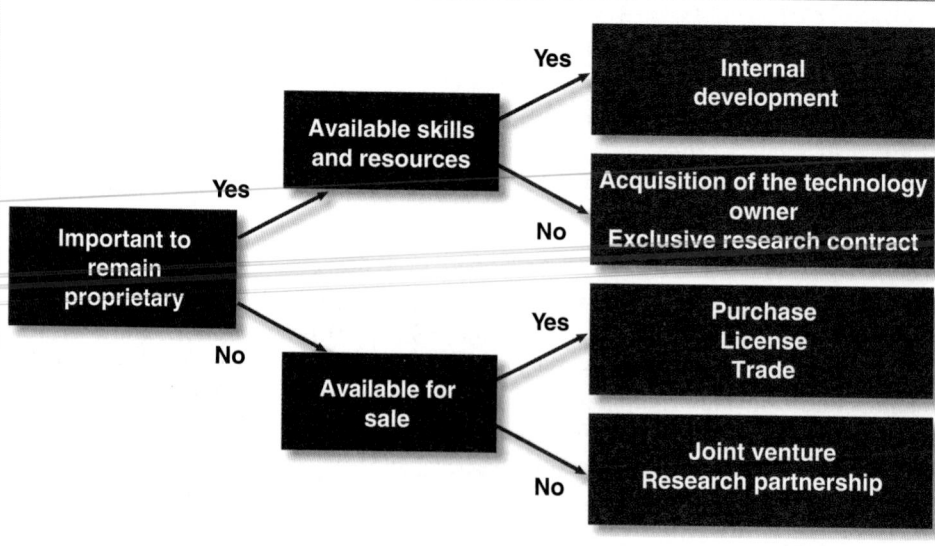

Technology and Managerial Roles

In organizations, technology traditionally has been the responsibility of vice presidents for research and development. These executives are directly responsible for corporate and divisional R&D laboratories. Typically, their jobs have a functional orientation. But increasingly companies are creating the position of **chief technology officer (CTO)**. The CTO is a senior position at the corporate level with broad, integrative responsibilities. CTOs coordinate the technological efforts of the various business units, act as a voice for technology in the top management team, supervise new-technology development, and assess the technological implications of major strategic initiatives such as acquisitions, new ventures, and strategic alliances.[24]

> **chief technology officer (CTO)**
>
> **Executive in charge of technology strategy and development.**

▼ FROM THE PAGES OF

BusinessWeek

Fighting for a PET Project Saves Lives

As one of the world's most famous scientists, Michael Phelps has done his share of mingling with the rich and the famous. But Phelps says that what really shaped his life were the boxing and brawling skills he perfected while growing up in a rough Irish neighborhood in Port Orchard, Washington.

Phelps delivered his knockout blow in 1974, when he and the postdoctoral student Ed Hoffman invented the first positron emission tomography (PET) scanner. Unlike X-rays, which display only the body's structure, PET reveals chemical and biological processes within the body. It shows, for example, how the brain remembers and thinks, how the heart beats, and how the pancreas synthesizes insulin.

The invention has saved thousands of lives. During a PET scan, a patient is injected with a tiny amount of radioactive glucose and then wheeled through the doughnut-shaped PET camera. As the glucose spreads through the patient's veins, heart, and tissue, the camera takes pictures. Because cancer cells gobble up sugar, an image showing a spot of glucose absorption could indicate a malignant tumor. The device can also spot Alzheimer's disease 15 years before the first symptoms occur, according to Phelps's most recent research.

Only major hospitals own PET scanners, which cost between $800,000 and $3 million, but some experts think the worldwide market for the device is about to explode. Already, pharmaceutical companies are using miniature PET scanners to test new drugs on mice.

Winning acceptance of the technology has been a challenge. Insurance companies refused for years to cover PET scans, which can cost about $2,500 and take as long as 90 minutes. By comparison, a regular computed tomography (CT) scan takes 15 minutes and generally runs no more than $500. But clinical studies show that PET scans have a higher accuracy rate than do traditional scans, depending on the disease and the patient.

In 1997, the government finally approved PET for detecting lung cancer in Medicare/Medicaid patients. Since then, PET has been approved for other diagnoses, thanks in part to years of lobbying by Phelps and supporters such as Senator Ted Stevens of Alaska. Stevens often tells a story about how he once missed a speech he was supposed to give because he was engrossed in a conversation with Phelps. "I was mesmerized," says Stevens about PET. "It seemed to me this was a breakthrough that could lead to other breakthroughs."

Phelps predicts that PET technology will be used to test drugs and bring them to market faster. First, medications will be tried out on genetically engineered mice to determine how they might react in humans. Later, PET could make human testing both safer and more accurate.

Speedy creation of drugs is still a dream; some would even call it a pipe dream. But Phelps likes to quote a friend. "Life has a natural curve," his friend told him. "You go up, you plateau, and you go down. The only way to change this is to be continually starting new curves and, in this way, always remain in a state of becoming." That's why Phelps continues to work seven days a week: He is training for his next fight.

SOURCE: Olga Kharif, "A Sharper Eye for Seeing Within," *Business Week Online*, July 30, 2002.

CTOs also perform an important boundary role: They work directly with outside organizations. For example, they work with universities for funding research to stay abreast of technical developments and with regulatory agencies to ensure compliance with regulations, identify trends, and influence the regulatory process.

Other people play a variety of critical roles in developing new technology. Recall from Chapter 7 that it is the *entrepreneur* who, in an effort to exploit untried technologies, invents new products or finds new ways to produce old products. The entrepreneur opens up new possibilities that change the competitive structure of entire industries.[25] For example, Steven Jobs started Apple Computer in his garage and launched the multi-billion-dollar personal computer industry.

Key roles in acquiring and developing new technologies are the technical innovator, product champion, and executive champion.[26] The **technical innovator** develops the new technology or has the key skills needed to install and operate the technology. This person possesses the requisite technical skills, but he or she may not have the managerial skills needed to push the idea forward and secure acceptance within the organization. This is where the product champion gets involved. Introducing new technology into an organization requires that someone promote the idea. The **product champion**—often at the risk of his or her position and prestige—promotes the idea throughout the organization, searching for support and acceptance. The champion can be a high-level manager, but often this is not the case. If the champion lacks the power and financial resources to make the required changes independently, she or he must convince people who have such authority to support the innovation. In other words, product champions must get sponsorship.

Sponsorship comes from the **executive champion,** who has the status, authority, and financial resources to support the project and protect the product champion. Without this support and protection, the product champion, and thus the new technology, could not succeed. Resources needed to develop the innovation would be unavailable, and without protection the champion would not be allowed to continue promoting the change.

technical innovator

A person who develops a new technology or has the key skills to install and operate the technology.

product champion

A person who promotes a new technology throughout the organization in an effort to obtain acceptance of and support for it.

executive champion

An executive who supports a new technology and protects the product champion of the innovation.

Organizing for Innovation

Organizing for innovation requires a balance between unleashing people's creative energies and capabilities and controlling the results to meet market needs in a timely manner.

Unleashing Creativity

As discussed in Chapter 7 ("New Ventures"), 3M has a strong orientation toward *intrapreneurship* and derives about one-third of its revenues from new products. 3M, and companies such as Merck, Hewlett-Packard, and Rubbermaid have well-established histories of producing many successful new technologies and products. What sets these and other continuous innovators apart? The one thing these companies have in common is an organizational culture that encourages innovation.[27]

Consider the 3M legend from the early 1920s of inventor Francis G. Okie. Okie dreamed up the idea of using sandpaper instead of razor blades for shaving. The aim was to reduce the risk of nicks and avoid sharp instruments. The idea failed, but rather than being punished for the failure, Okie was encouraged to champion other ideas, which included 3M's first blockbuster success: waterproof sandpaper. A culture that permits failure is crucial for fostering the creative thinking and risk taking required for innovation.

As strange as it may seem, *celebrating* failure can be vital to the innovation process.[28] Failure is the essence of learning, growing, and succeeding. Innovative companies have many balls in the air at all times, with many people trying many new ideas. A majority of the ideas will fail, but it is only through this process that the few big "hits" will emerge that make a company an innovative star.

> - **Set goals for innovation.** By corporate decree, 25 to 30 percent of annual sales must come from new products that are five years old or less.
>
> - **Commit to research and development.** 3M invests in R&D at almost double the rate of the average U.S. company. One R&D goal is to cut in half the time it takes to introduce new products.
>
> - **Inspire intrapreneurship.** Champions are encouraged to run with new ideas, and they get a chance to manage their products as if they were running their own businesses. 3Mers are allowed to spend 15 percent of their time pursuing personal research interests unrelated to current company projects.
>
> - **Facilitate, don't obstruct.** Divisions are kept small and are allowed to operate with a great deal of independence but have constant access to information and technical resources. Researchers with good ideas are awarded $50,000 Genesis grants to develop their brainstorms into new products.
>
> - **Focus on the customer.** 3M's definition of quality is to demonstrate that the product can do what the customer—not some arbitrary standard—dictates.
>
> - **Tolerate failure.** 3Mers know that if their ideas fail, they still will be encouraged to pursue other innovative ideas. Management knows that mistakes will be made and that destructive criticism kills initiative.

SOURCES: Company reports; R. Mitchell, "Masters of Innovation: How 3M Keeps Its New Products Coming," *Business Week*, April 10, 1989, pp. 58–63; T. Katauskas, "Follow-Through: 3M's Formula for Success," *R&D*, November 1990; and Thomas J. Martin, "Ten Commandments for Managing Creative People," *Fortune*, January 16, 1995, pp. 135–36.

TABLE 17.3
3M's Rules for an Innovative Culture

3M uses the simple set of rules listed in Table 17.3 to help foster innovation. These rules can be—and are—copied by other companies. But 3M has an advantage in that it has followed these rules since its inception and ingrained them in its culture. This culture is shared and passed on in part through stories. One such legend is about the 3M engineer who was fired because he refused to stop working on a project that his boss thought was wasting resources. Despite being fired, the engineer came to work as usual, finished the project, and demonstrated the value of his innovation. The engineer eventually was promoted to head a new division created to manufacture and market the innovation.

Bureaucracy Busting

Bureaucracy is an enemy of innovation. While bureaucracy is useful to maintain orderliness and gain efficiencies, it also can work directly against innovativeness. Developing radically different technologies requires a more fluid and flexible (organic) structure that does not restrict thought and action. However, such a structure can be chaotic and disruptive to normal operations. Consequently, companies often establish special temporary project structures that are isolated from the rest of the organization and allowed to operate under different rules. These units go by many names, including "skunkworks" (recall Chapter 7), "greenhouses," and "reserves."

In Japan, *angura is* an "underground research" policy that allows scientists to spend up to 20 percent of their time pursuing projects about which only the immediate supervisor knows.[29] When Apple developed the Macintosh, Steve Jobs took a small group of young engineers and programmers and set up operations apart from the remainder of the plant. They started from scratch, trying to rethink the personal computer completely. A pirate's flag was flown over their operation to demonstrate that they were not part of the regular bureaucratic operating structure and defied conventional rules. The result was a very successful new product.

Managerial systems can facilitate innovation. At steel companies such as Chaparral and Nucor, employees work in *cross-functional teams* to solve problems and create innovative solutions. These *flat structures* help create an enviornment that encourages collaboration and creativity. Teams focus on present issues and problems as well as future concerns and opportunities. In addition, teams work with outside partners to bring knowledge into the organization so that it can be integrated with existing ideas and information to create innovations. All the while, teams are supported by values of egalitarianism, information sharing, openness to outside ideas, and positive risk. The aim is to destroy the traditional boundaries between functions and departments in order to create less bureaucratic "learning laboratories."[30]

Implementing Development Projects

A powerful tool for managing technology and innovations is the **development project.**[31] A development project is a focused organizational effort to create a new product or process

development project

A focused organizational effort to create a new product or process via technological advances.

via technological advances. For example, several years ago Eastman Kodak launched a development project to create the FunSaver Camera. The concept was simple: to package film in an inexpensive plastic camera body so that after the pictures were taken, the consumer could simply drop the whole assembly with a photo finisher. While the FunSaver utilized existing design knowledge, it was developed on a unique computer-aided design and manufacturing (CAD/CAM) system. Two years earlier, Hewlett-Packard had initiated a development project of its own to design a new class of low-cost computer printers based on ink-jet technology. HP's Deskjet Printer was one of the company's first attempts to integrate manufacturing, marketing, and R&D. The development project allowed the company to achieve an unprecedented advantage in both cost and speed.

In general, development projects fall into one of four categories: (1) *research or advanced development projects* designed to invent new science for application in a specific project, (2) *breakthrough development projects* designed to create the first generation of a product or process, (3) *platform development projects* that establish the basic architecture for a whole set of follow-on projects, and (4) *derivative development projects* that are narrower in scope and are designed to provide incremental improvements to an existing product or process.[32]

Development projects such as these typically feature a special cross-functional team that works together on an overall concept or idea. Like most cross-functional teams, its success depends on how well individuals work together to pursue a common vision. And in the case of development projects, teams must interact with suppliers and customers frequently, making the complexity of their task that much greater. Because of their urgency and strategic importance, most development projects are conducted under intense time and budget pressures, thus presenting a real-time test of the company's ability to innovate.

Managers should recognize that development projects have multiple benefits. Not only are they useful for creating new products and processes, they frequently cultivate skills and knowledge that can be used for future endeavors. In other words, the capabilities that companies derive from a development project frequently can be turned into a source of competitive advantage. For example, when Ford created a development project to design an air-conditioning compressor to outperform its Japanese rival, executives also discovered that they had laid the foundation for new processes that Ford could use in future projects. Their new capability in integrated design and manufacturing helped Ford reduce the costs and lead times for other product developments. Thus, *organizational learning* had become an equally important criterion for evaluating the success of the project.

For development projects to achieve their fullest benefit, they should build on core competencies (recall Chapters 4 and 9); have a guiding vision about what must be accomplished and why (Chapter 12); have a committed team (Chapters 12 and 14); instill a philosophy of continuous improvement (Chapter 9); and generate integrated, coordinated efforts across all units (Chapters 8 and 9).

Technology, Job Design, and Human Resources

Adopting a new technology typically requires changes in the way jobs are designed. Often the way the task is redefined fits people to the demands of the technology to maximize the technology's operation. But this often fails to maximize total productivity, because it ignores the human part of the equation. The social relationships and human aspects of the task may suffer, lowering overall productivity.

The **sociotechnical systems** approach to work redesign specifically addresses this problem. This approach redesigns tasks in a manner that jointly optimizes the social and technical efficiency of work. Beginning with studies on the introduction of new coal-mining technologies in 1949, the sociotechnical systems approach to work design focused on small, self-regulating work groups.[33] Later it was found that such work arrangements could operate effectively only in an environment in which bureaucracy was limited. Today's trends in bureaucracy "bashing," lean and flat organizations, work teams, and an empowered workforce are logical extensions of the sociotechnical philosophy of work design. At the same time, the technologies of the information age—in which people at all organizational levels have access to vast amounts of information—make these leaner and less bureaucratic organizations possible.

> **sociotechnical systems**
>
> **An approach to job design that attempts to redesign tasks to optimize operation of a new technology while preserving employees' interpersonal relationships and other human aspects of the work.**

Managers face several choices regarding how to apply a new technology. Technology can be used to limit the tasks and responsibilities of workers and "deskill" the workforce, thus turning workers into servants of the technology. Alternatively, managers can select and train workers to master the technology, using it to achieve great accomplishments and improve the quality of their lives. Technology, when managed effectively, can empower workers as it improves the competitiveness of organizations.

However, as managers make decisions about how to design jobs and manage employees, they also need to consider other human resource systems that complement the introduction of new technology. Table 17.4, for example, shows how compensation systems can be changed to facilitate the implementation of advanced manufacturing technology. In the contemporary setting, the use of group incentives, salary, and skill-based pay systems helps reinforce the collective effort (recall the use of cross-functional teams), professionalism, empowerment, and flexibility required for knowledge work. If a company's pay system is not aligned with the new technologies, it may not reward behavior that is needed to make the changes work. Worse, existing reward systems actually may reinforce old behaviors that run counter to what is needed for the new technology.

Taken as a whole, these ideas provide a set of guidelines for managing the strategic and organizational issues associated with technology and innovation. In Chapter 18, we expand this discussion to focus on how organizations can reshape themselves to adapt to a dynamic marketplace. Managing change and organizational learning are central elements of what it takes to become a world-class organization.

Compensation Practices in Traditional and Advanced Manufacturing Firms

TABLE 17.4

Type of Compensation Practice	Traditional Factory	Integrated Manufacturing
Performance-contingent	Focus on *individual incentives* reflects division of labor and separation of stages and functions.	Extensive use of *group incentives* to encourage teamwork, cooperation, and joint problem solving.
Job-contingent	Use of *hourly wage* assumes that the differences in employee contribution are captured in job classifications and that performance is determined largely by the production system.	Use of *salary* assumes that employees' contributions transcend the job per se to substantially affect output. The distinctions between classes of employment are diminished.
Person-contingent	*Seniority pay* rewards experience as a surrogate for knowledge and skill in a stable environment and rewards loyalty to reduce uncertainty within the system.	*Skill-based* pay rewards continuous learning and the value added from increased flexibility in a dynamic environment.

SOURCE: Scott A. Snell and James W. Dean, Jr., "Strategic Compensation for Integrated Manufacturing: The Moderating Effects of Jobs and Organizationl Inertia," *Academy of Management Journal* 37, no. (1994) pp. 1109–40.

KEY TERMS

Chief technology officer (CTO),
    p. 535

Development project, p. 538

Executive champion, p. 536

Innovation, p. 520

Make-or-buy decision, p. 533

Product champion, p. 536

Sociotechnical systems, p. 539

Technical innovator, p. 536

Technology, p. 520

Technology audit, p. 527

Technology life cycle, p. 521

SUMMARY OF LEARNING OBJECTIVES

Now that you have studied Chapter 17, you should know:

The processes involved in the development of new technologies.

Forces that compel the emergence of a new technology include (1) a need for the technology, (2) the requisite scientific knowledge, (3) the technical convertibility of this knowledge, (4) the capital resources to fund development, and (5) the entrepreneurial insight and initiative to pull the components together.

How technologies proceed through a life cycle.

New technologies follow a predictable life cycle. First, a workable idea about how to meet a market need is developed into a product innovation. Early progress can be slow as competitors experiment with product designs. Eventually a dominant design emerges as the market accepts the technology, and further refinements to the technology result from process innovations. As the technology begins to approach both the theoretical limits to its performance potential and market saturation, growth slows and the technology matures. At this point the technology can remain stable or be replaced by a new technology.

How to manage technology for competitive advantage.

Adopters of new technologies are categorized according to the timing of their adoption: innovators, early adopters, the early majority, the late majority, and laggards. Technology leadership has many first-mover advantages but also poses significant disadvantages. The same may be said for followership. After that, technology that helps improve efficiency will support a low-cost strategy, while technologies that help make products more distinctive or unique will support a differentiation strategy. Determining an appropriate technology strategy depends on the degree to which the technology supports the organization's competitive requirements and, if a technology leadership strategy is chosen, the company's ability, in terms of skills, resources, and commitment, to deal with the risks and uncertainties of leadership.

How to assess technology needs.

Assessing the technology needs of a company begins by benchmarking, or comparing, the technologies it employs with those of both competitors and noncompetitors. Benchmarking should be done on a global basis to understand practices used worldwide.

Technology scanning helps identify emerging technologies and those still under development in an effort to project their eventual competitive impact.

Where new technologies originate and the best strategies for acquiring them.

New technologies can be acquired or developed. Options include internal development, purchase, contracted development, licensing, trading, research partnerships and joint ventures, and acquisition. The approach used depends on the existing availability of the technology; the skills, resources, and time available; and the importance of keeping the technology proprietary.

How people play a role in managing technology.

People play many different roles in managing technology. For example, the chief technology officer is the person with broad, integrative responsibility for technological innovation. In addition, the entrepreneur is the person who recognizes the competitive potential of the technology and finds new ways to exploit opportunities. The technical innovator has the key skills needed to develop or install and operate the technology. The product champion is the person who promotes the new idea(s) in order to gain support throughout the organization. The executive champion is the person with the status and resources to support the project.

How to develop an innovative organization.

Organizing for innovation involves unleashing the creative energies of employees while directing their efforts toward meeting market needs in a timely manner. Culture, structure, development projects, and job design are critical for building an innovative organization.

The key characteristics of successful development projects.

For development projects to achieve the fullest benefit, they should (1) build on core competencies, (2) have a guiding vision about what must be accomplished and why, (3) have a committed team, (4) instill a philosophy of continuous improvement, and (5) generate integrated, coordinated efforts across all teams and units.

DISCUSSION QUESTIONS

1. At the beginning of this chapter there is a quote from Francis Bacon that reads, "A wise man will make more opportunities than he finds." What does this have to do with technology and innovation? What does it have to do with competitive advantage?

2. What examples of technological innovation can you identify? What forces led to the commercialization of the science behind those technologies? Did the capability exist before the market demand, or was the demand there before the technology was available?

3. Thomas Edison once said that most innovations are 10 percent inspiration and 90 percent perspiration. How does this match what you know about technology life cycles?

4. Why would a company choose to follow rather than lead technological innovations? Is the potential advantage of technological leadership greater when innovations are occurring rapidly, or is it better in this case to follow?

5. If you were in the grocery business, who would you benchmark for technological innovations? Would the companies be inside or outside your industry? Why?

6. How would you see the executive champion, the chief technology officer, and the product champion working together? Could the roles all be played by the same individual? Why or why not?

Matsushita's Creative Destruction

When Kunio Nakamura became president and CEO at Matsushita Electric Industrial Co. in 1999, he had one big demand: to keep on doing what he'd been doing. As a senior executive at the world's largest consumer electronics conglomerate, Nakamura had reshaped almost everything he had touched. After successfully streamlining operations in the United States, he turned all 35 of Matsushita's money-losing Chinese subsidiaries into profitable units in two years.

When Nakamura assumed his new CEO duties, it wasn't surprising that he was given free rein. "I didn't want to be a CEO unless I could implement my own policies," he said. "My job is to instigate change."

Someone needed to. Matsushita had become a stodgy giant. With over 290,000 employees in 46 countries, it was becoming a slower mover in the information technology (IT) race. Matsushita's Panasonic brand was still immensely popular and the company commanded top market share in Japan for Net-capable phones, car navigation, and DVD products, but it had never produced a hit like Sony's Walkman. It also had been battered by falling profits on conventional products such as televisions and VCRs. In one year's time, consumer products profits at Matsushita fell a whopping 60 percent.

To be sure, Nakamura inherited a creaky machine. Matsushita's bureaucracy was mammoth, with too many business divisions— some 150 in Japan alone. Its stock was underperforming. A day after taking over, Nakamura pledged he would "empower" employees by rewarding talent—not age or seniority. That was a huge shake-up for employees at the 84-year-old company, who had long counted on career-length job security. "It'll be necessary for people to adjust their skills to the IT age," Nakamura said. As proof of his commitment, Nakamura pledged to invest $1 billion in information technology over the next three years. He also handed out 500 Net-ready cell phones to senior executives so that they could be reached anytime, anywhere.

To date, Nakamura has folded in five of Matsushita's divisions and laid off 13,000 employees. "The main aim is to eliminate duplication in product development," he said. When all is said and done, the company will have 14 product categories in four main

Kunio Nakamura attempts to remake Matsushita by consolidating divisions and beefing up the company's information technologies.

business divisions: audiovisual, home appliances, industrial equipment, and devices.

But in contrast to its competitors, Matsushita doesn't foresee moving factories to China, where labor costs are lower. "Japan is a country that needs its manufacturing base if it hopes to continue to grow," said Nakamura. "It has been pushing the edge of technology, manufacturing, and miniaturization ... So I'm not that worried about the Japanese losing our technological edge."

Nakamura hopes Matsushita won't either. In April 2002, the company reported it had fallen $3.4 billion in the red, its biggest net loss on record. Most of the costs were attributed to the restructuring.

Can Nakamura achieve the same kind of success companywide that he did in the United States and China? "No matter how beautiful a picture I paint, you're not going to believe me until I've actually accomplished something," he said candidly. And about that, the CEO is surely right.

QUESTIONS

1. Why is there a need for change at Matsushita?

2. What else can Nakamura do to improve the company's information technology strategies?

3. What do you think about Nakamura's plan to keep the company's production plants in Japan? How might that affect product development?

SOURCE: Patricia O'Connell, "Matsushita's Creative Destruction," *Business Week Online*, May 28, 2002; Irene M. Kunii, "Bold Mechanic for a Creaky Machine," *Business Week*, August 7, 2000, p. 58h.

17.1   Planning for Innovation

OBJECTIVES

1. To brainstorm innovative ideas for a company that has become stagnant.

2. To explore the elements of a good innovation plan.

INSTRUCTIONS

1. Read the Mason, Inc., scenario.

2. Individually or in small groups, offer a plan for encouraging innovation at Mason, Inc. Discuss staffing, rewards, organizational structure, work design, and any other facets of organizational behavior that apply.

3. In small groups, or with the entire class, share the plans you developed.

MASON, INC., SCENARIO

Mason, Inc., designs, develops, and manufactures personal grooming products. From 1950 to 1980 it was a leader in introducing new, profitable products into the marketplace. Its Research and Development Division grew from 20 to 150 professionals during

DISCUSSION QUESTIONS

1. What elements do these plans have in common?

2. How well do the plans follow the innovation process?

3. Do the plans incorporate provisions for fulfilling the various roles required for innovation?

4. What are the strengths and weaknesses of each plan?

5. What should be the components of an effective plan?

SOURCE: J. Gordon, *A Diagnostic Approach to Organizational Behavior* (Englewood Cliffs, NJ: Prentice-Hall, 1983), p. 654. Reprinted by permission of Prentice-Hall, Inc., Englewood Cliffs, N.J.

that time. Since 1980, however, the company has relied on its past successes and has failed to introduce any significant innovative product into the marketplace. Top management wants to reestablish Mason's reputation as the number-one innovator in the industry.

17.2   Innovation for the Future

OBJECTIVE

To look ahead into the future.

INSTRUCTIONS

Choose a partner. Together, develop an innovative product or service that will be popular in the year 2025. As you develop your product or service, ask yourselves the following questions:

1. What trends lead you to believe that this product or service will be successful?

2. What current technologies, services, or products will be replaced by your idea?

Present your idea to the class for discussion.

Operations Management in the New Economy

The business of a company—any company—is to take certain inputs and, by means of a process, transform them into outputs. Bringing these outputs (the product) to market cost-effectively will ensure the company's continued existence and well-being. The methods, systems, and mental framework by which a company transforms its inputs into outputs characterize its *operations*. A company maintains the health of its transformation process through *management* of these operations. *Operations management* is the analysis and implementation of this process.

Many varied factors impinge on a company's operations and managers. As company size increases, so do the number of variables. Effective management of the operation and its variables contributes in no small measure to the company's success, whether the company is small or large, diversified or devoted to core businesses, a network organization or a highly structured, centralized body. It holds true whether the company sells a tangible product (goods) or an intangible one (services), for in both cases, the customer is buying the object of a desire, or the satisfaction of a need.

EFFECTS OF CHANGE

We often read that operations management is in transition today. In actuality, it has always been in transition, because the world is always changing. Changes may take the form of new products (imagine the first traders bringing spices to Europe in the early Middle Ages), new distribution channels (Federal Express completely revamped our expectations about package delivery), alterations in the labor pool (women assumed many factory jobs during World War II, when men were at war), or new technologies (gunpowder altered all the rules of war in 14th-century Europe).

Characteristic of the current age is the quickening *rate* at which change occurs, placing pressure on individuals to adapt quickly and rewarding those able to shift mental gears, personal habits, and priorities easily. Indeed, survival of the fittest applies not only to physical attributes but also to mental agility. Operations managers must be among the most "fit" to function effectively in today's world.

THE CONTEXT OF OPERATIONS MANAGEMENT

What does it mean to be an effective manager of an operation? It means responding to the needs of diverse parties *within* the company, ensuring smooth movement through all stages of the transformation process. We can even take the viewpoint that, within the process, the "customer" is the department receiving the result of the preceding stage. For example, in a printing company, the operator of the press is the customer of the prepress area. An effective manager works with this awareness, ensuring that each area supplies what the next one expects.

Operations management also means satisfying parties in the *larger* arena. For example, investors may want to know how well a new product line is faring in the market or whether a new manufacturing process is delivering as promised. The community may want assurances that wastes from the production process will not cause quality of life to suffer. The government may demand an accounting of any number of activities covered by regulations. Thus, the manager of an operation does not exist in isolation but is part of an ongoing interaction among any number of parties.

In ages past, the world was home to many different societies or cultures, which were mostly different one from another, but each was more homogeneous than is the case today. Buyers in a given community needed the same products. Everyone knew what those products were, and common agreement on quality prevailed. Also prevalent was a common understanding of the entitlements of various social levels (what goods of what quality were the prerogative of the wealthy, for example). Because items were individually made, customization was the norm, for there was no other way to do business.

As the industrial age dawned in the 19th century, this situation changed. Suddenly the "customer" was no longer a few identifiable individuals, but a growing mass of less well-defined persons, any of whom, with money, could have what was formerly the prerogative of the few. With industrialization came mass production, and one product for all buyers became the norm, because there was no other cost-effective way to do business.

The modern-day corporation took shape against this background, and marketing was born. Now in the digital age, we are witnessing a phenomenon that once would have sounded like an oxymoron: mass customization. What are the implications for today's managers?

When the product is static or has few variations, operations management quite justifiably focuses on the product (and its cost). This perspective has produced the orientation of traditional operations management. With the ability to manufacture many variations of the same product, with access to increasing amounts of information, the focus today has shifted to the customer's *experience* of the product: how he or she perceives to have been served by the vendor. The customer assesses whether the product contains the desired characteristics and quality, at the best price. Management of an operation with this awareness probably will spell the success or failure of the company in today's environment.

But is today's customer truly different? Yes and no, for despite the fact that things change, things also stay the same. Human beings still engage in the same activities: They create community; they raise the next generation; they trade; they provide for themselves; and in the process, they learn, fight, and play. And today's managers still shuttle inputs through the transformation process into successful outputs. Most of the traditional notions about human activity still apply.

To explain any activity, however, one may use a variety of lenses (Galileo's lens was different from Ptolemy's, and so he derived a different explanation of the universe). A manager may view the process from the standpoint of product specifications, cost limitations, customer satisfaction, or any number of viewpoints. The lens chosen will reflect a particular view of the world and its priorities, as well as the company's priorities.

Sometimes there are no right or wrong choices, only consequences. The lens that adequately explained a given phenomenon at one time may not serve today. What is reflected through the lens will form the guidelines for decisions, however, and so the choice has far-reaching repercussions.

NEW PERSPECTIVES

From time to time, particular orientations or viewpoints burst onto the stage, altering perceptions and leaving changed priorities in their wake. Such is the case with W. Edward Deming's *total quality management*, now an article of faith for many of today's managers. The Japanese readily embraced Deming's principles, taking an enviable and now imitated approach to customer satisfaction (see Chapter 9 of the text for Deming's 14 points). Western nations paid scant attention until they saw the results of offering quality in a customer-oriented operation.

For most of us, quality is what we see in the end result (does the product meet manufacturing specifications?). In his lengthy essay *Zen and the Art of Motorcycle Maintenance*, Robert Pirsig associated achievement of quality with a state of mind: "Skilled mechanics and machinists of a certain sort . . . have patience, care and attentiveness to what they're doing, a kind of inner peace of mind that isn't contrived but results from a kind of harmony with the work . . ."[1] More characteristic of the Eastern mindset, this statement means that quality (good or bad) is not an attribute of the end product, but rather is inherent in the way an individual interacts with the subject of his or her attention.

To achieve good quality requires knowing what is good, and then having the mindset suitable for achieving it. This attentiveness is related to the Japanese *kaizen*, a willingness and desire to improve constantly. Since the 1980s, Japanese business practices have been the object of study and implementation by Westerners, from specific procedures (such as *kanban*, the basis of just-in-time inventory management) to general philosophies (the *kaizen* that is part of Japanese general operations strategy). A manager anywhere today would be ill served by neglect of these concepts.

Likewise, companies that involve employees in the process are on the way to understanding that the people interface with the product is crucial to their success. We will see how important this view is in a few pages.

CORPORATE ORGANIZATION

There are many ways to structure a company, and some of today's companies have taken their present form as a result of trends in the economy: mergers or acquisitions, diversification, alliances. With all, there are still certain functions identifiable in most corporate organizations. The operation of that function is what commands the attention of its managers. Let us consider how some of these common functions support the operations management system.

Strategic Planning   On the highest level, guiding the corporation from the broadest perspective is strategic, or long-range, planning. The firm's upper-level managers provide the corporation's direction, defining and refining its mission in the process. Management of this function entails answering questions such as: What business are we in? What business should or will we be in? Who are our customers? How can or should we serve them? Do we want to focus on core businesses or diversify? Answers to these questions will help develop corporate goals, which, filtered through the company's management levels, give direction to its operation.

As stated earlier, the world is always changing. Good strategic planning seeks to *anticipate* change and then plan for it. Good planners also foster a feeling of confidence about what is likely to produce success. During the 1990s, when the rallying cry of much of corporate management was to stick to core businesses, GE chief Jack Welch built a successful conglomerate of widely diverse businesses, finding people with the mindset to operate well within that structure, and achieving effective coordination of all functions through its many divisions.

Marketing   Of all the company's functions, marketing is closest to the customer. Its job is to identify customer needs (latent or manifest) and translate them back to the firm for its reaction. Its role in supporting the operations management system is therefore critical. Operations managers must then restate what marketing has communicated in terms that will bring about the needed response from the production mechanism. To support its efforts, marketing works with advertising to state the company's offerings in terms that are attractive to the buyer. Sales is a part of the marketing function also, salespeople being those who take action to sell within an identified market. This is the front line, the place where information about customer needs and desires penetrates and gains the attention of the company.

A story told in sales circles is about the ABC Company (a shoe manufacturer), whose marketing head visited a remote area of the world to assess the market. He returned to report to his boss, "There's no market; they don't wear shoes." The marketing head of competitor XYZ Company made the same trip for the same purpose, reporting to *his* boss: "It's a terrific market! They've got no shoes!" Marketing's response to a circumstance can take a firm into new areas.

Research and Engineering   Suppose the marketing function has identified a new need or potential market. Enter the design and engineering people, whose function is the development and refinement of the product and the processes that manufacture it. They design, develop, and test the product through all stages until it is ready for market launch. They interact with customers who participate in the testing of a new product prior to launching. They also interact with operations—the product attributes and the processes required to make them will become the responsibility of the operations management system. Even as a product is still on the drawing board, its design may change based on customer response, manufacturing procedures (i.e., what is feasible in the current setup), or prices of material or labor.

As researchers and developers, this part of the company is most in touch with what will be available in the future, and one of its functions is identification and implementation of solutions not currently in use. The end result of the designers' work will affect purchasing (of parts, equipment, materials), inventory management (quantities of items to keep on hand), shop floor operation (equipment may need rearrangement), capacity requirements (maximum rate of production), and human resources (human skills needed and cost of acquisition).

Human Resources

This brings us to the next function: human resources. A company *is* its people. They form the culture, produce the product, and deliver it. The human resources function must seek, attract, and keep individuals having the skills, human qualities, and experience required by the operations management system. Effective management of human resources thus directly affects the entire production process. Any company wishing to build a plant in a geographically desirable area would be foolish not to take into account the human component: educational level, work ethic, habits, and expectations of the labor pool.

Some believe that there are no bad employees, only employees placed in wrong positions. Effective use of employees will provide operations managers with a valuable source of innovation and productivity gains, for the employees are actually in contact with the product (and with the customer, in the case of a service business). They are the interface where quality is born. It cannot be stressed too heavily that one of the most valuable attributes of any employee is the ability to communicate: to articulate what's right about the work experience, what's wrong, and how to improve it. Dissatisfaction unexpressed is potential trouble; ideas not presented represent lost potential.

Purchasing

Just as human inputs matter, so do materials. Selecting inputs that will support the company's orientation and vision is the crucial role played by the purchasing function. Optimally, it is a source of expertise for the operations management system, providing information about the variety of materials and systems available for use by the production process. The performance of any operating division is ultimately dependent on goods and services supplied to it by purchasing. Will the materials produce the result intended by the design of the product? Will they allow themselves to be molded as intended by the production process? Will they support the level of quality promised?

Cost-effective supply of the right materials potentially represents enormous savings for the company. A purchasing manager was once heard to say: "The sales division would have to close $500,000 in new business to produce the money I just saved by changing suppliers."

Logistics

The logistics of moving inputs through transformation may or may not benefit from an overview of the entire process, for the flow may take different names, depending on its location in the process. It may be called inventory management as inputs arrive, scheduling while in the transformation process, and distribution when outputs are en route to the customer. Smooth or poor coordination of the flow from supplier of materials to delivery to the customer has repercussions throughout the channel. If materials are not ready for a specific section of the production apparatus at the right time, equipment and machinery sit idle (a drain on profitability). Delays in delivery to customers mean delays in payment received, and that has an impact on the company's cash flow.

Finance

This brings us to the finance area. This function serves as an interface between the firm's managers and the financial community: banks, investment firms, and stockholders. These entities have a stake in the company's success or failure, and at all times are poised to assist, advise, provide support, or withdraw it. Finance must explain the company's performance adequately to elicit the maximum amount of support from financial institutions. In so doing, it makes use of the accounting department. Not merely a mechanism for tracking costs, the accounting department provides information useful to managers in understanding the cost implications of their decisions. Such cost-monitoring information can help managers understand how their own costs compare with standard costs, for example. Accounting also can help derive the cost implications of introducing new equipment or technologies.

In another of its roles, the finance function must be knowledgeable about the firm's creditworthiness. Any decline in the company's ability to pay its bills will weaken its position vis-à-vis competitors. Finance also must monitor the creditworthiness of suppliers. If suppliers are not financially able to deliver what they promise, the operations management system will feel the impact immediately. The financial community watches the impact of all these decisions, basing its ratings (and therefore support) on the wisdom of the decision makers.

A Team Operation

The fineness with which one breaks down the preceding functions can vary, but it should be clear at this point that the operations management system is only one of those operating within the corporate context. In the best of all possible worlds, operations management works hand in glove with the other functions, alert to any harmful fragmentation or lack of communication. Communication is, of course, a two-way street, and just as operations people must be aware of the workings of the other functions, the latter must know what the operations management system perceives, needs, and expects.

Satisfying customer expectations is a corporate activity, the work of one body (from *corpus*, Latin for "body"), with the whole dependent on how well its parts work individually and how well they work together. Neglect of any one organ affects the body's ability to perform at optimum level.

PREPARING FOR THE FUTURE IN THE NEW ECONOMY

In addition to awareness of how the company is operating at present, every good manager will give thought to what *could* happen, what is likely to happen, and what is possible, both for the company as a whole and for his or her own sphere of influence. Stated another way, an effective manager has a sense of vision. This means being aware of changes or potential changes in customer demands and changes in the company's resources (technology, labor pool, financial support). A good manager must listen, being attentive to all facts, and then select the useful facts from among the many supplied. A manager must constantly ask, "What if . . . ?"

With good vision and a healthy curiosity, a manager will more adequately handle factors impinging on the operations management system. The objective is to develop a sense of vision adequate to anticipate conceivable consequences. Let us consider some of today's challenges in what is often referred to as the "**new economy**."

Globalization   A company's sphere of activity has always been what could be reached easily by current means of communication and transportation. What is reachable has constantly expanded. The entire world is today's operating arena, both for buying inputs and for selling outputs. This circumstance presents the operations management system with a new range of possibilities.

The possibility of outsourcing has always been present. That is, do we make a particular component of the product, or do we send it out for manufacture pursuant to our specifications? Today, a manager may outsource locally or to any facility in the world offering the capability of supplying the need. It takes a lot of information, as well as sound judgment, to know which part of the process would benefit from being handled out of house.

The success of producing elsewhere depends in part on the characteristics of the "elsewhere." In the 20th century, U.S. companies based in northern states sometimes would move certain manufacturing operations to the southern part of the country, taking advantage of lower labor costs. While this required some adjustment in expectations, the adjustment is slight compared to manufacturing in Pacific Rim countries or Latin America, for example. The reason is simple: Each culture handles things in a particular way. A wise manager will not assume that a different culture will respond to expectations in the same manner as an American labor force would, and this circumstance may work to one's advantage or to one's detriment. Those who can anticipate potential problem areas are ahead of the game in the decision to manufacture offshore.

Then there is the globe as *marketplace*. To sell globally requires product design that accounts for differing tastes throughout the world's cultures. A small manufacturer of skin-care products based on formulas from India began marketing her line in America some years ago. She reports that she had to make alterations to account for the fact that Americans would not use a product with an unusual smell, no matter how beneficial for the skin.[2] Nescafe markets its products all over the globe, but the instant coffee sold in Brazil does not taste like that sold in the United States—in each instance, the product must satisfy the taste of a different culture.[3]

The ease with which the operations management system can make these alterations has increased dramatically in the last few decades. Digital technology has made flexibility in manufacturing a much more attainable situation than was previously the case, offering enormous potential to vary the product.

Environment   Another challenge facing today's manager is the environment, meaning both the world and the milieu in which the company operates. In an earlier time, negative effects from a manufacturing process were absorbed unobtrusively by the surroundings. As population density increased and consumption skyrocketed, particularly in the Western nations, this ceased to be true. What occurs in one place on the planet has an impact on the rest of it. The manager's challenge is to care enough about the future without imperiling today's operations, and the decisions are not simple.

It is unfortunate that the issue of environmental responsibility traditionally has been cast in ethical terms. While this stance is valid, and ultimately *the* reason for being good stewards of the planet, it does not help managers handle all the information required to make good decisions or quantify what is needed for decision making. In addition, consumers are often inconsistent, demanding recycled paper, for instance, and then choosing to buy whiter paper that is not recycled.

Certainly the last few decades have witnessed significant progress in the handling of the most blatantly offensive effects of manufacturing processes (waste streaming, emissions control). But making the right decision is not a clear-cut path. Consider the simple example of the supermarket checkout stand. "Would you like paper or plastic for your groceries?" The environmentally responsible buyer must choose between less than desirable alternatives. Paper (even if recycled) uses trees; plastic uses hydrocarbons and is not as easy to recycle. Decisions faced by operations managers are infinitely more complex.

Furthermore, if managers do not see to their societal responsibility, others will demand compliance. A corporation is not its own island in community waters, for others are affected by its decisions: property owners, investors, the larger public, and tomorrow's adults. Surely we have learned by now that groups that do not police their own ranks effectively are sure targets for policing by others, be they governmental agencies or community organizations.

The alternatives for an operations manager are therefore to react or to take a leadership role, becoming knowledgeable about potential negative effects of the process managed by him or her and proposing ways to handle them. In the long term, if we are to manage our economy's activities for tomorrow rather than today, responsibility for the environment is not a choice.

Knowledge and Information   One of the features of the new economy is that in the transformation process, the major input is intellectual property: knowledge, research, information, and design. These inputs have supplanted (in value) the material inputs required to build physical units. When knowledge is the major raw material, launching the first unit of a product represents millions of dollars; the cost of the second and thereafter is minuscule.

The products themselves are of a different nature, and it often takes greater sophistication to use a new-economy product—thus, for example, people's reluctance to switch from a PC to a Mac, or vice versa. As a result, customers are not as likely to be swayed by advertising, but rather by their increasing knowledge of the product and its technology. Successful companies will be those that increase a customer's knowledge base in general, and skill with their own products in particular.

As the information explosion continues to feed today's consumers and today's workforce, the knowledge acquired gives rise to expectations. As we will discuss a few pages hence, today's consumers are far from being locked into only a few sources for their information. Rather, they swim in an ocean of facts, figures, perspectives, and opportunities.

Nor are today's employees like those of yesteryear. It is instead the case that, depending on his or her own personal needs or aspirations, an employee is drawn to (and will stay with) a specific job in a given company for two reasons: (1) the possibility of experiencing personal satisfaction or growth and (2) satisfaction in the human interaction prevalent at that company. The balance of these factors varies with the individual, but everyone draws from these two wells. Today's managers therefore must provide more than the means for an employee to put bread on the table. The company must offer ongoing professional development, opportunity for increased responsibility in the firm, and a satisfying place to work. Today's employees do not expect to be *supervised,* but rather *coached* along the path of success. Needless to say, the manager also must be knowledgeable and continue to grow, increasing in value as a mentor.

Technology   The challenge of technology will occupy us for the rest of these pages. Technology has always existed and has always been neutral. That is, just as a knife serves to feed the family or to kill an adversary, new technologies can be used to help or harm. As with any challenge, managers can view technological innovation as something to react to, something to anticipate, something to plan for, or something from which to derive potential improvements and growth.

Technologies exist in various stages of development; that is, some are ready and available for use by the operations management system, some will be cost-effective in 5 or 10 years, and some are in embryo. Any forward-looking manager will be aware of all three. Technology companies (those which market the latest of a given technology, e.g., cellular phones) must monitor technology on two fronts. They must be aware of similar products on the market, constantly assessing the limits of their own products. They also must be aware of technologies potentially usable by their own operations, just as any nontechnology company would.

In its development, a technology tends to move to the hands of the user. Take the clock as an example. At one time in history, the only clock in the community was the one in the town square. Then wealthier people could purchase large timepieces known as "grandfather clocks." By the middle of the 20th century most adults owned a wristwatch, often a special gift received at graduation. Today children and adults have access to many timepieces, from those on their wrists to the many in the home, office, or car. We could trace a similar progression for other technologies, such as engines and, of course, computers (where the transition from mainframes to portable PCs occurred within a few decades of the last century).

The shift of a technology to the user is not always smooth. One of the potential stumbling blocks when a company embraces a technology is to discount the human factor involved in its use. We see this in small businesses constantly. The local copy shop brings in the latest copying and finishing equipment, offering everything from double-sided, spiral-bound reports graced with photos to personalized, artistic party invitations. The resulting product, however, is in part dependent on the skill and experience of the operator and the availability of sufficient personnel to work with customers.

Larger industrial equipment offers a similar scenario. At an earlier time in history, the operator of, for example, a multistory printing press would have 30 years to become familiar with the operation of that equipment before a new generation came on stream. In today's offices, employees barely become proficient at using the current popular software before a new or different version of it comes out. These "improvements" provide fertile ground for inefficiencies, for in the final analysis, technology can advance only at the rate at which human beings can use it effectively.

With this knowledge, any effective operations manager will have some type of formal technology management in place—some means of looking ahead, preparing for the effects of new technologies. When envisioning the potential of new technology (or technology in embryo), the best human characteristics to bring to the table are:

1. Awareness (information plus perspective) and
2. Imagination (the ability to create new scenarios from existing ones).

Awareness is the easiest to acquire. In fact, it can be bought from the many consultants standing ready to assist corporations in preparing for the future. One must cultivate powers of imagination within oneself.

THE INTERNET

That brings us to the current challenge for one's imaginative powers: the Internet. Opportunities and pitfalls abound on the Web. What follows are some noteworthy experiences gained from successful and unsuccessful uses of the Internet. By the time this material sees print, much will have changed.

Three methods have emerged as options for exploiting an Internet operation. A regular "**bricks and mortar**" business can create its own in-house Web group, or it can partner with a dot-com company that will operate the Web end of its business for it. For example, when the three largest retailers in the country decided to jump on the "**e-tailing**" bandwagon in the late 1990s, their strategies differed: JC Penney and Sears formed their own in-house website divisions; Kmart, in contrast, contracted with a subsidiary, bluelight.com, to get its site up and running. Lastly, a business can elect to sell its products only on the Internet. Internet-only companies are referred to as "**pure-play**" operations. Amazon.com is an example.

Managers also have to figure out how to integrate Web activities seamlessly into their operations. Poorly integrated systems can wreak havoc within an organization. For instance, the first Christmas Toys 'R' Us did business on the Web, the company had to turn away customers because it couldn't fill the number of orders the site generated. To solve the problem, Toys 'R' Us formed an alliance with Amazon.com. Amazon handled the website and the online ordering process, and Toys 'R' Us managed inventory and shipping. Each company had expertise the other needed to sell toys online.

Alongside Web sales, retailers are in various stages of deploying new technologies to offer the benefits of online shopping at the retail site. For example, a kiosk on the shopping floor can make information available electronically, providing shoppers the information they need to make a buying decision. The Motorquest Automotive Group (parent of the car dealership chain) has refurbished existing locations to create a comfortable environment where customers can access all the information they want. At customer computers, buyers use MotorQuest's home page to wind their way through information from the various auto manufacturers, as well as options for pricing, loans, leasing, and reviews about the various makes and models.

Clicks versus Bricks: Ordering Hardware with Software

In e-tailing, it's getting pretty tough to hit the nail on the head, but it's especially tricky in home improvement and hardware. Few consumers want to buy lumber online because it would cost an arm and a leg to ship. Plus, scores of people make urgent trips to the store because the toilet is overflowing or they have a leaky faucet. They're not going to wait for the goods to be delivered before they make repairs. Indeed, online hardware sales make up only a tiny fraction of the $186 billion overall home-improvement market.

Established hardware companies have no dot-com delusions. They know the Internet isn't ideal for selling wrenches and table saws. Instead, they're finding savvy ways to use the Web to cut the inventory costs of stocking big-ticket items in stores and to reach new customers.

The Web may be just the ticket for luring buyers into old-fashioned stores. Home Depot, Lowe's, and Ace Hardware are using their websites to provide online hardware reference guides and how-to libraries, hoping this will help buyers make decisions. "I think online pure play isn't going to work," says market analyst Michael May. "But using the Net to enhance the offline experience is of real value to hardware stores."

Sears's research shows that its website influences 10 percent of all in-store major appliance purchases. The company says the home-improvement tips and product advice on its site attract potential customers, who then see promos for other products and come into the stores. Home Depot is using its Web strategy to attract big contractor-builders in addition to do-it-yourselfers. Ace also is hoping the Web will expand its customer base. Ace's in-store clientele is 70 percent male. That's where the company's minority stake in OurHouse.com comes in. More than 60 percent of the buyers at OurHouse are women. Ace supplies most of the goods for OurHouse.com and handles all fulfillment chores for the Web retailer.

For Victoria Stach, age 34, a regular e-shopper, buying a light fixture and some Christmas presents such as a George Foreman grill at OurHouse was a breeze. "It was easy, no stress, no hassle," says Stach, who regularly shops online because she doesn't have the time to wander through stores.

Another alternative is to bring the Net into the store. Ace, Sears, and Lowe's are all testing Web kiosks in their stores so that customers can get product information, comparison shop, and even buy items while avoiding long checkout lines. "We've had people tell us it's the fastest shopping they've ever done at Lowe's," says Thomas E. Whiddon, the company's executive vice president of logistics and technology.

Not that the remaining Internet-only hardware sites are ready to close up their tool sheds just yet. CornerHardware.com opened shop in February 1999 and offers more than 37,000 home-improvement products on its site. Still, lacking a partnership with a big bricks-based hardware retailer or a long-established online brand presence such as Amazon.com, pure-play e-tailers face an uphill climb.

Watching the growing Web presence of Home Depot and Lowe's, several analysis question CornerHardware's ability to survive. The privately held company insists it is doing fine despite the fact that its number of visitors declined while Lowe's and Home Depot's rocketed upward. It turns out that being a dot-com in the home-improvement market isn't always as easy as hitting the nail on the head.

SOURCE: Darnell Little, "Hammering Away at the Web," *Business Week Online,* February 19, 2001.

These retailers, along with others such as Nordstrom, Eddie Bauer, and Radio Shack, are building on brand-name presence and a familiarity already created at the mall, in the dealership, and through catalog sales—an advantage not enjoyed by companies operating exclusively on the Web.

An alliance with Amazon.com and redesigned stores featuring new departments are two steps Toys 'R' Us has taken to woo back customers.

Not long ago, the online auctioneer Ebay and a few companies that built e-stores for other firms were the only ones operating in the black. However, pure-play companies can be successful. Approximately one-quarter of the 200 public Internet companies that survived the dot-bomb shakeout are profitable now under standard accounting rules. The biggest moneymakers are online travel, software, and financial services. Why? Because they sell pure information products—there are no products to store or ship. But even Amazon.com, which has long operated in the red, is finally showing a profit despite the fact that every time someone buys a book on Amazon, the company must turn around and purchase a copy from the publisher. Also, once pure-play companies recoup their initial start-up costs, they don't need to spend much more money as sales rise. No additional stores need to be built to reach consumers, for example.[4]

Nonetheless, technology tricks and novel business ideas are not enough. Customers still want speed, convenience, quality, and good service. In this regard, the Web is no different from conventional stores and catalogs. Customers ultimately will cast their votes for the companies that provide the best product experience whether they see the product on the Web or can touch it in stores.

COMPANYWIDE RESONANCE

Sales and marketing data collection is turned on its head by the Internet, as companies record information about a user's habits during a website visit. For instance, if you buy a product on

Information Is Power

Until 2001, Mike Cripe set the prices at his three Ace Hardware stores near Chicago. He sold wheelbarrows, for instance, at $80 apiece. Then, in May 2001, Ace's corporate headquarters started issuing pricing recommendations to store owners. Among the suggestions: Drop the wheelbarrows to $50.

In the four months after the launch of the new pricing plan, Cripe sold eight wheelbarrows, compared with two in the preceding 12 months. "I made as much in four months on them as I did in a year before," Cripe marvels.

The key to this insight? Business intelligence (BI) software. BI programs help managers make smart decisions by extracting information from computer systems, running it through sophisticated math formulas, and delivering it in simple-to-understand reports. Ace Hardware uses the software to analyze price and sales data from its own stores and from competitors.

For Cripe, the result has been better margins—up to 39 percent from 32 percent, "With the data we're collecting, we can go back to the stores and say: 'Here's the money you're leaving on the table,'" says Mark Cothron, information technology manager at Ace's headquarters in Oak Brook, Illinois.

Success like that kept BI programs moving off the shelf even as the software industry stalled. BI software companies are prospering because they help their customers do a simple but vital task: make better sense of the information they already have in their computers and present it in a way that anyone from sales reps to chief executives can grasp. For years, companies have been using software to collect oceans of data. But navigating those seas has been tricky because data are stored on different types of computers that run various kinds of software.

Coty, Inc., in New York is a case in point. With more than a dozen different computer systems. Coty's managers had a tough time seeing and understanding all the sales data they were gathering. Coty had focused on its core business of makeup, devoting fewer resources to toiletries such as shampoo and shaving cream. After analyzing sales data by using BI software, executives realized they had missed potential profits. "Not only was [the toiletries sector] profitable, but it was better than a lot of other businesses," such as certain makeup lines, says Jim Shiah, senior vice president.

Another advantage of BI software: It's relatively inexpensive and can pay off quickly. Programs for generating sales reports and forecasts for a small business or department can cost as little as $10,000. Coty sees its $1.8 million investment paying off in two years.

SOURCE: Jim Kerstetter, "Information is Power," *Business Week Online,* June 24, 2002.

Amazon.com, during future visits, the site will make suggestions about similar products in which you might be interested. Many retailers are of the opinion that this type of **data mining** will make or break the operation in the future. That is, the ability to collect and use information from online customers will be crucial to successful marketing decisions.

Moreover, a company's Web page can make it easy or hard for the customer to get the information leading to a purchase. As some have learned the hard way, it is not enough to simply take images that are successful in print and place them on the Web, for each medium has its own characteristics.

The design of the company's website has a companywide impact. For example, if a customer on the Web can verify that an item is available, the chances of closing the sale are increased. If a customer can find out the expected delivery date of the product and the means, the chances of a sale are increased even more. In this scenario, front- and back-end operations touch, and delivering the goods is still key to success.

Mountains of Data   The purchasing function benefits from the Web through sheer availability of information, as well as ease of response to questions. Today, a purchasing manager need not wait for a visit from a sales representative. In fact, under the impact of the Web, businesses are seeing a realignment of the traditional relationships among producers, wholesalers, distributors, and retailers. In the business-to-business world, buyers previously faced a number of obstacles to getting the best deal: Suppliers were distant, research time was scarce, and intermediaries controlled most of the information. Enter FreeMarkets, a Web-based marketplace for industrial goods. Purchasing need only put out a contract on the Web, and a flood of bids from suppliers may be the response. In a sense, Web-based companies are becoming the new intermediaries, the conduit between producers and buyers.

Web shoppers can go to FreeMarkets for industrial goods, Seafax for seafood, National Transportation Exchange for trucking, Chemdex for biochemical supplies, and IMX Exchange for mortgage brokers to find loans, and this is only the start.

The Internet has also become the intermediary between employers and employees. Human resources departments can avail themselves of numerous Web-based tools to find candidates. Not only are there gigantic job exchanges such as Monster.com, but intranets exist to keep job searches within companies. Job seekers and potential employers can access one another's information based on geographic preference, salary range, or skill sets.

Logistics, scheduling, and distribution tasks increasingly are plugged into Web-based networks, benefiting from the ease of gathering weather data, traffic patterns, and late-breaking news. Tracking information about shipments can be downloaded from Federal Express. Zip codes are available online from the U.S. Post Office. These factors affect the company's ability to deliver the product on time and the availability of materials from suppliers, effects ultimately felt by the operations management system.

Changing Information Patterns   To reduce printing costs and make documents widely available, companies are digitizing information. In some instances, they are posting it on the Web. Different people residing in distant places can view the same information this way. Still, digitizing information is not without its obstacles. Not all people have the same hardware and software used for viewing and printing out information. Additionally, mis-

Companies can easily track their shipments by downloading the information directly from FedEx.

communications can occur that otherwise might not if all employees were working under one roof.

Corporations must take these circumstances into account when deciding how to make use of the Web, for the decisions affect each of the company's functioning units. Posting certain kinds of information does not usually cause problems. For example, providing company address(es), phone numbers, hours of operation, and the like, is more economically done on the Web than by a live employee answering the telephone. Many inquiries that in the print age were handled by mailing out an annual report, for example, may be handled more cost-effectively on the Web.

Supplying other types of information, however, might not be as free of repercussions as in the preceding examples. Depending on whether the company is a business-to-business or a business-to-consumer operation, buyers will want product information, forms and terms of payment, special sales, return policies, status of an order, shipping rates and turnaround, possibility of changing a current order, tracking information, or status of an order.

Providing and maintaining only one piece of this information—for example, change in an order—affects at least three departments: accounting, distribution, and marketing. Each department supplying the information must be aware of the consequences of making the information available and have a mechanism for handling changes. Coordination becomes an issue as well. For example, charges to a credit-card account must not occur before the merchandise is shipped. Whether selling to another business or to consumers, online operation requires new networks. Companies forge ahead nonetheless in this burgeoning technology, realizing that the potential advantages are well worth the temporary discomforts.

INTELLECTUAL PROPERTY

We have mentioned that a characteristic of the new economy is the nature of the product: knowledge, design, and engineering, rather than hard manufacturing. Let us look at an environmental engineering firm and how the Web affects its operation. The business of such a firm might include devising solutions to improve power-plant operation. The activities of firms involved in the plan-

ning of any such industrial facility are subject to compliance with government regulations. Handling engineering projects, for example, a new power plant, requires submission of an enormous amount of data to demonstrate that the firm has complied with and planned for all impacts on the community. A requirement might be, for example, that notification be given to every property owner within a certain radius of the plant. Downloading that information from title companies and then monitoring the notification process is only one of a multitude of tasks potentially manageable on the Web.

The firm must provide the information to the various parties in certain forms, which gives rise to new information needs. For example, one way to verify that it has indeed shipped the requisite print or CD-ROM copies is by downloading tracking information from Federal Express. It also can make its compliance documentation available in a read-only format on the Web, allowing printing of sections by those who wish to do so.

In preparing to build a plant, all federal, state, and local regulations must be accounted for. The firm must provide information on how its power plant will affect traffic patterns, cultural resources, schools, water supply, flora and fauna, and air quality. It also must state its plans for handling hazardous materials generated during the construction and operation of the plant.

Managing the enormous body of information to respond in the ways illustrated would have been a near impossibility before computer management of data.

PITFALLS

What have been the experiences of those who have succeeded in e-commerce and those who have failed, and what can we learn from them? We already mentioned Toys 'R' Us and its inability to fill its orders on the Web. In addition to losing business, it, along with other retailers such as Macys.com, CDNow, and Dbkids.com, was subject to Federal Trade Commission investigation and fines regarding rules for order fulfillment. The FTC regulation states that if retailers cannot meet promised deadlines, they must notify customers, giving them the option of canceling the order. Could the management of these companies have foreseen the inability to fill orders, and if so, how?

Confidentiality of information is an issue. A recent Gallup poll revealed that 66 percent of Americans favor new laws to protect their privacy amid the high-tech revolution.[5] Amazon.com found itself under fire after it began charging different consumers different prices on the basis of information it had collected on them. Toys 'R' Us was hit with a class-action lawsuit claiming that it allowed market researchers to access consumer data from its website. The retailer responded that it had hired the firm to analyze customers' data in order to improve their shopping experience. Although breach of confidentiality predates the Web, the enormity of any breach is compounded by the staggering amounts of digital data available for tapping. The Federal Trade Commission and Congress are attempting to pass laws and institute regulations to protect consumers.

Customer familiarity with the Web is another issue. Despite what seems to be a flurry of online buying, media reports suggest that many customers are not buying online at all, or only infrequently, or only certain products. As with catalog shopping, the online industry will mature as consumers become more familiar with offerings and as Web retailers improve in presentation and fulfillment.

Some customers are concerned about credit-card data transmitted online and are therefore hesitant to shop. The misuse of credit-card data is present, however, every time a clerk in a store records the data during a purchase. Although this is more a perception than a real problem, perception motivates people's actions, preventing some from making the leap into cybershopping.

Circumstances such as these are forcing the formation of new business models as companies grapple with all the variables, spurred on by the potential benefits.

NEW NEEDS AND DESIRES

Customers themselves are changing as it becomes possible to satisfy latent needs or desires. We have alluded to mass customization. Here are some specific examples of varying product features.

Setting up an assembly line or installing production equipment is part of the cost of manufacturing. Speaking of color choice in automobiles, Henry Ford once said: "They can have any color they want, as long as it's black." Alteration of a manufacturing process to vary a product feature was very costly. With the flexible manufacturing available in the digital age, manufacturers have the option of producing multiple flavors of bottled water, blue jeans tailored for different bodies, and a veritable artist's palette for automobile colors. Levi Strauss and Brooks now offer machine-customized garments, accommodating a vast array of body measurements. Barbie's friends can have hair and skin color, clothing, and even personalities picked by their young owners. Digital technology fuels the manufacturing capability; the Web spurs demand.

The result is that customers' desire for customization and personalization has been moved to a new level. Shoppers previously settled for a product that was mostly, or approximately, what they wanted. They are now beginning to see that sometimes they can have a product endowed with *precisely* the features they want. The experience of product acquisition is therefore changing.

THE VALUE OF HUMAN ATTRIBUTES

What are the implications of all this change for traditional operations management? Changes are remembered as negative or positive, depending on how well one has survived them. There is no reason to believe that technological change is any more threatening than other kinds of change. Traditional human qualities still serve: vision, awareness, alertness, imagination, courage, steadfastness, persistence, flexibility, attentiveness, and goodwill.

Today's managers must be aware, noticing shifts in trends, habits and customs, possibilities, and ground rules. They must have or develop the vision to foresee the range of possibilities, and then the imagination to create solutions. They must have the courage to strike out in new directions and be alert to adjustments required by the new direction. An effective manager will be flexible enough to make an adjustment and steadfast in the face of misunderstandings and mistakes. A manager will need to be persistent in following the chosen path, with attentiveness to all facets of the surroundings. Chances of success in any challenge are enhanced by goodwill.

Lastly, he or she will need luck. Some say "it comes to you," and some say "you make your own." Most think that both are true.

KEY TERMS

bricks and mortar, p. 547

data mining, p. 549

e-commerce, p. 547

e-tailing, p. 547

new economy, p. 546

pure-play, p. 547

DISCUSSION QUESTIONS

1. What is "mass customization"? How can products be mass-produced yet still be differentiated to appeal to individual market sectors? How has mass customization affected management's focus on the product?

2. Why was Deming's "total quality management" embraced by the Japanese long before Deming's philosophy became key to U.S. operations management? How does it relate to operations management?

3. How has the new economy changed operations management? What is the major input in the operations process as a result?

4. What must businesses consider in deciding to take advantage of new technology? How does new technology affect operations management decisions?

5. Why were many dot-com companies so short-lived at the end of the 20th century? Why would Amazon and Toys 'R' Us form an alliance? Which firm is likely to benefit more? Explain.

6. How can an Internet improve a firm's operations management?

7. What are the implications for operations management of customers being able to satisfy purchasing needs immediately by using the Internet? Have e-business functions fundamentally changed the way firms do business? Explain.

CHAPTER 18

Creating and Managing Change

The world hates change, yet that is the only thing that has brought progress.

—Charles Kettering

My interest is in the future because I am going to spend the rest of my life there.

—Charles Kettering

CHAPTER OUTLINE

Becoming World Class
Sustainable, Great Futures
The Tyranny of the *"Or"*
The Genius of the *"And"*
Managing Change
Motivating People to Change
Harmonizing Multiple Changes
Leading Change
Shaping the Future
Exercising Foresight
Learning Continuously
Creating Advantage
Creating the Future
Shaping Your Own Future

LEARNING OBJECTIVES

After studying Chapter 18, you will know:

1. What it takes to be world class.

2. How to manage change effectively.

3. How to create a successful future.

CHANGE AGENTS TALK ABOUT CHANGE

- "Want a tough job? Try leading an organization through major change . . . Almost without exception, executives claim it's the hardest work they've ever done."—T. A. Stewart, *Fortune*.
- "Anybody who says it can't be done: Wrong. Anybody who says it's easy: Also wrong."—Charles Lee, Verizon Communication.
- "If we're not failing 10 times more than we're succeeding, it means that we're not taking enough risks."—Mary Murphy-Hoye, Intel's director of IT strategy and technology.
- "We're on a journey that never ends. And the day we think we've got it made, that's the day we'd better start worrying about going out of business."—Rich Teerlink, CEO, Harley-Davidson.

- "Only the paranoid survive."—Andrew Grove, Chairman, Intel.
- "The capacity to change is a key success factor. You have to constantly reinvent yourself."—Edgardo Pappacena, partner, Arthur Andersen.
- "The brutal fact is that about 70 percent of all change initiatives fail."—Michael Beer and Nitin Nohria.
- At Corning's Sullivan Park research facility, "People say, 'we could revolutionize the world if we did this.' They don't say, 'We could make $100 million if we did this.'"—Adam Ellison.
- "In a world that keeps changing, perhaps the most valuable capability of all—for a company, for a team, for an individual—is the capacity for leading change. If you want to make a difference, you have to help your colleagues make change—in how they think, in how they behave, and in how they work together."—*Fast Company*.
- "You know how it is in the music business. Fickle! Here today, gone today!"—Chris Rock, comedian.

Companies need to improve constantly to achieve world-class excellence.

Sources: M. Gunther, "This Gang Controls Your Kids' Brains," Fortune, October 27, 1997, pp. 104–10; A. Grove, Only the Paranoid Survive, Currency/Doubleday, 1996; T. A. Stewart, "How to Lead a Revolution," Fortune, November 28, 1994, pp. 48–61; L. Kraar, Fortune, December 8, 1997, pp. 64–68; G. Imperato, "Harley Shifts Gears," Fast Company, June–July 1997, pp. 194–213; J. McCune, Management's Brave New World," Management Review, October 1997, pp. 11–14; C. Fishman, "Creative Tension," Fast Company, November 2000, pp. 358–88; M. Beer and N. Nohria, "Cracking the Code of Change," Harvard Business Review, May–June 2000, pp. 133–41; "Who's Fast," Fast Company, November 2001, p. 148; "Special Report: The Top Managers of the Year," Business Week, January 14, 2002, pp. 52–72; P. LaBarre, "Fresh Start 2002: Weird Ideas That Work," Fast Company, January 2002, pp. 68–71.

These executives—and Chris Rock—are all talking about the same things: the difficulties and challenges of creating change, and the need to improve constantly in order to achieve world-class excellence and competitive advantage for the future.

Change happens—constantly and unpredictably. Whatever competitive advantage you may have depends on particular circumstances at a particular time, but circumstances change.[1] The economic environment shifts; competitors pop up everywhere; markets emerge and disappear. The challenge for organizations is not just to produce innovative new products—it is to balance a culture that is innovative and that builds a sustainable business.[2] And for individuals, the ability to cope with change is related to their job performance and the rewards they receive.[3]

Becoming World Class

Managers today want, or *should* want, their organizations to become world class.[4] To some people, striving for world-class excellence seems a lofty, impossible, unnecessary goal. But it is a goal that is essential to survival and success in today's intensely competitive business world.

Being world class requires applying the best and latest knowledge and ideas, and having the ability to operate at the highest standards of any place anywhere.[5] Thus, becoming world class does not mean merely improving. It means becoming one of the very best in the world at what you do. Some have estimated that for most companies, becoming world class requires increasing quality by 100 to 1,000 times, decreasing costs by 30 percent to 50 percent, increasing productivity by two to four times, decreasing order-to-delivery time by a factor of 5 to 10, and decreasing new-product development times by 30 percent to 60 percent. And even if your firm realizes these dramatic improvements, it still will have to keep getting better![6]

World-class companies create high-value products and earn superior profits over the long run. They demolish the obsolete methods, systems, and cultures of the past that have impeded their competitive progress, and apply more effective and competitive organizational strategies, structures, processes, and management of human resources. The result is an organization capable of competing successfully on a global basis.[7]

Sustainable, Great Futures

Two Stanford professors, James Collins and Jerry Porras, studied 18 corporations that had achieved and maintained greatness for half a century or more.[8] The companies include Sony, American Express, Ford, Motorola, Merck, Marriott, Johnson & Johnson, Disney, 3M, Hewlett-Packard, Citicorp, Wal-Mart, and others. Over the years, these companies have been widely admired, been considered the premier institutions in their industries, and made a real *impact* on the world. Although every company goes through periodic downturns—and these companies are no exceptions over their long histories—these companies have consistently prevailed across the decades. They turn in extraordinary performance *over the long run*, rather than fleeting greatness. This study is reported in the book called *Built to Last*—which is what these great organizations were and are.

The researchers sought to identify the essential characteristics of enduringly great companies. These great companies have strong core values in which they believe deeply, and they express and live the values consistently. They are driven by goals—not just incremental improvements or business-as-usual goals, but stretch goals (recall Chapter 13). They change continuously, driving for progress via adaptability, experimentation, trial and error, entrepreneurial thinking, and fast action. And they do not focus on beating the competition; they focus primarily on beating themselves. They continually ask, "How can we improve ourselves to do better tomorrow than we did today?"

But underneath the action and the changes, the core values and vision remain steadfast and uncompromised. Table 18.1 displays the core values of several of the companies that were "built to last." Note that the values are not all the same. In fact, there was

3M	Innovation; "Thou shalt not kill a new product idea"
	Absolute integrity
	Respect for individual initiative and personal growth
	Tolerance for honest mistakes
	Product quality and reliability
	"Our real business is solving problems"
American Express	Heroic customer service
	Worldwide reliability of services
	Encouragement of individual initiative
Boeing	Being on the leading edge of aeronautics; being pioneers
	Tackling huge challenges and risks
	Product safety and quality
	Integrity and ethical business
	To "eat, breathe, and sleep the world of aeronautics"
Sony	To experience the sheer joy that comes from the advancement, application, and innovation of technology that benefits the general public
	To elevate the Japanese culture and national status
	Being pioneers—not following others, but doing the impossible
	Respecting and encouraging each individual's ability and creativity
Wal-Mart	"We exist to provide value to our customers"—to make their lives better via lower prices and greater selection; all else is secondary
	Swim up-stream, buck conventional wisdom
	Be in partnership with employees
	Work with passion, commitment, and enthusiasm
	Run lean
	Pursue ever-higher goals
Walt Disney	No cynicism allowed
	Fanatical attention to consistency and detail
	Continuous progress via creativity, dreams, and imagination
	Fanatical control and preservation of Disney's "magic" image
	"To bring happiness to millions" and to celebrate, nurture, and promulgate "wholesome American values"

TABLE 18.1
Core Ideologies in
Built-to-Last Companies

SOURCE: From *Built to Last* by James C. Collins and Jerry I. Porras, Copyright © 1997 by James C. Collins and Jerry I. Porras. Reprinted by permission of HarperCollins Publishers, Inc and Random House Group Limited.

no set of common values that consistently predicted success. Instead, the critical factor is that the great companies *have* core values, *know* what they are and what they mean, and *live* by them—year after year after year.

The Tyranny of the "Or"

Many companies, and individuals, are plagued by what the authors of *Built to Last* call the **"tyranny of the or."** This refers to the belief that things must be either A or B, and cannot be both. The authors provide many common

tyranny of the "or"

The belief that things must be either A or B, and cannot be both; that only one goal and not another can be attained.

examples:[9] beliefs that you must choose either change or stability; be conservative or bold; have control and consistency or creative freedom; do well in the short term or invest for the future; plan methodically or be opportunistic; create shareholder wealth or do good for the world; be pragmatic or idealistic. Such beliefs, that only one goal but not another can be attained, often are invalid and certainly are constraining—unnecessarily so.

The Genius of the *"And"*

In contrast to the "tyranny of the *or*," the **"genius of the *and*"** is the ability to pursue multiple goals at once. We discussed earlier in the book the importance of delivering multiple competitive values to customers; performing all the management functions; reconciling hard-nosed business logic with ethics; leading and empowering; and others. Authors Collins and Porras have their own list,[10] which includes:

genius of the "and"
The ability to pursue multiple goals at once.

- Purpose beyond profit *and* pragmatic pursuit of profit.
- Relatively fixed core values *and* vigorous change and movement.
- Conservatism with the core values *and* bold business moves.
- Clear vision and direction *and* experimentation.
- Stretch goals *and* incremental progress.
- Control based on values *and* operational freedom.
- Long-term thinking and investment *and* demand for short-term results.
- Visionary, futuristic thinking *and* daily, nuts-and-bolts execution.

You have learned about all of these things throughout this course and should not lose sight of any of them—either in your mind or in your actions. To achieve them all requires the continuous and effective management of change.

Managing Change

Every manager needs a clear understanding of how to manage change effectively. Organizational change is managed effectively when[11]

1. The organization is moved from its current state to some planned future state that will exist after the change.
2. The functioning of the organization in the future state meets expectations; that is, the change works as planned.
3. The transition is accomplished without excessive cost to the organization.
4. The transition is accomplished without excessive cost to individual organizational members.

People are the key to successful change.[12] For an organization to be great, or even just to survive, people have to care about its fate, and know how they can contribute. But typically, leadership lies with only a few people at the top. Too few take on the burden of change; the number of people who care deeply, and who make innovative contributions, is too small. People throughout the organization need to take a greater interest and a more active role in helping the business as a whole. They have to believe they can make a difference. And they have to identify with the entire organization, not just with their unit and close colleagues.

These important attitudes and feelings are not unusual in start-ups and very small organizations. Too often they are lost with growth and over time. In large, traditional corporations, they are all too rare. There needs to be a permanent rekindling of individual creativity and responsibility, a true change in the behavior of people throughout the organization. The essential task is to motivate people fully to keep changing in response to new business challenges.

Motivating People to Change

People must be *motivated* to change. But often they resist changing. For example, if your boss were to tell you, "We have to become world class," what would be your reaction?

Many people settle for mediocrity rather than aspire to world-class status. They resist the idea of striving mightily for excellence; they say things such as the following:

- "Those world-class performance numbers are ridiculous! I don't believe them, they are impossible! Maybe in some industries, some companies . . . but ours is unique . . ."
- "Sure, maybe some companies achieve those numbers, but there's no hurry . . . We're doing all right. Sales were up 5 percent this year, costs were down 2 percent. And we've got to keep cutting corners . . ."
- "We can't afford to be world class like those big global companies; we don't have the money or staff . . ."
- "We don't believe this stuff about global markets and competitors. We don't need to expand internationally. One of our local competitors tried that a few years ago and lost its shirt."
- "It's not a level playing field . . . the others have unfair advantages . . ."

To deal with such reactions, and successfully implement positive change, it is important to understand why people often resist change. Figure 18.1 shows the common reasons for resistance. Some reasons are general and arise in most change efforts. Other reasons for resistance relate to the specific nature of a particular change.

General Reasons for Resistance   Several reasons for resistance arise regardless of the actual content of the change.[13]

- *Inertia.* Usually people don't want to disturb the status quo. The old ways of doing things are comfortable and easy, so people don't want to shake things up and try something new. For example, it is easier to keep living in the same apartment or house than to move to another.
- *Timing.* People often resist change because of poor timing. Maybe you would like to move to a different place to live, but do you want to move this week? Even if a place were available, you probably couldn't take the time. If managers or employees are unusually busy or under stress, or if relations between management and workers are strained, the timing is wrong for introducing new

FIGURE 18.1
Reasons for Resistance to Change

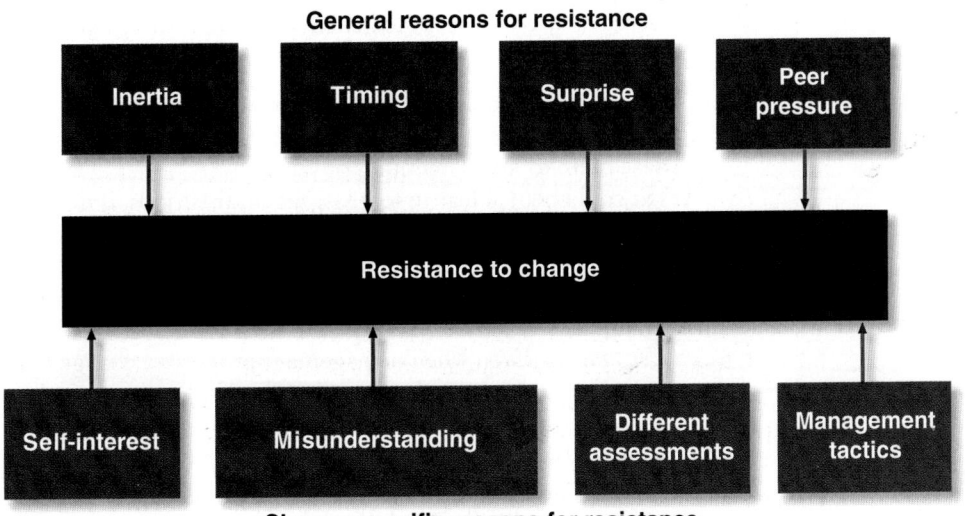

Fear of the unknown and mistrust can prompt resistance to change.

proposals. Where possible, managers should introduce change when people are receptive.

- *Surprise.* One key aspect of timing and receptivity is surprise. If the change is sudden, unexpected, or extreme, resistance may be the initial—almost reflexive—reaction. Suppose your university announced an increase in tuition, effective at the beginning of next term. Resistance would be high. At the very least, you would want to know about this change far enough in advance to have time to prepare for it.
- *Peer pressure.* Sometimes work teams resist new ideas. Even if individual members do not strongly oppose a change suggested by management, the team may band together in opposition. If a group is highly cohesive and has anti-management norms (recall Chapter 14), peer pressure will cause individuals to resist even reasonable changes.

Change-Specific Reasons for Resistance   Other causes of resistance arise from the specific nature of a proposed change. Change-specific reasons for resistance include:[14]

- *Self-interest.* Most people care less about the organization's best interest than they do about their own best interests. They will resist a change if they think it will cause them to lose something of value.

  What could people fear to lose? At worst, their jobs, if management is considering closing down a plant. A merger or reorganization, or technological change, could create the same fear. Despite assurances that no one will be laid off or fired, people might fear a cut in pay or loss of power and status under the new arrangement.
- *Misunderstanding.* Even when management proposes a change that will benefit everyone, people may resist because they don't fully understand it. People may not see how the change fits with the firm's strategy, or they simply may not see the change's advantage over current practices.[15] One company met resistance to the idea of introducing flexible working hours, a system in which workers have some say regarding the hours they work. This system can benefit employees, but

a false rumor circulated among plant employees that people would have to work evenings, weekends, or whenever their supervisors wanted. The employees' union demanded that management drop the flexible-hours idea. The president was caught completely off guard by this unexpected resistance, and complied with the union's demand.

- *Different assessments.* Employees receive different—and usually less—information than management receives. Even within top management ranks, some executives know more than others do. Such discrepancies cause people to develop different assessments of proposed changes. Some may be aware that the benefits outweigh the costs, while others may see only the costs and not perceive the advantages. This is a common problem when management announces a change, say, in work procedures, and doesn't explain to employees why the change is needed. Management expects advantages in terms of increased efficiency, but workers may see the change as another arbitrary, ill-informed management rule that causes headaches for those who must carry it out.

- *Management tactics.* Sometimes a change that is successful elsewhere is undertaken in a new location, and problems may arise during the transfer.[16] Management may attempt to force the change and may fail to develop employee commitment. Or it may fail to provide the necessary resources, knowledge, or leadership to help the change succeed. Sometimes a change receives so much exposure and glorification that employees resent it, and resist.

It is important to recognize that employees' assessments can be more accurate than management's; they may know a change won't work even if management doesn't. In this case, resistance to change is beneficial for the organization. Thus, even though management typically considers resistance a challenge to be overcome, it may actually represent an important signal that a proposed change requires further, more open-minded scrutiny.[17]

A General Model for Managing Resistance

Figure 18.2 shows that motivating people to change often requires three basic stages: unfreezing, moving to institute the change, and refreezing.[18]

In the **unfreezing** stage, management realizes that its current practices are no longer appropriate and the company must break out of (unfreeze) its present mold by doing things differently. People must come to recognize that some of the past ways of thinking, feeling, and doing things are obsolete.[19] Perhaps the most effective way to do this is to communicate to people the negative consequences of the old ways by comparing the organization's performance to its competitors'. As discussed in Chapter 15, management can share with employees data about costs, quality, and profits.[20] However, care must be taken not to arouse people's defensiveness by pinning the blame directly and entirely on them.[21]

An important contributor to unfreezing is the recognition of a performance gap, which can be a precipitator of major change. A **performance gap** is the difference between actual performance and the performance that should or could exist.[22] A gap typically implies poor performance; for

> **unfreezing**
>
> **Realizing that current practices are inappropriate and that new behavior must be enacted.**

> **performance gap**
>
> **The difference between actual performance and desired performance.**

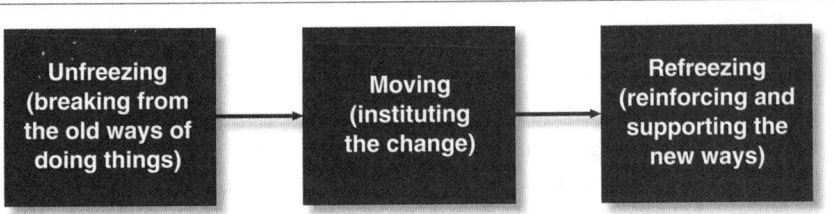

FIGURE 18.2
Implementing Change

example, sales, profits, stock price, or other financial indicators are down. This situation attracts management's attention, and management introduces changes to try to correct things.

Another, very important form of performance gap can exist. This type of gap can occur when performance is good but someone realizes that it could be better. Thus, the gap is between what is and what *could be*. This is where entrepreneurs seize opportunities and where companies that engage in strategic maneuvering gain a competitive edge. Whereas many change efforts begin with the negative, it often is more valuable to identify strengths and potential and then develop new modes of operating from that positive perspective.[23]

As an impetus for change, a performance gap can apply to the organization as a whole; it also can apply to departments, groups, and individuals. If a department or work group is not performing as well as others in the company, or if it sees an opportunity that it can exploit, that unit will be motivated to change. Similarly, an individual may receive negative performance feedback or see a personal opportunity on which to capitalize. Under these circumstances, unfreezing begins, and people can be more motivated to change than they are if no such gap exists.

moving

Instituting the change.

Moving to institute the change begins with establishing a vision of where the company is heading. You learned about vision in the leadership chapter and other sections of the course. The vision can be realized through strategic, structural, cultural, and individual change. Strategic ideas are discussed throughout the book. Changes in structure may involve moving to the divisional, matrix, or some other appropriate form (discussed in Chapters 8 and 9). Cultural changes (Chapter 9) are institutionalized through effective leadership (Chapters 12 through 15). Individuals will change as new people join the company (Chapters 10 and 11) and as people throughout the organization adopt the leader's new vision for the future.

refreezing

Strengthening the new behaviors that support the change.

Finally, **refreezing** means strengthening the new behaviors that support the change. The changes must be diffused and stabilized throughout the company. Refreezing involves implementing control systems that support the change (Chapter 16), applying corrective action when necessary, and reinforcing behaviors and performance (Chapter 13) that support the agenda. Management should consistently support and reward all evidence of movement in the right direction.[24]

In today's organizations, refreezing is not always the best third step, if it creates new behaviors that are as rigid as the old ones. The ideal new culture is one of continuous change. Refreezing is appropriate when it permanently installs behaviors that maintain essential core values, such as a focus on important business results and those values maintained by the companies that are "built to last." But refreezing should not create new rigidities that might become dysfunctional as the business environment continues to change.[25] The behaviors that should be refrozen are those that promote continued adaptability, flexibility, experimentation, assessment of results, and continuous improvement. In other words, lock in key values, capabilities, and strategic mission, but not necessarily specific management practices and procedures.

Specific Approaches to Enlist Cooperation   You can try to command people to change, but the key to long-term success is to use other approaches.[26] Developing true support is better than "driving" a program forward.[27] How, specifically, can management motivate people to change?

Most managers underestimate the variety of ways they can influence people during a period of change.[28] Several effective approaches to managing resistance and enlisting cooperation are available, as described in Table 18.2:

1. **Education and communication.** Management should educate people about upcoming changes before they occur. It should communicate not only the *nature* of the change but its *logic*. This process can include one-on-one discussions, presentations to groups, or reports and memos. For Amy Radin

Approach	Commonly used in situations	Advantage	Drawbacks
Education and communication	Where there is a lack of information or inaccurate information and analysis.	Once persuaded, people will often help with the implementation of the change.	Can be very time-consuming if lots of people are involved.
Participation and involvement	Where the initiators do not have all the information they need to design the change, and where others have considerable power to resist.	People who participate will be committed to implementing change, and any relevant information they have will be integrated into the change plan.	Can be very time-consuming if participators design an inappropriate change.
Facilitation and support	Where people are resisting because of adjustment problems.	No other approach works as well with adjustment problems.	Can be time-consuming and expensive, and still fail.
Negotiation and rewards	Where someone or some group will clearly lose out in a change, and where that group has considerable power to resist.	Sometimes it is a relatively easy way to avoid major resistance.	Can be too expensive in many cases if it alerts others to negotiate for compliance.
Manipulation and cooptation	Where other tactics will not work, or are too expensive.	It can be a relatively quick and inexpensive solution to resistance problems.	Can lead to future problems if people feel manipulated.
Explicit and implicit coercion	Where speed is essential, and the change initiators possess considerable power.	It is speedy and can overcome any kind of resistance.	Can be risky if it leaves people angry at the initiators.

TABLE 18.2
Methods for Managing Resistance to Change

of Citibank, "Getting buy-in across the organization takes a lot of education. If you have a core group of people who are focused only on e-commerce, then you've got to keep everyone else informed about what you're doing on the e-commerce front" (p. 363).[29]

2. **Participation and involvement.** Change requires reflection and dialogue,[30] as discussed in Chapter 15. It is important to listen to the people who are affected by the change. They should be involved in the change's design and implementation. For major, organizationwide change, participation in the process can extend from the top to the very bottom of the organization.[31] When feasible, management should use the advice of people throughout the organization.

As you learned in Chapter 3, people who are involved in decisions understand them more fully and are more committed to them. People's understanding and commitment are important ingredients in the successful implementation of a change. Participation also provides an excellent opportunity for education and communication.

3. **Facilitation and support.** Management should make the change as easy as possible for employees and be supportive of their efforts. Facilitation involves providing the training and other resources people need to carry out the change and perform their jobs under the new circumstances. This step often includes decentralizing authority and empowering people, that is, giving them the power to make the decisions and changes needed to improve their performance.

   Offering support involves listening patiently to problems, being understanding if performance drops temporarily or the change is not perfected immediately, and generally being on the employees' side and showing consideration during a difficult period.

4. **Negotiation and rewards.** When necessary, management can offer concrete incentives for cooperation with the change. Perhaps job enrichment is acceptable only with a higher wage rate, or a work rule change is resisted until management agrees to a concession on some other rule (say, regarding taking breaks). Even among higher-level managers, one executive might agree to another's idea for a policy change only in return for support on some other issue of more personal importance. Rewards such as bonuses, wages and salaries, recognition, job assignments, and perks can be examined and perhaps restructured to reinforce the direction of the change.[32]

   When people trust one another, change is easier. But change is further facilitated by demonstrating its benefits to people.[33] Janiece Webb, who creates change at Motorola, says that nobody wins unless everybody wins, and that you must demonstrate to others how your work benefits them.[34] Amy Radin of Citibank says, "One lesson that I've learned is to create a financial incentive so that business units will support an Internet initiative. We are planning to create a shadow P&L for our e-commerce efforts to track how everything is going. But the benefits, all of the revenues created, will be allocated to the operating units . . . You're helping people meet their own goals."

5. **Manipulation and cooptation.** Sometimes managers use more subtle, covert tactics to implement change. One form of manipulation is cooptation, which involves giving a resisting individual a desirable role in the change process. The leader of a resisting group often is coopted. For example, management might invite a union leader to be a member of an executive committee, or ask a key member of an outside organization to join the company's board of directors. As a person becomes involved in the change, he or she may become less resistant to the actions of the coopting group or organization.

6. **Explicit and implicit coercion.** Some managers apply punishment or the threat of punishment to those who resist change. With this approach, managers use force to make people comply with their wishes. For example, a boss might insist that subordinates cooperate with the change and threaten them with job loss, denial of a promotion, or an unattractive work assignment. Sometimes you just have to lay down the law: The game is changing, and you need to play by the new rules or play somewhere else.[35]

Each approach to managing resistance has advantages and drawbacks and, like many of the other situational or contingency management approaches described in the text, each is useful in different situations. Table 18.2 summarizes the advantages, drawbacks, and appropriate circumstances for these approaches to managing resist-

ance to change. As the table implies, managers should not use just one or two general approaches, regardless of the circumstances. Effective change managers are familiar with the various approaches and know how to apply them according to the situation.

Throughout the process, change leaders need to build in stability. Recall from the companies that were "built to last" that they all have essential core characteristics of which they don't lose sight. In the midst of change, turmoil, and uncertainty, people need anchors onto which they can latch.[36] This means keeping some things constant and visible, such as the organization's values and mission. In addition, strategic principles, discussed in Chapter 12, can be important anchors during change.[37] It can help further to maintain the visibility of key people, continue key assignments and projects, and make announcements about which organizational components will not change. Such anchors will reduce anxiety and help overcome resistance.

Harmonizing Multiple Changes

There are no "silver bullets" or single-shot methods of changing organizations successfully. Single shots rarely hit a challenging target. Usually, many issues need simultaneous attention, and any single, small change will be absorbed by the prevailing culture and disappear. **Total organization change** involves introducing and sustaining multiple policies, practices, and procedures across multiple units and levels.[38] Such change affects the thinking and behavior of everyone in the organization, can enhance the organization's culture and success, and can be sustained over time.

> **total organization change**
>
> **Introducing and sustaining multiple policies, practices, and procedures across multiple units and levels.**

A survey at a Harvard Business School conference found that the average attendee's company had five major change efforts going on at once.[39] The most common change programs were the things you have studied in this course: continuous improvement, TQM, time-based competition, and creation of a learning organization, a team-based organization, a network organization, core competencies, and strategic alliances. The problem is, these efforts usually are simultaneous but not coordinated. Things get muddled; people lose focus.[40] The result for the people involved is confusion, frustration, low morale, and low motivation.

Because companies introduce new changes constantly, many people complain about their companies' "flavor-of-the-month" approach to change. That is, employees often see many change efforts as just the company's jumping on the latest bandwagon or fad. The more these change fads come and go, the more cynical people become, and the more difficult it is to get them committed to making the change a success.[41]

In this context, it helps tremendously to avoid fads. If a change initiative is nothing more than a passing fad, why should people invest their energy and time in it? Before initiating change, management should ask:[42] Will it really make a difference in results? Will it help provide employees with information, knowledge, power, and rewards to become more fully involved in making the business succeed and thrive? Does it really help people add value throughout their work? Does it help us focus better on customers and the things they value?

Management also needs to "connect the dots"—that is, integrate the various efforts into a coherent picture that people can see, understand, and get behind.[43] You connect the dots by understanding each change program and what its goals are, by identifying similarities among the programs and identifying their differences, and by dropping programs that don't meet priority goals with a clear results orientation. Most important,

Survival after a crisis creates a need to change—a need to maintain anchors. Newly appointed CEO of Southwest Airlines, James Parker, had some serious decisions to make after 9/11. After choosing to pay $180 million in profit-sharing due 9/14, Southwest did not furlough or fire any employees. "We have a lot of people who have worked hard for more than 30 years so that they can have job security in hard times. Cutting jobs should be the last thing a company does rather than the first thing." *Fast Company*, May 2002, p. 62.

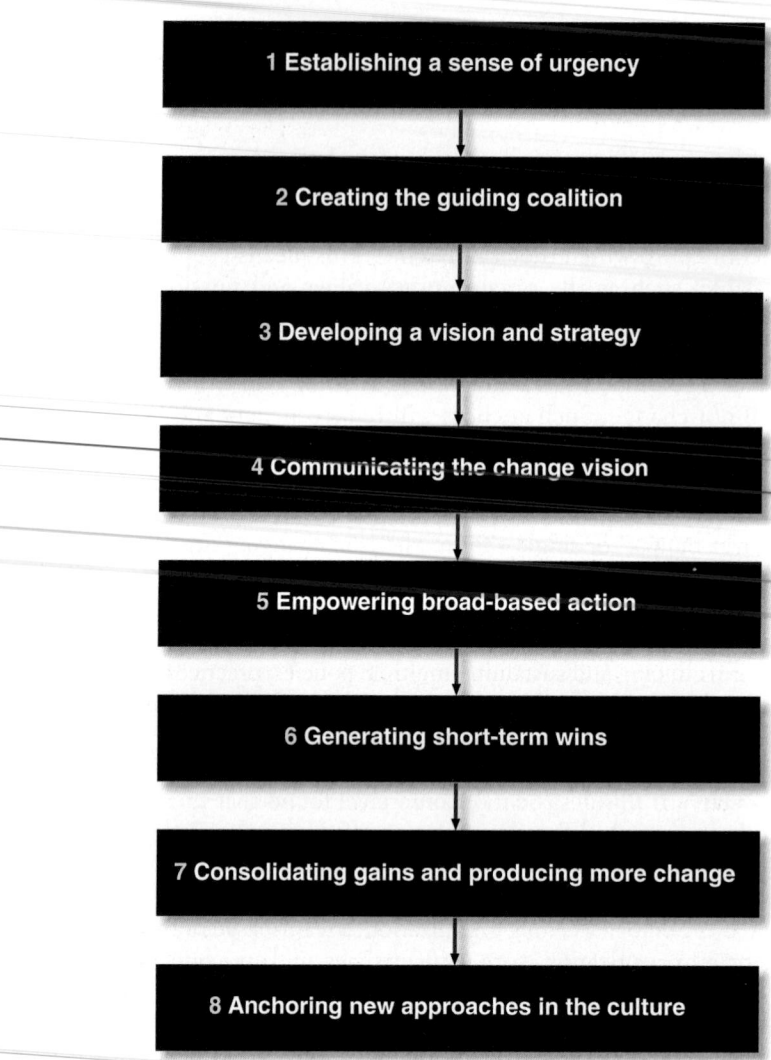

1 Establishing a sense of urgency

2 Creating the guiding coalition

3 Developing a vision and strategy

4 Communicating the change vision

5 Empowering broad-based action

6 Generating short-term wins

7 Consolidating gains and producing more change

8 Anchoring new approaches in the culture

FIGURE 18.3
Leading Change

you do it by communicating to everyone concerned the common themes among the various programs: their common rationales, objectives, and methods. You show them how the various parts fit the strategic big picture, and how the changes will make things better for the company and its people. You must communicate these things thoroughly, honestly, and frequently.[44]

Leading Change

Successful change requires managers to actively lead it. The essential activities of leading change are summarized in Figure 18.3.

A useful start for change leaders is to *establish a sense of urgency*.[45] This requires examining current realities and pressures in the marketplace and the competitive arena, identifying both crises and opportunities, and being frank and honest about them. This is an important component, in part because so many large companies have grown complacent.

Figure 18.4 shows some of the common reasons for complacency. To stop complacency and create urgency, the manager can talk candidly about weaknesses compared to competitors, making a point of backing up statements with data. Other tactics include setting stretch goals, putting employees in direct contact with unhappy

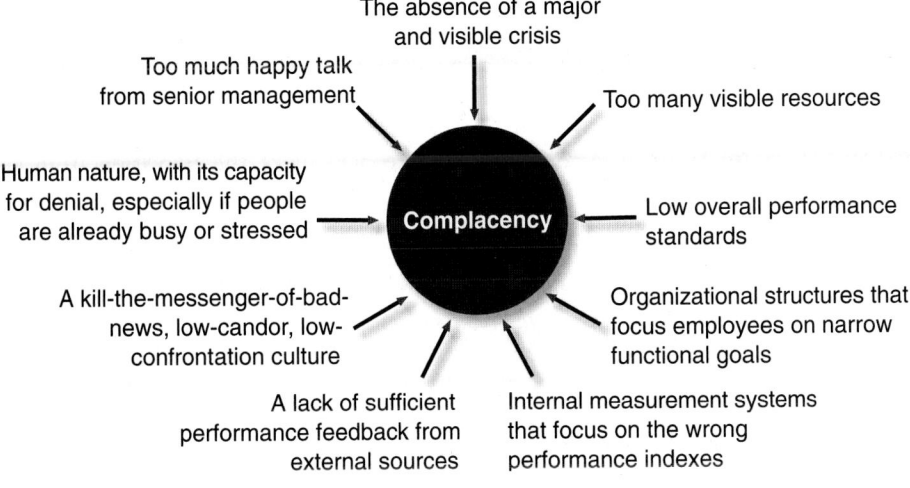

The absence of a major
and visible crisis

Too much happy talk
from senior management

Too many visible resources

Human nature, with its capacity
for denial, especially if people
are already busy or stressed

Complacency

Low overall performance
standards

A kill-the-messenger-of-bad-
news, low-candor, low-
confrontation culture

Organizational structures that
focus employees on narrow
functional goals

A lack of sufficient
performance feedback from
external sources

Internal measurement systems
that focus on the wrong
performance indexes

SOURCE: Reprinted by permission of Harvard Business School Press. From *Leading Change* by John P. Kotter, Boston, MA. Copyright © 1996 by the President and Fellows of Harvard College. All rights reserved.

FIGURE 18.4
Sources of Complacency

customers and shareholders, distributing worrisome information to all employees instead of merely engaging in management "happy talk," eliminating excessive perks, and highlighting to everyone the future opportunities that exist but that the organization so far has failed to pursue.

Ultimately, urgency is driven by compelling business reasons for change. Survival, competition, and winning in the marketplace are compelling; they provide a sense of direction and energy around change. Change becomes not a hobby, a luxury, or something nice to do, but a business necessity.[46]

To *create a guiding coalition* means putting together a group with enough power to lead the change. Change efforts fail when a sufficiently powerful coalition is not formed.[47] Major organization change requires leadership from top management, working as a team. But over time, the support must gradually expand outward and downward throughout the organization. Middle managers and supervisors are essential. Groups at all levels are the glue that can hold change efforts together, the medium for communicating about the changes, and the means for enacting new behaviors.[48]

Developing a vision and strategy, as discussed in earlier chapters, will direct the change effort. This process involves determining the idealized, expected state of affairs after the change is implemented. Because confusion is common during a major organizational change, the clearest possible image of the future state must be developed and conveyed to everyone.[49] This image, or vision, will be a target or guideline that can clarify expectations, dispel rumors, and mobilize people's energies. The portrait of the future also should communicate how the transition will occur, why the change is being implemented, and how people will be affected by the change. The power of a compelling vision is one of the most important aspects of change, and should not be underestimated or underutilized.

Communicating the change vision requires using every possible channel and opportunity to talk up and reinforce the vision and required new behaviors. It is said that aspiring change leaders undercommunicate the vision by a factor of 10, or even 100 or 1,000, seriously undermining the chances of success.[50] Chris Crosby, senior VP and director of Internet at Dain Rauscher Corp., advises you to "Draw pictures that take people where they want to go. Make the idea as tangible as possible. I had to take management out 18 months and say, 'Here's what the website will look like in a year and a half.' Once people could see it and touch it, they could understand it" (p. 358).[51]

Empowering broad-based action means getting rid of obstacles to success, including systems and structures that constrain rather than facilitate. Encourage risk taking and experimentation, and empower people by providing information, knowledge, authority, and rewards, as described in Chapter 13.

Generate short-term wins. Don't wait for the ultimate grand realization of the vision. You need results. As small victories accumulate, you make the transition from an isolated initiative to an integral part of the business.[52] Plan for and create small victories that indicate to everyone that progress is being made. Recognize and reward the people who made the wins possible, doing it as visibly as you can so people notice and the positive message permeates the organization.

Make sure you *consolidate gains and produce more change.* With the well-earned credibility of previous successes, keep changing things in ways that support the vision. Hire, promote, and develop people who will further the vision. Reinvigorate the organization and your change efforts with new projects and change agents.

Finally, *anchor new approaches in the culture.*[53] Highlight positive results, communicate the connections between the new behaviors and the improved results, and keep developing new change agents and leaders. Continually increase the number of people joining you in taking responsibility for change.[54]

Shaping the Future

reactive change

A response that occurs under pressure; problem-driven change.

proactive change

A response that is initiated before a performance gap has occurred.

Most change is reactive. A better way to change is to be proactive. **Reactive change** means responding to pressure, after the problem has arisen. It also implies being a follower. **Proactive change** means anticipating and preparing for an uncertain future. It implies being a leader and *creating* the future you want.

On the road to the future, there are drivers, passengers, and road kill. Put another way: On the road to the future, who will be the windshield, and who will be the bug?[55]

Needless to say, it's best to be a driver.[56] How do you become a driver? By being proactive more than merely reactive. By exercising foresight, learning continuously, creating advantage, and creating futures.

Exercising Foresight

If you think only about the present, or wallow in the uncertainties of the future, your future is just a roll of the dice. It is far better to exercise foresight, set an agenda for the future, and pursue it with everything you've got.

So, contemplate and envision the future.

If you and your bosses think you know what you need to do to succeed in the future, you probably need a dose of humility—it is impossible to know the future with certainty. But this does not need to be a reactive, defeatist view. It can be highly proactive, in a subtle but vitally important way. Managers may acknowledge that they don't know exactly what customers will want in the future, and what products they will have to deliver. But they *can* know that they have, or can acquire, the *capabilities* to deliver.[57] Thus, the focus is on identifying and building core competencies, as discussed in earlier chapters, and on improving continuously in the activities that will enable your firm to succeed in the future.

Learning Continuously

Continuous learning is a vital route to renewable competitive advantage.[58] To learn continuously, your firm (and you!) need (1) a clear, strategic goal to learn new capabilities and (2) a commitment to constant experimentation.

Companies and individuals striving for world-class excellence must improve constantly. Continuous improvement, the concept made legendary by Toyota Motor Company, is a relentless drive to be better in every way: to find faster, more-efficient,

- Lynne Franks is on a mission to help women entrepreneurs start businesses that are community-minded, values-driven, and family-friendly, through a global network of entrepreneurs who change the role of business all over the world.

- William Edwin Swing is founder of the United Religions Initiative (URI), an international interfaith organization. He had no idea how to create a global organization, but he did know that existing international interfaith groups included different religions but excluded each other. Each was trying to corner the interfaith market. He took an entrepreneurial approach, looking elsewhere to find knowledge on collaboration and organization design, including a business-school professor and a former banker. The URI now is a network through which organizations leverage one another's resources while pursuing both mutual and individual goals. "We're trying to change world history" (p. 236).

You could compare him with Thomas Edison, Alexander Graham Bell, or Henry Ford. He is Tim Berners-Lee and he invented the World Wide Web. Can you imagine what your life would be like without it?

- Ford Chairman William Clay Ford, Jr. maintains that the hydrogen-powered fuel cell will "finally end the 100-year reign of the internal-combustion engine" (p. 100). Ford and Daimler-Chrysler are in a joint venture to roll out fuel-cell cars by 2004, and most of the other auto companies have entered the race as well. *Fortune* calls the race an automotive Manhattan Project. More generally, some believe that fuel cells hold the potential to solve all energy problems. In homes and offices, they will keep the lights on and computers running even when energy grids cannot; in cars, they won't emit harmful emissions; the shift from fossil fuels would mean less global warming; and the United States and other countries would not be dependent on oil imports.

- Tim Berners-Lee, the "father of the World Wide Web," now envisions the next generation that will replace today's Web. The Semantic Web will be a smart network that understands human languages and will make working with computers very similar to working with other humans. Computers already are better than people at number crunching, of course. What if they were also better at language and reason? The Semantic Web "will help more people become more intuitive as well as more analytical. It will foster global collaborations among people with diverse cultural perspectives, so we have a better chance of finding the right solutions to the really big issues—like the environment and climate warming" (p. 98). Many doubt his vision, but "Tim has a gift for seeing the future and making it happen" (p. 98) says John Patrick, a retired IBM senior exec and a founder of the World Wide Web Consortium.

SOURCES: C. Dahle, "How to Make your Mark," *Fast Company,* December 2000, pp. 204–20; C. Salter, "William Edwin Swing," *Fast Company,* November 2000, pp. 230–38; D. Stipp, "The Coming Hydrogen Economy," *Fortune,* November 12, 2001, pp. 90–100; O. Port, "Special Report: The Next Web," *Business Week,* March 4, 2002, pp. 96–102.

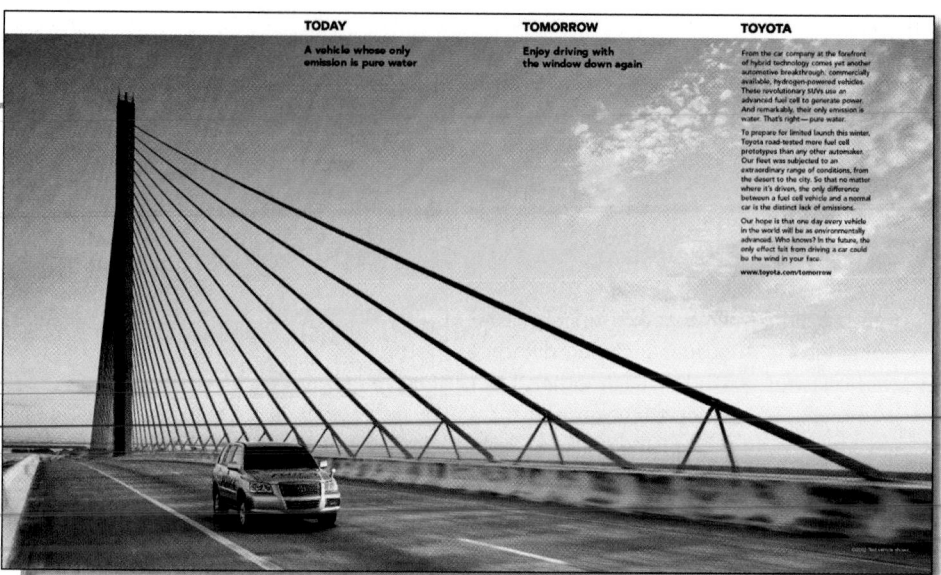

In the box "Envisioning the Future," Ford Chairman William Clay Ford Jr. states that the hydrogen-powered fuel cell will "finally end the 100-year reign of the internal-combustion engine." In this ad, Toyota promotes the fact it will launch their own hydrogen-powered fuel cell SUVs in the winter of 2002 whose sole emission will be water. Do you consider the development of these hybrid fuel cell autos a reactive change, or a proactive change?"

low-cost methods to develop new, high-quality products. When Toyota became so successful at making low-cost, defect-free cars, it set the quality standard.[59]

In an environment of continuous improvement, everyone engages in exploration, discovery, and action; continually learns what is effective and what is not; and adjusts and improves accordingly. Figure 18.5 elaborates. With this philosophy, and the appropriate approaches, your company *can* have it all: low cost, high quality, flexibility, responsiveness, innovation, and speed. This process also generates learning on a more individual level, generating personal growth and development.

As described in other chapters, experimentation means trying new things in the spirit of continuous improvement, investing in research and long-term development projects, encouraging risks, and tolerating failures. Companies like J&J, 3M, and Bally Engineering practice self-obsolescence. That is, they try to make their own products obsolete. Why? Because the products will become obsolete sooner or later, and it's better to replace them with their own new products than to have competitors beat them to it. Home Depot closed a single thriving store and opened two smaller ones in an effort to keep improving customers' shopping experiences.[60]

Similarly, Sony and Mitsubishi use "systematic abandonment" of their products.[61] When they introduce a new product, they establish a "sunset date" at which they will drop the product. Thus, they create a deadline for introducing a future product that will replace the brand new product, and begin those development efforts immediately. Their goal is to create three new products for every one they phase out: an incrementally improved product, a new product spin-off, and an entirely new innovation.

Creating Advantage

In a recent 10-year period, but prior to the recession, 17 companies in the Fortune 1000 grew total shareholder return by 35 percent or more per year.[62] How did they do it? They invented totally new industries, or completely reinvented existing industries. Harley-Davidson turned around by selling not just motorcycles, but nostalgia. Amgen broke the rules of the biotech industry by focusing not on what customers wanted, but

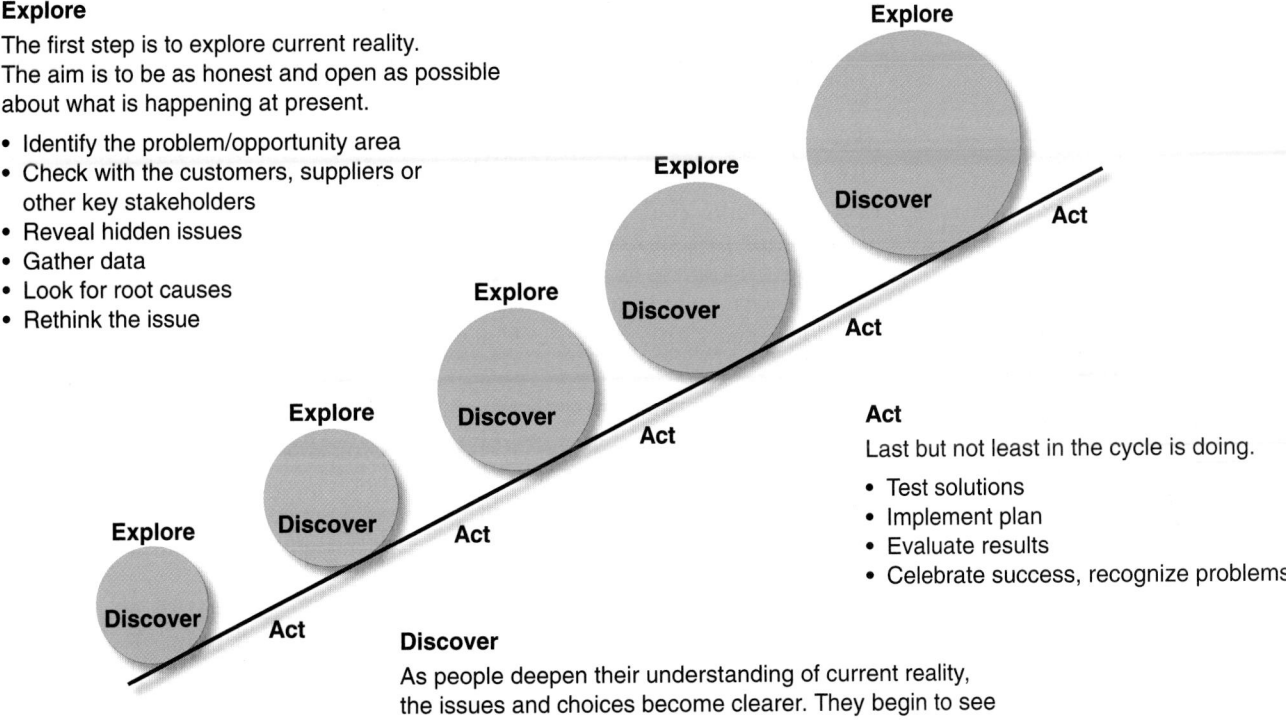

Explore

The first step is to explore current reality. The aim is to be as honest and open as possible about what is happening at present.

- Identify the problem/opportunity area
- Check with the customers, suppliers or other key stakeholders
- Reveal hidden issues
- Gather data
- Look for root causes
- Rethink the issue

Act

Last but not least in the cycle is doing.

- Test solutions
- Implement plan
- Evaluate results
- Celebrate success, recognize problems

Discover

As people deepen their understanding of current reality, the issues and choices become clearer. They begin to see with new eyes.

- Identify possible solutions
- Plan
- Anticipate problems

SOURCE: From *Leaning into the Future: Changing the Way People Change Organizations* by George Binney and Colin Williams; published by Nicholas Brealey Publishing Ltd., 1997. Tel: (0171) 430-0224, Fax: (0171) 404-8311. Reprinted by permission.

FIGURE 18.5
Learning Cycle: Explore, Discover, Act

---

on great science. Starbuck's took a commodity and began selling it in trendy stores. CarMax and other companies reinvented the auto industry.[63]

To create new markets or transform industries—these are perhaps the ultimate forms of proactive change.[64] Competing for the future thus involves creating and dominating emerging opportunities. Consider:

Instead of . . .	Why Not . . . ?
• fitting the firm to the environment	• change the environment to fit the firm
• preserving old advantages	• create new advantages
• locking in old markets	• create new markets
• investing in fixed assets	• invest in evolving/emerging opportunities

You need to create advantages. The challenge is not to maintain your position in the current competitive arena, but to create new competitive arenas, transform your industry, and imagine a future that others don't see. Creating advantage is better than playing catch-up through downsizing and reengineering. At best, such restructuring buys time; it cannot get you out ahead of the pack and buy world-class excellence.[65]

So, which should you and your firm do?

- Take the path of greatest familiarity, or the path of greatest opportunity, wherever that may lead?
- Be only a good benchmarker, or a pathbreaker?
- Focus just on product time to market, or on time to global preeminence?
- Be a product leader, or also a core competence leader?
- Place priority on short-term financial returns, or on making a real, long-term impact?
- Look to the past, or live for the future?
- Do only what seems doable, or what is difficult and worthwhile?
- Change what is, or create what isn't?
- Solve problems, or create entirely new opportunities?[66]

Creating the Future

adapters

Companies that take the current industry structure and its future evolution as givens.

Companies can try different strategic postures to prepare to compete in an uncertain future. **Adapters** take the current industry structure and its future evolution as givens. They choose where to compete. This posture is taken by most companies by conducting standard strategic analysis and choosing how to compete within given environments.

shapers

Companies that try to change the structure of their industries, creating a future competitive landscape of their own design.

In contrast, **shapers** try to change the structure of their industries, creating a future competitive landscape of their own design.[67] For example, Federal Express entered the mail-and-package delivery industry with a strategy of delivering overnight. FedEx almost went bankrupt in its first two years, but ultimately reshaped the industry. Its bet paid off hugely, forcing others like United Parcel Service to adapt.

To get ahead of the pack, create the future.

Creating Futures

- Helena Luczywo and Wanda Rapaczynski have turned a small underground newspaper in Poland into a local media empire, Agora SA. Theirs is one of the most remarkable success stories in postcommunist Europe. Says Luczywo, "I believe that our newspaper should stand for important things and should not avoid difficult topics. It should tell the truth, even when the truth goes against the popular grain, the government, or advertisers." Says Rapaczynski, "We aren't liked by everybody . . . We take seriously our role in this country as an institution of democracy." They both believe that the way to guarantee their independence as an agent of democracy is to become highly profitable, so as not to be vulnerable to outside economic pressure. States Luczywo, "If you want to be independent, then you must be financially independent."
- Ken Kutaragi of Sony knew that his company was behind in three hot, new digital markets: videogames, personal computers, and cell phones. Sony's historical strengths were in the analog technologies found in TVs, VCRs, and tape players. He went on a mission to convince senior management of the importance of computer entertainment, and to persuade them that Sony had to convert to digital. He threatened to quit if Sony didn't fund his R&D efforts in a videogame project, and promised he could create a platform for Sony's future growth. Two years later, the PlayStation was born. Kutaragi then led the engineering team for the PlayStation II, a $1 billion development project. In the wake of PlayStation II's success, Kutaragi broadened his sights. In Japan, he partnered with four ISPs to jointly run a high-speed online game service that he believes could become the world's largest broadband platform. If his vision prevails, Kutaragi could become Sony's next president.
- Fifteen years ago, the Fox network boldly took on all-powerful ABC, NBC, and CBS. Against all odds, it survived and now thrives because it rewrote industry rules— including what you can say and do on TV. It was the first network to brand itself, as the home for provocative shows aimed at young viewers. Recently Fox News became

number 1 in the ratings while branding itself as a conservative alternative to the liberal bias it alleges in its rivals. Fox pioneered the strategy of vertical integration in the media, as Rupert Murdoch bought Twentieth Century Fox studio, added stations, started the broadcast network, and then built cable networks from scratch. Instead of deciding between content and distribution, Murdoch bought both. *Fortune* calls Fox "noisy, unruly, brash, unpredictable, and impossible to ignore" (p. 137). Anyone who has seen Fox shows such as *The Chamber* (with John McEnroe)—which one critic called "the sickest, most brain-damaged, reprehensible show ever" (p. 137)—would probably agree.

Is creating the future necessarily a good thing?

SOURCES: G. Hamel, "Driving Grassroots Growth," *Fortune*, September 4, 2000, pp. 173–87; P. Kruger, "Helena Luczywo & Wanda Rapaczynski," *Fast Company*, November 2000, pp. 152–66; M. Gunther, "Will Fox Ever Grow Up?" *Fortune*, March 4, 2001, pp. 137–40; I. M. Kunii, C. Edwards, and J. Greene, "Can Sony Regain the Magic?" *Business Week*, March 11, 2002, pp. 72–80.

Creating the future is not for the faint-hearted; it requires high-stakes bets.[68] Eastman Kodak spent $500 million per year to develop digital photography products. The company *hoped* it would change fundamentally the way people create, view, and store pictures. But Hewlett-Packard is pursuing its own, competing vision for reshaping the industry, centered around photo processing done in the home rather than in shops. Which will win? Or will they both? Or neither?

Figure 18.6 illustrates the vast opportunity to create new markets. Articulated needs are those that customers acknowledge and try to satisfy. Unarticulated needs are those that customers have not yet experienced. Served customers are those to whom your company is now selling, and unserved customers are untapped markets.

Business-as-usual concentrates on the lower-left quadrant. The leaders who recreate the game are constantly trying to create new opportunities in the other three quadrants.[69]

When Gert Boyle's husband died of a heart attack, he left her with a debt-ridden company, and no knowledge of how to run it. Thirty-two years later, she and her son Tim Boyle have turned Columbia Sportwear Inc. into a successful outerwear company competing with the likes of Patagonia and North Face. Her first decisions were difficult ones, including firing nearly all of her roughly 55 employees, but Gert and Tim focused on listening to customers and innovating. Since 1984, sales have grown from $3 million to over $700 million.

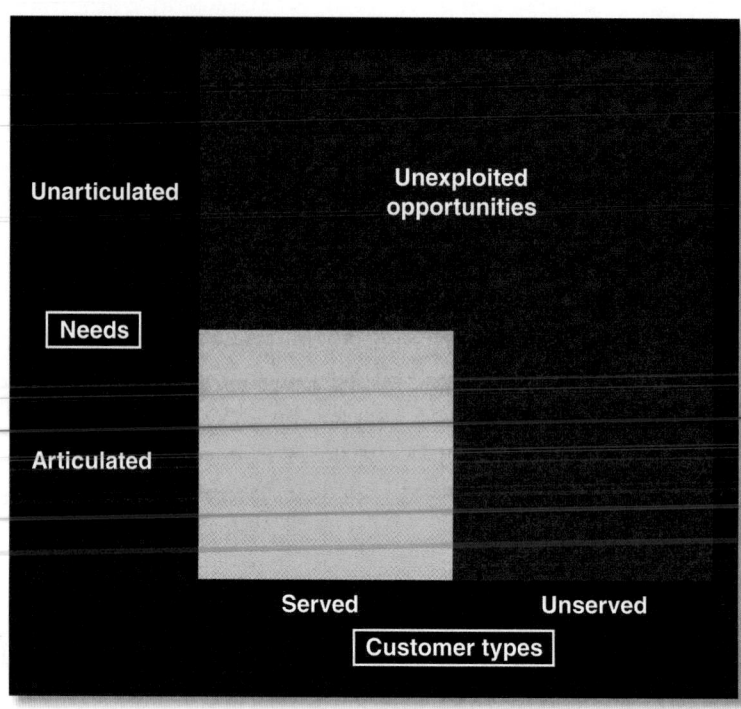

FIGURE 18.6
Vast Opportunity

For example, you can pursue the upper-left quadrant by imagining how you can satisfy a larger proportion of your customers' total needs.[70] Nike realized its customers didn't want only shoes and running apparel, but also specialized sunglasses, watches, and wearable MP3 music players. GE's Power Systems business learned that major electric utilities would pay not only for turbines and transformers, but also for a wide range of consulting and maintenance services, which have much higher margins.

Royal Dutch/Shell has institutionalized its "GameChanger" process to generate new businesses or new approaches to existing businesses, and GE Capital convenes annual "dreaming sessions." The company makes full use of its youngest managers to find business opportunities that their stodgier elders might miss.[71]

Shaping Your Own Future

If you are an organizational leader, and your organization operates in traditional ways, your key goal should be to create a revolution, genetically reengineering your company before it becomes a dinosaur of the modern era.[72] What should be the goals of the revolution? You've been learning about them throughout this course.

But maybe you are not going to lead a revolution. Maybe you just want a successful career and a good life. You still must be able to deal with an economic environment that is increasingly competitive and fast-moving.[73] Creating the future you want for yourself requires setting high personal standards. Don't settle for mediocrity; don't assume that "good" is necessarily good enough—for yourself or for your employer. Try to avoid companies and industries that are less competitive than the world norm.[74]

Table 18.3 helps you think about how you can continually add value to your employer, and also to yourself, as you upgrade your skills, your ability to contribute, your security with your current employer, and your ability to find alternative employment if necessary.

More advice from the leading authors on career management:[75] Consciously and actively manage your own career. Develop marketable skills, and keep developing more. Make career choices based on personal growth, development, and learning opportunities. Look for positions that stretch you, and for bosses who develop their protégés. Seek out environments that provide training and opportunity to experiment

TABLE 18.3
Adding Value, Personally

Go beyond your job description:

- Volunteer for projects.
- Identify problems.
- Initiate solutions.

Seek out others and share ideas and advice.

Offer your opinions and respect those of others.

Take an inventory of your skills every few months.

Learn something new every week.

Discover new ways to make a contribution.

Engage in active thought and deliberate action.

Take risks based on what you know and believe.

Recognize, research, and pursue opportunity.

Differentiate yourself.

SOURCE: Compiled from C. Hakim, *We Are All Self-Employed* (San Francisco: Berrett-Koehler, 1994).

and innovate. And know yourself: Assess your strengths and weaknesses, your true interests, and ethical standards. If you are not already thinking in these terms and taking commensurate action, you should start now.

Additionally: Become indispensable to your organization. Be happy and enthusiastic in your job, and committed to doing great work, but don't be blindly loyal to one company. Be prepared to leave if necessary. View your job as an opportunity to prove what you can do and increase what you can do, not as a comfortable niche for the long term.[76] Go out on your own if it meets your skills and temperament.

This points out the need to maintain your options. More and more, contemporary careers can involve leaving behind the large organization and going entrepreneurial, becoming self-employed in the "postcorporate world."[77] In such a career, independent individuals are free to make their own choices. They can flexibly and quickly respond to demands and opportunities. Developing start-up ventures, consulting, accepting temporary employment, doing project work for one organization and then another, working in professional partnerships, being a constant deal maker—these can be the elements of a successful career. Ideally, this self-employed model can help provide a balanced approach to working and to living life at home and with family, because people have more control over their work activities and schedules.

This can sound like the ideal world. It also has downsides. The independence can be frightening, the future unpredictable. It can isolate "road warriors" who are always on the go, working from their cars and airports, and interfere with social and family life.[78] Effective self-management is needed to keep things in perspective and in control.

Into the Future   Commit to lifelong learning. Lifelong learning includes being willing to seek new challenges and to reflect honestly on successes and failures.[79] Lifelong learning requires occasionally taking risks; moving outside of your "comfort zone"; honestly assessing the reasons behind your successes and failures; asking for and listening to other people's information and opinions; and being open to new ideas.

Honored as one of the best management books of the year in Europe, *Leaning into the Future* gets its title from a combination of the words *leading* and *learning*.[80] The two perspectives, on the surface, appear very different. But they also are powerful when pursued in complementary ways. Figure 18.7 captures the synergies of combining both leading and learning. Success in the future will come from shaping the future *and* adapting to the world; being clear about what you want to change *and* being responsive to others' perspectives; passionately pursuing your vision *and* understanding current realities; leading *and* learning.

This is another example of an important concept from the beginning of the chapter. For yourself, as well as for your organization, recognize and live the genius of the *and*.

Leading   **and**   **Learning**

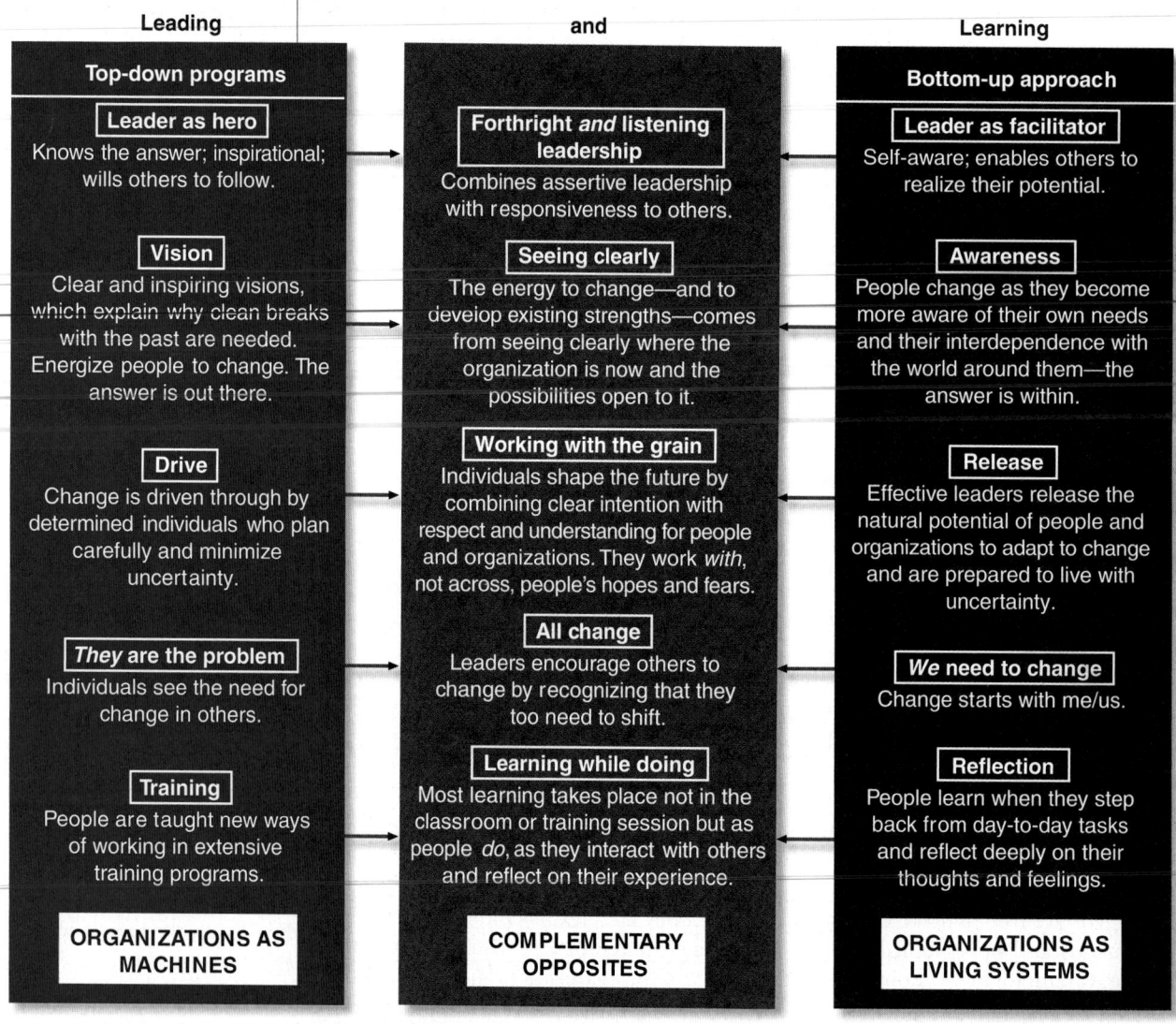

SOURCE: From *Leaning into the Future: Changing the Way People Change Organizations* by George Binney and Colin Williams; published by Nicholas Brealey Publishing Ltd., 1997. Tel: (0171) 430–0224, Fax: (0171) 404–8311. Reprinted by permission.

FIGURE 18.7

Leaning into the Future

KEY TERMS

Adapters, p. 570

Genius of the "and," p. 556

Moving, p. 560

Performance gap, p. 559

Proactive change, p. 566

Reactive change, p. 566

Refreezing, p. 560

Shapers, p. 570

Total organization change, p. 563

Tyranny of the "or," p. 555

Unfreezing, p. 559

SUMMARY OF LEARNING OBJECTIVES

Now that you have studied Chapter 18, you should know:

What it takes to be world class.

You should strive for world-class excellence, which means using the very best and latest knowledge and ideas to operate at the highest standards of any place anywhere. Sustainable greatness comes from, among other things, having strong core values, living those values constantly, striving for continuous improvement, experimenting, and always trying to do better tomorrow than today. It is essential to not fall prey to the tyranny of the *or*; that is, the belief that one important goal can be attained only at the expense of another. The genius of the *and* is that multiple important goals can be achieved simultaneously and synergistically.

How to manage change effectively.

Effective change management occurs when the organization moves from its current state to a desired future state without excessive cost to the organization or its people. People resist change for a variety of reasons, including inertia, poor timing, surprise, peer pressure, self-interest, misunderstanding, different information about (and assessments of) the change, and management's tactics.

Motivating people to change requires a general process of unfreezing, moving, and refreezing, with the caveat that appropriate and not inappropriate behaviors be "refrozen." More specific techniques to motivate people to change include education and communication, participation and involvement, facilitation and support, negotiation and rewards, manipulation and cooptation,

and coercion. Each approach has strengths, weaknesses, and appropriate uses, and multiple approaches can be used. It is important to harmonize the multiple changes that are occurring throughout the organization.

Effective change requires active leadership, including creating a sense of urgency, forming a guiding coalition, developing a vision and strategy, communicating the change vision, empowering broad-based action, generating short-term wins, consolidating gains and producing more change, and anchoring the new approaches in the culture.

Ideas for how to create a successful future.

Preparing for an uncertain future requires a proactive approach. Being proactive includes exercising foresight, learning continuously, creating advantages, and creating the future. You can proactively shape your own future by actively managing your career and your personal development, and becoming an active leader and a lifelong learner.

DISCUSSION QUESTIONS

1. Review the quotes on page xxx, describing "resistance to becoming world class." Why do some people resist the goal of becoming world class? What lies behind the quotes? How can this resistance be overcome?

2. Generate specific examples of world-class business that you have seen as a consumer. Also, generate examples of poor business practice. Why and how do some companies inspire world-class practices, while others do not?

3. How can you make the concept of continuous improvement useful to you in your personal life and your career?

4. Generate and discuss examples of problems and opportunities that have inspired change, both in businesses and in you, personally.

5. Choose some specific types of changes you would like to see happen in groups or organizations with which you are familiar. Imagine that you were to try to bring about these

changes. What sources of resistance should you anticipate? How would you manage the resistance?

6. Review the methods for dealing with resistance to change. Generate specific examples of each that you have seen, and analyze the reasons why they worked or failed to work.

7. How would you "exercise foresight" with regard to your personal life and career?

8. Develop a specific plan for becoming a "continuous learner."

9. Consider a business with which you are familiar and discuss some ideas for how it should pursue a growth strategy. What are some pros and cons to your ideas? How might the best ideas be implemented?

10. In your own words, what does the idea of "creating the future" mean to you? How can you put this concept to good use? Again, generate some specific ideas that you can really use.

Making Your Mark

This chapter was about creating change. Individuals create change, and make their marks. Making your mark means making a distinctive contribution, by making the most of your talents.

Neil Gershenfel is building "brains" for chairs, musical instruments, and other objects that up to now were considered inanimate. For example, he developed a computer for car seats that senses who is sitting in them so that they don't deploy potentially deadly air bags for small children.

Louis Monier invented Alta Vista, and therefore is one of the architects of the Web as we know it today. He was not one of the big financial winners, but he made his mark in a way that was far more important to him than just cashing in. With "my baby, my creation . . . I was able to see my experiment all the way to the end. I suppose I could have just taken one of the offers and joined another search engine or portal, and I would have been a lot richer today. It probably would have been less painful—and less interesting—than

sticking with Alta Vista. But I don't think I would have learned as much" (p. 216). "I'd rather do something interesting, solve an interesting problem, than do something boring and get rich" (p. 220).

Dean Jernigan, owner of the Triple A Memphis Redbirds, wanted to build a different kind of sports team, not dominated by greedy players and greedier owners. He believed a baseball team should be part of the soul of a community. The goal should not be maximum return to owners; the goal should be maximizing returns to the community. Conventional wisdom said to build a new stadium in the heart of Memphis's eastern-suburban sprawl. Jernigan took a risk and built it in the heart of downtown Memphis, creating a central-Memphis revival. And he registered his company as a nonprofit organization, with all income above expenses going to two local charities.

John Dooner of McCann-Erickson Advertising Worldwide lost the cherished Coca-Cola account in the early 1990s. He

Vice President of International Operations Heather Killen has turned Yahoo! into a truly global company.

vowed to win back the account. He didn't just work to get Coca-Cola back; he set out to change everything about the agency so that it would truly deserve Coca-Cola's business again. "I start out by asking what the dream is. What do I want, or what would my clients want? Then I talk about it. Then I write it down—that's a big part of the process. Then I imagine that the strategy or the situation has already happened. Then I put the strategy into action with the belief that I will never be denied that dream." He tore apart and rebuilt the agency, and got the Coca-Cola account back in late 2000.

Nick Riso is a Web guru who wants to help Nestlé USA "make e-business the way we do business." He says that putting the technologies into place is the easy part; the hard part is to get 17,000 people to change their thinking and behavior. "If our initiative is successful, e-business will permeate the company's DNA and all of our thought. We won't need e-catalysts. In the end, the term *e-business* has to disappear. I have to work myself out of a job."

Amory Lovins is a renowned expert on energy efficiency. He was a radical activist back in the 1970s, but now sees the private sector as the key to saving the planet. Lovins's latest venture: his nonprofit institute spun out a for-profit venture, Hypercar Inc. The company just unveiled a prototype body for a 99-mpg SUV that would be safe, fun to drive, and affordable. Says Lovins: "I never expected to be the chairman of a car development company. But life is full of surprises" (p. 106).

Ken Kutaragi, the developer of Sony's PlayStation whom you read about earlier, could have started his own videogame company, but he knew he wanted to leverage Sony's money, manufacturing capabilities, and marketing muscle. "If I had started this business as a venture outside a big company, it would have worked, but the moving speed would not have been

fast enough. Sony had great human resources, capital, and manufacturing capability, but it did not have a vision. My team had the vision" (p. 180).

Heather Killen is an evangelist and the ultimate global citizen, building a truly global Internet company. Under her leadership, Yahoo! has become not just a U.S. company with international operations, but a truly global company. She tells her colleagues, "Don't think about 'international' as being *part* of our business. It *is* our business!" Yahoo! attracts users outside the United States by generating content locally. Says Killen, "We don't squirt English-language news through a translation engine and then put it up on our China or Argentina sites. That would never work" (p. 194). Jerry Yang says of Killen, "She's our ambassador. Being a female executive in a global business can be very intimidating. But Heather is fearless, and she's found the right mix of showing respect yet not being a pushover" (p. 194).

Donald Winkler is dyslexic, and chairman and CEO of Ford Motor Credit Co. He struggles to process the world the way others do, but also he often sees the world in ways that others don't. A friend says that Winkler is motivated not by money but by success. "He always views himself as the underdog. He likes to surface from out of nowhere and win" (p. 266). Winkler's principles for effective leadership include: Set real priorities and real commitments; set and demand standards of excellence; and be willing to see failure as a stepping stone to success.

QUESTIONS

1. Consider the champions of change described here and in other parts of the chapter (for example, Lynne Franks, William Edwin Swing, Helena Luczywo, and Wanda Rapaczynski). Whom do you admire the most, and whom would you choose as a role model? Why? What do your choices teach you about yourself?

2. Choose any one individual from this group and generate an action plan for implementing the change he or she envisions.

3. What will be the mark *you* make? What is your plan for learning and leading the way to achieving your personal vision?

SOURCES: N. Stein, "Inventing Tomorrow Today," *Fortune,* March 6, 2000, pp. F-35–F-39; C. Dahle, "How To Make Your Mark," *Fast Company,* December 2000, pp. 204–20; G. Calkins, "Dean Jernigan," *Fast Company,* November 2000, pp. 170–84; A. Markels, "Heather Killen," *Fast Company,* November 2000, pp. 190–200; K. H. Hammonds, "Donald Winkler," *Fast Company,* November 2000, pp. 260–68; G. Hamel, "Driving Grassroots Growth," *Fortune,* September 4, 2000, pp. 173–87; F. Warner, "Change Agent—John Dooner," *Fast Company,* November 2001, p. 116; B. Breen, "Change Is Sweet," *Fast Company,* June 2001, p. 168; D. Stipp, "Can This Man Solve America's Energy Crisis?" *Fortune,* May 13, 2001, pp. 100–10.

18.1 A Force-Field Analysis

OBJECTIVE
To introduce you to force-field analysis of organizations and challenges facing them.

INSTRUCTIONS
Read the following force-field analysis, and come up with an organizational problem of your own to analyze.

Force-Field Analysis

A force-field analysis is one way to assess change in an organization. This concept reflects the forces, driving and restraining, at work at a particular time. It helps assess organizational strengths and select forces to add or remove in order to create change. The theory of change suggested by Kurt Lewin, who developed the force-field analysis, is that while driving forces may be more easily affected, shifting them could increase opposition (tension and/or conflict) within the organization and add restraining forces. Therefore, it may be more effective to remove restraining forces to create change.

The use of the force-field analysis will demonstrate the range of forces pressing on an organization at a particular time. This analysis can increase people's optimism that it is possible to strategize and plan for change.

Example—Trying to increase student participation in student government.

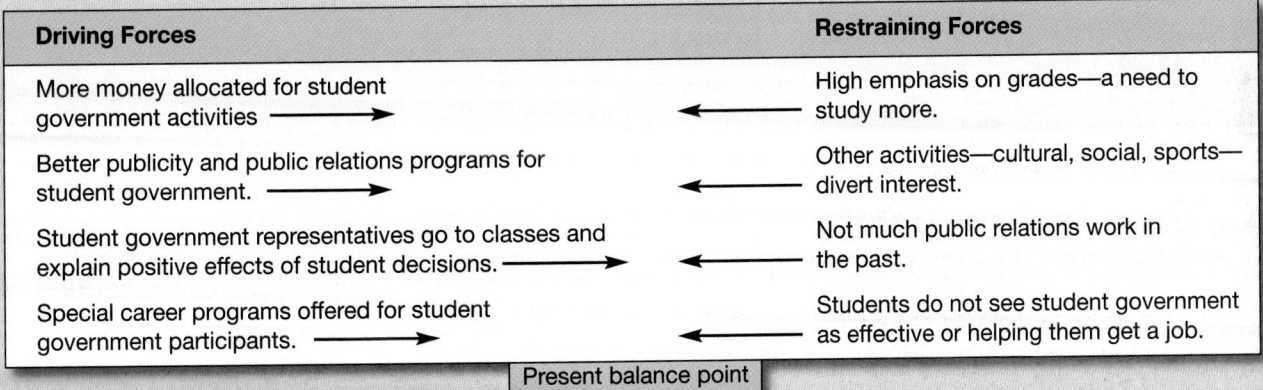

Driving Forces	Restraining Forces
More money allocated for student government activities →	← High emphasis on grades—a need to study more.
Better publicity and public relations programs for student government. →	← Other activities—cultural, social, sports—divert interest.
Student government representatives go to classes and explain positive effects of student decisions. →	← Not much public relations work in the past.
Special career programs offered for student government participants. →	← Students do not see student government as effective or helping them get a job.

Present balance point

Force-Field Analysis Worksheet

1. (10–15 min.) Choose an organizational change in process, complete the Problem Analysis section, and fill in the model.
2. (20 min.) In groups of three or four, discuss the driving and restraining forces in each person's problem.
3. (10 min.) Class discussion
   a. Why is it useful to break a problem situation up into driving and restraining forces?
   b. Would the model be used any differently whether applied to an individual or organizational problem?

PROBLEM ANALYSIS

1. Describe the problem in a few words.

_____

_____

_____

_____

_____

_____

2. A list of forces *driving* toward change would include:

a. _____

b. _____

c. _____

d. _____

e. _____

f. _____

3. A list of forces *restraining* change would include:

a. _____

b. _____

c. _____

d. _____

e. _____

f. _____

4. Put the driving and restraining forces of the problem on this force-field analysis, according to their degree of impact on change.

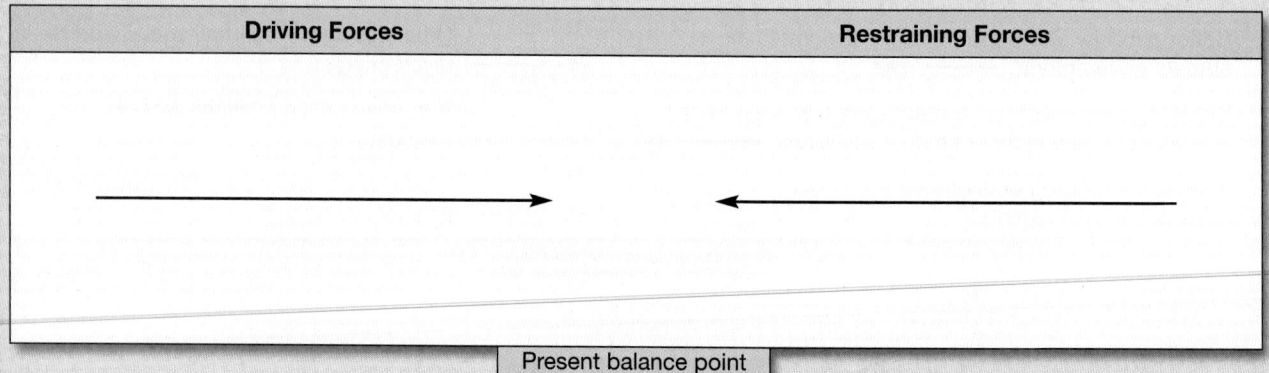

Driving Forces	Restraining Forces

Present balance point

SOURCE: Dorothy Hai, "Force-Field Analysis" in *Organizational Behavior: Experiences and Cases* (St. Paul, MN: West, 1986), pp. 259–61. Copyright © 1986. Reprinted by permission by South-Western College Publishing, a division of Thomson Learning.

18.2 Sears versus Kmart

OBJECTIVE

To analyze operations at two well-known retail firms, with a view to making recommendations for changes that will improve profitability, sales, and customer service.

INSTRUCTIONS

Your group, Fastalk Consultants, is known as the shrewdest, most insightful, and most overpaid management consulting firm in the country. You have been hired by the president of Sears to make recommendations for improving the motivation and performance of personnel in their operations. Let us assume that the key job activity in store operations is dealing with customers.

Recently, the president of Sears has come to suspect that his company's competitor, Kmart, is making heavy inroads into Sears's market. He has also hired a market research firm to investigate and compare the relative merits of products and prices in the two establishments, and has asked the market research firm to assess the advertising campaigns of the two organizations. Hence, you will not need to be concerned with marketing issues, except as they may have an impact on employee behavior. The president wants you to look into the organization of the two stores to determine the strengths and weaknesses of each.

The president has established an unusual contract with you. He wants you to make your recommendations based upon your observations *as a customer.* He does not want you to do a complete diagnosis with interviews, surveys, or behind-the-scenes observations. He wants your report in two parts.

Sears versus Kmart Worksheet

1. Given his organization's goals of profitability, sales volume, and fast and courteous service, he wants an analysis that will compare and contrast Sears and Kmart in terms of the following concepts:

Organizational Goals

Conflict? _____

Clarity? _____

Environment

Stable/Changing? _____

Simple/Complex? _____

Certain/Uncertain? _____

Size

Large? _____

Medium? _____

Small? _____

Personnel

Knowledgeable? _____

Well Trained? _____

Jobs

Variety? _____

Wholeness? _____

Interaction? _____

Freedom? _____

Time of Work? _____

Location of Work? _____

Horizontal Division of Labor

Formalized Policies? _____

Departmentalization? _____

Standardization of Rules? _____

Vertical Division of Labor

Number of Levels? _____

Span of Control? _____

Centralization? _____

Communication?

Direction? _____

Openness? _____

Leadership Style

Task Oriented? _____

People Oriented? _____

Employee Motivation

Type? _____

Intrinsic/Extrinsic? _____

Rewards? _____

Support? _____

Coordination? _____

Decision Making? _____

1. How do Sears and Kmart differ in these aspects? Which company has the best approach?

_____

_____

2. Given the corporate goals listed under part 1, what specific changes might Sears's management make in the following areas to achieve these goals (profitability, sales volume, fast and courteous service)?

  • Job design and work flow

_____

_____

  • Organization structure (at the individual store level)

_____

_____

  • Employee incentives

_____

_____

  • Leadership

_____

_____

  • Employee selection

_____

_____

3. Having completed your contract with the president of Sears, prepare a report for presentation to class. This should include specific recommendations you have considered in part 2.

SOURCE: Excerpted from Lawrence R. Jauch, Arthur G. Bedeian, Sally A. Coltrin, and William F. Glueck, *The Managerial Experience: Cases, Exercises, and Readings*, 5th ed. Copyright © 1989. Reprinted with permission of South-Western, a division of Thomson Learning, www.thomsonrights.com.

The Transformation at General Electric

Jack Welch Jr. was appointed chairman and chief executive officer of General Electric in April 1981. Recently, Welch retired. His tenure in the job was characterized by constant strategic and organizational change at GE. Among the initiatives with which Welch is associated are

1. *Changing the shape of the business portfolio.* Welch established two sets of criteria for redefining the business portfolio of GE. The first was to declare, "We will only run businesses that are number one or number two in their global markets—or, in the case of services, that have a substantial position—and are of a scale and potential appropriate to a $50 billion enterprise." Second, Welch defined three broad areas of business for GE: core, high-technology, and service businesses. As a result of these criteria, during the 1980s GE sold or closed businesses accounting for $10 billion in assets and acquired businesses amounting to $18 billion in assets. Divestment included Utah International, housewares and small appliances, consumer electronics, and semiconductors. Additions included RCA; Employers Reinsurance Corp.; Kidder Peabody Group; Navistar Financial; several new plastics ventures; Thomson's medical electronics business; and joint ventures with Fanuc (factory automation), Robert Bosch (electric motors), GEC (major appliances and electrical equipment), and Ericsson (mobile communications).

2. *Changing strategic planning.* Welch largely dismantled the highly elaborate strategic planning system that had been built up at GE over the previous decade. Documentation was drastically reduced, and the planning review process was made more informal—the central element was a meeting between Welch, his two vice chairmen, and top management of each SBU (Strategic Business Unit), which focused on identifying and discussing a few key themes. By 1984 the 200-strong corporate planning staff had been halved. The broad objective was "to get general managers talking to general managers about strategy rather than planners talking to planners."

3. *Delayering.* The changes in planning were one aspect of a more general change in the role of headquarters staff from being "checker, inquisitor, and authority figure to facilitator, helper, and supporter." This change involved a substantial reduction in reporting and paper generation and an increase in individual decision-making authority. These changes permitted a substantial widening of spans of control and the removal of several layers of hierarchy. In most of GE, levels of management were reduced from nine to four.

4. *Destaffing.* Divesting pressures, removing management layers, reducing corporate staffs, and increasing productivity resulted in enormous improvements. Between 1980 and 1990, GE's sales more than doubled while its numbers of employees fell from 402,000 to 298,000.

5. *Values.* A persistent theme in Welch's leadership was a commitment to values. Welch continually emphasized the importance of the company's "software" (values, motivation, and commitment) over its "hardware" (businesses and management structure). Welch's philosophy was articulated in 10 key principles and values:

Being number one or two in each business.

Becoming and staying lean and agile.

"Ownership"—individuals taking responsibility for decisions and actions.

"Stewardship"—individuals ensuring that GE's resources were leveraged to the full.

"Entrepreneurship."

"Excellence"—the highest personal standards.

"Reality."

"Candor."

"Open communications"—both internally and externally.

Financial support—earning a return needed to support success.

This emphasis on values was supported by a type of leadership that put a huge emphasis on communicating and disseminating these values throughout the company. Welch devoted a large portion of his time to addressing meetings of employees and management seminars at GE's Crotonville Management Development Institute.

NEW CULTURE, NEW SYSTEMS

During his first 5 years in office, Welch's priorities were strategy and structure. GE's business portfolio was radically transformed, and within its main businesses GE's strategies gave a much greater emphasis to local presence and global success and to the development and application of new technology. In terms of organizational structure, Welch's crusade against excess costs, complacency, and administrative inefficiencies resulted in a drastic pruning of the corporate hierarchy and a much flatter organization.

At the root of the "new culture" Welch sought to build at GE was a redefinition of the relational contract between GE and its employees:

"Like many other large companies in the United States, Europe and Japan, GE has had an implicit psychological contract based upon perceived lifetime employment ... This produced a paternal, feudal, fuzzy kind of loyalty. You put in your time, worked hard, and the company took care of you for life. That kind of loyalty tends to focus people inward ... The psychological contract has to change. People at all levels have to feel the risk-reward tension.

My concept of loyalty is not "giving time" to some corporate entity and, in turn, being shielded and protected from the outside world. Loyalty is an affinity among people who want to grapple with the outside world and win ... The new psychological contract, if there is such a thing, is that jobs at GE are the best in the world for people who are willing to compete. We have the best training and development resources and an environment committed to providing opportunities for personal and professional growth."[1]

Creating a new attitude requires a shift from an internal focus to an external focus:

"What determines your destiny is not the hand you're dealt, it's how you play your hand. The best way to play your hand is to face reality— see the world as it is and act accordingly ... For me, the idea is: to shun the incremental and go for the leap. Most bureaucracies—and ours is no exception—unfortunately still think in incremental terms rather than in terms of fundamental change. They think incrementally because they think internally. Changing the culture—opening it up to quantum change—means constantly asking, not how fast am I going, how well am I doing versus how well I did a year or two before, but rather, how fast and how well am I doing versus the world outside."[2]

Critical to building a new culture and changing the "old ways" of GE was not just the bureaucracy itself, but the habits and attitudes that had been engendered by bureaucracy:

"The walls within a big, century-old company don't come down like Jericho's when management makes some organizational changes or gives a speech. There are too many persistent habits propping them up. Parochialism, turf battles, status, "functionalities" and, most important, the biggest sin of a bureaucracy, the focus on itself and its inner workings, are always in the background."[3]

THE WORK-OUT PROGRAM— A GENERIC VIEW

GE's Work-Out Program was a response to the desire to speed the process of organizational change in GE. Welch conceived the idea of Work-Out in September 1988. Welch conducted a session at every class of GE managers attending Management Development Institute at Crotonville, New York. He was impressed by the energy, enthusiasm, and flow of ideas that his open discussion sessions with managers were capable of generating. At the same time, he was frustrated by the resilience of many of GE's bureaucratic practices and the difficulty of transferring the ideas that individual managers possessed into action. After a particularly lively session at Crotonville, Welch and GE's education director, James Braughman, got together to discuss how the interaction in these seminars could be replicated throughout the company in a process that would involve all employees and would generate far-reaching changes within GE. In the course of a helicopter ride from Crotonville to GE's Fairfield headquarters, Welch and Braughman sketched the concept and the framework for the Work-Out process.

A model for GE's Work-Out was a traditional New England town hall meeting where citizens gather to vent their problems, frustrations, and ideas, and people eventually agree on certain civic actions. Welch outlined the goals of Work-Out as follows:

"Work-Out has a practical and an intellectual goal. The practical objective is to get rid of thousands of bad habits accumulated since the creation of General Electric . . . The second thing we want to achieve, the intellectual part, begins by putting the leaders of each business in front of 100 or so of their people, eight to ten times a year, to let them hear what their people think. Work-Out will expose the leaders to the vibrations of their business opinions, feelings, emotions, resentments, not abstract theories of organization and management."[4]

A generic summary of the Work-Out Program reveals three interrelated purposes: to fuel a process of continuous improvement and change; to foster cultural transformation characterized by trust, empowerment, elimination of unnecessary work, and a boundaryless organization; and to improve business performance.

THE STRUCTURE OF THE WORK-OUT PROCESS

The central idea of the Work-Out process was to create a forum where a cross-section of employees in each business could speak their minds about how their business was managed without fear of retribution. Because those doing the work were often the best people to recommend improvements in how their work should be managed, such interaction was seen as a first step in taking

actions to remove unnecessary work and improve business processes. In January 1989, Welch announced Work-Out at an annual meeting of GE's 500 top executives. A broad framework was set out, but considerable flexibility was given to each of GE's 14 core businesses in how they went about the program. The key elements of Work-Out were

- *Off-site meetings.* Work-Out was held as a forum and to get away from the company environment. Two-to-three-day Work-Out events were held off-site.
- *Focus on issues and key processes.* There was a strong bias toward action-oriented sessions. The initial Work-Out events tended to focus on removing unnecessary work. This is what Braughman referred to as the "low-hanging fruit." As the programs developed, Work-Out focused more on more complex business processes. For example, in GE Lighting, groupwide sessions were held to accelerate new product development, improve fill rates, and increase integration between component production and assembly. In plastics the priorities were quality improvement, lower cycle times, and increased cross-functional coordination.
- *Cross-sectional participation.* Work-Out sessions normally involved between 50 and 100 employees drawn from all levels and all functions of a business. Critical to the process was the presence of the top management of the particular business.
- *Small groups and town meetings.* Work-Out events normally involved a series of small group meetings that began with a brainstorming session followed by a plenary session (or "town meeting") in which the suggestions developed by the small groups were put to senior managers and then openly debated. At the end of each discussion, the leader was required to make an immediate decision: to adopt, reject, or defer for further study.
- *Follow-up.* A critical element of Work-Out was a follow-up process to ensure that what had been decided was implemented.

THE RESULTS OF WORK-OUT

The results from Work-Out were remarkable. During its first 4 years, more than 3,000 Work-Out sessions had been conducted in GE, resulting in thousands of small changes eliminating "junk work" as well as much more complex and further-reaching changes in organizational structure and management processes. The terms *rattlers* and *pythons* were introduced to describe the two types of problem. Rattlers were simple problems that could be "shot" on sight. Pythons were more complex issues that needed unraveling.

As well as tangible structural changes and performance gains, some of the most important effects were changes in organizational culture. In GE Capital, one of the most centralized and bureaucratized of GE's businesses, one employee described the changes as follows: "we've been suppressed around here for a long time. Now that management is finally listening to us, it feels like the Berlin Wall is coming down.[5]

In 5 years, more than 300,000 employees, customers, and suppliers went through Work-Out sessions. A large variety of impressive and significant performance and efficiency improvements are reported in GE's internal documents, following introduction of the Work-Out processes. For example, the Gas Engine Turbines business unit at Albany, New York, reported an 80 percent decrease in production time to build gas engine turbines; Aircraft Engines at Lynn, Massachusetts, reduced jet engine production time from 30 to 4 weeks. GE's Financial Services Operation reported a reduction in operating costs from $5.10 to $4.55 per invoice, invoices paid per employee were up 34 percent, costs per employee paid fell 19 percent, and employees paid per payroll worker rose 32 percent. The Aerospace plant at Syracuse, New York, reported that as a result of the Work-Out Program, beyond achieving 100 percent compliance with pollution regulations, the production of hazardous waste materials was reduced from 759 tons in 1990 to 275 tons in 1992.

MANAGING WORK-OUT

Work-Out was intended as a bottom-up process in which (1) employees throughout each business would be free to challenge their leaders and (2) management's role was primarily to perpetuate the program and to ensure that decisions, once made, were implemented. But Work-Out could not be just a populist movement within the corporation. It needed to be directed toward creating the kind of corporation that GE needed to be to survive and prosper. To this extent Jack Welch saw his role as communicating and disseminating the principles, values, and themes that would permit GE's continued success.

In 1989 Welch crystallized his ideas about GE's management around three themes: speed, simplicity, and self-confidence:

> "We found in the 1980s that becoming faster is tied to becoming simpler. Our businesses, with tens of thousands of employees, will not respond to visions that have sub-paragraphs and foot-notes. If we're not simple we can't be fast . . . and if we're not fast, we can't win."

Simplicity, to an engineer, means clean, functional, winning designs, no bells and whistles. In marketing it might manifest itself as clear, unencumbered proposals. For manufacturing people it would produce a logical process that makes sense to every individual on the line. And on an individual, interpersonal level it would take the form of plain speaking, directness, honesty.

But as surely as speed flows from simplicity, simplicity is grounded in self-confidence. Self-confidence does not grow in someone who is just another appendage on the bureaucracy; whose authority rests on little more than a title. People who are freed from the confines of their box on the organization chart, whose status rests on real world achievement—those are the people who develop the self-confidence to be simple, to share every bit of information available to them, to listen to those above, below and around them and then move boldly.

But a company cannot distribute self-confidence. What it can do—what we must do—is to give our people an opportunity to win, to contribute, and hence earn self-confidence themselves. They don't get that opportunity, they can't taste winning if they spend their days wandering in the muck of a self-absorbed bureaucracy.

Speed . . . simplicity . . . self-confidence. We have it in increasing measure. We know where it comes from . . . and we have plans to increase it in the 1990s."[6]

BEST PRACTICES

One of the Work-Out Program's many impressive outcomes is that it's a catalyst for new improvement programs. One such program, Best Practices, is aimed at increasing productivity. The GE business-development staff focused on 24 credible companies from an initial pool of 200 that had achieved faster productivity growth than GE and sustained it for at least 10 years. From this list, one dozen companies agreed to take part in GE's proposal to send its employees to their companies to learn their secrets to success. In exchange, GE offered to share the results of the study as well success stories with the participating companies. This learning for the Best Practices program involved companies such as Ford, Hewlett-Packard, Xerox, and Chaparral Steel plus three Japanese firms.

GE was less concerned with the actual work done at the companies than with management practices and attitudes of the employees. The difference between Best Practices and traditional benchmarking is that the former does not require keeping score. The focus on learning alternative successful management practices and managing processes was identified as the most critical component for long-term productivity improvements. The basic assumption that through multiple exposure to alternative management practices, managers and employees will be stimulated to continuously improve their own practices, continues to guide the program. Best Practices has evolved into a formal course taught to at least one dozen employees and managers per month in each business unit.

QUESTIONS

1. Based on the information presented, describe the overall planned change approach and phases led by Jack Welch.

2. Identify and briefly describe the major characteristics of the Work-Out Program.

3. Discuss how the organizational culture changed. What caused the change? What effects did the culture change have on human behavior and organizational performance and effectiveness?

4. Assess the case using the models and concepts presented in the last chapter and other parts of the book.

SOURCE: This case was written by R. Grant and A. B. (Rami) Shani for classroom use. The case draws heavily on the following sources: N. M. Tichy and S. Sherman, *Control Your Destiny or Someone Else Will* (New York: Doubleday, 1992); R. Slater, *The New GE: How Jack Welch Revived an American Institution* (Burr Ridge, IL: Irwin, 1993); R. N. Ashkenas and T. D. Jick, "From Dialogue to Action in GE Work-Out," in W. A. Pasmore and R. Woodman (eds.), *Research in Organization Change and Development*, vol. 6. (Greenwich. CT: JAI Press, 1993), pp. 267–87; "Jack Welch's Lessons for Success," *Fortune*, February 25, 1993, pp. 86–90.

CASE INCIDENTS

Robot Repercussion

Victor Principal, vice president of industrial relations for General Manufacturing, Inc., sat in his office reviewing the list of benefits the company expected to realize from increasing its use of industrial robots. In a few minutes, he would walk down to the labor-management conference room for a meeting with Ralph McIntosh, president of the labor union local representing most of the company's industrial employees. The purpose of this meeting would be to informally exchange views and positions preliminary to the opening for formal contract negotiations later in the month, which would focus on the use of computer-integrated robotics systems and the resulting impact on employment, workers, and jobs.

Both Principal and McIntosh had access to similar information flows relevant to industrial robots, including the following. Unlike single-task machines, installed in earlier stages of automation, robots can be programmed to do one job and then reprogrammed to do another one. The pioneering generation of robots was mainly programmed to load machines, weld, forge, spray paint, handle materials, and inspect auto bodies. The latest generation of robots includes vision-controlled robots, which enable the machines to approximate the human ability to recognize and size up objects by using laser-beam patterns recorded by television cameras and transmitted to "smart" computers. The computer software interprets and manipulates the images relayed by the camera in a "smart" or artificially intelligent way.

Experts concluded that the impact of robot installation on employment would be profound, although the extent of the worker replacement was not clear. The inescapable conclusion was that robot usage had the capacity to increase manufacturing performance and to decrease manufacturing employment.

Principal walked down to the conference room. Finding McIntosh already there, Principal stated the company's position regarding installation of industrial robots: "The company needs the cooperation of the union and our workers. We don't wish to be perceived as callously exchanging human workers for robots." Then Principal listed the major advantages associated with robots: (1) improved quality of product as a result of the accuracy of robots; (2) reduced operating costs, as the per-hour operational cost of robots was about one-third of the per-hour cost of wages and benefits paid to an average employee; (3) reliability improvements, as robots work tirelessly and don't require behavioral support; and (4) greater manufacturing flexibility, because robots are readily reprogrammable for different jobs. Principal concluded that

these advantages would make the company more competitive, which would allow it to grow and increase its workforce.

McIntosh's response was direct and strong: "We aren't Luddites racing around ruining machines. We know it's necessary to increase productivity and that robotic technology is here. But we can't give the company a blank check. We need safeguards and protection." McIntosh continued, "We intend to bargain for the following contract provisions:

1. Establishment of labor–management committees to negotiate *in advance* about the labor impact of robotics technology and, of equal importance, to have a voice in deciding how and whether it should be used.

2. Rights to advance notice about installation of new technology.

3. Retraining rights for workers displaced, to include retraining for new positions in the plant, the community, or other company plants.

4. Spreading the work among workers by use of a four-day workweek or other acceptable plan as an alternative to reducing the workforce."

McIntosh's final sentence summed up the union's position: "We in the union believe the company is giving our jobs to robots to reduce the labor force."

Their meeting ended amiably, but Principal and McIntosh each knew that much hard bargaining lay ahead. As Principal returned to his office, the two opposing positions were obvious. On his yellow tablet, Principal listed the requirements as he saw them: (1) A clearly stated overall policy was needed to guide negotiation decisions and actions; (2) it was critical to decide on a company position regarding each of the union's announced demands and concerns; and (3) a plan had to be developed.

As Principal considered these challenges, he idly contemplated a robot possessing artificial intelligence and vision capability that could help him in his work. Immediately a danger alarm sounded in his mind. A robot so constructed might be more than helpful and might take over this and other important aspects of his job. Slightly chagrined, Principal returned to his task. He needed help—but not from any "smart" robot.

SOURCE: J. Champion and J. James, *Critical Incidents in Management: Decision and Policy Issues,* 6th ed. The McGraw-Hill Companies, 1989).

Implementing Strategic Change

James Fulmer, chief executive officer of Allied Industries, reviewed three notes he had exchanged with Frank Curtis, director of fiscal affairs, now president of a company owned by Allied. The two executives were going to meet in a few minutes to discuss problems that had recently surfaced. During the past decade, Allied had aggressively pursued a growth objective based on a conglomerate strategy of acquiring companies in distress. CEO Fulmer's policy was to appoint a new chief operating officer for each acquisition with instructions to facilitate a turnaround. Fulmer reviewed two of the notes he had written to Curtis.

Date: January 15, 2003.

Memorandum

To: Frank Curtis, Director of Fiscal Affairs, Allied Industries

From: James Fulmer, Chairman, Allied Industries

Subject: Your Appointment as President, Lee Medical Supplies

You are aware that Allied Industries recently acquired Lee Medical Supplies. Mr. John Lee, founder and president of the company, has agreed to retire, and I am appointing you to replace him. Our acquisitions group will brief you on the company, but I want to warn you that Lee Medical Supplies has a history of mismanagement. As a distributor of medical items, the company's sales last year totaled approximately $300 million, with net earnings of only $12 million. Your job is to make company sales and profits compatible with Allied standards. You are reminded that it is my policy to call for an independent evaluation of company progress and your performance as president after 18 months.

Date: September 10, 2004.

Memorandum

To: Frank Curtis, President, Lee Medical Supplies

From: James Fulmer, Chairman, Allied Industries

Subject: Serious Problems at Lee Medical Supplies

In accord with corporate policy, consultants recently conducted an evaluation of Lee Medical Supplies. In a relatively short period of time, you have increased sales and profits to meet Allied's standards, but I am alarmed at other aspects of your performance. I am told that during the past 18 months, three of your nine vice presidents have resigned and that you have terminated four others. An opinion survey conducted by the consultants indicates that a low state of morale exists and that your managerial appointees are regarded by their subordinates as hard-nosed perfectionists obsessed with quotas and profits. Employees report that ruthless competition now exists between divisions, regions, and districts. They also note that the collegial, family-oriented atmosphere fostered by Mr. Lee has been replaced by a dog-eat-dog situation characterized by negative management attitudes toward employee feelings and needs. After you have studied the enclosed report from the consultants, we will meet to discuss their findings. I am particularly concerned with their final conclusion that "a form of corporate cancer seems to be spreading throughout Lee Medical Supplies."

As Fulmer prepared to read the third note, written by Frank Curtis, he reflected on his interview with the consultants. While Fulmer considered Curtis a financial expert and a turnaround specialist, his subordinates characterized Curtis as an autocrat and better suited to be a Marine boot camp commander.

Date: September 28, 2004.

Memorandum

To: James Fulmer

From: Frank Curtis

Subject: The So-Called Serious Problems at Lee Medical Supplies

I have received your memorandum dated September 10, and reviewed the consultants' report. When you appointed me to my present position I was instructed to take over an unprofitable company and make it profitable. I have done so in 18 months, although I inherited a family-owned business that by your own admission had been mismanaged for years. I found a group of managers and salespeople with an average company tenure of 22 years. Mr. Lee had centralized all personnel decisions so that only he could terminate an employee. He tolerated mediocre performance. All employees were paid on a straight salary basis, with seniority the sole criterion for advancement. Some emphasis was given to increasing sales each year, but none was given to reducing costs and increasing profits. Employees did indeed find the company a fun place to work, and the feeling of being a part of a family did permeate the company. Such attitudes were, however, accompanied by mediocrity, incompetence, and poor performance.

I found it necessary to implement immediate strategic changes in five areas: the organization's structure, employee rewards and incentives, management information systems, allocation of resources, and managerial leadership style. As a result, sales areas were reorganized into divisions, regions, and districts. Managers who I felt were incompetent and/or lacking in commitment to my objectives and methods were replaced. Unproductive and mediocre employees were encouraged to find jobs elsewhere. Authority for staffing and compensation decisions was decentralized to units at the division, region, and district levels. Managers of those units were informed that along with their authority went responsibility for reducing costs and for increasing sales and profits. Each unit was established as a profit center. A new department was established and charged with reviewing performance of those units. Improved accounting and control systems were implemented. A management-by-objectives program was developed to establish standards and monitor performance. Performance appraisals are now required for all employees. To encourage more aggressive action, bonuses and incentives are offered to managers of units showing increased profits. A commission plan based on measurable sales and profit performances has replaced straight salaries. Resources are allocated to units based on their performance.

My own leadership style has probably represented the most traumatic change for employees. Internal competition is a formally mandated policy throughout the company. It has been responsible for much of the progress achieved to date. Progress, however, is never made without costs, and I recognize that employees are not having as much fun as in the past. I was employed to achieve results and not to ensure that employees remain secure and happy in their work. Don't let a few crybabies unable to adjust to changes lead you to believe that problems take precedence over profits. Does it mean that I am not people oriented if I believe it is unlikely that a spirit of aggressiveness and competitiveness can coexist with an atmosphere of cooperativeness and family orientation? Do you feel that we are obligated to employees because of past practices? Frankly, I thought I had your support to do whatever was necessary to get this company turned around. In our meeting, tell me if you think my approaches have been wrong and, if so, tell me what I should have done differently.

Just as Fulmer finished reviewing the third memorandum, his secretary informed him that Curtis had arrived for their scheduled meeting. He realized he was undecided about how to communicate to Curtis his ideas and beliefs regarding how changes in an organization can best be implemented. One thing he did know: He didn't appreciate how Curtis had expressed his views in his memorandum, but he recognized that he probably should set aside emotions and respond to the questions Curtis posed.

SOURCE: J. Champion and J. James, *Critical Incidents in Management: Decision and Policy Issues,* 6th ed. (Burr Ridge, IL.: Richard D. Irwin, 1989).

Glossary

360 degree appraisal Process of using multiple sources of appraisal to gain a comprehensive perspective on one's performance.

A

accommodation A style of dealing with conflict involving cooperation on behalf of the other party but not being assertive about one's own interests.

accountability The expectation that employees will perform a job, take corrective action when necessary, and report upward on the status and quality of their performance.

accounting audits Procedures used to verify accounting reports and statements.

activity-based costing (ABC) A method of cost accounting designed to identify streams of activity and then to allocate costs across particular business processes according to the amount of time employees devote to particular activities.

adapters Companies that take the current industry structure and its future evolution as givens.

affective conflict Emotional disagreement directed toward other people.

arbitration The use of a neutral third party to resolve a labor dispute.

assessment center A managerial performance test in which candidates participate in a variety of exercises and situations.

assets The values of the various items the corporation owns.

authority The legitimate right to make decisions and to tell other people what to do.

autocratic leadership A form of leadership in which the leader makes decisions on his or her own and then announces those decisions to the group.

autonomous work groups Groups that control decisions about and execution of a complete range of tasks.

avoidance A reaction to conflict that involves ignoring the problem by doing nothing at all, or deemphasizing the disagreement.

B

balance sheet A report that shows the financial picture of a company at a given time and itemizes assets, liabilities, and stockholders' equity.

barriers to entry Conditions that prevent new companies from entering an industry.

behavioral approach A leadership perspective that attempts to identify what good leaders do—that is, what behaviors they exhibit.

benchmarking The process of comparing an organization's practices and technologies with those of other companies.

bootlegging Informal efforts by managers and employees to create new products and new processes.

boundaryless organization Organization in which there are no barriers to information flow.

bounded rationality A less-than-perfect form of rationality in which decision makers cannot be perfectly rational because decisions are complex and complete information is unavailable.

brainstorming A process in which group members generate as many ideas about a problem as they can; criticism is withheld until all ideas have been proposed.

broker A person who assembles and coordinates participants in a network.

budgeting The process of investigating what is being done and comparing the results with the corresponding budget data to verify accomplishments or remedy differences. Also called budgetary controlling.

buffering Creating supplies of excess resources in case of unpredictable needs.

bureaucratic control The use of rules, regulations, and authority to guide performance.

business ethics The moral principles and standards that guide behavior in the world of business.

business incubators Protected environments for new, small businesses.

business plan A formal planning step that focuses on the entire venture and describes all the elements involved in starting it.

business strategy The major actions by which a business competes in a particular industry or market.

C

cafeteria benefit program An employee benefit program in which employees choose from a menu of options to create a benefit package tailored to their needs.

centralized organization An organization in which high-level executives make most decisions and pass them down to lower levels for implementation.

certainty The state that exists when decision makers have accurate and comprehensive information.

charismatic leader A person who is dominant, self-confident, convinced of the moral righteousness of his or her beliefs, and able to arouse a sense of excitement and adventure in followers.

chief technology officer (CTO) Executive in charge of technology strategy and development.

clan control Control based on the norms, values, shared goals, and trust among group members.

coaching Dialogue with a goal of helping another be more effective and achieve his or her full potential on the job.

coalition building Working with other organizations or groups of voters that share political interests on a particular legislative issue.

coalitional model Model of organizational decision making in which groups with differing preferences use power and negotiations to influence decisions.

cognitive conflict Issue-based differences in perspectives or judgments.

cohesiveness The degree to which a group is attractive to its members, members are motivated to remain in the group, and members influence one another.

collaboration A style of dealing with conflict emphasizing both cooperation and assertiveness in order to maximize both parties' satisfaction.

communication The transmission of information and meaning from one party to another through the use of shared symbols.

comparable worth Principle of equal pay for different jobs of equal worth.

competing A style of dealing with conflict involving strong focus on one's own goals, and little or no concern for the other person's goals.

competitive environment The immediate environment surrounding a firm; includes suppliers, customers, competitors, and the like.

competitive intelligence Information that helps managers determine how to compete better.

compliance-based ethics programs Company mechanisms typically designed by corporate counsel to prevent, detect, and punish legal violations.

compromise A style of dealing with conflict involving moderate attention to both parties' concerns.

computer-integrated manufacturing The use of computer-aided design and computer-aided manufacturing to sequence and optimize a number of production processes.

concentration A strategy employed for an organization that operates a single business and competes in a single industry.

concentric diversification A strategy used to add new businesses that produce related products or are involved in related markets and activities.

conceptual and decision skills Skills pertaining to the ability to identify and resolve problems for the benefit of the organization and its members.

concurrent control The control process used while plans are being carried out, including directing, monitoring, and fine-tuning activities as they are performed.

conflict Opposing pressures from different sources. Two levels of conflict are psychological conflict and conflict that arises between individuals or groups.

conglomerate diversification A strategy used to add new businesses that produce unrelated products or are involved in unrelated markets and activities.

contingency plans Alternative courses of action that can be implemented based on how the future unfolds.

continuous process A process that is highly automated and has a continuous production flow.

control Any process that directs the activities of individuals toward the achievement of organizational goals.

controlling The management function of monitoring progress and making needed changes.

cooperative strategies Strategies used by two or more organizations working together to manage the external environment.

coordination The procedures that link the various parts of an organization for the purpose of achieving the organization's overall mission.

coordination by mutual adjustment Units interact with one another to make accommodations in order to achieve flexible coordination.

coordination by plan Interdependent units are required to meet deadlines and objectives that contribute to a common goal.

core competencies The unique skills and/or knowledge an organization possesses that give it an edge over competitors.

corporate constituency programs Organizational efforts to identify, educate, and motivate individuals to take political action that could benefit the organization.

corporate governance The role of a corporation's executive staff and board of directors in ensuring that the firm's activities meet the goals of the firm's stakeholders.

corporate legitimacy A motive for organizational involvement in the public policy process. The assumption is that organizations are legitimate to the extent that their goals, purposes, and methods are consistent with those of society.

corporate social responsibility Obligation toward society assumed by business.

corporate social responsiveness The process companies follow and the actions they take in the domain of corporate social responsibility.

corporate strategy The set of businesses, markets, or industries in which an organization competes and the distribution of resources among those entities.

cost competitiveness Keeping costs low in order to achieve profits and be able to offer prices that are attractive to consumers.

culture shock The disorientation and stress associated with being in a foreign environment.

current ratio A liquidity ratio which indicates the extent to which short-term assets can decline and still be adequate to pay short-term liabilities.

custom-made solutions The combination of ideas into new, creative solutions.

customer relationship management A multifaceted process focusing on creating two-way exchanges with customers to foster intimate knowledge of their needs, wants, and buying patterns.

customer service The speed and dependability with which an organization can deliver what customers want.

D

debt-equity ratio A leverage ratio which indicates the company's ability to meet its long term financial obligations.

decentralized organization An organization in which lower-level managers make important decisions.

defenders Companies that stay within a stable product domain as a strategic maneuver.

delegation The assignment of new or additional responsibilities to a subordinate.

democratic leadership A form of leadership in which the leader solicits input from subordinates.

demographics Measures of various characteristics of the people who comprise groups or other social units.

deontology Focuses on rights of individuals.

departmentalization Subdividing an organization into smaller subunits.

design for environment (DFE) A tool for creating products that are easy to recover, reuse, or recycle.

development Teaching managers and professional employees broad skills needed for their present and future jobs.

development project A focused organizational effort to create a new product or process via technological advances.

devil's advocate A person who has the job of criticizing ideas to ensure that their downsides are fully explored.

dialectic A structured debate comparing two conflicting courses of action.

dialogue A discourse in which members explore complex issues from many viewpoints in order to come to a common, deeper understanding.

differentiation An aspect of the organization's internal environment created by job specialization and the division of labor.

differentiation strategy A strategy an organization uses to build competitive advantage by being unique in its industry or market segment along one or more dimensions.

discounting the future A bias weighting short-term costs and benefits more heavily than longer-term costs and benefits.

discussion A type of discourse in which each person attempts to win a debate by having his or her view accepted by others.

diversity training Programs that focus on identifying and reducing hidden biases against people with differences and developing the skills needed to manage a diversified workforce.

division of labor The assignment of different tasks to different people or groups.

divisional organization Departmentalization that groups units around products, customers, or geographic regions.

domain defense Activities intended to counter challenges to the organization's legitimacy.

downsizing The planned elimination of positions or jobs.

downward communication Information that flows from higher to lower levels in the organization's hierarchy.

dynamic network Temporary arrangements among partners that can be assembled and reassembled to adapt to the environment.

E

ecocentric management Its goal is the creation of sustainable economic development and improvement of quality of life worldwide for all organizational stakeholders.

economic responsibilities To produce goods and services that society wants at a price that perpetuates the business and satisfies its obligations to investors.

economies of scope Economies in which materials and processes employed in one product can be used to make other, related products.

egoism An ethical system defining acceptable behavior as that which maximizes consequences for the individual.

emergent strategy The strategy that evolves from all the activities engaged in by people throughout the organization.

empowerment The process of sharing power with employees, thereby enhancing their confidence in their ability to perform their jobs and their belief that they are influential contributors to the organization.

entrepreneurial orientation The tendency of an organization to identify and capitalize successfully on opportunities to launch new ventures by entering new or established markets with new or existing goods or services.

entrepreneurial venture A new business having growth and high profitability as primary objectives.

entrepreneurship The pursuit of lucrative opportunities by enterprising individuals.

environmental scanning Searching for and sorting through information about the environment.

environmental uncertainty Lack of information needed to understand or predict the future.

equity theory   A theory stating that people assess how fairly they have been treated according to two key factors: outcomes and inputs.

ERG theory   A human needs theory developed by Alderfer postulating that people have three basic sets of needs which can operate simultaneously.

ethical climate   In an organization it refers to the processes by which decisions are evaluated and made on the basis of right and wrong.

ethical issue   Situation, problem, or opportunity in which an individual must choose among several actions that must be evaluated as right or wrong.

ethical responsibilities   Meeting other social expectations, not written as law.

ethics   The system of rules governing the ordering of values.

executive champion   An executive who supports a new technology and protects the product champion of the innovation.

expatriates   Parent-company nationals who are sent to work at a foreign subsidiary.

expectancy   Employees' perception of the likelihood that their efforts will enable them to attain their performance goals.

expectancy theory   A theory proposing that people will behave based on their perceived likelihood that their effort will lead to a certain outcome and on how highly they value that outcome.

external audit   An evaluation conducted by one organization, such as a CPA firm, on another.

external environment   All relevant forces outside a firm's boundaries, such as competitors, customers, the government, and the economy.

extinction   Withdrawing or failing to provide a reinforcing consequence.

extrinsic reinforcers   Reinforcers given to a person by the boss, the company, or some other person.

F

failure rate   The number of expatriate managers of an overseas operation who come home early.

feedback control   Control that focuses on the use of information about previous results to correct deviations from the acceptable standard.

feedforward control   The control process used before operations begin, including policies, procedures, and rules designed to ensure that planned activities are carried out properly.

filtering   The process of withholding, ignoring, or distorting information.

final consumer   Those who purchase products in their finished form.

flexible benefit programs   Benefit programs in which employees are given credits to spend on benefits that fit their unique needs.

flexible factories   A system that calls for subassemblies and components to be manu-

factured in very small lots and delivered to the next stage of the production process just as they are needed.

flexible processes   Methods for adapting the technical core to changes in the environment.

forecasting   Method for predicting how variables will change the future.

framing effects   A psychological bias influenced by the way in which a problem or decision alternative is phrased or presented.

frontline managers   Lower-level managers who supervise the operational activities of the organization.

functional organization   Departmentalization around specialized activities such as production, marketing, and human resources.

functional strategies   Strategies implemented by each functional area of the organization to support the organization's business strategy.

G

garbage can model   Model of organizational decision making depicting a chaotic process and seemingly random decisions.

genius of the "and"   The ability to pursue multiple goals at once.

glass ceiling   An invisible barrier that makes it difficult for certain groups, such as minorities and women, to move beyond a certain level in the organizational hierarchy.

global organization model   An organization model consisting of a company's overseas subsidiaries and characterized by centralized decision making and tight control by the parent company over most aspects of worldwide operations. Typically adopted by organizations that base their global competitive strategy on low cost.

global start-up   A new venture that is international from the very beginning.

goal   A target or end that management desires to reach.

goal displacement   A condition that occurs when a decision-making group loses sight of its original goal and a new, possibly less important, goal emerges.

goal-setting theory   A motivation theory stating that people have conscious goals that energize them and direct their thoughts and behaviors toward a particular end.

grapevine   Informal communication network.

group maintenance behaviors   Actions taken to ensure the satisfaction of group members, develop and maintain harmonious work relationships, and preserve the social stability of the group.

groupthink   A phenomenon that occurs in decision making when group members avoid disagreement as they strive for consensus.

growth need strength   The degree to which individuals want personal and psychological development.

H

hierarchy   The authority levels of the organizational pyramid.

high-involvement organization   A type of organization in which top management ensures that there is consensus about the direction in which the business is heading.

horizontal communication   Information shared among people on the same hierarchical level.

host-country nationals   Natives of the country where an overseas subsidiary is located.

human capital   The knowledge, skills, and abilities of employees that have economic value.

human resources management (HRM)   Formal systems for the management of people within an organization.

hygiene factors   Characteristics of the workplace, such as company policies, working conditions, pay, and supervision, that can make people dissatisfied.

I

illusion of control   People's belief that they can influence events, even when they have no control over what will happen.

incremental model   Model of organizational decision making in which major solutions arise through a series of smaller decisions.

independent entrepreneur   An individual who establishes a new organization without the benefit of corporate sponsorship.

independent strategies   Strategies that an organization acting on its own uses to change some aspect of its current environment.

informing   A team strategy that entails concentrating first on the internal team process to achieve a state of performance readiness, then informing outsiders of its intentions.

innovation   A change in technology; a departure from previous ways of doing things.

innovation   The introduction of new goods and services.

instrumentality   The perceived likelihood that performance will be followed by a particular outcome.

integration   The degree to which differentiated work units work together and coordinate their efforts.

integrity-based ethics programs   Company mechanisms designed to instill in people a personal responsibility for ethical behavior.

intermediate consumer   A customer who purchases raw materials or wholesale products before selling them to final customers.

internal audit   A periodic assessment of a company's own planning, organizing, leading, and controlling processes.

international organization model   An organization model that is composed of a company's overseas subsidiaries and characterized by greater control by the parent company over the research function and local product and marketing strategies than is the case in the multinational model.

interpersonal and communication skills People skills; the ability to lead, motivate, and communicate effectively with others.

intrapreneurs New venture creators working in big corporations.

intrinsic reward Reward a worker derives directly from performing the job itself.

ISO 9000 A series of quality standards developed by a committee working under the International Organization for Standardization to improve total quality in all businesses for the benefit of both producers and consumers.

J

job analysis A tool for determining what is done on a given job and what should be done on that job.

job enlargement Giving people additional tasks at the same time to alleviate boredom.

job enrichment Changing a task to make it inherently more rewarding, motivating, and satisfying.

job rotation Changing from one routine task to another to alleviate boredom.

just-in-time (JIT) A system that calls for subassemblies and components to be manufactured in very small lots and delivered to the next stage of the production process just as they are needed.

K

knowledge management Practices aimed at discovering and harnessing an organization's intellectual resources.

Kohlberg's model of cognitive moral development Classifies people based on their level of moral judgment.

L

labor relations The system of relations between workers and management.

laissez-faire A leadership philosophy characterized by an absence of managerial decision making.

large batch Technologies that produce goods and services in high volume.

law of effect A law formulated by Edward Thorndike in 1911 stating that behavior that is followed by positive consequences will likely be repeated.

Leader-Member Exchange (LMX) theory Highlights the importance of leader behaviors not just toward the group as a whole but toward individuals on a personal basis.

leading The management function that involves the manager's efforts to stimulate high performance by employees.

lean manufacturing An operation that strives to achieve the highest possible productivity and total quality, cost-effectively, by eliminating unnecessary steps in the production process and continually strives for improvement.

learning organization An organization skilled at creating, acquiring, and transferring

knowledge, and at modifying its behavior to reflect new knowledge and insights.

legal responsibilities To obey local, state, federal, and relevant international laws.

liabilities The amounts a corporation owes to various creditors.

line departments Units that deal directly with the organization's primary goods and services.

lobbying Efforts to influence regulatory bodies, legislators, and their staff.

logistics The movement of the right goods in the right amount to the right place at the right time.

low-cost strategy A strategy an organization uses to build competitive advantage by being efficient and offering a standard, no-frills product.

M

macroenvironment The most general environment; includes governments, economic conditions, and other fundamental factors that generally affect all organizations.

make-or-buy decision The question an organization asks itself about whether to acquire new technology from an outside source or develop it itself.

management The process of working with people and resources to accomplish organizational goals.

management audit An evaluation of the effectiveness and efficiency of various systems within an organization.

management by objectives (MBO) A process in which objectives set by a subordinate and a supervisor must be coached within a given time period.

management myopia Focusing on short-term earnings and profits at the expense of longer-term strategic obligations.

management teams Teams that coordinate and provide direction to the subunits under their jurisdiction and integrate work among subunits.

managing diversity Managing a culturally diverse workforce by recognizing the characteristics common to specific groups of employees while dealing with such employees as individuals and supporting, nurturing, and utilizing their differences to the organization's advantage.

market control Control based on the use of pricing mechanisms and economic information to regulate activities within organizations.

mass customization The production of varied, individually customized products at the low cost of standardized, mass-produced products.

matrix organization An organization composed of dual reporting relationships in which some managers report to two superiors—a functional manager and a divisional manager.

maximizing A decision realizing the best possible outcome.

mechanistic organization A form of organization that seeks to maximize internal efficiency.

media richness The degree to which a communication channel conveys information.

mentors Higher level managers who help ensure that high-potential people are introduced to top management and socialized into the norms and values of the organization.

middle-level managers Managers located in the middle layers of the organizational hierarchy, reporting to top-level executives.

mission An organization's basic purpose and scope of operations.

monolithic organization An organization that has a low degree of structural integration—employing few women, minorities, or other groups that differ from the majority—and thus has a highly homogeneous employee population.

moral philosophy Principles, rules, and values people use in deciding what is right or wrong.

motivation Forces that energize, direct, and sustain a person's efforts.

motivators Factors that make a job more motivating, such as additional job responsibilities, opportunities for personal growth and recognition, and feelings of achievement.

moving Instituting the change.

multicultural organization An organization that values cultural diversity and seeks to utilize and encourage it.

multinational organization model An organization model that consists of the subsidiaries in each country in which a company does business, with ultimate control exercised by the parent company.

N

need hierarchy A conception of human needs organizing needs into a hierarchy of five major types.

needs assessment An analysis identifying the jobs, people, and departments for which training is necessary.

negative reinforcement Removing or withholding an undesirable consequence.

network organization A collection of independent, mostly single-function firms.

nonprogrammed decisions New, novel, complex decisions having no proven answers.

norms Shared beliefs about how people should think and behave.

North American Free Trade Agreement (NAFTA) An economic pact that combined the economies of the United States, Canada, and Mexico into the world's largest trading bloc.

O

one-way communication A process in which information flows in only one direction—from the sender to the receiver, with no feedback loop.

open-book management Practice of sharing with employees at all levels of the organization vital information previously meant for management's eyes only.

operational planning The process of identifying the specific procedures and processes required at lower levels of the organization.

opportunity analysis A description of the product or service, an assessment of the opportunity, an assessment of the entrepreneur, specification of activities and resources needed to translate your idea into a viable business, and your source(s) of capital.

optimizing Achieving the best possible balance among several goals.

organic structure An organizational form that emphasizes flexibility.

organization chart The reporting structure and division of labor in an organization.

organization culture The set of important assumptions about the organization and its goals and practices that members of the company share.

organizational behavior modification (OB Mod) The application of reinforcement theory in organizational settings.

organizing The management function of assembling and coordinating human, financial, physical, informational, and other resources needed to achieve goals.

orientation training Training designed to introduce new employees to the company and familiarize them with policies, procedures, culture, and the like.

outcome A consequence a person receives for his or her performance.

outplacement The process of helping people who have been dismissed from the company to regain employment elsewhere.

P

parading A team strategy that entails simultaneously emphasizing internal team building and achieving external visibility.

parallel teams Teams that operate separately from the regular work structure, and exist temporarily.

participation in decision making Leader behaviors that managers perform in involving their employees in making decisions.

path-goal theory A theory that concerns how leaders influence subordinates' perceptions of their work goals and the paths they follow toward attainment of those goals.

perception The process of receiving and interpreting information.

performance appraisal (PA) Assessment of an employee's job performance.

performance gap The difference between actual performance and desired performance.

planning The management function of systematically making decisions about the goals and activities that an individual, a group, a work unit, or the overall organization will pursue in the future.

plans The actions or means managers intend to use to achieve organizational goals.

plural organization An organization that has a relatively diverse employee population and makes an effort to involve employees from different gender, racial, or cultural backgrounds.

political action committees (PACs) Political action groups that represent an organization and make donations to candidates for political office.

positive reinforcement Applying consequences that increase the likelihood that a person will repeat the behavior that led to it.

power The ability to influence others.

principle of exception A managerial principle stating that control is enhanced by concentrating on the exceptions or significant deviations from the expected result or standard.

proactive change A response that is initiated before a performance gap has occurred.

probing A team strategy that requires team members to interact frequently with outsiders, diagnose their needs, and experiment with solutions.

procedural justice Using fair process in decision making and making sure others know that the process was as fair as possible.

product champion A person who promotes a new technology throughout the organization in an effort to obtain acceptance of and support for it.

profit and loss statement An itemized financial statement of the income and expenses of a company's operations.

programmed decisions Decisions encountered and made before, having objectively correct answers, and solvable by using simple rules, policies, or numerical computations.

project and development teams Teams that work on long-term projects but disband once the work is completed.

prospectors Companies that continuously change the boundaries for their task environments by seeking new products and markets, diversifying and merging, or acquiring new enterprises.

psychological contract A set of perceptions of what employees owe their employers, and what their employers owe them.

public affairs department A department that monitors key events and trends in the organization's political and social environments, analyzes their effects on the organization, recommends organizational responses, and implements political strategies.

punishment Administering an aversive consequence.

Q

quality The excellence of a product, including such things as attractiveness, lack of defects, reliability, and long-term dependability.

quality circles Voluntary groups of people drawn from various production teams who make suggestions about quality.

quality of work life (QWL) programs Programs designed to create a workplace that enhances employee well being.

R

reactive change A response that occurs under pressure; problem-driven change.

ready-made solutions Ideas that have been seen or tried before.

recruitment The development of a pool of applicants for jobs in an organization.

reflection Process by which a person states what he or she believes the other person is saying.

refreezing Strengthening the new behaviors that support the change.

reinforcers Positive consequences that motivate behavior.

relativism Bases ethical behavior on the opinions and behaviors of relevant other people.

reliability The consistency of test scores over time and across alternative measurements.

resources Inputs to a system that can enhance performance.

responsibility The assignment of a task that an employee is supposed to carry out.

return on investment (ROI) A ratio of profit to capital used, or a rate of return from capital.

right-to-work Legislation that allows employees to work without having to join a union.

rightsizing A successful effort to achieve an appropriate size at which the company performs most effectively.

risk The state that exists when the probability of success is less than 100 percent, and losses may occur.

roles Different sets of expectations for how different individuals should behave.

S

satisficing Choosing an option that is acceptable, although not necessarily the best or perfect.

scenario A narrative that describes a particular set of future conditions.

selection Choosing from among qualified applicants to hire into an organization.

self-designing teams Teams with control over the design of the team, as well as the responsibilities of autonomous work groups.

self-managed teams Autonomous work groups in which workers are trained to do all or most of the jobs in a unit, have no immediate supervisor, and make decisions previously made by first-line supervisors.

semiautonomous work groups Groups that make decisions about managing and carrying out major production activities, but still get outside support for quality control and maintenance.

sexual harassment Conduct of a sexual nature that has negative consequences for employment.

shapers Companies that try to change the structure of their industries, creating a future competitive landscape of their own design.

side street effect As you head down a road, unexpected opportunities begin to appear.

simultaneous engineering A design approach in which all relevant functions cooperate jointly and continually in a maximum effort aimed at producing high-quality products that meet customers' needs.

situational analysis A process planners use, within time and resource constraints, to gather, interpret and summarize all information relevant to the planning issue under consideration.

situational approach Leadership perspective proposing that universally important traits and behaviors do not exist, and that effective leadership behavior varies from situation to situation.

skunkworks A project team designated to produce a new, innovative product.

small batches Technologies that produce goods and services in low volume.

small business A business having fewer than 100 employees, independently owned and operated, not dominant in its field, and not characterized by many innovative practices.

smoothing Leveling normal fluctuations at the boundaries of the environment.

social facilitation effect Working harder when in a group than when working alone.

social loafing Working less hard and being less productive when in a group.

sociotechnical systems An approach to job design that attempts to redesign tasks to optimize operation of a new technology while preserving employees' interpersonal relationships and other human aspects of the work.

span of control The number of subordinates who report directly to an executive or supervisor.

specialization A process in which different individuals and units perform different tasks.

speed Fast and timely execution, response, and delivery of results.

staff departments Units that support line departments.

stakeholders Groups and individuals who affect and are affected by the achievement of the organization's mission, goals, and strategies.

standard Expected performance for a given goal: a target that establishes a desired performance level, motivates performance, and serves as a benchmark against which actual performance is assessed.

standardization Establishing common rules and procedures that apply uniformly to everyone.

stockholders' equity The amount accruing to the corporation's owners.

stonewalling The use of public relations, legal action, and administrative processes to prevent or delay the introduction of legislation and regulation that may have an adverse impact on the organization.

strategic alliance A formal relationship created among independent organizations with the purpose of joint pursuit of mutual goals.

strategic control system A system designed to support managers in evaluating the organization's progress regarding its strategy and, when discrepancies exist, taking corrective action.

strategic goals Major targets or end results relating to the organization's long-term survival, value, and growth.

strategic leadership Behavior that gives purpose and meaning to organizations, envisioning and creating a positive future.

strategic management A process that involves managers from all parts of the organization in the formulation and implementation of strategic goals and strategies.

strategic maneuvering An organization's conscious efforts to change the boundaries of its task environment.

strategic planning A set of procedures for making decisions about the organization's long-term goals and strategies.

strategic retreat Efforts to adapt products and processes to changes in the political and social environments while minimizing the negative effects of those changes.

strategic vision The long-term direction and strategic intent of a company.

strategy A pattern of actions and resource allocations designed to achieve the organization's goals.

structured interview Selection technique that involves asking all applicants the same questions and comparing their responses to a standardized set of answers.

substitutes for leadership Factors in the workplace that can exert the same influence on employees that leaders would provide.

subunits Subdivisions of an organization.

superordinate goals A style of dealing with conflict involving moderate attention to both parties' concerns.

supervisory leadership Behavior that provides guidance, support, and corrective feedback for the day-to-day activities of work unit members.

survivor's syndrome Loss of productivity and morale in employees who remain after a downsizing.

switching costs Fixed costs buyers face when they change suppliers.

SWOT analysis A comparison of strengths, weaknesses, opportunities, and threats that helps executives formulate strategy.

T

tactical planning A set of procedures for translating broad strategic goals and plans into specific goals and plans that are relevant to a distinct portion of the organization, such as a functional area like marketing.

task performance behaviors Actions taken to ensure that the work group or organization reaches its goals.

task specialist An individual who has more advanced job-related skills and abilities than other group members possess.

team A small number of people with complementary skills who are committed to a common purpose, set of performance goals, and approach for which they hold themselves mutually accountable.

team maintenance specialist Individual who develops and maintains team harmony.

team training Training that provides employees with the skills and perspectives they need to work in collaboration with others.

technical innovator A person who develops a new technology or has the key skills to install and operate the technology.

technical skill The ability to perform a specialized task involving a particular method or process.

technology The systematic application of scientific knowledge to a new product, process, or service.

technology audit Process of clarifying the key technologies on which an organization depends.

technology life cycle A predictable pattern followed by a technological innovation, from its inception and development to market saturation and replacement.

teleology Considers an act to be morally right or acceptable if it produces a desired result.

termination interview A discussion between a manager and an employee about the employee's dismissal.

third-country nationals Natives of a country other than the home country or the host country of an overseas subsidiary.

time-based competition (TBC) Strategies aimed at reducing the total time it takes to deliver a product or service.

top-level managers Senior executives responsible for the overall management and effectiveness of the organization.

total organization change Introducing and sustaining multiple policies, practices, and procedures across multiple units and levels.

total quality management An integrative approach to management that supports the attainment of customer satisfaction through a wide variety of tools and techniques that result in high-quality goods and services.

traditional work groups Groups that have no managerial responsibilities.

training Teaching lower-level employees how to perform their present jobs.

trait approach A leadership perspective that focuses on individual leaders and attempts to determine the personal characteristics that great leaders share.

transactional leaders Leaders who manage through transactions, using their legitimate, reward, and coercive powers to give commands and exchange rewards for services rendered.

transfer price Price charged by one unit for a product or service provided to another unit within the organization.

transformational leader A leader who transforms a vision into reality and motivates people to transcend their personal interests for the good of the group.

transnational organization model An organization model characterized by centralization of certain functions in locations that best achieve cost economies; basing of other functions in the company's national subsidiaries to facilitate greater local responsiveness; and fostering of communication among subsidiaries to permit transfer of technological expertise and skills.

transnational teams Work groups composed of multinational members whose activities span multiple countries.

two-factor theory Herzberg's theory describing two factors affecting people's work motivation and satisfaction.

two-way communication A process in which information flows in two directions—the receiver provides feedback, and the sender is receptive to the feedback.

tyranny of the "or" The belief that things must be either A or B, and cannot be both; that only one goal and not another can be attained.

U

uncertainty The state that exists when decision makers have insufficient information.

unfreezing Realizing that current practices are inappropriate and that new behavior must be enacted.

union shop An organization with a union and a union security clause specifying that workers must join the union after a set period of time.

unity-of-command principle A structure in which each worker reports to one boss, who in turn reports to one boss.

universalism The ethical system upholding certain values regardless of immediate result.

upward communication Information that flows from lower to higher levels in the organization's hierarchy.

utilitarianism An ethical system stating that the greatest good for the greatest number should be the overriding concern of decision makers.

V

valence The value an outcome holds for the person contemplating it.

validity The degree to which a selection test predicts or correlates with job performance.

value chain Sequence of activities that flow from raw materials to the delivery of a product or service.

vertical integration The acquisition or development of new businesses that produce parts or components of the organization's product.

vigilance A process in which a decision maker carefully executes all stages of decision making.

virtual office A mobile office in which people can work anywhere, as long as they have the tools to communicate with customers and colleagues.

virtue ethics A perspective that what is moral comes from what a mature person with "good" moral character would deem right.

vision A mental image of a possible and desirable future state of the organization.

voluntary responsibilities Additional behaviors and activities that society finds desirable and that the values of the business support.

Vroom model A situational model that focuses on the participative dimension of leadership.

W

work teams Teams that make or do things like manufacture, assemble, sell, or provide service.

Notes

Chapter 1

1. "A Dark Year's 25 Star Managers," *Business Week*, January 14, 52–72.
2. S. Finkelstein, "The Myth of Managerial Superiority in Internet Startups: An Autopsy," *Organizational Dynamics*, Fall 2001, pp. 172–185.
3. A. Bernasek, "Okay, Now What?" *Fortune*, June 11, 2001, pp. 98–106.
4. Finkelstein, "The Myth of Managerial Superiority."
5. P. Coy, "The Creative Economy," *Business Week*, August 21–28, 2000, pp. 76–82.
6. J. A. Byrne, "Management by Web," *Business Week*, August 21–28, 2000, pp. 84–96.
7. T. J. Mulaney, "Break Out the Black Ink," *Business Week*, May 13, 2002, pp. 74–76.
8. Ibid.
9. Ibid.
10. D. Rynecki, "Make Their Pain Your Gain," *Fortune*, July 9, 2001, pp. 158–159.
11. R. Hof and S. Hamm, "How E-Biz Rose, Fell, and Will Rise Anew," *Business Week*, May 13, 2002, pp. 64–72.
12. Ibid.
13. J. Useem, "Dot-coms: What Have We Learned?" *Fortune*, October 30, 2000, pp. 82–104.
14. J. Guyon, "The American Way," *Fortune*, November 26, 2001, pp. 114–120.
15. W. J. Holstein, "The Stateless Corporation," *Business Week*, May 14, 1990, pp. 98–105.
16. *The Executive*, November 1990, pp. 70–84.
17. A. Taylor III, "Imports to Detroit: Eat Our Dust." *Fortune*, June 11, 2001, pp. 150–154.
18. K. Capell, "MTV's World," *Business Week*, February 18, 2002, pp. 81–84.
19. B. O'Keefe, "Global Brands," *Fortune*, November 26, 2001, pp. 102–110.
20. P. Ghemawat, "Distance Still Matters: The Hard Reality of Global Expansion," *Harvard Business Review*, September 2001, pp. 137–147.
21. S. Rangan, "Profits and the Internet: Seven Misconceptions," *Sloan Management Review*, Summer 2001, pp. 44–53.
22. Coy, "The Creative Economy."
23. Ibid.
24. N. Gross, "Mining a Company's Mother Lode of Talent," *Business Week*, August 28, 2000, pp. 135–37.
25. S. Cranor, *The Management Century*, (San Francisco: Jossey-Bass, 2000).
26. M. Hansen and B. von Oetinger, "Introducing T-Shaped Managers: Knowledge Management's Next Generation," *Harvard Business Review*, March 2001, pp. 106–116.
27. "An E-Business Road Map," *Business Week*, May 13, 2002, p. 70.
28. Byrne, "Management by Web."
29. Ibid.
30. C. Loomis (Ed.) "Mr. Buffet on the Stock Market," *Fortune*, November 22, 2000, pp. 212–20.
31. Ibid.
32. M. Loeb, "How's Business?" *Fortune*, January 16, 1995, pp. 135–36.
33. L. M. Bellman, "Bricks and Mortar: 21st Century Survival," *Business Horizons*, May–June, 2001, pp. 21–28.
34. G. Hamel, "Avoiding the Guillotine," *Fortune*, April 2, 2001, pp. 139–144.
35. Ibid., p. 140.
36. R. I. Sutton, "The Weird Rules of Creativity," *Harvard Business Review*, September, 2001, pp. 94–103.
37. Hamel, "Avoiding the Guillotine."
38. L. Willcocks and R. Plant, "Pathways to E-Business Leadership: Getting from Bricks to Clicks," *Sloan Management Review*, Spring 2001, pp. 50–59.
39. D. Feeny, "Making Business Sense of the E-Opportunity," *Sloan Management Review*, Winter 2001, pp. 41–51.
40. H. L. Lee and S. Whang, "Winning the Last Mile of E-Commerce," *Sloan Management Review*, Summer 2001, pp. 54–62.
41. Taylor, "Imports to Detroit: Eat Our Dust."
42. D. A. Garvin, "Manufacturing Strategic Planning," *California Management Review*, Summer 1993, pp. 85–106.
43. Byrne, "Management by Web."
44. A. Muoio, "Should I Go.Com?" *Fast Company*, July 2000, p. 164.
45. Taylor, "Imports to Detroit: Eat Our Dust."
46. J. Simons, "Internet Survivors," *Fortune*, July 9, 2001, pp. 155–156.
47. E. Brown, "Heartbreak Hotel? *Fortune*, November 26, 2001, pp. 161–165.
48. M. Boyle, "What We Learned," *Fortune*, December 24, 2001, pp. 179–180.
49. Ibid.
50. J. Useem, "Dot-Coms: What Have We Learned?"
51. D. Kirkpatrick, "Now Everyone in PCs Wants to Be Like Mike," *Fortune*, September 8, 1997, pp. 47–48.
52. Ibid.
53. J. W. Cortada, *21st Century Business*, (London: Financial Times/Prentice Hall, 2001).
54. J. Collins, "Don't Rewrite the Rules of the Road." *Business Week*, August 28, 2000, pp. 206–8.
55. Ibid.
56. P. Shenon, "U.S. Agencies Seen as Slow to Move on Terrorism Risk," *New York Times*, May 12, 2002, pp. 1, 6.
57. J. Kahn and B. O'Keefe, "Best & Worst 2001," *Fortune*, December 24, 2001, pp. 139–144.
58. R. Webber, "General Management Past and Future," *Financial Times Mastering Management*, 1997.
59. H. Collingwood and D. Coutu, "Jack on Jack: The HBR Interview," *Harvard Business Review*, February 2002, pp. 88–94.
60. Q. N. Huy, "In Praise of Middle Managers," *Harvard Business Review*, September 2001, pp. 72–79.
61. C. Bartlett and S. Goshal, "The Myth of the Generic Manager: New Personal Competencies for New Management Roles," *California Management Review*, 40, no. 1, (1997) pp. 92–116.
62. L. R. Sayles "Doing Things Right: A New Imperative for Middle Managers," *Organizational Dynamics*, Spring 1993, pp. 5–14.
63. R. Katz, "Skills of an Effective Administrator," *Harvard Business Review*, 52 (September–October), pp. 90–102.
64. H. Mintzberg, "The Manager's Job: Folklore and Fact," *Harvard Business Review*, 53 (July–August 1975), pp. 49–61.
65. A. Deutschman, "The Trouble with MBAs," *Fortune*, July 29, 1991, pp. 67–79.
66. S. Lehrman, "Putting Management Potential to the Test," *Bryan-College Station Eagle*, December 8, 1985, p. 3F.
67. M. W. McCall, Jr. *High Flyers: Developing the Next Generation of Leaders* (Boston: Harvard Business School Press, 1997).
68. P. Cappelli, "Career Jobs are Dead," *California Management Review*, Fall 1999, pp. 146–67.
69. S. M. Jacoby, "Are Career Jobs Headed for Extinction?" *California Management Review*, Fall 1999, pp. 123–45.
70. W. Kiechel III, "A Manager's Career in the New Economy," *Fortune*, April 4, 1994, pp. 68–72.
71. Ibid.
72. K. Inkson and M. B. Arther, "How to Be a Successful Career Capitalist," *Organizational Dynamics*, Summer 2001, pp. 48–60.
73. Kiechel, "A Manager's Career in the New Economy."
74. S. Seibert, M. Kraimer, and R. Liden, "A Social Capital Theory of Career Success," *Academy of Management Journal*, vol. 44, 2001, pp. 219–237.
75. B. O'Brian, and G. Stern, "Nonstop Networking Propels an Accountant into U.S. Big Leagues," *The Wall Street Journal*, March 20, 1997, pp. 1, 2.
76. T. Peters, *Liberation Management* (New York: Alfred A. Knopf, 1992).

77. D. Brady, "Wanted: Eclectic Visionary with a Sense of Humor," *Business Week*, August 21–28, 2000, pp. 143–44.
78. T. Peters, "The New Wired World of Work," *Business Week*, August 21–28, 2000, p. 172–74.
79. Ibid.
80. J. Kotter, *The New Rules: How to Succeed in Today's Post-Corporate World*, (New York: The Free Press, 1995).
81. Ibid.

Appendix A

1. C. George, *The History of Management Thought* (Englewood Cliffs, NJ: Prentice-Hall, 1972).
2. Ibid.
3. A. D. Chandler, *Scale and Scope: The Dynamic of Industrial Capitalism* (Cambridge, MA: Belknap Press of Harvard University Press, 1990).
4. Ibid.
5. J. Baughman, *The History of American Management* (Englewood Cliffs, NJ: Prentice-Hall, 1969), chap. 1.
6. George, *The History of Management Thought*, chaps. 5–7; F. Taylor, The Principles of Scientific Management (New York: Harper & Row, 1911).
7. J. Case, "A Company of Businesspeople," *Inc.*, April 1993, pp. 70–93.
8. H. Kroos and C. Gilbert, *The Principles of Scientific Management* (New York: Harper & Row, 1911).
9. H. Fayol, *General and Industrial Management*, trans. C. Storrs (Marshfield, MA: Pitman Publishing, 1949).
10. George, *The History of Management Thought*, chap. 9; J. Massie, "Management Theory," in *Handbook of Organizations*, ed. J. March (Chicago: Rand McNally, 1965), pp. 387–422.
11. C. Barnard, *The Functions of the Executive* (Cambridge, MA: Harvard University Press, 1938).
12. George, *The History of Management Thought*: Massie, "Management Theory."
13. E. Mayo, *The Human Problems of Industrial Civilization* (New York: Macmillan, 1933): F. Roethlisberger and W. Dickson, *Management and the Worker* (Cambridge, MA: Harvard University Press, 1939).
14. A. Maslow, "A Theory of Human Motivation," *Psychological Review*, 50 (July 1943), pp. 370–96.
15. A. Carey, "The Hawthorne Studies: A Radical Criticism," *American Sociological Review*, 32 no.3 (1967), pp. 403–16.
16. M. Weber, *The Theory of Social and Economic Organizations*, trans. T. Parsons and A. Henderson (New York: Free Press, 1947).
17. George, *The History of Management Thought*, chap. 11.
18. D. McGregor, *The Human Side of Enterprise* (New York: McGraw-Hill, 1960).
19. C. Argyris, *Personality and Organization* (New York: Harper & Row, 1957).
20. R. Likert, *The Human Organization* (New York: McGraw-Hill, 1967).

21. L. von Bertalanffy, "The History and Status of General Systems Theory," *Academy of Management Journal*, 15 (1972), pp. 407–26; D. Katz and R. Kahn, *The Social Psychology of Organizations*, 2nd ed. (New York: John Wiley & Sons, 1978).
22. J. Thompson, *Organizations in Action* (New York: McGraw-Hill, 1967); J. Galbraith, *Organization Design* (Reading, MA: Addison-Wesley, 1977); D. Miller and P. Friesen, *Organizations: A Quantum View* (Englewood Cliffs, NJ: Prentice-Hall, 1984).
23. S. Crainer, *The Management Century* (San Francisco: Jossey-Bass, 2000).
24. Ibid.

Chapter 2

1. Catherine Arnst, John Carey, and Jack Ewing, "Where IMClone Went Wrong," *Business Week Online*, February 18, 2002, www.businessweek.com.
2. Amy Tsao, "This Time, Tech Will Follow, Not Lead," *Business Week Online*, November 12, 2001, www.businessweek.com; D. Kadlec, "The Nasdaq: What a Drag!" *Time*, October 23, 2000, 156, no. 17, pp. 72–73.
3. "Labor Force (Demographic) Data," U.S. Department of Labor, Bureau of Labor Statistics Web site, accessed September 23, 2002, www.bls.gov/emp/emplabl.htm; Judith J. Friedman and Nancy DiTomaso, "Myths about Diversity: What Managers Need to Know about Changes in the U.S. Labor Force," *California Management Review*, 38, no. 4 (Summer 1996), pp. 54–77.
4. "NRDC Report Finds Improved Fuel Efficiency Expands Consumer Choice," National Resources Defense Council press release, July 30, 2001, www.nrdc.org, accessed at ww.nrdc.org/media/pressrel eases/0107300aso.
5. Johnathan R. Laing, "Just Spiffy," *Barron's* 77, no. 12 (March 24, 1997), pp. 37–42; Matthew J. Kiernan, "Get Innovative or Get Dead," *Business Quarterly*, 61, no. 1 (Autumn 1996), pp. 51–58.
6. David J. Collis and Cynthis A. Montgomery. *Corporate Strategy: Resources and Scope of the Firm* (Burr Ridge, IL: McGraw-Hill/Irwin, 1997).
7. Roger Hallowell, "Southwest Airlines: A Case Study Linking Employee Needs, Satisfaction, and Organizational Capabilities to Competitive Advantage," *Human Resource Management*, 35, no. 4 (Winter 1996), pp. 513–34: Wendy Zeller, "Greyhound Is Limping Badly," *Business Week*, August 22, 1994, p. 32.
8. Brian K. Schimmoller, "Magicians Wanted," *Power Engineering*, August 2000, 104 no. 8, p. 3.
9. "Woods Is Fined By Actors' Union," *New York Times*, November 11, 2000, p. 7; Arthur Sherman, George Bohlander, and Scott Snell, *Managing*

Human Resources, 11th ed. (Cincinnati, OH: Southwestern Publishing, 1998).
10. Brent Schlender, "The Adventures of Scott McNealy: Javamtan," *Fortune*, 136, no. 7 (October 13, 1997), pp. 70–78.
11. P. Kotler, *Marketing Management: Analysis, Planning, Implementation and Control*, 9th ed. (Englewood Cliffs, NJ: Prentice-Hall, 1990).
12. Aaron A. Buchko, "Conceptualization and Measurement of Environmental Uncertainty: An Assessment of the Miles and Snow Perceived Environmental Uncertainty Scale," *Academy of Management Journal*, 37, no. 2 (April 1994), pp. 410–25.
13. Abdalla F. Hagen, "Corporate Executives and Environmental Scanning Activities: An Empirical Investigation." *SAM Advanced Management Journal*, 60, no. 2 (Spring 1995), pp. 41–47; Richard L. Daft. "Chief Executive Scanning, Environmental Characteristics, and Company Performance: An Empirical Study," *Strategic Management Journal*, 9, no. 2 (March/April 1988), pp. 123–39; Masoud Yasai-Ardekani, "Designs for Environmental Scanning Systems: Tests of a Contingency Theory," *Management Science*, 42, no. 2 (February 1996), pp. 187–204.
14. Sumantra Ghoshal, "Building Effective Intelligence Systems for Competitive Advantage," *Sloan Management Review*, 28, no. 1 (Fall 1986), pp. 49–58: Kenneth D. Cory, "Can Competitive Intelligence Lead to a Sustainable Competitive Advantage?" *Competitive Intelligence Review*, 7, no. 3 (Fall 1996), pp. 45–55.
15. Paul J. H. Schoemaker, "Multiple Scenario Development: Its Conceptual and Behavioral Foundation," *Strategic Management Journal*, 14, no. 3 (March 1993), pp. 193–213.
16. Robin R. Peterson, "An Analysis of Contemporary Forecasting in Small Business," *Journal of Business Forecasting Methods & Systems*, 15, no. 2 (Summer 1996), pp. 10–12; Spyros Makridakis. "Business Forecasting for Management: Strategic Business Forecasting," *International Journal of Forecasting*, 12, no. 3 (September 1996), pp. 435–37.
17. Irving DeToro, "The 10 Pitfalls of Benchmarking," *Quality Progress* 28, no. 1 (January 1995), pp. 61–63.
18. Martin B. Meznar, "Buffer or Bridge? Environmental and Organizational Determinants of Public Affairs Activities in American Firms," *Academy of Management Journal*, 38, no. 4 (August 1995), pp. 975–96.
19. David Lei, "Advanced Manufacturing Technology: Organizational Design and Strategic Flexibility," *Organization Studies*, 17, no. 3 (1996), pp. 501–23; James W. Dean, Jr., and Scott A. Snell, "The Strategic Use of Integrated Manufacturing: An Empirical Examination," *Strategic Management Journal*, 17, no. 6 (June 1996), pp. 459–80.

20. C. Zeithaml and V. Zeithaml, "Environmental Management: Revising the Marketing Perspective," *Journal of Marketing*, 48 (Spring 1984), pp. 46–53.

21. Willem P. Burgers, "Cooperative Strategy in High Technology Industries," *International Journal of Management*, 13, no. 2 (June 1996), pp. 127–34; Jeffrey E. McGee, "Cooperative Strategy and New Venture Performance: The Role of Business Strategy and Management Experience," *Strategic Management Journal*, 16, no. 7 (October 1995), pp. 565–80.

22. Richard A.D' Aveni, *Hypercompetition—Managing the Dynamics of Strategic Maneuvering* (New York, Free Press 1994); Michael A. Cusumano, "Strategic Maneuvering and Mass-Market Dynamics: The Triumph of VHS over Beta," *Business History Review*, 66, no. 1 (Spring 1992), pp. 51–94.

23. R. Miles and C. Snow, *Organizational Strategy, Structure, and Process* (New York: McGraw-Hill, 1978).

Chapter 3

1. T. Peters, *Liberation Management* (New York: Alfred A. Knopf, 1992).

2. M. Magasin and F. L. Gehlen, "Unwise Decisions and Unanticipated Consequences," *Sloan Management Review*, 41 (1999), pp. 47–60.

3. M. McCall and R. Kaplan, *Whatever It Takes: Decision Makers at Work* (Englewood Cliffs, NJ: Prentice-Hall, 1985).

4. B. Bass, *Organizational Decision Making* (Homewood, IL: Richard D. Irwin, 1983).

5. J. March, "Bounded Rationality, Ambiguity, and the Engineering of Choice," *Bell Journal of Economics*, 9 (1978), pp. 587–608.

6. D. Messick and M. Bazerman, "Ethical Leadership and the Psychology of Decision Making," *Sloan Management Review*, Winter 1996, pp. 9–22.

7. K. Olsson, "In Texas, the Best Kind of Failure Is Spectacular," *The Washington Post*, February 3, 2002, pp. B1, B3.

8. J. Kahn, "Stop Me Before I Pollute Again," *Fortune*, January 21, 2002, pp. 87–90.

9. D. Jones, "Playing the Weather Game," *USA Today*, December 11, 2001, pp. 1B–2B.

10. N. Carr, "On the Edge: An Interview with Akamai's George Conrades," *Harvard Business Review*, May–June 2000, pp. 118–25.

11. G. A. Garvin, "Building a Learning Organization," *Harvard Business Review*, July–August 1993, pp. 78–91.

12. McCall and Kaplan, *Whatever It Takes*.

13. K. MacCrimmon and R. Taylor, "Decision Making and Problem Solving," in *Handbook of Industrial and Organizational Psychology*, ed. M. D. Dunnette (Chicago: Rand McNally, 1976).

14. Q. Spitzer and R. Evans, *Heads, You Win! How the Best Companies Think* (New York: Simon & Schuster, 1997).

15. C. Gettys and S. Fisher, "Hypothesis Plausibility and Hypotheses Generation," *Organizational Behavior and Human Performance*, 24 (1979), pp. 93–110.

16. E. R. Alexander, "The Design of Alternatives in Organizational Contexts: A Pilot Study," *Administrative Science Quarterly*, 24 (1979), pp. 382–404.

17. P. Nayak and J. Ketteringham, *Breakthroughs* (New York: Rawson Associates, 1986).

18. A. R. Rao, M. E. Bergen, and S. Davis, "How to Fight a Price War," *Harvard Business Review*, March–April 2000, pp. 107–16.

19. Ibid.

20. J. O'Toole, *Vanguard Management: Redesigning the Corporate Future* (Garden City, NY: Doubleday, 1985).

21. McCall and Kaplan, *Whatever It Takes*.

22. Spitzer and Evans, *Heads, You Win!*

23. K. Labich, "Four Possible Futures," *Fortune*, January 25, 1993, pp. 40–48.

24. McCall and Kaplan, *Whatever It Takes*.

25. M. B. Stein, "Teaching Steelcase to Dance," *New York Times Magazine*, April 1, 1990, pp. 22ff.

26. D. Siebold, "Making Meetings More Successful," *Journal of Business Communication*, 16 (Summer 1979), pp. 3–20.

27. I. Janis and L. Mann, *Decision Making* (New York: Free Press, 1977): Bass, *Organizational Decision Making*.

28. J. W. Dean, Jr., and M. Sharfman, "Does Decision Process Matter? A Study of Strategic Decision-Making Effectiveness," *Academy of Management Journal*, 39 (1996), pp. 368–96.

29. R. Nisbett and L. Ross, *Human Inference: Strategies and Shortcomings* (Englewood Cliffs, NJ: Prentice-Hall, 1980).

30. R. Lowenstein, *When Genius Failed.* (New York: Random House, 2000).

31. Messick and Bazerman, "Ethical Leadership."

32. S. Pearlstein, and P. Behr, "At Enron, the Fall Came Quickly," *The Washington Post*, December 2, 2001, pp. A1–A11.

33. T. Bateman and C. Zeithaml, "The Psychological Context of Strategic Decisions: A Model and Convergent Experimental Findings," *Strategic Management Journal*, 10 (1989), pp. 59–74.

34. Messick and Bazerman, "Ethical, Leadership."

35. N. Adler, *International Dimensions of Organizational Behavior* (Boston: Kent, 1990).

36. K. M. Esenhardt, "Speed and Strategic Choice: How Managers Accelerate Decision Making," *California Management Review*, 32 (Spring 1990), pp. 39–54.

37. Q. Spitzer and R. Evans, "New Problems in Problem Solving," *Across the Board*, April 1997, pp. 36–40.

38. G. W. Hill, "Group versus Individual Performance: Are n + 1 Heads Better than 1?" *Psychological Bulletin*, 91 (1982), pp. 517–39.

39. N. R. F. Maier, "Assets and Liabilities in Group Problem Solving: The Need for an Integrative Function," *Psychological Review*, 74 (1967), pp. 239–49.

40. Ibid.

41. D. A. Garvin, and M. A. Roberto, "What You Don't Know about Making Decisions," *Harvard Business Review*, September 2001, pp. 108–16.

42. R. Cosier and C. Schwenk, "Agreement and Thinking Alike: Ingredients for Poor Decisions," *The Executive*, February 1990, pp. 69–74.

43. A. Amason, "Distinguishing the Effects of Functional and Dysfunctional Conflict on Strategic Decision Making: Resolving a Paradox for Top Management Teams," *Academy of Management Journal*, 39 (1996), pp. 123–48. R. Dooley and G. Fyxell, "Attaining Decision Quality and Commitment from Dissent: The Moderating Effects of Loyalty and Competence in Strategic Decision-Making Teams," *Academy of Management Journal*, August 1999, pp. 389–402.

44. K. Eisenhardt. J. Kahwajy, and L. J. Bourgeois III, "Conflict and Strategic Choice: How Top Management Teams Disagree," *California Management Review*, Winter 1997, pp. 42–62.

45. Cosier and Schwenk, "Agreement and Thinking Alike."

46. Ibid.

47. C. Knowlton, "How Disney Keeps the Magic Going," *Fortune*, December 4, 1989, pp. 115–32.

48. P. LaBerre, "The Creative Revolution," *Industry Week*, May 16, 1994, pp. 12–19.

49. J. V. Anderson, "Weirder Than Fiction: The Reality and Myths of Creativity," *Academy of Management Executive*, November 1992, pp. 40–47; J. Krohe Jr., "Managing Creativity," *Across the Board*, September 1996, pp. 17–21; R. I. Sutton, "The Weird Rules of Creativity," *Harvard Business Review*, September 2001, pp. 94–103.

50. A. Farnham, "How to Nurture Creative Sparks," *Fortune*, January 10, 1994, pp. 94–100; T. M. Amabile, "A Model of Creativity and Innovation in Organizations," in *Research and Organizational Behavior*, ed. B. Straw and L. Cummings, vol. 10 (1988), pp. 123–68.

51. R. Sutton and A. Hargadon "Brainstorming Groups in Context: Effectiveness in a Product Design Firm." *Administrative Design Quarterly*, 41 (1996), pp. 685–718.

52. Dean and Sharfman, "Does Decision Process Matter?"

53. K. Eisenhardt. J. Kahwajy, and L. J. Bourgeois III, "How Management Teams Can Have a Good Fight," *Harvard Management Review*, July–August 1997, pp. 77–85.

54. J. E. Jackson and W. T. Schantz, "Crisis Management Lessons: When Push Shoved Nike," *Business Horizons*, January–February 1993, pp. 27–35.

55. C. M. Pearson and I. I. Mitroff, "From Crisis Prone to Crisis Prepared:

A Framework for Crisis Management," *The Academy of Management Executive,* February 1993, pp. 48–59.

56. J. Hickman, and W. Crandall, "Before Disaster Hits: A Multifaceted Approach to Crisis Management," *Business Horizons,* March–April 1997, pp. 75–79.

57. G. Meyers with J. Holusha, *When It Hits the Fan: Managing the Nine Crises of Business* (Boston: Houghton Mifflin, 1986).

58. McCall and Kaplan, *Whatever It Takes.*

59. J. Dutton, P. Frost, M. Worline, J. Lilius, and J. Kanov, "Leading in Times of Trauma," *Harvard Business Review,* January 2002, pp. 54–61.

60. J. Useem, "What It Takes," *Fortune,* November 12, 2001, pp. 126–32.

61. H. Mintzberg, and F. Westley, "Decision Making: It's Not What You Think," *Sloan Management Review,* Spring 2001, pp. 89–93.

Chapter 4

1. J. Bracker and J. Pearson, "Planning and Financial Performance of Small Mature Firms," *Strategic Management Journal* 7 (1986), pp. 503–22; Philip Waalewijn and Peter Segaar, "Strategic Management: The Key to Profitability in Small Companies," *Long Range Planning,* 26, no. 2 (April 1993), pp. 24–30.

2. Aramark annual report, 1997.

3. "Y2K Planning Pays Off," *Government Executive,* February 2000, 32, no. 2, p. 9.

4. V. Viswanath and D. Harding, "The Starbuck Effect," *Harvard Business Review,* March–April, 2000; M. Hornblower, "Wake Up and Smell the Protest," *Time,* April 17, 2000; M. Gimein, "Right On: Starbucks Makes a Net Play," *Fortune,* March 6, 2000; L. Lee, "Now, Starbucks Uses Its Bean," *Business Week,* February 14, 2000; R. Papiernik, "Starbucks Starts Fiscal 2000 with 30% Profit Growth in 1st Q," *Nation's Restaurant News,* February 7, 2000; K. Holland, "Starbucks Thinks It Will Travel Well," *Business Week,* November 16, 1998; N. Weiss, "How Starbucks Impassions Workers to Drive Growth," *Workforce,* August, 1998; J. Reese, "Starbucks: Inside the Coffee Cult," *Fortune,* December 9, 1997; K. Strauss, 'Howard Schultz: Starbucks' CEO Serves a Blend of Community, Employee Commitment," *Nation's Restaurant News,* January 2000; "Interview with Howard Schultz: Sharing Success," *Executive Excellence,* November 1999; N. D. Schwartz, "Still Perking After All These Years," *Fortune,* May 24, 1999.

5. "Business: Fading Fads," *The Economist,* April 22, 2000, 355, no. 8167, pp. 60–61.

6. Steven W. Floyd and Peter J Lane, "Strategizing throughout the Organization: Management Role Conflict in Strategic Renewal," *Academy of Manage-*

ment Review, January 2000, 25, no. 1, pp 154–177. Don MacRae, "Seeing beyond Monday Morning," *Business Week,* November 22, 2000, online.

7. www.washingtonpost.com, accessed September 23, 2002; www.barnesandnoble.com, accessed September 23, 2002.

8. Arthur A. Thompson and A. J. Strickland III, *Strategic Management: Concepts and Cases,* 8th ed. (Burr Ridge, IL: Richard D. Irwin, 1995), p. 23.

9. Roger Hallowell, "Southwest Airlines: A Case Study Linking Employee Needs Satisfaction and Organizational Capabilities to Competitive Advantage," *Human Resource Management,* 35, no. 4 (Winter 1996), pp. 513–34.

10. Collis and Montgomery, *Corporate Strategy.*

11. Ibid.

12. www.att.com/quality, accessed September 23, 2002.

13. Robert C. Camp. "A Bible for Benchmarking, by Xerox," *Financial Executive* 9, no. 4 (July/August 1993) pp. 23–27. See also Dawn Anfuso, "At L. L. Bean, Quality Starts with People," *Personnel Journal* 73, no. 1 (January 1994), p. 60; Ken Stork, "Benchmarking: Analyze as You Go about Planning," *Purchasing,* October 19, 2000, 129, no. 7, p. 33.

14. Robert E. Hoskisson, "Corporate Divestiture Intensity in Restructuring Firms: Effects of Governance, Strategy, and Performance," *Academy of Management Journal,* 37, no. 5, (October 1994), pp. 1207–51; S. Gannes, "Merck Has Made Biotech Work," *Fortune,* January 19, 1987, pp. 58–64; Mark Maremont. "Why Kodak's Dazzling Spin-Off Didn't Bedazzle," *Business Week,* June 28, 1993, p. 34; Emily S. Plishner, "Eastman Chemical Spins Out of the Kodak Family Portrait," *Chemical Week,* 152, no. 24 (June 23, 1993), p. 7.

15. Stratford Sherman, "Why Disney Had to Buy ABC," *Fortune,* 132, no. 5, (September 4, 1995), p. 80.

16. M. Porter, *Competitive Advantage* (New York: Free Press, 1985), pp. 11–14.

17. John Huey, "Outlaw Flyboy CEOs," *Fortune,* November 13, 2000, 142, no. 11, pp. 237–250.

18. Anne Faircloth, "One-on-One Shopping," *Fortune,* July 7, 1997, pp. 235–236; Melanie Wells. "Are Dynasties Dying?" *Forbes,* March 6, 2000, p. 126.

19. R. A. Eisenstat, "Implementing Strategy: Developing a Partnership for Change," *Planning Review,* September–October 1993, pp. 33–36.

Chapter 5

1. K. Eichenwald, "Audacious Climb to Success Ended in a Dizzying Plunge," *The New York Times,* January 13, 2002, pp. 1–27.

2. L. J. Davis, "Enron? We're Missing the Point," *The Washington Post,* January 6, 2002, p. B1.

3. A. Bernstein, with B. Grow, D. Little, S. Holmes, and D. Brady, "Bracing for

a Backlash," *Business Week Online,* February 4, 2002, pp. 34–36.

4. A. Borrus, "Enron: Where Are America's CEOs?" *Business Week Online,* February 2002.

5. M. E. Guy, *Ethical Decision Making in Everyday Work Situations* (New York: Quorum Books, 1990).

6. O. C. Ferrell and J. Fraedrich, *Business Ethics: Ethical Decision Making and Cases,* 3rd ed. (Boston: Houghton Mifflin, 1997).

7. Ibid.

8. Guy, *Ethical Decision Making.*

9. Ferrell and Fraedrich, *Business Ethics.*

10. L. Kohlberg and D. Candee, "The Relationship of Moral Judgment to Moral Action" in *Morality, Moral Behavior, and Moral Development,* ed. W. M. Kurtines and J. L. Gerwitz (New York: John Wiley & Sons, 1984).

11. L. K. Trevino, "Ethical Decision Making in Organizations: A Person-Situation Interactionist Model," *Academy of Management Review,* pp. 601–17.

12. Ferrell and Fraedrich, *Business Ethics.*

13. J. Krohe Jr., "Ethics Are Nice, but Business Is Business," *Across the Board,* April 1997, pp. 16–22.

14. Ibid.

15. J. Badarocco Jr. and A. Webb, "Business Ethics: A View from the Trenches," *California Management Review,* Winter 1995, pp. 8–28.

16. G. Laczniak, M. Berkowitz, R. Brookes, and J. Hale, "The Business of Ethics: Improving or Deteriorating?" *Business Horizons,* January–February 1995, pp. 39–47.

17. S. Brenner and E. Molander, "Is the Ethics of Business Changing?" in *Ethics in Practice: Managing the Moral Corporation,* ed. K. Andrews (Cambridge, MA: Harvard Business School Press, 1989).

18. M. Gunther, "God & Business," *Fortune,* July 9, 2001, pp. 58–80.

19. R. T. De George, *Business Ethics,* 3rd ed. (New York: Macmillan, 1990).

20. J. B. Ciulla, "Why Is Business Talking about Ethics? Reflections on Foreign Conversations," *California Management Review,* Fall 1991, pp. 67–80.

21. R. E. Allinson, "A Call for Ethically Centered Management," *Academy of Management Executive,* February 1995, pp. 73–76.

22. R. A. Cooke, "Danger Signs of Unethical Behavior: How to Determine if Your Firm Is at Ethical Risk," *Journal of Business Ethics,* April 1991, pp. 249–53.

23. Krohe, "Ethics Are Nice."

24. K. Gibson, "Excuses, Excuses: Moral Slippage in the Workplace," *Business Horizons,* November–December 2000, pp. 65–72.

25. D. Messick and M. Bazerman, "Ethical Leadership and the Psychology of Decision Making," *Sloan Management Review,* Winter 1996, pp. 9–22.

26. Krohe, "Ethics Are Nice."

27. C. Handy, *Beyond Uncertainty: The Changing Worlds of Organizations*

(Boston: Harvard Business School Press, 1996).

28. Ciulla, "Why Is Business Talking about Ethics?"

29. A. Farnham, "State Your Values, Hold the Hot Air," *Fortune*, April 19, 1993, pp. 117–24.

30. Ibid.

31. G. R. Weaver, L. K. Trevino, and P. L. Cochran, "Corporate Ethics Programs as Control Systems: Influences of Executive Commitment and Environmental Factors," *Academy of Management Journal*, 42 (1999), pp. 41–57.

32. L. S. Paine, "Managing for Organizational Integrity," *Harvard Business Review*, March–April 1994, pp. 106–17.

33. F. Hall and E. Hall, "The ADA: Going beyond the Law," *The Academy of Management Executive*, February 1994, pp. 7–13; A. Farnham, "Brushing Up Your Vision Thing," *Fortune*, May 1, 1995, p. 129.

34. G. R. Weaver, L. K. Trevino, and P. L. Cochran, "Integrated and Decoupled Corporate Social Performance: Management Commitments, External Pressures, and Corporate Ethics Practices" *Academy of Management Journal*, 42 (1999), pp. 539–52.

35. Paine, "Managing for Organizational Integrity."

36. Krohe, "Ethics Are Nice."

37. J. L. Badaracco, Jr., "We Don't Need Another Hero," *Harvard Business Review*, September 2001, pp. 120–26.

38. Guy, *Ethical Decision Making*; D. Kirrane, "Managing Values: A Systematic Approach to Business Ethics," *Training and Development Journal*, November 1990, pp. 53–60.

39. J. Frey, "The Woman Who Saw Red," *The Washington Post*, January 25, 2002, p. C8.

40. C. E. Mayer and A. Joyce, "Blowing the Whistle," *The Washington Post*, February 10, 2002, pp. H1, H5.

41. R. P. Nielson, "What Can Managers Do about Unethical Management?" *Journal of Business Ethics*, May 1987, pp. 309–20.

42. L. Preston and J. Post, eds., *Private Management and Public Policy* (Englewood Cliffs, NJ: Prentice-Hall, 1975).

43. Ferrel and Fraedrich, *Business Ethics*.

44. Ibid.

45. D. Quinn and T. Jones, "An Agent Morality View of Business Policy," *Academy of Management Review* 20 (1995), pp. 22–42.

46. M. Witzel, "Not for Wealth Alone: The Rise of Business Ethics," *Financial Times Mastering Management Review*, November 1999, pp. 14–19.

47. D. C. Korten, *When Corporations Ruled the World* (San Francisco: Berrett-Koehler, 1995).

48. Handy, *Beyond Certainty*.

49. Quinn and Jones, "An Agent Morality View of Business Policy."

50. Handy, *Beyond Certainty*.

51. H. J. Reitz, J. A. Wall, Jr., and M. S. Love, "Ethics in Negotiation: Oil and Water or Good Lubrication?" *Business Horizons*, May–June 1998, pp. 5–14.

52. D. Turban and D. Greening, "Corporate Social Performance and Organizational Attractiveness to Prospective Employees," *Academy of Management Journal*, 40 (1997), pp. 658–72.

53. Handy, *Beyond Certainty*.

54. S. Waddock and N. Smith, "Corporate Responsibility Audits: Doing Well by Doing Good," *Sloan Management Review*, Winter 2000, pp. 75–83.

55. J. Collins and J. Porras, *Built to Last: Successful Habits of Visionary Companies* (London: Century Business, 1996).

56. Ibid.

57. R. Ackerman and R. Bauer, *Corporate Social Responsiveness* (Reston, VA: Reston, 1976).

58. M. B. E. Clarkson, "A Stakeholder Framework for Analyzing and Evaluating Corporate Social Performance," *Academy of Management Review*, 20 (1995), pp. 92–117.

59. J. S. Harrison and R. E. Freeman, "Stakeholders, Social Responsibility, and Performance: Empirical Evidence and Theoretical Perspectives," *Academy of Management Journal*, 42 (1999), pp. 479–85.

60. Ibid.

61. J. Gale and R. A. Buchholz, "The Political Pursuit of Competitive Advantage: What Business Can Gain from Government," in *Business Strategy and Public Policy: Perspectives from Industry and Academia*, ed. A. A. Marcus, A. M. Kaufman, and D. R. Beam (Westport, CT: Greenwood Press, 1987), pp. 31–41.

62. T. Parsons and C. Perrow, *Complex Organizations*, 2nd ed. (Glenview, IL: Scott, Foresman, 1979).

63. B. Baysinger, "Domain Maintenance as an Objective of Business Political Activity," *Academy of Management Review*, 9 (1984), pp. 248–58.

64. P. Andrews, "The Sticky Wicket of Evaluating Public Affairs: Thoughts about a Framework," *Public Affairs Review*, 6 (1986), pp. 94–105.

65. S. Lusterman, *The Organization and Staffing of Corporate Public Affairs* (New York: Conference Board, 1987).

66. C. Zeithaml, G. Keim, and B. Baysinger, "Toward an Integrated Strategic Management Process: An Empirical Review of Corporate Political Strategy," in *Strategic Management Frontiers*, ed. John H. Grant (Greenwich, CT: JAI Press, 1988), pp. 377–93.

67. J. Stephens, "Hard Money, Strong Arms and 'Matrix'," *The Washington Post*, February 10, 2002, pp. A1, A16–17.

68. A. Berenson and J. D. Glater, "A Tattered Andersen Fights for Its Future," *The New York Times*, January 13, 2002, sec. 3, pp. 1–11.

69. A. J. Hillman and M. A. Hitt, "Corporate Political Strategy Formulation: A Model of Approach, Participation, and Strategy Decisions," *Academy of Management Review*, 24 (1999), pp. 825–42.

70. A. Bernstein, "Too Much Corporate Power?" *Business Week*, September 11, 2000, pp. 145–58.

71. G. Keim and C. Zeithaml, "Corporate Political Strategy and Legislative Decision Making," *Academy of Management Review*, 1986, pp. 828–43.

72. S. L. Hart and M. B. Milstein, "Global Sustainability and the Creative Destruction of Industries," *Sloan Management Review*, Fall 1999, pp. 23–33.

73. P. M. Senge and G. Carstedt, "Innovating Our Way to the Next Industrial Revolution," *Sloan Management Review*, Winter 2001, pp. 24–38.

74. C. Holliday, "Sustainable Growth, the DuPont Way," *Harvard Business Review*, September 2001, pp. 129–34.

75. P. Shrivastava, "Ecocentric Management for a Risk Society," *Academy of Management Review*, 20 (1995), pp. 118–37.

76. Ibid.

77. Ibid.

78. M. Grunwald, "Monsanto Hid Decades of Pollution," *The Washington Post*, January 1, 2002, pp. A1–A17.

79. Shrivastava, "Ecocentric Management."

80. Ibid.

81. M. Russo and P. Fouts, "A Resource-Based Perspective on Corporate Environmental Performance and Profitability," *Academy of Management Journal* 40 (1997), pp. 534–59; R. D. Klassen and D. Clay Whybark, "The Impact of Environmental Technologies on Manufacturing Performance," *Academy of Management Journal* 42 (1999), pp. 599–615.

82. H. Bradbury and J. A. Clair, "Promoting Sustainable Organizations with Sweden's Natural Step," *Academy of Management Executive*, November 1999, pp. 63–74.

83. A. Fisher, "The World's Most Admired Companies," *Fortune*, October 27, 1997, pp. 40–58.

84. G. Pinchot and E. Pinchot, *The Intelligent Organization* (San Francisco: Berrett Koehler, 1996).

85. S. L. Hart, "Beyond Greening: Strategies for a Sustainable World," *Harvard Business Review*, January–February 1997, pp. 66–76.

Appendix C

1. P. Hawken, A. Lovins, and L. Hunter Lovins, *Natural Capitalism* (Boston: Little Brown, 1999).

2. F. Rice, "Who Scores Best on the Environment," *Fortune*, July 26, 1993, p. 114–22.

3. J. K. Hammitt, "Climate Change Won't Wait for Kyoto," *The Washington Post*, November 29, 2000, p. A39.

4. A. Brown, "Business Leaders Respond to Rio with Self-Regulation," *International Herald Tribune*, June 23, 1997, p. 17.

5. Ibid.

6. K. W. Chilton, "Reengineering U.S. Environmental Protection," *Business Horizons*, March–April 2000, pp. 7–16.

7. K. Dechant and B. Altman, "Environmental Leadership: From Compliance to Competitive Advantage," *The Academy of Management Executive*, August 1994, pp. 7–20.
8. R. Stavins, letter in "The Challenge of Going Green," *Harvard Business Review*, July–August 1994, pp. 37–50.
9. N. Walley and B. Whitehead, "It's Not Easy Being Green," *Harvard Business Review*, May–June 1994, pp. 46–51; C. J. Corbett and L. N. Van Wassenhove, "The Green Fee: Internationalizing and Operationalizing Environmental Issues, *California Management Review*, Fall 1993, pp. 116–33.
10. Walley and Whitehead, "It's Not Easy Being Green."
11. Stavins, "The Challenge of Going Green."
12. Ibid.
13. F. B. Cross, "The Weaning of the Green: Environmentalism Comes of Age in the 1990s," *Business Horizons*, September–October 1990, pp. 40–46.
14. "The Challenge of Going Green."
15. J. Singh, "Making Business Sense of Environmental Compliance," *Sloan Management Review*, Spring, 2000, pp. 91–100.
16. H. Ellison, "Saving Nature While Earning Money," *International Herald Tribune*, June 23, 1997, p. 18.
17. E. Smith and V. Cahan, "The Greening of Corporate America," *Business Week*, April 23, 1990, pp. 96–103.
18. M. E. Porter, "America's Green Strategy," *Science*, April 1991, p. 168.
19. A. Kleiner, "What Does It Mean to Be Green?" *Harvard Business Review*, July–August 1991, pp. 38–47.
20. D. C. Kinlaw, *Competitive: and Green: Sustainable Performance in the Environmental Age* (Amsterdam: Pfeiffer & Co., 1993).
21. Rice, "Who Scores Best on the Environment."
22. J. O'Toole, "Do Good, Do Well: The Business Enterprise Trust Awards," *California Management Review*, Spring 1991, pp. 9–24.
23. Rice, "Who Scores Best on the Environment?"
24. O'Toole, "Do Good, Do Well."
25. G. Hardin, "The Tragedy of the Commons," *Science*, 162 (1968), pp. 1243–48.
26. D. Kirkpatrick, "Environmentalism: The New Crusade," *Fortune*, February 12, 1990, pp. 44–55.
27. Ibid.
28. R. Carson, *The Silent Spring* (Boston: Houghton Mifflin, 1962); R. Paehlke, *Environmentalism and the Future of Progressive Politics* (New Haven, CT: Yale University Press, 1989), pp. 13–41, 76–143; R. Nash, ed., *The American Environment* (Reading, MA: Addison-Wesley, 1968); R. Revelle and H. Landsberg, eds., *America's Changing Environment* (Boston: Beacon Press, 1970);

L. Caldwell, *Environment: A Challenge to Modern Society* (Garden City, NY: Anchor Books, 1971); J. M. Petulla, *Environmental Protection in the United States* (San Francisco: San Francisco Study Center, 1987).
29. B. Commoner, *Science and Survival* (New York: Viking Press, 1963); B. Commoner, *The Closing Circle: Nature, Man and Technology* (New York: Bantam Books; 1971).
30. R. Paehlke, *Environmentalism and the Future of Progressive Politics* (New Haven: Yale University Press, 1989).
31. P. Shrivastava, "Ecocentric Management for a Risk Society," *Academy of Management Review*, 20 (1995), pp. 118–37.
32. Commoner, *The Closing Circle*.
33. Paehlke, *Environmentalism*.
34. Ibid.
35. Ibid.
36. P. Hawken, J. Ogilvy, and P. Schwartz, *Seven Tomorrows: Toward a Voluntary History* (New York: Bantam Books, 1982); Paehlke, *Environmentalism*.
37. Porter, "America's Green Strategy."
38. R. Y. K. Chan, "An Emerging Green Market in China: Myth or Reality?" *Business Horizons*, March–April, 2000, pp. 55–60.
39. S. Waddock and N. Smith, "Corporate Responsibility Audits: Doing Well by Doing Good," *Sloan Management Review*, Winter, 2000, pp. 75–83.
40. C. Morrison, *Managing Environmental Affairs: Corporate Practices in the U.S., Canada, and Europe* (New York: Conference Board, 1991).
41. Ibid.
42. Kleiner, "What Does It Mean to Be Green?"
43. K. Fischer and J. Schot, *Environmental Strategies for Industry* (Washington, DC: Island Press, 1993).
44. J. Howard, J. Nash, and J. Ehrenfeld, "Standard or Smokescreen? Implementation of a Voluntary Environmental Code," *California Management Review*, Winter, 2000, pp. 63–82.
45. Rice, "Who Scores Best on the Environment?"
46. M. P. Polonsky and P. J. Rosenberger III, "Reevaluating Green Marketing: A Strategic Approach," *Business Horizons*, September–October 2001, pp. 21–30.
47. Rice, "Who Scores Best on the Environment?"
48. Ibid.
49. Polansky and Rosenberger, "Reevaluating Green Marketing."
50. S. L. Hart and M. B. Milstein, "Global Sustainability and the Creative Destruction of Industries," *Sloan Management Review*, Fall 1999, pp. 23–32.
51. H. Ellison, "Saving Nature While Earning Money."
52. Dechant and Altman, "Environment Leadership."
53. Smith and Cahan, "The Greening of Corporate America."
54. J. Elkington and T. Burke, *The Green Capitalists* (London: Victor Gullanez,

1989); M. Zetlin, "The Greening of Corporate America," *Management Review*, June 1990, pp. 10–17.
55. Smith and Cahan, "The Greening of Corporate America."
56. Hart and Milstein, "Global Sustainability."
57. J. Stevens, "Assessing the Health Risks of Incinerating Garbage," *EURA Reporter*, October 1989, pp. 6–10.
58. A. Lovins, L. Hunter Lovins, and P. Hawken, "A Road Map for Natural Capitalism," *Harvard Business Review*, May–June 1999, pp. 145–58.
59. A. Kolk, "Green Reporting," *Harvard Business Review*, January–February 2000, pp. 15–16.
60. L. Blumberg and R. Gottlieb, "The Resurrection of Incineration" and "The Economic Factors," in *War on Waste*, ed. L. Blumberg and R. Gottlieb (Washington, DC: Island Press, 1989).
61. L. Blumberg and R. Gottlieb, "Recycling's Unrealized Promise," in Blumberg and Gottlieb, *War on Waste*, pp. 191–226.
62. Lovins, Lovins, and Hawken, "A Road Map for Natural Capitalism."
63. J. Elkington, "Towards the Sustainable Corporation: Win-Win-Win Business Strategies for Sustainable Development," *California Management Review*, Winter 1994, pp. 90–100.
64. Lovins, Lovins, and Hawken, "A Road Map for Natural Capitalism."
65. Dechant and Altman, "Environmental Leadership."
66. Brown, "Business Leaders Respond, to Rio with Self-Regulation."
67. H. Ellison., "Joint Implementation Promotes Cooperation on World Climate," *International Herald Tribune*, June 23, 1997, p. 21.
68. Corbett and Van Wassenhove, "The Green Fee."
69. Polansky and Rosenberger, "Reevaluating Green Marketing."
70. Corbett and Van Wassenhove, "The Green Fee."
71. R. D. Klassen and D. Clay Whybark, "The Impact of Environmental Technologies on Manufacturing Performance," *Academy of Management Journal*, 42 (1999), pp. 599–615.
72. Hart and Milstein, "Global Sustainability."
73. Ibid.
74. Polansky and Rosenberger, "Reevaluating Green Marketing."
75. N. Stein, "Yes, We Have No Profits," *Fortune*, November 26, 2001, pp. 183–96.
76. Hart and Milstein, "Global Sustainability."
77. Ibid.
78. Polansky and Rosenberger, "Reevaluating Green Marketing."
79. Ibid.
80. Elkington, "Towards the Sustainable Corporation."
81. F. S. Rowland, "Chlorofluorocarbons and the Depletion of Stratospheric Ozone," *American Scientist*, January–February 1989, pp. 36–45.

82. Elkington, "Towards the Sustainable Corporation."

83. Corbet and Van Wassenhove, "The Green Fee."

84. H. Ellison, "Joint Implementation Promotes Cooperation on World Climate."

85. Elkington, "Towards the Sustainable Corporation."

86. H. Ellison, "The Balance Sheet," *International Herald Tribune*, June 23, 1997, p. 21.

87. Ibid.

88. P. B. Gray and D. Devlin, "Heroes of Small Business," *Fortune Small Business*, November 2000, pp. 50–64.

89. S. Tully, "Water, Water Everywhere," *Fortune*, May 15, 2000, pp. 343–54.

Chapter 6

1. "Eúropean Foreign Policy: Unity by Machinery?" *The Economist*, March 2, 1996, pp. 46–47; "European Union: Wishful Thinking," *The Economist*, September 24, 1994, pp. 84–85; "Europe: Shaping the Union," *The Economist*, December 2, 2000, 375, no. 8199, pp. 49–51; "Leaders: Europe's Choice," *The Economist*, December 2, 2000, 357, no. 8199, pp. 20–21.

2. "EU: MNCs Face New Challenges as Frontiers Merge," *Crossborder Monitor* 2, no. 10, March 16, 1994, p. 1; Jane Sasseen, "EU Dateline," *International Management* 49, no. 2 (March 1994), p. 5; Andrew Martin and George Ross, *The Brave New World of European Labor: European Trade Unions at the Millennium* (New York: Berghahn, 1999); Robert A. Feldman and C. Maxwell Watson, "Central Europe: From Transition to EU Membership," *Finance & Development*, September 2000, 37, no. 3, pp. 24–27.

3. Robert W. Bednarzik, "The Role of Enterprenuership in U.S. and European Job Growth," *Monthly Labor Review*, July 2000, 123, no. 7, pp. 3–16; Wolf Sauter, *Competition Law and Industrial Policy in the Eu*, (Oxford, UK: Oxford University Press, 1998).

4. T. Peters, "Prometheus Barely Unbound," *The Executive*, November 1990, pp. 70–84.

5. Michael Shari, "Free Trade in Asia: Bogged Down Again," *Business Week*, December 4, 2000, 3710, p. 62; "Asia: Smaller Steps," *The Economist*, November 18, 2000, 357, no. 8197, p. 50.

6. James T. Peach, Richard V. Adkisson, "NAFTA and Economic Activity along the U.S.-Mexico Border," *Journal of Economic Issues*, June 2000, 34, no. 2, pp. 481–89.

7. Gail M. Gerhart, "Can Africa Claim the 21ˢᵗ Century?" *Foreign Affairs*, November/December 2000, 79, no. 6, p. 191; Michael D. White, "Land of Promise," *World Trade*, September 1999, 12, no. 9, pp. 58–60.

8. Evangelos O. Simos, "International Economic Outlook: The World Economy in 2009," *Journal of Business Forecasting Methods & Systems*, Fall 2000, 19, no. 3, pp. 31–35.

9. Roger Ahrens, "Going Global," *International Business* 9, no. 7, July/August 1996, pp. 26–30; Bill Javetski, "Old World, New Investment," *Business Week*, October 7, 1996, pp. 50–51.

10. Russel B. Scholl, "The International Investment Position of the United States at Yearend 1999," *Survey of Current Business*, July 2000, 80, no. 7, p. 46.

11. "Current International Trade Position of the U.S.: Imports Outpace Exports: Balance with Japan Improves," *Business America* 117, no. 6, June 1996, pp. 35–37.

12. James Barron, "Flower Power," *CIO*, September 15, 2000, 13, no. 25, pp. 108–12.

13. Anne-Wil Harzing, "An Empirical Analysis and Extension of the Bartlett and Ghoshal Typology of Multinational Companies," *Journal of International Business Studies* (2000), 31, 1, pp. 101–20; Don E. Schultz and Philip J. Kitchen, "Global Reach," *Adweek*, October 30, 2000, 41, no. 44, p. 51.

14. Steven E. Prokesch, "Making Global Connections at Caterpillar," *Harvard Business Review* 74, no. 2, March–April 1996, pp. 88–89; Laurie Freeman, "Caterpillar on a Roll," *B to B*, September 11, 2000, 85, no. 14, pp. 3, 44; Ian Buchanan, "The US Experience," *Asian Business*, May 1998, 34, no. 5, pp. 14–16.

15. Chang H. Moon, "The Choice of Entry Modes and Theories of Foreign Direct Investment," *Journal of Global Marketing* 11, no. 2 (1997), pp. 43–64; Isabelle Maignan and Bryan A. Lukas, "Entry Mode Decisions: The Role of Managers' Mental Models," *Journal of Global Marketing* 10, no. 4 (1997), pp. 7–22.

16. "Flying Solos Overseas," *Business Week Online*, May 28, 2002.

17. Maureen Nevin Duffy, "3M Lauds China Government Help," *Chemical Marketer Reporter* 251, no. 1, January 6, 1997, p. 19.

18. Charlene Marmer Solomon, "Staff Selection Impacts Global Success," *Personnel Journal*, January 1994, pp. 88–101.

19. Nancy J. Adler and Susan Bartholomew, "Managing Globally Competent People," *Academy of Management Executive* 6, no. 3 (1992), pp. 52–65; Cecil G. Howard, "Profile of the 21st-Century Expatriate Manager," *HRMagazine*, June 1992, pp. 93–100.

20. Scott A. Snell, Charles C. Snow, Sue Canney Davison, and Donald C. Hambrick, "Designing and Supporting Transnational Teams: The Human Resource Agenda," *Human Resource Management*, 1998: Charles C. Snow, Scott A. Snell, Sue Canney Davison, and Donald C. Hambrick, "Use Transnational Teams to Globalize Your Company," *Organizational Dynamics*, Spring 1996, pp. 50–67.

21. Donald C. Hambrick, James W. Fredrickson, Lester B. Korn, and Richard M. Ferry, "Reinventing the CEO," *21ˢᵗ Century Report* (New York: Korn/Ferry and Columbia Graduate School of Business, 1989).

22. Charlene Marmer Solomon, "Danger Below! Spot Failing Global Assignments," *Personnel Journal*, November 1996, pp. 78–85.

23. Reyer A. Swaak, "Expatriate Failures: Too Many, Too Much Cost, Too Little Planning," *Compensation & Benefits Review*, November/December 1995, pp. 50–52.

24. Howard, "Profile of the 21st-Century Expatriate Manager."

25. Nancy J. Adler, "Global Leadership: Women Leaders," *Management International Review*, 37, no. 1 (special issue, 1997), pp. 171–96; Nancy J. Adler and Fadna N. Israeli, "Competitive Frontiers. Women Managers in a Global Economy," *Organization Studies* 16, no. 4 (1995), pp. 724–25. See also Nancy J. Adler, "Pacific Basin Managers: A Gaijin, Not a Woman," *Human Resource Management* 26, no. 2 (1987), pp. 169–91; Hilary Harris, "Women in International Management: Opportunity or Threat?" *Women in Management Review*, 8, no. 5 (1993), pp. 9–11.

26. Gretchen M. Sprietzer, Morgan W. McCall, and Joan D. Mahoney, "Early Identification of International Executive Potential," *Journal of Applied Psychology* 82, no. 1 (1997), pp. 6–29; Ronald Mortensen, "Beyond the Fence Line," *HRMagazine*, November 1997, pp. 100–109; "Expatriate Games," *Journal of Business Strategy*, July/August 1997, pp. 4–5; "Building a Global Workforce Starts with Recruitment," *Personnel Journal* (special supplement), March 1996, pp. 9–11.

27. Gunnar Beeth, "Multicultural Managers Wanted," *Management Review*, May 1997, p. 21.

28. David Stamps, "Welcome to America," *Training*, November 1996, pp. 23–30.

29. Linda K. Trevino and Katherine A. Nelson, *Managing Business Ethics: Straight Talk about How to Do It Right* (New York: John Wiley & Sons, 1995).

30. Patricia Digh, "Shades of Gray in the Global Marketplace," *HRMagazine*, April 1997, pp. 91–98.

31. Charlene Marmer Solomon, "Put Your Global Ethics to the Test," *Personnel Journal*, January 1996, pp. 66–74.

32. Digh, "Shades of Gray"; Ashay B. Desai and Terri Rittenburg, "Global Ethics: An Integrative Framework for MNEs," *Journal of Business Ethics* 16 (1997), pp. 791–800; Paul Buller, John Kohls, and Kenneth Anderson, "A Model for Addressing Cross-Cultural Ethical Conflicts," *Business & Society* 36, no. 2 (June 1997), pp. 169–93.

Chapter 7

1. S. Shane and S. Venkataraman, "The Promise of Entrepreneurship as a Field of Research, *Academy of Management Review*, 25 (2000), pp. 217–26.

2. J. A. Timmons, *New Venture Creation* (Burr Ridge, IL: Richard D. Irwin, 1994).

3. G. T. Lumpkin and G. G. Dess, "Clarifying the Entrepreneurial Orientation Construct and Linking It To Performance," *Academy of Management Review*, 21 (1996), pp. 135–72.

4. R. W. Smilor, "Entrepreneurship: Reflections on a Subversive Activity," *Journal of Business Venturing* 12 (1997), pp. 341–46.

5. W. Megginson, M. J. Byrd, S. R. Scott Jr., and L. Megginson, *Small Business Management: An Entrepreneur's Guide to Success*, 2nd ed. (Boston: Irwin McGraw-Hill, 1997).

6. Timmons, *New Venture Creation*.

7. T. Peters, "Thrashed by the Real World," *Forbes*, April 7, 1997, p. 100.

8. D. Bricklin, "Natural-Born Entrepreneur," *Harvard Business Review*, September 2001, pp. 53–59.

9. G. Pinchot, "How Intrapreneurs Innovate," *Management Today*, December 1985, pp. 54–61.

10. A. Marsh, "Promiscuous Breeding" *Forbes*, April 7, 1997, pp. 74–77.

11. B. O'Reilly, "The New Face of Small Business," *Fortune*, May 2, 1994, pp. 82–88.

12. H. Aldrich, *Ethnic Entrepreneurs: Immigrant Business in Industrial Societies* (Newbury Park, CA: Sage, 1990).

13. P. Evans and T. S. Wurster, "Getting Real about Virtual Commerce," *Harvard Business Review*, November–December 1999, pp. 85–94.

14. J. Rose, "The New Risk-Takers," *Fortune Small Business*, February 15, 2002, fortune.com.

15. "How It Really Works: Introduction," *Business Week*, August 25, 1997, pp. 48–49.

16. P. Elstron, "It Must Be Something in the Water," *Business Week*, August 25, 1997, pp. 84–87.

17. T. Fuller, "Malaysia's Wired 'Supercorridor'," *International Herald Tribune*, November 15–16, 1997, pp. 1, 6.

18. M. Clifford and P. Engardio, "Asia's Future," *Business Week*, November 27, 2000, pp. 122–36.

19. J. Collins and J. Porras, *Built to Last* (London: Century, 1996).

20. Ibid.

21. K. H. Vesper, *New Venture Mechanics* (Englewood Cliffs, NJ: Prentice-Hall, 1993).

22. B. Schlender et al., "Cool Companies, Part 1," *Fortune*, July 7, 1997, pp. 50–60.

23. Ibid.

24. Vesper, *New Venture Mechanics*.

25. "The Top Entrepreneurs," *Business Week*, January 14, 2002, pp. 74–76.

26. T. Singer, "What Business Would You Start?" *Inc.*, March 2002, pp. 68–76.

27. E. Schonfeld, "The Space Business Heats Up," *Fortune*, November 24, 1997, pp. 52–60.

28. Ibid.

29. Ibid.

30. E. Schonfeld, "Going Long," *Fortune*, March 20, 2000, pp. 172–92.

31. Vesper, *New Venture Mechanics*.

32. "Do Universities Stifle Entrepreneurship?" *Across the Board*, July/August 1997, pp. 32–38.

33. Timmons, *New Venture Creation*.

34. Bricklin, "Natural-Born Entrepreneur."

35. M. Sonfield and R. Lussier, "The Entrepreneurial Strategy Matrix: A Model for New and Ongoing Ventures," *Business Horizons*, May–June, 1997, pp. 73–77.

36. Hisrich and Peters, *Entrepreneurship: Starting, developing, and managing a new enterprise*. Burr Ridge, IL: Irwin, 1994.

37. Ibid.

38. W. A. Sahlman, "How to Write a Great Business Plan," *Harvard Business Review*, July–August 1997, pp. 98–108.

39. Ibid.

40. Ibid.

41. Schlender et al., "Cool Companies."

42. Sahlman, "How to Write a Great Business Plan."

43. Ibid.

44. J. A. Fraser, "Do I Need to Plan Differently for a Dot-Com Business?" *Inc.*, July 2000, pp. 142–43.

45. R. A. Baron and G. D. Markman, "Beyond Social Capital: How Social Skills Can Enhance Entrepreneurs' Success," *Academy of Management Executive*, February 2000, pp. 106–16.

46. R. Balu, "Starting Your Startup," *Fast Company*, January–February, 2000, pp. 81–112.

47. Ibid.

48. S. McCartney, "Michael Dell—and His Company—Grow Up," *The Wall Street Journal*, January 31, 1995, pp. B1, B4.

49. A. F. Brattina, "The Diary of a Small-Company Owner," *Inc.*, May 1993, pp. 79–89, and June 1993, pp. 117–22.

50. L. Kroll, "My Partner, My Father," *Forbes*, June 2, 1997, pp. 66–70.

51. W. P. Barrett, "The Perils of Success," *Forbes*, November 3, 1997, pp. 129–37.

52. O'Reilly, "The New Face of Small Business."

53. C. Burck, "The Real World of the Entrepreneur," *Fortune*, April 5, 1993, pp. 62–81.

54. Serwer, "Lessons from America's Fastest-Growing Companies," *Fortune*, August 8, 1994, pp. 42–60.

55. P. F. Drucker, "How to Save the Family Business," *The Wall Street Journal*, August 19, 1994, p. A10.

56. S. Finkelstein, "The Myth of Managerial Superiority in Internet Startups: An Autopsy," *Organizational Dynamics*, Fall 2001, pp. 172–85.

57. Ibid.

58. Ibid.

59. Barrett, "The Perils of Success," p. 137.

60. Singer, "What Business Would You Start?"

61. Balu, "Starting your Startup."

62. B. Oviatt and P. P. McDougall, "Global Start-ups: Entrepreneurs on a Worldwide Stage," *Academy of Management Executive*, 9 (1995), pp. 30–43.

63. Ibid.

64. Ibid.

65. M. Hordes, J. A. Clancy, and J. Baddaley, "A Primer for Global Startups," *Academy of Management Executive* 9 (1995), pp. 7–11.

66. Ibid.

67. R. M. Kanter, *The Change Masters* (New York: Simon & Schuster, 1983).

68. D. Clark, "How a Woman's Passion and Persistence Made 'Bob,'" *The Wall Street Journal*, January 10, 1995, pp. B1, B8.

69. D. Kuratko, R. D. Ireland, and J. Hornsby, "Improving Firm Performance through Entrepreneurial Actions: Acordia's Corporate Entrepreneurship Strategy, "*Academy of Management Executive*, 15 (2001), pp. 60–71.

70. Collins and Porras, *Built to Last*.

71. D. Roth, "Now, for All You Net Potatoes, Here's NBCi," *Fortune*, March 20, 2000 pp. 156–60.

72. J. B. Quinn, "Outsourcing Innovation: The New Engine of Growth," *Sloan Management Review*, Summer 2000, pp. 13–28.

73. E. Nee, "Hewlett-Packard's New E-vangelist," *Fortune*, January 10, 2000, pp. 166–67.

74. Kanter et al., "Driving Corporate Entrepreneurship," *Management Review*, April 1987, pp. 14–16.

75. J. Argenti, *Corporate Collapse: The Causes and Symptoms* (New York: John Wiley & Sons, 1979).

76. Kanter et al., "Driving Corporate Entrepreneurship."

77. G. T. Lumpkin and G. G. Dess, "Clarifying the Entrepreneurial Orientation Construct and Linking It to Performance," *Academy of Management Review*, 21 (1996), pp. 135–72.

78. T. Bateman and J. M. Crant, "The Proactive Dimension of Organizational Behavior," *Journal of Organizational Behavior*, 1993, pp. 103–18.

79. A. E. Serwer, "Michael Dell Turns the PC World Inside Out," *Fortune*, September 8, 1997, pp. 38–44.

80. Lumpkin and Dess, "Clarifying the Entrepreneurial Orientation Construct."

81. Collins and Porras, *Built to Last*.

82. M. Arndt, "3M: A Lab for Growth?" *Business Week*, January 21, 2002, pp. 50–51.

83. C. Pinchot and E. Pinchot, *The Intelligent Organization* (San Francisco: Berrett-Koehler, 1996).

Chapter 8

1. Ronald N. Ashkenas and Suzanne C. Francis. "Integration Managers: Special Leaders for Special Times," *Harvard Business Review*, November–December 2000, 78, no. 6, pp. 108–16.

2. Andrew West, "The Flute Factory: An Empirical Measurement of the Effect of the Division of Labor on Productivity and Production Cost," *American Economist*, Spring 1999, 43, no. 1, pp. 82–87.

3. P. Lawrence and J. Lorsch, *Organization and Environment* (Homewood, IL: Richard D. Irwin, 1969).

4. Ibid.; Thompson, *The New Manager's Handbook*. Also see S. Sharifi and K. S. Pawar, "Product Design as a Means of Integrating Differentiation," *Technovation* 16, no. 5 (May 1996), pp. 255–64; W. B. Stevenson and J. M. Bartunek, "Power, Interaction, Position, and the Generation of Cultural Agreement in Organizations," *Human Relations* 49, no. 1 (January 1996), pp. 75–104.

5. Abbas J. Ali, Robert C. Camp, and Manton Gibbs, "The Ten Commandments Perspective on Power and Authority in Organizations," *Journal of Business Ethics*, August 2000, 26, no. 4, pp. 351–61; Robert F. Pearse, "Understanding Organizational Power and Influence Systems," *Compensation & Benefits Management*, Autumn 2000, 16, no. 4, pp. 28–38.

6. Susan F. Shultz, *Board Book: Making Your Corporate Board a Strategic Force in Your Company's Success* (New York: AMACOM, 2000); Ralph D. Ward, *Improving Corporate Boards: The Boardroom Insider Guidebook* (New York: John Wiley & Sons, 2000).

7. John A. Byrne, "The Best & the Worst Boards," *Business Week*, January 24, 2000, 3665, pp. 142–52.

8. A. J. Michels, "Chief Executives as Idi Ahmin?" *Fortune*, July 1, 1991, p. 13; C. M. Daily and D. R. Dalton, "CEO and Board Chair Roles Held Jointly or Separately: Much Ado About Nothing?" *Academy of Management Executive* 11, no. 3 (August 1997), pp. 11–20.

9. Tony Simons; Lisa Hope Pelled, and Ken A. Smith, "Making Use of Difference: Diversity, Debate, and Decision Comprehensiveness in Top Management Teams," *Academy of Management Journal*, December 1999, 42, no. 6, pp. 662–73; C. Carl Pegels, Yong I Song, and Baik Yang, "Management Heterogeneity, Competitive Interaction Groups, and Firm Performance," *Strategic Management Journal*, September 2000, 21, no. 3, pp. 911–21.

10. Shawnee Vickery, Cornelia Droge, and Richard Germain, "The Relationship between Product Customization and Organizational Structure," *Journal of Operations Management*, June 1999, 17, no. 4, pp. 377–91.

11. D. Van Fleet and A. Bedeian, "A History of the Span of Management," *Academy of Management Review*, 2 (1977), pp. 356–72.

12. Philippe Jehiel, "Information Aggregation and Communication in Organizations," *Management Science*, May 1999, 45, no. 5, pp. 659–69; Ahnn Altaffer, "First-Line Managers: Measuring Their Span of Control," *Nursing Management*, July 1998, 29, no. 7, pp. 36–40.

13. "Span of Control vs. Span of Support," *Journal for Quality and Participation*, Fall 2000, 23, no. 4, p. 15; James Gallo and Paul R. Thompson, "Goals, Measures, and Beyond: In Search of Accountability in Federal HRM," *Public Personnel Management*, Summer 2000, 29, no. 2, pp. 237–48; Clinton O. Longenecker and Timothy C. Stansfield, "Why Plant Managers Fail: Causes and Consequences," *Industrial Management*, January/February 2000, 42, no. 1, pp. 24–32.

14. E. Beaubien, "Legendary Leadership," *Executive Excellence* 14, no. 9 (September 1997), p. 20; "How Well Do You Delegate," *Supervision* 58, no. 8 (August 1997), p. 26; J. Mahoney, "Delegating Effectively," *Nursing Management* 28, no. 6 (June 1997), p. 62; J. Lagges, "The Role of Delegation in Improving Productivity," *Personnel Journal*, November 1979, pp. 776–79.

15. G. Matthews, "Run Your Business or Build an Organization?" *Harvard Management Review*, March–April 1984, pp. 34–44.

16. Russ Forrester, "Empowerment: Rejuvenating a Potent Idea," *Academy of Management Executive*, August 2000, 14, no. 3, pp. 67–80; Monica L. Perry, Craig L. Pearce, and Henry P. Sims, Jr., "Empowered Selling Teams: How Shared Leadership Can Contribute to Selling Team Outcomes," *Journal of Personal Selling & Sales Management*, Summer 1999, 19, no. 3, pp. 35–51.

17. Suzy Wetlaufer, "Organizing for Empowerment: An Interview with AES's Roger Sant and Dennis Bakke," *Harvard Business Review*, January–February 1999, 77, no. 1, pp. 110–23.

18. E. E. Lawler III, "New Roles for the Staff Function: Strategic Support and Services," in *Organizing for the Future*, J. Galbraith, E. E. Lawler III, & Associates (San Francisco: Jossey-Bass, 1993).

19. Michael Porter, *Competitive Advantage: Creating and Sustaining Superior Performance* (New York: Free Press, 1985).

20. Rob Cross and Lloyd Baird, "Technology Is Not Enough: Improving Performance by Building Organizational Memory," *Sloan Management Review*, Spring 2000, 41, no. 3, pp. 69–78; R. Duncan, "What is the Right Organizational Structure?", *Organizational Dynamics* 7 (Winter 1979), pp. 59–80.

21. George S. Day, "Creating a Market-Driven Organization," *Sloan Management Review*, Fall 1999, 41, no. 1, pp. 11–22.

22. R. Boehm and C. Phipps, "Flatness Forays," *McKinsey Quarterly* 3 (1996), pp. 128–43.

23. Bruce T. Lamont, V. Sambamurthy, Kimberly M. Ellis, and Paul G. Simmonds, "The Influence of Organizational Structure on the Information Received by Corporate Strategists of Multinational Enterprises," *Management International Review*, Third Quarter 2000, 40, no. 3, pp. 231–52.

24. Wilma Bernasco, Petra C. de Weerd-Nederhof, Harry Tillema, and Harry Boer, "Balanced Matrix Structure and New Product Development Process at Texas Instruments Materials and Controls Division," *R&D Management*, April 1999, 29, no. 2, pp. 121–31; J. K. McCollum, "The Matrix Structure: Bane or Benefit to High Tech Organizations?" *Project Management Journal* 24, no. 2 (June 1993), pp. 23–26; R. C. Ford, "Cross-Functional Structures: A Review and Integration of Matrix," *Journal of Management* 18, no. 2 (June 1992), pp. 267–94; H. Kolodny, "Managing in a Matrix," *Business Horizons*, March–April 1981, pp. 17–24.

25. David Cackowski, Mohammad K. Najdawi, and Q. B. Chung, "Object Analysis in Organizational Design: A Solution for Matrix Organizations," *Project Management Journal*, September 2000, 31, no. 3, pp. 44–51; J. Barker, "Conflict Approaches of Effective and Ineffective Project Managers: A Field Study in a Matrix Organization," *Journal of Management Studies* 25, no. 2 (March 1988), pp. 167–78; G. J. Chambers, "The Individual in a Matrix Organization," *Project Management Journal* 20, no. 4 (December 1989), pp. 37–42, 50; S. Davis and P. Lawrence, "Problems of Matrix Organizations," *Harvard Business Review*, May–June 1978, pp. 131–42.

26. Anthony Ferner, "Being Local Worldwide: ABB and the Challenge of Global Management Relations," *Industrielles*, Summer 2000, 55, no. 3, pp. 527–29; C. Bartlett and S. Ghoshal, "Matrix Management: Not a Structure, a Frame of Mind," *Harvard Business Review*, 68 (July–August 1990), pp. 138–45.

27. Jasmine Tata, Sameer Prasad, and Ron Thorn, "The Influence of Organizational Structure on the Effectiveness of TQM Programs," *Journal of Managerial Issues*, Winter 1999, 11, no. 4, pp. 440–53; Davis and Lawrence, "Problems of Matrix Organizations."

28. J. G. March & H. A. Simon, *Organizations* (New York: John Wiley & Sons, 1958); J. D. Thompson, *Organizations in Action* (New York: McGraw-Hill, 1967).

29. Paul S. Adler, "Building Better Bureaucracies," *The Academy of Management Executive*, November 1999, 13, no. 4, pp. 36–49.

30. J. Galbraith, "Organization Design: An Information Processing View," *Interfaces* 4 (Fall 1974), pp. 28–36. See also S. A. Mohrman, "Integrating Roles and Structure in the Lateral Organization," in *Organizing for the Future*, J. Galbraith, E. E. Lawler III, & Associates (San Francisco: Jossey-Bass, 1993); Barbara B. Flynn and F. James Flynn, "Information-Processing Alternatives for Coping with Manufacturing Environment Complexity," *Decision Sciences*, Fall 1999, 30, no. 4, pp. 1021–52.

31. Walden Paddlers, personal communication.

32. Galbraith, "Organization Design," Mohrman, "Integrating Roles and Structure."

Chapter 9

1. Rick Dove, "Agility = Knowledge Management + Response Ability," *Automotive Manufacturing & Production*, March 1999, 111, no. 3, pp. 16–17; Patrick M Wright, Lee Dyer, and Michael G Takla, "What's Next? Key Findings from the 1999 State-of-the-Art & Practice Study," *Human Resource Planning* (1999), 22, no. 4, pp. 12–20.
2. T. Burns and G. Stalker, *The Management of Innovation* (London: Tavistock, 1961).
3. Krackhardt and Hanson, "Information Networks: The Company behind the Chart," *Harvard Business Review*, July–August 1993, pp. 104–11.
4. B. Buell and R. Hof, "Hewlett-Packard Rethinks Itself," *Business Week*, April 1, 1991, pp. 76–79.
5. "Why Big Might Remain Beautiful," *The Economist*, March 24, 1990, p. 79; W. Zellner, "Go-Go Goliaths," *Business Week*, February 13, 1995, pp. 64–70.
6. "Chasing the Future," Microsoft Corporation essay (http://www.Microsoft.com/ISSUES/essays/07-10research.asp).
7. Linda L Hellofs and Robert Jacobson, "Market Share and Customers' Perceptions of Quality: When Can Firms Grow their Way to Higher versus Lower Quality?" *Journal of Marketing*, January 1999, 63, no. 1, pp. 16–25.
8. Keith H. Hammonds, "Size Is Not a Strategy," *Fast Company*, September 2002, pp. 78–82.
9. "The Choice: While Some Regionals Tout the Virtues of Merging, the Independent-Minded Still Flourish," *Investor Dealers' Digest*, May 28, 2001, p. ITEM0114900D.
10. W. Cascio, "Downsizing: What Do We Know? What Have We Learned?" *Academy of Management Executive*, February 1993, pp. 95–104; Sarah J. Freeman, "The Gestalt of Organizational Downsizing: Downsizing Strategies as Package of Change," *Human Relations*, December 1999, 52, no. 12, pp. 1505–154.
11. R. E. Stross, "Microsoft's Big Advantage—Hiring Only the Supersmart," *Fortune*, November 25, 1996, pp. 159–62; R. Lieber, "Wired for Hiring. Microsoft's Slick Recruiting Machine," *Fortune*, February 5, 1996, pp. 123–24; Ibid.: M. Hitt, B. Keats, H. Harback, and R. Nixon, "Rightsizing: Building and Maintaining Strategic Leadership and Long-Term Competitiveness," *Organizational Dynamics*, Fall 1994, pp. 18–31.
12. Cascio, "Downsizing"; Jack Ciancio, "Survivor's Syndrome," *Nursing Management*, May 2000, 31, no. 5, pp. 43–45.
13. K. Ohmae, *The Mind of the Strategist: Business Planning for Competitive Advantage* (New York: Penguin Books, 1982), Chap. 8; Harry Stern, "Succeeding in a 'Customer-Centric' Economy," *Foodservice Equipment & Supplies*, September 2000, 53, no. 10, pp. 27–28.
14. K. Ishikawa, *What Is Total Quality Control? The Japanese Way*, trans. David J. Lu (Englewood Cliffs, NJ: Prentice-Hall, 1985); Bob Lewis, "Instead of Focusing Solely on Internal Customers, Look at Customers as Well," *InfoWorld*, October 25, 1999, 21, no. 43, p. 104.
15. Bill Creech, *The 5 Pillars of TQM: How to Make Total Quality Management Work for You* (New York: Plume Publishing, 1995); James R. Evans and William M. Lindsay, *Management and Control of Quality* (Cincinnati: Southwestern College Publishing, 1998).
16. Mark Czarnecki, *Managing by Measuring: How to Improve Your Organization's Performance through Effective Benchmarking* (New York: AMACOM, 1999); Douglas Dow, Danny Samson, and Steve Ford, "Exploding the Myth: Do All Quality Management Practices Contribute to Superior Quality Performance?" *Production and Operations Management*, Spring 1999, 8, no. 1, pp. 1–27. See also, Janet Barnard, "Using Total Quality Principles in Business Courses: The Effect on Student Evaluations," *Business Communication Quarterly*, June 1999, 62, no. 2, pp. 61–73.
17. For more information about ISO 9000 (as well as newer programs such as ISO 14000 for environmental management), see the International Organization for Standardization's Web page: http://www.iso.ch/welcome.html.
18. J. Champy, *Reengineering Management* (New York: HarperBusiness, 1995). See also M. Hammer and J. Champy, *Reengineering the Corporation* (New York: HarperCollins, 1992).
19. Joan Woodward, *Industrial Organization: Theory and Practice* (London: Oxford University Press, 1965).
20. James H. Gilmore and B. Joseph Pine, eds., *Markets of One: Creating Customer-Unique Value through Mass Customization* (Cambridge, MA: Harvard Business Review Press, 2000); B. Joseph Pine, *Mass Customization: The New Frontier in Business Competition* (Cambridge, MA: Harvard Business School Press, 1992).
21. Erick Schonfeld, "The Customized, Digitized, Have-It-Your Way Economy," *Fortune*, September 28, 138, no. 6, p. 114–20.
22. Funda Sahin, "Manufacturing Competitiveness: Different Systems to Achieve the Same Results," *Production and Inventory Management Journal*, First Quarter 2000, 41, no. 1, pp. 56–65.
23. Subhash Wadhwa, and K. Srinivasa Rao, "Flexibility: An Emerging Meta-Competence for Managing High Technology," *International Journal of Technology Management*, 19 (2000), no. 7–8, pp. 820–45.
24. Jeff Green, "How Architects Are Giving Jeep New Traction," *Business Week*, October 2, 2000, p. 152H; Jeff Green, "Honda's Independent Streak," *Business Week*, October 2, 2000, pp. 152B–152H; Brett A. Peters and Leon F. McGinnis, "Strategic Configuration of Flexible Assembly Systems: A Single Period Approximation," *IIE Transaction*, April 1999, 31, no. 4, pp. 379–90.
25. A. Taylor III, "How Toyota Defies Gravity," *Fortune*, December 8, 1997, pp. 100–108; Gary S. Vasilash, "How Toyota Does It—Every Day," Automotive Manufacturing & Production, August 2000, 112, no. 8, pp. 48–49; Stephen R. Morrey, "Learning to Think Lean: A Roadmap and Toolbox for the Lean Journey," *Automotive Manufacturing & Production*, August 2000, 112, no. 8, p. 147; Funda Sahin, "Manufacturing Competitiveness: Different Systems to Achieve the Same Results," *Production and Inventory Management Journal*, First Quarter 2000, 41, no. 1, pp. 56–65; "Chrysler's Retooling Pays Off with Increased Productivity," *Knight-Ridder/Tribune Business News*, June 24, 2002, p. ITEM20175006; "Strategic Reconfiguration: Manufacturing's Key Role in Innovation," *Production and Inventory Management Journal*, Summer–Fall 2001, p. 9–17.
26. Sahin, "Manufacturing Competitiveness"; Gary S. Vasilash, "Flexible Thinking: How Need, Innovation, Teamwork & a Whole Bunch of Machining Centers Have Transformed TRW Tillsonburg into a Model of Lean Manufacturing," *Automotive Manufacturing & Production*, October 1999, 111, no. 10, pp. 64–65.
27. Chen H. Chung, "Balancing the Two Dimensions of Time for Time-Based Competition," *Journal of Managerial Issues*, Fall 1999, 11, no. 3, pp. 299–314; Denis R. Towill and Peter McCullen, "The Impact of Agile Manufacturing on Supply Chain Dynamics," *International Journal of Logistics Management* (1999), 10, no. 1, pp. 83–96; see also George Stalk and Thomas M. Hout, *Competing against Time: How Time-Based Competition Is Reshaping Global Markets* (New York: Free Press, 1990).
28. R. Henkoff, "Delivering the Goods," *Fortune*, November 28, 1994, pp. 64–78; Tony Seideman, "A&P Uses Transportation Software to Wring New Efficiency Out of Supply Chain," *Stores*, September 2000, 82, no. 9, pp. 172–74.
29. "2001 in Review: Logistics," *Traffic World*, January 1, 2001, 265, no. 1, p. 15; Morris A. Cohen, Carl Cull, Hau L. Lee and Don Willen, "Saturn's Supply-Chain Innovation: High Value in After-Sales Service," *Sloan Management Review*, Summer 2000, 41, no. 4, pp. 93–101.
30. Tom Stundza, "Buyers Ask Service Centers: 'What Happened to JIT?' . . . and a Few Other Things," *Purchasing*, May 6, 1999, 126, no. 7, pp. 60–70; Damien Power and Amrik S. Sohal, "Human Resource Management Strategies and Practices in Just-in-Time Environments: Australian Case Study

Evidence," *Technovation*, July 2000, 20, 7, pp. 373–87.

31. M. Tucker and D. Davis, "Key Ingredients for Successful Implementation of Just-in-Time: A System for All Business Sizes," *Business Horizons*, May–June 1993, pp. 59–65; Helen L. Richardson, "Tame Supply Chain Bottlenecks," *Transportation & Distribution*, March 2000, 41, no. 3, pp. 23–28.

32. John E. Ettlie, "Product Development—Beyond Simultaneous Engineering," *Automotive Manufacturing & Production*, July 2000, 112, 7, p. 18; Utpal Roy, John M. Usher, and Hamid R. Parsaei, eds. *Simultaneous Engineering: Methodologies and Applications* (Newark, NJ: Gordon and Breach, 1999); Marilyn M. Helms and Lawrence P. Ettkin, "Time-Based Competitiveness: A Strategic Perspective," *Competitiveness Review* (2000) 10, no. 2, pp. 1–14.

33. G. Hamel and C. K. Prahalad, "Competing for the Future," *Harvard Business Review*, July–August 1994, pp. 122–28.

34. G. Hamel and C. K. Prahalad, *Competing for the Future* (Boston: Harvard Business School Press, 1994).

35. R. E. Miles and C. C. Snow, *Fit, Failure, and the Hall of Fame* (New York: Free Press, 1994); Gillian Symon, "Information and Communication Technologies and Network Organization: A Critical Analysis," *Journal of Occupational and Organizational Psychology*, December 2000, 73, no. 4, pp. 389–95.

36. M. Lynne Markus, Brook Manville, and Carole E. Agres "What Makes a Virtual Organization Work?" *Sloan Management Review*, Fall 2000, 42, no. 1, pp. 13–26; William M. Fitzpatrick and Donald R. Burke, "Form, Functions, and Financial Performance Realities for the Virtual Organization," *S.A.M. Advanced Management Journal*, Summer 2000, 65, no. 3, pp. 13–20.

37. Miles and Snow, *Fit, Failure, and The Hall of Fame.*

38. Sherri Singer, "Diesel Engines Burn Leaner and Cleaner," *Machine Design*, October 7, 1999, 71, no. 19, pp. 64–69; P. P. Balestrini, "Globalization in the Automotive Industry: The Preferred External Growth Path," *Journal of International Marketing and Marketing Research*, October 2000, 25, no. 3, pp. 137–65; Eric Doyle, "Liberty Specifications Released," *Computer Weekly*, July 25, 2002, p. 30.

39. Pamela Harper and D. Vincent Varallo, "Global Strategic Alliances," *Executive Excellence*, October 2000, 17, no. 10, pp. 17–18.

40. R. M. Kanter, "Collaborative Advantage: The Art of Alliances," *Harvard Business Review*, July–August 1999, pp. 96–108; John B. Cullen, Jean L. Johnson, and Tomoaki Sakano, "Success through Commitment and Trust: The Soft Side of Strategic Alliance Management," *Journal of World Business*, Fall 2000, 35, no. 3, pp. 223–40; Prashant Kale, Harbir Singh, and Howard Perlmutter, "Learning and Protection of Proprietary Assets in Strategic Alliances: Building Relational Capital," *Strategic Management Journal*, March 2000, 21, no. 3, pp. 217–37.

41. P. Senge, *The Fifth Discipline* (New York: Doubleday Currency, 1990).

42. D. A. Garvin, "Building a Learning Organization," *Harvard Business Review*, July–August 1993, pp. 78–91; David A. Garvin, *Learning in Action: A Guide to Putting the Learning Organization to Work* (Boston: Harvard Business School Press, 2000); Victoria J. Marsick and Karen E. Watkins, *Facilitating Learning Organizations: Making Learning Count* (Aldershot, Hampshire, Gower Pub. Co, 1999).

43. Ibid.

44. Robert J. Vandenberg, Hettie A. Richardson, and Lorrina J. Eastman, "The Impact of High Involvement Work Processes on Organizational Effectiveness: A Second-Order Latent Variable Approach," *Group & Organization Management*, September 1999, 24, no. 3, pp. 300–39; Gretchen M. Spreitzer and Aneil K. Mishra, "Giving Up Control without Losing Control: Trust and Its Substitutes' Effects on Managers' Involving Employees in Decision Making," *Group & Organization Management*, June 1999, 24, no. 2, pp. 155–87; Susan Albers Mohrman, Gerald E. Ledford, and Edward E. Lawler III, *Strategies for High Performance Organizations—The CEO Report: Employee Involvement, TQM, and Reengineering Programs in Fortune 1000 Corporations* (San Francisco: Jossey-Bass, 1998).

45. R. Ashkenas, D. Ulrich, T. Jick, and S. Kerr, *The Boundaryless Organization: Breaking the Chains of Organizational Structure* (San Francisco: Jossey-Bass, 1995); R. W. Keidel, "Rethinking Organizational Design," *Academy of Management Executive*, November 1994, pp. 12–27; Ron Ashkenas, Todd Jick, Dave Ulrich, and Catherine Paul-Chowdhury, *The Boundaryless Organization Field Guide: Practical Tools for Building the New Organization* (San Francisco: Jossey-Bass, 1999).

Chapter 10

1. "The Importance of HR," *HRFocus*, March 1996, p. 14; John McMorrow, "Future Trends in Human Resources," *HR Focus*, September 1999, 76, no.9, pp. 7–9; Albert A. Vicere, "New Economy, New HR," *Employment Relations Today*, Autumn 2000, 27, no. 3, pp. 1–11.

2. Thomas O. Davenport, "Workers As Assets: A Good Start but . . .," *Employment Relations Today*, Spring 2000, 27, no. 1, pp. 1–18; Bruce Gilley, "Filling the Gap," *Far Eastern Economic Review*, September 14, 2000, 163, no. 37, pp. 44–46; "Filling the Skills Gap," *Business Europe*, May 17, 2000, 40, no. 10, p. 6.

3. Darin E. Hartley, *Job Analysis at the Speed of Reality* (Amherst, MA: HRD Press, 1999); Frederick P. Morgeson and Michael A. Campion, "Accuracy in Job Analysis: Toward an Inference-based Model," *Journal of Organizational Behavior*, November 2000, 21, no. 7, pp. 819–27; Jeffery S. Shippmann, Ronald A. Ash, Linda Carr, and Beryl Hesketh, "The Practice of Competency Modeling," *Personnel Psychology*, Autumn 2000, 53, no. 3, pp. 703–40.

4. Jeffery S. Schippmann, *Strategic Job Modeling: Working at the Core of Integrated Human Resources* (Mahwah, NJ: Lawrence Erlbaum Associates, 1999).

5. David E. Terpstra, "The Search for Effective Methods," *HRFocus*, May 1996, pp. 16–17; Herbert G. Heneman III and Robyn A. Berkley, "Applicant Attraction Practices and Outcomes Among Small Businesses," *Journal of Small Business Management*, January 1999, 37, no. 1, pp. 53–74; Jean-Marie Hiltrop, "The Quest for the Best: Human Resource Practices to Attract and Retain Talent," *European Management Journal*, August 1999, 17, no. 4, pp. 422–30.

6. Alex Daniels, "An Online Job War," *Newsbytes*, February 6, 2002, p. NWSB0203700E; Kerri Koss Morehart, "How to Create an Employee Referral Program that Really Works," *HR Focus*, January 2001, 78, no. 1, pp. 3–5; Keith Swenson, "Maximizing Employee Referrals," *HR Focus*, January 1999, 76, no. 1, pp. 9–10; "Are Your Recruiting Methods Discriminatory?" *Workforce*, May 2000, 79, no. 5, pp. 105–06.

7. "Pop Quiz: How Do You Recruit the Best College Grads?" *Personnel Journal*, August 1995, pp. 12–18; Shannon Peters Talbott, "Boost Your Campus Image to Attract Top Grads," *Personnel Journal*, March 1996, pp. 6–8; Cora Daniels, "Wall Street Says Please," *Fortune*, March 6, 2000, 141, no. 5, p. 420; Jean Buchanan, "Finding and Keeping Talent in a Shrinking Labor Pool," *Office Systems*, November 1999, 16, no. 11, pp. 42–46.

8. Malcolm Wheatley, "The Talent Spotters," *Management Today*, June 1996, pp. 62–64; Michael McDaniel, Deborah L. Whetzel, Frank L. Schmidt, and Steven D. Maurer, "The Validity of Employment Interviews: A Comprehensive Review and Meta-Analysis," *Journal of Applied Psychology* 79, no. 4 (August 1994), pp. 599–616; Michael A. Campion, James E. Campion, and Peter J. Hudson Jr., "Structured Interviewing: A Note on Incremental Validity and Alternative Question Types," *Journal of Applied Psychology* 79, no. 6 (December 1994), pp. 998–1002; R. A. Fear, *The Evalua-*

tion Interview (New York: McGraw-Hill, 1984); Pamela Mendels, "Asking the Right Questions," *Business Week Online*, October 13, 2000; Matthew T. Miklave and A. Jonathan Trafimow, "Ask Them If They Were Fired, but Not When They Graduated," *Workforce*, August 2000, 79, no. 8, pp. 90–93; Olivia Crosby, "Employment Interviewing: Seizing the Opportunity and the Job," *Occupational Outlook Quarterly*, Summer 2000, 44, no. 2, pp. 14–21.

9. Christopher E. Stenberg, "The Role of Pre-Employment Background Investigations in Hiring," *Human Resource Professional* 9, no. 1 (January/February 1996), pp. 19–21; "The Final Rung: References," *Across the Board*, March 1996, p. 40; Paul Taylor, "Providing Structure to Interviews and Reference Checks," *Workforce*, May 1999, Supplement, pp. 7–10; "Avoiding 'Truth or Dare' in Reference Checks," *HRFocus*, May 2000, 77, no. 5, pp. 5–6; "Fear of Lawsuits Complicates Reference Checks," *InfoWorld* February 1, 1999, 21, no. 5, p. 73; D. L. Hawley, "Background Checks on the Rise," *Legal Assistant Today*, May/June 2000, 17, no. 5, pp. 28, 40; David E. Terpstra, R. Bryan Kethley, Richard T. Foley, and Wanthanee Limpaphayom, "The Nature of Litigation Surrounding Five Screening Devices," *Public Personnel Management*, Spring 2000, 29, no. 1, pp. 43–54.

10. See also M. R. Barrick and M. K. Mount, "The Big Five Personality Dimensions and Job Performance: A Meta-Analysis," *Personnel Psychology*, 44 (1991), pp. 1–26; Daniel P. O'Meara, "Personality Tests Raise Questions of Legality and Effectiveness," *HRMagazine*, January 1994, pp. 97–100; Lynn A. McFarland and Ann Marie Ryan, "Variance in Faking across Noncognitive Measures," *Journal of Applied Psychology*, October 2000, 85, no. 5, pp. 812–21.

11. "Denny's Takes Drug-Free Policy Nationwide," *Employee Benefit Plan Review*, October 2000, 55, no. 4, pp. 34–36; "Fewer Employers Are Currently Conducting Psych & Drug Tests," *HRFocus*, October 2000, 77, no. 10, p. 8; Debra R. Comer, "Employees' Attitudes toward Fitness-for-Duty Testing," *Journal of Managerial Issues*, Spring 2000, 12, no. 1, pp. 61–75; "ACLU Report Debunks Workplace Drug Testing," *HRFocus*, November 1999, 76, no. 4, p. 4.

12. Patrick M. Wright, Michele K. Kacmar, Gary C. McMahan, and Kevin Deleeuw, "P = f(M × A): Cognitive Ability as a Moderator of the Relationship between Personality and Job Performance," *Journal of Management* 21, no. 6 (1995), pp. 1129–2063; Paul R. Sackett and Daniel J. Ostgaard, "Job-Specific Applicant Pools and National Norms for Cognitive Ability Tests: Implications for Range Restriction Corrections in Vali-

dation Research," *Journal of Applied Psychology*, 79, no. 5 (October 1994), pp. 680–84; F. L. Schmidt and J. E. Hunter, "Tacit Knowledge, Practical Intelligence, General Mental Ability, and Job Knowledge," *Current Directions in Psychological Science*, 2, no. 1 (1993), pp. 3–13; Mary Roznowski, David N. Dickter, Linda L. Sawin, Valerie J. Shute, and Sehee Hong, "The Validity of Measures of Cognitive Processes and Generability for Learning and Performance on Highly Complex Computerized Tutors: Is the G Factor of Intelligence Even More General?" *Journal of Applied Psychology*, December 2000, 85, no. 6, 940–55; Jose M. Cortina, Nancy B. Goldstein, Stephanie C. Payne, H. Krisl Davison, and Stephen W. Gilliland, "The Incremental Validity of Interview Scores over and above Cognitive Ability and Conscientiousness Scores," *Personnel Psychology*, Summer 2000, 53, no. 2, 325–51.

13. Winfred Arthur Jr., David J. Woehr, and Robyn Maldegen, "Convergent and Discriminant Validity of Assessment Center Dimensions: A Conceptual and Empirical Reexamination of the Assessment Center Construct-Related Validity Paradox," *Journal of Management* (2000), 26, no. 4, pp. 813–35; Raymond Randall, Eammon Ferguson, and Fiona Patterson, "Self-Assessment Accuracy and Assessment Center Decisions," *Journal of Occupational and Organizational Psychology*, December 2000, 73, no. 4, p. 443.

14. Lynn A. McFarland and Ann Marie Ryan, "Variance in Faking across Noncognitive Measures," *Journal of Applied Psychology*, October 2000, 85, no. 5, 812–21; David E. Terpstra; R. Bryan Kethley, Richard T. Foley, and Wanthanee Limpaphayom, "The Nature of Litigation Surrounding Five Screening Devices," *Public Personnel Management*, Spring 2000, 29, no. 1, pp. 43–54.

15. D. S. Ones, C. Viswesvaran, and F. L. Schmidt, "Comprehensive Meta-Analysis of Integrity Test Validities: Findings and Implications for Personnel Selection and Theories of Job Performance," *Journal of Applied Psychology*, 78 (August 1993), pp. 679–703.

16. Rocki-Lee DeWitt, "The Structural Consequences of Downsizing," *Organization Science* 4, no. 1 (February 1993), pp. 30–40; Priti Pradhan Shah, "Network Destruction: The Structural Implications of Downsizing," *Academy of Management Journal*, February 2000, 43, no. 1, pp. 101–12; Jennifer Laabs, "Has Downsizing Missed Its Mark?" *Workforce*, April 1999, 78, no. 4, pp. 30–38.

17. See *Adair v. United States*, 2078 U.S. 161 (1908); Deborah A. Ballam, "Employment-at-Will; The Impending Death of a Doctrine," *American Business Law Journal*, Summer 2000, 37, no. 4, pp. 653–87.

18. Anne Fisher, "Dumping Troublemakers, and Exiting Gracefully," *Fortune*, February 15, 1999, 139, no. 3, p. 174; Paul Falcone "Employee Separations: Layoffs vs. Terminations for Cause," *HRMagazine*, October 2000, 45, no. 10, pp. 189–96; Paul Falcone, "A Blueprint for Progressive Discipline and Terminations," *HRFocus*, August 2000, 77, no. 8, pp. 3–5.

19. See also John E. Lyncheski, "Mishandling Terminations Causes Legal Nightmares," *HRMagazine* 40, no. 5 (May 1995), pp. 25–30. Katherine A. Karl and Barry W. Hancock, "Expert Advice on Employment Termination Practices: How Expert Is It?" *Public Personnel Management*, Spring 1999, 28, no. 1, pp. 51–62.

20. *Employer EEO Responsibilities* (Washington, DC: Equal Employment Opportunity Commission, U.S. Government Printing Office, 1996); Nancy J. Edman and Michael D. Levin-Epstein, *Primer of Equal Employment Opportunity*, 6th ed. (Washington, DC: Bureau of National Affairs, 1994).

21. Robert Gatewood and Hubert Field, *Human Resource Selection*, 3rd ed. (Chicago: Dryden Press, 1994), pp. 36–49; R. A. Baysinger, "Disparate Treatment and Disparate Impact Theories of Discrimination: The Continuing Evolution of Title VII of the 1964 Civil Rights Act," in *Readings in Personnel and Human Resource Management*, ed. R. S. Schuler, S. A. Youngblood, and V. L. Huber (St. Paul, MN: West Publishing, 1987).

22. "Uniform Guidelines on Employee Selection Procedures," *Federal Register*, 43, no. 166 (August 25, 1978), pp. 38290–309.

23. Nicole Lee, "Learning How to Make the Best of Workplace Education," *The Financial Times*, August 19, 2002, p. 12; "Career Building Gets Put on Hold," *Crain's New York Business*, August 5, 2002, p.21; "Industry Report 2000: The Money," *Training*, October 2000, 37, no. 10, pp. 51–55; Skip Corsini, "The Great Training Robbery," *Training*, October 2000, 37, no. 10,p. 160.

24. A. P. Carnevale, *America and the New Economy: How New Competitive Standards Are Radically Changing American Workplaces* (San Francisco: Jossey-Bass, 1991); Marc Hequet, "Doing More with Less," *Training*, 31 (October 1995), pp. 77–82; Robert M. Fulmer, Philip A. Gibbs, and Marshall Goldsmith, "Developing Leaders: How Winning Companies Keep on Winning," *Sloan Management Review*, Fall 2000, 42, no. 1, pp. 49–59; "Most Training Dollars Spent on Trainers, and Not Materials," *HR Focus*, December 2000, 77, no. 12, p. 8.

25. Sandra N. Phillips, "Team Training Puts Fizz in Coke Plant's Future," *Personnel Journal*, 75, no. 1 (January 1996), pp. 39–42. See also George Bohlander and Kathy McCarthy, "How

to Get the Most from Team Training," *National Productivity Review*, Autumn 1996, pp. 25–35.

26. For more information, see Kenneth Wexley and Gary Latham, *Increasing Productivity through Performance Appraisal* (Reading, MA; Addison-Wesley, 1994).

27. Mark Edwards and Ann J. Ewen, "How to Manage Performance and Pay with 360-Degree Feedback," *Compensation and Benefits Review*, 28, no. 3 (May/June 1996), pp. 41–46. Also see Mary N. Vinson, "The Pros and Cons of 360-Degree Feedback: Making It Work," *Training and Development* 50, no. 4 (April 1996), pp. 11–12; John F. Milliman, Robert F. Zawacki, Carol Norman, Lynda Powell, and Jay Kirksey, "Companies Evaluate Employees from All Perspectives," *Personnel Journal*, 73, no. 11 (November 1994), pp. 99–103; R. S. Schuler, *Personnel and Human Resource Management* (St. Paul, MN: West Publishing, 1984).

28. G. W. Bohlander, S. A. Snell, and A. W. Sherman, Jr., *Managing Human Resources*, 12th ed. (Cincinnati, OH: Southwestern Publishing, 2001).

29. Garry M. Ritzky, "Incentive Pay Programs That Help the Bottom Line," *HRMagazine*, 40, no. 4 (April 1995), pp. 68–74; Steven Gross and Jeffrey Bacher, "The New Variable Pay Programs: How Some Succeed, Why Some Don't," *Compensation and Benefits Review*, 25, no. 1 (January–February 1993), p. 51; G. T. Milkovich and J. M. Newman, *Compensation* (New York: McGraw-Hill Irwin, 1999).

30. Theresa Welbourne and Luis Gomez-Mejia, "Gainsharing: A Critical Review and a Future Research Agenda," *Journal of Management* 21, no. 3 (1995), pp. 559–609; Luis P. Gomez-Mejia, Theresa M. Welbourne, and Robert M. Wiseman, "The Role of Risk Sharing and Risk Taking under Gainsharing," *Academy of Management Review*, July 2000, 25, no. 3, pp. 492–507; Denis Collins, *Gainsharing and Power: Lessons from Six Scanlon Plans* (Ithaca, NY: ILR Press, 1998); P. K. Zingheim and J. R. Schuster, *Pay People Right!* (San Francisco: Jossey-Bass, 2000).

31. J. Savage, "Incentive Programs at Nucor Corporation Boost Productivity," *Personnel Administrator*, August 1981, pp. 33–36; Anil K. Gupta and Vijay Govindarajan, "Knowledge Management's Social Dimension: Lessons from Nucor Steel," *Sloan Management Review*, Fall 2000, 42, no. 1, pp. 71–80; Elaine C. Hollensbe and James P. Guthrie, "Group Pay-for-Performance Plans: The Role of Spontaneous Goal Setting," *Academy of Management Review*, October 2000, 25, no. 4, pp. 864–72.

32. Kenneth W. Chilton, "Lincoln Electric's Incentive System: A Reservoir of Trust," *Compensation and Benefits Review*, 25, no. 6 (November 1994),

pp. 29–34. See also D. W. Meyers. *Human Management: Principles and Practice* (Chicago: Commerce Clearing House, 1986); James P. Guthrie, "Alternative Pay Practices and Employee Turnover: An Organization Economics Perspective," *Group & Organization Management*, December 2000, 25, no. 4, pp. 419–39.

33. Ellen C. Kearns and Monica Gallagher, eds., *The Fair Labor Standards Act* (Washington, DC: BNA, 1999).

34. Charles Fay and Howard W. Risher, "Contractors, Comparable Worth and the New OFCCP; Deja Vu and More," *Compensation and Benefits Review*, September/October 2000, 32, no. 5, pp. 23–33; Gillian Flynn, "Protect Yourself from an Equal-Pay Audit," *Workforce*, June 1999, 78, no. 6, pp. 144–46.

35. Bohlander, Snell, and Sherman, *Managing Human Resources*.

36. Eileen Henry, "Wage-Bias Bill: Study Panel Proposed," *Arizona Business Gazette*, February 28, 2002, pp. 2–4. Susan E. Gardner and Christopher Daniel, "Implementing Comparable Worth/Pay Equity: Experiences of Cutting-Edge States," *Public Personnel Management*, Winter 1998, 27, no. 4, pp. 475–89.

37. Alfred Lubrano, "Miners Live Life of Good Pay for High Danger," *Knight-Ridder/Tribune Business News*, August 13, 2002, p. ITEM02225012; T. Gup, "The Curse of Coal," *Time*, November 4, 1991, pp. 54–64.

38. Linda Kahn, *Primer of Labor Relations*, 25th ed. (Washington, DC: Bureau of National Affairs Books, 1994); A. Sloane and F. Witney, *Labor Relations* (Englewood Cliffs, NJ: Prentice-Hall, 1985).

39. S. Premack and J. E. Hunter, "Individual Unionization Decisions," *Psychological Bulletin* 103 (1988), pp. 223–34; Leo Troy, *Beyond Unions and Collective Bargaining* (Armonk, NY: M. E. Sharpe, 1999); John A. McClendon, "Members and Nonmembers: Determinants of Dues-Paying Membership in a Bargaining Unit," *Relations Industrielles*, Spring 2000, 55, no. 2, pp. 332–47.

40. Robert Sinclair and Lois Tetrick, "Social Exchange and Union Commitment: A Comparison of Union Instrumentality and Union Support Perceptions," *Journal of Organizational Behavior* 16, no. 6 (November 1995), pp. 669–79. See also Premack and Hunter, "Individual Unionization Decisions."

41. David Lewin and Richard B. Peterson, *The Modern Grievance Procedure in the United States* (Westport CT: Quorum Books, 1998); Steven E. Abraham and Paula B. Voos, "Right-to-Work Laws: New Evidence from the Stock Market," *Southern Economic Journal*, October 2000, 67, no. 2, pp. 345–62.

42. George Bohlander and Donna Blancero, "A Study of Reversal

Determinants in Discipline and Discharge Arbitration Awards: The Impact of Just Cause Standards," *Labor Studies Journal*, 21, no. 3 (Fall 1996), pp. 3–18.

Chapter 11

1. *2000–2010 Employment Projections* (Washington DC: Bureau of Labor Statistics, U.S. Department of Labor 2002), http://www.bls.gov/news.release/ecopro.nr0.htm.

2. Ibid.

3. *Employment Projections*, Bureau of Labor Statistics; *Highlights of Women's Earnings in 2001* (Washington DC: Bureau of Labor Statistics, U.S. Department of Labor, May 2002); Press release "Ask a Working Woman Survey, 2002," AFL-CIO, copyright 2002; Margaret Steen, "Male-Female Pay Gap Widened, Study Says," *Knight-Ridder/Tribune Business News*, September 1, 2002, pITEM02244014; Jennifer Laabs, "Celebrating National Business Women's Week," *Workforce*, October 2000, 79, no. 10, p. 32.

4. Toddi Gutner, "The Rose-Colored Glass Ceiling," *Business Week*, September 2, 2002; *Catalyst's* "2001 Census of Women Board Directors of the Fortune 1000"; Tami Lubhy, "Women Execs Narrowing Salary Gap," *Newsday.com*, June 24, 2002; Nacy Perry, "More Women Are Executive VPs," *Fortune*, July 12, 1993, p. 16; Jennifer Laabs, "Saturn Gets Female President, but Female Leaders Are Still a Corporate Oddity," *Workforce*, February 1999, 78, no. 2, p. 22.

5. "How to Shrink the Pay Gap," *Business Week*, June 24, 2002, p. 15; Tom Dunkel, "The Front Runners," *Working Woman*, April 1996, pp. 30–35, 72, 75; Rosemary Cafasso, "The Diversity Gap," *Computerworld*, June 1996, pp. 35–37; Laabs, "Saturn Gets Female President," p. 22; Rochelle Sharpe, "As Leaders, Women Rule," *Business Week*, November 20, 2000, pp. 74–84.

6. George Bohlander, Scott Snell, and Arthur Sherman, *Managing Human Resources*, 12th ed. (Cincinnati, OH: Southwestern Publishing, 2001); William Petrocelli and Barbar Kate Repa, *Sexual Harassment on the Job: What It Is and How to Stop It* (Berkeley, CA: Nolo Press, 1998).

7. Kipp Cheng, "Beyond Just the Numbers, What Counts as an Emerging Market?" *DiversityInc.com*, July 1, 2002; "Charting the Projections: 1994–2005"; Margaret Blackburn White and Joseph Potts, "Just the Facts: Women of Color in U.S. Corporations," *Diversity Factor*, Spring 1999, 7, no. 3, pp. 8–15; Alberto Davila and Marie T Mora, "English Fluency of Recent Hispanic Immigrants to the United States in 1980 and 1990," *Economic Development and Cultural Change*, January 2000, 48, no. 2, pp. 369–89; Milford Prewitt, "Immigration Eyed as Fix for Labor-Shortage

Woes," *Nation's Restaurant News*, October 2, 2000, 34, no. 40, pp. 1,68.

8. "Forgotten Men: The Continuing Crisis in Black Male Unemployment, and How to Remedy It," *The American Prospect*, July 15, 2002, pp. A36–A37; "GAO Looks at the Reality of Pay Equality," *Payroll Manager's Letter*, June 7, 2002, p. 7; Molly Prior, "Women and Minorities Still Exceptions to the Rule," *DSN Retailing Today*, May 20, 2002, p. 25; Asra Q. Nomani, "Labor Letter," *The Wall Street Journal*, November 7, 1996, p. A1. See also, G. Evans Witt, "In the Eye of the Beholder," *American Demographics*, October 1999, 21, no. 10, p. 24.

9. "On the Job," *Paraplegia News*, June 2002, pp. 41–42; "For the Disabled, It's Always a Depression," *Business Week Online*, December 5, 2001; "An ADA Checklist for Implementation and Review," *HR Focus*, July 1994, p. 19; Stephen Overall, "Firms Hire Fewer Disabled People in Unskilled Jobs," *People Management*, November 16, 1995, p. 10; James Jordan, *ADA Americans with Disabilities Act Compliance Manual for California* (Bristol, UK: Jordan Publishing, 1999).

10. "New ADA Enforcement Guides from the EEOC," *HR Focus*, December 2000, 77, no. 12, p. 2.

11. Gail Dutton, "The ADA at 10," *Workforce*, December 2000, 79, no. 12, pp. 40–46.

12. *Employment Projections*, Bureau of Labor Statistics.

13. Ibid.

14. "2001 AMA Survey: Basic Skills, Job Skills, and Psychological Measurement"; "Low Literacy," *Training and Development*, January 1994, p. 12; Ruth E. Davidhizar and Kenneth Brownson "Literacy, Cultural Diversity, and Client Education," *Health Care Manager*, September 1999, 18, no. 1, pp. 39–47.

15. Michael A. Verespej, "The Education Difference," *Industry Week*, 245, no. 9 (May 6, 1996), pp. 11–14; Teresa L. Smith, "The Basics of Basic-Skills Training," *Training and Development*, 49, no. 4 (April 1995), pp. 44–46; Teresa L. Smith, "Job Related Materials Reinforce Basic Skills," *HRMagazine*, July 1995, pp. 84–90.

16. Kenneth Labich, "No More Crude at Texaco," *Fortune*, September 6, 1999, 140, no. 5, pp. 205–12; *Good for Business: Making Full Use of the Nation's Human Capital* (Washington, DC: Federal Glass Ceiling Commission, 1995).

17. N. Adler, *International Dimensions of Organizational Behavior*, 3rd ed. (Boston: PWS–Kent, 1997); T. Cox and S. Blake, "Managing Cultural Diversity: Implications for Organizational Competitiveness," *Academy of Management Executives*, 5 (August 1991), pp. 45–56.

18. "America's 50 Best Companies for Minorities," *Fortune*, July 28, 2002; "Successful Companies Realize That

Diversity Is a Long-Term Process, Not a Program," *Personnel Journal*, April 1993, p. 54; Joan Crockett, "Diversity: Winning Competitive Advantage through a Diverse Workforce," *HR Focus*, May 1999, 76, no. 5, pp. 9–10.

19. Adler, *International Dimensions of Organizational Behavior*; Cox and Blake, "Managing Cultural Diversity."

20. Adler, *International Dimensions of Organizational Behavior*.

21. Audrey J. Murrell, Faye J. Crosby, and Robin J. Ely, *Mentoring Dilemmas: Developmental Relationships within Multicultural Organizations* (Mahwah, NJ: Lawrence Erlbaum Associates, 1999). See a review of this book by Mark L. Lengnick-Hall, "Mentoring Dilemmas: Developmental Relationships within Multicultural Organizations," *Personnel Psychology*, Spring 2000, 53, no. 1, pp. 224–27.

22. A. Livingston, "What Your Department Can Do." *Working Woman*, January 1991, pp. 59–60; Mary Dean Lee, Shelley M. MacDermid, and Michelle L. Buck, "Organizational Paradigms of Reduced-Load Work: Accommodation, Elaboration, and Transformation," *Academy of Management Journal*, December 2000, 43, no. 6, pp. 1211–34.

23. Leslie E. Overmyer Day, "The Pitfalls of Diversity Training," *Training and Development*, 49, no. 12 (December 1995), pp. 24–29; Sara Rynes and Benson Rosen, "A Field Survey of Factors Affecting the Adoption and Perceived Success of Diversity Training," *Personnel Psychology* 48, no. 2 (Summer 1995), pp. 247–70; Lynda Ford, "Diversity: From Cartoons to Confrontations," *Training & Development*, August 2000, 54, no. 8, pp. 70–71; "Diversity: A 'New' Tool for Retention," *HR Focus*, June 2000, 77, no. 6, pp. 1, 14: Lin Grensing-Pophal, "Is Your HR Department Diverse Enough?" *HRMagazine*, September 2000, 45, no. 9, pp. 46–52; John M. Ivancevich and Jacqueline A. Gilbert, "Diversity Management: Time for a New Approach," *Public Personnel Management*, Spring 2000, 29, no. 1, pp. 75–92.

24. Michael Burkart, "The Role of Training in Advancing a Diversity Initiative," *Diversity Factor*, Fall 1999, 8, no. 1, pp. 2–5.

25. Nancy L. Mueller, "Wisconsin Power and Light's Model Diversity Program," *Training and Development*, March 1996, pp. 57–60; Robert J Grossman, "Is Diversity Working?" *HR Magazine*, March 2000, 45, no. 3, pp. 46–50.

26. Phyllis Shurn-Hannah, "Solving the Minority Retention Mystery," *The Human Resource Professional*, May/June 2000, 13, no. 3, pp. 22–27; Gillian Flynn, "Firm's Diversity Efforts Even the Playing Field," *Personnel Journal* (January 1996), 56.

27. Barbara Durr, "Clubbing Together to Get Ahead," *Financial Times*, June 17,

2002, p. 11; Margaret Blackburn White, "Organization 2005: New Strategies at P&G," *Diversity Factor*, Fall 1999, 8, no. 1, pp. 16–20.

28. William G. Bowen, Derek Bok, and Glenda Burkhart, "A Report Card on Diversity: Lessons for Business from Higher Education," *Harvard Business Review*, January–February 1999, 7, no. 1, pp. 38–45; Bryan Gingrich, "Individual and Organizational Accountabilities Reducing Stereotypes and Prejudice within the Workplace," *Diversity Factor*, Winter 2000, 8, no. 2, pp. 14–19; Joan Crockett, "Diversity: Winning Competitive Advantage through a Diverse Workforce," *HR Focus*, May 1999, 76, no. 5, pp. 9–10.

Part Three Integrating Case

1. Gloria M. Curry, "Package Delivery Service: The Options Are Plentiful," *Office*, August 1989, pp. 60–62.

2. Charles Arthur, "The War in the Air," *Business* [U.K.], November 1989, pp. 60–66.

3. Erik Guyot, "Air Courier Fight for Pacific Business," *Asian Finance* [Hong Kong], July 15, 1990, pp. 22–23.

4. James T. McKenna, "Airline Boosts International Cargo Services to Protect Market Shares," *Aviation Week & Space Technology*, November 20, 1989, pp. 124–25.

5. Dean Foust, "Mr. Smith Goes Global," *Business Week*, February 13, 1989, pp. 66–72.

6. Frederick W. Smith, "Empowering Employee," *Small Business Reports*, January 1991, pp. 15–20.

7. Perry A. Trunick, "Leadership and People Distinguish Federal Express," *Transportation & Distribution*, December 1989, pp. 18–22.

8. "Federal Express Spreads its Wings," *Journal of Business Strategy*, July–August 1988, pp. 15–20.

9. Foust, "Mr. Smith Goes Global."

10. "Federal Express Spreads Its Wings," pp. 3–10.

11. Erik Calonius, "Federal Express Battle Overseas," *Fortune*, 1990, December 3, 1990, pp. 137–40.

12. Foust, "Mr. Smith Goes Global."

13. James Ott, "Board Decision Muddle Rules on Union Role after Merger," *Aviation Week & Space Technology*, August 28, 1989, p. 68.

14. Foust, "Mr. Smith Goes Global."

Chapter 12

1. W. Bennis and B. Nanus, *Leaders* (New York: Harper & Row, 1985), p. 27.

2. J. Petrick, R. Schere, J. Brodzinski, J. Quinn, and M. Fall Ainina, "Global Leadership Skills and Reputational Capital: Intangible Resources for Sustainable Competitive Advantage," *Academy of Management Executive*, February 1999, pp. 58–69.

3. Bennis and Nanus, *Leaders*.

4. Ibid., p. 144.

5. J. Kouzes and B. Posner, *The Leadership Challenge*, 1st ed. (San Francisco: Jossey-Bass, 1987).

6. Ibid.

7. Ibid.

8. J. Baum, E. A. Locke, and S. Kirkpatrick, "A Longitudinal Study of the Relation of Vision and Vision Communication to Venture Growth in Entrepreneurial Firms," *Journal of Applied Psychology* 83 (1998), pp. 43–54.

9. E. C. Shapiro, *Fad Surfing in the Boardroom* (Reading, MA: Addison-Wesley, 1995).

10. J. Kouzes and B. Posner, *The Leadership Challenge*, 2nd ed. (San Francisco: Jossey-Bass, 1995).

11. Ibid.

12. W. Bennis and R. Townsend, *Reinventing Leadership* (New York: William Morrow, 1995).

13. Ibid.

14. Kouzes and Posner, *The Leadership Challenge* (1987).

15. J. A. Conger, "The Dark Side of Leadership," *Organizational Dynamics* 19 (Autumn 1990), pp. 44–55.

16. J. P. Kotter, "What Leaders Really Do," *Harvard Business Review* 68 (May–June 1990) pp. 103–11.

17. A. Zaleznik, "The Leadership Gap," *The Executive* 4 (February 1990), pp. 7–22.

18. G. Yukl, *Leadership in Organizations*, 3rd ed. (Englewood Cliffs, NJ: Prentice-Hall, 1994).

19. R. House and R. Aditya, "The Social Scientific Study of Leadership: Quo Vadis?" *Journal of Management* 23 (1997), pp. 409–73.

20. R. D. Ireland and M. A. Hitt. "Achieving and Maintaining Strategic Competitiveness in the 21st Century. The Role of Strategic Leadership," *Academy of Management Executive*, February 1999, pp. 43–57.

21. R. E. Kelly, "In Praise of Followers," *Harvard Business Review* 66 (November–December 1988), pp. 142–48.

22. Bennis and Townsend, *Reinventing Leadership*.

23. R. Heifetz and D. Laurie, "The Work of Leadership," *Harvard Business Review*, January–February 1997, pp. 124–34.

24. Kelly, "In Praise of Followers."

25. J. R. P. French and B. Raven, "The Bases of Social Power," in *Studies in Social Power*, ed. D. Cartwright (Ann Arbor, MI: Institute for Social Research, 1959).

26. G. Yukl and C. Falbe, "Importance of Different Power Sources in Downward and Lateral Relations," *Journal of Applied Psychology*, 76 (1991), pp. 416–23.

27. Ibid.

28. Ibid.

29. R. M. Stogdill, "Personal Factors Associated with Leadership: A Survey of the Literature," *Journal of Psychology* 25 (1948), pp. 35–71.

30. S. Kirkpatrick and E. Locke, "Leadership: Do Traits Matter?" *The Executive* 5 (May 1991), pp. 48–60.

31. G. A. Yukl, *Leadership in Organizations*, 2nd ed. (Englewood Cliffs, NJ: Prentice-Hall, 1989).

32. Heifetz and Laurie, "The Work of Leadership."

33. J. P. Kotter, *The General Managers* (New York: Free Press, 1982).

34. S. Zaccaro, R. Foti, and D. Kenny, "Self-Monitoring and Trait-Based Variance in Leadership: An Investigation of Leader Flexibility across Multiple Group Situations," *Journal of Applied Psychology* 76 (1991), pp. 308–15.

35. D. Goleman, "Leadership that Gets Results," *Harvard Business Review*, March–April 2000, pp. 78–90.

36. J. Misumi and M. Peterson, "The Performance-Maintenance (PM) Theory of Leadership: Review of a Japanese Research Program," *Administrative Science Quarterly* 30 (June 1985), pp. 198–223.

37. Ibid.

38. G. Graen and M. Uhl-Bien, "Relationship-Based Approach to Leadership: Development of Leader-Member Exchange (LMX) Theory of Leadership over 25 Years: Applying a Multi-Level Multidomain Perspective," *Leadership Quarterly* 6, no. 2 (1995), pp. 219–47.

39. House and Aditya, "The Social Scientific Study of Leadership."

40. C. R. Gerstner and D. V. Day, "Meta-Analytic Review of Leader-Member Exchange-Theory: Correlates and Construct Issues," *Journal of Applied Psychology*, 82 (1997), pp. 827–44.

41. House and Aditya, "Social Scientific Study."

42. J. Wagner III, "Participation's Effect on Performance and Satisfaction: A Reconsideration of Research," *Academy of Management Review*, April 1994, pp. 312–30.

43. R. White and R. Lippitt, *Autocracy and Democracy: An Experimental Inquiry* (New York: Harper & Brothers, 1960).

44. J. Muczyk and R. Steel, "Leadership Style and the Turnaround Executive," *Business Horizons*, March–April 1999, pp. 39–46.

45. A. Tannenbaum and W. Schmidt, "How to Choose a Leadership Pattern," *Harvard Business Review* 36 (March–April 1958), pp. 95–101.

46. E. Fleishman and E. Harris, "Patterns of Leadership Behavior Related to Employee Grievances and Turnover," *Personnel Psychology* 15 (1962), pp. 43–56.

47. R. Likert, *The Human Organization: Its Management and Value* (New York: McGraw-Hill, 1967).

48. R. Blake and J. Mouton, *The Managerial Grid* (Houston: Gulf, 1964).

49. Misumi and Peterson, "The Performance-Maintenance (PM) Theory."

50. Tannenbaum and Schmidt, "How to Choose a Leadership Pattern."

51. V. H. Vroom, "Leadership and the Decision-Making Process," *Organizational Dynamics*, Spring 2000, pp. 82–93.

52. R. J. House, "A Path Goal Theory of Leader Effectiveness," *Administrative Science Quarterly* 16 (1971), pp. 321–39.

53. J. Howell, D. Bowen, P. Dorfman, S. Kerr, and P. Podsakoff, "Substitutes for Leadership: Effective Alternatives to Ineffective Leadership," *Organizational Dynamics* 19 (Summer 1990), pp. 21–38.

54. R. G. Lord and W. Gradwohl Smith, "Leadership and the Changing Nature of Performance," in D. R. Ilgen and E. D. Pulakos, eds., *The Changing Nature of Performance* (San Francisco: Jossey-Bass, 1999).

55. K. Brooker, "Can Anyone Replace Herb?" *Fortune*, April 17, 2000, pp. 186–92.

56. A. Bianco and L. Lavell, "The CEO Trap," *Business Week*, December 11, 2000, pp. 86–92.

57. B. M. Bass, *Leadership and Performance Beyond Expectations* (New York: Free Press, 1985).

58. Y. A. Nur, "Charisma and Managerial Leadership: The Gift That Never Was," *Business Horizons*, July–August 1998, pp. 19–26.

59. R. J. House, "A 1976 Theory of Charismatic Leadership," in *Leadership: The Cutting Edge*, ed. J. G. Hunt and L. L. Larson (Carbondale, IL: Southern Illinois University Press, 1977).

60. M. Potts and P. Behr, *The Leading Edge* (New York: McGraw-Hill, 1987).

61. S. Yorges, H. Weiss, and O. Strickland, "The Effect of Leader Outcomes on Influence, Attributions, and Perceptions of Charisma," *Journal of Applied Psychology*, 84 (1999), pp. 428–36.

62. Potts and Behr, "Leading Edge."

63. D. A. Waldman and F. J. Yammarino, "CEO Charismatic Leadership: Levels-of-Management and Levels-of-Analysis Effects," *Academy of Management Review*, 24 (1999), pp. 266–85.

64. House and Aditya, "The Social Scientific Study of Leadership."

65. D. A. Waldman, G. G. Ramirez, R. J. House, and P. Puranam, (2001). Does leadership matter? CEO leadership attributes and profitability under conditions of perceived environmental uncertainty. *Academy of Management Journal*, 44, 134–143.

66. J. M. Howell and K. E. Hall-Merenda The Ties that Bind: The Impact of Leader-Member Exchange, Transformational and Transactional Leadership, and Distance on Predicting Follower Performance," *Journal of Applied Psychology*, 84 (1999), pp. 680–94.

67. B. M. Bass, "Leadership: Good, Better, Best," *Organizational Dynamics*, Winter 1985, pp. 26–40.(b)

68. F. J. Yammarino, F. Dansereau, and C. J. Kennedy, (2001). A multiple-level multidimensional approach to leadership: Viewing leadership through an elephant's eye. *Organizational Dynamics*, Winter, 149–163.

69. D. I. Jung and B. J. Avolio, "Effects of Leadership Style and Followers'

Cultural Orientation on Performance in Group and Individual Task Conditions," *Academy of Management Journal* 42 (1999), pp. 208–18.

70. Bass, *Leadership*.

71. Bennis and Nanus, *Leaders*.

72. B. Bass, B. Avolio, and L. Goodheim, "Biography and the Assessment of Transformational Leadership at the World-Class Level," *Journal of Management*, 13 (1987), pp. 7–20.

73. K. Albrecht and R. Zemke, *Service America* (Homewood, IL: Dow Jones Irwin, 1985).

74. T. A. Judge and J. E. Bono, "Five-Factor Model of Personality and Transformational Leadership," *Journal of Applied Psychology* 85 (2000), pp. 751–65.

75. B. Bass, "Does the Transactional-Transformational Paradigm Transcend Organizational and National Boundaries?" *American Psychologist* 22 (1997), pp. 130–42.

76. G. Spreitzer and R. Quinn, "Empowering Middle Managers to Be Transformational Leaders," *Journal of Applied Behavioral Science* 32 (1996), pp. 237–61.

77. Ibid.

78. J. Huey, "The New Post-Heroic Leadership," *Fortune*, February 21, 1994, pp. 42–50.

79. W. Bennis, "The End of Leadership: Exemplary Leadership Is Impossible without Full Inclusion, Initiatives, and Cooperation of Followers," *Organizational Dynamics*, Summer 1999, pp. 71–79.

80. G. G. Dess and J. C. Picken, (2000). Changing roles: Leadership in the 21st century. *Organizational Dynamics*, Winter, 18–33.

81. Ibid, p. 22.

82. Ibid, p. 25.

83. Ibid, p. 31.

84. P. Block, *The Empowered Manager* (San Francisco: Jossey-Bass, 1991).

85. Ibid.

86. Kouzes and Posner, *The Leadership Challenge* (1995 ed.).

87. J. Beeson, "Succession Planning: Building the Management Corps," *Business Horizons*, September–October, pp. 61–66.

88. R. Fulmer, P. Gibbs, and M. Goldsmith, "Developing Leaders: How Winning Companies Keep on Winning," *Sloan Management Review*, Fall 2000, pp. 49–59.

89. M. McCall, *High Flyers* (Boston: Harvard Business School Press, 1998).

90. Ibid.

Appendix E

1. F. E. Fiedler, *A Theory of Leadership Effectiveness* (New York: McGraw-Hill, 1967).

2. P. Hersey and K. Blanchard, *The Management of Organizational Behavior* (Englewood Cliffs, NJ: Prentice Hall, 1984)

3. Yukl, *Leadership in Organizations*.

Chapter 13

1. R. Kreitner and F. Luthans, "A Social Learning Approach to Behavioral Management: Radical Behaviorists 'Mellowing Out,'" *Organizational Dynamics*, Autumn 1984, pp. 47–65.

2. D. Katz and R. L. Kahn, *The Social Psychology of Organizations* (New York: John Wiley & Sons, 1966).

3. C. A. Bartlett and S. Ghoshal, "Building Competitive Advantage through People," *Sloan Management Review*, Winter 2002, pp. 34–41.

4. E. Locke, "Toward a Theory of Task Motivation and Incentives," *Organizational Behavior and Human Performance* 3 (1968), pp. 157–89.

5. W. F. Cascio, "Managing a Virtual Workplace," *Academy of Management Executive*, August 2000, pp. 81–90.

6. R. H. Schaffer, "Demand Better Results—and Get Them," *Harvard Business Review* 69 (March–April 1991), pp. 142–49.

7. T. Mitchell and W. Silver, "Individual and Group Goals When Workers Are Interdependent: Effects on Task Strategies and Performance," *Journal of Applied Psychology* 75 (1990), pp. 185–93.

8. P. C. Early, T. Connolly, and G. Ekegren, "Goals, Strategy Development, and Task Performance: Some Limits on the Efficacy of Goal Setting," *Journal of Applied Psychology* 74 (1989), pp. 24–33; C. E. Shalley, "Effects of Productivity Goals, Creativity Goals, and Personal Discretion on Individual Creativity," *Journal of Applied Psychology* 76 (1991), pp. 179–85.

9. J. Main, "Is the Baldridge Overblown?" *Fortune*, July 1, 1991, pp. 62–65.

10. E. Thorndike, *Animal Intelligence* (New York: Macmillan, 1911).

11. A. D. Stajkovic and F. Luthans, "Differential Effects of Incentive Motivators on Work Performance," *Academy of Management Journal* 44 (2001), pp. 580–90.

12. R. Levering and M. Moskowitz, "The 100 Best Companies to Work For," *Fortune*, January 8, 2001, pp. 148–68.

13. Cascio, "Managing a Virtual Workplace."

14. S. Kerr, "Organizational Rewards: Practical, Cost-Neutral Alternatives That You May Know, But Don't Practice," *Organizational Dynamics*, Summer 1999, pp. 61–70.

15. S. C. Faludi, "At Nordstrom Stores, Service Comes First—but at a Big Price," *The Wall Street Journal*, February 20, 1990, pp. A1, A16.

16. K. Butterfield, L. K. Trevino, and G. Ball, "Punishment from the Manager's Perspective: A Grounded Investigation and Inductive Model," *Academy of Management Review* 39 (1996), pp. 1479–512.

17. S. Kerr, "On the Folly of Rewarding A While Hoping for B," *Academy of Management Journal* 18 (1975), pp. 769–83.

18. S. Pearlstein, "Executive Privilege?" *The Washington Post*, March 24, 2002, pp. H1, H4.

19. E. E. Lawler III, *Rewarding Excellence* (San Francisco: Jossey-Bass, 2000).

20. J. Weber, "Farewell, Fast Track," *Business Week*, December 10, 1990, pp. 192–200.

21. D. Leonard, "They're Coming to Take You Away," *Fortune*, May 29, 2000, pp. 89–106.

22. A. Bennett, "When Money Is Tight, Bosses Scramble for Other Ways to Motivate the Troops," *The Wall Street Journal*, October 31, 1990, pp. B1, B5.

23. V. H. Vroom, *Work and Motivation* (New York: John Wiley & Sons, 1964).

24. R. E. Wood, P. W. B. Atkins, and J. E. H. Bright, "Bonuses, Goals, and Instrumentality Effects," *Journal of Applied Psychology* 84 (1999), pp. 703–20.

25. Kerr, "Organizational Rewards."

26. A. H. Maslow, "A Theory of Human Motivation," *Psychological Review*, July 1943, pp. 370–96.

27. M. Wahba and L. Birdwell, "Maslow Reconsidered: A Review of Research on the Need Hierarchy Theory," *Organizational Behavior and Human Performance* 15 (1976), pp. 212–40.

28. F. Rose, "A New Age for Business?" *Fortune*, October 8, 1990, pp. 156–64.

29. G. Dessler, "How to Earn Your Employees' Commitment," *Academy of Management Executive*, May 1999, pp. 58–67.

30. Weber, "Farewell, Fast Track."

31. C. Alderfer, *Existence, Relatedness, and Growth: Human Needs in Organizational Settings* (Glencoe, IL: Free Press, 1972).

32. C. Pinder, *Work Motivation* (Glenview, IL: Scott, Foresman, 1984).

33. D. McClelland, *The Achieving Society* (New York: Van Nostrand Reinhold, 1961).

34. D. McClelland and R. Boyatzis, "Leadership Motive Pattern and Long-Term Success in Management," *Journal of Applied Psychology*, 67 (1982), pp. 737–43.

35. N. Adler, *International Dimensions of Organizational Behavior*, 2nd ed. (Boston: Kent, 1991); G. Hofstede, *Cultures and Organizations* (London: McGraw-Hill, 1991).

36. E. E. Lawler III and D. Finegold, "Individualizing the Organization: Past, Present, and Future," *Organizational Dynamics*, Summer 2000, pp. 1–15.

37. Ibid.

38. T. M. Amabile, "A Model of Creativity and Innovation in Organizations," in *Research in Organizational Behavior*, ed. B. M. Staw and L. L. Cummings (Greenwich, CT: JAI Press, 1988), pp. 10, 123–67.

39. C. M. Ford, "A Theory of Individual Creative Action in Multiple Social Domains," *Academy of Management Review* 21 (1996), pp. 1112–42.

40. G. Oldham and A. Cummings, "Employee Creativity: Personal and Contextual Factors at Work," *Academy of Management Journal* 39 (1996), pp. 607–34.

41. T. Amabile, R. Conti, H. Coon, J. Lazenby, and M. Herron, "Assessing

the Work Environment for Creativity," *Academy of Management Journal* 39 (1996), pp. 1154–84.

42. M. Campion and G. Sanborn. "Job Design," in *Handbook of Industrial Engineering,* ed. G. Salvendy (New York: John Wiley & Sons, 1991).

43. Lawler and Finegold, "Individualizing the Organization."

44. B. G. Posner, "Role Changes," *Inc.,* February 1990, pp. 95–98.

45. M. Campion and D. McClelland, "Interdisciplinary Examination of the Costs and Benefits of Enlarged Jobs: A Job Design Quasi-Experiment," *Journal of Applied Psychology* 76 (1991), pp. 186–98.

46. F. Herzberg, *Work and the Nature of Men* (Cleveland: World, 1966).

47. J. R. Hackman, G. Oldham, R. Janson, and K. Purdy, "A New Strategy for Job Enrichment," *California Management Review* 16 (Fall 1975), pp. 57–71.

48. T. Ehrenfeld, "Cashing In," *Inc.,* July 1993, pp. 69–70.

49. D. Fenn, "Bottoms Up," *Inc.,* July 1993, pp. 58–60.

50. R. Rechheld, "Loyalty-Based Management," *Harvard Business Review,* March–April, 1993, pp. 64–73.

51. D. Whitford, "A Human Place to Work," *Fortune,* January 8, 2001, pp. 108–18; 458–59.

52. G. Hamel, "Reinvent your Company," *Fortune,* June 12, 2000, pp. 98–118.

53. Levering and Moskowitz, "The 100 Best Companies."

54. A. Bianchi, "True Believers," *Inc.,* July 1993, pp. 72–73.

55. J. Finegan, "People Power," *Inc.,* July 1993, pp. 62–63.

56. Ibid.

57. T. Peters and N. Austin, *A Passion for Excellence* (New York: Random House, 1985).

58. Ehrenfeld, "Cashing In."

59. Finegan, "People Power."

60. Campion and Sanborn, "Job Design."

61. C. Argyris, "Empowerment: The Emperor's New Clothes," *Harvard Business Review,* May–June 1998, pp. 98–105.

62. R. Forrester, "Empowerment: Rejuvenating a Potent Idea," *Academy of Management Executive,* August 2000, pp. 67–80.

63. R. C. Liden, S. J. Wayne, and R. T. Sparrowe, "An Examination of the Mediating Role of Psychological Empowerment on the Relations between the Job, Interpersonal Relationships, and Work Outcomes," *Journal of Applied Psychology* 85 (2000), pp. 407–16.

64. Peters and Austin, *A Passion for Excellence.*

65. K. Thomas and B. Velthouse, "Cognitive Elements of Empowerment: An 'Interpretive' Model of Intrinsic Task Motivation," *Academy of Management Review* 15 (1990), pp. 666–81.

66. Price Waterhouse Change Integration Team, *Better Change* (Burr Ridge, IL: Richard D. Irwin, 1995).

67. E. E. Lawler III, *The Ultimate Advantage: Creating the High Involve-ment Organization* (San Francisco: Jossey-Bass, 1992).

68. G. M. Spreitzer, "Social Structural Characteristics of Psychological Empowerment," *Academy of Management Journal* 39 (1996), pp. 483–504.

69. O. Gadiesh and J. L. Gilbert, "Transforming Corner-Office Strategy into Frontline Action," *Harvard Business Review,* May 2001, pp. 72–79.

70. J. Kouzes and B. Posner, *The Leadership Challenge* (San Francisco: Jossey-Bass, 1995).

71. Price Waterhouse Change Integration Team, *Better Change.*

72. J. Jasinowski and R. Hamrin, *Making It in America* (New York: Simon & Schuster, 1995).

73. J. Adams, "Inequality in Social Exchange," in *Advances in Experimental Social Psychology,* ed. L. Berkowitz (New York: Academic Press, 1965).

74. G. Colvin, "The Great CEO Pay Heist," *Fortune,* June 25, 2001, pp. 64–70.

75. M. Bloom, "The Performance Effects of Pay Dispersion on Individuals and Organizations," *Academy of Management Journal* 42 (1999), pp. 25–40.

76. D. Skarlicki, R. Folger, and P. Tesluk, "Personality as a Moderator in the Relationships between Fairness and Retaliation," *Academy of Management Journal* 42 (1999), pp. 100–108.

77. J. Brockner, "Making Sense of Procedural Fairness: How High Procedural Fairness Can Reduce or Heighten the Influence of Outcome Favorability," *Academy of Management Review* 27 (2002), pp. 58–76.

78. W. C. Kim and R. Mauborgne, "Fair Process: Managing in the Knowledge Economy," *Harvard Business Review,* July–August 1997, pp. 65–75.

79. Ibid.

80. D. Henne and E. Locke, "Job Dissatisfaction: What Are the Consequences?" *International Journal of Psychology* 20 (1985), pp. 221–40.

81. D. Bowen, S. Gilliland, and R. Folger, "HRM and Service Fairness: How Being Fair with Employees Spills Over to Customers," *Organizational Dynamics,* Winter 1999, pp. 7–23.

82. Levering and Moskowitz, "The 100 Best Companies."

83. Whitford, "A Human Place."

84. R. E. Walton, "Improving the Quality of Work Life," *Harvard Business Review,* May–June 1974, pp. 12, 16, 155.

85. E. E. Lawler III, "Strategies for Improving the Quality of Work Life," *American Psychologist* 37 (1982), pp. 486–93; J. L. Suttle, "Improving Life at Work: Problems and Prospects," in *Improving Life at Work,* ed. J. R. Hackman and J. L. Suttle (Santa Monica, CA: Goodyear, 1977).

86. S. L. Robinson, "Trust and Breach of the Psychological Contract," *Administrative Science Quarterly* 41 (1996), pp. 574–99.

87. M. Gimein, "Sam Walton Made Us a Promise," *Fortune,* March 18, 2002, pp. 120–30.

88. E. W. Morrison and S. L. Robinson, "When Employees Feel Betrayed: A Model of How Psychological Contract Violation Develops," *Academy of Management Review* 22 (1997), pp. 226–56.

89. D. Rousseau, "Changing the Deal While Keeping the People," *Academy of Management Executive* 10 (1996), pp. 50–58.

90. E. Ridolfi, "Executive Commentary," *Academy of Management Executive* 10 (1996), pp. 59–60.

91. E. E. Lawler III, *From the Ground Up* (San Francisco: Jossey-Bass 1996).

92. Ibid.

93. S. Ghoshal, C. Bartlett, and P. Moran, "Value Creation: The New Management Manifesto," *Financial Times Mastering Management Review,* November 1999, pp. 34–37.

Chapter 14

1. E. C. Wenger and W. M. Snyder, "Communities of Practice: The Organizational Frontier," *Harvard Business Review,* January–February 2000, pp. 139–45.

2. S. Cohen and D. Bailey "What Makes Teams Work: Group Effectiveness Research from the Shop Floor to the Executive Suite," *Journal of Management* 23 (1997), pp. 239–90.

3. B. Dumaine, "Who Needs a Boss?" *Fortune,* May 7, 1990, pp. 52–60.

4. K. Wexley and S. Silverman, *Working Scared* (San Francisco: Jossey-Bass, 1993).

5. B. Dumaine, "The Trouble with Teams," *Fortune,* September 5, 1994, pp. 86–92.

6. E. E. Lawler III, *From the Ground Up* (San Francisco: Jossey-Bass, 1996).

7. Wexley and Silverman, *Working Scared.*

8. Lawler, *From the Ground Up.*

9. Ibid.

10. R. M. Kanter, "Championing Change: An Interview with Bell Atlantic's CEO Raymond Smith," *Harvard Business Review,* January–February 1991, pp. 118–30.

11. R. Heifetz and D. Laurie, "The Work of Leadership," *Harvard Business Review,* January–February 1996, pp. 124–34.

12. Lawler, *From the Ground Up.*

13. Dumaine, "Who Needs a Boss?"

14. D. Nadler, J. R. Hackman, and E. E. Lawler III, *Managing Organizational Behavior* (Boston: Little, Brown, 1979).

15. P. B. Paulus and H. Yang, "Idea Generation in Groups: A Basis for Creativity in Organizations," *Organizational Behavior and Human Decision Processes* 82 (May 2000), pp. 76–87.

16. M. Cianni and D. Wnuck, "Individual Growth and Team Enhancement: Moving toward a New Model of Career Development," *Academy of Management Executive* 11 (1997), pp. 105–15.

17. Cohen and Bailey, "What Makes Teams Work."

18. J. Katzenback and D. Smith, "The Discipline of Teams," *Harvard Business Review,* March–April 1993, pp. 111–20.

19. J. Zenger and Associates, *Leading Teams* (Burr Ridge, IL: Business One Irwin, 1994).

20. S. Cohen, "New Approaches to Teams and Teamwork," in J. Galbraith, E. E. Lawler III, and Associates, *Organizing for the Future* (San Francisco: Jossey-Bass, 1993).

21. Cohen and Bailey, "What Makes Teams Work."

22. Ibid.

23. R. Banker, J. Field, R. Schroeder, and K. Sinha, "Impact of Work Teams on Manufacturing Performance: A Longitudinal Field Study," *Academy of Management Journal* 39 (1996), pp. 867–90.

24. D. Yeatts, M. Hipskind, and D. Barnes, "Lessons Learned from Self-Managed Work Teams," *Business Horizons*, July–August 1994, pp. 11–18.

25. B. Kirkman and D. Shapiro, "The Impact of Cultural Values on Job Satisfaction and Organizational Commitment in Self-Managing Work Teams: The Mediating Role of Employee Resistance," *Academy of Management Journal* 44 (2001), pp. 557–69.

26. B. Kirkman and D. Shapiro, "The Impact of Cultural Values on Employee Resistance to Teams: Toward a Model of Globalized Self-Managing Work Team Effectiveness," *Academy of Management Review* 22 (1997), pp. 730–57.

27. B. Macy and H. Isumi, "Organizational Change, Design, and Work Innovation: A Meta-Analysis of 131 North American Field Studies—1961–1991," *Research in Organizational Change and Development* 7 (1993), pp. 235–313.

28. Ibid.

29. B. W. Tuckman, "Developmental Sequence in Small Groups," *Psychological Bulletin* 63 (1965), pp. 384–99.

30. C. Snow, S. Snell, S. Davison, and D. Hambrick, "Use Transnational Teams to Globalize Your Company," *Organizational Dynamics*, Spring 1996, pp. 50–67.

31. C. J. G. Gersick, "Time and Transition in Work Teams: Toward a New Model of Group Development," *Academy of Management Journal* 31 (1988), pp. 9–41.

32. J. R. Hackman, *Groups That Work (and Those That Don't)* (San Francisco: Jossey-Bass, 1990).

33. Zenger and Associates, *Leading Teams*.

34. R. Cross, "Looking before You Leap: Assessing the Jump to Teams in Knowledge-Based Work," *Business Horizons*, September–October 2000, pp. 29–36.

35. Dumaine, "The Trouble with Teams."

36. J. Case, "What the Experts Forgot to Mention," *Inc.*, September 1993, pp. 66–78.

37. A. Nahavandi and E. Aranda, "Restructuring Teams for the Reengineered Organization," *Academy of Management Executive*, November 1994, pp. 58–68.

38. J. Katzenback and D. Smith, *The Wisdom of Teams* (Boston: Harvard Business School Press, 1993).

39. Nadler, Hackman, and Lawler, *Managing Organizational Behavior*.

40. P. Petty, "Behind the Brands at P & G: An Interview with John Smale," *Harvard Business Review*, November–December 1985, pp. 78–80.

41. T. Peters and N. Austin, *A Passion for Excellence* (New York: Random House, 1985).

42. T. Kidder, *The Soul of a New Machine* (Boston: Little, Brown, 1981).

43. Nadler, Hackman, and Lawler, *Managing Organizational Behavior.*

44. Katzenback and Smith, "The Discipline of Teams."

45. Ibid.

46. C. Meyer, "How the Right Measures Help Teams Excel," *Harvard Business Review*, May–June 1994, pp. 95–103.

47. J. R. Katzenbach and J. A. Santamaria, "Firing Up the Front Line," *Harvard Business Review*, May–June 1999, pp. 107–17.

48. D. Knight, C. Durham, and E. Locke, "The Relationship of Team Goals, Incentives, and Efficacy to Strategic Risk, Tactical Implementation, and Performance," *Academy of Management Journal* 44 (2001), pp. 326–38.

49. B. L. Kirkman and B. Rosen, "Powering Up Teams," *Organizational Dynamics*, Winter 2000, pp. 48–66.

50. Lawler, *From the Ground Up.*

51. M. Erez, "Is Group Productivity Loss the Rule or the Exception? Effects of Culture and Group-Based Motivation," *Academy of Management Journal* 39 (1996), pp. 1513–37.

52. Katzenbach and Smith, "The Discipline of Teams."

53. P. Pascarelloa, "Compensating Teams," *Across the Board*, February 1997, pp. 16–22.

54. T. R. Zenger and C. R. Marshall, "Determinants of Incentive Intensity in Group-Based Rewards," *Academy of Management Journal*, 43 (2000), pp. 149–63.

55. R. Wageman, "Interdependence and Group Effectiveness," *Administrative Science Quarterly* 40 (1995), pp. 145–80.

56. Cianni and Wnuck, "Individual Growth and Team Enhancement."

57. Lawler, *From the Ground Up.*

58. R. Wellins, R. Byham, and G. Dixon, *Inside Teams* (San Francisco: Jossey-Bass, 1994).

59. Ibid.

60. J. M. Levine, E. T. Higgins, and H. Choi, "Development of Strategic Norms in Groups," *Organizational Behavior and Human Decision Processes* 82 (2000), pp. 88–101.

61. K. Jehn and E. Mannix, "The Dynamic Nature of Conflict: A Longitudinal Study of Intragroup Conflict and Group Performance," *Academy of Management Journal* 44 (2001), pp. 238–51.

62. J. O'Toole, *Vanguard Management: Redesigning the Corporate Future* (New York: Doubleday, 1985).

63. R. F. Bales, *Interaction Process Analysis: A Method for the Study of Small Groups* (Reading, MA: Addison-Wesley, 1950).

64. Katzenback and Smith, *The Wisdom of Teams.*

65. R. Wellins, R. Byham, and G. Dixon, *Inside Teams* (San Francisco: Jossey Bass, 1994).

66. C. Stoner and R. Hartman, "Team Building: Answering the Tough Questions," *Business Horizons*, September–October 1993, pp. 70–78.

67. S. E. Seashore, *Group Cohesiveness in the Industrial Work Group* (Ann Arbor, MI: University of Michigan Press, 1954).

68. Banker et al., "Impact of Work Teams on Manufacturing Performance."

69. B. Mullen and C. Cooper, "The Relation between Group Cohesiveness and Performance: An Integration," *Psychological Bulletin* 115 (1994), pp. 210–27.

70. D. P. Forbes and F. J. Milliken, "Cognition and Corporate Governance: Understanding Boards of Directors as Strategic Decision-Making Groups," *Academy of Management Review* 24 (1999), pp. 489–505.

71. T. Simons, L. H. Pelled, and K. A. Smith, "Making Use of Difference: Diversity, Debate, and Decision Comprehensiveness in Top Management Teams," *Academy of Management Journal* 42 (1999), pp. 662–73.

72. Seashore, *Group Cohesiveness in the Industrial Work Group.*

73. B. Lott and A. Lott, "Group Cohesiveness as Interpersonal Attraction: A Review of Relationships with Antecedent and Consequent Variables," *Psychological Bulletin*, October 1965, pp. 259–309.

74. B. L. Kirkman and B. Rosen, "Beyond Self-Management: Antecedents and Consequences of Team Empowerment," *Academy of Management Journal* 42 (1999), pp. 58–74.

75. Hackman, *Groups That Work.*

76. W. Bennis, *Organizing Genius* (Reading, MA: Addison-Wesley, 1997).

77. Cianni and Wnuck, "Individual Growth and Team Enhancement."

78. K. Jehn, "A Multimethod Examination of the Benefits and Detriments of Intragroup Conflict," *Administrative Science Quarterly* 40 (1995), pp. 245–82.

79. Wellins, Byham, and Dixon, *Inside Teams.*

80. D. G. Ancona, "Outward Bound: Strategies for Team Survival in an Organization," *Academy of Management Journal* 33 (1990), pp. 334–65.

81. Ibid.

82. L. Sayles, *Leadership: What Effective Managers Really Do, and How They Do It* (New York: McGraw-Hill, 1979).

83. Ibid.

84. S. Wetlaufer, "Common Sense and Conflict: An Interview with Disney's

Michael Eisner," *Harvard Business Review*, January–February 2000, pp. 114–24.

85. J. Chatman and F. Flynn, "The Influence of Demographic Heterogeneity on the Emergence and Consequences of Cooperative Norms in Work Teams," *Academy of Management Journal* 44 (2001), pp. 956–74.

86. R. T. Keller, "Cross-Functional Project Groups in Research and New Product Development: Diversity, Communications, Job Stress, and Outcomes," *Academy of Management Journal* 44 (2001), pp. 547–55.

87. Chatman and Flynn, "The Influence of Demographic Heterogeneity."

88. Keller, "Cross-Functional Project Groups."

89. D. Tjosvold, *Working Together to Get Things Done* (Lexington, MA: Lexington Books, 1986).

90. M. Blum and J. A. Wall, Jr., "HRM: Managing Conflicts in the Firm," *Business Horizons*, May–June 1997, pp. 84–87.

91. Ibid.

92. J. A. Wall, Jr., and R. R. Callister, "Conflict and Its Management," *Journal of Management* 21 (1995), pp. 515–58.

93. C. Tinsley and J. Brett, "Managing Workplace Conflict in the United States and Hong Kong," *Organizational Behavior and Human Decision Processes* 85 (2001), pp. 360–81.

94. K. W. Thomas, "Conflict and Conflict Management," in *Handbook of Industrial and Organizational Psychology*, ed. M. D. Dunnette (Chicago: Rand McNally, 1976).

95. K. W. Thomas, "Toward Multi-Dimensional Values in Teaching: The Example of Conflict Behaviors," *Academy of Management Review* (1977), pp. 484–89.

96. C. O. Longenecker and M. Neubert, "Barriers and Gateways to Management Cooperation and Teamwork," *Business Horizons*, September–October 2000, pp. 37–44.

Chapter 15

1. D. Yankelovich, *The Magic of Dialogue: Transforming Conflict into Cooperation* (New York: Simon & Schuster, 1999).

2. P. Senge, *The Fifth Discipline* (New York: Doubleday, 1990).

3. Ibid.

4. L. Penley, E. Alexander, I. E. Jernigan, and C. Henwood, "Communication Abilities of Managers: The Relationship to Performance," *Journal of Management*, 17 (1991), pp. 57–76.

5. W. V. Haney, "A Comparative Study of Unilateral and Bilateral Communication," *Academy of Management Journal*, 7 (1964), pp. 128–36.

6. M. McCormack, "The Illusion of Communication," *Financial Times Mastering Management Review*, July 1999, pp. 8–9.

7. R. Cross and S. Brodt, "How Assumptions of Consensus Undermine Decision Making," *Sloan Management Review*, 42 (2001), pp. 86–94.

8. S. Mohammed and E. Ringseis, "Cognitive Diversity and Consensus in Group Decision Making: The Role of Inputs, Processes, and Outcomes," *Organizational Behavior and Human Decision Processes*, 85 (2001), pp. 310–35.

9. S. Parker and C. Axtell, "Seeing Another Viewpoint: Antecedents and Outcomes of Employee Perspective Taking," *Academy of Management Journal*, 44 (2001), pp. 1085–100.

10. D. Tannen, "The Power of Talk: Who Gets Heard and Why," *Harvard Business Review*, September–October 1995, pp. 138–48.

11. Ibid.

12. Ibid.

13. L. K. Larkey, "Toward a Theory of Communicative Interactions in Culturally Diverse Workgroups," *Academy of Management Review*, April 1996, pp. 463–91.

14. C. Argyris, "Good Communication That Blocks Learning," *Harvard Business Review*, July–August 1994, pp. 77–85.

15. C. Deutsch, "The Multimedia Benefits Kit," *The New York Times*, October 14, 1990, sec. 3, p. 25.

16. T. W. Comstock, *Communicating in Business and Industry* (Albany, NY: Delmar, 1985).

17. J. Taylor and W. Wacker, *The 500 Year Delta: What Happens after What Comes Next* (New York: HarperCollins, 1997).

18. T. A. Stewart, "How Cisco and Alcoa Make Real Time Work," *Fortune*, May 29, 2000, pp. 284–86.

19. S. S. K. Lam and J. Schaubroeck, "Improving Group Decisions by Better Pooling Information: A Comparative Advantage of Group Decision Support Systems," *Journal of Applied Psychology*, 85 (2000), pp. 565–73.

20. M. Schrage, "If You Can't Say Anything Nice, Say It Anonymously," *Fortune*, December 6, 1999, p. 352.

21. B. Baltes, M. Dickson, M. Sherman, C. Bauer, and J. LaGanke, "Computer-Mediated Communication and Group Decision Making: A Meta-Analysis," *Organizational Behavior and Human Decision Processes*, 87 (2002), pp. 156–79.

22. R. Rice and D. Case, "Electronic Message Systems in the University: A Description of Use and Utility," *Journal of Communication*, 33 (1983), pp. 131–52; C. Steinfield, "Dimensions of Electronic Mail Use in an Organizational Setting," *Proceedings of the Academy of Management*, San Diego, 1985.

23. J. Solomon, "As Electronic Mail Loosens Inhibitions, Impetuous Senders Feel Anything Goes," *The Wall Street Journal*, October 12, 1990, pp. B1, B8.

24. B. Glassberg, W. Kettinger, and J. Logan, "Electronic Communication: An Ounce of Policy Is Worth a Pound of Cure," *Business Horizons*, July–August 1996, pp. 74–80.

25. Ibid.

26. Ibid.

27. N. B. Kurland and D. E. Bailey, "Telework: The Advantages and Challenges of Working Here, There, Anywhere, Anytime," *Organizational Dynamics*, Autumn 1999, pp. 53–68.

28. K. Edelman "Open Office? Try Virtual Office," *Across the Board*, March 1997, p. 34.

29. S. Shellenbarger, "Overwork, Low Morale Vex Office Staff," *The Wall Street Journal*, August 17, 1994, pp. B1, B4.

30. Ibid.

31. E. M. Hallowell, "The Human Moment at Work," *Harvard Business Review*, January–February 1999, pp. 58–66.

32. "Home Alone: The Job," *Collections & Credit Risk*, May 1997, p. 23.

33. "'Virtual Office' Not Yet Common," *Financial Executive*, March/April 2002, p. 10.

34. J. Stuller, "Overload," *Across the Board*, April 1996, pp. 16–22.

35. Taylor and Wacker, *The 500 year Delta*.

36. R. Tetzeli, "Surviving Information Overload," *Fortune*, July 11, 1994, pp. 32–35.

37. Ibid.

38. T. W. Malone, "Is Empowerment Just a Fad? Control, Decision Making and IT," *Sloan Management Review*, Winter 1997, pp. 23–35.

39. R. Sparrowe, R. Liden, S. Wayne, and M. Kraimer, "Social Networks and the Performance of Individuals and Groups," *Academy of Management Journal*, 44 (2001), pp. 316–25.

40. J. W. Medcof, "Challenges in Managing Technology in Transnational Multipartner Networks," *Business Horizons*, January–February 1996, pp. 47–54.

41. V. Govindarajan and A. Gupta, "Building an Effective Global Team," *Organizational Dynamics*, 42 (2001), pp. 63–71.

42. R. Lengel and R. Daft, "The Selection of Communication Media as an Executive Skill," *Academy of Management Executive*, 2 (1988), pp. 225–32.

43. J. R. Carlson and R. W. Zmud, "Channel Expansion Theory and the Experiential Nature of Media Richness Perceptions," *Academy of Management Journal*, 42 (1999), pp. 153–70.

44. L. Trevino, R. Daft, and R. Lengel, "Understanding Managers' Media Choices: A Symbolic Interactionist Perspective," in *Organizations and Communication Technology*, ed. J. Fulk and C. Steinfield (London: Sage, 1990).

45. J. Fulk and B. Boyd, "Emerging Theories of Communication in Organizations," *Journal of Management*, 17 (1991), pp. 407–46.

46. M. McCall, M. Lombardo, and A. Morrison, *The Lessons of Experience: How Successful Executives Develop on the Job* (Lexington, MA: Lexington, 1988).

47. C. M. Kelly, "Effective Communications—Beyond the Glitter and Flash," *Sloan Management Review*, Spring 1985, pp. 69–74.

48. J. A. Conger, "The Necessary Art of Persuasion," *Harvard Business Review*, May–June 1998, pp. 84–95.

49. D. Sull, "The Rhetoric of Transformation," *Financial Times Mastering Management Review*, December/January 1999/2000, pp. 34–37.

50. N. Nohria and B. Harrington, *Six Principles of Successful Persuasion* (Boston: Harvard Business School Publishing Division, 1993).

51. R. Ashkenas, D. Ulrich, T. Jick, and S. Kerr, *The Boundaryless Organization* (San Francisco: Jossey-Bass, 1995).

52. H. K. Mintz, "Business Writing Styles for the 70's," *Business Horizons*, August 1972. Cited in *Readings in Interpersonal and Organizational Communication*, ed. R. C. Huseman, C. M. Logue, and D. L. Freshley (Boston: Allyn & Bacon, 1977).

53. C. D. Decker, "Writing to Teach Thinking," *Across the Board*, March 1996, pp. 19–20.

54. M. Forbes, "Exorcising Demons from Important Business Letters," *Marketing Times*, March–April 1981, pp. 36–38.

55. C. Krauthammer, "Make It Snappy: In Praise of Short Papers, Short Speeches, and, Yes, the Sound Bite," *Time*, July 21, 1997, p. 84.

56. W. Strunk, Jr., and E. B. White, *The Elements of Style*, 3rd ed. (New York: Macmillan, 1979); H. R. Fowler, *The Little Brown Handbook* (Boston: Little, Brown, 1986).

57. G. Ferraro, "The Need for Linguistic Proficiency in Global Business," *Business Horizons*, May–June 1996, pp. 39–46.

58. P. C. Early and E. Mosakowski, "Creating Hybrid Team Cultures: An Empirical Test of Transnational Team Functioning," *Academy of Management Journal*, 43 (2000), pp. 26–49.

59. Ferraro, "The Need for Linguistic Proficiency."

60. C. Chu, *The Asian Mind Game* (New York: Rawson Associates, 1991).

61. Ferraro, "The Need for Linguistic Proficiency."

62. Comstock, *Communicating in Business and Industry*.

63. M. Korda, *Power: How to Get It. How to Use It* (New York: Random House, 1975).

64. A. Mehrabian, "Communication without Words," *Psychology Today*, September 1968, p. 52. Cited in M. B. McCaskey, "The Hidden Message Managers Send," *Harvard Business Review*, November–December 1979, pp. 135–48.

65. Ferraro, "The Need for Linguistic Proficiency."

66. *Business Horizons*, May–June 1993. Copyright 1993 by the Foundation for the School of Business at Indiana University. Used with permission.

67. "Too Many in the New Workforce Are Lacking Basic Skills," *Research Alert*, November 15, 1996, p. 5.

68. A. Athos and J. Gabarro, *Interpersonal Behavior* (Englewood Cliffs, NJ: Prentice-Hall, 1978).

69. "Have You Heard about Sperry?" *Management Review*, 69 (April 1980), p. 40.

70. J. Kouzes and B. Posner, *The Leadership Challenge* (San Francisco: Jossey-Bass, 1995).

71. G. Graham, J. Unruh, and P. Jennings, "The Impact of Nonverbal Communication in Organizations: A Survey of Perceptions," *Journal of Business Communications*, 28 (1991), pp. 45–62.

72. Ibid.

73. D. Upton and S. Macadam, "Why (and How) to Take a Plant Tour," *Harvard Business Review*, May–June 1997, pp. 97–106.

74. S. Wetlaufer, "Common Sense and Conflict: An Interview with Disney's Michael Eisner," *Harvard Business Review*, January–February 2000, pp. 114–24.

75. N. Adler, *International Dimensions of Organizational Behavior*, 2nd ed. (Boston: Kent, 1991).

76. Chu, *The Asian Mind Game*.

77. W. C. Redding, *Communication within the Organization: An Interpretive Review of Theory and Research* (New York: Industrial Communication Council, 1972). Cited in F. M. Jablin, "Superior-Subordinate Communication: The State of the Art," *Psychological Bulletin*, 86 (1979), pp. 1201–22.

78. Penley et al, "Communication Abilities of Managers."

79. A. Smidts, A. T. H. Pruyn, and C. B. M. van Riel, "The Impact of Employee Communication and Perceived External Prestige on Organizational Identification," *Academy of Management Journal*, 49 (2001), pp. 1051–62.

80. J. W. Koehler, K. W. E. Anatol, and R. L. Applebaum, *Organizational Communication: Behavioral Perspectives* (Orlando, FL: Holt, Rinehart & Winston, 1981).

81. J. Waldroop and T. Butler, "The Executive as Coach," *Harvard Business Review*, November–December 1996, pp. 111–17.

82. D. T. Hall, K. L. Otazo, and G. P. Hollenbeck, "Behind Closed Doors: What Really Happens in Executive Coaching," *Organizational Dynamics*, Winter 1999, pp. 39–53.

83. T. Judge and J. Cowell, "The Brave New World of Coaching," *Business Horizons*, July–August 1997, pp. 71–77.

84. J. Gutknecht and J. B. Keys, "Mergers, Acquisitions, and Takeovers: Maintaining Morale of Survivors and Protecting Employees," *Academy of Management Executive*, August 1993, pp. 26–36.

85. D. Schweiger and A. DeNisi, "Communication with Employees Following a Merger: A Longitudinal Field Experiment," *Academy of Management Journal*, 34 (1991), pp. 110–35.

86. J. Case, "The Open-Book Managers," *Inc.*, September 1990, pp. 104–13.

87. J. Case, "Opening the Books," *Harvard Business Review*, March–April 1997, pp. 118–27.

88. T. R. V. Davis, "Open-Book Management: Its Promise and Pitfalls," *Organization Dynamics*, Winter 1997, pp. 7–20.

89. R. Aggarwal and B. Simkins, "Open Book Management: Optimizing Human Capital," *Business Horizons*, 44 (2001), pp. 5–13.

90. W. V. Ruch, *Corporate Communications* (Westport, CT: Quorum, 1984).

91. W. Imberman, "Why Engineers Strike: The Boeing Story," *Business Horizons*, 44 (2001), pp. 35–44.

92. S. Verhovek, "Tentative Pact Made to End Boeing Strike," *The New York Times*, March 18, 2000, p. C1. Cited in Imberman, "Why Engineers Strike."

93. Ashkenas et al., *The Boundaryless Organization*.

94. Ruch, *Corporate Communications*.

95. A. Hutton, "Four Rules for Taking Your Message to Wall Street," *Harvard Business Review*, May 2001, pp. 125–32.

96. Koehler, Anatol, and Applebaum, *Organizational Communication*.

97. Ashkenas et al., *The Boundaryless Organization*.

98. D. K. Denton, "Open Communication," *Business Horizons*, September–October 1993, pp. 64–69.

99. N. B. Kurland and L. H. Pelled, "Passing the Word: Toward a Model of Gossip and Power in the Workplace," *Academy of Management Review*, 25 (2000), pp. 428–38.

100. R. L. Rosnow, "Rumor as Communication: A Contextual Approach," *Journal of Communication*, 38 (1988), pp. 12–28.

101. K. Davis, "The Care and Cultivation of the Corporate Grapevine," *Dun's Review*, July 1973, pp. 44–47.

102. N. Difonzo, P. Bordia, and R. Rosnow, "Reining in Rumors," *Organizational Dynamics*, Summer 1994, pp. 47–62.

103. Ibid.

104. Ashkenas et al., *The Boundaryless Organization*.

105. Ibid.

106. R. M. Hodgetts, "A Conversation with Steve Kerr," *Organizational Dynamics*, Spring 1996, pp. 68–79.

107. Ibid.

108. R. M. Fulmer, "The Evolving Paradigm of Leadership Development," *Organizational Dynamics*, Spring 1997, pp. 59–72.

109. Ashkenas et al., *The Boundaryless Organization*.

Chapter 16

1. James C. Collins, and Jerry I. Porras, *Built to Last: Successful Habits of Visionary Companies* (New York: HarperBusiness, 1994).

2. Keith Naughton, "Spinning Out of Control," *Newsweek*, September 11, 2000, 136, no. 11, p. 58; Christopher Palmeri, "California's Utilities Doth Protest Too Much," *Business Week*, January 15, 2001, 3715, pp. 42–43.

3. W. G. Ouchi, "Markets, Bureaucracies, and Clans," *Administrative Science Quarterly*, 25 (1980), pp. 129–41.

4. Robert Simons, Antonio Davila, and Robert S. Kaplan, *Performance Measurement & Control Systems for Implementing Strategy* (Englewood Cliffs, NJ: Prentice-Hall, 2000).

5. Elaine D. Pulakos, Sharon Arad, Michelle A. Donovan, and Kevin E. Plamondon, "Adaptability in the Workplace: Development of a Taxonomy of Adaptive Performance," *Journal of Applied Psychology*, August 2000, 85, no. 4, pp. 12–24; John H. Sheridan, "Lean Sigma Synergy," *Industry Week*, October 16, 2000, 249, no. 17, pp. 81–82.

6. J. T. Burr, "Keys to a Successful Internal Audit," *Quality Progress*, 30, no. 4 (April 1997), pp. 75–77; John E. Ettlie, "Surfacing Quality at GE," *Automotive Manufacturing & Production*, August 2000, 112, no. 8, pp. 44–46; Roy A. Maxion and Robert T. Olszewski, "Eliminating Exception Handling Errors with Dependability Cases: A Comparative, Empirical Study," *IEEE Transactions on Software Engineering*, September 2000, 26, no. 9, pp. 888–906.

7. Robert Della, "Harley Rides High on SPC Changes," *Quality*, January 2000, 39, no. 1, 40–43.

8. R. Henkoff, "Make Your Office More Productive," *Fortune*, February 25, 1990, pp. 40–49; R. Buchele, "How to Evaluate a Firm," *California Management Review*, Fall 1962, pp. 5–17.

9. George Ellis, "Feedforward for Faster Control Response," *Control Engineering*, October 2000, 47, no. 11, p. 104.

10. Vanessa Urch Druskat, "Effects and Timing of Developmental Peer Appraisals in Self-Managing Work Groups," *Journal of Applied Psychology*, February 1999, 84, no. 1, p. 58.

11. Sandra Waddock and Neil Smith, "Corporate Responsibility Audits: Doing Well by Doing Good," *Sloan Management Review*, Winter 2000, 41, no. 2, pp. 75–83; Lynn L. Bergeson, "OSHA Gives Incentives for Voluntary Self-Audits," *Pollution Engineering*, October 2000, 32, no. 10, pp. 33–34.

12. Janet, L. Colbert, "The Impact of the New External Auditing Standards," *The Internal Auditor*, December 2000, 5, no. 6, pp. 46–50.

13. G. A. Ewert, "How to Sell Internal Auditing," *Internal Auditor*, 54, no. 5 (October 1997), pp. 54–57; J. T. Burr, "Keys to a Successful Internal Audit," *Quality Progress*, 30, no. 4 (April 1997), pp. 75–77; Satina V. Williams and Benson Wier, "Value-Added Auditing: Where Are the Efficiencies Realized?" *Internal Auditing*, July/August 2000, 15, no. 4, pp. 37–42; David B. Crawford, "Levels of Control," *The Internal Auditor*, October 2000, 57, no. 5, pp. 42–45.

14. R. Henkoff, "Cost Cutting: How to Do It Right," *Fortune*, April 9, 1990, pp. 40–49.

15. Carol J. Loomis, "I Pay More in Income Taxes Than Cisco—So Do You," *Fortune*, December 18, 2000, 142, no. 14, pp. 44–46; Thomas G. Donlan, "Bridging the GAAP," *Barron's*, November 6, 2000, vol. 80, Iss. 45, p. 74.

16. P. C. Brewer and L. A. Vulinec, "Harris Corporation's Experiences with Using Activity-Based Costing," *Information Strategy: The Executive's Journal*, 13, no. 2 (Winter 1997), pp. 6–16; Terence P. Pare, "A New Tool for Managing Costs," *Fortune*, June 14, 1993, pp. 124–29.

17. K. Merchant, *Control in Business Organizations* (Boston: Pitman, 1985); C. W. Chow, Y. Kato, and K. A. Merchant, "The Use of Organizational Controls and Their Effects on Data Manipulation and Management Myopia," *Accounting, Organizations, and Society*, 21, nos. 2/3 (February/April 1996), pp. 175–92.

18. E. E. Lawler III and J. Rhode, *Information and Control in Organizations* (Pacific Palisades, CA: Goodyear, 1976); Anthony Ferner, "The Underpinnings of 'Bureaucratic' Control Systems: HRM in European Multinationals," *Journal of Management Studies*, June 2000, 37, no. 4, pp. 521–39; Marilyn S. Fenwick, "Cultural and Bureaucratic Control in MNEs: The Role of Expatriate Performance Management," *Management International Review* (1999), vol. 39, pp. 107–25.

19. J. Veiga and J. Yanouzas, *The Dynamics of Organization Theory*, 2nd ed. (St. Paul, MN: West, 1984).

20. L. Schiff, "Downsizing Workplace Stress," *Business & Health*, 15, no. 1 (November 1997), pp. 45–46; S. Albrecht, "Are Your Employees the Enemy?" *HRFocus*, 74, no. 4 (April 1997), p. 21.

21. Michael Scott, "Seven Pitfalls for Managers When Handling Poor Performers and How to Overcome Them," *Manage*, February 2000, 51, no. 3, pp. 12–14.

22. Henkoff, "Make Your Office More Productive"; see also, Peggy Anderson and Marica Pulich, "Recruiting Good Employees in Tough Times," *Health Care Manager*, March 2000, 18, no. 3, pp. 32–40.

23. Lawler and Rhode, *Information and Control in Organizations*; J. A. Gowan, Jr., and R. G. Mathieu, "Critical Factors in Information System Development for a Flexible Manufacturing System," *Computers in Industry*, 28, no. 3 (June 1996), pp. 173–83.

24. T. A. Stewart, "Do You Push Your People Too Hard?" *Fortune*, October 22, 1990, pp. 121–28.

25. S. Tully, "The CEO Who Sees Beyond Budgets," *Fortune*, October 22, 1990, pp. 121–28.

26. Robert W. Rudloff, "Casino Fraud," *The Internal Auditor*, June 1999, 56, no. 3, pp. 44–49; Mike McNamee, "Faster, Cheaper Trading—Can the Regulators Keep Up?" *Business Week*, August 9, 1999, 3641, pp. 84; Bill Zalud, "Conquering Digital Marks CCTV Innovations," *Security*, April 2000, 37, no. 4, pp. 43–44.

27. Gillian Flynn, "Out of the Red, into the Blue," *Workforce*, March 2000, 79, no. 3, pp. 50–52; Alison Stein Wellner, "Entrepreneurial HR," *HR Magazine*, March 2000, 45, no. 3, pp. 52–58.

28. Christopher Farrell, "Stock Options for All!" *Business Week Online*, September 20, 2002; Eric Wahlgren, "CEO Pay Tomorrow: Same as Today," *Business Week Online*, August 21, 2002.

29. S. A. Snell and J. W. Dean, Jr., "Strategic Compensation for Integrated Manufacturing: The Moderating Effects of Jobs and Organizational Inertia," *Academy of Management Journal*, 37, no. 5 (1994), pp. 1109–40; M. A. Youndt, S. A. Snell, J. W. Dean, Jr., and D. P. P. Lepak, "Human Resource Management, Manufacturing Strategy, and Firm Performance," *Academy of Management Journal*, 39, no. 4, Special Issue (1996), pp. 836–66; Peter Drucker, "Knowledge Work," *Executive Excellence*, April 2000, 17, no. 4, pp. 11–12.

30. Ken Moores and Joseph Mula, "The Salience of Market, Bureaucratic, and Clan Controls in the Management of Family Firm Transitions: Some Tentative Australian Evidence," *Family Business Review*, June 2000, 13, no. 2, pp. 91–106; Anthony Walker and Robert Newcombe, "The Positive Use of Power on a Major Construction Project," *Construction Management and Economics*, January/February 2000, 18, no. 1, pp. 37–44.

31. Peter H. Fuchs, Kenneth E. Mifflin, Danny Miller, and John O. Whitney, "Strategic Integration: Competing in the Age of Capabilities," *California Management Review*, Spring 2000, 42, no. 3, pp. 118–47; Mary Ann Lando, "Making Compliance Part of Your Organization's Culture," *Healthcare Executive*, September/October 1999, 15, no. 5, pp. 18–22; Kenneth A. Frank and Kyle Fahrbach, "Organization Culture as a Complex System: Balance and Information in Models of Influence and Selection," *Organization Science*, May/June 1999, 10, no. 3, pp. 253–77.

32. Ralph H. Kilmann, Mary J. Saxton, and Roy Serpa, *Gaining Control of the Corporate Culture* (San Francisco: Jossey-Bass, 1985); Kim S. Cameron and Robert E. Quinn, *Diagnosing and Changing Organizational Culture: Based on the Competing Values Framework* (Englewood Cliffs, NJ: Addison-Wesley, 1998).

33. Cameron and Quinn, *Diagnosing and Changing Organizational Culture*.

34. R. Leifer and P. K. Mills, "An Information Processing Approach for Deciding upon Control Strategies and Reducing Control Loss in Emerging Organizations," *Journal of Management*, 22, no. 1 (1996), pp. 113–37;

Scott A. Dellana and Richard D. Hauser, "Toward Defining the Quality Culture," *Engineering Management Journal*, June 1999, 11, no. 2, pp. 11–15; Don Cohen and Lawrence Prusak, *In Good Company: How Social Capital Makes Organizations Work* (Cambridge, MA: Harvard Business School Press, 2001).

Chapter 17

1. Robert A. Burgelman, Modesto A. Maidique, and Steven C. Wheelwright, *Strategic Management of Technology and Innovation,* (New York: McGraw-Hill Higher Education, 2000).
2. Donna C. L. Prestwood and Paul A. Schumann, Jr., "Revitalize Your Organization," *Executive Excellence,* 15, no. 2 (February 1998), p. 16; Carliss Y. Baldwin and Kim B. Clark, "Managing in an Age of Modularity," *Harvard Business Review,* 75, no. 5 (September–October 1997), pp. 84–93; Shanthi Gopalakrishnan, Paul Bierly, and Eric H. Kessler, "A Reexamination of Product and Process Innovations Using a Knowledge-Based View," *Journal of High Technology Management Research,* Spring 1999, 10, no. 1, pp. 147–66; John Pullin, "Bombardier Commands Top Marks," *Professional Engineering,* July 5, 2000, 13, no. 3, pp. 40–46.
3. Gary P. Pisano. *The Development Factory: Unlocking the Potential of Process Innovation* (Boston: Harvard Business School Press, 1996); Richard Leifer, Christopher M. McDermott, Gina Colarelli O'Connor, Lois S. Peters, Mark Rice, and Robert W. Veryzer, *Radical Innovation: How Mature Companies Can Outsmart Upstarts* (Cambridge MA: Harvard Business School Press, 2000).
4. Hugh M. O'Neill, Richard W. Pounder, and Ann K. Buchholtz, "Patterns in the Diffusion of Strategies across Organizations: Insights from the Innovation Diffusion Literature," *Academy of Management Review,* 23, no. 1 (January 1998), pp. 98–114; Everett M. Rogers, *Diffusion of Innovations* (New York: Free Press, 1995); Bernard Guilhon, ed., *Technology and Markets for Knowledge— Knowledge Creation, Diffusion and Exchange within a Growing Economy* (Economics of Science, Technology and Innovation (Volume 22) (Dordrecht, Netherlands: Kluwer Academic Publishing, 2000).
5. M. E. Porter, *Competitive Strategy* (New York: Free Press, 1980); "Ciba Specialty Chemicals Highlights Sustainable Growth through Innovation," *Chemical Market Reporter,* April 17, 2000, 257, no. 16, p. 5.
6. J. A. Schumpeter, *The Theory of Economic Development* (Boston: Harvard University Press, 1934); Kathleen DesMarteau, "Information Technology Trends Drive Dramatic Industry Change," *Bobbin,* August 2000, 41, no. 12, pp. 48–58.
7. Shaker A. Zahra, Sarah Nash, and Deborah J. Bickford. "Transforming

Technological Pioneering in Competitive Advantage," *Academy of Management Executive,* 9, no. 1 (1995), pp. 17–31; Michael Sadowski and Aaron Roth, "Technology Leadership Can Pay Off," *Research Technology Management,* November/December 1999, 42, no. 6, pp. 32–33.
8. Todd Wasserman, "Kodak, Polaroid to Duel in Malls over Gen Y Girls," *Brandweek,* January 31, 2000, 41, no. 5, p. 10; Joel Dreyfuss, "Pixel This: How to Choose a Digital Camera," *Fortune,* April 3, 2000, 141, no. 7, pp. 263–64.
9. Jared Sandberg, "Microsoft's Six Fatal Errors," *Newsweek,* June 19, 2000, 135, no. 25, pp. 22–28; "Leaders: Breaking Up Microsoft," *The Economist,* June 10, 2000, 355, no. 8174, p. 20.
10. Masaaki Imai and Gemba Kaizen, *A Commonsense, Low-Cost Approach to Management* (New York: McGraw-Hill, 1997); Masaaki Imai and Gemba Kaizen, *The Key to Japan's Competitive Success* (New York: McGraw-Hill, 1986).
11. Marc Bertucco, "FDA under Fire," *Psychology Today,* January/February 2001, 34, no. 1, pp. 10–11; Jill Wechsler, "Carrying a Big Stick," *Pharmaceutic Executive,* September 2000, 20, no. 9, pp. 24–27; Robin Goldwyn Blumenthal, "Next Thing You Know, the FDA Will Be Profitable," *Barron's,* November 22, 1999, 79, no. 47, p. 12.
12. P. A. Geroski, "Models of Technology Diffusion," *Research Policy,* April 2000, 29, no. 4/5, pp. 603–25; Louis A. Thomas, "Adoption Order of New Technologies in Evolving Markets," *Journal of Economic Behavior & Organization,* April 1999, 38, no. 4, pp. 453–82.
13. Ronald E. Oligney and Michael I. Economides, "Technology as an Asset," *Hart's Petroleum Engineer International,* September 1998, 71, no. 9, p. 27.
14. Scott Blake Harris, "Fixing Financial Standards," *Satellite Communications,* March 1999, 23, no. 3, p. 22; Lauren E. Burns, "Still Avoiding Flameout, Globalstar Learns Iridium's Lessons," *Aviation Week & Space Technology,* July 3, 2000, 153, no. 1, p. s23.
15. "Computing's Outer Limits," *Popular Science,* March 1998, 252, no. 3, p. 64.
16. Peter G. Neumann, "Missile Defense," *Communications of the ACM,* September 2000, 43, no. 9, p. 128; Nancy Gohring, "New Spectrum Up for Grabs," *Telephony,* May 24, 1999, 236, no. 21, p. 14.
17. Jimmy Carter, "Corporate Giving Is Part of the Solutions Equation; Philanthropy: When Business Works with Individuals, Government and Nonprofits to Do Good, Success Is Boundless," *Los Angeles Times,* February 19, 1998, p. B9; Nancy Walsh D'Epiro, "Targeting River Blindness," *Patient Care,* 31, no. 16 (October 15, 1997), p. 18; Joanne B Ciulla, "The Importance of Leadership in Shaping Business Values," *Long Range Planning,* April 1999, 32, no. 2, pp. 166–72.

18. Irene M. Kunii, "A Bold Mechanic for a Creaky Machine," *Business Week,* August 7, 2000, p. 58H; Sadanori Arimura, "How Matsushita Electric and Sony Manage Global R&D," *Research Technology Management,* March/April 1999, 42, no. 2, pp. 41–52; Richard Nathan, "Matsushita Hopes Silicon Valley Links Can Boost Its R&D," *Research Technology Management,* March/April 1999, 42, no. 2, pp. 4–5.
19. Rajiv Dewan, Bing Jing, and Abraham Seidmann, "Adoption of Internet-Based Product Customization and Pricing Strategies," *Journal of Management Information Systems,* Fall 2000, 17, no. 2, pp. 9–28; P. A. Geroski, "Models of Technology Diffusion," *Research Policy,* April 2000, 29, no. 4/5, pp. 603–25; Everett M. Rogers, *Diffusion of Innovations* (New York: Free Press, 1995).
20. Eric Von Hippel, *The Sources of Innovation* (Oxford, UK: Oxford University Press, 1994); Dorothy Leonard, *Wellsprings of Knowledge: Building and Sustaining the Sources of Innovation* (Cambridge MA: Harvard Business School Press, 1998).
21. Ibid.
22. John Hagedoorn, Albert N. Link, and Nicholas S. Vonortas, "Research Partnerships," *Research Policy,* April 2000, 29, no. 4/5, pp. 567–86; Sang-Seung Yi, "Entry, Licensing and Research Joint Ventures," *International Journal of Industrial Organization,* January 1999, 17, no. 1, pp. 1–24.
23. Joseph F. Kovar, "Readers' Choice: Scott McNealy, Sun," *Computer Reseller News,* November 13, 2000, 920, pp. 129–30; Peter Burrows, Michael Moeller, and Steve Hamm, "Free Software from Anywhere?" *Business Week,* September 13, 1999, pp. 37–38; Gary K. Jones, Aldor Lanctot, Jr., and Hildy J. Teegan, "Determinants and Performance Impacts of External Technology Acquisition," *Journal of Business Venturing,* May 2000, 16, no. 3, pp. 255–83.
24. Michael Vizard, "It's the CTOs Who Help to Drive the Changing Role of IT in the World of Business," *InfoWorld,* November 29, 1999, 21, no. 48, p. 91; Gary H. Anthes, "The CIO/CTO Balancing Act," *Computerworld,* June 19, 2000, 34, no. 25, pp. 50–51.
25. Melanie Warner, "The New Way to Start Up in Silicon Valley," *Fortune* 137, no. 4 (March 2, 1998), pp. 168–74; Leon Richardson, "The Successful Entrepreneur," *Asian Business,* July 1994, p. 71; Charles Burck, "The Real World of the Entrepreneur," *Fortune,* April 5, 1993, pp. 42–55.
26. D. L. Day, "Raising Radicals: Different Processes for Championing Innovative Corporate Ventures," *Organization Science* 5, no. 2 (May 1994), pp. 148–72; Clifford Siporin, "Want Speedy FDA Approval? Hire a 'Product Champion,'" *Medical Marketing & Media,* October 1993, pp. 22–28; Clifford Siporin, "How You Can Capitalize on Phase

3B," *Medical Marketing & Media*, October 1994, pp. 72–72. Eric H. Kessler, "Tightening the Belt: Methods for Reducing Development Costs Associated with New Product Innovation," *Journal of Engineering and Technology Management*, March 2000, 17, no. 1, pp. 59–92.

27. Edgar Figueroa and Pedro Conceicao, "Rethinking the Innovation Process in Large Organizations: A Case Study of 3M," *Journal of Engineering and Technology Management*, March 2000, 17, no. 1, pp. 93–109; David Howell, "No Such Thing as a Daft Idea," *Professional Engineering*, February 23, 2000, 13, no. 4, pp. 28–29.

28. Lisa K. Gundry, Jill R. Kickul, and Charles W. Prather, "Building the Creative Organization," *Organizational Dynamics* 22, no. 2 (Spring 1994), pp. 22–36; Thomas Kuczmarski, "Inspiring and Implementing the Innovation Mind-Set," *Planning Review*, September–October 1994, pp. 37–48; Robert D. Ramsey, "How an Optimistic Outlook Can Give You an Edge," *Supervision* (September 2000) 61 no. 9, pp. 6–8.

29. R. Neff, "Toray May Have Found the Formula for Luck," *Business Week*, June 15, 1990, p. 110.

30. Dorothy Leonard, *Wellsprings of Knowledge: Building and Sustaining the Sources of Innovation* (Cambridge MA: Harvard Business School Press, 1998); Dorothy Leonard-Barton "The Factory as a Learning Laboratory," *Sloan Management Review*, Fall 1992, pp. 23–38; Anil K. Gupta and Vijay Govindarajan, "Knowledge Management's Social Dimension: Lessons from Nucor Steel," *Sloan Management Review*, Fall 2000, 42, no. 1, pp. 71–80.

31. H. Kent Bowen, Kim B. Clark, Charles A. Holloway, and Steven C. Wheelwright, "Development Projects: The Engine of Renewal," *Harvard Business Review*, September–October 1994, pp. 110–20; C. Eden, T. Williams, and F. Ackermann, "Dismantling the Learning Curve: The Role of Disruptions on the Planning of Development Projects," *International Journal of Project Management* 16, no. 3 (June 1998), pp. 131–38; Mohan V. Tatikonda and Stephen R. Rosenthal, "Technology Novelty, Project Complexity, and Product Development Project Execution Success: A Deeper Look at Task Uncertainty in Product Innovation," *IEEE Transactions on Engineering Management*, February 2000, 47, no. 1, pp. 74–87.

32. Robert H. Hayes, Kim B. Clark, and Steven C. Wheelwright, *Dynamic Manufacturing: Creating the Learning Organization* (New York: Free Press, 1988).

33. E. Trist, "The Evolution of Sociotechnical Systems as a Conceptual Framework and as an Action Research Program," in *Perspectives on Organizational Design and Behavior*, ed. A. Van de Ven and W. F.

Joyce (New York: John Wiley & Sons, 1981), pp. 19–75; Alfonso Molina, "Insights into the Nature of Technology Diffusion and Implementation: The Perspective of Sociotechnical Alignment," *Technovation* 17, nos. 11/12 (November/December 1997), pp. 601–26.

Appendix F

1. Robert M. Pirsig, *Zen and the Art of Motorcycle Maintenance* (New York: William Morrow and Company, Inc., 1974).

2. Pratima Raichur, *Absolute Beauty* (New York: HarperPerennial, 1986).

3. Nescafe: Nestle (verified by Terril Haywood via 1/16/01 e-mail that Nescafe and Nesquik flavors are modified for the market in which they are sold).

4. Timothy J. Mullaney and Rober D. Hof, "Information Technology Annual Report," *Business Week Online*, June 24, 2002.

5. Jane Black, "The Fight for Privacy Has Just Began," *Business Week Online*, January 10, 2002.

Chapter 18

1. C. M. Christensen, "The Past and Future of Competitive Advantage," *Sloan Management Review*, Winter 2001, pp. 105–09.

2. M. Schrage, "Getting Beyond the Innovation Fetish," *Fortune*, November 13, 2000, pp. 225–32.

3. T. A. Judge, C. J. Thoresen, V. Pucik, and T. M. Welbourne, "Managerial Coping with Organizational Change: A Dispositional Perspective," *Journal of Applied Psychology*, 84 (1999), pp. 107–22.

4. C. Giffi, A. Roth, and G. Seal, *Competing in World-Class Manufacturing: America's 21st Century Challenge* (Homewood, IL: Business One Irwin, 1990).

5. R. M. Kanter, *World Class: Thriving Locally in the Global Economy* (New York: Touchstone, 1995).

6. T. G. Gunn, *21st Century Manufacturing* (New York: HarperBusiness, 1992).

7. Giffi, Roth, and Seal, *Competing in World-Class Manufacturing*.

8. J. Collins and J. Porras, *Built to Last* (London: Century, 1996).

9. Ibid.

10. Ibid.

11. D. A. Nadler, "Managing Organizational Change: An Integrative Approach," *Journal of Applied Behavioral Science* 17 (1981), pp. 191–211.

12. R. Teerlink, "Harley's Leadership U-Turn," *Harvard Business Review*, July–August 2000, pp. 43–48.

13. J. Stanislao and B. C. Stanislao, "Dealing with Resistance to Change," *Business Horizons*, July–August 1983, pp. 74–78.

14. J. P. Kotter and L. A. Schlesinger, "Choosing Strategies for Change," *Harvard Business Review*, March–April 1979, pp. 106–14.

15. D. Zell, "Overcoming Barriers to Work Innovations: Lessons Learned at

Hewlett-Packard," *Organizational Dynamics*, Summer 2001, pp. 77–85.

16. Ibid.

17. E. B. Dent and S. Galloway Goldberg, "Challenging Resistance to Change," *Journal of Applied Behavioral Science*, March 1999, pp. 25–41.

18. G. Johnson, *Strategic Change and the Management Process* (New York: Basil Blackwell, 1987); K. Lewin, "Frontiers in Group Dynamics," *Human Relations*, 1 (1947), pp. 5–41.

19. E. H. Schein, "Organizational Culture: What It Is and How to Change It," in *Human Resource Management in International Firms*, ed. P. Evans, Y. Doz, and A. Laurent (New York: St. Martin's Press, 1990).

20. M. Beer, R. Eisenstat, and B. Spector, *The Critical Path to Corporate Renewal* (Cambridge, MA: Harvard Business School Press, 1990).

21. E. E. Lawler III, "Transformation from Control to Involvement," in *Corporate Transformation*, ed. R. Kilmann and T. Covin (San Francisco: Jossey-Bass, 1988).

22. D. Hellriegel and J. W. Slocum, Jr., *Management*, 4th ed. (Reading, MA: Addison-Wesley, 1986).

23. P. Harris, *New World, New Ways, New Management* (New York: American Management Association, 1983).

24. Schein, "Organizational Culture."

25. E. E. Lawler III, *From the Ground Up* (San Francisco: Jossey-Bass, 1995).

26. Quy Nguyen, Huy, "Time, Temporal Capability, and Planned Change," *Academy of Management Review*, 26 (2001), pp. 601–23.

27. B. Sugarman, "A Learning-Based Approach to Organizational Change: Some Results and Guidelines," *Organizational Dynamics*, Summer 2001, pp. 62–75.

28. Kotter and Schlesinger, "Choosing Strategies for Change."

29. P. C. Judge, "It's Lonely on the Edge," *Fast Company*, September 2000, pp. 352–63.

30. Sugarman, "A Learning-Based Approach to Organizational Change."

31. R. H. Miles, "Beyond the Age of Dilbert: Accelerating Corporate Transformations by Rapidly Engaging all Employees," *Organizational Dynamics*, Spring 2001, pp. 313–21.

32. Nadler, "Managing Organizational Change."

33. D. Rousseau and S. A. Tijoriwala, "What's a Good Reason to Change? Motivated Reasoning and Social Accounts in Promoting Organizational Change," *Journal of Applied Psychology*, 84 (1999), pp. 514–28.

34. P. C. Judge, "Janiece Webb," *Fast Company*, November 2000, pp. 218–26.

35. R. B. Reich, "Your Job Is Change," *Fast Company*, October 2000, pp. 140–60.

36. C. F. Leana and B. Barry, "Stability and Change as Simultaneous Experiences in Organizational Life," *Academy of Management Review*, 25 (2000), pp. 753–59.

37. O. Gadiesh and J. Gilbert, "Transforming Corner-Office Strategy into Frontline Action," *Harvard Business Review*, May 2001, pp. 72–79.

38. B. Schneider, A. Brief, and R. Guzzo, "Creating a Climate and Culture for Sustainable Organizational Change," *Organizational Dynamics*, Spring 1996, pp. 7–19.

39. The Price Waterhouse Change Integration Team, *Better Change: Best Practices for Transforming Your Organization* (Burr Ridge, IL: Irwin, 1995).

40. M. Beer and N. Nohria, "Cracking the Code of Change," *Harvard Business Review*, May–June 2000, pp. 133–41.

41. N. Nohria and J. Berkley, "Whatever Happened to the Take-Charge Manager?" *Harvard Business Review*, January–February 1994, pp. 128–37.

42. Lawler, *From the Ground Up*.

43. The Price Waterhouse Change Integration Team, *Better Change*.

44. Ibid.

45. J. Kotter, *Leading Change* (Boston: Harvard Business School Press, 1996).

46. Lawler, *From the Ground Up*.

47. Kotter, *Leading Change*.

48. Schneider, Brief, and Guzzo, "Creating a Climate and Culture."

49. R. Beckhard and R. Harris, *Organizational Transitions* (Reading, MA: Addison-Wesley, 1977).

50. Kotter, *Leading Change*.

51. Judge, "It's Lonely on the Edge."

52. G. Hamel, "Waking Up IBM" *Harvard Business Review*, July–August 2000, pp. 137–46.

53. Kotter, *Leading Change*.

54. D. Smith, *Taking Charge of Change* (Reading, MA: Addison-Wesley, 1996).

55. G. Hamel, "Killer Strategies That Make Shareholders Rich," *Fortune*, June 23, 1997, pp. 22–34.

56. G. Hamel and C. K. Prahalad, *Competing for the Future* (Boston: Harvard Business School Press, 1994).

57. B. J. Pine, B. Victor, and A. Boynton, "Making Mass Customization Work," *Harvard Business Review*, September–October 1993, pp. 108–19.

58. J. W. Slocum, Jr., M. McGill, and D. Lei, "The New Learning Strategy: Anytime, Anything, Anywhere," *Organizational Dynamics*, Autumn 1994, pp. 33–37.

59. Pine, Victor, and Boynton, "Making Mass Customization Work."

60. W. Zellner and D. Griesing, "Go-Go Galiaths," *Business Week*, February 13, 1995, pp. 64–70.

61. M. J. Kierman, "The New Strategic Architecture: Learning to Complete in the Twenty-First Century," *The Academy of Management Executive*, February 1993, pp. 7–21.

62. J. O'Shea and C. Madigan, *Dangerous Company: The Consulting Powerhouses and the Business They Save and Ruin* (New York: Times Books, 1997).

63. Ibid.

64. Hamel and Prahalad, *Competing for the Future*.

65. Ibid.

66. Ibid.

67. H. Courtney, J. Kirkland, and P. Viguerie, "Strategy under Uncertainty," *Harvard Business Review*, November–December 1997, pp. 66–79.

68. Ibid.

69. Hamel and Prahalad, *Competing for the Future*.

70. R. Charan and G. Colvin, "Managing for the Slowdown," *Fortune*, February 5, 2001, pp. 78–88.

71. G. Hamel, "Reinvent Your Company," *Fortune*, June 12, 2000, pp. 98–118.

72. J. Kotter, *The New Rules: How to Succeed in Today's Post-Corporate World* (New York: The Free Press, 1995).

73. Ibid.

74. Ibid.

75. Lawler, *From the Ground Up*; Kotter, *The New Rules*.

76. Lawler, *From the Ground Up*.

77. M. Peiperl and Y. Baruck, "Back to Square Zero: The Post-Corporate Career," *Organizational Dynamics*, Spring 1997, pp. 7–22.

78. Ibid.

79. Kotter, *The New Rules*.

80. G. Binney, and C. Williams, *Leaning into the Future* (London: Nicholas Brealey, 1997).

Photo Credits

Chapter 1

1.1 AP/Wide World Photos; **1.2** © Chuck Nacke/Woodfin Camp & Associates; **1.3** Courtesy Intel Corporation; **1.4** AP/Wide World Photos; **1.5** Courtesy of Southwest Airlines; **1.6** Reuters/Toshiyuki Aizawa/Archive Photos/Getty Images; **1.7** © Mark Richards/Photo Edit; **1.8** Courtesy of Business Week; **1.9** AP/Wide World Photos

Appendix A

A.1 © Martin Rogers/Stone/Getty Images; **A.2** Stock Montage, Inc.; **A.3** Stock Montage, Inc.

Chapter 2

2.1 © David Young-Wolff/Photo Edit; **2.2** © AFP/CORBIS; **2.3** Photo by Honda/Getty Images; **2.4** © Harry How/Allsport/Getty Images; **2.5** © Reuters NewMedia Inc./Corbis

Chapter 3

3.1 BABY TREND, INC.; **3.2** © Stephen Dunn/Allsport; **3.3** Courtesy of Standard & Poors; **3.5** © Jeff Greenberg/PhotoEdit; **3.6** Courtesy of Rolf C. Smith, Jr.; **3.7** © Bettmann/Corbis; **3.8** Photofest; **3.9** AP/Wide World Photos

Chapter 4

4.1 © Richard Cummins/Corbis; **4.2** AP/Wide World Photos; **4.3** © Rob Crandall/Stock, Boston; **4.4** © Mark Richards/Photo Edit

Chapter 5

5.1 VCG/FGP International/Getty Images; **5.2** © Reuters NewMedia Inc./Corbis; **5.3** © Michael Newman/PhotoEdit; **5.4** Used with permission of the National Organization on Disability (www.nod.org <http://www.nod.org>); **5.5** Robbie McClaran; **5.6** DDB, Dallas Art Director: Carl Warner, Copywriter: Jim Hord; Stock photo by Getty Images; **5.7** Reuters/Keither B. Richburg/Archive Photos/Getty Images

Appendix B

B.1 Maillac/REA-SABA/Corbis

Chapter 6

6.1 Photo Courtesy of DaimlerChrysler AG/Getty Images; **6.2** Photo by Sean Gallup/Getty Images; **6.3** © Roy Ooms/Masterfile; **6.4** © Peter Oxley/Photo Japan; **6.5** © Houston Scott/ Corbis Sygma; **6.6** Loren Santow/Stone/Getty Images

Chapter 7

7.1 © Reuters New Media Inc./Corbis; **7.2** AP/Wide World Photos; **7.3** Wyatt McSpadden; **7.4** Courtesy of Finjin Software; **7.5** Courtesy of Kistler Aerospace Corporation; **7.6** MGM/Koball Collection; **7.7** Photo provided Courtesy of 3M

Chapter 8

8.1 AP/Wide World Photos; **8.2** © Spencer Grant/Photo Edit; **8.3** NASA; **8.4** © Keith Dannemiller/CORBIS/SABA; **8.5** © Rommel Pecson/The Image Works

Chapter 9

9.1 © Ed Quinn/CORBIS/SABA; **9.2** AP/Wide World Photos; **9.3** Photograph by Ansen Seale; **9.4** AP/Wide World Photos; **9.5** © Greg Whitesell/Getty Images; **9.6** © Tim Boyle/Getty Images

Chapter 10

10.1 Careerbuilder 2002; **10.2** © Ryanstock/Taxi/Getty Images; **10.3** © Gene J. Pusker-Pool/Getty Images; **10.4** © Reuters NewMedia Inc./CORBIS

Chapter 11

11.1 © Michael Newman/Photo Edit; **11.2** Courtesy of Xerox Corporation; **11.3** © Steven Rubin/The Image Works; **11.4** 8383/GAMMA Press USA; **11.5** AP/Wide World Photos

Chapter 12

12.1 AP/Wide World Photos; **12.2** AP/Wide World Photos; **12.3** © Phil Martin/Photo Edit; **12.4** © Bob Daemmrich/The Image Works; **12.5** From the personal archives of Rear Admiral Louise Wilmot; **12.6** AP/Wide World Photos; **12.7** © Flip Schulke/Stockphoto.com; **12.8** AP/Wide World Photos

Chapter 13

13.2 1983 ©Fujifotos /The Image Works; **13.3** © Joe Solem/Stone/Getty Images; **13.4** AP/Wide World Photos; **13.5** © Bob Daemmrich; **13.6** Copyright, State Farm Mutual Automobile Insurance Company, 1966. Used by permission.; **13.7** AP/Wide World Photos; **13.8** AP/Wide World Photos

Chapter 14

14.1 Zubin Shroff; **14.2** © Ronald Martinez/Getty Images; **14.3** © Mark Richards/PhotoEdit; **14.4** © Marc Pokempner/Stone/Getty Images; **14.5** Courtesy of American Arbitration Association

Chapter 15

15.1 © William Taufic/Corbis Stock Market; **15.2** © Sat Yip/SuperStock; **15.4** © Siemens Corporation; **15.5** Screen shot captured by Christine Shreid/© McGraw-Hill Higher Education, Inc.; **15.6** © Dick Luria/FPG International/Getty Images; **15.7** AP/Wide World Photos; **15.8** Courtesy of GE

Chapter 16

16.2 Charles Gupton/Corbis Stock Market; **16.3a** AP/Wide World Photos; **16.3b** © The Procter & Gamble Company. Used by permission.; **16.4** AP/Wide World Photos

Chapter 17

17.1 Steve Griffin/The Salt Lake Tribune; **17.2** Courtesy of Dr. Leslie Kay; **17.3** Photo by Mario Tama/Getty Images; **17.4** © Mark Richards/Photo Edit; **17.5** AP/Wide World Photos

Chapter 18

18.1 Jim Schnepf; **18.2** © Loren Callahan/Reuters/Getty Images; **18.3** Courtesy of Southwest Airlines; **18.4** Toyota Motor North America, Inc.; **18.5** AP/Wide World Photos; **18.6** Courtesy of Columbia Sportswear; **18.7** © James D. Wilson/Getty Images/Liaison Agency

Name Index

A

Abraham, Steven E., N-13
Abramson, Andy, 303
Ackerman, R., N-5
Ackermann, F., N-23
Adams, J., N-17
Adams, Scott, 83
Aditya, R., N-15
Adkisson, Richard V., N-7
Adler, Nancy J., 143, 345, 455, N-3, N-7, N-14, N-16, N-20
Adler, Paul S., N-9
Aggarwal, R., 477, N-20
Agres, Carole E., N-11
Ahrens, Roger, N-7
Ainina, M. Fall, N-14
Akasie, J., 211
Alaimo, Dan, 296
Albrecht, K., N-16
Albrecht, S., N-21
Alderfer, C., 406, N-16
Aldrich, H., N-8
Alexander, Clifford, Jr., 255
Alexander, E.R., N-3, N-19
Alexander, S., 310
Ali, Abbas J., N-9
Alix, Jay, 22
Allaire, Paul, 254
Allinson, R.E., N-4
Altaffer, Ahnn, N-9
Altman, B., 171, N-6
Amabile, T.M., N-3, N-16
Amason, A., N-3
Anatol, K.W.E., N-20
Ancona, D.G., N-18
Anderson, J.V., N-3
Anderson, Kenneth, N-7
Anderson, Peggy, N-21
Anderson, R., 155, 157
Anderson, S.F., 472
Andrews, C.E., 498
Andrews, F., 365
Andrews, P., N-5
Anfuso, Dawn, N-4
Anschutz, Philip, 254
Ante, Spencer, 52
Anthes, Gary H., N-22
Applebaum, R.L., N-20
Arad, Sharon, N-21
Aranda, E., N-18
Argenti, J., N-8
Argyris, Chris, 36, N-2, N-17, N-19
Arimura, Sadanori, N-22
Armstrong, Lance, 45–46
Arndt, Michael, 52, 63, 496, N-8
Arnold, Susan, 335
Arnst, Catherine, 270, N-2
Arther, M.B., N-1
Arthur, Charles, N-14
Arthur, Winfred, Jr., N-12
Ash, Mary Kay, 407
Ash, Ronald A., N-11
Ashcroft, John, 396
Ashkenas, Ronald N., 583, N-8, N-11, N-20
Athos, A., N-20
Atkins, P.W.B., N-16
Austin, N., N-17, N-18

Avolio, B.J., N-15
Axtell, C., N-19

B

Bacher, Jeffrey, N-13
Bacon, Francis, 518
Badaracco, J., Jr., N-4, N-5
Baddaley, J., N-8
Baden, Colin, 45–46
Bailey, D.E., N-17, N-18, N-19
Baird, Lloyd, N-9
Bakke, Dennis, 255, 397–398, 477
Baldwin, Carliss Y., N-22
Bales, R.F., N-18
Balestrini, P.P., N-11
Ball, G., N-16
Ballam, Deborah A., N-12
Ballard, L. Gregory, 13
Baltes, B., N-19
Balu, R., N-8
Banker, R., 430, N-18
Banta, Vivian, 335
Barker, E., 211
Barker, J., N-9
Barnard, Chester, 33, N-2
Barnard, Janet, N-10
Barnard, Kurt, 120
Barnes, Bear, 221
Barnes, D., N-18
Barnholt, Ned, 277
Baron, R.A., N-8
Barrett, A., 70
Barrett, Colleen, 334
Barrett, W.P., N-8
Barrick, M.R., N-12
Barron, James, N-7
Barry, B., N-23
Bartholomew, Susan, N-7
Bartlett, Christopher A., 18, 188, N-1, N-9, N-16, N-17
Bartunek, J.M., N-9
Baruck, Y., N-24
Bass, B.M., N-3, N-15, N-16
Bastien, Ernest, 287
Bateman, T., 394, 405, N-3, N-8
Battenberg, J.T., 187, 289
Bauer, C., N-19
Bauer, R., N-5
Baughman, J., N-2
Baum, J., N-15
Bayer, Ellen, 505
Baysinger, B., N-5
Baysinger, R.A., N-12
Bazerman, M., N-3, N-4
Beam, D.R., N-5
Beaubien, E., N-9
Beckhard, R., N-24
Bedeian, Arthur G., 27, 391, 478, 580, N-9
Bednarzik, Robert W., N-7
Beer, Michael, 128, 553, N-24
Beeson, J., N-16
Beeth, Gunner, N-7
Behr, P., N-3, N-15
Bellman, L.M., N-1
Bennett, A., N-16
Bennis, W., 429, N-14, N-15, N-16, N-18
Bentell, Nicholas J., 318

Berenson, A., N-5
Bergen, M.E., N-3
Bergeson, Lynn L., N-21
Berk, Michael, 278
Berkley, J., N-24
Berkley, Robyn A., N-11
Berkowitz, M., N-4
Berle, Adolf A., 246
Bernard, Betsy, 334
Bernasco, Wilma, N-9
Bernasek, A., N-1
Berner, Robert, 421, 516
Berners-Lee, Tim, 567
Bernhard, Wolfgang, 178
Bernstein, A., 137, 142, 149, 160, N-4
Berra, Yogi, 467
Bertucco, Marc, N-22
Bethune, Gordon, 125
Bezos, Jeffrey, 19
Bianchi, A., N-17
Bianco, Anthony, 389, N-15
Bickford, Deborah J., N-22
Biederman, P. Ward, 429
Bierce, Ambrose, 210
Bierly, Paul, N-22
Bigney, Frank, Jr., 273
Binney, George, 569, 574, N-24
Birdwell, L., N-16
Black, Carole, 5, 335
Black, Cathleen, 334
Black, Jane, N-23
Blake, Jim, 313
Blake, R., N-15
Blake, Robert R., 376
Blake, S., N-14
Blancero, Donna, N-13
Blanchard, Kenneth, 395, N-16
Blank, Dennis, 313
Block, P., N-16
Bloom, M., N-17
Blum, M., N-19
Blumberg, L., N-6
Blumenthal, Robin Goldwyn, N-22
Boehm, R., N-9
Boer, Harry, N-9
Bohlander, George, 305, 307, 317, 337, N-2, N-12, N-13
Bok, Derek, N-14
Bono, J.E., N-16
Bordia, P., N-20
Borga, Maria, 183
Borrus, A., N-4
Bossidy, Lawrence, 463
Bourgeois, L.J., III, N-3
Bourland, Greg, 519
Bowen, D., N-15, N-17
Bowen, H. Kent, N-23
Bowen, William G., N-14
Boyatzis, R., N-16
Boyd, B., N-19
Boyle, Gert, 571
Boyle, M., 5, N-1
Boyle, Tim, 571
Boynton, A., N-24
Bracker, J., N-4
Bradbury, H., 167, N-5
Brady, Diane, 24, 120, 137, 502, N-2, N-4
Braham, L., 421

Branson, Richard, 384
Brattina, Anita, 225, N-8
Breeden, Richard, 145
Breen, B., 429, 576
Brenner, S., N-4
Breteau, Fleur, 193
Brett, J., N-19
Brewer, P.C., N-21
Bricklin, Dan, 213, 219, N-8
Brief, Arthur, 143, N-24
Bright, J.E.H., N-16
Brinkley, Amy, 334
Brockner, J., N-17
Brodt, S., N-19
Brodzinski, J., N-14
Brooker, K., 365, N-15
Brookes, R., N-4
Brown, A., N-5, N-6
Brown, E., 149, 217, N-1
Brown, Lester, 176
Brown, P., 482
Browne, John, 155, 157
Brownson, Kenneth, N-14
Buchanan, Ian, N-7
Buchanan, Jean, N-11
Buchele, R., N-21
Buchholtz, Ann K., N-22
Buchholz, R.A., N-5
Buchko, Aaron A., N-2
Buck, Michelle L., N-14
Buell, B., N-10
Bulkeley, W., 290
Buller, Paul, N-7
Burbage, Tom, 429
Burck, Charles, N-8, N-22
Burgelman, Robert A., N-22
Burgers, Willem P., N-2
Burgstone, Jon, 234
Burkart, Michael, N-14
Burke, Donald R., N-11
Burke, T., N-6
Burkhart, Glenda, N-14
Burns, Lauren E., N-22
Burns, T., 274, N-10
Burr, Cameron R., 63
Burr, J.T., N-21
Burrows, Peter, N-22
Busey, Andrew, 224
Bush, George W., 182
Bussmann, Van, 186
Butler, T., N-20
Butterfield, K., N-16
Byham, R., N-18
Byrd, M.J., N-8
Byrne, A., 499
Byrne, John A., 247, N-1, N-9
Byrnes, Nanette, 120, 372, 389, 421

C

Cackowski, David, N-9
Cafasso, Rosemary, N-13
Cahan, V., N-6
Caldwell, L., N-6
Calkins, G., 576
Callister, R.R., N-19
Calonius, Erik, N-14
Cameron, Kim S., 93, 513, N-21
Camp, Robert C., N-4, N-9
Campion, James E., N-11
Campion, Michael A., N-11, N-17
Candee, D., N-4
Capell, K., N-1
Caplan, Betty, 303
Cappelli, P., N-1
Carey, A., N-2
Carey, John, N-2
Carlson, Ed, 473

Carlson, J.R., N-19
Carlzon, Jan, 385
Carnevale, A.P., N-12
Carr, Linda, N-11
Carr, N., N-3
Carrasco, Emma, 447
Carroll, Archie B., 148
Carson, Rachel, 169–170, N-6
Carson, Robert B., 163
Carstedt, G., 167, N-5
Cartada, J.W., N-1
Carter, Jimmy, N-22
Cascio, W.F., N-10, N-16
Case, D., N-19
Case, J., 477, N-2, N-18, N-20
Case, Steve, 367
Castagna, Vanessa, 335
Chambers, G.J., N-9
Chambers, John, 375
Champagne, Paul J., 422
Champion, J.M., 103, 360–361, 484–485,
      584–585
Champy, J., N-10
Chan, R.Y.K., N-6
Chandler, Alfred, 276, N-2
Chappell, L., 91
Charan, R., N-24
Chatman, J., N-19
Chen, Pehong, 10
Cheng, Kipp, N-13
Chilton, Kenneth W., N-5, N-13
Choi, H., N-18
Chow, C.W., N-21
Christensen, C.M., N-23
Chrysler, Walter P., 72
Chu, C., N-20
Chung, Chen H., N-10
Chung, Q.B., N-9
Churchill, Winston, 371
Cianni, M., N-17, N-18
Ciulla, Joanne B., N-4, N-5, N-22
Clair, J.A., 167, N-5
Clampitt, P.G., 462
Clancy, J.A., N-8
Clark, D., N-8
Clark, Kim B., N-22, N-23
Clarkson, M.B.E., 150, N-5
Clifford, M.L., 160, N-8
Cochran, P.L., N-5
Cohen, Don, N-22
Cohen, Morris A., N-10
Cohen, S., N-17, N-18
Cohn, L., 472
Colbert, Janet L., N-21
Cole, David, 193
Collingwood, H., N-1
Collins, Denis, N-13
Collins, Francis, 365
Collins, James C., 400, 554–556, N-1, N-5, N-8,
      N-20, N-23
Collis, David J., N-2, N-4
Colt, Sam, 139
Coltrin, Sally A., 27, 391, 478, 580
Colvin, G., N-17, N-24
Comer, Debra R., N-12
Commoner, Barry, 170, N-6
Comstock, T.W., N-19, N-20
Conceicao, Pedro, N-23
Condit, Phil, 471
Conger, J.A., N-15, N-20
Conlin, Michelle, 221, 303, 506
Connolly, T., N-16
Conrades, George, 69
Conti, R., N-16
Cook, Scott, 217
Cooke, R.A., N-4
Coon, H., N-16
Cooper, C., 198, N-18

Corbett, C.J., N-6, N-7
Corsini, Skip, N-12
Cortina, Jose M., N-12
Cory, Kenneth D., N-2
Cosier, R., N-3
Costakos, Christos, 365
Cothron, Mark, 549
Cotros, Charles, 110
Courtney, H., N-24
Coutu, D., N-1
Cowell, J., N-20
Cox, T., N-14
Coy, Peter, 132, N-1
Crainer, S., N-2
Crandall, W., N-4
Cranor, S., N-1
Crant, J.M., N-8
Crawford, David B., N-21
Creech, Bill, N-10
Crick, J.D., 463
Cripe, Mike, 549
Crispin, Gerry, 299
Crockett, Barton, 299
Crockett, Joan, 353–354, N-14
Crockett, Roger O., 270
Crosby, Chris, 565
Crosby, Faye J., N-14
Crosby, Olivia, N-12
Cross, F.B., N-6
Cross, Rob, N-9, N-18, N-19
Cull, Carl, N-10
Cullen, John B., N-11
Cummings, A., N-16
Cummings, L.L., N-16
Curry, Gloria M., N-14
Cusumano, Michael A., N-2
Czarnecki, Mark, N-10

D

Daft, Richard L., N-2, N-19
Dahle, C., 567, 576
Daily, C.M., N-9
Dalton, D.R., N-9
Dames, Peter, 425
Dammerman, Dennis D., 502
Daniel, Christopher, N-13
Daniels, Alex, 299, N-11
Daniels, Cora, N-11
Dansereau, F., N-15
D'Aveni, Richard, N-3
Davenport, Thomas O., N-11
Davidhizar, Ruth E., N-14
Davidson, Paul, 42
Davila, Alberto, N-13
Davila, Antonio, N-21
Davis, Clive, 211
Davis, D., N-11
Davis, J.W., 278
Davis, Keith, 271, N-20
Davis, L.J., N-4
Davis, S., N-3, N-9
Davis, T.R.V., 470, 477, N-20
Davison, H. Krisl, N-12
Davison, Sue Canney, N-7, N-18
Dawson, Peter P., 449
Day, D.L., N-22
Day, D.V., N-15
Day, George S., N-9
De George, R.T., N-4
de WeerdNederhof, Petra C., N-9
Dean, James W., Jr., 539, N-2, N-3, N-21
Dechant, K., 171, N-6
Decker, C.D., N-20
Deininger, Lydia, 177
Deleeuw, Kevin, N-12
Dell, Michael, 14, 217, 225, 227, 231
Della, Robert, N-21

Dellana, Scott A., N-22
Deming, W. Edwards, 280, 544
DeNisi, A., N-20
Dent, E.B., N-23
Denton, D.K., N-20
D'Epiro, Nancy Walsh, N-22
Der Hovanesian, Mara, 278
Desai, Ashay B., N-7
Descarpentries, Jean-Marie, 507
DesMarteau, Kathleen, N-22
Dess, G.G., N-8, N-16
Dessler, G., N-16
DeToro, Irving, N-2
Deutsch, C., N-19
Deutschman, A., N-1
DeVito, Denise, 55
Devlin, D., 217, N-7
Dewan, Rajiv, N-22
DeWitt, Rocki-Lee, N-12
Dickinson, Wood, 386
Dickson, M., N-19
Dickson, W., N-2
Dickter, David N., N-12
Difonzo, N., N-20
Digh, Patricia, N-7
Dillard, William, 254
Dionne, E.J., 160
Disney, Walt, 383
DiTomaso, Nancy, N-2
Dixon, G., N-18
Dixon, N.M., 451
Dodson, Peggy, 215
Donlan, Thomas G., N-21
Donnelly, J., Jr., 67
Donovan, Michelle A., N-21
Dooley, R., N-3
Dooner, John, 575
Dorfman, P., N-15
Dove, Rick, N-10
Dow, Douglas, N-10
Doyle, Eric, N-11
Drexler, Mickey, 253–254
Dreyfuss, Joel, N-22
Driscoll, D., 142
Droge, Cornelia, N-9
Drucker, Peter, 4, 40, 226, N-8, N-21
Druskat, Vanessa Urch, N-21
Dublon, Dina, 335
Duffy, Maureen Nevin, N-7
Dumaine, B., N-17, N-18
Duncan, R., N-9
Dunham, R., 137
Dunkel, Tom, N-13
Dunnette, M.D., N-19
Durham, C., N-18
Durr, Barbara, N-14
Dutton, Gail, N-14
Dutton, J., N-4
Dwer, P., 137
Dyer, Lee, N-10

E

Eads, Stefani, 107
Eagly, A., 375
Earle, Nick, 230
Early, P.C., N-16, N-20
Eastman, Lorrina J., N-11
Eaton, Robert J., 177
Echikson, W., 160
Eckes, George, 496
Economides, Michael I., N-22
Edelman, K., N-19
Eden, C., N-23
Edison, Thomas, 82
Edman, Nancy J., N-12
Edwards, Mark, N-13

Eggeris, Craig, 532
Ehrenfeld, J., N-6
Ehrenfeld, T., N-17
Einstein, Albert, 82
Eisenberg, D., 398
Eisenhardt, K., N-3
Eisenstat, R.A., 128, N-4
Eisner, Michael, 442, 467
Ekegren, G., N-16
Elkington, J., N-6, N-7
Ellis, George, N-21
Ellis, Kimberly M., N-9
Ellis, Leo, 450
Ellison, H., N-6, N-7
Ellison, L.J., 247, 253
Ellsion, Adam, 553
Elstron, P., N-8
Ely, Robin J., N-14
Engardio, Pete, 160, 273, N-8
Erez, M., N-18
Esenhardt, K.M., N-3
Ettkin, Lawrence P., N-11
Ettlie, John E., N-11, N-21
Euchenwald, K., N-4
Evans, David S., 348
Evans, James R., N-10
Evans, P., N-8
Evans, R., N-3
Ewen, Ann J., N-13
Ewert, G.A., N-21
Ewing, Jack, 243, N-2
Eyler, John H., Jr., 119, 420–421

F

Fagenson-Eland, E., 375
Fahrbach, Kyle, N-21
Faircloth, Anne, N-4
Falbe, C., N-15
Falcone, Paul, N-12
Faludi, S.C., N-16
Farnham, A., N-3, N-5
Farrell, Christopher, 139, N-21
Farrow, Vicky, 22
Fay, Charles, N-13
Fayol, Henri, 33, N-2
Fear, R. A., N-11
Feeny, D., N-1
Feldman, Robert A., N-7
Fenn, D., N-17
Fenwick, Marilyn S., N-21
Ferguson, Eammon, N-12
Ferner, Anthony, N-9, N-21
Ferrari, David, N-7
Ferraro, G., N-20
Ferrell, O.C., N-4, N-5
Ferry, Richard M., N-7
Fessler, Clyde, 256
Fidrych, Michael, 325
Fiedler, F.E., N-16
Field, Hubert, N-12
Field, J., 430, N-18
Figueroa, Edgar, N-23
Finegan, J., N-17
Finegold, D., N-16, N-17
Finkelstein, S., N-1, N-8
Finlay, J. Richard, 247
Fiorina, Carly, 230, 334, 375
Fischer, K., N-6
Fisher, Anne, N-5, N-12
Fisher, S., N-3
Fishman, C., 553
Fitzpatrick, William M., N-11
Fleishman, E., N-15
Floyd, Steven W., N-4
Flynn, Barbara B., N-9
Flynn, F. James, N-9, N-19
Flynn, Gillian, N-13, N-14, N-21
Foley, Richard T., N-12

Folger, R., N-17
Follet, Mary Parker, 33
Forbes, D.P., N-18
Forbes, M., N-20
Ford, Bill, Jr., 91
Ford, C.M., N-16
Ford, Henry, 32, 58, 91, 123, 385, 425, 551
Ford, Lynda, N-14
Ford, R.C., N-9
Ford, Steve, N-10
Ford, William Clay, Jr., 91, 567, 568
Forman, Craig, 447
Forrester, Russ, N-9, N-17
Foti, R., N-15
Foust, Dean, N-14
Fouts, P., N-5
Fowler, H.R., N-20
Fox, J., 389
Fraedrich, J., 139, N-4, N-5
Francesconi, Louise, 335
Francis, Suzanne C., N-8
Frank, Kenneth A., N-21
Franks, Lynne, 567
Fraser, J.A., N-8
Fredrickson, James W., N-7
Freeman, Laurie, N-7
Freeman, R.E., N-5
Freeman, Sarah J., N-10
Freivalds, J., 464
French, J.R.P., 370, N-15
Freshley, D.L., 466, N-20
Frey, J., N-5
Friedman, Judith J., N-2
Friedman, Milton, 147–148
Friesen, P., N-2
Frost, P., N-4
Fryer, B., 27
Fuchs, Peter H., N-21
Fulk, J., N-19
Fuller, Marce, 335
Fuller, T., N-8
Fulmer, Robert M., N-12, N-16, N-20
Fyxell, G., N-3

G

Gabarro, J., N-20
Gadiesh, O., N-17, N-24
Gaijin, A., N-7
Galbraith, J., N-2, N-9
Gale, J., N-5
Gallagher, Monica, N-13
Gallo, James, N-9
Galvin, Bob, 495
Gannes, S., N-4
Gantt, Henry, 32
Gardner, Susan E., N-13
Garfield, C., 167
Garry, Michael, 296
Garvin, D.A., N-1, N-3, N-11
Gates, Bill, 267
Gatewood, Robert, N-12
Gehlen, F.L., N-3
Geller, L.K., 451
Gendron, G., 215
George, C., N-2
Gerhart, Gail M., N-7
Germain, Richard, N-9
Geroski, P.A., N-22
Gershenfel, Neil, 575
Gersick, C.J.G., N-18
Gerstner, C.R., N-15
Gerstner, Lou, 5, 511
Gerwitz, J.L., N-4
Gettys, C., N-3
Ghemawat, P., N-1
Ghoshal, Sumantra, 188, N-2, N-9, N-16, N-17

Gibbs, Manton, N-9
Gibbs, Philip A., N-12, N-16
Gibson, J., 67
Gibson, K., N-4
Giffi, C., N-23
Gilbert, C., N-2
Gilbert, Jacqueline A., N-14
Gilbert, J.L., N-17
Gilbraith, J., N-9
Gilbreth, Dr. Lillian, 32
Gilbreth, Frank, 32
Gill, Jennifer, 52, 339–340, 506
Gilley, Bruce, N-11
Gilliland, Stephen W., N-12, N-17
Gilman, Thomas F., 177
Gilmore, James H., N-10
Gilmour, Allan, 288
Gimein, M., N-4, N-17
Gingrich, Bryan, N-14
Glaauszka, Peter, 516
Glain, S., 464
Glassberg, B., N-19
Glater, J.D., N-5
Glueck, William F., 27, 391, 478, 580
Goetzmann, Gordon J., 278
Gohring, Nancy, N-22
Goldberg, M., 447
Goldberg, S. Galloway, N-23
Goldberg, Stephanie B., 341
Golden, F., 365
Goldsmith, Marshall, N-12, N-16
Goldstein, Nancy B., N-12
Goldstein, Robert B., 278
Goleman, D., 377, N-15
Gomez-Mejia, Luis P., N-13
Goodheim, L., N-16
Goodman, Joshua, 182
Goodwin, James E., 5
Gopalakrishnan, Shanthi, N-22
Gordon, J., 39, 93, 542
Gorelick, Jamie, 335
Goshal, S., N-1, 18
Gottlieb, R., N-6
Govindarajan, Vijay, N-13, N-19, N-23
Gowan, J.A., Jr., N-21
Graen, G., N-15
Graham, G., N-20
Grandy, Fred, 337
Grant, Joseph M., 278
Grant, R., 583
Graves, Earl, 217
Gravett, Matt, 192
Gray, P.B., 217, N-7
Green, Jeff, 91, 178, N-10
Greene, J., 571
Greening, D., N-5
Greeno, J. Ladd, 166
Greenwood, A., 221
Grensing-Pophal, Lin, N-14
Griesing, D., N-24
Gross, Bill, 214
Gross, N., 457, N-1
Gross, Steven, N-13
Grossblatt, Harvey, 65
Grossman, Robert J., N-14
Grove, Andrew, 7, 13, 553
Grow, B., 137, N-4
Grunwald, M., N-5
Guilford, Roxanna, 243
Gundry, Lisa K., N-23
Gunn, T.G., N-23
Gunther, M., 553, 571, N-4
Gupta, Anil K., N-13, N-19, N-23
Guthrie, James P., N-13
Gutknecht, J., N-20
Gutner, Toddi, N-13
Guy, M.E., N-4, N-5
Guyon, J., 367, N-1

Guyot, Erik, N-14
Guzzo, R., N-24

H

Haben, Mary Kay, 335
Hackman, J. Richard, 410, N-17, N-18
Haddad, Charles, 529
Hagedoorn, John, N-22
Hagen, Abdalla F., N-2
Hai, Dorothy, 448, 578
Hainer, Herbert, 243
Hakim, C., 573
Hale, J., N-4
Hall, Alan, 522
Hall, D.T., N-20
Hall, E., N-5
Hall, F., N-5
Hall-Merenda, K.E., N-15
Hallowell, E.M., N-19
Hallowell, Roger, N-2, N-4
Hambrick, Donald C., N-7
Hamel, Gary, 8, 11, 290, 400, 571–572, 576,
    N-1, N-11, N-17, N-24
Hamermesh, R., 124
Hames, J., 360–361
Hamm, Steve, N-1, N-22
Hammer, M., N-10
Hammitt, J.K., N-5
Hammonds, Keith H., 576, N-10
Hamrin, R., N-17
Hancock, Barry W., N-12
Handy, Charles, 149, N-4, N-5
Haney, W.V., N-19
Hansen, M., N-1
Hanson, J., 275, N-10
Harback, H., N-10
Harbour, Ron, 289
Hardin, Garrett, 169, N-6
Hardin, Rusty, 498
Harding, D., N-4
Hargadon, A., 83, N-3
Hargrove, Buzz, 323
Harmon, C., 410
Harmon, Larry, 221
Harper, Pamela, N-11
Harrington, B., N-20
Harris, E., N-15
Harris, Hilary, N-7
Harris, Josh, 5
Harris, P., N-23
Harris, R., N-24
Harris, Scott Blake, N-22
Harrison, J.S., N-5
Hart, S.L., 167, N-5, N-6
Hartley, Darin E., N-11
Hartman, R., N-18
Hartmann, Tim, 323
Harzing, Anne-Wil, 188, N-7
Haspeslagh, P., 124
Hastings, D.F., 398
Hauser, Richard D., N-22
Hawken, P., 167, N-5, N-6
Hawley, D. L., N-12
Hawn, C., 27
Hayes, Robert H., N-23
Hays, L., 290
Hays, Scott, 341
Haywood, Terril, N-23
Heifetz, R., 451, N-15, N-17
Hellofs, Linda L., N-10
Hellriegel, D., N-23
Helms, Marilyn M., N-11
Helms, Susan J., 263
Helyar, J., 365
Henderson, David R., 159–160
Heneman, Herbert G., N-11
Henkoff, R., N-10, N-21

Henne, D., N-17
Henretta, Deb, 335
Henry, Eileen, N-13
Henwood, C., N-19
Hequet, Marc, N-12
Herbert, B., 160
Herman, Roger E., 130
Herr, Dave, 492
Herring, Laura, 202
Herron, M., N-16
Hersey, Paul, 395, N-16
Herzberg, Frederick, 408, N-17
Hesketh, Beryl, N-11
Hewlett, Bill, 216
Hickman, J., N-4
Higgins, Andrew, 218
Higgins, E.T., N-18
Hill, G.W., N-3
Hill, Vernon W., 278
Hillman, A.J., N-5
Hiltrop, Jean-Marie, N-11
Hipskind, M., N-18
Hirsh, S.K., 77
Hisrich, R., 222, N-8
Hitt, M.A., N-5, N-10, N-15
Hochwarter, W., 400
Hodgetts, R.M., 398, N-20
Hoenig, Jonathan, 10
Hof, Robert D., N-1, N-10, N-23
Hofstede, Geert, 200–201, N-16
Holden, Betsy, 334
Holden, James P., 178
Holder, Robert C., 270
Holland, K., N-4
Holland, Royce, 211
Hollenbeck, G.P., N-20
Hollensbe, Elaine C., N-13
Holliday, Chad, 155, N-5
Holloway, Charles A., N-23
Holmes, S., 137, N-4
Holstein, W.J., N-1
Holusha, J., N-4
Hong, Sehee, N-12
Honig, Barry, 329
Hoover, Gary, 218
Hopkins, Deborah C., 269
Hordes, M., N-8
Hornsby, J., N-8
Hoskisson, Robert E., N-4
House, Robert J., 379, N-15
Hout, Thomas M., N-10
Howard, Cecil G., N-7
Howard, J., N-6
Howell, David, N-23
Howell, J.M., N-15
Hudson, Peter J., Jr., N-11
Huey, John, 215, N-4, N-16
Hunter, J.E., N-12, N-13
Hunter, L., N-5
Huseman, R.C., 466, N-20
Hutton, A., N-20
Huy, Q.N., N-1, N-23
Hyatt, J., 217

I

Iacocca, Lee, 383, 385
Ibsen, Thor, 425
Ibuka, Masaru, 216
Imai, Masaaki, N-22
Imberman, W., N-20
Immelt, Jeffrey R., 388–389, 502
Imperato, G., 553
Inkson, K., N-1
Ireland, Christopher, 131
Ireland, R.D., N-8, N-15
Ishikawa, K., N-10
Israeli, Fadna N., N-7

Isumi, H., N-18
Ivancevich, John M., 67, N-14

J

Jablin, F.M., N-20
Jackson, J.E., N-3
Jacobson, Robert, N-10
Jacoby, S.M., N-1
Jager, Durk, 515
James, J.H., 103, 484–485, 584–585
Janis, I., N-3
Janson, R., N-17
Jarratt, Jennifer, 131
Jasinowski, J., N-17
Jauch, Lawrence R., 27, 391, 478, 580
Javetski, Bill, N-7
Jeffrey, Jim, 221
Jehiel, Philippe, N-9
Jehn, K., N-18
Jenkins, Darryl, 62
Jenkins, Peter, 65
Jennings, P., N-20
Jernigan, Dean, 575
Jernigan, I.E., N-19
Jick, Todd D., 583, N-11, N-20
Jing, Bing, N-22
Jobs, Steve, 140, 215, 253–254, 383, 532, 537
Johnson, Abigail, 334
Johnson, Clarence L., 434
Johnson, G., N-23
Johnson, Jean L., N-11
Jones, D., N-3
Jones, Gary K., N-22
Jones, T., N-5
Jordan, James, N-14
Jordan, Vernon, 254
Jorgensen, Barbara, 325
Joyce, A., N-5
Judge, P.C., 457, N-23, N-24
Judge, T.A., N-16, N-20, N-23
Juliber, Lois, 334
Jung, Andrea, 334, 365, 372
Jung, D.I, N-15

K

Kacmar, Michele K., N-12
Kadlec, D., N-2
Kahn, J., 20, N-1, N-3
Kahn, Linda, N-13
Kahn, R.L., N-2, N-16
Kahwajy, J., N-3
Kaizen, Gemba, N-22
Kale, Prashant, N-11
Kanov, J., N-4
Kanter, R.M., 292, N-8, N-11, N-17, N-23
Kaplan, Robert S., 114, N-3, N-4, N-21
Karl, Katherine A., N-12
Karom, S., 375
Katauskas, T., 537
Katen, Karen, 334
Kato, Y., N-21
Katz, D., N-2, N-16
Katz, R., N-1
Katzenbach, J.R., N-17, N-18
Kaufman, A.M., N-5
Kay, Leslie, 522
Kearns, Ellen C., N-13
Keats, B., N-10
Keegan, P., 215
Keeth, Fran, 335
Keidel, R.W., N-11
Keim, G., N-5
Kelleher, Herb, 383
Keller, R.T., N-19
Kelly, C.M., N-20
Kelly, R.E., N-15
Kennedy, C.J., N-15

Kennedy, John F., 383
Kenny, D., N-15
Kerr, Steve, 474, N-11, N-15, N-16, N-20
Kerstetter, Jim, 549
Kessler, Eric H., N-22, N-23
Kethley, R. Bryan, N-12
Kettering, Charles, 552
Ketteringham, J., N-3
Kettinger, W., N-19
Keys, Alicia, 211
Keys, J.B., N-20
Kharif, Olga, 519, 532, 535
Khermouch, G., 421
Kickul, Jill R., N-23
Kidder, P.J., 375
Kidder, T., N-18
Kiechell, W., III, 22, N-1
Kiernan, Matthew J., N-2, N-24
Killen, Heather, 576
Kilmann, Ralph H., N-21
Kim, Jeong, 270
Kim, W.C., N-17
King, Martin Luther, 383
Kinicki, A., 38
Kinlaw, Dennis C., 167, N-6
Kirkland, J., N-24
Kirkman, B.L., N-18
Kirkpatrick, D., N-1, N-6
Kirkpatrick, S., N-15
Kirksey, Jay, N-13
Kirrane, D., N-5
Kirsner, S., 425, 457
Kirwan, Peter, 447
Kitchen, Philip J., N-7
Klassen, R.D., N-5, N-6
Klein, Naomi, 303
Kleiner, A., N-6
Knight, D., N-18
Knowlton, C., N-3
Koehler, J.W., N-20
Kohlberg, L., N-4
Kohls, John, N-7
Kolk, A., N-6
Kolodny, H., 261–262, N-9
Korda, M., N-20
Kormann, Manuela, 382
Korn, Lester B., N-7
Korten, D.C., N-5
Kotkin, J., 215
Kotler, P., N-2
Kotter, John P., 561, 564–565, N-2, N-15, N-23, N-24
Kouzes, J., 367, 412, N-15, N-16, N-17, N-20
Kovar, Joseph F., N-22
Kozlowski, Dennis, 255
Kraar, L., 553
Krackhardt, D., N-10, 275
Kraimer, M., N-1, N-19
Krantz, Gene, 87
Krauthammer, Charles, 463, N-20
Krawcheck, Sallie, 335
Kreitner, R., 38, N-16
Krohe, J., Jr., 142, N-3, N-4, N-5
Kroll, L., N-8
Kroos, H., N-2
Kruger, P., 571
Kuczmarski, Thomas, N-23
Kummerow, J.M., 77
Kunii, Irene M., 193, 542, 571, N-22
Kuratko, D., N-8
Kurland, N.B., N-19, N-20
Kurtines, W.M., N-4
Kutaragi, Ken, 192, 570, 576
Kwon, B., 66

L

Laabs, Jennifer, N-12, N-13
LaBerre, P., N-3

Labich, Kenneth, N-3, N-14
Lacap, Jeffrey, 243
Lachnit, Carroll, 202
Lackow, Howard, 519
Laczniak, G., N-4
LaGanke, J., N-19
Lagges, J., N-9
Laing, Johnathan, R., N-2
Lalibert, Guy, 126
Lam, S.S.K., N-19
Lamarre, Daniel, 127
Lamont, Bruce T., N-9
Lampe, John, 91
Lanctot, Aldor, Jr., N-22
Lando, Mary Ann, N-21
Landsberg, H., N-6
Lane, Peter J., N-4
Lansing, Sherry, 334
Larkey, L.K., N-19
Larsen, Ralph, 253
Latham, Gary, N-13
Laurie, D., 451, N-15, N-17
Lavelle, Louis, 255, 389, N-15
Lawler, Edward E., III, N-9, N-11, N-16, N-17, N-18, N-21, N-23, N-24
Lawrence, P., 245, 266, N-8, N-9
Lay, Kenneth, 147, 472
Layne, A., 425
Lazarus, Charles, 119
Lazarus, Shelly, 334
Lazenby, J., N-16
Leana, C.F., N-23
Leand, Judy, 243
Leavene, Mike, 340
LeBoeuf, Michael, 402
Ledford, Gerald E., N-11
Lee, Charles, 553
Lee, Hau L., N-1, N-10
Lee, L., 160, N-4
Lee, Mary Dean, N-14
Lee, Nicole, N-12
Lehrman, S., N-1
Lei, David, N-2, N-24
Leifer, Richard, N-21, N-22
Lemonick, M.D., 365
Lengel, R., N-19
Lengnick-Hall, Mark L., N-14
Leonard, Bill, 299
Leonard, Dorothy, 77, N-16, N-22
Leopold, Aldo, 169
Lepak, D.P.P., N-21
Lepore, Dawn, 335
Leslie, Mark, 366
Lessig, L., 151
Levering, R., N-16, N-17
Levin, Gregg, 225
Levin, M., 149
Levine, J.M., N-18
Levin-Epstein, Michael D., N-12
Lewent, Judy, 334
Lewicki, R., 92
Lewin, David, N-13
Lewin, K., N-23
Lewis, Bob, N-10
Liden, R.C., N-1, N-17, N-19
Lieber, R., N-10
Likert, Rensis, 36, N-2, N-15
Lilus, J., N-4
Limpaphayom, Wanthanee, N-12
Lindblad, Cristina, 193
Lindsay, William M., N-10
Link, Albert N., N-22
Lipin, S., 290
Lippitt, R., N-15
Lippman, Helen, 331
Little, Darnell, 137, 548, N-4
Livermore, Ann, 334
Livingston, A., N-14

Locke, E.A., N-15, N-16, N-17, N-18
Loeb, M., 290, N-1
Loenard, Dorothy, N-23
Logan, J., N-19
Logue, C.M., 466, N-20
Lombardo, M., N-19
Longenecker, Clinton O., N-9, N-19
Longenecker, J.G., 204
Loomis, Carol J., N-1, N-21
Lord, R.G., N-15
Lorsch, J., 245, 266, N-8
Lott, A., N-18
Lott, B., N-18
Love, M.S., N-5
Lovins, Amory, 167, 576, N-5, N-6
Lovins, L. Hunter, 167, N-6
Lowenstein, R., N-3
Lower, Chelsea, 325
Lu, David J., N-10
Lubhy, Tami, N-13
Lubrano, Alfred, N-13
Luccock, Halford E., 424
Luczywo, Helena, 570
Lukas, Bryan A., N-7
Lumpkin, G.T., N-8
Lussier, Robert N., 220, N-8
Lusterman, S., N-5
Luthans, F., 356, N-16
Lyncheski, John E., N-12
Lyons, John, 278

M

Macadam, S., N-20
McAfee, R. Bruce, 422
McCall, Morgan W., Jr., 199, N-1, N-3, N-4, N-7, N-16, N-19
McCann, Bob, 65
McCann, Sara, 325
McCanse, Anne Adams, 376
McCarthy, Kathy, N-12
McCartney, S., N-8
McCaskey, M.B., N-20
McClelland, David, 407, N-16, N-17
McClendon, John A., N-13
McCollum, J.K., N-9
McCormack, M., N-19
McCracken, Mike, 495–496
McCrea, B., 215
MacCrimmon, K., N-3
McCullen, Peter, N-10
McCune, J., 553
McDaniel, Michael, N-11
MacDermid, Shelley M., N-14
McDermott, Christopher M., N-22
McDonald, John, 64
McDougall, P.P., N-8
McFarland, Lynn A., N-12
McGahan, Anita M., 247
McGee, Jeffrey E., N-2
McGill, M., N-24
McGinn, Richard, 269
McGinnis, Leon F., N-10
McGrath, Judy, 334
McGrath, R.R., Jr., 133, 162, 208, 297
McGregor, Douglas, 36, N-2
McKenna, James T., N-14
McKibben, B., 155
McKinnell, Henry A., 70
McKinney, J.A., 204
McKnight, William, 232
McMahan, Gary C., N-12
McMorrow, John, N-11
McNamee, Mike, N-21
McNealy, Scott, 534, N-22

McNerney, W. James, Jr., 232
Macy, B., N-18
Madigan, C., N-24
Magasin, M., N-3
Magner, Marjorie, 334
Mahoney, J., N-9
Mahoney, Joan D., 199, N-7
Maidique, Modesto A., N-22
Maier, N.R.F., N-3
Maignan, Isabelle, N-7
Main, J., N-16
Makhijani, M., 375
Makridakis, Spyros, N-2
Maldegen, Robyn, N-12
Malkin, E., 160
Mallaby, S., 149
Malone, John, 367, 460
Malone, Thomas W., 9, N-19
Mann, L., N-3
Mannix, E., N-18
Mansfield, Anja, 347
Manville, Brook, N-11
March, J.G., N-3, N-9
Marcus, A.A., N-5
Marcus, Bernard, 253
Maremont, Mark, N-4
Mark, Reuben, 5
Markels, A., 576
Markman, G.D., N-8
Marks, Michael, 273
Markus, M. Lynn, N-11
Marriott, J. Willard, 216
Marriott, William, 123
Marsh, A., N-8
Marshall, C.R., N-18
Marsick, Victoria J., N-11
Martin, Andrew, N-7
Martin, Casey, 338
Martin, Thomas J., 537
Martinez de la Vega, Francisco, 207
Maruca, R.F., 10
Maslow, Abraham H., 34, 405–406, N-2, N-16
Massie, J., N-2
Mathieu, R.G., N-21
Mathys, N., 400
Matthews, G., N-9
Mauborgne, R., N-17
Maurer, Steven D., N-11
Maxion, Roy A., N-21
May, Michael, 548
Mayer, C.E., 91, N-5
Mayo, Elton, 34, N-2
Means, Gardiner C., 246
Medcof, J.W., 460, N-19
Megginson, L., N-8
Megginson, W., N-8
Mehrabian, A., N-20
Melrose, Ken, 385
Mendels, Pamela, N-12
Merchant, K.A., N-21
Merritt, K., 457
Messick, D., N-3, N-4
Meyer, Andrew, 505
Meyer, Bruce, 325
Meyer, C., N-18
Meyers, D.W., N-13
Meyers, G., N-4
Meznar, Martin B., N-2
Michels, A.J., N-9
Mifflin, Kenneth E., N-21
Miklave, Matthew T., N-12
Miles, R.H., 290, N-2, N-11, N-23
Milkovich, G.T., N-13
Miller, Danny, N-2, N-21
Miller, Heidi, 335
Milliken, F.J., N-18
Milliman, John F., N-13
Mills, P.K., N-21

Milstein, M.B., 167, N-5, N-6
Mintz, H.K., N-20
Mintzberg, H., N-1, N-4
Mishra, Aneil K., N-11
Misumi, J., 373, N-15
Mitchell, Kevin P., 62
Mitchell, R., 537
Mitchell, T., N-16
Mitroff, I.I., 86, N-3
Moeller, Michael, N-22
Mohammed, S., N-19
Mohrman, Susan Albers, N-9, N-11
Molander, E., N-4
Molina, Alfonso, N-23
Monier, Louis, 575
Montgomery, Cynthis A., N-2, N-4
Moon, Chang H., N-7
Moore, Anne, 334
Moore, C.W., 204
Moore, Gordon, 529
Moore, P., 91, 389
Moores, Ken, N-21
Mora, Marie T., N-13
Moran, P., N-17
Morehart, Kerrie Koss, N-11
Morgan, M., 482
Morgeson, Frederick P., N-11
Morita, Akio, 400
Morrey, Stephen R., N-10
Morrison, A., N-19
Morrison, C., N-6
Morrison, E.W., N-17
Morrison, Sara, 55
Mortensen, Ronald, N-7
Mosakowski, E., N-20
Moskowitz, M., N-16, N-17
Mount, M.K., N-12
Mouton, J., N-15
Muczyk, J., N-15
Mueller, George, 218–219
Mueller, Nancy L., N-14
Muir, John, 169
Mula, Joseph, N-21
Mulaney, T.J., N-1
Mulcahy, Anne M., 333–334
Mull, J., 66
Mullaney, Timothy J., N-23
Mullen, B., N-18
Muller, J., 91
Muller, Jaye, 217
Muller, Joann, 178, 187, 289
Mullin, Leo, 253
Muoio, A., N-1
Murphy, A., 221
Murphy, Wendell, 221
Murphy-Hoye, Mary, 553
Murray, Paul, 171
Murrell, Audrey J., N-14
Murrell, Kenneth L., 256
Myhrvold, Nathan, 10

N

Nacchio, Joseph, 254
Nadler, D.A., N-17, N-18, N-23
Nahavandi, A., N-18
Najdawi, K., N-9
Nakamura, Kunio, 541
Nanus, B., N-14, N-16
Nash, J., N-6
Nash, Sarah, N-22
Nasser, Jacques, 5, 90–91
Nathan, Richard, N-22
Naughton, Keith, 91, N-20
Nayak, P., N-3
Nee, E., 457, N-8
Neeleman, David, 62
Neff, R., N-23

Neilson, R.P., N-5
Nelson, Katherine A., N-7
Nelson, Marilyn Carlson, 335
Neubert, M., N-19
Neumann, Peter G., N-22
Nevin, Joe, 366
Newcombe, Robert, N-21
Newman, J.M., N-13
Newstrom, John W., 271
Nguyen, Elena L., 183
Nguyen, Quy, N-23
Niblack, John F., 69
Nichols, Ralph G., 466
Nisbett, R., N-3
Nixon, R., N-10
Nohria, Nitin, 553, N-20, N-24
Nomani, Asra Q., N-14
Nooyi, Indra, 334
Norman, Carol, N-13
Norton, D., 114
Novak, David, 8
Nur, Y.A., N-15
Nussbaum, B., 83

O

Oberbeck, Steven, 519
O'Brian, B., N-1
O'Connell, Patricia, 542
O'Connor, Gina Colarelli, N-22
Ogilvy, J., N-6
Oh, Miriam Y., 348
Ohmae, Kenichi, 279, N-10
O'Keefe, B., 20, N-1
Okie, Francis G., 536
Oldham, G., 410, N-16, N-17
Oldham, Linda, 225
Oldham, Todd, 225
Oligney, Ronald E., N-22
Olim, Jason, 211
Oliver, Thomas R. 356
Olofson, C., 447
Olsson, K., N-3
Olszewski, Robert T., N-21
O'Meara, Daniel P., N-12
O'Neill, Hugh M., N-22
O'Neill Packard, K., 155
Ones, D.S., N-12
O'Reilly, B., N-8
Orfalea, Paul, 217
Organ, D., 394, 405
Orlov, D., 142
O'Rourke, J., 91
O'Shea, J., N-24
O'Shea, William T., 270
Osher, John, 515
Osorio, L.G., 160
Ostgaard, Daniel J., N-12
Otazo, K.L., N-20
O'Toole, J., N-3, N-6, N-18
Ott, James, N-14
Ouchi, William G., 490–491, N-21
Overmyer Day, Leslie E., N-14
Oviatt, B., N-8

P.

Packard, Dave, 216
Paehlke, R., N-6
Paine, L.S., N-5
Palmer, J., 91
Palmeri, Christopher, N-20
Papiernik, R., N-4
Pappacena, Edgardo, 553
Pare, Terence P., N-21
Parker, James, 563
Parker, S., N-19
Parsaei, Hamid R., N-11
Parsons, T., N-5

Pascal, Amy, 335
Pascarelloa, P., N-18
Patrick, John, 567
Patterson, Fiona, N-12
Patterson, Neal, 20
Patton, George, 385
Paul-Chowdhurry, Catherine, N-11
Paulus, P.B., N-17
Pawar, K.S., N-9
Payne, Stephanie C., N-12
Payson, William, 340–341
Peach, James T., N-7
Pearce, Craig L., N-9
Pearce, T., 417
Pearlstein, S., N-3, N-16
Pearse, Robert F., N-9
Pearson, C.M., 86, N-3
Pearson, J., N-4
Pegels, C. Carl, N-9
Peiperl, M., N-24
Pelled, Lisa Hope, N-9, N-18, N-20
Penley, L., N-19, N-20
Peretsman, Nancy, 335
Perlmutter, Howard, N-11
Perrow, C., N-5
Perry, Monica L., N-9
Perry, Nancy, N-13
Peter, Laurence J., 272
Peters, Brett A., N-10
Peters, Lois S., N-22
Peters, M., 222
Peters, Tom, 10, 24, 213, N-1, N-2, N-3, N-7, N-8, N-17, N-18
Peterson, M., 373, N-15
Peterson, Richard B., N-13
Peterson, Robin R., N-2
Peterson, Thane, 127
Petrick, J., N-14
Petrocelli, William, N-13
Petty, P., N-18
Petulla, J.M., N-6
Pfeffer, Jeffrey, 76
Phelps, Michael, 535
Phillips, Sandra N., N-12
Phipps, C., N-9
Picken, J.C., N-16
Piet, Johan, 166
Pinchot, C., N-8
Pinchot, E., N-5, N-8
Pinchot, G., 229, N-5, N-8
Pincus, L., 142
Pinder, C., N-16
Pine, B. Joseph, N-10, N-24
Pirsig, Robert M., 544, N-23
Pisano, Gary P., N-22
Plamondon, Kevin E., N-21
Plant, R., N-1
Plishner, Emily S., N-4
Podsakoff, P., N-15
Pollack, Elaine, 296
Polonsky, M.P., 167, N-6
Pomije, David, 226
Pope, Terry, 447
Popoff, Frank, 174
Porras, Jerry I., 400, 554–556, N-5, N-8, N-20, N-23
Port, O., 457, 567
Porter, Michael, 48, 258, N-4, N-6, N-9, N-22
Posner, B.G., 75, 367, 412, N-15, N-16, N-17, N-20
Posner, M., 464
Post, J., N-5
Pottruck, David S., 365, 417
Potts, Joseph, N-13
Potts, M., N-15
Pounder, Richard W., N-22
Powell, Colin, 371, 410
Powell, Lynda, N-13

Powell, Michael, 42
Power, Damien, N-10
Powers, William C., 247
Prahalad, C.K., 290, 451, 572, N-11, N-24
Prasad, Sameer, N-9
Prather, Charles W., N-23
Preidt, Robert, 522
Premack, S., N-13
Preston, L., N-5
Prestwood, Donna C.L., N-22
Prewitt, Milford, N-13
Prior, Molly, N-14
Probst, Jeannie, 382
Proctor, R.A., 124
Prokesch, Steven E., N-7
Prusak, Lawrence, N-22
Pruyn, A.T.H., N-20
Pucik, V., N-23
Pulakos, Elaine D., N-21
Pulich, Marica, N-21
Pullin, John, N-22
Puranam, P., N-15
Purdy, K., N-17

Q

Quinn, D., N-5
Quinn, J.B., N-8, N-14
Quinn, Robert E., 513, N-16, N-21

R

Raburn, Vern, 367
Radin, Amy, 562
Raggio, Louise, 217
Raichur, Pratima, N-23
Ramaswamy, V., 451
Ramirez, G.G., N-15
Ramsey, Robert D., N-23
Rancour, Tom, 495–496
Randall, Raymond, N-12
Rangan, S., N-1
Rao Srinivasa, K., N-10
Rapaczynski, Wanda, 570
Rapsas, Tom, 451
Raven, B., 370, N-15
Reagan, Ronald, 383
Rechheld, R., N-17
Redding, W.C., N-20
Redman, Margaret, 329
Reed, Alvin, 215
Reese, L., N-4
Reh, John, 506
Reich, R.B., N-23
Reinhardt, Andy, 270
Reinhardt, F., 155
Reitz, H.J., N-5
Renda, Larree, 335
Repa, Barbar Kate, N-13
Revelle, R., N-6
Rhode, J., N-21
Rhyne, Kristin, 234
Rice, F., N-5, N-6
Rice, Mark, N-22
Rice, R., N-19
Richardson, Helen L., N-11
Richardson, Hettie A., N-11
Richardson, Leon, N-22
Ridolfi, E., N-17
Rigas, John, 254
Ringseis, E., N-19
Rion, M., 142
Risher, Howard W., N-13
Riso, Nick, 576
Rittenburg, Terri, N-7
Ritzky, Garry M., N-13
Roberto, M.A., N-3
Roberts, Bert, 255
Roberts, D., 160

Robey, D., 261
Robey, Richard D., 491
Robinson, Janet, 335
Robinson, S.L., N-17
Robitaille, Suzanne, 329
Rock, Arthur, 224
Rock, Chris, 553
Roethlisberger, Fritz, 34, N-2
Rogers, Everett M., N-22
Rogers, Jim, 68
Romeril, Barry, 254
Ronkainen, Ilkka, 179
Rose, F., N-16
Rose, J., N-8
Rosen, Benson, N-14, N-18
Rosenberger, P.J., III, 167, N-6
Rosener, Judy, 375
Rosenthal, Stephen R., N-23
Rosnow, R.L., N-20
Ross, George, N-7
Ross, Gerald H.B., 511
Ross, L., N-3
Roth, Aaron, N-22, N-23
Roth, D., N-8
Roth, M., 142
Rothberg, Steven, 299
Rother, John, 339
Rousseau, D., N-17, N-23
Rowland, F.S., N-6
Roy, Uptal, N-11
Roznowaski, Mary, N-12
Ruch, W.V., N-20
Rudloff, Robert W., N-21
Russo, M., N-5
Russo, Patricia, 270, 334
Ryan, Anne Marie, N-12
Rynecki, D., 66, N-1
Rynes, Sara, N-14

S

Sackett, Paul R., N-12
Sadowski, Michael, N-22
Saffo, Paul, 234
Sage, Lee, 425
Sahin, Funda, N-10
Sahlman, W.A., N-8
Sakano, Tomoaki, N-11
Sales, C.A., 261, 491
Salkever, Alex, 46
Salter, C., 567
Sambamurthy, V., N-9
Samson, Danny, N-10
Sanborn, G., N-17
Sanchez, J., 198
Sandberg, Jared, N-22
Sandler, Marion, 335
Sant, Roger, 255, 397, 477
Santamaria, J.A., N-18
Sasseen, Jane, N-7
Satchu, Asif, 234
Sauter, Wolf, N-7
Savage, J., N-13
Sawin, Linda L., N-12
Saxton, Mary J., N-21
Sayles, Leonard R., 259, N-1, N-18
Schacht, Henry, 253, 269–270
Schaffer, R.H., N-16
Schantz, W.T., N-3
Schaubroeck, J., N-19
Schein, E.H., N-23
Schere, R., N-14
Schiff, L., N-21
Schimmoller, Brian K., N-2
Schippmann, Jeffery S., N-11
Schlender, Brent, N-2, N-8
Schlesinger, Leonard A., 561, N-23
Schmidt, Frank L., N-11, N-12

Schmidt, Warren, 377–378, N-15
Schnieders, Richard, 111
Schoemaker, Paul J.H., N-2
Scholl, Russel B., N-7
Schonbaechler, Christina, 382
Schonfeld, Erick, 367, N-8, N-10
Schot, J., N-6
Schrage, M., N-19, N-23
Schrempp, Jurgen E., 177
Schroeder, D.M., 526
Schroeder, R., 430, N-18
Schuler, Randall S., 318, N-13
Schultz, Don E., N-7
Schultz, Howard, 113, 215–216
Schultz, Susan F., N-9
Schumann, Paul A., Jr., N-22
Schumpeter, J.A., N-22
Schuster, J.R., N-13
Schwab, Charles, 20, 254
Schwartz, N.D., N-4
Schwartz, P., N-6
Schwarzenegger, Arnold, 385
Schweiger, D., N-20
Schwenk, C., N-3
Scott, Michael, N-21
Scott, S.R., N-8
Seal, G., N-23
Seashore, S.E., N-18
Segaar, Peter, N-4
Segars, A., 75
Seibert, S., N-1
Seideman, Tony, N-10
Seidmann, Abraham, N-22
Seifert, Kathi, 335
Sellers, P., 20, 375
Senge, P.M., 167, N-5, N-11, N-19
Serawop, Monette, 519
Serwer, A.E., N-8
Seybold, Patricia, 10
Shah, Priti Pradha, N-12
Shalley, C.E., N-16
Shane, S., N-7
Shani, A.B., 583
Shapiro, C., 151
Shapiro, D., N-18
Shapiro, E.C., N-15
Sharfman, M., N-3
Shari, Michael, N-7
Sharifi, S., N-9
Sharpe, Rochelle, 375, N-13
Shellenbarger, S., N-19
Shenon, P., N-1
Sheridan, John H., N-21
Sherman, Arthur W., 305, 307, 317, 337, N-2, N-13
Sherman, M., N-19
Sherman, Stratford, 583, N-4
Shiah, Jim, 549
Shinal, John, 270
Shippmann, Jeffery S., N-11
Shirvastava, P., N-6
Shockley-Zalabak, Pamela, 29
Shrivastava, P., N-5
Shurn-Hannah, Phyllis, N-14
Shute, Valerie J., N-12
Siebel, Thomas, 26
Silver, W., N-16
Silverman, S., N-17
Simkins, B., 477, N-20
Simmonds, Paul G., N-9
Simmons, Russell, 217
Simon, H.A., N-9
Simon, Herbert, 84
Simons, J., N-1
Simons, Robert, N-21
Simons, Tony, N-9, N-18
Simos, Evangelos O., N-7
Sims, Henry P., Jr., N-9

Sinclair, Robert, N-13
Singer, Sherri, N-11
Singer, T., 234, N-8
Singh, Harbir, N-11
Singh, J., N-6
Sinha, K., 430, N-18
Siporin, Clifford, N-22
Skarlicki, D., N-17
Skilling, Jeffrey, 5, 68, 472
Slater, R., 583
Sloan, Alfred P., Jr., 108, 242, 383, N-13
Slocum, J.W., Jr., N-23, N-24
Smidts, A., N-20
Smilor, R.W., N-8
Smith, Adam, 147–149
Smith, David, 131, N-17, N-18, N-24
Smith, E., N-6
Smith, Frederick W., N-14
Smith, Geri, 182
Smith, Gerri, 207
Smith, Ken A., N-9, N-18
Smith, N., N-5, N-6, N-21
Smith, Rolf, 82
Smith, Teresa L., N-14
Smith, W. Gradwohl, N-15
Snell, Scott A., 305, 307, 317, 337, 539, N-2, N-7, N-13, N-18, N-21
Snider, Mike, 193
Snider, Stacey, 334
Snow, Charles C., 290, N-2, N-7, N-11, N-18
Snow, John, 253
Snyder, W.M., N-17
Soares, Sunil, 457
Sohal, Amrik S., N-10
Solomon, Charlene Marmer, N-7
Solomon, J., 217, N-19
Sonfield, Matthew C., 220, N-8
Song, Yong I., N-9
Sparrowe, R.T., N-17, N-19
Spector, P., 198
Speir, Eddi, 221
Spindler, Mike, 296
Spitzer, Q., N-3
Sprecher, Jeffrey, 211
Spreitzer, Gretchen M., 199, N-7, N-11, N-16, N-17
St. Pierre, N., 66, 91
Stach, Victoria, 548
Stack, Jack, 477
Stajkovic, A.D., N-16
Stalk, George, N-10
Stalker, G.M., 274, N-10
Stallkamp, Thomas T., 177–178
Stamps, David, N-7
Stanislao, B.C., N-23
Stanislao, J., N-23
Stanley, A., 375
Stansfield, Timothy C., N-9
Stavins, R., N-6
Staw, B.M., N-16
Steel, R., N-15
Steen, Margaret, N-13
Stein, N., 576, N-6
Steinfield, C., N-19
Stenberg, Christopher E., N-12
Stephens, J., N-5
Stern, G., N-1
Stern, Harry, N-10
Stertz, Bradley A., 178
Stevens, Anne, 335
Stevens, J., N-6
Stevenson, W.B., N-9
Stewart, Martha, 13
Stewart, T.A., 553, N-19, N-21
Stewart, Thomas, 10
Stipp, D., 567, 576
Stogdill, R.M., N-15
Stoner, C., N-18

Stork, Ken, N-4
Straus, S., 77
Strauss, George, 259
Strauss, K., N-4
Strickland, A.J., III, N-4
Strickland, O., N-15
Strobel, Pam, 335
Stross, R.E., N-10
Strunk, William, 463, N-20
Stuller, J., 410, N-19
Stundza, Tom, N-10
Subramanian, Krishna, 10
Sugarman, B., N-23
Sull, D., N-20
Suttle, J.L., N-17
Sutton, Robert, 83, N-1, N-3
Swaak, Reyer A., N-7
Sweeney, Anne, 335
Swenson, Keith, N-11
Swiggett, Robert L., 366
Swing, William Edwin, 567
Symon, Gillian, N-11

T

Takla, Michael G., N-10
Talbott, Shannon Peters, N-11
Tannen, D., N-19
Tannenbaum, A., N-15
Tannenbaum, Robert, 377–378
Tata, Jasmine, N-9
Tatikonda, Mohan V., N-23
Taylor, A., III, 91, N-1, N-10
Taylor, Frederick, 31–32, 470
Taylor, J., N-19
Taylor, Paul, N-12
Taylor, R., N-3
Teegan, Hildy J., N-22
Teerlink, Rich, 553, N-23
Terpstra, David E., 305, N-11, N-12
Tesluk, P., N-17
Tetrick, Lois, N-13
Tetzeli, R., N-19
Thomas, K.W., 444, N-17, N-19
Thomas, Louis A., N-22
Thompson, Arthur A., N-4
Thompson, J., N-2
Thompson, K., 400
Thompson, Paul R., N-9
Thoresen, C.J., N-23
Thorn, Ron, N-9
Thorndike, Edward, 400, N-16
Thurow, R., 160
Tichy, N.M., 583
Tierney, Christine, 178
Tijoriwala, S.A., N-23
Tillema, Harry, N-9
Timmons, Heather, 278
Timmons, Jeffry A., 161, 213, 223, 235, 239, N-7
Tinsley, C., N-19
Tjosvold, D., N-19
Toben, Doreen, 334
Toffler, Barbara Ley, 499
Tome, Carol, 335
Tomlinson, Richard, 296
Touboul, Shlomo, 218
Towill, Denis R., N-10
Townsend, Robert, 368, N-15
Trafimow, A. Jonathon, N-12
Trevino, Linda K., N-4, N-5, N-7, N-16, N-19
Trist, E., N-23
Trott, Donald L., 119
Troy, Leo, N-13
Trunick, Perry A., N-14
Tsao, Amy, N-2
Tu, Howard S., 360
Tucker, M., N-11

Tuckman, B.W., N-18
Tulgan, Bruce, 303
Tully, S., 400, N-7, N-21
Turban, D., N-5
Turner, Phil, 367
Tyson, John, 254

U

Uhl-Bien, M., N-15
Ulrich, Dave, N-11, N-20
Unruh, J., N-20
Upton, D., N-20
Ursprung, Cecil, 470
Usachev, Yury V., 263
Useem, J., N-1, 389, N-4
Usher, John M., N-11

V

Vagelos, Roy, 150
Van, Sonny, 519
van der Hoeven, Cees, 295
Van Fleet, D., N-9
van Riel, C.B.M., N-20
Van Wassenhove, L.N., N-6, N-7
Vandenberg, Robert J., N-11
Varallo, D. Vincent, N-11
Vasilash, Gary S., N-10
Veiga, J., N-21
Velthouse, B., N-17
Venkataraman, S., N-7
Verespej, Michael A., N-14
Verhovek, S., N-20
Veryzer, Robert W., N-22
Vesper, K.H., N-8
Vicere, Albert A., N-11
Vickery, Shawnee, N-9
Victor, B., N-24
Viguerie, P., N-24
Vinson, Mary N., N-13
Viswanath, V., N-4
Viswesvaran, C., N-12
Vizard, Michael, N-22
Vlasic, Bill, 178
Vogel, D., 142
von Bertalanffy, L. , N-1
Von Hippel, Eric, N-22
von Oetinger, B., N-1
Vonortas, Nicholas S., N-22
Voos, Paula B., N-13
Vos, Ron, 211
Vroom, V.H., 375, 378–381, N-15, N-16
Vulinec, L.A., N-21

W

Waalewijn, Philip, N-4
Wachner, Linda, 20, 255
Wacker, W., N-19
Waddock, Sandra, N-5, N-6, N-21
Wadhwa, Subhash, N-10
Wageman, R., N-18
Wagner, J., III, N-15
Wah, Louisa, 354
Wahba, M., N-16
Wahlgren, Eric, 111, N-21
Walczak, L., 137
Waldman, D.A., N-15
Waldroop, J., N-20
Walker, Anthony, N-21
Wall, J.A., Jr., 377, N-5, N-19
Walley, N., N-6
Walton, R.E., N-17
Walton, Sam, 400, 418
Ward, Ralph D., N-9
Warner, F., 576
Warner, Melanie, 27, N-22
Wasserman, Todd, N-22

Watkins, Karen E., N-11
Watkins, Sherron, 147, 254, 472
Watson, C. Maxwell, N-7
Watson, F.H.C., 463
Watson, Thomas J., 298, 300, 383
Wayne, S.J., N-17, N-19
Weaver, G.R., N-5
Webb, A., N-4
Webb, Janiece, 562
Webber, R., N-1
Weber, J., N-16
Weber, Max, 34, 274, N-2
Weber, R., 482
Wechsler, Jill, N-22
Weiner, Edie, 130–131
Weiss, H., N-15
Weiss, N., N-4
Welbourne, Theresa M., N-13, N-23
Welch, David, 52
Welch, Jack, 17, 106, 253, 293, 388–389, 462, 474, 502, 544
Wellins, R., N-18
Wellner, Alison Stein, 132, N-21
Wells, Melanie, N-4
Wendt, Gary, 254
Wenger, E.C., N-17
West, Andrew, N-8
West, Maureen, 341
West, Tom, 434
Westley, F., N-4
Wetlaufer, Suzy, 398, 477, N-9, N-18, N-20
Wexley, Kenneth, N-13, N-17
Whang, S., N-1
Wheatley, Malcolm, N-11
Wheelwright, Steven C., N-22, N-23
Whetten, D., 93
Whetzel, Deborah L., N-11
White, E.B., 463, N-20
White, Margaret Blackburn, N-13, N-14
White, Michael D., N-7
White, R., N-15
Whitehead, B., N-6
Whitfield, Mary Brett, 295
Whitford, D., N-17
Whitman, Meg, 5, 334
Whitney, John O., N-21
Whybark, D. Clay, N-5, N-6
Wiebusch, Bruce, 313
Wier, Benson, N-21
Wildstrom, S., 457
Will, G.F., 400
Willcocks, L., N-1
Willen, Don, N-10
Williams, Colin, 569, 574, N-24
Williams, Satina V., N-21
Williams, T., N-23
Wilmut, Ian, 463
Wilson, A., 447
Winblad, Ann, 174
Winfrey, Oprah, 334
Winkler, Donald, 576
Winnick, Gary, 254
Wiseman, Robert M., N-13
Wissman, Geof, 295
Witney, F., N-13
Witt, G. Evans, N-14
Witzel, M., N-5
Wnuck, D., N-17, N-18
Woehr, David J., N-12
Woellert, L., 472
Woertz, Pat, 334
Wolfe, Rick, 41
Wong, Andy, 18
Woodward, Joan, 282, N-10
Worline, M., N-4
Wright, Patrick M., N-10, N-12
Wurster, T.S., N-8

Y

Yammarino, F.J., N-15
Yang, Baik, N-9
Yang, H., N-17
Yankelovich, Daniel, 137, N-19
Yanouzas, J., N-21
Yasai-Ardekani, Masoud, N-2
Yearwood, Carlton, 353
Yeatts, D., N-18
Yi, Sang-Seung, N-22
Yorgason, Daniel R., 183

Yorges, S., N-15
Youndt, M.A., N-21
Young, Jeffrey, 256
Youngblood, Stuart A., 318
Yukl, G.A., N-15, N-16

Z

Zaccaro, S., N-15
Zahra, Shaker A., N-22
Zaleznik, A., N-15
Zalud, Bill, N-21

Zawacki, Robert F., N-13
Zeithaml, C., 59–60, N-3, N-5
Zeithaml, V., 59–60, N-3
Zell, D., N-23
Zellner, Wendy, 63, 472, N-2, N-10, N-24
Zemke, R., N-16
Zenger, T.R., N-18
Zetsche, Dieter, 178
Zmud, R.W., N-19
Zuzich, Karleen, 354

Subject Index

A

AARP, 339
ABB, 154
Abbott Laboratories, 185
ABC, 499–500
Abercrombie & Fitch, 243
AccessAir, 62
Accommodation, 444
Accountability, 250–251, 352
Accounting audit, 498–499
Accu-Lube Manufacturing, 187
Ace Hardware, 548–549
Acer, 51
Achievement, 407
Achievement-oriented leadership, 379
Acordia, 230
Acquisition
    mergers and, 60, 84, 123
    new technology, 533–534
Activity-based costing, 499–500
ADA, 146, 310–311, 337–338
Adapters, 570
Adelphia Communications, 42, 254
Adhocracy, 512
Adidas, 243–244
Adjustment, mutual, 264–265
Administrative management, 33–34
Adobe, 11
Advantica Restaurant Group, 336
Adverse impact, 310
Advisory boards, 225
Advocacy skills, 431
AES Corporation, 255, 277, 397–398, 470
Aetna Life & Casualty, 144, 336, 350
Affective conflict, 81
Affiliation, 407
Affirmative action, 342–345, 348
Age Discrimination in Employment Act,
    310–311
Agilent Technologies, 277, 505
Ahold, 295
AIDS, 352
Akamai Technologies, 69
Alamo, 12
Alaska Air, 48
Allegiance Telecom, 211
Allen & Co., 335
Allen Bradley, 197
Alliances, 60, 230, 291–292
AlliedSignal, 463
Allstate, 124, 253, 336, 353–354, 502
Alta Vista, 575
Altra Energy Technology, 51
Amazon.com, 19, 119, 420, 530, 547–550
America Online, 8, 151, 224
America West, 48
American Airlines, 48, 71, 337
American Arbitration Association, 443
American Association of Retired Persons, 339
American Express, 255, 554
American International Group, 184
American Management Association, 306, 335, 505
American Society for Training and Development, 312
Americans with Disabilities Act (ADA), 146, 310–311, 337–338

Amgen, 253, 568
Amoco, 200, 470
Analysis
    competitor, 118
    cost-benefit, 170
    environmental, 53–56, 117–120
    financial, 120
    human resources, 118
    industry, 118
    internal resources, 120
    job, 304
    life-cycle, 172
    macroeconomic, 118
    market, 118
    operations, 120
    opportunity, 222–224
    political, 118
    regulatory, 118
    situational, 108
    social, 118
    SWOT, 116, 122–127
    technological, 118
Analyzer firm, 531
Andersen Consulting, 498–499
Angura, 537
Anheuser-Busch, 122, 167
Anticipated competency development, 530–531
Anticipated market receptiveness, 528–529
AOL, 185, 334, 367
APEC, 181
Apple Computer, 11, 14, 83, 140, 172, 231,
    253–254, 351, 429, 529, 532, 536–537
Applications, for employment, 305
Appraisals, of employees, 205, 252, 257,
    314–316, 397–398
Apria Healthcare, 253
Arbitration, 309, 321
ARCO, 172
Argus Management Corporation, 490
Arista Records, 211
Arthur Andersen, 137, 153, 553
Arthur D. Little, 166
Asea Brown Boveri Ltd., 7, 9, 180
Ashton Photo, 410
Asia-Pacific Economic Cooperation (APEC),
    181
Aspect Communications, 411
Assessment center, 306
Assets, 121, 500
Aston Martin, 186
Astrazeneca, 185
Atlantic Richfield Company, 110
AT&T, 41, 121, 196–197, 269, 277, 300, 306,
    334, 406, 458, 528
Auctioning, 51–52
Audioconferencing, 457
Audits
    accounting, 498–499
    internal, 496–497
    management, 496–497
    marketing, 120
    technology, 527
Authoritarianism, 379
Authority, in organizations, 247–250
Autocratic leadership, 374
Autonomous work groups, 430
Autonomy, 411
Avaya Inc., 270

Avis, 49, 368
Avoidance, 444
Avon Products, 333–334, 336, 343, 346, 365,
    372
A&W, 216
Awards, for quality, 280–281, 399, 495
Awareness building, 349

B

Babies "R" Us, 65
Baby's Dream, 65
BAE Systems, 492
Balance sheet, 500
Balanced scorecard, 113–114
Baldrige award, 280–281, 399, 495
Bally Engineering, 568
Bank of America, 184, 334
Bank One Corporation, 10, 335
Bankruptcy, 137
Bargaining, collective, 321–322
Barnes & Noble, 7, 117
Barr Laboratories Inc., 49
Barriers to entry, 49
Base technologies, 527
Baxter Healthcare, 352, 470
Bay View Capital Corp., 278
Bayer, 166
BBC, 13
BCG matrix, 123–124
Bean Stock program, 113
Bechtel, 199, 261
Behavior approach, to leadership, 372–377
Behavior modification, 400–402
Behavioral appraisal, 314
Behavioral description interview, 305
Behaviorally anchored rating scale (BARS), 314
Bell Atlantic, 123
Bell Labs, 533
Benchmarking, 55–56, 122, 527–528
Benefits, for employees, 319–320
Berkshire Hathaway, 184
Bertelsmann, 7
Best practices, 122
Best-case scenario, 54
Best-in-class, 56
Biases, psychological, 75–77
Board of directors, 248, 252–255
Boeing, 218, 261, 400, 426, 457, 471
Bombay Company, 291
Boo.com, 227
Bootlegging, 230
Border Environment Cooperation Commission
    (BECC), 181
Boston Consulting Group, 69, 124
Boston Warehouse Trading Corp., 65
Boundaryless organization, 293, 474–475
Bounded rationality, 84
Brainstorming, 82–83, 457
Breakthrough development projects, 538
Bribery, 43
Bricks and mortar business, 547
Bridgestone, 91
Bristol-Myers Squibb, 44, 172, 306
British Petroleum, 9, 184, 200
Broadvision Inc., 10
Broker, 291
Brooks Brothers, 291, 551

Browning-Ferris Waste Management Inc., 173
BSO/Origin, 174
Budgets
    activity-based costing, 499–500
    cash, 498
    cost production, 498
    defined, 497
    master, 498
    sales-expense, 497
    strategic, 129
    types of, 498–499
Buffering, 57–58
Built to last companies, 554–555
Bull and bear markets, 44
Bureaucracy, 34–35, 56, 537–538
Bureaucratic control
    approaches to, 494–495
    budgetary controls, 497–500
    control process, 491–494
    designing effective, 506–507
    downside, 503–505
    financial control, 500–503
    management audits, 496–497
Burger King, 121, 283, 348
Burr Group, 63
Business ethics, 138, 140–142
Business failures, 5–7
Business incubators, 215–216
Business models, 6
Business plan, 222–225
Business strategy, 125
Business-to-business (B2B) transactions, 51

C

Cafeteria programs, 319
Calvin Klein, 20, 83
Campbell Soup, 248
Cannondale, 12
Canon, 121
Capital
    human, 300
    intellectual, 9, 151, 300
Career planning, 21–24, 351
Carlson Co., 335
Carlyle Group, 20
CarMax, 569
Carmike Cinema, 257
Carrefour, 51
Carrying capacity, 169
Cases
    Biggest Grocery Store You've Never Heard
        Of, 295–296
    Boomerang Hiring: Maybe You Can Go
        Back, 325
    Diversity Is in Good Hands at Allstate,
        353–354
    Enter the Competition, 234
    Following a Legend, 388–389
    Group Meetings: Love 'em or Hate 'em, 447
    Lucent: Clean Break, Clean Slate, 269–270
    Making Your Mark, 575–576
    Many New Airlines Will Never Grow Old,
        62–63
    Matsushita's Creative Destruction, 541–542
    In Need of Motivation at Toys"R"Us,
        420–421
    Nike Controversies, 159–160
    Procter & Gamble Lets Go of the Reins and
        Goes for a Spin, 515–517
    Trying to Move On After a Crisis, 90–91
    Wal-Mart and Megastore Wars in Mexico,
        207
    What Lies Ahead, 130–132
    Would You Really Do It?, 477
    Would You Work Here, 26–27
Cash budget, 498
Catalytic skills, 431

Caterpillar Tractor, 193, 205
Caux Round Table, 147, 164
CBS, 5
CDnow, 211
Celera Genomics, 365
Centralized organization, 255
Cerner, 20
Certainty, 68
Change management
    becoming world class, 554–556
    creating advantage, 568–570
    creating the future, 570–572
    enlisting cooperation, 560–563
    harmonizing multiple changes, 563–564
    leadership and, 564–566
    learning continuously, 566–568
    motivating people, 557–563
    proactive, 566
    reactive, 566
    resistance to, 557–560
    shaping the future, 566–574, 572–574
Chaparral, 537
Charismatic leadership, 383–384
Charles Schwab, 6, 8, 254, 335, 365, 400, 411,
    416–417
Charts, organization, 244–245, 274–275
Chemical Manufacturers Association, 172
Chevron, 185, 197, 200, 334, 505
Chiat/Day, 458
Chief executive officer (CEO), 17, 248–249
Chief knowledge officer, 8
Chief learning officer, 474
Chief operating officer (COO), 17
Chief technology officer (CTO), 535
Childress Buick, 411
Chipshot.com, 12
Chiquita Banana, 173
Chrysler Corporation, 72, 121, 123, 152, 177,
    186–187, 283, 285, 499
CIBA-GEIGY, 174
CIGNA, 336
CIM, 284–285
Cirque du Soleil, 126–127
Cisco, 375, 451
Citibank, 561–562
Citicorp, 7, 125, 277, 554
Citigroup, 5, 125, 184, 278, 334
City National Bank, 278
Civil Rights Act, 310–311
Clan control, 491, 510–514
Clarke American, 281
Clean Air Act, 166–167
Clean Water Act, 167
Closeness of supervision, 373
CNN, 230
Coaching, 469
Coalition, 59
Coalition building, 154
Coalitional model of decision making, 84
Coast Gas of Watsonville, 406
Coca-Cola, 48, 51, 184, 190, 200, 314,
    352, 469
Codes of ethics, 143–145, 164–165
Coercion, 562
Coercive power, 369
Cognitive ability tests, 306–307
Cognitive conflict, 81
Cognitive development, model, 140
Cohesiveness, 344, 437–441
Colgate-Palmolive, 5, 173, 197, 253, 334
Collaboration, 9–10, 444
Collective bargaining, 321–322
Collectivism, 201
CollegeRecruiter.com, 299
Columbia Sportwear Inc., 571
Comerci, 207
Commerce One, 51

Communication, 450–485
    boundarylessness, 293, 474–475
    collaboration across boundaries, 9–10
    coordination by, 265–266
    defined, 452
    downward, 468–471
    effective supervision, 467
    electronic, 456–459
    formal and informal, 473–474
    horizontal, 473
    improving skills, 461–467
    interpersonal, 452–461
    mixed signals, 454–456
    networks for, 459–461
    nonverbal, 464–465, 478–479
    one-way versus two-way, 453
    oral, 456
    organizational, 468–475
    pitfalls, 453–454
    problems of, 344
    process, 452–453
    receiver skills, 465–467
    sender skills, 461–465
    skills for good, 20
    upward, 471–473
    written, 456, 493
Communications Collaborative, 325
Community response, 167
Compaq Computer, 11, 14, 80, 123, 205, 231,
    293, 458
Comparable worth, 319
Compensation and benefits, 319–320
Competency development, 530–531
Competing, 444
Competing in a space, 6
Competition, time-based, 285–286
Competitive advantage
    cost competitiveness, 13
    innovation, 11
    political environment and, 152
    quality, 12–13
    speed, 13
Competitive aggressiveness, 231
Competitive environment, 42, 48–53
Competitive intelligence, 54
Competitive position, 124
Competitor analysis, 118
Competitors, 48–49
Complacency, reasons for, 564–565
Complexity, environmental, 53
Compliance-based ethics programs, 145–146
Compressed workweek, 349
Compromise, 444
Computer Associates, 459
Computer-integrated manufacturing, 284–285
Con Edison, 336
Concentration strategy, 122–123
Concentric diversification, 123
Conceptual skills, 19–20
Concern for people, 373, 376
Concern for production, 373, 376
Concurrent control, 494
Confidentiality, 550
Conflict
    affective, 81
    cognitive, 81
    constructive, 80–81
    defined, 69
    styles, 444–445
    teams and, 442–445
Conglomerate diversification, 123
Conseco, 254
Conservation, 169
Consideration, 373
Consortium benchmarking, 55
Constituency programs, 154
Constructive conflict, 80–81
Consumer Product Safety Commission, 65

Container Store, 417
Contemporary approaches to management, 35–37
Content validity, 308
Continental Airlines, 125, 509
Contingency model, of leadership, 394–395
Contingency perspective, 36–37
Contingency plans, 72, 109–110
Contingent workers, 57
Continuous improvement, 280, 566–568
Continuous learning, 566–568
Continuous process technologies, 283
Contraction, 59
Control, 488–517
  bureaucratic
    approaches to, 494–495
    budgetary controls, 497–500
    control process, 491–494
    designing effective systems, 506–507
    downside of, 503–505
    financial control, 500–503
    management audits, 496–497
  clan, 491, 510–514
  concurrent, 494
  defined, 490
  developing systems for, 111
  feedback, 494–495
  feedforward, 494
  market, 491, 508–509
  resistance to, 504–505
  strategic, 129
Controlling, as a function of management, 16
Cooperative strategies, 58–59
Cooptation, 58–59, 562
Coordination, 245
Coordination by mutual adjustment, 264–265
Coordination by plan, 264
Coordination methods, 263–266
Coors, 315
Copeland-Griggs, 350
Core competencies, 121–122, 124, 289–290
Core values, 554
Corning, 122, 293, 300, 333, 509, 553
Corporate constituency programs, 154
Corporate ethical standards, 143–145, 164–165
Corporate governance, 246–247
Corporate legitimacy, 152–153
Corporate social responsibility; *See also* Ethics
  contrasting views, 147–149
  defined, 147
  reconciliation, 149–150
  responsiveness, 150–152
Corporate strategy, 122–125
Corrective action, 493–494
Cost competitiveness, 13
Cost production budget, 498
Cost reduction, 426
Cost-benefit analysis, 170
Costs
  activity-based, 499–500
  switching, 52
  transportation, 195
Coty, Inc., 549
Courage, 386
Covisint, 51
Cradle-to-grave, 156
Creativity, 81–82, 219, 344, 536
Crisis management, 85–87, 90–91
Criterion-related validity, 308
Cross-functional teams, 537
CSR1, 150
CSR2, 150
CSX, 253
Cultural integration, 345
Cultural issues, 200–203
Culture, organizational, 510–514
Culture shock, 200
Currency, foreign, 179–180

Current ratio, 503
Customer divisions, 260–261
Customer relationship management (CRM), 279–280
Customer responsiveness, organizing for, 279
Customer service, 10, 52–53, 125
Customers, 52–53
Customization, mass, 283–284, 551
Custom-made solutions, 71
Cyberjaya, 216
Cycle time, 286
Cyrix, 529

D

Daewoo, 186
DaimlerChrysler, 48, 51, 177–178, 184, 186, 292, 426, 489–490, 567
Dain Rauscher Corp., 565
Dana Corporation, 499–500
Danish Steel Works, 174
Data General, 434
Days Inn, 348
Decentralization, 56, 255–256
Decision making
  barriers to effective, 75–78
  characteristics of, 66–70
  decentralized, 56
  ethics and, 146–147
  fair process, 415–416
  groups, 78–82
  leadership, 374
  nonprogrammed, 67
  organizational
    constraints on, 83
    crisis management and, 85–87
    emergent strategies, 87–88
    models of, 84
    negotiations and politics, 84–85
  programmed, 66–67
  psychological biases, 75–77
  skills, 19–20
  social realities, 78
  stages of, 70–74, 109
  time pressures, 77–78
  types of, 67
  vroom model, 378–381
Declining stage, 431
Defects per million opportunities (DPMO), 495
Defender firms, 531
Defenders, 60
Delegation, 226–227, 250–255
Dell Computer, 9, 12, 185, 225, 304, 526, 529
Dell Webb Corp., 340
Deloitte & Touche, 300, 337, 350
Delta Air Lines, 48, 253
Demand forecasting, 301–302
Demar Plumbing, 221
Democratic leadership, 374
Demographics, 46–47
Deontology, 139–140
Departmentalization, 257
Derivative development projects, 538
Design for environment (DFE), 156
Deutsche Banc Alex Brown, 186
Development, of employees, 312–314
Development Dimensions International, 436
Development over time, 526
Devil's advocate, 81
DFC Intelligence, 193
Dialectic, 81
Dialogue, 452
Differential piecerate system, 32
Differentiation, 125, 244–245, 524
Digital Equipment Corporation, 315, 346–347
Digitization, 6
Dillards, 254
Directive leadership, 373, 379, 382

Disabilities, 146, 335–338
Discounting the future, 76–77
Discovery Communications, 367
Discrimination, 310, 342
Discussion, 452
Diseconomies of scale, 276
Disney Company, 5, 83, 125, 215, 217, 300, 372, 442, 467, 554
Distribution channels, 189
Diversification, 60, 123–125
Diversity, 328–361
  accountability, 352
  versus affirmative action, 342–345, 348
  age of workforce, 338–342
  assumptions, 345
  attracting employees, 347–349
  challenges of, 343–345
  cultivating, 346–352
  defined, 330–331
  gender issues, 332–336, 375
  history of, 330
  mentally/physically disabled, 335–338
  minorities and immigrants, 333–335
  multicultural organizations, 345–346
  organizational assessment, 347
  retaining employees, 350–352
  size of workforce, 332
  training, 314, 349–350
Divestiture, 60
Division of labor, 244–245
Divisional organization, 259–260
Dollar value of trade, 182–185
Domain defense, 152–153
Domain selection, 60
Domino Sugar, 283
Dow Chemical, 58, 121, 168, 199, 261, 300
Dow Corning, 58, 261
Dow Europe, 174
Downsizing, 277, 309
Downward communication, 468–471
Drive, 371
Drug testing, 306, 505
Drug-Free Workplace Act, 306
Dunn and Bradstreet, 335
DuPont, 121, 172–173, 406
Dynamic network, 291
Dynamism, 53

E

Early adopters, 523
Early majority, 523
Eastman Chemical, 124, 435
Eastman Kodak, 196–197, 253, 270, 316, 337, 343, 538, 571
eBay, 5, 8, 13, 334, 548
E-business, 6
Ecocentric management, 156–157
EcoMall, 173
E-commerce, 550
Economic nationalism, 189
Economic responsibilities, 147
Economic viability, 530
Economies of scale, 30
Economies of scope, 276
Economy
  environment and, 170
  global; *See* Global economy
  impact on entrepreneurs, 214–216
  macroenvironment, 44
Eddie Bauer, 48, 548
EDS, 290
Edward Jones, 277, 505
EEOC, 43, 310
Effort-to-performance link, 403
Egoism, 139–140
Electrolux International, 156, 167, 173
Electronic Data Systems, 278

Electronic mail, 458
Electronic manufacturing services (EMS), 273
Electronic media, 456–459
Eli Lilly and Co., 49, 185, 304
Emergent strategies, 87–88
Emerging technologies, 527
Emerson Electric, 506–507
Employee benefits, 319–320
Employee evaluation, 205, 252, 257, 314–316, 397–398
Employee involvement, 287
Employee Retirement Income Security Act, 320
Employment-at-will, 309
Empowerment, 56, 411–413, 510–514
Empresas La Moderna, 167
Enrichment, job, 408
Enron, 5, 76, 137–138, 140, 147, 211, 246–247, 254, 472, 498–499
Entrepreneurial initiative, 520
Entrepreneurial orientation, 231
Entrepreneurial strategy matrix, 220–221
Entrepreneurial venture, 213
Entrepreneurs
    business ideas, 216–219
    defined, 212
    global start-ups, 228
    hazards, 225–227
    information sources, 238–239
    myths, 212–213
    planning, 222–225
    reasons for becoming, 214
    role of economics, 214–216
    steps to success, 219–221
Entry modes, 194–197
Environment
    competitive advantage, 168
    conflicting views, 166–167
    cost-benefit analysis, 170
    economics, 170
    ethics and, 142–146
    implementation of programs, 172
    international perspective, 170–171
    legal issues, 167–168, 172–173
    life cycle analysis, 172
    marketing, 173
    natural, 47, 155–157
    operations, 173
    science and, 169–170
    social responsibility, 546
    strategic integration, 171–172
    sustainable growth, 168–169
Environmental analysis, 53–56, 117–120
Environmental complexity, 53
Environmental movement, 169
Environmental Protection Agency (EPA), 43, 156
Environmental response, organizing for, 279–282
Environmental scanning, 53–54
Environmental uncertainty, 53
Environmentalism, 169
E2open, 51
Equal employment opportunity, 310–311
Equal Employment Opportunity Commission (EEOC), 43, 310
Equal Pay Act, 319
Equitable Life Assurance Society, 347
Equity, 414–415
Equity theory, 413–415
e-retailing, 530
ERG theory, 406
ERISA, 320
Ernst & Young, 425
E-tailing, 547–548
Ethel M. Chocolates, 172
Ethical climate, 142
Ethical issue, 138
Ethical responsibilities, 147

Ethics; See also Corporate social responsibility
    bribery, 43
    business ethics, 138, 140–142
    corporate standards/codes, 143–145, 164–165
    decision making and, 146–147
    defined, 138
    environment, 142–146
    international, 164–165, 203–205
    moral philosophies, 138–140
    natural environment, 47, 155–157
    political environment, 152–154
    programs, 144–146
    systems, 138–140
Ethics Resource Center, 144
E*Trades, 365
EU, 179–180
Euro dollar, 179
European Community (EC), 282
European unification, 179–180
Evaluation, of employees, 205, 252, 257, 314–316, 397–398
Evolution of management, 30–37
Excite, 5
Executive champion, 536
Exelon, 335
Exempt employees, 319
Expatriates, 197–198
Expectancy, 403
Expectancy theory, 402–404
Expedia, 6
Expert power, 370
Exporting, 195
External audits, 496
External environment, 41–63
    competitive environment, 48–53
    defined, 42–43
    environmental analysis, 53–56
    influencing, 58–60
    macroenvironment, 42–47
    responding to, 56–60
External opportunities and threats, 117–120
External recruiting, 304–305
Extinction, 401
Extrinsic reinforcers, 407
ExxonMobile, 154, 172, 184, 277

F

Failure rate, among expatriates, 198
Fair Labor Standards Act, 319
Fairness, achievement of, 413–417
Family and Medical Leave Act, 311
Fannie Mae, 185, 335–336, 351
Fashion Cafe, 107
FBI, 306
Feasibility, 529–530
Federal Aviation Administration (FAA), 43
Federal Consumer Protection Agency, 207
Federal Express, 5, 12, 121, 221, 291–292, 356–360, 406, 426, 436, 543, 549–550, 570
Federal Hazardous Substances Act, 167
Federal Trade Commission, 550
Federated Department Stores, 336
Feedback, 316, 411, 434
Feedback control, 494–495
Feedforward control, 494
Fiat, 186
Fidelity Management & Research, 334, 365
Fiedler's contingency model, 394–395
Filtering, 454, 468
Final consumer, 52
Finance, 545
Financial analysis, 120
Financial ratios, 503
Firestone Tire, 85, 91
First Boston, 58
First Manhattan Consulting Group, 278

First Union Bank, 505
FishLogic, 234
Flaming, 458
Flarion Technologies, 276
Flat organizations, 537, 539
Flavor-of-the-month approach to change, 563
FleetBoston, 337
Flexible benefit programs, 319
Flexible factories, 283–285
Flexible processes, 58
Flexible work schedules, 349
Flextronics Corp., 273
FMLA, 311
Followers, 368–369
Followership, technology, 526
Food and Drug Administration (FDA), 44
Food Lion, 71, 507
Ford Motor Company, 5, 48, 51, 90, 122, 155, 178, 184, 187, 196, 283, 288, 292, 316, 335, 385, 425–426, 451, 554, 567–568, 576
Forecasting, 54–56, 301–302
Foreign Corrupt Practices Act, 204
Foreign currency, 179–180
Foreign direct investments, 183–185
Formal communication, 473–474
Formalization, 263
Forming, 431
Fortress Europe, 180
Fox, 570
Framing effects, 76
Franchising, 195–196
Fraud, 142–143
Free Trade Area of the Americas (FTAA), 182
Frito-Lay, 512
Frontier Airlines, 62
Frontline managers, 17–18, 112–113
FTP software, 227
Funco, 226
Functional integration, 257
Functional organization, 257–259
Functional strategy, 125–126

G

Gainsharing plans, 318
Gap, 115, 119, 243, 253–254
Garbage can model of decision making, 84
Gateway, 231, 526
GE Capital, 254
Gender issues, 332–336, 375
General Dynamics, 205
General Electric, 5, 9, 17, 58, 156, 184, 229, 249, 253, 261, 293, 300, 312, 386, 388–389, 406, 458, 462, 473–475, 499, 502, 544, 572
General Foods, 315
General Motors, 6, 12–13, 48, 51, 62, 91, 108, 121, 155, 166, 184, 186, 196, 256, 276–277, 283, 286, 288, 292, 312
Generalist, 21
Generally accepted accounting practices (GAAP), 499
Genetic testing, 306
Genius of the "and," 556
Geographic divisions, 260–261
Glass ceiling, 333, 343
GlaxoSmithKline, 9, 184
Global Crossing, 41, 254
Global economy
    Consequences of, 182–188
    EU, 179–180
    foreign direct investments, 183–185
    North America, 181
    pacific rim, 180–181
Global environment, 179–182
Global integration, 188–189
Global management; See International management

Global organization model, 190–191
Global start-ups, 228
Global strategic coordination, 189
Global strategy, 188–194
Globalization, 7–8, 186, 546
GlobalNetXchange, 51
GmbH, 187
Goal displacement, 79
Goals
    alternative, 108
    defined, 109
    establishing, 116–117
    evaluation of, 110
    operational, 113
    setting, 399–400, 434
    strategic, 112–113, 116–117
    tactical, 113
Goal-setting theory, 399
Golden West Financial, 335
Goodwill Industries, 337
Goodyear Tire & Rubber, 277, 413, 430
Gradual diffusion, 526
Grapevine, 473
Grease payments, 204
Great Plains Software, 411
Greenhouses, 537
Greyhound, 49
Gross national product (GNP), 181
Group culture, 512
Group maintenance behaviors, 373
Groups; See also Teams
    benefits of, 427
    decision making process, 78–82
    versus teams, 427–428
    working, 427
Groupthink, 79, 344, 438
Growth need strength, 411
Growth/share matrix, 123–124
Grupo Gigante, 207
G.S.I. Transcomm Data Systems, 408
GTE, 123

H

Hackman and Oldham model of job design,
    410–411
Hanna Anderson, 151
Hannaford Brothers Company, 435
Harassment, 333
Harbour & Associates, 186, 289
Hard Rock Café, 107–108
Harley-Davidson, 255–256, 411, 493, 528, 553,
    568
Harpo Entertainment Group, 334
Hasbro, 119
Hawthorne Effect, 34
Hawthorne Studies, 34
Hazardous Materials Transportation Act, 167
H.B. Fuller, 205
Hearst Magazines, 334
Heinz, 190, 497
Herman Miller, 171, 413
Herzberg's two-factor theory, 408–409
Hewlett-Packard, 122–123, 172, 217, 230, 273,
    275, 290, 334, 336, 349–350, 384, 386,
    473, 499, 524, 536, 538, 554, 571
Hi Frequency Marketing, 211
Hierarchical culture, 512
Hierarchical levels, in organizations, 249
Hierarchy of needs, 405–406
High-involvement organization, 293
Hilton International, 190, 195–196
Hitachi, 51, 176
Home Depot, 5, 119, 185, 253, 335, 548
Honda Motor Co., 7, 47, 186, 190, 256, 288,
    293, 316
Honeywell, 154, 249, 346–347, 351, 389, 426
Horizontal communication, 473

Horizontal structure, of organizations, 256–263
Horse trading, 229
Host-country nationals, 197
Hostile environment, 333
HotJobs.com, 299
Howard Industries, 347
Hsbc Holdings, 184
Human capital, 300
Human relations approach to management,
    33–34
Human resources management, 298–327
    analysis, 118, 120
    attracting employees, 347–349
    career development, 21–24, 351
    defined, 300
    diversity; See Diversity
    employee benefits, 319–320
    interviewing, 305–306, 309–310
    job analysis, 304
    labor relations, 320–323
    legal issues, 310–311, 319–320
    mentoring, 351
    operations management, 545
    performance appraisal, 205, 252, 257,
        314–316, 397–398
    planning process, 301–304
    pre-employment testing, 306–308
    recruitment, 299, 304–305, 347–348
    retaining employees, 350–352
    reward systems, 317–320
    selection, 305–308
    staffing issues, 304–311
    strategic impact of, 300
    technology impact on, 538–539
    termination, 309–310
    training and development, 200, 312–314,
        349–350, 435–436
    wages, 317–320
    workforce reductions, 308–311
Hummer Winblad Venture Partners, 174
Hyatt, 200
Hygiene factors, 408–409
Hypercar Inc., 576
Hyundai Motor, 186

I

IBM, 5, 14, 51, 53, 144, 172, 176, 184, 190, 217,
    224, 231, 246, 261, 276–277, 300, 316,
    336, 457–458, 509, 511, 567
ICF Kaiser, 174
Idealab!, 214
IDEO, 83
IKEA International, 156
Illusion of control, 76
Immigration, 47
Immigration Act, 310
Immunex, 401
Imports, 183
Inadequate delegation, 226–227
Incentive systems, 318
Incremental model of decision making, 84
Incubators, business, 215–216
Independent entrepreneurs, 214–228
    business ideas, 216–219
    defined, 212
    global start-ups, 228
    hazards, 225–227
    information sources, 238–239
    myths, 212–213
    planning, 222–225
    reasons for becoming, 214
    role of economics, 214–216
    steps to success, 219–221
Independent strategies, 58–59
Individual incentive plans, 318
Individualism/collectivism, 201
Industrial tourism, 55

Industry analysis, 118
Informal communication, 473–474
Information
    confidentiality and, 550
    real time, 78
Information overload, 468
Information processing, 265–266
Informing strategy, 441
Initiating structure, 373
Innovation; See also Technology
    creativity and, 536
    defined, 11, 520
    economic viability, 530
    feasibility, 529–530
    followership, 526
    leadership and, 524–526
    organizing for, 536–539
    process, 520–521
    product, 520–521
Innovators, 523
Inputs, 413–414
Inside directors, 248
Institute of Creative Technologies, 313
Instrumentality, 404
Insurance, unemployment, 319
Intangible assets, 121
Integration, 188–189, 244–246
Integrative skills, 432
Integrity, 371
Integrity tests, 306–307
Integrity-based ethics programs, 145–146
Intel Corporation, 7, 13, 184, 253, 529–530, 553
Intellectual capital, 9, 151, 300
Intellectual property, 550
Intellectual stimulation, 79
Intellectual Ventures, 10
Intercontinental Exchange Inc., 190, 211
Interface Corporation, 157, 167
Intermediate consumer, 52
Internal audits, 496–497
Internal development, of new technology, 533
Internal recruiting, 304
Internal resource analyses, 120
Internal strengths and weaknesses, analysis of,
    120–122
International Harvester, 374
International management, 176–209
    choosing a strategy, 189–194
    consequences of global economy, 182–188
    cultural issues, 200–203
    currency, 179–180
    dollar value of trade, 182–185
    entry modes, 194–197
    environment, 170–171
    ethics, 164–165, 203–205
    European unification, 179–180
    exporting, 195
    franchising, 195–196
    Free Trade Area of the Americas, 182
    global organization model, 190–191
    global strategy, 188–194
    international organization model, 189–190
    joint ventures, 196
    licensing, 195
    management across borders, 197–205
    multinational organization model, 190
    NAFTA, 181–182
    need theories, 407
    North America, 181
    pacific rim, 180–181
    skills of global managers, 197–200
    teams and, 431
    transnational organization model, 191–194
    wholly owned subsidiaries, 196–197
International Monetary Fund, 179
International Organization for Standardization,
    281–282
International organization model, 189–191

Internet
  auctions via, 51–52
  business venture failure, 5–7
  changes in, 6–7
  e-business, 6
  invention of, 567
  job hunting and, 299, 549
  online purchasing, 548
  pitfalls of, 550–551
  power of, 549–551
Interpersonal communication, 452–461
Interpersonal skills, 20
Interstate Commerce Commission (ICC), 43
Interviews, 305–306, 309–310
Intrapreneurship, 228–232; See also Entrepreneurs
Intrinsic rewards, 407–408
ISO 9000, 281–282
Ispat International, 9
Isuzu, 186
ITW Fluid Products, 187

J

Jaguar, 186
Java, 218
J.C. Penney, 48, 335, 547
J.D. Powers & Associates, 186
JetBlue Airways, 62
Job analysis, 304
Job description, 304
Job design, 407–413
Job enlargement, 408
Job enrichment, 408
Job hunting, via internet, 299, 549
Job maturity, 395
Job rotation, 408
Job satisfaction, 417–418
Job sharing, 349
Job shop, 283
Job specification, 304
Job survey, 423
John Thomas, 283
Johnson & Johnson, 85–86, 144–145, 184, 253, 386, 512, 554, 568
Johnsonville Foods, 413
Joint ventures, 60, 196, 534
JPMorgan Chase, 185, 278, 335, 337
Justice, procedural, 415
Just-in-time, 544
JVC, 184

K

K Shoes Ltd., 436
Kaizen, 280, 525, 544
Kanban, 544
KASPA, 522
Kaufman and Broad Home Corp., 447
Keefe Managers Inc., 278
Kellogg Company, 58, 116, 190
Key technologies, 527
KFC, 7
Kickbacks, 43
Kimberly-Clark, 253, 335
Kinko's, 217
Kistler Aerospace, 218
Kmart, 48, 119, 254, 547
Knight-Ridder, 299
Knowledge, 546–547
Knowledge management, 8–9
Knowledge workers, 216
Kodak, 121, 124, 190, 277, 344, 352, 436, 525
Kohlberg's model of cognitive moral development, 140
Kollmorgen Corporation, 366, 426
Korn/Ferry International, 383
Kovair Inc., 10
KPMG, 426

Kraft Foods, 185, 334–335, 409
Kroger, 51, 122
Kyocera Corporation, 426
Kyoto Protocol, 166

L

Labor, division of, 244–245
Labor force, 46–47
Labor laws, 320–321
Labor relations, 320–323
Labor supply forecasts, 302
Labor-Management Relations Act, 321
Labor-Management Reporting and Disclosure Act, 321
Laggards, 523
Laissez-faire, 374
Lakota Technologies, 519
Land Rover, 186
Landrum-Griffin Act, 321
Lands' End, 12, 48
Language, 463–464
Large batch technologies, 283
Law of effect, 400
Layoffs, 308–309
Leader-member exchange (LMX) theory, 374
Leaders, working, 18–19
Leadership, 364–395
  autocratic, 374
  behavioral approach, 372–377
  change management and, 564–566
  charismatic, 383–384
  contingency model, 394–395
  decision making and, 374
  defined, 366
  democratic, 374
  developing skills, 386–387
  directive, 373, 379, 382
  versus followers, 368–369
  function of management, 15–16
  gender issues, 375
  innovation, 524–526
  life cycle theory, 395
  low-cost, 524
  versus management, 368
  participative, 379
  path-goal theory, 379–382
  post-heroic, 385–386
  power and, 369–370
  relationship motivated, 395
  shaping the future, 572–574
  situational, 377–383, 394–395
  skills and strategies, 384–385
  strategic, 368
  style, 80
  substitutes for, 382–383
  supervisory, 368
  task-motivated, 395
  teams, 432–433
  technology and, 524–526
  traits approach, 371–372
  transformational, 384–385
  vision, 116–117, 366–368, 565
  Vroom model, 378–381
Leadership Grid, 376
Lean manufacturing, 285
Lean organizations, 539
Learning organization, 292–293
Least preferred coworker, 394
Legal issues
  compensation and benefits, 319–320
  environment, 167–168, 172–173
  human resources, 310–311, 319–320
  labor laws, 320–321
Legitimate power, 369
Leveling, 58
Lever Brothers, 173
Leverage ratios, 503

Levi Strauss, 199, 205, 406, 551
LG Electronics, 51
Liabilities, 500
Liberty Media, 367
Licensing, 195, 533
Life cycle, technology, 521
Life cycle analysis, 172
Life cycle theory of leadership, 395
Lifelong learning, 573
Lifetime Entertainment Services, 5, 335
Lincoln Electric Company, 318, 397–398
Lincoln Financial Group, 336
Line departments, 256
Liquidity ratios, 503
Listening, 465–466
Liz Claiborne, 336
L.L. Bean, 48, 122
LMX theory, 374
Lobbying, 153
Local content rules, 189
Local responsiveness, 189
Lockheed Martin, 218, 253, 335, 429
Locus of control, 379
Logistics, 173, 286, 545
Loral, 528
Lord Corporation, 413
Lotus, 214, 224, 290
Louis Galoob Toys, 291
Louisiana Pacific, 173
Louisville Gas and Electric, 173
Low-cost leadership, 524
Low-cost strategies, 125
Lowe, 548
Lubricating Systems, Inc., 187
Lucent Technologies, 13, 51, 253, 269–270, 276, 334
Lufthansa, 12
Lycos, 5

M

Maastricht Treaty, 179
McCann-Erickson Advertising Worldwide, 575
McClelland's needs, 407
McDonald's, 52, 121, 171, 195, 283
McGraw-Hill, 418
McLaughlin Group, 447
MacMillan Bloedel, 172
Macroeconomic analysis, 118
Macroenvironment, 42–47
Macys, 550
Maintenance behaviors, 374–376
Majority, 523
Make-or-buy decisions, 533
Malcolm Baldrige National Quality Award, 280–281, 399, 495
MaMaMedia.com, 447
Management
  administrative, 33–34
  classical approaches to, 30–35
  contemporary approaches to, 35–37
  defined, 14
  ecocentric, 156–157
  empowerment, 56, 411–413, 510–514
  evolution of, 30–37
  functions of, 14–16
  human relations approach, 33–34
  international; See International management
  knowledge, 8–9
  leadership; See Leadership
  levels of, 17–18
  open-book, 470–471
  operations, 543–547
  quantitative, 35
  scientific, 31–33, 470
  skills of, 19–20
  strategic, 17, 115–116, 300
Management audits, 496–497

Management by objectives (MBO), 314
Management by wandering around, 471–473
Management myopia, 503
Management teams, 428
Managerial control, 488–517
    bureaucratic
        approaches to, 494–495
        budgetary controls, 497–500
        control process, 491–494
        designing effective systems, 506–507
        downside of, 503–505
        financial control, 500–503
        management audits, 496–497
    clan, 491, 510–514
    concurrent, 494
    defined, 490
    developing systems for, 111
    feedback, 494–495
    feedforward, 494
    market, 491, 508–509
    resistance to, 504–505
    strategic, 129
Managers
    frontline, 17–18, 112–113
    middle level, 17–18, 112
    skills of, 197–200
    types of, 17–18
Managing across borders, 197–205
Managing diversity; *See* Diversity
Manipulation, 562
Manufacturing
    computer-integrated, 284–285
    continuous process, 283
    flexible, 283–285
    large batch, 283
    lean, 285
    mass customization, 283–284, 551
    modular, 288
    simultaneous engineering, 287–288
    small batch, 283
    value added, 287
Market analysis, 118
Market control, 491, 508–509
Market receptiveness, 528–529
Market share, 7
Marketing, 544
Marketing audit, 120
Markets
    barriers to entry, 49
    bull and bear, 44
    substitutes, 49–50
Marriott, 13, 554
Martin Marietta, 146
Mary Kay, 221
Masculinity/femininity, 201
Maslow's needs hierarchy, 405–406
Mass customization, 283–284, 551
Master budget, 498
Matrix organization, 260–263
Matsushita Electric, 51, 184, 531, 541–542
Mattel, 119, 200
Maximizing, 73
Mazda, 186
MBO, 314
MCI Worldcom, 504
Mechanistic organization, 274
Media richness, 461
Medtronic, 253, 400, 411, 417
Mentally disabled, 335–338
Mentoring, 351
Mercedes Benz, 123, 200
Merck & Company, 121, 124, 150, 184, 230,
        249, 302, 334, 336, 352, 524, 530, 536,
        554
Mergers and acquisitions, 60, 84, 123
Merit pay system, 318
Merrill Lynch, 65
Metro-Goldwyn-Mayer, 333

Metromedia Fiber Network, 255
MGM Grand Hotel, 227
Micro Warehouse, 253
Microsoft, 107, 184, 216–217, 224, 267, 273,
        276, 291, 505, 525
Microsystems, 293
Middle-level managers, 17–18, 112
Midvale Steel Company, 31
Midwest Hardware, 139
Miller Brewing Company, 435, 441
Minorities, 333–335; *See also* Diversity
Mirage Resorts, 300
Mirant, 335
Misperception, 454–456
Mission, 116–117
Misuse of funds, 227
Mitsubishi Motors, 186, 568
Mobile Oil, 351
Modular corporation, 291
Modular manufacturing, 288
Monitoring, 16
Monolithic organization, 345–346
Monsanto, 53, 156, 174, 199
Monster.com, 299, 549
Moody's Investors Service, 255
Moore's Law, 529
Moral philosophies, 138–140
Mortality, 226
Motivation, 396–423
    achieving fairness, 413–417
    change and, 557–563
    defined, 398
    demotivators, 404
    empowerment, 56, 411–413, 510–514
    expectancy theory, 402–404
    intrinsic rewards, 407–408
    job design and, 407–413
    job satisfaction, 417–418
    leaders and, 371
    of people to change, 557–563
    performance related beliefs, 402–404
    reinforcing performance, 400–402
    setting goals, 399–400
    teams, 435
    understanding needs, 405–407
Motivators, 409
Motorola, 200, 277, 280, 290, 447, 473, 495,
        528, 554, 562
Motown Records, 215
MountainBank Financial Corp., 278
Moving, 560
MSNBC.com, 230
MTV, 7
Multicultural organizations, 345–346
Multimedia Supercorridor, 216
Multinational organization model, 190
Mutual adjustment, 264–265
MyFamily.com, 13
MyWebGrocer, 296

N

NAFTA, 181–182
National Aeronautics and Space Administration
        (NASA), 55
National Association of Female Executives, 333
National Labor Relations Act, 320–321
National Labor Relations Board, 43, 320–321
National Oceanic and Atmospheric Administra-
        tion, 41
National Transportation Exchange, 549
Nationalism, 189
Natural environment, 47, 155–157
Natural Step, 156–157
NBC, 389
Needs
    assessment of, 312
    understanding, 405–407

Negative reinforcement, 401
Negotiation, 84–85, 562
Neiman Marcus, 125
Nestle USA, 7, 185, 576
Network organization, 290–291
Networks
    communication, 459–461
    human, 224–225
New Jersey Bell Telephone Company, 33
New ventures, 210–239
    independent entrepreneurs, 214–228
        business ideas, 216–219
        defined, 212
        global start-ups, 228
        hazards, 225–227
        information sources, 238–239
        myths, 212–213
        planning, 222–225
        reasons for becoming, 214
        role of economics, 214–216
        steps to success, 219–221
    intrapreneurship, 228–232
New York Stock Exchange, 7
New York Times Company, 335–336, 505
Nickelodeon, 7
Nike, 45, 159–160, 291, 572
Nippon Telegraph & Telephone Corp., 185, 216
Nissan, 7, 51, 167, 285, 288
Nokia, 185
Nonexempt employees, 319
Nonprogrammed decisions, 67
Nonverbal communication, 464–465, 478–479
Nordstrom, 48, 125–126, 221, 401, 510–511,
        548
Norfolk Southern, 253
Norming, 431
Norms, 436–437, 439–440
Nortel, 51, 269, 402, 426, 447
North America, 181
North American Free Trade Agreement
        (NAFTA), 181–182
North American Tool & Die, 401
Northwest Airlines, 62, 71, 404
NovaCare, 146
Novartis, 184
Novo Nordisk, 167
Ntt DoCoMo, 184
Nucor Steel, 318, 537

O

Oakley, 45–46
Observing, 467
Occupational Safety and Health Act, 320
Occupational Safety and Health Administration
        (OSHA), 43
Odwall, 411
Office of Federal Contract Compliance Pro-
        grams (OFCCP), 43
Ogilvy & Mather, 334–335
Old Navy, 215
OlympuSat, 215
One-way communication, 453
Online auctioning, 51–52
Online recruiting, 299
Open-book management, 470–471
Operational goals, 113
Operational level, 249
Operational managers, 17–18
Operational planning, 112–114
Operations analysis, 120
Operations management, 543–547
Operator control, 493
Opportunity analysis, 222–224
Opportunity obsession, 219
Optimizing, 73
Oracle Corp., 51, 216, 247
Oral communications, 456

Oral reports, 493
Organic structure, 56, 274
Organization culture, 510
Organization models
    international, 189–191
    multinational, 190
    transnational, 191–194
Organization structure, 242–271
    adapting to the environment, 56–58
    centralized, 255
    charts for, 244–245, 274–275
    for customer responsiveness, 279
    divisional, 259–260
    environmental response, 279–282
    flat, 537, 539
    functional, 257–259
    fundamentals, 244–246
    horizontal, 256–263
    for innovation, 536–539
    integration of, 263–266
    lean, 539
    matrix, 260–263
    mechanistic, 274
    monolithic, 345–346
    multicultural, 345–346
    for optimal size, 275–278
    plural, 345–346
    for speed, 285–286
    strategic response, 289–293
    technological, 282–289
    vertical dimension
        authority, 247–250
        decentralized, 56, 255–256
        delegation, 250–255
        hierarchical levels, 249
        span of control, 249
Organizational behavior, 36
Organizational behavior modification, 400–401
Organizational decision making
    constraints on, 83
    crisis management and, 85–87
    emergent strategies, 87–88
    models of, 84
    negotiations and politics, 84–85
Organizational learning, 538
Organizational suitability, 531
Orientation training, 312–314
Oscar Mayer, 83
OSHA, 320
Outcomes, 403–404, 413–414
Outplacement, 309
Outside directors, 248
Outsourcing, 303, 332, 546

P

Pacific Gas & Electric, 172
Pacific Rim, 180–181
Pacing technologies, 527
Parading, 441
Parallel teams, 428
Paramount Pictures, 313
Participation-in-decision-making, 374
Participative leadership, 379
Partnerships, 60, 225, 534
Path-goal theory of leadership, 379–382
Payless ShoeSource, 307
PC Data, 192
Peapod, 295
Peer pressure, 558
Peer reviews, 315–316
Penske Global Automotive, 286
People skills, 20
People's Bank, 349
PeopleSoft, 5, 386
PepsiCo, 8, 48, 185, 334, 344
Perception, 453–454
Perfect Curve Inc., 225

Performance; See also Motivation
    behaviors, 374–376
    evaluation of, 205, 252, 257, 314–316, 397–398
    expectancy theory, 402–404
    gaps, 559–563
    measuring, 492–493
    reinforcing, 400–402
    reviews for, 252
    standards of, 257, 491–493, 506
    of teams, 434
    tests to determine, 306
Performance-to-outcome link, 403–404
Performing, 431
Perkin-Elmer, 458
Personal observation, 493
Personality tests, 306
Personnel management; See Human resources management
Persuasion skills, 461–463
Pest Control Technologies, 221
Pets.com, 7
Pfizer, 69–70, 184, 253, 334
Philip Morris, 184
Phillips Petroleum, 156, 184, 191, 261
Phoenix Companies, 336
Physically disabled, 335–338
Pitney Bowes, 337
Pixelon.com, 227
Pizza Hut, 7
Planet Hollywood, 107
Planning; See also Strategic planning
    business plans, 222–225
    career, 21–24, 351
    defined, 108
    elements of, 222–224
    as a function of management, 15
    goals; See Goals
    human resources, 301–304
    levels of, 111–114
    operational, 112–114
    process of, 108–111
    scenarios for, 110
    situational analysis, 108
    strategic, 544
    tactical, 112–114
Plans
    contingency, 72, 109–110
    defined, 109
    evaluation, 110
    implementation, 111
    monitor and control, 111
    selection, 110
    single-use, 109
    standing, 109
Plant Closing Bill, 311
Plant visits, 55
Platform development projects, 538
Plural organization, 345
Policy manuals, 273
Political action committees (PACs), 153
Political and regulatory analysis, 118
Political environment, 152–154
Politics, impact on decision making, 84–85
Polycast Technology, 348
Positive reinforcement, 400–401
Post-heroic leadership, 385–386
Power
    empowerment, 411–413
    internet and, 549–551
    leadership, 369–370
    need for, 407
Power distance, 200
Pregnancy Discrimination Act, 320
Preliminary control, 494
Presentation skills, 461–463
President's Quality Award, 55
Price-Anderson Act, 152

Priceline, 6
PricewaterhouseCoopers, 83, 295
Principal Financial Group, 336
Principle of exception, 493
Privacy, 151
Pro Air Inc., 62
Proactive change, 566
Probing, 441
Procedural justice, 415
Process innovation, 520–521
Procter & Gamble, 10, 51, 166, 171, 173, 184, 190–191, 217, 220, 282, 335, 337, 350–351, 406, 434, 515–517
Product champion, 536
Product development, 521–523
Product divisions, 259–260
Product innovation, 520–521
Production budget, 498
Profit and loss statement, 500–503
Profitability ratios, 503
Profit-sharing plans, 318
Programmed decisions, 66–67
Project and development teams, 428
Promotions, 351
Prospect Associates, 411
Prospectors, 60
Protectionism, 189
Prudential Financial, 335–336, 343–344, 352, 502
PSA Peugeot, 51
Pseudo.com, 5
Psychological biases, in decision making, 75–77
Psychological contract, 418
Psychological maturity, 395
Public affairs department, 153
Punishment, 401
Purchasing, 51–52, 533, 545, 549
Pure-play operations, 547

Q

Quality
    awards for, 280–281, 399, 495
    continuous improvement, 280, 566–568
    defined, 12
    ISO 9000, 281–282
    service, 12–13
    six sigma, 389, 495
    TQM, 280–281, 544
Quality circles, 430
Quality of work life (QWL) programs, 417
Quantitative management, 35
Quid pro quo, 333
Qwest, 42, 254
QWL, 417

R

Radio Shack, 548
Rainforest Alliance, 173
Rational culture, 512
Raychem Corporation, 367
Raytheon, 335
RCA Corporation, 191, 195
Reach, 6
Reactive change, 566
Reading, 466–467
Ready-made solutions, 71
Real-time information, 78
Receiver skills, 465–467
Receptiveness, anticipated market, 528–529
Reconciliation, 149–150
Recruitment, 299, 304–305, 347–348
Reductions, in workforce, 308–311
Reebok, 291
Reengineering, 282
Reference checks, 306
Referent power, 369–370
Reflection, 465
Reflexite Corporation, 470

Refreezing, 560
Registry, 291
Regulators, 43
Regulatory agencies, 43–44
Rehabilitation Act, 310
Reinforcers, 400
Reinforcing performance, 400–402
Relationship motivated leadership, 395
Relationship oriented behavior, 375–376
Relativism, 140
Reliability, of employment tests, 307
Relocation Resources International (RRI), 202
Renault, 51
Research and engineering, 544–545
Research development projects, 538
Reserves, 537
Resistance to change, 557–560
Resistance to control, 504–505
Resource Conservation and Recovery Act, 167
Resources, 121–122, 124
Respond.com, 227
Responsibility, 250–251
Responsiveness, corporate social, 150–152
Results appraisal, 314
Resumes, 24, 305
Return on investment (ROI), 503
Reverse logistics, 173
Reward power, 369
Reward systems, for performance, 317–320
Rewards, 562
Rightsizing, 277
Right-to-Know Act, 167
Right-to-work, 322
Rigid bureaucratic behavior, 503–504
Risk, 68–70, 224
Risk society, 155–156
Roche Holding, 185
Rockwell International, 197
ROI, 503
Rolls Royce, 531
Rotation, job, 408
Royal Ahold, 51
Royal Bank of Scotland Group, 185
Royal Dutch/Shell, 172, 184, 190, 335, 572
Royalty payments, 195
R.R. Donnelley, 470
Rubbermaid, 290, 536
Ryder System, 286

S

Saab, 186
Safeway, 122, 295, 335
Saks Fifth Avenue, 125
Salaries, 317–320
Sales budget, 498
Sales practices, 189
Sanford C. Bernstein, 335
Sara Lee, 51, 430
Satisficing, 73, 79
Saturn, 286, 300
SBC Communications Inc., 184, 336
Scale economies, 276
Scandic Hotels, 156
Scanlon plan, 318
Scanning, 53–54, 528
Scenario development, 54
Scenarios, 54, 110
Scholastic, 336
Scientific management, 31–33, 470
Scorecard, balanced, 113–114
Scott Paper, 173
Seagate Technology, 51
Seagram International, 260
Sears, Roebuck and Co., 48, 51, 124, 142–143,
    253, 276, 304, 306, 336, 547–548
Securities and Exchange Commission (SEC),
    44, 174, 246

Seiko, 45
Selection, of employees, 305–308
Self-actualization, 405–406
Self-confidence, 371
Self-contained tasks, 266
Self-designing teams, 430
Self-managed teams, 429–430
Semco, 426
Semiautonomous work groups, 430
Sempra, 337
Sender communication skills, 461–465
Service quality, 12–13
Sexual harassment, 333
Shapers, 570
Sharp, 290
Shell, 172, 249, 261, 283, 386
Shenandoah Life Insurance Company, 426
Sheraton, 190
Side street effect, 219
Siebel Systems, 26–27
Siemens, 9, 180, 458
Simultaneous engineering, 287–288
Single-use plans, 109
Situational analysis, 108
Situational approach, to leadership, 377–383,
    394–395
Situational interview, 305
Six sigma, 389, 495
Size, organizing for, 275–278
SKF, 290
Skill building, 349–350
Skunkworks, 230, 537
Slack resources, 265–266
Small batch technologies, 283
Small business, 212–213, 217, 276–277; *See also*
    Entrepreneurs
Smith Kline Beecham, 459
Smoothing, 58
Social analysis, 118
Social facilitation effect, 435
Social issues, 47
Social loafing, 435
Social realities, 78
Social responsibility
    contrasting views, 147–149
    defined, 147
    reconciliation, 149–150
    responsiveness, 150–152
Social security, 319
Socialized power, 407
Society for Human Resource Management, 331
Sociotechnical systems, 539
Solectron, 51
Sony Corporation, 184, 191–193, 215–217, 313,
    335, 400, 531, 554, 568, 570
South of Boston Media Group, 325
Southwest Airlines, 5, 48–49, 58, 120, 125, 277,
    300, 334, 383, 413, 510
Span of control, 249
Specialist, 21
Specialist control, 493
Specialization, 245
Specification, job, 304
Speech-recognition software, 457
Speed to market, 13, 285–286
Spirit Airlines, 62
Springfield ReManufacturing Corp., 470, 477
SpringHill Greenhouses, 187–188
Spyglass, 300
Square D., 496
Staff departments, 256
Staffing, 304–311
Stakeholders, 117
Standard & Poor's, 72, 140
Standardization, 263–264
Standards
    defined, 491
    ethics, 143–145, 164–165

ISO 9000, 281–282
    performance, 257, 491–493, 506
Standing plans, 109
Starbucks Coffee Co., 113–114, 215–216,
    277–278, 510, 569
State Farm Insurance, 411
State Street, 336
Steelcase, 73
Stereotyping, 344–345
Stickiness, 6
Stockholders, 248
Stockholders' equity, 500
Stonewalling, 154
Storming, 431
Strategic alliances, 60, 230, 291–292
Strategic control system, 129
Strategic goals, 112–113, 116–117
Strategic intent, 116
Strategic leadership, 368
Strategic management, 17, 115–116, 300
Strategic maneuvering, 60
Strategic planning; *See also* Planning
    approaches to, 115–116
    barriers to, 128
    contingency plans, 72, 109–110
    defined, 112
    steps
        analysis of external opportunities, 117–120
        analysis of internal strengths, 120–122
        establishment of mission/vision/goals,
            116–117
        strategic control, 129
        strategy implementation, 127–129
        SWOT analysis, 116, 122–127
    strategic management, 17, 115–116, 300
Strategic response, organizing for, 289–293
Strategic retreat, 154
Strategic triangle, 279
Strategic vision, 116–117
Strategies
    business, 125
    cooperative, 58–59
    corporate, 122–125
    defined, 112
    differentiation, 125, 244–245, 524
    emergent, 87–88
    formulation of, 122–127
    functional, 125–126
    global, 188–194
    independent, 58–59
Strengths, weaknesses, opportunities, threats
    (SWOT) analysis, 116, 122–127
Structured interview, 305
Subaru, 186
Substitutes
    for leadership, 382–383
    threat of, 49–50
Sun Microsystems, 11, 22, 80, 216, 534
Sunoco, 173
Superfund, 167
Supervision, 467
Supervisory leadership, 368
Suppliermarket.com, 234
Suppliers, 50–52
Supply and demand, 302–303
Supply of labor, 302
Support groups, 350–351
Supportive leadership, 373, 379
Surface Mining Control and Reclamation Act,
    167
Surface Systems (SSI), 69
Survive and thrive, 23–24
Survivor's syndrome, 277
Sustainable growth, 168–169
Suzuki, 186, 256
Swiss Bank Corp., 174
Switching costs, 52
SWOT analysis, 116, 122–127

Sysco, 110–111
Systematic abandonment, 568
Systematic management, 30–31
Systems theory, 36
Systems thinking, 171

T

Taco Bell, 7
Tactical behavior, 504
Tactical goals, 113
Tactical managers, 17
Tactical planning, 112–114
Taft-Hartley Act, 321
Tangible assets, 121
Target Corp., 48, 51, 119
Tariff barriers, 195
Task identity, 411
Task performance behaviors, 373
Task specialist, 437
Task-motivated leadership, 395
Task-oriented behavior, 375
Team maintenance specialist, 437
Teams, 424–449
    benefits of, 427
    building effective, 434–441
    cohesiveness, 437–441
    conflict, 442–445
    contributions of, 426–427
    cross-functional, 537
    decision making, 78–82
    defined, 427
    failure of, 432–433
    global, 431
    versus groups, 427–428
    leadership of, 432–433
    managing lateral relationships, 441–445
    measuring performance, 434
    member contributions, 435–436
    motivating, 435
    parallel, 428
    process of becoming, 431–433
    pros and cons, 78–79
    roles of, 437
    self-designing, 430
    self-managed, 429–430
    setting goals, 434
    skills, 431–432
    top management, 225, 249, 428
    training of, 314, 435–436
    transnational, 431
    types of, 428–429
Technical innovator, 536
Technical skills, 19
Technological analysis, 118
Technological response, organizing for, 282–289
Technology
    anticipated competency development, 530–531
    assessing needs, 527–528
    defined, 282, 520
    development projects, 538
    diffusion of innovations, 523
    economic viability, 530
    feasibility, 529–530
    followership, 526
    framing decisions, 528–532
    internal development, 533
    job design and, 538–539
    leadership and, 524–526
    life-cycle, 521
    managerial roles and, 535–536
    operations management and, 547
    organizing for, 536–539
    sourcing and acquiring new, 533–534
    strategy development, 528
    trading, 534
Technology audit, 527

Telecommuting, 349
Teleconferencing, 456–457
Teleology, 139
Terminating stage, 431
Termination, 309–310
Termination-at-will, 309
Tests, pre-employment, 306–308
Texas American Bancshares, 278
Texas Capital Bank, 278
Texas Instruments, 129, 197, 253, 261, 304, 426, 430, 435, 441
Theory X and Theory Y, 36
Third-country nationals, 197
Threats, analysis of, 117–120
360 degree appraisal, 316
3Com, 11
3M, 11, 18, 173–174, 196, 232, 253, 290, 426, 512, 524–525, 531, 536–537, 554, 568
TIAA-CREF, 336
Time pressures, 77–78
Time to market, 13
Time-and-motion studies, 32
Time-based competition, 285–286
Top management teams, 225, 249, 428
Top-level managers, 17–18
Toro, 385
Toshiba, 51, 290, 532
Total organization change, 563
Total quality management (TQM), 280–281, 544
Totalfinaelf, 185
Toxic Release Inventory, 168
Toxic Substances Control Act, 167
Toyota Motor, 7, 9, 167, 185–186, 190, 285–288, 425–426, 566, 568
Toys"R"Us, 118–120, 343, 420–421, 547–548, 550
TQM, 280–281, 544
Traditional work groups, 430
Tragedy of the Commons, 169
Training
    diversity, 314, 349–350
    for international jobs, 200
    orientation, 312–314
    process, 312
    teams, 314, 435–436
    types of, 312–314
Trait appraisal, 314
Traits approach, to leadership, 371–372
Transactional leaders, 384
Transfer price, 509
Transformational leadership, 384–385
Transnational organization model, 191–194
Transnational team, 431
Transora.com, 51
Transportation costs, 195
Travelers, 125
Tribune Co., 299
Tricon, 7–8
TRW, 261, 277, 528
Two-factor theory, 408–409
Two-way communication, 453
Tyco, 255
Tyranny of the "or," 555–556
Tyson Foods, 254

U

UAL, 5, 62
UBS, 185
Uncertainty
    adapting to, 56–58
    avoidance, 201
    environmental, 53
    risk and, 68–69
Unemployment insurance, 319
Unfreezing stage, 559
Unification, 179–180

Unilever, 176, 185, 190
Union Carbide, 53, 85–86, 168
Union shop, 322
Unionization, 321
United Airlines, 48, 473
United Parcel Service, 80, 185, 570
United Technologies, 205
Unity-of-command principle, 262
Universal Security Instruments, 65
Universalism, 138
Upward communication, 471–473
Urban Broadcasting Company, Inc., 215
U.S. West, 347, 350
US Airways, 48, 62
USA Education Inc., 336
Utilitarianism, 139–140

V

Valence, 404
Validity, of employment tests, 308
Value chain, 257–258
Value of trade, 182–185
Value-added manufacturing, 287
Vanguard Airlines, 62
Variable pay, 318
Venture partners, 196
Verizon Communication, 184, 334, 337, 344, 553
Vertical integration, 123
Vertical organizational structure, 246–256
    authority, 247–250
    decentralized, 56, 255–256
    delegation, 250–255
    hierarchical levels, 249
    span of control, 249
VH1, 7
Viacom, 185, 334
Videoconferencing, 457
Vigilance, 74
Virgin Group, 384
Virtual corporation, 291
Virtual office, 458–459
Virtue ethics, 140
VisiCalc, 213, 219
Vision, 116–117, 366–368, 565
Vivendi Universal, 334
Vocational Rehabilitation Act, 311
Vodafone Group, 185
Volkswagen, 176
Voluntary responsibilities, 147
Volvo, 186
VooDoo, 12
Vroom model of leadership, 378–381

W

Wabash National, 470
Wages, 317–320
Wagner Act, 320–321
Walden Kayaks, 265
Walgreen's, 438
Wal-Mart, 5, 11, 16, 48, 51, 119, 121, 125, 173, 184, 207, 217, 276–277, 295, 400, 418, 420–421, 554
Walt Disney Company, 82, 121, 126, 221, 335, 429, 510
Warnaco, 20, 255
Warner-Lambert, 69
Washington Mutual Inc., 278, 336
Waste, elimination of, 286
WebMD, 7, 230
Websense Inc., 505
Wellmark Inc., 496
WellPoint Health Networks Inc., 336
Wells Fargo, 185, 337, 404
Wendy's, 121
Western Electric Company, 34
Westinghouse, 316, 397

Wetherill Associates, 146
Wetzel's Pretzels, 221
Weyerhaeuser Company, 53, 58, 77, 173
Whirlpool, 199
Whistle-blowing, 147, 309
Whole Foods Market, 112–113
Wholly owned subsidiaries, 196–197
WHYCO Chromium Company, 171
Wildcat strikes, 321
Williams Communication, 41
Wilson Sporting Goods Company, 437
Wine.com, 12
Winn-Dixie, 71
Wisconsin Power and Light, 349
Women, 332–336, 342, 348, 375
Work groups, 427, 430; *See also* Teams
Work teams, 428
Worker Adjustment and Retraining Notification
    Act, 311

Workers' compensation, 319
Workforce
    age of, 338–342
    diversity; *See* Diversity
    reductions in, 308–311
    size of, 332
Working leaders, 18–19
World Bank, 386
World class, 122, 554–556
World Health Organization, 530
World Trade Organization (WTO), 179
World Wide Web Consortium, 567
WorldCom, 137, 255
WorldWide Retail Exchange, 51
Worst-case scenario, 54
W.R. Grace, 172
Wrapping, 299

Writing skills, 463
Written communication, 456, 463, 493
Wyeth, 185

X

Xerox Corporation, 121–122, 167, 172, 190,
    254, 261, 277, 300, 316, 333–334, 347,
    350, 429, 505, 524

Y

Yahoo!, 5, 7–8, 230, 576
Yamaha, 256

Z

Zale Corporation, 305
Zenith, 191